The Workers' Opposition
in the Russian Communist Party

Historical Materialism Book Series

The Historical Materialism Book Series is a major publishing initiative of the radical left. The capitalist crisis of the twenty-first century has been met by a resurgence of interest in critical Marxist theory. At the same time, the publishing institutions committed to Marxism have contracted markedly since the high point of the 1970s. The Historical Materialism Book Series is dedicated to addressing this situation by making available important works of Marxist theory. The aim of the series is to publish important theoretical contributions as the basis for vigorous intellectual debate and exchange on the left.

The peer-reviewed series publishes original monographs, translated texts, and reprints of classics across the bounds of academic disciplinary agendas and across the divisions of the left. The series is particularly concerned to encourage the internationalization of Marxist debate and aims to translate significant studies from beyond the English-speaking world.

For a full list of titles in the Historical Materialism Book Series
available in paperback from Haymarket Books, visit:
https://www.haymarketbooks.org/series_collections/1-historical-materialism

The Workers' Opposition in the Russian Communist Party

Documents, 1919–30

Edited and translated by
Barbara C. Allen

Haymarket Books
Chicago, IL

First published in 2021 by Brill Academic Publishers, The Netherlands
© 2021 Koninklijke Brill NV, Leiden, The Netherlands

Published in paperback in 2022 by
Haymarket Books
P.O. Box 180165
Chicago, IL 60618
773-583-7884
www.haymarketbooks.org

ISBN: 978-1-64259-782-0

Distributed to the trade in the US through Consortium Book Sales and
Distribution (www.cbsd.com) and internationally through Ingram
Publisher Services International (www.ingramcontent.com).

This book was published with the generous support of Lannan
Foundation and Wallace Action Fund.

Special discounts are available for bulk purchases by organizations and
institutions. Please call 773-583-7884 or email info@haymarketbooks.org
for more information.

Cover art and design by David Mabb. Cover art is a detail of *Two Squares
9, Lissitzky drawing on Morris & Co design*, paint and wallpaper on canvas
(2008).

Printed in the United States.

10 9 8 7 6 5 4 3 2 1

Library of Congress Cataloging-in-Publication data is available.

Contents

Acknowledgements

My thanks are due to Sebastian Budgen and the other editors of the Historical Materialism Series for their interest in publishing the collected documents of the Workers' Opposition. While I gathered the documents in this book, my research was supported by the International Research and Exchanges Board (IREX), the U.S. Department of Education, the Hoover Institution at Stanford University, the U.S. State Department, and La Salle University. Aleksandr Shliapnikov's daughter Irina facilitated my access to archival collections about her father's life and the Workers' Opposition. The interlibrary loan staff at Connelly Library of La Salle University offered invaluable assistance. My PhD adviser at Indiana University Bloomington, Alexander Rabinowitch, and undergraduate adviser at the University of North Carolina at Chapel Hill, Donald J. Raleigh, have been inspiring mentors. More people than I can name have offered advice that improved this collection, but most of all, Simon Pirani carefully read the collection and offered detailed suggestions. Danny Hayward's meticulous copyediting vastly enhanced the manuscript. I am grateful to Brill for agreeing to permit me to use parts of my biography of Aleksandr Shliapnikov as a basis for the introductory essays in this volume, which I have updated through research into the library collection at University of Illinois, Champaign-Urbana. Last but not least, I owe much appreciation to Jennifer Obdam and Bart Nijsten at Brill and the typesetting team for their patience and close attention to the manuscript.

Explanatory Notes

Note about Translation

There are numerous Russian terms for trade unions or unionism. Two fairly equivalent terms are *obedineniia* [объединения] and *soiuzy* [союзы] for unions, although *soiuz* [союз] can refer to a type of union unrelated to trade unions. The term *professionalnye soiuzy* [профессиональные союзы] can be translated as professional unions or trade unions. Not only the white-collar type, but also industrial unions are encompassed under this term. There is also a narrower term for industrial unions, *proizvodstvennye soiuzy* [производственные союзы], which is literally translated as production unions. Sometimes the term *tred-iunionizm* [тред-юнионизм] is encountered. It is a transliteration of the English term trade-unionism into Russian, but it applies strictly to the reformist, non-revolutionary trade union movement.

Manual workers are *rabochie* [рабочие]. The term *rabotnik* [работник], which is often translated as worker, refers less to a manual worker and more to one who carries out organisational, agitation, or propaganda work for the political party or work on behalf of a government department. Therefore, I prefer to translate *rabotniki* [работники] as personnel or even activists. A *muzhik* [мужик] is a male peasant. Other terms relevant to the peasantry are *bednota* [беднота] or *bedniachestvo* [бедячество] for poor peasantry and *bedniak* [бедняк] for poor peasant, *kulak* [кулак] for rich peasant and *kulachestvo* [кулачество] for rich peasantry, and *seredniak* [середняк] for middle peasant. *Intelligent* (singular noun) and *intelligentsia* (collective noun) [интеллигент и интеллигентция] usually refer to radical leftist intellectuals.

Zavod [завод] is a factory and *fabrika* [фабрика] can be translated as factory, plant, or mill. Economy can be rendered in Russian as *ekonomika* [экономика] or *khoziaistvo* [хозяйство]. *Khoziaistvo* can also mean farm or peasant holding. *Narodnoe khoziaistvo* [народное хозяйство] distinguishes the general or national economy from smaller units.

Verkhi [верхи] and *nizy* [низы] refer to the power relationships between groups in society or in the political party. The terms translate literally as higher-ups and lower-downs or heights and depths. *Nizy* can also be translated as rank-and-file or grassroots. *Verkhi* might also be translated as leaders or bosses.

The term *samodeiatelnost* [самодеятельность] can be translated literally as self-activity, but other possibilities include initiative, enterprise, amateur activity, agency, independence, and self-organisation. In *The Russian Revolution in Retreat*, Simon Pirani argues that the term as used by the Russian Communist

Party and Soviet government evolved from 1917 to 1920 away from 'creativity' to 'voluntary worker participation in the tasks of economic construction – tasks that workers had no role in setting'.[1]

Note about Transliteration

This book follows a modified version of the U.S. Library of Congress transliteration system. It substitutes 'y' for the Cyrillic hard sign ъ and omits diacritical marks for the soft sign ь. Names ending in ий are transliterated with a 'y'. Names ending in ый are transliterated with 'yi'.

Note about Measurements

arshin [аршин] = 28 inches or 71 cm.
desiatina [десятина] = 2.7 acres.
pud [пуд] = about 36.11 pounds or 16.38 kilograms
sazhen [сажень] = 2.13 meters.

Note about St. Petersburg/Petrograd/Leningrad

Founded in 1703, the city of St. Petersburg replaced Moscow as Russia's capital in 1712. Affectionately, its residents called it Piter. After World War I erupted, authorities renamed it Petrograd in a patriotic gesture. The Petersburg Committee of the Bolshevik Party retained its name even after the city name changed to Petrograd, because the Bolsheviks opposed the war and resisted patriotic sentiment. The capital was returned to Moscow in 1918. After Lenin died in 1924, the city was renamed Leningrad to honour him. After the collapse of the Soviet Union, the name St. Petersburg was restored to it.

Note about Protocols and Stenographic Reports of Party Congresses and Conferences

Party congress proceedings were published either as protocols or stenographic reports. A stenographic report was usually a full record of the open sessions of

---

1 Pirani 2008, pp. 91–2.

a congress, although in exceptional cases, speeches were censored. Protocols often were abbreviated records, providing only major speeches and decisions, although sometimes they were more complete. In the early years of Soviet power, stenographic records of party congress and conference speeches were usually offered to speakers for correction before being entered into the official stenographic report. Some speakers opted to make corrections, while others did not. Speakers may have made changes in order to correct the stenographer's errors or to polish and perhaps even add to the recorded version of their oral presentations. The published stenographic reports reflect the fact that some speeches were corrected and others not. Where I have consulted the original uncorrected stenographic records, I have indicated so. I have also attempted to find complete versions of censored speeches and have indicated whether these are full versions.

Note about the Naming of the Workers' Opposition

According to some members of the Workers' Opposition [Рабочая оппозиция], Lenin or the Party Central Committee gave the group its name. Often, those who criticised the group referred to it ironically as the 'so-called' Workers' Opposition. In some original documents, Workers' Opposition is placed within quotation marks, perhaps ironically. I have chosen to omit the quotation marks, which editors may have inserted without consideration of the speakers' or writers' intentions. The group's name sometimes appears in lower case and other times in upper case in the documents. I have changed it to upper case consistently.

Note about Soviet Trade Union Organisational Structure

Within trade unions as within other Soviet organisations, there were several leading bodies. The presidium was the 'official' leading body. Its non-party members were a small minority, who had no real influence over the organisation's decisions. The presidium was formed out of the central committee of the union. Within the central committee, the communist faction held real power and it elected (with the Party CC's approval) a bureau as its leading body. Bureau members usually held dual posts in the presidium, so communists made up the majority of the presidium. In the early years of the Soviet state, unions also had a chair, but as the party exerted greater control over unions, its leaders preferred to substitute collegial bodies for elected chairs.

Abbreviations and Acronyms

CC	Central Committee of the Russian Communist Party
CCC	Central Control Commission of the RCP(b)
Cheka/VChK	All-Russian Extraordinary Commission for Combatting Counterrevolution and Sabotage
Comintern	Third Communist International
CP(b)U	Communist Party (Bolshevik) of Ukraine
ECCI	Executive Committee of the Communist International
Ekoso	Economic conference or council under Council of People's Commissars
GARF	State Archive of the Russian Federation
Glavki	VSNKh departments or directorates (literally 'chief committees') overseeing branches of industry; singular is Glavk
Glavtekstil	Main Administration of Textiles Industry
Gomza	State Association of Machine-Building Factories
Goskontrol	State Control
GPU	State Political Administration
Gubkom	Gubernia Committee
Ispolkom	Executive Committee
Komgosor	State Construction Committee
Narkomfin	People's Commissariat of Finance
Narkomindel	People's Commissariat of Foreign Affairs
Narkompochtel	People's Commissariat of Post and Telegraph
Narkomprod	People's Commissariat of Food Supply
Narkomtrud	People's Commissariat of Labour
Narkomvoen	People's Commissariat of the Military
Narkomzdrav	People's Commissariat of Health
Narkomzem	People's Commissariat of Agriculture
NKPS	People's Commissariat for Transportation and Communications
OGPU	Consolidated State Political Administration
Orgburo	Organisational Bureau of the CC of the RCP(b)
Politburo	Political Bureau of the CC of the RCP(b)
Rabkrin	Workers' and Peasants' Inspectorate
Raikom	Raion (district) Committee
RCP(b)/RKP(b)	Russian Communist Party (Bolsheviks), 1918–25
Registrud	Labour Registry
RGASPI	Russian State Archive of Socio-Political History
ROSTA	Russian Telegraph Agency

Sovkhoz	Soviet state-owned farm
Sovnarkhoz	Economic Council (local body of VSNKh)
Sovnarkom	Council of People's Commissars
STO	Council of Labour and Defence
TsA FSB	Central Archive of the Federal Security Service
TsAODM	Central Archive of Social Movements of Moscow
Tsentrobalt	Central Committee of the Baltic Fleet
Tsentrosoiuz	Central Union of Consumer Cooperatives
TsIK	Central Executive Committee
TsPTI	Central Board of Heavy Industry
Uchraspred	Registration and Distribution Department of the CC RCP(b)
VCP(b)/VKP(b)	All-Union Communist Party (Bolsheviks), 1925–52
Vneshtorg	Commissariat of Foreign Trade
VSNKh	All-Russian Council of National Economy
VSRM	All-Russian Union of Metalworkers
VTsIK	All-Russian Central Executive Committee [of the All-Russian Congress of Soviets]
VTsSPS	All-Russian Central Council of Trade Unions
Zhenotdel	Women's Department of the CC RCP(b)

Introduction

The Russian Revolution of 1917 unfolded in the context of war-induced economic crisis, which brought about the collapse of the imperial Russian state. The at first liberal then moderately socialist Provisional Government which replaced it was unable to extract Russia from the crisis successfully. The Bolsheviks, having seized power from this caretaker government, bore partial responsibility for the state's collapse, yet they assumed responsibility for the challenge of rebuilding the state as global war segued into civil war. Their dreams of empowering formerly oppressed industrial workers and poor peasants were tempered by the need to establish firm control over a vast territory populated by a few supporters, many who opposed their rule, and many others who simply sought to survive. Even some among the Bolsheviks (renamed the Russian Communist Party in 1918) feared that the 'proletarian dictatorship' was in danger of becoming a dictatorship of party and government higher-ups.[1] When the Bolsheviks took power, they had not fully resolved the relationship between the party, soviets, and trade unions. Winning the civil war at first took priority over organisational matters, but these arose again in 1919–20. Debate over trade unions' role in the economy and their relationship with the Communist party was fierce and produced distinct platforms identified with Vladimir Lenin, Leon Trotsky, and the Workers' Opposition.[2] Due to the contentious nature of the trade union debate, discussion was opened in December 1920 to party members as a whole.

The Workers' Opposition (1919–22) in the Russian Communist Party (Bolsheviks) was a movement of Communists in industrial trade unions who attempted to address problems of economic management that arose in the context of economic crisis that accompanied the Russian Civil War and of the Party's attempt to establish a dictatorship. Prominent leaders were Aleksandr Shliapnikov, Sergei Medvedev, Aleksei Kiselev, Ivan Kutuzov, Aleksandr Tolokontsev, and Iury Lutovinov. These individuals were skilled Petrograd metalworkers who had been union and party organisers before 1917. Bolshevik fem-

---

1 Far more has been written on these themes than I can accommodate in this footnote. Among the works that have most influenced me are: Rabinowitch 1976, Rabinowitch 2007, Raleigh 1986, Raleigh 2002, Burdzhalov 1987, Carr 1950–3, Fitzpatrick 1983, Hasegawa 1981, Koenker 1985, Koenker et al (eds.) 1989, Shkliarevsky 1993, Smith 1983, Thompson 1981, Wade 1984, Wade 2000.

2 Among the most important English-language secondary accounts of the trade union debates are: Daniels 1988 [1960]; Holmes 1990; Pirani 2008; Schapiro 1956; Sorenson 1969.

inist Aleksandra Kollontai mentored the group and supported it by speaking and writing on its behalf.[3] Thirty-eight leaders of trade unions and industry signed the final programme of the Workers' Opposition. Support for the Workers' Opposition was found in Moscow, Nizhny Novgorod, Samara, the Donbas, and other industrial centres, but each subgroup emphasised aspects of the group's programme differently. The group traced its ideological origin to the RCP(b) programme adopted in March 1919. Its opponents in the Party Central Committee labelled it 'Workers' Opposition'. This term was not a new one in party history. The history of the term 'workers' opposition' in the Russian Social Democratic Workers' Party dated as far back as 1900, when radical intellectuals (интеллигенты) used it to refer to uncooperative groups of workers in Ekaterinoslav and Kharkov. The Russian Jewish socialist movement saw tensions arise between workers and circle leaders in the 1880s and 1890s, especially over the relationship between political and economic goals. The term also was applied to Urals workers who in 1918 supported the anti-Bolshevik All-Russian Constituent Assembly Committee [Комуч] in Samara.[4] As a hostile term, the name drove a wedge between worker and *intelligent* socialists. It may be that Shliapnikov and his supporters did not choose this name for themselves, but that Lenin foisted it upon them.

Accused by party leaders of having created a dangerous faction, members of the Workers' Opposition came to emphasise the movement's informality and short life. There is no precise date on which the group coalesced. No conference or congress marked its founding. Scattered by the Civil War, Petrograd metalworkers at the forefront of Bolshevik organising in 1917 only began to reunite in the All-Russian Metalworkers' Union in late 1919, whereupon Shliapnikov's proposals for trade union management of the economy and workerisation of the party galvanised their support. His supporters arranged meetings by word of mouth. Attendance at the meetings fluctuated, which makes it difficult to tally the group's membership. Arguing that the Workers' Opposition was built upon currents of 'critical thought' that circulated among the 'masses' in the summer of 1920, Alexandra Kollontai emphasised its popular roots, yet she claimed that it formed a faction only after party leaders had done so. Shliapnikov later gave the impression that the Workers' Opposition came into being only after the Fifth Trade-Union Conference in November 1920.[5]

---

3 Biographies of Kollontai include Clements 1979, Farnsworth 1980, Porter 2014 [1980].
4 Wildman 1967, pp. 107–8; Mendelsohn 1965, 268, 277; Pavliuchenkov 2008, p. 59.
5 Kollontai 1921b, pp. 8–9; RGASPI, f. 589, op. 3, d. 9103, v. 5, l. 16, 17 June 1933, Shliapnikov's party purge session.

The programme of the Workers' Opposition assumed that trade unions representing industrial workers and engineers should lead economic recovery in order to ensure worker mastery over production rather than worker subordination to production. This goal rested on the assumption that workers and technical personnel had valuable knowledge and experience that could help resolve economic problems. The Worker Oppositionists regarded trade unions, which by 1920 were in Communist hands, as more worker-oriented and revolutionary than were many party committees. The party, they thought, needed a new influx of working-class members and leaders in order to restore its revolutionary character, which they thought had deteriorated during the Civil War. Contrary to opponents' charges, their programme was neither syndicalist nor anarchist, but was rooted in the multifaceted tradition of the Bolshevik party and of international Marxism.

The Workers' Opposition emphasised that its programme was based on principles laid out in earlier all-Russian trade-union congresses, but that it stemmed in particular from the economic section of the party programme, which was passed at the Eighth Party Congress in March 1919. The oppositionists complained that the militarisation of industry during the Civil War had forced trade unions into a role not accorded to them by party resolutions. In practice, the role of the trade unions in production had been relegated to that of 'an office of inquiry and recommendation'.[6] The Workers' Opposition blamed the marginal role of the unions in production on growing bureaucratisation. The only remedy for this unfortunate state of affairs was for unions to implement economic policy. Following the 1919 party programme, the plan called for trade unions to 'concentrate in their hands management of the entire economy as a single unit'. Reform had to begin at the lowest level and extend upwards to the central leadership. First, trade unions would immediately receive more staff and resources. Then, unions and factory committees would supersede state economic bodies in the organisation and management of the economy. Finally, unions would nominate, install and recall economic managers without interference from VSNKh.[7]

On all levels, union representatives would be elected, in order to ensure mass participation in economic management. Within the trade unions, higher levels would be accountable to lower ones through direct elections and periodic reporting, and lower levels would report to higher ones. Union representatives would assemble in all-Russian producer congresses for each branch

---

6 'Tezisy rabochei oppozitsii', *Pravda* (25 January 1921), p. 2.
7 'Tezisy rabochei oppozitsii', p. 3.

of the economy and for the economy overall. To facilitate such representation, management of industries would be rationalised 'according to production feature' (such as metalworking, mining, textiles, etc). A factory-level worker assembly, elected by 'organised producers', would be the basic organisational unit of the union. The proposals made clear that both manual workers and white-collar employees would elect management bodies. All separate leading bodies, including factory committees, wage-rates committees, shop committees and so on, would come together into one factory assembly to meet two or four times per month and decide all important questions facing the factory. The primary allegiance of each factory organisation, therefore, would be to the factory assembly rather than to higher organisations outside the factory. Finally, in order to improve the workers' standard of living and to raise their productivity, the Workers' Opposition recommended banning all payments-in-kind. Necessities, including clothes, food, transport and housing, would be provided for workers, but would not be distributed in place of actual regular wages.[8]

Having developed a well-organised and theoretically based attack upon the Workers' Opposition, Vladimir Lenin undercut its claim to legitimacy by arguing that point five of the party's 1919 economic programme would indeed be implemented, but not until trade unions were ready. He, Grigory Zinoviev and Nikolai Bukharin promoted the accusation that the Workers' Opposition fostered syndicalism, that it was 'an anarcho-syndicalist, petty-bourgeois deviation'. Party leaders also associated the Workers' Opposition with anti-Bolshevik forces, warning that it would allow non-party workers to manage production. By this time, Communists often understood 'non-party' to mean former Mensheviks, SRs or anarchists. Bukharin claimed that a congress of non-party metalworkers, mainly Mensheviks and SRs, had passed a resolution 'nearly the same as' that of the Workers' Opposition. Focusing on the Workers' Opposition's call for a 'congress of producers', party leaders claimed that a producers' congress would have meant allowing non- and semi-proletarian producers (that is to say, peasants and artisans) to exert influence over economic decisions. Insinuating that Shliapnikov's years of work in French trade unions had contaminated his Marxism, Bukharin scoffed that the 'Proudhonist' term 'producer' emerged from French syndicalism. Describing the 'mass' of the working class as 'peasant-oriented', Bukharin insisted that a congress of producers could not avoid channelling peasant perspectives into management of the economy.[9]

---

8 'Tezisy rabochei oppozitsii', p. 3; RKP(b) 1963, p. 366.
9 Lenin 1960–70, vol. 32, p. 50; *Pravda*, 27 January 1921, pp. 2–3; Tsentralnyi arkhiv obshchest-

Forced onto the defensive, Shliapnikov insisted that the Workers' Opposition was not anarcho-syndicalist because it did 'not repudiate political struggle, the dictatorship of the proletariat, the party's leading role, nor the significance of the soviets as bodies of power'. Moreover, it did not advocate decentralised ownership of production, which was at the core of syndicalism, as he pointed out. He tried to explain that by a congress of producers the oppositionists essentially meant 'an all-Russian congress of trade unions'. By 'producers' they meant 'factory and plant workers, white-collar staff, and all personnel necessary for production'. Peasants could not be included, he insisted, for at that time there were no peasant unions in the RSFSR. Furthermore, Shliapnikov claimed Marxist legitimacy for the term 'producer', for it originated with Engels. Lenin deftly retorted that Engels was speaking of communist society, not a society in transition, while class war was ongoing. Zinoviev asserted that the Workers' Opposition had employed the term cynically or carelessly 'in order to give their pro-worker platform a broader appeal'. Shliapnikov maintained that he only desired an inclusive term that would apply to all those who contributed to industrial production, whether through manual or intellectual labour. Unable to refute party *intelligenty* on theoretical grounds, he could only conclude with irony that no matter what term he used, his opponents would have twisted its meaning to exaggerate his alleged departure from orthodoxy. If he had used the term 'workers', rather than 'producers', he claimed that he would have been charged with Makhaevism.[10] At his purge in 1933, Shliapnikov seemed to have accepted that he had erred in the use of 'producer', for he recalled, 'When Lenin said to me that "producer" could be understood as "commodity-producer", I was indignant, but of course I cannot deny the fairness of such a rebuke'.[11]

Russian syndicalists did not recognise the Workers' Opposition as kindred to them, merely regarding it as part of a Bolshevik family feud. A strict definition of syndicalism truly did not fit the Workers' Opposition, because it accepted the Communist Party as equal to the trade unions and because its proposals depended on a centralist, rather than federalist structure. According to Wayne Thorpe, Western-European syndicalists were 'nonpolitical socialists' who 'repudiated political activity and organisation in favour of revolutionary action channelled through the workers' primary organisations, the trade uni-

vennykh dvizhenii goroda Moskvy (TsAODM), f. 3, op. 2, d. 2, ll. 3, 10, 15, sixth Moscow gubernia party conference, 19–21 February 1921; McNeal 1974, vol. 2, p. 122; RKP(b) 1963, pp. 222–3.

10   RKP(b) 1963, pp. 359–67, 380, 526–31; Sandu 2006, pp. 50–1.

11   Rossiiskii gosudarstvennyi arkhiv sotsialno-politicheskoi istorii (RGASPI), f. 589, d. 9103, vol. 5, l. 13.

ons, themselves organised ideally on a decentralised or federalist basis'. The Workers' Opposition shared the syndicalists' optimism about the potential of workers. Yet this only marked both groups as workerist [*ouvriériste*]. This meant that they had a working-class background, were active in trade unions and advocated the direct participation of the workers in creating a socialist manner of work and life. Granted, Wayne Thorpe, whose definitions are rooted in the context of French syndicalism, acknowledges that syndicalists varied by country and region.[12] A representative assembly based on delegates elected by vocation was not unique to syndicalists. This had been a component of corporatist theory. The idea was especially popular directly after World War I, although the leftist variant died out by the late 1920s. The congress of producers advocated by the Workers' Opposition had no political role, which their programme allocated to soviets. Moreover, the type of representation proposed by the Workers' Opposition for the congress and its scope of activity was significantly different from producer congresses proposed by many corporatists and syndicalists. Nevertheless, the anarcho-syndicalist label persisted, both in Soviet historiography and in many Western studies.[13]

The programme of the Workers' Opposition had no provisions on the nationality question. Other than advocating equal pay for women workers, Worker Oppositionists paid little attention to combating entrenched misogyny. The Workers' Opposition was primarily a movement of ethnically-Russian male metalworkers, whose leaders assumed that class-based priorities overrode ethnic and gender questions and that proposals to promote workers' decision-making would resolve the problems of women and national minorities. A sense that they were oblivious to the grievances of minority nationalities may have limited their programme's appeal to non-Russians and may have even raised suspicions that they were insensitive or even hostile towards some non-Russians. For example, both the Democratic Centralist leader, Rafail, and Emelian Iaroslavsky, later a party historian and leader of anti-religious propaganda, insinuated that the Workers' Opposition employed anti-Semitic rhetorical devices to stir up working-class anger against party intellectuals. In the wake of the Kronstadt uprising, Radek and other party ideologues linked members of the Workers' Opposition to Black Hundreds and White counterrevolutionaries, but these charges were patently ludicrous.[14]

---

12   Voline 1974, p. 437; Thorpe 1989, pp. xiii, 15, 28, 165.
13   Landauer 1983, pp. 1, 69; Shukman (ed.) 1988, p. 152; Sorenson 1969, p. 94; Ruble 1981, p. 10, and Ruble 1983, p. 3.
14   Fitzpatrick 1988, pp. 599–613, citing RKP(b) 1963, pp. 105, 263, 274; and Fitzpatrick 1992, p. 28; TsAODM, f. 3, op. 2, d. 36, l. 1.

My examination of Worker-Oppositionist rhetoric did not reveal anti-Semitism. In Shliapnikov's speeches and publications he took pains to emphasise his lack of ethnic chauvinism. The Workers' Opposition in Ukraine included members who were Ukrainian and Jewish, although Russians were in the majority.[15] When a worker named I. Makh (possibly Jewish), under investigation for illegal factionalism in 1923, was asked if he ever encountered anti-Semitism among members of the Workers' Opposition, he answered that he had not and that in his opinion they were far too ideologically 'conscious' Marxists to fall victim to such prejudice.[16] Nevertheless, such powerful rumours probably helped to discredit the Workers' Opposition among non-Russian and *intelligent* party members.

Hundreds of party members voted in favour of the programme of the Workers' Opposition, especially at trade union conferences, although far more voted for the platform endorsed by Lenin, which called for a long period of education for workers before they could manage the economy. Despite support in trade unions for the Workers' Opposition, Communist party leaders controlled material resources, directed state policy, and determined the fate of unions. Trade unions had large memberships, but they did not command the resources necessary to overcome the party. Also, Lenin's political strategy was more effective than that of the Workers' Opposition in gathering delegates for the Tenth Congress of the Russian Communist Party in March 1921, which decided the trade union question. Finally, the Kronstadt rebellion and worker protests in Petrograd on the eve of the congress made the Workers' Opposition vulnerable to accusations of heresy by party leaders. The Workers' Opposition was not only defeated at the congress, but also censured, and factionalism was banned. Nevertheless, some of its members continued to argue that the party was not doing enough to promote worker initiative. They participated in the intraparty factional struggles of the 1920s and promoted industrialisation. Purged from the party in the 1930s, many perished in Stalin's terror of 1937–8.

This collection builds upon my already published biography of Workers' Opposition leader Aleksandr Shliapnikov, for it provides in English translation entire texts of documents that I analyse in the biography.[17] Although several collections of documents of the Workers' Opposition and on the trade union debates were published in Soviet Russia in the 1920s, very few of these documents have been translated into English.[18] The editors of such volumes

---

15   Allen 2019; Shliapnikov 1982, p. 27.
16   RGASPI, f. 82, op. 2, d. 179, l. 86.
17   Allen 2015.
18   Anon 1922; Rudzutak 1927; Slepkov 1926; Zinoviev 1921a; Zinoviev 1921b; Zorky (ed.) 1926.

wanted to show that the Workers' Opposition was wrong and this goal influenced their selection of documents. Scholars and interested laypeople outside of the former USSR know of the group chiefly through Aleksandra Kollontai's 1921 booklet *Rabochaia Oppozitsiia*, for which other leaders of the Workers' Opposition refused to take responsibility.[19] For that reason and more importantly because the booklet has been published in translation many times, I have chosen not to include it in this volume. Less well-known documents authored by Kollontai are included. Since the collapse of the Soviet Union and opening of the archives, more documents have come to light, which demonstrate how the views of the leaders of the Workers' Opposition evolved with the introduction of the New Economic Policy and the mixed economy that it heralded. This translated collection of the group's documents is intended to draw attention to previously unpublished or published but untranslated documents, in order to illuminate little-known aspects of the Workers' Opposition's ideas, proposals, and tactics and how these evolved during the group's existence and after it formally disbanded. Providing scholars and activists with access to the original sources in translation may allow them to reassess previously held assumptions about the group's stances, which were tainted by being filtered through the interpretations of Russian Communist Party leaders.

One might legitimately ask whether a document collection of the Workers' Opposition should include materials from the period after the group officially ceased to exist. I have chosen to do so in order to shed light on the role that memory of the Workers' Opposition played in the intraparty debates of the 1920s. Although the Workers' Opposition formally disbanded after the Tenth Party Congress in March 1921 and its programme of 1920–1 was not entirely relevant to the context in which the New Economic Policy unfolded in 1921–8, some of its former members continued to defend the role of trade unions in administering the economy, the urgency of giving workers a predominant role in party committees, and the need for greater democracy and more open debate within the party. Some former Oppositionists, but also others who had not signed the group's programme, lodged an appeal with the Executive Committee of the Communist International (ECCI) in 1922, protesting that Russian Communist Party leaders suppressed workers' voices within the party.

Further, a few members of the Workers' Opposition joined the Workers' Group of the RCP(b) in 1923–4, but Gavriil Miasnikov, the leader of the Workers'

For more recently published collections of documents on the oppositions, see Felshtinsky 1990; and Vilkova 2004.

19   Among the languages into which Kollontai's booklet has been translated are English, French, German, Spanish, Swedish, Italian, and Chinese.

Group, had not supported the proposals of the Workers' Opposition about trade union management of the economy. He favoured a greater role for soviets over the economy. Although some former members of the Workers' Opposition met privately with members of the Workers' Group in 1923, the two groups could not come to a consensus about their positions. Still another group that arose in the period of intraparty debate in 1923–4 was Workers' Truth, which seems to have had nothing in common organisationally with the Workers' Opposition. Aleksandr Bogdanov's thought influenced this group's proposals, although Bogdanov disclaimed any responsibility for the activity of Workers' Truth.[20] A Russian philosopher, revolutionary, and novelist, Bogdanov was a lifetime rival of Lenin, for he offered an anti-authoritarian vision of Bolshevism that emphasised transformation of relationships among people to eliminate the distinctions between those who command and those who execute orders. Bogdanov founded the Proletarian Culture (*Proletkult*) movement, which produced a journal, organised a proletarian university and imagined a workers' encyclopedia.[21] Iury Milonov of Samara was drawn to implementing Bogdanov's ideas, but he left the Workers' Opposition after 1921 and his name does not figure in Workers' Truth or Workers' Group. Yet party authorities conflated the three groups, presenting all of them as dangerous phenomena deserving of repression.

Documents of Workers' Group or Workers' Truth do not belong in this collection, because their programmes differed significantly from that of the Workers' Opposition. For practical reasons, the collection heavily favours documents produced by Aleksandr Shliapnikov and Sergei Medvedev, who lived together with their families in the same apartment in the last half of the 1920s and collaborated politically. This slant reflects the parameters of my earlier research and the sources to which I have had access. I have attempted to include sources that I have located from other Worker Oppositionists, in order to convey how members of the group diverged politically after it was banned, yet my choices were circumscribed by having carried out research in central, Moscow, and Kiev archives and having had access only to the party control and Soviet security police files on Shliapnikov and Medvedev, not to the files of other Worker Oppositionists.

The name of the Workers' Opposition was often conjured during the intraparty debates of the 1920s. Some former leaders of the Workers' Opposition participated in intraparty debates or attempted to do so through the 1920s, until

---

20   For more on these groups, see Alikina 2006, Avrich 1984, Bordiugov 1995, Miasnikov 1995, Pirani 2008, and Vilkova 2004.

21   White 2018.

Stalin's turn toward collectivisation and intensive industrialisation. Lev Trotsky, Stalin, and their respective supporters claimed that the Workers' Opposition united or merged with the oppositions led by Trotsky, Grigory Zinoviev, and Lev Kamenev in 1925–8. The sources translated in this collection, which attempts to be as comprehensive as possible, show that the former Workers' Opposition never merged with the other oppositions. Distribution by the United Opposition of documents authored by Aleksandr Shliapnikov and Sergei Medvedev did not signify their endorsement of the United Opposition's proposals.[22] It cannot be excluded that other former Worker Oppositionists may have supported one or another of the oppositions, which were led by Trotsky, Zinoviev, and Kamenev. On the other hand, the secondary literature is incorrect to assert that Shliapnikov and Medvedev made peace with the Stalinists in the 1920s.[23]

The documents in this book are organised chronologically into four chapters: 1) chapter one representing the background to the trade union debate; 2) chapter two focusing on the height of the trade union discussion through the Tenth Party Congress; 3) chapter three surveying the period from the ban on factions through the Eleventh Party Congress closed session to consider expulsion of leading Worker Oppositionists from the party; and 4) chapter four, which covers the years until 1930, when the Workers' Opposition no longer existed as a faction, but its leading members still took critical stances openly within the party. The year 1930 marks the point at which they had ceased any oppositional politics, but after which false charges against them accrued to a greater degree than before. The collection does not proceed to examine the false case against the former Workers' Opposition which the NKVD concocted in 1935–7 on the basis of informers' reports from the early 1930s and confessions made under interrogation by Zinoviev, Kamenev, and their supporters. This is because, first, interrogation protocols differ significantly as sources from documents generated by oppositionists when their authorship was not mediated or interpreted by the secret police. Secondly, I would not want this collection to lend credibility to the fabricated case by creating any sense of continuity.[24]

22   Thatcher 2003 questions the true cohesion of the 'United' Opposition.

23   See Daniels 1988, p. 309, and Sorenson 1969, p. 232. For more on their oppositionist stances after 1922, see Allen 2015, Chapter Nine.

24   Those accused in March–April 1935 on the case of the 'Moscow counterrevolutionary organisation – the group of the "Workers' Opposition"' were: A.G. Shliapnikov, S.P. Medvedev, G.I. Bruno, S.I. Maslennikov, M.A. Vichinsky, V.P. Demidov, M.N. Ivanov, M.F. Mikhailov, I.I. Nikolaenko, M.I. Prokopenko, A.A. Serebrennikov, V.E. Tarasov, O.Kh. Prokopenko, K.M. Tarasova, A.A. Tikhomirov, N.I. Ruzhitskaia, Z.I. Akhmedova, and M.I. Dogadina (Iakovlev 1991, p. 104).

Background to the Trade Union Debate, March 1919–Autumn 1920: the Workers' Opposition in Formation

In the early months of Soviet rule, the Bolsheviks faced a fierce fight for the survival of their regime. While organising a government and army, they also aspired to craft a socialist society. Despite their increase in membership over the course of 1917, they were still a small urban party with no control over large swathes of the collapsing empire. To cope with developing crises and multiple agendas, the Bolsheviks often occupied multiple party, state and military posts and carried out divergent assignments in various parts of the country, shifting rapidly from one work assignment or geographic area to another. The Bolsheviks struggled to establish a government of an entirely new type while their enemies mobilised against them and the economy collapsed around them. The threat of counterrevolution overshadowed the Bolsheviks' new political, social and economic experiment, making their struggle more desperate.

In this unpredictable and rapidly evolving context, the Commissariat of Labour [*Narkomtrud*], under Shliapnikov's leadership, aspired to promote workers' welfare and collaborate with trade unions to organise and regulate industry. Challenges included the ambitions of the factory committees, the workers' interpretations of the state's responsibilities towards them, the need to ensure labour discipline and the intransigent leaders of non-Bolshevik unions. Bolshevik-controlled trade unions were called upon to supply personnel to assist the party, government, soviets and other bodies in vital work. The economic power of the unions was closely tied to Bolshevik decisions on how to hold onto political power.

Trade-union staff had expertise in the regulation of wages and working conditions and could replace Provisional Government bureaucrats who had gone on strike. The metalworkers', textile workers' and leather workers' unions (all controlled by Bolsheviks) contributed the most staff to Narkomtrud and had representatives in the commissariat's board (collegium). Trade unionists also entered into other commissariats and government bodies, for example the All-Russian Council of National Economy (VSNKh). In its first several months of existence, VSNKh was run by Left Communists like Valerian Obolensky (N. Osinsky), who favoured worker administration of factories, but when the Left Communists resigned from government in March 1918, VSNKh (under

Lenin's direction) revised its stance to advocate appointed factory boards supervised by workers' organisations.[1]

In January 1918, at the First Trade Union Congress, the debate over trade-union participation in government flared up dramatically. E.H. Carr wrote that the congress 'virtually settled the principle of the subordination of the trade unions to the state, which now remained uncontested ... for nearly three years'. Menshevik delegates regarded the introduction of trade unionists into state institutions as syndicalist. Chairing the congress, Shliapnikov declared in his opening speech that the unions should be equal to other governing bodies and should assume a primary role in the organisation of industry, as well as the economy as a whole. The congress declared 'organising production' to be one of the unions' major tasks, but seems to have left unresolved the exact relationship of the unions to government economic organs.[2]

Lack of clarity in the congress decisions probably reflected dissension among Bolsheviks, some of whom sided with Mensheviks on trade-union independence from government, such as David Riazanov, who had played a leading role in organising trade unions in St. Petersburg in 1905 and after the 1917 revolutions. Other Bolsheviks saw no need for unions under a socialist regime. Questions about the role of the unions in the transition to socialism would simmer until the trade-union debate of 1920–1.

Many of the questions Narkomtrud decided on in its first months of existence were related: the wage rates agreement, workers' control over industry, the nationalisation of enterprises and worker productivity. For workers' control to succeed, and for nationalised industry not to bankrupt the state, labour productivity had to be guaranteed. The deteriorating economy and conflicting political priorities undermined Narkomtrud projects. By March 1918, the Bolsheviks had largely captured the trade unions from the Mensheviks and soon the factory committees were subordinated to the trade unions.[3]

The Bolsheviks had nothing more than a vague commitment to nationalising industry when they came to power. Banks and important industrial sectors, such as oil, coal, sugar, metallurgy and transport, would be nationalised. However, no plan existed for how to accomplish nationalisation, or how quickly. Narkomtrud played a crucial role in recommending which factories to nationalise, with the hope that the nationalisation of industry would facilit-

1   Gosudarstvennyi arkhiv Rossiiskoi Federatsii (GARF), f. 130, op. 1, d. 1, l. 1, 15 November 1917; f. 382, op. 1, d. 17, ll. 1–4, 34; Shliapnikov 1922, 'K oktiabriu', *Proletarskaia revoliutsiia*, no. 10, p. 35; Obolensky 1918, pp. 11, 14; Oppenheim 1973, p. 15.
2   VTsSPS 1918, p. 3; Smith 1983, p. 217; Carr 1950–3, vol. 2, p. 111.
3   Shkliarevsky 1993, pp. 119–23, 128–9, 160.

ate the centralised coordination of workers' control of industry, halt Russia's economic collapse and rationalise the economy to make it stronger and more productive. Nevertheless, it made mistakes, including the hasty nationalisation of enterprises that turned out to be unprofitable.[4]

The decline of industry threatened to derail plans for workers' control and the nationalisation of industry. The decline in labour productivity in the railroad industry was especially dangerous for Soviet power.[5] The government re-introduced one-man management for railways on 26 March 1918, replacing colleges (boards) composed of two or more men, including union representatives. Government and union leaders hoped to help reverse economic decline by requiring workers to guarantee that they would turn out products.[6] Guarantees of productivity had been contentious before the revolution and continued to be so. The chief question was enforcement. Some officials called for tighter discipline and harsher punishments, including dismissal, to encourage workers to work harder. Others insisted that weakness from hunger, rather than lack of discipline, was to blame for the decline in productivity. The solution, they insisted, lay in 'higher wages, greater workers' control and moral suasion'.

Some Bolsheviks controversially called for the revival of piece-rates, as an incentive for workers to work harder. Riazanov deemed piece-rates an exploitative practice 'incompatible with socialism'. Practices such as piece-rates and Taylorism, however, were compatible with the views of some prominent members of the Metalworkers' Union, who composed the 'Platform of Labour Industrialism' group in early 1918. They imagined that socialist production would not only ensure a comfortable life for workers, but would also create a culture of labour and foster innovation. They were thus open to some capitalist methods designed to encourage innovation. In the 1917 wage-rates agreement between the Metalworkers' Union and factory owners, piecework pay had not been intended to replace designated wages, but to supplement them, accounting for no more than 25 percent of pay beyond normal wages.[7] Defenders of piece rates tried to justify their revival by arguing that workers' control would ensure that exploitation would not occur.

It proved impossible, however, for workers' control to become firmly established in the context of world war and civil war. Due to German military advances and the rise of counterrevolution, the Bolsheviks had decided to move Russia's capital to Moscow and to evacuate industry from Petrograd. This

---

4   Smith 1983, pp. 220–3; GARF, f. 382, op. 1, d. 17, l. 3.
5   Bunyan 1967, p. 20.
6   GARF, f. 382, op. 1, d. 17, l. 3.
7   Smith 1983, pp. 132–3; Sh[liapnikov] 1917, p. 3.

meant dismantling and relocating many of the factories that had attracted many of the most skilled and ideologically aware workers to Petrograd.

Although the Peace of Brest-Litovsk in March 1918 extricated Russia from World War I at the price of losing one-third of its European territory, organised, armed hostilities initiated civil war in May 1918. The Czech Legion, attempting to leave Russia via the Far East in order to join forces fighting Germany on the Western front, began an uprising on the Trans-Siberian Railway. In summer, former tsarist officers formed counterrevolutionary (White) armies along the periphery of the Russian Empire and Right SRs created governments in Siberia. Allied governments introduced troops into Russian ports and directed aid to White armies, hoping that a Bolshevik collapse would bring Russia back into the war against Germany. In organising a 'Red' Army, Communists faced the dilemma of attempting to create a new type of revolutionary military force while depending on former tsarist officers for expertise, since the Bolsheviks had little experience as military commanders. Improvising policies to cope with a whirlwind of crises, they were forced to utilise inherited tsarist structures and personnel. During the Russian Civil War, millions died from violence, disease and famine. Not only was combat brutal, but both sides perpetrated atrocities upon the civilian population.[8]

Suffused with militarism during the Civil War, the coercive and centralising variant of Bolshevism achieved ascendancy. Only later called 'War Communism,' Bolshevik economic policies in 1918–21 were often inconsistent and based on contingency, but usually entailed food requisitions, rationing, forced labour and state control of the economy and transport. Effective leadership became synonymous with being 'firm', yet this result was not preordained. Bolsheviks could have chosen from divergent paths in laying the foundation of their rule. Russian Communists felt they were fighting for the survival of their regime and of the socialist dream, the unfolding and expansion of which they believed hinged on their success.

Displeased with the Bolsheviks' repressive turn, workers in Tula, Sormovo, Iaroslavl and other cities demanded the right to strike, free elections to soviets, and independent unions. Having elected responsive Menshevik and SR candidates, workers saw the Communists disperse oppositionist soviets. In August 1918, workers rose up in Izhevsk and Votkinsk, centres of the armaments

---

8 Rabinowitch 2007 examined how objective circumstances shaped Bolshevik decision-making, while Raleigh 2002 showed how the Civil War set the stage for Stalinism to prevail over Bolshevik alternatives to it. For a survey of Civil War military operations, see Mawdsley 1987, who argues that the Russian Civil War began upon the Bolshevik usurpation of power in October 1917.

industry. Petrograd workers, upset about restrictions on trade and elections, went on strike in summer 1918, for which some were locked out of their plants. Discontent also simmered in Moscow factories. Worried Communist leaders pursued an inconsistent line in early 1919 against their socialist opponents, at first allowing free speech, then rescinding it and ordering mass executions. Needing the backing of the workers as the Civil War entered a crucial stage, they feared losing that support to rival socialist parties.[9] As the Civil War raged furiously in the borderlands, Communist leaders felt compelled to apply extreme coercion.

When the Soviet state targeted workers with harsh policies, some Bolsheviks in trade unions raised alarms. The best workers had left industry, which was in collapse. 'Bureaucracy' had taken hold in government institutions, of which VSNKh now asserted its ability to manage the economy. VSNKh's responsibilities had markedly expanded since spring 1918. With about six thousand personnel (most of whom were not Communists), it oversaw more than two thousand nationalised enterprises through its constantly growing *glavki* [главки], chief committees or directorates, each of which oversaw a branch of industry. By 1920 there were 179 *glavki*, subdivided into trusts, which were most concentrated in the textiles, metals, woodworking and the food-processing industries.[10] The state and party relied on 'specialists', who usually came from the pre-revolutionary intelligentsia, to run industry and staff governmental bodies. The goal of worker management of industry appeared to be seriously endangered. A new pessimistic attitude towards the proletariat in leading government and party institutions was worrisome, for it overlay a belief in the need to control and coerce workers. Striving to raise production, establish its power and win the Civil War, the Communist Party appeared to some to have abandoned the ideal of emancipating and empowering the proletariat.

An opportunity to redirect the party's attention towards the organised workers' ability to manage the Soviet economy came at the Eighth Communist Party Congress, held in March 1919, where a new party programme was adopted. Paragraph Five of the economic section became the linchpin of the programme of the Workers' Opposition, for it promised to 'concentrate in [trade union] hands management of the entire economy'.[11] Riazanov criticised Paragraph Five for being 'syndicalist and industrialist'. Marxism, he argued, gave trade unions no

9   Brovkin 1990, pp. 350–73; Rosenberg 1985, pp. 213–39; Pirani 2008. Aves 1996 discusses
      worker unrest in 1920–2, after Shliapnikov had developed a critical stance.

10   Oppenheim 1973, pp. 5, 9–11.

11   RKP(b) 1959, p. 403.

management role in production.[12] Further passages in the programme emphasised the unions' responsibility to mobilise labour and to ensure the productivity of the workforce. Encouraged by the results of the party congress, those who would become the Workers' Opposition rallied behind Shliapnikov, who made speeches and wrote articles criticising the actual situation in industry and in the trade unions, which he believed to be in stark disparity with the party programme.

The March 1919 congress also saw the rise of the Democratic Centralists, who carried the banner of democratic reform within the context of a one-party state. Led by Timofei Sapronov and N. Osinsky (Valerian Obolensky), the Democratic Centralists wanted 'democratic centralism and proletarian democracy' to replace the bureaucratic centralisation they perceived in the party. Specifically, they urged more frequent party committee meetings and party conferences at all levels. Because the Central Committee had become large and many of its members had duties that made it impossible for them to frequently meet in Moscow, the Eighth Party Congress created the Politburo from among their number, a smaller body that could hold more manageable discussions of important policy matters.[13] The Orgburo and Secretariat, also formed from the cc, would manage mundane organisational business. In reality, there was much overlap. At the very top, the Democratic Centralists insisted that the cc should be the main decision-making body, while the Politburo and Orgburo should only implement those decisions. The party would provide political leadership to soviets and trade unions, but should not interfere in their everyday work or in their preparation of draft proposals. The Democratic Centralists desired more open discussion of party matters in the press (without violating party unity), more workers in party committees and the revival of the party cell (the smallest unit of party organisation) as a forum for discussion of vital questions.[14]

Lenin and other leaders began to view with apprehension the remarks by Democratic Centralists and by Shliapnikov and his followers about the role of unions in workers' lives.[15] Some soviet and party leaders interpreted a greater role by unions as a threat to the party's role, as well as a dangerous incursion on the powers of soviets and economic councils. Key party leaders sided with

---

12   TsAODM, f. 3, op. 2, d. 34, l. 56.
13   Lenin, Trotsky, Stalin, Kamenev and Krestinsky were full Politburo members in 1919; Bukharin, Zinoviev and Kalinin were candidate members.
14   RKP(b) 1963, pp. 656–62; Pirani 2008 pp. 55–6; Priestland 1997, no. 2, pp. 37–61.
15   RKP(b) 1963, p. 367. The text of Shliapnikov's resolution is in RKP(b) 1933, pp. 869–70, fn. 137; see also *Pravda*, 27 March 1919.

VSNKh. Zinoviev, for example, warned trade unionists not to seek national economic leadership. Perceiving their ambitions as a threat to the Communist Party, he insisted that the party was 'the highest synthesis of all forms of struggle by the working class for its emancipation from capitalist slavery'.[16] Still, party leaders tried to reconcile with Communist trade-union leaders who they perceived to be overly assertive.

The Civil War reached its critical point in the autumn of 1919, when counter-revolutionary armies were at their height, numerically and organisationally, all along the periphery of the former Russian Empire. While the effective leadership and control of railway and telegraph hubs have been cited as factors in the Communists' victory, the Whites' political weaknesses seem to have been paramount. Not only could former tsarist generals not agree on a common political programme, they could not establish effective government in the areas they conquered. By January 1920 it was clear that the Whites' chances of victory had been lost.[17]

Perceiving that a crucial turning point in the Civil War had been reached, some Communists raised criticisms of the militarist party regime. The Democratic Centralists, for example, convinced the Eighth Party Conference in December 1919 to support their proposals to strengthen the soviets as independent institutions.[18] Shliapnikov promptly offered an assertive vision of the role of trade unions that presaged many points in the later programme of the Workers' Opposition.[19] His championing of the unions distanced him from the Democratic Centralists, who promoted the role of the soviets.

Trotsky's December 1919 proposals for organising the post-Civil War economy, which he sent to the CC for discussion, were published by accident or intent in *Pravda* (edited by Bukharin). His proposed 'labour armies', which would be 'run in military fashion', caused a stir within the party and trade unions, because they implied that the state would subsume the unions. Very many prominent Communists opposed Trotsky's ideas. Shliapnikov offered his opinions when he returned to Moscow in late December to meet with other leaders of the Metalworkers' Union. Developing an argument for a greater role for the trade unions in reviving the economy, he aired his views in such a way that these ideas left the confines of Moscow and circulated in the provinces, in places

---

16   Sandu 2006, p. 47; *Pravda* (18 September 1919), pp. 2–3.
17   Mawdsley 1987, pp. 194–6, 210–11, 219; Kenez 1977, p. xiii.
18   Pirani 2008, p. 56.
19   Tsentralnyi arkhiv Federalnoi Sluzhby Bezopasnosti Rossiiskoi Federatsii (TsA FSB), R33718, d. 499061, vol. 37, ll. 205, 210–12.

including Tula, the Urals, Nizhny Novgorod, Samara, and Perm. This prompted strong criticism from the Politburo.[20]

In January 1920, Shliapnikov sent to Lenin and to VTsSPS leaders his response to Trotsky's project. His proposals grew out of his earlier statements from autumn 1919. In a more extensive analysis of the problems facing Soviet Russia than in his earlier papers, Shliapnikov argued that Trotsky's plan for the militarisation of the economy would destroy workers' initiative. Shliapnikov emphasised that only the 'organised proletariat', workers represented by their trade unions, could successfully overcome the current 'ruin in industry and transport'. His proposals for supplying workers by means of horizontal economic relationships with peasant producers ran contrary to the trend promoted by the party of the centralised direction of the economy.[21]

Trotsky's ideas on post-Civil War economic reconstruction prevailed in early 1920 because they were supported by Lenin. Simultaneously, Lenin pressed a plan for one-man management of industry to replace the collegial system, in which trade-union representatives had participated alongside bureaucrats from state economic bodies. Both leaders found support among trade-union leaders. Abram Goltsman in the Metalworkers' Union, for example, saw the potential of militarised labour to create a class of managers from the working class 'without impairing efficiency'. For him, union participation in management was not necessary as long as management was composed of individuals from the working class. Most union leaders, however, were aligned against Trotsky and many also were alarmed by Lenin's plan for one-man management. Shliapnikov's confidante Alexandra Kollontai was a witness to this alarm and wrote about it in her diary.

Union leaders opposed to Trotsky were divided. Tomsky favoured the collegial management of industry but thought it premature to give workers control over production. His authority as VTsSPS chair and his moderate position won over many trade-union leaders. Tomsky argued that the typical worker could not handle the 'extraordinary nervous strain' accompanying administrative duties that would wear out even an *intelligent*. He claimed that workers were 'exhausted, fed up with War Communism'.[22] Less willing to challenge party leaders than Shliapnikov, Tomsky also seemed more pessimistic than he about the workers' potential. Standing behind Tomsky, the VTsSPS communist faction accepted his moderate proposals to continue collective management but

20   *Pravda* (17 December 1919): p. 1; Sorenson 1969, p. 94; RGASPI, f. 2, op. 1, d. 12106, l. 1; Sandu
       2006, pp. 52–61; RKP(b) 1960, pp. 591–2.
21   RGASPI, f. 2, op. 1, d. 12562, ll. 1–5; GARF, f. 5451, op. 42, d. 6, ll. 17–19; Aves 1996, p. 9.
22   RKP(b) 1972, pp. 179–81; Sorenson 1969, pp. 95, 97.

to accept one-man management in certain cases. Despite their caution and tact towards party leaders, VTsSPS leaders soon found that the CC insisted on asserting its leadership over the unions. Among its measures was sending CC members Nikolai Bukharin and Karl Radek to work in VTsSPS.[23]

Nevertheless, discord continued between party and trade-union leaders. While party leaders such as Zinoviev asserted that the party was superior to all other worker organisations and that in time the state would take over trade unions [огосударствление], Tomsky called for party leaders to trust trade unions and exercise party authority only through communist factions of unions. He supported the subordination of trade-union representatives in economic bodies to staff employed in the economic councils called *sovnarkhozes* [совнархозы], but called for a delineation of duties between unions and *sovnarkhozes*. Refusing to pipe down, Shliapnikov insisted that trade-union representatives in economic institutions should be responsible to the unions that sent them there and boldly proposed that unions elect VSNKh, with CC confirmation.[24]

Party leaders endeavoured to remove Shliapnikov from the scene during the discussion of Trotsky's plans for labour armies and one-man management. In March 1920, he was sent to Western Europe on a trade-union mission, from which he returned well after the Ninth Party Congress. Yet his supporters continued to campaign in his absence. Many of Shliapnikov's closest allies were from his pre-revolutionary circle of close comrades, with many years of experience organising party cells and trade unions and of Civil War service. Sergei Medvedev and Iury Lutovinov were Metalworkers' Union leaders and Lutovinov worked in VTsSPS. Lutovinov had also been a leader of the Communist Party of Ukraine. Ivan Kutuzov was chair of the Moscow Textileworkers' Union. Both Medvedev and Aleksei Kiselev, the chair of the Miners' Union, had served on the VSNKh Presidium.[25]

---

23 RGASPI, f. 95, op. 1, d. 5, l. 1, 23 January 1920; l. 89, 21 January 1920 VTsSPS communist faction bureau meeting; f. 17, op. 2, d. 27, l. 1; op. 3, d. 66, ll. 2–3; op. 2, d. 28, 6 February 1920; d. 30.

24 Sandu 2006, pp. 50–1, on a 7 March meeting of trade-union leaders, CC members and Moscow party officials.

25 Gambarov et al. (eds.) 1989, vol. 1, pp. 191–4, 253–5, 346; RGASPI, f. 589, op. 3, d. 9102, ll. 173–88; f. 2, op. 1, d. 8, l. 90, 7 January 1919. Kollontai identified the leaders of the Workers' Opposition as Lutovinov, Shliapnikov, Medvedev and two others whom she named only by initials ('T' and 'M'), all former workers (RGASPI, f. 134, op. 3, d. 34, l. 5, 23 February 1920 diary entry). 'T' was probably the artillery industry leader Alexander Tolokontsev. Lutovinov identified himself to Lenin as a founder of the Workers' Opposition (Lenin 1960–70, vol. 45, pp. 160–5).

At party and union meetings in March, these men echoed Shliapnikov's call for a separation of powers between the unions (economic power) and the party and soviets (political power). Lev Kamenev chided them for aiming to limit the party's power. CC members confronted them at a VTsSPS meeting scheduled to discuss one-man management versus the collegial management of industry. Although Tomsky and his supporters claimed to represent mainstream trade-union opinion, Krestinsky and Radek from the CC chose to attack Shliapnikov's views, which they insisted carried more weight among trade unionists. Kiselev, Kutuzov, and Medvedev rallied to defend Shliapnikov's positions as their own. The responses of CC members were extreme and scathing. Having the last word, Bukharin criticised Shliapnikov's proposals to hand over the management of the economy to the trade unions as heretically non-Marxist, arguing that there would be no trade unions in communist society.[26]

Lutovinov diverged from his fellow oppositionists and moved closer to Tomsky. Conceding that trade unions could not take control of production as it was then organised, he listed preconditions that included raising the masses' cultural level, introducing discipline into factories and unions, enforcing the wage rates agreement and workers' inspection. Nevertheless, he envisioned greater worker participation not only in the management of factory production but in all aspects of life in the Soviet republic. Finally deciding in favour of presenting a united front by union leaders at the party congress, Lutovinov praised Tomsky's position as one around which most trade unionists could rally. Tomsky discouraged anyone from comparing his and the VTsSPS position with that of Shliapnikov, which he implied had caused party leaders to suspect 'that trade unionists want to create a party within the party'. Riazanov also blamed Shliapnikov's 'sharp criticism' of the CC for having 'exacerbated' the misunderstanding between the party and the unions. On the eve of the Ninth Party Congress, VTsSPS and the Moscow city trade-union council expressed nearly unanimous support for Tomsky's position over that of Shliapnikov.[27]

Despite Lutovinov's vacillations (he supported the separation of functions, but not of power, between party, unions, and soviets), he presented Shliapnikov's proposals to the Ninth Party Congress, which met 29 March–5 April 1920 in Moscow. In these proposals, Shliapnikov addressed the relationship between the party, soviets and trade unions. Acknowledging the party's leading role in both economics and politics, Shliapnikov stressed that this leading role should not be exclusive, for unions and soviets also had important roles to play. Blam-

26   Sandu 2006, p. 52; GARF, f. 5451, op. 42, d. 3, ll. 7, 169, 171–4, 178, 205, 213–215.

27   GARF, f. 5451, op. 42, d. 3, ll. 116–17, 123–4, 142, 178; RGASPI, f. 95, op. 1, d. 5, l. 15.

ing the cc for meddling in the work of the unions and the soviets, and in his opinion thereby exceeding the responsibilities assigned to it in the party programme, he complained that the cc made policy towards workers without even consulting VTsSPS. Declaring the cc to be incompetent, he called for the cc to be 'workerised', which according to his interpretation would have meant a cc composed largely of union leaders.[28] Shliapnikov's call for a wholesale turnover in cc membership was a declaration of war, but one that resounded with those Communists who favoured a greater role for workers in leading party bodies.[29]

Refusing to engage Shliapnikov's criticisms, Bukharin, who gave the main report on trade unions at the congress, simply denounced the proposals as 'rot'. Lenin encouraged this abusive style of party discourse, which would only turn nastier. In effect, the response of the party congress to Shliapnikov's proposals was its decision to revise the section on unions in the party programme adopted at the Eighth Party Congress. Dropping the suggestion for the unions to manage the entire economy, the new programme specified that unions could organise but not manage production and would educate workers. Moreover, the communist factions of the local union committees would be subordinated to local party committees rather than to the communist factions of their unions' central committees, as the communist faction of VTsSPS would be subordinated to the cc. Finally, the congress resolved to flood unions with new staff composed of the 'most reliable and hardiest Communists', decisively rejecting Shliapnikov's wish that the most reliable worker Communists should inundate leading party and state organs.[30]

Lured by a strategic offer of compromise from Lenin, trade-union critics quickly retreated from their support for the collegial management of industry. The compromise allowed trade unionists to have a role in management either as assistants to a specialist director or as directors with specialist assistants. Tomsky did little to defend his own proposals. Even Lutovinov, while expressing disagreement with the party's policy, promised to support its implementation. Union leaders appeared to be swayed by assurances that one-man management would not exclude workers from management; rather, it would allow the limited number of qualified worker administrators to be assigned to a large number of factories, rather than congregate in collegia at a few factories.[31] Effectively, they traded balance of powers for upward personal mobility.

---

28   GARF, f. 5451, op. 42, d. 6, 1920, ll. 17–21.
29   RKP(b) 1960, p. 235; GARF, f. 5451, op. 42, d. 6, 1920, ll. 17–21.
30   Naumov 1991, p. 28; KPSS SSSR 1954, pp. 490–4; Schapiro 1956, p. 233.
31   KPSS SSSR 1954, pp. 483–4; Aves 1996, p. 27; Schapiro 1956, pp. 231–2.

After March 1920, and until the Tenth Party Congress, the CC consisted of: Andreev, Sergeev (Artem), Bukharin, Dzerzhinsky, Kalinin, Kamenev, Krestinsky, Lenin, Preobrazhensky, Radek, Rakovsky, Rudzutak, Rykov, Serebriakov, Smirnov, Stalin, Tomsky, Trotsky and Zinoviev. Petrovsky, Iaroslavsky, Muranov, Miliutin, Stuchka, Nogin, Gusev, Piatnitsky, Beloborodov, Zalutsky, Molotov and Smilga were candidate members. The increasingly important CC Secretariat was headed by Krestinsky, Serebriakov and Preobrazhensky, who also were Orgburo members.[32] VTsSPS was offered several places on the CC elected at the Ninth Party Congress. These were filled by Tomsky (who proved his loyalty at the congress), Rudzutak (a government man) and Andreev (aligned with Trotsky). An alternative list proposed by the Metalworkers' Union, which omitted Tomsky, was rejected. Lutovinov was nominated separately, but not confirmed by the CC. Subsequently, the CC changed the leadership of various trade unions, even subjecting the leadership of the Miners' Union to a wholesale reorganisation. In a move against Shliapnikov and an attempt to split his supporters, Lutovinov and Andreev were nominated as joint chairs of the Metalworkers' Union. Rejecting the nominations, the Metalworkers' Union retained Shliapnikov as chair. Finally, the CC sent several high-ranking members (Bukharin, Radek, Stalin and Kamenev) to guide the Third Congress of Trade Unions. Joined by Tomsky, Andreev and Rykov, they edited resolutions of both the communist faction and the congress and confirmed VTsSPS leaders.[33] The decisions of the Ninth Party Congress on trade unions thus prepared the way for the defeat of, and ban on, the Workers' Opposition that would take place at the Tenth Party Congress in 1921.

Shliapnikov's determined campaign to promote the role of workers' initiative was, in his opinion and that of his supporters, the only acceptable means for redressing the dire economic straits in Russia towards the end of the Civil War. They believed that rival programmes would necessitate abandoning the emancipatory goals of the revolution. Trotsky disagreed. Having identified the transport crisis as the main reason for food and fuel shortages and inadequate supply of the army, he advocated militarisation and compulsion to make railways work efficiently and smoothly. The CC's creation of Tsektran, which merged the unions of railway workers and water-transport workers, in late August 1920, was his initiative. As Tsektran chair, he planned to use it to implement his ideas on labour conscription. He chose to amalgamate the railway and water-transport unions and appoint their leadership because he did not trust elected

---

32   Schapiro 1956, pp. 262–4.
33   RGASPI, f. 17, op. 2, d. 29, ll. 1, 3; d. 30; f. 95, op. 1, d. 5, l. 144.

union leaders to use compulsion against workers. The actual implementation of the Tsektran merger began only in October 1920, due to opposition from high-ranking members of the water-transport union.[34] As the most controversial example of CC interference in union matters at this time, his measure inflamed discussion over the role of the trade unions in the post-Civil War economy. Shliapnikov and other union leaders feared the precedent Tsektran set for amalgamating unions, absorbing them into a centralised state administration and appointing leaders willing to follow CC orders. They suspected that Trotsky was preparing to extend militarisation of transport to all industry.

Until the Ninth Party Conference, which took place in Moscow on 22–5 September 1920, Trotsky and his supporters had great influence within the CC. Due in part to increasing worry in the party about conflicts between party leaders and activists, however, his influence began to wane on the eve of the conference. (In June 1920, CC secretary, Evgeny Preobrazhensky, warned of the danger posed by conflicts between the 'rank and file' [низы] and the 'higher-ups' [верхи] in the party and in early September the CC issued a circular on the topic.) Thus the conference presidium proposed by the CC included Lenin, Zinoviev, Tomsky and Bukharin, but neither Trotsky nor any of his more adamant defenders. Trotsky's supporters managed to add him and Radek to the presidium.[35] The focus of the conference was Russia's military situation, especially the Red Army's defeat in Poland, but intense debate ensued over the state of 'democracy' within the party and over Trotsky's plans for the militarisation of the economy.

An important watershed in the debate over the role of the trade unions and over party democracy, the Ninth Party Conference featured fierce exchanges between leaders of the Workers' Opposition and higher party leaders. Zinoviev undercut many of the opposition's demands by calling for greater criticism of party decisions, for more tolerance towards differing opinions among party members and for more frequently convened assemblies of party members. Due to growing concern over discord between party leaders and the rank-and-file, he and some other party leaders saw a need to tone down the harsh impression created by the policies Trotsky initiated and to extend a hand towards dissenters.[36]

Lutovinov was the main speaker for the Workers' Opposition. Having adopted a more radical position since the Ninth Party Congress in March, he delivered a speech so replete with criticism of party leaders that it was never

34 Bunyan 1967, pp. 188–9; Sorenson 1969, p. 107; Rosenberg 1989, pp. 349–73.
35 RKP(b) 1972, p. 3; Sandu 2006, p. 79.
36 RGASPI, f. 95, op. 1, d. 10, l. 202; Sandu 2006, pp. 71–2; Pirani 2008.

published in its entirety. Calling for 'radical treatment' for 'all the cancers [язвы] eating away the body of our party', his demands for reform included: 1) restoring leadership of the party to the CC rather than (as he implied) leaving it to the Politburo, 2) allowing soviets, party committees and trade unions to work without interference from higher party bodies and 3) ending the practice of appointments of party and soviet officials by central bodies.[37] Perhaps he was angered by the failure of the CC elected at the last congress to redress grievances.

In unpublished parts of his speech, Lutovinov insisted that the party should stop dispersing elected bodies and should step up efforts to include workers in party committees, soviets and trade unions. Even the Politburo and CC should hold a worker majority. Central officials who behaved in an authoritarian way would be sent to the provinces and replaced by 'fresh forces from the local level'. Workers, under party leadership, should discuss all policy matters. He warned that if such measures were not taken, workers would rise up against the party. Rumours arose that he advocated 'a third proletarian revolution'.[38] Indeed, Evgeny Preobrazhensky, a CC secretary and Trotsky supporter who responded to Lutovinov's speech, perceived a veiled threat in his words. From his perspective, the CC had insufficient staff to exert leadership, much less interfere in the work of other bodies.[39] Lutovinov's position, and the reaction to it, harkened back to the controversy over Shliapnikov's 1919 proclamations.

Others echoed Lutovinov's criticisms. Questioning Zinoviev's sincerity, Medvedev, Kutuzov and Kollontai demanded guarantees that workers would take up at least half of the places on regional party committees and that those who criticised would not be transferred from their positions. Their complaints provoked the wrath of Lenin, who retorted that in times of military danger there could be no question of discussion.[40] Nevertheless, the CC consensus of supporting Trotsky's policy on the militarisation of industry was breaking down. Shliapnikov and other dissenters thus had the opportunity to contribute towards building a new consensus.

In autumn 1920, the major factions in the debate over the role of the trade unions took formation in broad outlines; there were supporters of Lenin's position, those who stood behind Trotsky's proposals and the Workers' Opposition, led by Shliapnikov. Both Trotsky and Lenin were in the CC, which split in support for their platforms, while the Workers' Opposition had no CC pres-

37   Zorky 1926, p. 16; RKP(b) 1972, pp. 63–4.
38   RGASPI, f. 17, op. 71, d. 79, ll. 1–2.
39   RKP(b) 1972, pp. 172–3.
40   RKP(b) 1972, pp. 175–6, 186–90.

ence. Lines between Trotsky's supporters and his opponents in the CC were drawn more definitively in early November 1920. At the 8–9 November CC plenums, Lenin and Trotsky submitted separate proposals on the role of the trade unions. Sharp debate followed. While Trotsky wanted to subsume the trade unions into the state, Lenin's more moderate proposal opposed labour armies and allowed trade unions to be organisationally separate from the state, while strictly limiting their role to educating and preparing workers for their role in a socialist society. In attendance were Lenin, Trotsky, Zinoviev, Kalinin, Tomsky, Krestinsky, Serebriakov, Bukharin, Artem, Preobrazhensky, Dzerzhinsky, Andreev, Kamenev, Rudzutak, Rykov and Radek. In the absence of several key Trotsky supporters, Lenin won a narrow CC majority. Eight voted for Lenin's proposals, while seven voted for Trotsky's. Only four of Trotsky's supporters came out against Lenin's theses; the rest abstained. The CC created a commission composed of Lenin, Trotsky, Zinoviev, Bukharin and Tomsky to rework Lenin's proposals.[41] Given the close vote, some CC members called for a public discussion, but the majority sought consensus. Kamenev, Tomsky, Bukharin, Serebriakov, Sergeev, Dzerzhinsky, Radek, Krestinsky, Rykov and Zinoviev called for renewed discussion in the hope of creating a consensus. These 10 members, who included some supporters of Trotsky, were not identical with the 'Ten' who supported Lenin's platform on unions.[42]

Several other viewpoints in the CC gradually merged with Lenin's or Trotsky's position. Bukharin, for example, called for trade unions both to educate workers and to be gradually absorbed as an equal partner into the state system for administering industry, but by January 1921, he and Trotsky had agreed on common proposals. Tomsky and Rudzutak, representing the majority of the VTsSPS Presidium, favoured a greater role for the unions in economic management than under Lenin's plan, but rejected forceful subordination to state organs, proposed by Trotsky. They accepted the Party CC's sole right to make policy regarding workers, but advocated that it consider the opinions of the trade-union leaders. Representing VSNKh, Rykov favoured Nogin's proposal to eliminate all trade-union activities in areas already supervised by the state (such as in culture, wage rates, education and finances). It is hard to imagine that any role would have remained for unions under such a plan. By late January, VTsSPS and VSNKh leaders had aligned themselves with Lenin. This faction, forming a slight majority in the CC, was then referred to as the 'Ten' (Lenin, Zinoviev, Stalin, Tomsky, Rudzutak, Artem, Kalinin, Kamenev, Petrovsky and Rykov).[43]

---

41   RGASPI, f. 17, op. 2, d. 37.
42   RGASPI, f. 17, op. 2, d. 38.
43   Cohen 1980, pp. 103–5; Lenin 1960–70, vol. 32, p. 47; GARF, f. 5451, op. 42, d. 3, l. 43.

The Ten called for trade unions to educate workers in communism and mobilise labour for raising the level of production, but they deemed the absorption of
the trade unions into the state to be unwise, for it would interfere with their task
of educating workers. The remaining eight minority CC members supported
Trotsky's proposals (Trotsky, Krestinsky, Preobrazhensky, Serebriakov, Andreev,
Dzerzhinsky, Bukharin and Rakovsky).[44] Because representatives of absorbed
factions gave minority papers at debates on the role of trade unions, Medvedev
argued that the Ten attempted to sow confusion and create the impression that
only they represented stability.[45] The Workers' Opposition, which continued to
stand on its own platform, suffered from appearing to be one of many minor
platforms, rather than as the major alternative to Trotsky and the Ten.

The communist faction of the Fifth All-Russian Conference of Trade Unions (2–9 November 1920) offered a major forum for a discussion of the role of
the trade unions. Many trade-union leaders attacked Trotsky's proposals. In his
first major speech on behalf of the Workers' Opposition since returning to Russia from abroad, Shliapnikov spiritedly defended the Workers' Opposition and
skewered his rivals. Extolling workers for their heroism, he concluded that in
order to become true managers of production, trade unions had to seize control
of the Communist Party.[46]

In the wake of so much criticism within the closed communist faction, Trotsky's supporters in Tsektran brazenly (and atypically) aired his views to nonparty delegates and characterised his critics' speeches as 'demagogic'. Communist Party members usually conducted serious debate only within the communist faction, but did not air their disagreements in open forums, where
reports on benign topics were given. Therefore, Shliapnikov, Tomsky and others appealed to the CC to prosecute (in a party court) those who had violated
discipline. Relations between Trotsky's trade-unionist supporters on the one
hand, and those who supported Tomsky and Shliapnikov on the other, became
so contentious that the Party CC invited trade-union leaders into the commission it had already established to iron out differences among CC members on
the trade-union issue. Party leaders often used semi-formal commissions to
resolve conflict outside full CC sessions. Original members of the commission
were Zinoviev (chair), Tomsky, Trotsky, Rudzutak and Rykov, while Shliapnikov,
Lutovinov, Andreev and Lozovsky were added as union representatives.[47]

---

44   RGASPI, f. 17, op. 2, d. 56, l. 5. Piatakov, Larin, Sokolnikov, Iakovleva, and Goltsman (none
     of whom belonged to the CC) also signed (Daniels 1988, pp. 132–4).
45   TsAODM, f. 3, op. 2, d. 34, l. 54.
46   RGASPI, f. 95, op. 1, d. 10, ll. 1–44, ll. 113–17, 202–4.
47   RGASPI, f. 5, op. 2, d. 334, l. 5; RGASPI, f. 17, op. 2, d. 37; RGASPI, f. 95, op. 1, d. 10, ll. 145–6;
     RGASPI, f. 17, op. 2, d. 41; Pravda (13 November 1920), p. 2.

The trade-union commission quickly unravelled. First, Trotsky resigned before it even started to meet, as he had realised that its composition put him at a disadvantage. With Trotsky absent, the commission quickly took stances diametrically opposed to his. Shliapnikov seems to have hoped that the Workers' Opposition would be included in a consensus, but his distrust of Tomsky and frictions between him and Lutovinov undermined any such possibility. When Shliapnikov's suggestions (in his absence) were not incorporated in the commission's draft proposals, he resigned. Although Lutovinov remained, the commission's final proposals, formulated by a subcommission composed entirely of Lenin's supporters (Zinoviev, Lozovsky, Tomsky, Tsyperovich, Stalin and Kamenev), reflected only the point of view of the Ten. The final proposals were published under the initial 'Iu', creating the impression that Iury Lutovinov was responsible for the final formulation.[48] The surprised Lutovinov, frustrated by the commission's lack of practical results and by the way in which he had been manipulated, announced his intention to leave his leadership posts to resume factory work, but VTsSPS forbade him to do so. Trotsky agreed with Lutovinov that Lenin had employed the commission to bolster support for the platform of the Ten. Zinoviev, Tomsky, Rudzutak and Lozovsky signed the final proposals, but Andreev, Shliapnikov, Lutovinov, Rykov and Trotsky did not. Victor Serge, who saw Shliapnikov around this time, recalled him as 'a very bitter man'.[49] If Shliapnikov felt he had been manipulated, this would explain his resentment and anger. It remained for the Workers' Opposition to wage a campaign for support of its platform during elections to the upcoming Tenth Party Congress. But there was little time.

The Metalworkers' Union was potentially a powerful instrument for the advocacy and implementation of the Workers' Opposition's programme. It was led by a central committee, which elected a presidium and a chair (Shliapnikov). In addition, the union's central committee included a communist faction, which was led by a bureau. Shliapnikov chaired the bureau, which actually guided the union. Most members of the bureau belonged to the Workers' Opposition, but the Workers' Opposition had only a slight majority in the Metalworkers' Union's central committee (the minority was split between supporters of Trotsky and Lenin). After 38 leaders of trade unions and industry endorsed the proposals of the Workers' Opposition on 18 December, the bureau of the Metalworkers' Union central committee prepared a bulletin to mobil-

48   RKP(b) 1963, p. 379; Trotsky 1921, pp. 15–21; RGASPI, f. 5, op. 2, d. 288; f. 95, op. 1, d. 23, ll. 4–13; GARF, f. 5451, op. 42, d. 3, ll. 19–20, 25, 41–4.
49   RGASPI, f. 95, op. 1, d. 23, ll. 1, 4, 8; d. 5, l. 172; TsAODM, f. 3, op. 2, d. 34, l. 33; Serge 2002, p. 123.

ise support for these proposals among the union's regional branches. Of the five bureau members, four (Shliapnikov, Vladimirov, Lavrentev and Skliznev) belonged to the Workers' Opposition. Gurevich, a supporter of Trotsky, cast the lone vote against the dissemination of the circular and contested the bureau's decision to appeal to regional committees for support, without first seeking agreement within the union's central committee.[50]

In the bulletin, the bureau emphasised that communist workers should define the role the party would take within the state and urged that metalworkers participate more actively in party affairs, especially in the selection of delegates to the Tenth Party Congress. Scoffing at the platforms of Trotsky and the Ten on the role of trade unions, the bureau endorsed the platform of the Workers' Opposition as that closest in spirit to the section on the role of trade unions in the party programme adopted at the Eighth Party Congress. Carrying out economic policy through production unions, the bureau declared, would eliminate bureaucracy and draw workers back into production. Moreover, putting unions in charge of VSNKh would eliminate confusion sometimes caused by contradictory orders issued by the unions and by state economic bodies. To achieve acceptance of these goals, the bureau urged regional unions to elect supporters of the Workers' Opposition to the party congress.[51]

Nevertheless, the union was not prepared to carry out the bureau's assertive line, for at the end of 1920 trade unionists were still struggling for the return of staff that had been diverted to other work during the Civil War.[52] Considering that only a few months remained before the party congress, the bureau had hardly given its local committees time to do the type of work that would win them political domination of local party organisations. The fact that the Metalworkers' Union was only beginning to systematically attempt to muscle its way into local party leadership roles did not bode well for the chances of the Workers' Opposition in the coming struggle over the trade-union question.

---

50   RGASPI, f. 99, op. 1, d. 11, l. 20.
51   GARF, f. 5469, op. 17, d. 6, ll. 1–2.
52   RGASPI, f. 95, op. 1, d. 5, l. 176.

1   Economic Section of RCP(b) Programme, Point 5, Adopted at the
     Eighth Congress of the RCP(b), March 1919[53]

The organisational apparatus of socialised industry should lean for support
first and foremost on trade unions [*профессиональные союзы*]. They should
increasingly be freed of the narrow parochialism of guilds and be transformed
into large-scale production unions [*производственные объединения*], envel-
oping the majority, and gradually all labourers of each branch of production.

By Soviet law and established practice, trade unions already participate in all
local and central bodies that manage industry. Trade unions should further concentrate in their hands all management of the economy, as a single economic
unit. In this way they will secure an indissoluble link between central state
management, the economy and the labouring masses. Trade unions should to
the greatest extent possible attract the masses into directing the economy. The
participation of trade unions and through them the masses in directing the
economy is the chief means for struggle against bureaucratisation of Soviet
power's economic system. Moreover, it will make it possible to have actual popular control over the results of production.

2   A.G. Shliapnikov, 'Specialists'[54]

     Il n'est pas de sauveurs suprêmes,
     Ni Dieu, ni César, ni tribun,
     Producteurs sauvons-nous nous-mêmes!
          L'Internationale, Eugène Pottier, 1871

∴

---

53   RKP(b) 1959, p. 403. This point of the party programme, which was adopted at the Eighth
      Party Congress, served as the linchpin of the proposals of the Workers' Opposition.

54   'O spetsialistakh', *Pravda* (27 March 1919): 1. Shliapnikov, who had served as the first Com-
      missar of Labour under the Bolshevik regime, had recently returned to Moscow from
      serving in a military post in the Russian Civil War (he chaired the Revolutionary Milit-
      ary Council of the Caspian-Caucasian front, based in Astrakhan). Resuming his duties as
      chair of the All-Russian Metalworkers' Union, he renewed his focus on economic issues
      confronting the Soviet state and its main constituency of urban workers.

Attracting specialists is now one of our slogans of economic policy. Since its very inception, Soviet power collided with what was a typically hostile attitude from both educated and untrained[55] specialists, who initiated a most desperate struggle against it. Soviet power at its beginning acted in the same way that factory proletarians usually behaved during spontaneous[56] struggle against capital – that is to say, it hauled out all specialists on a wheelbarrow.

Now we're already moving away from that period when there was indiscriminate denial of the need to enlist specialists in our organising effort, but instead an extremely dangerous slogan – 'all to the specialists' – is replacing it. Already in many places speculation has begun upon the catchword 'specialists'. Such an effort to save the country, to redeem the difficult situation by means of specialists shows how firmly the foundations of bureaucratic thinking have gained a foothold among our soviet personnel. Office workers divorced from reality, obviously, propose that economic ruin intensified due to individuals' incompetent and stupid management. Thinking like bureaucrats, they want to redeem sins by replacing some people with others. The entire economic life of Soviet Russia suffers not so much from the personal unsuitability of certain personnel, as from the lack of a refashioned unified system. You won't get anything done by replacing some people with others. Our work is characterised by highly frivolous disdain toward the most elementary work systems, plans and procedures. And so, instead of struggling against this lack of systematisation by means of introducing a system, they've decided to change out people.

Along with the absence of systematic planning, at every step one can see irresponsibility. People lightheartedly take on responsible work, bulldoze ahead, and create spoilage, without taking any responsibility. It is necessary to stop this by deservedly punishing any who cannot carry out the work they've assumed.

Along with this, jovial carelessness flourishes. Improvident people very often head up institutions. Only criminal negligence and shortsightedness can explain those numerous 'catastrophes' in the area of supply, when towns and factories 'suddenly' are left without fuel, raw materials and so forth. Here the punitive hand of proletarian justice should render its effect. By this means it will succeed in significantly decreasing the growing careerism of talentless people and occasional adventurers.

Now we will investigate how much foundation there is for great expectations that many senior personnel place on specialists. What is a specialist in the cap-

---

55   Shliapnikov uses the adjective plural неучёные; the noun неуч is a colloquialism translating as 'ignoramus'.

56   Lars Lih prefers the translation 'elemental' rather than 'spontaneous' for the Russian word стихийный.

italist economy? This is usually a person brought up in an authoritarian system, intended for a certain workplace apparatus with clearly prescribed interrelations. From his first steps in our work he at once is deprived of the possibility to have such an apparatus and the interrelations with which he feels intimate. Brought up in the spirit of the past, in a system of capitalist relations, this specialist cannot bring into existing conditions a hundredth of the share of that usefulness, which he brought into capitalist relations.

In practically dozens of the largest enterprises of France, England, Germany, Belgium and America, I learned about the role of 'specialists'. Everywhere in the more organised enterprises there was no trace of 'specialists' in the sense of 'one who can do everything'. Everywhere, in labour as in management, they implemented a system of division of labour into the simplest operations. Even in such an apparently individualised specialty as work on inventions – even that was based on the division of labour. Dozens and hundreds of narrow specialties work on technical discoveries, on improvement, and so forth. Management of enterprises and trusts is extraordinarily simplified, thanks to a system of interrelations that has been decades in the making. Reception of orders, supply with raw materials, fuel, and financing are automated. Over everything reigns a centralised system of division of labour. We don't even have a trace of this system. In Europe as in America it is obvious that workers are brought into organisation of production through supervision, as masters, directors and so forth, over whole branches. Such is the practice.

Our management of affairs demands tremendous energy in the definition of extraordinary obstacles and unusual initiative in all areas. Only deeply devoted people confident of triumph and in the historical necessity of what we are creating can satisfy these demands. Do we have many of these people of conviction, not just paid-for specialists? The attraction of specialists, of so called technical forces and their actual work in Soviet institutions and in nationalised enterprises began from the first months of Soviet power. But these specialists prefer to work in offices and institutions and very reluctantly become active organisers. It is quite understandable why they do not believe in the durability and long-lasting nature of our work, and chiefly are far from being in agreement with its necessity and expediency. Now our country suffers not so much from lack of plans, construction and such technical considerations, as from insufficient organisers. Can appointed specialists be such organisers? Contemporary economic construction demands not only technical knowledge, but most of all confidence. This means confidence in the necessity and inevitability of a socialist order and confident direction of all energy to secure its success. Current specialists do not have this. It can't be a secret for anyone that our specialists at the current moment everywhere and in everything perceive the sign of the imminent fall of the existing order. They unequivocally point out the agony of our industry and the complete chaos reigning in our country. From this, they come to a funereal conclusion about our undertakings. Surely, these people can only be gravediggers, but not creators of a new order.

At the beginning of the October Revolution we all strove toward community with the working mass and actually leaned for support on its initiative. A year and a half ago, work assignments tore us away and separated us and our institutions from the direct activism of the masses. Only such isolation can explain the appearance of similar ideas of salvation through 'specialists'. The need for specialists is told of in the old proverb that nothing will come of it when the shoemaker will bake the pies, and the baker will stitch boots. But there is no foundation for drawing from this the conclusion that construction of the proletarian order can be assigned to specialists who have emerged from another world.

The building of socialism can succeed to the extent that it depends on the initiative of the working masses. Any effort to find a way out without initiative and without direct participation of the proletarian masses in creating the new – is idle intellectual chatter. Such a formulation of the matter speaks of distrust toward the masses and is a sign of one's own impotence. In our work we should rely upon the proletarian mass in minor matters as well as major ones. Since the first days of the October revolution, various worker organisations always utilised technical forces, meaning so-called specialists. The technical forces themselves, simply based on the natural need to exist, went under one or another pretext into institutions, unions and other organisations, which were in one way or another occupied with building an organisation. Their knowledge hasn't been and won't be lost. If the task of the slogan now proposed is to attract them not only as technical personnel, but to give them unlimited rights, then in this, it goes without speaking, is hidden a great danger, a danger of distrust coming from the workers themselves and the rural masses. When they will see that their organisations have been shoved aside and the reins of government have been entrusted to the delicate hands of bureaucratised specialists, undoubtedly, this will still further intensify the masses' dissatisfaction. Instead of relief from the existing situation, matters will get worse. We need to set up our creative work, so that the proletarian would feel and recognise that such a great matter as creation of a socialist structure depends on the nut, bolt or nail, which he has created.

Each hungry worker needs to understand that each *arshin*[57] of woven textile, each *arshin* of wood, pound of metal is necessary for receiving bread, meat and

---

57   *Arshin* [аршин] = Russian measure equivalent to 28 inches or 71 cm. Abandoned when the USSR adopted the metric system in 1924.

other food supplies. The everyday life of the leading masses needs to be closely connected to the work of our institutions, our organisations.

We should conquer all difficulties only through the masses and together with them. All other paths lead to bankruptcy.

3   A.G. Shliapnikov, 'Wages and Labour Productivity'[58]

Steady growth in the cost of living and food supply scarcities deeply agitate the proletarian masses, who direct all their attention to the regulation of wages. Dissatisfaction with the existing wage rates agreements delays the organisational work of factory, plant and other workers' committees. It also affects the activity of leading centres of the trade union movement.

At the last plenum of the All-Russian Central Council of Trade Unions (VTsSPS), representatives of various all-Russian unions heatedly criticised the current wage rates policy. However, a significant share of criticism by many comrades, especially representatives of the trade and industry office workers, was confined to parochial [цеховой] dissatisfaction with the rates of one or another group of personnel. Smaller unions protested especially loudly against the metalworkers' 'dictatorship' over wage rates and regulation.

The metalworkers' wage rates agreement is a model for the majority of industrial branches. It has been copied without compulsion. Neither the metalworkers nor the wage rates section of VTsSPS can be rebuked for this circumstance, which is not an accident but has roots in the economy. Here, there, and everywhere the metals industry is the basis of the economy, from which everything else originates. Petty outbursts against the 'bloodsucking ticks of steel' are attempts to break through the 'wage rates front', whose orderliness and unity serve as guiding principles when rates are worked out and decided upon. Such criticism has only suppressed the best aspects of the existing arrangement for handling wage rates. It has created confusion over trifling matters rather than examining actual blunders and mistakes in our system for regulating wages. Of course, there are mistakes. It would be a miracle if there weren't any mistakes in such a large and new matter as constructing the regulation of wages in production. This is new not only in Russia but in the entire world. But these insufficiencies are not at all of a 'parochial' nature. They are much deeper and more serious. Ignoring them threatens to radically destroy all

---

58   'Zarabotnaia plata i proizvoditelnosti truda', *Pravda* (27 April 1919): 1–2. The editors write, 'Published as a discussion article'.

efforts to raise the productivity of labour. The common misfortune of our wage rates policy is that since late 1917 it has not moved a step ahead. It has even managed to preserve all surviving characteristics from the period of capitalist relations. The collective agreement between the Petrograd Society of Factory and Plant Owners and the Petrograd Union of Metalworkers, which was concluded in the summer of 1917, continues to be a classic model. The ideas of naturalisation of wages remain unrealised, and the old basis of the wage rates – the minimum cost of living – is recognised only in theory. Trade unions have not created illusions among the worker masses about it being possible easily to catch up with rising prices by means of issuing paper rubles. Even during the *Kerenshchina* (under Kerensky), unions raised questions about intensely expanding production of household items, in order to raise reserves of goods and relieve the need for them in the towns and countryside. Now the chasm between the actual minimum cost of living and its monetary expression in the minimum rates in our wage rates agreements is greater than ever before. Existing research into workers' budgets directly cries out about this. However, not one union now advocates the 'simple' raising of rates, but they tie this raise to increasing the productivity of labour.

The ideas of levelling wages, having a tendency toward gradually lowering wages of skilled workers and raising wages of unskilled and trained workers, have as could be expected suffered complete failure, but nonetheless have succeeding in irreparably harming our economy. Because of the policy of wage rates, skilled workers in our industry, who are comparably few in number, but who play the most productive role in it, have left the enterprises for work in institutions or life in the countryside. This has lowered the productivity of workers in our enterprises. These are the results of such a wage rates practice.

Our trade unions' wage rates agreements err from lopsidedness. All their attention is consumed by parochial questions, as for example distribution of professions into groups and finding categories for each particular type of worker. The work is very respectable and some of our unions have learned the business thoroughly and deeply. But not even in one wage rates agreement is there the idea about needing to link wages to increased productivity of labour. True, almost all unions have rejected a hostile attitude to piece work, but vestiges of this negative attitude are present in all wage rates agreements.

The wage rates agreement of construction workers of Moscow and the central oblast (May 1918), recognising piece work in point 30, limits wages of workers to 25% over daily pay. The wage rates agreement of cartage (animal-drawn transport) workers and employees (July 1918) even limits the output norms under piece work to 25% above daily norms.

The Union of Food Processing Workers and Employees (August 1918 wage rates agreement) limits excess wages under piece work to not more than 20%, but provisionally, if the norm of piece work valuation has still not been set. The Union of Autoworkers of Moscow Oblast, in its wage rates agreement of 17 August 1918, 'to prevent [illegible word] of workers', limits exceeding piece work pay to 20% over hourly pay, and threatens to lower the rates if this norm is exceeded. The wage rates agreement of button and hook manufacturing workers and employees likewise categorically forbade excess hourly pay rates of more than 20% under piece work conditions. Strangely, the textiles industry wage rates agreement (September 1918) 'encourages' elevation of labour productivity in note 2 to point 3: 'In case of elevation of output norm in the course of a month to 20%, the worker receives additional payment in the amount of 10% from the set hourly pay'. Each textile worker, sensing that he was being 'taken advantage of' by 10%, of course, was wary of raising his output.

Even though the metalworkers' union is free from vestiges of the past, nonetheless in its new wage rates agreement this year, point 36 says that 'workers' wages under the usual system of piecework pay cannot exceed the set wage rate by more than 50%'. The difference between this and the previous agreement is not qualitative but quantitative. This wage rates agreement is a little kinder than others, but not much more so.

Such an attitude toward piece work at the current time in which we live is impermissible. It directly contradicts the effort of trade unions, factory committees, and Soviet power to raise the productivity of our industry.

Restriction of piece work wages to 50% or 'twice' that (100%) in relation to daily 'shop' pay, in the past, under capitalism, is understandable. Then rates were in the hands of the exploiter, who wished to take in as much as possible and pay out as little as possible. Now the situation should be different. Workers and technical personnel determine rates. The exploiter's grip is absent and the limitation of piece work norms by the system laid out above is harmful. Exhaustion should be struggled against not by rewarding the worker with less labour but by relieving the worker from worry about nourishment, sanitation, and related labour conditions.

Protecting workers' productivity under a piece work regime is criminal now when there is a goods shortage and lack of raw materials and fuel. Workers of factories and plants should be given more food than they are given now, but percentage limitations hinder this. No one is inclined to work for free, and still less so when they punished the worker for increased productivity with reduced wage rates. A more serious approach should be taken to piece work, its stability determined more strictly and precisely, based on production experience. Once a price has been assigned, it should not be removed without sufficient reasons. The enterprise needs to establish firm wage rates for a period not less than a year and to change them only if the work process changes, if there are innovations in processes or technology. But a firmly established pay rate is necessary to give full scope of activity to the worker. And that together with productivity will raise both the workers' pay and the profit of the republic. All parochial restrictions should be removed. Workers themselves in each case will determine where the boundary lies between piece work and sweatshop labour and they will not permit it to be transgressed. New percentage limitations will not guarantee against 'overexertion' and they should be discarded. The central committee of the All-Russian Metalworkers' Union took this point of view. Instead of pretending to have wise 'debates', workers should be emancipated from parochial restrictions. Then we will get both raised productivity and raised wages.

4   A.G. Shliapnikov, 'Production and Productivity'[59]

... A heroic proposal already exists, which is to temporarily be reconciled with a half-starving, semi-frigid, dirty and sick existence and not dream about better immediate prospects. War exhausted our economic reserves and consequently lowered the general cultural norm of existence. According to this proposal, we should not contemplate having diverse and grandiose buildings any time soon or expanding and developing production, but should limit ourselves to modest tasks to keep existing production and transport resources from further ruin. Further, according to this line of thinking, implementation of such modest assignments demands special measures of so-called 'economic dictatorship'. Comrade Ky's article in no. 65 of *Izvestiia VTsIK* is characteristic of such thinking.[60] The article takes a simple approach to the most important production tasks and attacks the proletarian masses. Its wretched conclusion is to establish 'dictatorship' over industrial workers. It is difficult to say what this smacks of, either nostalgic longing [тоска] for a 'master' or an intellectual's incomprehension of industry.

Comrade Ky asserts that 'if piecework pay and bonuses had been introduced promptly after the October revolution, then the goods famine would not have reached the current scale' and so forth. This assertion rests upon complete ignorance of the situation in which our industry was found before and after

---

59   'Voprosy proizvodstva i proizvoditelnosti', TsA FSB, R33718, d. 499061, vol. 37, ll. 207–8. Excerpts.

60   Ky, 'Ili diktatura ili gibel', *Izvestiia VTsIK*, no. 65 (26 March 1919), 8.

October. First of all, our industry began to demobilise after the October days, and then it had to adapt to peacetime demands. Wage forms could not have a decisive influence and the introduction of bonuses could have added nothing.

Rebuke against the leading stratum of the proletariat for narrowminded adherence to principle is likewise misplaced, for the most leading workers did not argue about wage forms. They argued about the essence of pay and already long ago struggled against wage-leveling tendencies and pay for doing nothing. Demobilisation intensified the collapse of transport and laid the foundation for the catastrophic state of the railways. This undermined the supply of enterprises with raw materials and fuel. Panicky, nonsystematic evacuation of enterprises with military significance ruined production links and condemned the largest enterprises to wandering, stagnation and desertion. Indiscriminate, poorly prepared nationalisation of enterprises, suicidal centralisation of economic life, and failure to secure the needs of enterprises suppressed initiative and led to the stoppage of entire branches of the economy.

If you take everything together then and now, the highest degree of short-sightedness turns out to belong not so much to the proletarian masses as to those leaders of ours who seem to have taken out a patent on economic ruin. Of course, the working class pays the cruel price for all of this. Comrade Ky asserts inaccurately that the government of the poor spoiled the workers by raising wage rates in accord with the rise of prices on goods and in this way stifled their interest in output norms. This would be justified, if goods prices depended on the will of the government. In fact it's possible to say that wage rates corresponded to the actual subsistence minimum only during the first six to eight months of Soviet power. Now workers' earnings are determined not by the subsistence minimum, but by the productive capability of the office for printing state currency. It is not the All-Russian Council of Trade Unions and People's Commissariat of Labour that create wage rates policy, but Sukharevka and comrade Krestinsky, who have jurisdiction over the printing press.

Beginning in 1917, long before the October days, there were 'enforced stoppages' of production, which did not depend on the will of owners or workers. Accordingly, the first wage rates agreement we concluded had a special point, which stipulated two weeks of wage payments during 'enforced stoppages'. The closer to October, the more frequent and longer lasting these enforced stoppages became. The main reason was lack of fuel. ... Now raw materials are also lacking. ... These enforced stoppages have a catastrophic influence on productivity. Workers have lost confidence in enterprises' stability and have become anxious about the future. The reduced pay during 'enforced stoppages' has driven away the most needed highly-skilled workers and specialists. ... The prevailing mood is lack of confidence in the future ... This destroys the work of proletarian organisations on labour discipline ... norm-setting in manufacturing ... the system of piecework. And the 'economic dictatorship' will do nothing and provide nothing in this area. ... heroic measures are needed ... to procure fuel and raw materials. But this least of all depends on workers and most of all on those in the centre who hold things up, so many of whom we have bred. ... Economic ruin and hunger have hurt workers, but chiefly lack of confidence in our 'bureaucratic' works has killed and is killing in the proletarians their 'living soul', pushing some on the path of dissatisfaction and others into apathy. Efforts and decisions are needed, but on a completely different plane (about this in another article).

5   A.G. Shliapnikov, 'Industrial Productivity'[61]

Many articles have appeared in economic literature lately about the drop in productivity in our plants and factories. A fair share of published material denounces our workers for low productivity, for lacking principles of labour self-discipline, and so forth. Many of these articles are old tunes, which are not even played in a new key, as the old proverb says. Past leaders of 'the fatherland's industry', who were inveterate capitalists, often and very gladly rebuked workers for laziness, disobedience, drunkenness, and similar such sins, which undermined capitalist wellbeing.

Using the data of Petrograd (Piter) factories, Comrade Strumilin produced the first attempt to approach scientifically the question about the decline in productivity and he refutes the prevailing vulgar accusations toward workers of lacking the desire to work. On the basis of the investigation's data, comrade Strumilin finds three main reasons, which contribute to lower productivity of labour, namely: 1) terms of pay for labour; 2) conditions of food; 3) quality of tools and raw material.[62] All these reasons lie outside the will of workers of our factory and plant enterprises.

Our leading organisations were extremely thoughtless when it came to wage questions. The effort toward leveling of pay for labour was elevated to the wisdom of wage rates policy. The principle of hourly pay, although approved by vague 'output norms', essentially was not connected with labour productivity.

---

61   'Voprosy promyshlennoi proizvoditelnosti', *Metallist*, no. 5 (15 June 1919): 2–3. *Metallist* was the journal of the All-Russian Metalworkers' Union and its audience included party members and nonparty workers and engineers.

62   Perhaps he means *Statistika truda*, vols. 1–2 (Narkomtrud, 1918–19), edited by Aleksandr Stopani and Stanislav Gustavovich Strumilin.

The leveling tendency reigned here, too: equal productivity of workers' labour is to the detriment of the producer. Acceptance of a simple system of piece-work on the basis of experience, as past and present practice has shown, fully solves the problem.

It is more difficult to solve the problem of food. Liberation from the constraint of procuring unregulated foodstuffs and the removal of defensive detachments will ease the situation of proletarian centres. But, independently from these individual measures, it is necessary to bring the minimum living wage closer to reality.[63] Outdated minimum rates and evasion of or deviation from them threatens to depopulate our enterprises. Economising in this instance will cost both workers and the Republic very dearly.

Worn-out machines, work benches and tools of production reverberate extraordinarily severely on the productivity of labour, as do insufficient instruments and auxiliary devices and the lack of materials that are suitable for their repair. Likewise, lower quality fuel slows down the pace of work and wastes many men, animals, and materials. All these chief reasons, which influence the decline in productivity, do not depend on the worker's personality, and so cannot be placed in rebuke of the worker.

Comrades, who are busy with questions of regulation of wages and norm-setting of labour, when confronted with facts about the drop in productivity, go along the line of least resistance, and chiefly take the route of concentrating pressure on labour. They invent special incentive schemes or they copy one or another system of bonuses, which are known in capitalist countries. This path will not give great results. It is necessary to expand the range of vision and leave no stone unturned in the search for productivity in the very organism of production.

The Russian worker's low productivity is a well-known fact. Already prewar statistics of world coal output in 1912, for example, gave the annual productivity of the Russian miner as 9,000 puds, the German as over 18,000 and the American as over 40,000 puds.[64] These numbers illustrate two systems of organising work: one founded on the 'cudgel' [дубинушка], and the other on the 'machine' [машинушка]. In processing industry the difference in productivity was even more marked, moreover at that time it fell to the lot of the unproductive Russian proletarian to have a longer working day, beastly discipline, and small earnings. Soviet power and workers' organisations should take the scientific

---

63   Денежный промежуточный минимум.

64   A *pud* [пуд] was a Russian unit of weight equivalent to about 36.11 pounds or 16.38 kilograms.

path toward organising our enterprises. It is necessary to do away with the 'cudgel' and really take up the 'machine', by which to bring our worker's productivity near to European norms. Obviously, technical transformation of our plants and factories cannot occur in a few months. Many years are demanded for this. However, we can already do much now in the branches that are more important for us, like repair of mobile stock, organisation of production of agricultural machines, tools and so forth. It is necessary already now to make our enterprises specialise in the manufacture of mass products of the same type. It is necessary to put an end to the habit of each factory and plant, taking up work on anything that turns up, dissipating energy on trifles, and not creating anything. Lack of foresight in this area strikes you in the face wherever you turn. So, in the majority of enterprises, repair of locomotives still goes on one by one, with different types and so forth. Dozens of different types of locomotives are encountered at any factory and in locomotive repair workshops. What an enormous economy of production there would be if repair were organised according to a mass route, of repair according to types, with similar features, and not according to the principle of possession and time of entering the queue.

One of the most important means of raising productivity is introducing into production the division of labour processes. This principle is studied and perfected in Western Europe and in America. The most complex and difficult work is divided into operations. At the Ford automobile factory the division of labour during automobile assembly is taken to such a level of perfection that driving a nail is one of the operations and employs a special worker. We should be working in this direction if we really want to raise our industry's productivity. The results of this work will be hundreds of times more fruitful than all kinds of bonus systems, calculated according to the worker's physical effort.

We still hold vocational training in disregard here. Meanwhile, the demand that modern technology makes on the worker outstrips that experience, which is passed on from generation to generation and which is accessible to our proletarians. The newest machines, workbenches and tools, besides general technical education, demand knowledge of the latest work methods, otherwise under old methods, new instruments will remain unused. To prepare skilled workers trained in specialties is a task of enormous importance. Capitalists have learned this. In all countries, they go to all lengths to encourage evening schools, factory and plant schools for apprentices. Moreover, they go beyond these to develop state technical institutes. Not only have we still done nothing, but according to statements from the provinces, Narkompros managed to destroy even the little that existed before it. Trade unions should take this business into their hands and only then will it go successfully.

We should allot as much strength and attention as possible to raising our industry's productivity. All successes of the workers' movement are linked to developing our country's productive forces. To give the country an abundance of industrial products means to reinforce, not in resolutions or words but in fact, all the socialist and revolutionary conquests achieved.

6   A.G. Shliapnikov's Report to a Meeting of the All-Russian
       Metalworkers' Union (VSRM) Central Committee, the All-Russian
       Central Council of Trade Unions (VTsSPS), and Other Union
       Personnel, Autumn 1919[65]

Theses of a report read at a meeting of members of the CC VSRM, VTsSPS, and union personnel in autumn 1919.

1.   With the crushing defeat of Kolchak, Iudenich, and Denikin, Soviet power
       is entering a new period of its existence.[66] ... For all the country's forces,
       the centre of gravity of work is shifting from the military to the economy.
       ... The party needs to ... implement ... the elevation of the role and signi-
       ficance of proletarian economic unions in the business of the country's
       economic rebirth. ... During wartime the best and most dedicated of the
       party were mobilised ... The party's organisational cohesion weakened
       significantly. Also, the party's outstanding principal core of party per-
       sonnel, those who were devoted to it, found their influence weakened
       over the entire course and character of party leadership. Systematic party
       cultivation of members either is completely absent or is arranged very
       unsatisfactorily. The business of propagandising communist conscious-
       ness among the broad masses is at a low level.
6.   Along with this, there has poured into the party, chiefly through soviet
       bodies, many of such an element which in the preceding period of
       struggle was either hostile to the party or in the best case stood apart from
       it. It was not at all linked with the struggle of the party and proletarian

---

65   TsA FSB, R33718, d. 499061, vol. 37, ll. 210–12. Shliapnikov is not identified as the author, but
       I concluded that he was, based on multiple references to this document elsewhere in the
       historical records. Excerpts are translated, because my notes do not contain a full version.
       Ellipses reflect omissions.
66   Nikolai Iudenich and Anton Denikin were White generals; Aleksandr Kolchak was a White
       admiral.

masses generally. By its spirit it is alien to the cause of organised party building. ...

8. The elements, which entered party institutions and took senior soviet posts, ... could not assimilate an understanding of the revolutionary spirit of this struggle, its goals, and its tasks ....

9. Such circumstances bring about the following:
    - the absence of a close living and organic link between party and soviet leading bodies and their local organisations;
    - insufficiently energetic and consistent implementation by leading party institutions of workerisation of all bodies of the republic in accord with the decisions of the Eighth Party Congress;
    - almost complete disregard and at times even a semi-hostile attitude toward these decisions by leaders of soviet bodies, who are only communists in name;
    - systematic disparagement by them of the role and significance of VTsIK and its presidium, as well as economic worker unions;
    - and formation around leading party and soviet bodies of dissatisfaction and an unhealthy atmosphere, thanks to the appearance in them of bureaucratism, careerism, personal influences, nepotism, and favouritism toward unsuitable and often hostile elements of the party.

10. These reasons explain leading party and soviet institutions' fear of individual party organisations and senior meritorious party personnel having independent opinions; the application to the former of the method of dispersal and to the second of exile by means of transferring them to work in other places in order to eliminate their influence over these institutions' activity; transformation of these methods into a system under the cover of demands for party discipline; systematic disregard of VTsIK and its Presidium and of economic proletarian organisations when deciding the most important questions of their existence and activity. ...

12. In order to best achieve the indicated tasks:
    a) it is necessary to more frequently convene gubernia, city, district and subdistrict conferences, and likewise periodic meetings of senior party and soviet personnel for businesslike resolution of all questions of current party life of a given organisation;
    b) it is necessary to eliminate the dispatch of party personnel as functionaries with assignments to various posts in the lowest-level organisations;
    c) in the interest of struggle against the penetration of people alien in spirit to the party and unsuitable for party and soviet work to senior party and soviet posts, establish a minimum length of time in the

party for occupation of these posts and approve these assignments by decisions of conferences or assemblies of senior party and soviet personnel of a local organisation;

d) it is necessary to have the best arrangement of inventory of all party members according to their party experience and length of time in the party, and to introduce special supervision and inventory of each party member's work.

7   A.G. Shliapnikov, 'Tasks of the Russian Proletariat's Economic Organisations'[67]

1. In the third year of revolution, the chief tasks of the economic organisations of Russia's working class are: 1) supporting (15/1/21 draft: 'raising') the republic's productive forces by all means at our disposal; and 2) struggle against economic ruin by means of systematic organisation of the economy. The efforts of proletarian production unions should be directed first of all toward reviving transport, procuring all types of fuel, and extracting raw materials.

2. These tasks should be put in a concrete framework of requirements. Production unions and likewise unions of transport and auxiliary workers should have definite programmes of implementation, proceeding on the basis of past experience.

3. The first All-Russian congresses and conferences of workers' unions resolved the questions of internal construction of workers' organisations, protection of labour, and regulation of wages. In the areas of organisation and management of industry these congresses could only schematically outline the policy of workers' organisations, not provide practical decisions.

4. Congresses during the third year of the proletarian dictatorship should define concrete tasks, which are the character of production unions and their order of activity. Through all worker unions should percolate the consciousness that without victory over ruin in industry and transport, it is impossible to actually improve the situation of workers and the poor.

---

67   'Zadachi ekonomicheskikh organisatsii Rossiiskogo proletariata', addressed to the Bureau of the VTsSPS Communist Faction, 20 January 1920. RGASPI, f. 2, op. 1, d. 12562, ll. 1–5. Draft from 15 January 1920 preserved in RGASPI, f. 2, op. 1, d. 12106. There are no significant differences between the two drafts; minor changes are indicated in the text by placing the original wording in parentheses or by inserting an explanatory footnote.

There is no other force than the organised proletariat, which is capable of conquering ruin and getting industry going. Proletarian organisations' two-year experience in the area of industrial construction should be utilised.

5. Trade union congresses of past years could not set concrete tasks partly because the Soviet Republic was deprived of the most important industrial regions, which were rich with food-stuffs, fuel and raw materials. Now the successes of the Red Army in the east, in Turkestan, and in the south significantly facilitate the building up of production. The victory of Red Arms should be reinforced by proletarian unions' organised work in the area of economic construction.

6. For the first time, Russia's production unions are confronted with the possibility of concrete elaboration of a production programme, which takes into account the reconstruction of all economic oblasts of the Republic into a unified whole. Definitively outlined for each branch of the national economy, the programme places before workers' unions the tasks of explaining demands for the labour force needed to realise the tasks set. First of all should be determined the work force demand, which is needed to extract all kinds of fuel, raw materials, and semi-processed products. Uninterrupted production in our plants and factories can only be put in place through procuring and ensuring timely supply for the manufacturing industry on a district by district basis.

7. The success of building the national economy on socialist principles now depends exclusively upon the degree of organisation (omitted from 15/1/20 draft: utilisation) of the workforce of the Republic. The proletariat's victory eliminated all private property barriers, which barred the way toward developing and utilising natural forces and resources. Toward these goals, production organisations should carry out registration of their skilled and unskilled workforces, using for this the registration data of union members, beginning since 1917, and likewise lists of personnel of industrial enterprises for that time.

8. The interests of struggle against economic ruin, and likewise the systematic distribution of the work force in the socialist economy, place industrial mobilisation on the agenda. All workers, both trained and untrained, but working in enterprises during war, should be registered. Those dispersed across the countryside, in institutions and in the army should be called to the workbenches, furnaces, mines and shafts. Workforce Distribution Sections should register all the able-bodied population of the Republic. Distribution of the workforce should be subordinated to the general economic plan. Industrial mobilisation should be implemented

through Military Commissariats, but under the supervision of Workforce Distribution Sections.

9. Satisfaction of workers, who are occupied in production, transport, fuel and raw materials procurement, with all types of allowances [money, clothing, etc.] is one of the powerful means for securing high productivity of labour, discipline and inflow of the work force into industry. A majority for workers' unions and cooperatives should be secured in collegia, which direct procurement and distribution of foodstuffs. With a view toward utilising local foodstuffs resources, produce bodies, together with unions and factory management, are to organise a natural exchange of labour in return for products of agriculture, market-gardening, cattle-raising and poultry farming. Repair and mending of the rural agricultural inventory and handmade items for it should be arranged, without loss to the main area of production. Workers' unions, likewise workers of separate enterprises, should be presented with the primary right to use former gentry estates and with a sufficient quantity of land, inventory, and resources for vegetable gardening and sowing grain.

10. VSNKh, as a body of VTsIK, is created on the basis of representation from production unions. Sovnarkhozes should be constructed on the basis of production, in such an order in which the production work force is organised. For realisation of their production programmes, unions should fully have at their disposal the state apparatuses, organising and regulating the national economy. The All-Russian Council of Trade Unions should become the responsible organiser of industry.[68]

11. Each production section of VSNKh unites all economic units, subject to it on the basis of their production, without considering interests of a proprietary nature, seniority, parochial bureaucratic interests, and other such pretensions. The artificial detachment of 'glavki' and bodies of management of production of separate objects and all sorts of creation of industrial columns, which are independent from sections, should not take place.

12. The Sovnarkhozes' work in the provinces is organised on the same principles as in the centre: local construction and management of plants, factories, workshops of industrial enterprises and so forth, are based on local departments of all-Russian production unions. Management of

---

68 The preceding two sentences came first in the paragraph in the 15 January 1920 draft. They were followed by the sentence beginning 'VSNKh ...'.

large and complex production units or their unions is guaranteed to responsible collegiums, represented by workers' unions.

13. Managing collegia are responsible before bodies, which appoint them, and are obligated to carry out periodic reporting to the bodies that appoint them. Besides that, with a view toward attracting the entire proletarian mass into the process of economic construction, the management of enterprises should make periodic reports and informational papers to workers directly occupied in enterprises managed by them.

14. Regulation [нормирование] of labour and wages should be subordinated to the basic task of organising industry. Wages, in money or kind, should be defined by a worker's productivity. With a view toward raising productivity, there should be implemented a system of bonuses, which would awaken interest in separate producers as well as in their groups. All kinds of improvement of methods and innovation that provide increases in productivity should be given an incentive in every way possible.

15. Evening technical classes for apprentices and trade union schools for children are necessary to organise broadly, with a view toward increasing cadres of metalworkers.

16. The interests of the proletarian revolution in Russia and of the international struggle of workers insistently demands establishment of the tightest connection between workers' unions of revolutionary Russia with workers' unions of all countries.

8   A.M. Kollontai's Diary Notes, January–February 1920[69]

13 January 1920.

Trotsky's proposals for militarisation of industry are the centre of conversations and attention. Yesterday he read a report to the party assembly. Debate was very lively. Trade unionists and sovnarkhozists (Tomsky, Riazanov, Rykov) spoke against the report. Al[eksandr] G[avrilovich Shliapnikov] always invents a '*bon mot*': 'Theses, that [two illegible words] – now with each' [remainder of the page is cut off]

---

69   RGASPI, f. 134, op. 3, d. 34, ll. 1–6, handwritten. Kollontai sometimes used abbreviations or initials for individuals well-known to her. I have expanded these in brackets where I can identify them. I have enclosed in brackets words of which I am unsure and illegible words. Parentheses are hers, except when I use them to indicate the Russian original of an English translation.

5 February 1920.

Al[eksandr] G[avrilovich Shliapnikov] just left. 'Labour army' is the general theme of conversations, discussions, and worries. A labour army in the hands of trade unions would be one thing. But a labour army in the hands of Znamenka and the government elite is unacceptable, of course.[70] Tr[otsky] wants to militarise the working class and to kill initiative [самодеятельность]. Lenin interprets this otherwise. He evidently doesn't completely share Trotsky's proposal, but he doesn't offer a counterslogan. Differences are growing in the party. Some are wholly with Tr[otsky]. Others are with Kalinin, Rykov and the sort for a course on the *muzhik*.[71] This tendency is against Tr[otsky's] theses. 'All for the army' is Trotsky's cry. The second tendency is to 'Remember the countryside, don't ruin her – she is the wet-nurse [кормилица]'. There is much that is healthy in it, there is [well-groundedness?] and economic farsightedness. Lenin supports them in much, but with reservations. Lenin is for creating unity, by all measures, between the proletariat of the town and the peasantry. That is why he is so interested in the section on work in the countryside. He is against 'excesses' in the sense of [illegible] the poor peasant [бедняк]; he is for consolidating the middle peasant [середняк]. Kalinin and his group have an S[ocialist] R[evolutionary] spirit. He himself goes about in felt boots [валенки] and in quite simple clothing – the peasants comprehend him and he is near to them.[72] He travels about on agitational trains and conquers the peasants' hearts. But they are dissatisfied – he always promises more than they want and than is possible. The Kalininist group is a deviation toward the peasantry. Trotsky and his followers stand for militarisation of Soviet everyday life and of the proletariat. But there is a third tendency – a group of workers, more truly former workers. They are Iury Lutovinov, Shliap[nikov], Medv[edev], T[olokontsev?], M[?] and such. There is much discontent among the worker masses with Tr[otsky's] course, which squeezes enterprise [самодеятельность], self-management, and initiative of trade unions, in a word 'militarisation'. This group considers that the countryside, not the urban industrial proletariat, won most of all from the revolution. Criticism grows. But in their dissatisfaction with Trotsky both these currents – that which groups around Kalinin and Shliap[nikov]-Lutov[inov] – are close and [Kalinych?] 'secretly'

---

70   Znamenka was the name of a street in Moscow, where the Revolutionary Military Council had its headquarters.

71   *Muzhik* [мужик] means male peasant.

72   *Valenki* [валенки] were traditional felt boots worn by peasants.

confers with them.[73] Al[eksandr] Gavr[ilovich Shliapnikov] showed me their theses. They're imprecise and rather weak, but they contain much true and sound criticism.

What a very intricate and complex bureaucratic machine of management we have built! Healthy criticism will not break through it. The initiative of workers' organisations is very compressed – everything is done through the 'apparats'. And in the apparatus there is still much rot and alien people. In 1917 we believed more in self-activity [*самодеятельность*], in the healthy class instinct of the masses.

6 February

... Often I see Anzh[elika] Balab[anoff]. Zinoviev secured her removal, she is no longer secretary of the Third International. He does not tolerate around himself anyone who is popular abroad. This is an enormous mistake and harmful for the Third Int[ernational]. His policy encourages colourless quantities [*величины*] but for that 'obedient' in everything. A repulsive type. Zinoviev. And a coward ...

23 February

... We sit in session at my place. Mariia Ilinichna is a sensible editor. She and Inessa have strained relations. M.I. hates Inessa (for an understandable reason!). Nad[ezhda] K[onstantinovna] on the contrary is always affectionate with Inessa, emphatically affectionate. Inessa always looks a little humble and guilty in N.K.'s presence (all this is typical). The work of our editorial board proceeds smoothly in general.

... At the TsIK session the opposition of workers revealed itself. They criticised and beat upon the government for the present course of policy, with which we will have not state socialism but state [illegible word]. They exposed facts that it is not workers who manage enterprises, but specialists [*спецы*]. Workers are only 'under them'. Of course, this current met rebuff and was called 'syndicalism'. They have begun to punish the opposition by means of dispersal. He who is stronger, who is unbending, they send further away to the most difficult sectors of work, where in the masses there is much dissatisfaction and no

---

73   This is the only source I have seen where it is alleged that Shliapnikov and his supporters
      met with Kalinin and his in order to determine common interests. I am not sure if it is
      trustworthy, given the possibility that Kollontai later revised her memoirs.

way to help so far. Inevitably relations become aggravated between the party's envoy and the worker masses.

The oppositionist sees in practice how difficult it is to conduct what is planned. Many have already surrendered in such a way. Others, who are weaker, more pliable, are on the contrary brought into useful 'bodies' and in such a way are attached 'to the higher-ups'. All sins are assigned to him and he is isolated from the masses. This is V.I.'s tactic.

11 March

... Al[eksandr] Gavr[ilovich Shliapnikov] left for Norway on party business. ....

[Further she expresses disappointment about the frictions between trade unions and the women's departments or sections (zhenotdels). Then she opines on how the revolution has changed attitudes toward manual labour, which has ceased to be despised. Some final thoughts of this section (ll. 12–15) dwell on the dangers of trying to create change by forceful methods.]

9   Speeches by Iu.Kh. Lutovinov and A.S. Kiselev at the Ninth Congress of the RCP(b), March–April 1920[74]

Session two.

Lutovinov (pp. 59–62). In his report, comrade Lenin drew a contrast between one-man management and collegiality, but I will not dwell on this. Generally, Comrade Lenin recently has spoken about one-man management wherever he has been presented with the opportunity to do so. If comrade Lenin greeted some congress of trade unions, then he found it obligatory to begin and end with one-man management. This is on our agenda and we will return to it later, but now I want to dwell on the report about the CC's activity.

There is not much to say about the first part of the CC's report, which is about political work. The very fact of soviet power's existence and its growing strength is the best way to determine how correct the political line of our party is and always was.

The party's political line now plays first violin in the international movement and one cannot say that it suffers from spinal curvature and needs straightening. Our party always excelled in this, which is its greatest service to the whole

---

74   RKP(b) 1934.

world. I am convinced that at this congress we will not find even one eccentric [чудак], who would dare to assert the opposite. Well, if someone were found from among the left communists or from among the backward type of old social democrats, who in October 1917 shied away from the party, then they would be looked at as if they were a rarity from across the sea, and of course they will not express the opinions of any groups at all.

But the matter of practical implementation of this political line is a far cry from the above. Here it is possible to say without exaggerating that we are lame in all four legs. Having observed for an entire year the work of the highest body of our party, the CC, which should be able to lead in all areas no matter how diverse (party, soviets and unions), unfortunately, we have to state that we haven't had such a leading body. Organisations at the local level were always left to their own devices. If, in the majority of cases, in the provinces everything didn't run off the rails, we owe this not to the CC, but exclusively to old experienced personnel, who work at the local level. Frequently, I have heard complaints from local personnel about this. This probably will be confirmed in speeches later on.

The CC, especially its Orgburo, has been transformed from the highest leading body into an executive body of the most petty, insignificant little matters, as for example, assigning to some sort of institution a commandant to direct the economic section and so forth. On this it wasted 8/10 of its time. To test my assertion's validity, comrades, I suggest that you examine protocols of the Orgburo sessions, where you will find for the course of 15–16 sessions discussion of one question about assignment of one and the same comrade. I can introduce an innumerable multitude of such facts, but, unfortunately I must limit myself due to insufficient time.

Now I want to dwell on comrade Krestinsky's accusation against trade unionists of 'counterrevolutionary' efforts to usurp the CC's power. In his report, Comrade Krestinsky anticipated attacks on him from trade unionists, who he injured quite sufficiently with his tactless interference, so he defended himself by going onto the offensive.

He asserted here that trade unionists wanted to create some sort of chief committee [главк] of trade unionists and set it up in opposition to the CC. The basis of comrade Krestinsky's assertion is the 'Proposal about the VTsSPS communist faction', in which he, reading between the lines of course, uncovered trade unionists' criminal schemes, if not to destroy the CC, then at least to identify VTsSPS and the CC RCP as one and the same. At one time there were more than a few debates about and fights over this question. The Politburo examined the proposal. There comrades Lenin and Trotsky convinced comrades Krestinsky and Kamenev that in this proposal there was not even a shadow or an insinuation of such horrible schemes by trade unionists. After that, it seemed that the question had been exhausted. Yet for some reason comrade Krestinsky had to speak about this and to seek a scapegoat.[75]

Comrades, I think that you will be interested in knowing more about this 'Proposal about the VTsSPS communist faction' and about these alleged counterrevolutionary schemes by trade unionists, so that you can figure out who are the aggressors and who is capable of leading the party. I will permit myself to cite several paragraphs here:

1. The VTsSPS communist faction is the leading party organisation of the entire Russian trade union movement, the work of which the Party CC directly supervises and leads.

2. The first task of the VTsSPS communist faction is to expand and strengthen the party's influence by unifying and attracting broad masses of workers into the communist party.

3. In order to coordinate the actions of the all-Russian production unions and to implement more successfully and in a better-organised way a unified communist party line in the trade union movement, all communist factions now existing in the all-Russian production unions, as well as those arising in the future, shall be directly subordinated to the VTsSPS communist faction.

In my opinion, any commentary would be completely superfluous. Maybe only the question about the *glavk* should be addressed. It is very possible that to some comrades a VTsSPS communist faction will seem similar to a *glavk*. But where is the misfortune in this? Indeed the CC created *glavki*, which exist under it. There are *glavki* for youth, for women, for the *muzhik* (the section on work in the countryside), so why should there not be a *glavk* of trade unions? Even more so, in that the trade union movement is such a complex movement that the CC still has not became familiar with it.[76]

For the CC, the trade union movement is a book with seven seals. Of course it's necessary to say with all sincerity that the CC cannot lead this movement in all its manifestations. As proof of this, I will introduce one very characteristic fact. Comrade Kamenev, who is one of our party leaders and is not less competent than comrade Krestinsky, posed the question: 'For what purpose does the wage rates agreement exist, why are wages still not equalised?' Indeed

---

75   The Russian phrase is сваливать с больной головы на здоровую.

76   *Glavk* is the singular form and *glavki* is plural.

such leaders are a real treat. And they, if I may say so, lead! Although this leadership is more similar to pulling at strings fastened to unfortunate personnel. These leaders, who do not understand basic things about the trade union movement (not to speak of details), curse us as syndicalists, 'trade-unionists' [in the English sense], individualists, and Mensheviks.[77] To put it concisely, they say whatever comes into their heads from what they have read about the trade union movements of various countries.

I can provide another fact to prove that they jerk us around. Comrade Krestinsky cursed us for Ukraine's wage rates agreement, which after [General Anton] Denikin's departure turned out to be 2–3 times higher than that in Moscow, but not by our fault. In order to emerge from the situation that had been created, trade unionists elaborated a draft for a new wage rates agreement and sent it to the Politburo for examination. In this draft project we proposed to level the difference in the wage rates according to a system of zones and to make a transition to partial naturalisation of wages in order not to raise the wage rates and not to consolidate a firm rate. There in the Politburo they indecently cursed us out. Now after 2–3 weeks have passed, comrade Trotsky has presented us with the same thing, just dressed up differently as 'competition'. Yet his proposal is treated as if he discovered America, and we are sure that it will be accepted. What is this, if not being jerked around on a string? As my time has expired, I should conclude by refuting comrade Iurenev's declaration.

Comrade Iurenev stated that the CC used exile as a method of struggle against party members it found unsuitable and he stated that comrade Shliapnikov was exiled abroad. I declare that this time the CC did not exile comrade Shliapnikov. Trade unionists, among whom I personally participated, sent him abroad. But I do confirm that exile has been broadly applied toward comrades in general and several times toward comrade Shliapnikov specifically.

A.S. Kiselev (pp. 66–8). Comrades, I will say a few words regarding agitation, which the annual report about the CC's activity touched upon too little. Both the presenter of the report and the second speaker comrade Krestinsky pointed out just the same that we accomplished extraordinarily little in the area of agitation and propaganda. Our party centre was reproached here for having addressed too little attention to such activity, for the entire success of consol-

---

77   Mensheviks were the more moderate faction of the Russian Social Democratic Workers'
     Party, in comparison with the Bolshevik faction. The factions formed after the Second Congress in 1903, but did not rigidify until 1912. Even so, there was much practical cooperation
     among individuals belonging to the factions until after the Bolsheviks seized power in
     October 1917.

idating our revolution depends wholly on the extent to which broad working masses will be attracted to work and attracted into our ranks for building communism. Unfortunately, this is true. Not long ago I went out to the provinces. If you look now at the provinces, then you will see that comrades in the provinces waste an enormous amount of time on starting courses in party work. There is an enormous need for personnel. If you take a bird's eye view, then you will see that in all the gubernias it is especially difficult for personnel to compose a curriculum. They must rummage and search for books and curricula in all the libraries. At the same time these curricula are amateurish and unsatisfactory. Here I will note that the Party CC did almost nothing to help with this. It could have economised a great deal, because we have good programmes and many literary forces. It would have been simple to create a uniform curriculum and various types of schools, in order to alleviate the situation of comrades in the provinces and so aid the growth of our party.

Now, comrades, I want to turn attention to the question about how our party centre did not implement in our country all that the Eighth Party Congress assigned to it. This partially relates to the debate at the Eighth Party Congress about the struggle against bureaucratism.

Bureaucratism has set upon and tormented us everywhere and all the time. The Eighth Party Congress found the following exit from it: in order to air out this stagnant atmosphere, it is necessary to workerise those very centres, which are stuffed to the gills with functionary [канцелярский] bureaucratism. If we cast a glance toward this area, then we will see that everything has remained here almost as it was in olden times. VTsIK paid sufficient attention to this question and from its discussion it brought forth worker-peasant inspection. We pointed to some defects in CC policy, especially in relation to Narkomprod, which answers for all our commissariats (comrade Krestinsky at least declared resolutely that produce policy is our policy), and we pointed to the exit, which is the need to workerise this entire area.[78] Nevertheless, nothing has emerged from this.

Moving on, recently it has become noticeable that in our country our centres are going to great effort to kill, reduce, or weaken any kind of party idea in the provinces. The business has currently gone so far in implementing the party line in our country that right here and now certain decrees put constraints on me, so that I am restricted to defending the CC's line. Other delegates say exactly the same thing about the obligation laid upon them. But

---

78 Narkomprod was the People's Commissariat of Food Supplies.

when the cc's line fluctuates, as it does now, what will we defend? All this is extraordinarily difficult. There are such moments, when steadfast courage and the manifestation of independence can play an enormous role in history. Yet our opinions are reduced to nothing within the party. We have to point this out here. I hope that the congress will struggle against that which happens when people start trying to defend the positions of the Eighth Party Congress and for that are declared anarchists, syndicalists, and Makhaevists.[79] In our programme it says that trade unions should actually concentrate in their hands all management of the national economy, but when there was an attempt to lean for support on this point and defend it, well the most intense demagogy was raised against it. It is not surprising that many comrades present here took great fright.

Further, it's necessary to talk about the Eighth Party Congress resolution, which says that careerist elements infiltrate us. I should say that I have had the honour to come into contact with the military sphere. Here is the kind of thing that happens there. They convene an assembly. A new communist, who does not like the assembly, says that he should deliver a report at it. If you don't allow him to do so, then he threatens to disperse the assembly. A newly fledged communist wants to disperse an assembly of 300 communists.

Now I want to dwell on the pettiness of our cc, which busies itself with minor disputes with VTsIK. For example, the latter directed to close the ill-fated newspaper of Rosta. The article, for which they closed the newspaper, says something about specialists [ellipses] (Laughter, noise, chair's signal). In this article it says: 'To be a spets is profitable and pleasant'. [ellipses] (Reads excerpts from the newspaper.) The VTsIK presidium decreed the closure of Agit-Rosta, since it conducted an antiparty line.[80] If comrade Lenin and comrade Trotsky had read these articles, then they probably would have been horrified, but the cc nevertheless countermanded VTsIK and decreed to let the newspaper come out. That was because the Orgburo saw its authority undermined in this VTsIK resolution. Not having become familiar with the article and with the resolutions, the Orgburo placed the VTsIK presidium, a worker organisation, under suspicion and did not allow it to work. Comrades, I declare that the resolutions

---

79   Among Russian communists, 'Makhaevist' was a pejorative term referring to alleged followers of Jan Waclaw Machajski (1866–1926), a Polish revolutionary whose ideas were influenced by both Marxism and anarchism and who seemed to elevate workers above intellectuals in the revolutionary movement.

80   Rosta was the abbreviation for Russian Telegraph Agency, which was the post-revolutionary state news agency in the RSFSR. Agit-Rosta was the section of Rosta responsible for agitation and the name of a newspaper it published.

of the Eighth Party Congress have not been implemented. Of course, maybe this is a misunderstanding, but you yourselves will agree that such facts force us to ponder matters.

∴

Session 6.

Lutovinov (pp. 253–7). In my opinion, comrade Rykov is very poorly informed about the trade unions' internal world. Therefore, he went too far and too harshly evaluated comrade Riazanov's role in the Russian trade union movement. I fully agree with him that comrade Riazanov's presence in the bosom of the trade union movement offers nothing essential. Still less will be the loss for trade unions if comrade Riazanov will not work in them. But it does not follow from this that he should be exiled from the trade union movement in his old age. I am not speaking of Iakutka, which already haunts comrade Riazanov. Comrade Riazanov is a trade unionist of modest stature with a very small amount of influence upon and authority among trade unionists. Therefore, he is not dangerous enough to be sent to Iakutka, even now after his speech. It would be too much of an honour for comrade Riazanov! In order to eliminate the danger that comrade Rykov perceives, the best thing would be to leave comrade Riazanov in peace.

As a matter of fact, of what does this danger consist? A supplementary report? In a supplementary report, one can promise the moon and the stars![81] There is no danger in it for anyone at all, except for the presenter of the supplementary report. Trade unionists are too literate to lose their way in Riazanovist mazes. We have all become quite accustomed to comrade Riazanov. Therefore, we have ceased 'to take fright' at all kinds of unexpected things, which are often unforeseen even by comrade Riazanov himself. That which for many seems to be a danger is for us an unexpected amusement, even a very merry one.

What has comrade Riazanov delivered to us in his supplementary report? The same ill-starred independence of trade unions, only in a somewhat different shell, but the essence has remained Menshevist-SR-petty bourgeois, against which we struggled in the most embittered way for two whole years. Now when we have emerged victorious and the independents of various colours have lost all credit among the masses, comrade Riazanov resurrects it. He spoke here about the tasks he assigns to trade unions, including organisation of unions, the wage rates agreement, protection of labour and so forth, but not in any case pro-

---

81   The phrase he used was семь верст до небес и всё лесом.

duction. Already at the First Congress of Trade Unions, Riazanov spoke against statisation [огосударствление]. Indeed who from among the independents will refuse to endorse this? Today, in his supplementary report, he was very careful and did not say a word from among those he shouted with all his voice at sessions of the VTsSPS communist faction, the Moscow Committee of the RCP, and at other meetings in the Moscow districts, where he spoke about defending the interests of the proletariat. [ellipsis] Comrade Riazanov, what do you mean when you speak of defending the interests of the proletariat? From whom does the proletariat need its interests defended? Do they need defending from soviet power, which is flesh from the proletariat's flesh and bone from the proletariat's bone?[82] Comrades, I ask you: can there be a worse kind of independence? I affirm that there is not! But no matter where independence comes from, it does not frighten us.

Comrade Molotov is in solidarity with comrade Riazanov's point in his supplementary report about unions' role in production. He and comrade Riazanov both earnestly recommended the removal of unions from production. It is understandable when a newly reforged independent such as comrade Riazanov says this, but not so with comrade Molotov. How is it possible to remove unions from production, when they are the only producers in a given area of manufacturing? To propose this means to understand nothing! Maybe they are talking about management of enterprises and institutions. But we did not promote this. We always repeated that unions cannot interfere in management, for this is the job of the special body of factory management. A distinction must be drawn between these two elements, or else you'll get a mishmash [каша]. [ellipses] How do we trade unionists conceive of unions' participation in production and how do we define participation? By participation in production we mean the active and conscious participation by an entire production union of a given branch of industry by means of introducing the strictest union discipline, elevating the cultural level of the producers, steadfastly implementing the wage rates agreement, and protecting and organising labour. Only the production union can be the senior figure in each branch of industry, in our opinion. Only VTsSPS can be the senior figure over all branches of industry in their entirety. It cannot be otherwise!

Comrade Tomsky declared that he would not make a supplementary report to comrade Bukharin's report, since there is agreement in their basic principles and positions. Yes, there is agreement, because hardly anything has remained from comrade Bukharin's theses. Comrade Bukharin made his report from

---

82   This adapts language from Genesis 2:23 (Old Testament).

comrade Tomsky's theses, against the basics of which, of course, not one trade unionist will object. But it's necessary to dwell on the details, which in practice stifle trade unions. Comrade Bukharin rushed through one of the details, which is an accursed question for trade unionists. This is the matter of trade union interrelations with the party along horizontal and vertical lines. Instead of using his report to ground his proposals in the context of the trade union centre's relations with its periphery and trade union relations with the party from top to bottom, comrade Bukharin instead was busy criticising an immense amount of rot that was written before the congress. Incidentally, he dragged in comrade Shliapnikov's proposals, which are neither here nor there.

It needs to be noted that the most demagogic methods were used to struggle against trade unionists before the congress in Moscow. During disputes about the tasks of trade unions, they stopped at nothing. They especially tore to shreds comrade Shliapnikov, who supposedly wrote terrifying theses. Who spoke against the trade unionists? Who considered it his duty to speculate on the basis of these theses, which barked at comrade Shliapnikov? Not one orator could avoid doing so. Comrade Bukharin did not refuse to do it! I am not about to defend comrade Shliapnikov or his theses here, for these theses are not about the tasks of trade unions. They were written for another goal. Moreover, comrade Shliapnikov does not need a defence. But since comrade Bukharin struck a blow against comrade Shliapnikov, who is not here and so cannot deliver the obligatory rebuke, I consider it my duty to at least partially deflect undeserved blows at his head. Those points comrade Shliapnikov made, for which comrade Bukharin kicked him, are in the main remarkably correct! His proposals about the interrelations of the party, soviets, and trade unions render concrete the role and functions of these organisations. They precisely define what trade unions should do and how they should do it [ellipses]. The proposals outline the correct transition away from dilettantism and the jack-of-all-trades approach[83] toward the narrow specialisation of all organisations! [ellipses] This is completely correct, it cannot be otherwise! We still don't have the kind of personnel or organisations, which could do everything. Now all organisations and individual persons try to do everything, but they essentially cannot do anything. When they say that trade unions want to seize power into their hands, a bitter smile involuntarily appears on all our faces. What's this for? Who needs this? Enough demagogy!

---

83 He uses the term мюр-и-мерилиз which refers to a department store that existed in Moscow on Petrovka street in the late nineteenth and early twentieth centuries. It was founded by Scottish partners Andrew Muir and Archibald Mirrielees.

Getting back to the proposals about which comrade Bukharin reported, it's necessary to underline the point saying that the resolutions of VTsSPS should be implemented in the provinces, if they do not contradict the resolutions of the CC RCP. To say this is to say almost nothing. At the same time, this is the most urgent question, which we are breaking our necks upon. The party committees, which sometimes have no understanding of the trade union movement, meddle inopportunely in the trade unions' business. Here we need to establish precisely and definitively the conditions and limitations under which they may enter into the competency of trade unions. In the provinces [на местах], the highest party body is the local party committee. It is the inalienable right of local party committees to form trade unions' governing boards and councils, to determine their direction, to supervise them, and so forth. But in specifically trade union areas of work, as for example the wage rates agreement, the protection of labour, the organisational question, financing and so forth, we must say outright to the local party committees – hands off! For there cannot be any unified line in the trade union movement while it is under the closest 'leadership' of provincial party committees, most of which do not wish to recognise any resolutions of VTsSPS or trade union congresses. As evidence I can introduce some anecdotal examples. We know some cases, when party committees dispersed unions just for having steadfastly implemented VTsSPS resolutions, which the CC had confirmed. We recently received from one union such a complaint: the local party committee, which did not wish to recognise the wage rates agreement that VTsSPS had confirmed, demanded that the union urgently send it 'graceful rates' [грациозные ставки]. Finally, after long conversations, the trade unionists guessed that the party committee simply meant 'graduated rates' [градационные ставки]. Such know-nothing party committees pretend to leadership. Such facts call for a guarantee to be given to trade unions. Otherwise there can be no talk of any work.

In conclusion I want to respond to comrade Bukharin about one-man management. Comrade Bukharin turns the attention of the congress toward inspiring trade unionists not only to obey but also to implement the congress's decisions about one-man management. I think and declare that I express the opinion of all trade unionists about this. While the question of collegiality and one-man management was not resolved, we struggled to vindicate collegiality, but as soon as there was a decision it became law for us. In the history of our practical work, there has not been a case when we sabotaged a resolution of a congress or of the CC. We always were and will be the most efficient and dependable conductors [проводники] of our party's will. Despite the diverse points of view on this question and despite the fact that we are convinced that our point of view is correct, now we will consistently implement one-man management wherever necessary, in accord with the congress's decision. We will do so not from fear, but from good conscience! [ellipses]

10   A.G. Shliapnikov, 'Relations between the Russian Communist Party, the Soviets, and Production Unions'[84]

Presented to the congress by Lutovinov, because Shliapnikov did not attend.

1.   The three-year experience of the Russian Revolution shows that the proletariat is the sole force, which consciously fights to organise society on communist foundations.

2.   The petty rural commodity producer, the poor peasants and middle peasants, and the urban artisan have supported the proletariat in its struggle against the landlord and the large capitalist. But because their position is that of property owners, their support has constantly fluctuated and still does. Only the direct threat of a relapse to the past has restrained and is restraining these masses from outright betrayal of the cause of the proletarian revolution.

3.   The intelligentsia, as a privileged social estate in Russia in relation to the suppressed worker and peasant masses and thus imbued throughout with the ideas and system of the ruling exploiter class, has met the emancipatory struggle of the proletariat in an openly hostile manner and has refused any collaboration with it. A significant part of it went over to the side of the counterrevolution. Thanks only to long and tenacious struggle, the proletariat has succeeded in attracting part of it to participate in construction.

4.   During armed struggle and creative construction, the working class has resolutely been the only class capable of managing industry and the state and of defending its homeland from class enemies in an organised manner.

5.   In its struggle the proletariat has created three forms of political and economic associations:

    1)   the Russian Communist Party

    2)   soviets of workers and peasants

    3)   production workers' unions

---

84   GARF, f. 5451, op. 42, d. 6, 1920, ll. 17–21.

The Russian Communist Party

6. The Russian Communist Party (RCP), as recent history indicates, is the only revolutionary party of the working class. It leads class war and civil war in the name of Communism.

7. The RCP unifies the more conscious and resolute part of the proletariat around the revolutionary communist programme of action and draws to the Communist banner the more leading elements of the rural poor. Therefore, all higher leadership of building communism and general direction of the country's policy must be concentrated in the RCP.

8. The RCP, being in power, must realise its supreme leadership through its local committees and cells, but by no means over their heads. The party must realise and implement all decisions involved in administering the country and the national economy through mass bodies created in the process of revolution: Congresses of Soviets, the All-Russian Central Executive Committee of the Soviet (VTsIK), local councils of the All-Russian Central Council of Trade Unions, production unions and local union councils.

The Soviets

9. Created by the revolution, the soviets of workers and peasants and their congresses have turned out to be the only form of political union of the urban proletariat with the rural poor. As bodies of political power, soviets serve as guides to the dictatorship of the proletariat and realise it in fact.

10. As bodies of the centralised system of power, soviets manage the country by means of all labourers' direct participation. All bodies of power are directly responsible and accountable to the workers' and peasants' elected representatives.

The Unions

11. During struggle to seize industry and manage it, the Russian proletariat created numerous associations of workers in the form of production unions, which unify all production workers without exception.

12. Production associations, in the countenance of all their unions, central committees and the All Russian Central Council of Trade Unions, recognise the RCP's political and economic leadership and reject the independence of the trade union movement from the political party, no matter under which slogan this would be carried out (equality, self-sufficiency, anti-statism, and so forth).

13. The part of the RCP programme concerning the emancipation of trade unions from a narrow guild mentality has been fulfilled. The whole trade

union movement is included in the production framework. All workers, no matter what their professions, are union members.

Interrelations

14. For 2½ years of the existence of the dictatorship of the proletariat, the following interrelations have been outlined between the above-named mass organisations of all labourers:
    i. The RCP is the sole responsible political leader of worker and peasant masses' revolutionary struggle in construction
    ii. Soviets have become the sole form of political power in the country.
    iii. Unions are the sole responsible organisers of the national economy and are a school for the workers in managing the state economy.
15. During mutual work, the boundaries of each organisation's activity and responsibility have been demolished. The organisations' decrees have become intertwined, have hampered and disorganised work, and have had harmful reverberations upon the common cause. These circumstances urgently demand the definition of boundaries and of the character and order of work of all organisations named above.
16. Establishing the rights, obligations and order of work of our Party Central Committee will significantly put things in order.

The Party Central Committee

17. According to the 20th point of the RCP charter, the Congress is the supreme body of the RCP. Although the statutes do not indicate so, it is obvious that the Congress's rights should belong to the Central Committee during the periods between congresses. The Central Committee of the RCP realises the dictatorship of the organised Proletariat in the epoch of the communist revolution that we are experiencing.
18. In accord with the meaning of the 24th point of the RCP charter, the CC should realise the leadership of central soviet and social organisations through their communist factions. In such a way, the Party CC realises the leadership of external and internal policy through VTsIK and its bodies.
19. The RCP CC should firmly and resolutely carry out the party programme in regards to the economy, especially that part demanding the transfer to production unions of the management of the republic's entire national economy.
20. The Party CC should carry out the programme of building industry through the production worker unions or through their all-Russian centre. The CC decides policy related to workers with the direct participation of the leading centre of the trade union movement.

21. With the full power of its authority, the CC should support all mass organisations and bodies of power, which the revolution created, but it should not assume their functions. Work of VTsIK, as the supreme body for mass management of the republic, should be placed at its requisite high level. The same should be the case in regard to local soviets and executive committees.

22. The CC is obligated to lead the work of local organisations, encouraging at the same time all kinds of useful party initiative in the centre as well as on the local level. It should lead by giving clear, definite directives and instructions and it should not descend to petty intrusion into organisations' life and activity.

23. The CC should carry through directives of the Congress and conferences about workerising state management bodies, not only by including individual workers in collegia as a formality but also by bringing mass worker organisations into the bodies of management, according to the spirit of the RCP programme. These measures should be carried out first of all in management of the Republic's economy – industry, transport, provisions, agriculture and so on.

24. The distribution of party forces is especially important and significant at the present time. The CC should regard this matter especially carefully. It should carry out registration and characterisation of all personnel and systematically distribute them in all branches of work. Candidates, who prove through their activity dedication to the revolution, must be nominated to senior political posts. Elements that were hostile to the working class in the past may be merely clerical staff, but by no means may they be senior leaders of government institutions.

25. When implementing the party programme as it relates to using the cultural inheritance of the bourgeoisie in the form of specialists in various branches of science, technology and art, the CC should utilise these specialists through the appropriate associations of workers. Only by direct cooperation with workers can specialists and scientists be thoroughly and expediently utilised. Their detachment into a privileged ruling caste, bypassing and against the will of workers' unions, can develop patronage, adventurism and the effort to use such a position to further interests alien to those of the workers' revolution. The government should place this stratum of personnel in material conditions which promote the display of full efficiency and initiative.

26. The inefficiency of central governing bodies and the flourishing of bureaucracy and sabotage in them attest to the incapacity of the CC's organisational sector to cope with the tasks of directing these institutions' activ-

ity. Because the CC absorbed itself in trifling matters (ex. distribution of apartments and rooms, payment on suppliers' accounts, and assignment of building superintendents), it could not master the more important apparatuses of power (ex. Narkomprod, Narkompros, Narkomput, Goskontrol, and Narkomvoen), which in fact are in the hands of those who are alien to the interests of the working class.[85]

27. The history of party work for the past year has proven that those currently composing the CC are not capable of leading complex party work in governing. Therefore party comrades are confronted with the task of putting together a more efficient CC at the approaching RCP Congress. To advance the implementation of the policy of workerising state management bodies, this workerisation must begin with the Party CC.

28. To protect the party from the rush into it of alien careerist elements and to straighten out the revolutionary line in the provinces, it is necessary to set up contacts between all workers who are old party people. A majority of delegates elected to the Ninth Congress need to be party members who are workers.

11   Speeches by Iu.Kh. Lutovinov, S.P. Medvedev, I.I. Kutuzov, and A.M. Kollontai at the Ninth Conference of the RCP(b), September 1920[86]

Session five. 24 September, evening.

Chair. Comrades, the presidium has received a note signed by ten delegates, asking to allow a third presenter [apparently Degtiarev] to take the floor. The

---

85   The abbreviations are for the Commissariats of Food Supplies, Enlightenment, Transportation, State Control, and Military.

86   Sources are the officially published protocols and the archival stenographic report: RCP(b) 1972, pp. 163–4, 175–6, 186–7, and 187–8; RGASPI, f. 44, op. 1, d. 4, ll. 49–51 and 86–8; d. 6, ll. 106–8, 110 (accessed by me at the Hoover Institution Library & Archives). First published as a shortened version in 1920, the stenographic report of the Ninth RCP(b) Conference 'became a bibliographical rarity' (inside title page). The version published in 1972 was based on the full stenographic report preserved in Communist Party archives, but both published editions omitted some material from the speeches of Lutovinov, Medvedev, and Kutuzov. From the archived complete stenographic reports, I have restored portions of the Lutovinov, Medvedev, and Kutuzov speeches which were omitted from the published protocols. The restorations are designated by bracketed text below. In footnotes, I indicate places where versions of the complete stenographic report differ.

presidium suggests giving the presenter twenty minutes. Besides that, the presidium suggests shortening the time to ten minutes for orators who will participate in debate.

Lutovinov. When orators begin repeating themselves, debate can be cut short, but as long as this does not happen, there is no reason to curtail debate time.

Voice from the hall. I think that there is no reason to listen to a third presenter. We already heard out two of them. Although ten signed a request, I heard nothing new from comrade Sapronov, unfortunately. I fear that we will not hear anything new from a third. It would be better to allow comrades to engage in debate already.

Chair (conducts vote). A third presenter is rejected; time for orators is limited to ten minutes. Comrade Lutovinov has the floor.

Lutovinov. [Comrades, no matter how strange it seems, there is a great kinship between the CC and the Russian peasant. There is a Russian proverb: 'The *muzhik* will not cross himself until thunder booms'. Until events bashed the CC in the skull, the CC not only did not take any measures to prevent the decay in our party, but by its attitude, it objectively strengthened this decay.[87]

Indeed, only now has everyone, including the CC, started talking about our party's decay, when the party has started, as comrade Lenin put it in relation to trade unions, 'to smell bad'. Well, where was the CC several months ago? Indeed, the decay began a long time ago. We in good time warned the CC about all that has just been experienced, about which Comrade Zinoviev spoke here. How did it react to this? Did it take any measures? I affirm that none were taken. Except for angry growls at 'Makhnoists' and 'Makhaevists' and for the cruelest retribution against the opposition, nothing was done.][88]

Comrades, now the CC and comrade Preobrazhensky have raised in their letters this question about demoralisation of the party and our liberal comrade Zinoviev has acknowledged in his report the existence of such phenomena. Therefore, I think it is necessary now to reject old methods of struggle against opposition and eliminating discontent. Now it is necessary to reveal, not hide, all those ulcers which are eating away the body of our party, and to set about

---

87   The word Lutovinov uses, разложение, can also be translated as 'demoralisation'.

88   'Makhnoists' refers to alleged supporters of Nestor Makhno, a leader of an anarchist or anarcho-communist peasant army in Ukraine.

radical treatment, if not healing.[89] What are the chief reasons for the demoralisation of our party? Efforts to uncover these reasons are found in comrade Preobrazhensky's letter, comrade Zinoviev's report and, finally, in proposals of the liberal-gubernia [liberal-governorial] opposition. Although they solemnly uttered several bitter truths, they have not discovered the chief reasons.[90] For a long time we have known about those things going on in the provinces and those about which comrade Zinoviev so vividly and clearly spoke in his report. At one time we frequently warned the cc about these things, but they are not the reasons. For me it is completely unimportant how individual comrades display themselves, independently of whether they occupy minor or major posts. For me the system is important. The system truly brings about the appearance of such characters and inescapably leads to such actions.[91]

[Comrade Zinoviev asked workers in Rostov why they have not yet taken power into their hands. If I had been in the place of those Rostov workers, I would have asked Comrade Zinoviev, 'Why is it that workers in Petersburg, under you, have still not taken power into their hands?' Why is it that when Petersburg workers tried to do this, by expelling Zinoviev's lackeys from the old Petersburg Committee (pc) and bringing old, tried-and-true comrades trusted by the masses into a new committee, Comrade Zinoviev sabotaged this pc? And why was this pc disbanded? Because a system exists, under which it will always be so. It is necessary to talk about this system. This is the main reason for the demoralisation in the party.][92]

In the party, we see the sway of party specialists. [*This line stands in place of an entire paragraph in the stenographic report*: Just as the civil war bitterly raged, we created a strong [?] party, and soviets and trade unions, which now have ceased to exist in our country. Instead of them, party specialists have appeared. These specialists are far worse than those about whom Comrade Zinoviev spoke here. Our party specialists do not just mutter through clenched teeth, when speaking with workers, but lie to the utmost about their party comrades. (Applause.)]

89 According to the stenographic report in RGASPI, f. 44, op. 1, d. 6, l. 106, he said 'rational' instead of 'radical'.

90 According to the stenographic report in RGASPI, f. 44, op. 1, d. 6, l. 106, this was 'minor regrettable truths', not 'bitter truths'.

91 The stenographic report in d. 6, l. 107 indicates that he specified characters such as 'Khlestakovs, commissars'.

92 After World War I began, the name of the Russian capital, St. Petersburg, was changed to Petrograd, but the Bolshevik Petersburg Committee did not change its name. In early 1918, the Bolsheviks moved the capital to Moscow, which was more distant from invading German armies.

[Instead of soviets, we have at best chairmen of gubernia executive committees, who settle accounts vindictively left and right, just like here in the centre,
for they are required to carry out the centre's line without deviating. Instead
of a committee, we have secretaries who are far from suitable for their posts
and who have only recently come into our party. Biographical questionnaires
[анкеты] are proof of this. This also occurs in Ukraine and in Donbas.[93] And
what does the CC represent?]

The CC long ago stopped being just a guiding body. It gradually turned into
a body of management and executive function. [Take the VTsIK, VTsSPS, any
People's Commissariats, or economic organisations. Indeed, they only work
according to CC directives, independently carrying out the line defined by the
CC. Nothing of the sort. The CC interferes in everyone's work and in such a situation, it is impossible to lead correctly. Therefore,] It is necessary to strictly limit
the CC's functions, transform it into a guiding body, and restore the soviets to
their rights, so that they could work self-sufficiently without any interference.[94]

[So that in the soviets, not specialists but the masses would decide all questions of high principle.[95] It is necessary to involve the masses, so that they
would feel at home in the soviets.]

Further, comrade Zinoviev spoke about appointees. He said that we send
from the CC to a post a comrade with a recommendation and we say: 'We
recommend this administrator to you; verify him and appoint him to some
work or other'. But indeed if this were so, then there could be no objections.
In practice the matter stands completely differently. These characters, who are
sent with the broadest mandates to the provinces on CC assignment, deal with
people like a cook with potatoes.[96] [The masses, who are chased out of the soviets and committees, start to react in their own way. Seething at congresses and
conferences, they choose and send forth their own people, who carry out their
views. How does the CC act in such cases and with the support of gubernia
committees? Just simply, they disperse such congresses and conferences. So it
was in Ukraine, in Rostov, and in many places in Russia. In Rostov, for example,
Beloborodov dispersed a conference for having elected to the presidium two

---

93   In d. 6, l. 107, after 'Donbas' the sentence continues, 'where there are clusters of party per-
     sonnel, who do not participate at all in work thanks to not being able to arrange work with
     soviets of deputies committees. In many party organisations, there are party specialists,
     who need to get it in the neck'.

94   In d. 6, l. 108, the stenographer types 'all organisations' instead of 'soviets'.

95   In d. 6, l. 108, the stenographer types 'party specialists', not just 'specialists'.

96   1920 editors wrote in parentheses that Lutovinov here 'introduces examples of pressure
     on party assemblies in provincial towns'. They cut these examples from the 1920 edition
     and the 1972 editors do not include them here. I have restored them in brackets.

comrades who disorganised work. But why the whole conference? Indeed, does this resolve the problem? When you break up a conference, the masses are forced to seek another outlet. Some leave the party in batches, while others take revenge, as for example the Finns with their CC. Also, it is finally no longer a secret that Makhno forms his detachments in Ukraine out of communists and command posts in the detachments are taken by our former district military commanders and leaders. This takes place, thanks to that system, which is still practiced in the centre.] As long as those in the centre don't disavow this system, of course, the system will not essentially change.[97]

[Comrade Zinoviev very readily described the situation in other places, but he did not say what is done under him in Piter and nearby the CC here in Moscow. Indeed, the local satraps, the 'Belenkys and Piatnitskys' (there is no other name for them) went so far as to expel people from the party for an assembly, which in their opinion was illegal.[98] Of course, this only intensifies demoralisation. Today, I was shown the decision of a committee, which forbids comrades acquitted by a court for illegal assemblies to communicate with or appear on the territory of the district, where they earlier worked. And Comrade Belenky in the district threatened to shoot workers for illegal assemblies. Yes, indeed, these are monstrous things. No matter how many thoughts you pour out here about abnormal blunders, until you destroy the system, it will be impossible to eliminate them. In order to do away with decay and to make our party healthy, the following measures are necessary: (reads a resolution). If these proposals will not be accepted, then the workers, who have now reached the summit of their indignation, undoubtedly will carry out this work themselves and then it will already be too late to set it right.]

Medvedev. At all recent congresses, Comrade Bubnov frequently has emphasised the presence of the 'Workers' Opposition'. He has not overlooked this question at our current conference. Comrade Bubnov has been in our ranks since before October.[99] As long as I have known him, he was always in 'opposition',

---

97   1920 editors wrote in parentheses that Lutovinov concluded by 'introducing some proposals and said that if these proposals would not be accepted, the masses will do this work themselves'. Neither edition listed the proposals. The proposals must have been in the resolution referenced as read by Lutovinov in the next paragraph, which was censored from the published protocols.

98   In d. 6, l. 110, the stenographer references 'Belenky, Bubnov, and Volin' rather than 'Belenky and Piatnitsky'.

99   In d. 6, l. 110, the stenographer records Medvedev as first calling Bubnov 'Lord' [Господа], then correcting himself by saying 'Comrade'.

but he has never proposed anything that would really have guaranteed implementation of those fine measures, which our past conferences and assemblies set forth.

We have many reasons to be satisfied that the question about our party's illness has been put on the agenda. Everyone has been allowed to say what he thinks about it. According to Vladimir Ilich's report, we will confront not less intense but more intense struggle in the future. [He said that we now are transitioning toward struggle against all of international imperialism.] This struggle will demand from us even greater strength, even greater cohesion. But this cannot be achieved [in that period of time, which international imperialism allows us], if we don't seriously explain how to guarantee that all our beautiful measures will be implemented. In order to make our party healthy, it is necessary not only to outline measures, which were in the CC's letter, but also to seriously implement freedom to criticise the work of all our party committees, including the CC. There has been no such criticism up to now. Why hasn't there been? There really have accumulated in our party many military commissars, who we should have swept out from our ranks a long time ago. But the matter is also about what we should say right now, that there is too much of a new element in our party institutions and too little of that old element, about which comrade Kalinin spoke. To wed this new element to the old in our committees is very difficult. But we should do this no matter what. As long as this is not done, we will not resolve the questions worrying us. Until then we will witness the same squabbles, fights and wrangling, which we observe right now. But in order to achieve the correct combination of personnel, the CC should first of all know the personal composition of the party. We carry out more than a little reshuffling, but not all of it guarantees friendly work in the committees. One must know how to select personnel with a conscious intention [and not be guided, as often happens, by tale-bearing, as a result of which, such things happen. Today you are unanimously elected to one or another senior post. You set to work and suddenly the CC transfers you to another place. What calls this forth? It's unknown. We begin to clear it up and it emerges that someone somewhere informed something to someone.] Right now the CC and its apparatus do not know the personal composition of committees and they are little interested in the actual length of service and party record of personnel. It is necessary to eliminate this insufficiency.

Of the measures which comrade Zinoviev proposed here, we think that two are new. These are freedom of criticism and ending repression. Up to now they tried to convince us of just the opposite. That means that we were not told about the actual situation. [If the CC now is presenting great freedom for exchanging opinions, it is clear that this will make our work significantly healthier in the provinces.] We already had and have now to a significant degree all the remaining measures, such as establishment of regular general assemblies, creation of commissions and so forth. Looking in part at the Kuban, we have very many assemblies and commissions, but they do not give rise to that which comrade Zinoviev proposes. [Comrade Zinoviev said that in many places we have assemblies, which are painstakingly created and so forth, but they happen less often. Why? This began to happen when that opposition, which we see, began to grow. Thanks to this, it is possible to take account of the growing opposition not only here, but also in the provinces. The picture has unfolded before the CC that these assemblies have become rarer. It is easier to say to invite to the assembly all rank and file party members, but indeed they will demand discussion, they will interfere in resolving our problems, and you cannot refuse them this.] Comrades Bubnov and Sapronov declared that 'workerisation' of our committees will not immediately cure our party's illnesses and that in the nearest future it will not weaken this unhealthy phenomenon we have all recognised. Nevertheless, I think it will and I assert that half of all the staff positions in gubernia committees should be secured for workers.

Kutuzov. Comrades, when I heard comrade Zinoviev's report here, well I thought that if comrade Zinoviev had made a similar report a week ago in some district party committee of Moscow, then he would have been forced to leave the party long ago [and probably they would have clubbed him to death somewhere]. But comrades, as you see, the report was so important and so remarkable that, in all probability, all comrades present here can come to agreement around it. I think that if the party conference will accept Comrade Zinoviev's proposals, then they must be implemented not just on paper, but in fact. Then we will see what will happen. Further, comrades, each senior staff person and each district party committee should gather communists 'from below', both workers and nonworkers without distinction, and make [such meritorious] reports and lectures to them. If a person will speak, then he will say: 'Don't conduct demagoguery. Get out of here. This resolution is not needed. We need one like that which comrade Zinoviev read'. Then you will see good material from the provinces. Then the CC would not have to bring forth this resolution just today. Already long ago it would have brought forth such a resolution. Comrades, I propose, therefore: communist comrades need to be assembled as often as possible not only by districts, but also by institutions. Then say, Aleksei Ivanovich, now then, comrades, what do you specialists do here.[100]

---

100   It's possible 'specialists' was a typographical error and that the intended word was 'socialists'.

Now they will tell us where it is good and where it is bad, but we don't have this [fashion] in the institutions.

Further, comrades, I should dwell on those unpleasant incidents, which happen here, there, and everywhere. Of course, the big wheels are constantly lording it over unlucky communists, but in one way or another it has to be said, comrades, that some phrases can be fair.[101] [I will take myself as an example. According to Comrade Trotsky's instructions, inasmuch as he said that it is necessary to search our souls, I want to engage in some soul-searching before you. Earlier I did not have a clue. Comrades, I will speak with a reservation. The worker as such has to be preoccupied during his work with such chatter about who eats butter, who eats fish, who rides on an automobile. There's no time. I declare this up front. But nevertheless, when I became a higher-up [убер-кондуктор], then I took on a servant, although there is no such thing. Today I brought butter, tomorrow some bread, and the day after tomorrow, well, one day leads to another and it comes to the point that people haul sugar by the sacks. Now, about the automobile. Of course, not one worker, no one has ever said that I used an automobile without any purpose, although of course, who is not guilty? But when I desired one evening to take my family and the lads along for a ride, it was not with enormous hats. We, including your humble servant, we go for a holiday drive and not in the evenings, but on the holiday, when all people sit and watch.]

Comrades, I should likewise say also that your obedient servant has strayed a little from the line he took three years ago. They made me a military commissar, but even now I live in factory housing. Under the bourgeois social order, it happened that you would go to your pals.[102] [Then it would happen that you would go to visit your lads – and now I live in factory housing, but the Bankom kicked me out because I said to it that the Bannyi district committee defends horrible people.][103] They would say: 'Answer, comrades, why do you summon us to struggle?' I would say because the situation, in which we find ourselves, cannot be tolerated. As they say, a threat hangs over us. Look, isn't it so, you just walk past some military nitpicker and he'll give you a kick just because. You'll

101   In parentheses, the editors of the 1920 edition explained that 'Kutuzov gave some examples of how easily the psychology of a person can change, when he comes from a worker environment and lands in a senior post. This change can occur thanks to how easy it can be to overstep the bounds of what is permissible'. The editors of the 1972 edition did not restore these examples to the text. I have done so in the following passage to the best of my ability, but at times the uncorrected transcript offers no clear meaning.

102   The word 'bourgeois' does not appear in the stenographic report, which seems to indicate that Kutuzov was describing circumstances under Soviet power, not before the revolution.

103   Bankom must refer to the Bannyi District Party Committee.

start talking and gradually get round to what we are struggling for, which is for freedom, finally, so that plants would be in our own hands, and for our own Soviet republic in the end. Speaking before workers is more difficult nowadays, and some comrades try to avoid it.[104] [Indeed, who wants to go to a dirty place? I would rather go where it is clean, tidy, and well cared for.] Workers request footwear, bread, and clothing. Comrades, when you go to an assembly, workers ask: 'When will there be bread?' I say to them, 'There will not be bread'. 'Why?' 'The situation is serious'. 'Well, comrade Kutuzov, if they don't give us bread, then after labouring quite righteously we have to go to the nearest countryside, work extra there, or exchange something for ten pounds, and carry it to the plant mill, where they deduct a quarter of a pound [four pounds] for the cost of the grinding'. I say, 'This is a firm decision. It is the centre's order. You should give up a quarter of a pound [four pounds] for grinding'. [And it turns out that we do not give them anything, but we only take from them].

Comrades, they ask me: 'Comrade Kutuzov, what about apartments?' Indeed, comrades, we should say outright that the workers' housing question is far from resolved. [And so we see that if a worker somewhere by mistake, by following our former decrees, got in the way, then he is sent out.] At the same time, if we say that some manufacturer needs to be evicted from a dwelling, then all of our central institutions rally behind him, say that he is a comrade, and they don't have the right to evict him. Here, there, and everywhere Kutuzov planted such comrades in institutions. Comrades say that I hate [the old][105] spetses. Yes, that is correct, I will die still hating them. But in what respect? I understand the matter about specialists thus: as long as they do not become accustomed to working together with us in close proximity and they don't overcome adversities together with us, it is necessary to hold them in an iron grip, just like they held us. [But we became soft, yes we give them highly responsible work, in order that they would talk various nonsense to worker representatives, who go out of our institutions and carry only contagion against Soviet power. I should likewise point out that workers as such, communists, they do not get much good fortune from us. What does communist mean? Indeed we are all worker communists, especially recently, at the books and going to lectures, yet in fact if I go along the street and see that four noncommunists are humiliating a communist, I nevertheless roll up my sleeves and bang! It means worker communists are a strike force.

---

104 The stenographic report records a series of colloquial phrases, which appear to be summarised accurately here.

105 There were ellipses in the published text in place of 'the old' in the uncorrected transcript.

Comrades, it's necessary to say truthfully that here, there and everywhere, when we summoned workers and said it's for the sake of your interests and your Soviet Republic, they went forward. When we begin to turn away a little from the workers, then they retreat from us.

Dear comrades, what are we doing now pretty often among communists? Last year, when Comrade Trotsky talked about a hatchet, well what happened? Some of our lads began to carry around hatchets. If we came to the centre and saw that here they wore 'frenchi' service jackets or carried whips, well they go back home so. Especially in the provinces, in party committees and local organisations where I work, there are sonny boys. As soon as a critical moment arrives, these sonny boys run away. We have documents, which show that no one remained in a town, with the exception of several workers. Everyone ran away and very many of them were communists. Also due to the economic situation, they departed from us. Their souls need to be looked into.]

Chair. The presidium offers the floor out of turn for five minutes to comrade Kollontai, who has just recovered from illness. (Applause.)

Kollontai. Comrades, all of us here welcomed comrade Zinoviev's speech, especially that part where he speaks about the need for freedom to criticise. We all know how much we need this freedom of criticism. Too many of our problems have festered and become painful. Although we welcome this point in comrade Zinoviev's speech, nevertheless I would say that this point has not been developed to the end. Freedom of criticism, but what kind? Comrades, there should be a guarantee, that if we really will criticise thoroughly that which has become painful, then he who criticises will not be sent to nice hot places to eat peaches. Now, comrades, this is not a rare phenomenon. I pose the question about the need to secure guarantees that none of those criticising will go to eat peaches. Criticism is allocated not only to the CC. The Central Committee issues decrees, which are implemented through the gubernia party committees (gubkoms). When gubkoms implement these directives, they modify CC decisions somewhat by applying them to local conditions, and they do not allow their actions to be criticised. Criticism is not allowed. Therefore it is important that this point about criticism be stated clearly and precisely. Long live criticism, but without the need to eat peaches after it! (Applause.)

12   Iu.Kh. Lutovinov's Proposals to the Ninth Conference of the
      RCP(b), September 1920[106]

1.   Immediately transform the CC from a body of management into a guiding body.
2.   Restore to their rights the organisations (party committees, soviets, and trade unions) and replace the party specialists with actual party committees, soviets, and trade unions.
3.   Revoke appointmentism and allow it only in exceptional cases, when local organisations are not in the condition to nominate candidates from their own midst.
4.   Eliminate the dispersal of congresses, conferences, and committees. In exceptional cases, when it will be necessary, transfer the evidence of dispersal to a court.
5.   Attract broad masses of workers into management not just in words, but also in deeds, both in the centre and in the provinces.
6.   Redistribute from the centre to the provinces those who have sat too long in the centre and those who have never left it, and not just for tours by popular comrades, but for work, and extract personnel from the provinces to fill their positions.
7.   As much as possible, require permission of local organisations to transfer senior personnel.
8.   Increase the circulation of newspapers and party news at the expense of Narkompros-published literature, which nobody needs.
9.   Before the Tenth Party Congress, increase the permanent cadres of the CC instructors for constant maintenance and study of all party organisations by sending them on circuits.
10. At the Tenth Congress, compose the CC with such a reckoning that there would be representatives of all the most important areas of work, who would remain in place for work in the CC, while remaining CC members would travel the provinces by uninterrupted circuit. Moreover, a prevailing number of places in the CC would be guaranteed for workers.

---

106   RGASPI, f. 44, op. 1, d. 6, l. 109 (accessed by me at the Hoover Institution Library & Archives).

13   N. Kopylov, 'That Which Needs to be Destroyed: "Higher-Ups" and "Rank-and-File"'[107]

When senior personnel of the Zamoskvoretsky district met, one prominent party comrade asserted that the abnormalities in our party, which have been the subject of especially intense conversation recently, are no more than small pimples on the body of the organism. As they say, there is nothing especially to raise a fuss about.

This is deeply incorrect in essence. The question about 'higher-ups' and 'rank-and-file' shows all the signs of a chronic illness, although it is not especially strongly evident externally. Nevertheless, the most serious methods of treatment are needed against it.

1.   *History of the Illness*
The first symptoms of the illness relate to the time when our party was transforming from a party of opposition into a ruling party. The centre of gravity of party personnel transferred from chaos into state building. Little by little, a thin stratum of our communist bureaucracy was worked out in our country. Unnoticeably, gradually, it began to depart from the masses. Moreover this departure was not always accompanied by the [illegible word] of party work. Comrades who specialise in soviet work, if it is can be expressed so, began to regard themselves as their own type of [illegible word] 'spetses', they adopted all of the latter's basic methods of work, forgetting that the 'spets' is organiser-[illegible word] in his own area of work, dealing with workstations, machines, and people, which in the production process also are not more than separate parts of the mechanism, by which it is possible and should [illegible phrase], arrange them in one or another order, apply norms, and regulate their work completely as the pace of the clock is regulated. The 'spets' is right in his own area. It would be ridiculous and awkward to arrange parliaments in workshops, request legislative approval for each technical instruction.

It is impossible, however, to justify the actions of the soviet spets, who blindly transfers all methods of technical management into the area of party building. The party is not a mill with automatic work stations, where under the pretext of military necessity it is possible to hold complete command, without asking the opinions of the entire workforce. But nevertheless, this can be seen in some places, unfortunately. Individual comrades, who hold high adminis-

---

107   'To, chto nado unichtozhit: k voprosu o "verkhakh" i "nizakh"', *Pravda*, 30 September 1920, no. 217.

trative posts, began to strive to concentrate in their hands the entirety of power both in the party and in the soviets. Having accrued this power, they ceased already to take account of the will of the organisation. They started to regard the party through the viewpoint of the 'spets', as if they were looking at raw material, from which something or another can be molded, but only accounting for it to the extent that the technical spets generally takes consideration of raw material. An extreme form of new bureaucratism flourished on this soil, both in soviet and in party work. The party in fact lost control over soviet work in the provinces, since those very same 'soviet specialists' or their dumb, impersonal creatures, who cannot take even one step resolutely and independently, entrenched themselves in the gubkoms. Instead of self-activity within the party and instead of work to cultivate and prepare new members to actively participate in soviet and party building, the bosses busied themselves with one main task, which was to create their own solid, obedient majority, which would serve as [illegible word] for their actually irresponsible activity. When distributing personnel, the main [illegible word] became to appeal not to the capability of one or another comrade in a given branch, but to his ability to be an obedient [illegible word], a blind weapon in the hands of comrades who stand above him.

Little by little, the organisations in the provinces (for some places I can definitely vouch) assumed some sort of terrible ceremonial, closed-up character, I would say. Within a quite strong organisation, which is forged with iron discipline, there are triumphal, ostentatious sessions on the current moment and current events. The main thing, which is uninterrupted, organising life of each individual [illegible words] living organism of the party, was absent. There is no broad mass participation in soviet building by party members. Draft projects and proposals about worker-peasant inspection remained only draft projects and proposals. Sections continue to exist apart, without any link with the masses. Personnel are assigned to posts on account of services, of which the merits are unknown to any organisation and it is unclear to whom these are known. Then they made haste to surround themselves personally with an obedient element, which disorganises work rather than reinforcing it. The party undoubtedly cannot be reconciled to such a situation. Healthy reaction against bureaucratising comrades' demoralising tactics, which to put it mildly are excessive, gave birth to the division into 'heights' and 'depths', with which we cannot help but wage most resolute struggle, for it contradicts all the basic principles of our party. The situation was exacerbated even more by the unhealthy circumstance, which comrades standing here and there in power created by in fact exiling the opposition, under the pretext of various sorts of mobilisations.

2. What is 'Makhaevshchina'?

The opposition to the situation which is being created was lavishly christened with the epithet 'Makhaevshchina', which did not at all correspond to the truth. Are there really Makhaevists, who are enemies of the intelligentsia and even of Marxism, in our Party? I know very many comrades, who have been indiscriminately accused of 'Makhaevism', but I assert that each of them is as much an enemy of Makhaevshchina, as any fully irreproachable Marxist. Accusation of Makhaevshchina is built on the external similarity of struggling elements and outward correspondence to those signs, according to which genuine Makhaevists separated sheep from goats and workers from intelligentsia.

Intelligenty lead the majority of gubernia committees and gubernia executive committees; workers really make up the core of the opposition to their attitude toward party and soviet work. But does this mean that the Workers' Opposition is directed not against certain methods of work, but against the party and nonparty intelligentsia? No, and a thousand times no. I know a mass of cases, when people who were old *intelligenty* from head to toe came to stand at the head of the 'opposition'. Likewise, I know of some 'highly placed' workers, who became cut off from the masses. There have been many cases of both workers and intelligents assimilating all the bad habits, which are inevitable when one becomes estranged from the masses.

This 'Makhaevshchina' is only a trump card in the hands of those who, by bandying this term about and speculating on it, want to shame the opposition and preserve first place for themselves.

What they call 'Makhaevshchina' is actually nothing else than the healthy current in our party, which is directed not only against intelligentsia but also against workers, who have broken off from the masses, ossified in their excessive bureaucratism, and retreated into shell of their department and their office. It stands to reason that there is no guarantee that this opposition of the most steadfast and conscious elements of our party, when in the future it is reflected back from among the more backward, raw strata, will not assume any kind undesirable, sickly forms, which might extend all the way toward rebirth of genuine Makhaevshchina, which had been dead. Indeed, it depends on the party itself to take measures in a timely manner to destroy the illness and its causes.

3. Opposition Needs to Be Destroyed

Given those enormous tasks which confront our party, these oppositions and divisions into 'heights' and 'depths' should be destroyed, for they are impermissible, in order not to weaken by one iota the unity of the party of international revolution, which is forged with an iron will striving toward communism, and bonded by a deluge of the blood of proletarians, who perished in countless battles on all fronts and barricades. We do not observe any differences of principle within our party. Minor practical disagreements generally are unavoidable in such an enormous business as building communism in the conditions of merciless civil war, but these disagreements are eliminated in the process of work. The party is healthy. The party enjoys colossal authority among labourers of the entire world. Moreover, resolute measures are needed against the ferment of looming demoralisation, which so far has still not been spent, but which cannot be allowed to multiply, become stronger, cause inflammation, and cost the organism of our party dearly.

The Party CC's letter about 'heights' and 'depths' and the Moscow Committee's theses make a big step forward in the area of reviving work in the provinces and making it healthier, but it must not be forgotten that the best law, when it falls into the hands of a poor executive, transforms into a scrap of paper.

Without weakening the tempo of militant 'shock work', cultural-educational work in the masses needs to be made a thousand times stronger. It's necessary to attract into soviet work as broad strata of the party as possible and to transform each member of the organisation into an activist. Our soviet and party clubs should be transformed so that they would discuss many questions of principle in addition to hearing reports about the current moment and about the party's history, and programme. Strengthening the party's control over the clerks, departments, and work of the soviets, it is necessary at the same time that the strictest responsibility for assignments be born not by the collective, but by the one who proposes the given candidacy. The CC needs to carry out more frequent audits of the gubkoms' work and to create auditing commissions in the provinces, which are independent from the gubkoms not in words but in fact. The character and essence of any opposition should be researched thoroughly, for only under this condition is it possible to eliminate the causes of its absorption. All mobilisations should be taken under the CC's control. The electoral principle needs to be preserved and expanded at all levels of party work. The question about dispersing committees needs to be regulated one way or another. It would be possible, for example, to introduce as an obligatory rule a court, which would try cases of dispersed organisations, with the right of appeal to the CC. Such courts would right away put an end to squabbles and to settling personal accounts under the banner of discipline and responsibility for the general direction of work.

Besides that, party courts composed of old party members are a good thing in general. They could try any sort of offence which falls between the cracks, thanks to lack of clarity in party jurisdictions.

All these measures, it needs to be supposed, kill at the root any opposition, besides a small, insignificant group of talentless people, who were removed from posts for their lack of talent or excessive bureaucratism and isolation from the masses. These very measures in the most beneficial way do not delay also to tell on the condition of our soviet work, which the party's forces carry out.

14   A.M. Kollontai's Diary Notes, Circa October 1920[108]

2 October [she writes the year as 1921, but it surely should be 1920]

The party conference … That which I said regarding criticism was witty and elicited laughter, but it seems V[ladimir] I[lich Lenin] was dissatisfied. He furrowed his brow. I said that a guarantee should be given, that 'if you criticise, then let them not send you away to "eat peaches" for this' (this regarding the transfer of T[omsky?] to Turkestan).[109] They laughed loudly. Criticism went along the line that we're turning the party into an instrument of Soviet state policy, contrary to the direct line to communism. … Lenin was sincere. He said outright that now 'no kind of criticism is permissible, Russia is surrounded by enemies, we are under siege, it's necessary to keep silent, endure and obey. We will not give you freedom of criticism'.[110]

15   Theses Presented to Some Party Cells and to the Central Committee of the All-Russian Metalworkers' Union in the Autumn of 1920[111]

1.   Three years of intense struggle for existence both at home and abroad, which was accompanied by only the passive support of the West European proletariat, undermined the material and spiritual strengths of

---

108   RGASPI, f. 134, op. 3, d. 37, ll. 29–30, among materials for 1921–2. Kollontai used initials for persons mentioned. The bracketed additions are mine. The parenthetical remarks are hers. I cannot remember whether the ellipses are hers or mine.

109   Tomsky was sent to work in Turkestan in summer 1921, which would seem to confirm that this dates to October 1921, but she made the 'eat peaches' remark in a speech at the September 1920 Ninth Party Conference. The fragment was found among her diary entries for 1921–2.

110   RGASPI, f. 134, op. 3, d. 37, ll. 29–30.

111   TsA FSB, R33718, vol. 37, ll. 215–16.

Soviet Russia, which was forced to make a priority of military tasks and to subordinate to them the economic and political management of the Republic.

2. Unceasing attacks from international capital and the blockade of Soviet Russia hindered economic development and contributed to the country's material impoverishment. Communist achievements did not go beyond the bounds of equalising the distribution of consumer goods.

3. Soviet Russia is entering its fourth anniversary under the staggering blow of a difficult economic crisis (lack of food, fuel, raw materials, working hands and so forth), which puts a brake on political and economic construction and threatens the failure of all socialist undertakings.

4. Broad circles of the working masses have endured deprivations, burdens, and disasters. They have an insignificant sense of communist achievements. All this, together with the transition to authoritarian (so called military) methods of management and organisation, have created in the masses indifference and distrust, which cross over to hostility toward organisations and the system of power.

5. General decline and demoralisation also overwhelm the family of our party. The cohesion and unity of old are gone. Dissatisfaction grows and it is accompanied by the departure from the party of proletarian elements. Party members have become confronted with the task of seeking out measures, which will help overcome the crisis we are experiencing, and with it all disasters, ruin, and demoralisation.

6. Domestically, the ongoing crisis is deepened and broadened by: a) the country's general economic backwardness, the primitivity and weak productive capacity of extracting and processing industries; b) the disruption of the organic link between industry and agriculture and between city and countryside; c) the country's exhaustion by many years of imperialist slaughter and continuing civil war; d) the lack of an actually well-considered system for organising the economy of the Republic, which gives rise to abnormalities and failure to maintain well the interrelations between separate parts of the economy; e) irrational bureaucratic centralisation, which performs exclusively on paper, without taking account of industry's backwardness and geographic particularities and without actually forging creative activism among local forces.

7. As a consequence of economic crisis, we see the collapse of the organised, largescale industrial economy and the effort to transition from factory work to handicrafts and from mills to cottage industry. Due to this, the overall production of wares decreases and the rapacious expenditure of raw materials grows.

8.   In agriculture, small property owning on a reactionary basis of levelling and consumption is cultivated intensively. Arable land is reduced in area and it declines in quality. Cattle raising decreases. Profitable interest in farming is paralysed. The peasant farmer strives to limit productivity of farming to the needs of his family.

9.   The difficult situation of the Republic's economy, the catastrophic impoverishment of the broad masses of the labouring population, and the threat of cold, hunger and degeneration peremptorily dictate the immediate implementation of a system of measures, which would give broad scope to individual and collective initiative, enterprise, and creativity in all areas of economic life.

10. First of all, the intensivity of political activity of RCP members should be made healthier and raised up. Authoritarian methods of work should be eliminated. The communist party as built on the foundations of democratic centralism, absorbing all activist elements of the working class, should be the brain, heart, and will of all socialist work. It should be the inspiration and leader of all organisations acting in various branches of construction.

11. The RCP realises its supreme and systematic leadership of the activity of government bodies and workers organisations through factions of the given institutions. This leadership should not stoop to transforming the party organisation into the technical appendage of one or another body of government administration or slip into petty tutelage over worker organisations.

12. In the area of economy building and management of the national economy, the RCP depends for support upon the production unions, which are connected with the broad proletarian masses and concentrate within themselves collective and economic experience.

13. The respite, which we received thanks to a break in the fighting with Poland, should have been used to extend economic construction by strengthening and reinforcing trade unions and economic bodies both in the centre and in the provinces. Moreover, this reinforcement should go along the entire line, taking into attention that the principle of 'shock work' in relation to separate branches or localities disrupts the organic link and the integrity of an economic whole.

14. In the interests of attracting all labourers into managing the economy, it is necessary to have a broad scope for workers' self-activity. Toward these goals, it is necessary to revive the activity of soviets, as proletarian bodies, which embrace all government questions, carry out all government construction, and support the political activism of the masses.

15. An end should be put to political tightrope-walking and the particular-istic quest to seek a fulcrum of support, sometimes on the 'poor peasants', at other times on the 'middle peasant', and finally on the 'spetses'. Mass organisations of workers, that is unions and soviets, should be the buttress of support for soviet policy. Relations between the city and the coun-tryside should rest on the economic interest of both sides.

16. The policy of proletarian power in relation to the countryside should be a policy of 'good husbandry', not one of mechanically destroying the eco-nomic wellbeing of the peasantry or stooping to petty bourgeois charity, such as dividing out property among heads of families. Our activity in the countryside should go along the line of class stratification and unification of the propertyless into large production associations, while remember-ing that the path to introducing socialism in the countryside is via the machine and collectivism.

17. In the interests of expedient and full use of the workforce, it is necessary to get each individual worker and likewise their collectives in the form of brigades and groups to feel invested in the work they execute. Wage rates policy should be built on the interests of developing labour productiv-ity and should combine monetary pay and pay-in-kind so as to secure for workers a minimum for subsistence. Trade unions and economic bodies should coordinate not only food resources but also the Republic's monet-ary fund according to the needs of the economy.

18. All attempts to introduce the expansion of work hours into the system of elevating the productivity of labour should be rejected as reactionary measures that do not contribute to achieving the actual goal. The sys-tem of administrative punishment should be transformed into a judicial system, with an institution of judges who are elected by the labourers themselves.

19. Soviet legislation for the protection of labour, motherhood and infants, children, and invalids, should actually be carried out and violators of it should be punished.

20. Our leading slogans should be to defend the interests of the working class by intensifying its economic and political might within the country, to give armed rebuff to the imperialism of all countries and in all its forms, and to mount an ideological offensive against the capitalist West.

16   Iu.Kh. Lutovinov, Letter to Ukrainian Comrades, 23 October 1920[112]

[Labeled: 'Letter of Iu.Kh. Lutovinov, representative of the Ukrainian opposition, about his speech at the All-Russian party conference'. Typed text with no signature. Lutovinov's urgent advice to oust specific leaders of the Communist Party of Ukraine brought his letter to the attention of party leaders in Moscow. According to Trotsky, Zinoviev delivered Lutovinov's letter to the CC.[113] The Orgburo investigated the letter after leaders of the Communist Party of Ukraine complained about it.[114]]

Dear comrades,
     On behalf of those who share my view, I answer your letter by informing you of the following:
1.   My speech at the All-Russian conference was not just mine personally, but was in the name of and with the full approval of a whole group of comrades, who were not only Muscovites, but from some other cities.
2.   Regarding your inquiry as to whether I called for a third proletarian revolution, not only was the character of my speech not 'insurrectionist', but on the contrary it was precautionary in warning about the inevitability of an outburst among broad worker masses, if the current policy of the CC RCP will not change.
3.   Our point of view about current events and means of struggle against the situation-in-the-making coincides with yours, judging from your letter. For comparison, I list in summary the demands, which I put forth at the All-Russian conference in the name of our group:
      a)   Promptly transform the CC from an executive body of management into a leading body (one that instructs).
      b)   Renew the rights of the Soviets, the party committees and trade unions.
      c)   Destroy appointmentism of both party and Soviet specialists, allowing it only in those cases, when the provinces cannot nominate from their midst candidates to one or another post. Then a comrade will be dispatched from the centre, but under no circumstances will the centre foist a candidate into any post. The centre will only make a recommendation.

---

112   RGASPI, f. 17, op. 71, d. 79, ll. 1–2.
113   RGASPI, f. 5, op. 2, d. 288.
114   RGASPI, f. 17, op. 112, d. 100, l. 6.

d) Do away with the dispersals of committees, conferences, congresses and central bodies elected at them (such as the CC CPU [Communist Party of Ukraine]. If dispersal is necessary, a court, formed especially with this goal, should consider and decide the case.

e) Attract broad masses of workers not just in words, but in fact, installing them in party committees, soviets, and unions.

f) Transfer to the provinces all those who have sat too long in their posts and who throw their weight around, and so make it possible to attract fresh forces from the provinces to the centre.

g) Transfer discussion of all questions through party committees and meetings to the broad masses of workers.

h) The composition of the VTsIK [All-Russian Central Executive Committee] and Party CC must be changed in such a way so that the overwhelming number would be workers.

Those are all the demands [ellipses in text]

You can clearly imagine our line [ellipses in text]. There should always be resoluteness and certainty. Under no circumstances enter into a compact with any vacillating and uncertain elements. When the opportunity arises, make use of them but do not introduce them into one's organisations, otherwise their hesitation will doom the cause. Now it is necessary to turn the most particular attention to party organisations by working in them and explaining to the masses their role and significance in the revolution and the present situation. At re-elections of committees, try to enter into new committees and bring with oneself midlevel people [середняки], while gradually pushing aside all sorts of commissars and satraps [держиморды].

[Ellipses in text]

At the all-Russian conference it's necessary to attempt to toss Rakovsky, Iakovlev, Epshtein, Kassior, and the like out of the CC, as well as out of all institutions, stopping at nothing.

17   Remarks by I.N. Perepechko, Antonov, and G.E. Zinoviev at the
       Fifth Conference of the Communist Party (Bolshevik) of Ukraine
       (CP(b)U), 17–22 November 1920, Kharkov[115]

Excerpt from Perepechko's Supplementary Report to the Fifth All-Ukrainian Party Conference

Which organisations at the present time can express most fully this proletarian class essence? Trade unions are the most suitable at the present moment. Even if they have many prejudices, they nevertheless fundamentally bring out the proletariat's class essence.

Which other organisations bring out the proletariat? The communist party does. But comrades, we need to turn special attention to the petty bourgeois element, which is pouring into our party. It brought into our midst all those psychological prejudices that are deeply hostile to the proletariat. It brought bourgeois methods of work into our party. These elements cannot represent the class essence of the proletariat.

The soviets are the next organisations which should bring out the class essence of the proletariat. The proletariat's isolation from management and the congestion of the party with alien elements are the main reasons for that crisis, which we, that is the party and Soviet power, are experiencing.

Excerpts from Debate

Perepechko. We threw out the proletariat, which is all we can depend on in the proletarian revolution. Merger with Borotbist elements contributes to this passion for committees of poor peasants.[116] They don't lean for support on the proletariat, because these right SRs aspire to lean for support on the petty bourgeois peasantry.

Antonov. The CC just wrote a report, where on its first page it completely overlooked the Ukrainian proletariat, which numbers here 900,000. What is this? 'The most important, greatest work, which lay before Ukraine', it says, 'was to stratify the countryside'.

And the proletariat? It is not a coincidence that the report says nothing about trade unions! They've forgotten the chief task, which is to turn the main attention to the working class, which created the dictatorship of the proletariat.

---

115   Zorky (ed.) 1926, pp. 80, 88–9.
116   *Borotbist* comes from the word for 'fight' or 'struggle'. They were a group of Socialist Revolutionaries of Ukraine before eventually joining the Communists. Some sources see them as leftist Socialist Revolutionaries, rather than 'right SRs', as Perepechko describes them.

... [ellipses in text] We well know that already in 1907 comrade Lenin wrote a letter about work in the countryside. Then attention was still paid to work in the countryside. But comrades, we say that our CC has not even fulfilled that work, although it sold the proletariat to the peasantry for a mess of pottage.

Zinoviev: Comrade Antonov considers himself to be very leftist, but he does not notice that he speaks in the most ordinary Menshevik prose. This is a fact. Of what has comrade Antonov rebuked us today? He used such a phrase: 'You sold workers to the peasants for a mess of pottage'. If it had been so, then he should have shaken the dust from his feet and run from this party, which sold workers to the peasants. Why does he not run? Because all this is said for effect. The devil is not so black as he is painted!

He defends workers from us and against the peasants. So do Mensheviks. They shift from one foot to the other all the time. Now they represent themselves as workers and demand that workers should not make a concession to the peasants, and then they start to defend peasants from workers and protest that we are taking bread from the countryside. In Germany there is such a picture. German Mensheviks also act as if they defend workers from peasants. Comrade Antonov, in thinking that he speaks in a very 'leftist' way, repeats the usual Menshevik banalities.

Endnotes to This Set of Excerpts

The Fifth Conference of the CP(b)U took place in Kharkov in November 1920. The speeches, excerpts of which are provided above, were pronounced in debates on comrades Rakovsky's and Kassior's reports about the work of CC CP(b)U.

Perepechko spoke at the conference as leader of the Workers' Opposition group. Later he spoke in the name of the Workers' Opposition at the Tenth Congress of the RCP (in response to the reports by comrades Lenin and Krestinsky).

Antonov also spoke at the Fifth Conference as official spokesman for the opinions of the Workers' Opposition.

Zinoviev participated in the work of the conference as representative of the CC RCP(b).

During the vote on resolutions about the CC's reports, 23 voted for the resolution proposed by Antonov (out of 316 taking part in the voting).

∴

Compare the above to the speeches below from the archival record of the Fifth Conference of the Communist Party (Bolshevik) of Ukraine, November 1920.[117]

Perepechko: In my opinion, the political report of the CC CP(b)U which was delivered here is as evil a parody of the CC's entire political line [as one can imagine]. At a time when our Ukrainian reality demanded something completely different, much was said about a CC political line that could only be sensed here in Kharkov. There were big parades. They were busy with problems on a union and worldwide scale. I am expressing my modest opinion. The international situation, to which Rakovsky devoted 90% of his speech, had nowhere near that degree of influence on our internal life. This is my deep conviction, which corresponds to our experience. The CC had the wrong political line, which shows up in its occupation with the highest affairs on an international scale and its aloofness from Ukraine's real circumstances. It hurls itself from one direction to another.

Comrade Rakovsky did not state by chance that the proletariat which arose here is the only one we can depend on for support in carrying out the proletarian revolution, for without this proletariat no social revolution is possible. The CC lacks a principled base on which to build its policy. It does not rely on the proletariat for support, but is distracted by committees of poor peasants, which have become the basis of its policy. The proletariat is not driving the car, but sits in the back seat. This facilitates merger with Borotbist elements, because these Right SR Populists aim to rely on the petty bourgeois peasantry for support. But experienced communists who sit in the CC should not follow this practice. This remoteness from the main base, on which social revolutions should depend, created the absence of a healthy base of the type which our policy in Ukraine should have held onto for support. And from this we get the entire organisational muddle, which has existed in our CC.

Methods of punitive exile entered the system as an actual practice. Any free thought within the party organisation was forbidden, and those who protested were exiled. The practice of appointments found a place for itself. There were some individual representatives of the CC who tried to suppress this practice of appointments. Dispersal of committees also became part of the system. Significantly, there is no city in Ukraine where there has not been a dispersal and where the practice of appointments has not been implemented. When the sys-

---

117   Tsentralnyi derzhavnyi arkhiv hromadskykh orhanizatsii Ukrainy (TsDAHO), f. 1, op. 1, d. 42, ll. 61–2, 65–9, 164–8.

tem of appointments and punitive exile became the method of party work, the expression 'sent to eat peaches' entered into usage. This system suppresses the expression of free will and thought within the party organisations. Although comrade Rakovsky promises to permit such in the future, we will not accept his charity.

We know that this absence of a base on which political principles were built forced organisational policy to be built by chance upon completely harmful methods in the policy of our Communist Party which essentially have not been fully thought through. In this regard it is significant that we did not have a basis on which to build a principled line for our CC. We needed to conquer the countryside, which could occur only with maximum initiative within party organisations. When the front demanded great initiative and we defeated Wrangel, we were only victorious then thanks to the mass initiative of the proletariat and the semi-proletarian countryside.

It needs to be said that the last congress of soviets accepted a resolution about abolishing gubernia soviet executive committees and replacing them with a five-man body. In fact, this abolition led to complete isolation in the provinces, for it transformed them into revolutionary committees, which did not depend on the worker masses for support. CC members are mistaken in thinking that they can summon a colossal exertion of strength from the working class by means of a personal base. In all its activity, the CC lacks a definite, firm communist base, on which our policy should be constructed. Constant fluctuations in one or another direction carry with them absolute harm for our party.

The CC RCP issued a resolution and the all-Russian party conference made decisions about the tasks of trade unions. From these, one concludes that it is necessary to set about implementing democracy not only within the party but also within mass worker organisations. But the CC's resolution did not find a foothold at a moment when our forces were greatly exerted, so the CC could not reveal its political line. This decision cannot come to be under any circumstances. Comrade Rakovsky said here that the share of the proletariat among the population fell. That is not exactly true. [Elected] gubernia soviet executive committees were replaced by revolutionary committees composed of appointees. Such managers are completely cut off from the worker masses, partially due to objective reasons, but even more so thanks to the methods of work, which the CC carried out. We most resolutely distance ourselves from all those work methods which were cultivated, for they are not suitable for anything anywhere. We'll never build a communist party with such methods.

Antonov: We just heard out the CC's report. Now we should ask if the CC of Ukraine is responsible before this congress or not. Maybe it is not responsible to this congress, but to the RCP, for the first CC, which was elected at the Fourth Party Conference, was later evacuated to Moscow. Not only is the CC not responsible to the present assembly, but it is not responsible to the RCP. There was a directive that registration should be carried out in Ukraine in a month, but it has not been so for six months. So the CC evidently is not responsible [illegible lines follow].

Anyone who does not comply with the RCP should be tried by a court.

This is one side of the question, now the other side, which is the main one. In the report it wrote, the CC forgot to mention the Ukrainian proletariat, which now numbers about 900 thousand. What is this? It says that the most important and greatest work confronting Ukraine is to socially stratify the villages. Indeed, isn't the proletariat the most important? (laughter).

Audience: This is correct. We should be for the proletariat.

Antonov: The proletariat stratifies the villages. Proletarian organisations stratify the countryside. In October, proletarians of Russia achieved the dictatorship of the proletariat and the proletariat poured into the Red Army.

Petrovsky: We are the proletariat.

Antonov: We are also the proletariat. I know you, comrade Petrovsky. I know that you are a worker. At this time, when they are making the chief work out to be in the countryside, factory workers are going on strike. In Donetsk gubernia, there are 320 thousand miners, who right now are digging black gold for Soviet Russia. The Party leaders are taking all kinds of measures to raise productivity in the Donetsk basin (Donbas) for the Soviet Republic. The dictatorship of the proletariat will be successful when we will fulfill the most important production tasks.

It is not an oversight that this report says nothing about trade unions. They forgot that the most important task is to pay the chief attention to the working class, for it created the dictatorship of the proletariat. Right now we don't see the trees for the forest, so understandably various strikes break out in our country, not only here in Ukraine, but they are starting even in Moscow. Not long ago comrade Lunacharsky came back from Kolomna to report to the Moscow Committee about a factory where 70 thousand people worked. Comrades, he said, I have not seen a worse factory. What does this say? It says that comrade Lunacharsky, while sitting in his office, has not observed the mood of the working class, and right now he is tied up in knots.

Not in vain do Batka Makhno and his staff fan out among worker populations in the mills and factories and do tens of thousands stand in line for his assemblies. What does this say? In October, when we returned from our sentences of hard labour, comrade Lenin said that if there is an unhealthy element in the proletariat which is attracted to anarchism, it means that the Communist Party is operating poorly. Maybe now we need to say that the Communist Party operates poorly among the Ukrainian proletariat. The RCP definitely states in the most recent issue, the 24th issue [of *Pravda*?] that the October Revolution in Ukraine has still not been completed, that the Ukrainian Communist Party has still not carried out the October Revolution.

Comrades, the CC was wrong to turn all its attention to the countryside. The CC should have said outright that we are a proletarian organisation and not a populist party of the Maximalist type, which now daily swell in size. They are heroes for the crowd. Why do populist parties exist right now in Ukraine at the first stage of revolutionary development? The populists completed a march to the countryside – that is old history from the 1850s. We say that a campaign to the countryside is necessary, but our chief task is among the proletariat and urban working class. Only after that do we work together with the villages, without separating them out. Fragmentation [раздробление] needs to be carried out in the countryside to attract rural proletarian elements into our proletarian party milieu. That is the task of the Communist Party. We know well about work in the countryside, for Lenin wrote about it already in 1907. Already then attention was paid to work in the countryside. But, comrades, we declare that our CC did not fulfill this work. It sold the proletariat for a mess of lentil soup to the peasant.

Now comrades, in his report, Comrade Kasior talked more than anyone else about how the CC CPU sent very few people to Russia and that it should have sent many more. (From the audience: Nothing of the sort!) Comrades, here is something significant. Some comrades were exiled from Moscow to Odessa. The old party activist Comrade Petroplavsky was exiled from the Kremlin. When he went to Odessa, he told of how Comrade Shumsky came there and packed the Odessa committee wholly with former Borotbists. This tells of protectionism. Protectionism became an everyday occurrence in the communist party. One hand washes another. This everyday phenomenon harms the entire course of our construction.

Comrades, we do not say that the CC did not produce any work. We do say that when the CC used the method of dispersal, it was the type of method as when the blind climb onto the throne in the kingdom of the crippled. It should not be that everyone is forced to keep quiet. Some who came here have pointed out to us not to cast judgement. But comrades, we should say right now that in the future our work should assume a different character. Right now the doors have been flung widely open to criticism. Even Comrade Zinoviev, who did not want to permit any criticism at all, was just harnessed in a troika together with Shliapnikov and Lutovinov (applause) at the last All-Russian Congress of Trade Unions.

Zinoviev from his seat: 'That's understood'.

Antonov: I say that our future task is more now than ever to weigh the pros and cons as to what we have that is unhealthy. The Marxist pros and cons. Marxists say that there are no absolute truths [законных истин]. If we and the communist party will seek in the process of criticism to build our future socialist society, then we now more than any time before should turn attention to this side of the question. Maximum effort needs to be exerted to create a large militant organisation of the working class. Only then will the ranks of the proletariat start to fling themselves into fulfilling the task of differentiating the countryside (applause).

Perepechko: I speak, comrades, in the name of a group of delegates, primarily workers, who call themselves the Workers' Opposition. Comrade Zinoviev's analysis of the reasons for the crisis, which our party and the entire Soviet apparatus of soviet power are experiencing, is completely wrong. Comrade Zinoviev's approach is not Marxist, but psychological in essence. Comrade Zinoviev's psychological analysis is an attending circumstance. Comrade Zinoviev said that the main reasons were our party's shortcomings as it transitioned from the old organisational tasks of the underground into a ruling party. People with completely different experiences moved onto new ground and they felt completely different. Comrade Zinoviev concludes from this that this is the reason for those grouping, about which he spoke here, but this is basically wrong. The psychological moment which defines the transition of old people to new ground is not the decisive factor. The question should be posed not about the psychological moment, but about how much the party expresses the will of the class, not just of its individual representatives.

It is about how much this party basically expresses and carries out correctly a class line in the sense of the country's organisational management and of the party's internal organisation. Here is the main premise, which comrade Zinoviev [illegible word]. He also points out that people being pulled away for the front contributes to a crisis. This is not true, because there were more than a few people who previously struggled against the tsarist government. People from the working class are dislodged in Moscow. Trade unions were able to bring forward more new forces, who came to replace others and who nevertheless implemented the class line of the proletariat. Therefore those comrades who refer to the depopulation of worker organisations are essentially wrong. This premise also only demoralises our party.

The question needs to be posed about what is the current nature of our revolution and what forms has our communist party assumed. We see that the forms of the dictatorship of the proletariat were united. The proletariat's forms lean for support on broad [illegible phrase] of revolution. No one will deny that during the early period of the Russian Revolution, our soviet organisations attracted broad masses [illegible]. Then, [illegible] in this first period, all the agents of revolution gave moral support to the communist party which led this revolution. But as things went further, more bourgeois people started to enter the forms. This occurred because the proletarian masses were isolated from management. All this to nothing [illegible]. Therefore as the basis of the main moment, influencing the crisis of our party, it comes to place this unanimity on the proletariat which in fact progressed and which all the more progresses and those traditions which here comrade Zinoviev put forth to us representatives of the Workers' Opposition with palliatives and insufficiently. Understandably, of course those comrades are not correct who represent the exposure of the class will of the proletariat in individual circumstances. Maybe sometimes this is good. Those comrades are not correct who quietly substitute this for the basic essence of the proletarian revolution. Trade unions are currently the most suitable organisations to bring the class proletarian essence out into the light.

Let's allow that they have many prejudices, but basically they nevertheless reveal the class essence of the proletariat. What other organisations express it? The Communist Party reveals it. But, comrades, we need to pay special attention to the petty-bourgeois element, which is flowing into the party. They brought to us psychological prejudices, all of which are deeply hostile to the proletariat. They brought us bourgeois methods of work into our party. These elements cannot represent the class essence of the proletariat. The next organisations, which should reveal the class essence of the proletariat are the soviets. You don't have to be told how much the soviets are important for us and here having described this class character of the revolution we should say that this isolation is fundamental. This is the main reason for the crisis, which we in the party and Soviet power are experiencing. Comrade Zinoviev says that the worker position represents from itself something that is cut off. Indeed do Ian, Drobnis and others like them try to represent the worker position? Nothing of the sort. These comrades are not correct when speaking about us, because Makhaevism is a negative policy and we stand fully on the party line, we fully understand our positions.

They are not correct and they speculate on this, when they try to present the Workers' Opposition as the enemies of the intelligentsia. We are not the enemies [illegible word] intelligentsia, but we declare, that if you want to preserve the proletarian class essence, then act like a proletarian. From these basic suppositions it emerges that the Workers' Opposition right now at this conference and elsewhere when it appears and can make demands plays the main role in making our party and soviet power healthy. It depends on the proletariat for support. Let's say the proletariat has many prejudices, but basically it occupies a firm communist line. Let's say that in some places the proletariat displays localist tendencies, but mainly the proletariat is correct. If it makes mistakes, they are partial and do not constitute a hundredth part of those mistakes, which soviet power commits when it stands far away from the proletariat. We think that the crisis of the party and of soviet power can be eliminated only by creation of a body for class renewal of the proletariat in order to connect our party with the working class, so that each beating of the pulse of the working class would reverberate upon the Communist Party, so that each pulse beat of the working class would be taken account of.

It is necessary to restore the trade unions to their rights. I repeat that at the All-Russian Conference of Trade Unions and at its faction, Vladimir Kossior, who in the past year played at opposition now plays [illegible phrase]. This is said from a feeling of being beyond defence by the CC.[118] Inasmuch as now the task of the communist party is to revive trade unions, there is no reason for us to be afraid of them. We never feared them and do not fear them. The second moment which we observe in practice and through which we consider possible to make the party and soviet power healthy is the regeneration of the soviets. We think that the restoration of soviets should became exactly now the first priority task. In my opinion, it is a deep mistake when comrade Zinoviev imagines that soviets at the present time should not be renewed, because danger exists. No matter how great the danger, it can be overcome only by the proletariat's colossal effort, strength, and activity. How is this expressed? This can be politically expressed only in the soviets of soldiers and workers deputies and not in various manifestations of individual enthusiasm among workers and [missing word or phrase].

If circumstances now are difficult, if circumstances demand strength and effort, then it is necessary to create such circumstances in which each proletarian would not feel as if he is in exile, and so that he would feel himself to be a master and as the master could talk about that which he finds unbearable.

---

118   Это говорится из чувства сверх защиты ЦК.

This is not the case right now. Comrade Zinoviev wanted to go around this, declaring that when military circumstance will end and we will then renew the soviet. Right now the Soviets .... [ellipses in text], because to overcome all obstacles is possible only under the effort of all strength and will of the proletariat, and this effort of all forces can be found only through the soviets and not through any other sorts of organisations. The third moment for making the party healthier, we think necessary, is to once and for all to put an end to that bureaucratism and careerism which firmly made a place for itself in some central bodies of our party. Comrade Zinoviev proposed to us a control commission. I spoke with a member of a control commission from Nizhny Novgorod. When I asked how are things with you, he said that we do not know the regulations. Who is a controller-inspector and what is it for ... [in text] At the Politburo session, we so timidly asked the secretary if we can exist or not and they made a declaration to us. Personally speaking, he said, there is no reason for you to be present, because you have a mass of discord and so forth. This honest guy wanted to stop the music and go back to his place. This is not a method for healing our party. What is needed is to organise party masses by means of the most merciless self-criticism.

18   Letter from G.E. Zinoviev to I.N. Perepechko, 26 November 1920, with Excerpts from Perepechko's Letter to Zinoviev[119]

I regret that I could not meet with you and your friends, for I had to leave Moscow quickly. You find that my speech against the Workers' Opposition was merciless and unjust. I acknowledge that I hesitated for a long time before I finally decided to speak against the Workers' Opposition group in that very tone, which you called merciless. But after some reflection, I could not in good conscience act differently. I know that among you supporters of the Workers' Opposition there are wonderful proletarians, who sincerely suffer the party's pains, and I declared so at the conference as well as in the press. But when I saw what this is degenerating into, I said to myself that it's necessary to say everything up to the last word.

Just think about what you, Kuznetsov and Antonov said. I could not believe my ears. Antonov went so far as to talk as if our party sold out the working class to the wealthy and middle peasantry for a mess of pottage. You talked about our party's autocracy. Together with Kuznetsov you depicted our party as an organ-

---

119   TsA FSB, R33718, d. 499061, vol. 39, l. 124.

isation rotten to the core. You stated in theses that the party does not have a line on the national, agrarian and other questions. You announced that those workers who abandoned the party are the best workers and so forth and so on. You overly exaggerated those illnesses from which our party suffers. Yes, even in your letter, which I received after my speech, you write for example, 'and isn't it clear that what we have in the party, in the soviets, and in the trade unions has absolutely no influence on the revolution of the proletariat as a class and far from guarantees it' (underlined by you).

Just think, comrade Perepechko, what you said here. Our organisations are constructed, in your opinion, as if the proletariat as a class has no influence on the revolution. Indeed this is a scandalous lie. This is a monstrously unprecedented exaggeration, which helps only the Mensheviks, SRs and other opponents of ours. You write further in your letter, 'Why did you in your answer not touch upon the basic question, which I raised? Should proletarian worker organisations built on initiative play the main role and define the essence of the proletarian revolution, or should chiefs and personalities do so?' (underlined by you)

You call this question the main one. In my opinion, it was not worth talking about this seriously at the party conference. When and by whom among us has it been asserted that 'chiefs and personalities' and not proletarian organisations should define the essence of the revolution? You again exaggerated by a thousand times the abnormalities existing in our party.

How could I not have spoken out against all this? If you had seen the dozens of notes passed to me from delegates during your speech, you would have understood how much indignation you, Kuznetsov, and Antonov summoned forth from many delegates who were present.[120]

You are making a mountain out of a molehill.[121] You paint such a picture of our party's inadequacies that any unsophisticated worker who listens to you will decide that he needs to run away from this party without looking back. In this sense your agitation unintentionally introduces far more demoralisation into our ranks than any bureaucratism does.

That is why, comrade Perepechko, party duty obligated me to speak out mercilessly, as you express it.

I want to believe that you yourself see your mistake. Let's struggle together within the party against bureaucratism and against ossification of some of our

---

120   See Albert 2014 for an analysis of political notes [записки] passed to speakers at meetings in the 1920s.

121   The literal expression translates as 'an elephant out of a fly'.

party organisations. But don't you help the Mensheviks and Makhnoists out by making the kind of 'criticism' which throws out the baby together with the bath water.

Give up creating a special faction or grouping. This will inevitably lead you where you don't want to go. We don't need any Workers' Opposition. Our party is entirely a workers' party. The CC will meet healthy criticism halfway and will lead the charge against bureaucratism. One should work to raise mass initiative and lift up mass proletarian organisations not by grumbling and not with the kind of 'criticism' of the party which like rust eats away faith in the party itself. One should work with one's feet on the ground by going into the very thick of the masses. Let's do this kind of work together.

19   A.G. Shliapnikov, 'Tasks of Workers' Unions'[122]

I.

We have just discovered yet another new crisis, which like all the others threatens to end in yet another catastrophe. The newspapers abound with articles and speeches about the illnesses of the Russian trade union movement. Toward the end of the fourth year of their existence, contemporary production unions have turned out to be afflicted with a fatal disease. There still is not a single analysis of this illness. Some assert that unions and the personnel within them were incorrectly transplanted and need a good shaking up. Others say that unions have been reduced to nothing and are busy with what is neither necessary nor desirable. A third group simply and briefly declares that workers' unions and all sorts of committees and committee people are not necessary for us. Accountability and clarity need to be brought into this dispute, which for the first time is opening up so broadly. For this we should not behave like one who has forgotten his origins, but should turn to our experience, take a glance back, evaluate our work in the past, and by its lessons learn how to construct the present. The future also is subject to illumination, but the path to it lies through the present, that is through that crisis, which all forces of the republic are called upon to destroy.

The contemporary Russian trade union movement is the child of revolutionary storms.[123] All our large production unions arose in the first weeks after

---

122   'O zadachakh rabochikh soiuzov', 13 December 1920, published in Zinoviev (ed.) 1921b, pp. 287–304; and in Rudzutak (ed.) 1927, pp. 175–87.

123   The term used here for 'Russian' is Российское, which implies identification with the state or its multiethnic citizenry rather than the nation, which the word Русское would convey.

the February revolution. But our unions are the offspring of the revolution not only chronologically, but also in their very essence. In the annals of the Russian trade union movement there is not one moment which was not dictated by the interests of revolution and that was not synchronised with them in a fundamental way. Besides that, our unions for a short time, from February to October, completed a revolution within themselves. For these several months of struggle, having no historical examples, trade unions assumed such flexible organisational forms, that they are a model in principle for unions of the whole world.

In their work under capitalist conditions, that is from March to the end of 1917, and for a few even further, our unions could not use the international experience of the trade union movement. The West's last word in 'trade union politics and technique' was reduced to class peace, to agreement between workers and capitalists. Wartime events and working masses' revolutionary actions excluded the possibility for agreements in our country. The condition of the economy, managed by capitalists, was at a precipice. All attempts of a certain party of 'revolutionary democracy' to extract the country from its dead end by agreement with capitalists was not for the best, but on the contrary, wildly spreading predatory interests daily worsened the condition of the economy, and together with it the situation of the working class.

From the first days of their existence, trade unions together with factory committees advanced demands for government regulation of the economy and for workers' control.[124] In practice our factory committees began to fulfil economic responsibilities from the moment of their appearance. The February Revolution 'scared off' many directors, owners and administrators, who from fear of the red banner abandoned enterprises. Committees, created by the will of revolutionary workers, led many enterprises already at that time. Since that time conflicts between workers' committees and factory administration on the grounds of 'interference' in the rights and responsibilities of factory administration have not ceased.

Under the revolutionary pressure of working masses and organisations, the coalition government was forced to go along the path of democratising various military-industrial, economic, regulating centres. Representatives from various social and administrative-economic institutions, such as the soviets of workers' and soldiers' deputies, town governments, cooperatives, societies of entrepren-

---

124   I have translated as 'factory committees' his term фабричные и заводские комитеты, which literally is 'mill and factory committees'. The term I have translated here as 'workers' control' can also be translated as 'workers' supervision', because it consisted more of oversight than command.

eurs and trade unions, were permitted into state economic bodies created by the bourgeoisie, such as the Council for State Defence, factory councils, and councils for fuel and metals distribution. When government representatives vacillated, worker representatives sometimes even received a majority in many regulating centres. But this partial seizure of the administrative apparatus of state regulation, just as the seizure of separate enterprises, could not change the capitalist system. Capitalism turned out to be so flexible and tenacious that it tried to use the revolution, as it was being created, to reinforce itself. Many owners knew how to use worker committees as their envoys and as fixers for getting hold of resources and raw materials. So, in the process of revolutionary struggle, having begun with regulation of wages, reduction of the work day, and safeguarding worker health, trade unions changed their tasks, adapting to the demands of the time.

The slogan of state regulation of the economy, supported by even the most moderate economists, did not satisfy worker committees and trade unions. The naked formula 'state regulation' demanded supplements. All disputes of that time turned around which class would regulate the economy: the bourgeoisie or the workers? The Mensheviks and Socialist Revolutionaries leaned for support on the capitalist experience of Western Europe and proposed to thrust the principles of regulation of the economy on our native bourgeoisie. We Bolsheviks disputed our bourgeoisie's capability to cope with this business, and the possibility to regulate the economy and industry in the interests of the labourers by means of the bourgeoisie's hands. In practice, in everyday work, trade union organisations and worker committees of that time were convinced of the need for a proletarian dictatorship, solely capable to organise and regulate the economy in the interests of the entire state. This explains the largest trade unions' direct struggle for Soviet power. The logic of leadership of the class struggle inescapably led to the desire not only for temporary successes in this struggle, but also to the effort to gain full victory in the interests of its class.

The October seizure of power was not unexpected for our country's trade union movement. Already for a long time prior, our production unions were ideologically prepared for the soviets' seizure of power. Unions were not limited only to ideological readiness, but also for many months of practical work had involved activist worker elements in economic bodies. Thanks to this work, workers' unions and committees at the moment of the seizure of power could assign a significant quantity of personnel to economic-administrative posts and in this way strike a decisive blow against resistance and sabotage by the capitalists, intelligentsia, bureaucrats and office personnel. Such was the path of the Russian trade union movement from the February days to October.

II.

The October seizure of power opened a new page in the history not only of the Russian trade union movement. At that time, when the soviets of workers, soldiers and peasants were winning authority in the whole country, trade unions conducted struggle for the working class's dictatorship over the economy. The struggle on the economic front was as difficult and complex as the victory by armed workers and soldiers against the bourgeois government was easy. On the economic field of struggle, the bourgeoisie mobilised all its best forces and decided to make its last stand. The capitalists and a significant share of technical and administrative personnel answered the victory of the working class with a strike and sabotage. Numerous central and local boards of directors and factory management, with the entire office staff, left their work to protest the working class's seizure of power. The bourgeoisie, jointly with the clerical staff of banks, government, private and social institutions, formed a united capitalist front. This front was set off against the front of proletarian, organised initiative, led by trade unions and factory worker committees. The forces of the latter succeeded in supporting the work of enterprises, preserving valuable buildings, and so on. All those who made the October revolution will remember their own organisations' work to revive economic institutions' activity. So, in the process of proletarian struggle, new tasks stood before the trade unions of Russia's workers. Instead of 'defending the working class's economic, legal and moral interests' by strikes and other means, trade unions had to head up individual manufactories and entire branches of industry and transport, under the most difficult conditions. But since that time, the springtime of proletarian authority, three years have passed, the work of which should now be taken into account.

Now, near the end of the fourth year of the existence of trade unions, which have completed colossal revolutionary work, the terrible question is posed: to be or not to be. All those approaching the trade union movement of our country critically, are inclined to regard it as a thing in itself, and completely isolated from the whole sum of Soviet conditions. Both those who are observing the activity of our trade unions, encountering them in the course of work, and those active elements, working within unions, are dissatisfied with trade unions' current lot. The old scope in union activity of late 1917 and early 1918, after three years, has led us to a death knell.

The whole sum of criticism of trade unions' current condition and activity can be reduced to the following three tenets:

1)   vagueness of tasks, uncertainty about unions' position and role,
2)   disparity of leading centres' personal composition,
3)   outdated methods of work.

On the first point, regarding tasks, we can turn to trade union and party congresses and find there an exhaustive answer.

The First All-Russian Congress of Trade Unions in January 1918 first defined tasks of the trade union movement of the new epoch. In the resolution accepted on comrade Zinoviev's report, in point six it says precisely that 'the centre of gravity of trade unions' work at the present moment should be carried over into organising the economy. Trade unions, as class organisations of the proletariat, constructed according to the production principle, should assume the chief work in organising production and reconstruction of the country's undermined production forces.

At the second congress, in February 1919, in the resolution on comrade Tomsky's report, it was said that 'trade unions transitioned from supervision over production to its organisation, participating actively in management of separate enterprises, as well as in the entire economic life of the country'.

The end of this resolution linked trade unions with the entire state in such a way: 'participating directly in all areas of soviet work, forming government bodies and assigning their own personnel to work in them, trade unions should, by means of attracting into this work both their own organisations and broad masses of workers, cultivate workers and prepare them for the business of managing not only production, but also the entire government apparatus'.

The idea of basing all government soviet bodies on worker unions is revealed very clearly in this point. The idea to 'unionize' those very government bodies is counterposed to efforts toward the statisation of trade unions, that is, their transformation into a technical executive appendage of governing economic bodies.

The resolution about tasks of trade unions, which the third congress accepted, said very much about the correctness of the positions accepted at both preceding congresses, but the old precision, clarity and perspectives are missing. Instead of prominent tasks, the resolution contains a series of modest wishes and recommendations to the unions, about how they should behave themselves in regard to bodies of state power.

III.

Despite the diplomatic fog of the third congress's resolution, it can't be said that our unions did not have concrete tasks. If we turn to our programme, which the Eighth Party Congress accepted and presented as the guiding direction for all policy, then there, under the heading 'In the economic area', in point five, there is a sufficiently bold indication of the trade union movement's goals: 'By Soviet law and established practice, trade unions already participate in all local and central bodies that manage industry. Trade unions should further concentrate in their hands all management of the economy, as a single economic unit'.

The positions brought forward fully suffice to put an end to criticism that the trade union movement's tasks are 'vague and imprecise'. Both the congresses' resolutions and the party programme sufficiently clearly defined not only the tasks, but also the place of trade unions in the worker government. These tasks were not invented, but were dictated by life itself, just as was the appearance of the very system of Soviet power.

The clearer resolution about trade unions' tasks was accepted two months after struggle began for the proletariat's dictatorship. During these months, unions displayed maximum energy, and comrade Zinoviev's report summed up their experience and their work.

If now again the question is raised about 'tasks of trade unions', this occurs not because tasks confronting unions are obscure. Some critically thinking comrades simply do not agree with the resolutions and programmatic positions about trade unions' tasks. They are frightened by the assignment of these tasks to unions, since they do not believe in the strength, consciousness and capability of workers' organisations to fulfil programmatic tasks. They wrap their distrust in foggy phraseology about the vagueness of the trade union movement's tasks and do this just in order to interpret and revise them.

For these three years in fact, struggle was waged to implement the tasks designated by the congresses. The stages of this struggle were stamped in the resolutions of the same congresses. The first and better defined of them was accepted already at that time, when our plants, our factories were billowing smoke. Afterwards, the economic situation of the republic worsened with each month, and for the past few years the country has experienced an unusual economic crisis. Civil war and imperialists' attacks pushed economic tasks to the back burner. Along with this, trade unions' role and actual significance declined. This explains the fact that the second and third trade union congresses were occupied only with bowing and scraping before decisions of the first congress. The basic positions of the first congress were transformed into a trade unionist prayer, departing further and further from reality.

Thus, our unions' illness consists not at all in that they do not know what they are supposed to do, but in that the work given to them does not correspond to the tasks put before them. But this type of illness is related not only to the trade union movement, but to our entire structure. We now are experiencing an impressive streak of disagreement between that which is written or said, and that which is implemented and how it is implemented. The annihilation of this contradiction will heal our ailments in the trade union movement.

IV.

There is little to say on the second point of disagreements, about disparities in the personal composition of trade unions' leadership. Our unions during these years have experienced a streak of permanent shaking up. Not one leading centre is nominated and elected by the congresses of our unions, the majority of which are led by communists. In this regard the tutelage of unions by the secretary of the CC of our party was so petty, that it extended even to selecting central committees' personal composition. Our congress delegates, embodying the entire unionised masses' collective experience, knowing one another and their leaders through work, were deprived of the right of using their experience, and because of party discipline, were forced to elect those who were recommended in the name of the highest party centre. It is obvious that such tactics don't at all promote the strengthening of trade unions and the lifting-up of their work. The results of such a system for selecting 'leading personnel' soon told on a whole series of extraordinarily important unions, like with the railway workers and water transport workers. A system of 'shaking-up' manifested especially energetically in organising these unions' centres, as a result of which unions were reduced to the condition of complete breakdown. The leading centre of the railway and transport workers' union 'Tsektran', created according to the last word in shaking-up technique, turned out to be a general command without an army, deprived of influence and authority. The incongruency of this union's personal composition of leaders with tasks placed before them is brilliantly proven by the summing up work put together at the December conference, breaking up the union into a whole series of groupings [группировки].

In the interests of trade unions' revitalisation and unity with broad union masses, it is necessary to stop repeating such mistakes. Union members and their representatives should have the freedom to make known their collective experience. Only under this condition can unions be authoritative, leading bodies of the proletarian masses.

It is also necessary to approach carefully the 'obsolescence' of our trade unionists' methods of work. Russian trade unions' work flows in conditions of extreme deprivation and lack of technical, auxiliary resources. Our unions undoubtedly suffer from these insufficiencies. The absence of technical means explains also the obsolescence of work methods. However, proletarian democratism lies at the foundation of methods for implementing union work. On it is built the union's entire life, and if they consider this system of work to be 'obsolescent' and counterpose to it 'military methods of work', as the latest means to heal trade unions' lingering illness, then one must argue with this. When civilians speak about military methods of work, then they subsume under this concept speed, assiduousness, self-sacrifice, responsibility and similar such good words. But just superficial familiarity with the work of any worker union or cell, allows one to state that all the enumerated qualities – speed, assiduousness, responsibility and self-sacrifice – were accepted and implemented long before babblers [крикуны] about military methods appeared. The final result of all these useful things depends on technical resources. If unions had an abundance of telephones, telegraph equipment, automobiles, trains and similar such good things, which the military has, then the speed of work and assiduousness in business would have significantly benefited. As concerns responsibility and self-sacrifice, the life of worker organisations is full of these qualities, and they saturate the existence of all conscious workers.

But civilians are mistaken. Military methods do not at all lead to the things enumerated above, but have particular qualities, which up to now still have not caught on among worker organisations. These particularities, good in military matters, are like bayonet thrusts in the management of collectives. Giving orders, executing them, unconditional obedience and so forth, are of little use for managing worker masses. These methods are not new: capitalists of all countries practised them long before the war, they practice them now. We did not construct our work on the principles of simple obedience, but we try to master the consciousness of worker masses and, basing it on this, manage them with the help of their own will.

Of course, our old methods are significantly more difficult than the new 'military' ways. It is far easier, sitting in offices, to dash off orders and offer them for execution. But what will happen if a small 'I don't wish to' arises between those giving the orders and those carrying them out? History has many lessons to offer about this, and we would not like to assimilate them.

It was very difficult to convince Russian workers and peasants to take up the club and drive away the tsar. For many decades the best forces of the country worked upon this. They built political parties, worked in the underground, and perished by the thousands, but anyway they forced the whole working class to rise up and overthrow the Romanov court. It was also difficult for our party to wage struggle to topple the bourgeois order, but, using old methods of drawing into our struggle the broadest worker and peasant masses, the party was victorious.

Now it happens that it is very difficult to persuade and direct worker masses along the path needed, but we will overcome these difficulties by old methods, which any kind of worker can understand. We will seek support in his consciousness and his interests. During the course of our struggle, we have become convinced that our method of work is correct. Each step we take ahead teaches us that only that which is thought through and implemented by the working mass itself becomes firmly established. These methods do not do away with discipline, unconditional execution, and obedience to the accepted directive. But before it is an order for execution by the broad masses, the matter is decided and then firmly conducted in a revolutionary way and resolutely by millions of worker masses. This tactic is justified not only in struggle, but also in building the economy. If we suffer, then it is not because we hold to these principles of activity too zealously, but on the contrary we suffer from insufficient forces, which are capable of fully embracing work.

v.

In order to conclude the survey of all methods for healing the all-Russian sickly trade union movement, it is necessary to devote a few words to that liquid, which they pump into it from all around, that fluid known by the short title 'merger' [сращивание]. Subjecting it to a sort of chemical breakdown, we receive the following explanation. It is known how exceptionally and 'suddenly' the crisis of the trade union movement was revealed. Just as unexpectedly it was shown that dualism [двойственность] exists in the management and organisation of our economy. Three years have passed since an equal footing in the management of industry and organisation of the economy was established in our republic. Unions and economic councils [совнархозы] are in charge of industry and the economy. Special regulations define the rights of those and others. However, the existence of two bodies is extremely abnormal, and often their work overlaps and stirs up conflicts. To escape the latter a new means was invented, in the form of 'merger' of union bodies with the apparat of the Council of the National Economy (VSNKh). Also proposals and constitutions are written about the rights of plants and factories. There exist such 'vanguard' people. It is decided to make our factory committees happy by including their representatives as assistants to the directors of enterprises and so forth. But one cannot escape dualism in the essence of work by all these measures.

Our healers take the very idea of 'merger' of two sources of authority from German opportunist leaders who struggled against Bolshevism. Opportunists of all countries of Europe now seek such a form of organisation, which could lead working masses out of that pauperisation to which the war and the opportunists' policy led them. And they found a lucky way out: in merger of worker organisations with government and proprietary organisations on the grounds of 'socialisation' [социализация]. There is no such country where merger of opportunists with capitalists was not practiced, but this cannot serve as an example for us. Of course, with us the matter is about 'merger' within a single worker state, but all the same such a formal approach to a great matter, yes still with baggage from an alien camp, is evidence of poverty. Come on, comrades, exert yourselves, can't you find your own experience in your baggage, which you obtained during the revolution. Search for it.

Yes, the trade unions' crisis is apparent. It has existed for a long time, from the beginning of our industry's crisis. Its expression is in production worker associations' activity, in the centre as well as in the localities, which becomes narrower as each month passes. Worker organisations' enterprising, creative activism is dying away. Surgical measures are demanded in order to impart freshness and revolutionary intensity to trade unions' activity.

For these preceding three years of revolution, trade unions have gradually, but unswervingly and resolutely, been supplanted by a body, the foundation for which was laid by unions and worker committees. Its name is VSNKh.

Created on the basis of mass worker organisations, VSNKh departed further and further from its creators with each year and lately has made an unswerving effort to completely subjugate trade unions, make them into simple technical appendages of its apparat. But this would not be terrible, if the business of developing our country's productive forces demanded such a type of construction of economic bodies. In fact the abolition of production worker organisations or the destruction of their initiative threatens to completely ruin the business of industrial construction. The past and current situation of trade union affairs speaks loudly of this. The current and past activities of VSNKh likewise show, that for these three years it has not managed to set up industry, despite enormous resources and forces that the government has put at its disposal. Of course, a three year period is extraordinarily small, but also in the system of work there are sins, which facilitate failure.

The essential indicator of those abnormal paths that VSNKh took is the effort to push away proletarian initiative and to build walls of 'noninterference' to cut itself off from workers' organisations. The existing dualism in economic construction is just a small illustration of that mistaken direction. But the way out from such a situation lies not only in organisational measures, but also in our party policy. Having a wonderful programme on trade union activity, our party allotted very little attention to developing the activity of trade unions and government bodies to draw closer to that moment, when the unions 'should concentrate in their hands all management of the economy, as a single economic unit' (RCP(b) programme).

Our party in fact should finally decide by which paths it will implement its policy of economic construction. Will it be through workers' organisations or by the old method adopted from the bourgeois epoch, which is through bureaucratically constructed apparats?

In our opinion, the further continuation of governing economic bodies' isolated existence will lead to a break with production workers, who are the main creative force for moving ahead. An equal footing, which is now being implemented, does not satisfy anyone positively. Dualism actually brings a loss to the very business of organising production.

If one would now at least look through protocols of the sessions of our more powerful unions' central committee presidiums, then one would find that 9/10 of all questions decided by them are directly connected to production. Thanks to union work's isolation from production work, wage regulation questions are decided completely abstractly. This leads to the fact that our wage rates agreement, instead of stimulating productivity, becomes a brake on its development. From the other side, our factory budgets, confirmed by regulations of an office character, completely ignore the modern effort to naturalise, at least partially, workers' wages. The interests of the living workforce are not served in budgeting; the question was not even posed in such a way up to now. But difficult living conditions force our factory committees and factory management to take the path of servicing some of workers' needs at the enterprise's expense. In some places factories gave workers electric light, arranged shoe repair shops and so forth. In a word, they try to serve the elementary inquiries and needs of workers by their own initiative, without loss to the fundamental work of the enterprises. But all this is committed illegally, and our comrades live under the constant threat of punishment for violating budgetary rules and such. This phenomenon likewise indicates the breach between managing bodies and managed enterprises, at which thousands of producers are employed.

Now, when we are confronted by the question about intensifying our activity toward increasing the country's productive might, it is necessary first of all to resolutely eliminate contradictions and frictions within our [governing] bodies. This is possible to achieve only by implementing economic policy directly through proletarian organisations and placing production unions at the head of industrial branches. Resolution of the question in this direction will cause, of course, some 'revolution' also in the construction and interrelations of the economic departments, and maybe will demand some changes in our Soviet constitution. But these are likely formalities, which cannot halt the resolution of the matter itself.

VI.

Communists of all countries think of the socialist economy as the systematic organisation of production. In our programme and in congresses' decisions there are very many fine directives about a single economic plan. But in our practice all kinds of exceptionalism and emergency measures flourish and grow stronger, in place of a system. Instead of well-considered and planned works, we continue to chase after miracles. We employ petty stinginess [крохоборство] according to whether it is the straw that will break the camel's back.[125] Demand gives birth to supply. Specialists of a dubious type appear on the field of industry. They self-advertise and receive mandates for making miracles. New methods for organising the economy are invented, which lead to the transfer of military-strategic templates to industrial construction. Today everyone is summoned to transport, and tomorrow they rush to the Donbas. One type of shock work replaces another. Shock work itself is now divided into levels. It is time to put an end to such a promotional approach to the economy and to look the truth in the eye, for our whole existence has become shock work. There is no area of the economy which now would not be in an extra-important position. Chaotic shock work and rushing everyone here today and there tomorrow, as has been implemented up to now, is of no use. One needs to remember that the industrial economy is too closely connected by the general chain of mutual dependence. During recent years it would have been possible to take an organised approach toward putting together a circle of tasks to lift up industry and so exclude the periodic appearance of catastrophes, crises, and panicky summons. But our bureaucratic VSNKh apparat could not realise this work, which is obvious for anyone directly engaged in production. There is no personal blame to be assigned here, this phenomenon is the result of the system.

When we struggled for soviet power [власть], then we set the soviets, as mass bodies of power of proletarian democracy, off against the bureaucratic authority of the capitalist government. In the course of our struggle we piled up such a large quantity of governing bodies that they became estranged from the masses, so that we were forced to place on the agenda struggle against bureaucracy [бюрократизм]. Under the very concept of bureaucracy we subsume various understandings. For some bureaucracy is reduced only to excessive red tape of various sorts. But this is only one side to bureaucracy, which is easy to overcome by means of internal organisation of the apparat's work. The most dangerous aspect of bureaucracy is the fetishism of apparatuses of state power; it is in their effort to regard themselves as the centre of the earth, around which turn the sun, moon and soviet planets. From here, from such a position, emerges a formal attitude toward business, callousness, narrow-mindedness, and other evil. It is possible to get the better of this evil only by constructing our power apparatus on a system of worker organisations, where proletarian initiative and enterprise would penetrate easily.[126] Overcoming bureaucracy

---

125   The Russian phrase is выдержит ли кишка Ильи Муромца нашу нагрузку.

126   Shliapnikov uses the words инициатива and самодеятельность, both of which can be translated as 'initiative'. Самодеятельность can also be translated as 'self-activity', but I have chosen here to translate it as 'enterprise' to convey the nuances that he seems to have intended.

in economic bodies is possible only by drawing worker unions into creatively organising our industry and by granting to them the corresponding rights to do so.

At the present time all participation of worker organisations in the business of organisation and management of our industry is reduced to unions' service as suppliers of personnel for VSNKh. In remaining areas of practical work, we have continuous frictions and conflicts, which reverberate severely on the sickly body of our economy. This is possible to escape only by destroying trade and industrial worker unions or by destroying VSNKh's complacency and subordinating its work to production worker organisations. The matter is not about simple subordination of the chiefs, personnel shake-ups or transfers, but about implementing two mutually exclusive systems.

Our existing system of industrial organisation gave birth to bureaucracy and dualism, and pushed aside the working masses from enterprising influence on production. With the transition of the entire business of industrial management to unions, bureaucracy will be destroyed, dualism will disappear, and workers will be attracted into building the economy. Our unions' production forms of organisation, which profitably harmonise broad democratism and centralism, will be able to create flexible conditions for involving each worker, each educated engineer and specialist in the business of reviving our industry. Then it will not be demanded to create artificial bodies 'of production propaganda' fabricating pictures, which elicit smiles or spiteful innuendo from workers. Production propaganda then will be produced in the business, in the process of work. Unions will know how to connect the producer's most minor work with general government work and will transform workers from accessories to the machine into conscious creators of communism, creating it on the foundations of economical division of labour.

Only when unions manage industry can our country's scientific and technical forces be used expediently and harmoniously. Implementing this system will extricate our technical and administrative personnel from the ambiguous position in which they are constantly found, when the union line departs from the line conducted by the economic centres. Only when the entire business will be united in production unions will it be possible to implement democratic forms of enterprise management and to introduce an elective basis for all administration, not just managing individual enterprises, but also whole branches of industry. Likewise the question about specialists [спецы] will disappear, since they will be members of a single economic family and in their activity will not be placed in opposition to the worker masses.

The task of unions' organisational mastery of the republic's industrial economy places before factory communists the business of directing all our party policy, from small cells to the highest body, toward reinforcing our worker unions with people and resources. It is necessary to return to unions those forces which were removed from trade union posts. This will allow some trade unions to put on their agenda right now the transition from 'organisation of labour and its protection' to organisation and management of industry.

A general demarcation should take place in that very trade union movement. Up to now unions have been organised by the 'jack-of-all-trades' principle.[127] Many people have an extraordinarily original understanding of the production principle, which for them coincides with departmental [ведомственный] and economic division. Unions should be demarcated into two types: production unions and those serving them. The latter should not acquire their own factories or create their own departmental economic policy, but should perfect the business of their specialty. This will make it possible to actively implement the principle of concentration of production and expedient use of resources.

Besides that, 'unionisation' [осоюзнение] of our economy will radically do away with the division of our industry into departments and shops [цехи] that exists to this day. Our more important metals industry up to now is in a fragmented condition. In other branches the same tendency is observed. Departmental and proprietary influences are at the heart of the existing bureaucratic system for managing our economy.

The transition from unions' current work to management of industry should be completed by means of attracting broad union masses to new tasks confronting them. All union conferences should in the first place discuss this question and carry out its resolution at general assemblies of workshops [цехи и мастерские], factories and plants. The fourth congress of each production union should be prepared in this direction. Congresses should make known their collective experience, give direction and infuse into the composition of central committees people corresponding to the new tasks. Such work should be carried out at the local level. Our All-Russian Congress of Trade Unions should also fulfil such work.

Before us is an unprecedentedly difficult task – to lead the country out of disintegration and collapse onto the path of building communism. The success of this work depends wholly on the activism, enterprise and productivity of our country's worker masses. The task of foreseeing and creating such forms and conditions, which can facilitate the enterprise of all and each, rests on the conscious representatives of these masses. These conditions are created by attracting production unions to the business of building industry. On this

---

127   The Russian phrase is швец, и жнец, и в дуду игрец.

depend victory over bureaucracy and the triumph of communism, which will occur as the result of the new organisation of labour, which will be incarnated in our production-labour unions.

20   Circular of the All-Russian Union of Metalworkers Communist
      Faction Bureau about Organising Party Cells in the Provinces,
      Moscow, 16 December 1920[128]

Dear comrades!

Six weeks have passed since the last conference of our union, at which it was decided to organise a Russian Communist Party faction throughout the entire union. This decision already is being implemented and the Bureau is receiving protocols from the provinces about organisation of factions in our departments and sections [отделы и отделения]. From the first protocols, it is still difficult to judge the scope of party work among members of our union, but it's possible to say that we have left behind us the time when our party comrades were isolated from political work.

Some comrades supplement the protocols they send with requests to provide the provinces with information about the political life of the centre. We understand this need and will try to meet it however we can. We will inform and enlighten our factions about the activity of the centre. However, we should qualify this by saying that the party press is responsible overall for reporting about and shedding light on party life and policy both in the centre and in the provinces. Therefore, our information will be only a supplement to that of the party press and will concern chiefly the trade union movement and economy building.

The basic tasks of our party cells in the provinces should be: 1) attracting the entire union masses into political work, 2) attracting workers into the RCP(b), 3) setting up the closest connection between union and party work, 4) distributing party work among leading cells, and likewise distributing personnel among union and economic bodies, and 5) taking inventory of party members in all enterprises.

We are experiencing a period of transition from military tasks to economic work, and so we should strengthen our party activity in two directions: expand our party influence over the worker masses and intensify the influence of the

---

128   GARF, f. 5469, op. 17, d. 6, ll. 1–2, no. 1, copy.

party mass of union members on the economy building, which we see unfolding. We should not limit our activity only to distributing union work among members of our party, but should strive to approach the entire sum of government activity of our party from the point of view of the communist who is directly engaged in production.

The role and significance of metalworkers in the first and second (October) revolutions were enormous, but their party activity was noticeably weak. The most advanced workers of Russia are the metalworkers, but up to now they are represented very poorly in our party. Our cells should turn the most serious attention to this circumstance. The most recent reports note not an influx of new members into the party, but actually an outflow. An end must be put to this disgraceful phenomenon among metalworkers. Minor dissatisfactions or the bad behaviour of some 'communist' who has overstepped the mark or just conveniently attached himself to the party should not serve as a pretext to leave the ranks of our party. It's necessary to arrange things so as not to lose members, but to acquire new ones, sweeping away the dirt that has stuck to the party.

Intensification of party activity by trade unions generally and by members of our union in particular is especially important at the current time. The Tenth Party Congress is scheduled to begin on 6 March 1921. The congress will discuss some very important questions about policy toward the economy and toward unions. In these matters, the metalworkers' words should carry much weight. The crux of discussion is the future of trade unions. About the tasks of trade unions, three tendencies have taken shape. The first takes the point of view that everything that exists is wonderful and one shouldn't dream or wish for something better. The second position (of the sovnarkhozists and Tsektranists), despite all their 'liberal' phrases and declarations of love for trade unions, proposes such forms of organisation and methods of work as in fact would subordinate our unions to economic bodies. The third point of view promotes to first place the implementation, in relation to unions, of our party programme that was accepted by the Eighth Congress. In the interests of eliminating bureaucratism, isolation of workers from production, the dualism [двоевластие] that exists in the economy, and the relationship of parity between unions and economic councils, our economic policy should be implemented through production unions. By bringing this situation about, unions will take charge of the bodies of the Council of the National Economy and thus the dualism that exists now will disappear. Besides that, it will become possible in practice to attract broad proletarian masses into economy building and management of industry. The majority of the presidium of the central committee of the All-Russian Metalworkers' Union supports the last point of view and proposes to comrades in the provinces to use their economic experience to define the current tasks of trade unions.

The communist factional bureau of the All-Russian Metalworkers' Union is taking measures to supply the provinces with materials, which expound more fully all views that exist on the question about the trade union movement.

The commission on the trade union movement that was selected by the Party CC and supplemented by those chosen by the Fifth Conference of Trade Unions is publishing a discussion collection, which is devoted to this question. Upon receiving it, the bureau will promptly distribute it to the provinces.

However, comrades should not delay discussion of our economic and trade union policy until they receive from us the materials, but should discuss these questions right away. Discussion of these questions should have the practical goal of preparing for the Tenth Party Congress. To this congress we should send as many representatives as possible who support our point of view. Political personnel and metalworkers should come out of their shells, close ranks, and join party work. In such a way, the Eighth Party Congress's decision will secure victory.

As reports from the provinces accumulate, the factional bureau will attempt to create a general summary of the experience of local work and share it with all our cells.

With communist greetings, the factional bureau of the All-Russian Union of Metalworkers comrades Shliapnikov, M. Vladimirov, Lavrentev, Skliznev.

The Trade Union Discussion, December 1920–March 1921: the Workers' Opposition as a Fully-Formed Legal Faction

Even as the Civil War was coming to an end, Russian Communist Party leaders faced many challenges. The policies of War Communism, especially grain requisitions, were becoming unsustainable and increasingly difficult to justify. Just as the Whites were defeated, peasant rebellions seemed to threaten the Communist hold on power and discontent among workers and soldiers weakened the Communists' support base.[1] While the population chafed at requisitions and goods shortages, tensions grew between party leaders and rank-and-file members over apparent elite privileges, as well as a lack of 'democracy' in the party. When a CC consensus over Trotsky's approach to rebuilding industry evaporated, the discussion of the role of the trade unions could no longer be contained within the confines of the leadership of the party and the union. With debate opened in late December 1920 to include all party members, Shliapnikov and his comrades resolved to struggle (as the 'Workers' Opposition') for acceptance of their programme at the 1921 Tenth Party Congress. The congress was held as Kronstadt sailors and Petrograd workers, who had been among the most militant forces of the revolution, rose up in rebellion against party policies. Party leaders used this rebellion to tar dissenters belonging to the Workers' Opposition, the Democratic Centralists and other groups. Not only was the Workers' Opposition defeated and censured at the Tenth Party Congress, but factionalism was banned, which also had implications for groups like the Democratic Centralists. The ban on factionalism was not such a crucial turning point as is sometimes supposed, for it only changed the terms of intraparty struggle. More significantly, the new economic policies adopted at the congress radically changed the debate over the role of the trade unions.

By December 1920, the group's programme had been signed by 38 leaders of the trade unions and industry. Hundreds of party members voted in favour of it, especially at trade-union conferences. The Workers' Opposition came to incorporate groups of Communist workers that arose independently, such as the Bauman group in Moscow and followers of Efim Ignatov.[2] The Democratic

---

1 Malle 1985; Figes 1989; Aves 1996.
2 For more on the Bauman and Ignatov groups, see Pirani 2008, pp. 50–69, 117–26, 195, 237–

Centralists and the Workers' Opposition attempted to unify on the basis of a common platform, but they could not agree on the exact relationship between the party and the unions. While the Democratic Centralists talked of the degree to which the party should influence unions, the Workers' Opposition saw the question in terms of union influence over the party.

Leaders of the Workers' Opposition tried to mobilise grassroots support among communist trade-union members, but the evidence of how much support they received is fragmentary. Although the Workers' Opposition enjoyed a majority in few party organisations, support for it was considerably stronger in industrial trade unions. Many well-known members of the Workers' Opposition had the support of local union organisations that they led. Certain local party and union organisations had made reputations as hotbeds of dissent and were associated, in one way or another, with the Workers' Opposition. Among these were industrial areas of Kharkov, the Donbas, Odessa, Nizhny Novgorod, Samara, Omsk, Riazan, Krasnodar, Vladimir and Moscow. Still, support in the unions for Lenin's views was also strong and Trotsky had some followers there as well.

Almost the entire Kharkov regional committee of the Communist Party of Ukraine stood for the Workers' Opposition. A party conference held in Kharkov in November 1920 witnessed a fierce conflict between advocates of the Workers' Opposition, such as Ivan Perepechko, and Zinoviev, who represented the Russian Party CC. After Zinoviev castigated them for repeating allegedly 'Menshevik' criticisms, the resolution of the Workers' Opposition received only 23 of the 316 votes cast.[3] Conversely, the communist faction of the Kharkov regional Metalworkers' Union voted in favour of the Workers' Opposition's proposals, without even considering those of the Ten. Trotsky had a few supporters. Nevertheless, the union's chair viewed with pessimism the metalworkers' prospects for taking over the party, since his organisation had frequently changed leadership and lost many staff during the Civil War. Once union leaders gathered their forces in November 1920 and urged metalworkers to be more active in party organisations, they met with hostility from local party leaders, who branded them as 'syndicalists'. Metalworkers prevailed among party members in the dis-

---

52. Pirani maintains that the groups 'had their own political identities' (Pirani 2008, p. 61), whereas I see less rigid boundaries between workerist groups in the party, with movement of individuals between groups and joint action at important moments, much as socialist activists of various parties behaved before the revolution.

3 Zorky (ed.) 1926, pp. 88–9. The main speakers at the conference were Rakovsky and Kassior, who were members of the CC of the Communist Party of Ukraine (in his 23 October 1920 letter to Ukrainian comrades, Lutovinov had urged that they be ousted).

trict of Petinsky, where the union was centred, and party leaders there feared being overwhelmed. The union chair was forced onto the defensive, insisting that his organisation never intended to challenge 'the party's ideological leadership'. In other regions of Ukraine, such as Ekaterinoslav, there was a more typical pattern of divergence between union organisations and party committees.[4]

Samara, where Iury Milonov had led the party organisation since late 1920, was one of the few areas in which the Workers' Opposition had a majority among party members. In late January, its provincial party committee voted by eight to four for the Workers' Opposition's programme over that of the Ten. By late February, the Ten had gathered their forces. A majority of provincial party-conference delegates voted for the platform of the Ten. Nevertheless, delegates elected a provincial party committee, of which two-thirds were supporters of the Workers' Opposition. Thus, prominent adherents of the Workers' Opposition still enjoyed much trust among communists in Samara. Milonov asserted that the Workers' Opposition had constituents in largely working-class districts, not those populated by peasants or soviet staff.[5] Perhaps because of Milonov's strong attachment to Bogdanov's philosophy, the documents of the Samara group of the Workers' Opposition emphasise proletarian cultural revolution more so than documents issuing from Worker Oppositionists in trade union organisations in the centre, Moscow, and Kiev.

If the Workers' Opposition could not win a majority for its platform in Samara, where it had the support of local party leaders, it faced an uphill struggle winning in other areas, where it did not have the local party's support. It came close to winning a majority at a party conference in the Krasnodar oblast, where it collected 30 votes but was edged out by the Ten's 33 votes (nine delegates voted for Trotsky's platform). The Workers' Opposition assembled 15 votes at the Riazan uezd party conference, but the Ten prevailed with 30. Even in Ivanovo-Voznesensk gubernia, which had a long tradition of working-class unrest, the party conference resulted in an overwhelming win for the platform of the Ten, which secured 99 votes, against 12 for Trotsky and nine for the Workers' Opposition.[6]

In the Uralsk Metalworker Union's communist faction, a majority of 13 against four approved the platform of the Workers' Opposition. (One member opposed the transfer of production to unions because he feared workers

---

4   GARF, f. 5469, op. 17, d. 10, ll. 82, 85; TsA FSB, R33718, d. 499061, vol. 36, ll. 36–8, 44; vol. 37, l. 425.

5   Holmes 1990, p. 15; RKP(b) 1963, p. 84.

6   Spencer 1981, p. 169.

would regard unions as bosses.) The Workers' Opposition scored another victory in the communist faction of the Orenburg-Turgaisk regional section of the Metalworkers' Union, where 10 members backed 'comrade Shliapnikov's proposals', as opposed to five voting for 'comrade Lenin's proposals'. In Ekaterinburg in the Urals, the trade-union debate prematurely opened in early December, when the newspaper *Uralsky rabochy* aired support for Trotsky's views. But on 18 December, trade unionists in Ekaterinburg responded publicly with support for the Workers' Opposition.[7]

A discussion of the role of the trade unions also opened early in Nizhny Novgorod, an old Russian industrial centre and a source of the strength of the Workers' Opposition. Shliapnikov travelled there in late 1920, apparently in an attempt to rally support, although published records reveal nothing about speeches he might have made for the Workers' Opposition. Andrei Chernov-Grechnev, director of the Sormovo factory, had endorsed the programme of the Workers' Opposition. The Workers' Opposition won a large majority at the party faction of the Nizhny Novgorod provincial trade-union council in early March. The communist cell of an important artillery factory, Kovrovsk Pulzavod, there unanimously approved its programme. The most support for the Workers' Opposition in Nizhny was in the Beregovoi, Sormovo and Gorodskoi districts. There was also strong support for the Workers' Opposition in artillery factories, which were under Tolokontsev's direction, in areas of armaments production, such as Tula and Izhevsk, and in the Armavir Metalworkers' Union in the southern Krasnodar region. Industrial areas of southern Russia showed strong backing for it.[8]

The most extensive records about support for the Workers' Opposition at the local level are from Moscow. As elsewhere, the Moscow party was polarised between activists in worker districts and city and district leaders. Moscow party-committee leaders favoured the Ten, but Trotsky also commanded very strong support among Moscow communists. The Workers' Opposition inspired intense devotion in worker districts, especially the Bauman district, where in August 1920 tempers flared over a rift between party leaders and rank-and-file activists. Trade unionists had tried to put a new district party committee in place, headed by Kutuzov. At a November 1920 Moscow Gubernia Party Conference, the Workers' Opposition formed a bloc with other opposition groups, including followers of Efim Ignatov, who favoured a role for the soviets, as well as the trade unions, in managing production. The bloc proposed its own list of candidates for the Moscow party committee and even met separately 'in an

---

7   RGASPI, f. 99, op. 1, d. 12, ll. 33, 47; Sandu 2006, pp. 84–5.
8   Holmes 1990, pp. 15, 24–5; Sandu 2006, pp. 86, 72, 81; RGASPI, f. 99, op. 1, d. 12, ll. 27–9.

adjoining hall'. When the opposition bloc got a large minority of delegate votes, it requested proportional representation. At this point, the CC intervened to ensure that only supporters of Lenin were selected. Consequently, delegates from several worker districts of Moscow expressed a lack of confidence in the Moscow party committee. Arguments over proportional representation were endemic during debates leading up to the Tenth Party Congress. All factions accused their rivals of rejecting or supporting proportional representation for motives of self-interest, but Lenin's faction manipulated representation most effectively.[9]

The Bauman case also highlights the reprisals against oppositionists. Having received reports that Bauman party leaders and activists held illegal assemblies and broached the topic of armed struggle, the Moscow party committee resolved to expel many of them from the party. When informed that direct threats of armed struggle had not been made, Moscow leaders decided only to remove the accused from their posts until they changed their behaviour. When the accused attended delegate assemblies in defiance of the Moscow party leadership, they were tried before a party court and deprived of membership in district party committees. Representatives from worker districts accused the Moscow party committee of having overreacted to rumours and being out of touch with the districts and with trade unions.[10]

The Moscow case shows how support for the Workers' Opposition was sometimes rooted more in communist workers' dissatisfaction with local party leaders than with national party leaders. This undermined the attempts by Shliapnikov and the Workers' Opposition to galvanise opposition to national party leaders, especially to Lenin, who enjoyed much respect among communist workers across Russia and who controlled more resources than did Shliapnikov and his allies. In the Sokolniki district of Moscow alone, Lenin supplied fifty agitators with literature and a car in order to propagandise the views of the Ten. He met personally with oppositionist workers to persuade them to abandon the Workers' Opposition. Lenin appeared on short notice at the Congress of the Miners' Union to attack the Workers' Opposition as a 'syndicalist deviation' from communism. This discredited Shliapnikov, who in his keynote address had just defended the proposals of the Workers' Opposition as a fulfilment of the party programme written by Lenin. Lenin's intervention brought an overwhelming victory for the Ten. Andreev remarked later that the Ten had brought out the 'heavy artillery' (Lenin) against Shliapnikov at this congress.

---

9   Sandu 2006, pp. 66–7, 74–6; Spencer 1981, pp. 136–7; Shliapnikov 1921, 'O nashikh vnutri-
      partiinykh rasnoglasiiakh', *Diskussionyi listok* no. 1, p. 13; TsAODM, f. 3, op. 1a, d. 2, l. 5.

10   TsAODM, f. 3, op. 1a, d. 2, ll. 16–17, 25.

The Miners' Union Congress was held in Moscow from 22 January to 2 February 1921. The Ten received 137 votes over 61 for the Workers' Opposition and 8 for Trotsky.[11] Lenin's charisma and tactics undermined the oppositionists' mobilisation of supporters in preparation for the Tenth Party Congress. Yet the oppositionists did not give up hope that Lenin might be convinced to support their views, especially if they could demonstrate the depth of their support through open debate and through the election of congress delegates.

Not only had the efforts of party leaders to resolve differences privately failed by mid-December 1920, but all factions had actually begun debating at the local level even before the CC officially opened debate on 24 December and Trotsky immediately addressed a meeting of trade unionists and delegates to the Eighth Congress of Soviets. The major factions first clashed openly in the communist faction of the Eighth Congress of Soviets on 30 December. Zinoviev gave the main speech for the Ten, arguing in favour of limiting the role of trade unions to organising and educating workers, and against the unions managing production. Shliapnikov forcefully declared that the trade-union debate boiled down to whether, during the transition to socialism, the Communist Party would put 'canonised bureaucrats and specialists' in charge of implementing economic policy or whether the party would implement economic policy directly through the workers, organised into unions. He asserted that to make unions into disciplinary bodies, as Lenin intended, was unnecessary because 'comrade courts' could perform this role. (In fact, Donald J. Raleigh has found that comrade or party courts only weakly disciplined party members in cases of drunkenness and unreliably enforced discipline when a party purge was not in process.)[12] Most radically, Shliapnikov concluded that the trade-union crisis was part of a broader soviet and party crisis, the resolution of which demanded a purge of the CC at the Tenth Party Congress.[13] No doubt, his chief goal was to rid the CC of those like Trotsky who supported the militarisation of industry. Nevertheless, many high-ranking party members must have realised that a 'shake up' of the CC was inevitable, due to the deep and close split growing within it.

Soon the Ten, working through staunch Zinoviev supporters in the Petrograd party organisation, attempted to take control of the trade-union discussion. Towards this goal, the Petrograd organisation sent a letter to the CC offering to 'organise' the party-wide discussion on trade unions. Although the

---

11 Sandu 2006, p. 92; Shliapnikov 1921, 'Politika Tsektrana i nash sindikalizm', *Biulleten vtorogo vserossiiskogo syezda gornorabochikh*, no. 1, p. 4 and no. 2, p. 3; RGASPI, f. 95, op. 1, d. 24, l. 20.

12 Raleigh 2002, p. 138.

13 RGASPI, f. 17, op. 2, d. 48; f. 95, op. 1, d. 5, l. 46; d. 19; Naumov 1991, p. 32; Zinoviev 1921a.

Moscow party committee immediately objected, Lenin endorsed the Petrograders' step as a healthy sign of lower-level initiative to heal the party from factional struggle. The party's Central Control Commission (CCC) did not agree. Created at the Ninth Party Conference in September 1920, the CCC's role and responsibilities would be defined at the Tenth Party Congress in 1921. Among its early leaders were Dzerzhinsky and Iaroslavsky. Both were Old Bolsheviks who had spent much time in prison and exile. Although one of the CCC's chief responsibilities was to try ethical infractions by party members (drunkenness, nepotism, physical abuse, sexual harassment etc) it also became an important tool to discover and punish intra-party factionalism. (Local and regional control commissions were also formed.)[14]

The CCC warned that the Petrograd organisation's appeal threatened a party split, but it also criticised the CC for its avoidance of a leadership role, which created the impression 'that we do not have a party but only separate political groups which will struggle among themselves at the party congress'. The CCC recommended that the CC take control of the trade-union discussion and conduct it 'only in the form of comradely principled explanation and not factional struggle accompanied by elements of a split'. Implicitly, this was strong criticism of the CC and Lenin for declaring the debate 'open'. Nevertheless, the CC ignored the CCC's advice when it marginally approved voting for congress delegates by platform. Lenin, Zinoviev, Stalin, Tomsky, Rudzutak, Artem, Kalinin and Kamenev voted for Zinoviev's proposal. Voting against were Trotsky, Bukharin, Krestinsky, Dzerzhinsky, Serebriakov, Preobrazhensky and Andreev.[15] The CCC's pronouncements conveyed its leaders' support for top-down management of the party, rather than broader democratic decision-making.

As the trade-union debate developed, Shliapnikov tried to dispel insidious rumours about the radical nature of the proposals of the Workers' Opposition, assuring his audiences that the group's platform was based on the party programme and was the product of practical experience. Dismissing other proposals as 'office reflections', he painted the supporters of Trotsky as being remote from workers. Rather than attacking the Ten directly, he attacked those VTsSPS leaders who had joined it, as unreliable proponents of strengthening trade unions. His strategy was to capture supporters from their camp. As an example of the ineffectiveness of the VTsSPS leaders, he cited long delays in publishing union journals, which rendered obsolete their news and advice to workers.

---

14   TsAODM, f. 3, op. 2, d. 23, l. 6; Lenin 1960–70, vol. 32, p. 48; David-Fox 1997, pp. 115–16.

15   RGASPI, f. 5, op. 2, d. 150, ll. 1, 3, 5 January 1921; f. 17, op. 2, d. 55.

Moreover, the attempts of VTsSPS to ensure a role for the unions in production had so far amounted only to the delegation of union representatives as 'hostages' to state-regulatory bodies. Union representatives, who were a minority in the state organs, had no real decision-making power and so lost touch with the workers.[16]

Shliapnikov's opponents could be found even among communists in the Metalworkers' Union, some of whom leaned towards Trotsky. Shliapnikov formally presented the proposals of the Workers' Opposition at the 21–3 January Metalworkers' Union central-committee plenum. Its communist faction formally discussed the role of the trade unions on 24 January 1921. While 11 voted for the proposals of the Workers' Opposition, seven came out for proposals based on Trotsky's and two stood for 'Lenin's theses'. (Those for the Workers' Opposition were: Vladimirov, Shliapnikov, Lavrentev, Skliznev, Rozental, Budniak, Solovev, Pleshkov, Kariakin, Medvedev and Tolokontsev. Medvedev, Tolokontsev and Solovev were candidate members. In favour of Trotsky's proposals were: Goltsman, Gurevich, Andreev, Lutsuk, Denisov, Tarygin and Vainberg. Gorbachev and Lepse voted for the Ten's theses. Lepse became union chair in 1922.)[17] The slight majority for the Workers' Opposition was hardly auspicious, considering that this union was its anchor. Shliapnikov and his allies had thus not managed to win the support of an overwhelming number of their own union members on the eve of the Tenth Party Congress.

Although the platform of the Workers' Opposition was signed on 18 December 1920, *Pravda* editor Bukharin along with other party leaders delayed its publication in *Pravda* until 25 January 1921, later than the proposals of any other faction. This postponed the VTsSPS communists' discussion of the trade-union question. When the VTsSPS communist faction finally took a stand in the trade-union debate, it was anti-climactic. Only representatives of the Ten and of Trotsky spoke.[18] There was no report from the Workers' Opposition. Shliapnikov was supposed to have spoken but was absent. By then, he must have realised that he had little chance of success in this arena. Lutovinov flatly stated his expectation that the assembly would vote for the platform of the Ten, but he urged delegates to hold a 'real debate' anyway. The majority voted not to debate, with one delegate insisting that he had heard enough at the local level. The Ten received

---

16   TsAODM, f. 3, op. 2, d. 25, ll. 1, 35–7.
17   Fomichev 1984, vol. 10, p. 3; RGASPI, f. 99, op. 1, d. 8, l. 1.
18   RGASPI, f. 95, op. 1, d. 23; d. 24, l. 1, 4, undated stenographic report of VTsSPS communist faction session, chaired by Lutovinov and probably occurring on 28 January (despite a delo label of 23 January), given Tomsky's reference to Kollontai's 28 January *Pravda* article as having been published that same day.

70 votes, Trotsky 23 and the Workers' Opposition 21. Supporters of the Ten dominated a commission selected to rework the platform. Riazanov and Lutovinov refused to fill the minority positions, with Lutovinov exclaiming: 'I cannot be a puppet in someone else's hands'. At the end of January, VTsSPS accepted his resignation from its leadership and approved his request to work abroad.[19]

Unlike Lutovinov, Shliapnikov continued the struggle by addressing communists in Tula and other cities outside of Moscow, with steadily declining results. (He, Kamenev and Trotsky spoke to Tula party representatives on 25 January. Kamenev won 587 votes for the Ten, while Trotsky gathered 272 and Shliapnikov only 16.)[20] Other comrades of his also fought against the current, but they were increasingly pessimistic. When Kiselev spoke to a Moscow Gubernia Party Conference, he assessed the role of the workers in the Soviet economy as not significantly better than their role under capitalism. He suffered a heavy loss. (The Ten received 217 votes, the Trotsky-Bukharin group 52 votes, the Workers' Opposition 45 votes and the Democratic Centralists 13.)[21] Unsuccessful in winning over VTsSPS and Moscow gubernia, the Workers' Opposition faced gloomy prospects. Meanwhile, unrest grew among workers. In early February in Moscow a conference of Bolshevik, SR, and politically unaffiliated (nonparty) metalworkers convened. Delegates decried unequal rations that privileged 'higher-ups' and demanded the end of grain requisitions. Many regarded the party's increasing concentration of power in its hands as detrimental to the interests of the workers. Resentment was also high against *glavki* and specialist management of industry.[22] In the increasingly tense climate, leaders of the Workers' Opposition faced dissatisfaction from workers who identified them with Communist Party policy, pressure from VTsSPS leaders to bring rebellious metalworkers into line and efforts by party leaders to smear them by association with workers who had SR and anarchist sympathies.

One final anecdote from the campaign is instructive. Communists working in the artillery industry represented a significant source of support for the Workers' Opposition. Aleksandr Tolokontsev, chair of the Central Board of Artillery Factories, was a prominent member of the Workers' Opposition. Nevertheless, among artillery-industry communists, the vote was very close. The Workers' Opposition, represented by Shliapnikov, garnered 25 votes and the Ten, represented by one of its less prominent members, Mikhail Rykunov, received 24. Although members of the Workers' Opposition dominated the

19   RGASPI, f. 95, op. 1, d. 22, ll. 35–6, 208; d. 24, ll. 22–8.
20   *Pravda*, 27 January 1921, p. 4.
21   TsAODM, f. 3, op. 2, d. 2, ll. 3, 14–21.
22   Pirani 2008, pp. 74–8.

commission elected to write a resolution, it could not agree.[23] This failure represented a marked turnaround from Shliapnikov's angry and determined speeches at the opening of the debate in December 1920.

The Tenth Communist Party Congress was in session in Moscow from 8–16 March 1921. As the first party congress since the end of the Russian Civil War, it marked the transition from War Communism to the era of the New Economic Policy, of which the cornerstone was a tax-in-kind on grain to replace requisitions. Featuring stormy debates on internal party democracy and the relationship between the party, the soviets and the trade unions, the congress culminated in the passage of resolutions condemning the Workers' Opposition and putting a lid on the future expression of dissent within the party. Nevertheless, such harsh results were not preordained in the minds of Shliapnikov and his supporters. By the time the congress met, the Workers' Opposition had reached a consensus on the importance of working strictly within party institutions to achieve its goals.[24] Of 694 voting delegates, the Ten held the majority. Approximately 45 were from the Workers' Opposition.[25] This small number decreased even more during the congress, but Shliapnikov and key comrades stubbornly persisted. The congress provided an important forum for their views, which they hoped would eventually prevail. More practically, the opposition hoped to gain some concessions for its platform in the resolutions adopted by the congress.

Desperate to seize the attention of congress delegates, Shliapnikov appealed to Kollontai. Admiring her passion and skill at swaying audiences, he and other members of the Workers' Opposition asked her to write something about the group. The result was her famous booklet, *Rabochaia oppozitsiia*, published in 1,500 copies only for delegates to the Tenth Party Congress, but having fallen into foreigners' hands, it eventually was translated into many languages.[26] This

---

23   RGASPI, f. 99, op. 1, d. 12, l. 45, Third All-Russian Conference of Artillery Factories, 21 February 1921. Gurevich spoke for the Trotsky-Bukharin group, for whose platform nine delegates voted. One delegate did not cast a vote.

24   TsA FSB, R33718, d. 499061, vol. 42, ll. 297, 299; RKP(b) 1963, pp. 3–6, 765.

25   At least 46 delegates belonging to the Workers' Opposition attended a meeting of it on the eve of the congress (TsA FSB, R33718, d. 499061, vol. 42). Kollontai wrote in her diary that there were 60 members of the Workers' Opposition at the congress, all of whom were workers. 45 were full delegates and 15 had a consultative vote (RGASPI, f. 134, op. 3, d. 37, l. 1). In 1931 Shliapnikov informed the Marx-Engels-Lenin Institute (upon its query) that up to 60 supporters of the Workers' Opposition were initially present at the Tenth Party Congress, but he declined to name them (TsA FSB, R33718, d. 499061, vol. 43, l. 142, 14 January 1931).

26   RKP(b) 1963, pp. 100 and 866, note 66.

has been treated as the chief document of the Workers' Opposition. Yet the group's leaders did not endorse the booklet; they only signed the proposals of the Workers' Opposition that were published in *Pravda*. Shliapnikov in fact emphasised that Kollontai's publication was not authored or endorsed by the Workers' Opposition; rather, it was a tract about the Workers' Opposition. He consistently refused to answer for it before the party.[27]

An early confidante of members of the Workers' Opposition, Kollontai was an *intelligent*, not a trade-union leader or worker, but the views of the Workers' Opposition accorded with her values. In private meetings of the Workers' Opposition, she assumed a role like that of a mentor. Shliapnikov also prevailed upon her to agitate for them. Due to illness and her work in the Women's Department (*Zhenotdel*), she only began to speak out in late 1920. In her view, the spirit of Bolshevism, based on worker creativity, had decayed since 1917. Her language in print was stirring yet incendiary, more inflammatory than Shliapnikov's proposals. She emphasised the grassroots of the Workers' Opposition. Her claims that the membership of the Workers' Opposition was growing rapidly, especially in major industrial centres, and that it was rooted among 'broad worker masses', were provocative. In hyperbolic prose, she asserted that the Workers' Opposition was 'organically' linked to widespread mass discontent present in the country, thus enhancing its vulnerability to accusations of collusion with 'counterrevolutionary forces'.[28] Shliapnikov had been careful to insist that the Workers' Opposition attempted to calm unrest among workers and redress their complaints within the framework of party regulations.

Kollontai's propositions for reform mostly repeated those enumerated by the Workers' Opposition, but she placed a greater emphasis on reducing 'bureaucratisation'. Calling bureaucracy 'a direct negation of mass activity', she explained that the greatest defect of a large bureaucracy was the extent to which it hindered local initiative and made all activity dependent on receiving orders from the centre. Enlivening Shliapnikov's call for drawing the working masses to directly participate in management of the economy, she wrote: 'the task is clear: to stir the masses' initiative and self-activity' and then not to frustrate this initiative by means of red tape and bureaucracy. Implying that the current ruling elite had betrayed the principles of the revolution, she concluded by paraphrasing Marx and Engels: 'building communism can only be the affair of the working masses themselves'.[29] Her concrete proposals differed little from

---

27   RGASPI, f. 589, d. 9103, vol. 5, ll. 12–13.
28   RGASPI, f. 134, op. 3, d. 34, l. 4; Kollontai 1921a, p. 1 and 1921b, p. 5.
29   Kollontai 1921b, pp. 36–47.

those of the Workers' Opposition, but her publication was far more severely attacked. Her brochure quickly fell into the hands of non-communists, and its language conveyed much harsher criticism of the party and CC than did Shliapnikov's language. Most significant in making Kollontai and the Workers' Opposition vulnerable to charges of irresponsibility and of aiding counterrevolution, however, was the Kronstadt mutiny, which unfolded simultaneously with the 1921 party congress.

Located on an island in the Gulf of Finland, Kronstadt was the base for the Baltic Fleet and it guarded access to Petrograd. Its sailors had been at the forefront of revolution in 1917. Influenced more by the SRs than by the social democrats in 1917, they supported soviet power. By 1921, Kronstadt sailors were angered by Bolshevik grain requisitions and the repression of workers and peasants. A large strike had started in Petrograd in February 1921, on the eve of the Kronstadt revolt in March. Neither workers nor sailors were opposed to socialism; rather they were dissatisfied with the policies of the Communist dictatorship. Workers decried food and fuel shortages. The Kronstadt sailors sympathised with them and with peasant uprisings across Russia. They called for new elections to the soviets by secret ballot; freedom of the press for socialists, workers, and peasants and other measures to end Communist repression against those who made the revolution and in whose name it was made. Fearing that the uprising could lead to their loss of power, leaders of the Communist Party ordered that it be suppressed; they had already imposed martial law on Petrograd. The Red Army and Cheka stormed the fortress, crushed the uprising and killed more than one thousand rebels.[30] Party leaders including Radek spread propaganda that SRs, reactionaries and foreign agents had instigated the uprising, knowing full well this was not true. Opponents of the Workers' Opposition discredited the movement by linking it to the events in Kronstadt.[31] The revolt and its suppression loomed large against the background of the March party congress.

Opening the attack on the Workers' Opposition at the congress, Lenin dismissed it as 'a syndicalist deviation' and belittled the significance of the trade-union debate. Depicting the party of the proletariat as besieged in a country mostly populated by peasants, he declared that the programme of the Workers' Opposition threatened party unity and the party's hold on power. Shliapnikov responded vigorously, shifting the blame for disrupting party unity onto the party leadership; this in turn gave rise to the Workers' Opposition. He insisted

---

30   Avrich 1970; Getzler 1983; Iarov 1999.
31   TsAODM, f. 3, op. 2, d. 36, l. 1.

that the party had lost the 'organic link between party members and their leading bodies', because the centre did not trust local organisations to make decisions. Challenging Lenin to recall the enthusiasm and comradeship in the party during the underground years and the revolution, he advised that hurling insults at the Workers' Opposition could not create unity nor prevent workers from leaving the party. He warned: 'Do not go too far in struggling against us. Here, perhaps, you will suppress and smash us; but from this you will only lose'.[32] Delegates applauded him.

Kollontai also charged that the CC had not tried sufficiently to resolve the crisis confronting the country and the party. Turning the tables on Lenin, she admonished him for not discussing the Kronstadt uprising in his report. Lenin again took the floor and crashed hard upon the Workers' Opposition, constructing a link between it and petty-bourgeois, anarchist counterrevolution. He lambasted Kollontai's booklet as the best example of this link and accused the Workers' Opposition of irresponsibility and of violating party unity in submitting it to the printers, even as they were aware of the outbreak of the Kronstadt mutiny. Fulminating that a person who would present such a booklet to the congress was 'playing games with the party', Lenin challenged the Workers' Opposition to produce a defence solidly grounded in theory. Referring to the Moscow Gubernia Party Conference, where adherents of the Workers' Opposition had broken off and met separately, he intimated that the Workers' Opposition was bent on fracturing the party. Returning to Kollontai's booklet, he exclaimed that it contained the same slogans as did the speeches of Kronstadt rebels.[33] Kollontai wrote emotionally in her diary of the effect that Lenin's vitriolic attack on her brochure had upon delegates.[34]

The members of the Workers' Opposition seemed unsure and divided as to how they should evaluate the Kronstadt uprising and worker unrest in Petrograd. On the evening of 9 March, when a majority of delegates accepted a CC resolution on Lenin's report, 45 delegates still voted for the alternative resolution of the Workers' Opposition. The resolution, which Medvedev presented, criticised the CC for having failed to carry out resolutions of prior party congresses on the rejuvenation of the party and on worker democracy, to take measures against bureaucracy and to implement workerisation. The rhetoric of the party leaders became fiercer. Bukharin made the astonishing accusation that the Workers' Opposition 'was complicit in peasant opposition to the Soviet

---

32   RKP(b) 1963, pp. 27–40; RKP (b) 1963, pp. 71–6.
33   RKP(b) 1963, pp. 100–3; pp. 112–24.
34   RGASPI, f. 134, op. 3, d. 37, ll. 1–2.

regime'. Just because Shliapnikov had been a worker, he proclaimed, did not mean that his politics were correct.[35]

The Workers' Opposition soldiered on. After Bukharin gave the majority report on party organisation and the Democratic Centralists responded with their views, an ally of the Workers' Opposition, Ignatov, made several proposals, with which Shliapnikov agreed. Attributing the crisis within the party to an influx of careerist elements during the Civil War and to the 'transfer of military methods of rule into everyday practice of the party', Ignatov saw the solution partly in a party purge, with automatic expulsion of all non-peasant/non-proletarian members who entered after mid-1918. Further, he recommended the imposition of a one-to-two year wait before non-proletarian party members could hold party posts. On the other hand, he would have exempted workers from needing a recommendation to be admitted into the party. Finally, he would have required party members to carry out 'no less than three months of physical labour' annually and to show proficiency in some peasant or proletarian job or skill. The point was for communists not of working-class origin to understand the 'labouring proletarian psychology'. When the vote on party organisation was taken, only 23 votes were recorded for the Workers' Opposition, which represented a marked drop in the number of delegates voting for the group's proposals. Some of its supporters went to Kronstadt to battle rebels (which did not redeem them in the eyes of party leaders), while others may have left for home.[36]

Shliapnikov attempted to salvage what he could from the programme of the Workers' Opposition. Defiantly rejecting the charge of syndicalism, he nevertheless conceded that the programme of the Workers' Opposition could be implemented in stages, the first of which should ignite workers' initiative by allowing voting on major questions of economic management at factory assemblies. The last stage would have to await the mechanisation of agriculture. He stubbornly asserted: 'no matter what platform you accept here, life will dictate not what is written by you, but what is fixed in our platform'.[37]

Despite his retreat (or perhaps because of it), his opponents continued to flog him mercilessly. Asserting that a party congress would decide that trade unions had sufficiently prepared themselves to take over the economy, Lenin nevertheless reached out a hand to the Workers' Opposition, requesting the

---

35   RKP(b) 1963, 136–7, 222–3.

36   RKP(b) 1963, pp. 234, 243, 334, 652–4. On a list of those who left the congress for Kronstadt were at least four Worker Oppositionists, including Mikhail Chelyshev (RKP(b) 1963, 765–8).

37   RKP(b) 1963, pp. 359–67.

assistance of its members in fighting bureaucracy. In the end, the party congress resolved that the unions would be considered 'ready' for the administration of the economy when they were free of a 'narrow guild outlook' and when all workers were unionised, a slight but significant rewording of the paragraph on trade unions in the 1919 party programme. The position of the Ten on the trade-union question won a large majority. Only 18 voted for the proposals of the Workers' Opposition. Despite the low vote for the Workers' Opposition, the congress included Shliapnikov in the commission responsible for writing the final version of the resolution, but he could not have any influence on it in isolation.[38]

The final business of the congress included laying the foundations for party unity by inhibiting future organised criticism within it. Lenin and Bukharin worked together to accomplish this goal. Despite Lenin's harsh rhetoric, he had been cajoling his supporters behind the scenes to include a few oppositionists in the CC. Lenin also seems to have conducted private negotiations with leaders of the Workers' Opposition. Bukharin, meanwhile, initiated the proposal to ban factions, which would become the basis for persecuting dissenters within the party. Floored by Bukharin's proposal, Shliapnikov announced that the Workers' Opposition would not make any nominations from its group to the CC unless the leaders of the congress majority would renounce a ban on factions.[39]

Meeting privately on the eve of the congress's final session (16 March), the Workers' Opposition understood that there would be a censure of the opposition but were not yet sure what form it would take. Some members wondered if oppositionists should join the CC and other leading party bodies. Some thought it possible to work fruitfully with party leaders from other factions, while others feared a swindle, and still others questioned the motives of those who would enter the leadership. Given such disagreement, Shliapnikov offered the option of personal refusal. Kollontai asked whether the opposition would disband after the congress. Shliapnikov firmly stated: 'There is no reason for us to disband', and said that the Workers' Opposition would 'conduct work on a new basis'. Others agreed, with varying levels of enthusiasm, to continue work, but

---

38   RKP(b) 1963, pp. 369–71, 380, 399; McNeal 1974, vol. 2, pp. 121–3. The total number of votes (404) was far less than the total number of delegates attending the congress (694). By this time, around two hundred of the congress delegates had left for the Kronstadt front. Even so, around 90 delegates must have abstained from voting, if they had not left the congress for other reasons.

39   Cohen 1980, p. 106; RKP(b) 1963, p. 790; Mikoian 1970, pp. 139–43; TsA FSB, R33718, d. 499061, vol. 42, l. 285.

not under the name of the 'Workers' Opposition'. Some were enthusiastic that their views would eventually prevail.[40] It seems that they did not expect a resolution specifically aimed at them.

Two anti-factionalist resolutions passed easily at the final session. The resolution on party unity did not explicitly attack the Workers' Opposition, but its concluding clause (which Stalin made public only in 1924, at the Thirteenth Party Conference) allowed the CC, by a two-thirds vote, to demote or expel CC members who conducted factional activity or who violated party discipline. The second resolution, condemning the 'syndicalist and anarchist deviation in our party', was aimed directly at the Workers' Opposition. It hinged on Shliapnikov's use of the term 'producer' as a non-Marxist term. The resolution explicitly underlined that the Communist Party could 'unify and organise' the avant-garde of the proletariat and lead 'all parts of the proletarian movement, including all labouring masses'. This was one of Lenin's contributions to Marxism. The resolution made further advocacy of the basic tenets of the Workers' Opposition's programme impossible.[41]

Responding with outrage to the two resolutions, Shliapnikov characterised the resolution on the anarcho-syndicalist deviation in the party as unprecedentedly 'demagogic and slanderous'. Strongly objecting to 'the proclamation of punitive measures' in the resolution on party unity, he and his supporters offered an alternative resolution, which stipulated that the congress reject the 'leading party bodies' [policy of] distrust of the creativity of the working class'. They repeated their call for a purge of 'careerist groups and socially alien elements' from the party and the 'workerisation' of the party and soviets. Further, all party members should be required to struggle against the suppression of dissent within the party. Only under such conditions would it be appropriate to abolish party factionalism. A mere 26 delegates voted for this final resolution, evidence that the Workers' Opposition was haemorrhaging members.[42]

Lenin presented the inclusion of members of the Workers' Opposition in the CC as a peace offering. Shliapnikov was elected to the CC as a full voting member.[43] He was also appointed to lead a commission on improving workers' living conditions and to the Central Purge Commission; other members of

---

40   TsA FSB, R33718, d. 499061, vol. 42, l. 285.

41   RKP(b) 1963, pp. 573–5, 773–4, 778; KPSS SSSR 1954, vol. 1, pp. 529–33; RKP(b), pp. 573–5. Twenty-five delegates voted against the resolution 'On the Unity of the Party' ['Ob edinstve partii'] and 30 delegates voted against 'On the Syndicalist and Anarchist Deviation in our Party' ['O sindikalistskom i anarkhistskom uklone v nashei partii'].

42   Zorky (ed.) 1926, pp. 27–9; RKP(b) 1963, pp. 526–7.

43   RKP(b) 1963, p. 402. Shliapnikov received 354 votes out of 479. Medvedev and Kiselev were made candidate members of the CC.

the Workers' Opposition joined regional purge commissions. Their inclusion was a message from party leaders that the purge should rid the party of 'petty-bourgeois elements'. Lenin even suggested that Shliapnikov, as a member of the commission on editing the resolutions, might find a way of softening their language. Finally, he proposed that the congress not accept any resignations. Agreeing with him, a majority passed a resolution obligating all members of the Workers' Opposition to remain in their posts. Moreover, the CC delegated Zinoviev, Bukharin and Kutuzov to write a letter to local party organisations, instructing them to smooth over differences and work together with members of former factions.[44] Shliapnikov and other leaders of the Workers' Opposition expected to continue their campaign at upcoming trade-union congresses. They were optimistic that, through the unions, they could still win the party.

1   A.G. Shliapnikov's Speech at the Eighth Congress of Soviets, Moscow, 30 December 1920[45]

[Supplementary paper by Shliapnikov at the 30 December 1920 joint session of delegates of the Eighth Congress of Soviets, All-Russian Council of Trade Unions (VTsSPS), Moscow City Council of Trade Unions (MGSPS), and RCP members.]

Comrades! We have heard already four presenters about one of the most fundamental questions of our party work and our upcoming activity in the trade union movement.

But I think that I will not be alone in this hall, especially among trade unionists, if I will say that our leading comrades did not give concrete business-like instructions about what we need to do tomorrow in the trade union movement. They did not and cannot provide this. Comrade Lenin was right, when he indicated that in discussing this question we need to proceed from our three years of practical work experience. Unfortunately, our comrades did not do this.

We who work in economic and trade union organisations can be grateful to comrade Zinoviev for having exposed very well here the petty-bourgeois essence of new work methods, which our trade union hussars advocate. He did likewise with those corrections which comrade Bukharin, as Tomsky's polit-

44   RKP(b) 1963, p. 538; KPSS SSSR 1954, vol. 1, p. 533; RGASPI, f. 17, op. 2, d. 62, l. 2. According to Naumov 1991, Lenin convinced Shliapnikov to withdraw his resignation (Naumov 1991, p. 39).

45   Zinoviev (ed.) 1921a.

ical commissar, introduces into the business of the trade union movement. The means and paths recommended by these comrades will not lead us to the desired goal.

First of all here, I should protest resolutely against those insinuations and accusations of syndicalism, 'trade-unionism' and similar sins, which our heroes advance against me and my comrades.[46] Our work was never 'trade-unionist' nor syndicalist, neither before nor during the war.[47] Only someone who is an utter ignoramus of the history of our workers' movement can say so. We can say to comrade Trotsky, who very often and generously flings these reproaches, that in the past we always saw his friends going against us. They rebuked us not for 'trade-unionism', but for splitting the Russian trade union movement by introducing politics into it. I ask comrade Trotsky to remember once and for all that in the trade union movement, in both legal and illegal times, we worked as social democratic Bolsheviks and communists, and we strictly carried through our party line. If you want to beat us, then don't beat around the bush, but get right to the point[48] and beat also the party, its line and the Central Committee. There's no cause to smear, ridicule, and poke fun at us.

We won over the trade union movement in 1917. Despite all sorts of obstacles, we accomplished this work and so secured our October days victories. Everyone knows our work during the July days and the October days. We were the second line of the proletarian trenches then. If trade unions really were 'trade-unionist', vulgar syndicalists, and supporters of neutrality, we would not be sitting with you here and Trotsky would not be a presenter.

There you have a short history of our work. Now we need to direct the political line of our party down that path, along which it always went in the trade union movement. This right now is especially important because attracting broad circles of worker and peasant masses into economic work stands on the agenda. This work cannot be fulfilled without professional production organisations or apart from them.

Comrade Zinoviev emphasised that it is impossible to achieve the goal by those methods with which innovators now approach it, and he is completely right. I can give thousands of examples, when thanks to these new methods

---

46   He uses here the English term 'trade unionism [тред-юнионизм]'.

47   Shliapnikov and others usually use the term профессиональные союзы when referring to the organisations that in English are translated as 'trade unions', but the Russian term literally is 'professional unions'. By using the English term 'trade-unionism' he specifically means organisations that defend workers' everyday interests, but that do not seek political revolution as an ultimate goal.

48   Бейте не по оглоблям, а бейте прямо по коню.

an abyss opened up between the worker masses and our party organisations. There was nothing with which to fill up this abyss and it can only be filled with illegal sr and Menshevik organisations, owing to workers' attempt to save their own skins from these methods.

However, it is insufficient just to reject methods of work. Proper attention also needs to be paid to the very essence of the work. The question about how our party should build the economy deserves to be posed as a matter of high principle. On this question, we in the Workers' Opposition, who are accused of syndicalism and 'trade-unionism', have a proposal, which is based on the experience of our personnel and of entire organisations working with the masses. We think that reviving and developing our country's productive forces is possible only if the whole system for organising the management of the national economy is changed. For a long time we have said much about attracting broad worker and peasant masses into the business of economic construction, but in fact it hasn't gone any further than production propaganda, pictures and speeches. We need to move away from this standstill. The future party congress should put on its agenda the review of our whole system of managing our national economy and, first of all, industry. The essence of the debate can be reduced to the means by which our communist party, in the current transitional period, will conduct its economic policy: through worker masses organised in unions, or over their heads by a bureaucratic path, by means of canonised bureaucrats and specialists [спецы].

The methods of bureaucratic construction have already failed. The three-year experience of our work confirms this.

In the area of organisation and management of the economy we have unconcealed dualism, which harms the business of organising the economy along its entire line. We'll turn to what is happening with us. Up to now our economy has been organised and managed, on the one hand, by VSNKh along a bureaucratic line of functionaries and of dubious specialists and, on the other hand, by professional and production unions along the whole line. Unions took upon themselves all that concerns worker policy, the organisation of labour, norm-setting, and wages. All the rest was left in the hands of VSNKh. This speaks of incomprehension of the matter, for tell us what is organisation and management of industry or of the economy in general? First and foremost, this is management of worker masses employed in production. There is no other means of managing machines, technical resources and raw materials. Only by immersion in the thick of production is it possible to build and manage the economy. Comrade Trotsky here, who so generously makes various prescriptions, has he given us anything new, even with the collaboration of Goltsmans and Kassiors? No, they promise only the discipline of the rod and forced labour. But these means

are extraordinarily inconvenient for producers' organisations and for attracting worker masses into economy building. It's necessary to look at the matter
from the perspective of everyday experience. Let's take our factories. What are
they in need of and what interferes with them organising business? Let's get
down to business, like practical people. I personally made the circuit of some
factories and had many meetings with comrades from factory committees and
factory management in the provinces. The comrades declared to me that it is
impossible to continue in this way. The union instructs us to do one thing, the
factory management another. We agree with the union's policy, but we cannot
fulfil it. In the provinces I happened to observe a curious phenomenon, [miss-
ing word] everyone considers, that there in the enterprise where the director is
strong, he has subordinated to his influence the factory committee. If it is the
contrary and the director is weak, and this happens in 90% of cases nowadays,
he is subordinated to the factory committee. Thanks to this, there is neither
one-man management nor organised collegial work in the area of managing
enterprises, but a complete mess. The business of organising industry suffers
extraordinarily from such disorder. From here it is necessary to approach and
develop the picture further. It's necessary, therefore, to destroy dualism and
to begin to organise and manage our industry, our economy, along the line
of organising the working class. By this route we go around that which interferes with us now creating a single will in the area of organisation of industry.
It is ridiculous to talk about statisation or, as comrade Nogin puts the question, that it is now necessary to partially transfer to the soviets and their bodies
some functions of management of industry. Comrades, it should not be forgotten that before us stands the task to organise a unified economy, but this is
impossible to realise by fragmenting leadership and by 'partially' transferring
management of the economy into the hands of trade unions. In this regard our
group, the Workers' Opposition, is more consistent than all the rest. We connect the tasks of unions with the economic plan and we unite leadership in one
body. Comrade Nogin's proposal is a thorough misunderstanding. In our practical work in recent years we have become sufficiently convinced, that unity
of management is the basis for organising the economy. If we accept comrade
Nogin's proposal, then we will not organise any kind of industry, any kind of
economy. Our economic bureaucrats, to whom statisation is so dear, understand it to mean subordination of workers' unions to state bodies, meaning the
glavki and the VSNKh sections (departments). To this we answer that organised producers have no interest in subordinating themselves to bureaucrats,
but want exactly the opposite, which is to use the economic apparatus and any
other state apparatus in the interests of all labourers. In this regard it would
be more correct not only to say but also to do what is necessary not to make

unions part of the state, but to unionise the state, that is to saturate our state bodies at least to a small degree and in essence with the proletarian spirit.

The system now existing of dualism and of equal footings, gives birth to complete lack of coordination in work. I personally tried to verify what kind of influence our unions' work has on industry, and can declare, that there is complete lack of co-ordination between the practical work of factories, plants and the management bodies of both.

We verified some trade union work in practice, as it is reflected in the so-called lifting of productive forces, and we find that trade unions' isolation from real leadership and initiating influence on the activity of enterprises gives rise only to conflicts. Our directions, especially in the area of wage rates policy, run contrary to demands to revive productive forces and often become outright reactionary. In some factories, which are large trusts, our imposition of maximum limits on wages are followed by lower productivity. As an experiment, we removed the limitation on wage-norms for piecework in Piter. Afterwards, productivity of labour there rose higher than 30% on average. In other places experiments were also performed, and in individual cases, productivity of labour rose up to 200%. These illustrations I bring from our direct large-scale practical work in the provinces. It can't continue further in this way.

Many sing to us the song of 'merger' [сращивание], but two mutually exclusive systems confront us. One ignores the initiating mass participation of workers and attempts to build and manage everything by means of bureaucracy. The other attempts to put in place and interest workers, meaning the entire family of producers together with office workers and scientists, in organising and managing the economy. Just try to merge the two systems. Take Comrade Nogin's proposal 'to merge'; in fact it seems that our trade union cell, the plant or factory committee, will 'augment' the director. In such a situation, VTsSPS would simply be subordinated to VSNKh. Here is the ideal picture Nogin paints. Comrade Trotsky proposes merging in this same spirit, but just by a different amount. In general their argument is only about quantity, but not quality, and there are no differences between them in principle. Such a merger will yield nothing positive.

We want for the party, as personified by the congress and CC, to examine our work in the trade union movement and, as it did earlier, to recognise and declare that our work in the trade union movement is communist work. It is possible to hope that this will be so, and that unity in this direction can be created among us. Then there won't be those frictions which we see now. In the meantime, things are wretched at the present. We don't have any industry or central directorate [главк], which has no conflicts with worker organisations. In the final accounting, the Party CC Orgburo decides how to organise industry and resolves questions about the composition of factory management and so forth, without consulting unions and contrary to their wishes. If it has already gone so far, if you want to 'merge' everything, then go ahead and transfer everything directly to the Orgburo. Then merger will find a synthesis and God's grace will reign in all regards. But I think that the Orgburo will not cope with this task, as it has not coped with many others.

Comrade Trotsky here declares that there are no workers who can command the economy and therefore, in order to manage industry, it is necessary to cultivate and create these people. This statement is untrue. Capitalism created such people and used them very well in its interests. We should also bear this in mind. Our protégés in particular, who are workers and union members, manage to a significant degree our most important industries – metallurgical, metalworking, machinebuilding and electrical – and they don't manage so poorly. Along with this, we will recall something else. Comrade Lenin forgot about decrees, but we don't forget decrees, including also the decree about comradely courts. We even use comradely courts for raising labour discipline. We arrange public trials and we have valuable results. This method of work yields better results than do prison holding cells, the train cars with bars on the windows, which comrade Trotsky's collaborator Goltsman advocates. Our comrades in Sormovo used some measures to struggle against violations of labour discipline.[49] Their measures included comradely courts and they decreased the percentage of absenteeism at work from 32% to 10%. These were old methods, which were tested in the history of our underground work and during the first stage of the revolution, and which consist of the know-how to convince people by word and deed of the necessity and usefulness of measures. Reproaches are often cast at us, the worker group, especially by Trotsky that we are so primitive that we want right now, by means of publishing a decree, to make unions happy and arrange it so that everything would go well. This is not true; we think that it's necessary to carry out great preparatory work before crossing over to that manner of organising work, which we promote. Neither the Orgburo nor Trotsky and his collaborators will carry out this work, but we, who you call Makhaevists and syndicalists, will do so, together with thousands of workers organised in unions.

No one else will cope with this. Comrade Trotsky won't cope, just as he did not cope with the railway workers and water transport workers.[50] Experience

---

49 Sormovo was a metalworking centre near Nizhny Novgorod, about 400 kilometers east of Moscow.

50 This is a reference to Trotsky's attempt to merge railway workers and water transport workers in the transport union Tsektran.

has shown that his methods not only do not facilitate the attraction of nonparty broad masses into the party, but instead demoralise the party ranks. Knowing this, we do not want to repeat Trotsky's mistake, so we will build both unions and their work from below, attracting in each case the deepest layers of the working class. This is our main divergence from comrade Trotsky.

If you turn to trade unions' contemporary practice, then it will not be difficult to judge the character of their work from reading one list of agenda items, which I took at random from an agenda packet of the presidium of the central committee of the Union of Metalworkers.

I will read to you protocol no. 68 of the session of the presidium of the central committee of the All-Russian Union of Metalworkers from 27 November 1920.

Agenda:
1.   Approval of presidium protocol no. 67 from 23 November, protocol no. 52 of the section for organisation of production from 25–6 November, the directive of the section of norm-setting from 19 November about conditions of pay for senior personnel who are transferred to other districts.
2.   About the procedure for distributing bonuses in kind.
3.   About additional vacation days in especially dangerous sectors of production.
4.   Statute on disciplinary courts.
5.   Instruction for maintaining personnel books and for uniform accounting of working time for those working at factories of the metals industry.
6.   Instructions to security guards in entrance points to factories and in workshop storehouses of the metals industry.
7.   Instructions to the director of facilities improvement of metals industry factories.
8.   Instructions to the director of security of metals industry factories.
9.   Comrade Vladimirov's report on his trip to Briansk factory.
10. About a conference of electrotechnical personnel in Moscow.
11. Routine business:
     a.   about a circuit trip by members of the presidium of the central committee around some districts of VSRM.
     b.   about N. Etna factory management in Nizhny Novgorod.[51]
     c.   About comrade Kariakin's vacation.

---

51   Currently there is a 'Red Etna' (after Aetna) factory in Nizhny Novgorod. The original factory was founded in Riga in 1896 and evacuated to Nizhny Novgorod in 1915. A.B. Fradkin and son bought it out in 1916 and renamed it 'New Etna'. The Bolsheviks nationalised it

From it you see that 90% of the questions, which unions now discuss, are very closely connected with our national economy and with industry. In all 24 all-Russian unions, you can see such a state of things. The entire misfortune is that these matters are only 'discussed', but we do not have initiating influence on the course of work. Those people who we give to VSNKh for its sections and glavki are not responsible to us and they conduct policy through their organisation along a bureaucratic line. We can say that from our point of view it is expedient to introduce one or another measure. We can say that abuse of overtime hours is unprofitable, that it is unreasonable to make from them a system for raising productivity, and that one should remember old lessons, which taught us that a long working day is less productive than an eight-hour working day. But we are deprived of the possibility to act usefully and with initiative in each case. Referencing the resolution of the Ninth Party Congress and the resolutions of the Third Congress of Trade Unions, they tell us that this is not your business, don't interfere, but just observe what we do. Now such a situation is being created in the factories, in which the factory committee is in charge of everything that is unpleasant in the organisation of labour, like struggle against absenteeism, exerting pressure [подтяжка] on workers, and everything concerning wage rates policy. In our time of poverty these are the most terrible and unpleasant questions. On the other hand, the enterprise director, plenipotentiary, or manager is in charge of everything that concerns boons and the workers get the picture that the factory committee which they elected is 'a bogeyman' [бяка], that it is busy persecuting workers, and the manager is a benefactor who sometimes can even increase the ration and give bonuses and so forth. Some extraordinary plenipotentiaries bring with themselves train cars full of manufactured goods, such as clocks and clothing, and distribute them for free according to their own discretion. In a word, such debauchery ensues that not a trace remains of union policy. Such a bacchanalia takes place as breaks all our wage rates and norm-setting instructions and creates such chaos and a hostile attitude to our factory committee that our factory committee members, who are the best comrades, flee from this work back to the workbenches. So if we do not want to demoralise the worker masses for good and completely scare our comrades, our best comrades, away from economic work, we need to change the methods for cultivating 'productivity'.

Only the party congress can decide how the party should lead its economic policy. Only the congress can direct the CC to carry out its policy on organising

---

in 1918 and renamed it Red Etna in 1922. This information is from *Vikipediia* (ru.wikipedia .org), which cited the company's website, but there is no longer a history section on the website.

industry through trade unions, which for their whole existence, both before the revolution and now, have proved that they lead communist work in our revolution by leaning on the broadest layers of workers for support. We often are extraordinarily perturbed by that distrust, which shows through the decisions of our centre in regard to trade union movement personnel. It is necessary to overcome and destroy this dualism in policy, just like the dualism in the economy, where all are on an equal footing, such as that which exists between VSNKh and unions, and quickly begin preparation for unification of work at the depths. The main forces should be directed, first of all, toward strengthening and reinforcing our factory committees, which bear the entire burden of implementing our common economic plan. We should direct our attention there first of all. The principal work should be performed there, leaning for support on the collective experience of the entire worker mass, which will be expressed in congresses of production unions. On this foundation we can build the summits [верхушки].

Comrade Trotsky is not satisfied with VTsSPS. We also are dissatisfied with VTsSPS.

I criticise it strongly and angrily, especially when I am together with Tomsky. We know his weakness perfectly well and criticise him for this. When comrade Trotsky swears at individual people for the weakness he sees in them, isn't he again making scapegoats of others?[52] But it is easy to refute him on this basis, just by asking, who is that sage who assembled VTsSPS? The guilty party sits here. He is comrade Krestinsky, who is from the exact same majority to which comrade Trotsky belongs. (Krestinsky from his seat: 'I would not have assembled it so poorly'.) But comrade Tomsky makes no objection and comrade Krestinsky's denial does not disprove the truth. Here is where the chain leads. Neither the congress nor the collective experience of personnel in the trade union movement put through these weak comrades. They were elected not even by those who are responsible for the poor work of VTsSPS, but by cooks [стряпухи] from our CC Orgburo. Comrade Trotsky, you should direct your blows upon it.

You see here how pitifully the CC majority behaves even in our common party and economic work. Therefore we need to beat this majority and not VTsSPS. We think that the upcoming party congress in March will produce the necessary purge even of the CC. Will comrade Bukharin really permit me to extend that same 'workerisation', of which he became a supporter, even to the Party CC? Comrade Trotsky rebukes us with primitivity, syndicalism and sim-

---

52   Не бьёт ли товарищ Троцкий опять по оглоблям, а не по коню.

ilar sins, especially when we promote the slogan 'unionise the government'. But here his best supporter, comrade Bukharin, uttered the same thought and declared that there is nothing to fear here, that this is genuine Marxist truth. Comrades Trotsky and Bukharin, you are from the same camp and you came to an agreement. You at first should have aligned your front, for with such a fragmented front you can neither damage nor vanquish us. In this work which confronts us, it is necessary first of all to close the ranks of personnel in the provinces. We are confident that these ranks, when united on the basis of economic tasks, will go our way and that our supporters at the forthcoming congress will be significantly stronger.

Comrades! Remember that the crisis, which our trade union movement is experiencing, is a crisis not only of trade unions. It is just one aspect of a general party and soviet crisis. You see also very well that this crisis in part ran through the sessions of communist factions and of the very congress. It is not necessary to tear asunder our jobs one from another. Military, trade unionist, economic and other jobs should not be separated or pushed away from one another. One job can't be torn away from another, since these are parts of one and the same party whole. If one part is sick, it means that the whole organism is unhealthy. To heal our illness, we need to re-examine our entire experience and to build new systems of work on its foundation. We should accomplish this work and, by leaning for support on our accumulated experience, try to correct both the policy and work of our party. To such work we also summon workers who are falsely called Makhaevists and syndicalists. Closing the ranks everywhere as worker groups, we will be victorious.

In the name of the 'Workers' Opposition', I have the following proposals to make about what we are to do today and tomorrow:

[Begins reading text entitled 'Organisation of the national economy and tasks of unions. Guiding principles.']⁵³

2   Theses of the Workers Opposition: Tasks of Trade Unions⁵⁴

[Translated from the version published in the stenographic record of the Tenth Party Congress and checked against the *Pravda* article.]

---

53   See document 4 in this chapter, A.G. Shliapnikov, 'Economic Organisation and Unions' Tasks'.

54   First published in *Pravda*, 25 January 1921, pp. 2–3; also published in RKP(b) 1963, 685–91; RKP(b) 1921; Zorky (ed.) 1926, pp. 235–43; Lenin *1926–35*, vol. 26 (1920–1), pp. 563–9.

General Tenets

1. The role and tasks of trade unions in our transitional period have been precisely and clearly defined by recommendations [*Pravda*: resolutions] of the All-Russian Congresses of Trade Unions. The First All-Russian Congress of Trade Unions in January 1918 defined the tasks of trade unions thus: 'the centre of gravity of unions' work at the present time should be transferred to economic organisation. As class organisations of the proletariat, built according to the production principle, trade unions should assume the main work in organising production and reconstructing the country's undermined productive forces'.

    The Second Congress of Trade Unions in February 1919 declared that 'in the process of joint practical work with Soviet power on strengthening and organising the national economy, trade unions have passed from supervision [контроль] over production to its organisation, taking active part both in the administration of separate enterprises, and in the entire economic life of the country'.

    The end of that same resolution states: 'Participating directly in all areas of soviet work, advancing their own nominees, and forming state bodies, trade unions should use this work to attract into it not only their own organisations, but also the broad working masses, in order to cultivate and prepare them for managing not only production, but also the entire state apparatus'.

    The Third Trade Union Congress, which took place in April 1920, formally confirmed the basic decisions of both previous congresses. Having given concrete instructions and recommendations to unions on how they should participate in organising the national economy, it essentially narrowed the volume of tasks, which resolutions of the first and second congresses had defined. The RCP programme, which the Eighth Party Congress accepted in March 1919, especially precisely and clearly defined the practical tasks of trade unions.

    In the RCP programme, in the section 'In the economic area', we find in point five the following: 'The organisational apparatus of socialised industry should lean for support first and foremost on trade unions'. ...[55] 'By Soviet law and established practice, trade unions already participate in all local and central bodies that manage industry. Trade unions should further concentrate in their hands all management of the economy, as a single economic unit'.

---

55   Ellipses in text.

2. The transition from military tasks to economy building and from militar- ised methods of work to democratic methods revealed a crisis in profes- sional workers' unions. This crisis was expressed in the disparity between the content of unions' everyday work and those tasks, which were defined in the congresses' resolutions and fixed in the party programme. The prac- tice of party centres [*Pravda*: congresses] and state bodies for the past two years has systematically narrowed the framework of trade unions' work and has reduced almost to zero the influence of workers' unions in the Soviet state. Trade unions' role in organising and managing production in fact has been reduced to the role of an office of inquiry or recom- mendation for placing staff in administrative posts. There is no agreement between state bodies and unions, and conflicts overload party organ- isations. A report about the condition of the trade union press clearly illustrates the situation of unions. Unions still have neither a printing press nor paper. Journals of large unions come out with a delay of several months. The state printing press hardly even accepts work from unions, even as the lowest priority.

3. This decline of the role and significance of trade unions occurs at that time when the experience of three years of proletarian revolution shows that unions wholly and faithfully carried out a communist line and led behind them broad circles of nonparty worker masses. To all and each it is clear that the realisation of the RCP programme in our country, where the overwhelming majority of the population is made up of petty com- modity producers, demands a strong, authoritative, mass worker organ- isation, which would be accessible to the broad masses of the proletariat. The disparagement of the significance and actual role of professional organisations (trade unions) in Soviet Russia signifies the manifestation of bourgeois, class hostility toward the proletariat and should be quickly eliminated.

Trade Unions' Immediate Tasks and Activity

4. The first real possibility of a respite for the labourers' republic from bloody armed struggle against internal and foreign counterrevolution makes it possible to concentrate all forces and resources of the country primar- ily on struggle against economic ruin and on the utmost elevation of our republic's productive forces. The experience of the four-year period of revolution and three and one-half years of Soviet building and struggle teach that the realisation of tasks put forth was successful only insofar as the broadest layers of the working masses participated in implementing them. We must consider this experience and construct our activity so that

it now would be directed toward attracting worker masses into directly managing the national economy.

5. Victory over ruin and the renewal and lifting of our country's productive forces is possible and achievable only if the existing system and methods of organising and managing the republic's economy will be radically changed. The system and methods of construction, which now rely upon an enormous bureaucratic machine, exclude any kind of creative initiative and enterprise of producers organised into unions. The system of conducting economic policy by a bureaucratic path over the heads of organised producers, along a line of functionaries, appointees, and dubious specialists, has given birth to dualism in economic management and entails constant conflicts between factory committees and enterprise management and between unions and economic bodies. This system has given birth to an entire sum of conditions, which delay the manifestation of enthusiasm for production among the broad worker masses and hinder their attraction into actual and systematic participation in overcoming economic ruin. Such a system should be resolutely repudiated.

6. The effort now observed to evade implementing programme decisions of the party congress about trade unions' tasks and role in the Soviet government attests to outright distrust toward forces of the working class. Conscious leading elements of the working class, who are organised communists, should direct all energy toward overcoming this distrust and the bureaucratic stagnation existing in the party. The system currently in existence needs to be annihilated. Trade unions need to educate and ideologically prepare huge masses of producers. The real defence of producers' class interests in our times is in the victory over economic ruin and in the renewal and elevation of productive forces of the republic. The very existence of the working class of our country depends on the successful execution of these tasks. The currently existing bureaucratic approach to economy building hinders the achievement of maximally productive results, which introduces discord, distrust and demoralisation into workers' ranks.

7. Our country's difficult economic situation, the shortage of metals and fuel, and the lack of equipment and raw materials demand immediate heroic measures, which would be capable of warding off the approaching catastrophe. Productivity can be raised chiefly by conducting the economic policy of workers' organisations along the line of professional and production unions and by presenting to them decisive influence in state economic bodies which extract and distribute the country's material resources. Management of the national economy is simultaneously

management by worker masses. Introduction of a system of organisation and management of the national economy through production unions creates a single leadership, destroys the setting off of worker masses against specialists, and in this way creates a broad scope of organisational and administrative activity for people of science, theory and practice.

8. Professional and production unions of workers are the heart of organisation of collective economic experience, and they are built on the principles of workers' democracy, elections, and accountability of all bodies from the bottom to the top. While they have existed, unions have acquired sufficient experience and people with administrative and economic capabilities and talents. Whole branches of our military, machinebuilding, metallurgical and other industries are managed by worker administrators. Many hundreds of complex industrial enterprises are led by collegia or separate worker-managers. But, as representatives of unions and economic bodies, these leaders of enterprises are neither responsible nor accountable to the organisations which appointed them. They are not even subject to recall, but they answer only to the economic body. Unification of industrial leadership in unions will destroy this harmful phenomenon.

9. It is necessary to accomplish in an organised way the transition from the currently existing bureaucratic management of the economy, which is cut off from labouring masses' enterprise, and start strengthening the primary cells of professional and production unions, the factory and plant workers' committees and those higher up, setting as the goal their preparation for direct management of the economy, in order to ensure the success of the transition of workers' unions from currently passively assistanting national economic bodies, to their active, conscious, enterprising and creative participation in managing the country's entire economy. To accelerate this transition, the following measures need to be implemented:

a. Create boundaries between separate unions on the basis of their production characteristic.

b. Immediately begin reinforcing unions with personnel, technical and other material resources, with the goal of adapting them to new tasks.

c. Select personnel of union and workers' committees from the standpoint of their suitability for realising the tasks confronting unions. This selection must proceed from below and under unions' supervision.

d.   All areas where there is currently parity between VSNKh and VTsSPS on unions' participation in managing and organising the economy should expand toward increasing the rights and advantages of workers' organisations.

e.   No one should be assigned to an economic administrative post without the union's knowledge.

f.   All candidates nominated by the union cannot be rejected and should be considered obligatory for VSNKh and its bodies.

g.   All personnel appointed or nominated by unions are responsible to unions and can be recalled by them at any time.

h.   Those unions, which VTsSPS recognises as sufficiently strong to organise direct management of entire branches of industry, are to realise this right, independently of other unions' degree of readiness for this.

10. The entire sum of union attention and work should be transferred to plants and factories, enterprises and institutions, and should be focused on developing the producer's activism and consciousness in the very process of his activity. This should be the role of unions as schools of communism. Developing the consciousness of the emancipated producer in the process of and on the basis of production, the union should organise work so as to transform the worker from an appendage of a dead economic machine into a conscious creator of communism, which should be created according to the principle of expedient and economical division of labour. Each bolt maker's screw, each weaver's thread, each blacksmith's nail, and builder's brick should serve as the clamp, coupling and foundation of new relations of production. Communist education should occur on this basis.

Management of the National Economy: General Theses

11. Forms of organisation for managing industry developed in their finished condition, and likewise the definitively built system of interrelations of diverse economic bodies, should bring existing organisations of producers, organised in the form of production and professional unions, in the republic toward concentration in their hands of all management of the national economy, as a unified economic whole.

12. This concentration of management of the unified economy of the republic will be achieved by such an organisational arrangement, under which representatives of organised producers will elect all bodies of management of the national economy in the centre as well as in the provinces. In this way, they will create unity of will, which is necessary to organise the

economy. Likewise, the broad masses' initiating influence on the organisation and development of our economy will actually become possible.

13. Organisation of management of the entire economy will belong to an All-Russian Congress of Producers, who are united in professional production unions, which will elect a central body to manage the entire economy of the republic:

   a. All-Russian congresses of production unions of separate branches of the economy will elect bodies managing production economic sections and branches.

   b. Oblast, gubernia, uyezd, district, and similar bodies of management are to be instituted by corresponding local congresses of professional and production unions. By this route, a combination of production centralism with local initiative and enterprise will be achieved. Sections of oblast, gubernia, uyezd, district and such bodies of economic management will be formed by the corresponding union in each case.

14. Enterprises related according to production feature are to be unified into groups [куст, главки] with the goal of making the best use of technical resources and materials. Similar enterprises, which are located in the same city or village, are to be united under a common management, which would be created by the union as a routine matter. The management of unified enterprises, which are territorially dispersed, is to be created by congresses of workers' committees of the given enterprises. The union would convene such congresses.

Organisation of Workers' Committees Managing Enterprises

15. All workers and employees, who are employed at all enterprises and institutions of the republic and who are members of professional and production unions, should actively and in an organised manner participate in managing the economy, with the goal being the fastest possible organisation of labour and production on socialist foundations.

16. All workers and employees, without distinction to post and profession, who work in individual economic units such as plants, factories, mines, pits, in all enterprises, institutions, and transport services, and in connection with all types of agriculture, are the direct superintendents of property located within their jurisdiction and are answerable to all labourers of the republic for its safekeeping and expedient use.

17. Being participants in organising the enterprise's management, workers and employees occupied in factories, plants, workshops, and institutions and services of transport and communications, land and other specific

economic units in given locales, are to elect the body leading their enterprise. This leading body is the workers' committee.

18. The workers' committee is the primary organisational cell of the union of a given area of production and is formed under the leadership and supervision of the corresponding union.

19. Among the tasks of the workers' committee is management of the given factory or economy, which includes:

    a. leadership of the production activity of all workers and employees of a given economic unit;

    b. care for all needs of the producers.

    In accord with the union's statutes and instructions, committee members are to distribute among themselves their work on economic leadership in such a way that each member's personal responsibility should be precisely defined, alongside their collective responsibility, which first of all rests on the chair.

20. All activity of the enterprise, its programme of work, and its internal routine, within the bounds of existing legal statutes and the assignments it has received, are to be elaborated and confirmed by the labourers who work in the given enterprise, under the responsibility and leadership of the workers' committee and union.

Organisation of Workers' Everyday Life

21. One of the necessary, indispensable conditions of lifting up our national economy is the systematic implementation of naturalisation of wages, as a measure which would ensure increased productivity of labour and improvement of producers' everyday lives. All measures introduced below should be connected with the wage rates system and enter into the general sum of natural wages:

    a. Abolition of payment in rations, household goods, and consumer goods, which are allotted to workers by ration cards and orders of state food supplies bodies.

    b. Abolition of payment in the form of lunches for workers and their families.

    c. Abolition of payment in the form of public baths, trams, theatres and so on.

    d. Abolition of payment for apartments, heat and electricity.

    e. In places where the housing question is severe, consolidate soviet and military institutions in order to present apartments to workers.

    f. Organise repair of workers' living quarters using enterprise resources, conditional upon the guarantee by the enterprise of fulfilling its basic production tasks.

g. Recognise as a matter of first-degree importance the construction of workers' settlements and workers' communal homes, and include a maximum programme for construction of workers' housing in the programme of the State Committee for Construction (Komgosor) for the upcoming construction period.

h. Organise special workers' trains and trams, timing their movement to coincide with the end and beginning of works in the enterprises.

i. Take measures for preferential supply of workers with consumer goods.

j. Simplify and speed up the order for receiving work-clothes, and likewise basic and bonus payments in kind.

k. For serving factory workers' needs, attach to factories or especially organise shoe and clothing repair shops; moreover, enterprises should render support and help these workshops both in organisation of equipment and in supply with the necessary material to the extent possible.

l. When enterprises have communal cultivation of land for gardens and so forth, equip the communal farming with technical inventory and resources at the expense of the enterprise.

m. In enterprises, which are in close proximity to the countryside, organise the repair of agricultural machines.

n. Take into account the need for the factory to carry out the measures enumerated above, when drawing up financial and production estimates for factories.

22. All the measures indicated above should be carried out first of all in nationalised enterprises. In privately owned enterprises and handicrafts enterprises, they can be carried out with the trade union's permission in each separate case. Measures bearing a collective all-factory character should be carried out in factories depending on the progress of their work. Measures having personal significance for an individual worker should be carried out in the form of incentives, starting with the most successful workers.

Chair of the Central Committee of the All-Russian Union of Metalworkers A. Shliapnikov. Assistant Chair M. Vladimirov. Secretary S. Skliznev. Members: I. Kariakin, V. Pleshkov, S. Medvedev.

Central Board of Artilleries Factories. Member of Central Committee and Chair A. Tolokontsev. Members: P. Borisov, G. Bruno, Ia. Kubyshkin.

Assistant Chair of the Council of Military Industry K. Orlov.

Director of the Directorate of Aviation Factories (Glavko-Avio) Mikhailov.

Director of State Machine-Building Factories (Gomza) A. Vasilev.

Chair of the Central Board of Heavy Industry I. Kotliakov.

Chair of Chief Board of the Association of Mid-sized Machine-Building Factories I. Barulin.

Chair of the Board of Sormovo Factory Chernov-Grechnev.

Member of the Committee of the Moscow section of the All-Russian Union of Metalworkers N. Ivanov.

Chief of the Production Propaganda Section of the All-Russian Union of Metalworkers N. Kopylov.

Chair of the Central Committee of the All-Russian Miners' Union A. Kiselev. Members: M. Mikov, S. Losev, V. Sivert, S. Arutiuniants, A. Gorbachev, A. Storozhenko.

Member of the Central Committee of the Miners' Union and member of the Collegium of the Mining Council of VSNKh V. Voronin.

Chair of the Usolsk subdistrict of the Board of the Miners' Union V. Strokin.

Chair of the Kizelovsky District Committee of the Miners' Union I. Ialunin. Members: S. Rychkov, A. Mironov, I. Lagunov, P. Fedurin, A. Zaburdaev.

Chair of the Central Committee of the All-Russian Union of Textile Workers I. Kutuzov.

Chair of the Central Committee of the Farm and Forest Workers' Union N. Kubiak. Member Khitrov.

Chair of Kursk Gubernia Commission on Workers' Supply Izvorin.

Member of the Party Control Commission under the Central Committee of the Russian Communist Party Chelyshev.

18 January 1921[56]

3   Iu.Kh. Lutovinov, Report to the All-Russian Trade Union Council
         (VTsSPS) on the Work of the November–December 1920 Trade
         Union Commission[57]

[Some of those present argued that discussion of the trade union question should be postponed, since attendance was low. Allowing that half a dozen unions were not represented at this meeting, Tomsky held a vote, which favoured postponing the trade union discussion.]

Lutovinov: Comrades, you know that disagreements about the trade union movement took shape long before the Fifth All-Russian Conference of Trade Unions. These disagreements were most prominent and defined at the Fifth Conference and especially at its communist faction. These disagreements divided the trade union movement not just into two parts, but also into groupings, among which there were various points of view and nuances. By this time the civil war had already ended. With its end, the trade union movement, which had been busy chiefly with serving the front with foodstuffs and transport, had to transfer the centre of gravity of its work and its forces from the fronts. It had to outline other tasks, which were linked neither with production nor with the basic tasks of trade unions, as they had been defined by congresses and conferences.

At this very conference and afterwards, the Central Committee detached a trade union commission. The commission's first charge was defining and concretising the tasks assigned to the trade union movement. Its second charge was to strengthen the trade unions' entire apparatus. At the communist faction of the Fifth All-Russian Conference, several trade unionists were selected to enter this commission. They included comrades Shliapnikov, Lozovsky, Andreev and Lutovinov. This commission was created to reflect those tendencies and nuances, which had been present in the trade union movement up

---

56   The theses were signed on 18 December 1920, but the Workers' Opposition claimed that
         Bukharin delayed their publication in *Pravda* until all other platforms had been published.
57   RGASPI, f. 95, op. 1, d. 23, ll. 4–24, stenographic report of VTsSPS RCP(b) faction session,
         17 January 1921.

to that time. There were representatives of the VTsSPS majority, the Workers' Opposition, Tsektranism, and members of the cc. In this commission, these representatives were to summarise all disagreements and elaborate some kind of common, well-defined theses, which would unite all trade unionists. This very commission was given the urgent task to strengthen VTsSPS materially.

As soon as the commission gathered, attrition among its members began. At its first session, it lost the most prominent representative of the so-called Tsektranist point of view, which is comrade Trotsky. At first he justified this on the basis of personal reasons, because the commission included subjective elements, with whom he could not work. Subsequently this turned out to be nonsense. Comrade Trotsky refused to work not for personal reasons, but simply because he was convinced from the very beginning that it would be absolutely impossible to achieve any agreement in this commission. From the very beginning of the commission's work, Andreev was absent and Goltsman replaced him.

Then work seemed to go amicably. There were no differences of principle. It appeared that the contradictions which separated the two main tendencies could have been eliminated in the course of joint work and that as a result unified theses would be agreed upon. But when discussion turned to the main questions, which were questions of principle, then comrade Rykov broke away. He represented the VSNKh point of view and it was because of him that this commission arose. You know that Rykov belongs not to the Trotskyist point of view and not so much to the sovnarkhozist, both of which are very closely related, but only constructed a little differently. During the commission's work, comrade Rykov defined the point of view that was most unacceptable to the majority of the commission. At that time the commission had still worked completely in solidarity. Comrade Rykov had been present at all sessions of the commission and did not object to some purely practical questions. When it came to matters of principle, however, Rykov departed second after Trotsky.

The greatest unanimity in the commission's work was achieved at the next stage, when we were preparing for the Eighth All-Russian Congress of Soviets. The commission then included people representing various nuances among the VTsSPS majority, the Party cc majority [Цекисты], and the Workers' Opposition, of which Shliapnikov and Lutovinov held slightly different views. There was full unanimity against Tsektranism, against which from the very beginning we unanimously spoke out at the Fifth All-Russian Conference and at all sessions of the faction. We distributed among ourselves all the work, without taking account of our different views. By the middle point of the Eighth Congress, we had divided the theses into various parts relating to practice and principle.

These parts were supposed to lay the foundation for a single set of common theses, but from this moment the different points of view appeared.

Shliapnikov was not present at the session, where we discussed the foundations of the future theses. Therefore, the theses of the Workers' Opposition were not taken into consideration at this session; they were crossed out. A group of trade unionists from Petrograd were invited to participate. It was they who prepared very many of the practical proposals signed by the Ten. Because the theses of the Workers' Opposition not only were not included, but were not even discussed, comrade Shliapnikov demonstratively departed from the following session, and essentially abandoned the commission. The commission continued to work, but after having lost representatives of three different views. By this time Andreev had abandoned the commission. At least, I did not encounter him during discussion of the final theses. He neither introduced any of his own theses, nor theses of the group to which he belonged. He only made some objections to proposals, which were put forth at the session.

Then the trade union commission convened especially for reconciling and unifying the various points of view and distilling them into a single set of theses. Those who remained were representatives of the VTsSPS majority and Lutovinov supplemented them. At the beginning of my report today, I did not mention the personal composition of the commission and the number of its members. Everyone knew, for it was published that the commission was not the same as the Ten. Some senior comrades were attached to the commission, including commissars and CC members, to give it greater conviction.

After all these proposals had been summarised, the theses were something like a thick book, which consisted not only of principled proposals, but also of practical considerations and maybe even several instructions on various questions. They were transferred to a subcommission composed of people who could write well (literary forces), so that they could extract from this large quantity of material the most necessary parts for writing up in a literary way. This subcommission included comrades Zinoviev, Lozovsky, Tomsky, Tsiperovich, Stalin, and Kamenev [?] and it decided to publish theses under the signature Iu.[58] They summoned me only when these theses were already prepared to go to press. When I read them, I was convinced that the trade union commission's work had not at all resulted in eliminating practical disagreements or those of principle. I did not sign these theses. Thus, the theses presented by 'Iu' were composed and signed in final form by only one certain tendency of those who shared common views, without any nuances. The Tsektranist point of view

---

58   In Russian, the letter Ю represents the sound made by the combination 'Iu' in English; this is the first letter of Iury Lutovinov's given name.

and that of the Workers' Opposition are completely missing. These theses did not eliminate disagreements but on the contrary deepened them still further and most acutely.

That is all I have to report about the political side of the trade union commission. I have more to say about its practical aspect, which relates to materially strengthening the VTsSPS apparatus and the central committees of all-Russian unions. The trade union commission at first was of undoubtedly enormous significance. The commission accomplished in several minutes that which we could not achieve through the CC in the course of several months. All our suggestions, demands and estimates were confirmed unanimously in the commission without the slightest debate. But if the matter depended only on this commission's approval, then we probably already would be rich with all the resources we now need. We would already be settled in one enormous building and would already be able to expand our work. But the commission had no executive authority.

Despite all the trade union commission's efforts, we have so far received nothing from the relevant institutions. The commission got the CC's approval very quickly, but the further stages so tormented us that we lost any hope of receiving anything at all. It should be said outright that it took enormous effort to extract promises from some institutions to deliver the material resources we need so much. The unbelievable resistance, red tape, and bureaucracy of these institutions don't allow us to actually receive anything. Well they curse us for still not having an apparatus and not getting down to work. But neither the Fifth Conference of Trade Unions nor the trade union commission has helped us get anything, not even the building we need and which we long ago already identified. The Little Sovnarkom confirmed that this building should go to us; now we wait Sovnarkom's confirmation.[59]

These endless transfers from one institution to another cause so many delays that many things are not worth either the trouble or the time. I give you one example, there is a building on Solianka [?] no. 12, which looks like a small provincial town. In this it would be possible to settle VTsSPS, the central committees, and the gubkoms. Obviously the request for this building will be granted. We received also four [машин].[60] That is all that we received from the trade

---

59   Sovnarkom was the Council of People's Commissars, while the Little Sovnarkom was a
      smaller body that was supposed to deal with matters that were not of high political signi-
      ficance. While Lenin usually chaired Sovnarkom, less prominent people chaired the Little
      Sovnarkom.

60   I am not sure of what kind of machines he was speaking, if they were not automobiles or
      typewriters.

union commission. We have no typewriters, office equipment, or paper. There are no necessary transport vehicles, there are no automobiles. Only today did the commission deliver to us paper for our daily newspaper. That is what we have to strengthen our apparatus. All our demands were approved, but not one institution has done anything. We were not refused outright but instead just got promises, no matter where we went. Thus, work is delayed and all our reinforcement consists of receiving four [машин] and the pie in the sky building at no. 12 Solianka [?]. These are the resources, which we received to strengthen the apparat of the trade union movement.

Tomsky: Lutovinov makes frequent mistakes in the political part of his speech. If these are entered in the stenographic report, then we will be accused of errors. One of these was about comrade Rykov. As you know, both at the faction and at the conference we treated the sovnarkhozists a little rudely. They interpreted our resolution as a vote of no confidence. On this basis, a group of sovnarkhozists resigned. But comradely criticism is not at all a vote of no confidence. In our resolution there is no vote of distrust. There was and will be no proposal to overthrow authority. ...[61] Comrade Rykov posed the question in such a way, that the trade union commission should state that the VSNKh presidium correctly fulfilled the resolution of our Ninth Party Congress about trade unions. Even given all our goodwill toward Sovnarkhoz, we found it extraordinarily difficult to say in such an ultimative form that the presidium of Sovnarkhoz fully implemented the resolutions of the Ninth Party Congress.[62] ... We finally agreed to the following formulation ... We both praised and cursed one another, saying that the VSNKh presidium and VTsSPS to an equal degree fulfilled the resolution of the Ninth Party Congress. As VTsSPS representative in this commission, I personally considered that this praise and censure were identical and that we fulfilled the resolution of the Ninth Party Congress no worse than Sovnarkhoz. ... And the opposite is true. Sovnarkom did no worse than VTsSPS. ... Concerning comrade Rykov's departure, comrade Lutovinov made an error. Just because he was not present at commission meetings did not mean he had quit it, only that he had left for Briansk. Comrade Miliutin took his place in the commission. ... Although Miliutin replaced comrade Rykov, the position of the Sovnarkhozists and the position of comrade Rykov remained completely unclear, but your position is completely clear. On the one hand, comrade Rykov appears to support Nogin's well-known theses, but on the other

---

61   I am not sure if these and following ellipses were in the text or if I omitted something, probably the former.

62   Sovnarkhoz here seems to be a synonym for VSNKh.

hand we have not heard from him objections of principle against our theses. The only point of disagreement is in making trade unions responsible to the government and bodies of Soviet power for the functions they fulfill. In this the commission found only one opportunist, this is I, whose formulation is that trade unions are responsible only for those functions and state power which they receive from the government and only are responsible to higher-up bodies. For example, when VTsSPS accepts an assignment from the Council of Defence, it answers only to the Council of Defence ... Conversations about trade union irresponsibility should cease, because we are not at all irresponsible toward the government. ...

Comrade Lutovinov's assertion that comrade Andreev did not introduce any theses at all is incorrect. When he was asked, comrade Andreev declared modestly and without emotion that he proposed acceptance of comrade Trotsky's theses as the basis for the common ones. We just didn't pay attention.

I should say a couple of words about comrade Lutovinov's statement that other tendencies were absent. This is very sad. I do not understand, unfortunately, how comrade Lutovinov can say that comrade Trotsky's line was not expressed in these theses. ... You can't pose the question like the Petrograders put it. Many of you ... remember how the Petrograders put the question, and how we turned red. Really, we presented our demands somewhat excitedly. The Little Sovnarkom rejected them, but this is such an institution, which cannot just give out 15 automobiles, but has to inquire where they are and only then give them out. Not even comrade Safronov can do this ...

Andreev: I did not resign from the commission, but remained within it and attended two sessions. I proposed at the second session to accept comrade Trotsky's theses as the basis for the common theses. ... Although I was a member of the commission, I was not presented with the final draft and I did not have the opportunity to introduce any corrections into the practical part. ... I was ready to write a protest to the commission that its members had not been informed of the final result. For purely coincidental reasons I did not write the statement, but right here and now I protest this ...

Medvedev: On behalf of comrade Shliapnikov, allow me to make a statement about his departure from the commission.

Tomsky: Shliapnikov can make a statement himself. There is a proposal to close the debate. Who wants to give Comrade Lutovinov a word?

Medvedev: Then I also will speak.

Lutovinov: I should respond to the remarks addressed toward me.

A majority votes to give Lutovinov three minutes.

Lutovinov: I never said that Andreev demonstratively walked out of the meeting (or left the commission). But in fact it was so. He had no theses. When the theses of the Ten were voted upon, one needed to know how to defend them in order to introduce them. The comrade, like a bump on a log, said nothing.[63] [Lutovinov reads decision of Little Sovnarkom about supplies, which elicits laughter. Someone says this is mockery of the assembly.] Little Sovnarkom makes a decision 'to give' but we get nothing.

[Discussion continues at length about supplies and Little Sovnarkom. Glebov proposes a resolution to bring the matter of supply to the Party CC.]

Lutovinov: Comrades, when the CC has made a decision to issue something, then it needs to be given. In the military, when it was necessary to give to the front, just one CC decision was all that was needed. Then all measures were taken to satisfy requests, when it was necessary for the front. No matter how high-up an organisation, if it didn't fulfil the CC's assignment on time, people were put in jail. If the business concerned supply, people could be shot. The reinforcement of VTsSPS is given only formal support and we cannot let the matter rest so. I support fully this resolution, for it is impossible to sit in the VTsSPS office while Krol, the leatherworkers, the metalworkers, and woodworkers come and declare that they will resign their positions, if in the course of a week they haven't received anything. Such a situation is abnormal. We have not a thing. We have neither typewriters, nor paper, nor an office building. Today we were refused publication of our daily newspaper. This is sabotage or something like it. Such a situation is impermissible and it doesn't help much that the CC issued a resolution or that Little Sovnarkom issued a resolution more than once. The question about sabotage must be definitively addressed to the VTsIK. Will those institutions, which are instructed to reinforce VTsSPS, give us something or not? Yet this resolution only urges the CC. The acceptance of resolute measures toward satisfying VTsSPS needs to be forced, otherwise we'll get nothing.

[Tomsky votes Glebov's resolution, and then proceeds to other matters. Lutovinov and others debate the organisation of VTsSPS departments.]

---

63   Literally, the expression is 'like cats lying in the sun' [кошки на солнышке].

Chair: Regarding the trade union commission's report, a group of comrades, including Skliznev, Tolokontsev, Chirkov and others, signed a proposal to assign comrade Lutovinov to implement comrade Glebov's resolution. I support it. Let's vote. The majority approves. [This seems to be a vote of low confidence in Tomsky's ability to defend Glebov's resolution]

Tomsky: If you wonder why I support this, it is because when comrade Lutovinov became secretary three months ago, he said to me (the chair) that he would be in charge of organising the apparatus. So I say to him: God bless you, have at it. He is in charge of this, so his knowledge of it is more current than mine. You see, if I come to the CC and say it's necessary to shoot people for sabotage and put people in jail, they will ask who in particular. I would have to answer that I don't know, Lutovinov knows.

[They agree to discuss the trade union question the following week and to invite the Moscow City Council of Trade Unions. At that meeting there didn't appear to be speeches by any Worker Oppositionists, only by Tomsky and Andreev.]

4   A.G. Shliapnikov, 'Economic Organisation and Unions' Tasks: For Discussion'[64]

Guiding Principles
1.   Building communism should be based on a single economic plan, which would begin to utilise and lift up the country's productive forces in an organised way. In a planned economy, there is expedient utilisation of the human work force, of technical equipment and resources, and of organised distribution of food supplies for a special purpose. Distribution is organised both between individual branches of industry and communications and between individual producers and consumers.
2.   Conducting a single economic plan in present conditions means first of all reviving our industry, raw materials and fuel extraction, all branches of manufacturing, communications, and land husbandry [земельное хозяйство] in all its diversity. Definite boundaries should be placed on the plan to revive the republic's productive might, according to time and

---

64   'Organisatsiia narodnogo khoziaistva i zadachi soiuzov: k diskussii o zadachakh profsoiuzov', Luch (*Organ Muromskogo i Melenkovskogo Uispolkoma i Uyezdkoma* RKP) 8 (194), 29 January 1921; also published in RKP(b) 1963, pp. 819–23.

the programme of execution. Our main practical goal for the foreseeable future should be achievement of productivity that is no lower than that in 1913.

3.   A single economic plan excludes anarchic shock work and extraordinary measures. Calculations of the extraction of raw materials, fuel, and production programmes of enterprises should be based on an accounting of material resources and should be developed systematically, in proportion to their accumulation. Both capitalist experience and the experience of our three years of work to organise the country's new economy should be used to realise this plan.

4.   Indispensable conditions to facilitate the implementation of a single economic plan are unification of enterprises according to their production feature, centralisation of the utilisation of technology, and concentration of management in one body. This will put an end to currently existing narrow departmental politics, which rend into parts the single economic organism of the country.

5.   Likewise, implementation of a single economic plan demands practical unification and leadership of the activity of all bodies, which are directly connected to organisation and management of the economy, such as: VSNKh, NKPS, NKF, Narkomzem, Narkomprod, and Narkomvneshtorg.[65] This unification will be realised within VTsIK.

6.   Management of the entire national economy of the RSFSR should be built on the principles of workers' centralism and elections. All management bodies up and down the hierarchy should be responsible, in organising the national economy, to organised producers and all labourers.

7.   Forms of organisation of economic management, as developed in their final shape, and likewise the definitive construction of a system of interrelations of various economic bodies, should lead existing organisations of producers in the Republic, in the form of production and professional unions, to concentrate in their hands all management of the entire national economy, as a single economic whole.

8.   This concentration of management of the unified economy of the Republic will be achieved by means of establishing such an organisational order, in which all bodies of management of the national economy, both in the centre and in the provinces, are to be elected by representatives of organised producers. This will create unity of will, which is necessary to

---

65   The abbreviations are for the All-Russian Council of the Economy, the People's Commissariats of Communications, Finances, Agriculture, Food Supplies, and Foreign Trade.

organise the national economy, and really make it possible for the broad working masses to show initiative in the organisation and development of our economy.

Organisation of the Management of the National Economy

9. Organisation of the management of the national economy belongs to an all-Russian congress of producers who are unified in trade and production unions. The congress elects a central body to manage the entire national economy of the Republic.

10. All-Russian congresses of production unions of individual branches of the economy elect bodies managing production and economic departments and branches.

11. Bodies of administration at the levels of the oblast, gubernia, uyezd, raion, and so on are elected by the corresponding provincial congresses of professional and production unions. This will combine production centralism with local initiative and enterprise.

12. The corresponding production unions elect sections of oblast, gubernia, raion and such bodies of management of the economy.

13. The transition of the currently existing system of bureaucratic management of the economy, which is isolated from the enterprise of the labouring masses, is necessary to complete in an organised way. This should begin with reinforcing the primary cells of professional and production unions, such as factory and plant committees and higher, in view of preparing them for direct administration of the economy.

14. In the interests of haste, it is necessary to precisely set out the gradual development and order of the transition of workers' unions from rendering completely passive assistance to national economic bodies, to their active and enterprising participation in managing the entire economy of the country. For this it is necessary to:[66]

    a. Create boundaries between separate unions on the basis of their production characteristic.

    b. Immediately begin reinforcement of unions with personnel, technical, and material resources, with the goal of adapting them to new tasks.

    c. Select personnel of union and workers' committees from the standpoint of their suitability for realising the tasks confronting unions.

---

66 The following list (a-h) is exactly the same as in the theses of the Workers' Opposition published in *Pravda*.

This selection must proceed under unions' supervision and from below.

d. Workers' organisations' rights and advantages should expand in all areas where there is currently parity between VSNKh and VTsSPS on unions' participation in managing and organising the economy.

e. No one should be assigned to an economic administrative post without the union's knowledge.

f. None of the union's candidates may be rejected and should be considered obligatory for VSNKh and its bodies.

g. All personnel appointed or nominated by unions are responsible to unions and can be recalled by them at any time.

h. Unions which are recognised by VTsSPS as sufficiently strong to organise direct management of entire branches of industry are to realise this right, whether or not other unions are ready for this.

Organisation of Workers' Committees Managing Enterprises
[Further the text continues just as in the theses published in *Pravda* on 25 January 1921.]

5   A.M. Kollontai, 'Time to Analyse'[67]

We are experiencing a typical phenomenon to which each thoughtful comrade should direct the most serious attention. All one has to do is meet a comrade from among the party higher-ups, from among senior personnel. The first question is 'for which theses are you? Trotsky's? Zinoviev's? Bukharin's?' There is not a sound about the Workers' Opposition. It is like the elephant in the room that no one wants to talk about.[68]

The question changes if you happen to find yourself among the party masses or trade union rank and file: 'Are you for our position or against it?' They debate and discuss the nuances of other platforms, but passions run high only when the matter concerns the Workers' Opposition.

This is characteristic, portentous and revealing. The masses' healthy class instinct allows them to 'sense' when among the 'higher-ups' takes shape a dangerous deviation toward accommodation or 'opportunism', as this was called in the old times of the underground. Higher-ups can divert the working class onto

---

67   'Pora proanalizirovat', *Pravda* (28 January 1921): 1.
68   Величина не стоящая внимания.

a false path when the masses are passive, silent and only 'follow'. So it was during the imperialist slaughter. But when the masses are in a state of unrest, they begin fervently to champion their class tasks, if not always skilfully and eloquently. Then it's necessary to know how to listen to their voice. Then the party should rely less upon the experience of 'refined politicians' and listen more to the healthy voice of the working masses themselves.

The main class task of the proletariat is the creation of a unified planned communist economy. Who can introduce greater creativity into implementing this main point of the communist programme? Through its class organisations, the production unions, the working class can. What does the Workers' Opposition want? 'To establish unions' gradual and orderly transition from being the currently passive assistants to economic bodies into participating actively and with initiative in managing the country's entire economy' (Shliapnikov's theses). The Workers' Opposition proposes to transfer the organisation of economic management to a body elected by an all-Russian congress of producers who are united in production unions. If we add to these two positions the principle of electing bodies of management and supervision by unions when assigning persons to leading administrative posts in production, then these proposals contain the essence of the point of view of the Workers' Opposition.

What does our party find unacceptable about the opposition's positions? What forces our comrades among party higher-ups either to condescendingly dismiss it or to consider it 'politically dangerous' (comrade Trotsky's words at discussions of the Moscow Committee)? Is it the spirit of syndicalism? But if the 'syndicalist line' pertained to the dispute about emancipating unions from our party's influence, the debate would have revolved especially acutely around the points of 'shaking up and appointmentism'. Yet exactly these points drop to second place. Theses opposing the Workers' Opposition seem diverse, but have a mutual spirit. All defenders of other theses make some concessions to democratism. The Workers' Opposition has never called for weakening the party's influence over unions. The root of disagreement must be sought elsewhere. Who will bring creativity into our national economic life, which we are building now on the foundations of communism? Will it be an organisation which is working-class in composition and which bears the spirit of creativity of the rising class, or will it be a state body with a mixed social composition, which includes a significant number of those who emerged from the bourgeois world? These holdovers [выходцы] from the past might be irreplaceable implementers and technical forces in the broadest sense of the word, but permeated as they are by the bourgeois world view, can they be trusted with the great creative work of communism?

Opponents of the Workers' Opposition object, 'Pardon me, but how could you have a more class-based organisation when all our soviet bodies are in the hands of workers!' This is not true. If the matter stood so, there would be no disputes and no conversations about 'merging'. But the misfortune is that class-oriented worker organisations are proposed to 'merge' with state bodies where the leading authority is in the hands neither of workers nor of communists. Instead, the leading authority flows beyond the realm of proletarian-communist influence as technical tasks become more complex and as petty property-owning peasants make more insistent requests.

Our misfortune is that our government is a 'worker government, in which the peasant population prevails, and with bureaucratic perversion' (comrade Lenin's article in *Pravda*, 21 January). The leading party, which manages the whole complex mechanism of the state, has to take into account the intersecting, mutually exclusive interests of three main social groups. The first is workers and the second is the peasantry. The third comprises the bourgeois intelligentsia, the specialists [*спецы*] and pseudo-specialists in all areas of economy and government building who are declassed, but who are inescapably drawn toward the buttresses of the past.

To whom should our party show greater trust from among these three groups? It stands to reason that it should show greater trust to workers, the proletarian masses. Without the flesh and blood of the proletariat, there is no communism.

But in fact it is not so. No matter how the nuances differ among our comrades' numerous theses (now each 'self-respecting' senior person has his own theses), all of them can be reduced to one thing. This is lack of trust in the rank and file workers, and obvious trust in the creative talents of bureaucratic apparats, allowing for a mixed social composition in building the communist economy. 'Workers have still not matured sufficiently to manage the economy', they say. Workers should still sit at unions' school desks. They should pass according to the system of old-fashioned pedagogy, by studying construction of the communist economy not through practice, experience, or creative exercises, but by copybook and edification by 'experienced pedagogues' from VSNKh.

If we had employed the same wise caution and gradualism in 1917, our party would not have led us on the straight though rocky path that shortened the way to communism, but would have led us astray on well-trod roads into the swamps and forested thickets of history.

That which the Workers' Opposition now tries to vindicate is exactly the distinct, uncompromising class line, which distinguishes the programme of the communists and which made our party, under comrade Lenin's leadership, a first-rate force. Not in vain does the organiser of the masses [массовик] from the Workers' Opposition believe, 'Ilich will join us'.

Either the party will join the side of timeservers and so will depart from the broad worker masses who have politically matured during these years, or it will stand for conscious creative construction of the communist economy by means of elected bodies of producers, who are imbued with and inspired not by a departmental soviet spirit, but by the revolutionary Bolshevik spirit of communism.

A. Kollontai

6   A.M. Kollontai's Corrections to the Theses on Party Building[69]

Corrections to Theses on Party Building

Point 11: **After the words:** International situation, **insert:** Toward this goal, elections are needed to verify the appointment of all leading party bodies and to abolish appointmentism and 'plenipotentiaries'. Only comrades elected as leaders of party bodies by the Congress or conference can be plenipotentiaries (for example, members of the CC, gubkom, uyezdkom).

Point 14. Keeping in mind: first, that all genuinely revolutionary elements from a nonproletarian milieu entered the party in the initial period of the October Revolution and that according to the degree by which Soviet power became stronger there began to pour into the party petty-bourgeois, careerist, unsteady elements from the nonproletarian milieu, second ... [ellipses in text].

Point 17. **After the words:** bodies of the party **insert:** 'workerisation' of the CC and gubkoms is necessary, that is, the guarantee of workers' overwhelming influence.

Point 17a – new. Toward strengthening party centres of such a kind, which actually would be bodies of ideological supervision over Soviet bodies and would lead the latter in a consistent class spirit, and likewise toward strengthening party work, it is necessary that at least one-third of the available personnel of members of party centres personally would not combine party and soviet work.

---

69   RGASPI, f. 134, op. 3, d. 37, l. 56, undated.

7   A.G. Shliapnikov, 'Our Intraparty Disagreements'[70]

[On page one, the editors write, 'In accord with the decision of the all-party conference, we are issuing a "Discussion Leaflet". The editors consider it their duty to print, if possible, all articles which were received. The current issue does not include only those articles and notes which, first, have exclusively an individual character and represent essentially personal complaints; and second, those which were received too late. The latter will be included in further issues of the "Leaflet", for to have included them would have meant the further delay of this edition's appearance in print'.]

There is unrest in our party ranks. For a long time there has been talk that there is mutual struggle here and there in the party ranks. Dissatisfaction grows and the old party cohesion is gone. In some places this dissatisfaction turns into open protests, in the form of individual or mass departures from the party. Not only novices abandon the party, but also workers who can claim credit for many years of underground experience. It's becoming obvious that an illness consumes the party. However, as yet this situation has not been brought to light in the party press or at assemblies.

Only in the beginning of September, an appeal appeared in no. 21 of *Izvestiia TsK RKP* which posed 'higher-ups and rank-and file' as a burning topic, which was rending our ranks.[71]

The September 1920 All-Russian Party Conference paid much attention to the party's situation, but a significant part of this attention was superficial. Debate led to acceptance of a resolution that attempted to solve painful questions by a formal route. The whole matter was reduced to the desire to strive toward greater equality. There were proposals to eliminate some 'rough patches' and calls to arrange party assemblies 'as often as possible'. The higher-ups were invited to 'go to the people'[72] and to associate with the masses in all sorts of ways. The delegates dispersed, having gained confidence that friction had been overcome and the party had set out on the path of recovery.

---

70   'O nashikh vnutripartiinykh raznoglasiiakh', *Pravda: Diskussionyi listok*, 1 (January 1921): 13–14.

71   Here and throughout, Shliapnikov employs the terms верхи и низы, which have been translated variously. While Lars T. Lih prefers 'higher-ups' and 'lower-downs', Simon Pirani uses 'the tops' and 'the ranks'. I translate the terms as 'higher-ups' and 'rank-and-file'. Another possible translation for низы would be 'grassroots'.

72   This phrase reminds one of the 1870s populist movement in Russia.

For the past few months, however, some things have shown clearly that the All-Russian Party Conference did not eliminate disagreements. In October the Fifth All-Russian Conference of Trade Unions, by the very nature of its activity, turned into a party conference of economic sector personnel and of trade unionists. At this conference questions arose that divided our ranks into two and even three parts.

The Moscow Gubernia RCP Conference also took place under the omen of intraparty frictions and disagreements. All these things attest that the All-Russian Conference of the RCP did not solve the tasks given it at the time, so urgent problems break out everywhere possible. Leading party bodies are obligated to find an organised way out of the situation that is being created, in order to allow party members 'to unloose their tongues', as they say in the districts, to make it possible for all party members to talk about and clarify the questions agitating them, and in such a way to move toward the strengthening and unification of party ranks.

Now we'll move on to those questions, which disturb broad circles of party comrades and push them into opposition to the existing official course.

I personally met with oppositionist elements of our party in various workers' cities and settlements and also became acquainted with those visiting Moscow. Old acquaintanceship through party work during the old times of the underground and personal friendship allows comrades to share with me all that troubles their proletarian minds and agitates their best revolutionary feelings. In a series of articles, I propose to briefly summarise those questions, which alarm minds and hearts and to which they seek answers.

But those who expect me to provide an exhaustive classification of the opposition's views should not read this article. I don't aim to draft a 'new' programme, but only to sum up the disagreements that have taken shape. Up to now I have not met anyone who proposed a ready-made scheme or a new platform of action which would embrace the entire complex combination of party and government work. All comrades approach the great questions from their own personal or collective experience, which they have obtained during these three years of struggle and construction. Their experiences taken separately are limited by the character, time, and place of their work. But the questions or proposals they raise do not lose any value because of this. The bygone versatile, multifaceted party worker gave way to the practician limited by time and place. The party should assemble and make use of these practicians' uncoordinated experience.

All disagreements which have been revealed so far can be separated into two parts. Differences of a tactical character belong to the first part. The second part embraces some positions which possess a principled character.

Tactical differences have often been revealed in all communist faction sessions of the Republic's leading collectives (VTsIK, VTsSPS, party conferences, trade union conferences and so on). First of all, the methods and nature of our party work have been severely criticised. In many places, there has been seen a rupture in the relations between leading party collegia and the masses of party members. The spirit of comradely understanding and solidarity has been gelded from party organisations and automatic acknowledgement and obedience have taken its place. By this path they killed enthusiasm, creativity, and the vital work of a united party organism which was united in a comradely way. The party, as a managing, creative collective, has turned into an unwieldy bureaucratic machine. The masses' party work has been reduced to fulfilment of a few very easy obligations, such as voluntary work Saturdays [субботники], manning a desk, standing guard, and so forth. Protests and conflicts have met such impoverishment of party activity. Then the relevant party centres interfered in these conflicts. In most cases the centres' interference did not resolve the situation, but only increased the number of conflicts and, in the best case, drove the illness within.

The last few weeks of party life in Moscow have clearly illustrated for us the unsuitability of such methods for implementing the centre's organisational policy. Members of the Moscow organisation of the RCP(b) have expressed distrust toward the actions of the Moscow Committee. The Moscow Committee met this distrust with hostility. Our disagreements grew on the soil where the Moscow Committee's work was evaluated. The Moscow organisation's members' modest desire to elect a new committee, which would respond to the party masses' demands and inquiries, elicited the CC's rebuff and interference. This interference was expressed in a whole system of pressures and struggle against comrades, who are dissatisfied with the inactivity of the Moscow Committee. In those districts where the opposition turned out to be in the majority, they forced proportional distribution of delegates according to the number of votes received. Where supporters of the old Moscow Committee turned out to be in the majority, no proportionality was allowed. Such tactics for mechanical suppression of intraparty disagreements by means of organisational circumventions must be halted. The interests of the harmonic development of the party and its unity demand that the party masses be given full freedom to choose their leaders.

Our party grew, became stronger, struggled, and achieved victory by depending for support on the activity and revolutionary initiative of broad proletarian and peasant masses. For the past two years, they have recalled this at especially difficult times, but now they resort to mass activity only for piling on burdens.

The old slogan promoted at one time that 'even a cook must learn how to govern' has turned out differently in practice. All of recent time is known for the persistent reduction of students of state management. In reality, the principles 'don't interfere' and 'it's none of your business' are implemented. We've gone so far along this path that we've annulled factory workers' assemblies and reduced to nothing the activity of communist cells, the work of general assemblies and so forth. Instead of attracting everyone all the way to the last cook into the work of management, in fact it has turned out differently. Our statesmen have become cooks, who prepare such dishes, which are supposed to make many millions of labourers rejoice. So it is not surprising that religious moods grow among the backward masses. There is only one step from passively waiting to be rescued by a hero toward hope in God. The party should bring to life the deep meaning of the international anthem that 'no one will grant us deliverance, neither god, nor tsar, nor hero.' This principle should be applied not only during voluntary Saturdays and while cleaning streets, but also in political and economic construction of the state.

The organisational policy of the leading party centre should in fact attract all party members into building communism, and together with them and through them the entire labouring population of the Republic.

Our revolutionary course has created organisational forms for this, but they are wasting away. Party activity is directed along other paths. The Soviet government, instead of trying to be a 'thorough and comprehensive form of worker organisation', has turned into a government managed by a bureaucracy, which in reality excludes from state management the mass participation of worker organisations. Such tactics lead mechanically to all kinds of conflicts.

The questions of centralism and regionalism [местничество], higher-ups and rank-and-file, heroes and masses, will not cease to confront party organisations. The organised proletarian masses don't want to be a formless lump of clay, from which individual political artists mold figures. The party should consider this and set up its work so that clashes between higher-ups and rank-and-file would be impossible.

8   A.G. Shliapnikov's Speeches to the Communist Faction of the
       Second All-Russian Congress of Mineworkers

A.G. Shliapnikov, 'Tsektran Policy and Our Syndicalism', 23 January 1921[73]

I would like to remind Vladimir Ilich that not only have individual CC members
'taken the Tsektranist approach' to trade unions, but that the entire CC is to
blame for this. I will remind you of that period which preceded the Ninth Party
Congress. Vladimir Ilich took a quite definite position in regard to the 'political sections' in the worker movement. Comrade Tomsky probably remembers
that period, when he opposed this system. Anyway, despite this, the system
which gave birth to Tsektranism [Цектрановщина] came to life and brought
with it political harm. Its political harm is rather well-known. It is expressed
in Tsektran. What were the economic results, we still do not know. The harm
of this system, of course, is difficult to take into account. It would be necessary to compose a special commission to clarify how such a policy would have
had an impact on the repair of railway stock. We objected that such methods
of building political sections in the trade union movement are impermissible.
Instead of fracturing trade unions, it's necessary to reinforce trade unions and
strengthen each cell so that our trade unions will be the political backbone of
our work.

We were accused of syndicalism, but such accusations have ceased to
frighten us. Fear of possible splits has stopped scaring us. We agree with Vladimir Ilich that now we need to be more ideologically and organisationally unified than at any other time in the past. But we should not muddle the question,
precisely in the interests of our strength and the unity of the entire working
class and especially of our party ranks. The working class, organised in all its
forms (the vanguard of the proletarian dictatorship, party, and trade unions),
must be strong. In order to strengthen its organisations, we need to carry out
those very measures, for which we the Workers' Opposition have been struggling for more than a year already.

First of all, I must repudiate all accusations of syndicalism, which have been
made against us. We'll see how Trotsky 'killed us' in his proposals, as comrade
Lenin declared. 'Syndicalism is understood as the effort of trade unions, meaning workers' organisations in capitalist society, to seize control of production
without the proletarian party and aside from it'. To what measure this relates

73   Bulletin no. 1 of the Second All-Russian Congress of the Union of Mineworkers, Tuesday,
        25 January 1921, p. 4.

to us, you yourselves can judge. This point does not require clarification. Vladimir Ilich was at one session where he was told that if you want to rebuke Shliapnikov for syndicalism, then you need to take a look in the mirror. It needs to be acknowledged who gave Shliapnikov the basis for his syndicalism.

Are we going against the party programme?

Vladimir Ilich wrote our party programme, which states: 'The organisational apparatus of socialised industry should depend for support first and foremost on trade unions'. This is from the programme. But indeed do your observations and experiences on every day of your practical work remind you in any way at all of the programme's position? Further along, this position is even keener: 'By Soviet law and established practice, trade unions already participate in all local and central bodies that manage industry. Trade unions should further concentrate in their hands all management of the economy, as a single economic unit. In this way they will secure an indissoluble link between central state management, the economy and the labouring masses. Trade unions should to the greatest extent possible attract the masses into directing the economy. The participation of trade unions and through them the masses in directing the economy is the chief means for struggle against bureaucratisation of Soviet power's economic system. Moreover, it will make it possible to have actual popular control over the results of production'.

We placed these two points here at the foundation of our syndicalism. It's necessary to be consistent. Comrade Riazanov says that in order to finish off the Workers' Opposition for good, the ground needs to be removed from beneath its feet by eliminating these two points in the programme. If the congress so decides, I will submit to its decision. I think that our position no more resembles syndicalism than does comrade Lenin's position. First of all, I must declare that I waited to see what they would say to us about the concrete tasks and rights that we have in the trade union movement. I am not speaking of the nonparty masses, but we all agree about the point of the programme that speaks of the need to attract the broadest circles of worker masses into the business of organising our national economy. But neither the first nor the second presenter gives us such rights and responsibilities. On the contrary, we have to share our own experience with them. This will render a service to Vladimir Ilich and others, so that they will define more precisely their position on this matter.

Our party is a unifying centre:

Despite the fact that they consider us now to be syndicalists, their statements have sometimes differed. Workers in a Moscow district asked Kamenev, 'If you had to choose between the Workers' Opposition and Trotsky, which programme would you vote for?' Comrade Kamenev answered, 'What kind of position does Trotsky have? At least Shliapnikov has a position. Of course, I'd do better to vote for his position than for Trotsky'. So comrade Kamenev is voting for us. In another district, they posed the same question to Trotsky. 'Well of course', says he, 'what kind of line and platform do those signing the programme of the Ten have? There is no practical way out at the local level. Of course, I would vote for the Workers' Opposition'. Thus we constitute the unifying centre which brings these two camps together. They depend on us to unite them at the local level and cease this cockfight, which we observe now in many districts. (Applause.)

The difference between them is not large. The closer you look, the more closely they converge. Now comrade Trotsky says that he has retracted his idea about shaking us up. So unions turned out to be strong and he had to reject the shaking-up method, but on the rest they agree with what is written in the brochure signed by Vladimir Ilich and by Zinoviev. Let's take the position of our Ten. Vladimir Ilich personifies this position, which especially recommends Rudzutak's proposals forgotten by all. No. 11 of the proposals, which Vladimir Ilich recommends, informs us about 'Economic sections':

1. Systematic study and generalisation [обобщение] of economic bodies' work.
2. Inspection and control functions.
3. Participation in elaborating an economic plan, allotting economic tasks, and drawing up production programmes.
4. Study of the technical aspect of labour processes.
5. Participation in forming economic bodies.

You see how triumphantly this is said. Further, about economic sections of trade unions: 'These need to be turned in actuality into quickly acting powerful levers for unions' systematic participation in organising production'. Here you see how powerful these levers are in the practical platform. Vladimir Ilich is a good defender of that from which we began. Vladimir Ilich defends that very thing from which the illness comes. Here it is necessary to heal not by out-patient means, but maybe some surgery is demanded. You want to carry out a 'surgical operation' 'on syndicalism', but I think you will not succeed in this. You will not go far on our 'syndicalism'. We are not dreamers in this regard, as V.I. says. No, we observe that our bureaucracy's three years of mastery in the area of construction, especially in building the economy and industry, has led us to catastrophe. You know perfectly well what kind of fuel crisis we are experiencing in Donets. But comrades, we should tell you that despite our unbelievable fuel crisis, we could significantly reduce the use of fuel that is expended irrationally. We have become aware that right now we expend ten times more fuel than we could if the matter were arranged differently. It is only getting worse.

Turning to our demands for raw materials and foodstuffs, we find that this situation is also extraordinarily difficult. Our total sum of experiences provides the possibility to say that the matter is not about 'merging', as some propose to do. Others declare that this has been going on for a long time and they propose introducing the kind of system which would make such unexpected catastrophes impossible. We need to put a stop to bureaucratic methods of management.

We are not federalists.

Neither I nor anyone else here advocates any kind of federalism. We are centralists and we struggle against economic federalism. We want for unions in each area of production to participate actively and directly in managing our national economy. Sincerely speaking, comrades, for three years we have pushed away from ourselves not only workers' organisations like unions, but also our communist comrades. Now a strange phenomenon can be observed in some of our institutions. They say that if you go there and announce that you are a communist, then the door is closed to you and your initiative is demolished. That's what we've come to by putting the stake on whatever is convenient, only not on the workforce and not on the communist party. We need to correct this decidedly. Comrades, I think that you at each step have observed on your own that the management of our economy is in great disorder. The party congress decided on one-man management. Comrades, I am certain that you visit the factories and the mines. What do we have there? Is it one-man management or collegiality? I regard one-man management with great doubt, for the technique of management requires creation of bodies for regulation, valuation (determining wage-rates), and supply. This depends on the complexity of the enterprise. In any case, there are some managing bodies, which directly influence how productivity of a given enterprise develops. I must declare to you that if an individual chief stands at the head of such an enterprise and there is a factory committee, which is a cell of our union, then this is what happens. If the chief is strong and possesses knowledge, authority, and political experience, then he can arrange business so that he subordinates the factory committee to himself and makes it the instrument of his work. But in the majority of cases the reverse occurs. The factory committee turns out to be stronger and essentially a new collegiality begins, except that it has an amorphous character. In result, you have a mess. We know economic bodies. They are created by means of bureaucratic selection. A senior person appears, an apparat is created, and the apparat begins to command along a bureaucratic line. On the other hand, you created an existing apparat, which is your congress. You also elect a central committee, which commands to a certain degree. Don't forget, comrades, in wage rates policy each directive is a command. This is especially felt in any productivity policy that encourages bonuses-in-kind, for it has lost touch with production, often brings irreparable harm to our industry, and is even reactionary. It's necessary to put a stop to this state of dual command. How can a stop be put to it? Here is where we start to differ.

Our differences:

In comrade Trotsky's opinion, the matter is resolved simply by not having dualism and by attracting worker masses into participation. This interests us insofar as we would be able to draw broad groups of worker masses into work so that they not only sprinkle sand but also use their strengths in the production process. Taking into account the type of training and cultivation our proletarians have, however, it is necessary to speak in their language, meaning the language of the masses. But what do comrade Trotsky and others recommend to us? How do they propose to attract the masses into directly participating in production? Putting it succinctly, he recommends personnel transfers. I think that this conjures up any kind of association except for that of attracting the worker masses. In principle all these measures are being implemented, although I don't know in what quantity. But this is not changing anything, for the workers who back us do not consider it important who sits in what chair. We know that unions have always known how to put together factory committees that were favourable to our unions and there were no conflicts about principles. It is not true that now we want to convince Vladimir Ilich or to slip him a piece of paper. It's not true that it's all in the bag. No, Vladimir Ilich, first of all it's necessary to regroup trade unions and create internal demarcations among them. Much work has to be done in this regard. I have five minutes left, so I will not enumerate all the measures. We will call a conference of our personnel who directly manage factories and tell them what we have to do. We will discuss it with them. But we don't want to mark time in the place where we are now, from which VTsSPS drags us and from which we try with all our strength to break away. This work has to start from the bottom, not like comrade Trotsky began it, with transfers of personnel from one chair to another.

Both comrade Trotsky and Vladimir Ilich agree about this. No matter what each contributed to his own business, they agree on a certain political programme. It depends on us to impart to this programme one or another character. In conclusion, I should answer Vladimir Ilich about producers. Our definite opinion is that producers, who should be united in trade unions, are not to be confused with commodities producers (товаропроизводители). We do not have a union of commodities producers. Vladimir Ilich doesn't allow commodities producers to organise such a union. I think that this misses the mark.

Competent economic management is necessary:

In conclusion, I should say that our proposals are not fantasy, but are observation that sums up the experiences not only of our trade union personnel, but also of our administrators. Now the line of command goes not through the bourgeoisie. I have come to the conclusion that the bourgeoisie is not so stupid as simply to sabotage us, but instead it stands on the position of supporting all our enterprises. You know that thanks to some enterprises, factories have raised our productivity higher in some cases than it was in the prewar time. According to the data of our wage rates section, our metalworkers' labour productivity never falls lower than 50% on average. If you sum up this productivity, then it emerges that workers have given 50% of their energy and in result are creating 8% of former productivity. How is this so? To a significant degree this can be laid at the feet of incompetent economic management and on inexpedient use of the workforce. This runs contrary to that line we see now of our bureaucratic management.

We want for the party to manage Russia's mining through us. No one will allow it to be said that you represent a federation in the Russian miners' movement. We want for everything to be organised through us, so that everything that concerns mining would go through this assembly or through the central committee standing in for it, and would not be built on the principle of bureaucratic patronage.

A.G. Shliapnikov, concluding remarks, 24 January 1921[74]

Comrade Trotsky painted my portrait. Comrade Trotsky is a great artist of the word and he executed this masterfully. I should point out, however, that this is not my portrait, but Trotsky's self-portrait. He says that I pursued such and such a line and sang in such a choir, with which I never showed any degree of solidarity. For the same reason, which Ilich spoke about, which is that I see in this a cockfight and not a principled disagreement, they say that I took such a tone in this cockfight that it singles me out. From this they make a conclusion about our position. But I should say that not only we but even the CC cannot sing to the same tune. Comrade Trotsky pursued this, but in painting me he painted a self portrait. Of course, we shed blood over our proposals. We are not great writers. We are weak people in this sense. Nevertheless, you cannot rebuke us for not having a businesslike approach. Your position and that of the

---

74   Bulletin of the Second All-Russian Congress of the Union of Mineworkers, no. 2, 26 January 1921, p. 3.

Moscow Committee and of others proved to us that you depart from the class line for the benefit of other interests. You place your bet on the specialists or on anyone convenient, just not on workers' organisations. This position is clearly unhealthy. Among us there are no sick people. We very carefully choose our friends. Our proposals are made carefully and are based on our three years of experience. When supporters of comrades Trotsky and Zinoviev speak against us, they say that we have a line. Thank you for this. At some point we will have the opportunity to discuss this line more extensively than now. We do not say that we want to destroy the *glavki* right now. We will see. We will move gradually. Maybe we will break up some *glavki*. We do not approach this question as if it is the goal of our life or our work. We have no democratic prejudices at all in this sense. You have said here that workers are stealing soap and matches. If we were to examine why they steal, then there would be less theft. There are comrades here who want to do everything right away. We propose to carry out great work. We want to approach this after having discussed each step and what follows from it. Tomsky wants to splice us together with Trotsky. As you see, he succeeds at this 'brilliantly'. He declares that I want the same thing as Tsektran. Tsektran wanted to select personnel by the shaking up process. Now it howls that this should not be done. In this sense it is closer to Tomsky than to us. We say in point nine (reads). Here is the main thing that separates us from comrade Trotsky, because he began without the union, bypassing it. In vain does comrade Trotsky try to deny this again.

Comrade Tomsky also noted point thirteen, which is about the authority of trade union congresses. Tell us, comrade Tomsky, is this congress sufficiently authoritative to manage the mining industry? Say so directly and sincerely. Comrades, we are confronted with questions which place new tasks before us. Comrade Tomsky said that the entire trade union movement is ceasing to be what it should be. This is all the same to us, comrade Tomsky. Our Republic is not the same as it was a year ago. As we live, we grow and change. We are not afraid of being better than we were yesterday. In this sense we do not travel the same path as you, comrade Tomsky. Regarding practical measures, it was said here that it's needed to place here so many people and from here take so many. But we say that this policy of jerking workers around and placing them in inconvenient conditions is foul in the provinces. If we look at our government's administrative line, then we will see that the part of the organism that eats rations grows bigger and the parts that work and think grow smaller. The resulting picture is of a huge stomach with very slender arms and legs and a tiny head. This stomach will crush us in the end. We must put an end to this abnormal growth. But this is possible only by introducing trade union representatives into management of the entire economy. There is no other recipe for this. Comrade Tomsky states incorrectly that I am the reverse side of comrade Nogin's system. Comrade Nogin proposes to conclude this in such a way that unions will be proclaimed part of the state and factory committee members will be appointed as factory chiefs. But we propose to make a production technical apparat from all these economic bodies. We would be masters of the technical apparat of production. I repeat that in the end comrades Lenin and Trotsky will meet on the same page. Maybe they will be left without tails from this cockfight, but the practical position will essentially not be more principled than it is now.

9   N. Kopylov, 'Mistake or Urgent Task?'[75]

Many of those who do not desire to investigate more seriously the Workers' Opposition's methods for solving the crisis in the trade union movement are inclined to call the platform of the Workers' Opposition on the role of trade unions either a mistake or a deviation toward syndicalism, 'lacking business-like content, and so forth and so on'.

It's as if this platform fell down from the sky or was only a work of fiction by a handful of 'syndicalist' comrades.

We will investigate those 'irregularities' and mistakes, for which the Workers' Opposition is blamed. Let's just take comrade Zinoviev's article in no. 17 of *Pravda* on 27 January. Comrade Zinoviev blames the Workers' Opposition for: 1) incorrectly analysing trade unions' actual situation; 2) making wrong conclusions about specialists; 3) mistakenly formulating the question about management of the economy; 4) and other 'contradictions'.

Comrade Zinoviev is perplexed. On the one hand, the Workers' Opposition recognises that trade unions currently are weak and that the party and soviet bodies have ignored them. On the other hand, it proposes to transfer to them management of economic bodies. Between the first and the second, he sees no interval. The first element directly emerges from the last. Not only comrade Zinoviev poses the question so. Others of our opponents also have posed the question so at numerous discussion meetings. But in fact it is not so. The Workers' Opposition does not propose to transfer management of the economy to trade unions in their current state. Moreover it does not suggest managing production by means of that pitiful technical apparatus, which trade unions now possess. In such a situation, when the central committee of the Metalworkers' Union has only two or three typists, no automobiles or horses, and absolutely

75   'Oshibka ili neotlozhnaia zadacha', *Pravda: Diskussionyi listok* 2 (February 1921): 12–13.

no resources for publishing activity, it's impossible to manage not only our entire metals industry, but even any individual factory. It is obvious that unions, first of all, should receive personnel and resources, and second, take for the basis of management that apparatus, which our *glavki* already have.

'But in such a case', writes comrade Trotsky in his brochure ('Role and Tasks of Trade Unions', 14), 'you would get not unilateral seizure of production by a trade union, but something very much approximating merger'.[76]

It's not at all so. We are against 'a simple massive raid on production' and are against 'merger' in that form, in which comrade Trotsky carries it out. To transfer management of production into the hands of trade unions does not mean only for the presidium of the central committee of metalworkers to move into the premises of the metals department. It means bringing not only the trade union higher-ups but also the masses closer to the business of management. Broad production propaganda, production conferences and production cells, organisation of proposals and of worker production newspapers and other measures for involving the masses in the process of production will help unions to smash the bureaucratism of our glavki not 'by means of a simple raid', but by using the organised influence of the masses. There is no contradiction between unions' weakness, which is conditioned by their current abnormal situation, and their readiness (again, not of all trade unions and not 'tomorrow', not perfunctorily, but by means of the masses' systematic involvement in the business of management) to take management of production into their hands. The question about spetses as formulated in the theses of the Workers' Opposition (putting an end to the placing of worker masses in opposition to specialists) likewise leads comrade Zinoviev into reflection (as if this is all a fairy tale). I will cite just one example. We metalworkers have a little experience arranging production propaganda. Production propaganda is essentially a mass action, in which both engineers and worker masses are involved. It has been possible to see how the juxtaposition of workers to engineers and vice versa have abated through the experience of this work. Contradictions between workers and spetses can be explained not only by the spetses' 'bourgeois character' [буржуазность], but also by the lack of understanding of production tasks of those at the bottom who have lost touch with production. In the future, when the workers, not in words but in deed, will master the production process, the contradictions between spetses and workers will be smoothed over to a greater degree.

---

76   This was Trotsky's draft resolution for the Tenth Party Congress, 14 March 1921. See Bunyan
          (ed.) 1967, pp. 221–45.

We will not dwell, however, on comparatively trivial questions. If you wish, of course, you can find a mass of shortcomings and omissions in the theses of the Workers' Opposition. From the practitioner's point of view, there even are weaker and more vulnerable spots than those which comrade Zinoviev noticed, but the matter is not in this. Indeed, the theses are not instructions, and you won't be able to say everything there.

Now, I will say a little about the supposed removal of the party from leadership of economy building. How unreliable are these objections is evident just from the fact that the party managed to become the actual leader of the entire state structure of the republic. Its authority is indisputable not only for non-party workers, but also for the multitudes of the petty bourgeois peasantry. With transfer of management of production into hands of trade unions, the party will be far from in the situation of the Moor, who has done his duty and can leave.[77] It should increase tenfold its agitational and educational work, actually involve millions of labourers in active construction, correct their mistakes, and through communist factions lead all of production and economic policy.

Well, and what if trade unions will not follow the party? The fear is serious, but 'without trade unions', as comrade Lenin correctly said more than once, 'our dictatorship would not have lasted even two weeks'. (See comrade Zinoviev's speech at the discussion on 30 December 1920.) It means that this is a general question. The party's influence and leadership inside unions is already necessary right now, as a guarantee of preservation of the dictatorship of the proletariat, and it will remain so with the transfer of economic functions to unions. The split of the party from unions is the death of the proletarian dictatorship. But it is naïve to try to avoid this split by advocating disparagement of trade unions' rights and transforming unions into a school of communism and seven million proletarians into first-grade school pupils.

The school of communism, which is our paraphrase of comrade Zinoviev's paraphrase, rings out as a proud-sounding phrase! According to what kind of communism, however, can the trade unions learn in current conditions? How, by what kind of activity? Is it by how the district committees issue certificates for rations or funeral benefits? Or, maybe, by its wage rates policy, which in practice leads not to an increase, but to a decrease of productivity? Comrade Bukharin correctly indicated that any school, first of all, should have definite subjects of instruction. Until recently the trade unions did not have such

---

77   This expression seems to be from a German play by Friedrich Schiller, *Die Verschwörung des Fiesco zu Genua* (1783).

subjects and 'a programme of instruction'. The masses became accustomed to regard the union as some imponderable being that beyond the boundaries of the factory committee takes on some kind of secretive, mysterious appearance.

Now unions begin to present production propaganda. Production propaganda is the only means of contact between union higher-ups and the masses. Beginning with production cells and ending with all-Russian congresses of producers, the entire mass of proletarians is promoted into the movement. (No matter how amusing this seems to comrade Zinoviev, we understand the term producers to mean not only workers as such, but to include all participants of production processes.) Before each worker, there opens the widest prospect of developing his initiative and applying it to organisation of production. To advocate the theory of evolutionary merger and a limited production charter means to knowingly distrust the creative and organisational forces of the proletariat. Production propaganda is currently almost the only subject of instruction in the union school of communism. A school of communism where workers only listen, discuss, and make generalisations about the real world, will remind one only of a school for children with a talentless sexton for a teacher. This sexton is ignorant of how to teach his pupils any wisdom, except for his own bureaucratic mediocrity.

We reject 'sudden raids' and an anarchic lack of organisation. If the union is not prepared to take production into its own hands, we do not propose 'to break its spine' by foisting onto it functions of management. If you want, we also are for merging trade unions with economic bodies, but for such a merger, under which the *glavki* do not swallow up unions, but on the contrary, unions absorb the *glavki* into themselves and transform them into its own bodies of worker management.

It seems to me that in our time it has become an axiom of truth that the development of labourers' initiative is the best medicine against bureaucratism in all its forms. The development of workers' initiative in production will create such a powerful foundation of socialist construction, which will ease by many times the process of socialisation [обобществление], even of agriculture, and will bring closer the moment when the state withers away as a special form of management.

10   **N.M. Tikhonravov, Supplement to the Theses of the Workers'**
        Opposition about the Tasks of Trade Unions[78]

1.   The impending period of the Russian Revolution, as a proletarian revolu-
        tion, as it transitions from a period of war to a focus on the economy,
        demands a precise clarification of this economic moment, as it pertains
        to the further development of the revolution, and a definition of the role
        of the working class.

2.   Three aspects of this economic moment need to be taken into account:
        1) production forces and the material basis of production; 2) organisation
        of production and its management; and 3) the level of Russia's economic
        development.

3.   The first aspect poses the task of increasing production forces, given their
        extremely steep decline, and elevating production from a state of extreme
        ruin. The resolution of this task does not emerge directly from the revolu-
        tionary process and relates to the purely material side of the economic
        process.

4.   The second aspect poses the task of restructuring production relations, as
        a social, public process. Resolution of this task directly emerges from the
        flow of the revolutionary process and is directly linked with it.

5.   The third aspect, which represents the particular conditions of the (Rus-
        sian) revolution, counterposes to the minority of the proletariat a signi-
        ficant majority of small property-holding producers. This creates special
        difficulty for implementing the proletarian dictatorship, since the prolet-
        ariat has to hold out against the pressure of petty bourgeois social forces.

6.   The economic moment of the revolution presents colossal difficulties,
        which must be overcome by a source of active strength. This source can
        only be development of the revolutionary process in the sense of expand-
        ing and deepening primarily socialist means of revolution. Moreover, the
        force of the state apparatus, in exercising exclusive influence from above,
        cannot achieve the goal. It will put a brake on revolution and lead toward
        rupture with it. This will increase difficulties and danger for the revolu-
        tion.

7.   In Soviet Russia, an extreme degree of centralisation in the system of
        organising state economic bodies has taken shape and put a brake on
        expanding the revolution into a socialist one. This system represents a

---

78   Aleksandrov R.V.Ts, Gosudarstvennaia tipografiia no. 5, 11 February 1921. Republished in
        RKP(b) 1933. Tikhonravov wrote that these were 'in development of the theses, approved
        by Comrade Shliapnikov' but Shliapnikov did not approve his supplement.

conservative force, which transforms Soviet government, as a form of proletarian democracy, from a flexible, transitional organisation that is subordinated to the proletariat as the leading part of society, into a self-sufficient organisation, which stands above all of society, including the very proletariat.

8. With the cessation of military struggle, all attention of the worker masses has turned to social organisation and its economic foundations. Within the proletariat, as a class imbued with class instinct, there ripens a certain demand for socialist organisation of society and production and an effort to further expand the revolution. Therefore, the current conservative course, which only looks toward production and uses government to bring society out of production ruin, creates an oppositionist attitude in the worker masses and incites them onto a path of active protest.

9. The third aspect of the economic moment of the revolution is the manifestation of activism by the small property-owning milieu. By weakening the proletariat, such a situation creates a direct threat to the revolution. If the production crisis intensifies, such activism can lead to anarchy and unleash counterrevolutionary forces.

10. Such a state of things poses with special acuteness the question about organisation of the working class and the concentration of its revolutionary creative energy. Its energy should fix upon restructuring economic relations on socialist foundations. Thus, there emerges the question about the role and tasks of trade unions. This question should be clearly and definitely decided by clarifying the relations between the party, soviets, and trade unions and their role in the era of proletarian dictatorship.

11. The party, as the political organisation of the proletariat, is the highest form of its organisation. Without transforming into a body of government power, it realises the dictatorship of the proletariat through the soviets as bodies of proletarian dictatorship. The party can fulfil this without losing touch with the revolution, if it draws its strength from the proletariat, is supported by its will, and apprehends its class strivings.

12. In a political sense, the working class does not represent a homogeneous mass, but is united by a single common class feeling in relation to the bourgeois stratum or its separate elements, which remain after the revolution. The working class unites through its class organisations. Trade unions, which manifest the will and class strivings of the working class, are the direct support and source of strength for the party in realising its proletarian dictatorship. From trade unions the party derives class will and class ideology. Otherwise the party risks turning into one that transcends class.

13. The soviets are a form of proletarian democracy and an apparatus of proletarian dictatorship, but they are ceasing to be a proletarian class organisation. Because of the conditions of the Russian Revolution, the soviets unite the entire labouring population, among which the proletariat composes an insignificant and nonexclusive minority in the soviet organisation.

14. In view of the above-stated particularities of the upcoming period of the Russian Revolution, the trade unions acquire special significance as an exclusively class organisation of the proletariat. Both in the preceding and upcoming periods of the Russian Revolution, the proletariat and its party should place the significance and role of unions higher than that of the soviets and closer to the party than the soviets are.

15. But the proletariat as a class is based on production, which composes the economic foundation of its social and revolutionary strength. Its dictatorship will be strong, firm and realisable under the condition of its unification into powerful organisations on this foundation, welding its proletarian discipline into a steadfast force. Then the party will be capable of accomplishing the dictatorship of the proletariat and maintaining it, especially in connection with the looming pressure of petty bourgeois social forces.

16. This final struggle against petty bourgeois pressure will be protracted. Pressure in the form of economic conflict will occur and will transition into political pressure within the soviets. Here the proletariat should carry out its economic dictatorship. Trade unions, which are based in production, should be bodies of this economic dictatorship, which the party will carry out through the soviets.

17. From this it follows that trade unions should stand not along side government bodies. Trade unions should not mingle or merge with government bodies or be subordinated to them, but should stand above them. The revolution demands that trade unions be brought quickly to this state.

18. The stated correlation of trade unions and soviets and their government bodies do not subordinate soviets to trade unions. Here the correlation should be the same as the party and the soviets. Like the party, trade unions with all their organisation and significance, stand higher than soviets, which remain the apparatus of the proletarian dictatorship. Trade unions are under the leadership of the party and together with it, they carry out the dictatorship of the proletariat. Trade unions, as class organisations, are the base of the party.

19. A tendency toward such a direction took shape in decisions of the First and Second Congresses of Trade Unions and of the Eighth Party Con-

gress, but it remained insufficiently clearly formulated within the party's outlook. The Ninth Party Congress treated trade unions like an auxiliary apparatus of the soviet government and gave an impetus to development of a tendency within the party to subordinate trade unions to soviet bodies.

20. Only inasmuch as trade unions assume the fulfilment of government tasks do they come under the leadership of the government in this regard. Inasmuch as they participate in organising government bodies and generally represent the organised proletariat, they carry out its class will. Trade unions are higher than government bodies and higher than soviets.

21. Given such a role by trade unions, their task in the nearest time frame is to seize production. By seizing separate branches of production, they will arrive at seizure of the entire economy. Trade unions will seize government economic bodies and so come under the leadership of soviets in this regard. Economic sections of trade unions are to unite with other soviet economic bodies. VSNKh, as a section of VTsSPS, unites within VTsIK with other central economic bodies – the people's commissariats. Such are the relations of economic councils (sovnarkhozes) and local executive committees (ispolkoms). In this way, the government will retain decisive influence over economic tasks.

22. During the transition prior to the seizure, trade unions will unify the central economic body. Management of industry will comprise VSNKh, trade unions possessing separate branches of industry, and the management apparatus (sections or *glavki* of VSNKh). They will unite their activity within the bounds of VSNKh and work under its directives, without transforming entirely into a body subordinated to VSNKh.

23. The current crisis of trade unions is part of the general crisis of the entire apparatus of the proletarian dictatorship and may be overcome when the entire course of the party's policy is changed.

24. Alongside objective reasons for the crisis of trade unions (the war and mobilisation) there exist subjective reasons, which hinder an exit from the crisis and demand immediate elimination. Clear subjective conditions are:

   a) As government economic bodies grew and became stronger and more bureaucratic, VSNKh bodies and agents ignored trade unions and edged them out of production. Definitely, they attempted to destroy trade unions by subordinating them and absorbing their apparats. This was the source of origin of the conservative state theory for restoring the country's production forces;

b)   Leading party circles ignored these manifestations and did not suffi-
      ciently press for the need to implement congress resolutions
      without deviating. Resolutions of the Ninth Party Congress gave
      cause for deviation away from resolutions of previous congresses
      toward the state conservative side of things. This turned out to be
      in leading party circles' implementation of a 'hard line' of shaking
      up [перетряхивание], restructuring, reshuffling appointments to
      posts, and the like.

25.   This deviation in the party course needs to be resolutely ended by return-
      ing the party to a revolutionary policy of implementing the proletarian
      dictatorship and building socialism.

11   Polosatov's and Kuznetsov's Speeches at the Fourth CP(b)U Conference of Donetsk Gubernia, 16–18 February 1921[79]

[Evdokimov gave the report on the role of trade unions under the Soviet government on 17 February. Following it, [A.] Pavlov gave a supplementary report
in the name of the Workers' Opposition while Pikel spoke on behalf of those
supporting Trotsky's proposals. A majority of 79 voted for the proposals backed
by the Ten, 21 voted for the Workers' Opposition's programme, and Trotsky's
proposals garnered two votes. I did not find Pavlov's speech in the records.
According to the chair, Polosatov spoke on behalf of fifteen delegates. Both he
and Kuznetsov are responding to a speech by Piatakov.]

Polosatov:[80] Comrade Piatakov's entire report, comrades, definitely reflects
support for the positions taken in Trotsky's bloc with the CC. His entire report
is constructed so as to carry out struggle against the Workers' Opposition. The
proposals published in the press prove this.

We are now confronted with the task of reviving the economy, which we can
only fulfill if we take account of and analyse the present conditions in which
we find ourselves. Correctly defining our task to revive the economy depends
on a definitive accounting and analysis of the present social composition of the
Communist Party and of the methods which have guided the Party.

According to Comrade Piatakov, the Communist Party needs unanimity in
order to revive the economy. I will not argue to the contrary. What Piatakov did

---

79   TsDAHO, f. 1, op. 20, d. 453, ll. 7–11.
80   Polosatov's speaking style here is very repetitive and wordy. For the reader's convenience,
      I have tried to make the translation more concise than the original.

not talk about, and which I will discuss, is about whether the Communist Party has had a single line up to now. Has a group held its own line about reviving the economy and spoken out about it outside of the boundaries of the Communist Party? Yes, a group has done so, and it was not the Workers' Opposition, but Trotsky's group.

Comrade Piatakov, who constructed his report in order to struggle against the Workers' Opposition, did not refer to those measures, which a certain group has taken outside of the Communist Party's boundaries. But, if you look at all the practical activity in the Donbas, here you will sense the manifestation of a definite group following Comrade Trotsky, composed of the 'godfather' comrades in the Central Board of the Coalmining Industry (TsPKP). The decisions made by the Fifth Party Conference do not guide the actions to revive the coal industry.

When Comrade Piatakov was speaking about the role and tasks of trade unions, he acknowledged that there is a crisis. Thank you kindly, comrades. The Workers' Opposition has a similar evaluation, which you found to be groundless. But then let's discuss the means by which to put an end to this crisis. The policy of the Communist Party has been to subordinate itself to the petty bourgeoisie and to give incentives to the petty bourgeoisie, but not to try to satisfy the working masses.

The Communist Party, which is the avant garde of the working class, gave nothing to this working class during three years of the civil war and did not hold the working class in high regard either. Our policy was not to become closer to the working class but to lose touch with the worker masses. I do not want to say that there were no objective reasons. During the civil war, we had to fight against the world bourgeoisie and to suppress internal counterrevolution, so we had to attract a certain stratum to our side. Together with 80% of the petty bourgeoisie, we defended what we gained from the October Revolution. So we had to attract the petty bourgeoisie to help us accomplish the tasks which confronted us. Therefore we had to step back from what we could give directly to the workers. So we deviated toward the side which is against the workers.

Comrade Piatakov touched upon the matter of social composition. We should not close our eyes to what is the actual composition, which we have in our party. Eighty percent of those in our ranks are a petty bourgeois element.

In as much as the communist party drew in the worker element and the petty bourgeois element, we see that the task of reeducating this entire element has sharply braked. This element is everywhere now.

Comrade Piatakov just pointed to young communists. This is not important. If we want to establish a unified party policy, we need to wage struggle against an element such as engineers and technicians like Polivanov who find their way into the Communist Party.

Comrade Piatakov constructed his report along the line of struggle against the Workers' Opposition. He said that right now all our strength needs to be directed against the Workers' Opposition, which is a genuinely revolutionary element.

The Workers Opposition stands for the principle of directly leaning for support on the working class and on union bodies of the working class. These have the most interest in the gains of the revolution, more so than the peasants who make up a certain part within the party. The Workers' Opposition is a healthy element, which raises the business of directly attracting the masses into party building and into the entire political and economic life of the country.

Yet Comrade Piatakov wants to struggle against our opposition. Comrade Piatakov should explain how this opposition arose. Was it inevitable that it arose in the Communist Party and how to emerge from this situation? I think that if we were to take account of the circumstance that 80% of the Russian Communist Party is composed of peasants and similar outsider elements, then it stands to reason that there would be groupings within the Communist Party, which manifest one or another line. This line is defined by prevailing private interests. Since from this [outsider] grouping a harmful ideology emerges, we should fight against it and direct struggle against it.

Inasmuch as part of the worker core is in this grouping, we need to fight twice as hard against it.

The revival of the economy will be possible when our communist party will define its line, taking into consideration our recent experience, and will attract the broad worker masses into actively solving questions. I think that it is possible to achieve this through applying a democratic principle, about which comrade Piatakov very briefly spoke. The more extensive the economic ruin and crisis, the greater the efforts demanded for cohesion and unity of actions to revive the national economy. Only by attracting the broad masses to create a new economy and consolidate the gains of the revolution can this unity of actions be achieved.

Therefore, naturally when we pose the question about reviving the national economy, we say that it is necessary to restructure our party groupings. We should place the question definitively as to how we will lead the workers to attract the worker masses to follow along the path of our trade union, soviet, and party work. Our entire party personnel and organisation is needed to attract a large cadre of the working class to fulfill practical tasks to directly involve the worker masses toward effect. About party building, the avant-garde of the working class should find familiar all those questions raised before us. All questions around economy building should be discussed not only by the avant-garde of the working class, but also by the entire working class at the local level. If we will implement this decision not only in words but also in deeds, then we will have the right link with the masses and achieve the correct accountability before the masses, then can general assemblies and collectives be set up. Only in this way will our work get results.

Likewise trade unions should focus all efforts to attract broad worker masses into reviving the economy. This way the party's work will not suffer, but will certainly benefit, for the party will retain leadership of unions' work. The party will guide the trade union movement. The gubernia party committee carries out political work, while the gubernia council of trade unions arranges production work. These two bodies need a connection in order to find a way out of the current situation. The executive committees of the soviets should also participate actively to restore the economy. Only by connecting these three bodies of power will we achieve a positive effect.

We do not yet actually have united action in these three bodies. It is harmful to have such a divide between these parts of the working class's associations. To avoid this and to correctly define the tasks of the party building, the question about destroying groupings needs to be resolved. It is not Trotsky's group but the Workers' Opposition that has done the party a service in making noise about this.

Comrade Piatakov noted that the Party CC is not a very united leading body of our party, that a split can be seen among its members, and that the CC has not provided the needed positive results in its practical activity.

Therefore, I conclude that this abnormality needs to be eliminated. Comrade Piatakov, do not forget that the Workers' Opposition was not in the CC, so how will you explain this split and violation of unity? From what we have observed in practice, it happened when supporters of Comrade Trotsky began to work in the area of reviving our industry.

This is not unity of the centre and the locale. If you ask about struggle against internal groupings, then you need to talk about struggle against Trotsky's group.

No matter how much you would struggle against one or another grouping, there have been and will be such in the party. If you look at the entire history of party life, both in the West and in Russia, such groupings existed and remained connected with the party through party discipline.

A party grouping should not be destroyed right away. For a long time certain groupings and currents will exist in the party. It is not a Marxist approach to talk about destroying party groupings.

The Workers' Opposition has never talked about splitting the Communist Party, as was mentioned here.

The Workers' Opposition must have some strength, because if not, then Comrade Piatakov would not have talked about struggle against the Workers' Opposition.

Comrades, I should say that conjecture about a split in the party speaks definitively about struggle against the Workers' Opposition having been set out. Rather than striking down the Workers' Opposition, such a method of struggle can direct the blow against yourselves.

Now when we are confronted with restoring our economy, it's necessary especially to talk about unification, to understand the appearance of the Workers' Opposition, and to understand those tasks which confront us. When you analyse these tasks, which are brought forward by exposure, by understanding these tasks, then we can really emerge from the situation which has been created. Only by attracting broad masses into the most energetic work of trade unions, party and soviet apparatuses, will the task of reviving the economy be resolved.

Workers, from whom we demand sacrifices and who die at their posts, have not participated in the party and economic life of the country. The working class has been estranged from those tasks which now confront soviet power. By being connected with workers, we should attract them into peaceful economy building.

The comrades who are present here will understand that we can only resolve the tasks which confront us by attracting the broad worker masses into the communist party, the soviets, and the trade union movement. In this way, we will secure the revival of the economy and the development of the worldwide socialist revolution.

Kuznetsov: Comrades, I will dwell a little on comrade Piatakov's theses. With paternal admonition, Comrade Piatakov approached the matter of getting rid of the party's illness. He spoke a very long time on this question. Unfortunately the lecturer himself was very ill. Comparing the CC CP(b)U theses with of Comrade Piatakov, it needs to be said that 90% of the latter suffers from factionalism.

I will move on to the essence of those disagreements which we have in our party. We are confronted by the task of party building and of worker democracy. I will dwell on this plane to the extent to which I have understood this question.

Comrades, the crisis of the party cannot be regarded as a crisis apart from some of our other institutions. The party crisis is closely linked with the crises of trade unions and soviets. We cannot examine the party crisis in isolation because the trade unions are experiencing a larger crisis. The soviets are also experiencing such a crisis. They say to us that this crisis occurred because the civil war left us a completely ruined economy. Turning trade unions and party bodies around was an unavoidable consequence of civil war.

When military approaches were past, we received a breathing space. At this moment it is necessary to develop the three apparats. We say that we should use the breathing space in order to turn over and stand finally on firm legs. But for four months we have done nothing on this matter. Now we are busy altering methods of work, we have disputes about theses, and we criticise party bodies. Can we continue to exist in such a way?

In the factories, there are eight communists for 8,000 workers. Let's look at whether this phenomenon is the consequence of all our policies. The party masses' isolation from the main communist backbone is obvious, for we know that the worker by his internal substance is a communist. And if we tear him still further away from the basic backbone of the communist party, well here is where our illness lies.

We now should move on to the broadest attraction of broad worker masses into state building. Only by such an attraction can we lay a strong foundation under current communist production. We cannot leave the party in such a condition. We should work out a method of fusing the Communist Party with the mass of workers. The masses who have lagged behind need an opportunity. Those petty bourgeois masses, which latched onto the body of the Communist Party, need to significantly broaden their horizon. We say that further leaving the party in such a condition threatens great danger.

By what means will we approach this matter? We set forth three basic questions and methods. We say that only by attracting broad masses of workers we will able to absorb that 80% which is petty bourgeois peasantry and to put the business of restoring the economy onto that path, which we demand for the good of our homeland. It is necessary not in words but in deed to attract broad worker masses into state building. We perform this enormous work by uniting workers in trade unions. Trade unions should expand their activity and render indispensable service to the party in the matter of attracting worker masses. From trade unions, or more accurately through trade unions the party will derive new communist forces.

So, to expand the work of trade unions is the most vital necessity.

Now, regarding the development of soviets, which were once a mighty political parliament but have come down to a troika. The soviets need to be developed. In developed form the soviets will have new content. Soviets likewise will have new tasks in the conditions of our more prolonged breathing space. To the extent that these two auxiliary bodies, both trade unions and soviets, will develop we will find it possible to capture the entire labouring mass and attract it into party life.

By making such demands of the soviets and trade unions, the Workers' Opposition sets opposition as its task, but not just for the sake of opposition, but so as to eliminate those illnesses within our party. We say that all these disputes cannot help but have significant influence on the entire course of party life. If our advice is not followed, our party will become completely isolated and its crisis deepened.

12   Documents from Samara about the Debates over Party Building, Culture, and the Tasks of Trade Unions, February 1921[81]

Telegram to the CC RCP(b), Kremlin, Moscow, undated but probably 11 February 1921.

Having discussed the report of the Fifteenth Samara City Party Conference, on 9[?] February the delegates' assembly of the first district of the Samara city organisation decided to join the protest of the 76 delegates, who believe that the delegates for the gubernia conference were incorrectly elected at the city-wide conference. The opinion of 44% of the delegates, who are a significant part of the Samara organisation, was suppressed.

The bureau [?] of the first district committee asks the CC to take urgent action, for only twelve days remain until the gubernia conference begins on 23 February.

The first district has 2,500 members and the overall city organisation has 5,080 [or 5,030 or 5,060?]. Of those present at the meeting of the first district, 83% voted to accept the decision [to ally with the protest of the 76 delegates].

Secretary of the Raikom [no signature]

∙∙
∙

To Krestinsky, CC RCP(b), Kremlin Moscow
From Samara

1.   Having heard the CC RCP(b) Orgburo's 17 February telegram, signed by comrade Krestinsky, which annuls the Fifteenth Samara City Party Con-

---

81   RGASPI, f. 17, op. 84, d. 199, ll. 1–18. For more on the Samara group of the Workers' Opposition, see Kaliagin 2003; Sandu 2006; Holmes 1990.

ference vote for delegates to the Eighth Samara Gubernia Party Conference and proposes to hold voting again but on the principle of personal representation, the Samara City RCP(b) committee, in a plenary session, declares the following:

a)   The 21 January decision of the CC plenum about the character of pre-congress discussion, which was published in *Pravda* on [?] February, states in point four that local organisations can allow voting for delegates to the RCP(b) Congress to take place by platforms, if they find this necessary and useful. It recognises as the indisputable right of each organisation to propose to the party such platforms, which transfer the centre of gravity from the role of trade unions to other questions of the day. The Party Central Committee makes recommendations but leaves the final decision to local organisations.

b)   In its telegram, the CC Orgburo does not recommend, but instead directs and proposes to immediately carry out elections to the gubernia conference, according to the principle of proportional representation.

c)   According to point twelve of the RCP(b) statutes, local organisations may act autonomously to resolve local questions.

2.   Thus, in relation to the Samara organisation, the CC Orgburo violated, first of all, the basic principle of democratic centralism in point twelve of the statute and point four of the CC plenum's decision.

3.   The plenum of the Samara party gubernia committee (gubkom) expresses complete confusion regarding the Orgburo's violation of the CC plenum's decision and of party statutes in relation to the Samara organisation.

4.   Taking into account all that has been set forth here, the Samara gubernia committee decides:

a)   To protest to the CC plenum against the Orgburo's decisions foisting proportional voting upon the Samara organisation, in spite of this plenum's decision.

b)   To consider that resolving the question about revoting should belong not only to the leading party bodies, which for the Samara organisation is the gubkom, no matter how authoritative is this body, but chiefly to the masses of party members. In consequence, the final resolution of the question will be transferred to the general city assembly of the Samara RCP(b) organisation.

c)   To inquire of the CC what motives guided the Orgburo in repealing the elections of the Fifteenth City Conference and violating the decision of the CC's 19 February plenum.

Kazakov
Secretary of the Samara RCP(b) gubernia committee

∴

To all RCP(b) organisations of Samara Gubernia.

Honorable comrades,

At the Fifteenth Samara City Party Conference, which just concluded on 7 February, the view of the Workers' Opposition, which guided the gubernia committee, gained the upper hand on all the main questions (role and tasks of trade unions, party building, etc.). In the resolutions it accepted about party building, the role and tasks of trade unions, and the content of our cultural work, the majority of the conference distinctly opposed not only the 'conservatism' (their opinion) of the party [illegible word], but also our party's entire general line and the overwhelming majority of its members. Like a red thread, the thought runs through the accepted theses and resolutions that up to now the party's general line has been incorrect, that it favoured 'fellow travelers' and the petty bourgeoisie, that right now this line needs to be changed, and that some kind of 'new course' needs to be taken. Almost all speeches by gubkom representatives and their supporters in the majority of the conference were replete with hounding of senior personnel and the cultivation of division within the party into 'higher-ups' and 'rank-and-file'.

The minority of the conference defended the points of view of Zinoviev, Lenin, Tomsky, and others. During various votes, this minority composed from 25% to 45% of the general number of participants in the conference. During votes for delegates to the gubernia conference, which is to take place on 23 February, this minority was suppressed. It did not even receive one seat. The proposal of proportional voting by platforms, which the minority introduced with 70 signatures in support, was rejected by a majority of 97 against 76.

As a sign of protest, 76 comrades who voted for proportionality refused to participate in elections and declared that they would protest the elections to the Party CC and to the gubernia conference.

We bring to the attention of all organisations of Samara gubernia that the 51-person delegation to the gubernia conference, which was elected by the majority of the Fifteenth City Conference, in no way reflects the actual correlation of groupings and tendencies of party thought within the Samara city organisation. Insofar as the composition of the city delegation has decisive significance for the gubernia conference and its composition and opinion are predetermined, its opinion will not correctly reflect the correlation of tendencies in the gubernia. Further, insofar as the gubernia committee chose to pressure the minority and violate democracy in the city in order to secure itself a majority in the gubernia, it is to be expected that it will continue to implement the same line and correspondingly will fabricate both the composition of the gubernia's delegation to the Tenth Party Congress and the composition of the future gubkom.

By assignment of the city conference's minority, we appeal to all Samara gubernia organisations to protest the compulsion used against the minority and [illegible phrase].

Illegible signatures

∴

To the CC RCP(b) [excerpts]

By assignment of a group of members of the Fifteenth Samara City Party Conference and a significant number of members of the Samara RCP(b) organisation, we notify the CC about the absolutely impossible working situation, which now exists in the Samara party organisation ....

The Samara gubkom, which earlier held a vaguely oppositionist stance toward the CC and now has definitively turned toward the Workers' Opposition, constantly carries out within the organisation a policy of setting the 'rank-and-file' in opposition to the 'higher-ups' and a definite policy of persecuting senior personnel who support a different point of view and defending those who make jests.

Demagoguery and the line of the Workers' Opposition in general have enjoyed such comparatively great success in Samara's organisation, chiefly because of the longtime presence of the Turkestan Front Headquarters and its institutions here. Thus, there were readily available the most vivid bureaucratic and militarist perversions, in the worst sense of this word, and enormous inequality between the worker population and the headquarters and military personnel. Likewise, [illegible] Soviet bodies were weak and inefficient.

Further, as a very typical vulgar, petty bourgeois centre of the Republic, Samara has always had the most favourable soil for all sorts of extreme [illegible word] and pseudorevolutionary tendencies and moods. They enjoyed influence here in 1918.[82] Right now the Workers' Opposition tendency rises to the top

---

82   Former members of the Constituent Assembly formed an anti-Bolshevik government in

by depending for support chiefly upon the enormous discontent and unhealthy anarcho-petty bourgeois mood of the most backward members of the organisation.

At the Fifteenth City Party Conference, which just ended, the gubkom had to acknowledge in its report that it did almost nothing. It laid responsibility for its inactivity on the 'opposition', meaning chiefly soviet senior personnel, who did not share the gubkom's political line and who intentionally 'sabotaged' its work, as the presenter put it. By a majority (101 against 54), the conference accepted a resolution, which approved the gubkom's general line and recognised its work as unsatisfactory, but laid responsibility upon 'saboteurs' ....[83] It proposed that the gubkom take resolute measures against them, including even expulsion from the party. Yet they did not name even one 'saboteur' at the conference. ...

On the role and tasks of trade unions, Shliapnikov's platform was accepted by 74 votes against 63 for the platform of the Ten.

On the content of our cultural work, the same majority confirmed a curious set of theses about building proletarian culture, the need to immediately reconstitute the abolished Moscow Proletarian University, and creating a network of similar universities across the entire Republic, under general leadership of the Academy of Socialist Sciences. ....

[complains of the majority's rejection of proportional representation]

... We insist that the CC immediately undertake energetic intervention and influence, otherwise the complete collapse of both the Samara organisation and of all work is inevitable. .... We request that the CC send an authorised member, who would explain here on the spot the actual situation of things and would carry out under his or her guidance the re-election of delegates to the gubernia conference and who would attend that same gubernia conference.[84]

Samara in 1918. There was also extensive activism by anarchists and Socialist Revolutionary Maximalists in Samara in that year. See Smith 2011.

83   The ellipses here and below probably signify my omissions when taking notes.

84   In the archival file, there are two more sets of theses between the preceding set and the following set. One set is entitled, 'Theses accepted by a group of members of the Samara RCP(b) organisation about disagreements within the party and about the condition of the Samara gubernia party organisation'. These appear to have been approved by the minority, who protested to the CC the decisions accepted by the majority. The document is over five pages long, typed, and single-spaced. The other set is entitled, 'Theses on Party-Building'. It is a very poor quality copy and is signed by M. Khataevich (Rosta, Samara), who I believe

13   [A.D.] Sirotin, 'Theses for the Report about Party Building', Eighth
        Samara Gubernia RCP(b) Conference, January 1921[85]

a)   The party's current tasks
b)   Prerequisites for fulfilment of these tasks
c)   Content of the party
d)   The party's line of development (prerequisites for regeneration)
e)   Conditions for improving the party's health

A.   Tasks of the R.C.P.(b)

1.   As one of its first tasks, the party should prioritise organisation of the
        Republic's military forces for defence and, if it is demanded, then
        also for attack on imperialist governments. Following right after
        partial demobilisation of soldiers for building peace, the intensi-
        fied reorganisation of the army should begin in order to apply it
        in the conditions, which are being created, of partial armistice on
        the front of the war with capital. Having been reduced numerically,
        the army should improve qualitatively in all regards. The Republic
        should have the iron fist of the Red soldiers ready for the moment
        when pressure comes upon us.

2.   The party's second priority should be thorough technical revolu-
        tion as a means of struggle against economic reaction. If we do
        not reorganise the technology of production (electrification, stand-
        ardisation of locomotive repair, Taylorism and the like), then our
        production forces will turn toward smallscale handicrafts produc-
        tion. This will lead to the failure of communist production relations.
        The economic structure of the Soviet government will fall under the
        pressure of large capitalist production relations from abroad and
        small capitalist production relations of the speculative-amateurish
        type from within.

3.   The third task: 'Cultural revolution is a revolution of ideological
        forms'. For organising communist society, both technological revolu-
        tion and ideological revolution are necessary. Until now, cultural
        revolution was accomplished spontaneously. The proletariat spon-
        taneously destroys old ideological norms (just like it spontaneously

---

belonged to the minority. I did not think it necessary to translate either set for this collection.

85   R.V.Ts. Samara. Sovnarkhoz printshop no. 5. 600 [?] copies printed.

destroyed the bourgeois state machine), family supports are collapsing, the old marriage links are disintegrating, old petty bourgeois morality and ethics are becoming obsolete, and bourgeois art is losing value. In place of all that is spontaneously destroyed, however, nothing or almost nothing that is purely proletarian has been (consciously) created so far. From spontaneous formation of a new ideology, we need to move on to consciously building culture.

4. With partial victory on the fronts of technical and cultural revolution, the party will set the fourth task for the proletariat: 'Reorganising the Soviet economy'. This means changing the forms of state management and production management. Defects in our economy can be eliminated in words and in actual fact only by making a technical revolution and a cultural revolution, and by having achieved significant results in both. The defects are bureaucratism, speculation, labour desertion, red tape, bribery, protectionism and the like. For this reason, the party and the working class are currently forced, first of all, to extend technical and cultural revolution, and secondly, to begin to eliminate minor defects in our economy. Otherwise the words of revolution 'about struggle against bureaucratism' and so forth will be thrown into the wind.

5. The party's fifth task will be 'Increasing its ranks and inundation by communists of all cells of production, distribution, administration, and culture'.

6. The task of the RCP(b) is to organise the worldwide uprising of the proletariat. The course of the party toward world revolution not only does not change, but on the contrary now is greater and more steadfast than at any time.

B. Prerequisites for fulfilling the appointed tasks.

1. For resolving its historical tasks via the Soviet apparatus and worker organisations, the Communist Party as a whole and its protégés in various government posts should have the active support, trust, and moral sympathy of broad strata of the proletariat and peasantry. If the party in power will not depend on broad strata of labourers, then it will become bankrupt, like some conciliationist and bourgeois parties became bankrupt in our country and in the West. For gaining the trust and sympathy of the labouring strata, the party of communists must be cruel toward all elements, which have leeched onto the party and onto the Soviet apparatus. There should be severe and just punishment for theft, bribery, bureaucratised functionaries,

self-supplying shop-assistants, and in general anyone who renders harm to workers and peasants through criminal acts or negligence at work.

2. To swiftly resolve its tasks, the party should be united, disciplined, and free to transfer its forces without hindrance, whenever, wherever, and however much is demanded in each given instance. To ease the transfer of communists from one locality to another, it is expedient for the government to provide them with the elementary comforts of life and work, so that valuable time and resources would not be spent on finding a place to live and on securing for oneself and one's family firewood, food and similar items, which so far a majority of our cities does not have.

3. To realise the dictatorship of the proletariat in all its work without hindrance, the party of communists should be free from petty bourgeois and petty bourgeois-intelligentsia elements, whose presence fetters revolutionary initiative and narrows the scope of work.

C. The Party's Content

In the RCP(b), it is possible to single out the following main groups, which by the content of their work (by their daily life, social position, and work experience) have some distinguishing features.

1. The proletariat, which has not become isolated from production

2. The proletariat, which is found in the apparatus of state management

3. The peasants, who produce agricultural products

4. The peasants, who serve in soviets and on committees

5. Minor soviet office workers

6. Outstanding, highly-qualified intelligentsia

In subdividing our party into such groups, we can be accused of dividing the party, which would lead to a split and so forth. But only people, who find it profitable to lie for some reason or who are political ignoramuses can make such an argument. The attitude cannot be the same toward one and the other. If the former need to be exposed as political charlatans, then the latter need to be proven their error in a comradely manner.

D. The Party's Line of Development

1. Along with our party's absolute growth, its worker and peasant core decreased in its relative percentage of the whole. Likewise, each reregistration tossed overboard more workers than soviet employees or senior personnel. The reasons for the leakage of workers from the party and for the influx of Soviet employees and senior personnel, who follow the Marxist school, should be seen not in insuffi-

cient ideological preparation, but in the substructure of being. This means, in other words, in the conditions of material existence. Some personnel of food supply depots, directors of soviet economic institutions, employees of soviet shops, senior personnel, and so forth, who enter into the party ranks, do so from motives of material interest and for a membership card. Some of these elements can be used by appointing them to privileged positions. Workers and peasants who haven't broken with production can have only one motive for entering the party ranks, which is the desire to struggle with all their strength against enemies and ruin. The revolutionary need to struggle for the interests of labourers is created. The result of this is that the party becomes rebalanced, with a greater weight of people serving the proletariat and the peasantry and a smaller proportion of people who produce value.[86]

2.   a)   Working in a state where agricultural producers prevail, the Communist Party is forced to depend upon the petty bourgeois private-property owning peasantry.

b)   Not having in its ranks a sufficient number of specialists (spetses) and outstanding administrators of the economy, the Party resorts to the services of spetses who are alien to communism, and to the services of senior personnel who are guilty of offences.

c)   Pressure is exerted upon our Soviet economy from without by capitalist production relations and the financial capital of the Entente countries and by speculative, trading capital from within.

d)   Having not yet completed deep cultural revolution and being forced to use broadly the weapons of bourgeois culture and science, the party often unnoticeably [illegible] veers 'To the Right'. But the aggregate of these and many other conditions leads to the unswerving degeneration of the party of the proletariat into a party with some petty bourgeois nuances. Under the pressure of foreign and domestic factors, the RCP(b) lost its proletarian cast of mind and dressed itself in the rags of fellow travelers to the proletariat. The Party dictatorship of the proletariat will slowly but steadily degenerate, if it will

---

86   Here I have broken up a very long run-on sentence into separate sentences with the goal of achieving greater clarity.

not eliminate spontaneous [стихийные] growth conditions in favour of consciously attracting healthy proletarian elements, and if it will not transfer the party's centre of support from the highest element (the 'aristocracy') to the proletarian core. Diverse social groups will sweep the party away. This degeneration is dangerous. It is just completely impossible that deformation of classes should be permitted in Communist society. If it does not wither away during the transition under the dictatorship of the proletariat, it will appear in the most extreme forms. Under the dictatorship of the proletariat, its political party should be completely free from fellow travelers. Otherwise they will loaf around, whine, and hinder work.

3. As the party's composition changed, the tactics of its leading centres changed, too, and for self justification found confirmation in the correlation of forces within the party. The more 'fellow travelers' in the organisation and the more actively they display their will, then the more the leading centres turn the wheel 'To the Right', the more they find justification for orienting toward the highest aristocratic strata, and the less they listen to the opinion of the party's worker core.

4. The ideology of each group in the party forms in dependence upon the conditions of existence.

The first group (of the proletariat in production), which finds itself in conditions of material scarcity, lives by concepts of 'distracted [отвлеченной] need'. It starves in the present and survives on hope for a life of plenty in the future. Although it lives in conditions of deprivation, it observes 'excessive indulgence' at the top. All this puts a stamp on consciousness, which seeks less support from realistic activity. Instead, consciousness either depends more on idealistic fanaticism or, if it finds neither real nor abstract-idealistic support, then consciousness suffers failure and its bearer abandons the ranks of the party. The abstraction of the idea can and should be eliminated. The party leadership can give real support to the consciousness of this core group in the party, by drawing closer to it through factory work, at meetings, in theatres, in housing, and so forth. This needs to be done. Otherwise, the party loses its main base, which is its steel proletarian spine.

The second group is the proletariat in the state management apparatus. The majority of it lives their lives in the most realistic activism.

a) Members of this group actively participate in organising the republic's human and animal workforce to resolve tasks of material construction, organisational tasks, and cultural tasks.
b) Members of this group use objects of material and cultural value on a large scale.
c) All these conditions of their existence form a more sensible ideology, from the communist point of view.
d) Members of this group are more armed with Marxist knowledge and their consciousness is less soiled by abstract-idealistic concepts.
e) Such strata of our party periodically need to be let loose in the plants and factories, where they will introduce a realistic spirit and will serve as a buttress for the consciousness of those who vacillate. Besides that, a change in their labour conditions will invigorate their consciousness and their psyche.

Into the third group go minor Soviet employees, Soviet shop clerks, directors of economic unit depots, directors of dairy farms, Soviet work-shops, and the like. They live in conditions, which most of all corrupt consciousness. Communists of this group do not create value, but distribute it. Inasmuch as distribution is not regulated, in it can come to light some cases of individual initiative of distributing according to the bad habit of individual gratifications. Many preconditions are on hand for corruption of proletarian ideology and abuses, which with time can lead to crimes. This group yields the largest percentage of accused at party courts and tribunals. Of course, it is not because people of this group have especially criminal or selfish inclinations, but because these people live in conditions, which nudge them toward violating proletarian morals.

Consciousness depends on existence. In order to make the perverted consciousness of this group's party members healthier, they need to be sent to do physical work periodically or for good. Their individual initiative in distributing objects of value needs to be forged together with collective initiative. Individual gratifications need to be replaced with equal distribution. Pay above the norms needs to be regulated according to the principle of who deserves it on the basis of carrying out special work, for example to necessary spetses, senior personnel, and so forth. It is not necessary to dwell upon the ideology of the third, fourth, and sixth groups, because the most valuable groups in the party are the first, second, and part of the fifth.

E.   Conditions to Make the Party Healthier

Among the unhealthy phenomena in our party are the following:

1)   The party's tendency to degenerate in favour of fellow travelers.

2)   The party ideology's pollution with individualist norms and petty bourgeois ideals and prejudices.

3)   The rupture of the comradely cohesion within the party, the tendentious orientation of some party leading bodies, which incline toward the fellow travelers to the working class, and the leading bodies' insufficiently attentive attitude toward healthy instructions offered by the party's worker core.

Degeneration can be ended through mass attraction of healthy proletarian elements into the party and expulsion of 'fellow travelers'. 'Fellow travelers' can be defined by the criterion: 'Incapacity for self-sacrifice for the sake of the proletariat's victory, use of a party membership card for personal self-interest, and patronage for petty bourgeois elements'. Cleansing the party can be assigned to the gubkoms and the ukoms in contact with party control commissions, which are elected at party conferences, and under the supervision of general party assemblies.

Cultural revolution can eliminate ideological pollution. The Main Political Education Committee (Glavpolitprosvet), together with its local bodies, can be a good weapon in the struggle for new forms of proletarian culture, but only a weapon.[87] Besides a weapon, new personnel are needed with a new method of cultural work. The proletariat needs help in studying new sciences about building (tektology).[88] The tektological perspective needs to be applied to recasting the morals of norms and of sciences, beginning with the social sciences, continuing, and ending with the rest of the sciences.

The rupture of comradely cohesion within the party can be seen in the absence of discipline, the distrust of broad party strata toward leading bodies, petty squabbling, and petty intrigues. Such defects result from the monopoly of party leadership by a small circle of people and from excessive burdens on the party rank and file. More protracted, palliative measures can alleviate the problem. Workerisation of party bodies needs

---

87   For more on Glavpolitprosvet, see Brandenberger 2011, pp. 11–12, 15.

88   Here the theses show the influence of A.A. Bogdanov's thought. See Bogdanov 1980 and Pavlov and Rowley (eds.) 2015–.

to be one of these palliatives. More precisely, this is the airing out of a stagnant, monopolistic atmosphere by means of fresh forces emerging from the party grassroots, broadly informing party members about the activity of party committees, discussing important questions at general assemblies, and so forth.

More radical measures need to be taken, such as circulating party forces within the party organism, as they did in Piter, when 300 comrades were sent from senior posts to plants and factories. It would be best if personnel were shifted by initiative of the lowest-level cells. It would be expedient to receive the sanction of general assemblies, when candidates are nominated for transfer, so that motives of personal interest and favouritism would take a back seat to motives of businesslike necessity. Comrades who have committed an offence should set themselves right at their places of work in the eyes of the organisation and of workers, who have shown dissatisfaction with the behaviour of those who have done wrong. An upsurge of labour enthusiasm of the broadest strata of the proletariat and peasantry is needed in order to resolve historical tasks. Therefore, the party should hold the course toward those who produce value, rather than toward the strata, which serve the state. The party should become the party of the ruling class, not the party of the managing stratum. Whoever will not understand this is doomed to failure, like many of the conciliationist parties. Neither past meritorious services nor the worthless authority of pitiful political ignoramuses in the present such will save them from political death.

14   Iu.K. Milonov, 'Theses: the Content of our Cultural Work', Eighth Samara Gubernia RCP(b) Conference[89]

1.   The history of past social revolutions speaks of how a revolution in social relations interweaves with a revolution in social consciousness. In other words, the economic revolution intertwines with the ideological and cultural revolution.

2.   The relationship between these two processes is defined so that restructuring of society forms and creates a new culture. Then the new culture regulates and directs the life of the restructured or still just restructuring society.

---

89   These were published in Samara at sovnarkhoz printshop no. 5 in a print run of 600 copies.

3. The mechanism of such a cultural revolution is defined by the features, which follow. The class, which is actively restructuring society or preparing such a restructuring in the process of this work, forms its class cultural point of view, which reflects its social existence. Then from this point of view, it regards the cultural heritage of the old society or class and so creates its own world view and its own culture.

4. Specimens of these past cultures and world views are the *Old Testament*, which was created by patriarchal organiser-prophets and was thoroughly steeped in the authoritarian[?][90] point of view, and likewise *L'Encyclopédie*, which French bourgeois revolutionary scholars created and imbued throughout with an abstract individualist point of view.

5. The cultural point of view of a class, first of all, saturates its views toward social relations, where the direct clash of class interests is strongest of all.[91] Culture defends these interests in the literal and direct sense of this word. Then, on the path to a single world view and its own culture, views about nature and consciousness [насознание] penetrate culture. At various times, the ideology of class can consist of a combination of diverse cultural elements.

6. Along with restructuring social relations, the ongoing proletarian social revolution also revolutionises culture.

7. A proletarian cultural point of view, which is collectivist-labour and free from fetishism and idol-worshiping, already has taken shape. It has already saturated the views of the proletariat and of society, but in everything else the proletariat remains under the influence of the old culture (views toward nature and consciousness). Its ideology consists right now of a combination of diverse cultural elements (feudal and bourgeois).

8. The proletariat's cultural dependency interferes with it coming forth as the independent organiser of society. It is forced to use the services of people of the old culture and regime. Inevitably, it falls under their influence. This interferes with building a new society.

9. Specimens of the proletariat's cultural dependence are the bureaucratism of public employees [общественные работники] who emerge from the ranks of the working class, the strength of petty bourgeois prejudices

---

90   The Russian word in the text is авторитетный, but Milonov probably meant авторитарный.

91   The Russian text has the word либералы where I chose 'interests', but I think this must have been a misprint, especially because интересы is in the next sentence.

among workers, eclecticism, and the desultory world view of the majority of the proletariat.

10. The task of the conscious part of the proletariat and of the party of communists, for the time being, is to deepen the cultural revolution, which has already begun. It will be in the form of a complete reevaluation, from the collective-labour point of view, of the entire cultural inheritance of the old society and the creation of an independent proletarian culture.

11. However, leading circles of our party disclaim this task entirely.

12. Opponents of proletarian culture are delineated into three groups.

13. One group denies that proletarian culture is possible while the bourgeois order still exists to any degree. In their opinion, the proletariat has neither the strength nor the time to create its own culture. Socialist culture, to which they juxtapose proletarian culture, coincides with full realisation and consolidation of socialist society.

14. The second group limits the capacity of proletarian culture to fall only within the boundaries of the social sciences, leaving the so-called precise sciences outside of it.

15. The third type of opponent thinks that proletarian culture will be developed by adapting working-class consciousness to industrial wage rates and norm-setting categories.

16. The position of the first category of opponents does not hold up to criticism from the Marxist point of view. The very position of the proletariat in capitalist society makes it a carrier of socialist ideas and a fighter for the socialist idea. So it already fills in the foundation of socialist culture in volume but not in essence. The first group is more thoroughly saturated with the collective-labour point of view.

17. The position of opponents of the second type is based on limiting the capacity of scientific communism. The roots of this phenomenon lie in the limitation of their thought, which cannot be reconciled with Marxism.

18. The third position is based on the fetishisation of the role of technology in social life and the lack of accounting for the influence of economics and ideology. This fetishism is irreconcilable with Marxism.

19. Thus, there is no basis for denying the task of creating independent proletarian culture, aside from mistaken arguments and reasoning. This task persists and demands to be resolved.

20. One of the basic goals, which will help resolve it, is to create a *Proletarian Encyclopedia*, which would formulate the whole, consummate world view of the proletariat.[92]

---

92   Iury Milonov wrote more about the Proletarian Encyclopedia in his article, 'Na puti k

21. In order to achieve the projected goal, the organisational form for this will be the creation of a network of united proletarian universities across the entire republic. Constructed according to the model of the Moscow Proletarian University, these universities would stand at the centre of a socialist Academy.[93]

22. That is how the contours are drawn of this cultural revolution, which needs to be placed on the practical agenda.

15   Iu.K. Milonov, 'Trade Unions and Their Role in the Economic Life of the Country: Theses of a Report to the Eighth Samara Gubernia Conference of the RCP(b)'[94]

1. For the Tenth All-Russian Party Congress, local organisations should not elaborate their own platforms on the trade union movement, but are supposed to select one of those which have already come together. This is necessary so that the role of trade unions will be decided at the forthcoming congress as an outcome of struggle between those tendencies which have already taken shape. In such circumstances, elaborating one's own platform would mean isolation and would be tactical nonsense.

2. To correctly select a platform, one should evaluate, from the perspectives of theory and practice, these tendencies' answers to the main questions of the trade union movement, which are tasks, methods, and organisation of trade unions. From these perspectives, one should compare and sort the arguments of platforms that have already taken shape.

3. Three platforms are on hand: Trotsky's, Zinoviev's, and Shliapnikov's.

4. Trotsky's platform answers three basic questions of the trade union movement thusly:

   a)   Trade unions' tasks are not limited to cultivating the masses in the spirit of communism and to supplying personnel for military and food supply organisations, but extend to seizing production, raising the productivity of labour, and organising workers for production.

---

rabochei entsiklopedii', which was published in Bogdanov 1921, pp. iii–xxiv. See document #3.35 in this collection.

93   The proletarian universities were a vision of the Proletkult movement. For more on it, see Mally 1990, and Sochor 1988.

94   These were published in Samara at sovnarkhoz printshop no. 5, on 23 January 1921, in a print run of 600 copies.

b)   Methods for executing these tasks are defined as participating in production, improving technology, reeducating the masses so that producers will adopt the spirit and attitude of organisers of production, and getting the masses to take interest in the work of trade unions.

c)   Organisation of trade unions means producer democracy. Personnel will be selected on the basis of their practical experience and skills in the economy. There will be statisation of trade unions. At first, there will be mutual representation in trade union bodies and leadership bodies of the national economy. Worker democracy will be combined with extraordinary measures.

5.   Zinoviev's platform answers these basic questions differently:

a)   Unions' task is to cultivate the masses in a communist spirit and turn over to them the wheel of the organised proletarian movement, realise the role of a conveyor belt from the government to the masses, and defend the interests of the proletariat from the worker-peasant government and from its bureaucracy.

b)   Methods for resolving such a task are help from unions for the Soviet government, help from the Soviet government for unions just the same as it provides to military organisations, independent work free from pressure and from government harassment, government's use of the union struggle against bureaucratism to defend the workers' material and spiritual interests.

c)   The organisation of trade unions should remain as of old. Unions' merger with government bodies should be partial and gradual.

6.   Shliapnikov's platform formulates these answers in these ways:

a)   The task of trade unions consists of concentrating in their hands all management of production and of improving workers' living conditions.

b)   Methods for implementing this task are defined as: increasing the rights and privileges of professional workers' organisations, transitioning from shock work to purposefulness and regularity of economic work, repealing payments by means of consumer goods, organising workshops supplying workers' needs, adapting the means of transport to workers' needs, construction works and the like, and applying bonuses on a large scale.

c)   Trade unions are to be organised in the following manner. Unions elect economic bodies; unions' boundaries are correctly delimited; strong personnel are selected; economic bodies do not reject candidates nominated by unions for economic posts; unions already prepared for this work cross over to it; the apparatus is built on the foundation of worker centralism, that is, the elective principle and responsibility of bodies; and through local union bodies, all worker enterprises speak and act as active participants in the organisation of production.

7. Supporters of Zinoviev's platform raise the following arguments against Trotsky's platform:

   a) Production democracy is empty, incorrect, and leads to errors. It slides toward appointmentism. Production democracy is an incompatible combination. Workers' democracy is more accurate.

   b) You can't realise the dictatorship of the proletariat directly through the masses, which essentially appear purely proletarian.

   c) The reality of the transition period needs to be taken into account. We do not have a purely worker government, but a worker-peasant government, and indeed even with bureaucratic distortions.

   d) Unions defend the interests of the proletariat from this government.

   e) Mutual representation, as a method of merger, is simply a bureaucratic fib.

   f) Statisation of unions into a government, which has not been cleansed of bureaucratism, will hinder the communist cultivation of the proletariat.

   g) Trotsky's and Bukharin's theses are thoroughly tactless and thoroughly abstract. They are the policy of bureaucratic harassment of trade unions.

   h) It's necessary to study practice and not argue about theory.

8. Supporters of Trotsky's platform have the following objections to Zinoviev's platform:

   a) A turning point in the role of trade unions should be recognised not only in words but also in deeds.

   b) A new attitude of the producer toward production needs to be created. Essentially, this is an organiser's attitude.

   c) Plenipotentiaries and appointees will remain until unions make an enormous step forward in the business of seizing production.

   d) Right now, trade unions constitute small groups of people, who are connected with union work by having an interest in it, against the background of a mass membership, which is united in a completely mechanical way.

   e) In the workers' government, the basis for the existence of trade unions can and should be only participation in production and the organisation of workers for production.

f) Their objections to all the other positions on the role of trade unions come down to these being too conservative:

i) Riazanov proposes to preserve for trade unions in the workers' state such a position as 'trade unions' occupied and occupy in the capitalist state. This is Soviet 'trade unionism' [of the English type].[95]

ii) Against a practical argument from the party programme (gradual but resolute statisation of trade unions, by merging them with the government) Tomsky juxtaposes his own point of view, which is very different from such arguments. This is also a variety of Soviet 'trade unionism'.

iii) Shliapnikov proposes to unions to take the existing apparatuses of industrial management under their leadership, in order to approach merger, but his proposal does not lead toward a greater role for unions in economic life. As a result, you get in the best case organisational chaos and in the worst case a mass raid on production. Shliapnikov's position bears the stamp of syndicalism. It is akin to Soviet 'trade unionism' in its conservatism, which can be seen in its failure to understand the need to radically restructure unions and to reeducate them in order to match the tasks of production.

9. Shliapnikov's argument against all other positions is difficult to understand, because his platform has no polemical section. The stenographic report of his speech at the meeting about this question has not been published anywhere.

10. Upon evaluating all three platforms, one has to make the following conclusions:

a) The essence of Trotsky's arguments against Zinoviev's platform comes down to trade unions being either bodies of struggle or bodies of construction, but nothing in between. This is correct, both theoretically and practically. Such are the theoretical notions. By its nature, the petty bourgeoisie cannot play the leading role in a social movement. Therefore, even in the worker-peasant government, its organiser is the working class in the person of all its organisations. These worker organisations cannot play the role of fighters against

---

95 The sentence uses two terms for trade unions: профессиональные союзы and тред-юнионы, the former of which was applied to Soviet trade unions and the latter reserved as a pejorative for reformist unions in a bourgeois, capitalist state (according to the Soviet Communist definition of such). I've placed the pejorative usage in quotation marks.

the government, the role of passive observers, or the role of simple solicitors. In practice, as the matter stands in the present, incongruous moment and situation, trade unions are slowly rotting. They are transforming into talking-shops and scribbling offices.

b) Trotsky's argument against Shliapnikov's platform is that the effort to seize the apparatus for managing production obscures from view the main thing, which is the creating in producers a new attitude toward production. This argument simply does not correspond to reality. Shliapnikov defines the main task as workers' active participation in the business of management, which just exactly means the creation of a new attitude by producers toward production.

c) The essence of Zinoviev's arguments against Trotsky's platform comes down to unions defending the working class from the bad bureaucracy of a good government and independently educating it in the spirit of building communism. Theoretically, here is how the matter stands. The workers' state should defend the interests of the proletariat from bureaucracy. It should educate it in the spirit of building communism. Practically, unions' defence of the working class against government's bureaucratic perversions puts them in the position of bodies struggling against it. When it is isolated from construction, education becomes an empty phrase and a blank space. Thus, these arguments are theoretically and practically incorrect.

d) But Zinoviev's argument that mutual representation of bodies is a bureaucratic fiction is both theoretically and practically correct. Theoretically, a new attitude by the masses toward production can't be built on the basis of merging bodies. Practically, such a merger, or more accurately almost such a merger, has still not yielded anything.

11. Proceeding from these practical comparisons of the three platforms about the trade union movement, the following needs to be said:

a) It is necessary to accept Trotsky's criticism of our trade unions' contradictory situation (they are neither here nor there) and to agree with him that this contradiction should be resolved toward transforming trade unions into organisers of the national economy.

b) It is necessary to accept Zinoviev's and Lenin's reproofs against the bureaucratic character of Trotsky's practical proposals (mutual representation) and to decline the plan of organisation.

c) Shliapnikov's platform, which has neither the sin of bureaucratism (involvement of masses) nor that of excessive theorisation (actual unionisation of many government bodies), should be accepted as the basis [for a resolution].

12. Having accepted Shliapnikov's platform as the basis [for a resolution], it should be discussed as widely as possible, in order for the masses to initiate from below valuable practical corrections and additions to it.

16 Speeches, Resolutions, Materials, and Declarations Relating to the Workers' Opposition at the Tenth Party Congress, March 1921[96]

Speeches of Worker Oppositionists: Shliapnikov: 71–6; Milonov: 82–5; Perepechko: 90–2; Kollontai: 100–3; Shliapnikov: 125; Medvedev: 135–6; WO remarks: 233–4; Ignatov: 234–43; Medvedev: 269–72; Kiselev: 281–3; Rybak [?]: 296–8; Kollontai: 298–300; Ignatov: 316–21; Shliapnikov: 359–67; Kutuzov: 373–5; Medvedev: 383–5; Shliapnikov: 385–9; Medvedev: 526–30; Shliapnikov: 530–2; Ignatov: 534–5; Kiselev: 543–4

Resolutions Relating to the Workers' Opposition: 'On Party Unity', 571–3; 'On the Syndicalist and Anarchist Deviation', 574–6; 'On Members of the Workers' Opposition Elected to the CC', 577

Materials Relating to the Workers' Opposition: Resolution on Party Building proposed by the Workers' Opposition, 651–6; Tasks of Trade Unions proposed by the Workers' Opposition, 685–91 [see text above]; List of delegates voting against the party unity resolution and abstaining, 773–4; List of delegates voting against the resolution on anarcho-syndicalist deviation and abstaining, 778;

Declarations Relating to the Workers' Opposition: Tuntul, Pykhtin & Kondrakov on Medvedev's claims, 787–8; Declaration of the Workers' Opposition to Zalutsky, 790; Shliapnikov's 'Organisation of the Economy and Tasks of Trade Unions', 819–23.

∴

Session 1, morning of 8 March 1921. Chaired by Vladimir Lenin.

[Summary: Lenin delivers the opening speech. The presidium is elected. The mandate commission is selected. They hear greetings from foreign communist parties.]

---

96 RKP(b) 1963. Excerpts of some speeches were published in Zorky (ed.) 1926.

• •
•

Session 2, evening of 8 March 1921. Chaired by Lev Kamenev.

[Summary: Lenin gives a report on the cc's political work. Krestinsky gives the report about the cc's organisational work. Solts speaks about the work of the Control Commission.]

• •
•

Session 3, morning of 9 March 1921. Chaired by Mikhail Tomsky.

[Skvortsov (Stepanov) speaks about the reports of the previous day.]

Shliapnikov (pp. 71–6): Yesterday, from this tribune, Comrade Lenin flung a question at us representatives of the Workers' Opposition: do all comrades from the Workers' Opposition share the opinion of some workers that right now we need maximum cohesion? I can state that among us there is not one who would deny the need for this unity. In order to prove this graphically, we have our own example, this will prove our unity. But only formal recognition of the need for unity means little to us, comrades. We should state that, despite formally existing unity, we in the party do not have an organic link between members of the party and its leading bodies. This I can say not only from my personal experience, but also by citing the situation in the provinces, and each of us knows this perfectly well. We, Vladimir Ilich, do not have in our party that former cohesion, which we had in past moments of our party's life, in the prerevolutionary period, which were not less difficult. It is strange, comrades, that this organic feeling of being cut off takes place at that moment when the party has full disposal of all the technical resources: radio, postal system, telegraph, thousands of party personnel, and the Soviet apparatus! But anyway, despite these perfect resources, within the party there is not that cohesion which we observed, let's say, not so long ago, both in 1914 and in 1917. Do you remember, Vladimir Ilich, when our leading centre was not even in Russia, it had insignificant resources available, and then each word, each published illegal leaflet, each scrap of paper, brought by our party organisations to worker centres – Piter, Moscow, Donetsky basin, Urals, how they were met then, despite the fact that we were deprived of all technical resources. Then both cohesion and unity of thought and feelings, all of it was present. Now it is not. This, comrade Lenin, is what gave birth to what you call here the 'Workers' Opposition'.

We do not have differences regarding our main internal and international policies. We accept this aspect of comrade Lenin's report. But we have many differences regarding tactical questions and methods of realising our general political line. Because of this, the broad labouring masses of the town and countryside often noticeably turn against us. Not only do methods of work assimilated during the civil war not allow us to realise the programme's demand to attract broad groups of the proletariat into Soviet construction, but they definitely push them away from us and our party. This spurs those of us who stand very close to broad circles of proletarians in plants and factories to loudly announce the threatening danger of being cut off from the masses.

During the party pre-congress discussion, we heard everything it was possible to hear. Those labels, double entendres, and insinuations, which ring out here in our direction, do not trouble us. We know ourselves and we know well who we're dealing with.

Facing difficulties confronting us, we should first of all bring our Russian Communist Party into a healthy state and more tightly close the ranks of the revolutionary vanguard. But the path that comrade Lenin has taken does not lead us to the unity desired by all. If you, Vladimir Ilich, in your analysis will obviously confuse the Workers' Opposition with petty bourgeois elements, the purest syndicalism, and anarchism, and if you will heap up all this and connect it with us, then you will not create unity in our party on such grounds, and you will instil very much bitterness into the hearts of those workers who are here in person, and through them you will alienate those in the plants and factories who support us.

Comrades, the matter is not as comrade Lenin paints it. We recommend to you to very carefully, more strictly and more seriously analyse each phenomenon of the moment we are experiencing. Comrade Skvortsov was correct, when he pointed out this insufficiency. Those who lump together anarchic elements and the Workers' Opposition are not correct. Such an approach compromises those speaking, does not help elucidate the main reasons for the phenomena observed by us, and confuses the whole business by turning thoughts to the snare of contradictions. In the presenter's opinion, it emerges that petty bourgeois elements turn up in the glory and pride of the revolution, in Kronstadt. No one else but the proletariat of Piter yields to its influence, that proletariat, which not so long ago served as advertising for comrade Zinoviev and others who declared that the Piter proletariat was free from any kind of opposition, and especially from the Workers' Opposition. The proletariat of Piter, Red Army soldiers and sailors, 'the pride of the revolution', should bear all the imprints of actual proletarian thought and action, but even in this centre it's not there. What do we see there? We see that this leading proletariat turned out to be subject to influence, true, not of the Workers' Opposition, no, but of petty bourgeois anarchist elements. It's necessary to approach these phenomena a little more carefully.

The organic illness, which can be seen in our party, consists of the isolation of our centres from party masses and of the entire party apparatus from the working masses. The CC itself carries traces of this illness. Those reproaches, which were flung at the Workers' Opposition, that 'you behaved badly during the party discussion about the trade union movement, you infected the party with syndicalism and similar such sins,' we should resolutely return to the sender, reminding you that we wrote our theses just one time and for the final time, but you, CC members, wrote theses first and in great abundance. It wasn't we who started the discussion. We only followed in your footsteps, but we brought something of our own here, safeguarding the further advancement of the revolution. Let's discuss this here, but it is unworthy to brand us without substantiation as syndicalists, as anarchists! To link us with those or other uprisings or discontent, which now seethes in worker quarters, is not only senseless, but also unscrupulous and demagogic. Comrade Iakovleva, secretary of the Moscow committee, will tell you who significantly aggravates these disturbances in worker quarters, and likewise who they call upon in the most important incidents. She will tell you, that very often the Workers' Opposition helps out. The Workers' Opposition appears in the capacity of a firehose, so also in this case it is necessary to be fair. We can tell you that the reasons for that discontent, which we observe in Moscow and in other worker cities, lead us not to the Workers' Opposition, but to the Kremlin. A number of factors point to this. Some circumstances of these misunderstandings force us to demand that someone be put on trial, exactly those people who enjoy here general 'respect'. This is how the business appears, given the smallest attempt to elucidate all the circumstances.

Questions posed here by comrade Lenin and comrade Krestinsky are extraordinarily important. A few minutes are not enough to take them in. I think that our comrades who follow will also allot to them the required attention. Here Vladimir Ilich spoke about the difficulties of the transition from wartime to peace and pointed to the necessity of maneuvering in internal policy.

The Workers' Opposition understands perfectly well all the difficulties of this policy, but we should declare: when comrade Lenin spoke about mistakes, that it is said that food supply resources were clumsily distributed, well this simple assertion does not satisfy us. We know and have known for a long time that in Narkomprod all is not well. We pointed this out to our centres many times, but without success. Our trade union comrades, who work in Narkomprod, have shouted about this for more than a year. There in Narkomprod, not only were our resources incorrectly distributed, but also were criminally stockpiled and allowed to rot.

But allow me to ask: has Tsiurupa been tried before a court? No, he still has not been. If he will be tried before a court after this party congress, I do not know, but this would be instructive for many others.

Maybe this policy brought in its wake the intensification of that petty bourgeois anarchic element, in which we are so frivolously implicated. An analogously catastrophic situation also arose with fuel. This also is no secret for anyone. But there is no Workers' Opposition in these bodies. We were not able to bring our anarchism there, but we know that henceforward it will be just the same, because these bodies more than all others shunned workers' organisations.

These bodies were afraid of workers' control and here we have now right in front of us the fruit of this policy. If we will analyse the facts, then probably we will not have those differences which now exist in the evaluation of phenomena. Maybe in your concluding remarks, Vladimir Ilich, you will introduce more nuances into your positions?

Many times, Comrade Krestinsky emphasised data about the proletarian composition of our party and, as a model, cited the personal composition of our gubkoms. I permit myself to doubt the accuracy of his conclusions. Some phenomena in the provinces indicate the opposite of what comrade Krestinsky proposes to recognise as indisputable. The CC attempts to refute that which is known to all and each, namely that our party is being reborn; in our party is a marked influx of an element alien to us. The social composition of the party is sharply changing. This threatens us not only with the intensified influence of the petty bourgeois element in our party, but also that this petty bourgeoisie [мелкобуржуазность] will slip a rather hefty brood into our party. There is sufficient evidence of this on hand.

We'll turn to the facts and numbers. We'll see, for example, how many in famous Piter, about which they so loved to speak earlier (now they're silent about it), how many members of our party are there among metalworkers, as the most advanced and revolutionary workers. There aren't even 2%. I have some data about the party complement among Moscow metalworkers in 41 metals industry factories, which embrace about 22,000 workers. What do you think, how many party members do we have there among these factory workers? We have 4%. That's how the matter stands in the most important branches of industry, proletarians of which always were the leaders of the revolution, and now they give us such an insignificant percentage of our supporters. Particular attention should be turned to this, and not to beating up the Workers' Opposition. You have to know how to attract workers into the party and not just those who call themselves workers, but those, who at the present time are tightly connected with our plants and factories.

Our CC, knowing that the matter in this regard is far from successful, not only was unable to attract new proletarian members, but even could not hold onto those, who were drawn into our party by the efforts of many thousands of workers in all corners of our extensive country. No, it seems, there is not one proletarian town, not one gubernia, where there has not been a mass exit of the worker element from the party. What has the CC undertaken in order to paralyse this phenomenon? No measures at all have been taken. The CC somehow brushed aside this phenomenon and, printing reports about numerical growth, tried only to show that we grow, grow … [ellipses in text] But this growth was one of quantity at the expense of quality. Here the CC, speaking through comrade Krestinsky's mouth, answers that in the party we have peasants and office workers, but almost no one of bourgeois origin. Really, if we are to judge by questionnaires, filled out by the interested parties, this is so, if you please, but when you dig more deeply into this data, then you will see that among these 'peasants' and 'office workers' numbers a not entirely safe [благополучный] element.

Methods of party work likewise need radical change. It is necessary quickly to put an end to individuality [единоличие] in party work, to stop putting stake on plenipotentiaries. The CC constantly conducts struggle against the provinces with the help of appointmentism and plenipotentiaries. The CC never helped the provinces and did not teach personnel of the provinces. To further arrange the matter just as they do so now, by exploiting plenipotentiaries and appointees, should not be done. You can discover what kind of results there are from this policy from those whom you are exploiting. Maybe comrades Smilga and Beloborodov will tell you from this tribune about their experience. Such an arrangement of matters creates the situation, in which at the heights of the party and Soviet apparatus we see a very thin layer of people, who are worn-out and overburdened with work, who are transferred from one place to another, and individual people from this layer are moved about from one chair to another. Very many talk about involving the rank and file, about utilising local experience and new forces, but they do little in this direction. Comrade Stepanov said that we intensely depopulate the provinces. This is true, but only with a reservation: we depopulate the provinces, but in order to make personnel from the provinces into clerks or couriers.

Here you have part of those illnesses, which we propose to heal. Here there have been attempts to speculate on party discipline. Among us there still hasn't been a case when it was violated, and when the CC gives us an order, we answer: 'I obey'. We recognise and find necessary this formula of discipline, which is unity, but we want for there to exist among us not only a formal connection, but also that same organic link, which was in our party earlier. It is not underground romanticism that speaks in me, but simple practical proletarian gumption [сметка] that demands this. Visiting plants, factories, receiving delegates from various ends of the country, who have come on union work, I very often sense this, but instead of running in a panic to the office to speak with Vladimir Ilich, as do many timid comrades, we propose practical measures to make our ranks healthy and to make our interrelations more fit. If you want to lose touch with the broadest masses, if you want to break it off with the revolutionary element, then, please, continue to act just like you have acted up to now. Add to this, moreover, persecution of the Workers' Opposition and insinuations against us. We also think that to turn your back upon that proletarian element, which is exploited by the counterrevolutionary element, means only to lose. We should not turn our back on that element, which has free rein across Russia, but should study it, and maybe we will find its culprits in our very methods, in our central apparatuses.

Vladimir Ilich touched upon a little question about our foreign relations. I already have said many times, and comrades, you know that foreign relations are not in the hands of the Workers' Opposition, and we can't be accused of having spoiled something there. I and many comrades have had the opportunity to come into conflict with our representatives abroad. I have already said more than once, that these representatives discredit us and they discredit our revolution abroad. More than once we had to declare there, when we were abroad: 'Don't judge our Republic by these people'. Comrade Lenin said that we must order machines, resources and tools of production from abroad. Superb. But what do they now order in return for hard currency? In my briefcase there are some facts, which do not go to the Control Commission, and comrade Solts eloquently convinced you, why they shouldn't go there. So from abroad they order bay leaf, pepper, red whortleberry tea, a motor car and similar such things. But comrade Avanesov, who keeps these little documents, instead of taking someone to court for such an act, maybe, will add still more to the millions being stolen.

There, comrades, that's how the business stands. Vladimir Ilich, if we will direct all our efforts to struggle against these phenomena and elements not only abroad, but also here within our country, then probably the Workers' Opposition will very firmly and unanimously be with you. But don't stir up struggle against us. Here, perhaps, you will overwhelm and defeat us, but you will only lose from this. (Applause.)

[Osinsky and Sosnovsky speak.]

Milonov (pp. 82–5): Comrades! It is extraordinarily difficult in the course of 15 minutes to give a full evaluation of the CC's activity. Therefore I must limit myself to some remarks on behalf of the majority of the Samara organisation. In our general evaluation of the activity and direction of the line of the CC of the party we almost fully agree with comrade Shliapnikov and especially with that evaluation, which comrade Kollontai gives to this line in her brochure *Rabochaia oppozitsiia*. We think that the Party CC overlooked the most important and basic thing, which is that the party now is experiencing a deep party crisis. The essence of this party crisis, in our opinion, is that our party, being in the situation of a petty bourgeois country, is getting clogged up with elements alien to it. The peasantry and intelligentsia are not terrible in and of themselves, but they enter into our party without having accepted fully the point of view of the working class and without having fulfilled that principal condition, which is placed in our party programme. Healthy worker elements pour out of the party. Party personnel from the provinces know how this is spontaneously revealed during our re-registrations, which are carried out on purely formal grounds. In the background of all this, there occurs the hardening of the very highest stratum, which is being transformed into a caste-like [кастовый] stratum. In connection with these changes in the organisational aspect of our party life, the party's tactical line is modified somewhat. Authoritarian methods of leadership from the centre are preferred over the initiative of the masses. These unhealthy phenomena remain outside the field of vision of the Party CC. We agree with comrade Shliapnikov and with comrade Kollontai in their evaluation of the situation, but we consider it necessary to accentuate some basic features more prominently and more vividly. First of all, those defects which have been pointed out here and others not yet noted relate more to our entire party organisation than to the Party CC. The shortcomings, which are seen here in the CC's activity, should not be transformed into a platform. In the provinces, these insufficiencies are turning into a platform, in defence of which cruel struggle proceeds against the group, which bears the name Workers' Opposition. Now is the time to speak about defects, which relate to the entire party organisation. It needs to be noted that all these circumstances are, of course, not a personal or a subjective fault and not the fault of individuals, but an objective misfortune which strikes our party. Here I can only dwell only on one aspect. On the other hand, it is necessary to evaluate that which calls itself the tendency of the Central Committee.

Comrade Lenin so categorically, it is possible to say 'by administrative procedure' and without any kind of evidence, stuck the label of syndicalism on the

Workers' Opposition. Psychologically this is not difficult to understand. Comrade Lenin, as Sovnarkom chair, guides our Soviet policy. It is obvious that any kind of movement, no matter from where it would come, interfering in this work of management, is perceived as a petty bourgeois movement and as an extraordinarily harmful movement. (Noise, laughter.) I think that this laughter is extraordinarily revealing. This tendency within the party approaches questions of party life from the point of view of people who have accumulated the fixed, narrow, specialised experience of party personnel, mostly gubernia committee personnel, who defend the point of view of the CC, and of personnel in Soviet institutions, who are isolated from the thick of the broad masses. This circumstance forces them to approach questions of party life from the point of view of people from a certain branch of party experience. Therefore some phenomena show through, which would have been impossible to perceive, if approaching the question from another point of view. It is presented to us that now groupings within the party are not simply a manifestation of the 'perniciousness' of some sort of Shliapnikov and the Workers' Opposition, but a manifestation of comrades' isolation from one another and frequent inability to reach an understanding. Up to now three groupings have struggled in the party: the CC grouping, the Democratic Centralism grouping and the grouping of the Workers' Opposition. The Workers' Opposition grouping tries to certify [оформить] the experience of those party personnel, who move in the very thicket of the worker masses. (Laughter.) From below, all insufficiencies are much more visible. The opposition of the CC grouping expresses the experience of personnel of the leading centre, who see many interruptions of work, but who cannot cast a glance from below at them, and instead regard them from a leading, high-up position. The Democratic Centralism grouping expresses the party and soviet experience of that sector of the party, which unites in its hands work in the provinces. Personnel of this group sit in Soviet institutions and see, until they pass out from it, all insufficiencies, which do not measure up to developed centralism. If we approach the question from the present point of view, and this is possible to do only when we try to reveal the social base of these tendencies, we see that all these groupings are not the ill will of individuals, but an expression of how in the party there begins such stratification, such differentiation, that these points of view cannot be entirely reconciled with one another.

Now about syndicalism. Lenin poses the question thus: the peasantry has a petty bourgeois orientation, it is not with us. We cannot lean for support on it. The working class is falling under a petty bourgeois influence.

It is necessary to agree that the Workers' Opposition leans for support on the working class. In Samara we have three worker districts. The district where

Soviet personnel predominate is not with us. Those uyezd organisations, where peasant elements predominate, are not with us. Those uyezd organisations, in which worker elements predominate, are with us. The same thing can be seen, of course, in the entire Republic (Noise, laughter, cries of exclamation: 'Nothing of the sort!')

Chair (Kamenev). Maybe you will decline to characterise our congress and Moscow?

Milonov. The experience of a significant part of gubernia organisations confirms that the Workers' Opposition leans for support on worker strata. I can give an example: first, Samara gubernia, and second, part of Ukraine, part of the Kuban and part of Donskaia oblast. (Protests from the hall.) How to resolve such a problem? Since the peasantry is not with us and since the working class falls under the influence of various petty bourgeois anarchist elements and is inclined to move away from us, on what can the Communist Party now depend? Here a way out must be sought in two directions. Either it is necessary to say, as say some people in the provinces, that in revolutionary and political struggle and socialist construction the working class is self-seeking and can't be depended upon – and they have invented such a theory – or we need to say that no one can be depended upon, as comrade Osinsky tried to point out. An awkward situation results: we seem to be over an abyss, between the working class, which is infected with petty bourgeois prejudices, and the peasantry, which is essentially petty bourgeois. Is it impossible to depend only upon Soviet and party officialdom? Of course, it is impossible to depend on it. Here it is necessary to establish the isolation of certain parts of our party from the working class. Our party ceases to be a worker party. This usually is overlooked. This is the most principal anomaly in the work of our CC, and not so much of it specifically, as chiefly of that tendency, which up to now reigns in the party. And it is not an accident that the majority of comrades here laugh, when you talk about how the Workers' Opposition leans for support on healthy worker elements of the party. They laugh, because their experience forces them to perceive these phenomena differently. Of course, it is possible to laugh, but there is danger, not to laugh too much and not to keep laughing until the party stands before a crisis in acute form. Then it is necessary to remember that 'he who laughs last, laughs best'. We also think that it is too early now to laugh at the Workers' Opposition. Now it is necessary to recognise that the party is in a condition of the most serious crisis and that the Party CC does not see this crisis and the tendency reigning in the party. This question about the crisis ought to be placed at the head of the line and it's necessary to get busy curing it.

[David Riazanov speaks.]

Ivan Perepechko (pp. 90–2). I consider it my duty, mildly speaking, to clarify that untrue information, of which comrade Sosnovsky informed us. According to him, the electrical station in Moscow, where comrade Shliapnikov spoke, accepted a resolution demanding to purge the intelligentsia from the party. Here before me is this resolution (Reads).[97] There is no demand in it about the purge of the party.

Comrade Lenin, in his political report, indicated that the CC asked about struggle against bureaucratism, and this struggle was partially carried out. Comrade Krestinsky, in order to show the successful results of this struggle for improving the party's health, indicated that in the gubkoms almost 80% are workers. This makes it seem as if comrade Krestinsky is saying that there's no reason to engage in workerisation any more, when workers sit everywhere. I should say that it is primitive to formulate the question as did comrade Krestinsky in the struggle against bureaucratism. Those measures, which the CC applied to improve the party's health, were only a first attempt to struggle against bureaucratism. These were mostly words. The CC did not go further than attempts, words, and drawing incredible pictures depicting the crisis of the party. Recommendations include such measures as registering those arriving at and departing from sessions, publishing the names of those who committed offences, and other even more elementary things. There were no concrete measures, nor was there any serious struggle. To this day we have the soviets, which should bring out the collective will, the class will of the proletariat, being replaced by separate bureaucratic departments [ведомства]. This tendency, to replace the collective will and class essence of the Soviets continues to exist, develop, and become stronger. Because of this, the struggle against bureaucratism hasn't gone further than pitiful, insignificant attempts of a purely technical character. There was no serious resolution of the problem. Bureaucratism is a painful problem for our party. It is the source of the alienation of Soviet power and the entire soviet apparatus from the broad worker masses.

The CC's other task is improving the party's health. This problem also was not fully resolved. Very much was also said about abnormal phenomena in our party, but on that the matter ended. Comrade Zinoviev very colourfully painted a picture of the abnormalities, which appear as a result of isolation from the rank-and-file, but further than this and aside from such purely technical meas-

---

97   The editors of the 1963 volume write in a footnote that the resolution has not been preserved.

ures, no serious attempts for remedying the evil have been carried out. Yes, workers are the majority in our gubkoms. Undoubtedly, we have such industrial centres as the Donbas and Ivanovo-Voznesensk, where the intelligentsia have no sway. But the entire misfortune is that the entire political system of both soviet and party bodies was directed not toward connecting the leading centres of the party [with the masses],[98] so it led to still greater estrangement. As a result of this, it is possible to speak directly and definitely of isolation [from the masses].[99] Comrade Shliapnikov already gave us figures, to which could be added even more horrifying numbers. This shows that between our party and the worker masses there snapped that connecting thread, which made our party strong in the past and allowed it to give tried and true leaders to the masses. The replacement of the enterprise [самодеятельность] of the broad masses with the enterprise of a bureaucratic departmental [ведомственный] apparatus is not a discrete phenomenon, but a whole system, a whole policy. If it will remain so, then it can lead to even more.

Comrade Osinsky spoke here and said that the Workers' Opposition is decentralism. Although I know perfectly well the activity of the Workers' Opposition in various places, I do not know of one fact, which would support Osinsky's statement. For clarification I will read a brief bit of information from comrade Osinsky's concluding remarks at the Third Tula Gubernia Conference. Here are the desires and moods, which guide comrade Osinsky (reads): 'So, for example, they talk about the initiative of worker masses,' says comrade Osinsky, 'when the intelligentsia with the greatest effort drags behind it the hungry, tired working class. It is the foremost vanguard, which pulls along everyone, and at this time to speak about initiative of the masses is called dancing on a grave'.[100] (Osinsky from his seat: 'Nothing of the sort! This is a distorted stenographic report!') If, comrades, this is counterfeit, then those who submitted this stenographic report must be tried before a court.

If you will look at the theses of the Democratic Centralism group, then you will see that this is a decaying, half-rotten tendency. The Tenth Congress will finally smash it. This group obviously sees no other tasks before the party, except for having comrades Sapronov and Osinsky in the vanguard of the party. It seems that further there is nowhere to go. It is clearly evident what the group of Democratic Centralism strives for. This group wishes to create a scarecrow out of the Workers' Opposition and by means of this invented scarecrow, the

---

98   1963 edition editors' insertion in brackets.
99   1963 edition editors' insertion in brackets.
100   На похоронах в дудочку играть.

Workers' Opposition, it tries to frighten people. This group in fact moves toward the same bureaucratism and centralism, which it frivolously disowns.

The Workers' Opposition, said comrade Sosnovsky, sees the improvement of the party's health in the struggle against the intelligentsia. If the Workers' Opposition really saw the chief means of making the party healthy in struggle against the intelligentsia in our party, then, indeed, we would need to take down the sign Workers' Opposition. But, thank god, neither we nor any other party member will take this path. It is the profoundest mistake to say that our party and bodies of Soviet power can be made healthy only through struggle against *intelligentshchina* and so forth. We formulate the question differently. The worker masses must be made cohesive and connected with the party and with Soviet bodies in such a way that they are not only connected through workers' inspection. Workers there are turning into agents and inspectors, who are sent to investigate, but who themselves can offer nothing new.[101]

In so far as the Soviet revolution leans for support on the proletariat and in so far as the hegemon is the RCP, which calls itself the vanguard of the proletariat, then to that extent the role of the proletariat in its class organisation in the social revolution should not be reduced to the role of a simple object, with which they do whatever they wish. The role of the working class should be completely different. We want and will secure it so that the working class would not be a weak-willed creature in the hands of the bureaucratism of a departmental apparatus, but so that the working class would really be that hegemon, of whose leadership our programme says so much.

[Minin and Rafail speak.]

Kollontai (pp. 100–3). Comrade Riazanov here called the Workers' Opposition by the name *Pugachevshchina*. Involuntarily one recalls the epoch of Pugachev and wants to remind Riazanov: doesn't he remember that in that time there was likewise a special type of people, who were called minstrels [скоморохи].[102]

Comrade Riazanov pointed to still another fact, that right now we find it acceptable to publish brochures and write on them: 'Only for members of the

---

101   Perepechko must be speaking about the People's Commissariat of Workers' and Peasants Inspection (*Rabkrin*), which existed from 1920 to 1934 and oversaw the work of the state administration in order to ensure it functioned effectively and that decrees were implemented. It was merged with the Party's Central Control Commission in 1923 and replaced by the Commission for State Control in 1934. See Rees 1987.

102   Emelian Pugachev was a Cossack rebel who led a large-scale popular rebellion in 1773–5 against Empress Catherine II of Russia (see Avrich 1976). Скоморохи were pagan minstrels (see Zguta 1978).

Communist party', 'all rights remain with the author' [на правах рукописи], yet publishing them in an unbelievable quantity of copies. On the cover of the brochure *Rabochaia oppozitsiia*, published by the State Publishing Company, a note claims that it was published in the quantity of 1,500,000 copies. That is, they added an extra three zeroes, and so it seems that the brochure *Workers' Opposition* has an enormous distribution, such which no other official brochure of ours has ever had. But essentially it was published in a total of 1500 copies, and that was published with difficulty. (Noise.) Comrade Riazanov further indicated that comrade Kollontai 'went to the people'. Our cause would be poor, if those comrades, who in a literary way express simply their opinion or the opinion of those who are like-minded, had to 'go to the people'. This would be a clear indicator that a gulf exists between party higher-ups, who conduct a certain line, and the rank-and-file, concerning whom it is necessary to go 'to the people'.

Then comrade Riazanov said that the brochure points out the disgracefully pitiful existence of workers in our country. Comrades, each of us who works in the provinces among the masses knows that it falls to our lot to encounter horrifying pictures of conditions, in which our worker comrades live, and you can't be silent about this, not for any reason. On the contrary it is necessary to uncover this illness and to show that still there is too little attention paid to this. Distracted by some big, serious tasks, we have not dwelled deeply on this basic question of improving workers' living conditions in connection with the rebirth of our national economy.

Now, comrades, I will move on to the Central Committee's report. Now I think I can say that we all have an excellent feeling in the depth of our hearts toward Vladimir Ilich. Despite this, we cannot help but say that his report yesterday satisfied hardly anyone. Even if no one here said so, nevertheless those comrades present here expected from him a response to those threatening and consequential events, which are happening in our Soviet labouring Russia. We expected that in a party milieu Vladimir Ilich would open up, reveal the entire essence, and would say what measures the CC is taking, so that these events would not be repeated. Vladimir Ilich skirted the question about Kronstadt and the unrest in Piter and in Moscow. He did not answer any of these questions.[103] Maybe he will shed light on it in his concluding remarks. No one, comrades, will deny that we are experiencing a difficult crisis. I think that the CC will agree that it said so several times in its resolutions. If this were not so, the CC would not have said anything about this and would not have brought this question

---

103   The editors refer the reader to pp. 33–4.

to a party congress or to conferences. From these resolutions we clearly see that we are experiencing right now a difficult transitional period, a fracture in the party itself. What has called forth this sudden change, this crisis? On the one hand, external reasons called it forth. Some difficulties arose before us. On the other hand, internal reasons led to crisis. First of all among these was the changing composition of our party. Indeed, no one suspects comrade Smilga of supporting the Workers' Opposition, but not even the 'Pugachevist' Workers' Opposition dares to make such sharp remarks about what is done now to us within the party. Comrade Smilga says that in our country the old type of ideological personnel has disappeared and that now the managers and the managed have appeared. One stands above and the other below. He points out other examples, which I am not about to bring up to you, but in which he most mercilessly criticises the situation within the party. The most important thing, comrades, is that the party recognises this crisis. It recognises that alien elements have attached themselves to us. Resolutions about purification of the party are accepted only on paper and are not implemented. I would like to ask the CC, why has the decision of the Eighth Party Congress regarding a purge from our party of elements alien to it still not been implemented? Why has the decision of the September conference to stop dispatching to far off places comrades, who from the point of view of the CC are like-minded to us, not been implemented? We know that behind the scenes comrades are definitely evaluated, in order to assess who should remain and who should be sent further from those masses, on whom they exert influence.

Here comrade Lenin said that we did not know how to take stock of fuel and food crises in a timely way. But when we cite these very words, women workers ask with complete justification, 'how is it that you are the government, if you don't know how to take stock of the political situation, if you don't understand the economy, and if you are not able to sufficiently calculate supplies, so as not to reach such a crisis in two or three stops down the line?!' Here, comrades, it needs to be said what is the CC's deviation and why these deviations exist. It is necessary to look around and recall that the Central Committee is an ideological, political, guiding body. Should the CC guide all our Soviet institutions, ideologically improve them, and direct them in a class spirit? Undoubtedly it should! Theoretically and in principle, we recognise this, but in reality? In fact the petty bourgeois social composition of our labouring Russia is predominantly peasant, with an enormous quantity of alien elements, who have emerged from the bourgeois world and ensconced themselves in soviet institutions. At first they influence soviet bodies and then indirectly the Central Committee. The Central Committee has to adapt to them and maneuver, instead of clearly and distinctly carrying out its line. We sense a deviation and accommodation in the question about interrelations with trade unions and in the international question. We know that a bureaucratic element[104] exists in our party. But again I ask the CC: what did it do in order to create conditions under which the initiative of the masses would be possible? At each party congress and conference, they speak about mass initiative and issue resolutions. Already at the September conference, Comrade Zinoviev put himself out on behalf of mass initiative. But what did the CC do in order to make it possible to realise this initiative in the provinces and in order to make it easier to carry out this initiative not only for the broad masses, but for party personnel? Are there circulars and explanations? Did you comrades from the CC send appropriate letters, which would point out the necessity of rapidly taking measures to create conditions to facilitate the display of initiative? Have you shed light on this question in the press? Have you pointed openly to that deviation, which now characterises our party? In this regard there has been nothing, except official articles, which have given no practical measures for creating conditions, which would allow the masses to display initiative.

But the main misfortune, comrades, is that we sense hidden distrust toward the broad masses. We sense that the masses recoil from us. At assemblies it happens that if you point to a communist who enjoys the trust of the masses, they say about him that he does not look like a communist, because he is trusted, so he is not like the others. This, comrades, shows clearly that in our country, communists are one thing and the masses are another.

So we need to search out where the blame rests. We should say here outright: the CC is obligated to itself to review its own positions, its policy and its line. The CC should straighten out its line on class policy. We demand that the CC should remember that initiative should be not just in words but also in deeds and that we need to create the conditions for this initiative. Before anything else, we need to cleanse the party from elements alien to it. Finally, comrades, we need to straighten out the line within the party in actual fact. Then we won't have to call for unity. Unity will be created of its own accord. It is the same with unity between the party and the working class.

At this congress it depends on us to create such a position [положение], which will strengthen this unity in actual fact, instead of just talking about it.

---

104   The word she uses, начало, can also mean a beginning, a source as of a river or stream, principles, or a basis.

[Summary: Iaroslavsky and Krestinsky speak. Lenin speaks, pp. 112–24. Part of his speech is devoted to Shliapnikov, Kollontai, and the Workers' Opposition. Osinsky speaks.][105]

Shliapnikov (p. 125). Comrades, I received from our Party CC the stenographic report, against which comrade Osinsky protests. They went to Tula and received this material from the party gubernia committee in Tula. There in the gubkom there was no Workers' Opposition. Comrade Artem can confirm this. There, he is nodding his head affirmatively.

Now allow me to answer a personal question about Tsiurupa. You would like to try me before a court. Please, I will even be glad to appear. A week ago, all our trade unionists who work in Narkomprod came to us, deeply indignant about the arrangement of work in Narkomprod as well as in the provisions bodies [продорганы] in the provinces. Frequently, they have appealed to us to support them. We then accepted that resolution, part of which I read aloud,[106] in which it indicates that we are in a catastrophic state. Comrade Tomsky knows that they demand from us that this question be posed at a plenum of VTsSPS. The Central Committee removed this question from the agenda, and now it dares to declare that I did not do everything that I should have done. We do all that is possible. But we don't always encounter that which we should have encountered. If it pleases you to prosecute me in court, then go ahead. I'm standing here. But my colleagues and I think that a significant share of the blame for that breakdown, which we have, rests on Narkomprod.

[Riazanov and Tomsky speak for a similar amount of time as did Shliapnikov.]

∴

Session Four, 9 March, evening. Iaroslavsky and later Kamenev chair.

[There is procedural discussion of whether to vote a resolution on the Control Commission's report. Olminsky speaks. Iaroslavsky reads aloud a resolution on the CC's report, and then Bubnov reads aloud the Democratic Centralists' resolution on the CC's report.]

---

105   Translations of Lenin's speeches from December 1920 to August 1921 can be located in his *Collected Works*, volume 32.
106   Editors write, 'In the stenographic report the reading aloud of the resolution is not recorded. Its text is not among the documents of the congress'.

Medvedev (135–6). On behalf of the congress delegates who are affiliated with the platform of the Workers' Opposition, I offer the following resolution:

> Having heard the cc's report, the Tenth Congress of the RCP declares:
>
> 1) Since the Ninth Congress, the cc has not carried out the measures which the Eighth Congress already pointed out for rendering the party healthy by cleansing it of alien elements which were starting to dash into it, especially after the suppression of the Left SR uprising and the disintegration of petty bourgeois parties;
>
> 2) The Central Committee did not conduct sufficient measures and did not create within the party conditions, which would ensure the actual initiative of the mass of party members and their communist education [воспитание]. The Central Committee did not protect and did not in fact implement in the party ranks the principles of party democracy, responsibility, and accounting of leading bodies before the party rank-and-file, and broad publicity [гласность] of opinions on all questions of building the party and communism;
>
> 3) The Central Committee likewise did not carry out actual measures of struggle against the bureaucracy that is getting fat off our entire soviet apparatus, which rouses the indignation of broad masses of workers and the poorest peasant elements. The Central Committee did not workerise leading soviet bodies in the centre or in the provinces;
>
> 4) Even within the Central Committee itself, the cc did not create an efficient and lively apparatus, which would be capable of serving the needs of the party in all the diverse branches of its activity;
>
> 5) In the most important areas and on the most important questions of building communism, cc policy deviated toward distrust in the creative strengths of the working class and toward concessions to the petty bourgeoisie and to the bourgeois-functionary castes;
>
> 6) Resolutely condemning the cc's vacillating policy, the Tenth Party Congress finds that eliminating the deviations stated above and achieving victory over all difficulties of economic and soviet building are possible only if the party will be organically and unbreakably connected to the maximum with the broad proletarian and semi-proletarian masses of the town and countryside, through soviets and trade unions;
>
> 7) The Tenth Congress believes that only actual realisation of the measures stated above will facilitate the elimination of intraparty dis-

agreements, will allow achievement of mutual trust between guiding bodies and party masses, and will facilitate actual and full party unity.

[Summary: There is discussion and a vote on the resolutions. Then Preobrazhensky, Lunacharsky, Riazanov, and Iaroslavsky speak.]

∙∙

Session Five, morning of 10 March. Kamenev and briefly Voroshilov chair.

[Summary: I.A. Ivanov, Krasikov, and Gusev speak. There is discussion about voting. Stalin speaks about the nationality question. Safarov, Zatonsky, Mikoian, and Burnashev debate, there is a vote, and Stalin has the final word.]

∙∙

Session Six, 11 March, morning. Iaroslavsky chairs.

[Summary: Bukharin speaks, pp. 217–33. Presents theses on party building and criticises theses of others on party building.]

Chair (pp. 233–4). We have several presenters of supplementary papers. The Workers' Opposition group should have presented 40 votes. It did not submit a statement signed by 40 people. The presidium does not object to giving the right to speak to its supplementary presenter, if the congress does not object. Who is for giving the floor to its supplementary presenter? Accepted. Next, comrades, the Democratic Centralism group likewise did not present a signed declaration with the full number of votes. It collected 34 votes. Comrades from this group explain that there was not enough time to collect more, but the presidium also does not object to giving their representative the floor. (The proposal is voted and accepted.) Also a statement, which was signed by 43 votes, has come in about a supplementary paper by comrade Smilga. The comrade signatories have full right to a supplementary presenter. Comrade Shliapnikov, who did not present 40 signatures, objects to giving the floor to comrade Smilga. The statement about a supplementary report by the latter is so signed: 'From a group of comrades, supporting the point of view of the need for an analysis of the Workers' Opposition and Democratic Centralism'. (Laughter, noise, voices: 'This belongs in the debate!')

Smilga (p. 234). The fact is that here at the congress there is a large group of delegates, who think that the resolution on party building, which will be accepted, should include an analysis of the opposition which exists in our party. This is not in the resolution which was distributed today. Besides that, this group proposes to introduce corrections into the resolution, which comrade Bukharin defended here. We are not presenting a separate resolution. We decided to put forth a supplementary presenter and introduce corrections.

Shliapnikov (p. 234). I object to the delivery of this report for the following reason. Presentation of a corresponding platform is necessary, which the Democratic Centralism group did, despite the fact that it did not have the sufficient quantity of signatures. We did not collect our signatures, not because we don't have the necessary number of people, but because the question was placed impromptu. As concerns comrade Smilga's supplementary report, well this essentially is debate on the platforms we have, and not a new platform.

Chair (p. 234). Comrades, the presidium does not have the right to violate the regulations. The congress, I think, will not violate the regulations according to those frivolous notions, which comrade Shliapnikov uttered here. (Noise.) Who objects to giving the floor? An insignificant minority. The floor is given to the supplementary presenter from the group, which supports the need for an analysis of the Workers' Opposition. (Noise.) Comrades, you are behaving completely impermissibly. The congress is turning into a gathering of rowdies [сходка]. Comrade Ignatov, you have the floor for a report from the Workers' Opposition.

Ignatov (pp. 234–43). Comrades, it was not so long ago at party assemblies in Moscow districts, when we intensely debated with comrade Bukharin about whether there is a crisis in the party or if the party is experiencing only some painful events, as was said then. Now Bukharin, when speaking here, indicated that the party is experiencing a crisis. It means that now everyone acknowledges the assertion and evaluation which was first made by us. Therefore, now it is possible to move directly to an explanation of the reasons why this crisis appeared. Comrades, on the one hand, the crisis in our party is called forth by external objective reasons, which lie outside the party's influence and elimination of which does not depend on the party. But along with these conditions, the reasons for the crisis also lie in intraparty phenomena, which are conditions that do depend on the party and which can and should be eliminated. If we turn to external reasons, then we will say that uninterrupted civil war and the onslaught of White Guard elements from without helped this crisis develop. On the other hand, the collapse of the national economy during this period also significantly promoted this crisis and to a certain degree accelerated it, of course. These are objective causes, which of course could not depend on the party and of course they should be dealt with as such. Further, besides this, our party has to rule in a country that is economically backward, where the working class is an insignificant minority,[107] and the majority of the population is peasant. The party has to maneuver and adapt its policy to diverse tendencies. First, these are communist tendencies of the working class. Second, they are the needs of the petty bourgeois masses and the peasantry. Third are the needs of the functionary bourgeois caste. These clashing circumstances have promoted the intensification of the crisis.

But, comrades, in noting here these objective reasons, it is necessary to address those, which lie in the sphere of the party's influence and which can be eliminated. During that circumstance, when the party was forced to adapt and maneuver, it had its own line, but its class line was insufficiently clear and consistent. In this regard, our party's policy departed from that position in our Comintern's decision, where it shows that the clarity of the proletarian line should not depend on the soviets' departmental [ведомственной] politics. On the contrary, soviets should adapt to the proletarian class line. Next, let's address external reasons. Because of military need, our party had to absorb an atmosphere of militarisation and military methods, which contributed to a breakdown in communications between the party's higher-ups and its proletarian rank-and-file. This breakdown intensified the crisis. It needs to be said that now the matter seems terribly acute in this regard. Despite having been immersed in civil war for this period, the party raised an enormous number of rank-and-file members, who learned and developed. Those clamps, which up to now were put on their initiative, are breaking under their pressure. In connection with the transition to the economic front, this became even more greatly revealed and expressed as crisis.

The crisis in the party began around the time of the Eighth Congress, where measures for eliminating these things were pointed out. But it needs to be said that the decisions of the Eighth Congress and those immediately following did nothing serious to eliminate these painful things.

The Soviet Republic and our Communist Party, in as much as it was strengthened and internally reborn, lost that uniform composition, which it had before the October Revolution. It especially started to swell when alien elements came into our party. Without having broken with their old ways of thinking and working, they began to pour into the party, after the suppression of the Left SR uprising and the liquidation of petty bourgeois parties. Of course, this circumstance in its turn, contributed to the party's loss of contact with the masses, on the one hand, and on the other hand, made the party all the more

---

107   Note that he used the same words ('insignificant minority') that Iaroslavsky as chair used in referring to the Workers' Opposition.

diverse internally. Here it should be said, of course, that the conditions cited above only facilitated the making of a special type of Soviet bureaucrat in our communist party and milieu. This was a bureaucrat, who did not assimilate the earlier communist way of thinking and who could not adequately be educated in the circumstances of civil war. On the contrary, he was cultivated in wartime and from him was created a type of functionary-bureaucrat [чиновник-бюрократ], who cannot understand communist psychology, because it is alien to him. It is completely understandable how this circumstance gave a certain direction to new groups, which poured into the party. Under other conditions, our party could have coped with this, but not in the context of civil war. When the party's most valuable proletarian element perished on the fronts, the ill-assorted new element could not be recast in a new mold. Due to this, heterogeneous groups appeared inside the party. These groups were just as alien to one another. Gradually, the party lost contact with its class, which aggravated the crisis. When we turned to economy building, we saw that our party was experiencing a deep crisis. Our party was losing authority within the working class. From essentially having been the vanguard of the working class, it is ceasing to be connected with it. We can see evidence of this in strikes, when workers force communists out of factories. Moreover, the mass departure of workers from the ranks of our party proves that our party really is experiencing a crisis. If we will think back upon the July resolution of the Comintern, we can see indications that after the communist party would break the resistance of the ruling classes and remove from them the means of force – schools, newspapers and so forth, then the infusion of the working class into the party would go at a more intense tempo. Finally, at the end, the party would include in its ranks almost all, if not all, workers. Yet now, when we see that counterrevolution has been suppressed inside the country and there are no outright attacks from the outside, we see simultaneously that the party is not attracting workers, as it should have happened. Instead, the party pushes them away. The reason for this is in those things, to which I indicated here. In this is concealed the fundamental mistake and here it is necessary to seek answers to the basic question.

Comrades, these unhealthy things and the crisis, which has now taken shape here in our country, set before us completely clearly and definitively serious tasks, which the party undoubtedly needs to consider. The party needs to accept pressing measures. It seems to us that in this regard, the party should in the first place create such conditions [for the working class],[108] under which it could again absorb its class and begin to lead it. In fact, the party should

---

108   Brackets in published text.

become the sole leader of this class. Indeed, now giant tasks confront us and we have to take into account the mood of the peasantry, which no longer faces a direct threat of losing its land at the hands of White Guard generals. Given the situation in which the working class now finds itself, it needs to be said that we essentially are losing touch with our main base. If this will continue in the future, then we will not be able to guide communist policy, because we are being cut off from this main base of ours, meaning the working class. In this regard, the main task is to pay attention to this circumstance and to create such conditions, under which this could not happen and under which the party could depend on its base and on its class, and could go forward. This is an immediate and principal task.

Besides that, it needs to be said that when the party first attempted to raise the masses' creativity and initiative, when it tried to directly involve the masses – and only by direct involvement is it possible to win over the proletariat, when we made the first very timid attempt at our September conference, well this attempt was not implemented. It could not be implemented, because the 'higher-ups' of the party instinctively, and maybe even not instinctively, did not trust the growth of consciousness of the 'rank and file'. The reason for the significant growth of this crisis, which we now observe, rests in this distrust toward the growth of the 'rank and file' and toward their consciousness. It must be said that the party should resolutely support the principles of worker democracy, cast off petty tutelage, and put its trust in the consciousness of the grassroots. In this is the way out from the crisis. We will not climb out of this crisis, without the initiative of communist grassroots and proletarian masses. If we only rely upon circulars, instructions, and so forth, the crisis will deepen and expand, no matter how many eloquent speeches there will be. It needs to be said very clearly and definitively that we need to get on the path of worker democracy. In this regard, comrades, the mood of the September party conference was very characteristic and instructive. We first took the path of worker democracy then, when the Republic and the party experienced one of the most dangerous situations they had faced. Probably, comrades attended the conference then and heard the report of comrade Trotsky, who pointed out the situation on the red front near Warsaw, when our Red Army bore, in his words, a historically unprecedented defeat. The party then found the courage to look in the eyes of reality and take a definite course. Now we should say that the party should not be afraid. It should resolutely take the path of worker democracy, not only when there is peace and quiet everywhere, but also when there is unrest all around. Comrades, it should not be forgotten that our party and our Soviet power can only go forth to victory and to the full triumph of communism, when the broad proletarian masses will be with us. If they will break away still further from us, as is now seen, then we, having retired into an even narrower shell, will risk remaining in this shell. Then we will not have to think about any communist society, for to build communism without the proletarian masses is impossible, and this we must firmly remember.

Comrades, I already noted here that our party, having taken in a colossal mass of alien elements, to whom the psychology of the proletariat is alien, has become significantly weaker, and it is necessary to turn special attention toward this. Under such conditions, workers will not come into our party like they should have done. By now we should have counted in our ranks a colossal number of workers, but instead we observe the reverse phenomenon. Some workers declare, 'I would have gone into the Communist Party, but it has far too many of that sort of people, with whom I do not know how to talk and who I do not understand'. This cannot be forgotten, comrades! Comrade Bukharin already made a leap forward, toward the understanding that it is necessary to more seriously and more soberly look reality in the eyes.

The Communist Party is supposed to be the vanguard of the proletariat. In it should be the most steadfast, conscious, and mature representatives of the proletariat. It's necessary to tell the truth. If we apply these terms, then it turns out that we don't have so many of such an element in the party.

Comrades, we think that to eliminate the crisis it is necessary to carry out extraordinary measures in the party. First of all, the party should be uniform in its class composition. The party needs to be cleansed from all the class-inconsistent elements. We can't help but say that in the ranks of our party, there are rather many of such elements. I already indicated how this happened. Some entered the party in order to fish in troubled waters and others because there was nowhere else to go. This process intensified after we crushed the Left SRs and the petty bourgeois parties. Now it is necessary to set the task to make the party more uniform and to cleanse it from all unsuitable elements. Here comrade Bukharin has stepped forward, which he did not do a week and a half ago. He points out that it's necessary to throw out that which is unhealthy in a class sense and unsuitable for the party. We think that it is necessary to halt the access into the party of all those holdovers [выходцы] from the bourgeois strata, who haven't worked in our party or in parties, which were revolutionary, before the Left SR uprising. Further, a thorough purge of the party needs to be carried out. The purge should leave in the party only the most healthy and viable from among the nonworker and nonpeasant elements, only those elements who have fully adopted the point of view of the working class and of the communist revolution. A thorough and exacting purge should be carried out.

Communist education [воспитание] needs to be carried out in the party. This communist education should mean not only that workers would understand Marxist theory from books, when they already understand it well in practice, but also that the nonworker element, which entered the party ranks, would understand the labouring proletarian psychology. There should be a dual path to education. First, any nonworker or peasant elements that enter our party should be obligated to work for a certain amount of time as a labourer at a plant or factory. They should study the simplest processes of physical work. In order that our party would not degenerate due to being in power, all party members need to serve regularly for a certain period at factories and plants. (Voice: 'And in the army'.) This is useful, since all party members are considered to be revolutionaries. (Voice: 'Were you in the army?') About the army, I should say that I was in the army back in those days when there were still no ribbons or chevrons, and when the commissar was at the front lines together with the Red Army soldier. (Voice: 'And now?') Now the CC has called me away from the army. If they send me back, I will go. We know well that there is also inequality in the army, where it is even more vivid and distinct. (Voice: 'This is demagoguery'. Noise.) There is no demagoguery here. This can be proven with as many facts as you like. Anyone who was in the army knows that in regard to equality, you see no communism either in the army or behind the lines. This we should say without any demagoguery, because anyone understands the difference between the communist at command headquarters and the one in the trenches. He who exclaims about 'demagoguery' just wants to conceal this difference by not talking about it.

But we will move on to the essence of the problem. We thought that many precautions should surround acceptance of nonworker elements into the party. Recommendations alone are insufficient. Nonparty working masses need to know who comes into our party. For this, lists of new entrants' surnames need to be posted in plants and factories in advance. These may seem to be trifling matters, but they really do have state significance. Thanks to our inattention to such trifles, very many alien elements have wormed their way into the party. Labour education is extraordinarily important. The way it will be is that each person will know that he will have to work in a factory or plant for a certain period of time each year. Very many, right now, not only do not go into the factories, but flee the party voluntarily.

Further, appointmentism to party posts needs to be abolished without any conditions. This institution of having plenipotentiaries and appointees must be ended! Plenipotentiaries can be chosen by a congress or by an appropriate conference. Besides that, it is necessary to make it so that each person entering the party would undergo a certain preliminary probation period. For nonworkers and peasant elements, a two-year probationary period is needed in order to receive senior work assignments and a year for junior work assignments.

Besides that, it needs to be pointed out that an organisation can be disbanded only if this organisation takes a decision, which contradicts the decision of a congress or an order of the highest bodies resulting from a congress decision. In those and other cases, higher standing bodies should convene appropriate conferences, where they would carry out reelections of committees or reregistration of members. In order to make the 'higher-ups' healthier, systematic changes in the composition of leading bodies is necessary. We consider it necessary that all leading bodies be infused with a majority of workers, who have not become cut off from the workbench and who are connected with the broad proletarian masses. On the one hand, this will make it possible to connect more closely with the masses. On the other hand, it will allow as many appropriate personnel as possible to enter through the workplace and moreover, will not allow cadres of bureaucrats to settle down in place. Despite how everyone says that the course needs to be held toward worker democracy, such bureaucratic cadres are still in the party. You still find here at the congress comrades who stand lost in thought and say: 'We are at a turning point here and don't know where to direct our path'. And this after the September conference!

The party needs to direct all work of our state apparatuses, so that our soviet comrades in charge of certain work would be more or less under the party's supervision and would sense its leadership. A certain number of party comrades who work in party bodies need to be fully freed from any other work. They should not hold more than one office [совместительство]. We think that up to half of the complement of communists should be freed for this work. Then comrades who will exclusively carry out party work will find it possible to take into account the mood of the broadest masses. They will be current in all their work. At the same time, they will make sure that our comrades who hold soviet and administrative positions will not deviate. This measure needs to be put through, for we have paid great attention to distributing all our comrades through certain institutions and giving them suitable portfolios, but we have completely forgotten about party work and about the masses. Now we see the results of this and we are staggering to and fro in search of a way out.

In order to cleanse the party and make it healthier, in the sense that the party would be uniformly composed and that it would have a tight connection with and influence upon the nonparty masses, the centre of party work needs to be transferred to the cells. Comrades, it needs to be said completely clearly that the cells are in no situation to attract to us the broad proletarian masses and for us to enjoy their trust. Such is the complete and clear reality. A month ago, the Moscow Committee still had not said a word about this. Well, presently it clearly indicates that the centre of gravity must be transferred to the cells. In this regard, we think that the congress should charge the CC with working out instructions for strengthening the work of cells. All cell members should actually make an accounting of the specific party work they have carried out in a certain area. This would ensure accountability and responsibility. Our party needs to make a resolute step forward in this regard. Otherwise, communists will become as scarce as hen's teeth and you will have no idea at all where they work and what they do. I do not doubt that the congress will charge the new CC with fulfilling work in the direction indicated. Practical steps toward this should be taken not only in words on paper, as it has been so far, but also in actions.

Further, comrades, I will say a couple of words about subbotniks (voluntary Saturday workdays). So far, we have placed extraordinarily great hopes on these subbotniks. We hoped that subbotniks would bring about equality among party members and that they would attract a significant number of nonparty comrades into communist labour. In fact, it has turned out that subbotniks reveal most vividly the inequality among party members. At the end of it all, subbotniks became an empty formality.

It needs to be said that subbotniks have not lost their value as a communist idea for drawing broad nonparty proletarian masses into communist labour, but they need to be carried out in such a way as to demonstrate that subbotniks really are communist labour, which is joyous labour and not a burden. Up to now, they have been a burden for very many people. When we have mentioned subbotniks in the Moscow districts, workers often have ardently dismissed them. When you figure out how to arrange subbotniks so that they would be instructive, so that specialists would be used at them, and so that they would bear a certain significance at a certain time in the form of definite political campaigns, then it would be sufficient for them to be carried out once per month and maybe even less often.

Besides that, we think that in connection with the new situation and new conditions of work, the congress needs to charge the CC with reworking our statutes. To a significant degree, our statutes bind together our organisation. Therefore, they demand to be reshaped, after which they need to be circulated to the appropriate gubernia organisations and presented for confirmation at the next upcoming party conference. So, in this matter too, certain steps forward need to be taken.

Comrades, I will conclude by pointing out that the crisis in our party will not be overcome until two things have happened. First, our party must take active measures toward becoming internally homogeneous and must cleanse itself of those elements which are alien to the proletariat and to the communist revolution. Undoubtedly, we have such elements. Second, definite steps must be taken toward establishing a process of labour education [воспитание]. Then our party will find it possible to actually strive toward equalisation of our party ranks. We cannot say that we now have equality in the party. Inequality creates frictions within the party. Moreover, inequality has an effect upon the relationship between the party and nonparty masses. Generally speaking, worker democracy needs to be carried out not just in words, but by actions. We will not emerge from the current crisis and earnestly tackle economic tasks, without the vital and creative enterprise of the proletarian masses. Our party should think about these basic positions. It should make the appropriate conclusions and go forward resolutely. Maybe then, having overcome this crisis, the party of the proletariat will again sense the support of its class base, we will have no more unhealthy things, and we will carry out work more calmly and earnestly. Then each proletarian and member of the nonparty masses will recognise in good conscience and not from fear that the Communist Party is the chief leader of this class and that it works to carry out policy in the interests of this class. Then we will overcome not only this internal crisis, but also our general economic crisis. Otherwise, we cannot emerge from the crisis and will not build communist society.

[Maksimovsky and Smilga speak.]

∴

Session seven, 11 March, evening. Tomsky chairs.

[Iaroslavsky and Zavialova speak.]

Medvedev (269–72). Comrades, during our discussion of the congress's agenda items, our opponents advanced many accusations against us, but most of all they accused us of syndicalism regarding the trade union question, which we have yet to discuss, and of Makhaevshchina in relation to party building. Now comrade Zavialova, who no doubt represents here a 'proletarian' gubernia, Stavropol it seems, advanced against us a new accusation. She accused us of defending the masses![109] A strange business it proves to be. If you go to the trouble of studying the documents which have emerged from the ongoing discussion, you will see that whenever our opponents wanted to set about practical resolution of any problem, they invariably borrowed from us. This

---

109   He is being sarcastic. Stavropol was a centre of trade and agriculture, but not industry at that time.

includes the question now under discussion. They took everything from us that was essential and then called us Makhaevists.

Today you received draft proposals about party building, which the Party CC promotes. Why did they accuse us of Makhaevshchina? Ask yourselves, examine the documents and you will see. It is because we asserted that in our party there are many alien elements, which are alien to proletarian discipline and to proletarian tactics. Even according to comrade Zinoviev's statement at the September conference, these elements prevail over workers by 48% to 42%. We asserted this the whole time and the facts supported us. Now for this they call us Makhaevists.

They say to us that we agitate against the intelligentshchina and that we want to build a 'worker' communist party.

However, we read in the theses that it is extremely necessary to resolutely direct the reins of policy toward cleansing the party ranks from noncommunist elements. (Voice: 'The conversation is about you'.) Thus, the facts demonstrate every time that when our opponents accuse us of Makhaevshchina right around the same time when they are trying to make the party healthy, they offer our proposals as if they were a new discovery.

Further, they accused us of Makhaevshchina for wanting to build our party apparatus so that there would be more workers in it in the provinces. We want to end such things as, for example in Ekaterinburg gubernia, which is supposed to be a worker gubernia, there hasn't been even one worker in the gubkom. (Voice: 'There were'.) Now, under the pressure of the 'Workers' Opposition', you elected workers to it, but until then they weren't there.

Thus, we strove to struggle against this evil, the consequences of which harmfully reverberate upon our party's policy in all the most essential questions and in all the most important areas of building communism. We tried everywhere to promote the building of fences around those elements, toward which we sustain obvious distrust. For this you can accuse us of being petty bourgeois and so forth. But we promoted the demand to build our party apparatus, so that it would be organically linked with the party rank and file and through them with all the worker masses. We advanced these demands, for which we were called Makhaevists or were awarded all the other kinds of epithets, which they could think up on this account. Yet what do we read in Bukharin's theses, which accused us of Makhaevshchina? He writes that nonworker comrades, who are elected to senior posts, need to have had at least a year of party experience. We maintain that this was copied off of us.

I shall attempt to show you the very same thing regarding other vital measures for making our party healthy. We have constantly asserted that our party has broken down into 'higher-ups' and 'rank and file'. The factors giving rise to this sharply agitate our communist rank and file, not the broad worker masses, but communists. We did not speak of this today, but one of our opponents, comrade Smilga, said that 30% of communists are against us and 40% are not for us. The Workers' Opposition did not have the opportunity to say one word, because its supporters cleared out of there. This was in Petrograd among the proletariat, which used to be at the vanguard all of the time. The talk was about Petrograd workers (Voice: 'About Kronstadt sailors'.) Among sailors, we did not have supporters of the Workers' Opposition. We can confirm this. There were Zinoviev's supporters, who were always held up as an example to other organisations. These things take place in our party. We spoke about how to treat these things. They can be treated only, as Bukharin writes, by resolutely turning the reins of party policy toward recruiting workers into the party ranks. We also say that it is necessary to turn the reins toward the creativity and initiative of the party rank and file. We constantly insisted upon this. We thought that we could overcome reservations such as those insisting that nothing should be done that might 'interfere with the military position' and so forth. We thought that if would put the actual decisive stake on the initiative of our party rank and file and reject all that rubbish, which we have to discard, then we could emerge victoriously from the current situation and as recognised leaders of the worker masses. As Bukharin said, distribution of personnel needs to be businesslike and expedient. Moreover, higher party bodies should assign and send comrades to be at the disposal of lower bodies as qualified personnel, but they should not receive any special plenipotentiary mandates and the like. We constantly said that this needs to be carried out, for only then will each party member sense the scope for his initiative, when he will see that responsibility for the party lies on him. Then we will awaken in each the awareness that he cannot remain passive at difficult moments. Again, for this we were called Makhaevists. They said that we introduce disagreement everywhere. Now it turns out that our Party CC has endorsed the medicines we proposed.

In this case, too, comrades, we assert that the Workers' Opposition proposed earlier everything that is proposed here. This 'Workers' Opposition', which they call syndicalist, anarchist, and now a new label, which is petty bourgeois, already proposed these medicines. Comrade Bukharin and the Party CC think that a shortcoming of the party needs to be recognised. This is that up to now we have not known how to nominate the forces we have to appropriate posts and did not know how to give sufficient scope to their development. We maintain that there are sufficient creative forces in our party ranks. We always said that these forces exist and that they are capable of reviving our influence among the proletariat, so that our party would again become the actually recognised vanguard of the working class. We were rebuked of making an error. We were told of the need to strictly observe forms of party organisation, which conform to the present time. (Voice: 'You are now defending Bukharin's theses'.) I repeat that here we see that these theses copy those practical measures, which we constantly proposed in order to make the core of our party healthier. In this case, we should say exactly the same, which is that we do not have to bring up the rear. We do not propose anything else. Examine our speeches, and you will see this. Comrade Bukharin, who is in such good spirits today, asked us at the Moscow conference: 'Do you have anything else to present?' To this we answered: 'That is all that we propose'. Then after the Moscow conference, comrade Bukharin said: 'Then we agree with you'. We ask: will comrade Bukharin now go along with us? (Laughter. Applause.) We see that all this is now inserted in comrade Bukharin's theses.

We are not afraid to say that comrade Bukharin copied from our theses much that he proposes. But when they started to fire heavy artillery at us regarding syndicalism, then he hid in the bushes. Now comrade Bukharin is not frightened, I hope, and will not hide in the bushes those proposals which they call Makhaevshchina? You are the author of these theses, comrade Bukharin.

Chair. You have two minutes remaining.

Medvedev. I will finish now. We cannot help but insist upon one measure. We suppose that any party member and any congress delegate cannot brush aside our proposed measure for communist education of members of our party.

How do we educate our members in a communist way? By writing proclamations, by listening to reports, by talk and only talk. We say now that a stop must be put to this. Any time, when we spoke in defence of our theses, they shouted at us, 'You want to draw attention to yourself at the workers' expense'. We maintained that we need to lean for support on the rank and file of the working class. You talked then about demagoguery. Of demagoguery we were accused by those elements, which never were and never could be imbued with the factory spirit. We want to set about the education of all our party members in a communist spirit and in a practical way. We maintain that our party and our workers should be educated in a communist spirit. But those who accuse us of Makhaevshchina are not educated in a communist spirit. We propose and will insist upon introducing yet one more measure, which is not part of comrade Bukharin's theses. We propose that not less than three months out of every year, each party member should serve at compulsory labour in a factory, plant, mine, or on a railroad. This is so that he, having arrived from there, would know how workers live now. These workers, who lived in terrible conditions under tsarism, who slept on wooden slats then, now do not even have these wooden slats. Then these party members will also say that they are supporters of the Workers' Opposition.

[Rafail, Shatskin, and Iakovleva speak.]

Kiselev (pp. 281–3). Comrades, it falls to me to start from the speech of the last orator [Iakovleva], who mentioned that the Workers' Opposition separates our party into classes. We should declare that we, the Workers' Opposition, took as our foundation the decisions of the congress and the party conference, so many of which have been accepted and then rarely remembered. Allow me to remind you of the resolution of the Eighth Party Congress, in order to deflect all that which is being dumped on us at the current time. At the Eighth Congress, when the question about cleansing the party was raised, it was proposed not to allow nonworker and nonpeasant elements into the party.

The resolution stated: 'Nonworker and nonpeasant elements should be received into the party very selectively'. It said that doors need to be opened as widely as possible to worker and worker-peasant youth. The theses of the Second Congress of the Third International say approximately the same thing. Nonworker and nonpeasant elements should be accepted very selectively. If you examine the decisions of the September conference, you see that there also it states that the obstacles to entry into the party of the nonproletarian element should be increased to the maximum extent possible. So, they link these proposals with us completely in vain. It just needs to be said that usually we completely forget about that, which for one or another reason comrades find it necessary to forget. We consider it our duty to recall those points of the programme, which were accepted at the congress. We talked a lot about what line we need to mark out to heal our illnesses, and for this we were called by very many epithets.

Here are the Central Committee's theses. These theses already reflect that about which we spoke. Today, comrade Bukharin even gave us an advance on it. They consider it possible to take from us that which they consider healthy and acceptable. But what do you think? Did some kind of revelation finally dawn upon our CC, perhaps? Bukharin's answer is curious. He says, 'The theses have partially become outdated'. Then here it was said more concretely what the shifting fault line is. I would have said briefly instead: 'The peasant only crosses himself after he hears thunder'.[110] We already said long ago that in our

---

110   According to Krylov 1973, p. 46, the proverb is literally 'If thunder doesn't sound, the peas-

country the broad worker masses and even the party masses depart from us and that the Communist party departs from the masses, but no one paid any attention to this. Now we just want to indicate that they should have listened to the voice of the Workers' Opposition and not simply waved their hands as if to say, 'Okay, Egor, Ivan, and Sidor are talking over there, let them talk'.[111] My observation relates to the lower cells, where our voices are never heard. If they had listened to the voice of the Workers' Opposition, then of course it would have been possible to avoid many defects in our party, in building the economy and soviets, and elsewhere. But, unfortunately, this was not so. You did not notice these defects, and only now is our voice beginning to be heard.

Here they accuse us of being a petty bourgeois party. When I was in the provinces, it was a little strange to me to hear such speeches. They said to me, 'You yourself are a petty bourgeois'. A certain gubkom secretary said so. I was surprised. Where did such a contagion come from? It turns out that it comes from the CC. I say so, because today from comrade Bukharin's mouth we heard the very same thing, about how 'this petty bourgeois element rots, it passes through the proletariat, and a great danger lies in this'. On the other hand, workers currently have dispersed, the working class at the present time constitutes a thinner stratum, and therefore they say here how there is a great danger in this. We already proposed earlier to cleanse the party. They beat us up for it. Now Bukharin finds that we need to cleanse our party from various undesirable elements that demoralise our party from within. There is chaos [стихия] within the party, there is petty bourgeois chaos in the Workers' Opposition. Now I look everything over and I think, it seems that we don't have people with a proletarian spirit. Surely those with a proletarian spirit are not those soviet young ladies [барышни] who are in the party? Maybe they are not really a petty bourgeois element, but a real communist foundation on which our party can be built? Comrade Bukharin, of course, does not think so, but from what Bukharin says to us, from what the defenders of the CC's point of view ascribe to us, I should conclude that there is not any element on which our party could lean for support.

Look at what kind of medicine is suggested. Here they suggest, 'It is finally necessary to begin to systematically realise the resolutions of the Eighth Party Congress about posting personnel, who have long been at soviet or party work, to the workbench and the plow', but again, the proletariat is supposed to go

---

ant doesn't cross himself'. Krylov translates it idiomatically as 'The time to lock the barn door is not after the horse has been stolen'.

111   These are just typical Russian names, not necessarily the names of any Worker Oppositionists in particular.

there, while other elements should be educated in communism. Comrade Medvedev already put forth points indicating the need to send all party members to plants and factories to study labour. We likewise propose another series of measures. Comrades can be elected to elective posts only under the condition that they will go through a probationary period of physical labour. They can occupy a responsible post not more than a year, after which they should return to physical labour again. With this will begin communist re-education precisely of those elements, which we need to educate. The link of the Communist Party will be established with broad communist masses. That hostility toward non-worker elements, which we have noticed among worker-communists who are manual labourers, will be eliminated.

[Danishevsky, Vareikis, Radek, and Lozovsky speak.]

∴

11th session, 13 March, evening. Kamenev chairs.

[Riazanov speaks.]

Rybak (pp. 296–8). Comrades, here we constantly see comrades flinging themselves upon the Workers' Opposition, especially those from the sector about which Riazanov spoke so passionately. Here in the higher party body at our party congress, they try to prove that the Workers' Opposition is very nearly counterrevolutionary. We have to remember how we work in the provinces and how similar comrades regard us in the provinces. When we speak in the provinces about how a certain imprint is laid upon methods of work in our party committees, thanks to some conditions, partially thanks to petty bourgeois elements in our party, who are often more developed than the worker masses, they persecute us as Makhaevists there in the provinces just like they do here. Understandably, we should say to comrades, who do not understand what kind of situation we are experiencing or what kind of things we observe in the party, and who do not understand how the party's composition is changing, that those theses which Bukharin presents in the CC's name take certain steps toward us. Indeed, maybe these comrades easily believed our opponents. When they will realise that Bukharin said the same thing that we did, then maybe they will also call Bukharin a Makhaevist and will persecute and crucify him. We should also say how up to now all resolutions, which were accepted at congresses and conferences, were not carried out in the provinces. Now when we will come to the provinces and will demand realisation of resolutions accepted here, repeating Bukharin's words about obstructionism within the party, there is no guarantee that they will not defame us. Those very ones, who will not implement the accepted resolutions, will call us Makhaevists. If we had statistics, then we could say that a large number who came from petty bourgeois parties are in the provincial committees. Very many of that sort is there. Also, we should say that Bukharin advanced inadequate theses here. Not only is it necessary to cut off the entry into the party of careerist elements, who are not our kind of people, but it is also necessary to create great responsibility. A probationary period is needed in order not to allow further soiling of the party. The question about cleansing it needs to be posed. We say that it became dirty. In the provinces, they think that they are defending the cc's line by suppressing all that is healthy in the party organisation. Here at the congress, some organisational measures needed to deliver us from this in the future were boldly illustrated. We should say that our future cc, which will guide by means of the theses which the congress accepted, should also make sure that these positions will be implemented in the provinces. They should not just remain within the cc or within the archives of all party organisations, beginning from the cc and ending with the cell.

Besides that, we should say that the report points out some steps toward reviving the activity of cells in enterprises, but in our opinion these proposals are insufficient. Both Riazanov and Smilga oppose presenting these rights to cells. Well, we should say that we, who work practically all the time, know that cells conduct only political-educational work. Essentially they fairly often do nothing. In the best case, they are busy having meetings and holding concerts. We should say that cells of factory enterprises need to know the objective reality and the heart of the enterprise, in which they work. In order to work as necessary and to educate and attract the masses to participate in production in a politically conscious way, cells should be up-to-date. They should demand an accounting from enterprise managers and they should know what is being done in enterprises. But now, neither rank and file workers nor communists know what is done in the factory. They don't know what they should work for and they cannot exert any kind of influence on the course of production. We say now, as we said earlier, that cells exist not only to unite communists. They should know what is done in enterprises and they should render influence on the course of work. Of course, it is impossible to say that the cell would interfere directly in production. Obviously, no one demands this and will not begin to demand it, but we say that the cell should know what is done in the factory, in order to know what to say to the worker masses. If the manager will not make reports and give an accounting, then of course the cell cannot carry out its main work, which is production propaganda. If the question will be placed otherwise, then the cell will be doomed to a barren existence. We should say that in gubernia committees and in the lowest uyezd committees, we see an effort to break away from the masses, to enclose themselves, and to lead work without contact with the masses. Maybe this is an extraordinarily good thing, when it is possible to lead by telegraph, but this is completely impermissible in party work. We see this fairly often in our country, and any attempt by party members, who are from the healthy proletarian part, to break free from this is interpreted as demagogic Makhaevshchina and as an insult against the bosses. Thus, no matter how much comrade Riazanov and others here might shout, no matter how much they might call us syndicalists, our party knows how to evaluate their words and will know how to separate off the healthy efforts of workers who are drawn into party building and economy building.

Kollontai (pp. 298–300). Comrades, we have to re-examine the question about our party building in a charged atmosphere [сгущённое электричество]. We have to regard this question especially attentively precisely at this moment. Party building should be thought out along with current revolutionary tasks, as comrade Bukharin completely correctly said. We agree with comrade Bukharin about one thing, which is that organised forms should not be perennial. They should not be fixed once and forever, but instead they should be flexible. We do not agree with him, however, about another thing. We do not agree with him that known forms can be modified, depending on external conditions. In his preface to his theses, Comrade Bukharin definitely says that the military-bureaucratic system was fully acceptable at one time. Comrades, there is an enormous difference between the military-bureaucratic system and the purely bureaucratic system which has reigned in our country recently. The Workers' Opposition acknowledges party discipline, but discipline does not exclude self-activity, and bureaucratism is a concept which excludes this self-activity. We need to pay attention to how wrong is comrade Bukharin, when he says to us that during the most difficult period we carried through a definite military system, which essentially degenerated into a bureaucratic system, and that it was the most expedient at that time. It is not true, comrade Bukharin, as you will recall. What did the party do at the most acute moments, when Iudenich and Denikin mounted offensives, and when Petrograd, Lugansk, and other cities were attacked? At these times, it summoned the broadest party rank and file to initiative. It expected not just discipline from them. Not even one representative of the Workers' Opposition ever spoke against party and class discipline. Let comrade Bukharin recall that at that moment we depended for self-defence on conscious participation by the broad party rank and file. At the present time, we are encountering more than one Kronstadt. We know that petty bourgeois chaos [стихия] unfolds around us and enemies of the working class and workers' revolution try to use this mood against revolution and against communists. At that moment, one needs to say to oneself that self-activity should be the main system, not only when there is the opportunity for a breathing space, but also when there is danger. So we do not agree with comrade Bukharin that right now in the face of terrible danger, we should somehow change those theses, which comrade Bukharin expounded to us. In his speech, at least, he said that the situation had changed slightly and that some positions have to be reformulated. In point eight of the theses of the Workers' Opposition, it says definitely that we should implement a system of broad all-out democracy, not only during a respite but precisely at the moment of danger.

Comrade Bukharin flung against us here a certain reproach, which also can be felt in his theses. It is that the Workers' Opposition is a petty bourgeois party or grouping. Comrades, first of all, I would like to recall again, have any of you proved this without a doubt? A phrase was tossed out. If Comrade Bukharin finds that the Workers' Opposition is a petty bourgeois grouping, then why did he himself say in his speech that the party now is making concessions to the peasantry and that it is forced to maneuver? Indeed, he says the same thing that I wrote in my brochure, against which there were so many attacks. Comrade Lenin especially was up in arms against it, forcing one involuntarily to recall the saying, 'Jupiter, if you are angry, it means you are wrong'.[112] At this moment, we see that the petty bourgeois element [стихия] really is flogging the party to death and influencing it from within. At this time the Workers' Opposition more articulately than any one else puts forth some positions, which we formulated. We propose a programme of party building, through which we try to gather the working class around our communist party slogan. Here again we differ with comrade Bukharin. It seems to him that the entire question is about cleansing the party. We go hand in hand with comrade Bukharin in this. Some of our points, on which I will not dwell, more sharply delineate how to cleanse the party. But we also say something else. We speak not only about how the party must be cleansed from within, but we point out that groupings within the party constantly influence it. Through the soviets, these very groupings demoralise our party. At times, they force to deviate toward petty bourgeois

---

112   A popular phrase in Russian, it is based on the Russian translation of a phrase supposedly said by Prometheus to Jupiter in a satirical work by an ancient Greek writer Lucian: 'Jupiter, you are seizing thunder [or a lightning bolt] instead of giving an answer, it means you are wrong.'

tendencies. At other times, they force it to turn toward those currents, which seem to us to be groupings. More accurately, they are separate ones, which are not outwardly connected, but they are internally welded together by representatives of the bourgeois world. These bourgeois representatives now hold posts in soviet institutions and so exert pressure on the very party with their psychology, their tendencies, and their deviation in a certain direction. Therefore, our theses make a point that in order to cleanse the party from these influences and more accurately to secure the party against alien elements, we need to make it so that in each party committee there would be at least one-third ... [ellipses in text] (Voice from seat: 'Two thirds'.) You are not saying the right thing, comrades, precisely one third! You think this is workerisation. No, workerisation in and of itself ... [ellipses in text] The question is about one-third of comrades, who would not combine party and soviet work. They would be comrades and leaders, who stand aside from soviet work. Thus, at the moment of need, they would be capable of calling to order those who submit to the influences of alien elements from without, who from purely departmental [ведомствен-ных] conceptions introduce into the party proposals, which from a class point of view should not be defended. Our Workers' Opposition firmly insists that it is necessary not only to reorganise the entire apparat (this we do, for we have some points, which supplement those in comrade Bukharin's theses; we already pointed out that the Workers' Opposition earlier proposed what comrade Bukharin has offered), but it must be said firmly and clearly that not just at a moment of respite, but at all times, we need a system of broad expansion of democracy, of trust in the masses, and of securing freedom of opinions for comrades. We need this not only on paper, but also in fact. For this reason, we introduce the point about freedom of discussion. Party tendencies and representatives of various tendencies must have the right to arrange discussion and the possibility to defend their views, for example to use CC funds to publish such a 'harmful' brochure as my brochure, 'Workers' Opposition'. We insist upon the need to actually be able within the party to defend that which we consider true and correct. Don't forget, comrades, that the Workers' Opposition is connected with the broad worker masses. (Voice from seat: 'And with Kronstadt'.) Comrades, you know that there was never a case, when the Workers' Opposition refused work and did not go where it was sent. Who first responded to Kronstadt, who first went there, if not representatives of the Workers' Opposition? It was certainly not the Red General Staff who went there, but representatives of the Workers' Opposition who did. That's who went first.[113]

---

113   On a list of those who left the congress for Kronstadt were at least four Worker Opposition-

(Laughter.) I repeat: when necessary, we know how to obey the party and fulfil our duty in the name of communism and in the name of the worldwide worker revolution. We demand therefore also the right, as a distinctly working class party, to defend the interests of the proletarian revolution. (Noise.)

[Mashatov, Tskhakaia, Murakhin, Smilga, and Maksimovsky speak.]

Ignatov (pp. 316–21). Comrades, comrade Bukharin defined the Workers' Opposition as a peasant opposition. His reason behind his opinion was that, in defending the principles of broad democracy in the party, it defends the slogans of an enormous number of the peasant element, which can be found in the ranks of the proletariat. Comrades, if you examine this question more deeply, then you need to say that when we in Moscow discussed trade unions and party building, then comrades who were CC members went out to broad party assemblies and drew attention to that which is the thorn in the flesh of the Workers' Opposition. They pointed out that the party now has a single base of support, which is the working class. We have no other base of support. Essentially, comrades, this is true. If we notice right now that there is a significant number of peasants in the working class, then comrades, we should know that there is not very much of a purely proletarian element in the working class in Russia, and we have to deal with that working class, which we have. With the help of this working class, we made the October Revolution. With the help of this working class we still up to now have defended this revolution victoriously. If you reject this and say that our working class is a peasant class, then it emerges that our party has nothing to depend on. Indeed it is impossible to depend on those party masses, which partially consist of workers who have long left the workbench and partially of elements, which entered the party not from the working class but in many cases, as comrade Bukharin indicated, after the disintegration of petty bourgeois parties. By entire groups, an ill-assorted, vulgar, petty bourgeois element was infused into us. Besides that, we have an element, which has diffused throughout the Soviet apparatus and has turned it into a bureaucratic apparatus. It has to be said that if right now we cannot depend on

---

ists, including Mikhail Chelyshev (RKP(b) 1963, pp. 765–8). Shliapnikov later requested that Medvedev, Kiselev, and other Old Bolsheviks with pre-revolutionary experience in Petrograd enter a commission to investigate the February–March events in Kronstadt and Petrograd. He did not trust one composed of people who did not know Petrograd workers. He also challenged Zinoviev to prove his allegations that Worker Oppositionists, instead of suppressing the Kronstadt rebels, had attempted to win over workers to the platform of the Workers' Opposition (RGASPI, f. 82, op. 2, d. 173, l. 13, 7 April 1921).

the working class and that the peasantry is untrustworthy, then you have to say doubly that you also cannot lean for support on Soviet young ladies. (Bukharin from his seat: 'I am not about to lean on young ladies for support'. Laughter.) It emerges so that you can't lean for support on anyone, for workers are a peasant mass and the rest ... [ellipses in text] the rest you can count on your fingers. It is possible to administer questionnaires and see what kind of elements come to us, but our working class is peasant. Well then, I don't know, who supports our revolution? If it is supported by the working class, in which there are peasant elements to a significant degree, then comrades, I suppose that we have to take the working class such as it is, for this is a historical perspective, and you won't go far with such arguments, with which comrade Bukharin loves to entertain us.

Comrades, further I should say a few words to comrade Maksimovsky, who said that the harm of the Workers' Opposition is that it creates division within the party, which intensifies the crisis. We have had to dwell very frequently upon this question. Often we were reproached for creating division within the party. But comrades, he who will abandon this demagoguery and will seriously examine the matter will say that the resolutions of the Eighth Congress repaired this division within the party. By this accounting, anyone could find definite instructions, even in the point about reregistration. If we reinforce this boundary by means of a purge, which comrade Bukharin also favours, well this is not meant to intensify the crisis, but to cleanse the party of unsuitable class elements, which have not assimilated the proletarian psychology. The purge should make the party uniform and close its ranks, rather than stratify them as comrade Maksimovsky imagines. So his assertion is nonsense. Further it needs to be pointed out that comrade Maksimovsky sees a crisis not of the party, but a crisis of the party apparatuses. Of course the misfortune would not be great, if it were a crisis only of party apparatuses. But the matter is more serious. This illness is not only in party apparatuses. It is expressed precisely in that obstructionism [засоренность] within the party, about which I spoke. The entire party is experiencing a crisis and not just the apparatuses alone. It would be easier just to cope with the apparatuses. Here you have to look at the question deeply. More rational methods of treatment need to be applied.

But I should say that comrade Smilga missed the mark here most of all. Comrade Smilga actually comes here and starts his speech with how great everything had been, before the party turned in a new direction in September, for from this came all the misfortunes, and so forth. (Smilga: 'Nothing of the sort!') Read your own brochure. In this regard I should cite the authority of comrade Lenin, who recently pointed out that if we had not made this turn at the September party conference, then maybe in November we wouldn't have been around any more. That psychological state, through which Smilga regards the moment we are experiencing, needs to be evaluated from this point of view. It is not so important how Smilga himself regards it, but it is important that this is not just Smilga's personal view. We pointed out some important but cautious measures, which the all-Russian party conference accepted, which could have eliminated this crisis. Then we encountered a whole group of comrades blocking our way and intentionally opposing implementation of these resolutions. Yet it was we who were charged with demagogy.

Just read what Smilga writes in his brochure about the failure to implement the September conference's decisions (he reads): 'It would be very good, if the matter were limited only[114] to nonimplementation of this resolution. Unfortunately, this is not so. The masses were offered a false demagogic slogan, which aggravates a small wound on the party's body into a large, gaping one.' Before this he points out that carrying this through would have brought about the death of the entire revolution. Further, if the party tossed out slogans like 'levelling' in order to come closer to the masses, well it seems to Smilga that the party demands a heroic deed from senior personnel. I should say that now we all must carry out a great deed for the revolution. Not only the party demands it, but also the proletariat demands this revolutionary feat from party members. Smilga here indicates (reads): 'So it was not especially pleasant for an old communist to have received an extra piece of bread for a workday with no limit.' Now after the conference's resolution, which pointed out the very impermissibility of combining jobs and so forth, now it is said that this is completely bad. It needs to be said that in the republic's situation now, there is a limit to these payments, of which the special feature is that they exert influence on the psychology of the worker masses. When nonparty masses point out that communists should provide an example, you should provide it. If we won't do this and say that we can't do it, then we can't demand it from hungry workers. I would not recommend to Smilga to write such things. Comrade Smilga accuses us also of conducting an opportunist line in the party and he indicates that we can be united only along a Marxist line. No one will object to a Marxist line. Indeed, we call on the party not to depart from a Marxist path, but we insistently object to a bureaucratic line. When Smilga points out the need to exclude from the party all those who belong to factions, I say, first of all it's necessary to exclude those who intentionally fail to implement the party conference's decisions. Smilga's speech serves as evidence of the existence of

---

114 In the stenographic report, this word is italicised, as if for emphasis.

this tendency, which is the root of the deepening crisis in the party. The party conference accepted some measures, which would help clear away this crisis, but this did not happen, thanks to the views of comrades like Smilga. Instead, the crisis developed further. It needs to be said in this regard that the decisions of both the September Conference and the Eighth Congress remained only on paper. This results in such a situation, when what is written on paper is not actually implemented. We object most resolutely to such verbal concessions. Having made the decision to take the path of worker democracy, one needs to proceed along it and not put up barriers. At the end of it all, barriers will embitter the party rank and file and contribute to communists stopping right at the halfway point at the crucial moment. Smilga pointed out that we need to consider the mood of Kronstadt communists. He claims that among them 30–40% are neutral and part of them are against us. He wants to take account of the mood among worker masses. But he concludes that it's necessary to grasp the wheel more firmly, to tighten up, and to put pressure on. But who will put the pressure on? It needs to be said that such pressure will not help the matter. We can manage the peasantry and that whole petty bourgeois element which now encroaches upon us from all sides, only with the active support of the working class. When they conclude from this that we need democratism in words but bureaucratism in fact, then there is no way out.

It's also impossible to leave cells in such a situation, where they essentially have no rights but only obligations. The cell has lost any authority and only transmits that which is dictated from above. Cells have not shown initiative, except in isolated cases and with little impact.[115] So, the cell has been discredited in the eyes of the nonparty masses. The party can be strong only if its cells will work together with the masses and if the masses will see that these cells really work for them and together with them. Therefore, the rights of these cells need to be clarified and expanded. We point out in our theses that the congress should charge the CC with elaborating instructions on the basis of these positions. Further, it's necessary to state definitively that the crisis which the party and the Republic are experiencing will not be overcome as long as the party does not take serious measures. These measures, first of all, should consist not only of purification, but also of turning the party's exclusive attention toward the working class, so that the latter would again raise its creative initiative and self-activity. Only under this condition can our party lead these worker masses forward. Comrades, don't practise self-deception on this account. Apathy among the working class is great now. Comrades who speak

---

115   He employs the phrase 'a voice crying out in the wilderness'.

at Moscow plants and factories know this well. They know that even where we put through our resolutions, they were accepted by an insignificant majority and most workers did not even vote. Workers need to be led out of this apathy. They can be awakened if we will firmly take the course toward worker democracy, if our party will appeal to the working class and to its self-activity, and if we will draw the working class into active construction. We should not be afraid in this regard, as we have been afraid of initiative among our communist rank and file. He who will lead people onto the path of fear will bring about an intensified crisis and the collapse of our party.

Now I will say two words about comrade Iakovleva. She accuses the Workers' Opposition of not implementing party centres' decisions. (Voice: 'Correctly!') This is completely untrue. Comrade Iakovleva cannot find even one incident in Moscow when this really took place. (Voice: 'At the gubernia conference'.) I should say that here in Moscow, of course, the matter was sometimes more acute than in other places, because we are located under the CC's wing. It needs to be said that when the MC (Moscow Committee) feels a bit under the weather, it calls right away for the CC's help. The CC helps with agitation, speeches and so forth, but when this is insufficient, sometimes there are other histories, such as what took place in Zamoskvoretsky district. Delegates' assemblies were not allowed to elect delegates to the conference. Before the November conference, this was a fact. But on the other hand, we should say that where district committees supported our point of view, it turned out that the leading group of the MC held illegal assemblies, as if they were delegates' assemblies, in order to put through its lists at official delegates' assemblies. It was so in Sokolniki. In Gorodskoi district, when we said, 'Let's put together a conciliatory list', they answered: 'We will not talk with you, for the only conversation with you is that of the sword'. (Voice: 'They offered us three people and 80 for them'.) If you disagree, let's go ask the delegates' assemblies. Then this heavy artillery, this sword, was presented in the person of comrade Bukharin. True, he received one-third there and appealed to us for proportional representation, to which we agreed. During the trade union discussion, the CC and MC were asked about illegal troikas, which were created in the districts to lead the election campaign. They did not answer.

How you implement decisions of higher bodies needs to be examined. When the decision benefits you, you chatter about the need to carry it out, but when it doesn't benefit you, illegal troikas are created. (Voice: 'There, where it is useful to do so'.) So, before making accusations against others, you need to talk about this.

I will not dwell upon comrade Smilga's evaluation of the Workers' Opposition. In my opinion, comrade Smilga himself gave a sufficiently clear evaluation of that line which he defends. I do not doubt that the congress will appropriately evaluate his attempt to convince that the conference's resolutions are not obligatory, because there are already statutes, a programme and so forth. I think that the congress will indeed say something about this. If necessary, it will exclude someone from the party. First in line will be he who sabotages these decisions. Now allow me to read forth the resolution, which we propose to you. (Reads draft resolution.[116]) We said little about cells ... [ellipses in text].

Chair (p. 322). You took 20 minutes beyond the time permitted. It's comrade Bukharin's turn to speak.

[Bukharin speaks.]

Chair (pp. 333–4). Discussion has concluded. We will move to a vote on the draft resolutions. There are only three draft resolutions: the draft resolution proposed by the CC and defended by Bukharin, the second is the theses of the Workers' Opposition group defended by Ignatov, and the third is the draft defended here by comrade Maksimovsky from the Democratic Centralism group. I will hold the vote in that order. The results of the voting are 369 for comrade Bukharin's theses, 23 for the theses of the Workers' Opposition, and 9 for the theses of the Democratic Centralism group; with two abstentions from voting. Thus, comrade Bukharin's theses are accepted as the basis. (Voice: 'The count is not accurate'.) In view of the fact that voices ring out about inaccuracy of the count, I request you to take into consideration the following. More than 700 comrades in all came to the congress. About 130–40 with a full vote departed, so 710 minus 140 equals 570. 400 participated in the voting. Besides that, the Petrograders departed.

So the voting has ended. We move on either to create a commission or to introduce corrections. Does it suit the congress to give the resolution to the commission, without introducing corrections now? We move on to the composition of the commission.

Tuntul (p. 334). A commission is proposed consisting of Bukharin, Ignatov, Sokolov, Iakovleva, Maksimovsky ... [ellipses in text] (reads.) It is obvious that the commission has the right to draw in comrades needed for work. Besides that, all comrades possessing materials and practical proposals can address the commission.

---

116   See pp. 651–6 of the published stenographic report.

Ignatov (p. 334). I propose to reinforce the representation of the Workers' Opposition in the commission. Of eleven places on the list that was accepted, two belong to the Workers' Opposition. This is insufficient. Therefore I propose to give seven places to comrades sharing the point of view that got a majority and four to representatives of the minority.

Chair. I put comrade Ignatov's proposal to a vote. A majority is against it. There is a proposal to confirm the list as it was read. A majority approves. The list is accepted.

Bukharin (pp. 334–5). I ask the chair to put to a vote the proposal that Popov's resolution[117] would be accepted in connection with the theses on party building and that the congress would assign final elaboration of this resolution to the commission which will study the question about party building. The congress's resolutions should secure the congress's demand that we should not have factional groupings after the congress ends. This question relates to party building, therefore I pose it right now. As concerns a concrete formulation, well it is the business of the congress to accept, confirm or introduce corrections.

Chair (p. 335). Allow me to speak against this. It is completely unclear what kind of resolution comrade Bukharin wants to accept. (Voices: 'It is clear'.) Let those to whom this is clear make a show of hands. I assert that the congress does not know what resolution you are talking about or in what connection. Is it in connection with condemning syndicalist deviation, about which comrade Lenin spoke, or is it in connection with party unity? We do not have a draft resolution. Each group has the right to bring to the congress its resolution on any matter. Comrade Lenin declared openly that he has such a resolution to introduce. We don't have it yet, and it is early to propose anything now to this commission. I propose to make no decisions in advance about this problem. When a resolution will be introduced, we will elect a commission and decide. Who is for Bukharin's proposal? A minority.

Comrades, you will recall that, upon Dzerzhinsky's suggestion, a meeting of the Samara and Saratov delegations was convened and it resolved, 'All delegates of the congress from Samara and Saratov gubernias, with the exception of four (two from each gubernia), should depart the congress for home right away'. The presidium confirmed this decision. I bring it to the comrades' notification. Comrade Rafail has the floor for a personal question.

---

117   Editors: 'The text of the resolution has not been preserved among the documents of the congress.'

[Rafail and Kirillov speak.]

Artem (p. 336). All supporters of the platform of the Ten should remain for a meeting.

[The chair calls the session to an end and announces that the congress will reconvene on the next day at 10 a.m. to discuss the trade union question.]

∴

Session twelve, 14 March, morning. Kamenev chairs.

[Riazanov, Tomsky, Zinoviev, and Trotsky speak.]

Shliapnikov (pp. 359–67). Comrades, today you are deciding a matter of the greatest importance. Should our Republic's trade unions be under the influence of our Communist party in the future or, despite comrade Trotsky's and comrade Zinoviev's travels with their platforms around the country's outlying districts, should they adopt the form of Menshevist, SRist and other trade unions? We disagree with both platforms presented here, but by no means do we disagree with them about the dictatorship of the proletariat, the dictatorship of its vanguard our party, or whether trade unions have a party spirit [партийность]. These questions have already been answered, in our minds. We will not raise them again here. We do not recommend either to re-examine or to resolve them. Therefore, we think our comrades are wrong when they claim that we regard negatively or have reservations about whatever we did not stipulate in our platform. This is completely absurd.

The existing economic situation dictates to us our position on the role and tasks of trade unions. Comrades, we are only motivated by the critical situation of our economy and by the desire to get broad proletarian circles involved in production, which accords with the programme approved by our Eighth Party Congress. So, proceeding from these two considerations, we advance our programme. Earlier, comrade Zinoviev and before him comrade Lenin spoke here. They chiefly objected to our use of the term 'producers'. In an issue of *Pravda*, Comrade Zinoviev mocked this word in what he probably thought was a witty manner. He said that in this case we are hunting for a fashionable turn of phrase. I should say that we did not invent the word 'producer'. This word appears in our Marxist literature fairly often; Engels is its author. (Voice from seat: 'Is he the leader of the Workers' Opposition?' Chair: 'Comrades, I ask you not to interrupt'.) Engels has the following phrase in his book *The Origin of the*

Family, Private Property and the State: 'Society, which organises industry anew on the basis of the free and equal association of all producers' and so forth.[118] That is what guided us, when we inserted the word 'producer' into our theses. (Noise.)

Therefore all comrade Zinoviev's tricky efforts to distort this word and his questions about why we did not say simply 'workers' instead of 'producers' are in vain. But I should say that if we had followed Zinoviev's advice, we would have been called 'Makhaevists'. The concept of 'producer' is broad. By narrowing it, you will push us into Makhaevshchina. By using this word, we embrace the aggregate of all people, who are employed in production. In our platform, there is not even a hint that we understood this word 'producer' to mean commodities producers [товаропроизводители]. So far, commodities producers, who are peasants, are not organised into trade unions here in our country. We will hope that our party will not organise them. We're talking about those trade unions that we have now, which include the entire aggregate of those people who are employed in production in our industry and who are embraced by our trade unions as producers. We categorically reject any speculation regarding our use of this word.

Now the second question is about our syndicalism, about which very much has been said. At one meeting, Trotsky even defined the degree of our deviation in this direction. He found not more than two degrees. Lenin probably will say it is more. But I want to say to you, the majority of whom are sufficiently literate – nearly the majority of you have a high school education ... [ellipses in text]. (Laughter, noise.) The mandate commission will tell us precisely. So, I think that before broaching the word syndicalism and inclining to use it, you will investigate what it is. I will not tell stories about this question, but I will read an excerpt about it from Trotsky's theses, 'Trade unions and their further role', where he defines syndicalism. I completely agree with him on this point. There he says, 'By syndicalism is understood the effort of trade unions, that is workers' organisations in capitalist society, to seize production without and apart from the proletarian party and the proletarian government'. This is how Marxists have understood syndicalism up to now. If it suits you to discover in 1921 a new variety of syndicalism, you can do this, but it will not be convincing.

---

118   Editors' endnote: He cites F. Engels's work *Origin of the Family, Private Property and the State*, where in Chapter Nine, 'Barbarism and Civilisation', it says, 'Society, which organises anew production on the basis of free and equal association of producers, directs the entire state machine to the place where it belongs: to the museum of antiquities, alongside the spinning wheel and the bronze ax' (K. Marx and F. Engels, *Sochineniia*, 2nd edition, volume 21, p. 173).

Up to now syndicalism has meant a certain essence [суть] and a certain world view. Judge this for yourselves. How similar to syndicalists are we communists, who fulfil the role of guides to communism in our trade union movement? How are we similar to such syndicalists who hope for worker-producers to take possession of the national economy without a proletarian state and without a proletarian dictatorship? I think that this name cannot be applied to us in any circumstances.

What moves us now to oppose our existing confused system of organising our country's economy? First of all, the current condition of our economy pushes us toward this. To the current bureaucratic management of the economy, we counterpose a strictly disciplined system of attracting all workers into active and enterprising participation in the organisation of our national economy. That which we now observe in our economy results not only from objective factors that do not depend on us. In that breakdown, which we have witnessed, a share of responsibility falls upon the system that we have adopted.

Comrade Zinoviev, relying on VTsSPS data, spoke here about the Metalworkers' Union's weak influence on production and on the organisation of production. He also spoke about the supposed gradual decline in the significance of this union and of its role in organising the metals industry. I must declare loudly that this is wrong. Of those questions which we examine at each of our sessions (we meet two or three times per week), 90% of the questions relate exclusively to organising the national economy. But the way in which we work is completely different from that of others. We conduct preparatory work by sections, the protocols of which we examine in the presidium. The section for organising production is in charge of matters relating to the metals industry, the secretariat is responsible for internal organisation, and other appropriate sections lead cultural-educational activity, production propaganda and many other matters.

We send protocols to VTsSPS in the following way. A report, let's say, of our secretariat is one question and the report of the section of organisation of production is a second one, but VTsSPS remains unaware of the content of these reports and of the number of questions. What was examined in each of these sections? Questions of an organisational character and of a production character were examined. Comrade Zinoviev's statement results from VTsSPS's ignorance of the diagram of our organisation and of its work. Similar evidence attesting to a supposed decline in the quality of our work is fundamentally untrue. No, the pace of work changes in order to accelerate the handling of those questions, which pile up at each session. This attests to the fact that we are up to our necks in work, but we divide it in a reasonable way among members of our central committee. We do not always have to consider each point of the agenda in session, but instead we can transfer it for preliminary elaboration. Sometimes we assign it to an individual to work up. As to which trade unions are more closely linked with the worker masses and where, we can say that this link is weaker with those very trade unions, which in comrade Zinoviev's opinion are at the top. Namely these are the Petrograd unions, including the unions of metalworkers, textile workers and chemists. I became convinced of this at the conference of the Metalworkers' Union. This is our misfortune. But we will only become weaker if we remain on that same path, which we have taken up to now.

Now the broadest nonparty masses make reprimands, but what do you think they are about? They are about unions' inactivity. In what area is this inactivity? Many may think that these are reprimands about inactivity in the sense of defending their economic interests or, as it is sometimes expressed, their selfish interests. No, our workers (at least it is possible to confirm this regarding the majority) have got accustomed to the idea that their economic situation depends on the general welfare of the entire Republic. At any assembly, you'll encounter a lively response and agreement with this from the mass of workers. If there are objections and indignation, then they are against the unfair distribution of our meager resources or because workers see that the fruits of their labour are wasted, thanks to that bureaucratic system which we assimilated over the three and a half years of our economic policy. We are accused of doing little to improve our economic situation. Today it depends on you to establish the course for economy building, toward which our party policy will be directed.

Up to now, we have built our national economy without drawing broad worker masses or even worker organisations into this construction. At the first session, Comrade Lenin already said very much about a 'congress of producers'. He attempted to impart a different meaning to congress of producers. Speaking about a congress of producers, we have in mind an all-Russian congress of trade unions. How is the national economy organised now? It is not representatives of trade unions who meet, vote, and decide. Sometimes it is not even even communists working in gubernia sovnarkhoz sections who do so. Instead, those who decide are the functionaries who lead these sovnarkhoz sections. Most of these functionaries are not connected to production and, as I already said, they are not always communists, far from it. So this congress of representatives of sections decides our industry's organisational fortunes. Anyone who knows how our gubsovnarkhozes are assembled will understand how abnormal our industry's situation is. We are making corrections to this abnormal situation.

Our platform comprises two parts. The first part says what should be done now. The second part is about management of the national economy after car-

rying out the first preparatory part (beginning from point 11 to point 20 inclusively). This section is about forms for organising the economy that have been
developed in their final form. Developed.[119] It follows that much preparatory
work must be carried out, which we write about in the first part of our platform. Preparatory work should make it possible to draw the broad masses and
trade unions into organising the national economy and not with that glacial
slowness [китайская постепенность], about which Vladimir Ilich speaks in
one of his little books, so that it would take until the end of the 25th century.
According to his proposal, everything depends on how rapidly large-scale agriculture will be organised in our country, in other words, how quickly we will
transition from the wooden plow to tractors with multiple plowshares [много-
лемешным тракторам]. Clearly, this task will take many decades. (Laughter.)
You laugh at your own ignorance. We metalworkers make tractors and we don't
promise them to you soon. You will not easily get them from American capital.
We suppose that now we should already apply to organising our large-scale
industry those methods of involving workers, to which Vladimir Ilich agrees
under the condition that in most of the country large-scale agriculture will
be organised. Only then, in his opinion, will it be possible to pose this question. Comrade Zinoviev is not correct, when he flings at us the demagogic
rebuke that 'right now' and forthwith 'in two weeks' we want to completely
master the economy. First of all, not one of us has ever posed the question
in such a way. The question is not about convening the congress 'right now'
or 'in two weeks'. We [in the Workers' Opposition] have in mind a definite
programme of action: what to do right now, what to do tomorrow, the day
after tomorrow and so forth. But we put the emphasis on 'doing' and not just
idle talk, of which all workers have had enough. We [party members gener-
ally] have much to say about a school of communism and about attracting
broad masses into production, but we do nothing in this direction. Maybe this
satisfies comrade Riazanov, but it does not satisfy the working masses in our
union.

Right now we propose first of all to strengthen our trade unions. In our platform you will find precise instructions as to the order in which all this needs to
be done. The matter also concerns whether we preserve in all their beauty and
grandeur those bureaucratic forms of government which now flourish. We put
in **here** [тут] very major changes, but we don't make fetishes of these forms.
Comrade Trotsky accused us of making a fetish of workers' democracy. This

---

119   Italicised for emphasis in the text.

is not true. You make a fetish out of deformed bureaucracy, but we don't. If we see that here or there a government body is harmful, we propose to you to destroy it. We propose to the congress to do away with the bureaucratic method for managing the economy, which exists now in our country, which led us to the current crisis and which delivered our whole economy into the hands of elements alien to us, into the hands of the enemy. I will read to you the description of our economic bodies which I took from our central press organ *Pravda*, no. 24, Friday, 4 February (reads): 'We lose sight of the internal enemy, which is a clandestine and very dangerous enemy, who has ensconced himself into our soviet institutions, having seized control of our production, distribution, accounting, and supervisory [контрольные] bodies'. This is stated in *Pravda*, and it is comrade Frumkin who writes so. Our central press organ writes about this and I completely agree with it, for if our friends were in our economic bodies, then you and we would not be confronted by a fuel supply catastrophe. You know that before this catastrophe fell upon us, in all of Russia the press was full of articles about the wonderful state of our fuel supply, so how can the result be that we have to stop our factories' operations. The VSNKh press organ *Ekonomicheskaia zhizn*, no. 27 declares that 'the fuel supply crisis was entirely unexpected for the majority'. That's what we've come to, under such a system for organising the economy. Further comrades, when this crisis developed, countless commissions were created to investigate the reasons for it, as is the custom here in Soviet Russia. Once I had the luck to be at a session of one such commission. There I heard Avanesov make a report about a counterrevolutionary organisation that sets as its task to introduce people into our economic and other bodies under the soviets, in order to play dirty tricks, impede, and spoil our work in all ways possible. It seems sufficient for a pair of good conspirators to appear in order for the whole bureaucratic system of work to turn against us. This is what you get under this bureaucratic system. We feel and see this and we propose a different system, which rules out the possibility of counterrevolutionary dirty tricks and the appearance of catastrophes, because the proletariat and its organisations will supervise development and management of the economy all the way down the line. We firmly insist on this and no one can accuse us of demagogy or syndicalism. The programme, which our party adopted at the Eighth Congress, is the foundation of our alleged syndicalism. It speaks rather eloquently about the tasks of trade unions and we develop it in that spirit, which secures the maximum involvement of the working masses in the economic life of the Republic. Without this, we assure you most stubbornly, you will not set things right with the economy. I think that at least one-tenth of comrades who can be found here are familiar with the state of things in our factories and workshops. They all recognise that in our country people often govern, or more accurately try to make do in governing, without the workers. This calls forth great dissatisfaction from workers and alienates them from trade unions.

Comrades say, 'How is it possible to allow the electoral principle in factories?' It exists here in Moscow, comrade Trotsky. Recently workers at the electrical station demanded, 'Drive away such and such a director', so we recalled him and put in place a more desirable candidate. This is the worst type of election, but we were forced to do this. We propose to have organised elections. Again, not right away, not today, and not even in two weeks. (Chair's bell rings.) I want to use the right of one giving a supplementary report on the same basis as did the preceding two 'democrats' [Zinoviev and Trotsky].

Riazanov: Give him four more minutes [to speak] against Trotsky.

Chair: How much time do you need?

Shliapnikov: As much as you gave the others.

Chair: Zinoviev, in my absence, spoke an extra eight minutes. Who is for giving comrade Shliapnikov an extra eight minutes? The majority approves.

Shliapnikov: Let's turn our attention to our practical work in factories. How are our factories managed now? Unfortunately, I was not present at the last congress, because I 'journeyed along the fjords'. But now I have the good fortune to be present here and to say that at that time they settled the completely scholastic debate about the problem of one-man management and collegiality. I assure you that we did not treat collegiality then as a matter of principle. Long before that, as the Ninth Congress gathered, we created glavki, one-man, and collegial bodies through our unions. Wherever it was necessary to have a manager, we put one person in place. For certain production groups, where it was necessary to legislate, we formed collegia. Why? This was because there were no people in charge, who alone could grasp the complexity of a given enterprise or factory. We selected two or three suitable chiefs. Realising that Ivanov knows a certain area well, Stepanov another, and Egor such and such a part of it, we formed a unified whole from these three. When we had collective leadership and management, it was also united. Now, when we in principle have accepted one-man management, no matter what, this single management does not exist, nor does collegiality. What do we have? Take a factory or a plant. There are bodies, which manage the enterprises. The first and most official is the factory board, then the factory and plant committee, the rates commission, the party cell, the managers of workshops, the masters, the representatives of the union, and various commissions. All these are bodies which also manage, to one or another degree, the factory or the plant. If the factory committee is strong, authoritative and popular among workers, and if the director or manager sent to the plant is an engineer or worker of weak character, maybe one who is insufficiently developed or ignorant of how to get on good terms with workers, then having wound up in this factory, he is forced to obey the factory committee and falls under its influence. Essentially we have a managing body: the director plus the factory committee. Wherever they appoint a solid, energetic person, with much experience as a communist, sometimes the reverse happens. He subordinates the factory committee to himself and the latter carries out his will. Wherever these figures are equal, when both the factory committee and the director are on a high level, we often encounter conflicts. Sometimes neither we, nor VTsSPS, nor VSNKh can resolve these conflicts, but only the Orgburo can. Those are the kinds of things we observe in practice. It is harmful to approach business without taking accurate stock of our experience. By your approach you will not settle the business, but will only make it more complicated and confusing. You will not resolve the tasks that lie before us by accepting the theses of the 'Ten'. Based on the experience of the provinces, we propose practical measures, which have been accepted by conferences of representatives of our factory managers and factory and plant committees.

Not so long ago, in fact it was just a month ago, we had a conference of managers and factory committees from all the artillery factories of our Republic. These are the most complex enterprises in our country's metalworking industry. We argued there about trade unions in a heart-to-heart way ... [ellipses in text]. There were Leninists, but supporters of the 'Workers' Opposition' turned out to have one vote more. Very few Trotskyists were there. When the business touched upon practical questions about how to organise production and about how to put an end to that mess which exists in the organisation of the national economy, then there was complete unanimity among us. We proposed to organise in these enterprises a special factory council (soviet) alongside the executive body, which is the factory management or the board of directors. This council comprises factory management, our factory committee, the rates commission, the chiefs of individual shops, and shop representatives in union departments. We want to link this apex of management with the entire periphery of the factory. We propose to assemble this factory council two, three or four times per month. We propose to investigate at these assemblies each major event in the enterprise and plan and discuss a programme of action for the entire enterprise, as well as for each shop taken separately. By this route we think we will arrive at a situation in which we will manage the entire economy through production unions.

We very strictly take into account each major and minor experience of our union and of its departments. In this regard our platform is just a completion [завершение], resulting from our many years of experience in organising industry. I say to you that no matter what platform you accept here right now, life will dictate not that which you write down, but what is fixed in our platform. (Applause.)

[Summary: After Shliapnikov, Drobnis speaks briefly, Tomsky gives a longer speech, and then Bukharin presents. All three say much about the Workers' Opposition, Shliapnikov, and trade unions.]

I.I. Kutuzov (pp. 373–5). Comrades, when the trade union discussion began, we trade unionists thought that the moment had finally come when our comrades wanted to turn attention to trade unions' work, role, and tasks. I thought that finally we will feel at ease. At that moment I had no idea that discussion would divide us into hostile camps. Instead, I thought that our party had correctly calculated the moment as the necessary time to pay deep attention to the trade union movement. I thought that it was already obvious to the party that the working class was beginning to take a passive stance toward all our institutions. And so what have we given to trade unions in the course of three months of discussion, with the most senior dear comrades having participated in discussion? Nothing. What will there be further? After Trotsky's paper, I think that we'll have to renew work over and over again in those conditions, under which we worked earlier.

What must we do, comrades? How are we to engage the masses who relate to us passively? They take this stance not only toward sovnarkhozes, but even toward some trade unions. You can't turn a blind eye to evil. The masses do not perceive broad initiative in trade unions. The worker does not see that the business of trade unions advances both to improve the situation both of the country and of workers. Earlier, unions said to factory committees, 'Comrades, we need to sack any swine under our employment who oppressed workers'. Who said this then? Communists said it. Who protested against it? The Mensheviks, srs, and the owners and their stooges protested against it. The masses were for us. The masses supported us. We communists said that kitchens [очаги], crèches, hospitals, and schools need to be organised. Why weren't these in the factories earlier? Who interfered and protested? It was those same elements who struggled against workers and who said that it is still not time for workers to take factories into their hands. Then the working class was behind us. Now what do we see? We built a lot of institutions, yet the factory committees and cells of these institutions or local gubkoms either play no role at all or play an infantile role in these institutions. This shouldn't be hidden. These institutions – clubs, nurseries, and schools – came under the jurisdiction of commissariats, which started to send people who were alien to us to manage them. I practically had to chase out from these institutions the kind of elements that our commissariats appointed. For example, former mill owners were appointed as school super-intendents and principals. The management of a factory club was entrusted to a former proprietress of this factory. It goes on and on. Factory committees and cells could not cope with this. Comrades, one should not close one's eyes to the fact that there are commissariats, which give orders to use good loca-tions for proposed facilities such as 'future' infectious diseases wards. Then the premises stand unused, while at the same time workers sometimes live in a room of six square arshins. Moreover 40–50 people are housed in this room, where there are no stools, no tables, absolutely nothing. Workers sleep on bare boards. Instead of pillows, they have logs to lay their heads upon.

I had to take measures. I had to put out fires when workers demanded the Constituent Assembly or free trade. You say to them, 'Fellows, why are you talk-ing nonsense? Come on, what is the matter?' They say, 'The fact of the matter is that we have nothing to sleep on. That's what needs attention'. I answer, 'I will call the attention of such and such a union central committee to it. It will help'. But what kind of help is there? No matter where you go or to whom you write, everywhere the most natural-born [натуральный] bureaucrat, pardon my expression, denies your request. Those comrades who settled down and made a place for themselves in the economic bodies don't have time. They work in commissions. They place in charge of departments those who are alien to the working class. In my opinion, at each institution needs to be placed a worker who would receive workers and would talk to them in their own lan-guage, at least for the sake of decorum or window dressing, that is. Otherwise the factory committees say, 'When you arrive at an institution, they laugh at you.'

Incidentally, comrades, I should state what are my views about the word 'producer'. I don't know how well those of you here understand Shliapnikov. But tell me, please, what does producer mean? I understand it to mean those workers, who work in plants and factories. In fact, what do they do now? Now they convene conferences and elect their leading body. Why can they not elect a body to manage the economy? They can do so through their union. We say that those representatives, who were chosen by trade unions, need to report back to trade unions. Along with this, comrades, I should point out that people now happen to laugh when speaking about producers. I have gone through struggles. See here we have the Chief Administration of Handicrafts, Small-scale Industry, and Cottage Industry (Glavkustprom),[120] where natural-born small proprietors sit in the administration and conduct counterrevolutionary agitation. Workers complain. You send a telegram, 'Indeed comrades, don't you have the revolutionary courage to disperse these swine?' They are dispersed. But they just go somewhere else and renew this counterrevolutionary nest. So who defends petty bourgeois producers? Not the Workers' Opposition. I don't know how everyone in his own way understands the word producer, but I understand it my way. Comrades, you should not in any case make fun of those very theses, which the Workers' Opposition puts forth. They have within them much that is healthy. If their proposals cannot be put in force right now, in particular after comrade Trotsky's report, nevertheless we should approach and train all trade unions for this. At this moment we should say that the Party CC should be obligated to reinforce trade unions and not VSNKh with personnel. I should declare outright that I have not received recently even one staff person from among those assigned to VSNKh and the Chief Committee of Textiles (Glavtekstil). It has to be said that we should be helped.

[Riazanov, Lenin, Andreev speak in turn.]

Medvedev (pp. 383–5). Comrades, today some of our opponents declared that the Workers' Opposition is not as bad as it has been depicted so far, especially at the beginning of the discussion. Now they try to talk about the 'Congress of Producers' as if it will happen in just two weeks. You all received our platform. We convinced the CC to allow everyone to become familiar with it. All delegates to the congress and all party members received our proposals, so that untrue assertions could be refuted as quickly as possible. We suppose that this will satisfy the CC. But what we need to point to here is that to which comrade Tomsky objected, when he told us that our ideology is that of the very top stratum and that it grew out of industrialism and syndicalism. This bogey [жупель] has been repeated many times. There is no need to especially dwell upon it. If anyone else had said this, then it would be possible to ignore it. But comrade Tomsky did say it and he knows personally all trade union personnel who are guilty of syndicalism and of industrialism. Comrade Tomsky will not dare to say that these comrades support the platform of the Workers' Opposition. Instead, they are in Trotsky's camp. These people are comrade Goltsman

---

120 Главное управление по делам кустарной, мелкой промышленности и промысловой кооперации.

and other comrades, with whom we work, but they do not support us. Comrade Tomsky knows them splendidly well.

Comrade Trotsky tells us that the Workers' Opposition fetishises the principles of workers' democracy. We will easily parry this blow, if you are just a little familiar with the documents of our discussion. Who put forth the 'holy' slogan of democracy? The Workers' Opposition? No. Comrade Bukharin, who now supports the same platform as Trotsky, advanced this slogan. As we have frequently declared here, we do not regard democratism as the holy of holies. Nothing of the sort! We all subordinate ourselves to the interests of the revolution and our whole platform takes this path. This accusation can in no way serve as a rebuke of our platform.

In just the same way, Tomsky resorts to the very latest methods when he indicates that it is possible to gather votes among workers with our platform. Think back, comrade Tomsky: is this so? Does our platform gather votes? This has not been completely proven. We know that there are not as many workers in our party as there once were. Workers are not the prevailing element in it. But there are still a lot of workers in our party and the majority of them support the platform of the Workers' Opposition. Concerning collection of votes, it must be said that our platform cannot gather votes. It is being persecuted, because it runs contrary to all those platforms, which were signed by well-known names. They gamble on their fame, but they do not develop the consciousness of party members. Comrade Trotsky himself frequently emphasised: 'It is not the platform of the Ten, but Lenin's platform'. This card trumps all others and brings in votes. But we are innocent of this.

Comrades, we must say that what comrade Zinoviev communicated to us here is really not that new. Up to now he has not said that if we have any organisations which have preserved a living link with the masses, then these organisations are trade unions. We now hear this from comrade Zinoviev in categorical form. But we have asserted this all the time and have made the corresponding conclusions from our assertion. If we have organisations, which more than others are linked with broad circles of worker masses, then these are trade unions. We say that it's necessary to link together with these unions so firmly that no events could tear us apart. (Moreover, think about this, what happened in that place where there is no Workers' Opposition, where comrade Zinoviev's rule has complete sway, and where the Workers' Opposition had no opportunity to present reports, make speeches, and join the struggle?)[121] We say just the same, that connecting with workers by means of unions insures our

---

121   This section was enclosed in parentheses in the published report.

party against a rupture with the working masses, but it cannot be a simple matter of good intent. We already said many times that our party should connect with the working class, but in reality we have done nothing. Comrade Kutuzov said to us here that the most painful places in workers' everyday life are ignored. When we wrote in our platforms about the department for organising workers' daily life, we met with derision. They said, 'You are presenting demands.' Yet today they say that greater priority should be given to the needs which we pointed out. This means that clearly the Workers' Opposition is not as bad as comrades said before.

Chair (p. 385). Comrades, debate has ended. We are moving on to the final speeches. Since we have cut orators' speaking time, the presidium proposes to have done now with the question about trade unions. Are there no objections? Comrade Shliapnikov has the floor.

Shliapnikov (pp. 385–9). When they try to disprove our positions, they have to resort to all sorts of dubious documents, because their arguments are so weak. Not only comrade Bukharin does this, and he has just acquired much experience in this at the congress, but so does comrade Tomsky, who recalled something that happened two years ago in a closed session. But since he began it, then allow me to end it by way of explanation. There was a closed session of senior personnel. Of course, if we speak about closed sessions in attempting to discredit an opponent, then we won't have any secrets at all. But if our opponent makes use of this, then I think that I also have the right to violate a small part of this secret. At this secret session, the matter concerned a place where some people spoke with workers using the language of machine guns. I said then loudly to all comrades that we cannot talk to workers in such a way (at that point the word 'Tsektranshchina' had still not been invented). Then, as often happens now too, they flung at me the accusation that I want to strut at the head of the discontented worker masses. To this we answered, 'If only it were so!' What does it mean to appear at the head of those who are dissatisfied? In our opinion, it means that one does not ignore that element of dissatisfaction which exists. If you don't want them to take forceful action from below, then take action from above to do away with those outrages which give birth to chaos and dissatisfaction in our factories. All the same, I recommend not to speculate regarding a special connection between the current platform and that session and secret communications.

The ideas of industrialism were always alien to us. I never supported them at all. Tomsky, however, personally supported them and brought supporters of these ideas into VTsSPS. All industrialists are the most active personnel in VTsSPS, both in the presidium and in its departments. If we are to speak about this, then it's necessary to observe how comrade Tomsky acts at home. It is curious that the chair of the International Council of Trade Unions has brought to you here nothing but trivial gossip and that he has accused me of not visiting Moscow factories. I chair the All-Russian Union of Metalworkers. There are two thousand factories. If I had to visit each factory personally, I would need at least five or six years just to travel from one factory to another. But these thoughtless people from VTsSPS propose to us to correct our ways and start busying ourselves with this! We don't even have enough time to speak with comrade-delegates who come from the provinces. (Voice: 'But will you go to the mill to work for three months per year?') Not just for three months per year, but we would go for good. Working in mills and factories has never frightened us. But now this is not so easy to do, since we bear responsibility for the entire union. We will not differ from you on this. We will go to the factories sooner than you. There are no disagreements on this point. Tomsky forgets that until a certain moment we and he were on the same path, and he forgets when disagreements began. On the whole, we often had disagreements with Tomsky, when the matter was about whether to implement the policies of our party congress, party conference, and union congresses. Tomsky, as Riazanov characterised him, is a spineless type of person. Not only Trotsky but anyone can get the better of him just over the telephone. The crisis is in that up to now there has been no firm will in VTsSPS in making organisational and production decisions. We did not see from him any leadership or any direction. We had no help in solving those problems which union leading bodies were supposed to resolve. Even in this area we did not enjoy the aid of VTsSPS. This, if you please, is worse than any gossip, which you collect against the Workers' Opposition.

Now, regarding 'shaking up' [перетряска]. Let comrade miners from the provinces remind you how they were 'shaken up' at the Congress of Miners. The Ten used their factional sessions and everything possible. They even made splendid use of those methods, which comrade Trotsky recommended. In this regard your camps have a lot more solidarity against the worker part of the party than there are differences between you.

Bukharin mentioned here some theses, which supposedly were approved by Shliapnikov.[122] Bukharin was forewarned that this leaflet was the fruit of provincial creative work. I myself hold to such a rule: if I agree with and approve something, then I sign my name to it. So it needs to be taken into consideration that I only approve that which has my name under it. Trotsky, who sat

---

122   Bukharin's reference in a speech published in RKP(b) 1963, p. 371 was to the Tikhonravov pamphlet published in translation in this volume.

beside me when Bukharin read these theses, finds much similarity between these very theses and those of the Ten. Bukharin's theses can be interpreted subjectively as well. Something from his theses can be taken out of context and ridiculed. The method of unscrupulous polemics should be avoided at party congresses. Why is it necessary to criticise one's opponents by referring not to their own documents, but to other, dubious documents? I suggest that you become more closely acquainted with that which we actually propose.

Our platform is founded on a completely different principle than are the other platforms advanced here. We feel that our trade union movement is weak because our activity does not have the required buttress of support among the rank and file. Each union member will say so. Many say here that our work should be the business of education and that unions should become a school of communism. Well then, show us this school's curriculum. This school should be distinguished somehow from just a labour school, a workers' department [of a higher educational institution], and other educational bodies. This school is and should be about production. A practical school of communism should draw into and join with production each proletarian who works at the bench. With screws and casters [винтики и колесики], cogwheels and rollers [шестерни и валы], the practical school of communism should connect the proletarian with communism and with building and managing the entire state. Trotsky's platform will not solve this problem and even less so will the platform of the Ten solve it.

Comrade Lenin spoke and declared that many members of the Workers' Opposition need to be sent into struggle against bureaucratism and be placed at those machines, which are especially intended for struggle against bureaucracy. We declare that this will not lead to anything good. One should struggle against bureaucratism not by playing at musical chairs but by contraposing a special system to this bureaucratic system. We offer a different system for organising the national economy, a system which from top to bottom depends entirely for support on proletarian enterprise. No matter how they might shout at us that this is 'committeeism' [комитетчина], this is all a trifle. We do not cultivate any committeeism. We strive for the creation at each factory of a single body, which would organise production and would manage the factory. I would like to know, since when have we become enemies of 'committeeism'? At the congress of unions, we will elect a managing body. In regard to the national economy, we also propose the following method. We will convene representatives of trade unions through communist factions, of course, as we always do. Then we will nominate those people, who we consider to have more experience and better qualifications to manage the national economy than those who are nominated now. That is what we want. For organising our national economy, we want to use the experience of many millions of people, who can be found in all corners of our country.

No other system proposes this. All comrades who have spoken here have concentrated all their suggestions on the apparat. In criticising us, what does comrade Andreev propose? He says, 'Office practices are bad'. Undoubtedly, Comrade Zinoviev also will talk about office management, typewriters, and automobiles, but will go no further than this. We transfer the centre of our attention to plants and factories. Our economy has to be organised starting there. It's from there, from below, from plants and factories that our organisation has to begin. There we can strengthen our influence on our national economy. There are no other proposals here. They only propose some corrective relief to that which already suffocates us. I think that I do not declare in vain that the following problem confronts us. Either our trade unions will remain under the ideological and spiritual leadership of our party or, if you will mark time in the same place where you are now, we will be overwhelmed by chaos [стихия], and communist trade unionists will quit trade unions, as is seen in the factories. Right now communists are being chucked out from factory committees. The factory committees are the foundation of our unions and they are becoming nonparty, comrades, thanks to the fact that we present only insignificant rights to our union cells and our party cells. We observe an even worse thing. We heap on them all that is unpleasant, and the masses are confronted with the following problem. The cell and the factory committee are like enemies to them, while the chief, who is often a former factory owner or engineer who worked at this factory earlier, is a good master [барин], who can raise wages, give good rations, and make it easier to take leave from work. That is the correlation of things that exists in the provinces. This harmful phenomenon undermines our existence and our economy. Worker unions, factory committees, and party cells need to be given more rights and the possibility to supervise the organisation of our national economy.

[Summary: Trotsky speaks, then Zinoviev. Voting is recorded and a commission is elected for final elaboration of the resolution on trade unions (pp. 399–400). They schedule a 13th session to elect members to the cc.]

. .
.

Session 13, evening of 14 March.

[The session was closed (p. 401) and its stenographic report was not published.]

• •
•

Session 14, morning of 15 March, chaired by Zinoviev.

[Summary: Results of voting for CC announced. Lenin speaks on tax in kind.]

• •
•

Session 15, evening of 15 March, chaired by Rakovsky.

[Summary: They discuss the need to end the congress on this day, by midnight or 1 a.m., because many delegations need to return to the provinces. Kamenev speaks about relations with capitalist governments. Commissions make reports. Kamenev takes the chair and says the decision to end the congress has been rescinded, but it has to end on the next day. What remains is to hear the reports of additional commissions, including the commission on the trade union question and the commission on party building, both of which seem to have been meeting during this congress session.]

• •
•

Session 16, morning of 16 March. Kamenev chairs.

[Summary: Zinoviev delivers the Comintern's report. Lenin speaks regarding the resolution, 'On Party Unity.' Kamensky follows him with criticism of the draft resolution as providing for 'unity in form' but not 'unity in essence'.]

Medvedev (526–30). Although these two resolutions, of course, are almost inseparable from one another, I will permit myself to touch upon just one resolution, 'On Party Unity'. Both of them are directed exclusively against us.[123] This is clear to us and we do not in the least deceive ourselves on this account. We also do not deceive ourselves regarding comrade Lenin's hint that an enormous, overwhelming majority of the current congress will approve the resolutions, which he proposed. We have no doubt of this. It can't be otherwise, given the class composition of our party, with the prevalence within it of petty bourgeois

---

123   He is speaking about the resolutions 'On Party Unity' and 'On the Anarcho-syndicalist Deviation in our Party'. These are on pp. 571–6 of the published stenographic report. English translations have been published in Daniels (ed.) 1993, pp. 109–111.

strata, of which an enormous number of representatives are at the current congress. But all the same, we have not lost hope that at the last minute there will be found, among the overwhelming majority here at the congress, comrades who try to examine closely and attentively and think deeply about that proposal, which comrade Lenin defends here. Each one should be guided not by blind faith in authorities, albeit meritorious ones, but should proceed from facts and should consciously defend the actual interests of the proletariat and its party.

I will move on now to the main question, which is the resolution. We already spoke and clearly emphasised the reasons for the disagreements that have taken shape in our party about the most important problems of our communist policy and our party building. We already talked about this and I will not repeat myself. This resolution takes the position that our party should show full unity before the whole world, which is hostile to us. How does comrade Lenin's resolution 'On Party Unity' help us resolve debate? It demands that our party should show complete unity in the face of forces hostile to us. Given this demand, the resolution proposes to achieve complete unity not by creating conditions that will secure internal party unity and permit the weakening if not elimination of the severe intraparty crisis, which everyone senses and which takes exacerbated forms in the provinces. No, the resolution proposes to achieve complete unity only by formally proclaiming the need for unity and by announcing punitive measures toward transgressors. The resolution, which comrade Lenin defends, does not ensure actual internal unity. On the contrary, its content patently contradicts those theses on party building, which comrade Bukharin defended here in the name of the CC. Here, the resolution on party building recognises for each party member the right to his own opinion, although it may differ from the opinion of the CC or of leading party bodies generally.

The resolution instructs that criticism should go through the appropriate leading bodies. What will this mean in practice?[124] We knew, for example, about the case with the Odessa gubkom of our party, separate members of which, as it turned out, were linked to the grande bourgeoisie. Former members of this gubkom spoke against us here. As comrade Zinoviev told us at the September conference, the Central Committee dispersed this gubkom. If we had tried to criticise this gubkom for its link with the grande bourgeoisie through that very gubkom itself, then what good would such criticism be? Such criticism will not help the matter. Besides that, the punitive intentions of comrade Lenin's resolution certainly threaten party unity. We don't close our eyes to the fact that this

---

124   I moved the preceding two sentences from the end of the previous paragraph.

part of it will be directed exclusively against the Workers' Opposition. Likewise, I think that you cannot deceive yourselves by thinking that punishments will help you avoid a new and even crueler crisis. You cannot overcome crisis by engaging in such struggle, but will only deepen it further. That's where this resolution leads, in our opinion. Because we evaluate this resolution as an effort to achieve only formal unity, we propose another resolution, which leads to actual unity of the party. I ask you to listen to it attentively. (Reads resolution.)

The Tenth RCP Congress, taking into account the entire pre-existing experience and result of party activity and summing up its work, directs all party members to pay special attention to the following:

1) Currently, there are again threats to the proletarian dictatorship and the existence of our Republic, which are not less important than when we had armed struggle against Kolchak, Denikin, Iudenich, Vrangel and others.

2) Given the colossal destruction of industry and all branches of the national economy, the extremely difficult situation of the working class, the enormous ruin of backward small-scale peasant agriculture and the consequent growth of revolts and banditry among peasant masses, the party is confronted by the most difficult task of struggle against economic ruin and against the danger of peasant revolts and banditry.

3) In order to fulfil the tasks indicated above, our party should become more powerful and more cohesive than it has been up to now. The party should indissolubly and organically connect with nonparty mass proletarian trade unions through the party's disciplined and resolute cadres, who are conscious in a communist sense. This is necessary in order for the party to preserve cadres' full trust and, with their aid, to become the complete and acknowledged leader of the entire working class, the proletarian masses of our Republic.

Therefore the Tenth Congress of the RCP resolves:

1) All party leading bodies and party members should resolutely condemn and repulse leading party bodies' policy that deviates toward distrust in the creative strengths of the working class, for this policy has made workers distrust the party.

2) The CC should prepare and implement the party's cleansing of all careerist, bureaucratic groups, and socially alien elements who adhere to the party for mercenary reasons.

3) To steadfastly and resolutely implement principles of workers' democracy throughout the party's internal structure from below to above and in all areas of its activity.

4) Just as staunchly and resolutely to implement workerisation of leading soviet bodies and to struggle against the bureaucratism which rots our

soviet apparat, exasperates broad worker and labourer masses of the Republic, and calls forth from among them distrust toward the party.

5)   All leading party bodies and party members are charged with the obligation to struggle resolutely against any attempts to apply any direct or concealed repression against dissenting party members, who do not violate in their party work the principles of worker democracy and the resolutions of party congresses and conferences.

6)   Along with this, the Tenth Congress considers that the obligatory and actual implementation of the measures indicated above will create all the necessary conditions for each party member's display of creativity, initiative, enterprise, and real, active participation in resolving all problems of party life and will effectively eliminate distrust between the mass of members and leading party bodies and ensure full party unity, which is especially necessary at the current very difficult time for the party.

7)   Under these conditions, the congress considers that organisational consolidation of special groups or factions within the party, along with the formation of leading factional centres and demands for group or factional discipline, will lead unavoidably to the weakening of amicable party work, which is especially necessary now. It will also lead to deeper disagreements on individual questions and possibly to the conditions for a party split and for the downfall of the dictatorship of the proletariat.

Therefore, the Congress instructs the CC to steadfastly implement the conditions laid out above, which will ensure party unity, and to resolutely struggle by all means with the organisation of such groups and factions, even by excluding them from the ranks of our party entirely'.

This is the resolution which we propose in place of that, which comrade Lenin introduced and defended, which does not say anything about what conditions are needed for actual party unity. Our resolution tells about the conditions necessary for real unity. We completely agree with comrade Lenin regarding interpretation of the word 'deviation' [уклон], but we speak about the danger of a deviation toward distrust in the strengths of the working class. We mean that deviation which undermined the working class's trust in our party and in the future is capable of bringing about an outright breach within the party.

We fully accept in this sense comrade Lenin's interpretation of this word 'deviation'. There you have the remarks, which we find it necessary to add.

Shliapnikov (pp. 530–2). The question about party unity is posed utterly from a different direction. Vladimir Ilich lectured you about how unity cannot be achieved. Neither in my twenty years in the party nor during the course of my entire life, have I seen or read anything more demagogic and slanderous than this resolution. Beginning from the first lines, the resolution claims that who else but the Workers' Opposition is a throng of Mensheviks and White Guards of all types! But look at the signatures under our theses and likewise at the list of comrades, who were at the private meeting. Among 41 people who share our point of view [единомышленники], 16 people entered our party before 1905 and the remaining 25 entered before the war. Among them there is not one Menshevik. There is not even one who disavowed another party before joining us. You probably know this already. Likewise, there are no signatures of Mensheviks under those theses, which we published. (Voice: 'There is! Arutiuniants entered the party in 1920.') There is not one!

Now I will say a few words about 'producers' and about point 13 of our theses. Twelve points precede point 13. You can't in good conscience criticise a whole set of theses by excerpting from it one thesis and putting paramount importance upon it. Such a victory is too cheap! Before the 13th thesis, we have point 11, which says, 'fully developed forms of economic management'. Only after point 11 comes point 13 about how, in our opinion, such forms of economic management should be fully developed. This does not mean that we propose now, immediately, without preliminary work, to begin realising point 13. Therefore the formulation about 'anarchist deviation' provided in the resolution is completely demagogic. As concerns the word 'producer', well it is not used less often in that discussion collection, which comrade Zinoviev edited or in articles written by his closest collaborators, yet no one finds there an 'anarchist deviation'. We don't have peasant trade unions. When we speak here about 'producers', we have in mind not small-scale commodities producers, but factory workers, employees and all personnel necessary for production. If we had been talking only about workers, without having in mind all other participants in factory labour, then both comrade Lenin and comrade Zinoviev would have been correct to call us Makhaevists. We are not Makhaevists and so we adopted a word that in our opinion was broader.

Next, the beginning of the resolution is not at all connected with its end. The sixth point proposes to you to condemn that which the second section suggests only to discuss. There it is said, 'A place should be allotted for thorough exchange of opinions by party members on all questions indicated'. One understands from this that opinion on this question is not completely certain and that an exchange of opinions is still needed. But at the same time, they propose right away to 'condemn'. You cannot tie these two ends together. Comrades, there is no hiding it, we should declare to you that acceptance of this resolution will introduce into our party not unity, but a split. Comrades who told me so today are members of districts where ¾ of the organisation consists of supporters of the Workers' Opposition. When they receive this document in the provinces, it will produce an impression of schism and will sow dissension. We ask you to reject the proposed resolution.

In the name of the Workers' Opposition group, I am here to read the following declaration:

'The group of delegates of the Tenth RCP Congress who support the platform of the Workers' Opposition, having heard the draft resolution "On the Syndicalist and Anarchist Deviation in our Party", declares that:

1) The resolution as introduced bears a clearly demagogic and impermissible character, for it introduces into the worker milieu of our party a schism, and it sets the petty bourgeois bureaucratic elements of the party against the worker part.

2) The point of view of the Workers' Opposition about the trade union movement and organisation of the national economy is diametrically opposed to anarchism and syndicalism. The Workers' Opposition does not contrapose economics to politics, does not reject political struggle, and does not reject either the dictatorship of the proletariat, or the leading role of the party, or the significance of Soviets as bodies of power. The Workers' Opposition, just like the Group of Ten, the Group of Eighteen and others, tries to conduct and realise its line through our RCP, but not aside from it and against it.

3) By means of point 3, "Organisation of management of the entire national economy belongs to the All-Russian Congress of Producers, united into professional and production unions, which elect a central body managing the entire national economy of the Republic", the Workers' Opposition proposes to make a reality of the soviet system in the management of the national economy, in counterweight to all-consuming bureaucratism. The word "producers" embraces all persons who are employed in factories and industrial plants. It does not mean the peasantry, since we have no trade unions of peasants.

4) Up to now, despite the bogeys [жупели] and thunder expended against us, no one has proven to us that our views are mistaken. The situation of the national economy and likewise the practice of hundreds and thousands of workers, who are old party personnel, only confirms our basic thought and position on the need to attract the proletariat into economy building.

5) In the interests of intraparty unity, the Workers' Opposition proposes rejection of the unworthy resolution. If it is accepted, all those who support the views of the Workers' Opposition will be forced to refuse entry

into the CC RCP, possibly to resign from all other senior positions, and to transfer discussion of dishonorable methods of struggle against the Workers' Opposition to the court of the international communist proletariat'. It stands to reason, comrades, that once you stick to me the name 'anarcho-syndicalist', even with the great reservation that it is a 'deviation', I cannot be an authoritative member of the CC. I offer you my resignation.

[Radek speaks next.]

Ignatov (pp. 534–5). Comrade Lenin asserted that we require in our ranks the greatest possible cohesion and unity at this difficult time for the Republic. Comrade Radek emphasised and intensified this idea. But comrades, I have to tell you not in my words but in the words of a comrade who is present here, who supports comrade Lenin's point of view on the trade union question, and who having emerged after comrade Lenin's concluding speech on the CC report, said, 'On the trade union question I agree with you, but I declare that after such a resolution is accepted there will be no workers in our party'. These are the words of a comrade, who supported comrade Lenin on the trade unions, together with you. (Voices from seats: 'Name names!') If it is demanded, I can name names. Comrades, I have to say that the resolution here essentially talks about formal unity, but not about actual unity. If you attentively follow this entire resolution point by point, then it is clear that it provides a new slogan, so to speak, a new sign that the demagogy which we have had in the party will assume monstrously exaggerated forms. This, comrades, we should not forget! Both comrade Lenin and comrade Radek point out that we need now maximal unity and cohesion.

Comrade Radek indicated that the CC might make mistakes, but it's necessary for the party to implement them. No one objects to the need to implement a decision of our party centre. But I should point out that in Moscow before the September conference, **rank-and-file comrades** [italicised in text] started to raise a protest against the CC position then, these protests found expression in the resolution of the September conference, and comrade Lenin authoritatively declared, 'If this had not happened then in September, we would have been derailed.' But with the resolution proposed now, you eliminate the possibility to discuss any problems within the party. Here everything gets tossed in a heap. Instead of real principles of worker democracy, you get suspension of any discussion and cessation of any vital idea within the party. That is why it is necessary to take note of this and talk about it. If comrades think that condemnation of groupings, deviations, syndicalism and so forth is necessary, then it is necessary to talk about this in general form. No one will be for syndicalism! But you can't conclude from this that one part of the party should be set against another part, for this is what the proposed resolution leads to. Comrades, I appeal to members of the congress. He who really wants unity and does not want separate groups stirred up against one another will reject this proposal. If deviations and so forth need to be condemned, then let's talk about it in a different way. You can't talk about unity by proposing to set one section of the party against another section. I hope that comrades who are members of the congress will regard this question with extraordinary seriousness.

[Summary: Lenin gives the concluding speech. The chair turns to voting the resolutions presented by Lenin and Medvedev. Various people take the floor to offer corrections or supplements. The vote is taken.]

Kiselev (pp. 543–4). Comrades, you just accepted the resolution 'On Unity', in which it says that CC members, candidate members, and the Control Commission, if necessary, will exclude members of the CC and of course party members. It turns out that 2/3 of votes in the CC are required to exclude someone. Comrades, yesterday here I was elected as a candidate. Now, comrades, I find myself in an extraordinarily embarrassing position, because here we have no way of tying the two ends together. Maybe the congress will explain it to me. Vladimir Ilich said that we will not have to apply this point, he hopes, but nevertheless the point remains. Vladimir Ilich picturesquely expressed the need to 'set up machine guns'. So out of 30 or 45 people, I alone will sit behind the machine gun and probably will have to shoot. I will have to shoot from this machine gun, not at comrades from the Ten, of course, but I will have to shoot at those who either adhered to the Workers' Opposition or who are representatives of other groups which are inclined toward opposition. (Noise, voices from the seats: 'Tolstoyan!') Allow me, comrades, to say the following. Here you accepted point four, where it says: '… It is necessary that each party organisation should most strictly ensure that there be no factional speeches or acts'. When comrade Riazanov suggested a correction, Vladimir Ilich explained that he does not exclude the possibility of elections on the basis of platforms, meaning factional acts. He rejected comrade Riazanov's correction. But now they ask in what position will the 'machine gunners', meaning those people you elected, be placed? How will they regard the fact that there will nevertheless be platforms? But in fact, obviously, there will be only one platform and no others. I will be forced, obviously, to shoot at all those who offer a different platform. Comrades, I cannot agree to play the role of a 'machine gunner' in such conditions. Therefore I resign my candidacy and I hope … [ellipses in text] (Noise. Chair: 'Comrades, calm down. Comrade Kiselev, I cannot …' [ellipses in text]) I don't know what, am I at a peasant congress, where peasants have dragged me across the floor? I hope that the congress will pay heed to such a declaration. Despite its resolution, it will not force me to shoot at my comrades from a machine gun. (Noise.)

[Summary: Lenin then spoke briefly (p. 544), apologising for using the term 'machine gun' and promising Kiselev that neither he nor anyone else would be forced to shoot. Then Ignatov proposed to vote on two resolutions about party unity and said he could not support Lenin's resolution as it was formulated. The chair clarified that those who vote against Lenin's resolution are not voting against unity, but for Medvedev's resolution. Then there is discussion of the voting method and a mention that 200 members are absent and were also absent from the CC election. Tomsky gives the report of the trade union resolution commission and subcommission. Trotsky makes a few observations. Shliapnikov (p. 546) says, 'The attitude of the Workers' Opposition to the reworked theses is the same as it was before, which is negative, it follows.' The vote is held. The next business is Bukharin's report on the work of the commission on party building. He speaks briefly. Ignatov says, 'Comrade Bukharin said that there were no essential disagreements in the commission. I should state that all corrections of a principled nature which I introduced, received just one vote, which was mine. The commission accepted some corrections, which were suggested to us. We think that the resolution improves upon the earlier draft. Undoubtedly this is a step forward. Therefore, we will abstain from voting.' Shliapnikov followed with, 'This resolution is not good enough to vote "for" it'. The vote is held. Some other brief reports are given and voted upon. Zinoviev and Medvedev (p. 549) make brief remarks about the Odessa party organisation. Lenin delivers the concluding speech. The congress ends.]

Resolutions:

'On Party Unity', 571–3;
'On the Syndicalist and Anarchist Deviation in our Party', 574–6.[125]

On Members of the Workers' Opposition elected to the Party CC (p. 577):
The congress calls on all members of the dispersed group the Workers' Opposition to submit to party discipline. It obligates them to remain in the posts entrusted to them, without making any resignations.

---

125   English translations were published in Daniels (ed.) 1993.

Materials:

Resolution on Party Building proposed by the Workers' Opposition (pp. 651–6).

1. In view of the crisis, which the RCP is experiencing, the Tenth RCP Congress finds it necessary to expound upon the causes of this crisis and to immediately eliminate those which are susceptible to the party's direct influence. Both **external** [italicised in published text] causes, which lie outside the party's influence, and **intraparty** [italicised in published text] causes bring forth the crisis. The latter causes can and should be eliminated by correcting and supplementing the party building that we have had so far. Conditions relating to the economy and to everyday life belong to the objective causes, which create special difficulties when the programme of the Russian Communist Party is brought into life:

    a) the circumstances of the country's complete economic breakdown, which are deepened by the onslaught of world imperialism and White Guardism;

    b) bringing communism to life in a economically backward country, where capitalism has still not succeeded in completing the full circle of its development;

    c) the social diversity of the population and the numerical predominance of the peasantry and petty bourgeoisie over the working class, which result in the need for the party to reconcile three heterogeneous political tendencies: workers' communist policy, peasants' petty bourgeois expectations, and the large-scale capitalist aspirations of the bourgeois-functionary caste.

    The party's adaptation to contradictory social interests, which has entailed inconsistency and concessions first to one and then to another social group of the population, becomes intensified according to the degree to which the party identifies with soviet executive apparatuses. The Second Congress of the Third International accepted a resolution about the role of the communist party in the proletarian revolution, where it says definitively, 'he, who proposes to the communist party to "adapt" to the soviets and who sees in such accommodation the strengthening of the 'proletarian character' of the party, delivers a well-meant action that has the opposite effect [медвежья услуга] on the party and the Soviets; that person understands neither the significance of the party nor the significance of the Soviets'. The Communist Party should be so strong and well-defined by class that it will not adapt to the soviets, but will exercise most resolute influence on their policy by forcing the Soviets to reject accommodation with the bourgeoisie.

2. The reasons for the crisis that have an intraparty character are the following:

a) the tense atmosphere of civil war, which entailed the transfer of military methods of management into the everyday practice of party, soviet, and trade union building and the removal of party masses from active participation in the party, which provoked the isolation of leading party bodies from the broad worker masses and created the grounds for the development of bureaucratism;

b) the Republic's existence under constant threat from world imperialism, which weakened the democratic development of organisational forms of party building and gave birth to the disparity between outmoded forms of party apparatuses and the demands of the masses, based on their stronger political consciousness, to exercise their own initiative to create the foundation of communist society;

c) the influx into our party ranks of petty bourgeois, careerist elements, people who emerged from the bourgeois and petty bourgeois strata, without having broken with their old worldview; this surge especially intensified after the liquidation of the Left SR uprising and the disintegration of petty bourgeois parties, whose members entered our party as entire groups.

As a consequence of having lost in the civil war the best advanced workers, the party could not integrate the socially heterogeneous elements surging into it. On the contrary, the alien elements entering the party, having assimilated the habits which were cultivated in the party by the circumstances of civil war, became isolated from the worker masses. They brought into the party a parochial [ведомственная] bureaucratic psychology, they impeded the education of the masses in the spirit of taking initiative, and they delayed the replacement of the system of 'management from above' and petty tutelage [опёка] of the higher-ups over those lower down by comradely leadership. The crisis was made even more intense by party leaders' obvious underestimation of and distrust toward the workers' creative talents and political maturity.

3. All these reasons have led to the following:

a) curtailment in the party of conditions for showing **enterprise** [italicised in published report], given the extreme limitations placed on party members' initiative;

b) the flourishing of bureaucratism, which **obstructs cultivation** [previous two words italicised] of the masses' enterprise and makes empty verbiage of the slogan 'self-activity';

c)   the absence of responsibility of higher-up leaders to the party masses;

d)   broadly distributed command over the workers lower down;

e)   the practices of intimidation and excessive compulsion in trade unions as well as soviet organisations, which demand strict execution of orders, party discipline, self-sacrifice, and devotion from party members;

f)   the absence of openness [гласность] and democratic means of resolving the most important problems of the party and of soviet policy, which result from party leaders' obvious distrust of rank and file members;

g)   the decline of the party's authority and the loss of its popularity among proletarian masses, to which attests the mass departure of workers from the party, strikes and other such things that come to pass;

h)   non-implementation of the decisions of congresses and conferences.

4.   Taking into account all these unhealthy, abnormal phenomena, which hinder the development of the revolution's successes, the Tenth Party Congress finds it necessary to outline some practical measures to restore the party's health. It proposes to all party members to exert every effort to overcome the crisis in the party as soon as possible and to ensure intra-party unity. The preservation of the existing state of matters threatens to consolidate the crisis and to impart to it a longlasting character, which would be very dangerous for the revolution.

5.   Taking note that the period of the revolution is still not over, that the RCP still has to realise communism while under capitalist encirclement, and that at the given time of transition to commercial relations [торговые сношения] with bourgeois-capitalist governments, world capitalism attempts by roundabout ways to capture and subordinate the Soviet republic to itself, the 10th Congress indicates that the following positions should serve as the basis for practical measures, which serve to restore the party's health and to reinforce its class might and revolutionary steadfastness.

The Tenth Congress proposes:

1)   to radically cleanse the party and to do so in accord with the definition accepted at the international Comintern congress, namely: 'the Communist party is the most leading, most conscious, and therefore most revolutionary part of the working class; the Communist party is created by means of selecting the best, most conscious, most selfless, and most farsighted workers';

2) to create conditions for party bodies that favour and facilitate development and strengthening of self-activity by rank and file party members in
all areas of class creativity and building communism; to confirm the resolution of the All-Russian conference[126] and to establish that the party
masses' growing consciousness makes it possible and necessary to implement and preserve the principle of worker democracy not only in peacetime, but also when tensions are heightened at home or abroad; keeping
in mind the working class's difficult situation, which was born from the
global breakdown of production and the economic disorders of the transition period, the party congress instructs that only the vital initiative and
enterprise of the proletarian and semiproletarian masses, without being
inhibited and constrained at every step by a hierarchy of permissions and
directives, can create new forms of production and ensure free range for
raising the country's production forces;

3) to unite by comradely leadership broad masses around practical tasks
of economy building and improvement of workers' daily living conditions, realised through trade unions, having grouped in such a way around
the party the well-defined class core of the proletariat, capable not only
of creating a new system of production and of communist forms of the
economy, but also with an interest in deflecting the blows of counterrevolution from within and from outside the labourers' Republic toward the
goals of class self-defence;

4) to take account of the mood of the broad peasant masses, who are confronted by the direct threat of losing their land to White Guard forces, and
to strengthen work in rural cells;

Proceeding from the basic positions explained above, which are supposed to
make our party healthy, the Tenth Congress suggests to immediately carry out
the following practical measures.

Practical Measures:

With this goal the Tenth Party Congress directs:

1. To cleanse the party of all noncommunist elements and to create from
it an actual vanguard of the working class, as our programme and the
Comintern's resolution demand. Taking into consideration the following:
a) that all genuinely revolutionary elements from a nonproletarian milieu

---

126 The editors write that this refers to the Ninth All-Russian Conference of the RCP(b), 22–
25 September 1920.

entered the party in the initial period before the October revolution and that as Soviet power became consolidated, more and more petty bourgeois, careerist, and inconsistent elements from a nonproletarian milieu poured into the party; b) that the bourgeoisie attempts to demoralise our party by entering it; c) that these elements that are alien to us bring into the party a spirit that is also alien to us, which makes it difficult to create class unity in the party and which introduces into it habits and concepts that are distinctive to the bourgeoisie and which debauch workers, the congress directs to cease access to the party by nonproletarian and nonpeasant elements, with the exception of those who worked in it before the liquidation of the Left SR uprising, that is up to mid-1918.

2.   With the aim of removing from the party all careerists and hangers-on, all nonworker and nonpeasant elements who entered the party later than the time indicated in point one should be subject to reregistration within the party not later than a month after the closing day of the congress. Those who entered the party after the time indicated in point one will automatically quit the party with the right to appeal for readmission after three months. For reregistration each party organisation should create special commissions and troikas, which will be composed of party personnel who entered before the October Revolution, with two representatives from a higher party organisation and one from the local organisation. Comrades who recommend one or another nonworker or nonpeasant for party membership will bear responsibility for any negligence and harm they cause to the Communist party or to Soviet power.

3.   Lists of candidates for party membership from a nonworker milieu should be publicised in advance (through the press or by means of lists posted in enterprises and institutions) a month before the candidates' acceptance into the party. The Central Committee should work out the period, during which one bears responsibility for actions of a person whom one has recommended for party membership. Each party member from a nonproletarian milieu will be permitted to assume senior party positions not earlier than two years after admission to the party; in not less than one year after admission shall such a party member occupy less senior positions. To attract worker masses into the party and to ease entry into it, the obligatory recommendation will be annulled and will be replaced with discussion of the worker's candidacy for the party at the party cell assembly.

4.   Each party member is obligated to be employed in physical labour in plants, factories, mines, pits, railways, agriculture and similar work for not less than three months per year. Each party member is obligated to

study one or another simple type of factory work or other type of work indicated in the previous point, in accordance with his predilection or by instruction of economic bodies and by sanction of party organisations. Party members, while carrying out physical labour as their party duty, are obligated to live in the same general conditions as all workers who do the same type of labour in the same place. No party member can be chosen for any party or soviet position before carrying out physical labour as his party duty. Party members cannot hold senior leadership positions more than one year without fulfilling the duty of carrying out three months of physical labour. Only party members who have physical shortcomings can be freed from physical labour; all others will execute physical labour in accordance with their strength and health.

5. During acceptance of a new member into the party, the opinion and references not only of party members and candidate members, but also of nonparty workers who sympathise with the Communist Party and Soviet power, must be taken into consideration.

6. Actual realisation of developed forms of worker democracy within the party is demanded in order to achieve the goal of ensuring the initiative of party masses. The following measures are needed in order carry this out:

    a) Unconditional election of all leading bodies without appointmentism or plenipotentiaries. Appointment is allowed only as an exception. The corresponding party body will inform the upcoming conference or congress about all appointments, so that the appointment will be confirmed or revoked. Only comrades, who are chosen by a congress or conference (members of gubkoms, partkoms, uyezdkoms), can be plenipotentiaries. Introduction of a system for the transfer and distribution of party forces and for guiding them through local organisations.

    b) Subordination of all party and political work territorially to the local organisation and subordination of all party members working in a given territory to the supervision and leadership of the local party organisation.

    c) Regular accounting by all party members who are employed in elected posts to their electors and at broad party assemblies.

    d) Freedom of criticism within the party as applied to the actions of individual party members as well as to resolutions passed by the majority, under the condition that all are obligated to implement the decisions of the highest authorities within the party.

e)   Ensuring that freedom of discussion is possible; recognise for intra-party tendencies the right to arrange discussions and give representatives of tendencies the material resources they need to defend their views;

f)   Acceptance of more resolute measures for implementing conferences' decisions about equalising party members' material situation as well as the party obligations they bear.

7.   To reinvigorate our higher party authorities, to strengthen the link with the masses, and to draw broad strata of the proletariat into party building and policy leadership in a consistent class spirit, the congress proposes workerising and airing out all leading party bodies, regularly replacing the majority of their membership, and introducing into all these leading bodies an overwhelming number of proletarians who have not lost touch with production work and who are linked with broad party and nonparty masses.

8.   In order to create the kind of party bodies, which really would be bodies of ideological supervision over soviet bodies and would lead the latter in a consistent class spirit, and likewise in order to strengthen party work, at least one third of the available membership of party centres should not combine party and soviet work in the same person.

9.   Higher party bodies may disperse lower organisations only in cases when the latter have clearly violated either decisions of the party congress or instructions and circulars issued with the aim of elaborating upon congress decisions. In all remaining cases the higher body will convene, at the appropriate level, a conference or delegates' assembly, which would resolve a brewing conflict. A lower body should not halt or delay the implementation of a decision of the highest party body, until resolution of the conflict according to the procedures indicated here.

10. In order to educate rank and file party members in communism, and likewise in order to strengthen party influence over the nonparty working masses, the centre of gravity of party work needs to be transferred to the cells.

11. The role of the cell in the work and life of enterprises or institutions needs to be strengthened. It participates in elaborating and implementing the production plan. It nominates candidates to all senior and elected posts and guides them through the corresponding stages.

[Published here according to the text published in the book *Desiatyi syezd RKP: stenograficheskii otchet* (Moscow, 1921)]

Tasks of Trade Unions, proposed by Workers' Opposition (pp. 685–91)

[Printed here according to the text of the brochure published separately for delegates of the congress; translated above]

List of delegates voting at the congress against or abstaining from the vote on the resolution 'On Party Unity' (pp. 773–4)

Voting against:

Name		Mandate #	Notes
1.	Alekseev, M.G.	91	
2.	Antonov, I.P.	239	
3.	Barchuk, V.	683	
4.	Burovtsev, M.V.	608	
5.	Gorsky, Z.P.	180	Submitted two 'no' votes
6.	Zubov, S.E.	381	Also submitted a 'yes' vote[127]
7.	Ivanov, I.A.	636	
8.	Ignatov, E.N.	609	
9.	Ionov, A.M.	96	
10.	Kiselev, A.S.	628	
11.	Korzinov, G.N.	610	
12.	Krutov, P.P.	682	Also submitted a 'yes' vote
13.	Kuranova, E.Ia.	137	Submitted two 'no' votes
14.	Manevich, D.M.	623	
15.	Meleshchenko, A.I.	337	
16.	Nikolaenko, I.I.	684	
17.	Perepechko, I.N.	218	
18.	Rivkin, R.G.	245	Also submitted 'yes' vote and on the 'no' form wrote: 'Consider my "yes" vote a "no" vote' [but he was included among the 'yes' votes anyway]

---

127 Those who are noted as voting both 'yes' and 'no' also had their names listed under the 'yes' votes.

(cont.)

Name		Mandate #	Notes
19.	Rybak, D.I.	635	
20.	Sergeev, N.K.	607	
21.	Sirotin, A.D.	621	
22.	Tikhonravov, N.M.	68	
23.	Chigrin, N.A.	264	Submitted two 'no' votes
24.	Shliapnikov, A.G.	629	
25.	Shtanko, A.M.	253	Also submitted a 'yes' vote

Delegates who abstained from voting:

1.	Zarzhevsky, G.P.	316	
2.	Lobanov, V.A.	643	
3.	Meerzon, Zh.I.	3	

List of delegates voting at the congress against or abstaining from the vote on the resolution 'On Anarcho-Syndicalist Deviation' (p. 778)

Voting against:

Name		Mandate #	Notes
1.	Alekseev, M.G.	91	
2.	Antonov, I.P.	239	
3.	Barchuk, V.	683	
4.	Burovtsev, M.V.	608	
5.	Gorbunov, A.I.	685	
6.	Gubelman, M.I.	698	
7.	Zubov, S.E.	387	Also submitted 'yes' vote
8.	Zyrin, P.P.	187	
9.	Ivashchenko, N.S.	80	
10.	Ignatov, E.N.	609	
11.	Ionov, A.M.	96	

(*cont.*)

Name		Mandate #	Notes
12.	Kiselev, A.S.	626	
13.	Kozlovsky, B.N.	221	Submitted two 'no' votes
14.	Korzinov, G.N.	610	
15.	Korshunov, S.I.	463	
16.	Krivov, T.S.	499	
17.	Legotin, M.E.	131	
18.	Manevich, D.M.	623	
19.	Neizhmak, A.N.	274	
20.	Nikolaenko, I.I.	684	
21.	Obolensky, D.I.	422	
22.	Pakhomov, N.I.	406	
23.	Perepechko, I.N.	218	
24.	Rivkin, R.G.	245	Submitted two 'no' votes
25.	Sapozhnikov, G.L.	64	
26.	Sergeev, N.K.	607	
27.	Tikhonravov, N.M.	68	
28.	Shilin, P.P.	181	
29.	Shliapnikov, A.G.	629	
30.	Shtanko, A.M.	253	Also submitted 'yes' vote

Delegates abstaining:

Name		Mandate #	Notes
1.	Gorsky, Z.P.	180	
2.	Zarzhevsky, G.P.	316	
3.	Sirotin, A.D.	621	
4.	Podkorytov, P.V.	301	On the back of his 'yes' vote on the resolution on party unity, he wrote that he abstained from voting on the resolution on the anarcho-syndicalist deviation. The editors of the 1963 published report

(*cont.*)

			speculate that the counting commission did not notice his note.

Delegates submitting indecipherable ballots:

1.	Boiarshinov, P.A.	668	Wrote on the form for the 'no' vote an unclear notation: '2 democ. centr'.
2.	Vainer, R.A.	481	Wrote on two forms for the 'no' vote an unclear notation: 'no. 2–3'.
3.	Meleshchenko, A.I.	337	Wrote on the form for the 'no' vote an unclear notation: 'resolutions Lenin's 2nd, for Medvedev's resolution'.
4.	Rybak, D.I.	635	Wrote on the form for the 'no' vote an unclear notation: '1 ... about deviation'.

Declarations

Statement by comrade Tuntul (pp. 787–8)

To be attached to the protocol

During debates on the party building question, comrade Medvedev, employing the reasoning typical of some 'representatives' of the so-called Workers' Opposition, gave the congress the news that supposedly there was not one worker in the Ekaterinburg gubkom.

As a member of the last three compositions of the Ekaterinburg gubkom, I declare that this assertion is absolutely untrue. In that composition of the gubkom, about which Medvedev speaks, five out of seven members who serve continually were workers.

Likewise comrade Medvedev is not guilty in the slightest degree of 'work-erising' the Ekaterinburg gubkom. The gubernia conference (22 February) is in no way obligated to comrade Medvedev, aside from the minor pleasure of sacrificing two or three hours to observe Russian syndicalism in its natural state.

Statement of comrades Pykhtin & Kondrakov (p. 788)

We ask the presidium to make known the declaration below

In his speech, comrade Medvedev declared that in Ekaterinburg, the prolet-arian centre of the Urals, the entire gubkom of the old composition was made up of *intelligenty*. This is at best a most unpardonable lie. We, the signator-ies below, have been members of the gubkom plenum for more than one year and we know its composition superbly well. Of 19 members of the gubkom, only six were intellectuals, more accurately semi-intellectuals, and the rest were all workers. Therefore we categorically protest against comrade Medve-dev's unfounded declaration, which is characteristic of the demagogic methods employed by representatives of the Workers' Opposition. Comrade Medvedev's assertion that workers were introduced into the new composition of the gub-kom by means of his group's influence is completely untrue, for despite the presence of Medvedev himself in Ekaterinburg, to no degree whatsoever was the Workers' Opposition able to exert influence on the conference, since their group was an insignificant minority. The genuine Workers' Opposition could not firmly establish its influence even among its supporters at the gubernia conference. The following fact attests to this: comrade Iushkov, a member of the Metalworkers' Union central committee, who their group elected to the Tenth Congress, who was one of the most visible trade union personnel and leaders of the Workers' Opposition group, abandoned comrade Medvedev and with him the Workers' Opposition.

   Delegates of the Tenth Congress from Ekaterinburg gubernia comrades Pykhtin and Kondrakov.

Editors note that the text published here duplicates that published in the book *Desiatyi syezd RKP(b): Protocols* (Moscow, 1933) and was verified against the original stored in the archive of the Institute of Marxism-Leninism (now RGASPI).

Declaration of Representatives of the Workers' Opposition to comrade Zalut-sky (p. 790)

To answer your request, in the name of your supporters, 'to notify you of the list of those comrades, who supporters of the Workers' Opposition intend to recommend as members of the Party CC', we inform you:

1. We do not think it possible to nominate our comrades for membership in the Central Committee, until we will know exactly whether leaders of the overwhelming majority of the current congress will back away from their intention 'to carry through a special resolution condemning the tactics employed in the party by supporters of the Workers' Opposition', as comrade Bukharin declared in his concluding speech on party building.
2. If this intention will be removed, we could provide the names of those comrades, who our delegates' group has selected for these posts.
3. We resolutely reject any other way of including supporters of the Workers' Opposition among CC members. If an attempt were made to bypass this routine and include them in the CC anyway, then those concerned would resolutely refuse to have their names on the ballot for election to membership in the Central Committee.

A. Shliapnikov, I. Perepechko, Medvedev, Ignatov

The editors note that the document above is published according to the text published in the book *Desiatyi syezd RKP(b): stenograficheskii otchet* (Moscow, 1921) and verified against the original held in the IML archive (which is now RGASPI).

A.G. Shliapnikov's 'Organisation of the Economy and the Tasks of Trade Unions', 819–23.

This is identical to document #2.4 above entitled, 'Economic Organisation and Unions' Tasks'.

The editors of this 1963 volume note that the original manuscript is dated September–October 1920 and that Shliapnikov read it aloud on 30 December 1920 at the communist faction of the Eighth Congress of Soviets. There is much overlap between this and the theses of the Workers' Opposition that were published in *Pravda* in January 1921.

17   Iu.K. Milonov, 'Assembly of Former Underground Party Members
       during the Tenth Party Congress'[128]

The documentary record of an exclusively important speech by V.I. Lenin has
not been preserved for history. Protocols of the Tenth and Eleventh Party Congresses only mentioned it in references, which are incomprehensible to anyone
who did not hear this speech.

At the sixteenth session of the Tenth Party Congress, Vladimir Ilich indulged
in irony, when he expressed regret for having used the graphic phrase, 'to put
machine guns in place'. He jokingly gave a solemn promise that henceforth he
would not use such words, even as a figure of speech, for those who do not
have a sense of humour. He made it clear to A.S. Kiselev, who showed such
incomprehension, that no one is preparing to shoot anyone from any machine
gun and that no one should expect to be shot. However, there is no mention of
machine guns in any of Lenin's speeches at the congress or in the pre-congress
discussion.

But Lenin really did joke about machine guns at a private conference of
former underground party members. This meeting was mentioned before the
twelfth session of the congress ended. Also, Lenin referred to it in his concluding speech after debates were held on the resolution, 'About Party Unity'.
This conference took place on Lenin's initiative. Formally, the congress presidium decided to hold it on 14 March 1921, before the thirteenth session, which
was devoted to CC elections and was held in the evening. The conference met
in Mitrofanevsk Hall, with about 200 people in attendance. A congress presidium member chaired the meeting, but a protocol of it was not kept. The only
documentary traces of this conference are the first drafts of the resolutions,
'About Party Unity' and 'About the Syndicalist and Anarchist Deviation in our
Party'.

Vladimir Ilich spoke twice at the conference. He gave introductory and concluding speeches.

Lenin began his introductory speech by stating that the rise in the party of
groups such as the Workers' Opposition and Democratic Centralism, which had
special platforms and attempted to a certain degree to create tight circles and
their own group discipline, demanded 'frank conversation' about a split and
party unity. He categorically declared that the party is not a discussion club.
He indicated that vacillations by the petty bourgeois element were summon-

---

128   'Soveshchanie byvshikh podpolshchikov vo vremia X syezda partii' in Petrov et al (eds.)
        1963, pp. 595–7.

ing greater danger within the country than had Denikin and Iudenich from without. Therefore, the party needed something deeper than just formal unity. Having emphasised the need for quick and resolute liquidation of factionalism, which is fatal for the party, Lenin uttered the demand that anyone who voices criticism of deficiencies in soviet and party work should also propose the means by which to achieve their elimination and should participate personally in practical work to help correct these shortcomings. Having read aloud both resolutions, Lenin then turned to the groups of the Workers' Opposition and Democratic Centralism, which displayed impermissible factionalism. He proposed to them to talk, without any demagogy, about what actual shortcomings they see in work and what kind of duties they will assume, in order to correct these deficiencies.

After this, representatives of the oppositionist groups were allowed to speak, but the floor was not given to the 'ideologists' who, being blinded by factional struggle, lost the capability to objectively evaluate the situation that had been created and in their polemical fervour [азарт], as they say, would take the bit between their teeth and gallop away [закусили удила]. Speakers were representatives of leading collectives of these groups, who carried out practical work in the soviet apparatus. For history, it does not bear special significance to name those to whom the conference presidium gave the floor.

They were given enough time to speak, in order to answer Lenin's two questions thoroughly and in detail. However, these orators' speeches showed that they did not carry away any lessons from the debates, which the congress had held on the reports about the Party CC's work, party building, and tasks of trade unions. They lacked all comprehension of the cautionary significance, which the Kronstadt rebellion posed. Having repeated, in still more condensed form, the rebukes and pretensions of their groups, which we had already heard at the congress, they did not introduce any businesslike, practical proposals and did not assume any responsible personal commitments, although they recognised the harm of factionalism in rather indefinite form.

In conclusion, Vladimir Ilich noted that evasive statements by representatives of oppositionist groups could not satisfy the party and that they would not be permitted to violate party unity. He emphasised the need for a guarantee that party unity actually could not and would not be violated. Such a guarantee, V.I. Lenin said, was the seventh point of the resolution about unity which, in cases when discipline would be violated and factionalist offences would reoccur a second time, gives the CC the authority to apply all measures of party penalties, all the way up to exclusion from the party. If CC members committed violations, they would be demoted to candidate status and as an extreme measure excluded from the party.[129] It was at this point that Lenin figuratively referred to this point of the resolution as a machine gun, which needed to be put in place, loaded, and even aimed, so that one could 'fire it at the splitters', in case they would violate decisions about disbanding factions and ceasing factional work.

This conference remained in my memory very well, because it played the decisive role in my departure from the Workers' Opposition, the views of which I shared until Lenin delivered these speeches. His persuasive line of argumentation, compared with the flimsy arguments of those who had been my like-thinkers just a few hours previously, forced me to break with this group. Despite my vivid impressions, however, I cannot hold everything in my individual memory and reconstruct important details with all the necessary precision.

Those participants in the 14 March 1921 conference of underground party members, who have survived to the present time, are faced with the task of reconstructing Vladimir Ilich's unrecorded speech, with all possible precision. This is our duty to the party and to history.

---

129   Editor's footnote: See *KPSS v rezoliutsiiakh i resheniiakh syezdov, konferentsii i plenumov TsK*, part 1, edition 7, 1954, p. 529.

From the Ban on Factions through the Eleventh Party Congress, 1921–2: Former Worker Oppositionists Respond to the New Economic Policy and to Repression against Them

After eight years of world war, revolution and civil war (1914–21), Russia's economy was exhausted and its urban population reduced. Communist leaders therefore reluctantly resolved to retreat from War Communism and compromise with the peasantry in order to restore the economy and repopulate the cities. Lenin's announcement at the Tenth Party Congress, that Civil War-era agricultural requisitions would be replaced with a tax-in-kind, led to a series of economic and social changes, which resulted in a mixed economy with small private enterprise allowed. Under the New Economic Policy (NEP), which unfolded in the months after the congress had ended, the tax on grain was set at a sufficiently low level to ensure that peasants had a surplus, which they could sell at market prices. Because most peasants could not easily travel to markets, intermediaries (derisively called 'speculators') were allowed to transport produce to cities for sale. Later changes allowed private traders to sell consumer items to peasants. Reassessment of prior Soviet economic policy also led to a reversal of the nationalisation of industry. The state retained control of banking, foreign trade, transport, communications, and large industry (the 'commanding heights'), but it denationalised small-scale manufacturing, retail, handicrafts and services, which could be held in private hands.[1] Some communists, including former members of the Workers' Opposition, feared that NEP would facilitate the bourgeoisie's revival and so undermine the revolution. They voiced concerns on early NEP initiatives as these developed and offered proposals to modify discrete aspects of NEP. VSNKh, which initiated many of the new policies, was an early target of their ire.

NEP fundamentally changed the debate over the role of organised workers in economic management. Former Worker Oppositionists still believed that trade unions should dominate government and the party, as they were best suited to protect and empower workers. Throughout 1921, political struggle over the rela-

---

[1] Koenker 1985, pp. 424–50; Carr 1950–3, vol. 2, pp. 269–357.

tionship between party and unions continued. The decree of the Tenth Party Congress banning factions did not make them disappear. Despite creating an impression of unity at the top by promoting prominent former opposition-ists to certain key positions, party leaders transferred and removed individual oppositionists from other leadership positions and dispersed entire party and union organisations. Lenin guided this policy of administrative reprisals, which nevertheless stopped short of criminal prosecution or even the purging of leading figures from the party. Party leaders removed Shliapnikov as chair of the Metalworkers' Union and packed its leading bodies with more tractable men. The former Worker Oppositionists responded in a variety of ways: nego-tiation, appeal, evasion and confrontation. Some like Perepechko and Pani-ushkin broke with the party, while others attempted to promote trade unions without risking charges of factionalism. Struggles at the top took place in a context of widespread confusion about the implications of the New Economic Policy, worry about the workers' low living standards and famine in rural Rus-sia.

NEP had ended grain requisitions and in some areas encouraged peasants to sow more land. Nevertheless, the enduring consequences of Bolshevik policies, Civil War conditions and drought had led to poor harvests and famine, which especially afflicted the Volga region. Despite aid from abroad, most notably via Herbert Hoover's American Relief Administration, millions died of starvation and more than twenty million people suffered from malnutrition.[2]

As the Tenth Party Congress ended, Workers' Opposition members charged Shliapnikov and Medvedev to compose a critique of NEP. Nevertheless, for sev-eral reasons they were slow to develop it. First, they had to be careful not to violate party discipline. In addition, they wanted to make the analysis a col-legial effort. Finally, the main features of NEP developed gradually. Shliapnikov and his key like-minded comrades therefore reacted to NEP decrees in a piece-meal way. They said little about the tax-in-kind on peasant production, not only because the party congress had backed it, but also because they likely understood that taxation could facilitate rational economic planning more than could arbitrary, coercive requisitions. Shliapnikov's greatest ire was dir-ected towards the revival of private trade and the privatisation of small enter-prises, which came as an unpleasant shock to him, since he had guided many of the decrees on the nationalisation of industry in early 1918. When VSNKh decided in principle to allow the leasing of large enterprises ('concessions')

---

to private individuals, including foreigners, the former Worker Oppositionists and many other communists feared that capitalists would regain a dangerous foothold in Soviet politics and society. Resentful at what they perceived as VSNKh's failure to give workers a significant role in implementing new policies, the former Worker Oppositionists expressed their views orally and in writing to one another and to trade-union and party organisations.[3]

By April 1921 NEP was beginning to take shape in broad outlines. At first, the former Worker Oppositionists voiced concern to trade union audiences about concessions to foreign industrialists, but they offered indirect criticisms and attempted to avoid the appearance of principled opposition to party policy. They worried about capitalists suppressing worker agency and writing into contracts a guarantee of their profit no matter what happened to the enterprise they leased. Trade union audiences were receptive to their demand that the unions have final approval over all concession contracts (to safeguard worker interests). In fact, few foreign concessions came to fruition because few foreigners trusted the Soviet government to protect their investments. (Of 42 concession agreements, 31 actually operated, and most of those were in the timber industry.)[4] The problem of how to find capital to develop Soviet industry plagued the USSR through the 1920s. Imposed after 1928, Stalin's solution, one that until then had never seriously been contemplated by any Bolshevik leader, would wrench capital forcibly from peasants and cause tremendous loss of life and damage to health among peasants and workers to achieve rapid, large-scale industrialisation.

By early May, the former Worker Oppositionists' concerns had grown. Shliapnikov, Medvedev, Kutuzov, and Kubiak requested a special Politburo session on economic issues, which was held before the trade-union congresses and the Tenth Party Conference met that month. Proposals Shliapnikov wrote and the others endorsed heavily criticised VSNKh's plan for the denationalisation of industry.[5] VSNKh leaders mocked their inattention to the ruinous situation of the peasantry at a time when famine raged across the agricultural regions of Russia.[6] Although Shliapnikov carefully avoided the appearance of opposition to party policy, his conjecture upon the nature of NEP and how it accorded with the party's professed goals hit at the core of what Lenin considered to be a necessary retreat. Shliapnikov insisted on government control

---

3   TsA FSB, R33718, d. 499061, vol. 41, ll. 153, 157; Nove 1984, pp. 83–5.
4   GARF, f. 5451, op. 42, d. 29, ll. 60–3; Nove 1984, p. 89.
5   RGASPI, f. 2, op. 1, d. 20219, ll. 1–2; f. 17, op. 3, d. 160; TsA FSB, R33718, vol. 38.
6   RGASPI, f. 2, op. 1, d. 20219, ll. 3; f. 99, op. 1, d. 9, l. 7.

of key industrial sectors, including 'all large enterprises, mining and processing industry' and all power plants. Most importantly, he proposed that the state rely on organised workers' initiative to rebuild industry. He called for trade unions and collectives of workers and staff to operate large enterprises.[7] This emphasis on workers' initiative showed continuity with the ideas of the Workers' Opposition. Shliapnikov saw a greater reliance on trusts and industrial combinations both as a useful means to revive the most vital branches of industry and as the next step in building a socialist economy. Calling to expand the territory of state farms (*sovkhozes*), he recommended organising mutual supply networks between individual sovkhozes and industrial enterprises. In that way, the proletarian state would become independent of smallholder peasants. The Politburo responded to the former Worker Oppositionists' recommendations conciliatorily by asking for more details and urging VSNKh to collaborate with them.[8]

Due to the introduction of NEP, the party underwent a heightened exodus of members. Workers asked party leaders when the tax-in-kind would be applied to them. Commissar of Agriculture, Osinsky, after a trip round the provinces, reported to the CC that many people perceived NEP as a departure from socialism, while others suspected that it was a political ruse that would soon be abandoned. He called for an extraordinary party conference to clarify NEP tasks. At the ensuing Tenth Party Conference in late May, Lenin explained the theoretical basis for NEP as rooted in the variegated social structure in Russia that had existed even before civil war had weakened the proletariat. In his view, the tax-in-kind, industrial concessions and cooperatives would restore the peasant economy, revive industrial enterprises and improve workers' living conditions. Asserting that Communists could learn much from 'bourgeois specialists', he warned that the Mensheviks and SRs, in 'non-party' guise, were attempting to mislead workers about NEP and spread demoralisation. Only partially mollified, delegates aired concerns about early NEP initiatives; they especially worried that leaders, in their 'haste', had not sufficiently 'thought through' the implementation of their policies. Osinsky assured them that NEP would require 20–5 years to unfold (Lenin revised this to 5–10 years) and that the transition from 'bourgeois relations' to socialism would take place not by means of 'order and compulsion' but by means of 'enterprise directed towards the general good'.[9]

---

7 RGASPI, f. 2, op. 1, d. 20219, ll. 3–5.
8 RGASPI, f. 2, op. 1, d. 20219, ll. 5–6; f. 17, op. 3, d. 162.
9 Tsakunov 1994, pp. 52–7. Lenin's report echoed points he had made a month earlier in a brochure on the tax-in-kind (Lenin 1960–70, vol. 32, pp. 329–65).

The response of VSNKh to criticisms and doubts was to accelerate its planned economic changes. Despite the Politburo's instruction, VSNKh did not incorporate any of the former Worker Oppositionists' proposals into its own plan for resolving Russia's economic crisis. Instead, in early July VSNKh issued several decrees that supported small industry and the lease of enterprises to entrepreneurs. These included a 17 May 1921 decree revoking the nationalisation of small-scale industry, a 5 July decree allowing the leasing of enterprises, and a 7 July decree permitting privatisation of handicraft production and small manufactories. Unrelenting, Shliapnikov and Medvedev responded to the new decrees with a scathing letter of protest to the Politburo and VTsSPS. VSNKh's focus on the peasant producer as the main figure in the economy greatly disturbed them; they suspected that this elevation of the peasant concealed a bias in favour of the peasantry as a social class.[10]

Despite the attempts of party leaders to clarify the nature and time span of NEP, much confusion persisted – particularly over what the role of the unions should be in the mixed economy that was developing. The Fourth All-Russian Congress of Trade Unions, which met on 17–25 May 1921 in Moscow, faced contentious issues such as party-union relations, the competition between production unions and gubernia trade-union councils for the direction of VTsSPS and whether the supply of workers should be tied to productivity. Discontent from below, and the Politburo's dissatisfaction with trade-union leaders, threatened a shake-up of the VTsSPS leadership. Production-union congresses were usually held immediately before the All-Russian Congress of Trade Unions. Rumours circulated that the Workers' Opposition would first consolidate its strength at production-union congresses, then attempt to take control of the All-Russian Congress of Trade Unions. To outmanoeuvre them, the Politburo brought forward the date of the all-union congress so that it would fall before individual union congresses. The Metalworkers' Union opposed the change to no avail. From the perspective of VTsSPS leaders, the Politburo's step was inconvenient and worrisome, for it gave them little time to plan for the all-union congress.[11]

Animosities among trade-union leaders and their divergent opinions on party-union relations prevented them from presenting a united front against party interference in their affairs. Shliapnikov agreed with party leaders that Trotsky's supporters should be ousted from the VTsSPS leadership, while Tomsky was reluctant to displace them. While Tomsky feared that Shliapnikov and

---

10   Nove 1984, pp. 83–5; RGASPI, f. 5, op. 2, d. 340, l. 81; f. 17, op. 84, d. 175, ll. 94–6.
11   TsA FSB, R33718, d. 499061, vol. 41, l. 195; RGASPI, f. 99, op. 1, d. 9, l. 1. Communist faction sessions ran from 16–24 May. For details of the confusion resulting from the Politburo's decision, see Allen 2002.

the Politburo were colluding to replace him, Shliapnikov blamed Tomsky for having helped remove supporters of the Workers' Opposition from their posts and for inadequately defending the interests of unions and workers in CC plenums.[12]

Shliapnikov led a group of production-union delegates, who were the best organised group at the congress. Representing eight production unions, they included many former members of the Workers' Opposition who advocated distinct views on the role of trade unions and on NEP. Union leaders who had supported Lenin in the trade-union debate also joined. The most prominent of these was the chair of the Miners' Union, and CC member, Artem (Fedor Sergeev). Aiming to increase the influence of production unions over VTsSPS, these union leaders were particularly angry about recent VTsSPS attempts to centralise trade-union administration by giving trade-union councils greater authority over production unions at all levels. Production union leaders feared that VTsSPS would weaken production unions by diverting their staff to trade-union councils. They believed that this would lead to trade unions becoming a branch of government. The production-unions group proposed a list of candidates for the congress leadership who included many former members of the Workers' Opposition.[13] By wresting control of VTsSPS, the production-union group would seek to extend the influence of production unions over state economic policy and to preserve some degree of proletarian democracy in production unions.

While production unions had a pre-revolutionary history in Russia, the gubernia trade-union councils, the delegates of which constituted a rival interest group, were creations of the Soviet era. These delegates felt that production unions and profession-based unions had too much influence over VTsSPS. They wanted central trade-union leaders to show greater sensitivity to their concerns, which meant extending more authority and resources to them. They were not united behind any one leader and seemed to differ quite a lot on specific policies. Some appeared to follow the Tsektranist line, represented by Efim Bumazhnyi, which favoured a military-style administration of industry, the appointment of trade-union leaders and the incorporation of the trade unions into the state system of administering industry. Tsektranists (or Trotsky supporters) could be found in a broad array of bodies: trade-union councils, various union central committees and in the central staff of VTsSPS. Other gubernia trade-union council delegates were weary of factional infight-

---

12   TsA FSB, R33718, d. 499061, vol. 41, ll. 195–6, 200–1.
13   TsA FSB, R33718, d. 499061, vol. 41, ll. 201, 208.

ing and intrigues that had occupied top party and union leaders. In a perhaps unintentionally ironic twist on the political term 'opposition', these delegates were referred to as a 'business-like opposition' [деловая оппозиция].[14]

Given the Politburo's dependence on Tomsky to carry out a shake-up of the VTsSPS leadership he had put in place, preparations could not go smoothly. Unexpected developments included Riazanov's election to the congress's temporary presidium. Riazanov was well regarded by Russian communists for his command of Marxist theory, for his historical writings on the socialist movement and for his extensive experience working in the trade unions. Nevertheless, he had a troubled history with party leaders, who had expressly told Tomsky that he should not be elected to the presidium. When Riazanov's resolution criticising both VTsSPS and the Politburo passed through the communist faction, party leaders became alarmed.[15]

Tomsky's report to the communist faction revealed the strain that he was under. Maintaining that the VTsSPS bureau had to 'indisputably obey' party leaders, he channelled the party leaders' distrust of workers and union leaders when he voiced the view that trade unionists' daily work with factory workers made them susceptible to the same 'vacillations' that plagued the deprived 'working masses'. Both Shliapnikov and Riazanov fiercely criticised VTsSPS leaders, but Riazanov also attacked the CC (unlike Shliapnikov, who was now a member of it). Blaming VTsSPS leaders for their lack of leadership ability, which led to excessive dependence on the CC and allowed regional party committees to disrupt trade-union work, Shliapnikov proposed that trade unionists should participate more in party organisations, that the roles of the party and the unions should be clearly demarcated and that the control of the production unions over VTsSPS and the trade-union councils should be strengthened. Lashing out at Tomsky for allowing the CC to hold VTsSPS in a stranglehold, Riazanov complained that party leaders did not take unions seriously, failed to consult them except in the most peremptory way and ordered them to sign off on decrees that were obligatory regardless of whether they approved. Moreover, he said, VTsSPS leaders did not resist when party leaders actively quashed the attempts of unionists to strengthen their organisations.[16] Riazanov thus staked out the clearest position on proletarian democracy, which motivated an overwhelming majority of delegates to vote for his resolution. Attributing the poor work of VTsSPS to the CC's excessive and 'petty' interference, he called on the party to end its meddling in the 'routine' work of VTsSPS. Most importantly, he called

---

14   TsA FSB, R33718, d. 499061, vol. 41, ll. 205, 213–15.

15   RGASPI, f. 17, op. 3, d. 157, l. 3; TsA FSB, R33718, d. 499061, vol. 41, ll. 199, 202, 213–15.

16   RGASPI, f. 17, op. 84, d. 217, ll. ll. 6–10, 30–3, 48; and f. 95, op. 1, d. 23.

for the election of union leaders by communist trade-union members themselves, free of party interference. He also wanted to end non-party conferences of industrial workers because he thought they disrupted trade-union work.[17]

Riazanov's past year of tense relations with party leaders set the mood for his tempestuous outburst. In 1920 the communist faction of the Third Congress of Trade Unions had adopted his resolution that all *Narkomtrud* functions should be transferred to VTsSPS (effectively abolishing *Narkomtrud*), instead of the CC's resolution. Considerably embarrassed, the CC resolved not to bring Riazanov's resolution to the Third Congress of Trade Unions plenum and to exclude him from trade-union work on account of his 'undisciplined speeches' at the congress. He was only re-admitted to work in the unions in December 1920. Riazanov blamed Tomsky and the rest of the VTsSPS leadership for failing to appeal against his exclusion.[18]

The vote for Riazanov's new resolution forced party leaders to take control of the Fourth Congress of Trade Unions and to investigate how his resolution passed.[19] The investigative commission was made up of CC members Mikhail Frunze (chair), Stalin, Kiselev and Dzerzhinsky. Frunze had commanded the Eastern front during the Russian Civil War and was renowned for his brutality in Turkestan. A rising star in party politics, he died in 1925 while undergoing an operation ordered by Stalin. He and Stalin were aligned with Lenin on trade-union matters. Kiselev, former chair of the Miners' Union, had belonged to the Workers' Opposition; in spring 1921 he was a candidate member of the CC, a member of the CCC Presidium and chair of Little Sovnarkom (which handled prosaic matters unrelated to policy). Dzerzhinsky, head of the Cheka, had been aligned with Trotsky during the trade-union debates.[20] The unpublished transcript of the commission's investigation illuminates personal rivalries and policy differences among trade-union leaders, as well as evolving methods of control over communist assemblies.

Under questioning, both Shliapnikov and Artem harshly criticised Tomsky for ineptly organising the congress and for showing greater concern with

---

17   TsA FSB, R33718, d. 499061, vol. 41, ll. 208, 214. I could not find an exact vote count in the stenographic report of the congress. Riazanov later claimed that his resolution passed by 1500–30 votes (RKP(b) 1961, p. 262). He also referred to a 945–500 vote to keep him in the trade-union movement. A vote taken at another session shows that at least 856 communist delegates were in the faction (RGASPI, f. 17, op. 84, d. 217, ll. 203–4). The discrepancies may reflect flaws in the congress's organisation.

18   RGASPI, f. 17, op. 2, d. 30.

19   RGASPI, f. 17, op. 2, d. 65, 18 May 1921; TsA FSB, R33718, d. 499061, vol. 41, ll. 195–216.

20   Gambarov et al. (eds.) 1989, Chapter 1, pp. 191–4 and Chapter 3, 191–3; TsA FSB, R33718, d. 499061, vol. 41, ll. 195–216.

his personal reputation than with creating a strong organisation. Shliapnikov aspired to remove Tomsky as chair, but he agreed with other witnesses that Tomsky had not conspired against party leaders. Having concluded that there was no evidence of 'conscious cooperation' between Tomsky and Riazanov to pass Riazanov's resolution, the commission nevertheless recommended Tomsky's removal as VTsSPS leader due to his mistakes.[21] Stalin and Frunze were perplexed as to why no one took the 'usual' measures to ensure that Riazanov's resolution did not pass; these included halting the proceedings and excerpting and combining the three resolutions offered. When Tomsky claimed, in his defence, that he did not perceive the CC's disapproval of Riazanov's candidacy as a 'directive', Frunze pointedly replied: 'But you had the definite opinion of the [CC] commission. I think it's the same with us as with the military – opinion is equal to directive'.[22] This told of the Civil War's influence on party politics.

There was so much discontent with central party and union leaders among delegates, the source of which few of the leaders seemed to understand, that unexpected events were inevitable. Perhaps all factional leaders were so immersed in the politics of their causes that they did not understand how deeply dissatisfied delegates were with factionalism and how strongly delegates felt that their leaders did not understand the challenges of carrying out everyday work at the regional and local level. The party's decision to rush the congress had not only made the work of VTsSPS leaders more difficult, but had rushed the delegates' preparations as well.

During the remainder of the congress, Shliapnikov cooperated with party leaders to diminish Tsektranist influence over VTsSPS. When the communist faction of the trade-union congress reconvened without Tomsky in charge, party leaders had already constituted a new congress presidium, which included Shliapnikov and at least four others from the former Workers' Opposition, as well as Artem. As a presidium member, Shliapnikov enforced CC decisions that were rejected by a majority of the communist faction of the congress. One such matter concerned wage rates and the supply of workers with food and other goods. The communist faction had approved a resolution linking pay and provisions to worker productivity, despite being aware that the CC had already rejected this Tsektranist approach. The faction majority remained steadfast, despite the Politburo revoking its decision and its approval of alternative proposals that did not tie the provision of food to worker productivity.[23]

---

21   RGASPI, f. 17, op. 84, d. 217; TsA FSB, R33718, d. 499061, vol. 41, ll. 215–16.
22   TsA FSB, R33718, d. 499061, vol. 41, ll. 198–9.
23   RGASPI, f. 17, op. 84, d. 217, l. 214.

Shliapnikov, who favoured the alternative proposals, announced that he and other presidium members would vote against the faction's decision at the congress's open session. His declaration emerged from genuine conviction, since he strongly opposed basing the provision of food and clothing to workers on their productivity. Nonetheless, his decision directly contradicted his overall stance against party leaders dictating to communist factions. Bumazhnyi sarcastically rejoined that Shliapnikov should 'learn the party statutes'. Molotov, speaking for the CC, offered a compromise. To preserve the appearance of party unity, individual communists could abstain from voting. Shliapnikov instead proposed that the faction meet again to reconsider its vote. Delegates accepted his proposal.[24] In the meantime, he and other presidium members convinced a majority to change their minds. After delegates' positions shifted, the communist faction voted to decouple worker productivity from the supply of workers with food and other goods. Key delegations speaking in favour of these proposals were those of the Miners' Union and the Donbas region trade-union delegations, over whom the former Workers' Oppositionists had much influence.[25]

However, Shliapnikov's good working relationship with the Politburo was not to last, for party leaders next turned to replacing supporters of the Workers' Opposition in the leadership of the Metalworkers' Union with new men who were loyal to the CC majority. At the Fourth Congress of the Metalworkers' Union in May 1921, the union's communist faction resisted the Politburo's changes and re-elected all those rejected by the Politburo. This set the stage for a direct confrontation. There was little indication before the congress that its proceedings would degenerate into a stand-off between the union's communist faction and the party Politburo. Even when the communist faction of the union's central committee met to prepare for the congress, its discussion seems to have been non-political.[26]

Despite the innocuous nature of the metalworkers' recorded statements on the eve of the congress, tensions must have been high when the communist faction of the Metalworkers' Union Congress first met on 26 May. Almost all those elected to the important bureau and presidium were former members of the Workers' Opposition. On the same day, the Politburo organised a commission to lead the congress. Attending that Politburo session were Lenin,

---

24   RGASPI, f. 17, op. 84, d. 217, ll. 164–7, 183.

25   RGASPI, f. 17, op. 84, d. 217, ll. 184–5, 190–1, 203–4, 212; f. 5, op. 1, d. 231, l. 4.

26   Shliapnikov 1921, 'K chetvertomu syezdu VSRM', *Metallist*, nos. 3–4, p. 1; RGASPI, f. 99, op. 1, d. 8, l. 4, 25 May 1921. The account of the proceedings by Sorenson 1969, p. 169, appears to be based on a 6 August 1921 *Izvestiia* article.

Zinoviev, Bukharin and Molotov; they set the terms of the struggle against the former Workers' Opposition. The commission they constructed included only Shliapnikov from the former Workers' Opposition. All other members, including Bukharin, supported the line of the Politburo.[27] Thus the battle lines were drawn in the struggle for control of the Metalworkers' Union.

The first conflict came over the union's leadership. Shliapnikov's supporters and those of the party leaders presented separate lists of candidates for the new central committee of the Metalworkers' Union. Henceforth termed the 'Moscow list' for the sake of brevity, Shliapnikov's list was endorsed by major regional organisations of the Metalworkers' Union, including Moscow, Nizhny Novgorod, Kharkov, Tula and the Urals. The Petrograd Metalworkers' Union, which was manipulated by Petrograd soviet chair Zinoviev, offered a rival list. As was standard practice, the standing leadership of the Metalworkers' Union had to approve a list of candidates before presenting it to the communist faction. The recent All-Russian Trade Union Congress, however, had not followed this procedure.

Communist faction leaders on the central committee of the Metalworkers' Union discussed the lists. Shliapnikov chaired the meeting, which other members of the Party CC commission (except Bukharin) attended. Nearly all metalworkers in attendance were former members of the Workers' Opposition. Only the leader of the Petrograd Metalworkers' Union (Grigory Fedorov) supported the Petrograd list. CC commission members immediately pronounced the Moscow list unacceptable because it was so heavily skewed towards the Workers' Opposition. Nevertheless, nearly all metalworker leaders present demonstrated their independence by accepting it. Later that day, Bukharin announced to the communist faction of the Metalworkers' Union congress that the Politburo wanted the list of the Petrograd delegation to be passed. Nevertheless, the faction voted for the Moscow list.[28]

The Politburo promptly ordered the faction to endorse the Petrograd list. In protest, Shliapnikov resigned his membership of the CC's commission on the congress. He also demanded to withdraw his name from the Petrograd list. The Politburo rejected his resignation and refusal. Instead, it authorised the commission to reconcile the two lists. This created the appearance of compromise.

---

27   RGASPI, f. 99, op. 1, d. 7, ll. 7–8; f. 17, op. 3, d. 170, 26 May 1921.

28   RGASPI, f. 17, op. 84, d. 220, l. 3, 28 May 1921. Attending the faction's 28 May session were 164 delegates with a deciding vote, 30 with consultative vote and three members of the CC's commission on the congress – Chubar, Shmidt and Uglanov. The faction accepted the Moscow list over the Petrograd list 122–40. Two delegates abstained from voting (RGASPI, f. 99, op. 1, d. 7, l. 10). I could not find a complete stenographic report of the debate.

The commission met later that day with the bureau of the communist faction of the Metalworkers' Union. The majority (minus Bukharin) rejected the former members of the Workers' Opposition as union central committee members, but Shliapnikov voted for them. The majority of the CC commission did not hide the fact that candidates were unsuitable precisely because they had been in the Workers' Opposition, which moved Shliapnikov to object that this violated the ban on factional struggle passed by the Tenth Party Congress. He managed to salvage a few candidacies from certain large industrial areas. Under his influence, the faction's leaders refused to endorse the commission's modifications.[29]

Faced with such determined resistance, the Politburo allowed many former members of the Workers' Opposition to be nominated for the union's new central committee. At the union's communist faction, Bukharin announced that a majority of the union's central committee must consist of those who followed the CC's line, but that a minority of seats could go to former Worker Oppositionists. Thereupon, a delegate defended 'democratic' methods of election in the union by interjecting that the faction had no right to go over the heads of union organisations that had nominated candidates to the Moscow list. Attempting to preserve the pretence of democracy, Bukharin persistently urged the faction to discuss the list. A majority of delegates refused to discuss it, rejecting Bukharin's political game. Abandoning any pretence, Bukharin declared that discussion would be held 'as a party directive'. Shliapnikov could not actively resist a party directive, but he could refuse to participate in a political charade. Feeling that he personally had been 'systematically discredited', he requested to remove his candidacy from the commission's list and some other candidates demonstrated solidarity with him. Medvedev Vladimirov, Pavlov, Chernov, Lobanov, Tolokontsev, Mitin, Bruno and some others also requested to resign. Bukharin insisted that the Party CC would not accept any resignations.[30]

Many impassioned comments by and even tears from Shliapnikov's supporters ensued. Most of these reflected a sincere feeling that the Metalworkers' Union was being intentionally and permanently disempowered.[31] Emotions ran so high that the faction postponed discussion until the next day. In the meantime, Shliapnikov appealed to the Politburo.

Unsurprisingly, the Politburo confirmed Bukharin's order. The union's communist faction accepted the Petrograd list as a party directive, but it rejected the directive to 'discuss' the list. Faction members instead wanted to debate

---

29   RGASPI, f. 17, op. 3, d. 171, 28 May 1921; op. 84, d. 220, ll. 1–3; f. 99, op. 1, d. 7, ll. 12–13.
30   RGASPI, f. 17, op. 84, d. 220, l. 4.
31   RGASPI, f. 17, op. 84, d. 220, l. 4; f. 99, op. 1, d. 7, l. 14.

the legality of the Politburo's directive, but this was not allowed. The CC commission offered dissident metalworkers the possibility to appeal, through their new leadership, to the Party CC, the CCC or the next party congress. Distrusting their new leaders' commitment to this right to appeal, the majority resolved to obligate them to complain both to the CC and to the CCC that the Politburo had violated the decree of the Tenth Party Congress. If leading bodies rejected the complaints, then they would have to appeal to the Eleventh Party Congress. A member of the CC commission attempted to dilute the content and soften the language of the resolution, which delegates rejected. Upon the commission's demand for a roll-call vote, Shliapnikov resisted this obvious attempt to bully the faction. He allowed faction members to choose whether they would go on record by writing a note to the union secretariat.[32] Commission members dropped their demand.

The Politburo confirmed the union's new central committee (as composed by the commission). Neither Shliapnikov nor any of his supporters were allowed to resign. The next step was to eliminate Shliapnikov's influence over the union, of which he had been chair since late 1917. To marginalise him, the Politburo resolved to replace the position of chair with a 'secretariat' (a secretariat had just been introduced in VTsSPS). Molotov was appointed to carry out the Politburo's instructions. Such a significant modification inevitably met resistance at the 31 May communist faction meeting of the union's new central committee. In the presence of communist faction members and Molotov, Shliapnikov regretfully intoned that it would be the last time he would serve as chair. Before proceeding, he asked Molotov whether the CC wished to make any announcements. Molotov replied that he would introduce 'modifications' to the faction's decisions as became necessary. Thus, he conveyed the faction's reduced status from the outset. As soon as the election of leaders was brought up, a few faction members immediately proposed to replace the chair and presidium with a secretariat, as in VTsSPS. Shliapnikov retorted that the Metalworkers' Union had set the precedent of having a chair, and that it should be directed not only by VTsSPS statutes but also by its own decrees and directives. Molotov interjected that since the Party CC favoured a secretariat, the metalworkers should organise one. Shliapnikov's supporters continued to resist, offering a resolution to retain the old leadership structure.

---

32 RGASPI, f. 17, op. 84, d. 220, ll. 5–7, 30 May 1921; f. 99, op. 1, d. 7, l. 22, 30 May 1921. Only Chubar, Shmidt and Uglanov attended from the commission (Bukharin was absent). According to the record, Medvedev's resolution passed 132–53, with three abstentions. On the next day, Shliapnikov gave a slightly different breakdown: 134 for; 39 against and nine abstentions (RGASPI, f. 99, l. 1, d. 8, l. 4, 31 May 1921).

Molotov countered with a motion for a three-person secretariat. While only 10 voted for Molotov's solution, a majority of 14 voted for the old system.[33] This was startling, since Bukharin was supposed to have assured a majority of 14 loyalists against 10 Shliapnikov supporters. Molotov, perhaps taken aback and unsure how to proceed, did nothing.

Despite this small victory, Shliapnikov's tenure as leader was over. Although Lenin's supporters, led by Ivan Lepse, head of the Petrograd Metalworkers' Union, favoured retaining Shliapnikov in the presidium, he would have been in a minority, together with his supporters, Vladimirov and Tashkin. Shliapnikov asked to withdraw, declaring that he was 'not in the condition to work' in the presidium; Vladimirov and Tashkin joined him in resigning. Having recovered his composure, Molotov declared that no one, especially not a Party CC member (meaning Shliapnikov), could withdraw his own candidacy. Shliapnikov, with an air of exasperation, replied: 'I must declare that we have one refuge remaining, one right – this is the right to refuse and no one can take this away from us'. Chastising Shliapnikov for putting factional interests over those of the party, Molotov ordered him and Vladimirov to enter the new presidium, but conceded that Vladimirov could take sick leave (he did not require Tashkin to serve). Despite Molotov's order, a majority voted to allow the three men to resign. Complaining of factionalism, Molotov declared that the Politburo would examine the vote.[34]

When the communist faction of the Metalworkers' Union central committee reconvened, Molotov announced that the Politburo had decided to retain a presidium, but to create a secretariat to lead it. The Politburo acquiesced to Shliapnikov's refusal to serve in the presidium, but retained in it Vladimirov, who was highly valued for his administrative and organisational skills. Shliapnikov then orchestrated a vote in the faction to appeal to VTsSPS and to the Party CC concerning the Politburo's 'persistent violations' of party unity (it passed 14–10). Molotov cut discussion short, declaring that the new presidium would discuss all further questions on the agenda, due to the faction's 'accidental composition'. Medvedev had the last word, sarcastically questioning how the faction could be 'accidental' when the Politburo had selected it.[35] Since the faction had proven unreliable, the secretariat and presidium handled the union's business until a new central committee could be elected.

33   RGASPI, f. 17, op. 3, d. 172; op. 65, d. 21, l. 205–6; f. 99, op. 1, d. 8, ll. 4–5.
34   RGASPI, f. 99, op. 1, d. 8, l. 5.
35   RGASPI, f. 17, op. 3, d. 173; op. 65, d. 21, l. 208; f. 99, op. 1, d. 8, l. 7, 1 June 1921. Fedorov, Ianson and Gurevich comprised the secretariat. The new presidium was finally composed of Fedorov, Ianson, Gurevich, Sergeev, Bukhanov, Vladimirov, Vasilev and candidate members Tarygin, Lepse and Rozental.

Lenin and other Politburo members had thus removed Shliapnikov from his longstanding position as elected chair of the Metalworkers' Union. This was a decisive defeat. According to Shliapnikov, Lenin had regarded the Metalworkers' Union as 'the party organisation of the Workers' Opposition'. Lenin worried that there were more workers in the union (five hundred thousand) than in the party, so he resolved that Shliapnikov could not remain as chair. Nevertheless, Shliapnikov did not concede that his cause was lost, merely that it had suffered a major setback. He advised a supporter that because of events at the trade union congresses, it was necessary to start organising again from the ground up. Believing that Lenin's factional politics violated the directives of the Tenth Party Congress, he was determined to resist. He was optimistic that methods such as the party purge still offered the opportunity to reform the party and bring it closer to workers.[36] This optimism also underlay his refusal of his 25 May 1921 appointment to work in VSNKh. On 16 June 1921, the Politburo fulfilled Shliapnikov's formal request to resign from VSNKh. In letters to supporters, Shliapnikov confirmed that his own response to the leaders' 'factional intrigues' was to refuse to take on work. That was one of the reasons why he rejected his assignment to VSNKh; he said another was the incompatibility of his views with those of its leaders.[37]

Some of his former comrades in the Workers' Opposition were not so optimistic and had already directed 26 letters to Shliapnikov, Medvedev, and other sympathetic comrades in Moscow about reprisals that had been carried out against them in the provinces. In response, Shliapnikov and Medvedev registered protests to the Politburo, Orgburo and the CC in April, May and June 1921. The Politburo at first seemed conciliatory, for it asked the CCC to investigate the incidents. Key former supporters of the Workers' Opposition were included in the deliberations on how to attract both party and non-party workers to work in the soviets. Finally, the Politburo instructed the CC Secretariat to re-emphasise to local party organisations their obligation to observe the CC's memorandum on party unity.[38] These attempts were made in April 1921, before the trade-union congresses discussed above were held.

Shliapnikov's harassed appellants saw few results from the Politburo's attentions. Several – Vasily Paniushkin, Ivan Perepechko and Flor Mitin – took extraordinary initiatives to combat reprisals. Paniushkin, who in mid-March

---

36   TsAODM, f. 88, op. 1, d. 168, l. 66; TsA FSB, R33718, d. 499061, vol. 40, l. 124; vol. 41, l. 158.

37   RGASPI, f. 17, op. 3, d. 176; TsA FSB, R33718, d. 499061, vol. 40, l. 124 and vol. 41, l. 157.

38   RGASPI, f. 17, op. 3, d. 156, 28 April 1921; f. 99, op. 1, d. 8, l. 5; f. 48, op. 1, d. 14, ll. 52–3. Sandu 2006 discusses in more detail reprisals against provincial oppositionists.

1921 had renounced his Communist Party membership due to the decisions of the Tenth Party Congress, formed a splinter group called the 'Worker-Peasant Socialist Party', which called for 'power to soviets, not parties'. Describing the Communist Party as 'full of non-worker elements', Paniushkin and his supporters agitated for the election of more workers to the soviets in April 1921; they also supported political participation by non-Bolshevik left socialists. Shliapnikov and Medvedev understood Paniushkin's mood, but they strongly opposed his decision to form a new party, which Shliapnikov compared to the SRs. Paniushkin castigated them for political 'indecisiveness', but after the Cheka crushed his own party, he returned to the RCP(b) and made amends with those Worker Oppositionists who had never left it.[39]

Paniushkin was not the only former oppositionist to air grievances against Shliapnikov and to call for active resistance to the persecution of workerist Communists. Ivan Perepechko (separately from Paniushkin) may have authored a letter to members of the former Workers' Opposition in late spring or early summer 1921. The letter lambasted Shliapnikov, Medvedev, and other former Worker Oppositionists in Moscow for failing to resist the party leaders' reprisals and called on oppositionists to respond to these reprisals in kind. Shliapnikov objected strongly to the accusation that he had not resisted reprisals, calling it 'superficial and frivolous' and the result of misinformation. By the time former members of the Workers' Opposition re-assembled in early 1922, Perepechko had reconciled with them.[40]

In contrast to their disapproval of Paniushkin's and Perepechko's actions, Shliapnikov and Medvedev endorsed Mitin's initiative in circumventing the reprisals. Mitin's method involved transferring those targeted to a low-level position in a different geographical area, and then to a higher-level position in yet another geographical area. In so doing, he had preserved his comrades' ability to continue working in responsible positions. Mitin avowed that his long-term plans including placing 'our people' in key factory committees, getting control of factory cells, then regional party committees and so on, up the hierarchy. Nevertheless, Mitin expressed uncertainty as to what 'our ideological world view' was and what route to take 'out of our dead end'. He concluded: 'All oppositions seem to be a game in comparison with that tragedy which is being played out here, at the local level, among industrial workers'.[41] Party leaders were appalled by Mitin's tactics, which struck at the heart of their attempts to

39 TsA FSB, R33718, d. 499061, vol. 40, ll. 124, 234–5; vol. 41, l. 22; Aves 1996, p. 179; Pirani 2008, pp. 105–6.

40 RGASPI, f. 17, op. 71, d. 77, ll. 1–3; TsA FSB, R33718, d. 499061, vol. 40, l. 145; vol. 41, l. 157.

41 TsA FSB, R33718, d. 499061, vol. 41, ll. 153–7.

manipulate cadres to serve political purposes, and excluded him from the party at the Eleventh Party Congress in 1922.

Petitions to higher party bodies to defend former Worker Oppositionists against persecution produced few positive results. More ominously, the reprisals extended, by association, to worker-communists who were not oppositionists. Aleksandr Medvedev reported that in Briansk gubernia many trade-union leaders and staff were transferred to other posts. Those who replaced them, he said, were completely discredited among union members and consequently were unable to carry out useful work. Mitin agreed that retaliation caused widespread disillusionment among worker-communists, who ceased to participate in elections after seeing their elected bodies dispersed. When, for example, the gubernia conference in Mitin's area was disbanded because it had selected Shliapnikov as a delegate to the Metalworkers' Union congress, workers were so disillusioned that they did not vote in the elections for a new gubernia conference. Such cases caused Shliapnikov to worry that acts of vengeance against the opposition undermined the authority of the trade unions among workers. To convey the seriousness of his concern about the leaders' 'factional intrigues', he requested (and received) Politburo permission to resign from his recent appointment to work in VSNKh (he also held views incompatible with those of VSNKh leaders).[42]

Yet Shliapnikov still attempted behind-the-scenes negotiations with Zinoviev and Lenin. In late June, he met with Zinoviev to ascertain the possibility of an agreement to empower workers, develop industry and return the Metalworkers' Union to its former leadership. In what was likely an empty threat, he warned of a split from the party if 'the official course' continued unchanged. Zinoviev acted amenable to negotiations and reported that 'the old man' (Lenin) was 'tired of quarrelling'. Shliapnikov made five conditions for a 'ceasefire'. These included: 1) a special party instruction to end attacks on the former 'Workers' Opposition'; 2) easing up on repression against workers; 3) convocation of a conference of the Metalworkers' Union and the validation of all the decisions made by the communist faction of the union's congress; 4) inclusion of 'worker representatives' in VSNKh and other leading state economic bodies; and 5) reorienting economic policy towards intensive investment in heavy industry and the assigning a percentage of industrial products to workers for barter with the peasantry. Lenin and Zinoviev delayed talks, ostensibly because the Comintern congress was meeting.[43]

---

42   RGASPI, f. 17, op. 3, d. 176; f. 589, op. 3, d. 9103, vol. 3, ll. 99, 102; TsA FSB, R33718, d. 499061, vol. 40, l. 124; vol. 41, l. 157.

43   TsA FSB, R33718, d. 499061, vol. 41, ll. 157–8; vol. 42, l. 128.

While Shliapnikov and Medvedev negotiated with party leaders, they pressed Kollontai to inform the Third Comintern Congress (meeting in Moscow,
22 June–12 July 1921) about dissent within the Russian Communist Party over
NEP. Addressing the Comintern congress on 5 July, Kollontai warned, on behalf
of a small minority in the party, that NEP threatened to disillusion workers,
to strengthen the peasantry and 'petty bourgeoisie' and to facilitate capitalism's rebirth. In their replies, Trotsky and Bukharin devastated Kollontai,
using gender-coded language in their attack on her. Trotsky derided her as an
'Amazon', his acolyte Radek helpfully translating this to 'Valkyrie' for German-
speaking delegates. Bukharin attacked her Menshevik past, ignoring Trotsky's
similar background, and faulted her arguments for being illogical and incoherent. In the end, the congress expressed its approval of NEP. After her speech,
other Bolsheviks accused Kollontai of having violated party discipline and
many were outraged that she had involved foreigners in Russian party affairs.
When she objected that these 'foreigners' were 'delegates of fraternal parties'
who 'should know the truth', one of her interlocutors rudely replied: 'We'll give
them the truth, but what you and the shitty Workers' Opposition think is harmful to distribute. It plays into our enemies' hands'.[44]

The only effect of Kollontai's speech on foreigners was to lead some foreign
communists, who resented the Russian Communist leadership's iron hold over
the Comintern, to think that they had potential allies in the Workers' Opposition. In late August, a prominent member of the Communist Workers' Party
of Germany (KAPD), which had split from the Communist Party of Germany
(KPD) in autumn 1919, wrote to Shliapnikov soliciting the participation of the
Workers' Opposition in the foundation of an 'international union of all revolutionary leftist political groupings', which would be an alternative to the Comintern. At the Third Comintern Congress in summer 1921, the KAPD called for the
Comintern to be autonomous 'from the Russian state policy system'. In reply,
Shliapnikov insisted that the Workers' Opposition had never been a 'special
party'. He denied that it continued to exist after the Tenth Party Congress and
wrote that he frowned upon a split in the Third International.[45] Despite his

---

44   *Kommunisticheskii internatsional* 1922, pp. 367–73, 379–83; Carr 1950–3, vol. 3, p. 381;
      RGASPI, f. 134, op. 3, d. 37, ll. 15, 21–4.
45   Carr 1950–3, vol. 3, pp. 145, 393; TsA FSB, R33718, d. 499061, vol. 41, ll. 1–2; RGASPI, f. 2, op. 1,
      d. 24625. Ruth Fischer, who was expelled from the Communist Party of Germany in 1926,
      claimed in her memoirs that Shliapnikov, Lutovinov and Gavriil Miasnikov, on early 1920s
      trade missions to Germany, had attempted to convince German leftists to split from the
      Communist Party of Germany (Fischer 1982, pp. 181–3, 311–12). But Fischer was not in dir-
      ect contact with any of the three and was most probably mistaken, at least in regards to
      Shliapnikov.

grievances, he did not want to leave the party. Shliapnikov found it suspicious that when he reported the solicitation, the CC was uninterested. He concluded that the proposal was a Russian Cheka attempt at entrapment, but party leaders laughed down his suspicions.[46]

After the Comintern congress ended, Lenin scheduled a meeting with Medvedev on 19 July but it had few results. By mid-summer 1921, party leaders paid far less attention to complaints about harassment and demotion of former Worker Oppositionists. Although CCC members visited some gubernias, repression continued in most cases. While some former Worker Oppositionists in Moscow reconciled themselves to their loss of power in trade unions, others continued to criticise and envisioned taking further appeals to the party conference and congress.[47] Party leaders feared that they were prepared to take their struggle to a broader audience within Russia and began preparing more radical prophylactic measures, including a trial of Shliapnikov for remarks he allegedly made in a factory party cell meeting.

There was a long tradition of holding party courts to judge party members. (Non-Communists were tried in judicial trials for political offences. The first large-scale judicial political trial would be that of the SR leaders in June 1922.) Party members had been tried on suspicion of being police informants before the revolution. Both before and after the revolution, party courts were held to settle charges of defamation by one party member against another or to determine whether a party member was guilty of violating party discipline. Shliapnikov's trial in August 1921, however, differed from most previous trials of party members, in that the 'court' was composed of the CC and CCC, which would decide whether to expel an elected member of the CC from that body. The trial would send a significant political message, for this was the first case in which a CC member would be tried on charges of having violated the Tenth Party Congress directive banning factionalism. Shliapnikov's conviction would cast a pall on the discussion of political and economic issues among party members and would set an example for reprisals against supporters of minority views within the party.

As Russian Communists consolidated their one-party dictatorship, they gradually created party cells in most workplaces. While the party 'faction' had helped decide important policies, the cell increasingly served to educate and mobilise the rank-and-file. Prominent communists often served as mentors for

---

46   RGASPI, f. 48, op. 1, d. 14, l. 59. On 9 March 1922, someone who purported to represent the
      KAPD again asked him to participate in the formation of a fourth international (RGASPI,
      f. 17, op. 3, d. 280, l. 15). Shliapnikov suspected that this was also a Cheka provocation.

47   RGASPI, f. 2, op. 1, d. 19867; TsA FSB, R33718, d. 499061, vol. 40, l. 124.

party cells. Appointed by the Moscow party committee to mentor the party cell of the Moscow Hydroelectrical Station (MOGES), Shliapnikov later recalled having had good relations with both party members and non-party workers at MOGES. When the station's communist cell met in late July 1921 to discuss rumours that the station was to be 'let out for concessions', its members resolved to invite Shliapnikov, their party 'mentor', to advise them. No protocol survives from the 26 July meeting where he spoke, but a cell member (K. Frolov) was moved to denounce him to the CC for having uttered the phrases: 'they are guilty for leading the workers to thievery' and 'our entire party – with the exception of the Workers' Opposition, has become petty bourgeois'. Shliapnikov later admitted that he had spoken impulsively at the cell but denied having criticised the party's policy or leadership. Rather, he had spoken against VSNKh's proposals, which in his opinion were 'capitalist' and 'deeply anti-party'. The informer's motives are unknown, but could have included concern for party discipline or careerism. The denunciation passed through the hands of Gleb Krzhizhanovsky, who at the time chaired both the State Committee for Planning (Gosplan) and the State Commission for Electrification of Russia (and thus had jurisdiction over MOGES). An old comrade of Lenin, Krzhizhanovsky forwarded the document to party leaders.[48]

Still unaware of the denunciation, Shliapnikov spoke on 29 July to a communist assembly in Bauman district, which was heavily populated by textile workers and whose administration contained many supporters of the Workers' Opposition. In response to his call for a greater role for the unions in production, a majority of 20–10 voted in favour (with five abstentions). Earlier that month, party leaders had attacked Kollontai at the Comintern congress for defending Shliapnikov's views. Nearly two weeks had passed since his comrade, Medvedev, met with Lenin to discuss his proposals. Shliapnikov still hoped to come to create accord with Lenin; perhaps he hoped the Bauman district vote would demonstrate that workers supported his views. But Lenin preferred other methods. Upon receiving Frolov's charges, the CC scheduled a special session to try Shliapnikov for having violated party discipline and the directives of the Tenth Party Congress banning factionalism.[49]

Determined to vindicate Shliapnikov, his supporters scrambled to refute the accusations against him. At the request of S.P. Vasilev, secretary of Zamoskvoretsky district Metalworkers' Union, the MOGES communist cell met in spe-

48   RGASPI, f. 2, op. 1, d. 20251; f. 589, d. 9103, vol. 5, ll. 12, 77; TsAODM, f. 267, op. 1, d. 4, ll. 29, 32; Gambarov et al. (eds.) 1989, ch. 1, pp. 234–6.

49   Sandu 2006, pp. 148–9; RGASPI, f. 5, op. 2, d. 320, l. 1, 31 July 1921; f. 17, op. 2, d. 67, l. 93; f. 589, op. 3, d. 9103, l. 266, 8 August 1921 (morning).

cial session just hours before Shliapnikov's trial to discuss whether the allegations carried any weight. Representing the Zamoskvoretsky District Party Committee, Rozaliia Zemliachka, who had a well-deserved reputation as a harsh and rigid defender of the party line, attempted to guide the cell in determining the depth of Shliapnikov's guilt. Disregarding her, the cell sided with Vasilev and, in a 'lively debate', proceeded to assess the veracity of the charges. Cell members conceded that Shliapnikov had called VSNKh's draft proposals anti-proletarian. Nevertheless, they rejected the most serious charge, namely that Shliapnikov had made anti-party statements. Finally, cell members concluded that Shliapnikov had made no factional statements in his speech.[50] Despite his popularity with cell members, the real determination of whether he had violated party discipline was up to the CC and the CCC.

The CC and the CCC met on the afternoon of 9 August 1921 to decide Shliapnikov's fate. These bodies resolved to allow him to remain in the CC but to reconsider his expulsion if he were to make any more statements, outside of CC sessions, that criticised either party policy or specific decisions reflecting the 'opinion' of the party congresses. Significantly, the second stipulation expanded the definition of factionalism and gave him less room in which to express dissent. Those present voted unanimously for this decision, with three abstentions. Despite the decision to retain him in the CC, those assembled voted to remove him from his work in the Central Purge Commission, to which he had been appointed at the Tenth Party Congress in March 1921. Shliapnikov's election to this commission had been one of the more significant concessions made to the Workers' Opposition. Seven CC members voted for his exclusion from the commission, but three opposed it. A CCC majority (four against two) voted to keep him in the purge commission, probably so as not to disrupt its work. This disagreement caused concern among Politburo leaders, but the plenum resolved to table the differences between the two bodies for later discussion.[51] Shliapnikov retained nominal membership in the commission.

Although Shliapnikov avoided expulsion from the CC, opponents of the former Workers' Opposition took advantage of his disgrace to intensify attacks on its former supporters, which was most evident in Moscow. In autumn 1921 some communists complained to the Moscow Party Committee that district party committees had taken advantage of Shliapnikov's 'trial' and censure to 'commence rabid persecution' of former members of the Workers' Opposition. The Moscow Party Committee did not restrain the district committees but

---

50   TsAODM, f. 267, op. 1, d. 4, l. 32; RGASPI, f. 589, op. 3, d. 9103, vol. 3, l. 104.

51   RGASPI, f. 17, op. 2, d. 69; f. 589, op. 3, d. 9103, l. 267.

encouraged them and even enforced the purge of oppositionists from the Bauman District of Moscow.[52] In the context of 1921, this meant the removal of individuals from leading positions and possibly from party membership, but not yet execution, criminal exile or imprisonment.

Some Worker Oppositionists, however, thought that continuing to fight would lead to success. Those in the Metalworkers' Union had hoped to convene an extraordinary congress of the union in autumn 1921 to recapture it, but VTsSPS refused their request.[53] Rather than violate party discipline by calling an extraordinary congress without permission, they turned to the October plenum of the union's central committee and especially to its communist faction. The communist faction met for the first time since the May 1921 congress, where the Politburo had replaced Shliapnikov as chair with a more compliant secretariat.

Seizing the floor at the communist faction meeting, Shliapnikov and his allies heaped criticism on the union's new leaders for neglecting important questions such as the role of the workers and the unions under NEP and for becoming too greatly immersed in administrative minutiae. The new leaders blamed former members of the Workers' Opposition for hindering their work. Vladimirov, the only former member of the Workers' Opposition in the union's presidium, declared that the new leadership was paralysed. In his view, when it appointed the unions' leaders, the Party CC had destroyed both the authority of the union central committee and its organisational links with the regions. Vladimirov called for the election of new leaders who 'could firmly carry the metalworkers' banner and disperse the fog of appointmentism'. A vote on the work of the union's presidium demonstrated that a majority (13–9) of faction members remained defiant towards their union's Politburo-appointed leadership.[54]

After the vote had shown support for his views, Shliapnikov scathingly criticised union leaders for failing to influence the work of the VSNKh Metals and Electric Departments. Agreeing with him, a majority of faction members resolved to form a commission to make proposals regarding the Metals Department. Despite their disagreement over the relationship between union, party and state, leaders of the Metalworkers' Union found common ground in their opposition to foreign concessions. The focus of discussion was whether to allow a group of American workers to lease the Nadezhdinsky factory in Kuzbas coal-mining region. The Council of Labour and Defence (STO) supported the

52   TsAODM, f. 3, op. 2, d. 18, ll. 23–5; RGASPI, f. 589, op. 3, d. 9103, vol. 3, l. 104; Pirani 2008.
53   RGASPI, f. 17, op. 84, d. 219, l. 24.
54   RGASPI, f. 99, op. 1, d. 8, ll. 11–14.

project, which had been endorsed by well-known labour leaders Bill Haywood and Tom Mann, but the Metalworkers' Union and the VSNKh Metals Department objected to it as 'utopian'. Unanimously, the otherwise warring faction members in the Metalworkers' Union rejected an American workers' colony in Kuzbas.[55]

Despite this momentary agreement, discord resurfaced in the vote for a new presidium. A majority (13–9) endorsed a list composed almost entirely of former members of the Workers' Opposition, while a VTsSPS-proposed list that gave a minority of seats to the former Workers' Opposition was defeated. The Politburo promptly annulled both the vote for a new presidium and the vote against the American workers' colony; instead, it approved a presidium not dominated by former members of the Workers' Opposition. In response, faction members voted unanimously against the Politburo's decision to approve the American project, demonstrating that this issue could drive a wedge between party leaders and their most loyal supporters in the trade unions. Faction members acquiesced to the Politburo's directive on their leadership, but a majority refused to support those leaders. The former Worker Oppositionists would make another attempt to retake control of the Metalworkers' Union at its March 1922 congress.[56]

After the Tenth Party Congress, divisions grew between former oppositionists at the centre and at the local level, between advocates of the trade unions and proponents of the soviets as bodies better suited for the democratisation of Soviet life, and between those who thought it necessary to remain within the Communist Party and those who wanted to create a new, improved workers' party. Significantly, there was even disagreement over the relative merits of the Soviet courts versus the unions in defending workers under NEP. Yet all were united by their perception that the role of workers within the Communist Party was diminishing and by their dissatisfaction with this situation. Ironically, given the frictions within the Russian Communist Party, a December 1921 CC plenum announced a campaign to create a united front of revolutionaries with non-revolutionary European workers to struggle against the bourgeoisie.

Some key former Worker Oppositionists felt that a February–April 1922 political conjuncture offered the opportunity to air their grievances against some features of NEP and to convey their sense that party-worker relations were troubled. The meetings, rather close to one another in time, of the Comin-

55   RGASPI, f. 99, op. 1, d. 8, ll. 15–18, 24; GARF, f. 5667, op. 5, d. 226, l. 6; Zhuravlev 2000.
56   RGASPI, f. 99, op. 1, d. 8, l. 19, 23; d. 9, l. 12; f. 17, op. 3, d. 220, l. 21; and d. 223, l. 8.

tern Executive, the Fifth Congress of the Metalworkers' Union and the Eleventh Party Congress meant that a small group could obtain the attention of a large audience (Russian and foreign communists and Russian metalworkers) for its views. In addition, it was legitimate, within the framework of party statutes, to appeal to these forums. Shliapnikov, Medvedev, Kollontai, and others therefore chose this time to act, but members of the Comintern Executive proved resistant to their message and party leaders undertook to punish them for their bold move. The methods used by party leaders reflected their increasing intransigence towards comradely dissent within the party, to which party members reacted in a range of ways. Debates at open and closed congress sessions and political manoeuvring behind the scenes revealed much about the evolving meaning of party discipline and the limits of internal political discussion and disagreement.

In February 1922 several private meetings were held of former Worker Oppositionists in the Metalworkers' Union to discuss their tactics, goals, and a course of action at the upcoming Fifth Congress of the Metalworkers' Union and the Eleventh Party Congress.[57] Participants held diverse views, but were closely connected to the former Workers' Opposition. Eight had signed the Workers' Opposition programme, while nearly all had supported it.[58] The chief exception was Gavriil Miasnikov, a Russian metalworker from Perm in the Urals, whose ideas departed significantly from those of Shliapnikov. Miasnikov had polemicised with Lenin regarding the former's call for freedom of speech and press for all from 'monarchists to anarchists'; later, he qualified these freedoms as only for workers and peasants. He differed from Shliapnikov in advocating soviet control of production and peasant unions. Because Miasnikov was a worker, Shliapnikov engaged in dialogue with him, despite their differences, and often interceded on his behalf with higher party leaders.

The first meeting in mid-February 1922 was devoted to discussing workers' political opinions as expressed at the local level, the role of unions under NEP, the proposed workers' united front and the group's further plan of action. According to all participants, a dismal mood had settled upon communist and non-party workers. Party and union life was dead, discussion was often forbidden and many communists and unionists no longer tried to make proposals or discuss important questions because they felt it did not matter. In Perm, reportedly, everyone was afraid of the Cheka and in Ekaterinburg unionists

---

57   TsA FSB, R33718, d. 499061, vol. 41, ll. 68–9, Sergei Medvedev's handwritten notes, dated 10 or 16 February 1922; and vol. 40, ll. 127–8. Medvedev organised the meetings and took notes.

58   RGASPI, f. 17, op. 71, d. 3, ll. 1–2.

were afraid of publishing anything. Entire cells of communists were leaving the party, some enticed back only by gifts of boots from party leaders. Apathy prevailed among Moscow worker communists and many were indignant at the Soviet government for ordering industrial products from abroad rather than subsidising their production within Russia.[59]

The oppositionists blamed one another for missed opportunities. Supposedly in Ukraine, oppositionists could have taken over the Metalworkers' Union leadership if only their most prominent spokesmen had rallied and spoken. Local representatives blamed those in the 'centre' (Moscow) for not showing enough direction and for allowing a gulf to develop between leaders of the opposition and potential supporters. The situation in Nikolaev, where purportedly an already existing 'underground' organisation existed, was instructive. An overwhelming majority of delegates (84 out of 100) to a local trade-union congress had voted for the Workers' Opposition. When the congress's oppositionist majority clashed with the majority in the gubernia union committee supporting the Ten, central party leaders sent CC member, Dmitry Manuilsky, to Nikolaev; he transferred about 90 prominent supporters of the Workers' Opposition elsewhere. Some in Nikolaev continued to organise, but they reportedly resented Shliapnikov for not taking a lead or rendering aid. He refused to consider providing leadership for the Nikolaev group, although he found it acceptable to organise such groups.[60] He thus tacitly encouraged his supporters to form groups at the local level, but refused to set up a centralised network of leadership as it would bring charges of factionalism from party leaders.

Responding to criticism that he was a weak leader, Shliapnikov responded that he had sensed no support from the regions. He rebuked his supporters for not working closely enough with factory workers, for providing insufficient material for a political platform and for offering little concrete information about the moods, desires and life of workers at the local level. The problem lay not only at the local level. He admitted that the opposition itself had to a certain extent become demoralised.[61] Despite their dejection, Shliapnikov and his supporters attempted to explore where their perspectives coincided and to develop the group's future tactics. The most important issue was the role of the unions under NEP.

Miasnikov's views on the role of the unions and the soviets in the management of production sounded a discordant note. Like the Worker Oppositionists,

---

59   TsA FSB, R33718, d. 499061, vol. 40, ll. 68, 127.
60   TsA FSB, R33718, d. 499061, vol. 40, ll. 128, 143; vol. 41, ll. 68–9.
61   TsA FSB, R33718, d. 499061, vol. 40, ll. 127–8.

he had suffered at the hands of party leaders for his outspoken criticism of the diminishing role of workers in the party and in managing the economy. But they had disagreed on precisely how to manage production: Miasnikov advocated soviets, the Workers' Opposition advocated unions. Shliapnikov harshly criticised Miasnikov's plan for management through soviets, saying that, in essence, it meant the 'organisation of peasant unions'. He concluded: 'The working class should not organise a unit hostile to it'. Most of Shliapnikov's supporters agreed with him that Miasnikov's proposal to give management of production to the soviets could further strengthen the peasantry's influence over state policy. Later in the meeting, Shliapnikov expressed the fear that the Communist Party was degenerating and falling into the hands of 'a peasant element aspiring to become the complete master of Russia'.[62]

A dialogue about the management of production led to a more general conversation on what role the unions should assume in the face of their exclusion from an important supervisory role in production (whether by soviets or by state economic bodies). All participants saw NEP as a setback for the revolution. One point of view was that if unions were not allowed to manage production then they should resume their pre-revolutionary role as defenders of workers' rights in the workplace. Nevertheless, they acknowledged the harsh reality that without strike funds, trade unions could not carry out strikes, the ultimate method of pressure against employers.[63]

The final question on the meeting's agenda concerned further tactics. Views ranged from the creation of a new 'worker' party to unspecified 'strong means' to heal the party. Between the two extremes was a proposal to create 'circles with a leading group' within the Communist Party. Some wanted Shliapnikov and Medvedev to prepare a platform for discussion, but Medvedev objected that a platform had to be the product of collective work. He did not think there was enough agreement within the group to write a platform. Further, he commented sardonically that some of those demanding a platform feared to 'write anything that would diverge from CC decrees'. Shliapnikov flatly called a platform 'impossible'.[64] Not only would it violate the ban on factionalism passed by the Tenth Party Congress, but his supporters had not provided enough information about workers to include in a platform.

Nevertheless, against Shliapnikov's protests, his supporters voted to assign him and Medvedev to elaborate a political platform that they would discuss at a future meeting and present to the Eleventh Party Congress. Archival records

---

62   TsA FSB, R33718, d. 499061, vol. 40, ll. 127–8.
63   TsA FSB, R33718, d. 499061, vol. 40, ll. 127–8.
64   TsA FSB, R33718, d. 499061, vol. 40, ll. 127–8.

indicate that the two men did not formulate a platform but a set of proposals. These were discussed at a subsequent meeting, but never presented to the party.[65] The fact that Shliapnikov's colleagues would instruct him and Medvedev to prepare a platform and that they would ignore that order and write a different type of document, perhaps even for an audience different from the one that the others at the meeting had in mind, testifies to the chaotic relationship between Shliapnikov and those who shared his concern about a role for the workers in socialist society.

In the end, 22 of those who had attended the meetings decided to appeal to the Comintern, as the highest court in the international communist movement, about the persecution of dissenters within the Russian Communist Party.[66] Although there is no evidence that Kollontai attended any meetings of the original signatories in February 1922, she shared their concerns, their hopes about the Comintern's impartiality, and their sense that appealing to it was the only route that remained. A persuasive speaker, she might sway an international audience.

Lenin and Zinoviev had authored the guiding 21 Points (or conditions), adopted by the Comintern in 1920. One of the points stipulated that individuals belonging to any member party had the right to appeal to the Comintern as the highest body of the international Communist movement, either separately or collectively, if their grievances were not satisfied by the leading organs of their national party.[67] Thus, an appeal to the Comintern was 'legal', according to its founding document. An expanded Comintern Executive was to meet from 24 February to 4 March 1922 to discuss the proposal for a 'united front', which was to unite all revolutionary socialists (including anarchists and syndicalists) and social-democratic workers in the struggle against international capital and reformist socialist leaders.[68] In fact, the leadership of the Russian-dominated Comintern intended to centralise the international communist movement under its leadership. The efforts of the 22 to reveal deep disagreements within the RCP(b) thus undermined Russian party leaders' campaign for a united front.

The 22, joined by Kollontai and Zoia Shadurskaia, presented their petition to the Comintern Executive on 26 February 1922. The original signatories were:

---

65   TsA FSB, R33718, d. 499061, vol. 40, l. 128, ll. 133–9.

66   RGASPI, f. 17, op. 71, d. 1, l. 10.

67   Chase and Staklo (eds.) 2001, pp. 11–19. Lars Lih argues that the use of the term 'rarefaction' [разжижение] in the '21 conditions' highlights how Zinoviev was the main author of the document (Lih 2011, p. 52).

68   Humbert-Droz 1967; Tivel and Kheimo (eds.) 1967.

M. Lobanov, N. Kuznetsov, A. Polosatov, A. Medvedev, G. Miasnikov, V. Pleshkov, G. Shokhanov, S. Medvedev, G. Bruno, A. Pravdin, I. Ivanov, F. Mitin, P. Borisov, N. Kopylov, Zhilin, M. Chelyshev, A. Tolokontsev, A. Shliapnikov, I. Barulin, V. Bekrenev, A. Pavlov, and A. Tashkin. Shadurskaia was a close friend and comrade of both Kollontai and Shliapnikov; she shared their ideals and their concern that the revolution was taking a wrong course. Before approving the Russian party leaders' plan for a united front in Western Europe, the petitioners called on the Comintern to 'heal the rift' between workers and party leaders in Russia. They found it unlikely that the Russian Communist Party could lead an international effort for a 'united workers' front' when there was so much disunity and a reduction of the role of the workers within the Russian party itself. The signatories complained that 'bourgeois' elements had flooded into the party, diluting the influence of 'proletarian' members and fostering the suppression of dissent among worker Communists. The trend away from participatory democracy within trade unions and towards unilateral decision-making by the 'party and trade union bureaucracy' had disillusioned communist workers, who were leaving the party. Finally, the signatories expressed their support for an international workers' united front, but first asked that the Comintern intervene to 'eliminate the threat of a schism hanging over our party'.[69]

When Kollontai attempted to speak before the Comintern Executive on 26 February on behalf of the views expressed in the appeal, Russian party leaders (most notably Trotsky and Zinoviev) on the presidium of the Comintern conference removed her name from the list of orators. In a private meeting with Kollontai, they urged her not to speak. Zinoviev insisted that support for the united front was a party directive that the entire Russian delegation had to pursue without reservations. When she proved recalcitrant, Trotsky forbade her to speak and issued a decree, in the name of the CC, that ordered all members of the Russian delegation to 'obey party directives'. Both Trotsky and Zinoviev thus stifled criticism in the name of party discipline. Other presidium members were Radek and Bukharin (Russia), Brandler (Germany), Souvarine (France), Terracini (Italy), Kreibich (Czechoslovakia) and Carr (née Ludwig E. Katterfield, USA).[70]

The Politburo delegated Zinoviev and Trotsky to convince the Comintern Executive that the 'Letter of the 22' contained distortions and was a factionalist statement of the former Workers' Opposition. The Executive, as elected at the July 1921 Comintern Congress, consisted of: Zinoviev, Bukharin, Radek,

---

69   RGASPI, f. 17, op. 71, d. 3, ll. 1–4; RKP(b) 1961, pp. 749–50; Anon 1922, p. 16.

70   RGASPI, f. 134, op. 3, d. 37, ll. 33–5.

Lenin, Trotsky (Russia), Gehert and Frohlich (Germany), Souvarine (France), Burian and Kreibich (Czechoslovakia), Terracini and Gennari (Italy), and seventeen other members. The extended session in late February–early March 1922 was attended by 105 participants from 36 countries. To investigate the letter, the Comintern created a commission composed of Clara Zetkin, the French Communists Ludovic-Oscar Frossard and Marcel Cachin, the young Italian Communist Umberto Terracini, Arthur MacManus of Great Britain, Kreibich of Czechoslovakia, and Vasil Kolarov of Bulgaria.[71] According to Kollontai, the commission only 'hastily' questioned her and Shliapnikov. Then it sat in a long session with Trotsky and Zinoviev, after which it roundly condemned the letter and its signatories. Kollontai suspected that Radek had authored an 'accusatory, prosecutorial' speech by one commission member. Disappointed, she blamed Zinoviev for cultivating in the Comintern leadership 'lackeyism' and 'cowardice'. The commission censured the 22 and warned them not to make such an appeal in the future. No protocol was recorded at the 3 March session when the Comintern commission interviewed Kollontai and Shliapnikov, but one of the commission members later restored it from memory.[72] Zinoviev and other leaders of the Russian Communist Party held the Comintern so tightly in rein that it could only be a 'court of appeal' for those whose goals coincided with the interests of Russian party leaders. The recourse of the 22 to it signified that they had already been backed into a corner. Yet their strategy required taking a principled stand.

A few days after the 22 Russian communists had presented their appeal to the Comintern, the Fifth Congress of the Metalworkers' Union convened. Before the congress began, certain former Worker Oppositionists had determined to wage, in the union's communist faction, a campaign to reassume the leadership of their union. But since the last session of the union's central committee in October, others of them had vacillated in their support. In addition, the Politburo had intervened in the selection of congress delegates. On the eve of the congress, the former Worker Oppositionists were uncertain of their strength. Vladimirov had apparently withdrawn from the struggle. Those who remained decided that their primary goal at the congress would be to give 'rebuff' to the 'coalition of fools and careerists' in the union leadership. If they could win a majority of the faction, they would demand the implementation of their decisions. If half of the faction were with them, they would push for proportional representation in the union's leadership. If they had a 'resolute' large minority, they would carry the struggle to 'lower bodies' of the union.[73] They did not address what to do if they had a majority, but the CC (or Politburo) struck down their decisions, as had occurred at the last congress, when Shliapnikov and many of his supporters submitted to party discipline.

Meanwhile, the Politburo prepared for a confrontation at the congress. On Lenin's initiative, it created an Orgburo commission (comprising Tomsky, Andreev and S. Syrtsov) to compose the new central committee of the Metalworkers' Union and instructed gubernia-level party committees to select union leaders at their level. In preparation for the congress and its communist faction, which met 2–8 March 1922, only CC-endorsed proposals were presented (by Lepse) to the communist faction of the Metalworkers' Union's central committee. Of 16 voting members present, eight had formerly supported the Workers' Opposition. Nevertheless, 11 of the 16 voted for Lepse's proposals, indicating that several of the former Worker Oppositionists had shifted allegiance.[74] When the communist faction of the congress convened, conflict immediately surfaced over who would lead the congress. The Orgburo had approved one list of nominees for the congress presidium, while another originated from the former Workers' Opposition. Although the names of a few nominees were on both lists, they quickly asked to be removed from the rival list, attesting to the intractable nature of the dispute within the union over its leadership and direction. Shliapnikov urged delegates not to be influenced by accusations swirling around the 'Letter of the 22'. Yet, perhaps recognising that he did not have majority support, he even withdrew his name from the list put forward by his supporters. This signified his resignation from the struggle to resume control of the union. When voices from the floor rang out in support of him, Nikolai Ianson, a loyal member of the union's 'new' leadership, rejected their calls and disparaged Shliapnikov. He scoffed: 'It is possible to bandy one's name about, to be a noisy cart, but to do little in everyday work'. Ianson put forth Vladimirov's name as an example of a diligent and hard worker.[75]

In refusing his nomination to the presidium, Vladimirov spoke as passionately as he had at the previous congress. He declared that he had never yearned for high-ranking posts, but had worked hard 'because I sensed the vibrancy of this work'. Nevertheless, he said, for the preceding six months, he had suffered more at his job than he had in tsarist prisons. Furthermore, he maintained that he would refuse to hold a post in the union's central committee, even if he were to be charged with violating party discipline. Vladimirov concluded: 'I am

---

73   TsA FSB, R33718, d. 499061, vol. 43, l. 148.

74   RGASPI, f. 17, op. 3, d. 271, l. 4; f. 99, op. 1, d. 8, l. 33.

75   RGASPI, f. 99, op. 1, d. 2, ll. 1–6.

thankful for your trust in me for four years, but this time I ask you to leave me in peace'. Lepse questioned Vladimirov's loyalty to the party, but the faction allowed him to resign. By a small majority (85–76), the faction endorsed the Politburo-approved list. These proceedings showed disarray among the former Workers' Opposition members. Some (Skliznev and Kiselev) still put up a fight, but others (Shliapnikov, Vladimirov, Tashkin, and G.F. Tarasov) refused to participate in such a charade.[76]

The debate on the role of the Metalworkers' Union under NEP revealed subtle differences between Shliapnikov and his comrade Medvedev. Addressing the role of the unions in defending workers under NEP, Medvedev called for the right of workers in capitalist enterprises to strike and for the union to create strike and unemployment funds; for without these, the capitalists would not abide by collective agreements. Significantly, he wanted to extend this discussion to consider the unions' defence of workers not only in capitalist enterprises, but also in state enterprises, alluding to his doubts that the 'proletarian state' actually ruled in the interests of the 'proletariat'. Although he clarified that he was not calling for the independence of the unions from state power, as did the Mensheviks and the SRs, one of the new Politburo-approved leaders labelled his proposals 'anti-Marxist' and declared that it was no longer necessary to use 'antiquated methods' of trade-union work. Shliapnikov retorted that pre-revolutionary methods would not be necessary only if 'everything in our government had changed'. Unfortunately, he continued, the current policy was not new in relation to capitalism. Nevertheless, he differed with Medvedev on strikes, advocating instead that 'state laws and courts' be used to enforce collective agreements between concessionaires and unions.[77] Aware that no funds would be available for strikes, Shliapnikov staked his hopes on the law and Soviet judges.

Attempting to influence the delegates' vote for the new central committee of the union, both sides highlighted controversial issues. Tomsky (restored to VTsSPS leadership) informed them of the Politburo's highly critical view of the 'Letter of the 22', which prepared the way for Ianson's proposal of a list for the union's new central committee that excluded those who had led the appeal to the Comintern. Shliapnikov then accused Tomsky of provoking a split. Contrary to Ianson's proposal, Medvedev (who was only allowed to address the congress after 42 delegates signed an appeal) urged delegates to elect a 'strong,

---

76   RGASPI, f. 99, op. 1, d. 2, l. 5; d. 7, l. 24. Schapiro 1956 assumed that Kiselev 'had broken with the opposition' (Schapiro 1956, pp. 332–3), since he did not sign the Letter of the 22, but he still actively attempted to regain control of the Metalworkers' Union.

77   GARF, f. 5469, op. 17, d. 3, ll. 1–11; RGASPI, f. 99, op. 1, d. 2, ll. 23–5, 76; d. 7, l. 42.

authoritative central committee' that would exert influence on such vital questions as the 'necessity to stop orders abroad for equipment that could be made at home'.[78] Foreign orders stirred the emotions of the delegates, because they were a concrete example of the Soviet economic leadership's distrust of the Russian workers' capabilities.

During the debate over the elections to the new central committee, the history of party and trade-union relations came into play. Shliapnikov's sympathisers criticised the central committee that had existed between the fourth and fifth congresses for having accomplished nothing, because, as appointees, its members had no credibility. Arguing that 'appointmentism' was a legitimate tradition in the history of Communist (or Bolshevik) relations with the trade unions, Lepse erred in referring to Shliapnikov as an appointee in 1917. Shliapnikov rejected this attempt to revise party history, recalling that when the CC assigned him to win over the Metalworkers' Union in 1917, he was the sole Bolshevik in the bureau leading the union. When he and his comrades won the union, he insisted: 'We consistently did so by means of elections'. His response drew applause from the delegates.[79] Appointmentism [назначенство] would be a prominent theme in the party discussion of late 1923.

Predictably, this applause for Shliapnikov notwithstanding, the Politburo-approved list for the union's new central committee won, by 99 votes to 84, over that proposed by his supporters.[80] Given this small margin of victory, the Politburo moved to consolidate its victory by engineering a vote in the faction on the 'Letter of the 22'. Surprisingly, the faction voted unanimously (with five abstentions) to 'caution' those who signed the appeal 'from further such acts'. Thus, nearly all of those delegates who had formerly supported the Workers' Opposition voted in favour, perhaps finding it necessary to recognise the Comintern as the highest party court. Those former Worker Oppositionists who still refused to surrender proposed proportional representation in the union's central committee. Unable to decide, the faction asked the CC to rule. The Politburo, in the CC's name, rejected proportionality, characterising the majority's list as sufficiently representative. Moreover, it cast aspersions on the rival list as composed of people who had been censured by the Comintern.[81] The Fifth Congress of the Metalworkers' Union thus ended without a single victory for Shliapnikov and those who shared his views. The new leadership of the union had managed to

78   RGASPI, f. 99, op. 1, d. 2, ll. 26, 35–7.
79   RGASPI, f. 99, op. 1, d. 2, ll. 49–52, 148.
80   RGASPI, f. 99, op. 1, d. 2, ll. 104–7. This total exceeds the number of 161 delegates attending the congress; I cannot explain the discrepancy.
81   RGASPI, f. 99, op. 1, d. 7, ll. 28–31; f. 17, op. 3, d. 277.

eke out a majority among delegates. Nevertheless, the large minority of votes received by Shliapnikov and his fellows at this late date testifies to the depth of their support among rank-and-file metalworker unionists and to the difficulty the party and new union leaders had in extinguishing it.

The Politburo and Narkomtrud decided many of the questions raised at the Metalworkers' Union Congress in spring 1922 and announced these decisions as policy at the Fifth All-Russian Congress of Trade Unions in September 1922. Trade unions were not to strike in defence of workers, for they should support the goal of the party and the state to rebuild the economy, which required increased productivity from workers. The 1922 Labour Code had been prepared by Narkomtrud without consulting the broad trade-union movement, only VTsSPS, which was bypassed when the final revisions were made. Trade-union critics, such as Riazanov, censured the code for weakening the enforcement of collective agreements between management and workers, for allowing employers to arbitrarily refuse employment to workers hired through labour exchanges, for failing to protect workers who were not paid on time or at all and for failing to enforce the maximum working day and holiday time. With Tomsky's support, however, the code took effect by the end of 1922. In the meantime, the Eleventh Party Congress had already approved Lenin's resolution clarifying that trade unions could not aspire to a management role, but should serve as mediators between workers and managers of state industry.[82]

Some party leaders wanted to go further than the Comintern's decision and to prosecute the 22 for factionalism. There was real concern that pressure from the former Workers' Opposition, together with widespread economic grievances, would lead to a split in party ranks.[83] The Soviet press thus used the Comintern's decision as fodder to attack the signatories and other former supporters of the Workers' Opposition for factionalism and violating party discipline. The party press impugned the signatories as ideologically tainted by Menshevism, anarchism and all other political associations especially repugnant to Russian communists at that time. Forced on the defensive, the 22 had to explain repeatedly in writing and in person what had compelled them to appeal to the Comintern. As the Eleventh Party Congress drew nearer, prominent figures among the 22 faced the prospect of exclusion from the Communist Party.

Bukharin, who edited *Pravda* in 1917–29, surely helped lead the press campaign against the 22. Kollontai named Radek as another principal author of the

82   Sorenson 1969, pp. 174–6; Pirani 2008, p. 156.
83   Kvashonkin et al. (eds.) 1996, p. 243.

press campaign to 'smear' the 22. Lenin could not have been actively involved in it, since for much of March 1922 he was outside of Moscow, recuperating from illness. Although Bukharin would not have undertaken the campaign without Politburo approval, he had his own reasons to press it. He was strongly opposed to factionalism within the party, was increasingly identified as a chief advocate of NEP and finally had developed an argument to justify the party's dictatorship, claiming that the proletariat was incapable of generating an 'intellectual elite' from its own ranks with the ability to organise 'all of society'. In his opinion, the proletariat had been unable to do this because of 'bourgeois' control over education in capitalist society.[84] The former Worker Oppositionists undermined Bukharin's interpretation both because of what they stood for and who they were: self-educated proletarians who had proven to be capable organisers and administrators during the Civil War and early NEP.

Despite furious accusations against them in the press, Shliapnikov and Medvedev still received letters of encouragement from individual worker communists and party cells scattered across Russia. These letters, no doubt, boosted his morale in the trying month of March 1922. Support came chiefly from old party members who knew them well. In expressing their solidarity with the 22, those defenders overcame enormous pressure from party leaders to condemn the appeal to the Comintern; but as one informed Shliapnikov, there were few like them left. Many oppositionist workers had left or been hounded out of the party; most of those who remained readily participated in ritual condemnations of the appeal of the 22. In his diary, a detached observer wrote of apathy among Moscow workers towards the appeal, but acknowledged that at higher levels in the party there was a large measure of sympathy for the 22, even among their opponents.[85]

Opponents of the former Workers' Opposition not only used the Letter of the 22 to condemn them, but also made allegations regarding what Shliapnikov and Kollontai had said to the Comintern commission. In a letter to the CC, Shliapnikov decried distortions in the press of his statements to that commission, denying that he had threatened 'worker uprisings', insisting that he had only pointed out that worker dissatisfaction was so deep that sometimes it 'erupted in the form of strikes'.[86] The party-press campaign also utilised any flaws, real or apparent, in the political background of those among the 22. Miasnikov, who had also signed the 'Letter of the 22', was expelled from the

---

84   Pipes 1994, p. 457; Cohen 1980, pp. 142, 156; RGASPI, f. 134, op. 3, d. 37, l. 36.
85   TsA FSB, R33718, d. 499061, vol. 41, ll. 22–4, 84–5; Pirani 2008, pp. 120–4; Kovalchenko (ed.) 1993, vol. 4, pp. 108–9.
86   RGASPI, f. 17, op. 71, d. 1, ll. 5–8, March 1922.

Communist Party by the Politburo on 20 February for 'repeated violations of party discipline' and for attempting to create a faction within the party. His exclusion and his signature on the 'Letter of the 22' were cited to discredit the letter and those who had signed it.

Given the press campaign's limited effectiveness, party leaders applied other measures at their disposal. Stalin used his new powers as CC secretary against sympathisers with the 22 in the provinces. For example, in Omsk, communists who supported the 22 had taken over the gubernia party committee. The Siberian party bureau (*Sibbiuro*), the Omsk Gubernia Cheka and the Orgburo cooperated to remove the oppositionists from power. Stalin, as CC secretary, sent a 'threatening telegram' in which he accused them of factionalism. He authorised the Sibbiuro to conduct a re-registration of the entire Omsk gubernia organisation and to expel from the party those who had 'conduct[ed] agitation for leaving the party'. In May and June, members of the party, the soviets and the trade unions were verified in Omsk, resulting in a few expulsions, reprimands and about twenty transfers. By the end of 1922, Sibbiuro transferred more than one hundred party functionaries to establish firm control over the Siberian organisation.[87] Nevertheless, such methods were still a far cry from the criminal prosecutions that would be applied against dissident Communists in 1923.

Political pressure became so great that some of Shliapnikov's comrades considered relinquishing their party-appointed positions and returning to manual labour. Medvedev for example drafted a 9 March 1922 letter to the Orgburo (which was perhaps not sent) in which he stated that due to the party leaders' lack of trust in him, he would not accept future CC work assignments but instead would work in a metals factory. (A copy found its way to Medvedev's CCC file after a party member accidentally discovered it in a library book he borrowed in December 1922.)[88] Some of their nervous tension emerged from the belief that party leaders were resorting to provocation. For example, Shliapnikov reported to the Politburo that on 10 March 1922 a woman who identified herself as Goldstein and claimed to represent the KAPD personally invited him and the 'Workers' Opposition' to participate in a conference of a fourth international. When he denied the existence of the Workers' Opposition and disagreed with attempts to split the Third International, she allowed that a faction within the KAPD also disapproved of the creation of a new international. Reinforcing his suspicion, she then asked him to write out an answer to her

---

87   Olekh 1994, pp. 107, 115–18; Demidov 1994, pp. 8–9. S.V. Kossior served as Sibbiuro secretary
      from November 1922.
88   RGASPI, f. 589, op. 3, d. 9102.

invitation and to discuss the position of the Workers' Opposition in the German press. Shliapnikov refused. (Together with Dutch and Bulgarian oppositionists, the KAPD formed the Communist Labour International in April 1922.)[89] Her methods mirrored those of secret-police provocateurs.

Party leaders used not only the press (and possibly the Cheka) but also the CCC against the oppositionists. The first step in the CCC's investigation was a formal letter from Timofei Krivov, CCC secretary, to Shliapnikov, as the presumed leader of the 22, requesting that he present in writing his evidence for accusing party centres of a 'struggle against proletarians with their own opinions'. Krivov also required Shliapnikov to explain why he did not present his evidence to the party before submitting it to the Comintern and, more provocatively, if he thought that his accusations could 'lead to a party split'. Suggesting ominously that the 'Letter of the 22' violated the Tenth Party Congress's resolution on party unity, Krivov asked whether Shliapnikov would comply with the Comintern commission's ban on future appeals.[90]

Shliapnikov prefaced his answers to Krivov with the comment that he considered it 'unusual' for the CCC to become involved in an exclusively political matter. Moreover, since the Comintern, as the highest court in the communist movement, had already made a decision on the affair, he considered it inappropriate for the CCC, as a lower court, to re-examine it. Nevertheless, he cited numerous examples of persecution and then added wryly: 'I have no doubt that in your files there is rather more material than I have in my memory'. In reply to Krivov's second question, Shliapnikov wrote that he had tried unsuccessfully to convince the CC to discuss his grievances. As to whether his accusations could weaken the party, he declared forcefully that in the past the Bolsheviks had never feared discussing their faults. Rather, the elimination of the causes of these faults would strengthen the party. He declared emphatically that the appeal had not violated the Tenth Party Congress's ban on factionalism, but that he did not intend to violate the Comintern's ban on future appeals.[91] Moreover, he rejected the CCC's designation of him as the 'leader' of the 22, insisting that he did not speak for others who had signed. He thus avoided confessing to factionalism but enhanced the probability that others of the 22 would be interrogated.

When the CCC met with the 22 on 17 March, its investigators assured the signatories that their only goal was to ensure healthy 'party life'. Nevertheless,

89   RGASPI, f. 17, op. 3, d. 280, l. 15; Schapiro 1956, pp. 330–1.
90   RGASPI, f. 17, op. 71, d. 1, l. 9.
91   RGASPI, f. 17, op. 71, d. 1, l. 10; Heywood 1999, p. 1921; Heywood 1992; Anderson et al. (eds.) 2007, vol. 2, p. 45.

they could not guarantee that criminal prosecutions would be avoided. After all, the 'Letter of the 22' had fallen into the hands of enemies of the revolution. (CCC members present were Krivov, A.A. Solts, Z.Ia. Litvin-Sedoi, K.A. Ozol and S.N. Smidovich. Most of the 22 were present. At least one, Polosatov, had been questioned earlier and was not present.) Medvedev responded that the fault for this lay with those party leaders who had published it in *Pravda*. Ignoring for the moment his ironic jibe, the CCC proceeded to question each signatory individually, but in the presence of all. This saved time and was less formal than individual interrogations. Yet the presence of a stenographer made some of them uncomfortable. Each emphasised his own particular reasons for signing. Genrikh Bruno had become disillusioned when he witnessed central bodies restore to the party 'alien elements' purged by the gubernia purge commission in which he worked. Tolokontsev claimed that agreements made to buy locomotives abroad, rather than to produce them in Russia, drove him to sign the 'Letter of the 22'. Despite his high positions of authority, he said, he could not remain silent in the face of 'actions that kill the proletariat'. According to historian Anthony Heywood, the Worker Oppositionists failed to appreciate the broader diplomatic and economic context for orders of railcar equipment from abroad. Yet in 1926, Tolokontsev still complained that the decision to buy locomotives abroad rather than build them in the RSFSR had delayed the recovery of the metals industry. Kollontai was most concerned, she said, with the 'mass departure of workers from the party'. Acknowledging that she would obey the Comintern's directive, she added that she would not remain silent if nothing changed. Mitin stated that he too would continue to air grievances as an individual, although perhaps not in a collective appeal again.[92]

CCC members responded with condemnation rather than comradely discussion. One urged the signatories to recant; another warned them that they were on the road to factionalism. The level of tension was high. When Medvedev was asked bluntly if he thought that current CC and CCC members had no right to sit in these bodies, he replied tersely: 'The [Tenth Party] Congress elected you; I did not vote'. His answer only annoyed the questioner. At this point, the stenographer was dismissed and the rest of the meeting was not recorded. The CCC either desired less formality or wanted no record of defiant remarks. As a result of its investigation, the CCC recommended that those members of the 22 who had been 'guilty of frequent, systematic violation of the Tenth Party Congress's decree on party unity' be expelled, but it did not specify whom, perhaps

---

92   RGASPI, f. 589, op. 3, d. 9103, vol. 3, ll. 97–106.

indicating disagreement within it.[93] This investigation set the stage for a commission of the Eleventh Party Congress to make specific recommendations on whom to ask the Congress to expel.

At the Eleventh Party Congress (27 March–2 April 1922), those who signed the Letter of the 22 defended themselves against charges of having violated party unity with their appeal to the Comintern. Their opponents accused them of having continued to organise themselves as the 'Workers' Opposition' and of having pursued a line contrary to party policy. Because of the party leadership's campaign in the winter of 1921–2 to remove supporters of the former Workers' Opposition from their organisational bases, only a handful of those who had signed the programme of the Workers' Opposition had returned as voting delegates at the Eleventh Party Congress. Nevertheless, many delegates were dissatisfied with some features of NEP and with the expanding powers of the party control commissions. The 22 thus stood some chance of benefiting from the delegates' mood, especially since two high-ranking leaders were absent or had a reduced presence at the congress. Lenin, whose charisma and persuasive powers could sway delegates, missed some sessions due to his poor health. Bukharin and Radek, highly effective speakers and critics of the 22, were in Berlin for talks on the united front.[94] Because the congress's open proceedings were published and have been analysed in secondary literature, my discussion of it will emphasise what is to be learned from the unpublished records, including the record of the closed session where delegates discussed and voted upon the exclusion of Shliapnikov, Medvedev, Kollontai, and others.

Aware of his supporters' numerical inferiority at the congress, Shliapnikov attempted to appeal to a broad range of delegates. He aimed, at the very least, to convince them that the party's relationship with workers was truly troubled and in need of repair. In open session, he denied that the Workers' Opposition had continued to function as a group. He asserted that party leaders would rather blame the party's troubles on a scapegoat, on a conspiracy of malcontents, rather than address genuine problems. He warned that worker discontent posed a real threat to the party because workers were saying that it was 'better to lose power now, in order to take it anew in 10 years'. Contesting Lenin's claim that the Russian proletariat had ceased to exist as a class in the Marxist sense, Shliapnikov, with customary irony, congratulated congress delegates 'on being the vanguard of a non-existent class' (the proletariat). In a more serious vein, he insisted that Communists needed to work with the industrial proletariat that

93   RGASPI, f. 589, op. 3, d. 9103, vol. 3, ll. 97, 103; f. 48, op. 1, d. 14, l. 3.
94   Schapiro 1956, pp. 334–8; Sorenson 1969, pp. 171–2; Daniels 1988, pp. 163–5; Cohen 1980, p. 151.

existed. He did not share the view that the Russian proletariat had degenerated; rather, he thought that this perspective was a 'justification for political
manoeuvres, searches for support in other social strata' (such as soldiers who
emerged from the peasantry). He insisted: 'Another and "better" working class
we will not have, so we should accept the one we have'.[95]

Ever fond of militaristic metaphors, Lenin had accused the 22 of having created panic in the party ranks with their appeal. Expanding the metaphor, he
reminded delegates that in a real army those who created panic during a retreat
were shot 'and correctly so'. Gamely retorting that the Comintern was 'not a
manoeuvreing army', Shliapnikov also questioned the basis for prosecution,
since all of those who signed had already accepted the decision of the Comintern. He uttered the opinion that comradely relations among party members
were fading and that this posed a danger to the party's very existence. If the
party turned its back on its core constituency of workers, he believed, it would
lose its right to rule. He warned that the atmosphere in the party reminded him
of that in 1907 when *intelligenty* abandoned the workers and showed apathy
towards the cause of revolution. He reminded delegates that he and his supporters were not alien political elements weakening the Communist Party but
belonged to the party's core constituency. At the congress, Zinovy Litvin-Sedoi
had smeared Medvedev as a Menshevik. Defending his comrade, Shliapnikov
remembered that in 1914, when Sedoi enlisted in the French army as a volunteer, Medvedev was on his way to Siberian exile for organising a protest against
the arrest and trial of anti-war Bolshevik deputies in the Duma. 'That is the
irony of fate', Shliapnikov drily added. He concluded dramatically: 'Do not forget that we came from [the working class] to this tribune, and back [to the
working class] we will return'.[96]

Certainly some party leaders wanted to exclude Kollontai, Shliapnikov and
Medvedev from the party and perhaps even prosecute them criminally. But
other party leaders hesitated to risk such a step for fear of stirring up congress
delegates who, although they did not approve of the appeal to the Comintern, sympathised with the grievances expressed in it. Kollontai sensed 'vacilla-
tion' and a 'wait-and-see attitude' at the top. She was aware that the congress's
commission appointed to investigate the 22 had no members sympathetic to
the opposition, yet she believed that even they hesitated to vote for exclusion. (The commission had 19 members, among whom the most prominent

95   RKP(b) 1961, pp. 103–4.
96   RKP(b) 1961, pp. 24, 187–8. Litvin-Sedoi disputed Shliapnikov's accusation (RKP(b) 1961,
      p. 190), but his autobiography does not clearly define his stance towards the war (Gam-
      barov et al. (eds.) 1989, Chapter 3, pp. 30–1).

were: D.Z. Lebed, G.I. Petrovsky, E.M. Iaroslavsky, S.M. Kirov, L.M. Kaganovich, Z.Ia. Litvin-Sedoi, G.E. Zinoviev, I.V. Stalin and F.E. Dzerzhinsky.)[97] Lenin did not take a firm stand.

The Eleventh Party Congress met in a special closed session on 2 April 1922 to consider the recommendations of the congress' commission, which had been formed to investigate whether members of the 22 had violated the Tenth Congress's ban on factionalism. The commission's report determined that there were ideological and organisational links between the former Workers' Opposition and meetings of those who signed the 'Letter of the 22', but the appeal alone did not constitute factionalism. The commission found evidence of 'constant long-term factional work' in Mitin's July 1921 letter, in which Mitin referred to meetings of the former Workers' Opposition after the Tenth Party Congress and to his tactics (discussed earlier) for taking over the Donbas party organisation.[98]

Singling out Shliapnikov, Medvedev, and Kollontai as those most guilty of having continued 'factional work', the commission recommended their expulsion for an indefinite period for having violated the Tenth Party Congress's directives on unity and against factionalism. Of the remaining signatories, the commission recommended to expel only Mitin, for the actions described in his July 1921 letter and for having hidden his Menshevik past, and Nikolai Kuznetsov, for misrepresenting his social origins and length of party membership. (An Old Bolshevik commission established that Kuznetsov had entered the party during World War I rather than in 1904, as he claimed, and before the war had worked as a grocer, not a metalworker.) This was the same Kuznetsov who in 1923 would join Miasnikov's 'Workers' Group'. Those signatories who were not targeted for exclusion proclaimed their solidarity with Shliapnikov, Kollontai and Medvedev (but not with Mitin and Kuznetsov), announcing their intention to resign from the party if those three were expelled. The CCC warned that they were in possible violation of party discipline.[99]

Shliapnikov, Kollontai and Medvedev were permitted to speak in their own defence. Kollontai, who spoke first, steadfastly denied that the 22 had formed a faction. All three denied the existence of a faction. While Kollontai asserted the party could only benefit from private discussion by members of issues of vital importance, Shliapnikov asserted that the true factionalism was on the other side, among the opponents of the Workers' Opposition, including those at the

---

97   RGASPI, f. 134, op. 3, d. 37, l. 37; RKP(b) 1961, pp. 178, 702–10.
98   RGASPI, f. 48, op. 1, d. 14, ll. 3–7; Zorky (ed.) 1926, pp. 51–3.
99   RKP(b)1961, p. 710; RGASPI, f. 48, op. 1, d. 14, ll. 9–13.

very top in the Kremlin and were possibly motivated by lack of concern for the working class. Medvedev, too, spoke defiantly with sarcastic notes.[100]

Following the three oppositionists' speeches, four well-respected and long-standing party members debated the proposal to exclude them. Two, Nikolai Kubiak and Vladimir Antonov-Ovseenko, opposed exclusion of Shliapnikov, Kollontai, and Medvedev; and two, Dmitry Manuilsky and Grigory Petrovsky, did not take a clear position. A former Workers' Opposition supporter, Kubiak reminded delegates of the long history of 'struggle' between *intelligenty* and workers in the party. He recalled how students edged workers out of party-leadership posts because, students claimed, workers were illiterate and could not make speeches. There had been a 'workers' faction', of which Kubiak was a member, at the Third Party Congress in London in 1905, where elevating the role of workers in the party was discussed and the first worker entered the CC. Kubiak also referred to the 1906 Fourth Party Congress in Stockholm as having been 'called by the workers' party'. Presenting party history in this light, he legit-imised the efforts of the Worker Oppositionists to provide a 'worker' perspect-ive on party policy and to increase the role of workers in the party leadership. He argued that the party leaders' acknowledgement that the 22 had the right to appeal to the Comintern contradicted their simultaneous condemnation of its appeal. Both Kubiak and Antonov-Ovseenko downplayed the factional sig-nificance of Mitin's letter. Manuilsky charged that the 22 had worked towards the formation of a liberal workers' party and he spoke for 'strong measures' against the oppositionists. Petrovsky criticised the oppositionists for poor judg-ment, but neither he nor Manuilsky came out for exclusion. Antonov-Ovseenko assured delegates that he had not sensed any underground, anti-party work when he had worked with members of the former Workers' Opposition in Samara. Both he and Manuilsky left the door open for letting the oppositionists off with a warning.[101]

After debate there ensued a complicated series of resolutions, amendments and votes, reflecting evolving opinions within the party on how to treat dis-sent. A majority of delegates resisted going on record with a roll-call vote. The final outcome was to exclude Kuznetsov and Mitin from party member-ship, but Shliapnikov, Kollontai and Medvedev were allowed to remain in the party pending further violations of party unity.[102] The controversy around the 'Letter of the 22' to the Comintern was crucial to the process by which the

100   RGASPI, f. 48, op. 1, d. 14, ll. 14–24, 50–64, 126–31.
101   RGASPI, f. 48, op. 1, d. 14, ll. 65–7, 70–8.
102   RGASPI, f. 48, op. 1, d. 14, ll. 78–84.

party defined the meaning of party discipline and the limits of political discussion. The Eleventh Party Congress delegates' narrow vote signified that many within the party still supported the right to air critical views. Lenin's reluctance to call outright for their expulsion may have emboldened other delegates to resist that option. Many congress delegates wanted to observe communist 'legality', according to which the Comintern's decisions prevailed over those of member parties. Rather than risking defeat, party leaders allowed delegates to choose lesser measures, yet by 1922 the possibility of criminal prosecution for dissent had entered the party's political discourse. Most old party members probably understood that Lenin was speaking figuratively when he referred to using 'machine guns' against opponents within the party. As newer members recruited during the Civil War increasingly replaced 'Old Bolsheviks' at party congresses, the intensely violent language of the leaders came to be understood more literally.

Crucial policy matters also led congress delegates to sympathise with the 22 and to resist the proposal to exclude Shliapnikov, Kollontai and Medvedev from the party. Many in the party felt guilt and discomfort over the ideological compromise that NEP entailed and they feared that concessions to the peasantry posed a danger to urban and industrial worker hegemony. Nevertheless, this very compromise with the peasantry and the consequent vulnerability of the 'proletarian party' drove hardliners to insist that the party close ranks and stifle heterodoxy in order to survive the transition to socialism through NEP. Events surrounding the 'Letter of the 22' were thus a defining moment in the transitional stage between an era of relatively open discussion within the party and one in which party members could be vilified, stigmatised and isolated for expressing opinions that differed from the Politburo's line.

1   A.M. Kollontai's Diary Entries, March–April 1921[103]

23 March 1921

The Workers' Opposition spoke out as an official group. There were forty-five delegates in all with a deciding vote and fifteen with a deliberative vote. All are workers. My brochure was published hastily .... About 2,000 copies were issued. The Workers' Opposition decided to get places in the presidium. Shl[iapnikov]

---

103   RGASPI, f. 134, op. 3, d. 37, ll. 1–7. In this translation, the parenthetical material is Kollontai's. I inserted bracketed text. The ellipses may belong to the original text or may indicate my omissions in note-taking.

is at the head. But I hate Medvedev's cunning. The brochure circulates from hand to hand. Many like it.

But the atmosphere is heavy and difficult. A few days before the congress, the Kronstadt uprising, the mutiny of sailors, began. ... In Petrograd there is worker unrest. People arriving from Petrograd say, 'This is all [because of] Zinoviev's and Lashevich's lording about. They went too far. The workers are embittered and hungry'. The sailors demand re-election of the Kronstadt soviets. There are our party members in Kronstadt, but they also favour re-elections.

The congress proceeds under the mark of difficult events. Our people will have to pacify our own people. ....

My brochure is in Lenin's hands. He very quickly leafs through it and shakes his head disapprovingly. ... Lenin's speech routs ¾ of the Workers' Opposition [на три четверти громит], but my brochure is the main thing. I sit with [Jacques] Sadoul [?]. V[ladimir] I[lich Lenin] approaches. 'Do you understand what you have done? Indeed, this is a summons to a split and the platform of a new party. For this you all should not only be excluded [from the party], but also shot! And at such a time! This is syndicalism. I will place your brochure before a court of the International!' Those who had only just grabbed the brochure would not offer their hands ... All around there was emptiness and coldness. The most terrible was that our people from the opposition, those who insisted that I write it, Shl[iapnikov] and Medv[edev], suddenly start to avoid me! This I did not expect at all! Didn't I express their theses and thoughts in it? Wasn't it the fruit of much discussion? Didn't they get angry with me, because I did not speak together with them at meetings? (I had no time.) They nearly accused me of cowardice, yet now at the congress, after V[ladimir] I[lich]'s speech, they go into hiding. Well okay, maybe right now is not the time for the W[orkers'] O[pposition], but indeed we were in it all together. You can't just pretend that I alone 'managed to do' [осилила] all this?!

In the evening the 'CC convenes a private meeting' of its underground Bolsheviks. I am not an underground Bolshevik, according to Shl[iapnikov] and Medv[edev], so they go without me ... The meeting was devoted to my brochure. I do not and cannot disavow my opinions, but this hurts. Just what is this, to have been betrayed by those who were in this together with me, those who seemed to sincerely want to correct the party line, who shout from below: this is how we feel!

Shl[iapnikov] and Medv[edev] disavowed the brochure. Medv[edev] even said: 'I did not read it!' ... Then the entire opposition met. I stated the problem point-blank. The matter is not about my brochure, but about proposing something real to the congress. We need to demand the removal of Zinoviev and Lashevich from Petrograd, until the reasons for the mutiny are investigated. But my proposal fails. There is no longer any unanimity. There are three different proposals, but nothing well-defined.

They read out the resolution censuring the Workers' Opposition and the conditions for their candidates to enter the CC. Our people, Shl[iapnikov] and Kutuzov, enter. The opposition is destroyed.

When they read the resolution, Lenin attentively listened and gazed upon our group. He nodded his head as a sign of approval. After the proclamation, no one even asked to say a word. Before the resolution was pronounced, Shliapnikov said, 'It remains to don one's cap and depart'. But he did not budge, since there was already an 'understanding'. Factions and groupings are forbidden. The workers, who sincerely wanted to do something and to change something, are dismayed and perplexed. I went home with a heavy heart. I do not forgive Shl[iapnikov] and Medvedev for their betrayal. They abandoned me and all the responsibility fell on me.

The events in Kronstadt push everything into the background. But the reasons need to be investigated! Pavel said that it was possible to avert fratricidal slaughter. He proposed to go as an envoy to the sailors. Trotsky forbade it. Trotsky sent a demand to the Kronstadters: 'surrender, then we'll pardon you'. This only embittered them more. Trotsky behaved insolently and cowardly. There's nothing to say about Zinoviev. His automobile stood ready night and day by the 'Astoria'. Everyone saw and knew this. 'If not for Stalin, nothing would have been done', said Pavel.[104] But Trotsky is embittered against Stalin for having known how to stop the [illegible] uprising ...

Such was the situation. Lenin negotiated with the 'leaders' of the opposition Shl[iapnikov] and Med[vedev]. They are offered two places in the CC.

All this is very, very difficult. I don't go to visit Shl[iapnikov]. We meet on the stairs: 'Why won't you drop in on me?' 'I have no time A[leksandr] G[avrilovich]'.

There was an Orgburo session. Molotov had replaced Krestinsky. With him [Molotov] it is easier. He more keenly perceives our needs and inquiries (of Zhenotdel). Kr[estinsky] is a dry crust [сухарь] and [two illegible words].

But there was much blood. Kronst[adt] cost 3,000 lives of communists alone! It is hard for me ...

At the congress, there was personal struggle along with political struggle. Around trade unions and between Tr[otsky] and Zinoviev. Zinoviev was very malicious and petty. During elections for the CC, Zinoviev came in at 18th place and Trotsky at sixth. This is all characteristic. The popularity of both is waver-

---

104   She crossed through 'Pavel' and wrote 'comrade'.

ing. The half-intelligentsia composition of the congress is also characteristic. There are many new communists, who are not workers.

It is funny that the 'apparat' immediately changed its attitude. I remain in Zhenotdel. But I cannot get a car when I call to the garage or to the auto depot. They gave me a special order for invalid rations and then refused to issue the special ration and everything of this sort.

But this does not hurt! Disappointment in my comrades and in such a friend as Shl[iapnikov] is painful. Well okay, he understood that he acted incorrectly and that opposition is not needed. But then why enter the CC 'from the opposition'? Why not say directly at the congress: I erred and will not have anything more to do with oppositionism. It is harmful and so forth. But no! I know that in the evenings they gather in Shliapnikov's room and again 'criticise' and again 'crack jokes' ...

If you want to set right the party's line, it's necessary to have the courage to do so openly.

[Writes about trade, about the tax in kind]

Now, after the congress, it is impossible even to begin discussion. Lenin sees salvation in party unity: 'Only a firmly welded party, which is united and not disconnected even on one question, can cope with the situation'.

But indeed many have doubts. Much is not understood or not as it should be. It's impossible without criticism and without mass initiative! ...

27 March 1921

Pavel returned from Kronstadt. He was in a lively mood and had an Order of the Red Banner. Pavel is a suppresser of the sailors' mutiny ... Life is so full of incompatibilities. It seems that Pavel carried out feats of courage. He, like others, curses Trotsky and praises Stalin. Stalin goes against the military spetses from Trotsky's apparat.

I gaze at Pavel and think how can it be so? At Kronstadt, maybe there were your comrade-sailors [матросня] from Tsentrobalt?[105] Really, are they all enemies? 'This was necessary to save the Soviet Republic. We were within a hair's breadth' ... Yes, yes, of course. But really in the depth of your soul, Pavel, doesn't a 'little worm' [of doubt] stir?

---

105   Tsentrobalt was the Central Committee of the Baltic Fleet.

Revolution is a cruel thing. Lenin is right. It's impossible to do in white gloves. But all this is hard.

Pavel was appointed commandant in Kronstadt.

But why don't our newspapers write about him? Or are Dybenko's old 'transgressions' still not forgotten?[106]

I go to meetings at plants. It feels as if right now there is not the same attitude toward us communists that there still was in the autumn. In our presence, they don't converse among themselves. Cells [ячейки] have been nicknamed 'bloodhounds' [ищейки].[107] For 900 workers in the factory, there are only 15 communists. When an orator criticises us, they laugh loudly and applaud. This is so in many places. Especially where there are more male workers. With women it is easier and better. ...

Not long ago, when a resolution was voted, 27 hands were raised in favour. Who is against? No one. Who abstained? Two hands. And as for the rest? They laugh loudly. 'We're not participating'. These are all bad symptoms. We have become isolated from the masses. Something needs to be done. Something is going [awry?].

Yesterday 233 voted for us and 203 for the Mensheviks. Not because the Mensheviks proposed something smart and useful, but only because they are 'against' us.

1 April 1921

[It was her birthday]. The Workers' Opposition has collapsed. It has disintegrated. Shl[iapnikov] is intoxicated by his rank as a CC member. We see one another infrequently.

[Further, she writes about Zhenotdel.]

2   **Appeals of the Worker-Peasant Socialist Party Led by Vasily Paniushkin, Early 1921[108]**

[On 14 March 1921, Vasily Paniushkin directed a letter to the RCP(b) committee of Gorodskoi district in Moscow, with copies to the CC and the Moscow Com-

---

106   In April 2018 Dybenko was dismissed from his post as Naval Commissar and court martialed for mistakes made in the defence of Petrograd from German troops' advance in February 2018.

107   The Russian words for party cell and bloodhound sound very similar.

108   RGASPI, f. 5, op. 1, d. 2572, l. 52; TsAODM, f. 3, op. 2, d. 18, ll. 2–3.

mittee, in which he asked that he no longer be regarded as a member of the Russian Communist Party. At the time, he was a member of the Gorodskoi District Party Committee. His decision to leave the party, he said, was motivated by decisions of the Tenth Party Congress, which from his perspective signified that the party no longer defended the interests on which the October Revolution was built. His letter was accompanied by a statement of his group, which referred to themselves as a group of activist revolutionary worker-activists of Moscow and Russia. Their March statement called on revolutionary workers to participate in elections to the soviets. It remarked that the Communists kept the date of elections secret for a long time, before finally calling them for 13 April and providing only two days in which to conduct elections. The March letter stated that his group opposed inclusion in the soviets of 'Guchkovs, Miliukovs, Mensheviks, SRs, and anarchists', but complained that the Communist Party was full of nonworker elements.[109] Unfortunately, my notes from the Central Archive of the FSB are only summaries of the above-mentioned documents. Below are two other documents, which emerged from the group, courtesy of Simon Pirani.]

1.   *Announcement*[110]
Dear comrades.

The unhealthy atmosphere which has been created in the RCP around political and organisational questions, especially about the situation of the worker element in the party, has reached the height of evil, perversion, patronage, favouritism, and simply dishonesty and shameless bragging (Khlestakovshchina)[111] of all sorts and types. The overwhelming influence of an element alien to the workers has made it impossible to wage struggle against all these things. Consequently, many honest worker comrades, who do not wish to become reconciled to this, have felt compelled to abandon the ranks of the party. We workers who have left the RCP remain communists ideologically and do not wish to suffer a political death. We hold dear the interests of the proletariat and its achievements in October 1917. Because power currently has transferred in concealed form to the bourgeoisie, which only calls itself communist, we have organised into a group of activist revolutionary workers of Moscow and Russia, who now have transformed into the Worker-Peasant Socialist Party (WPSP). We summon all workers and peasants who hold dear the October Revolution, the

---

109   TsA FSB, R33718, d. 499061, vol. 40, ll. 234–5.
110   RGASPI, f. 5, op. 1, d. 2572.
111   Khlestakov was a character from Gogol's play *The Inspector General*.

interests of the proletariat, and the very fate of the proletariat to enter into the ranks of our party, which is young in age but old in ideas, in order to help the great cause of struggle for liberation of labourers of towns and countryside from both bourgeois and state capital. We order all worker comrades who have departed from the RCP for one or another motive to enter into the WPSP for organised struggle against the bourgeoisie. Long live the Socialist Revolution! Long Live Soviet Power and the greatest achievement of the October Revolution! Long Live the Revolutionary Proletariat!

Temporary bureau of the WPSP

2. *Worker-Peasant Socialist Party*[112]
Proletarians of all countries, unite

Declaration to the first plenum of the Moscow Soviet of Workers' and Peasants' Deputies convening on 31 [May?]

Nearly four years have gone by in the proletarian revolution. At the cost of enormous losses, the proletariat of the towns and countryside took power from the bourgeoisie. Yet the ruling party of communists, by means of diverse machinations and tricks, has shoved the proletariat aside from management of the Republic and reduced it to the situation of a citizen, who is deprived of rights and at times is even regarded as [politically] 'unreliable'.

The soviets are the greatest achievement of the October revolution. They transformed from bodies, which bore and expressed the will of the proletariat, into a screen for communists who act like guardians for a minor and into a blind weapon in these guardians' hands. These guardians now ruthlessly and cynically trample upon everything for which the proletariat once struggled and spilled its blood. The elections to the Moscow Soviet serve as a vivid example of the above. It is no wonder that at the plenum of the Moscow Soviet, we see so few genuine representatives of the revolutionary proletariat. Class struggle, as the consequence of proletarian social revolution, is still not finished. It only enters a new period of its development. Having lost the possibility to smash the Soviet Republic from without, the bourgeoisie together with the Menshevik

---

112 TsAODM, f. 3, op. 2, d. 18, ll. 2–3, May 1921?. According to Pirani 2008, p. 105, the appeal translated here (from photocopies provided by him) was directed to nonparty members of the Moscow soviet. Pirani writes that members of Paniushkin's group achieved a small victory when they convinced a meeting of Moskomgosor employees to denounce actions Kamenev had taken to politically undermine nonparty members of the soviets (p. 105).

and SR parties, which are branded with the mark of Cain and support it with lackeyism and servility, apply new methods of struggle against the proletariat. The effort to shatter the power of the proletariat from within is becoming too obvious and insolent. Unfortunately, we should establish as a fact here that the bourgeoisie meets with faithful assistants from the party of communists, which is poisoned by petty bourgeois types who are alien to the proletariat. Likewise, having broken off from and lost connection with the proletariat and having become filled up to about 75% with a bankrupt element, the party of communists set foot on a false and harmful path for the social revolution. This was the path of concessions to the kulakry, to speculators, and to predatory capitalists of the world, which incurs a loss to the interests and strivings of the proletarian masses of the cities and countryside. Given such a situation, all conquests of the October Revolution are threatened by inevitable obsolescence.

The business of saving the revolution is that of the proletarians of town and countryside themselves, as they are closely bound by mutual interests and unconstrained by any casuistical laws of soviet guardians. Only when the proletariat of the towns and countryside directly participates in all events of the life of the republic is it possible to find the exit from the dead end and to realise socialism by deepening and broadening the achievements of October.

Being representatives of workers in the Moscow Soviet and invested by their trust to defend the interests of proletariat, we members of the Worker Peasant Socialist Party and nonparty supporters of the social revolution declare:

We went into the Soviet not for idle chatter, but for stubborn daily work in order to correct old and new mistakes and to lay the path for future socialism. We intend for our work to be guided by the achievements of the October Revolution and by the paths it has marked out, namely:

Because the soviets should express the will of the proletariat and so should be proletarian soviets, it is necessary to eliminate from the soviet the alien element, which at times is hostile to the proletariat, although it conceals itself behind a communist mask. A new harmful phenomenon is causing the idea of Soviet power to degenerate. This phenomenon is executive committeeism [исполковщина]. Soviet power must be restored quickly to that form in which it appeared to the proletariat in the time of October. The chair of the soviet and of the executive committee cannot be the very same person; one cannot simultaneously be the superviser and the supervised. This measure needs to be compulsory, considering that secret affinities and personal sympathies can be concealed. We will especially insist upon it during discussion about organising the construction of soviets.

It needs to be noted that our country's difficult economic situation, when metals and fuel are scarce and there are insufficient equipment and raw materials, demands rapid heroic measures in building the economy, in order to avert an impending catastrophe. The chief means capable of raising productivity is implementation of economic policy through workers' organisations. Professional organisations and production unions should be presented with decisive influence in government economic bodies, which obtain and distribute all kinds of material resources. Introduction of a system of organisation and management of the national economy through production unions will create unified leadership, will eliminate the setting of worker masses off against specialists, and so will create broad scope for people of science, theory, and practice to be organisers and administrators. Besides that, it will eliminate irresponsibility and lack of accountability by individual leaders of many complex industrial enterprises.

To successfully implement the proposed measures, it is necessary to reinforce the primary cells of professional and production unions, which are mill and factory worker committees. They and higher bodies should be prepared to directly manage the economy. In order to involve them in the conscious, initiating, and creative participation in this management, it follows:

a) to carry out demarcations among individual unions on the basis of their role in production.

b) to not make assignments to administrative-economic posts, without involving the union.

c) to not reject candidates of unions and to consider them mandatory for VSNKh and its bodies.

d) that all personnel appointed or nominated by the union are responsible to the union and can be recalled by it at any time.

Unity of will, which is necessary to organise the national economy, can only be created by concentrating management of the whole economy of the republic in the hands of the production unions. This will make it actually possible to initiate the broad worker masses' influence over the organisation and development of our economy.

Organisation of workers' daily life is closely tied to economy building. The following measures need to be implemented without deviation:

a) Struggle resolutely against all illegal issuance of rations and complete elimination of specialist rations for anyone, no matter what position they occupy.

b) Cease the practice of paying for specialists' labour by means of bonuses in kind and replace it with cash remuneration.

c) Take measures for preferential supply of workers with consumer goods.

d)   Simplify and hasten the procedure for receiving work clothes and likewise basic and bonus stores of goods.

e)   In those localities, where housing is an acute problem, consolidate soviet and military institutions toward the goal of presenting apartments to workers.

f)   Organise repair of workers' housing on the resources of enterprises, under the condition that the enterprise will guarantee fulfillment of its main production assignments and will transfer homes exclusively to the workers of a given enterprise.

g)   Organise special worker trains and trams, timing their movement according to the beginning and the end of work in enterprises.

h)   Attach to factories or specially organise workshops for repair of footwear and clothing in order to service the needs of workers of factories; the enterprises should render all kinds of support and aid to these workshops, both in organising equipment and supplying them with necessary materials to the extent possible.

i)   When an enterprise has communal gardens and the like, communal farms should be equipped with technical inventory and resources at the expense of the enterprise.

j)   Enterprises, which are located in direct proximity to the countryside, should organise the repair of agricultural machines.

k)   Urban services and utilities need to be improved to an adequate level.

l)   Serious attention must be turned to schools, nurseries, and so forth.

The Moscow Soviet should mark out a firm policy and attitude toward the peasantry in the sense of strengthening close ties between the urban proletariat and the poor and middle peasants; first of all, the inventory needs of the countryside should be satisfied.

Recognising the right to a free existence in a free republic for all truly revolutionary parties, which have participated in emancipating the proletariat from the yoke of capital, we demand political rights for all parties, which have not betrayed the cause of the proletariat, the liberation of these parties' representatives from prisons, if they are not guilty of criminal violations, and the full repeal of the death penalty, with the exception of certain enemies of the proletariat, against whom struggle should be waged most resolutely.

Recognising that the Moscow Soviet is confronted with enormous and crucial work, which may be carried out successfully only when delegates are directly and closely united with their electorates, who should be constantly kept informed of the creative work of the Soviet through weekly reports of delegates about the situation, the Worker Peasant Socialist Party calls upon the proletarian masses of Moscow city and gubernia to close their ranks and wage resolute battle with economic dislocation on the path toward the end goal of worldwide socialism.

Long live the power of the Soviets, which is the greatest conquest of the October revolution

Long live the world socialist revolution

Long live the revolutionary proletariat of the city and countryside

The Worker-Peasant Socialist Party

3   A.G. Shliapnikov, 'To the Fourth Congress of the All-Russian Metalworkers' Union (VSRM)'[113]

The Fourth Congress of the All-Russian Union of Metalworkers will be held on 25 May.

Representatives of our country's metals industry will assemble from all ends of immense Soviet Russia, in order to summarise the results of past activity and to mark signposts for future work.

The extensive agenda embraces all questions that worry metalworkers, not only as members of the steel industry family, but also as leading revolutionary warriors, who in recent years carried out enormous work and resolutely struggled to defend our worker fatherland.

Senior representatives of metalworking Russia will listen to papers and reports about the condition of our union, the situation of industry, and its prospects.

The Congress has to resolve some organisational problems, make a final decision about wage rates in the new economic circumstances, and state its authoritative word about the fate of our industry.

In summarising past results and outlining future work, the congress should take account of all particularities of the time we are living through.

Worker-Peasant Russia emerged as the victor on all fronts against counterrevolution. As a result of these victories, our international position got stronger and for the first time, after three years of uninterrupted bloody struggle, our

---

113   'K chetvertomu syezdu VSRM', *Metallist*, nos. 3–4 (April–May 1921): 1–2.

country's workers and peasants can count on the possibility of free and peaceful economy building.

But the general backwardness of our country and the prevalence of the petty bourgeoisie and of handicrafts [ремесленные] economic forms make the path of economy building extraordinarily complicated.

The basis of socialist construction is large nationalised industry, which is experiencing a phase of crisis. The exhaustion of government resources and the general ruin of the country do not allow large enterprises' work to develop to its full speed. The crisis we are experiencing has an especially severe impact on our industrial base, which is metallurgy and metalworking industry. Productivity of our blast furnaces fell to 2.5% of the prewar level. At the factories, business also goes poorly. It should not continue this way. Our union, which unites more than 500,000 workers, is vitally interested in reviving metals industry. The revival of the entire national economy, the welfare of the working class, and the realisation of socialist goals depend on the work of our blast furnaces, our factories and workshops.

Therefore, the congress should pay special attention to the future of our metals industry.

Working in wartime conditions, we found it difficult to take stock of our experience and to seek new forms of proletarian labour unions, which would be capable of reviving workers' slumbering creativity, getting them to take an interest, and utilising their labour self-activity.

Now, with the transition to economy building, all members and personnel of our congress should direct their efforts to this aspect of the business.

Reports and papers will conclude with some practical proposals.

The congress should accept those which will secure for the workers' Republic the development of its productive forces, the revival of its destroyed economy, and maximum wellbeing for the working class.

The position of our industry's workers is extraordinarily difficult.

Because of this, the attraction toward the land and toward vegetable gardens has prevailed up to now. Our best and most essential cadres of skilled workers have been dispersed. They have turned into tillers of the soil, market-gardeners, and representatives of other 'free' professions.

It will be necessary to struggle against this phenomenon. The congress should point to such measures, which could halt the dispersal of the work force and create a reverse inflow of workers to our plants and factories.

Our wage rates policy should use the entire experience of four years of work. This experience is extraordinarily instructive. First of all, it teaches that wage rates policy cannot be built on the principles of consumer equalisation [потребительская уравнительность] and of dogmatic 'unity' of wage rates, which renders unity only on paper.

The wage rates table should account for all particularities of industry and separate districts [районы] and should be tailored earnestly to each enterprise. A single wage rates table should be created. It should emerge only from concrete conditions and should be based on the minimum of resources necessary to support and revive the work force.

A completely new question for our union is on the agenda of the congress. This is about cooperative societies. Permission for free trade and the development of handicrafts [ремесло и кустарничество] will confront us with the need to utilise this means to reinforce our wage rates practice.

Along with these questions, the congress has to resolve the problem of our union's participation and activity in the International Federation of Metalworkers' Unions. The opportunist big shots of the International Central Committee distribute false information about our organisation. They counterpose to it some supposedly 'free' unions of metalworkers of Soviet Russia. Delegates from various districts of our country will expose the conciliationists' unworthy counterrevolutionary method and will show that the metalworker family of Russia is united and that **there are no other metals organisations in our country, aside from the All-Russian Union of Metalworkers.**[114]

This congress of all metalworkers of our republic will demonstrate not only its organised unity, but also its unity of thought and will.

After the Fourth Congress, our proletarian family will be even more tightly cohesive, even more united, and ready with all its strength to defend the conquests of the October Revolution.

4   A.G. Shliapnikov, 'Our Economic Policy and Practice'[115]

Shliapnikov, Kutuzov, Medvedev, and Kubiak brought these points to the 11 May 1921 Politburo meeting about economic policy.

1.   All government economic bodies, trade unions, factory managements and similar proletarian organisations determine our economic condition to be catastrophic. The catastrophe is that the government is deprived of circulating resources of raw materials, provisions, and fuel, causing plants, factories, and railroads to spontaneously come to a halt. Such an economic state undermines the basis of the proletarian dictatorship, disorganises workers, atomises the proletariat, deprives it of a material base,

---

114   The text was underlined for emphasis.
115   RGASPI, f. 2, op. 1, d. 20219, ll. 1–6; and TsA FSB, R33718, d. 499061, vol. 38, 'K voprosu o nashei khoziaistennoi politike i praktike', handwritten by Shliapnikov.

throws it from industry into agriculture and cottage industry, and brings it under the power of petty industry and speculation.

2.   Our economic policy and practice up to now have had the following basic features. All large industry, communications, and transport are the property of the Republic. Local state bodies command a significant share of the most important small and mid-sized industrial enterprises. State bodies regulate and supply cottage industry. The interrelations of urban industry and agriculture were regulated in the war period by requisitions, which were replaced in the current year with the tax-in-kind [продна-лог], which is based on government taking a share of peasant production for its benefit and free disposal of the remaining amount. To the peasants, the government presents manufactured goods and government services 'at fixed prices' and often completely free.

3.   In order to determine the correct line of economic policy and practice, the preceding three and a half years of experience building the economy need to be considered. According to our economic bodies' official data, the imminent catastrophe is the consequence of the following three basic reasons:

    a.   Soviet government has had to manage a huge mass of very diverse enterprises, but it did not have sufficient resources to serve them;

    b.   lack of organisation and planning in supplying workers with provisions, everyday and special clothing, and consumer goods;

    c.   no link between provisioning workers and workers' labour productivity, which is low.

4.   Such assertions are deeply incorrect in essence and harm not only the business of internal economic construction, but also the interests of international revolution.

    a.   The quantity and variety of nationalised industrial enterprises cannot explain the catastrophe. All the enterprises so indicated have turned a profit for their owners and served as a material basis for the predominance of the capitalist class. Proletarian power should have used these enterprises to reinforce its strength and to attract material resources from the broad mass of consumers.

    b.   The second assertion about the lack of correlation between provisioning and productivity likewise is not well-grounded. Not one factory in the Republic has been supplied regularly and fully even at half the minimum required for subsistence. Struggling to survive, workers were forced to seek a way out through disorganised barter with the countryside and secret work for the private consumer, which ruined them.

c. The third reason refers to workers' low labour productivity. Its formulation attests to a dangerous, bourgeois deviation of thought and attitude toward well-known facts of the relationship between productivity and working conditions. Never has the situation of the proletarian who has not had recourse to agricultural support been so horrible as now in our time. Despite this, the output of basic items of production (metals, mining, and textiles) significantly exceeds the sum of value that workers have used. Data from the Donbas show that in 1920 a miner's labour to produce one pud of coal cost 35% less than in 1914. The productivity of labour is not the main reason for the catastrophe. Instead, it is a consequence of the material conditions in which workers live.

All these apparent 'reasons' are only consequences of our soviet bodies' uneconomical use of the equipment and resources of powerful socialised production.

5. The basic reason for the imminent catastrophe is that Soviet power, which is the power of the organised industrial proletariat, after having nationalised the railroads, other means of transport, all large and mid-sized industry, part of small-scale industry, and some town holdings [город-ские хозяйства], then presented all this free-of-charge for use by the peasantry, the bourgeoisie and the urban petty bourgeoisie. Chiefly the workers maintained the state as a social organisation, while the urban petty bourgeoisie and the peasantry made comparatively insignificant contributions. Instead of using socialised resources and equipment to create a system to reinforce the dictatorship of the proletariat and to improve its material situation, these resources were presented to the peasantry and to bourgeois and petty bourgeois elements of the cities under the slogans of implementing apparently socialist measures, without almost any compensation for their value. The inevitable result was and is the exhaustion and atomisation of the Republic's raw materials, fuel, and food supplies. Meanwhile, these resources were wasted not so much on satisfying the direct needs of the working class as on serving chiefly the interests of peasants and the petty bourgeois population of the towns. The direct conclusion that follows from this is that the use of socialised resources and production equipment should be built upon the principles of economic reckoning and aimed first of all toward securing fully and in a multifaceted way the vital needs of the working class.

6. The decisions of the Tenth Congress and the May conference of the RCP about questions of economic policy have not given a concrete, precise

and final instruction about the mistakes of prior economic policy. Instead, they have introduced confusion and conflict into party members' thought and into the work of party, economic and trade union organisations. They have made more difficult the correct assimilation of the content of the new course and its implementation, and are still understood by many party personnel as contradicting the party programme. It is necessary to clearly indicate how the new course of our economic policy agrees with the basic positions in our party programme.

The RCP programme defines the basis of our economic policy in the following way:

a.   to unwaveringly continue and bring to a conclusion the expropriation of the bourgeoisie and the transformation of the means of production into the property of Soviet power, which means the common property of all labourers. These processes have already begun and mainly have already concluded.

b.   The wholesale elevation of productive forces is the main thing in defining the entire economic policy of Soviet power. Because the country has experienced the most severe destruction, the amount of goods needed by the population must be increased quickly and by whatever means necessary. This is the practical goal to which everything else must be subordinated. [preceding is underlined] ('RCP programme', part on the economy, points 1 and 2)

7.   The RCP(b) Tenth Congress and May conference decided to outline a new point of economic policy (tax-in-kind, barter, support of petty and handicrafts industry, cooperatives, private leasing and so forth). This point is contradictory only in form, but in essence coincides with the programme's directive as it is expressed in the second point of the same proposal. At the current time, not only the correlation of the country's internal economic forces, but also the Republic's international situation dictate this new course of economic policy.

8.   When implementing the new course of economic policy, it is necessary to avoid those mistakes, which were committed at the beginning, with the socialisation and arrangement of the management of our industry and entire national economy. Without giving in to panic, it is necessary to carry out a system of measures, which would ensure for the working class the maximum of actual participation in the economy, in the epoch when petty economic forces are growing.

In the first place, our economic policy needs to be turned definitively toward serving the demands [запросы] of agriculture for items of industrial production. This demands the hasty re-examination of all basic production programmes and the maximum reduction of work toward general government needs, such as transport, army, and navy. [preceding paragraph is underlined]

Available state resources should be concentrated on the largest enterprises of general state significance. In regards to the remaining large, middle, and small enterprises outside of state supply, the following measure should be accepted. All enterprises are subject to leasing on negotiated conditions, under the supervision of trade unions, collectives of workers, and technical personnel of given enterprises, according to the principle that they will use their own finished products for organised barter with agricultural producers.

9. The dictatorship of the working class can exist only under the nonnegotiable condition that the main branches of the industrial economy, of all large enterprises, mining and processing industry are kept in the hands of the workers' state. Likewise and especially, all central and local power-plants [силовые установки] must be concentrated under state bodies.

The government's available provisions and supplies are insufficient to fully realise this plan. However, the country has sufficient resources to support workers. Proof of this is evident. By means of work in the countryside and barter, workers of those nationalised enterprises, which for three years state bodies supplied very irregularly and incompletely, independently found the resources they needed for survival. This should be considered, when organising foodstuffs and raw materials for industry. Earlier capitalists and now workers show that industry on its own has sources for maintaining the workforce. The state should take this path and use the initiative of workers' organisations in the business of organising and restoring industry.

10. There should be energetic struggle against widespread illusions that delivery from the imminent catastrophe will come from creating small industry and developing handicrafts. Anyone who has studied the economy of our country knows that small industry and handicrafts were only insignificant supplements to the main branches of industry.

Just as mistaken are reckonings about the delivery of the proletariat's power through private-entrepreneur leasing. Russian lessors-entrepreneurs will make their base in the countryside, using its foodstuffs and the Republic's raw materials. Important aid can be rendered only by using concessions to attract foreign capital that is capable of giving working capital. Instead of supporting private-entrepreneurial, speculative leasing, the state needs to support workers' artels, workers' cooperatives and other such collective leasing by the workers themselves, according to the principle of presenting to the government a certain percentage of manufactured products, or an appropriate amount of labour hours.

11. The route of forming trusts and combinations of large and midsized enterprises, according to the principles of the material interest of the workers in the enterprise's running and exploitation, is a more reasonable and healthy resolution of the problem and a means of reviving the industrial economy. This can be achieved by rational distribution of state production, foodstuffs, and financial capital within each branch of industry, with such a reckoning that enterprises of government-wide significance are secured fully within the limits of the minimum for subsistence established by the trade unions. Other enterprises issuing goods for use in agriculture and consumer goods are to organise supply by deducting a certain percentage of fabricated goods issued by the enterprise in a quantity not less than that share, which lay in the wages of the workers as a percentage of the overall output under capitalist management. Deducted manufactured goods are to enter into a barter fund and sale, for the satisfaction of the workers.

12. Focusing all its resources on large industry, the government should try to free itself from its old dependence on the small producer of products of food and raw materials, by organising large mechanised farming and concentrating the inventory of the existing sovkhozes on the largest acreages of land. To achieve these goals, it is necessary to attach sovkhozes, cultivated land, meadows and forests to plants and factories.

13. The renewal and development of Soviet Russia's national economy is impossible without establishing economic ties to the world economy. Taking into consideration the predominance of the capitalist economic system in other countries and the backwardness of our economy, the forms of links between Soviet Russia and other states can be trade agreements based on barter and granting of concessions for exploiting our country's natural resources.[116]

---

116   The copy in RGASPI omits point #13, but the copy in the TsA FSB includes it.

5   Speeches Protesting Against Party Appointment of Metalworkers'
     Union Leaders; Protocols of the RCP CC's Commission, the Bureau
     of the Communist Faction, and the Communist Faction of the
     Congress; and Other Materials Relating to the Fourth Congress of
     the Metalworkers' Union in May 1921[117]

Session of the RCP(b) faction of the Fourth All-Russian Congress of the Metalworkers' Union, 26 May 1921.[118]

168 delegates present. Shliapnikov chairs.

Decided:

1)   To elect a Bureau of the RCP Faction composed of the following seven
     comrades: Shliapnikov, Skliznev, Mitin (Donbas), Tashkin (Urals), Barsky
     (Nizhny), Fedorov (Piter), Tarasov (Moscow). Congress delegates who are
     communists with a consultative vote have the right of a full vote at the
     sessions of the faction. ...

2)   To elect a Presidium of the Congress composed of 13 comrades, of whom
     11 are communists and two are nonparty delegates. From the faction, to
     elect the following comrades: Shliapnikov, Vladimirov, Skliznev, Tarasov,
     Maslennikov (Tula), Tashkin, Brykov [?] (Briansk), Fedorov, Mitin, Barsky,
     Plokhotnikov (Kharkov).

[Confirms the Congress's regulations and agenda, both with corrections. Elects
a mandate commission.]

.•.•

Session of the RCP(b) Central Committee Commission on conducting the
Fourth All-Russian Congress of Metalworkers, 28 May 1921.[119]

Attending: comrades Shmidt, Chubar, Uglanov, Shliapnikov; members of the
Congress of the All-Russian Union of Metalworkers RCP(b) Faction Bureau.
Chair: comrade Chubar.

Heard: Discussion of those removed by the Petrograd delegation of metalworkers from the list of All-Russian Metalworkers' Union central committee mem-

---

117   RGASPI, f. 17, op. 84, d. 220; f. 99, op. 1, d. 7, d. 8.
118   RGASPI, f. 99, op. 1, d. 7, l. 8, protocol no. 1.
119   RGASPI, f. 17, op. 84, d. 220, ll. 1–2, protocol.

bers, which was accepted by a majority of the Bureau of the Faction of the RCP(b) of the Fourth Congress of the All-Russian Metalworkers' Union. Fourteen comrades were removed as full members of the union central committee and seven as candidate members.

Comrade Shmidt proposes comrade [Nikolai] Ianson in place of comrade Medvedev, because comrade Ianson is an old trade union movement worker [работник] and it's desirable to bring him into the new central committee as a worker [работник] from the provinces. Comrade Medvedev worked in the central committee earlier and his line of behaviour in it speaks for itself that he should not enter its new composition.

Decided: three members of the commission vote to remove comrade Medvedev, while one is against.

Heard: Comrade Shliapnikov speaks out for bringing comrade Medvedev into the central committee as an old trade union activist, who can be of much use to it.

After the vote, comrade Shliapnikov declares: From the time of the Tenth RCP(b) Congress there have been no groupings and there are none now. There is no Workers' Opposition. The commission's actions are guided by concern about groupings that no longer exist. Therefore I propose to affix my statement in the protocol.

Comrade Shmidt speaks out against Skliznev, indicating that he needs to be replaced by comrade [Aleksandr] Gurevich, who works more in the central committee.

Decided: Three vote to remove comrade Skliznev and replace him with comrade Gurevich, while one votes in favour of comrade Skliznev.

Heard: Comrade Shliapnikov advocates bringing comrade Skliznev into the central committee as a young and promising worker [работник] He points to the need to send comrade Gurevich to work at the district level.

Comrade Chubar speaks out against comrade Chernov, pointing out that he should remain at economic work.

Decided: The commission by three votes does not object to bringing comrade Chernov into the central committee, but he should remain at economic work. Comrade Uglanov abstains.

Heard: Comrade Shliapnikov speaks in favour of bringing comrade Chernov into the central committee and argues that it should decide where comrade Chernov should work.

Comrade Shmidt voices opposition to introducing comrade [Mikhail] Lobanov into the central committee, since he is weak and cannot be of use to it.

Comrade Shliapnikov states that since the Southern delegation has nominated comrade Lobanov, it is necessary to include him. Concerning comrade Shmidt's indication that Lobanov is weak, well we should make him strong by bringing him into the cc.

Decided: Three are for removal, while one is for including comrade Lobanov in the central committee.

Heard: Comrade Chubar says that we will remove comrade Solovev, because there are other candidates. He proposes to fix in the protocol right now that three favour removal of Solovev, while one is against.

Decided: three favour removal of Solovev and one is against.

Heard: Comrade Shliapnikov declares: The chair, in proposing removal in the name of the three, does not put this to a vote. Moreover, none of the three know comrade Solovev, who is nominated by the delegation of Vyksa urban region [округ]. Therefore, I consider this wrong.

Comrade Chubar declares that the proposal to enter the votes without formality is because three members of the commission spoke out unanimously in favour of removing comrade Solovev.

Comrade Chubar: We are voting against comrade Solovev.

Comrade Shmidt proposes to replace comrade Kariakin from the Urals with comrade Sulimov.

Decided: To transfer to the Uralsk delegation for resolution.

Comrade Shmidt proposes to replace comrade Stolbov from Nizhny [Novgorod] with comrade Bukhanov from Kolomna.

Decided: Three favour comrade Stolbov remaining and one abstains.

Heard: Comrade Shliapnikov speaks out against such a replacement, because Kolomna had a small number of members. Nizhny has 40,000 members and needs to be given one place. The Nizhegorod delegation personally nominates comrade Stolbov.[120]

Heard: Instead of comrade Brykov from Briansk, comrade Shmidt proposes to bring into the central committee comrade Zheltov.

Decided: two are for Zheltov and one for Brykov. Comrade Chubar abstains.

Heard: Comrade Shliapnikov says that because the Briansk delegation nominated comrade Brykov, he needs to be introduced into the central committee, all the more since comrade Zheltov will work in the presidium of the Moscow Soviet.

Comrade Chubar speaks out against electing to the central committee comrade Liull from Kharkov, since he is not known there.

Decided: three favour removal of comrade Liull and one is against.

Heard: Comrades Shliapnikov and Pavlov point out that comrade Liull has worked for a long time as secretary of the Kharkov Metalworkers' Union and they propose to make him a central committee member.

Comrade Uglanov declares that the Petrograd delegation proposes to remove comrade Rozental from the central committee.

Decide: one is for removing him and three favour bringing him into the central committee.

Heard: Comrade Shmidt proposes not to bring comrade Vasilev from Gomza into the central committee, but to leave him among the candidate members.

---

120   Nizhny and Nizhegorod are both abbreviations for Nizhny Novgorod.

Decide: One favours bringing him into the central committee, but three favour leaving him among the candidates.

Heard: Comrade Shliapnikov proposes to bring Comrade Vasilev into central committee membership, because he leads a large metalworking *glavk* and is a good economic manager.

Heard: The same about comrade Tolokontsev.

Decided: The same.

Heard: The same about comrade Bruno.
    Decided: One is for central committee membership, two favour candidate membership, and comrade Chubar abstains.

Comrade Uglanov proposes to replace comrade Ignatev from Izhevsk with comrade Krupin. Three favour bringing comrade Ignatev into the central committee, while one is against.

Comrade Shliapnikov: Comrade Ignatev was unanimously elected by the Izhevsk delegation. Therefore, it is necessary to bring him into the central committee.

Comrade Shmidt proposes to make comrade Shats a central committee member. Comrade Shliapnikov proposes to leave him among the candidate members. Three favour bringing comrade Shats into the central committee and one wants to keep him as a candidate.

Comrade Shliapnikov proposes to make a candidate member of comrade Ivanov from Moscow, since only comrade Tarasov is going from Moscow into the central committee, after the commission removed comrade Ivanov, who has worked a long time in trade union organisations.

One votes to make comrade Ivanov a candidate, but two are opposed and one abstains.

Comrade Uglanov speaks against making comrade Shipillo a candidate member, because he does not have a well-defined line of behaviour and is inconsistent. Two oppose making Shipillo a candidate member, one is in favour, and one (Shmidt) abstains.

Comrade Barsky, in refuting what has been indicated, says that comrade Shipillo worked as secretary of Nizhegorodsky district committee, distinguished himself as a good trade union activist and has not shown any inconsistency.

The question about comrade Parov from the Urals will remain open and will be transferred to the Urals delegation for discussion.

Comrades Chubar, Shmidt, and Uglanov speak against introducing comrade Kharitonenko from Briansk into the candidate central committee members, because there are already two representatives from Briansk district on the list [two illegible names].[121]

It is not possible to reconcile the two lists, the first from the Bureau of the RCP(b) faction of the Fourth Congress and the second from the Petrograd delegation, and create one list. Disagreements arose between the majority of the commission of the CC RCP(b) and the Bureau of the RCP(b) faction of the Fourth Congress of the All-Russian Union of Metalworkers. Therefore, this question will be taken for discussion to the Politburo of the CC RCP(b), while the commission's work is regarded as finished.

∴

Session of the Bureau of the RCP(b) Faction of the Fourth Congress of the All-Russian Union of Metalworkers, 28 May 1921.[122]

Present: Bureau members comrades Shliapnikov, Mitin, Barsky, Tashkin, Skliznev, Tarasov, and Fedorov. Members of the Commission of the CC RCP(b) on conducting the congress comrades Chubar, Shmidt, and Uglanov.

Comrade Shliapnikov chairs.

Heard: About central committee candidates. In the bureau of the faction, says comrade Shliapnikov, two lists were introduced. One was from Moscow, Nizhegorod, and other delegations, and the second was from Petrograd. These two lists are not read aloud here.

---

121   In f. 99, op. 1, d. 7, l. 12, it reads that they object to him because 'they do not know him'.

122   RGASPI, f. 17, op. 84, d. 220, l. 3, protocol.

Comrade Chubar, speaking about the list introduced by the Moscow delegation and others, points out that this list is unacceptable, because it consists of one line of conduct. He proposes reconciling these two lists into one.

Comrade Shmidt also speaks in favour of this.

Comrade Uglanov, speaking about a certain line of conduct behind the composition of the list of the Moscow delegation and other delegations, indicates that this is a hidden line [определённость] and a threat for the party. The party rejected this line, in view of which I propose not to accept this list and to reconcile both lists.

Comrade Mitin proposes to fix comrade Uglanov's words in the protocol.

Comrade Fedorov, in the name of the Petrograd delegation, removes from the Moscow and other delegations' list 14 comrades as central committee members and seven as candidates.

Decided: To accept as the basis the list proposed by the Moscow and other delegations (six votes for and one against).

One vote for and six vote against the removal of 14 comrades as central committee members and seven as candidates, as proposed by the Petrograd delegation.

∴

Session of the RCP(b) Faction of the Fourth Congress of Metalworkers, 28 May 1921.[123]

Attending are 164 delegates with a full vote, 30 with a consultative vote, and three members of the CC commission on leadership of the All-Russian Congress of Metalworkers comrades Chubar, Shmidt, Uglanov.

Mitin chairs.

Heard: Discussion of candidates for the central committee of the Metalworkers' Union. Comrade Shliapnikov notes that two lists came to the Bureau of

---

Factions. One list was from the Moscow, Nizhny Novgorod, Kharkov, Tula, Urals and some other delegations, and the other was from the Petrograd delegation. Then there is read aloud the protocol of the Bureau of the RCP(b) Faction about the list of candidates to the central committee, the protocol of the commission and the list. Further, comrade Bukharin reads aloud the Politburo protocol regarding the list of candidates for the central committee and the list of the Petrograd delegation, which the Politburo suggests to make the basis.

Decided: Having heard all the information, protocols, and after a lively exchange of opinions, the faction votes on the lists. The list composed by the Moscow and other delegations is accepted by a majority of 122 with a full vote and 28 with a consultative vote. Forty with full votes and two with consultative votes voted for the list of the Petrograd delegation.

On the question about the motives guiding the faction in confirming the list of candidates to the central committee of the All-Russian Metalworkers' Union, which was proposed by delegations and introduced to the Bureau of Faction, the following resolution is accepted by an overwhelming majority (against the votes of the Petrograd delegation and part of the Tula delegation).

1. Confirming by 122 votes against 40 the list of candidates for the central committee of the All-Russian Metalworkers' Union which the Bureau of the faction accepted, the faction considered it necessary to establish close and efficient links between the new central committee and the most important districts and leading bodies of metalworking industry and to impart to it great businesslike capability for firm leadership of all union activity, given present circumstances, which are most difficult for the union.

2. In accepting this, the faction took under consideration:

   a/ that the candidates named on the list accepted by the faction were party members, no matter what internal grouping they belonged to before the Congress, and that as party members, in all their work they are obligated unconditionally to implement all decisions of the Tenth Congress about the role and work of trade unions and likewise all directives of corresponding party bodies.

   b/ that during the reading aloud, name by name, of all candidates on the list and discussion of it either in the commission of the Party CC or in the faction itself, no one made presented any reasons for rejection of or objections against the nominated comrades, either as party members or as trade union personnel, for not obeying or not carrying out party decisions.

••
•

Session of CC RCP(b), 28 May 1921.[124]

Heard:

9.   About the makeup of the central committee of metalworkers. Comrades
     Fedorov, Barsky and Tarasov attended.

Decided:

9.   a/   The Politburo acknowledges that such an institution as the Metal-
          workers' Union's central committee cannot be composed uniformly
          in the sense of nuances [оттенки] corresponding to former factions,
          neither from the formal party point of view nor from the general
          political point of view.

     b/   To take the list put forward by the Petrograd delegation as the basis
          for appointing candidates to membership in the central committee
          of the Metalworkers' Union. Preserving for the Party CC commission
          the right to make partial changes in the list, the Politburo empowers
          the commission to not stop before partial changes of this list on the
          basis of information, which may be acquired as a result of negoti-
          ations with the faction, the Bureau of the faction and with delegates,
          for the commission should confirm the final list and present it as the
          list of the CC.

     c/   Reject both comrade Shliapnikov's resignation from the Party CC
          commission on the Congress of Metalworkers and his refusal to
          include his name on the above-indicated list for the central com-
          mittee of the Metalworkers.

Signed by Molotov

Sergei Medvedev's statement to the Bureau of the Faction of the Fourth All-
Russian Congress of the Metalworkers' Union, 28 May 1921.[125]

Declaration (about a personal matter):

Not wishing to drag out the session of the faction with a statement about a personal matter, I consider it necessary to make one, however. I ask the Bureau to

---

124   RGASPI, f. 99, op. 1, d. 7, l. 13, protocol excerpt.
125   RGASPI, f. 99, op. 1, d. 7, l. 20.

air this statement at the next session of the faction, and likewise to attach the following declaration to the protocol of the current session:

When raising an objection to me, Comrade Evdokimov demagogically distorted the meaning of my allusions to the outrage taking place in the faction of the Fourth Congress of Trade Unions. He tried to foist on me the thought that I supposedly talked about outrages committed by the Central Committee of the Party.

Speaking about outrages taking place in the faction of the Fourth Congress of Trade Unions, I had in mind the speeches of some members of VTsSPS and of some Party CC members, which called forth the internal demoralisation of the faction and disorganisation of the course and work of the congress itself. I had it in mind to emphasise such things, as when comrade Tomsky, in my opinion not without the knowledge of Politburo members, and Riazanov, by agreement with Tomsky, conducted provocational persecution there against some trade union personnel and party members, who during the pre-congress discussion shared the platform of the Workers' Opposition. They shifted the dispute with them away from disagreements about the essence of questions of the trade union movement, which had been under discussion, and exclusively toward their having supported the platform of the Workers' Opposition in the period leading up to the congress. It is just the same here, where members of the CC commission conduct debate about candidates to the central committee of the All-Russian Metalworkers' Union not from the perspective of their practical experience in union or economic work or of their party discipline, but again exclusively from the standpoint that a large number of the candidates, who were nominated on the list of the Bureau of the faction, supported the platform of the Workers' Opposition during the pre-congress period.

In the faction of the Fourth Congress of Trade Unions, those trade union personnel who had shared the platform of the Workers' Opposition were persecuted. Tomsky and Riazanov introduced the deepest demoralisation and, in so doing, completely disorganised the work of the congress. Precisely the same thing has happened here, too. The character of the debate from Party CC commission members and individual delegates of the Petrograd delegation will bring demoralisation into our faction. It inevitably will entail disorganisation of the course and work of our congress. Besides this, it will also demoralise the Communist milieu of our union and will disorganise all its work both in the centre and in the provinces.

Delegate of the Fourth All-Russian Congress of the Union of Metalworkers Medvedev. 28 May 1921. 11:00 p.m. Hall of the session of the faction.

∙ ∙
∙

Session of the RCP(b) Faction of the Fourth All-Russian Congress of Metalworkers, 29 May 1921.[126]

Attending are members of the CC commission on conducting the Fourth All-Russian Congress of Metalworkers, comrades Bukharin, Chubar, Shmidt, and Uglanov.

Comrade Shliapnikov chairs. Comrade Vasilev is secretary.

Agenda: About election of candidates of the central committee of the All-Russian Union of Metalworkers.

Bukharin: Yesterday the faction did not accept as the basis the list proposed by the CC commission, nor did it accept the principles by which it was composed. The CC transferred its authority to the commission of the CC on the matter of the list's composition. The commission once again thoroughly re-examined the list and confirmed its earlier decision. The commission agrees to compromise to the maximum degree. The question concerns the numerical relationship of former nuances [оттенки]. Out of 24 members of the All-Union Metalworkers' Union central committee, 14 places would be given to those who are Orthodox and support the CC's point of view, and ten places to comrades belonging to what was called the Workers' Opposition before the Tenth Party Congress. The commission does not refuse to re-examine the candidates once more, person by person, in the framework of the given numerical relationship. The CC commission composed the list of candidates for the central committee of the All-Russian Metalworkers' Union according to the following principles: 1) the need to set up absolute contact between the CC RCP(b), VTsSPS and the All-Russian Metalworkers' Union central committee; 2) arrange communications with the provinces and businesslike work within the union; 3) discrediting no one, of course.

Tarasov (from the Faction Bureau): Delegates from the provinces made nominations to the list of candidates, which the Faction Bureau proposed for the All-Russian Metalworkers' Union central committee. The basic principles for composing the list were to make the central committee businesslike and effi-

---

126   RGASPI, f. 17, op. 84, d. 220, l. 4, protocol no. 3.

cient and to ensure its links with the provinces. The Bureau of the Faction discussed the list of candidates to the central committee and did not find it possible to accept the list proposed by the Party CC commission, since rejection under the flag of belonging to the former Workers Opposition is unacceptable for the Faction Bureau, carries the obvious stamp of discreditation, and shows distrust from the CC toward old party personnel. Besides that, such a selection and appointment to leading posts of the Union of Metalworkers, in bypassing the will of the provinces and of the overwhelming majority of the faction (3/4), disorganises both the unions and party work among metalworkers, about which the Bureau warns the commission of the CC RCP(b).

Pavlov: Let's take a look at the list, which the CC RCP(b) proposes. There you'll find from Kharkov comrade Ivanov, who no one knows, and so on. It is completely futile to rearrange candidates person by person into the indicated numerical proportions. The opinion of the faction is clearly and precisely expressed. If the list of the CC will be carried through as a party directive, well, party directives are not subject to discussion. From the Moscow delegation, I declare that in the conditions being created, when they give birth to distrust toward the main mass of the communist proletariat, meaning the metalworkers, who bear all the work and all the burden, there is no reason to waste time in the faction by subjecting any such list to discussion.

Bukharin: I propose to the faction to discuss the list, since I think that it's possible to create conviction during the course of discussion.

They vote about whether to discuss the list. 106 voting delegates say not to discuss the list and 56 delegates vote for discussion of it.

Bukharin: Given the faction's refusal to discuss the proposed list of candidates, the CC commission is forced to carry it through as a party directive. I propose to the faction to discuss whether it considers it possible to make one or more changes in the personal selection of candidates.

Shliapnikov: I ask the CC commission to remove my candidacy. The composition of the central committee is an extremely serious matter. The most important tasks confront the central committee of the All-Russian Metalworkers' Union. After what we have endured and heard here from representatives of our Party CC, I do not feel I am either in the physical or moral condition to continue working under these conditions. Having been systematically discredited, I cannot accept assignment to the central committee of the All-Russian Metalworkers' Union and cannot work in it, given its new composition.

Medvedev: I declare on behalf of myself, Vladimirov, Pavlov, Chernov, Lobanov, Tolokontsev, Mitin, Bruno, and others, that we are in wholehearted solidarity with comrade Shliapnikov's declaration. We appeal to the CC RCP(b) to free us from the obligations laid upon us.[127]

Pavlov: In supplement to comrade Medvedev's statement, I request that the faction remove my candidacy.

Semkov: I am not on either of the lists. I am a simple member of the Congress. I think that the question is one of extraordinary importance and that the CC RCP(b) has not taken into account here the political responsibility, which it will bear for its decision on this matter. Indeed, the future central committee of the All-Russian Metalworkers' Union will bear responsibility for all of metalworking industry and all this now will be transferred to the Party CC. It is necessary to come to an agreement. I suppose that comrades should remain on the list and get to work, and we in the provinces should carry out production work.[128] Comrade Vladimirov's theses have a basis for mastery of production, on which industry is built. We will implement this, but how can the Petrograd delegation carry it out, for its basic line departs from this? Will the CC RCP(b) and the Petrograd delegation agree to carry out the line we've designated?

Fedorov: I verify that hardly anything is left from the list of the Petrograd delegation. It is ridiculous to point out to the Party CC that it should bear responsibility for the work of the All-Russian Metalworkers' Union. The CC knows this perfectly well and it's not for us to be its teacher. I consider it completely futile to say much here. Once a CC directive is given, then it has to be taken under advisement and as guidance. Each person, of course, has the right to appeal about being relieved of obligations placed upon him. I feel and see that demoralisation more and more takes root in our faction. It's necessary to halt debates and declarations and recognise our obligations to fulfil the Party CC's directives.

Chernov: For us, party members, of course, Party CC decisions are obligatory to accept and implement. As true executors up to now of the decisions of the

---

127   In RGASPI, f. 99, op. 1, d. 7, l. 14, there is an extra sentence in Medvedev's statement that does not appear in f. 17, op. 84, d. 220, but I could not comprehend it.

128   In RGASPI, f. 99, op. 1, d. 7, l. 14 at this point, the following phrase is typed and then crossed out: 'and the Petrograd delegation, standing on Zinovievist graves, should carry out the same production line'.

Tenth Congress, we will remain so in the future and further will grip strongly the banner of communism. We emphasise that we have not broken up and split our party and our work.

Brykov: I was a delegate to the Tenth Party Congress. When I went to the Fourth Congress of Trade Unions and to the Fourth Congress of Metalworkers, I knew that we have no factions at all. There are no groupings. So I am surprised by Bukharin's statement about the existence of groups and the central committee being composed of three groups of some kind. We composed the list of candidates from comrades, who were nominated by the delegations. I consider it completely impossible to work in such a Metalworkers' Union central committee as was composed by the commission. Therefore, I request to withdraw my candidacy.

Beldeev (from Kharkov): The Kharkov delegation attests that the Vasily Ivanov of Kharkov, who figures on the list of the commission, doesn't work at all in the Kharkov district committee of Metalworkers, but only in the gubernia committee. He is completely unknown to the worker masses. Because of this, the entire faction of the district committee will resign, upon returning to Kharkov.

Tolokontsev: I think that it needs to be said clearly and openly that the central body of the All-Russian Metalworkers' Union is not elected, but appointed. In my opinion, the Eleventh Party Congress should set down in writing that such bodies as the central committee of the All-Russian Metalworkers' Union are not elected, but appointed by the Party CC. At our Fifth Congress, we will not even assemble delegations by districts to nominate candidates. Like all other comrades, I verify that after the Tenth Party Congress all kinds of groupings and congresses disappeared, yet here a representative of the Party CC, comrade Bukharin, incites us to think about groupings and the like.

Vladimirov: I am among those, who are on the commission's list. I am an old communist and am obligated to carry out the will of the highest organisation. I am sorry to my core that our organisation, to which I gave all my strength, as have many others, now can fall apart and completely die (comrade Vladimirov began sobbing and could not continue his speech).

Tashkin: I verify, as have many other comrades, that in the Urals we did not have strong groupings before the Tenth Congress. If there were any, then it was not a significant number. Personally I did not carefully examine the list of candidates to the central committee with the goal of trying to ascertain or remember who belonged earlier to which grouping. Further, I am pained by all that has occurred here just now. I declare that those of us who were elected by delegates to the central committee and who are also on the commission's list, have become appointees, not elected representatives.

Shcherbin (Kharkov): After the Tenth Party Congress, all groupings in our district disappeared and died out. Then friendly joint work began in our district, so it turns out that everything was extinguished in the provinces, but the fire still rages here in the Party CC.[129] Here at the Fourth Congress of Trade Unions, I saw that the CC decided to push us toward that which we already overcame and outlived. I am surprised. I cannot understand why they raise all this anew. Obviously this does not have an effect upon the CC, but I should say that in the provinces this does strongly reverberate upon work and on the workers and it terribly impedes work.

Medvedev: I want to remind you that at our plenum we have to conduct one more party obligation. The nonparty delegates want to demand for themselves proportional representation in the central committee, and so all party members should appear tomorrow at the plenum. On the question about the Revision Commission, a majority has decided to bring into it one nonparty delegate, and the rest will be named by the bureau of the faction.

∵

Session of the RCP(b) Faction of the Fourth All-Russian Congress of the Metalworkers' Union, 30 May 1921.[130]

Members of the RCP(b) CC commission are present at the faction: comrades Chubar, Shmidt, Uglanov.

Heard: About the introduction of nonparty candidates to the central committee of the All-Russian Metalworkers' Union.

Decided: Reject the request of the nonparty delegates. Inform the group of nonparty delegates that the Metalworkers' Union central committee considers it inexpedient to organise on the basis of party membership or of being nonparty.

---

129 In f. 99, op. 1, d. 7, l. 14, an additional phrase is handwritten in here, but I could not make it out.

130 RGASPI, f. 17, op. 84, d. 220, ll. 5–6, protocol no. 4.

Heard: About candidates to the central committee of the All-Russian Metal-workers' Union. Comrade Shliapnikov's notification about the commission's and the Politburo's confirmation of the commission's 29 May decision about the composition of the central committee of the All-Russian Metalworkers' Union.

Decided: Not to discuss the list and the notification, but to take it under consideration.

Heard: Comrade Shliapnikov reads the statement of the commission of the CC RCP(b), which submitted it just as the session of the faction met. 'Due to the fact that the faction of the congress at its 29 May 1921 session refused to discuss the list for the Metalworkers' Union central committee, which the CC RCP(b) proposed, and accepted it as a party directive, the commission of the CC RCP(b) considers it superfluous to convene the faction to discuss an already accepted decision. Since the Bureau of the Faction regards the Politburo's decision as a deviation from the decision accepted by the Tenth Congress, the commission proposes to the Bureau to protest against that decision to the Plenum of the CC RCP(b), to the Control Commission, or to the Party Congress. The commission proposes to not convene the faction'.

Comrade Medvedev introduces a proposal that the faction appeal the commission's and Politburo's violation of the decisions of the Tenth Party Congress. Having heard once more the proposal of the CC commission, the faction of the Fourth All-Russian Congress of Metalworkers regards the attitude of the commission and of the Politburo toward the Faction of the Congress as an obvious violation of the decision of the Tenth Party Congress, which obligated party organisations to especially carefully implement normal methods of proletarian democracy, especially in trade unions, where more than anywhere else leaders should be selected by the organised masses themselves. Therefore the Faction considers it necessary to appeal and it obligates the faction of the newly composed central committee of the Metalworkers' Union to appeal this violation of the decision of the Tenth Party Congress to a plenary session of the Party CC and to the Party Control Commission. In case the Party CC plenum will reject the faction's request, the new central committee's faction must appeal to the upcoming Eleventh Party Congress.

Comrade Shmidt's proposal: The Faction of the Congress, having observed in the decision of the Politburo a retreat from the decisions taken by the Tenth Party Congress, assigns the Bureau of the Faction of the Metalworkers' Union central committee, in the name of the faction of the Congress, to protest against this decision to the cc rcp(b) plenum, to the Control Commission, or to the Party Congress.

Decided: Comrade Medvedev's proposal is accepted by 132 against 53, with three abstaining. Comrade Shmidt's proposal is rejected, with only three voting for it.

Heard: Comrade Shmidt's statement: As a directive from the cc rcp(b), the commission of the rcp(b) demands roll call voting on comrade Medvedev's proposal.

Decided: In response to comrade Shmidt's demand for roll call voting, comrade Shliapnikov proposes to not violate the congress's course of work, but instead to propose to each party member to submit a signed note to the Secretariat about his attitude toward the decision taken by the Faction.

Resolution of the rcp(b) Faction of the Fourth All-Russian Congress of the Union of Metalworkers about the attitude of the Commission and the Politburo of the Party cc toward the Faction of the Congress.[131]

Having heard once more the cc commission's proposal, the faction of the Fourth All-Russian Congress of Metalworkers regards the attitude of the Commission and Politburo of the cc of the Party toward the Faction of the Congress to be an obvious violation of the decision of the Tenth Party Congress, which obligated party organisations to especially carefully implement normal methods of proletarian democracy, especially in trade unions, where most of all leaders should be selected by the organised masses themselves. Therefore, the faction considers an appeal to be necessary and obligates the faction of the newly composed central committee of the Metalworkers' Union to appeal this violation of the decisions of the Tenth Party Congress to a plenary session of the Party cc and to the party control commission. In case the cc plenum will reject the faction's request, it must appeal to the forthcoming Party Congress.

Vote (handwritten): 132 for, 53 against, and three abstentions.

∙∙
∙

---

131   RGASPI, f. 17, op. 84, d. 220, l. 7.

Session of the faction of the plenum of the central committee of the All-Russian Metalworkers' Union, 31 May 1921.[132]

Present: Shliapnikov, Vladimirov, Gurevich, Ianson, Fedorov, Tarygin, Tashkin, Rozental, Vasilev, Stepanov, Tolokontsev, Mitin, Brykov, Mikhailov, Lepse, Ignatev, Ivanov. Candidate members: Klinov, Chubar, Pavlov, Medvedev, Lobanov, Parov, Orlov, Budniak, Chernov, Bruno.

Attending from CC RCP(b): Molotov.

Chair: Shliapnikov.

Because six members of the central committee are absent, six candidate members (Klinov, Chubar, Pavlov, Medvedev, Lobanov, Parov) replace the absent comrades. As the plenum opens, comrade Shliapnikov asks comrade Molotov if he has any statements to make from the CC RCP(b). Comrade Molotov informs the plenum that he has none. Further, comrade Shliapnikov informs about the results of the roll call vote in the faction of the congress on comrade Medvedev's resolution: 134 delegates were for the resolution, 39 were against, and nine abstained without explaining a motive.

Comrade Tarygin, a central committee member, proposes to discuss the formation of a secretariat in place of a presidium.

Heard: About the structure of the presidium; Comrade Tarygin's proposal about formation of a secretariat in place of a chair.

Comrade Shliapnikov explains that this type of question falls within the competency of the congress, which should decide it.

Comrade Gurevich considers it possible to decide this question at the plenum, based on the precedent that the plenum eliminated the position of treasurer.

Comrade Shliapnikov: I want to make a factual correction to what comrade Gurevich said. The plenum did not eliminate the position of treasurer, but only appointed to the position a senior staff member, not a member of the central committee.

---

132   RGASPI, f. 99, op. 1, d. 8, ll. 5–6, protocol no. 1.

Medvedev: I remind you that no one raised this question, either at the congress or at the faction.

Lepse thinks it possible to implement a secretariat, but not a chair, on the basis that until 1920 the metalworkers did not have a chair.

Gurevich: Our abnormal statutes, which VTsSPS confirmed, do not stipulate the internal structure of the union. The congress of trade unions did not examine this problem. Yet nevertheless, a structure with a secretariat at the head is to be implemented.

Shliapnikov: Comrade Lepse forgot something. The Union of Metalworkers was the first union, which introduced a chair. I think that our work should be guided not only by what VTsSPS accepted, but also by our own decisions and positions.

Molotov: Having listened to many comrades, I have not heard strong arguments for the existence of the old system. The CC RCP(b) discussed this question and came out in favour of organising a secretariat. I propose that the faction of the central committee of the All-Russian Metalworkers' Union address the faction of VTsSPS on this matter. If the latter will have no objections, then it's necessary to organise a secretariat.

Vladimirov: We metalworkers have a completely different character of work than they have in VTsSPS. In our work it is necessary have an individual person [лицо], who would unite all work and lead it.

Medvedev: I propose the following: [not included here].

Molotov: I propose to support the organisation of a secretariat of three people, to request the opinion of the VTsSPS faction about this, and in case of its objection to ask the CC RCP(b).

Decided: To accept comrade Medvedev's proposal. Fourteen voted for Medvedev's proposal. Ten voted for the proposal of comrades Tarygin and Molotov.

Heard: About the personal composition of the presidium.

Comrade Lepse proposes the following composition for the presidium: Shliapnikov, Fedorov, Tashkin, Ianson, Sergeev, Vladimirov, and Sukhanov.

Comrade Shliapnikov's declaration: I was very serious when I declared at the faction of the congress that I am in no state to continue working in the central committee of the All-Russian Metalworkers' Union.

Comrade Tashkin: I am surprised by the thoughtlessness of those who put forth my candidacy for the presidium of the central committee of the All-Russian Metalworkers' Union. I have worked in one godforsaken place [медвежьий уголок], where work is on a small scale. I absolutely cannot immediately transition to and take on such enormous work in the central committee. My presence here would be of absolutely no benefit. Taking all this into consideration, I withdraw my candidacy. I will not work in the central committee presidium.

Molotov: No one has the right to withdraw his candidacy, especially not members of the Party CC.

Shliapnikov: I should state that we have one refuge and right remaining, which is that of refusal. No one can take this away from us.

Vladimirov: I declare the same thing as comrade Shliapnikov, and moreover for a personal reason besides. My physical condition is such that I require a lengthy holiday. If the plenum will not give this to me, then I [does not continue].

Lepse: I think that the statements of comrades Tashkin and Vladimirov are without basis.

Shliapnikov: I think that he who does not want to kill comrade Vladimirov will honour his statement.

Comrade Molotov's statement: In the name of the CC RCP(b), I declare that voting is occurring in a purely factional manner and that this has a terribly harmful effect on work. Not one member of the old composition has entered into the newly composed central committee. It is necessary to begin to work together amicably. Continuity between the old central committee and the new one needs to be established. I emphasise one more time that the meeting is taking place in a purely factional way and a member of the CC does not have the right to vote against a directive of the CC RCP(b). The same is true of others, who vote together with them. Comrades Vladimirov and Shliapnikov will join the new central committee for the sake of communications. Shliapnikov does not have the right to vote against this, since the CC supports this candidacy. Moreover, as a member of the VSNKh presidium, Shliapnikov should work in the presidium of the central committee. Comrade Vladimirov will receive a holiday. Upon returning from holiday, he will set to work in the presidium.

Shliapnikov: Comrade Molotov's statement that my candidacy is required surprises me. When the plenum opened, I asked comrade Molotov if he had any statements from the CC RCP(b), to which he answered that there were none at all. If this presidium, as it has been put forward, is a directive of the CC RCP(b), then we should not have bothered to vote. Concerning Molotov's words about group interests, well comrade Molotov knows that he and I together built the party and that the interests of the party are dearer to me than perhaps to others. By continuing persecution, you are acting in a way that does not strengthen our party, but demoralises it. Now I understand that the centre supports the persecution, which flourishes in the provinces. I also understand why I was dismissed when I went to the CC RCP(b) to complain about persecution of comrades from the former Workers' Opposition. By maintaining such an attitude toward us, discrediting us, and undermining party trust both at the Congress of Trade Unions and at the Congress of Metalworkers, the CC RCP(b) or more accurately the Politburo has made it completely impossible for us to work. Personally, I have neither the moral nor the physical strength to work. You will not see me either in the All-Russian Council of the Economy (VSNKh) or in the All-Russian Metalworkers' Union. This seventh point of the resolution of the party congress is your punishment of the disobedient.

Medvedev: I am surprised. Why did Comrade Molotov not immediately declare to us that in his pocket he has an order regarding the composition of the presidium? If I had known that there was such a thing, then of course I would not have voted.

Decided: Set the composition of the presidium at seven people.

Voting for comrade Lepse's list:
Shliapnikov: 11 for; 13 against
Vladimirov: 11 for; 13 against
Ianson: 10 for; none against; 14 abstain
Fedorov: 9 for; none against; 13 abstain[133]

---

133   Fedorov did not vote.

Sergeev: 10 for; none against; 13 abstain
Tashkin: 10 for; 11 against; 3 abstain
Bukhanov: 10 for; none against; 14 abstain
Elected: Ianson, Fedorov, Sergeev, and Bukhanov.

Because only four were elected, the plenum supplements the list with the fol-
lowing comrades: Stepanov, Tarygin, Lepse, Gurevich, Rozental, and Stepanov.
Stepanov: 8 for; none against
Lepse: 7 for; none against
Gurevich: 12 for; none against
Rozental: 5 for; 10 against
Tarygin: 3 or 5 for
Elected: Gurevich, Stepanov, Lepse, Tarygin.

The presidium comprises: Ianson, Fedorov, Sergeev, Bukhanov, Gurevich,
Stepanov, Lepse; and Tarygin as a candidate member.

Comrade Molotov's statement: Again I emphasise the existence at the plenum
of a special factional compact, which has a harmful impact on the work of the
central committee of the All-Russian Union of Metalworkers. Taking this into
account, I protest the election and will appeal for a second discussion of this
question by the Politburo.

Comrade Fedorov's statement: I consider it impossible to work in the central committee, given the conditions that have been created when 14 people
abstained during the vote for my candidacy. I will bring this to the attention
of the central committee of the All-Russian Metalworkers' Union and to the
attention of the cc rcp(b).

Shliapnikov: Why did comrade Fedorov not protest at the session of the faction
of the congress, when only 40 voted for and 122 voted against the list they put
forward?

Heard: About Comrade Vladimirov's holiday.

Decided: To present to Comrade Vladimirov a three-month holiday (unanimous).

∴

Session of the faction of the plenum of the central committee of the All-Russian Metalworkers' Union, 1 June 1921.[134]

Present: central committee members Shliapnikov, Vladimirov, Gurevich, Ianson, Fedorov, Tarygin, Tarasov, Tashkin, Rozental, Vasilev, Stepanov, Tolokontsev, Mitin, Brykov, Mikhailov, Lepse, Ignatev, Ivanov; candidate members Klinov, Chubar, Pavlov, Medvedev, Lobanov, Orlov, Budniak, Chernov, Bruno; CC RCP(b) member Molotov.

Chair: Shliapnikov.

In view of the absence of seven central committee members, seven candidates (Klinov, Chubar, Pavlov, Medvedev, Lobanov, and Orlov) will replace them.

Heard: Protocol no. 1 of the 31 May session of the faction of the plenum of the union central committee.

Resolved: Confirm it, adding that during voting, comrade Stepanov asked to withdraw his candidacy.

Comrade Molotov's statement: I find that the protocol contains minor editing errors. For example, comrade Shliapnikov's expression 'order' [приказ] is replaced by the word 'statement', and so forth.

Heard: Comrade Molotov's information about the CC RCP(b) decision about the structure and personal composition of the presidium, which is proposed as an outright directive of the CC RCP(b):
a) Confirm a three-member secretariat for the central committee of the Metalworkers' Union. Ask the opinion of the VTsSPS faction about this question. In the case of a formal objection from the VTsSPS faction, the question will be placed before the CC RCP(b) a second time for discussion.
b) Confirm the presidium of the central committee of the Metalworkers' Union in the following composition. Secretariat: Fedorov, Ianson, Gurevich (name crossed out) Sergeev, Bukhanov, Vladimirov, Vasilev. Candidate members: Tarygin, Lepse and Rozental.
  Decided: Having heard the information and obligatory directive of the Party CC about changing the structure and personal composition of the

---

134   RGASPI, f. 99, op. 1, d. 8, l. 7, protocol no. 2.

Presidium, take the decision into consideration (and implementation). Along with this, the Plenum RCP(b) Faction obligates the Faction Bureau to demand convocation of the VTsSPS faction and deliver to the VTsSPS RCP(b) faction a protest against the insistent repeated violations by the Party CC Politburo of the decisions of the Tenth Congress of the Party and to insist upon the delivery of its protest to the Plenum of the Party CC. Fourteen voted in favour and ten voted against.

Heard: Statement of the Central Board of Artillery Factories regarding comrade Tolokontsev's candidacy as director of TsPTI [Central Board of Heavy Industry].

Comrade Molotov's proposal: I propose to withdraw the question from discussion and transfer it to the presidium for resolution.

Comrade Shliapnikov asks Comrade Molotov if this is his proposal or a directive of the CC RCP(b).

Comrade Molotov: Yes, the directive of the CC RCP(b) is to withdraw all questions from discussion by the faction of the plenum and to transfer them to resolution by the bureau of the faction.

Comrade Shliapnikov's statement: The presidium discussed this question and transferred its resolution to the plenum.

Comrade Molotov's statement: I repeat once more that the directive of the CC RCP(b) is to withdraw all questions from the plenum faction's discussion, in view of its accidental composition.

Comrade Medvedev's statement: I declare that this (supposedly) accidentally composed plenum was appointed by the CC RCP(b) itself (and not in any measure) can be considered an accidental composition.

Resolved: In view of Comrade Molotov's proclamation of the directive of the CC RCP(b), the faction of the plenum is closed.

6   A.M. Kollontai's Speech to the Third Comintern Congress, 5 June
       1921[135]

[Lenin read a report, followed by debate. Among the speakers were Radek, Kollontai, Trotsky, and Bukharin. A resolution followed.]

Kollontai: Comrades! I speak here not in the name of the Russian delegation, but on behalf of a small minority of the Russian Communist Party. In our opinion, we communists have higher obligations than those which party discipline places upon us. These are discipline and obligations toward the whole Communist International. I speak here so that comrades from other countries would know that in the ranks of our RCP there are certain people who regard with great apprehension Russia's current policy and the turn in its internal policy. We consider it our duty to share our apprehensions with comrades from other countries.

The first and chief question is whether this turn and policy actually serve to strengthen and develop the new communist economy in Russia? Indeed, we as communists know that only a new communist system of production really is capable of moving ahead and facilitating the development of productive forces. As long as the old system of production exists, meaning the capitalist method of production, with its various scales and various calculations, the growth of productive forces is still not possible, and their further development still can't be expected. Comrades! We start from the assumption that the capitalist system and the capitalist social order all over the world has reached the limit of its resources. Likewise, we know that social revolution is conditioned by this very circumstance: either all humankind will perish for good, or the rising new class will create a new, more perfect method of production. So, observing Russia now and looking closely at how relations are taking shape, we should ask ourselves a question. Won't this turn in internal policy help revive the old capitalist system of production? We do not want to hide the fact that the new economic policy makes it possible for capitalism to regain its footing and be reborn in Russia.

The question is do we help productive forces to develop and Russia's economic life to flourish, by enabling the revival of capitalism in Russia? Will we find a way out from economic ruin by restoring capitalism? We think this is a false assumption. Thanks to freedom of trade, it is now possible for private property to revive in Russia. The rise and legal recognition of small enterprises,

---

135   *Kommunisticheskii International* 1922, pp. 367–9. John Riddell's translation of Kollontai's speech is published in Riddell (ed. and trans.) 2015, pp. 679–82. My translation does not differ substantially in content from his.

which exist in parallel with our central economic bodies, facilitate the revival of capitalism. This acknowledges the possibility of certain concessions to capital. We are aware that Russia's population is still not uniform and that three social strata still influence our policy. Peasants compose a large part of our population. Next is the dying bourgeoisie, which is transforming now into our bureaucracy and into specialists who are affiliated with the bourgeoisie and are connected with foreign capital, not materially but spiritually, of course. Finally, third, the working class is the chief social force and the chief social stratum.

Indeed, is it really the proletariat, which demands the revival of the old capitalist system of production in general and in its entirety? Is the proletariat really calling for the turn to our new economic policy? Aren't those who call for this turn actually the petty bourgeoisie and peasantry, who are steeped in their old traditions, their ideas of private property, and their love for a little plot of land, which the peasant regards as his property? Don't we sense here the force of foreign capital, which has its ideological agents, so to speak, here in Russia, and is influencing our policy through them? Comrade Lenin does not deny that we are now concluding a union with the Russian peasantry. But what kind of union is it? Isn't it, properly speaking, an enormous concession of all our economic policy to the Russian petty bourgeoisie? Yes, we should say honestly that it is a concession. Comrade Lenin and others acknowledge that this is a concession, but they say that we have no other way out! We are forced to make these concessions, in order to have the opportunity to wait out the situation, until our foreign comrades will complete the social revolution. But it is exactly during the time before our foreign comrades complete the social revolution when the greatest danger threatens Russia from these concessions, especially if this period will extend for a few years and if the social revolution in other countries will not happen soon enough.

Of course, I am convinced that it will come earlier, but if it will slacken, what will these concessions bring to us, in that case? They will bring the recognition that those communist principles, on which our policy was built, deceived our hopes and turned out to be bankrupt. This acknowledgement demoralises workers. On the contrary, the concessions give birth to the conviction among peasants that they are the ones on whom our whole economic golden age rests and whose fate it is to render strong influence on our policy.

Finally, these concessions remove from the worker masses their trust in communism. They deprive workers of faith in their ability to create a new communist economic system by means of their own enterprise. I strongly fear that if we will continue this policy of concessions, we will reach the point when it will be too late when social revolution breaks out in other countries, for then we will not have a real, sound, conscious proletarian core, on which revolution could lean for support. By that time, the peasantry and the urban petty bourgeoisie [мещанство] may become so politically and economically strong that one more worker revolution will really have to be carried out in Russia against these alien social forces, in order to bring about communism. Very many of our comrades have this fear. Therefore, I consider it my duty to command your attention for a few minutes more.

Comrade Lenin spoke here about there being no other way out. I know that many of our comrades share this point of view. But why, in searching for an exit, do we constantly forget that in Russia there exists still one great force, which still has not been fully utilised? This force is the creative energy of our working class. Comrades will say, but indeed the working class already has the possibility to prove itself! Comrades! You yourselves know that precisely in recent times this creative force was not sufficiently utilised. If, in the first years of revolution, broad masses of workers really participated creatively in common work, well now they are edged out more and more by a whole number of social forces that are alien to us, which in Russia are acquiring a quickly growing influence over our whole life.

Is it characteristic that comrade Lenin, who in his theses attaches such great significance to mechanical strength and to its development in the business of renewing industry in Russia, nowhere indicates in what way the creative working class, that new living force, exerts influence on the development of production by creating new production methods? There is not a word about how to cultivate workers and how to stimulate them to create a new system of production. No attention at all is turned to these questions. Moreover, it is precisely the creative living force of the proletariat that is capable of creating new methods of production and new productive forces.

But for the proletariat to be able to create, it should have sufficient freedom. It should have the possibility to show its initiative, yet the latter is paralysed more and more in our country, thanks to our current system. We should think about actually changing this system, not just on paper, in order to cultivate a new spirit in the masses. As long as we don't do this, we will always need to search for a new force to lead us out of calamity.

Comrades! The attitude practiced toward the creative energy of the proletariat in our country will become clear to you from a few examples. But we will take one illustrative example as to how little thought we give to cultivating and encouraging the proletariat's creative energy.

At the present time, as you know, intense famine rages in our country. Here in Russia, instead of drawing workers into rendering aid to the starving and making it possible for them to organise toward this goal, a committee is created to aid the starving peasantry and proletariat. Leading the committee are alien elements that are politically hostile to us, including for example, Kuskova, a type of Russian Beatrice.[136] We are reconciled to this, instead of directing all our attention toward strengthening workers' faith in their own strength and to intensifying, in this way, the link between workers and peasants. We also forget that at the same time when we are completing a new turn in our economic policy, we also are immediately destroying all our work.

We should not forget that workers already have become accustomed to the new system, which has replaced taxation and has secured for them receipt of all that is necessary from the state. They already became attached to this system. Also, their psychology and their views have changed and have adapted already to communism. Workers said, 'If we do engage in speculation, then this essentially is a crime, which we are forced to commit only because the government does not supply us sufficiently and because our rations are still insufficient'. But they already have begun to understand the idea of social property and of the common good. This, actually, is a great victory of our revolution.

We are forgetting the task of cultivating the proletariat's new creative energy in order to create a new person who will help us to actually bring the new social order into existence. We sacrifice this task, owing to the turn in policy. Of course, this turn may help comrades to raise Russia's productive forces for a certain period of time, but only within certain limits, which are not especially large in capitalist society. But even if we achieve this, if we temporarily save Russian industry, anyway at the same time we are threatened by a great danger of losing the trust of the worker masses toward our party. Here is why we think that one should not sympathise with this policy as much as we see many comrades doing. On the contrary, we should take a critical stance toward it, so that our comrades from other countries, which so far are still capitalist, could extract from this a lesson for themselves. Our sole salvation lies in preserving in our party a strong nucleus, which would stand for our old steadfast principles and which would be capable of revealing itself at the moment when revolution breaks out abroad. If the turn in all of Soviet policy will develop further, and if our communist republic will turn into one that is simply soviet but not communist, then this nucleus of steadfast communists will take into their hands the red banner of revolution, in order to secure the victory of communism in the whole world.

---

136   Possibly she refers to the character Beatrice in Dante's *Paradiso*.

7   A.M. Kollontai's Diary Entries, July–August 1921[137]

28 July 1921

[She hasn't touched her diary for over two months, she writes.] ... Three months in a revolutionary year is an epoch! And the epoch was rich and vivid. The International Congress of the Comintern, the Third Congress of the International only just ended. .... Where to begin?
   ... [She writes about an international scandal involving Zhenotdel.]

30 July 1921. Chaika.

'Did you have to speak during the Congress? You violated discipline'. 'Why bring foreigners into our affairs?' 'What kind of foreigners are these? They are all our people, delegates of fraternal parties. They should know the truth'. 'We'll give them the truth, but that which you and the shitty Workers' Opposition think is harmful to distribute. This plays into our enemies' hands'.
   We debate in such a tone with comrades daily at teatime and at lunch. Many are cold towards me; they are hardly on speaking terms with me. It is difficult.
   I try to think about the women's conference. This was a success and it produced results. ... Among women it is always easy for me. Among them I know how I need to behave, what will help work along, and what should be avoided. And the attitude toward me is warm. ... So why did I speak out? Everything was so good after the women's conference. Now how will everything be further? What will happen to the zhenotdels?
   [She'll go to be with Pavel Dybenko in Odessa in three days.] ... Pavel understood that I had to speak at the congress. 'Your Shliapnikov is a coward and a dishrag [тряпка]', writes Pavel. 'You really told it as it is. The party should not be afraid of the truth'.

2 August 1921. Moscow.

My speech. Now I ask myself if I had to do this. Didn't I just serve as a Don Quixote? Why, when I sensed that this would not yield results? Why spoil the relations that had just been put so right after the women's conference?
   But again 'my friends' put me into a spot. Shl[iapnikov] and Medv[edev] badgered me: 'Is it possible you won't speak? You really won't say that not

---

137   RGASPI, f. 134, op. 3, d. 37, ll. 11–32.

everyone shares the course toward NEP? That we see the danger of a return to capitalism?' I stood in the hall and agonised over this. Is my duty to speak or to hold my tongue before the International?

Lazzari and his tears urged me on …[138] Isn't it simply 'cowardice' to keep silent? Especially now, especially after they have become pleased with me?

I approached V[ladimir] Ilich. 'V.I., I want to violate party discipline and say a word'. 'Violate party discipline? And you are asking my blessing for this? Those who do this don't talk about it in advance'. 'I take you at your word, Vl. Ilich, I don't ask, but I am putting my name down'. So far we were joking. But when V. Ilich saw that I went up to Loriot to register, he led me aside and started to dissuade me from speaking.[139]

'You'd do better to take an automobile and go for a ride …. Drive around and take a look at what we are doing, how we are turning things around in Kashirka.[140] All your doubts will fall away'.

Bukharin interjected, 'This is an implication. If A.M. is to speak in the spirit of the Workers' Opposition, we will send her to eat peaches'.

Vl. Ilich did not like this. 'I did not say this', he said. Again he tried to dissuade me from speaking. But I had already registered my name.

I was wearing a white dress of Swiss embroidery. It was rather old and I had handsewn it, but it was clean and freshly ironed.

I seemed to myself very small on this big stage before so many eyes concentrated on me. What did I say? I tried not to be strident. The essence was to be 'in sympathy' with criticism of the turn toward NEP, but I became agitated and spoke more harshly than I wanted. Lenin listened attentively and now and then a strange smile ran across his face. There was sadness in it, but about what? Tr[otsky] and Bukharin whispered to one another.

When I finished, there was weak applause. I had expected grave silence.

First, Trotsky spoke against me. He polemicised not against my speech, but against my brochure. I could not contain myself. 'Comrade Trotsky. This relates to the discussion at the Tenth [Party] Congress, but that discussion ended'. They laughed. Tr[otsky]: 'You are right'. But he continued to thunder against my brochure. Then Bukharin [spoke], and after him Radek. Trotsky

---

138   At the Third Comintern Congress, Lenin accused Constantino Lazzari (Italian Socialist Party) of 'disorganising the revolution' through his speeches at the congress. This was after Lazzari had lamented accusations of treason to the international revolution made against him and his comrades. See Riddell (ed. and trans.) 2015, pp. 339, 352.
139   Fernand Loriot chaired sessions six and 17 of the congress.
140   Kashirka was an outlying district of Moscow.

flung out the phrase, 'Kollontai went on the attack like an Amazon'. Radek drowned him out, 'Like a Valkyrie!'

Bukharin built his speech on the basis that 'Kollontai was a Menshevik'. But what about Trotsky and Lozovsky? 'Kollontai's position is not monolithic. At this congress she is unique'. After him, Roland Holst [took the floor]. What will she say? Of course she did not agree. Even in its new tactics, the Russian Communist Party remains 'leftist' [reporting Roland-Holst's view].[141]

Lenin made a wry face. He purposely moved forward, when Roland-Holst began to speak, in order to hear better. He expected something from her and went away disappointed.

But on the next day in the commission, Lenin emphasized, 'We are not leftists and are not rightists. In vain does comrade R.-H. want to drag us to the left. We simply are the party of realistic politics and of the expediency of "common sense"'.

The polemics against me and the speeches ended. I went across the hall toward the exit. No one noticed me. I knew that this would be so. But it was painful, very painful.

The Congress continues. I am present, but already there is not that enthusiasm for me, the joy of capture.

The French now converse with me. But the rest stand aside. And our people are very, very dissatisfied. Many rebuke me, 'Why did you speak?'

And this is the most incomprehensible thing. Shl[iapnikov] and Medvedev declared to me, 'You were in a hurry. You needed to speak so that they would have supported you'.

And what is this already?! ...

I said that which I considered to be my duty. But 'to prepare the act [выступление] of a group', no, you shouldn't expect this from me.

And now I am even more alone. Yesterday I took leave. They gave it enthusiastically. It is calm in the Zhenotdel. [Further, she writes about Zhenotdel matters.]

---

141   According to the published stenographic report of the congress Henriette Roland-Holst spoke before Bukharin took the floor. F.L. Kerran (Britain) and (Jan Appel) Hempel spoke between Trotsky and Roland-Holst. Radek spoke immediately before Kollontai and made interjections during later speeches. See Riddell (ed. and trans.) 2015, 674–97.

8   Letter from A.G. Shliapnikov to S.P. Medvedev, 28 June 1921[142]

Dear Sergei,

I am sending you this letter and some Comintern materials with a comrade from Mineralnye Vody, about whom I told you and whose letter to V.I. I read to you.

On Sunday I had a lengthy conversation with Grigory [Zinoviev]. I consider it awkward to write in detail in a letter sent via someone else. I posed questions directly, point-blank – 'war or peace', under definite conditions. He himself supported 'peace'. Yesterday (Monday) he met me at the Comintern and informed me that the old man [старик] [Lenin] also agrees and supports conclusion of an agreement, since he's tired of fighting.

I dashed off five conditions, of which the main things are:

1)   Cease struggle against the Workers' Opposition;
2)   Cease the policy which was expressed in the attitude toward the Congress of the All-Russian Metalworkers' Union; convene for this a conference, at which all wishes of the congress's faction will be carried through.
3)   Actually put our stake on heavy industry and the proletariat in economy building policy.

This matter will be definitively settled in a few days. I don't know what will emerge from the final negotiations, but we need to continue the line we've begun.

The draft plan for the party purge has been accepted with a large dose of the proposals we made at the congress and before it.

I would like to take a rest, but unfortunately it seems I will have to go abroad.[143]

Say hello to Mariia Ivanovna [Medvedev's wife]. I shake your hand.

Your Aleks[andr].

---

142   TsA FSB, R33718, d. 499061, vol. 42, l. 128, handwritten and signed. Shliapnikov was in Moscow and Medvedev was in Mineralnye Vody. The letter was sent through a comrade rather than through the mail. Russians used the word оказия to signify dispatch of a letter through a personal courier.
143   I have not found a record of a trip abroad by Shliapnikov in summer 1921.

9   Letter from A.G. Shliapnikov and S.P. Medvedev to the Politburo
     and VTsSPS, July 1921, Protesting VSNKh Decrees[144]

To the Politburo CC RCP(b) and to VTsSPS

We are sending you our thoughts about the essentials of the 11 July 'Decision of
the VSNKh Presidium' about questions related to the new economic policy.[145]
     S. Medvedev, A. Shliapnikov[146]

[Their criticisms appear to correspond numerically to the points in the VSNKh
presidium decision.]

Point 1.
a)   It begins with recognition of 'an acute crisis, into which we entered in
      May'. But several lines later, it only speaks 'about a worsening of the eco-
      nomic situation that is taking shape.'
      All this is written on 11 July, but on 11 May these same 'commanders of the
      economy' delivered theses about one of the most important branches of
      industry being in 'a state of full crisis.'
      Obviously there was a state of full crisis. Then, toward the beginning of the
      11 July theses, 'we entered into the state of acute crisis'. Finally, toward the
      end of the first point of these theses, we happily arrived at 'an economic
      situation which is getting worse'.
      This decision is a model of deliberation and gravity.
b)   It seems that from the moment the new economic course was proclaimed,
      we have observed the most dangerous lag between our economic policy
      and the new economic course.[147]
c)   There is clarity in only one regard: 'full speed toward implementation of
      the new economic policy'. We see further along in the resolution how they
      understand this.

---

144   RGASPI, f. 17, op. 84, d. 175, ll. 94–6 [incomplete] and f. 5, op. 2, d. 340, ll. 78–81 [com-
      plete].
145   Excerpts of the 11 July 1921 VSNKh decree are published in Fedorov and Tyrin 2016, pp. 79–
      80.
146   Given the writing style and sarcastic tone in this document, Sergei Medvedev may have
      been the primary author, with Shliapnikov adding his name in support.
147   They use a phrase which I cannot translate: чем это хуже, знаменитого обезглавления
      головы и носа.

Point 2.

a)   The basic flaw in our current economic policy turns out to be the absence
     of an economic subject [субъект]. It means that he who holds power
     gives the orders.[148]

     It is pleasant to hear such an authoritative confirmation from the mouth
     of such an authoritative body that no matter where you go, there is no
     place in the economy for the proletariat. There is no economic subject.

b)   In this melancholic longing for an 'economic subject', the Presidium
     splendidly reflects the sign of the current times in the life of our soviet
     republic. The peasant, who operates in a private economy, appears at
     centre stage.

c)   Here's something strange. On 11 May, representatives of VTsSPS, who were
     members of it for the first time, attended a session of the Politburo of the
     CC RCP(b), where they expressed surprise at how little they thought we
     knew about the actual state of industrial management and rates [став-
     кой]. They earnestly recommended to us that we read *Ekonomicheskaia
     Zhizn*, where we would find 'direct answers to all the accursed questions'.
     We comfort ourselves with the awareness that the current 'managing sub-
     jects' are beginning to grasp the gospel truth, which is that 'everything
     flows, everything changes'. But it seems unlikely that they will grasp it for
     long.

     And how do they manage the economy? Well, we will see further.

d)   It turns out that in the view of these louts, workers have been supplied
     with provisions through 'theft from factories and enterprises'.

     Oh, of course, these managing subjects will not allow theft. No. They write
     in point five that it is impossible to sustain industry on the basis of supply
     by the state. The government should present to enterprises a larger por-
     tion of their own production in order to sustain industry. We dare to think
     that that includes proletarians and the restoration to them of their 'civil
     rights'.

e)   If you take these 'managing subjects' seriously, it turns out that almost all
     bodies of Soviet power have only been busy supplying the proletariat and
     that they have supplied it with food, work clothes, and everyday clothing.
     Moreover, they have supplied it even without taking workers' productiv-
     ity into account, only their needs. Production has fallen, yet supply has
     been abundant. This is how the matter still stands, according to the cal-
     culations of the 'managing subjects'.

---

148   Кто палку брал тот и был в хозяйстве у нас капрал.

In actuality, everyone knows that there is no industrial proletariat, which is hungrier and poorer than this one supposedly well-supplied by all the bodies of the Republic. This supply of the proletariat, which the 'managing subjects' have demoted in importance and which does not exist in reality, well what does it express? Only that these subjects conceal within themselves a deep class prejudice. They harbour an unstated yet absolute condemnation of the working class, because they believe that too much has been given to the proletariat.

f)   The 'managing subjects' soften this spirit of condemnation with the ridiculous and ignorant explanation that our proletariat's supply must be conditional upon the Republic's situation being comparable to a 'military camp'. It turns out that 'in besieged fortresses they try to supply everyone as equally as possible'.

It's good that they at least found a way to swallow such a bitter pill. On the other hand, it must be regretted that this circumstance interfered with the development of an approach to supplying workers presently ruined by 'the managing subjects' in VSNKh [хозяйствующих в вснх субъектов].

Point 3.

a/   'We discard a mass of foodstuffs and other resources'. Who do these subjects have in mind when they say this? Who does not know that the proletariat was supplied at not more than 25% of the subsistence minimum? Who discarded a large quantity of foodstuffs and other resources?

We categorically assert that it was not the proletariat, but the rural peasantry, the urban townspeople, and the petty bourgeois strata. Soviet bodies sated them and they misappropriated all these resources, often with the benevolent permission of the current 'managing subjects'.

b/   It speaks of the complete 'nebulousness [расплывчатость] of our economic management'. But who is responsible? Indeed the current 'managing subjects' were also in VSNKh in the past.

Indeed, they first plumbed the depths there.[149] About whom are they talking? If about themselves, then why do they remain there?

Point 4.

a/   'The government does not give anything to anyone for free'. Let's say, for example, here in Moscow fare for proletarians on railways and steam ships or trams is equivalent to the fare for the peasant who lives near Moscow and hauls to the bazaar on his back half a million berries at a

---

149   Ведь дни знались там первыми.

time, or for the Moscow speculator, who goes to buy these berries in the countryside for 2,000 rubles per pound [фунт] and sells them in Moscow for 4,000 rubles per pound, thus earning in a day up to 200,000 rubles cash.

The government neither gave nor gives anything away for free to the workers of factories and plants. Each time the government issued something to a factory worker, the government made him its employee [работник] and demanded fulfilment of certain obligations and labour equivalents.

On the contrary, the government, acting through the hands of the 'managing subjects', distributed and still distributes to the rural peasant, hundreds of billions worth of livestock, implements, seeds, provisions, urban manufactured goods, and the like, by current calculations.

Equating the factory and plant workers to the 'citizens' of our Republic in general is undoubtedly a manifestation of the equality that is so sacred to the petty bourgeoisie.

Point 6.

A strikingly expressive point.

a/   This is the angry cry of the private-owners who crave the implementation of the decree about leasing out enterprises. The VSNKh Presidium is the mouthpiece for these longings in this point, which contains the basic motive for the entire decision.

The tone becomes more strident with each paragraph of this point. But in these paragraphs, there is no concern about emancipating the 'apparat'. Oh no, far from it. Here you find the insolent pressure of cravings [вожделений].

This is the crux of the entire decision. It saturates the entire decision. But how the emancipation of the 'apparat' from small factories and enterprises develops and gets accepted becomes obvious in the seventh point of the decision.

Point 7.

This point directly follows from the preceding one, both by numeration and conception. It is fully coordinated with it and places itself above all political and economic aspirations of the current 'managing subjects' in the VSNKh Presidium.

Here you find concern 'about small-scale production', about bringing it into cooperative organisations [кооперирование], about raising its productivity, and even about combining [комбинирование] it with largescale industry. The latter obviously means simply its upkeep at the expense of industry.

We see how in point six, they express the passionate and ardent desire to 'emancipate the apparat' from smallscale factories and enterprises. But it bears reading to the end of point seven, where this passion suddenly transforms into a call for 'all bodies of the Presidium of managing subjects', and even all bodies of Soviet power to encourage to the utmost the development of trading (bourgeois-kulak) cooperatives.

The chief content of the decision concludes with this point.

Grand total.

1. a) There was no managing subject.
   b) The proletariat received supplies from absolutely all bodies of Soviet power and gave an insignificant return. Besides that, it 'stole' from the factories and enterprises.

2. Smallscale enterprises need to be transferred over to leases as quickly as possible. It's necessary to organise the smallscale producer, to bring him into the cooperative movement, and combine him with largescale industry.

3. All bodies of Soviet power need to be forced to render powerful aid to trading (read bourgeois-kulak) cooperatives. Speaking in general and concisely, such are the efforts now of the subjects managing industry. The effort is patently anti-proletarian. Moreover, there is not one proposal about who, in their opinion, should be 'the managing subject' in the current matter of preserving industry and in its eventual rebirth. By which methods or forces does the Presidium of VSNKh, suddenly feeling nostalgia for the 'managing subject', think to preserve and then give rebirth to industry, which was reduced almost to a state of complete collapse?

What does it think about doing, in order to preserve the exhausted proletariat of now-halted factories and plants? What does it think to do with these factories and plants? Does it want to revive them and make them again hearths of revolution and communism?

What role does it allot in all this tragedy to the forces of the proletariat itself?

We do not find answers to these questions in this decision.[150]

The entire decision is saturated with antiproletarian tendencies, which indicate that the VSNKh Presidium, as it is currently composed, is not a transmitter of the proletarian dictatorship in the area of building the national economy, but yields to the influence of private-property owning desires and petty bourgeois interests.

---

150 This line underlined for emphasis.

10   Letter from [A.G. Shliapnikov] to Comrade [N.S.] Mamchenko,
        6 July 1921[151]

Dear friend,

Much of what you've been told about Moscow is not true. Part of this concerns the Worker-Peasant Party. I should inform you that its organiser is one of those comrades who you met at our congress sessions. This comrade is Paniushkin. The decision of the Tenth Congress and the struggle against the Workers' Opposition that began after it, so acted upon him that he left [the party]. Together with him departed some of the workers of that district in which he had connections. They formed not more and not less than a Worker-Peasant Party. Essentially they took the SR path to a significant degree. As concerns Ignatov, well he is not at all mixed up in this affair and now is in Poland as our representative on matters concerning prisoners of war.

During the months after the congress, rather much that was new and exceptional happened to us. I think that you already know the history of the Congress of Trade Unions. I think that someone told you about the All-Russian Congress of Metalworkers. The result of all this is that in the provinces our people are forced to get organised all over again. I don't know how this policy of factional struggle is reflected within the bounds of our gubernia,[152] but we have information about an organised campaign in the remaining parts of the Republic, from the Urals to the South. Therefore, we naturally took up defence against this campaign. Several times I placed this question before the CC. Individual members of the Party Control Commission went to some gubernias. Some measures were taken in some places to eliminate [the campaign], but in general the picture remains the same.

There is no doubt that the centre sets the tone. The key to all this, as events at the congress indicated, is to be found in our CC. Now we put this question before the CC itself and did so, without fearing the exacerbation of the economic situation of the Republic. We cannot allow squabbles to develop. We cannot allow our centre to disorganise the Revolution instead of organising it. We cannot allow this at all. Therefore, we are taking all measures so as either

---

151   TsA FSB, R33718, vol. 40, l. 124. Typed, unsigned. This was found among materials which
        the NKVD confiscated from Sergei Medvedev in 1935. Based on the content of the letter, I
        believe the author was A.G. Shliapnikov.
152   He is probably referring to Vladimir gubernia, where Shliapnikov's and Mamchenko's
        hometown of Murom was located.

to completely do away with such a policy and to force the CC to reject it, or to place such an intraparty policy and practice before all members of our party for discussion.

My refusal to actively work in VSNKh and other institutions is closely connected with such a policy. I cannot bear to feel that I am in the position of a functionary [чиновник]. I don't find it possible to agree with such a course and I will not take upon myself any work until this basic party question is elucidated. There is complete confusion in economic policy. Rather quickly and noticeably, we are adapting to the demands of the petty bourgeoisie and are constructing our government according to its interests, having forgotten the most elementary defence of workers. This especially clearly appears in industry in all sorts of places in the provinces. The way they talk about the need for small-scale industry in some places is to focus work on handicrafts.

There is still much that is interesting. True, it's not new. But I will provide more details about this when I will be home. I suppose that after the 15th, I will be free for some time and will come to Murom.

With comradely greetings,
[no signature]

11   Letter from F.A. Mitin to S.P. Medvedev, Summer 1921[153]

[The translation below is based on different versions published in 1922 and 1926 edited collections. The 1926 publication omitted a large section of Mitin's letter dealing with the tactics he followed to circumvent reprisals from above against former members of the Workers' Opposition. This section was included in the 1922 publication. I have italicised that section in the translation below. Some minor differences between the archival and published versions may be due to misspellings by Mitin, which editors corrected.]

Esteemed comrade Medvedev, excuse me for my immodesty, but nevertheless I should say to you and comrade Shliapnikov: What's the matter? Why do you keep quiet? Do you really have no questions, or has God's grace brought about a state of serenity?[154] Secondly, I remember that at our last meeting you and

---

153   Published in Anon 1922, pp. 10–12; and in Zorky (ed.) 1926, pp. 51–3; also located in TsA FSB, R33718, vol. 41, ll. 153–6.

154   Mitin places three question marks in the archival version (typed, not signed). I did not copy by hand the entire letter that is in the archive, only excerpts.

Shliapnikov were assigned to evaluate and make conclusions for us about the New Economic Policy. But enough time has passed. There is no information from you. Using an opportunity to send a letter through a person traveling to Moscow, that is, comrade Polosatov, I would like to revive our close contact and to receive at least a little recent news about all your machinations.[155] Moreover it's important that our CC seems to have choked on something. Therefore, it is silent. Not one word is heard, as if there is a void there.

I admit that we received here one typed letter from Ivan Perepechko, which was a heartrending cry from his soul against the CC RCP(b), but it doesn't give us anything essential. It was rather like our Paniushkin.[156] But the main thing it contains is an explanation of how the metalworkers limited themselves at their congress to just proletarian methods, that is, they broke down in tears and so forth. Our lads were about to discuss it, but I sent this letter, the person who wrote it, and him to whom it was addressed to the lowest level of hell,[157] because I regard I. Perepechko as a very shady piece of work.[158] Indeed, the lads agreed with me.

There you see what kind of news from the centre can turn the provincial head of a weak brotherhood. Therefore, contact is also needed. Indeed, it is just as important to know about your fate and that of comrade Shliapnikov. Where and with whom do you pass your time?

Now I will try to briefly set forth what we are doing here in the famous Donbas.

The chronological approach is a good thing, but it is devilishly long and our brother-master does not have patience to write. Therefore, excuse me for writing in condensed form.

First of all, I'll tell you that as soon as I appeared in the Donbas after the congress, I already sensed that 'heroism[159] was in the air'. For the Gorlovsky Factory District Party Committee (raipartkom) took the initiative to drive out from management our comrade Mikhailov and the factory committee chair, as members of the 'former' (they're afraid of a shadow) Workers' Opposition[160] and replace them with their own people. Naturally the case went to the gubernia committee (gubkom) and to us in the district committee (raikom). The first

---

155   The Russian phrase is свежесть из ваших кухонь.

156   In the archival version, it appeared as if he wrote 'your Paniushkin'.

157   Literally 'to all devils'.

158   The published version had the word штучка here. In the archival version, it appeared that he wrote тучка instead of штучка. Тучка is a diminutive of туча, which is a rain cloud or storm cloud.

159   In the archival version, it appeared that the word was 'horizon' [горизон].

160   The archival version had the parenthetical phrase '(what kind of members?)'.

battle began.[161] *forget comrade Kviring (?).*[162] *Of course, I tried to prove it was all an absurdity, but the gubkom nevertheless decided on a recall and instructed the raikom to assign another manager. I declared categorically that I don't have such a storehouse where I can pick and choose them like objects and having secured one,*[163] *then discard him [or the rest?]. The gubkom insisted that I provide a manager. I personally took the following tactic. If the raipartkom will assign a manager, then I will relinquish responsibility for production. If it charges me to assign one, then of course I again assign the same comrade Mikhailov, because the raiparkom did not assign that same Mikhailov, who up to now occupies the post.*[164] *This is the first thing.*

The second thing is that also before my arrival, the Enakiev raiparkom removed several members of our Enakievsky podraikom, in connection with which some took sick leave and some simply departed.[165] *In such a way a situation was created which forced preparation for re-elections. Here I have to go back a little, to Lugansk. There, still under fresh impressions of posts*[166] *of former Workers' Opposition, a victim of which became Fokin (Shliapnikov knows him), the Lugansky raipartkom excluded him from the party, but in Bakhmut in the gubkom we succeeded in making a stand. Then it was decided to transfer him from Lugansk to Iuzovka to work at the bench. As soon as I arrived from Moscow, before me stood the Enakievsky picture indicated above. I agreed with the gubkom to send Fokin to Enakievo. Since the factory strongly felt an insufficiency of skilled workers, the gubkom agreed (it did not know what I had in mind). Fokin moved. On the third day, I go to Enakievo and enter the raiparkom to nominate candidates for the Enakievsky podraikom of metalworkers.*

Naturally, we nominate old trade union personnel. I nominate Tretiakov from Tula. Knowing in advance that he will not come, I say that the new central committee of the Metalworkers' Union recommends him. We bring forward Fokin as a

---

161   The entire italicised section below was omitted from Zorky (ed.) 1926. It was included in Anon 1922, but there were differences between it and the archival document.

162   Archival version: 'Don't forget that our gubernia committee secretary is comrade Kviring'.

163   The published version used the Russian word 'обеспечив', but the archival document had what appeared to be обезличив, which means to depersonalise, deprive of individuality or personal responsibility.

164   I find the verb tenses employed by Mitin here to be confusing. They are the same in the archival document as in the published one. The Mikhailov to whom he refers here most likely was not the same Mikhailov who figured more prominently in the Workers' Opposition in Moscow.

165   The podraikom was a subcommittee of the raikom.

166   Archival version: not 'under fresh impressions of posts', but 'under fresh impressions of the Tenth Party Congress, there were ardent attempts to remove former Worker Oppositionists from posts'.

candidate. And so, the list was composed, elections were held, but there is no Tre-
tiakov. So of course, Fokin enters into the podraikom and becomes its secretary.

That is how the second attempt at chucking out [вышибание] ended, but
unsuccessfully. Today, the 29th, the representative of the Makeevsky podraikom
arrived with official papers and declared that the raiparkom of Enakievo removes
comrade Primerov, chair of the metalworkers' podraikom, and sends him to be
chief of the labour section (otdel). It also removes the secretary and sends him
to the housing subsection (podotdel). Another scandal. The devil knows what is
going on. A sense of doom hangs over us.[167] *Just recently the board [правление]*
of the gubernia union (gubsoiuz) (of cooperation) and the gubkom were re-elected
here. The Ispolkom rejects our Kuznetsov.[168] *We posed the question at the fac-*
tion of metalworkers and then transferred it to the union council (sovprof). It
turned out in the second case like it did in the first case. Kuznetsov was installed
in the gubsoiuz board, but the gubkom decided to reject him and brought it to
the congress faction. At the faction of the congress, secretary Kviring held forth
in an accusatory speech and Mitin spoke in defence. It turned out that Kuznetsov
was unanimously voted into membership in the board. After the faction's decision,
Rukhimovich, as Ispolkom chair, says to me, 'what is to be done?' My answer is,
'comply with Moscow'. In a strange phenomenon, the gubkom bureau, which two
days ago decided to recall Kuznetsov after the congress faction meeting, resolved
to confirm him as a member of the board.

By then I already had no idea what to make of all this.[169] *Well there you have so*
far what takes place in our backwater [захолустный] town. [published version
resumes] Now a couple of words about how I think about and conduct work.

1. Reinforce factory committees with our lads,[170] no matter what, and
through them win over factory cells. Conduct work along this line, that is,
through them, up to the district party committee (raipartkom), to the conference, and so forth. The only line tactically possible is from bottom to top.
I tried to take the heights here, meaning to conquer the gubsoiuz, sovnarkhoz, our sovprof (I'm chair). In the sovnarkhoz, however, it broke down, not
because I was incapable, but because people don't suffice, damn it.[171] If I had

---

167   Чёрная нить тянется без конца.

168   This is probably not the same Kuznetsov who signed the Letter of the 22, was expelled
      from the party, and joined Miasnikov's Workers' Group.

169   Ни черта не понял, *что сие значит.*

170   The published version uses the Russian term наши ребята, while the archival version uses
      свои ребята, both of which mean the same thing. After this letter became known to party
      leaders, they would grill Shliapnikov and other former members of the Workers' Opposi-
      tion as to what 'our lads' meant.

171   The literal translation is 'devil take it'.

succeeded in carrying this out, the Donbas would be ours. But what does it mean to be ours? What is our ideological worldview? Of what does the contradiction truly consist? The main question is what are the paths out of that dead end, in which we have got stuck? These questions arise in an agonising way here in the provinces. There are no provisions. Workers' wives bring their children to the factory committees and say, 'Feed them or send them wherever you want. There is no clothing'. It is excruciatingly difficult when you see the fiery mass go and flow, and nearby stand emaciated workers worn out by malnutrition, without shoes, and blood mixed with soot and rust. Moreover, you know the gloomy prospects for provisions in July and August. Then you completely lose your self-possession.

The danger is desperate. Everything, all opposition, seems a game when compared to that tragedy, which you see here in the provinces among industrial workers.

In connection with the lack of provisions, they threaten to flood the mines. Then it will be even harder and more difficult to get out of our economic impasse. Factories will have to be closed, because there will not be enough coal for the railways, which already now requisition that 1.8-million pud reserve, which is exchanged for goods with STO's approval.

On the whole the provisions situation in the Donbas is the most desperate. June and August are even more threatening. A whole series of strikes has arisen. Many people quit work simply due to malnutrition. Coal output has fallen to 60 percent. If the situation does not improve, they threaten to flood the mines. All these economic material factors, it would seem, should make the party specialists [партийные спецы] understand that former people of the Workers' Opposition bore all this burden themselves, but alas. Today is the first (I write the letter with interruptions) and I heard from the Iuzovsky podraikom that the raipartkoms have been persecuting people and accusing them of syndicalism, deviation and sins committed before the Tenth Party Congress. All these facts clamor about one thing, which is that that our political Kolupaevs and Razuvaevs cannot master those difficult conditions in which our comrades work.[172]

And so a request, have you elaborated anything about self-defence, in abbreviated form at the very least? Also, maybe you have carried out that instruction which the meeting gave you? Well then, how are you doing in general, has

---

172   Kolupaev and Razuvaev were characters created by Russian satirist Mikhail Saltykov-Shchedrin (1826–89) in *The Haven of Mon Repos* [Убежище Монрепо] to represent capitalists. The names translate as scratchers and shoe-removers.

Shliapnikov left the CC? Finally, how about the trip abroad and what are the Politburo's views on the subject of our shaking-up [перетряска]?

Greetings to all.

With respect,
[Mitin's signature]

12   Letter from A.G. Shliapnikov to F.A. Mitin[173]

Secret party document.

Dear comrade Mitin,

I received your long letter from the first, obviously dated mistakenly as in June. I completely agree with the tactics you outline and are carrying out. [missing part] We've frequently brought before the CC the struggle against the Workers' Opposition. [missing part] We thought the same as you about Perepechko's letter – that it's superficial and frivolous. He obviously received information about our congresses and our position from an unreliable source.

Sergei [Medvedev] went away on holiday for awhile. Soon he will return, probably before the 15th of this month. Then I'll try to get some 'holiday'. I have thought much about the work which was assigned to us [missing part], but have not finished [missing part]. I need very much to consult with our closest comrades [missing part]. I am continuing the same tactic, which we outlined at the congress and about which I spoke publicly at the session of the faction. Until the time when all factional squabbles, as a form of revenge, will not be officially and resolutely rejected, I will not take on any kind of work. Therefore I turned down work in VSNKh. Another reason I refused work in VSNKh was my desire not to be mixed up with those people who now attempt to lead the affairs of the national economy of our Republic.

Not so long ago, in fact a week ago, I had a discussion with Grigory Z[inoviev] and asked some point-blank questions. The main thing came to the following.

---

173   TsA FSB, R33718, vol. 41, ll. 157–8, early July 1921, typed, unsigned, undated. This is not translated in entirety, because brief parts were not transcribed in my notes. I also cannot say with 100% certainty that Shliapnikov wrote this letter. But references to it in other documents make it appear that the author was Shliapnikov rather than Medvedev, who is referenced in the letter as having departed Moscow.

Are we going to introduce mutual struggle, will they declare war against us, or is some kind of agreement still possible in the interests of the revolution and party unity? In our discussion, which extended about two hours, we as old acquaintances exchanged quite candid opinions about questions relating to the party and the republic [missing part] I declared [missing part] that the official course does not satisfy us and that it conceals within itself the danger of a split. There is deep dissatisfaction among workers, which is expressed among communist proletarians. [missing part] We can now turn out to be significantly stronger than we were in the era of the pre-congress discussion. But we understand perfectly well that this will tell heavily on the general course of affairs. Nevertheless, if the party centre will not reject those practices which it has adopted since the Tenth Congress, this step will be necessary in the interests of saving the working class, the workers' movement, and its organisation.

My suggestions are:
1. Cease persecution of the Workers' Opposition and issue a special circular on this subject.
2. Adopt a circumspect attitude to repressive measures which are directed toward workers.
3. Reconsider the case of the faction of the All-Russian Metalworkers' Union congress by fully satisfying its last decision and convene a conference in the upcoming month.
4. In VSNKh, STO and other economic bodies of the republic, include our worker representatives, who possess economic experience and initiative.
5. Direct economic policy toward restoring large-scale industry, focusing on it all attention and resources of the republic. Accommodate industry to the demands of the internal market, by presenting to workers such an amount of foodstuffs and industrial goods as could secure their existence by means of goods exchange with the countryside. [missing part] In the metalworking industry [missing part] this will be expressed on average at 40% of manufactured goods being placed at the disposal of our cooperative societies.
[missing part]

Comrade Zinoviev agreed with my formulation of the question and declared that he supports reconciliation most resolutely. He promised to talk this question over with Ilich, who he said likewise supports the need for agreement, but the very process of agreement has been delayed for a few days, due to the work of the congress.

I hope you got news of the Central Committee's decision about the purge of the party. [missing part] The commission [missing part], Orgburo and Politburo accepted a significant share of those practical proposals, which we put forth in the pre-congress era and which officials at that time regarded as Makhaevist. [missing part] It follows first of all to protect against the possibility that clever sirs [господа] will not use this purge for a settling of accounts with the workers. The CC's decision, which was published on 30 June, makes it possible for workers, who are old party members, to take this matter in hand. Work should begin on this everywhere.

Your information about the situation in the Donbas alarms me very much. [missing part] More information is needed [missing part]. I am sending you materials about the Congress of the Comintern.

13   Protocol and Resolution from a Meeting of RCP(b) Members Who Had Belonged to the Workers' Opposition, 8 July 1921

Protocol of a meeting of RCP(b) members, 8 July 1921.

Comrade Pravdin (VTsIK) chairs.

Attendees: comrades Shliapnikov (CC RCP), Kutuzov (CC RCP), Chelyshev (CCC), Perepechko (VTsSPS), Lutovinov (VTsIK), Samorukov (VTsSPS), Borisov (Central Board of Artillery Factories), Skliznev (ZhAKO factory), Polosatov (CC Metalworkers' Union), Barulin (State Moscow Metallurgical Factory – GOMO-MEZ), Kiselnikov (CC Textileworkers' Union), Budnik (Moscow Metalworkers' Union), Semenov (Moscow Metalworkers' Union), Lebedev (Avisoklad), Fishel (CC Printers' Union), Matrosov (Cable factory), Tarasov (Moscow Metalworkers' Union), Poberezhsky (Gubernia Trade Union Council).

Comrade Shliapnikov suggests that the agenda for the session should include hearing informational reports about the work of representatives of the Workers' Opposition in the CC; a report by CCC member Chelyshev about his trip to the provinces; and comrade Lutovinov's report about the situation in Germany.

Comrade Kutuzov proposes to introduce into the agenda the item of more exact communications in the future, at least among personnel in the centre.

Comrade Lutovinov finds that the agenda should not be confined only to informational reports, but that today it is necessary to discuss further tactical behavior, the stance toward the CC, and so forth. He proposes, after having heard informational reports, to single out special questions for discussion.

Comrade Perepechko proposes that after having heard informational reports, debate should be opened and then appropriate conclusions made.

(Comrade Perepechko's proposal is accepted.)

Shliapnikov: Comrades, the communications we began setting up during the pre-congress discussion have still not been broken off. We correspond with districts in the South, the Urals and other oblasts. It is true that mostly individual people rather than organisations write to us. Moreover, those who write to us include Trotskyists, who appeal to us as the only representatives to whom they can turn about local abuses of power and matters of principle. Comrades who have left the party write to us at the same time when they write to comrade Lenin. These are the types of communications we have, either through letters or by people coming here for temporary work assignments [ходоки]. This is despite the fact that after the Tenth Party Congress the opposition officially has not existed. Recent events have made communications develop and become stronger:

1) persecution of the Workers' Opposition is developing all over Russia, leading to greater organisation of the masses; and

2) the RCP leaders have departed from the line of the proletarian dictatorship.

The vividly exposed policy at the Fourth Congress of Trade Unions and the All-Russian Congress of Metalworkers forced us to set the need anew to organise within the party as a worker group in order to strengthen and reinforce our party's influence over the working class and to straighten the party's line, which departs from defending the working class. For example, the party's line on the economy has been much too cluttered by petty bourgeois interests.

I should inform comrades that Kiselev, Chelyshev, Kutuzov and I have frequently asked the CC about its current economic policy. Vladimir Ilich's brochure about the tax in kind on grain frightened us. Of course, this is not because of how the question is generally posed, but because there are places in it which definitely point to harmful deviations by our party. As a result of this brochure, the threat arose of the misappropriation of large-scale industry. Workers began to send delegates asking for workbenches, anvils, and forges in order to set up small workshops. Later at the Politburo's session, representatives from the provinces, such as Saratov and Gomel gubkom secretaries, posed the question much more acutely than did comrade Lenin. They declared outright that there's no reason to bother with largescale industry, but that all must be staked on aid to handicrafts and smallscale industry. We then protested that this was a harmful deviation. We are very confident that because of our criticism they convened the All-Russian Conference, at which leading comrades tried to flesh out the policy of making large scale industry our base. But then a fly spoiled the honey.[174] In Vladimir Ilich's speech on page five of the 'Bulletin of the All-Russian Conference', we read, 'Small-scale industry must be restored in order to seriously revive large-scale industry to any extent'.

This demonstrates a complete lack of understanding of the role and significance of small-scale industry in Russia. Anyone who has studied the economic and industrial development of our country at all knows that it did not experience a gradual transition to large-scale industry. Small-scale industry did not have the same significance in our country as it had in other countries. Now small-scale industry will be revived at the expense of our large plants and factories. Comrade Kutuzov will tell you that in the textiles industry, Trekhgornaia manufacturing company can take the place of all of handicrafts textile industry. There cannot be any indiscriminate approach in this regard. For example, we will need to apply another method in woodworking and other areas which are based directly on peasant-produced raw materials.

In the provinces, all this is settled in distinctive ways. In the newspapers, for example, you can find paragraphs about the squandering of our enterprises in connection with VSNKh's circular on the 7 June decree. Naturally those old economic managers, most of whom still sit in our enterprises, facilitate plunder and disorder in our economic life. There you have it. All this taken together forced us, comrades, to be on our guard and to raise this question frequently in the CC.

Second, we should dwell on repression against the Workers' Opposition and the working class. We know now that it is chiefly workers who sit in prison for crimes. The wage rates policy under implementation drives workers into prison. When we raised these matters in the Politburo, we encountered the desire to meet halfway in relation to the Workers' Opposition. They forwarded our statements to the CCC and telegrams were sent places. They made it appear that they agree with us that nonproletarian elements cannot be allowed to take revenge.

But immediately after this, we saw at the congresses of VTsSPS and the Metalworkers' Union that they were hiding a clear policy of suppression against us behind this outward appearance of agreement. This policy emerged from the

---

174 Но и здесь была влита солидная ложка дёгтя.

Politburo. Many comrades at the VTsSPS congress did not understand how the situation was taking shape. We understood it only after we became acquainted with materials of the interrogation of Tomsky and others, which clarified their roles. These materials made it obvious that with the permission of the CC, Tomsky decided to ally with Tsektranists to wage struggle against the Workers' Opposition. In order to do so, Tomsky united with Riazanov and prepared to get me excluded. He constructed his report so that if you want to criticise the activity of VTsSPS, then you are criticising our leading body the CC. Riazanov had prepared an attack on the CC. I said that we did not see these comrades in opposition to the CC at the party congress and that here they are playing a game. I branded Riazanov's speech and the resolution as independently oriented. As a result of all that happened, Tomsky was derailed [на всей этой истории слетел].

Then there was the Congress of the Metalworkers' Union. At it the CC, perceiving the Union of Metalworkers as our organisational centre, decided to shake it up. All these events served as extra confirmation that we were simply amusing when we went to complain to the CC about its very own policy. We discussed these questions at some separate meetings and decided to outline an organisational path of struggle. First of all, we decided that in the provinces it is necessary to more closely link with unions and party cells. We gave some practical instructions, which we printed up and distributed.

Further, after negotiations with some comrades, we decided to pose this question to our opponents. We did not fish for an appointment, but for example comrade Zinoviev, seeing our militant mood, was constantly seeking opportunities to talk things over with us. Once he made an appointment to see me, but because we both were busy, this meeting did not take place. But finally ten days ago, we conversed for a whole two hours. We gathered like two old acquaintances from illegal times. I posed the question categorically: are we at war or will we come to a peaceful agreement? I said that we wage struggle, we are organising and will continue to organise, and that if he knows the situation of the party and the workers' mood, then he should know that workers will be with us. He agreed that the mood is such that a significant portion of them will follow us and not them. I said that if you make it necessary for us to leave the party, then you should remember that we will not be nonparty. Then I asked whether the CC and the party as a whole will discredit us and systematically disparage us all the way down to the cells, for if so, then we will seek trust in the masses. We'll go even further into the rank and file. Clearly, when we will be in the rank and file, the higher-ups will not hold out for long. Here Zinoviev got completely out of hand and characterised people such as Shmidt as holding onto their places for that small policy role which they are given. He said that the difference between them and us is that we carry out politics and they don't. The practical conclusion from the conversation was my proposal to cease mutual struggle under the condition that we will become party members with equal rights and will struggle for our opinion just the same as they. A circular should go out to all organisations that the Workers' Opposition nowhere served as a source of discord. Attention should be paid to repressions against workers, who are sentenced to prison for having carried off a pud of potatoes and for sharp criticism of the gubkoms. I asked for review of the decision regarding the central committee of the Metalworkers' Union. A conference of metalworkers should be convened, at which the central committee should be elected and then it should carry out all that was outlined by the faction of the Congress of the Metalworkers' Union. Further, Sovnarkom and STO bodies should be formed with the most lively participation by trade unions. Zinoviev agreed with everything, saying that he would speak with Ilich. On the next day, he summoned me and said that Ilich also stated that he is tired of war with us and that he wants to reconcile, but that he insists on a precisely worked out agreement. This business was postponed until the present congresses have ended.

Of course, I have very little trust in all this. It goes without saying that these people will not succeed in devouring us. We now stand on the unanimous opinion that we need the proletarian people to close their ranks and get organised without fearing this notorious point seven. Without unity, people such as Paniushkin grow out of the soil of that lax discipline, which existed after the Tenth Congress. Such cases are not isolated. The Ekaterinburg organisation decreased to 16,000; it was primarily workers who left. We should impede this departure, the more so that now those principles, which not so long ago were called 'Makhaevshchina' are now published as the last word from the CC on the purge of our party.

Zalutsky, when presenting about the party purge, acknowledged that our party's composition does not favour the working class and that more than 50 % of our party is a nonproletarian element. Now it would be desirable to use the purge to unify the proletarian element and put it at the head of this purge. During discussion of our existing tactical line, which has a historical connection, we should not pass over this business of the party purge. As much as possible, we should provide our own people for this work.

Chelyshev – I completed a circuit of a portion of the party organisations and now I want to share impressions with you. First of all, the majority of organisations have intrigues, which are often of a subjective character. They try to implicate members of the Workers' Opposition in these intrigues, or more accurately to create a provocation around them. Our people, often without taking stock or calculating, get into groups not based on a principled platform but on friendship, which catches them up. Therefore, when you arrive somewhere as an official in order to investigate some repression, then you find a tangle of evidence. True, in some places the provocation is evident, but in general it is difficult to prove. The CC knew this very well and took it into account. Even the Nizhegorod business did not yield positive results, since all sorts of elements were dragged into it. Second, I need to note that when I appeared in worker districts, even representatives of the 'Ten' saw in me a deliverer. They clustered round and said that I should make them healthy. They wanted me to eliminate the existing situation in which the cell is completely cut off from the highest bodies, which hide everything from them. For example, they asked me how strong is Paniushkin's party and raise the point that there is a declaration which they are not allowed to read. When a gubkom representative comes to the cell, they often do not allow him to speak. In general, organisational life is poor. There is complete stagnation in petty bourgeois circumstances. Calmly and routinely they carry out work, without involving the masses at all. Cells are very dissatisfied with the people who occupy posts. The latter are often drunk and do no work. It is most unpleasant that there is nepotism and drunkenness from above to below.

In some gubernias, peasant communism stands out in sharp relief. There is the strong desire in such places to give all smallscale industry to the peasantry. In Simbirsk, for example, they directly declare that I do not understand the situation of the peasantry and that I incorrectly interpret the new policy. They say that it's necessary to lean for support on the peasants. Characteristically, all disgraceful things which exist in organisations are regarded from the party point of view and not from the legal point of view. All party people in our country became lawyers. In order to carry out any decision, all facts must be proven by evidence. Under the force of this, any swine such as our Shpitsbergers and Krasikovs arrange everything from a juridical standpoint so that often they become accusers against the bodies which judged them. For example, a colonel with his daughter entered the party and he was appointed director of distribution. I attended his exclusion from the party. They told me in one place that a land captain was the chair of a certain cell.[175] I asked how they could let this happen to which they replied that they could not do anything against the cell's recommendation. On the whole, of course, all this work creating control commissions absolutely leads to nothing. They sit in judgement over weird

---

175 As one of a series of counterreforms, Tsar Alexander III introduced land captains in 1889 to provide administrative control over peasant communities. Usually from the nobility, they could veto the decisions of peasant councils. The position was abolished in 1917.

Sidor, who, having drunk up half a bottle, goes to show the entire world his great strength. Having inveighed against somebody, he takes leave from the party.

Lutovinov. – Comrades, I was abroad for the first time and therefore I cannot compare its present state with the past. But in general my impression was stupefying. I expected from the information of the CC and certain individuals that neither transport nor factories exist there and that people die off just the same as in our country. But in Germany, I found complete restoration of politico-economic might. Of course, one cannot speak about Germany's influence among other countries until it is fully free of the military threat from the Entente and minor states. Only creation of a solid military base, which could repulse attack, can make it free. Creation of a military base is possible only in another country, from which it could haul off everything at the necessary moment. This forces Germany to seek a country, with which it could conclude illegal agreement. Russia is such a country, in which Germany could place its military industry and its production capital. Germany can be said to have now emerged from crisis and to have resolved its worker question. Unemployment so far is large, but in any case this unemployment has stopped growing. Workers are fed. Of course, they eat not as well as before the war but in any case they have a firmly set ration [определённый твёрдый паёк]. Transport has revived to the level of before the war, which is sixty trains per hour. Therefore Krasin's information several months ago that Berlin was practically a ghost town absolutely doesn't hold up to criticism. The proletariat is better fed and clothed than ours, which significantly degree dampens the prospects of revolution. So our bets on revolution are not justified. Moreover, in Germany communists definitely are persecuted. Not only communists but also their sympathisers are kicked out of unions. About this they usually say at the factory that the union does not answer for the actions of so and so. After this, repression follows. Our Comintern and union work is absolutely not noticeable there. Our leadership and directives come down to chowing down at congresses.[176] German workers who belong to the party essentially are functionaries who work for Soviet power. The party still has not established membership dues, while declaring that charging dues would be exploitation of the working class. If we stopped right now sending money to Germany, then the party as it is now there would cease to exist. This was proven in the March days, when there was a silent directive to come forward. At that time our commissars, who are kicked out from here and sent there, looked only to Russia. As a result the blood of the proletariat was spilt unnecessarily. Our role is not far off from that of a provocateur in

---

176   He uses the word for feeding animals.

that we give money, we send people who are incapable of leading, we raise an uprising, and the result is beatings. Considering our superficial inspection of all the missions in Revel, Kovno and elsewhere, the one in Berlin was where we uncovered the most confirmed thieves and swindlers.[177] At their head stood the famous Kopp. In the trade mission were definite black marketeers (Schiebers), who were called 'old party personnel'. When I went to Berlin, I was told that all my proposals will be accepted, yet right now, despite our investigation, Kopp has again been appointed to Berlin and obviously has restored to their places the employees who worked with him. Right now we are at war against the CC for this reason. We asking whether we should resign or whether we should try in court those blackguards who sold off the interests of the RSFSR wholesale and retail.

In my opinion, if this system under which they put a worker in prison for a pud of stolen potatoes and set free a scoundrel who has spent millions will not be extinguished, we should immediately declare war and wage it completely openly. Comrades, you remember how much time it took for legal action against Gukovsky. At first I thought that a clique/camarilla in the CC simply was making decisions according to its sympathies. It is nothing of the sort. We now have become convinced that there is a whole system like a chain from which not one link can be removed. They have to defend the most despicable acts, for they support one another. A logical conclusion needs to be made. This is why I proposed at the beginning of this session to talk about tactics and information completely independently. Inasmuch as we have heard Shliapnikov's information, now let's express our opinions and recognise that it's necessary to bring to the CC's attention that its actions are completely intolerable and are pushing us to struggle. We henceforth are reviving the Workers' Opposition and will struggle as much as is legally possible. In the future we cannot be limited to accidental meetings. The question of organisation on an all-Russian scale has definitely already matured completely. Without putting communications in good order, we will waste time. I support the proposal for an all-Russian conference, which could coincide with one or another congress or conference at which representatives from all corners of the republic could gather.

Perepechko – Comrades, I want to note that clearly our party's social composition has changed. Those who follow the press probably read in reports that some gubernia organisations are composed of up to 60% of a nonproletarian element. This undoubtedly influences the relations between the party and the working class. The party's leadership is no longer correctly communist but is

---

177   Revel (alt. Reval) was the Russian name for the Estonian city Tallinn.

being transformed simply into command. In my opinion, the CC considers that its line of behavior toward the Workers' Opposition is completely correct. The Workers' Opposition reflected the mood of the leading part of the proletariat. Inasmuch as the Workers' Opposition led a significant part of trade unions, it is in the interests of the CC to carry out expulsions.

As concerns Zinoviev's promise to Shliapnikov, well I don't believe even one iota of it. The most striking fact to confirm this is the story of the Nizhegorod metalworkers, where because the faction did not pass the gubkom's list of candidates, exclusions from the party were proposed. This is right near Moscow. So what is done in the remote areas? Now we should make two conclusions: first, we need to get better organised, to communicate in a more organised way, and to place as the next task convocation of an all-Russian conference, since we still do not have a common line and experience. Secondly, in the area of tactics our group should proceed from the experience of our old illegal struggle, since our task is the strictest discipline. There should not be any outright explanations of our organisational line, such as to some extent Shliapnikov's act of defiance.

Kutuzov – Comrade Lutovinov's speech was not completely correct. It is correct that it is hard to find a greater disgrace than what is going on with our foreign trade, but when comrades start to criticise Kopp, then it's necessary to think about that which is done in our own ranks. After the Tenth Party Congress, those who were formerly with us renounced us, declaring that they were with us by mistake. Were they with us then only because they hoped to receive comfortable positions?

We constantly raised giving more initiative to the provinces and trusting them. In fact we have seen that when some Sidorov or Petrov comes to Narkomvneshtorg, he is told to first dot all the i's [разрисуй], and then he'll get work, for he is not ready. But some sort of Nolde arrives, 'dots all the i's', and sets about managing. Comrades, I think that we now should insist that if they will not place communists at the head of factories and other places and will not allow initiatives, then our cause is lost [пропащее]. Where various swine sit in management, our unions are discredited on all accounts, and we did everything we could to train them.[178] Old workers regard everything passively and the young ones get drunk and engage in debauchery. There is even great slovenliness among those who have been and still are with us. When you place them in the factory and then they behave the same way, then they discredit you. We need first of all to arrange communications as they should be. We need to send out feelers [щупальцы], and then already it will be possible to wage open struggle.

---

178   мы их же воспитали на своей шее.

Samorukov – I would like to note some facts. The play 'Buf' is being staged now.[179] The Comintern spent 11,500,000 rubles at the same time as the same sum was denied for restoration of Volsky cement industry. Or take K's three articles in *Ekonomicheskaia zhizn*, which are simply disgraceful. They elevate specialists, about whom it is said that salvation of everything depends on them.

Our tactics should be especially careful and we should not swallow Zinoviev's bait for any reason. He is arranging all this in order to keep up morale to a certain extent. There should be the strictest selection in our grouping. A continually functioning body needs to be selected. As concerns our party's social composition, Zelensky stated at the gubernia conference that in the previous two months workers left the party and more than 50% of those who entered were peasant and petty bourgeois elements. When I asked him if I could use this report, I was told that these numbers can't be disclosed.

Our tactics should be to wage struggle and to pay the most serious attention to the working class, because now attention is turned to the peasantry. Their farms are improving while nothing is done for workers. Work needs to be carried out as conspiratorily as possible, not by driving up in automobiles as today several arrived all at once.

Rybak – Before talking about any organisational forms, we need to speak about our principled platform. Our disorganisation after the Tenth Party Congress resulted from that crossbred resolution which was accepted. In the provinces, it was a result of that healthy protest which is observed. If we now turn to economic policy, then we will see that everything now leads to revival of small-scale industry. If you take our old newspapers and the current ones, then you will see such an enormous difference. Now they're only talking and writing about the peasants and revival of farming here, there, and everywhere. But workers are mentioned nowhere, except for Shliapnikov's notorious commission. So it is possible to say that right now there is a definite effort to bypass the working class. In order to begin to do something as it should be done, we first of all need to agree about a definite position of principle, and then to talk about organisational forms. I already proposed at one meeting that we have more conspiratorial methods and urgently elect a bureau. In my opinion, this is necessary to do.

Pravdin – We as the Workers' Opposition find ourselves in a contradictory situation. I think that until representatives of the Workers' Opposition will sit in senior posts beside others, they will receive all blows fully upon themselves.

---

179   Vladimir Maiakovsky's play 'Mystery-Bouffe'. It premiered on 7 November 1918, the anniversary of the Bolshevik seizure of power. A second revised version opened on 1 May 1921.

We have until now made very little effort. Right now it's necessary to resolve the business of our behavior and our role in the Soviet organism. If we have become convinced that in occupying senior posts we are powerless to influence anything, then it's necessary to decide whether to go on another path again. Having decided this question, all the remaining questions we have will take on a real foundation. In the provinces we have no platform. There the party of functionaries and of peasant bourgeoisie demoralises the worker masses. It directs their thoughts to simple dissatisfaction, as of any petty bourgeois. This poisons the worker idea, which does not rise to pose the question politically, for it wallows among narrow-minded rumours. Even more prepared comrades lose contact and are swallowed up by this swamp. We need now to collectively decide our behavior.

Polosatov – About those gathered here it is possible to say, "They lock the barn door after the horse has run away."[180] After the Tenth Party Congress they dispersed, having believed something, and now they again begin questing after some kind of platform. If they are searching out new platforms, then this group simply is a crowd of dissatisfied individuals. The Workers' Opposition brought to light definitively its own line of conduct and its own platform. Now the question can only be about whether this line of conduct was correct or not. I think that those views we held during the pre-congress period remain correct, despite the fact that we have now already raised the question of whether it is possible to transition from defense to attack. Our immediate task is seizure of the party within its existing bounds. First and foremost, it's necessary to seize the communist cells and trade unions, which will be the supportive base for the implementation of our line.

Regarding an all-Russian conference, I find that this question has still not matured. The main tasks are elections to a bureau which should communicate with the provinces and in the area of tactics to begin the transition to an offensive along the entire front.

Chelyshev – Here a split and convocation of all-Russian conferences and other questions were raised. But first it's necessary to think about in what situation the group will be then. We should behave just as politically, as they behave toward us. Maybe somewhere sometime there will come a time to have a talk. Here were uttered some positions of principle, which should be taken into consideration. In all branches of work we will have to work out some definite positions, without which it will be difficult to carry out work. It will be necessary to assemble and group together our forces. We should certainly implement

---

180   Гром не грянет – мужик не перекрестится.

all the discipline which we will elaborate. It would be incorrect to move immediately toward a split and for all to leave the party, because first of all practical
impediments will arise.

Shliapnikov – The comrades gathered here are not only personnel in the
centre, but also those from the provinces, from the grassroots, and from the
party cells. It's very bad that we do not hear their voices. Regarding a split and
so forth, I should say that it can't be forced. We can always create a split. If we
compare the very first disagreements between Mensheviks and Bolsheviks to
our disagreements, well they both rested in the organisational-practical area.
Organisational-tactical disagreements are taking shape right now between the
Workers' Opposition and the semi-peasant party. Right now we haven't heard
even one proposal of a programmatic character. Everything can be reduced to
practical questions.

I still would like to make some remarks regarding selection of a centre. At the
faction of the Tenth Party Congress was selected a centre, which has constantly
guided work. About electing a bureau I hear conversations at each meeting and,
you must agree, that a new centre cannot be elected at each meeting.

The comrade's objection that our ranks have thinned is incorrect. We are
much stronger now than earlier. Comrades, I think that we can all come
together right now on the need to expand our work. It's necessary to link up
with the cells and with union bodies and to consolidate ourselves organisationally. To force it is not necessary. On the contrary, we should show that we are
ready for agreement in the interests of the party's unity. I think that it's necessary to negotiate with Zinoviev, in order at the right moment to show that we
are not responsible for the collapse.

Borisov – I find that inasmuch as we have gathered here, we should now clarify whether we still have our former program (since we're gathering here under
the flag of the Workers' Opposition) and if everyone agrees with it. When comrades here raise the question about a centre, I should say that first it's necessary
to ask about what we will unite around. Will it be around discrete ugly facts in
the missions and in Moscow, or will we begin in another way. In my opinion,
the fundamental problem is to reveal our face and then to begin preparing for
the next party congress. The situation with the trade union movement in our
country has not improved, but has gotten worse. Soviet and party building have
also worsened. We have lost around a year and need to begin again. Our centre
should now accept measures to reveal ourselves to get ready for the future Eleventh Party Congress.

Skliznev – Here some comrades express their dissatisfaction regarding those
outrages which they see and they propose a split as their conclusion. Others
more diplomatically suggest essentially the same thing by calling this an all-

Russian conference. I want to ask such comrades if we gathered here to speak seriously, or are the interests of the party and revolution for us dependent on Kopp or the staging of a mystery having roused our indignation? We are not taking the bull by the horns; party and soviet building should now unite us. Instead of speaking about all-Russian conferences, we need first of all to take up fulfillment of our program, which is fixed on party and soviet building. We do not need to elect a centre, because we already have it – Shliapnikov, Kutuzov, and Chelyshev. This centre just needs to work. Now about the party purge, it's necessary to direct a letter all up and down the line so that our people would not ignore the party reregistration but would organise the purge.

We should unify here not on the basis of disagreements with the main line but with methods of implementing this line. I think that we cannot reject the line taken by the Tenth Party Congress. In my opinion it is a truth that small-scale industry and agriculture need to be revived in order to revive largescale industry. Comrades here are not correct when they say that while they do not object to the main line of state capitalism, they shake with fear at that capitalism which grows out of this policy. As concerns the basic line of conduct of the CC in relation to the trade union movement, I find that this line is incorrect. I am convinced that they chuck out of the trade union movement not just the Workers' Opposition but workers in general, who sit there and who are the only ones capable of holding out against inevitable clashes in the coming age. Our CC has now taken the line of expelling from the trade union movement those capable of leading it. I think that this line is destructive, that it will lead toward collapse, and that our main task is struggle against this line and against bureaucracy, which is spreading in our trade union movement. We can only help strengthen the trade union movement and help avert the growing conflict of the petty bourgeoisie with the working class.

To speak about a split, I repeat, is not warranted, because it is necessary to not forget that any kind of forces acting at the current time outside the communist party are counterrevolutionary forces. Right now it is necessary to begin to explain the break in our economic policy. For I categorically affirm that the majority of party members from among workers are leaving the party now because they cannot understand this change in our policy. Paniushkinism [Панюшковщина] now is growing larger and this is a tragedy of the working class. Our party bureaucracy is afraid to go into cells and explain the course that has been engaged, and demoralisation proceeds from this. Our task is to go to the masses and organise them on the basis of an inevitable turn.

Poberezhsky – It seems to me that we are now experiencing the very same tragedy as at the Fifth Conference [Congress] Of Trade Unions, when worker democracy was the centre of attention and when Zinoviev spoke out as defender of our point of view. It seems to me that right now comrades approach the question incorrectly. Comrades were at the Tenth Party Congress and should have foreseen that which is now being done, but they overlooked even such facts as expulsion from central places, for example, in the Metalworkers' Union. Our representatives in the CC need to ask at the CC plenum about the behaviour of the leading group at the Congress of the Metalworkers' Union. What have they undertaken in this regard? This was the central crux [гвоздь], around which a campaign needed to be raised. Why was there this beautiful gesture at the Tenth Party Congress about how if they will not change the resolution about the anarcho-syndicalist deviation, then we will not enter the CC? Our main task should be struggle against the CC's tactics in implementing one-man management [единоличие]. Against this it is necessary to struggle and on the basis of democracy it is necessary to organise the broad party masses. It is early to speak of a split. A split is created through struggle. It is not just made.

Lutovinov – Now it is necessary to recognise one thing out of two. Either the proletariat should defeat the demagnetized party intelligentsia or it should depart on its own. In accord with this, the first task should be to create an organisationally largescale group with a leading centre. Comrade Shliapnikov says that there is a centre and that there is no need to elect it at each assembly. There were objections here against an all-Russian conference. I do not put forward a conference as the first priority. It goes without saying that organisational work must be carried out before a conference. I emphasise that it's necessary to organise cells. Comrades here proposed to implement our program. I ask how will you implement it, when our party is 65% petty bourgeois? I took Kopp as a typical representative of a certain part of our party. They beat the proletarian at each step. The trade union movement and other questions are partial. The main question is proletariat or intelligentsia. The main question is if the proletariat will be drawn into management or will various swines, who only arrived yesterday, sit there? First of all, an organisation is needed to realise this. It is all the same whether it is in the form like we have now or by seizing institutions in which there are none of our comrades. Then we need to send our representatives to all corners of Russia, having organised a conference as a result of this preparatory work. In coming days it is necessary to assemble and ask ourselves about tactics and to see how we ourselves approach the question. Maybe we will have a split even within the Workers' Opposition itself.

Kutuzov – When comrades say that there is absolutely no contact, it is not the truth, because we have somehow assembled even here. There have been results from the group's work, it goes without saying. Although they laughed at it, the CC now implements that which the Workers' Opposition proposed. Of course, you can't especially place your hopes on Kutuzov, Chelyshev, and others, because we are only for window dressing. But I should say that great dissatisfaction now ripens not only among our representatives, but also among those who have supported the 'Ten'. Both those on the left and on the right are transferred and dissatisfaction grows. We need to skilfully carry through our influence. For this it is necessary to be in the course of things and to see one another often. I propose that in each district we should have at least three constant people, who would serve for information and contacts.

Tarasov – We all agree that we have no differences of principle. But nevertheless this obviously does not satisfy us. The careful methods proposed by Shliapnikov and Skliznev give us a guarantee that in the ranks of the party, where 65% are of a nonproletarian element, that which is outlined in a principled way will be carried out correctly. If there is even the smallest guarantee, then obviously there's no reason to prepare for creation of a parallel party, but probably this lack of confidence forces to place the question about organised rebuff to petty bourgeois element. If now in the Moscow Party Committee can be posed the question about giving them an extra pound of bread and a jar of preserves in order to hold back the communists, then what will this lead to? It will lead to everyone who is honest being dispersed. Dissatisfaction in the broad masses pushes sometimes the most honest communists to disorganised outbursts. If we now will not organise the masses by some means, then we will continued to be confronted by a party composed 90% of petty bourgeoisie. We now need to organise the communists who have remained in the party.

Lebedev – Comrade Shliapnikov was interested in knowing what those from the provinces will say. I can inform that in the provinces the cells are in a state of neglect. Work has completely come to a standstill. We are not in the condition to do anything, because when we tried to speak out, even in defense of proposals, we received a very strong rebuke. After my speech in favor of Shliapnikov's theses, a special person came to us at each assembly, in order to keep track of what I would say. After this, I could either keep quiet or leave the party. Without definite leadership from the centre here, we cannot do anything. I spoke with individual party cell members who agree with me, but we don't have an organisational plan to carry out. There was a lot of talking here, but there's still no definite plan. Without directives from here, I cannot undertake anything.

Kopylov – I think that it's time for us to begin living like adults, but at all our meetings we only seek and grope for that which will unite us. Here comrades stood for a split. I ask what is a split for? Is the goal to fish out the swindlers, or to form a concrete party to seize political power? It's necessary to speak and to agree on definite conclusions. If workers will take power, then can they organise themselves and struggle better than is done now? It's clear that the dissatisfaction which one hears is the reverberation of general insecurity. Will we be able to eliminate this and win over the masses' sympathy not with eight jars of preserves but with the more suitable project of building a state, which will destroy con men and will feed the hungry? You can't just force a split only on the basis of Shliapnikov's genius foresight. There were some proposals here about how to work. In my opinion, comrades lost sight of one small advantage which we received after the Tenth Party Congress. This is the possibility of bringing exposure to our theoretical views via the press. On the basis of the exchange of opinions in literature, we would accumulate some experience and we could come forth with more serious preparation. Comrade Shliapnikov is correct that the masses support us. But the masses don't know what to do. We need to meet them halfway and help them to figure out what to do.

Shliapnikov – The comrade who indicated that we did not react to what happened in the Metalworkers' Union is incorrect. Apart from how in the faction itself we began with 100 votes and ended with 138, we frequently raised this question to the CC. Regarding our tactics, a split is a political means for comrades Perepechko and others, but for us a split is the result of definite work and alignment of forces. We say that we have no major differences according to written documents, resolutions, and programs, so for now there is still an element which unites us with this 65% mass of petty bourgeois element. The time will come when we do not have a common language and the appropriate conclusion will be made from this. But it is insufficient to organise now only on the basis of indignation and dissatisfaction.

Proposals are introduced to hold the next meeting as soon as possible, and that the Bureau make use of the material of the current assembly. [end]

Resolution accepted either at the meeting above or at a subsequent meeting:

We have discussed the Politburo's line of conduct toward relations between the party and the trade unions and toward party members who spoke out before the congress as supporters of the platform of the Workers' Opposition. The Politburo's line was demonstrated at the Fourth All-Russian Congress of Trade Unions and especially so at the Fourth All-Russian Congress of Metalworkers. Further, we pay heed to the following:

1. This line with especial clarity was expressed in depriving the Union of Metalworkers of the right to freely elect the union's CC in full and by making appointments to it on the basis of personal arbitrariness from above, which fundamentally violates the decision of the Tenth Party Congress about the party's relation to the trade unions.

2.   Both at the faction of the Congress of Trade Unions and especially at
      the faction of the Congress of Metalworkers when it was discussed how
      to compose the union's new central committee, Politburo representat-
      ives openly, insistently and especially provocatively divided delegates of
      the congress and the candidates for the new leading bodies of the trade
      union movement and of the Metalworkers' Union into two sharply differ-
      ent camps of those who had supported the CC RCP and those who had
      supported the Workers' Opposition before the Tenth Party Congress.

3.   At these congresses, Politburo representatives just as openly, insistently,
      and provocatively tried to discredit delegates and party members who
      nominated candidates to leading bodies of the trade union movement
      and the union and who had supported the platform of the Workers'
      Opposition before the congress. They acutely emphasised that the CC
      RCP did not have confidence that these delegates, who are party mem-
      bers, would carry out decisions of the Tenth Party Congress. Yet they did
      not confirm their lack of confidence with even one insignificant fact that
      any of those who had defended the platform of the Workers' Opposition
      before the congress had violated any directives of the party.

4.   For the same motives, the Politburo introduced the same division and
      into the plenum faction of the All-Russian Metalworkers' Union central
      committee when making nominations to its presidium, having deman-
      ded from it in the form of an order that it violate its own statutes on the
      very structure of the presidium of the central committee of the union.

5.   Thus the Politburo took the path of open intraparty factional struggle
      by dividing without any factual basis the delegates of the congress, as
      party members, into two categories and demanding from the faction of
      the Congress of Metalworkers a firm majority in the new Metalworkers'
      Union central committee of fourteen supporters of the Politburo and ten
      who had supported other tendencies.

6.   With all this the Politburo a) made morally and physically absolutely
      impossible any coordinated, comradely, and friendly work within the
      party; b) disorganised for the long term all party and union work both
      in the centre and in the provinces; and c) caused open and deep distrust
      among trade union personnel toward leading party bodies. The effects are
      fatal on future relations between unions and the party. All this once again
      split and disorganised the party.

Therefore the party members gathered here find it urgently necessary:

1.   To work energetically in all party bodies, at party meetings, and among
      individual party members, especially and chiefly among its proletarian
      elements, to explain the entire political danger given the current interna-

tional and domestic political and economic conjuncture of the Politburo's positions a) blatantly pushing trade unions toward a split with the party and the party toward splitting into pre-congress intraparty groupings; b) deliberately supporting open persecution, which the petty bourgeois elements, political careerists, and political scoundrels who have latched onto the party systematically carry out within it, against party members who spoke out before the congress in support of the platform of the Workers' Opposition; c) threatening, along with this, to apply to the latter measures of retribution of a party character and of the Soviet regime against any of their attempts to defend themselves from persecution.

2. To conduct on an all-Russian scale, until the Politburo repudiates the position it has taken of distrust and persecution toward trade unions and party members who share the views of the former Workers' Opposition, work to rally party-proletarian elements by explaining to them the greatest political danger of that laid out above and the special need right now: 1) to elevate proletarian elements' active role and participation in deciding all matters of party, soviet, union, and economic policy and practice; 2) to ensure for these very elements maximal self-activity and the most attentive accounting and use of their experience in these matters.

3. To show solidarity and to organise energetic protests and counter actions to the maximum extent in all forms possible within the party against any attempts to continue the intra-party persecution, political murder or reprisals of a party character or of a soviet regime against those who only spoke before the congress in support of the Workers' Opposition.

4. Because individual Party CC members have made exaggerated threats in party circles to apply to Comrade Shliapnikov, who is a member of the Party CC and who spoke before the congress openly and very energetically in defence of the platform of the Workers' Opposition, the punitive point of the resolution of the Tenth Party Congress about party unity over his resolute refusal to carry out at the Congress of the Metalworkers' Union the Politburo's line, those gathered here likewise find it necessary that if this measure is applied to Comrade Shliapnikov, to categorically demand from the other full and candidate members of the CC and CCC who were brought into these bodies by the Congress as hostages from the Workers' Opposition, immediate departure from these institutions with an open letter to the Party CC about the reasons for their departure.

5. Due to provincial party members having insufficiently and with difficulty assimilated the general character and content of the party's new economic policy and to the need to precisely explain the new tasks of the proletariat dictated by this policy in the area of the trade union movement,

those gathered here likewise find it necessary to obligate the comrades remaining in Moscow to clarify these questions and to systematically inform those working in the provinces about everything they've noticed anew in this area.

6.   Those assembled here likewise obligate all those working in the provinces to systematically inform Moscow comrades about all aspects of party, soviet, union and economic life in the provinces and about questions arising in these areas which demand the attention of all party members.

The following material may have been a resolution or instructions passed or proposed at a meeting around this time:

1.   The activity outlined can give the desired results only under one sure condition – if it will be implemented systematically and in an organised way, quietly, steadily, insistently, politically and tactically restrained and in a consecutive manner. Patience is needed. Noisy demonstrations without results should be avoided. One should not surrender to any provocations.

2.   No organised activity is possible without systematic leadership and an apparatus to carry it out. Therefore the first thing necessary is to select one to three comrades and charge them with regularly informing comrades in the provinces about the most important events and phenomena of party, soviet and economic life, explain its significance, correspond with comrades, and so forth.

3.   We also need to pay attention to how we may use the trade union apparatus (district committees, subdistrict committees, and factory committees) to broadly and systematically develop the activity outlined above within their districts, and if necessary in neighboring districts.

4.   If this is not possible now, then all forces should be exerted so that the possibility will exist as soon as possible. Each comrade here should situate himself so as to achieve the tasks set, to assume work which he has not yet fulfilled, to change the area of his work, and so forth.

Toward those goals, the following measures should be carried out:

On Unions:

5.   Occupy all the most important posts with maximal unity in district committees and subdistrict committees; thoroughly use their technical apparatus and resources; direct all influence toward strengthening such unity in the factory committees and setting up the closest links with them and the same with personnel of economic bodies and factory management; and use their resources to the maximum.

6.   Resolutely and actively counteract all sorts of petty tutelage and micromanagement, and the foisting of special observers as authorized rep-

resentatives, permanent instructors, senior personnel and so forth, both from the CC and from oblast bureaux assigning them.

7. Resolutely refuse to enter these bureaux, if you are not guaranteed in them a decisive or sufficiently strong influence (for example: 2/3 or 2/5 think like we do with one wavering or undecided); and if there is not such influence to refuse individual senior posts and transfer all our forces directly to the districts and the factories.

8. Resolutely refuse and protest demands from the CC or Bureau to send for work personnel or intentionally reshuffle them for reasons of party intrigues.

9. Unfailingly resolve all these matters in the faction of the union branch or section, if its composition is satisfactory, and to expand its composition by adding factory committee representatives in special circumstances and when it is desirable to impart special significance to its resolutions.

10. Insistently, resolutely, and thoroughly prepare for upcoming conferences to elect oblast bureaux and to use them in the indicated way.

11. Systematically observe protocols (of the main and economic centres and businesslike evaluation and criticism of their activity) with obligatory notetaking of these evaluations in protocols of your sessions and carrying special resolutions on individual matters.

12. Systematic illumination before conferences at factories, in the district and similar places of unsatisfactory aspects of the activity of the union central committee and likewise of oblast bureaux.

13. All forces and the centre of attention of the district committee should be directed toward systematic and regular convocation of factory, district and gubernia conferences and assemblies on all matters of the activity of the district committee, the section of the union and so forth or individual matters of the wage rates agreement, cooperative work, payment in kind [натурфонд], cultural and educational work or on improvement of workers' living conditions. All these conferences or meetings should be organised and arranged exclusively by our forces.

14. Along with this internal union activity it is likewise necessary to decisively counteract any attempts by petty bourgeois elements from the gubernia trade union councils to interfere in the internal work of the union in wage rates agreements, improvement of living conditions, payment in kind, cooperative work, and so forth.

15. Establish the closest contact with gubernia departments of other production unions and rallying their personnel on this basis and on a party-political basis around ourselves.

On Economic Bodies: glavki, district boards, gubernia economic councils:

16. Select and unite senior personnel of the body and of the factory boards under it.

17. Special circuit by the leader of the body, dispatch of a suitable comrade or a small commission with a corresponding business assignment to the provinces; and along with this, systematic summons of personnel from the provinces for information on matters of impending activity and clarification with them of its possible forms.

18. Convocation of meetings with them likewise on separate questions, connected with the course of production, and posing at them questions of union policy and practice, outlined by decisions of the Fourth Congress of the Union and of the Tenth Party Congress.

19. Comprehensive assistance by means of all the body's resources to the district committee and section of the union in the activity outlined for it.

14   Resolution Offered by Aleksei Sovetov to the Delegates' Assembly of the Bauman District RCP(b) Organisation, 29 July 1921[181]

Having heard the report about the economic situation, the delegates' assembly recognizes as correct comrade Shliapnikov's thesis, which explains the reasons for the extraordinarily difficult economic condition of the republic, in that we for the entire existence of Soviet power have not been able to use the expropriated material wealth [благ] of the bourgeoisie for the improvement of the situation of the working class and to strengthen the dictatorship of the proletariat, by distributing this wealth free of charge even among groups not giving in exchange for this state valuables. Likewise is correct the line of economic policy facilitating the preservation and strengthening of the proletariat, presenting to workers' associations upon agreed upon principles command of production, with direct participation of trade unions, instead of transfer of enterprises to purely private enterprising, speculative lessees, which do not make use of the forces of the collective creativity of the proletariat.

---

181   TsAODM, f. 63, op. 1, d. 44, l. 28. The resolution was read but not voted upon. At this assembly, Aleksandr Shliapnikov presented a report about the New Economic Policy, but the text was not available for inclusion in this collection. Sovetov's resolution is courtesy of Simon Pirani's notes. Pirani 2008 notes that the assembly did not vote on Sovetov's resolution and that Shliapnikov's report was only taken under consideration (p. 125, notes).

15   Letter Received by Ukrainian Comrades in 1921 from a Former
      Member of the Workers' Opposition, perhaps Ivan Perepechko[182]

Dear comrades!

The turn in economic policy and chiefly the CC RCP(b)'s measures to implement the 'party' line at trade union congresses forced some comrades from the
former Workers' Opposition to ask themselves whether to be or not to be in the
party. Others busied themselves with self-reproach. A third group calmly and
dispassionately evaluated the Party CC's acts.

It is possible to state generally and fully that the latest events in the party
stimulated and forced one to think about the further fate of the Workers'
Opposition, which in fact ceased to exist after the congress.

In this letter I will not touch upon the new course of economic policy and
its evaluation. I think it needs to be done at another time. I will just dwell upon
those facts, which actually served as the reason for unrest, if it is possible to call
it so, in the ranks of the Workers' Opposition.

Also, I don't consider it necessary to dwell upon what happened at the congress of unions, since the events at it were not decisive. The CC RCP(b) uncere-
moniously, insolently, and cynically cast out the Workers' Opposition from the
central committee of the Metalworkers' Union. Its zealous followers declared
that the Workers' Opposition needs to be chucked out now not only from the
raikoms, but even out of the wage rates [расценочные] commissions. This is a
cynical fact. 'Not just any politically degraded person can attain such a degree
of cynicism', because decisions of the Tenth Party Congress conceal this clearly
factional policy and designate it as policy on party unity.[183] By this act, the Party
CC transforms the party into a herd of sheep, to which it is possible to bring
unconcealed factionalism stuffed in resounding phrases about unity.

Actually, this fact has revealed nothing new. It only clearly illuminated the
factionalism within the party, which the CC cleverly has carried out up to now.
It is possible to cite hundreds of facts from various places around Russia and
from the CC's direct activity. Both before the Tenth Party Congress and especially after it, the CC expelled the 'Workers' Opposition' from all places where it

---

182   Published in Anon 1922, pp. 12–14; and in Zorky (ed.) 1926, pp. 54–6. Typescript preserved
       in RGASPI, f. 17, op. 71, d. 77, ll. 1–3. Although the signature is indecipherable, it seems clear
       that the author was neither Shliapnikov nor Medvedev. Judging from references in other
       documents, I believe that the author was most likely I. Perepechko. Pirani 2008, p. 124
       identifies the author as Perepechko.

183   I am not sure from where Perepechko takes this quotation.

was linked with the activity of the worker masses. It obligingly presented places in bureaucratic institutions to the comrades whom it had chucked out. The act with the metalworkers emerged in an especially glaring way, because they were dealing not with individuals but with an enormous collective there.

How did our comrades respond to this? The response was Tolstoyan, yes, and even a caricaturish form of it.[184] The CC began with the blatantly cynical policy of expelling them from their base, and these people [публика] offered up tearful petitions. But Tolstoyan doctrine teaches that if you're struck on one cheek and you offer the other, then there's no need for tearful begging. Our comrades not only offered their cheeks, but their entire selves up to the insolent blow. A tearful petition shows how honest, sincere, and infinitely devoted are our comrades to the party, the revolution, and union institutions, but at the same time it shows that the comrades fail to understand fundamental political factors. With honesty and sincerity alone, you'll always end up looking like a fool before a person who understands the meaning of politics.

Politics concentrates the good and the bad, the cynical and the honest; he who has mastered this mechanism can make policy. If they use insolent tricks against you, respond with the same. If self-defence demands an offensive with an admixture of bad methods, which we cannot carry out by our class nature, use them anyway.

In the case of the metalworkers, our comrades displayed lack of understanding of the basic rules of politics. We, as a collective, should struggle against it. The CC will chuck out the Workers' Opposition from wherever it is linked with the masses and with its class. 'Even from the wage rates commissions', as they already declared. The metalworkers fell first and will do so in the future, because among them we were the most firmly grounded. The CC ousts them because it thinks that in the future the Workers' Opposition can be the nucleus of opposition to what is now taking shape as the party's petty bourgeois policy, which emerges from the New Economic Policy.

In the nearest future, we should struggle against the Party CC's factionalism in politics; against new, open, insolent and clever forms of repression (removal from mass work and transfer to office work); for democracy within the party and unions, which, despite the Tenth Congress's decision, still doesn't exist; and against the scourge[185] of union leading bodies. But this is not the main thing. Our group should revive as a group first of all to create the new course of economic policy and to expose the attitude toward it of the worker part of

---

184   This refers to the Russian writer Leo Tolstoy, who became a religious pacifist.
185   The term is literally 'shaking up with sand' [перетряхивание с песочком].

the communist party. The new course is correct. To oppose it in any form is to commit an act of black reaction. This course, despite its unavoidability and the need to help it along, does not mean that the policy of the worker part of the communist party should be the same as is now the official line, much of which betrays pure Bolshevism and Marxism and turns us into opportunists of the latest brand.

My brief evaluation of the new course should not force you to conclude that this is my final outlook. No, my own attitude toward the new course is still just forming. If the group as a whole will get busy with clarifying its position on this question, then I think that undoubtedly we will elaborate a common line. The Party cc leads a campaign against us, proceeding from the assumption that we are obviously the nucleus of those who will understand the New Economic Policy in a proletarian way.

You won't justify by means of any other arguments the senseless persecution of us. Our tasks are to elaborate our world outlook and to struggle against deviations away from the proletariat, which the Party cc commits. Answer insolence with insolence. Respond to attack with organising and going on the offensive. Just avoid introducing into politics sentimental things, as was done by our comrades at the Congress of Metalworkers. They proved their infinite devotion to the revolution and communism by means of this sentimentality, but simultaneously they revealed their complete lack of understanding of politics.

With comradely greetings,
[indecipherable signature]

16   Letter from Levit of the *Kommunistische Arbeiter-Partei Deutschlands* (KAPD) to A.G. Shliapnikov, 30 August 1921, and Shliapnikov's Signed Response, 31 August 1921[186]

Letter from Levit, secretary of the KAPD delegation, to Shliapnikov, 30 August 1921. Excerpts.

[Encloses materials from his party's press about attitudes toward the Third Comintern Congress and toward the Workers' Opposition.]

---

186   TsA FSB, R33718, vol. 41, ll. 1–2; RGASPI, f. 2, op. 1, d. 24625.

Our party congress will be on 11 September. It will finally decide the matter of our membership in the Comintern and the creation of an international union of all revolutionary leftist political groupings. ... This will mean a split of the Third International ...

We would appreciate the sympathy of the Russian Workers' Opposition toward us, even the more so since we recognise the significance of Soviet Russia among the world's proletariat.

Therefore we ask you to voice your definite attitude toward our congress and the appeal we forwarded to you, and if possible to address our congress in writing ....

[not signed]

⋮

Shliapnikov's letter in response, 31 August 1921, with a copy sent to the CC RCP(b) on the same day.

Dear comrades!

In response to your inquiry, I inform you that the Workers' Opposition did not constitute a special party, but was a part of the unified RCP(b). Chiefly a grouping of old underground party members, it enjoyed the support and sympathy of advanced industrial workers. Its base was in the All-Russian Union of Metalworkers, the All-Russian Union of Miners, and the Union of Textileworkers. It had many supporters in other trade unions.

After the Tenth Congress, the Workers' Opposition disbanded. It has no centre. Therefore, my answer to your questions bears exclusively a personal character. However, knowing the mood and opinions of those who think like me, I can say that the majority of them share my point of view.

1.   My attitude toward the creation of a Fourth Comintern is negative.
2.   We oppose a split of the Third International. Therefore, and likewise taking into account that which is set forth above, we do not propose to make any greeting from the Workers' Opposition to the Congress of the KAPD.

31 August 1921

    A. Shliapnikov

Note follows: Comrade Lenin, on comrade Molotov's instruction, here is a copy of comrade Shliapnikov's answer, for your information. CC office manager [*Управделами цк*].

17   Excerpts from Speeches at the All-Russian Union of Metalworkers
       Central Committee Plenum, 17–21 October 1921[187]

Protocol of 17 October 1921 session of faction of plenum of central committee
of the All-Russian Union of Metalworkers.

Attendance:
cc Members: Shliapnikov, Ianson, Fedorov, Rozental, Lavrentev, Vladimirov,
Bukhanov, Lepse, Tarygin, Ignatev, Tashkin, Vorobev, Sergeev, Stepanov, Mitin,
Brykov and Tarasov.
Candidate members: Klinov, Budniak, Medvedev, Orlov, Chernov, Pavlov.
TsPK members: Polosatov, Khamlianen (?).
Senior staff: Dybets, Lutsuk, Mandelstam.
Senior union staff: Prosolov, Izakov (Donbas), Zdekhovich (Siberia), Vasilev,
Budniak (Moscow), Skliznev (Iuzhbiuro).
Chair: Fedorov.

Agenda: Debates on the presidium's report.

P.F. Lavrentev indicates that the central committee's work recently has produced a dispiriting impression. Upon becoming acquainted with the presidium's and secretariat's work, according to their protocols, it turns out that
during the time covered by the report, the presidium and the secretariat in large
part were composed of one and the same. The secretariat composed more than
half of the presidium. The protocols make it clear that the secretariat and the
presidium did not take part in the most essential questions of the day. They
passed by these. Their time discussing economic questions fell sharply. They
spent far more time discussing minor organisational and administrative questions. The participation of senior union personnel in the presidium's work fell
significantly. In the provinces, no directives were received during this time. Our
union organisation is falling apart. Objective conditions alone cannot explain
all this. It must be recognised that part of the blame falls upon the central committee.
    Dybets remarks upon the weakness of the reports of the presidium and its
sections and indicates that the central committee's representatives in the economic bodies sense no leadership from it. At the current serious moment, what
is needed is not criticism so much as a serious attitude toward work, because
the question is about the preservation of the proletariat.

---

187   RGASPI, f. 99, op. 1, d. 8, ll. 10–24. Ellipses signify omitted parts.

Semkov declares that the central committee has not sufficiently shown the union line, as a result of which there appeared statutes, which the Department of Metal [of VSNKh] suggested and which were reminiscent of [A.P.] Meshch-ersky's project.[188] It is necessary to regard the situation seriously and to outline a programme for the future.

Tashkin (Urals) points to the situation being created in the Urals, where over the heads of union bodies and without any participation by them, such things occur as the transfer of Motovilikhinsky factory to the Council of Milit-ary Industry without any preparation. The same thing is done with Kyshtymsky factory. There are rumors about the lease of Nadezhdinsky factory.

Ia. A. Klinov (Petrograd) points out that the presidium of the central com-mittee is not to blame for its weak work. The fault lies on those central commit-tee members, who being located in the provinces and partly in Moscow, have rendered it no help. Considering the current criticism irrelevant, he proposes to make practical proposals about how to construct work in the future.

Medvedev talks about those especially difficult conditions, in which metal-workers have come to be found. Moreover, the metals industry has experienced intense demoralisation. Under these conditions, the unification of all union forces was necessary, first of all. Union masses needed to be united around the central committee not mechanically, but with a militant ideology binding them. Besides that, you can see everywhere the full isolation and alienation of the central committee from the district committees. The central committee has not led the district committees in implementing all the most important meas-ures of the current time.

[missing lines]

Ia. D. Rozental informs that at a session of the Bureau of the VTsSPS Faction, comrade Fedorov presented the report of the presidium of the central com-mittee, describing the situation in the central committee, indicated that an

---

188   In 1916, A.P. Meshchersky had proposed an 'Association of the Engineering Industry' as a
         more rational way to fulfill orders for industrial goods through the private sector rather
         than the state sector. This project made only a small impact before the February Revolu-
         tion toppled the tsarist government, but after the October Revolution, Meshchersky nego-
         tiated with VSNKh (upon Shliapnikov's invitation) to form a 'National Association of
         Engineering Enterprises'. Negotiations ended in April 1918, due to several objections. These
         included Meshchersky's inattention to trade unions, contention over the degree of 'work-
         ers' control', concern about the large degree of ownership German companies would have
         in the enterprises, and Communist ideological objections to 'state capitalism'. See Gatrell
         1995, pp. 7–14.

obstacle to work was the continuing line of the Workers' Opposition, which exists and carries out its own work. He thinks that the reason for the central committee's inactivity was not the policy of the Workers' Opposition but primarily the irrational structure of the central committee, and secondarily the lack of desire of some members of the presidium (Sergeev, Ianson) to work in the central committee, which they frequently have asserted.

Comrade Vorobev finds that the weakness of work at the present time cannot be explained by the lack of desire of individual personnel to work. Work has slowed down exclusively due to the complex conditions of the great turning point in our whole policy. ...

Tarasov indicates that since a production centre exists, then it should realise leadership of the district committees' work. In regard to inter-union organisations, the Union of Metalworkers until this time has held to the slogan 'seize the gubernia trade union councils'. At a session of the VTsSPS Presidium, Comrade Fedorov proposed the slogan, 'emulate the gubernia trade union councils'. Further, he reads a resolution which was accepted at the Moscow district committee plenum.

Comrade Mitin says that the central body's task is to capably and energetically lead and direct the entire organisation's work, despite difficult and complex objective conditions. At the Fourth Congress of Unions, there was talk of the danger posed by the petty bourgeois element. The central committee was called upon to struggle against this element and to instruct the provinces about this struggle. Now life confronts us with the lease of government enterprises. There are no directions from the central committee as to whether we can lease out large enterprises ... Collective supply is promoted ... There are no instructions from the central committee. In the provinces, they had to decide some important questions without directions from the central committee. It was necessary to find both new organisational forms and, with pain in one's heart, to withdraw factory committees from production. Earlier it was difficult to say where is the factory management and where is the factory committee, for the line between them blurred. It is impossible to work under circumstances when the central committee does not lead. The Ukrainian conference recognised this and found it necessary to convene a special Congress for the re-election of the central committee.

Comrade N.D. Brykov (Briansk) points out that the work of the central committee completely confirms what results appointmentism can have. As a consequence of this, in the provinces the party and inter-union bodies completely disregard the Metalworkers' Union. He reminds us that the line shown by the Politburo at the Fourth Congress on elections for the central committee did not end with that. Terrorisation of personnel who were suspected of belonging to the Workers' Opposition, forced furloughs, and mobilisation into food requisitions work began in the provinces. All this knocked personnel off course [выбило из строя] and destroyed union organisations. Mobilised personnel were not used. It's necessary to take stock of the experience of the central committee's work and point out to the Politburo that it allowed a fundamental mistake.

P.A. Skliznev (Southern Bureau of VSRM) informs that after the Fourth Congress there has not been a united union. After that experiment, which was carried out, there is no unified metalworkers' organisation. Discord exists in union life. This has also extended to the south, despite the fact that in the Southern Bureau of the union were individuals who enjoyed the trust of Southern union organisations. Currently in each town they have their own methods of resolving all the most important questions. The greatest obstacle to the production unions' normal work is the decision of the Fourth Congress of Unions about organisation. If this decision will continue to be realised, then by the Fifth All-Russian Congress not even one production union will remain. Replacement of the higher-ups alone will not change anything. In the South, this line resulted in conflicts and litigation with the city trade union councils of almost all cities.

Fedorov: ... The central committee was immediately deprived of many senior experienced personnel, who after the Congress intentionally abandoned the CC ... The conditions of work under NEP were not suitable for implementing the decisions, which the Fourth Congress accepted. ... Convocation of an extraordinary congress of the Metalworkers' Union, which some comrades suggest, will not change the situation, which is being created. Here at the plenum, it's necessary to find a way out and to create businesslike circumstances for further work.

Prosolov: ... An extraordinary congress is needed in order to elect a central committee which could put an end to conflicts within the party and inter-union organisations ... Each district committee is under attack and falls under the suspicion of these organisations, each of which interprets the resolutions of the Fourth Congress in his own way.

Budnik [Savva]: ... Not only the remote Donbas, but also nearby Moscow did not sense leadership from the central committee ...

Budniak: ... The central committee's main fault is that it doesn't participate in the work of economic bodies and doesn't have its own representatives in such important body as Gosplan. Moreover, the fate of the entire metals industry is decided not in the Metals Department and other corresponding bodies, but in Gosplan. There the majority consists of former shareholders and factory owners, who are closely linked with international capital. ... We need to call a congress.

Chernov: The union's one basic line, which it should never forget, is the seizure of production. ... The central committee's line has been insufficiently flexible and energetic. ... Gubernia trade union councils have strongly impeded the work of the union. ... The trade unions should be the masters of that production which they organise ...

Andreev is surprised that all the criticism is directed against the presidium ... The VTsSPS appointed a special group of inspectors to investigate the central committee and it turned attention to the work of sections of the union in the provinces. The VTsSPS secretariat heard the information gathered and the reports of the gubernia trade union councils, which attest to the very weak work of the sections of the union of metalworkers in the provinces. Objective circumstances are at fault. There are too few personnel. There are factory stoppages in the Urals, the south and other places. After the Fourth Congress of the Metalworkers' Union, departure of former activist personnel noticeably intensified, as if it were intentional. Union life in general has lagged behind other turns of our policy. Therefore it should not have been demanded that the central committee manifest its own definite line. ... The composition of the presidium needs to be reexamined and supplemented with fresh forces. Then a conference of district committee representatives should be convened to strengthen links to the provinces. Convocation of a special congress would provide nothing but conversations. The organisational line that was accepted at the Fourth congress does not need to be changed.

M.P. Vladimirov: This plenum should recognise that the presidium, as currently composed, is unable to work. In conversation with comrade Lenin, I told him that the decision of the CC RCP(b) at the Fourth Congress did not make it possible to strengthen the Metalworkers' Union, but the contrary. Earlier the central committee of the All-Russian Union of Metalworkers was a seething stream, to which all of metalworking Russia was drawn, as if to a magnet. Now there is no link to the districts and there is no life in the central committee itself. Such a crisis as we have now, I have never seen before in the central committee. I find it extremely difficult for me to go somewhere to a union organisation and to speak not as an elected, but as an appointed central committee member. In order to exit from this situation, we need to elect from our midst a presidium, which could firmly carry the banner of the metalworkers and disperse the fog of appointmentism. For this it is not necessary to convoke an extraordinary congress, but to speed up the convocation of a conference.

Sergeev finds that frictions, which were called forth by arguments, can be divided into two parts: 1) unnecessary rebukes, which do not move business ahead, but which are only in the realm of conversations; and 2) an important organisational question, about where the entire centre of gravity of work should be concentrated, whether in production or in an inter-union body. Concerning the second question, accusations against the presidium are completely unfounded. In the protocols of the presidium, you can find some decisions about NEP, wage rates, and other questions. If you can rebuke the presidium, it is for putting insufficiently firm pressure upon VTsSPS. Rozental criticised the last presidium just as he did this one, but he himself brings nothing new. He doesn't differ from the majority of the presidium when deciding important questions. He is a two-faced person.

Ianson (concluding word): The presidium hasn't had its own line, because it has carried through the line of the Communist Party.

Mitin's resolution is accepted by 13 votes against nine.

∴

Second session of communist faction of the central committee plenum of All-Russian Union of Metalworkers, 18 October 1921.

Agenda: debate on reports of economic bodies.

[No notes from the speeches of Semkov and Ryskin-Rysko]

Chernov points out that the entire structure and operations of the Metals Department are directed toward destroying the self-sufficiency of those glavki which are under its jurisdiction. Here you have the crudest centralism. The Metals Department attempts to take everything into its hands, but is incapable of doing anything. In order to receive any kind of satisfactory decision to supply Gomza factories, you have to wait a whole month in line at various echelons of authority [инстанции] in the Metals Department. ... When finally the programme enters the factory, then the Metals Department starts to inundate you with such changes that in two months you can't recognise the programme. As a result, there's no rationality behind work in the factories. So, the highest levels of government ignore the Metals Department and make decisions without consulting it. The Gomza factories have been transferred to collective supply. But workers have still not received their wages in this system of collective supply. The Metals Department has still not given any instructions on how to go over to self-financing [расчёт себестоимости].

[No notes from the speeches of Vorobev and Mandelshtam]

Shliapnikov says that the reports of the Metals Department and of the Electric Department cannot be considered satisfactory. But of course, it is not those comrades who the central committee sent there who are guilty of weak reports. A significant share of the blame falls upon the central committee. Never before now has such a breach between the central committee and the economic bodies been observed. In order to avoid this in the future, union bodies need once and for all to refuse those tasks, which are formulated with the instruction 'get further away from production', which the central committee gave to the representative of Bezhitsky district committee. For by such a path, we will not create a foundation for socialism.

It is a fact that the squandering [разбазаривание] of factories can be seen in the metals industry. Local management bodies of the metals industry do not receive timely directions and instructions from the centre. The centralisation of leadership (which is necessary) needs to be separated from direct management. Moving on to the plan for building metals industry, he points out that the Metals Department has not attempted to co-ordinate its programmes with the basic tasks of electrification and aid to agriculture, with which the last congress of soviets proposed to restore the entire economy. Realisation of this plan is the only way out for our metals industry, which needs variable [переменный] capital and circulating capital [оборотные средства].

Of course, the squandering [разбазаривание] of southern factories, which was pointed out here, is understandable. It results from the Metals Department not trying to find this circulating capital [оборотные средства] within production. Speaking about the activity of the Metals Department, you can't be silent about the unification of military industry in the Metals Department, which should have been realised in accord with the decision of our Fourth Congress. Comrade Orlov rather merrily declared that this decision was not carried out. It should have been implemented, since it definitely was accepted not only within the union but also within the party, that is, at the communist faction of the congress. It is also completely incomprehensible how the most important questions of the metals industry could be decided without the participation of the Metals Department. The central committee, which should not have permitted this, shares a portion of the blame. It is guilty from both a union and a party standpoint [порядок].

Shliapnikov explains why he had to refuse work in the Metals Department, to which he had been appointed. He does not think it possible to carry out work in an economic body, given the lack of close cohesion of all workers' organisations around the metals industry, especially taking into account the pressure of international capital on this industry. He finds that the plenum should give the future collegium of the Metals' Department a mandate [наказ], which would clearly outline the perspectives and tasks of its work.

Budniak ... argues with Semkov's characterisation of the Metals Department.

[No notes from the speeches of Ianson, Rozental, Vladimirov, Dybets, Kuibyshev, Klinov, Orlov, and Fedorov]

Tarygin points out that individual comrades cannot be blamed if work did not go right in the Metals Department. Without broad support, not one economic body can work. Comrade Shliapnikov can be rebuked here for his lack of desire to work in the Metals Department. Such comrades should be forced to go to work. He who is capable of managing industry should work, rather than watch from the sidelines. In order for the Metals Department to work, we need to set a condition to reject minor enterprises and focus attention on large enterprises of mass production. The plenum should say that gubernia metals departments also are weak and that the centre binds them together. It is necessary to give the gubernia metals departments more rights. It is impossible not to agree with the theses, which the Metals Department presented. The Metals Department needs to be instructed to review all enterprises and to determine all resources, which it's possible to have. We should send comrade Shliapnikov to work there. In the name of the plenum, we should force him to work.

[No notes from the speeches of Lepse, Veprintsev, Maslov (Chair, Ukrainian Metals)]

Baryshov: The blame falls on the presidium for the problem with the work of the Metals Department. Regarding the Electric Department the blame falls on the prior presidium, because it didn't pay attention in time to what was going on in the Metals Department.

Medvedev points out that an analysis of the Metals Department's report reveals that the problem is that union bodies are pushed aside and take a back seat. They do not participate at all in decisions about the metals industry. Our union should actually become the leading body of the metals and electric industries. It's not true that in the provinces, there's an empty place. There are forces, but they are still not unified. We need to gather them, prepare them, and push onward to resolve the basic questions of renewing the metals industry. Former economic bodies proved their unsuitability. The union trusted too much in supervision by the communist party. Union representatives did not justify the tasks placed upon them. The Metals Department's proposals prove this. They don't correspond at all to workers' spirit. The proprietary spirit [фирменность] needs to be squeezed out of the economic bodies. The conditions in which our representatives have to work there need to be changed.

Lavrentev: Many superfluous accusations have been showered upon our comrades from the Metals Department here. What could our representatives change when there are five people in the collegium? They could not exert influence on the entire course of work. ... The matter is worse with the Electric Department. It's no secret that a clique of proprietors [фирменники] has gathered there. ...

The plenum votes to form a commission to elaborate a resolution about the Metals Department's report, statutes, and theses. The commission comprises: Vladimirov, Fedorov, Shliapnikov, Mitin, and Medvedev.

●●
●

Session of the 20 October 1921 plenum of the faction of the central committee of the All-Russian Metalworkers' Union.

Agenda: Lease of Kuznetsky basin and Nadezhdinsky factory to a group of American workers.

Rutgers' report: Americans will bring enough food for a long period and will pay for their own transport. They ask only $300,000 for machinery.

Vladimirov: STO decided this question and only afterwards did it come to the central committee of the All-Russian Metalworkers' Union. STO decided it, without the participation of the central committee and of the Metals Department. The Metals Department protested STO's decision and brought it to the central committee for examination. The presidium of the central committee didn't agree with STO's decision, but representatives of the group of American workers demanded that the question be put before a plenum of the central committee.

Dybets: I would say that this effort of American workers and STO constitutes extortion, if the project were not signed by such names as Haywood, Tom Mann, and others we respect and trust ... But I must say that the comrades have let themselves get carried away. They propose a utopia.

Shliapnikov, dwelling on the proposed project, points out that having been abroad (in Germany), he had the occasion to observe how some adventurers, and likewise the most honest communists, lure workers to relocate to Russia, in order to help Soviet Russia. Some of them do so from adventurist motives, while others actually want to help Russia. It's necessary to take account of what kind of political significance such a massive resettlement can have. The larger contingent of such workers is recruited from the unemployed. Consequently, the accumulation of revolutionary forces weakens in the country from which they come. Besides that, these same workers, having returned from Russia, distribute about it rumours which are outright counterrevolutionary. Instead of bringing the revolution in their own country nearer, such facts of resettlement only weaken it.

There have already been colonisation attempts, which have yielded nothing positive, but workers returning to their homelands have filled the counterrevolutionary camp. If it were possible to give each Russian worker 100 dollars, then our industry would thunder away. If foreign comrades really want to help us, let them buy up shares from capitalists who take our concessions. But there is still the matter at hand, on which it is worth dwelling. Without a doubt, such comrades as Haywood, Mann, Rutgers and others enjoy our trust, but these comrades are speaking as individuals. They are not speaking in the name of or as delegated by their trade unions. The comrades are deeply mistaken in promising to quickly raise industry and so forth. All the same, they will not be able to fulfil their promises once they have encountered reality.

Klinov: If they really want to help, let them lease small enterprises. We'll try to run the large ones ourselves.

Mandelshtam agrees with Shliapnikov.

Rutgers: ... This project was approved by the Urals trade unions ... If we knew there would be opposition from Russian workers' organisations, then we wouldn't have made the proposal ... The comrades say that with money and bread, they themselves could set production right, but the matter is not only in this. Organisation and a system are needed.

Kolbert: They are not talking about sending masses of the unemployed, but highly qualified engineers and technicians, who can earn high salaries.

... Semkov's resolution is accepted unanimously. ... They accept Fedorov's theses on organisational tasks under NEP ... A future presidium is to elaborate the theses into special instructions for the provinces.

Election of the presidium:

Skliznev's list: Shliapnikov, Vladimirov, Lavrentev, Brykov, Vorobev, Medvedev, Tarasov; candidate members: Chernov, Pavlov, Bruno, Evreinov.

VTsSPS faction bureau's list: Lepse, Brykov, Vladimirov, Vorobev, Mikhailov, Ianson, Lavrentev.

Skliznev's list receives 13 votes. Nine vote for the VTsSPS-proposed list. One abstains.

Theses on the organisational question are accepted.

⋮

Session of 21 October 1921 plenum of the central committee of the All-Russian Metalworkers' Union.

The faction of the plenum hears Medvedev's information that the Politburo has confirmed a presidium composed of those names presented by the VTsSPS bureau of the faction [the list that the faction rejected in favour of Skliznev's list]. Comrade Ianson confirms Medvedev's news, which the plenum records.

Regarding the proposal to form 'An Autonomous American Colony of Workers' in the Kuzbass, with the addition of Nadezhdinsky factory and other enterprises, the plenum voted to reject the project as utopian and unsuitable from the point of view of the republic's economic interests. The plenum assigned the presidium to formulate the principled stance of the central committee of the All-Russian Union of Metalworkers about this matter and to publish it in the press.

18   Iu.Kh. Lutovinov's Speech to the Eleventh Party Conference,
        19–22 December 1921, and Related Party Documents[189]

To Comrade Molotov (Top Secret).

In accord with the CC RCP(b) Secretariat's 1 March 1922 instruction to investigate how Comrade Lutovinov's speech came to appear in the foreign press, I
report the following:

   We printed the stenographic record of the speech at the party conference in
six copies. Having been printed, all copies went (as is always done) to the next
higher editor for correction. After correction, the stenographic records were
transferred to the senior distributor for distribution to newspapers, bulletins,
and the archive.

   If part of the stenographic record is withdrawn, then it is not distributed
and all six copies are sent to the archive. Stenographic sheets (that which stenographers type) are destroyed.

   That is the general practice. It was the very same at the last party conference.
Comrade Lutovinov's speech was withdrawn, according to the decision taken
by the presidium of the conference (see sheet no. 1). And really **all six** copies of
Comrade Lutovinov's speech turned out to be in our archive.

   Among these six copies, one copy was corrected by Comrade Lutovinov's
hand. Upon investigation, it turned out that Comrade Lutovinov, before his
departure for Berlin, requested of Comrade Morshchiner (she who maintains
our archive) to give him his speech for correction for a future stenographic
report.

   Further, it turned out that Comrade Lutovinov dictated his corrected speech
to a typist and took with himself retyped copies of his speech, while he returned
the corrected original to Comrade Morshchiner for the archive.

   If Comrade Lutovinov's speech appeared in a newspaper in the form of a stenographic record, then only one supposition can be made. Comrade Lutovinov
himself gave his speech to the press (which I personally do not assume) or he
transmitted it to someone to read, or he accidentally lost his retyped speech.

   In any case, our archive committed a blunder, in that the speech was given
to the author for correction and so this gave Comrade Lutovinov the possibility
to retype his speech. In the future, of course, it will be most strictly forbidden
to show withdrawn stenographic records to anyone.

---

189   RGASPI, f. 47, op. 1, d. 1, ll. 146–59 (accessed by me at the Hoover Institution Library and
      Archives).

I attach to this all six copies of the stenographic record of Comrade Lu-tovinov's speech, which I request be returned when the need for them expires.

With comradely greetings,
A. Enukidze

[There follows a decision handwritten on CC RCP(b) letterhead to censor parts of Lutovinov's speech. Zinoviev, Rudzutak, Petrovsky, Iaroslavsky, and Voro-shilov signed the unanimous decision.]

∴

Lutovinov's speech to the Eleventh Party Conference, incorporating his correc-tions and including parts designated for censorship by party leaders:

I will not spend time analysing whether Comrade Kamenev correctly shed light upon the reasons for the transition from our old economic policy to a new one. Some comrades dwelled on this here and explained it. I could add much. My point of view is completely different. I think that it was not only those objective reasons, which Comrade Kamenev enumerated, which led us to such a life, meaning to a decline, but also many other reasons about which Comrade Kamenev did not speak here. These reasons include our wasteful-ness, our clumsiness, and our attitude toward the proletariat. Here you have the main reasons for that which led us inevitably to the New Economic Policy. I think that this cannot be disputed, because the New Economic Policy is an absolutely inescapable factor. I do not think that any comrades here would object to the New Economic Policy. There was no reason for Comrade Kame-nev to spend an entire hour and a half on a report about the New Economic Policy.

It would have been better if Comrade Kamenev had told us how he and the rest of the Central Committee conceive of the practical implementation of this New Economic Policy. Comrade Kamenev did not pose any of these basic ques-tions, which are the most essential questions of life and death at the present time, but he went round them, sliding along the surface. We should now pose in the broadest way some questions connected with this New Economic Policy. Presently I am interested in the rights of trade unions, the organisation of trusts, and the restoration of the country's economic wellbeing. But the report says not a word about any of this.

I have not read Comrade Kamenev's theses, but having listened very attent-ively to his report, I can say that this speech is like the shaft of a wagon, for it goes wherever you turn it.[190] That is not how the question should be posed. What forms will you choose to carry out the New Economic Policy? Comrade Kamenev did not dwell on this. Comrade Kamenev or the Central Committee should tell us how they think to carry out the New Economic Policy. Will it be by means of trusts headed by speculators, or by proletarian organisations? Will the proletariat continue to receive in the future, as it does now, 28 kopecks average wages per day for a skilled worker, as at the steam engine building factory in Kharkov? Will the proletariat participate at least somewhat in carrying out this New Economic Policy? Or will it continue to get boxed on the ears, just as it has up to now?

Will you keep smashing the trade unions, although you say at each turning point that you can't do without them? Will you give broad rights to trade unions, or will you keep carrying out incursions upon them, like those plundering forays and raids at the All-Russian Congress of Trade Unions and at the Congress of Metalworkers, just like when responsibility was taken away from the communist faction of the Profintern Congress. During voting for its executive committee, our delegation not only could not discuss the candidates it sent to the Ispolkom, but did not even know them, until Comrade Bukharin or someone else brought a list and said 'here, vote, and don't argue'. There turned out to be people in the Profintern who not only were unconnected to the trade union movement, but who even now do not participate in it. Will you also in the future carry out a murderously consistent line to destroy the trade union movement, or will you actually give trade unions a break to catch their breath?

Now capitalism is arising and it is not state capitalism, of course. That is nonsense and rubbish. You won't deceive anyone with this now. What kind of state capitalism is there? Entrepreneurial capitalism is being born. With our own hands, we are delivering nanny capitalism. Do you want right now to give trade unions the right to resuscitate the old forms of unions under new entrepreneurial enterprises? Would you like to make it possible for trade unions to revive the old organisations of struggle, to organise strike funds, to go on strikes in struggle against capitalists, and to organise labour and protection of labour. In general do you want to allow some necessary things, without which in a few months we can break our own necks? Or will you use the courts, with which Comrade Melnichansky is so captivated, as an intermediary to regulate interrelations between the working class, speculators and employer-entrepreneurs, for whom this means nothing? I think that questions about the trade union movement are very acute now. Such questions include attracting trade unions

---

190   Как дышло, куда повернул, туда и вышло.

to participate in trusts and in organisation of trusts. Another question concerns destruction of speculators. At a time when workers are getting 20 kopecks, speculators receive tens of millions and sell Russia both wholesale and retail. I witnessed this when I was abroad. You don't say anything about this.

If you will try to escape this question this way, it means that your economic policy is still not completely thought through. You still don't know what will happen tomorrow. You don't even mark any signposts [вехи], yet you put hope on a lucky accident. Comrades, we have broken our necks often enough and life has taught us enough lessons, so let's be more concrete. I will move on to the final point, which is about monopoly of external trade and of trade in general. Comrade Kamenev declared here that no matter what, we should open some kind of airhole, without which we will choke to death, but at the same time he informed us that foreign trade is being nationalised. Then how can there already be an agreement? I don't know about one, does Comrade Kamenev know about it?

There is talk about an agreement with the object of including Tsentrosoiuz as an organisation which will trade abroad. Moreover, still others would trade abroad through this organisation. Who are these others? Well, you know who. It follows that these would be entrepreneurial employers, who have been born and who we are in no condition to feed right now. They will make their way abroad, drag away valuables from here, and beat down the market there. The very same demands and orders made by several people will artificially raise prices on the market. You almost did this once, but why did Comrade Kamenev not say so?

Either you will carry out economic policy with all your heart and soul as each situation demands, or you'll provide some concrete positions. I spoke out here not just to criticise or to attack, but with the hope of posing some questions, which comrades would grab onto and develop further, chiefly in order to achieve an explanation from Comrade Kamenev about this question. Now I will move on to the question about our new economic policy as it pertains to organising production.

I think that it is impossible to organise our industry by those methods, which we have already tested sufficiently up to now and which have revealed their incapability. You can't do so only with the aid of these trusts, which seem to be the same old glavki, but significantly larger and significantly more bureaucratic than they were up to now. You can't only count upon them and you can't just begin again anew. These trusts don't seem to have their original form and goal. The goal was to attract some foreign capital, some nongovernmental capital, maybe even some of our own native capital, and combine it into a trust, so that industry gradually would include new employer-entrepreneurs with their capital and [illegible] force our industry to turn around. But what happened after that when we even [illegible] announced our desire to make payments on the old tsarist loans. [Illegible phrase] to some degree. We still have not received even one large speculator. In trusts or in new glavki, there still are not entrepreneurs or capitalists, who would contribute their own capital and so ease our situation.

So what is the work of these trusts now supposed to lead to? Will it be exactly like the work of those same glavki, those centres, which essentially were busy doing nothing? They were not even capable of accounting for what we amassed by robbing the bourgeoisie and that which we took from the capitalists. If in the future, we will busy ourselves with setting up production in such a way, and at the same time we will isolate and destroy trade unions [illegible], we undoubtedly [illegible] ourselves in the neck. Comrade Bogdanov's and Comrade Smilga's declaration that we live in friendship is nonsense and rubbish.

You can talk as much as you want from the tribune, you can be too fond of talking, but in essence do they understand anything about trade unions' participation in production? No. Any trade union will confirm this, even VTsSPS, which recently they ceased to take into consideration as an organisation. In the end of it all, they want to transform the entire trade union movement into a single trade union. This is at that time when production trade unions, such as the metalworkers and textile workers, are more qualified, conscious, and united than ever before. Right now is especially the time to be vigilant and just lean for support on certain ones. Should they be mixed together with those petty bourgeois swine, which outnumber production unions by tens of times over?

Your disagreements [разнобой] will be directed not at party members, who unquestioningly fulfil your demands whether they agree or not, but at the non-party masses and at the Menshevik-SR element, who work in the trade union movement. That is the kind of perspective we get from Comrade Kamenev's report. I think that Comrade Kamenev will answer these questions.

19   Undated Minutes from a Meeting of the Workers' Opposition or the
        22[191]

[This meeting might have occurred not long after the Tenth Party Congress ended, for Vladimirov is still a member. Or, it might have occurred during the

---

191   TsA FSB, R33718, volume 42, l. 104.

October 1921 meeting of the central committee of the Metalworkers' Union. This could be a fragment that is related to other fragments elsewhere in the notes]

Mitin:
1.   At the Donetsk conference, the CC's theses were put forth as not subject to discussion in principle.
[No notes taken from speeches by Miasnikov and Budniak][192]

Tolokontsev:
1.   Changes in our government policy result from the internal weakness of our international revolution, which did not arrive. The government's working capital [оборотные средства] is wasted. An influx of foreign capital is needed. NEP is correct about this.
2.   Who will implement NEP? Will it be those interested in preserving soviet power or its enemies?
3.   Trade unions should manage the state economy. If we will be cast off, we will advocate struggle by all means for better conditions for the workers.
4.   The RCP(b) has become the enslaver of the working class. The bench worker does not enter the ranks of the RCP(b). He does not see it as his leader.
5.   It's necessary to regard very carefully the formation of underground organisations. Their presence will be the first step to a split.
[No notes taken from speeches by Miasnikov and Goldberg]

Vladimirov:
1.   Decay (marasmus) is conditional upon the weak development of the proletariat's consciousness and the retreat from developing it further.
2.   The Workers' Opposition group has to be disbanded and a new group with a new platform or programme has to be created.
3.   How platforms are formulated.

Pravdin:
1.   The party's practical policy is coming to be in obvious contradiction to the theoretical world-view of Marxism. This is where decay (marasmus) comes from.

---

192   I do not recall whether the original notetaker did not note down what they said, or if I chose not to transcribe it.

2.   Is our policy really Marxist? Is our party really communist?

3.   The party is regenerating (or degenerating) not by the days but by the
      hours.

20   **A.G. Shliapnikov's Letter to the Politburo about the Genoa
        Conference, February 1922**[193]

[Analysis of the reasons for 'capital's current victorious offensive against the
working class'.] .... We must make use of the contradictions and struggle among
the four main capitalist powers, which are America, England, France, and Japan
... but we should not do so in any way similar to the Brest negotiations. ... [The
Genoa Conference] must also be used for agitation, but not just for declaring
our rejection of the capitalist world. It must have a businesslike character. There
must be clarity concerning emergence from the world crisis ...

... The commission's 21 February 1922 decision on preparing for the conference directly rejects not only a businesslike attitude, but even a simple understanding of the current state of matters in Europe. For Russia, the European
market doesn't possess those five billions of gold which our programme proposes as the maximum.[194] Krzhizhanovsky's phantasmagoric proposals (points
2, 3, and 4) are a political and technical rejection of private-property ownership
interests. Therefore, they cannot serve as a 'basis' for negotiations.

It would have been more correct to prepare materials on the organisation of
the largest industrial associations [объединения], both in mining as well as in
processing, in which the partial participation of foreign capital would be desirable. We can meet the pretensions of individual capitalist firms, each wishing
the renewal of 'its rights', with the more alluring prospect of a large trust, which
would be without competition or rivals within the country for raw materials
and fuel and which would allow for technical perfection in order to achieve
steadily improving productivity and consequently larger profits.

For the capitalists, the Genoa Conference offers the possibility to create a
'united front' against us ... we must be prepared for this ... Of all countries
France has the most financial interest in our past ... so-called small investors in
France have interest in 20 billion out of 53 billion francs ... such smallholders
consist of about 1.7 million persons ... it is possible to weaken capitalist France

---

193   TsA FSB, R33718, d. 499061, vol. 40, ll. 154–7. Partial notes taken from this. Ellipses signify
       omissions, while brackets signify paraphrased material.

194   It is unclear what unit of gold is being spoken of here.

by way of counterposing small holders against large magnates of capital .... England is less interested in our past. All its interests are of an industrial nature ... To have a country of many millions as one's market, to use German finished products [фабрикаты] as the means of realising gold in place [возмещение] of war reparations [контрибуции] is an alluring prospect for English capital. ... so there is open conflict between England and France. Our task is to deepen this conflict.

... America seems 'indifferent' to Russia, but our moves in the Far East can defeat this tactic. Attracting American capital to developing this region's industry can be a winner against Japan. ... When maneuvering around the debt question, we should not in any case claim a share of German war reparations. We regard France's war debt as financing of a definitely militarist enterprise, for participation in which our country lost a large amount of gold and human lives, and paid with the loss of property and land, and with the devastation of several oblasts. The Versailles peace and its profitable return are the results of this militarist enterprise. We do not share in its profits, and our losses are not covered.

2) In the question about our exit from the war, there are impermissible references to how the Entente supplied us with unsuitable military materials. These materials can serve as justification for nonpayment of war debts and as explanation for the failure to achieve 'victories'.

3) It is impermissible, untrue, and politically harmful to give international capital the direct or indirect impression that it could conveniently take advantage of us (that is, the communist government) in the business of exploiting our country's natural resources.

21 **Protocol of a 10 February 1922 Meeting of a Group of 25 Delegates to the Fifth All-Russian Congress of Metalworkers and Other Minutes from Meetings of Those Who Would Sign the Letter of the 22**[195]

Chair: Bruno.

Agenda:
1. Information of delegates from the provinces.
2. About a platform and tactics.

---

195 TsAFSB, R33718, d. 499061, vol. 40, l. 127; vol. 41, ll. 68–9. Ellipses indicate omissions. Similar notes from this meeting are in volume 42, ll. 103–4.

Reports by delegates from the provinces:

Mitin (Donbas): Regarding discussion of [the CC's] theses, Shmidt reported on the role and significance of trade unions at a conference in Bakhmut, where Antipov, Vorobev and Skliznev were present. Shmidt declared that the theses are a obligatory directive of the CC RCP(b) and therefore, they were not subject to discussion. At a conference in Kharkov, comrade Bulkin spoke in favour of rejecting the theses, for which the Politburo excluded Bulkin from the party. The conference's communist faction demanded Bulkin's restoration as a party member, but the Politburo of the Communist Party of Ukraine did not pay heed to this. It deprived Bulkin of any work, except in cooperatives. Party life is completely dead. At meetings, reports are not discussed and no proposals are introduced. In Nikolaev there is an underground organisation, but it has no leadership. I can verify that trade union work is completely dead also. Everything is accepted according to directives and without any discussion.[196]

Miasnikov (Urals): The mood in Perm gubernia is just as downtrodden as in the Donbas. They fear the Cheka. In Ekaterinburg the mood is also depressed. They are afraid to publish anything. The role and tasks of the trade unions was discussed in the bureau of the cell of the printers. Zalutsky presented a report. In my speech, I dwelled chiefly on the unions being chased out of production and the need to discuss democratisation. In Ekaterinburg, they asked me if I will agitate within the party. Everywhere you look, there are departures from the party. Cells are being split up. Entire cells are leaving. In Perm, I convinced three cells not to leave. At enterprises in Ekaterinburg, all kinds of measures are taken to keep people in the party. The result is that having received boots or *valenki*, some stay in the party. In the provinces, there are no leaders, but there is huge discontent. I think that if such a mood will be contained for a long time, it can erupt in a stormy explosion. This could be an uprising or a strike, which can turn into an uprising against Soviet power. I consider it necessary to precisely formulate everything that comrades in the provinces feel and make known.

Goldberg (Kharkov and Nikolaev): In Nikolaev, there was no group work for two months. From Kharkov, I sent some instructions about creating groups, a committee, and links with the uyezd. In Nikolaev, 56 workers wrote a statement

---

196   Bakhmut and Kharkov were cities in eastern Ukraine. Nikolaev was in southern Ukraine, near the Black Sea.

about departure from the party. Their motive was that work was being carried out incorrectly. The plenum of the gubernia committee, together with Andreev, passed the decision that there would be no repression and that none of those who signed would be sent away from the gubernia. At the Gubernia Congress of Trade Unions in Kharkov, Bulkin proposed to the congress plenum not to accept the CC's decision, because it contradicted the decision of the Tenth Party Congress. For that, Bulkin was purged from the party. The faction decided unanimously to reexamine Bulkin's case. I attest that Lobanov, Mitin, and Skliznev let everything slip through their fingers in Ukraine, so they missed their chance at the party conference. There were 152 people against the presidium there. It would have been possible to win them round, but they did nothing. So Nikolaenko, Ugarov, and that sort wound up in the CC. They're getting ready for the Congress of Trade Unions of Ukraine in a month. Nikolaevskaia gubernia sent 24 delegates. Of those, 16 are our people. Our people did not deliver any speeches at the congress, for there was no cohesion. Our group didn't even gather once. Kolesnikov's behaviour was to blame [ниже всякой критики]. I formed the impression that we do nothing but hold conversations. We're doing nothing practical, yet without organisation you can't do anything.[197]

Shokhanov (Moscow): The Party's general mood is one of apathy. The working masses regard elections to the Moscow Soviet of Workers' Deputies as a formality. There is a great sense of being downtrodden. Even more despondent is the mood of enterprise personnel about the new theses on the trade unions. The spetses [спецовская публика] feel they are the masters of the situation and have led the attack against the trade unions. Ordering manufactured goods from abroad is not in the interests of our country's proletariat. The proletarian part of the party will very actively and in an organised way counterpose its opinion to our leading policy.

Resolved: Take the reports from the provinces under consideration.

Agenda item #2: Report on platform and tactics (Comrade Shliapnikov).

Shliapnikov: Even we feel demoralised at times. The absence of our group's work contributes to the party's fatal weakening [замирание]. In connection with the bourgeois development of the New Economic Policy, the opinion appears in the party ranks that our old revolutionary economic policy was

---

197   TsAFSB, R33718, d. 499061, vol. 41, ll. 68–9.

mistaken. At the last All-Russian Party Conference, the very prospects of our revolution were distorted. Our group did not speak at this conference because we did not see any political meaning in speaking before people alien to our revolution. Indeed, we did not sense support for us in the provinces. Lobanych [Lobanov] in Kharkov is angry, because we don't write to him, but he does not keep up communications with us.

The destruction of our party on the one hand, and the new direction in regard to the trade unions on the other, demand ideological links and cohesion among us. To a significant degree, these theses are a concession not only to the specialists, but also to international capital. It remains to be seen what kind of consequences our party's policy will have for the working class and its dictatorship. Our party thought that the socialist revolution can take place within the enormous expanse of Russia's territory, even when there is a capitalist system in other countries. According to the newspapers, our country can develop now only in a capitalist way. This situation demands discussion.

Mistakes we made earlier in class struggle were exploited by other classes. The bourgeois element made greater use than did the proletariat of almost all achievements of the revolution. We constantly fed bread to eight million proletarians and 35 million nonproletarians. A large portion of industrial production (4/5) went to the countryside. Most of all, classes alien to the proletariat exploit the current turn in economic policy. What are the conclusions? Since the leaders have become bankrupt, the party cannot further allow unchecked leadership of policy. It is necessary to demand that broad circles of personnel discuss questions of general policy and tactics.

The Eleventh Party Congress is being prepared in silence. It's been decided to conduct as little discussion as possible. This phenomenon is fundamentally impermissible. The party needs to be made healthy, because the elements of its degeneration are obvious. The party is not talking, for it is afraid to speak. A peasant element, which wants to become the complete master of Russia, appears in the party. Our domestic policy is subordinated to the interests of foreign policy. Today we are confronted with resolving the question of how we are to unite on a firmer foundation. We should discuss organising a club or seizing a district.

Debate opens on Shliapnikov's report.

Miasnikov (Urals): In preparation for the Eleventh Party Congress, we need to decide the main question, which is whether NEP is acceptable. To develop productive forces in a petty bourgeois country, the large industrial base must be

strengthened and free range given to small industry. Management of nationalised industry and of the government should remain in the hands of the proletariat. We can't speak of a united international workers' front, for it means a path
toward agreement with socialist parties. This means that in Germany they will
create a ministry with a communist appendage. In the era of bourgeois revolution, we had to ally with the Mensheviks. In the era of proletarian revolution,
we can't unify with conciliationist parties. In the era of proletarian dictatorship,
not unions but soviets should manage production. It is desirable that Comrade
Shliapnikov and Comrade Medvedev would prepare a definite platform.

Medvedev: We don't propose today any definite platform, because we want to
achieve a work created collectively, which would be easier to write. Comrade
Vladimirov suggested that we liquidate ourselves. Others propose not to write
that, which would depart from the CC's decisions. This is the result of the decay
[маразм], which surrounds us. By ignoring the so-called 'yellow' unions and
parties, we push away the working masses, which support these associations.[198]
Communist organisations have come to be isolated from the working masses.
The All-Russian Union of Metalworkers was even excluded from the international union. In the international arena, new paths must be sought to set up
links with the proletarian masses of all countries.

The fate of the dictatorship of the proletariat in Russia demands deep investigation. In the newspapers, you find such phrases: 'the proletarian state can
allow competition of commodity-capitalist relations to certain limits, without
violating its essence'. Under the proletarian dictatorship, there cannot be a proletarian organisation which would not be the bearer of government power to a
certain degree (see Bukharin's book on the proletarian dictatorship).[199] Under
tsarism, there was a coalition between the bourgeoisie and gentry landowners, who used government power to further their own goals. Analogous to this,
the nullification of trade unions' significance means liquidating the proletarian
government.

The theses on trade unions need to be evaluated from this point of view. In
these proposals, the party expresses petty bourgeois instinct. The political line

---

198   'Yellow' unions are generally understood to be company-controlled unions for workers,
      but my sense is that the revolutionary socialists sometimes used the term for any labour
      organisation, which they did not term 'revolutionary'.
199   This could be a reference to Nikolai Bukharin and Evgeny Preobrazhensky, *The ABC of Com-
      munism*, Part Two: Practical – The Dictatorship of the Proletariat and the Building Up of
      Communism (Moscow, 1920).

strongly depends on elements sitting in leading posts. Great unemployment may result from much of the gold being sent to fill the capitalist purse of Western Europe. Will we accept NEP in the form of enriching West European capital, of creating conditions for the appearance of new, gentry landowners and for removing trade unions from production? The proletariat can achieve diminishing returns, if it will be removed from state power and from production. The task of practical politics is to strive not for independence, but to deflect any attempts to cast out the proletariat from power.

Budniak (MRO of All-Russian Metalworkers' Union): Until August, remnants of the old revolutionary policy were still felt. A transition to state capitalism was suggested. Now in the new theses, trade unions are completely removed from management of production. Even in 1917, representatives of trade unions entered into bodies regulating industry. Now the unions are pushed back. They say that unions should recommend candidates. However, the last word lies with the economic bodies. Clearly, if the union will send activist personnel who will fulfil the union's will, such candidates will be unacceptable. Essentially, only those union representatives, who will carry out the new policy, will turn out to be acceptable. Likewise, the purchase of various items (locomotives) from abroad is not in the interests of Russia's working class at a time when we have unemployed, who are in no condition to learn a different type of production.

The situation of workers in private industry is more difficult, it is worse than in state industry. When the union put forward a minimum of seven million for private industry, the workers themselves asked to lower it to five million, since the owner will not agree to such pay for labour and would close the enterprise.[200] Manufactured goods are being sold for gold currency [золотая валюта], yet workers are being paid with paper. Policy on this question should be aligned. Some congresses are coming up. Metalworkers should be organised and disagreements with our leading bodies should be outlined.

Tolokontsev: Our policy changed after our party came to understand that international revolution has not been vindicated. Considering our poverty and ruin, the course on NEP is correctly taken. In the near future, no more than 200–300 million can be taken from the muzhik.[201] These resources are insufficient. The question is who will carry out NEP? The proletariat cannot relinquish its leading role. The theses about the trade unions are very vague and contradictory.

---

200   I am not sure what unit is being referenced here.
201   I am not sure what unit is being referenced here.

They should be corrected. If the union assigns managers, this means it does not manage. If unions don't manage production, they should defend the interests of their members.

The CC RCP(b) is guilty of a policy of satrapies [держиморда]. Unions are to blame for a wage rates policy, which supports the line of the executioners of the working class and of being afraid to raise their voices in defence of the working class. Thus the revolution significantly improved the situation of the peasantry and worsened the situation of the working class. Before the revolution, people went from the countryside to the city for earnings, but after the revolution the working class was dispersed across the countryside. In connection with NEP, it is necessary to guarantee the leading role of the proletariat. This goal should be followed when getting organised. An organisation already exists in Nikolaev. It is necessary to discuss whether a split is needed. Do we need our own workers' organisation, or should measures be set forth to create a workers' party?

Miasnikov (Urals): We should have the courage to have our own opinion. However, industry should be managed through the soviets of workers' deputies, as bodies of state power. An international bloc with the Scheidemanns should not be created, even if the majority of the working class supports them.[202] In the beginning of 1917 in Russia, the Mensheviks had a majority, by July they had half, and by October already less than half. We created a bloc with the Mensheviks only to struggle against the autocracy. After that, our path departed from theirs. Trade unions should not be disrupted. What's needed is a united workers' front, not a united socialist one. Socialist parties entering into the Second International are the chained dogs of capital. The working class cannot have unity with the bureaucracy.

Goldberg: Right now what's needed is to equalise the policy line. It is necessary to carry out struggle against party methods taken individually. Comrade Miasnikov sets unions against soviets. Independence is incorrect since it worsens the workers' situation. There's no reason to place hopes on strikes. There are no strike funds. Today a factory closes, and tomorrow there's nothing to eat. In state enterprises the seizure of production is necessary, and in private ones supervision over production. This is a united workers' front, not a socialist front.

We should also strive toward unity of the front in the international workers' movement, keeping in mind that not the entire workers' movement supports

---

202   Philipp Heinrich Scheidemann (1865–1939), a politician who belonged to the Social Democratic Party of Germany, helped found and lead the Weimar Republic in Germany.

the communists. We'll move toward unity of the front. We need to write down the points which we can sign off on. At the present time, a split is still unthinkable, because differences have not been revealed. There is neither preparation nor organisation. While preserving party unity, we should organise circles with a leading group. We need to review our ranks and to prepare reserves for attack along the entire front for victory or for a split.

Vladimirov (All-Russian Metalworkers' Union central committee): Here the condition of our party has been called decay [маразм]. Really, there is no active work. Reaction has set upon us. The concessions, which the party is making, have a demoralising effect. We need to establish who and what we are, as party personnel. Some distinctly try to prove that it's necessary to leave the party, while others suggest that we should disband the Workers' Opposition as an official group. It is necessary to reveal a platform. We began to organise for the congress too late. A party platform should be prepared very soon.

Chelyshev: Comrade Miasnikov wants to hand over management of production to the soviets, which means that he wants to present full freedom to the muzhik, knocking aside [отшибая] the proletarian base. Our party as a whole exerts very weak influence over general policy. Leading groups of two or three people decide questions everywhere. The remaining senior personnel, who carry out their line, feel as if they have no responsibility.

Pravdin: Right now the party's practical politics diverge from theory. General confusion [растерянность] emerges from this, especially among those who understand practical questions. Theoretical questions need to be proposed for discussion. How is it that in a proletarian state, the proletariat is removed from management of the country? Obviously, the party has degenerated. Is the Communist Party really the party of the proletariat? Why is the proletarian party overthrowing the proletariat? Light must be shed upon these questions. Miasnikov's advice is not well-considered. The essence of the question is in the party itself. Exclusively strong means are necessary to heal it.

Shliapnikov (concluding word): There is little material from the provinces. Comrade Miasnikov speaks of managing through the soviets. The country's entire circulating [оборотный] capital is squandered, it is not distributed to the benefit of the proletariat. The crux of comrade Miasnikov's proposal is the organisation of peasant unions, which must be opposed most resolutely. The working class should not organise a unit, which is hostile to it. It is not true that we are surrendering the proletariat to the Scheidemanns by organising a united worldwide workers' front. Engels was a member of the Social Democratic Party of Germany and Marx praised it. The German working class has absorbed this party's traditions. In Germany, they have only 300,000 communists, who don't even pay membership fees, for their party is maintained by Russian resources. That policy, which the Communist Party carries out on an international scale, has placed the party outside of the international proletariat. Two months ago, comrade Vladimirov proposed our self-liquidation. Now he is inclined in the opposite direction, which does not speak well of his political vision [прозорливость]. It is impossible to demand a prepared platform from us. Those in the centre should not be rebuked for being isolated, for there has been no support from the provinces.

The basic question is still the same: the role of the working class in the subsiding revolution [в идущей на убыль]. Tolokontsev and Pravdin lead central directorates (glavki), but whose interests do they carry out? Industry's situation is not outstanding and resources have been squandered. The proletariat is blamed for all mistakes, which are actually mistakes of policy. In the newspapers they write that the country is more prepared for capitalism than for communism. Our party's old affirmations that our country can have a social revolution, in the absence of proletarian revolutions in other countries, have been completely justified. It's necessary to come to an agreement about the limit to concessions.

The party can become so demoralised that as a result of maneuvers nothing might remain of the party. Not long ago, Comrade Kamenev boasted that we are the least expensive government in the world. This economising takes place at the expense of the proletariat. In Western Europe a struggle is occurring over who will pay for the bourgeoisie to revive its economy. In our country more so than anywhere else, economic revival will occur at the expense of wages. This question should be carefully analysed. The cc's theses on the role of trade unions contain some contradictions. They point out the need to prepare red directors, yet some following points are directed against them. The directors are set against the working masses. The question about specialists in the theses is incorrectly illuminated. The example of an engineer's suicide points to the unsettled nature [неналаживание] of relations between the working masses and the state.

If each of those present were closer to the working masses and had led political work in the factories, then at today's session it would have been possible to glean more materials for a political platform. The trip to Genoa can bring much benefit to the working class. If earlier it was possible to come to agreement with the Society of Factory Owners, then now it is possible to take part in the work of the Genoa Conference and negotiate with a worldwide society of factory owners. If the conditions will be usurious, then my attitude to the treaty will be made known in Russia. The conference's success for us depends on the unity of the workers' movement within Russia and on the development of the proletarian movement in Western Europe.

The All-Russian Union of Metalworkers presently counts for nothing on the international scale. In Russia, no one takes the union into account. A mandate from it carries no weight. For the proletariat to make international conquests, kindred elements of the workers' movement in the world must be united. There's nothing bad in groups organising in our country in particular. There hasn't and can't be a condemnation of the Nikolaev comrades. The organisation of a special club in Moscow for us is desirable and completely possible.

Decided:
A) Consider it necessary, in the name of the struggle against the decay that has seized the party, to arrange discussions on political questions and to prepare a platform for the Eleventh Party Congress.
B) Assign comrades Shliapnikov and Medvedev to work out a common political platform by 20 February 1922. Convene a preliminary meeting on the 20th to discuss the theses.
C) The platform should answer the following questions:
1. What are the tasks of the party and the role of proletarian elements in the revolution?
2. What are the tasks and the role of trade unions?
3. Is the current course of policy a dictatorship of the proletariat?
4. The Genoa conference?
D) Materials of today's session should be used in composing the theses. All comrades who have additional materials should present them to comrades Shliapnikov and Medvedev.
E) Require those present to participate actively in elections to the Eleventh Party Congress.
F) Assign the Moscow Committee of the All-Russian Union of Metalworkers to come to agreement with comrade Shliapnikov regarding convocation of a special meeting of delegates of MRO VSRM at the All-Russian Congress of Metalworkers to examine the tasks of unions.
G) Assign comrades Pravdin, Borisov and Bruno to organise a club for the group.[203]

---

203 TsA FSB, R33718, d. 499061, volume 40, ll. 127–8.

Handwritten note from Chelyshev to Medvedev: Sergei, we need to put an end to the session, for it is at least an hour's journey from here. Signed Chelyshev.[204]

Medvedev's Notes, Undated

Lobanov: ... After these theses, many worker-communists will leave the party.

[No notes from comments by Pavlov, Chelyshev, and Tarasov]

Petrov: At the top there is no trust toward the proletariat. Strikes, Italian strikes, theft, and so forth don't dispose them toward it.

Tarasov: ... Productivity is usually totaled and divided equally among all those working, as well as those who have been absent for many years. Because of this, productivity appears to have decreased. ...

Bruno: The unacceptability of leveling-distributive wages needs to be emphasised. ...

[No notes from comments by Baranov, Polosatov, and Ignatenko [?]]

Kutuzov:
1. All intrigues are the result of our party being the prevailing one (Not true. The social composition of the party)
2. All trade unionists involved in economic planning who have become economic directors, wage struggle against us (depravity of workers).
3. Mainly it was our comrades who carried out the party purge. Struggle occurs inside our cells on the basis of inequality. (Not true. Introduction of [parochialism?])
4. There's no need to fight for portfolios and lead to a split. (Why is the slogan 'All to the factories, plants' not true?)
5. The purge struck us as well. At the congress there will be stronger blows against the cc.
6. Fellows quickly get ruined by finding themselves in positions of power. (Need to speak very carefully about this)
7. In the provinces only workers (men and women) are arrested. Hunger forces them into protest.[205]

---

204   TsA FSB, R33718, d. 499061, volume 40, l. 132.
205   Here Medvedev records Kutuzov's points and inserts his own opinions in parentheses.

Maslennikov:

1. We are not clearly explaining to worker cells what we want.
2. The purge in Bauman district perverted its purpose.

[No notes from comments by Mitin]

Baranov: Workers don't elect us because we speak as communists (As whom does comrade Baranov think of speaking?)

Information about the Donbas.

1. After the Tenth Party Congress we lost clarity in our further behaviour within the party organisation.
2. With the new economic policy, all preceding positions shifted definitively. The 'Workers' Opposition' faded away in regard to the trade union question and there was no clear and consistent line.
3. Persecution against supporters of the Workers' Opposition had a significant impact. Entire organisations were dispersed.
4. Discussions of former supporters of the 'Workers' Opposition' continue, but there is no clarity in behaviour.

Information about the Nikolaev organisation.

1. Seeks a way to restore health to our provincial organisation, led to the creation of a troika, its connection to trade unions.
2. At the congress of trade unions we turned out to be in the overwhelming majority, 84 out of 100. This led us to conflict with the gubernia committee.
3. As a result, comrade Manuilsky arrived and the organisation was completely routed by mobilising 90 people who were chiefly supporters of the Workers' Opposition.
4. The general opinion of those who share our views is that: a) they blame Moscow comrades for everything that has gone wrong, meaning the complete lack of leadership and of help in deciding the most important questions of the economic and political crisis; b) like-minded individuals who are strong and capable of leadership and of work need to be sent to the Nikolaev organisation to seize it anew.

1. Meeting with representatives of party, trade union, and economic bodies of Moscow, the Donbas, Briansk, the Caucasus, Rostov-on-Don, Nikolaev, the Urals, Kharkov.
    – Subjects of discussion – debates
    – Decisions of the meeting

2. New facts of the CC's old policy.
    a) Dispersal of supporters of the Workers' Opposition (Shliapn[ikov], Baum[an], Briansk)
    b) Commission – letters from the south.
    c) New trends and policy toward trade unions (draft of wage rates agreement)
    d) New attacks on the presidium of the central committee of the Metalworkers' Union
    e) Completely ignoring the trade union and even VTsSPS
        i. leases (concessions) with America
        ii. Glavmetall collegium and so forth
3. a) Purge of the party – some results – 10 gubernias
    b) Purge of the party – in Moscow
4. Expanded Plenum of VTsSPS

[No notes from comments by Nikolaevsky]

Prasolov:
1. Comrade Shliapnikov should have told us: i) circumstances, ii) tasks, and iii) tactics.
2. There should have been far more communications between comrades Shliapnikov and Trotsky.

[No notes from comments by Perepechko]

Pavlov: It does not benefit our revolution or the international workers' movement to pose the question of a split and of creation of a Workers' Communist Party.
1. Clarify our attitude toward our group in the CC.
2. Establish firmer links between it and the provinces.
3. Make it obligatory to not only talk about our work but also to carry it out.
4. Open a resolute campaign for consolidation of links with the masses by means of persecuted comrades departing for the workbenches.
5. Resolutely wage struggle against persecution, all the way up to insubordination toward gubernia committees' decisions.
6. Resolutely conduct a campaign of protests against courts and investigations, slander, and so forth.
7. Prepare for the Eleventh Congress. Convene an assembly.[206]

---

206   Points 2, 3, 4, and 7 have check marks to the left of them. TsA FSB, R33718, d. 499061, volume 40, ll. 133–145, all notes appear to be in the handwriting of Sergei Medvedev.

Two Sets of Theses, Undated and Unsigned

The first set of theses appears to be a set of points summarising the discussion at one of the February 1922 meetings attended by Shliapnikov and Medvedev.[207]

[omission] ... on the Politburo's line of behaviour toward the question about the interrelations of party and trade unions and toward party members speaking on behalf of the Workers' Opposition in the period before the congress ... [omission]

1.   The Politburo expressed this line especially harshly toward the Union of Metalworkers, when it (Politburo) deprived the Congress [of the Metalworkers' Union] of the right to freely elect the entire central committee of the union. Instead, the Politburo appointed its members from above on the basis of arbitrary personal motivations, which fundamentally violates the decision of the Tenth Party Congress about the party's relationship to trade unions.

2.   Politburo representatives to the factions of the Congress of Trade Unions and of the Congress of the Metalworkers' Union ... [omission] divided delegates ... [omission] into two camps, which were supporters of the CC and supporters of the Workers' Opposition.

3.   The Politburo representatives openly, insistently, and provocatively tried to discredit supporters of the former Workers' Opposition at these congresses, without producing one piece of evidence that even one supporter of it had violated decisions of the Tenth Party Congress.

4.   The Politburo also separated people into camps when it constituted the new presidium of the central committee of the All-Russian Congress of Metalworkers, which violated the union's statutes .... [omission]

5.   Thus, the Politburo and the Ten chose to wage openly factional intraparty struggle against the remaining tendencies.

6.   Moreover, the Politburo has created absolutely impossible moral and physical conditions for any concerted and friendly, comradely work within the party. For a long time, it has disorganised all party and union work both in the centre and in the provinces. Its actions have given rise to open and deep distrust among trade union personnel toward leading party bodies. This distrust brings new disruptions and will have a disastrous impact upon further interrelations of unions with the party.

---

207   TsA FSB, R33718, d. 499061, volume 40, 146–149. They are 'first' according to the order in which I found the two sets of theses in the archival papers.

Therefore, the party members who are gathered here consider it urgently necessary:

1) To carry out energetic work in all party bodies, at party meetings, and among individual party members, especially and chiefly among proletarian elements of the party, to clarify the entire political danger, considering the current international and domestic political and economic conjuncture, of that position, which the CC Politburo has taken on the questions indicated above, positions which:

    a) overtly break up the party into intraparty groupings and push trade unions toward a split with the party;

    b) consciously support open persecution against party members who spoke out in support of the platform of the Workers' Opposition during the pre-congress period; petty bourgeois elements, political careerists, and political scoundrels who have latched onto the party carry out systematic persecution within it;

    c) threaten to apply to those who supported the Workers' Opposition retributional measures of a party character and of a soviet regime, in case they attempt to defend themselves from persecution.

2) To conduct work on an all-Russian scale to unite proletarian elements in the party, in order to make the Politburo reject its position of distrust and persecution toward trade unions and party members who share the views of the former 'Workers' Opposition'. This work should proceed on the basis of explaining:

    a) how immensely politically dangerous it is;

    b) how especially necessary it is presently: i) to elevate activist participation of proletarian elements in deciding all questions of party, soviet, union and economic policy and practice; and ii) to secure for these elements the maximum initiative and the most careful accounting and use of their experience in these questions.

3) To energetically protest and oppose, in all intraparty forms of solidarity and organisation possible, any attempts to continue intra-party persecution, political murder, or retribution of a party character or of a soviet regime against those, who vocally supported the Workers' Opposition in the pre-congress period.

4) In party circles, certain individual Party CC members have foamed at the mouth with threats to apply the punitive point of the Tenth Congress resolution about party unity against Party CC member comrade Shliapnikov, for having spoken out openly and energetically in defence of the Workers' Opposition platform in the pre-congress period and for his resolute refusal to implement the Politburo's line at the Congress of Metalworkers.

In case this measure will be applied against comrade Shliapnikov, those gathered here believe it necessary to categorically demand from those who were brought as hostages from the Workers' Opposition into the CC and CCC, as full and candidate members, to promptly resign from these institutions and to openly appeal to the Party CC about the motives for their departure.

5) Party members in the provinces still assimilate the general character and content of the New Economic Policy with difficulty and insufficiently. In this new context, the new tasks of the proletariat in the trade union movement and economy need to be clarified precisely. With this in mind, those gathered here think it necessary to require the comrades remaining in Moscow to clarify these questions and to systematically inform those working in the provinces about everything new that is taking shape in this area.

6) Those gathered here likewise obligate all those working in the provinces to systematically inform Moscow comrades about all manifestations of party, soviet, union and economic life in the provinces and questions arising in these areas, which demand that all party members' attention be paid to them.

∵
•

Second set of theses.[208]

1) The projected activity can yield desired results only under one unalterable condition, which is if it will be implemented systematically and in an organised way, without clamorous sound effects, but unswervingly, insistently, and in a politically and tactically mature and consistent way. Patience needs to be accumulated. Noisy demonstrations without results should be avoided and one should not yield to any provocation.

2) No organised activity is possible without systematic leadership of it and without an apparatus for its fulfilment. Therefore, the first thing that needs to be done is to choose one, two or three comrades and assign them to regularly inform local comrades about the most important events of party, soviet, union, and economic life, to explain their significance, to conduct correspondence with comrades, and so forth.

3) Also, we need to pay attention to whether we can use trade union apparatuses (district committee, sub-district committee, and factory committee),

---

208   TsA FSB, R33718, d. 499061, volume 40, ll. 150–2.

in order to broadly and systematically develop planned activity within the boundaries of their districts and if necessary, in those adjoining them.

4) If it is not possible now, then try to create conditions so that it will be possible soon for each comrade to assume work which he has so far not fulfilled, to change the area of his work, and so on and so forth.

The following must be done, in order to achieve the following results.

In the unions:

5) There must be maximal unity in district committees and subdistrict committees. All the most important posts in them must be occupied. Thorough use must be made of their technical apparatus and facilities. All influence should be directed toward strengthening such unity in factory committees and to establishing the closest link with them, just as with personnel of economic bodies and of factory management. Their resources and facilities must be used maximally.

6) Resolute and active opposition to any manifestations of petty tutelage [опёка], small-minded supervision, and foisting of special supervisors in the guise of plenipotentiaries, permanent instructors, senior personnel, and the sort, both from the union central committee and from oblast bureaus assigned to them.

7) Resolute refusal to enter into these bureaus, if there is no guarantee of a decisive or sufficiently strong influence in them. For example, 2/3 or 2/5 would consist of those who think like us, with at least one fluctuating. In the absence of the latter condition, we must refuse to occupy individual senior posts in them and should transfer all our forces directly to the districts, to the provinces, and to the factories.

8) Resolute refusal and accompanying protest in cases when the central committee or bureau demands dispatch of individual personnel or reshuffling of them for the purpose of intrigue within the party.

9) Certain resolution of all these questions at the faction of the union section [отделение], under the condition that it have a satisfactory composition. In the case of special circumstances and with the desire to attach to its decisions great significance, it is necessary to expand its body with representatives of factory committees.

10) Insistent, resolute, and thorough preparation for upcoming conferences to elect oblast bureaux and use them as already indicated.

11) Systematic supervision of protocols of main and economic centres, businesslike analysis and criticism of their activities, obligatory recording of these analyses and criticism in the protocols of their sessions, and pronouncement of special resolutions on individual questions.

12) Prior to conferences at factories, in the district, and so forth, systematically illuminate the unsatisfactory aspects of the union central committee's activity, and likewise that of the oblast bureaus.

13) All forces of the district committee and the centre of its attention should be directed toward systematic and regular convocation of factory, district, and gubernia conferences and assemblies on all questions relating to the activities of the district committee, sections of the union, and so forth, or about individual questions of the wage rates agreement, cooperative movement, items for barter [?] [натурфонд], cultural-educational work, or improvement of workers' everyday lives. All these conferences or assemblies should be maintained [обслуживаемый] exclusively by our forces.

14) [omission] ... We also need to oppose attempts by petty bourgeois elements in the gubernia trade union councils to interfere in the internal work of trade unions in the areas outlined in point 13.

15) The establishment of the closest contact with gubernia sections of other production unions and unification of their personnel on this and likewise around ourselves on a party-political basis.

On Economic Bodies:

16) Select and unify senior economic council personnel in the glavki, the district councils, gubernia councils, and the factory managements, which are subordinated to them.

17) Share information and discuss imminent actions and their forms, summon personnel systematically from the provinces and arrange special circuits by the body's leader, or dispatch into the provinces a suitable comrade or a small commission with a suitable businesslike purpose.

18) Likewise, convene meetings about individual questions, which are connected to the course of production, and about questions of union policy and practice, which have been outlined by decisions of the Fourth Congress of the Union and by the Tenth Party Congress.

19) Assist the district committee with all the resources and facilities at the disposal of the body to [be directed to] the section of the union for its projected activity.

∴

Notes apparently taken from a meeting attended by people who later signed the Declaration of the 22.[209]

---

209   TsA FSB, R33718, volume 42, ll. 214–16.

Baranov: A slogan that the masses can understand is needed, about the need to struggle resolutely to re-elect the district party committees (raikoms) and to struggle against petty bourgeois elements in the party. They need to be told that they have no influence in the party.

Mikhail Ch[elyshev?]: 1. An introduction to our proposals is absolutely indispensable. Without this, broad circles of workers will not understand us. 2. We should again promote workers' occupation of all leading posts in the gubernia party committees (gubkoms). Principles of workers' democracy should actually be implemented. The Central Committee theses should be acknowledged as blatantly distancing unions from the national economy. Our theses need to be finalised.

Kuznetsov: 1. An evaluation of our international situation needs to be added to our theses, which do not provide an economic analysis of NEP. 2. The 'command-style' [командирская] arrogance of those who are the leaders of our economic policy and speculative bedlam [спекулятивной свистопляски] also need to be pointed out.

Kutuzov. 1. Our theses are appearing too late. They will be defeated just the same as if we had not written them. The Eleventh Congress will be dead. 2. Danger began to threaten us in 1919, when they staked their bet on the 'specialists'. The only one of the Central Committee's theses that I do not share is the one about the specialists. 3. Our theses should be distributed among broad worker-communist circles. 4. We take no interest in placing food supplies in trustworthy hands. Our enterprises have been removed from state supply. 5. Even earlier the trade unions [illegible word] confirmation of their candidates. Now it is necessary to give up talk about unions' seizure of production and instead defend workers' interests.

[No notes from comments by Babkin]

Bruno: 1. We will not succeed in influencing bodies of state power in the nearest future. We need to rally communists around us.

Pravdin: 1. Do we come alive only before the congress? Clearly not.

Vladimirov: 1. Soviet power's economic policy is insufficiently outlined. It's not consistent from day to day. 2. It's necessary to [illegible word] our views on matters relating to the authorities' inevitable capitulation before capital, after having leased to it all that, which comrade B has indicated. 3. Our group needs to be formed at the congress .... [makes 9 points in all].

[No notes from comments by Kubyshkin and Kutuzov]

Protocol of a private assembly of party members and of a comradely exchange of opinions on the most important questions of intra-Comintern and intra-party policy, 26 February 1922.[210]

23 present.

Introduced: Suggestions to exchange opinions on questions: a) 'about the need to realise an actual united front within the RCP' and b) 'On appeal to the ECCI plenum with an explanation of the actual situation within the RCP', in order to create a guarantee to implement actual unity within the RCP. c) on the coming Fifth Congress of the Metalworkers' Union and about possible pressure on [text breaks off]

S.P. Medvedev's notes about this meeting:

For the meeting's agenda:[211]
1.   A letter to the ECCI plenum about the 'United Front'
2.   Our behavior at the upcoming Congress of Metalworkers [crossed out]
3.   Exclusions from the party (Miasnikov, those in Briansk).
4.   Behaviour of comrades Vladimirov and Lavrentev.

From Shliapnikov's remarks about the United Front:
1.   From the moment when the Communist International lost initiative in leading the international movement, we now reach for an anchor [якорь] of salvation, for all proposals, which emerge from the Second and Second-and-a-half Internationals.
2.   In the international context, this tactic summons forth great bewilderment. So Frenchmen only just carried out a split with the social conciliators. They produced colossal work. They undermined the trust of the working masses toward them. Now they propose to them to return to their former position.

---

210   TsA FSB, R33718, d. 499061, volume 43, ll. 147–50, handwritten document, incomplete.
211   'Pavlov' is written in the top left corner.

3. Given a cursory familiarisation of the representatives with the actual state
    of things within our party, their bewilderment will only increase.

Given such an evaluation of the Comintern's activity, despite knowing that in
it the decision lies with the Politburo CC RCP(b) members who belong to the
Ispolkom, nevertheless we decided to appeal to the ECCI plenum.

About the tactics at the Congress of Metalworkers:

Lobanov: Has our situation changed in comparison with last year?

Unnamed attendee:
1. The most resolute rebuff must be given to the attempt to expel the more
    recalcitrant from the union's leading body, leaving in place a coalition of
    fools and political careerists.
2. If we have a majority in the faction, then carry through all which it will
    decide.
3. If we have half of the faction, then go for proportional representation.
4. If we have a significant and resolute minority, then go into the union's
    primary (lowest) bodies.

List of names with notations:[212]
1.   c.[213] Shliapnikov [checked and marked through with blue pencil]
2.   c. Medvedev [checked and marked through with blue pencil]
3.   c. Chelyshev [checked and marked through with blue pencil]
4.   c. Bruno [checked and marked through with blue pencil]
5.   Tolokontsev [checked and marked through with blue pencil]
6.   Borisov [checked and marked through with blue pencil]
7.   Pravdin [checked and marked through with blue pencil]
8.   Budniak
9.   Kubiak
10. Miasnikov [checked and marked through with a blue pencil]
11. Tashkin [checked and marked through with blue pencil]
12. Chernov

---

212 Names 1–7, 10–11, 13–18, 21, 23, and 29 were checked off and struck through with a blue
     pencil by an unknown hand, which could have been Medvedev or someone else at the
     meeting, an NKVD investigator in the 1930s, or someone who later consulted this file while
     considering a rehabilitation inquiry.
213 Abbreviation for 'comrade'.

13. Lobanov[214] [checked and marked through with blue pencil]
14. Kolesnikov [checked and marked through with blue pencil]
15. Mitin [checked and marked through with blue pencil]
16. Polosatov [checked and marked through with blue pencil]
17. Zhilin [checked and marked through with blue pencil]
18. Pavlov[215] [checked and marked through with blue pencil]
19. Tarasov
20. Deulenkov
21. Mikhailov [checked and marked through with blue pencil]
22. Vasilev
23. Kuznetsov[216] [checked and marked through with blue pencil]
24. Babkin
25. Kutuzov[217]
26. Fabb
27. Ignatev
28. Kubyshkin
29. Barulin [checked and marked through with blue pencil]
30. Mikov
31. [no name]

22 **Letter of the 22 to the Comintern, Signed by Shliapnikov, Kollontai, et al[218]**

Dear comrades!

From our newspapers we have learned that the Executive Committee of the Communist International (ECCI) is discussing the 'United Workers' Front'. We consider it our communist duty to inform you that in our country the 'United Front' is in bad shape not only in the broad sense of this term, but even in its application toward the ranks of our party.

At a time when the forces of the bourgeois press upon us from all sides and when they even infiltrate our party, the social composition of which (40%

---

214 A notation groups Lobanov, Kolesnikov, and Mitin together in some way.
215 A notation groups Pavlov, Tarasov, Deulenkov, Mikhailov, and Vasilev together in some way.
216 A notation groups Kuznetsov and Babkin together in some way.
217 A notation groups Kutuzov and Fabb together in some way.
218 RKP(b) 1961, pp. 749–50.

worker and 60% non-proletarian) favours this, our leading centres wage a relentless, demoralising struggle against everyone, especially proletarians, who permit themselves to have their own opinion. They apply all kinds of repressive measures against those who express their own opinion within the party.

They call this attempt to bring the proletarian masses closer to the government 'anarcho-syndicalism'. They persecute and discredit its advocates.

In the trade union movement, there is the same picture of suppression of worker enterprise and initiative and struggle using all means against heterodoxy. The unified forces of the party and trade union bureaucracy, taking advantage of their position and authority, ignore our congresses' decisions about laying the foundations of worker democracy. Our union communist factions, even factions of entire congresses, are deprived of the right to manifest their will in the election of their own centres. Bureaucracy's petty tutelage and pressure has gone so far, that party members are directed under the threat of exclusion and other repressive measures to elect not those who the communists themselves want, but those who the dismissive higher-ups want. Such methods of work lead to careerism, intrigues, and servility. Workers respond to this by leaving the party.

Sharing the idea of the United Workers' Front as it is interpreted in point 23 of the theses, we appeal to you with the sincere wish to end all these abnormalities, which stand in the way of the unity of this front, first of all within our RCP(b).

The situation within our party is so difficult, that it impels us to turn to you for help and in this way to eliminate the impending threat of a split in our party.

With communist greetings, members of the RCP(b):

M. Lobanov	No. 136308	party member since	1904
N. Kuznetsov	No. 142506	"	1904
A. Polosatov	No. 878225	"	1912
A. Medvedev	No. 645186	"	1912
G. Miasnikov	No. 259002	"	1906
V. Plashkov	No. 223167	"	1918
G. Shokhanov	No. 137425	"	1912
S. Medvedev	No. 225136	"	1900
G. Bruno	No. 213618	"	1906
A. Pravdin	No. 478149	"	1899
I. Ivanov	No. 160022	"	1899
F. Mitin	No. 466543	"	1902
P. Borisov	No. 223045	"	1913
N. Kopylov	No. 224098	"	1912

Zhilin	No. 175089	"	1915
M. Chelyshev	No. 210009	"	1910
A. Tolokontsev	No. 212226	"	1914
A. Shliapnikov	No. 225383	"	1901
M. Borulin	No. 222955	"	1917
V. Bekrenev	No. 644158	"	1917
A. Pavlov	No. 136024	"	1917
A. Tashkin	No. 587158	"	1917

I support [this appeal]. A. Kollontai No. 225025 party member since 1898
I support the declaration of the 22 comrades. Zoia Shadurskaia.[219]

23 Comparison of Those Signing the Letter of the 22 and the Theses of the Workers' Opposition[220]

	Letter of the 22	Year of party entry		Theses of the Workers' Opposition	Year of party entry
1.	M. Lobanov	1904 (metal-worker)			
2.	N. Kuznetsov	1904	1.	M. Vladimirov, vice chair, A-R Metalworkers' Union	
3.	A. Polosatov	1912 (metal-worker)	2.	S. Skliznev, secretary A-R Metalworkers' Union	
4.	A. Medvedev	1912	3.	I. Kariakin, member A-R Metalworkers' Union	
5.	Miasnikov	1906	4.	Ia. Kubyshkin, member artillery industry board	
6.	V. Pleshkov		5.	Pleshkov, member A-R Metalworkers' Union	1918
7.	G. Shokhanov	1912			
8.	S. Medvedev		6.	S. Medvedev, member Metalworkers' Union	1900
9.	G. Bruno	(metalworker)	7.	G. Bruno, member artillery industry board	1906
10.	A. Pravdin	1899	8.	K. Orlov, assistant chair military industry council	
11.	I. Ivanov	1899	9.	Mikhailov, director of Aviation Industry Board	

---

219 Shadurskaia was also a party member, but the year she joined was mistakenly omitted from the document.

220 RGASPI, f. 17, op. 71, d. 3, ll. 1–2.

(cont.)

Letter of the 22	Year of party entry	Theses of the Workers' Opposition	Year of party entry
12. F. Mitin	1902 (metal-worker)		
13. P. Borisov	(metalworker)	10. P. Borisov, member artillery industry board	1913
14. N. Kopylov	(metalworker)	11. Kopylov, Komsomol propagandist	1912
15. Zhilin	1915		
16. Chelyshev	(metalworker)	12. Mikhail Chelyshev, member Party CCC	1910
17. Tolokontsev	(metalworker)	13. A. Tolokontsev, chair artillery industry board	1914
18. A. Shliapnikov		14. A. Shliapnikov, chair Metalworkers' Union	1901
19. M. Borulin	1917	15. I. Barulin, chair glavpravobzavsr. mashstroi	
20. V. Bekrenev	1907–19/1917	16. A. Vasilev, director State Machinebuilding Factories	
21. A. Pavlov	1917	17. I. Kotliakov, chair Central Board of Heavy Industry	
22. A. Tashkin	1917 (metal-worker)	18. Chernov-Grechnev, chair of the board of Sormovo factories	
& A. Kollontai	1898	19. M. Ivanov*, member committee Mosc. Metalworkers' Union	
& Z. Shadurskaia	no date (was a party member at the time)	20. A. Kiselev, chair A-R Miners' Union	
		21. M. Mikov, member A-R Miners' Union	
		22. S. Losev, member A-R Miners' Union	
		23. V. Sivert, member A-R Miners' Union	
		24. S. Arutiuniants, member A-R Miners' Union	
		25. A. Gorbachev, member A-R Miners' Union	
		26. A. Storozhenko, member A-R Miners' Union	
		27. V. Voronin, member A-R Miners' Union, VSNKh	
		28. V. Strokin (Sorokin), chair Usolsk prav	
		29. I. Ialunin, chair Kizelovsky raikom of Miners' Union	
		30. S. Rychkov, member Kizelovsky raikom of Miners' Union	
		31. A. Mironov, member Kizelovsky raikom of Miners' Union	
		32. I. Lagunov, member Kizelovsky raikom of Miners' Union	
		33. P. Fedurin, member Kizelovsky raikom of Miners' Union	

(*cont.*)

Letter of the 22	Year of party entry	Theses of the Workers' Opposition	Year of party entry
		34. A. Zaburdaev, member Kizelovsky raikom of Miners' Union	
		35. I. Kutuzov, chair CC A-R Textile workers' Union	
		36. N. Kubiak, chair CC Vserabot-zem	
		37. Khitrov, mbr CC Vserabot-zem	
		38. Izvorin, chair Kursk gubernia workers' supply committee	

24   Selected Speeches at the Meeting of the RCP(b) Faction of the Fifth Congress of the Metalworkers' Union, 2–7 March 1922[221]

[Because the stenographic record was uncorrected, it is difficult to determine the precise consecutive order of the speeches. Moreover, parts of the record are preserved in different archives (GARF and RGASPI). Here I have weighted the selection toward speeches by former members of the Workers' Opposition.]

Ianson: In the name of the bureau of the communist faction of the central committee of the Union of Metalworkers and in the name of the Piter [Petrograd], Tula, Nizhny [Novgorod], Vyksa, and Donbas delegations, the following list of candidates for the presidium is offered (reads). In composing this list, comrades, we thought that our congress presidium should represent all major regions, so that there would be a close, direct connection between the presidium and the largest delegations.

Skliznev: The Moscow, Ekaterinoslav, Kharkov, Kiev, Aleksandrov, Nikolaev, Crimean, and Vyksa delegations and 16 delegates from the Donbas have appointed me to announce the following list (reads).

Shliapnikov: Comrades, I have some proposals for you. I propose, comrades, that you should not be guided by the dispatch of the letter to the Comintern and should not raise this question when you are voting for the presidium. We

---

221   GARF, f. 5469, op. 17, d. 3; RGASPI, f. 99, op. 1, d. 2, d. 7.

cannot discuss it here. Let's keep in mind that we did not put it on the agenda. We are interested in discussing it, but not here, for such a large assembly cannot resolve it. We will not have time to examine it thoroughly. Let's postpone it until the commission which the Comintern chose decides it. Let's respect its decision as authoritative. Therefore, when we elect the presidium of the current congress, I propose that we vote individually for each of the candidates, so that frictions will not be permitted to grow on the basis of these two lists.

Chair: Each of those proposing a list should read it aloud twice. Six or more orators spoke about each list, therefore I consider this question exhausted and will not allow anyone else to speak about it. We'll move on to the vote. [ellipses in text] Because three comrades removed their candidacies from one or the other list, it is not reasonable to vote by lists. Therefore, we are left with Shliapnikov's proposal to vote on individual candidacies.

[83 favour voting by list, while 76 support voting by the name of each individual candidate.

85 vote for the list announced by Ianson, while 76 support the list, which Skliznev read aloud.

Tarasov requests to withdraw his candidacy. The majority of delegates support the bureau's proposal to replace him with Bukhanov from Kolomna.]

Ianson: I nominate comrade Vladimirov for the following reasons. Comrade Vladimirov has worked nearly from the founding of the Metalworkers' Union. He has been one of the most dedicated – (voices from the floor say 'Comrade Shliapnikov') – I'm talking about Comrade Vladimirov. There is no point in comparing names of people when it comes to union work. You can bandy your name about and be a noisy cart, but do little in everyday work. But you can work behind the scenes and assume a heavy burden of work. Comrade Vladimirov is exactly one of those, who is not seen and who does not raise a fuss, but who works. We need such a comrade.

Vladimirov: I worked not in order to be in the presidium and in the central committee [of the union], but for the sake of the work itself. I have suffered such torment for the past six months, which I never experienced during hard labour under the tsarist regime. No one now can force me to work in the central committee. Even if called to account under party discipline, I would say, 'No, I can't.' I am thankful for having been trusted for four years with this work, but now I ask to be spared.

Chair: Comrade Vladimirov has refused twice. I suggest to the comrades that a man sometimes has heartfelt hesitation and it's worse if this happens in the ranks of the Communist Party (noise). Therefore, Comrade Vladimirov needs permission to get over these worries. There's nothing else to do.

[The chair proposes Gurevich in Vladimirov's place and the majority approves.]

Kiselev: I think that the opinion of certain regional (oblast) delegations needs to be considered. Therefore, our Urals delegation has decided how to construct the presidium. We chose not to squabble like many have here. Instead, we unanimously chose Comrade Tashkin. The Urals is not Perm alone. Therefore, we categorically protest against the introduction of a delegate only from Perm. We nominate Comrade Tashkin.

Chair: Comrade Balandin was nominated by the bureau of the faction of the central committee and was supported by the delegations from Tula, the Donbas, Petrograd, and Nizhegorod.

Tashkin: I withdraw my candidacy for the same reasons which Comrade Vladimirov gave.

[Ianson and Skliznev propose different lists of nominees for the mandate commission. 88 vote for Ianson's list and 63 for Skliznev's.

Matrozov from the Nizhegorod delegation raises the Letter of the 22 to the Comintern and requests that Tomsky, as a representative from the CC RCP(b), provide information about it. Tomsky objects that Matrozov has no right to raise this question. A delegate from Petrograd voices support for Matrozov.]

Shliapnikov: I am one of those who signed this appeal. I want to put a stop to all sorts of misunderstandings among you. Why make insinuations, when everyone knows who signed it and what was signed? A statement to the CC, which regarded some abnormalities noticed in our party, was signed. A special commission was created about this. I see nothing criminal in this action. An official decision has been recorded about it. There was no need to raise this question just out of desire to discredit someone. There was no reason to take up your work time.

[The chair announces that 87 oppose and 67 support giving Tomsky time to speak about the statement that some metalworkers made to the Comintern. Then Tomsky clarified that he was not present as an official CC representative but from VTsSPS. He proceeded to say that too many workers were learning about the appeal to the Comintern, particularly through an assembly in Moscow of representatives from some metalworking factories. He also regretted that for the first time in the history of the Metalworkers' Union, there were two rival lists for the presidium of the congress from two different groups of delegations.]

[Further, there were reports from Glavmetall, Promvoensovet, and Glavelektro, and debate upon the reports.]

Polosatov: In my report, I did not touch upon one question, which is connected with the composition of the central committee at our last congress of the Metalworkers' Union. Since then we have seen in fact that the presidium of the central committee was appointed. There was an incident at each of its two plenums, which had an impact upon the provinces. I was in the Donbas on inspection at the time when this line began to be implemented there. It was right after delegates from this congress of the Metalworkers' Union arrived there.

At the same time when I was in Iuzovka on inspection, the party uyezd committee demanded a report from the subdistrict committees of the Metalworkers' Union. The party secretary suggested to me that I go to this session, so I went there. There was a report about the enormous work carried out by the subdistrict committee. Debates on this question were interesting. They asserted that in reality the work of the district committee is to carry out merger (using Trotsky's expression) and that this reflects the influence of the Workers' Opposition. Briefly, that characterises the report from the bureau of the communist party. I declared that there should be no such interference and that such an approach emerges not from the activity of the party committee, but reflects the Fourth Congress of the Metalworkers' Union. As a result, the party committee recognised the activity of the district committee to be satisfactory.

The second case was when I was in Perm recently. I saw all the members of the district committee. There had been seven, but two people remained to carry out work. Comrade Balandin will not deny what I say. Such things did not happen before. I know each member personally and I know to which group he belonged. Comrade Balandin did not belong to the Workers' Opposition. He is a member of the presidium of our congress. He told about how it is impossible to work when the bureau of the faction sends a political commissar to work beside him. I set the task as exit from the union. Comrade Balandin will not refuse to confirm this, although he is not from the Workers' Opposition. From this moment, special attention was turned to [text breaks off].

Medvedev: The plenum of our union's central committee previously discussed those theses, which Comrade Lepse defended. The examination of them there demanded a further exchange of opinions, because they were accepted by a narrow margin of twelve votes against ten. This fact attests that a significant part of the central committee did not find them satisfactory. Some comrades who have managed to become acquainted with them have found them unsatisfactory. First of all, we are not satisfied with the role which these theses accord to the union. We also are dissatisfied with how the theses define the role and tasks of unions in our changing internal circumstances. We are satisfied neither with the explanation nor the approach to this question, for the theses do not explain the actual situation as it currently exists. Therefore, they cannot correctly outline further behaviour in these circumstances.

For these reasons, 42 comrades assigned me to speak to you about what we had earlier decided to say about the role and tasks of trade unions. For us, it is no secret that the question about the role and tasks of the union arose as a consequence of the new circumstances in which we have lived for an entire year. The New Economic Policy has essentially changed our entire economic structure. Until the New Economic Policy was implemented, we had state industry, which was the only master in our government. As you know, the situation has changed quite a lot since the New Economic Policy was implemented. Already now, we have a significant amount of private capitalism, which counts significant cadres of hired workers in its enterprises. These hired workers are exploited most cruelly. As you know, not long ago in Moscow there were so called demonstrative courts about this exploitation. They revealed the entire disgraceful picture of the cruel exploitation in these purely capitalist enterprises.

Both meager wages and a long working day, which are the most horrifying circumstances of this exploitation, resulted from the New Economic Policy.

Another circumstance connected with the New Economic Policy is that our state industry was significantly reorganised on new foundations. Most of our state economy was cast off state supply and transferred to so-called commercial foundations or, as they say, an economic foundation, which essentially is the same thing. This means that surplus value is received from these enterprises. True, the state benefits from this. It also means that the structure of our state economic enterprises significantly changed in comparison to what we had until recently. Now that our state economy has gone over to commercial principles, which means profitmaking, it will need to establish its existence on a firm foundation and further develop its manufacturing product by competing on the free capitalist market with capitalist enterprises.

An enormous number of state economic enterprises have been removed from state supply and transferred to supply exclusively by means of struggle on the market and successful extraction of national resources. Self-management of state economic holdings goes in the direction of expanding the laws and independent management of state enterprises. This applies to administration, technical organisation, and labour conditions. Of course, all this is connected with the need to bitterly compete with private capital on the market. This is the foundation for the role and influence of unions on the direction of management at state enterprises. We are confronted with the clear picture that the situation of the working masses in these enterprises will depend very much on reigning market conditions. If our state enterprises were technically equipped significantly better than private capitalist, concessionary, and leased enterprises, we could hope that the state economy would not be bound by competition, so workers in these enterprises would not be exploited more or have a significantly more difficult material situation than in the private capitalist economy.

In fact, this is not so. Technical equipment in our state enterprises differs from the technical equipment in leased enterprises and even more so from that in enterprises working under concessions. In order to successfully compete with the private capitalist free market, they will be forced to sell their production output on the free market under the competitive conditions. There are two paths of competition: 1) lowering the cost of manufacturing output by improving manufacturing technology; or 2) intensifying workers' productivity. This confronts our unions with new circumstances right now and forces them to set tasks in a new way in order to defend the interests of the working masses. Here we encounter the question of how one can conceive of the successful defence of the working masses' interests in the state economy, in an economy with government participation (the concessions form), or in a capitalist economy?

How can a defence be mounted? The theses, which were accepted by a majority of just two votes, say too little about this. Besides we think that our defence should be not only in words but also in actions in state enterprises, purely capitalist enterprises, and in mixed ones. We cannot be limited now to the same methods, to which our union has been confined up to now. Therefore, we think that now there is a great danger that in state industry, which has been made dependent on the market and has to compete on the market to a significant extent, there will come to light more frequent violations of workers' interests than before. One may conclude that the role and influence of the

Metalworkers' Union and of unions in general should be strengthened in state enterprises in order to protect workers' direct interests. This must be done to the utmost and with all the means that are at our disposal.

In order to understand all the conditions, which are being created in state enterprises, I will cite a *Pravda* article, 'The Food Industry on New Foundations'. At first, they saw beneficial results, including higher labour productivity, better food supplies, reduced work absenteeism, and improved methods. All this made it possible to estimate the real subsistence wage in this industry, but this did not continue for long. Personnel reductions on the one hand and the furious growth in market prices on food supplies on the other hand reduced the initial beneficial results to nothing. So the result is the following: all measures for improving workers' living conditions presently amount to nothing. (Reads article.) These are the conditions, which the transition to new principles has created in the state economy. Clearly, if our influence is reduced, it may come to the point that women can no longer feed their children. We should change these conditions by introducing a different system of work.

The union's role and influence on the organisation of the economy and its direct management should be made stronger. The union should be given decisive influence. We cannot limit ourselves only to writing theses, but should exert actual influence over industry. For this to happen, we need to say to the new central committee that it needs to create for itself a decisively significant role in the metals industry in all things, upon which the successful work and life of the worker depend. There will be agreements (about which yesterday Comrade Lenin spoke), which will make the state a participant. Such economic forms will be semi-state, semi-capitalist. The state is the owner and the master of the enterprise. Other negotiated economic forms will be semi-capitalist and the private employer-entrepreneur will be the master. Of course, the union cannot participate in directly aiding the interests of private capital; it cannot feel satisfaction at the enrichment of the private owner (West European capitalist). The influence of the union upon our economic organisations should be more decisive and more profound than it has been up to now.

There can be no dispute, however, that the theses do not treat the capitalist economy satisfactorily. In a capitalist economy, workers can defend themselves from exploitation by means of struggle through strikes. One must clearly admit that currently the working class cannot carry out strike actions in private capitalist enterprises, because right now the proletariat is like a beggar. We should create strike funds and unemployment funds, which could make it possible to realise a sufficient amount of strike actions. The absence of a fund aggravates workers' difficulty, because it does not allow the union the powerful option of going on strike to prevent economic exploitation of the working masses. Also, there is little hope for a collective agreement to be concluded with capitalists, who would violate it. Without a fund, there can be no resort to a strike to ensure the conscientious fulfillment of the collective agreement.

It needs to be said definitively that the union should be given decisive influence over regulating private-capitalist production and labour conditions in the bodies in charge of regulation (Narkomtrud, Sobes, workers' insurance). We can successfully struggle within the private capitalist economy only if we have such a presence in soviet power's lawmaking bodies that will allow us to defend the worker masses from inevitable/unavoidable exploitation. Here are the basics of the position, which we should hold. In some places in our country, a line of independence has taken shape in regard to the methods of action to defend workers in these economic forms. Our political enemies the SRs and Mensheviks preach this old hackneyed independence, which follows logically from their mode of thought. They think that under the rulership of the Communist Party, Soviet Russia is now giving the workers less than they got from private capitalism and less than would the restoration of complete private property on democratic foundations. They think that the development of a capitalist economy in our impoverished Russia will give the worker more. Therefore, they say to the workers that only this path can protect them and keep them secure. This SR and Menshevik element is the most harmful, disorganising one, which has slipped in here. Each union needs to hold the most acutely negative attitude toward this position, for given the damage done to our metals industry and our general weakness, such independence would lead to not to unions' independence from the government, but to unions' complete loss of influence over government bodies.

Those are the main things, which I consider it necessary to draw your attention to, without promoting any special theses on this fairly routine question. But that is what we propose for the role and tasks of unions. We think that unions should be given a more decisive role and influence now over the state economy than at any time in the past, for this economy is now under the pressure of capitalist desires. These desires were manifested in our government bodies, so that we were presented at one of the latest plenums with such a project, that would declare all of metalworking industry to be a private trust. This runs through all conversations about agreements with Soviet power – how will it supply this or that and what will it do. True, the plenum rejected this, but this is an indicator of the situation in which our metals industry is found. In mixed enterprises, where the government is only a participant, we will not participate directly. There we demand only the strengthening of our role and influence in those bodies, which regulate the conditions of labour. Unions should be given a decisive say in these bodies. All bodies of soviet power should be used exclusively in private capitalist firms, for hopes on strike struggle cannot give us sufficient resources, in order to successfully protect workers from that most cruel exploitation about which I told you.

[Gurevich says that Medvedev's position cannot easily be criticised, because he hasn't submitted written proposals, although a week has passed since the plenum. Nevertheless, he says that Medvedev's conclusions are not Marxist.]

Medvedev:[222] I should express regret that I am speaking late. I asked to register to speak, but I was too late. Here some are allowed to sign up easily and speak as much as they want (noise, protests). This is what I want to say here. The debate was waged around the organisational question and the procedure for creating the central committee, about the activity of which comrade Vorobev reported. We could not permit ourselves to be limited to this question. Why did the central committee's report not say a word about our current situation, the union's activities, productivity, union organisation, how to unite the union, and what is its role and plan. In Vorobev's report, there were no instructions.

In order to correctly decide the task, we should think about past experience. The central committee should set the task so that the whole point of the question would be reflected. The situation of the metals industry needs to be examined in the conditions of the New Economic Policy. It was necessary to begin from this and to show what is the situation. This situation was formulated at the Fourth Congress as if the metals industry is a complete failure. There were many reasons for the catastrophe. These include inadequate food supplies, raw materials, auxiliary materials, and so forth. After the Fourth Congress, the metals industry experienced the deepest shock, which threatened to bring about its final downfall. After this shock, phenomena followed in connection with the New Economic Policy, but here not a word has been said about this.

Speaking about the central committee's work, it must be asked to what degree the central committee was able to protect the union from that terrible ruin, which afflicted the metals industry? This is the fundamental question. Our answer is that the union had absolutely no role in or influence upon economic policy. Maybe Comrade Vorobev will evaluate this in his concluding word, but I will attempt to prove that I am correct. We are confronted with the possible closure of largescale metalworking factories – those where loco-

---

222   It is unclear whether this speech follows or precedes the one above.

motives and train cars are built. Do you know why this question confronts us? It is because we made enormous orders abroad. Supposedly, we don't have adequate resources to breathe life into these colossuses, so to speak, but we do have gold in order to make orders abroad. Right now, the metals trust refuses to accept even those train cars which have already been manufactured, it says, because foreign locomotives are on the way. The picture that results is that we drove our very own factories to death and sent gold to Sweden and other countries. Where was our central committee at this time? Those of us who were unable to give warning are not guilty. It is the reigning economic system that is guilty. The guilt is in the improvisations and harebrained schemes of some rogue that led us into an extremely difficult situation. The central committee gave no notice about the death and atomisation of metalworkers of this largest branch of metals industry.

I should talk about the supply of the metals industry. Since we work for the government, we should find resources. What did the central committee do in this area? It has done absolutely nothing. It's necessary to propose the abrogation of orders sent abroad, so that gold would go into the centre of the life of the communist revolution. Shliapnikov made such an attempt, but they began to persecute him. The union with its current leadership had no role or influence.

We do not have gold for the metals industry of Russia, but there is gold for providing for 100 American workers, who will work in the Kuznetsk basin. The central committee did nothing in this regard and could not do anything, because it was composed not according to how well or poorly it resolves the organisational question or by how it understands the union's interests, but by how well it implements the bosses' orders. Clearly, the condition of the central committee, its line for conducting economic policy, and the newly created conditions do not help the metals industry emerge from its current state of disorder, which is the greatest ever. If we want for our union to be a strong body, which influences economic policy and pushes it ahead, then we should not elect this central committee, because its activity is accidentally defined. It is weak in that it lacks a method for moving forward which would be possible to implement. Circumstances are not such that the party could create such a method. There can be no leadership, because there is no Metalworkers' Union representation at gubernia trade union councils. If they do go, they are busy with underhanded dealings [крючкотворство]. The central committee cannot speak sincerely with trade union personnel about how to quickly emerge from such a situation in order to finally began fruitful work. Leadership needed to be systematic and correct and provide methods to build the trade union movement and start rolling. We have not seen such an approach. We saw only that one section of our party is thought to be true commanders and another section to be disloyal; one section does not believe the other section. Such a situation is abnormal.

They spoke to us about new theses. We understand wonderfully what such new theses are. At the end of the congress, we will have to elect a central committee. This needs to be seriously considered. We should elect a central committee, which always and everywhere will be authoritative, strong, firm, and have sufficient communist courage, in order to lead our trade union movement so that it would be noticed all up and down the line. But there is no leadership. There are only blunders in work. Leadership should be such that all trade union personnel would learn under this leadership. What will happen in our country in the spring? Clearly, private trade and industrial capital will grow and concentrate. We should not hide from our communist faction that soon private capital will have contact with spetses, and then there will turn out to be a really Menshevik atmosphere. Right now it is not so terrible, but when private capital will set up contact with spetses, then the Menshevik atmosphere will be very strong in all enterprises.

[Tarasov asks to remove his name from the list nominated by the central committee. Tarygin makes a request regarding his candidacy. Alekseev complains about unbusinesslike conversations.]

Medvedev: Comrades, because of comrades from the Nizhegorod organisation, a question has been raised that is not on the agenda of our congress. I was among those who signed the statement that the heterodox are thoroughly persecuted at our congresses, including right now. You are being called onto this path. They want you to give them the right to persecute all those who signed that statement, in which the Party cc found nothing worth prosecuting. Clearly, what we are dealing with here is a measure prodding you toward a split. We appealed to you, because our party matters are so difficult that we are moved to appeal for help to you in order to eliminate the threat of a split hanging over the party. We suppose that you will follow Comrade Tomsky's summons.[223] If you will read our discussions with the Mensheviks at the First All-Russian Congress of the Metalworkers' Union, you will see that they said that the government organises the economy, which is its affair, and that we defend the workers' interests. No one can dare to say that we can strengthen the dictatorship of the proletariat by means of a strike. Trying to use a strike to correct our bureaucratic perversions would be an incitement against the dictatorship of proletariat.

---

223   It is uncertain whether the following lines are from Medvedev's speech.

[Andreev speaks. Then Tomsky calls for an end to political games and to group struggle at the congress for the sake of the union, of which nothing might remain if such struggle continues. He says that the Eleventh Party Congress will discuss the Letter of the 22, which should be off limits for this congress. Sidorov speaks. Lepse accuses Shliapnikov, Medvedev, and others of trying to push through the platform of the Workers' Opposition under a different name. He says he has 'a greater right to be called a worker, because I began to work in the central committee as one called from a factory committee, while you, Comrade Shliapnikov, were appointed to the union's central committee in 1917, so you shouldn't talk about appointees'.]

Shliapnikov: I very much regret that I could not participate in the nuances of the activity of your central committee, all the more so since I organised it. (The chair protests, declaring that he earlier participated in this). Nevertheless, I belong to those who organised the central committee, and to me each step in the development of our union is dear. I heard Andreev's speech, in which he rebuked me with the very serious accusation that I used the union like an arena for political struggle (cries: it is true) but it is worth remembering what took place yesterday, in order to say exactly the reverse. I took the stenographic records home to examine, so that I could present evidence to the commission with which I sat in session, as to who is waging a thuggish policy against us. We are not the ones who brought up here those matters related to disagreements in party life. Who was it who first came to this tribune and read the letter? We do not deny the letter's existence, but anyone with the slightest sense of justice will say that neither I nor any of our comrades took this path. At the Fourth Congress last year in this hall, someone created a squabble by proposing a list which did not find support. Only 40 were for this list while 136 were against in a roll call vote. The initiators were Rudzutak and Co., who are the very ones who rebuke me (Rudzutak protests). If not Rudzutak, then his second edition. This is not important, but I want to place a period there where they would not have placed it.[224]

[Gurevich speaks about how in some gubernias after the reregistration in the party, some comrades decided 'spontaneously' to reregister union members. This was due to 'confusion', he says. 'It happened differently in each district. In some districts, workers were excluded because they do not share the platform

---

224   The speech either ends here or there is an interruption in the stenographic record.

of Soviet power. This is incorrect. We include people in the union no matter
what their religious and political convictions are.']

Shliapnikov: Comrades, there was a time when we all complained that there
were too many theses. It seemed that they were brought forth at all times of
the day. Comrade Medvedev does not propose theses, but bitter experience
has taught us that any theses can be regarded as a platform or a political association. This time the only theses were those released by the Party CC and
the central committee of our union and in these they expressed apprehension about some future deviation against which protective measures need to
be taken. Take Comrade Gurevich, who points out that our country's economy
has radically changed and says it would be wrong to maintain the old methods
of work. This would be correct, if everything had changed in our government.
According to the central committee's theses, the new policy introduces some
changes into the situation of the working class in Russia, but the essence of
the working class does not change. Comrade Gurevich, you should make a
case about whether or not to change the existing situation. Your attitude is
not Marxist, but is reactionary. You take the situation not as it is but as it has
been fabricated. Making a generalisation about capitalist relations, you attribute them to the masses. Essentially you propagandise outright independence
and you say that trade unions should be independent in relation to separate
bodies of the economy. To speak so means to play us for fools. No one can do
this. Only enemies of the proletariat can say this, but the proletariat will send
them to hell. If you can speak so, then any person can say that he is carrying
out the will of the proletariat. Correcting these mistakes by means of strikes
would be wrong. We should review our work, but not as you suggest, because
this would be an ace in the hands of the Mensheviks.[225]

   In the first point, he writes: 'the military need to defend proletarian power
created an economic policy of universal nationalisation'. In fact, this is not true.
The war resulted from our power, from our new economic policy in October,
and our attitude toward the old capitalist economy. Our current new economic
policy is not really new, but is very similar to the old policy. Therefore, let's
call the policy that was new in relation to capitalism the new one and not our
current policy, which they say is new. If you look at our discussion with the
Mensheviks at the First Congress of the All-Russian Metalworkers' Union, then
you will see that they said that the government organises the economy. That is

---

225   The section which follows may or may not be from Shliapnikov's speech. It may come from
      one of Medvedev's speeches.

its business, while we defend the workers' interests. We told them in relation to this that the working class cannot have another defence besides the organisation of the national economy and struggle against ruin. No one will dare to say that we can strengthen the dictatorship of the proletariat by means of a strike. If we will try to correct our bureaucratic distortions by means of a strike, this will be a blow against the dictatorship of the proletariat.

Therefore, we should adopt different methods of struggle and work on the plane of improving workers' daily living conditions than those you propose. The economy right now is going in three directions. First, there is state industry, which we are protecting in all kinds of ways. For it, we demand from the government maximal resources, in order to secure for these enterprises all their first priority needs. We send the best comrades to bodies which manage state industry, in order to strengthen our influence, for our largescale industry is the single thing of value that we have for strengthening the proletarian dictatorship. If the participation of foreign capital is taken into account, the rest of industry also will be great. Further, there is the leased sector of our industry, the concessions sector, and the combined sector. This last one is the sector where both government and West European capital will participate. That is what is taking shape in our country right now in the area of the new economic policy that applies to the metals industry. In relation to each of these groups, we should determine in advance our methods of work, struggle, and participation.

We will have a different attitude toward lessees. We will haul the lessees onto the bench of the accused. We will use those government resources which we have for struggle against it. There will be another method in relation to the concessionaire. He, as a foreigner, will not so easily be seated on the bench of the accused. But of course we should arrange it so that all of them should obey our legistation. By means of collective agreements, we should accept some measures, which would impose upon the concessionaire certain obligations. Further, there are enterprises, which combine a government share and West European or American joint-stock company. How will we behave in relation to these? State power should keep sight of and extend to them regulation if not administration.

The experience of 1917 taught us that without regulation of industry we cannot set up our economy. Even backward Russian capitalists were convinced of this. You know what kind of bodies were created in our country for distributing raw materials, fuel, and such goods. It should be arranged so that trade union workers would have a large and serious representation in government regulating bodies related to these enterprises. We should increase our influence in these government bodies, just not in the management of the combined enterprise, where we cannot send our comrade to clash directly with capital in defence of workers' interests.

These basic signposts are not marked out in these theses, but there are some dangerous places. I have just two minutes remaining, in which I cannot show all the dangers, but I especially warn the comrades about point #15 and parts further down, where it tells of the need to evenly distribute victims among individual production groups.

At one time we were busy distributing work clothing and bread, yet right now we want to distribute only victims. During the past few years, some objective conditions, of which the main thing was that we were chiefly government and military industry which satisfied the needs of the state and not the needs of the private market, we metalworkers were deflected away from questions of wages and wage rates. But some formulations in the theses say to pay metalworkers by taking away from textileworkers and leatherworkers. Comrades, we should dissociate ourselves from these formulations. Neither in the past nor in the present have we resorted to such measures in our struggle as to take away from Peter in order to give to Paul. To take from one and give to another means to set workers of other specialties and other unions against us. This will undermine the authority we have at our disposal in the trade union movement and among workers of other professions (weak applause).

[Nikolsky criticises Medvedev's supplementary report, and seems to say that Shliapnikov contradicts what Medvedev said. Lobanov speaks.]

Skliznev: I should eliminate the vagueness introduced by Nikolsky, who distorted Shliapnikov's meaning. Shliapnikov did not say that the New Economic Policy did not introduce any changes. He did say that it transformed the situation of the working class to a certain degree. But it does not follow from this that the form of the proletarian state changed. One should not garble facts. [He proceeds to discuss Gurevich's speech.]

[Polosatov speaks and offers part of his time to Shliapnikov. Semkov and Prasolov speak. Pages follow where it is unclear who is speaking.]

Kiselev: We think that the old central committee did not work in contact with the provinces. Nevertheless, we see that the old central committee gave a certain amount of leadership and we sensed this leadership in the provinces. But this central committee, which was constructed by the Fourth Congress, its faction, and the party, did not provide leadership because its personnel lacked practical experience. I will not speak about our industry, because our leading body was such that our district committee did all the construction. Moving on to the electrical industry, we see that according to Glavelektro circulars, the Sovnarkhoz, which is led by spetses, constructs all the gubernia electrical sections.

[Lepse, Nikolsky, and Vorobev speak.]

Skliznev: The Moscow delegation has authorised me to nominate candidates from the following delegations: Moscow, Ekaterinoslav, Nikolaev, Kharkov, the majority of the Urals delegation, and part of the Donetsk delegation. The list is composed according to the following principles. First of all, the aforesaid delegations think that the list for the central committee needs to be composed so that it would fully reflect the mood of the current congress. Second, the list for the central committee should eliminate any possibility of any internal comradely reticence [недомолки] in the further work of our union. Third, given our union's current difficult conditions and the role which it, as the leading union, inevitably should again occupy, we think that there is no way that our old union guard can be put back in place. Fourth, it is necessary to compose a central committee which would have good basic core of personnel for steady work and would be linked to the maximum extent with the provinces in its practical work.

In our list, along with individuals from the centre and from the engineers' section of the union, we thought it reasonable to allot 15 places to individuals from our largescale metalworking districts. The people on the list are the following: Tarasov (Moscow), Klinov (Piter), Tarygin (Tula), Volkov (Nizhny), Korolev (Vyksa), Kubyshkin-Maltsev (Donbas), Fofenko (Ekaterinoslav), Brykov (Kharkov), Potaskuev (Central Urals), Parfutin (Urals), Klimenko (Perm), Firfov (Briansk), Zaitsev (Povolzhe), Kaigorov (Izhevsk), Shliapnikov (CC), Tolokontsev (CC), Lepse (CC), Vorobev (CC), Lobanov (the South), Andreev (VTsSPS), Vladimirov (CC), Ianson (CC), Skliznev (the South), and Evreinov (Section of Engineers). The candidate members proposed are: Mitin (Iugostal), Kuibyshev (Elektrootdel), Medvedev (CC), Zheltov, Khararez (CC), Kharitonenko (Briansk), Luka (Donbas), Bukhanov (Kolomna), Deulenkov (Moscow), Pavlov (Petrograd), Maslennikov (Tula), Samarin (Vyksa), and Ustanov (Urals).

[In the name of the Party CC, Tomsky proposes that the faction vote unanimously at the plenum of the congress.]

99 vote for Vorobev's list, while 84 are for Skliznev's list.

Shliapnikov: In the presence of Comrade Tomsky, the chair of VTsSPS, I appeal for the need to find a path to agreement. Clearly, those on the list approved by the majority cannot depend on the entire organised masses in their work. The reverse is also true. A path toward understanding and agreement needs to be found. The only expedient path toward agreement is to award places on the basis of proportional voting. The commission, which can involve Comrade Tomsky, can decide this. A commission composed on an equal footing will pass a decision and will carry it through our delegations. Then a final decision will be arrived at.

[Tomsky says that such a commission would not arrive at the 'necessary results'. A central committee based on 'proportional' representation would see 'political work' waged within it. It would not be able to carry out trade union work.]

Shliapnikov: Comrade Lepse accused me of having been the Party CC's appointee when our union was organised. I declare that this was not so. In view of extraordinary difficulties for our party in April 1917, the CC assigned me and some other comrades to conquer the Metalworkers' Union, which was in the hands of the Mensheviks. In the bureau where I landed, there were three people. Two were Mensheviks and I was the sole Bolshevik. I was confronted with the task of winning over this union. Together with other comrades, we did so. Moreover, everywhere and always, we did so by elections (applause).

∴

S.P. Medvedev's resolution, which he presented to the RCP(b) faction of the Fifth Congress of the All-Russian Metalworkers' Union.[226]

Having heard the exchange of opinions about the role and tasks of trade unions at the current time, the communist faction of the Fifth All-Russian Congress of Metalworkers decides:

1) In its work, the union's new central committee should achieve decisive influence both in state economic bodies, which manage the metals industry, and in direct management of production in state metals enterprises. The interests of metalworkers will be defended to the maximum degree possible, only if the state metals industry's interests are defended more successfully. The successful defence of the metals industry's

---

226   RGASPI, f. 99, op. 1, d. 7, l. 34.

interests is impossible, without the maximal strengthening of the role and influence of the union in all government economic bodies, which organise the state economy.

2) In the mixed metals economy, where the government will partner with private capital, the union must have the decisive influence in all questions regulating and defining the conditions of labour.

3) In the private capitalist economy, the union is confronted with the urgent task of most resolutely defending the direct interests of the metalworkers by using all means, which the current moment dictates.

4) The internal structure of all union bodies in the centre and in the provinces should be reorganised and adapted, in order to more successfully fulfill tasks to defend the direct material interests of metalworkers from the cruelest exploitation of them in private capitalist enterprises.

5) Taking into account the impoverished material situation of the working class in our country, which results from many years of war and terrible destruction of the country, the central committee and the union as a whole can successfully defend the direct interests of metalworkers in government-owned, mixed, and privately owned enterprises at the present time only if the role and influence of the union is reinforced to the maximum extent in all bodies of Soviet power (Narkomprod, Narkomfin, Narkomtrud), which regulate, condition, or supervise labour conditions and the implementation of Soviet labour law.

6) The faction also finds that so-called 'union independence' in production should be condemned and rejected, for in fact it inevitably leads to actual independence of economic bodies of state power from the influence of the proletariat and of its trade unions, which inevitably weakens the proletariat's political supremacy.

∴

S.P. Medvedev's resolution on the report of the central committee of the All-Russian Union of Metalworkers, 3 March 1922.[227]

1) Since the Fourth Congress concluded, the central committee of the union has been unable:

a) to protect the interests of the metals industry, to secure its renewal and development in new economic conditions, and to win receipt of necessary government resources for this;

---

227 RGASPI, f. 99, op. 1, d. 7, l. 36.

b)   to raise and secure metalworkers' real wages at least to a level, which would save them from outright physical extinction and guarantee satisfaction of the material demands most necessary for their survival;

c)   to set right its own activity and to establish and set right a living organic link at least with the district committees of large metalworking districts.

2)   This complete ineffectiveness of the union's central committee in all the above-indicated areas of union work directly resulted from its personal composition being forced on the union, contrary to the will of the overwhelming majority of the faction of worker communists of the Fourth Congress. Its majority turned out to be incapable of leading any union work at the current time.

3)   Because the central committee was personally selected and composed in a way that was contrary to the will of the overwhelming majority of the faction of the congress, friendly and fruitful work is clearly impossible even in the very central committee itself. This inevitably leads to the complete disorganisation and deep demoralisation of the central committee and of the entire union.

4)   Taking this experience into account, the RCP(b) faction of the Fifth All-Russian Congress of the Metalworkers' Union believes it necessary for the union's new central committee to be formed by selecting its personal composition both in full and individually by candidate according to the will of the congress's communist faction, its individual delegations, and groups of the largest districts of the metals industry. Only under this condition can the faction find it possible to move past that disorganisation and deep demoralisation of the central committee and the entire union, which led them into a state of complete impotence and internal feebleness in all areas of union work.

Signed and verified by S.P. Medvedev, 4 March 1922.

∴

Statement from a group of comrades to the presidium of the Fifth Congress of the All-Russian Metalworkers' Union, asking permission for S.P. Medvedev to deliver a supplementary report.[228]

---

228   RGASPI, f. 99, op. 1, d. 7, l. 42.

We, the signatories below, who are delegates to the Fifth All-Russian Congress of the Metalworkers' Union, declare the need to put forth a supplementary speaker on the tasks of the unon at the current time. We nominate comrade Medvedev as the supplementary speaker.

Signed by (name and delegate number):

1.	Fokin	39	22.	Ivanov	88
2.	Safronov	95	23.	Sukhanov	137
3.	Tarasov	96	24.	[illegible]	109
4.	Poplavsky	41	25.	Petrov	83
5.	Fisenkov	108	26.	Romov	112
6.	Rogozhinsky	26	27.	Sidorov	40
7.	Makhnevich		28.	Shokhanov	
8.	Safatinov	61	29.	Gorunenko	93
9.	Markov	60	30.	Kuninko	239
10.	Komissarov	55	31.	[illegible]	216
11.	Bolshakov	70	32.	[illegible]	151
12.	[illegible]	143	33.	Parov	85
	[illegible][229]	203	34.	Lukka	
13.	Uvarov	140	35.	Zhilin	55
14.	Kosov	131	36.	Brykov	81
15.	Petrov	80	37.	Kondratev	
16.	Sobolenko	31	38.	[illegible]	
17.	[illegible]	38	39.	[illegible]	
18.	[illegible]	57	40.	[illegible]	
19.	[illegible]	46	41.	[illegible]	
20.	Deulenkov	152	42.	[illegible]	
21.	[illegible]	142			

∴

A.G. Shliapnikov's speech to the 6 March 1922 RCP(b) faction of the Fifth Congress of the All-Russian Metalworkers' Union.

Comrades, having worked with me for many years, you were probably very surprised by the entirety of comrade Zinoviev's speech constructed against me. I already warned you, comrade Zinoviev, against both your tone and your inter-

---

229   The name here was not numbered in the original manuscript.

pretation of the essence and thoughts of the testimony I gave. As I just said, insufficient attention was paid to making an accurate stenographic record of each word comrade Kollontai and I said, unfortunately. For this I am punished by here having to refute much of that which has been said.

Here are the particulars of how our case was handled. The Comintern commission of seven invited us, I think, on Friday at noon, but the session began only at 3 p.m. Comrade Zinoviev will probably remember that some comrades were at his session of the Comintern and could not participate in the work. I came to him then at the session and said that I did not want to speak without our comrades. I resolutely insisted that he would come. He declared that he could not do so without an invitation. I went and strongly requested of comrade Kolarov that I would like comrade Zinoviev to be present in order to avoid misunderstandings. But comrade Kolarov said that they didn't want this. So I could not do anything. I just requested that a protocol would be kept. But yesterday I learned that the protocol was not kept and that each comrade, according to his impressions, entered some words in his notebook. I will begin from the end. Those matters which we put in the letter and which we transmitted to each comrade in writing in all languages were not discussed. The Workers' Opposition was discussed on the basis of those documents which have been published abroad. Maybe for the sake of struggle against leftists in international politics, against whom I spoke very resolutely when I was abroad in 1920, it is possible to sacrifice not only 22 people, but maybe far more. Maybe the Communist International demands the staging of such a theatrical production. But if there is not such a need, then it's necessary to be fair and say that the case went awry. So I will tell you how the matter was. In writing this letter, we proceeded from the desire to put an end to all those pains which bother everyone. To say that within our party everything is alright means to hide the actual situation. Comrade Zinoviev rebuked us for not having appealed earlier to the Control Commission and for having acted behind the back of the CC. But he forgets that at the Tenth Party Congress we said that we retain the right to go to the arena of the Third Communist International and the Third Communist Congress about the problem which worries us and which in our opinion you are attempting to solve incorrectly. Then the workers demanded this. I received a series of signatures in particular from workers of the town Nikolaev demanding this be placed at the Third Congress. Then we did not do this because we did not want to confront the Third Congress with a small fissure within the party.

About our work. We sat in session from 3 p.m. to 4:30 p.m., because we could not go any longer, since comrades needed to get a bite to eat, for at 5 p.m. there was already another commission. Comrade Kolarov probably will confirm this. An hour and a half was devoted to our case. I asked the comrades if it suited them for me to fill them in on all sorts of facts or to describe the general state of affairs of our party, without touching upon our Soviet policy. They proposed the latter to me. I said that we are trying to warn the party against the danger of losing its unity with the proletariat. I illustrated this with the point that we are a very exhausted country. There is a basis for dissatisfaction in the poverty of the people. We cannot study Russia only by means of the parades which are arranged in our country. I began with this. Yet Comrade Zinoviev set this at the end. You see what my meaning was and how it turned out in the depiction by Comrade Zinoviev. I said that unity takes shape where the workers assert themselves. But I did not say that an insurrection or a movement against the government is growing somewhere. I never uttered such a thought anywhere. I developed the explanation that in our country there are taking shape abnormal relations with an enormous mass of nonparty workers, who live in extraordinarily difficult conditions, whose wages do not exceed 20% of those before the war. There is a colossal basis for dissatisfaction. In a businesslike way I approached without any ambiguities those problems which have been placed before us.

2. (*Reads*) I introduced documents on this subject. I have a list of 33 gubernias. Comrades, you know that the gubkom secretary is the face and the brain of the organisation. It turned out that among 33 secretaries of gubkoms, only three were workers. Indeed, during these years of revolution and underground struggle have we not brought up a sufficient quantity of workers with superb experience who could take the party apparatus into their hands? The party could only win from this. But in fact this is not the case. The explanation for this is that the majority of our party is not proletarian. In this regard we have the report of the cc for 1920, the statistics of which speak precisely about this. These are the data I possessed and what I pointed to without any equivocations.

3. and 4. (*Reads*) You sit here, personnel from many cells. Am I not correct, comrades that each of us has to struggle against this? It is not true that we incite many comrades, who write or come personally on this matter or send delegates. This is a thing, to which we especially turn the attention of the cc. I have pointed this out often and for a long time. To totally eliminate this, we propose (reads points 3–4) That is what we proposed. As you see, debate and impressions, which were received from our conversations, are reflected in the resolution in a completely different manner. I do not want to reproach anyone from the members of the commission, if it was necessary to do so, okay. But we did not at all want the unfair trial [судилище], which was held. We wanted a solution to these painful questions, which you will not receive a solution to if you expel 22 or 40,000 people and these painful questions will not cease to confront you as they do now. If our Comintern commission had resolved the

question as it stands in the resolution, we of course would submit to this, but we should say that the illness will not be cured with this.

Now let's move on to the essence of comrade Zinoviev's speech. He accused me and comrade Medvedev of having conceived and fulfilled premeditated intentions to lead us to a split. All these rebukes that we want to create a special party, all this has been known for a long time. We have often said that we are against this. All comrades know how we warned against such proposals sometimes at the price of being discredited, and that they were done in more than one town. This is also known to comrades. If they say that we organised a faction, well I retort that there was no faction. If comrades who are interested in one question gather today at my place, tomorrow at Ivan's place, is this a faction? Indeed, comrades, in the Kremlin you have sessions for a cup of tea, for blini and other wonderful things, and no one says that this is a faction. What is a faction? It comprises a bureau, a joint fund, one's own agents, and so forth. We have nothing of the sort. Comrade Zinoviev said, by the way, that I have a smile on my face, that I speak with a smile and so forth. What's there to do, sometimes you have to laugh when you see how little connection there is between that which is said and about whom it is said. Comrade Zinoviev said that I laughed when he said that we want to create a faction. My answer to this: if we had wanted to create a faction, those 22 comrades who signed and those comrades who are still only thinking it over, well you tell me, with our experience in all kinds of conspiracy, could we have done it? We did not do this, but you are provoking us. Comrade Tomsky's speech at the Fourth All-Russian Congress was an attempt to create around me the Workers' Opposition, an attempt for which he paid somehow. Such an attempt was made also at the Congress of Metalworkers, which stood on the point of view of the Tenth Party Congress and did not carry out any special policy. It wholly followed behind the CC in the area of implementing its policy and you remember the results: the CC was supported by 40 people versus 136. This means a policy nudging toward organisation. Further about a fourth international. Here are jeers from comrade Zinoviev. You are the ones who should be jeered, comrades, not we. More than once I was confronted with possible expulsion from the party. Of course, if my political death is necessary, and if it can bring benefit to the party, well I have nothing against this. But I know that this will not heal our party. A whole series of measures need to be taken in order to heal it.

So the matter is not in this. The question about a fourth international stood on such a plane one time. I told you exactly this at the CC plenum in the autumn of last year, when you presented a paper. At the conference you also gave a paper and you said that we answered by refusing this invitation to a fourth international. This invitation was organised by Cheka agent Rumynov, who compared a party representative to the stenographer [female form] of a commission, which investigated the activity of Vneshtorg, and a secretary [female form] of Zhenotdel under the CC. A metalworker comrade was also drawn into this game. I was at this time outside of Moscow and was extraordinarily surprised, having received this letter. I spoke generally against splits of any kind in our party or abroad and against any attempts to discredit the Third International. I spoke out against independent internationals. I answered that I am resolutely against and said why, and I sent a copy to our CC RCP. What was my surprise when I arrived in Moscow and this entire picture was exposed before me. Obviously, someone needed to organise this and if it did not succeed to organise the Workers' Opposition on an all-Russian scale, well it was necessary to organise it internationally and our participation here was necessary. Such work, comrades, will not lead to unity. The fact that the label of oppositionist or professional splitter is hung on us leads to them allowing themselves to appeal to us for assistance of a very dishonourable character. Here I will remind Rudzutak and Tomsky and others, who worked in Turkestan together with Safarov, of their conversations with me on 9 September, when they acquainted me with their mutual relations and asked me to speak out as disinterested person against the candidacy of Safarov. I said to them that you have Pravdin. And Pravdin said to them exactly the same thing: why should I do this? If you have something against him, then have the courage to say this. Nevertheless Pravdin wrote a memorandum, while Rudzutak and Tomsky kept quiet, and they set us up. There you have the general conditions which are created for our work.

Now regarding Lutovinov's speech. Lutovinov delivered a speech which was deleted from the stenographic report. If there is a direct connection with White Guards in your apparatus, then you need to cleanse it and examine it. I regard Lutovinov's speech negatively, for it was a pure muddle.

They said to us that we are in the opposition simply because we are failures and careerists and want to earn more. **If we had wanted to make careers for ourselves, we needed only to play up to you. This is the best path.**

Here there can be all kinds of misunderstandings. I am not such a brilliant speaker [говорунъ] of French. As concerns comrade Cachin, well he does not have this in his notebook. I looked at it.

Now regarding the confiscated letters. I was asked what kind of situation I have in the party. I answered that it is not brilliant. The following circumstance can serve as evidence of this. A CC member's correspondence is insufficiently safe in our country. I know a case when a courier who carried a letter addressed to a CC member was arrested, and this letter was sent to the person about whom the letter complained. This I have introduced as an illustration.

Now you should remember the history of the locomotives. This is the most important thing – a party question. We achieved nothing here in a political sense and we lost hundreds of millions which Swedish capitalists put in their pockets.

Now about the party purge. They spoke as if the CC had ruined everything. Here is a sheer misunderstanding. Actually, a purge was our slogan. For this slogan they called us Makhaevists and whatever else suited them. But we dare to declare that this was our slogan. We put forth the purge and I said how many of us are purged. I approved the purge and Comrade Kolarov will confirm this. What concerns Tsaritsyn is a sheer misunderstanding. I spoke about Tsaritsyn and illustrated with a protocol the sad situation of our old personnel in our party. This protocol said that the uyezd representatives participated in the gubernia commission on the party purge. There it doesn't say that these party members were in the gubkom's livestock pen [загон]. This illustrates the attitude toward a certain part of our party members. Remember likewise the history of the gubkom secretaries.

Now regarding Miasnikov's case. As concerns literature, well it is clear that the entire world looks to us and therefore we treat our literature with the greatest discipline. We should do everything that depends on us so that this literature would not bring harm to us. But we will hardly come to anything with such methods. Miasnikovist literature is distributed. I negatively regard it, which comrade Zinoviev knows. I was one of the first who spoke out against the creation of a peasant union, when this question was put to the CC.

I will say that there are CC members who support this Miasnikovist position and who use their situation to exert pressure on the party, yet they are not excluded. I can even name a name – this is comrade Osinsky.

About the case of Miasnikov; here I have a letter of the gubkom (reads). That is how the matter stands, but if in international interests we need to punish Miasnikov for this, then we will punish him but go ahead and say so, that a certain condition forces such an act. But why say that which is not and was not so? If I roast Miasnikov, it is only for his attitude toward the peasant union. There is no greater enemy of a peasant union than I. I can bring to the CC a series of statements and fill out questionnaires which you comrade Zinoviev also answered. I resolutely at all times was against organisation by our opponents. That's how I place the question. So please, without any deviation in this regard, I will not allow anyone on this account to play games with my name.

Regarding Kollontai's addition about strikebreaking, well I was present when comrade Kollontai spoke and as far as I remember she spoke about how right now the Red Army has organisations everywhere in the Soviet economy and that this means that a share of labour falls upon it. Foreign comrades probably bent its interpretation in such a way as to say that the army doesn't participate in economic life at all, but if it participates then it does so as strikebreakers.

In what sense I spoke about a parade and indignation and so forth, I already explained. Comrades, I will finish with this and I think that I have sufficiently shed light on our position in this matter and mine personally. I should say that I appeared before this commission only as one of the signatories and did not pretend to represent all the 22. Comrade Kollontai attended to translate, in case the Commission demanded this. I think that some of those 22 comrades who signed will have a chance to speak. Let them say what they think about what has been said here and why they signed this well-known letter. But if we want to extract a lesson from this, then we should be more conscientious toward one another. If comrade Zinoviev regards us as he has said so here, that we did this with premeditated intent, then we will not arrive at anything and will not come to an agreement. By this very thing he violates here the resolution elaborated by this Commission. We never left the ranks of our party even at its most difficult moments, which were many. I never left, even when some sitting in the Politburo incited me to this. When we diverged about participation of socialists, Left SRs, I supported the opinion that it's necessary to attract them, but when the question stood about departing from work, then I said go to hell, but I will work. This was in the office of the Petrograd Ispolkom in the Tauride Palace and Comrade Kamenev initiated this question. That is the form which this question takes.

25 Letter from Z.L. Shadurskaia to the Politburo, 8 March 1922[230]

... I protest against the transformation of an accidental transmission of a sheet with my signature, together with a page of the statement of 22 comrades to the conference of the Comintern, into a pretext for attacks against comrades who signed this statement.

The supplementary sheet for those expressing solidarity with the statement of the 22, where my signature stood (even unfinished, without indication of my party membership number and the year I joined the party), was not supposed to be submitted to the conference. Comrade Kollontai notified the CC RCP(b) and Comrade Zinoviev about this in writing and in a timely manner.

---

230   RGASPI, f. 17, op. 3, d. 280, l. 15.

... My signature is neither in the official copy of the statement of the 22, which the CC received, nor in translations of it, which were given to the conference. Because my signature is not finished, this serves as a pretext to treat me not as a comrade, not as an RCP(b) member, but as an 'unknown individual', for the sake of wittiness and polemical convenience. Moreover, those who do this are people who cannot help but recall that I was brought in on the case of the Bolsheviks in 1917. Together with Radek, Ganetsky, Kollontai, Zinoviev and others, I was branded 'a German spy' by Aleksinsky, who was settling accounts with me. This is because in Paris I was one of the judges, who presided over Aleksinsky's trial for informing on comrades Trotsky, Lunacharsky, Rakovsky, and other internationalists.

Member of RCP(b) No. 244527, Zoia Shadurskaia, 8 March 1922.

26   Letter from S.P. Medvedev to the Orgburo, 9 March 1922[231]

[The letter below was found in a library book and delivered to the CC (see further documents below the letter). I do not know whether Medvedev had delivered the letter himself to the CC earlier, if he only circulated a draft among like-minded comrades, or if the letter below was lost or misdirected.]

Respected comrades!

The period of leave from work, which you granted me, expired on 1 March.

My request to you for leave from work arose from the utmost necessity for me to receive dental treatment, which demanded a long period of time.

I still haven't finished my dental treatment, due to the lack of materials. Also, it is proving difficult to receive appropriate treatment in the Kremlin outpatient dental clinic, as well as in the State Institute of Dentistry, which is where comrade Semashko recommended and directed that my teeth be treated.[232]

The Fifth All-Russian Congress of the Metalworkers' Union took place through 1–8 March. As a member of the union's central committee, which had to account for its work, I had to participate in the congress and I did so. This

---

231   RGASPI, f. 589, op. 3, d. 9102, unnumbered pages. Stamped as received by Bureau of the Secretariat of the CC RCP(b), 12 January 1923.

232   Old Bolshevik Nikolai Aleksandrovich Semashko (1874–1949) served as Commissar of Health, 1918–30.

deprived me of the possibility to meet with you in person on 1 March and to explain the motives for my absence.

As one of the 22, I signed the 'Appeal to Members of the International Conference of the Comintern'. In connection with this, I read in the 7 March issue of our central party organ *Pravda* such a characterisation of my personal qualities and of my party-political behaviour, which leads me to conclude that I clearly cannot expect any party-political and personal-comradely actual trust whatsoever from the Party CC and its bodies. Given this condition, I feel it morally impossible to accept any assignments in the future from the bodies of the Party CC. I consider it necessary to notify you that in the near future, I intend to return to work in my specialty at one of the metalworking enterprises of Moscow or in one of the metalworking regions.

With comradely greetings,
Party member S. Medvedev.
Moscow, 9 March 1922

Excerpt of protocol of closed session of the presidium of Nizhny Nikolaevsky RCP(b) gubernia committee (gubkom), 9 January 1923 (copy).

Heard: 3. Statement of 62nd Regiment Red Army soldier and party member Nudolin about how, upon checking out the book *Russkaia Istoriia* (*Russian History*) from the Zakamensky party district committee (raikom) library, he found in it a letter signed by Medvedev, who was a member of the group of '22' of the Workers' Opposition. The letter was addressed to an unknown person. Inquiries were made and it was determined that the book had at one time been in the possession of party member Pigilev, secretary of Cherepanovsky RCP(b) uyezd committee.

Resolved: To send the original, as a historical document, to the CC RCP(b) and to keep a copy in the gubkom.

Comrade Ravdel will have a talk with comrade Pigilev, upon his arrival.

Letter to State Political Directorate (GPU) representative in the 62nd Novorossiisk Artillery Regiment, signed by Nudolin, 6 December 1922 (copy).[233]

---

233   In February 1922, the State Political Administration (GPU) replaced the Cheka, and then became the OGPU in 1923 with the creation of the USSR. Lower-level political police

I am sending to you a letter written by Medvedev in Moscow. He is one of the 22 of the Workers' Opposition from the Tenth RCP(b) Congress. I found the letter in a book, which I checked out on 3 November from the library of the Zakamensky raikom. The title of the book is volume 4 of *Russian History* by Pokrovsky, third edition, published by Tovarishchestvo Mir.[234]

Nudolin, RCP(b) member, 62nd Regiment, 6 December 1922.

27   A.G. Shliapnikov's Correspondence Regarding the 22, March 1922

Statement by A.G. Shliapnikov about the Letter of the 22 to the Comintern[235]

In order to prevent unscrupulous interpretations of information, which I provided to the Commission of the Comintern, I briefly exposit here the basic features of what I said at the session on 3 March of this year.

I appeared at the commission at noon, as was suggested. However, a simultaneous session of the Executive Committee (Ispolkom) permitted the commission's session to open only around 3 p.m.

Immediately upon the opening of the commission's session, I declared that I am not a representative of the 22 signatories and that I would only speak on my own behalf, as one of those who signed. Besides that, I requested that the commission invite a member of our party's CC, who has been especially appointed to conduct the case on the declaration of the 22 comrades. The first statement was taken under consideration, but the second request was categorically rejected, despite my insistent wish.

Before moving on to the essence of the problems, which we posed in the letter, I explained in the following way the reasons impelling us to take this path of appeal to the Comintern:

1)   In appealing to you about the problems worrying us, we want to avoid discussion and its consequences, which in current circumstances can

---

administrations were still called GPU. See Hagenloh 2009, Glossary and pp. xvii–xviii. The term GPU was often used interchangeably with OGPU.

234   Mikhail Nikolaevich Pokrovsky (1868–1932), a Russian Marxist historian, wrote a five-volume history of Russia while in exile in France. It was first published as *Russkaia istoriia s drevneishikh vremen* (Moscow: Mir, 1910–13). A second edition was published in four volumes in Moscow and Petrograd in 1922–3 by Gosudarstvennoe izdatelstvo. I am not sure to which edition Nudolin was referring. For Pokrovsky's biography, see Enteen 1978. Pokrovsky's history has been published in several English translations.

235   RGASPI, f. 17, op. 71, d. 3, l. 5.

weaken our party, and likewise accusations of creating a pre-Congress 'platform', factionalism, and so forth.

2) We consider it necessary to warn the International Communist centre about the troubled state of the united front within our party and through this to achieve painless settlement of intraparty disorders, without drawing the broad masses of party members into struggle.

After this explanation, the conversation led to arranged questions about 'goals of our appeal to the conference of the Ispolkom of the Comintern'. On each point I gave explanations, and likewise answered the questions of commission members.

On the first point, about how our party is threatened by loss of its unity with the proletariat, I pointed to the enormous difficulties in which we landed because of the protracted character of the development of the international revolution. The position of the broad masses of the proletariat is extraordinarily difficult. Wages in enterprises of heavy industry fluctuate at around 20% of those before the war. On this basis, dissatisfaction grows and strikes occur. The New Economic Policy deepens this dissatisfaction. Moods of workers in the factories and plants differ from those, who you see at our festive assemblies and parades. Such a condition among workers is a direct threat to the United Workers' Front in our country.

On the second and third points, I pointed to the dangerous phenomena of the noticeable social degeneration of the RCP(b). I illustrated the personal composition of the party by using statistical data from the materials of the CC Secretariat.

In order to illustrate the decline of the role of the proletarian element in the RCP(b), I provided data about the composition of gubernia committees (gubkoms) and secretaries of gubkoms, which I received from the CC's organisational section. These data point to the outright physical ouster of workers from leading party bodies. Information on the RCP(b) purge supports the same impression. I introduced the protocol of the meeting of chairs of party verification commissions in Tsaritsyn gubernia, which I just happened to have. The slogan 'proletarians to the work benches' creates an analogous situation for workers, who work in state bodies in elected or appointed positions. Many Soviet institutions are losing their last few remaining proletarian personnel.

On the last point, which related to the party's internal life, I introduced some facts both from my personal practical experience and from our common knowledge about the decline of party work and of interest in the party and its affairs, about the bureaucratisation of work, about the struggle against heterodoxy, and about persecution for simple expression of disagreement with one or another action of accountable party bodies.

After this, I read aloud four points of practical proposals, after which I was asked some questions. I make note of the two most important ones.

The first question concerned my attitude to the New Economic Policy. My answer can be summarised as recognition of its necessity, but simultaneously I declared that I observe an insufficiently attentive attitude to large state industry. As proof of the latter, I introduced incidents known to me of giving orders abroad for manufactured goods, which could have been performed significantly less expensively in our country. I declared that I consider such an attitude toward the needs of our industry, which exists without circulating capital, as undermining our economy and as graphic evidence of the absence of workers' influence over the economy.

The second question addressed my situation within the party and in the CC RCP(b). To this I answered by stating the facts of my removal from trade union work, the distancing of me from party work, the trial for my speech at a factory cell, and the Moscow Committee's ban on inviting me to assemblies. Belonging to the CC RCP(b) does not guarantee that my letters are not intercepted and seized. I informed them of an incident of which I had learned regarding the search of a courier, confiscation of a letter addressed to me, and its conveyance to an interested person by the bodies of the Cheka.

Following me, comrade Kollontai briefly gave some information. I resolutely deny that she said what was attributed to her, about 'strikebreaking by Red Army soldiers', about boycott of elections and so forth. I did not hear such speeches at the commission's meeting.

With comradely greetings,
A. Shliapnikov

∴

Letter from CC member A.G. Shliapnikov to the CC RCP, Moscow, [7?] March 1922.[236]

Declaration

In view of the fact that the appeal to the Comintern about the problems relating to our intraparty abnormalities has assumed the character of a 'trial [процесс] of the Workers' Opposition', I bring to the attention of all members of the Central Committee the following:

---

236   RGASPI, f. 17, op. 71, d. 3, l. 8, copy.

1) There is no organised faction behind the appeal to the Comintern. I was personally invited to the commission and there I declared that I do not represent the remaining comrades. I gave explanations personally on my own behalf.

2) My explanations touched only upon those questions, which were published in *Pravda*, under the title 'Goals of our Appeal and so forth'.

3) I resolutely deny that odious character, which is imparted to some of my answers to the commission's questions. I spoke of no uprisings. I spoke only about how the grounds for dissatisfaction are enormous and it sometimes pours out in the form of strikes.

4) There was no talk about a search of me. This is an obvious misunderstanding. I informed that there was a search of a courier, who was bringing a letter to me, a member of the CC RCP(b), that the letter was seized, and that many letters have been lost. This illustrates the absence of mutual trust.

5) The question about locomotives emerged in response to their question regarding my attitude toward the New Economic Policy. I declared that I acknowledge its necessity, but I think that we don't worry enough about our large industry. Having made concessions to the peasant, the speculator and the lessor, we do not fortify industry with circulating capital. Instead, we send abroad large-scale orders, which could be fulfilled at less cost in Russia.

6) I have not yet obtained the protocol of the testimony.

7) They rejected my proposal to hear me in the presence of a CC representative.

∙ ∙
∙

A.G. Shliapnikov's statement, Moscow, 10 March 1922:[237]

Yesterday evening, citizen Rumynov visited me and brought with him a German comrade, who introduced herself as Goldshtein.[238] I know Rumynov as a person who took part in the 'knocking together' [сколачивание] of a fourth international (personally I'm not acquainted with him). Considering his role

---

237 RGASPI, f. 17, op. 3, d. 280, l. 15, 13 March 1922.

238 The grammatical forms Shliapnikov uses to refer to Goldshtein have feminine endings. 'Citizen' was a form of address applied to those who were not Communist Party members ('comrades').

in this affair rather reprehensible, I did not receive either of the arrivals and I suggested to Rumynov that they leave my room.

Today, 10 March, yesterday's guest came to me, but alone this time. She declared that the KAPD sent her here in November of last year to make contact with the 'Workers' Opposition'. Along the way, her mandate was taken away from her.

She informed me in conversation that an international conference of a fourth international is expected very soon. Representatives are expected from Holland, England, Bulgaria, Yugoslavia, Canada, and South Africa. The 'Workers' Opposition' is also invited. To this invitation, I answered orally that there is no 'Workers' Opposition'. The tendency which they know abroad and which occurred before the Tenth Congress is neither a special faction nor a special party. It never existed as an organisation. I emphasised again my own negative personal stance toward a split in the Third International.

At this Comrade Goldshtein informed me that within the KAPD there is also a tendency which opposes the creation of a fourth international. She asked me to answer her question in writing. She also expressed the wish that I should clarify the matter of the Workers' Opposition in the press, so that the Germans should not have false ideas concerning us. To this I answered that I could write only with the permission of my party's CC. I also refused her invitation to communicate and correspond with organisations, which are hostile toward the Third International.

A. Shliapnikov

∴

Letter to A.G. Shliapnikov from CCC Secretary Krivov, 22 March 1922.[239]

Comrade Shliapnikov,

The CC requests that you answer the questions, which follow below, in the course of two days. On the basis of your signature on the appeal of 22 comrades to the Comintern:

1) What kind of data did you have for presenting accusations against leading centres of our party of waging unrelenting demoralising struggle particularly against proletarians, who permit themselves to have their own

---

239   RGASPI, f. 17, op. 71, d. 3, l. 9, copy.

opinion, and of applying repressive measures against them for expressing their opinion in a party milieu?

2) Why did you not pose this question to your party, the RCP(b), for preliminary discussion?

3) Doesn't each of the [22] comrades think that such an indiscriminate accusation against the leading centres will weaken the party and lead to its split?

4) Are those who signed the appeal going to obey the Comintern's decision condemning this act and how do they understand this decision?

5) Don't the comrades think that such an appeal in fact and formally is a group appeal and don't they think that it is a violation of the Tenth Party Congress decision about party unity, points 2, 4, and 5?

With communist greetings,

Comrade Krivov

∙ ∙
∙

A.G. Shliapnikov's answer to Krivov's letter.[240]

To the CCC RCP(b)

Dear comrades!

On the evening of 22 March, I received your suggestion to provide written answers to questions, which relate to the appeal of 22 comrades to the Comintern. I make haste to satisfy your desire fully on each point, but at the same time I consider it my duty to point out that the CCC is taking on a matter unusual for it, one which bears an exclusively political character. Besides that, the case of the 22 has already been decided by the Comintern and thus is not subject to re-examination by lower courts.

On the first point, I can indicate many cases of persecution, which I can remember, namely:

1) dispersal of delegates of the Tenth Congress and of entire organisations, which supported the platform of the Workers' Opposition at the Congress; 2) the behaviour of the CC during the Fourth All-Russian Congress of Unions; 3) the division of metalworker communists at the Fourth All-Russian Congress

---

240 RGASPI, f. 17, op. 71, d. 3, l. 10, undated copy.

of Metalworkers into 'loyal' and 'disloyal', which was totally unjustified, and struggle against workers who were 'former supporters of the Workers' Opposition'; 4) dispersal of personnel of Nizhegorodskaia gubernia for 'heterodoxy'; 5) dispersal of Petersburg personnel (Uglanov and others) for disagreement with Zinoviev; 6) dispersal of Briansk personnel and persecution of worker-communists of other uyezds in the same gubernia; 7) dispersal of Nikolaevsky personnel for dissenting from the CC of the Communist Party of Ukraine; 8) The case of the Kiev metalworker union personnel, who were removed for speaking out at a party assembly; 9) Lobanov's information at the metalworkers' congress about persecutions in Donbas, about the annulment of the elections to the conference, about the Cheka participating in elections and meetings, and so forth; 10) The case of Bauman district, the dispersal of personnel, the defamation and searches of an apartment where communists were gathering to celebrate the new year; 11) the case of Safarov and others; 12) Miasnikov's case. I suppose this is enough. Undoubtedly you have in your files many more materials than I have in my memory.

Reports about the course of the RCP(b) purge also gave us much data, but you also know this information well.

To the second question I can inform you that I both personally and jointly with others tried to place some questions before the CC RCP(b), but we did not meet with the attitude we desired. I personally considered it inexpedient to appeal to the party rank and file, for it could have entailed discussion and accusations of the desire to create a 'platform'.

On the third point, I can say that the Bolsheviks never were afraid to reveal their sore spots. The accusations are rather concrete. Elimination of the reasons, which call them forth, will help the party to become stronger and more unified.

Fourth point. I never violated the decisions of congresses either of our party or of the Comintern. I understand it as it is written.

To the fifth question, I can answer that I don't consider the fact of appeal as violating the decision of the congress about unity. Even a collective appeal does not signify the creation or the existence of a faction or of a closed group with its own platform. Each communist has the right to appeal to the party and to the highest international centre, both separately and together. In my opinion, this cannot serve as a violation of the second point. Even less can you speak of a violation of the fourth point. Our letter was not a platform. It was not our fault that there was no discussion leaflet and the like. It is the same regarding the fifth point of the resolution. There is faction, just as there is no factional criticism.

In addition I attach a letter regarding the declaration of the 22, which was sent to supplement the materials of the Comintern. I still have not seen the protocol of my conversation with the commission. They say that it does not exist. Besides that, I am sending an excerpt from the register of the Central Commission on Improvement of Workers' Lives (Tsenkomuluchbyt) listing files sent to you, in order to refute the 'slander' published in the CCC's name in *Pravda* on 7 March, as if I did not appeal to you. This does not include the cases and statements of comrades, which I personally sent to you. Also these do not include the Nizhegorodsky, Briansk and other cases. I think that the CCC will correct its mistake and will place a retraction in *Pravda*.

With communist greetings,
A.G. Shliapnikov

∴

Letter to the Comintern referenced in A.G. Shliapnikov's letter above, undated copy.[241]

Goals of our appeal to the Conference of the Executive Committee (Ispolkom) of the Comintern

To warn the CC RCP(b) that the policy it is implementing threatens the party with the greatest dangers.
1.   Loss of the party's unity with the proletariat.
2.   Weakening of the role and influence of the proletariat, both in the party and in the bodies of government power.
3.   The full social degeneration of the party, as an inevitable consequence of these phenomena. Degeneration is already noticeable within the party.
4.   To caution the CC RCP(b) that the procedures [режим] established within it in fact lead, in current circumstances and given the current social composition of it, to workers' mass departure from the party and to amplification of the role and influence of nonproletarian elements in it.
Toward the goals of protecting the party from the dangers indicated above, we propose that it is urgently necessary:
1.   To secure for the proletarian composition the leading posts in the party and soviets and actually carry out mass attraction of nonparty workers into direct government work.

---

241   RGASPI, f. 17, op. 71, d. 3, l. 12.

2. To propose to the CC RCP(b) to actually implement the decisions of the Tenth Congress and worker democracy in the party and trade union movement.

3. To secure actual freedom for intraparty criticism, without which it will be impossible to revive party life, develop self-activity, inculcate initiative, and raise the general level of consciousness and of conscious discipline of party members.

4. To cease persecution for displaying heterodoxy both in the party and in official soviet procedures; also stop discrediting worker communists by categorising any worker's disagreement with decisions from above as 'anarcho-syndicalism'.

28   **Party Central Control Commission (CCC) Questioning of the 22, 17 March 1922**[242]

Krivov asks those present the following questions:

1) What kind of information did you have for accusing leading party centres of waging unrelenting demoralising struggle?

2) Why did you not pose this question before the RCP for preliminary discussion?

3) Doesn't each comrade think that such an indiscriminate accusation against the leading centres will weaken the party and lead to its split?

4) Do the comrades who signed the appeal support the Comintern's decision condemning this act?

5) Do the comrades think that such an appeal in fact and formally is a group appeal and do they think that it violates the congress's decision or that it is a means of unifying our party?

6) Why didn't the comrades appeal beforehand to the CC or CCC?[243]

Solts: Is it possible to explain precisely how the comrades understand subordination to that decision, which the Comintern made? Is it in the sense of forbidding them to further speak out and defend that which they defended, or will they just take this decision into consideration and nothing more?

Krivov: Polosatov stated that he submits to the Comintern's decision but considers it incorrect. If necessary, he thinks it will be possible to speak out in

---

242   RGASPI, f. 589, op. 3, d. 9103, vol. 3, ll. 97–106, partial transcript. It is not clear how many signatories attended this meeting.

243   These same questions were asked of Shliapnikov earlier (see above).

defence of this appeal. Therefore the CCC could not comprehend how this could be obedience to the Comintern's decision.

Medvedev: I do not understand why all of us were summoned, if you are asking questions of each one separately. It should have continued as you began, by summoning each in turn, because it makes no sense for for us to sit and listen to how each comrade will answer. If you think that you need to set up an interrogative process of each in turn in the presence of all, then it is one thing. If you think that this CCC session has as its goal discovery of a criminal offence, then let's exchange opinions on those questions which were put forth. We have no basis for keeping silent rather than answering, if only the first question, but if you attach a judicial evidentiary character to your session, I will refuse to answer the first question, because I think that if you take the criminal point of view, then this is one path, if [line missing]. I would like for this session not to bear the character of a judicial investigation.

Sedoi: ... Tell us your concrete accusations.

Ozol: I think one person can answer the first question. The other questions are clear enough that it will take two words to answer ... As concerns the character of this session, let's allow that this is an interrogation, but indeed the CCC is the highest body, which can compose questions.

Medvedev: in criminal acts.

Ozol: There's no criminal act here. The question concerns party life. The CCC conducts comradely conversations with all comrades.

Krivov: We invited you all here so as not to drag out the questioning. We invited a few separately, because they were from the provinces and had to leave. This is a party matter, not a criminal one. You can answer orally or in writing, as you wish.

Smidovich: ... Our goal is not to punish but to investigate party life and the reasons why such a phenomenon appears and from where the dissatisfaction emerges. ... We'll take such paths so as to avoid a split.

Medvedev: If Smidovich's answer is that of the entire commission, it satisfies me. I have no reason to hide anything.

Kuznetsov: Inasmuch as comrade Smidovich poses the matter so, then the CCC's questions fall away, for we have already advanced your inquiries in the area of party life. If we were not defendants here, then we would not be asked questions and they would have fallen away. Here the matter should be set up differently. There should be a different approach toward illuminating the question that interests everyone and forces us to make a statement.

Solts: We are the CCC, which the Congress authorised to worry about party unity. Maybe you also worry about this, so you made a statement. ... The difference between us and you is that the congress assigned this to us ... We discuss what kind of foundations you had, if there is a basis and so forth. The circumstances in which we carry out conversation, as comrade Medvedev said in his opinion, is criminal. We clarify the question as the CCC, not like a group of comrades accidentally gathering who would like to discuss this question. ... Comrade Shliapnikov told us that you are not a group and that each one of you answers for himself. We are interested in knowing the opinion of each of you. ...

Borisov: I think that each word spoken here is not just in the character of a simple conversation, but bears significance on a scale that goes beyond Russia. Therefore, I want first of all to get to the essence of things and to clarify if I correctly understand the questions posed here.

Medvedev: Comrade Solts's statement about how the CCC wants to clarify the question personally from those who submitted the statement, places this question on the plane of either an accusation or a clarification. If it is an accusation, then there is nothing for us to talk about. Like Comrade Borisov, I'm interested in knowing if the CCC wants in a clarification of the motives behind the declaration. Do you think that there is a crime here, because we supposedly disorganised the unity of the party and violated the decision of the Tenth Congress?

Solts: If we already had a definite opinion, we wouldn't have called you here. ...

Krivov: Let the comrades answer the main questions here orally, then in detail in writing .... We never decide in advance of calling comrades if they have violated party discipline ....

Medvedev: They tell us that we made the declaration contrary to the usual order, that we bypassed the CC by going directly to the Comintern. Here you can sense some sort of accusation. I should say that these questions were clear to us from the very beginning. We knew that giving our declaration to the Comintern does not to any degree violate party discipline or party unity. Confirmation of this is the CC's decision, which says that it does not contend the right of individual comrades to appeal to the Comintern as to the highest court [инстанция]. We understand that any member of the party has the right to make a statement to the CC, without fearing any violation of party discipline and party unity. We also think that our statement characterising the Party CC's methods of work and some aspects of its policy cannot in any degree be a violation, since it is addressed to the highest communist court. The Politburo's decision is confirmation that we are not making a mistake. Regarding the second question, if by making this appeal we had by one iota violated the decision of the Tenth Congress about unity, we would not have made this step. Personally I was very sure that nothing of the sort could be seen in our appeal to the Comintern. If you saw in this a violation, you should have informed the commission of the Comintern about this. We regard submitting such a statement to the Comintern as in no way violating the unity of our party, since we appealed to the highest body. You say that the very content of the letter weakens the party and provides the possibility to use it for counterrevolution. It's necessary to say that our appeal was directed to the Comintern. If it was printed in *Pravda*, where everything is printed with the consent of the leading centres, who found this possible to print, well we cannot be judges as to how necessary this was or was not. This is the business of the Party CC. It allowed publication, and it was not we who gave the counterrevolution the opportunity to print our statement. We did not have in mind that it would become accessible to the entire world. The CCC wants to clarify what foundations did we have and materials. If we had collected all the materials, we undoubtedly would have been transformed into an apparat, but in that is the misfortune that we cannot formally collect materials. We collect them in a very haphazard way, but even so the materials are very weighty. I will allow myself to introduce one such piece of material: 'General assembly of RCP members of the Railway District'. It says that here, from 7:30 p.m. until the morning, debates were held, in which senior comrades members of the gubkom, and the presidium participated. As a result, they accepted a resolution, which rejected the accusation against us of sympathy for anarcho-syndicalists and which confirmed that the facts set forth in our letter are true. But numerous facts could prove that intransigent opponents of the Workers' Opposition are expelling dedicated workers for heterodoxy. They declared that each RCP member should confirm that the facts laid out in the Letter of the 22 actually exist. Here is confirmation of that which we accurately wrote in our letter. I personally have even more very clear confirmations, which could be sufficient material. Contrary to our desire, our appeal has descended to the very depths of the party. We received from those depths [низы] that which I just read to you here.

Our party political practice serves as material attesting to how leading centres conduct intransigent, demoralising struggle. Why stick your heads in the sand? Indeed, don't you know what was done in Zamoskvoretsky district when Zemliachka was there? She struggled against the heterodox. I would like to say more regarding our attitude toward the decision of the Comintern. For me, I think that it is unconditionally obligatory as a decision of the highest communist court, and I think that other comrades unanimously will confirm the same to you.

Tell me why the decision of the highest communist court does not satisfy a lower court, which wishes to talk more and outline measures. We heard that a directive has been prepared and given about excluding us from the party. This does not scare us one iota. I declare this for myself personally and on behalf of others. Our attitude is that we all think this decision is obligatory. How can we say what reasons could force us not to carry it out? We will do so until we are excluded from the communist party. But while we remain members of the party, we consider the demand of the Third Communist International to be obligatory for us.

Kuznetsov: I have almost nothing to add to Medvedev's statement. The comrades have the facts. Well, what more reasons could there be? You do not want to study them. What is being done in the Donbas, what was done with the Briansk organisation, where 10 years were spent on the creation of an organisation? It was literally dispersed in the most unceremonious way. An old organisation was reduced to complete ruin.

Solts: Who reduced it?

Kuznetsov: Two or three cc representatives. We don't need to furnish documents. It is not at all difficult to obtain them. Comrade Medvedev can vividly paint the picture why we cannot be patient any longer. Do you really think that one should be indifferent to the departure of workers from the party? We are not indifferent to this. It was a matter of indifference for those sent from the cc to the provinces. As concerns your statement about presentation of materials, well we of course cannot present to you statistical materials, since we are not a formal organisation. We can talk on the basis of personal experiences. Take me, I was torn away from the grassroots [низы] and sent to Tsentrosoiuz. This cannot help but act in a [illegible] way. This served as a reason for submitting the declaration. I signed knowing the decision of the Tenth Congress. In all seriousness, I will say that I could not help but do this. For me, as an old member of the party, the Comintern's decision is obligatory without hesitation. I had to sign the statement, although this was against discipline. Here is why we did not go through the authorities [начальство]. We heard this expression very many times. They say the idea is correct, but you didn't go through the authorities. Right now workers are withdrawing and we could not pass by this in silence. Those who in the past were dilettantish, parasitical elements have made their way [докатились] to the very top, among the bosses [верхушки]. We see especially often in the provinces a person, who never created anything, but who is promoted up among the bosses and begins to command. Take the experience of the [L]ugansk organisation. The best comrades don't want to work in the Communist Party. This could not help but act upon our psyche and force us to make a statement. Take the Congress of Metalworkers in April and May. Maybe the CC does not know what was done there. If undesirable communists landed there, then in various ways the election of desirable persons was achieved. Some such phenomena took place not long ago in the Donbas, where there was the gubernia conference of metalworkers, thanks to the fact that elements undesirable to the gubernia party committee ended up at the congress ... Such suppression of a certain part of the heterodox cannot be passed by in silence. I spoke out in Gorodskoi district and on the next day everyone was talking about it and pinning labels. All it takes is for a comrade to point out those mistakes which are made in our party, for tongues to start wagging. We are worn out physically and morally.

Solts: Do the comrades think it possible to continue to defend that which they wrote ....? Can they say that they consider their statement to have been a mistake?

Borisov: In view of the fact that comrade Solts finds that the questions are essentially not being answered, I think that the question needs to be posed in such a way: will we retract that letter, which we signed? Is this the opinion of the entire commission or not?

Solts: I don't demand that you retract it. I want to know what you mean when you say the Comintern's decision is obligatory ....

Bruno: Comrade Solts indicated that the CCC was created to support the party's unity. But each member of the party should put his mark [обозначивать] upon it. When the question surfaced about signing the statement, it was this way for me personally. We all worked in good conscience on the party purge during the past year, in accordance with the party's decision. Yet when I arrived here, I was crestfallen. I saw that everying that was written about the purge just remained in writing. When I see workers and I see what is done within the party, I know that there is a difference in our party. There are alien elements in the party and we in the provinces purged them. I was sure that we were conducting the purge from a class point of view, in order to get a core of more class-united people in the party. This was not fulfilled. They told me not to approach the instructions in a formalistic way, when I referred to its points as correct. No matter whom you meet with in economic work, everywhere there is the same opinion. Recently our party members have found the most severe conditions for work. In the Donbas and in Nikolaev, you can see workers departing. I feel that if it will continue so, that the best will leave the party. That is the reason why we did not carry out purge work to the end. As concerns the question about higher ups who engage in intrigues, I know that this is cultivated in the provinces more than anywhere else. Our leading centres have paid insufficient attention. Some personnel became bankrupt and they were transferred to another place. In signing the declaration to the Comintern, I thought that the question should be examined in the main leading bodies, rather than carry it to those further down, in view of the general difficult position in our country, so this was done. When I read reports about the Comintern in the newspapers, I saw that all parties but ours were analysed. So I considered it necessary to issue a warning, so that the Comintern would seriously and impartially discuss this question. I thought that we worked as much as possible. I thought that many party bodies in the provinces were violating instructions and deviating from them on the purge, but were supported in this. I thought that once the phenomenon would become [line missing] to the proletarian elements the leading role in all our life. The attitude toward our statement brought about dissension. I see abuse of our comrades, who have been activists for decades. Agents in the provinces carry out such a policy. If there will be such a policy, discussion will yield no results. Polemics brought about fatal dissension. From my point of view, the Comintern did not pay sufficient attention to the views of all comrades who signed the declaration; some aspects remain unilluminated. Nevertheless, I consider it obligatory. We did not conduct any kind of factional policy. I stated this everywhere. What does this decision mean? Indeed we should be mummified. If they will persecute each of us, then I don't know what we will do. Must we close our mouths for good? I don't know then. The third point indicates that this will lead to a split. It is absolutely not so. After publication in *Pravda*, there was a split, but this is not our fault. This cannot worry us.

A. Medvedev: Longtime party personnel have noted the demoralisation of our party organisations in the provinces. Already in 1920 in Briansk district, there was such extensive disintegration that in October Stilmkhovich and I submitted a statement to the gubkom and the Party CC. But declarations lay on top of each other and did not go anywhere. This statement pointed to the violation of union discipline, about assignment of deputy commanders (zamkoms) and secretaries of entire districts and about the creation of district committees (raikoms) just in order to put in place their own leaders. Glebov just recently started to write here to the centre. I appeared as a member of the town verification commission. Suddenly I was removed from the commission without the agreement of the gubernia verification commission. Moreover, it was proposed to replace me with another. The gubernia verification commission directed the opposite. All work was re-examined. They appointed another member of the verification commission, but with the same result. When 11 comrades submitted a statement, they were suspected of disloyalty. Right away, the gubernia committees (gubkoms) were mobilised. A statement was sent for the signature of about six comrades. The majority of workers did not belong to any kind of Workers' Opposition. Therefore, it is impossible to speak about how a certain tendency is here. Here we depicted in detail the situation of the Briansk organisation and asked to send a commission there. With great difficulty, we achieved dispatch of the commission. It reached the gubkom from the railway station. It held a session. After two or three days, without having reached the worker cells, it went back to Moscow, having acknowledged that we are troublemakers [склочники] and so forth. Following right behind our mobilisation, a campaign began against the rest. You should receive a statement by Kozlov, who left the party. He depicts how a campaign was waged against the factory committee (zavkom). The gubkom and uyezd committee (ukom) were displeased with him and replaced him against the wishes of the masses. Here is a copy of the statement of the authorised person [уполномоченный] in the ukom. /reads the statement/ from the CC of the Metalworkers' Union. The ukom decided on 9 February to reject the petition. When comrade Kozlov was rejected, he petitioned about entering Briansky [factory], yet they sent him to a different factory. Further, there is Slabkov's [sp?] statement about departure from the party, only because he was mobilised. He submitted to mobilisation, but the CC decided to return him to the factory. For this, they started to consider him nonparty. Bylychev states similarly that they all remain not only beyond the bounds of the party, but also of the factory. Next come reprisals. Comrades leading the gubernia verification commission exclude eleven members of the party for anarcho-syndicalism [reads decision of Lizdrinskaia [sp?] organisation]. The CCC reinstated three and directed them to the Kirgiz republic. Material about work in Briansk gubernia could not be gleaned in full, but in any case there is enough to characterise the situation there. At our gubernia party conference in the beginning of 1921, workers were in the majority. As a result, some personnel were transferred. Comrades Stankov and Gutin were sent to other places. Contrary to the will of the conference, two other comrades remain. The party organisation decided to send Deniukhov [sp?] to the workbench, but instead, with the help of comrade --ykov [illegible], he was assigned the task of working out a three-year programme in our district. A definite campaign was waged to disrupt all the work of the gubkom. Zorin, upon arrival, first of all began to divide people into groups. Moreover when composing lists, he said that certain types could not be members of the gubkom. He declared that if Medvedev will be elected, then the CC will not confirm the gubkom. Zorin did not set up work right, so they sent Glebov, and you know what he did. Where to turn? Statements were directed to the CC RCP and to the CCC. The result was that the Briansk organisation was destroyed. Instead of 800 [?] party members, there remained 25 [or 125?] and those submitted their resignation, because it was impossible for them to consider themselves party members any longer. As a result, theses will not pass. They do not believe any statements about democratism. Comrades who were selected to the gubernia level do not know how to get work going again. I am leaving you a copy of my statement about the reasons why I signed the declaration to the Comintern.

Borisov: All the questions posed were posed in general. I should say that the Comintern's decision is binding for me and I submit to it. That formulation, which here was commented upon, shows some differences between the original version and that which was published.

Solts: [asks something difficult to decipher]

A. Medvedev: It was incorrectly translated [?].

Borisov: On 7 March, the press wrote that a small group [кучка] of people had gone too far, had lost everything, and so forth, and that any honest worker should say if he is with them or with the RCP and the Comintern. At that time, the CCC had still not decided whether we are a small group of people who have gone too far and the like. Therefore, the Party CCC and CC should say that this is not completely true yet. The CCC wants us to clarify whether we became confused and what was the reason. But indeed, the CCC adds to our concerns, when it declares that honest workers should say who they are with, a small group of people who have gone too far or with the RCP and Comintern. Comrade Sedoi talks about a faction. I ask myself, does any assembly that gathers to discuss a matter without informing party bodies bear a factional character? While the party has been legal and in a leading position, I have known and still feel I know that any meeting of communists to clarify any question is not factional as long as it does not call itself a faction or act like a faction. Therefore, I think that CCC members should declare outright that we are a faction. If they want to clarify something, well they push in a certain direction. Is there a definite, formed opinion behind your questions about our statement, or do you actually want to find out our motives from the materials in hand? I cannot imagine how you could ask about submission to a decision, which has already been taken by the Comintern. If it were otherwise, we would have come and said that we are leaving the party. That is how I can answer comrade Solts's question about how we understand submission to the decision.

Kollontai: The first basic question was about what moved us to submit the declaration. It seems to me that our conversation today already shows that the declaration pursued the goal of making our comrades seriously think about the difficult situation, which exists now. The CCC will answer that it is wonderfully well-informed about the situation, that they already knew long ago everything in the declaration of the 22 in general features. Just in the declaration, it is laid on thick [сгущаются краски], but it is nothing new. Yet what made the declaration necessary was that our higher-ups lack the desire and will, despite being well-acquainted with what is happening. In our own party, such a regime has been established that our ideologically conscious comrades often lose the possibility to direct their own party. If 22 comrades decide to make a declaration to the Comintern, it means that something wrong has built up in our party. As one joining in solidarity, I speak for myself and I think that I express the opinion of all comrades, in saying that I signed because I thought that they are spokesmen about the sore spot that is in our party. Obviously our comrades already tried out some measures, before they had to resort to submitting a declaration. This appeal was brought forth by the desire to force our party higher-ups to think long and hard about what kind of situation there is. I dread to think that our conversation here will not be in a comradely manner and that the entire question of the signatories has already been decided in advance. If it is not predetermined, then I should state that the declaration was called forth by the necessity to warn our party and by such urgent measures to force attention to be turned to the troubles [нелады] in our party. There are the definite points about what summons this. Why was our party raised against these 22 comrades? Did they formally violate the decision of the Tenth Congress? As an ECCI member, I have seen a party minority appeal to the Comintern many times. In the Comintern, we have often investigated relations among various parts of a party. This led not to the split of a party, but to its unity.

Appeal to the Comintern usually did not signify an effort to bring about a split, except for those instances when the Comintern itself considered it necessary to cleanse a party of some element or another. So formally there was no violation here. What's the matter? What called forth our comrades' dissatisfaction? It seems to me that the entire problem is that in our party the regime has become so entrenched that even in one's own circle it is impossible to state those facts, about which we talk separately. If I came individually to CCC members and employed just the same expressions, all of them would have acknowledged separately that there are such facts, that there are intriguing higher-ups, and that they struggle against this. The CCC struggles with this. It has sufficient materials in order to remove these higher-ups. It means that the matter is about more than just such facts. The entire question is about the extent to which the entire party regime and its atmosphere support these dark phenomena. The party struggles against them, but something is not right in the party's regime. Our declaration pointed to the mass departure of workers from the party, which means workers' influence on the party is declining. Statistics say that workers are 44% of the party in the majority of industrial gubernias. Indeed this shows that something is not right in the party. We need to investigate this together, yet we have reached the point that when we gather to meet, we are suspected of threatening to split the party and undermine its authority. If we had in fact carried out the decision of the Tenth Congress about freedom of criticism and worker democracy, then this declaration would not have come to be. Next, regarding the question about party unity, was there an effort toward a split? Obviously, if there had been such an effort, would it really have been necessary to the Comintern? We sought another path, because of our fear that dissatisfaction grows in our party. It's necessary to reflect upon this and investigate it together.

Comrade Krivov interrupts and asks if the question was discussed in advance in the party.

Kollontai: The declaration was made in one or another form, not in the form of materials, but as separate facts. Each of the comrades, just as I, had made appeals. Struggle was waged by speaking at conferences. Comrades spoke out separately, not like a group, for such a group does not exist. There was no such group. You pose the question as if a group existed. I joined in solidarity with the full conviction that it was necessary to appeal to the Comintern, as to the highest court [инстанция]. If the appeal had been to the CC of the party, the CC would have examined it and pronounced a general phrase, 'we know this better; we know all these facts'. I thought that the CC, having recognised that all this is so, does not make it possible to delve thoroughly [углубиться] into these questions, to investigate and discuss them. Someone's influence was needed in order to show how serious is the situation. These means were supposed to turn deeper attention to all these questions.

Regarding the last question about the attitude to the Comintern's decision, each separate party member must take account of this as an accomplished fact. Frankly [по совести], I think that the decision was accepted hastily. I also declared in the Comintern that they should return the question for reexamination, since I think the decision is premature. But since it already took place, I will submit, inasmuch as each member of the party supports a decision taken by the party, although he does not agree with it. But the fact that we submit to an individual decision does not mean that this problem is overcome. For me, this is too serious to force us not to speak on this question. For me it is most important that the declaration should serve as a stimulus toward a more serious attitude toward the questions we have raised.

Pravda has published articles about how young people end their lives due to being cut off from the masses. The masses do not strive to enter the party as if it were their home. This does not happen. Something needs to be done. Each of us should think and speak. Closed mouths are not needed. There is no need to say that the party has split or that people who speak up are a faction. They are thinking about what needs to be done and how to do this. If everything remains just as it was, can I be silent? No. If the Comintern will demand from me that I fall silent, I will answer no. I will always struggle against what we see as wrong. You cannot demand this. Our own party demands active interference in all types of incorrect phenomena. At large assemblies, of course, I will not speak out and struggle against the decision of the Comintern. But I will continue to struggle against any fact of that type to which our declaration pointed, if it will take place within the party.

Solts: .... Any party member has the right to appeal directly to the Comintern. But we ask them to act in the party's interests.

Mitin: First of all I will answer the question, which comrade Solts posed regarding my supposed entry in 1902. I should say that beside my signature on this declaration, I wrote that I have been a revolutionary since 1902, but I wrote in the declaration that I formally joined the RSDRP Bolsheviks in 1920. ... I have just come from the Donbas, where I worked two years without interruption. I have seen leading bodies, including local gubernia organisations, behave in a demoralising way. During the party purge, it was proposed to exclude some prominent personnel. One of them carried out a definite line of the Tenth Congress and won over the masses, so his exclusion from the party was raised. The motives for excluding him were that this party member, who is a worker, has great influence over the nonparty masses and leads these masses. An old party comrade said this. The gubernia commission excluded him from the party. But then he was reinstated and transferred to economic-administrative work.

Solts: About whom are you speaking? Who did they want to exclude?

Mitin: Me. I speak about facts from the Donbas. Because of intrigues, they exclude a longtime communist from the party. Instead of this, he remains chair of the local cell. At a general meeting, no one speaks out in favour of shedding light on the question. They remain silent when faced with each question. They send a certain comrade to work in the economy as a factory manager. The local gubkom chair does not accept him, because such people are not needed in his gubernia. Kalnin, the Chair of the Miners' Union, reached the point that he published a circular letter to all enterprises, instructing them to seize the party organisation. They decided to exclude him from the party. We did not know the reasons.

Very longstanding party members constantly wave their hands declaring that elections for the presidium of trade unions are never held and people are elected according to directives. For example, Shliapnikov was elected as a delegate to the All-Russian Congress of Metalworkers. Because of this, they dispersed the gubernia conference. Completely in despair, workers already did not participate in the second elections. I submitted a declaration to the CC of the Communist Party of Ukraine and did not get any result.

I don't think that our declaration will lead to a split, for I think that each split is counterrevolutionary. But an underground organisation exists in Nikolaev, no matter how sad this is. You ask if I feel bound by the decision of the Comintern and how so. Comrade Solts asks: will these comrades again submit a declaration, will they act out as a group, and will there be groupings? Maybe from tactical considerations such a grouping will not act out, but the unhealthy phenomena which we have in the party demand to be brought to the attention of the commanding part. I signed the declaration in full awareness, for I saw the impact of this upon all work in the Donbas.

Tolokontsev: If you will recall how the meeting proceeded, there was definitely discussion of whether this step will entail a split of the party. Everything here was weighed and reckoned. We decided that from our point of view, this step would not lead to the party's split, but instead would strengthen the party. We did not at all expect that this matter would be revealed to the nonparty masses. I will not dwell on the political part of the question, since I participated more in economic organisation. They say that the party is degenerating and that proletarian elements are not attracted to it. I have a document about 22 foreign agreements, which are unprofitable orders for the Russian Republic. These are orders for locomotives and so forth. How would you regard such things? It should be from the point of view of the worker, who in 1920 asked to give him leave to return to the work bench. And who is [кто-же] Lomonosov? This matter has colossal significance for us. This is one of the most enormous inadequacies of our general political work, when the question is posed whether give the order to Russian factories or foreign ones. If they will say that this is a political maneuver, well it is an unjustified one. In Europe, there is not only industrial capital but also commercial capital. I saw that 35 million gold rubles were overpaid in two weeks. With such a policy, is it really possible to create a proletariat? Indeed, because of this agreement we transferred two years of our production programme abroad. This was at the same time when our factories stood still. Indeed at some point we will not have circulating capital. This decision deprives 100 Russian factories of the right to repair locomotives. We had to go to great efforts recently to occupy the Commissariat of Transport (NKPS) factories with this. All the same, I do not make such statements at mass assemblies. We are not called upon to lead high policy, but to those of us who have a close-up perspective on such business, it hurts very much when we see that this policy does not strengthen the proletariat. We lose heart. Our point of view is that first of all, manufacture in Russian factories needs to be proposed. Only if that is not possible, then transfer it abroad, but we are circumvented. With the excessive gold expenditures, it would be better to buy necessary food supplies for the proletariat and so strengthen it. Indeed, with our money they give orders to nonexistent factories, which demoralises the party. Indeed, I am not an aggrieved person. I have many ranks [чинов], but when the question concerns actions, which kill the proletariat, then I can't keep silent. How can you ask what kind of materials we have, when overpay for foreign orders is equal to 70 million puds of bread? I appealed to the Politburo through [P.A.] Bogdanov.

Beklenev and Borolin think it sufficient to answer in written form.

Smidovich: ... You speak of agreements concluded in 1920–1. Our party aims to strengthen the dictatorship of the proletariat on a worldwide scale. We have always been concerned about the global interests of the proletariat. If we only followed the interests of our country, then we would not be communists. ... We do not suspect you of desiring a split, but you act just like you want one. The fact of going to the Comintern did not violate discipline, but it is important how you did so. Going there with such a note as yours is committing a political mistake. Comrade Kollontai knows how necessary is our party's prestige in the international movement, that it unites and rallies foreign parties. To instil doubt in our party by giving the impression that it is demoralised reduces the revolutionary character [революционность] of foreign parties. ... You ask why it was published. Yes, indeed, it should not have been published. What kind of impression will this give women workers, among whom comrade Kollontai enjoys such influence? How will your declaration act upon such people? ... We know some workers are leaving the party. The main danger we face is that we had to make an economic retreat, and many don't understand this necessity. Therefore, there is disillusionment in the party. This is why they leave the party, yet you explain it differently. In Samara, there was the Workers' Opposition, and how did it behave? It jailed its opponents. We retreated and our link weakened. At this moment, it was necessary to be especially careful. ....

Sedoi: Indeed, we've worked closely with comrade Chelyshev for eleven months. Not once have we heard a word from him, until suddenly this happens. What is this? This path leads to the creation of special groupings and factions. The group of comrades behaved impermissibly among us in relation to other comrades. They make accusations against small organisations and what happened there in Samara? We did not publish this. Responsibility to the party forced us not to publish it. Why should they curse the CC, because Milonov of Samara demoralised the party to such an extent that only 3000 of 13,500 remained? I saw the result of this. For six months after the congress, nothing was done there. People were put in prison there. What happened in Perm and in Vyksa with comrade Solovev? They say he was removed. Removed how? When I, your humble servant, arrived from Nizhny Novgorod, I left him in place. Chelyshev signed my decision about Samara, Nizhny Novgorod, and Vyksa. I think that those groups, which were closer to Moscow and which knew how struggle is conducted, intentionally did not inform comrades, in order to submit a declaration. If I were in your place and had thought that the higher-ups demoralised the party, I would not have sat together with them. There was a faction here. It was necessary to create the atmosphere of a minority.

Solts: ... If you had said that our CC took bribes for orders made through Lomonosov, then it would be another matter. They made a mistake, they were wrong. They went to the Politburo, which did not understand and signed an unprofitable agreement, but what relation does this have to the Comintern? There are no secrets. ... We have not even had one disagreement with Chelyshev. They say the higher-ups create intrigues, they talk about Piatakov. But what did he do that was criminal? He thinks that these higher-ups interfere with the development of a production programme .... Your statement is a political act against the party. We have not had such an incident in the party. Our way has been to eliminate our misunderstandings among ourselves. ... You knew that your declaration would be a political scandal. You could not seriously count upon receiving an answer to the questions which cause us pain. ... You should have foreseen that you would gain nothing from such a declaration to the Comintern, but would only compromise the party. How could you not understand that this would harm the party? They spoke here about Nizhny Novgorod. At the gubkom session, they were all workers. Comrade Korshun was such a worker. I told him that he acts incorrectly. How is it possible to speak here about some kind of higher-ups? Here two groups of workers were involved. The committee likewise evaluates the act [выступление] of the railway workers. In my opinion, it was not necessary to insist upon transfer. Indeed, two groups of workers often struggle so. But you make it sound like 60% of party members are intelligentsia and that higher-ups from the intelligentsia aimed to exclude workers from party command posts. In Briansk, likewise, two worker groups struggled against one another. ... For example, we sent a group of workers exclusively from the Workers' Opposition to Poland. It spent 1 ½ months there and carried out there such a bag of tricks, so as not to take second place to anyone else. You don't say anything new. We say that it's necessary to find places for workers and you say the same thing. ...

Ozol ... The comrades say that there are some serious flaws in the higher bodies, but they don't offer one word on how to correct them .... From the CCC archives, I could extract a mass of similar material, more than you could imagine. From your statement one can conclude not that we struggle against flaws, but that we create them.

Medvedev: You shield the system which leads to such facts.

Ozol: You think that we here have no right to sit in the CC and CCC.

Medvedev: The Congress elected you. I did not vote.

Ozol: I said at the Tenth Party Congress that you can't correct Medvedev and Kollontai by means of the Congress's decrees. This is temporary compulsion. ...

Comrade Kollontai says that she will not obey and that she will unmask [speak out]. The other comrades say that she is right.

[Text ends here, but it is not clear if the session ends.]

29   Letter from V.L. Paniushkin in Support of Shliapnikov and Medvedev, on the Eve of the Eleventh Party Congress[244]

... When I left the ranks of the party during the time of the Tenth RCP Congress, a mistake which I have since acknowledged ... comrades S.P. Medvedev, A.G. Shliapnikov, Pravdin and others at that time categorically condemned my departure. Criticising me severely but in a comradely way, they pointed out to me my senseless step .... When I had already left, they called on me to return, pointing out to me the harmfulness of my act, as a symptom of a party split, the unity of which they always considered the chief bulwark of the revolution. ... Then I parted ways with them. I condemned comrade Shliapnikov and others for their ... indecisiveness[245] ... I thought it important to state this, now that these comrades are being discussed.

30   N. Kopylov, 'For a United Party'[246]

Unexpectedly for those who signed it, the appeal of 22 comrades to the Executive Committee of the Comintern about the United Front within the RCP(b) was treated as no better than 'high treason'. All you have to do is look over the Comintern's resolution or the lead article in the 7 March edition of *Pravda* to dispel any doubt. But really, did the '22' (and there were not only 22 of them) intend to discredit and undermine the authority of the RCP(b)? Was there any deliberate slander in this 'complaint', as our appeal to the Comintern is classified over and over and with calculated intent?

I think that no one should deny that a serious and well-considered appeal by a group of workers to the highest body of the international proletariat, which is organised in a communist way, should be taken more seriously.

---

244   TsA FSB, R33718, d. 499061, volume 41, l. 22, handwritten, signed, undated. Excerpts translated here. The letter was directed to the Eleventh Party Congress commission investigating the 22.

245   A letter from him was published in the newspaper *Rabochy*, no. 11.

246   The CC RCP(b) published this among other articles in a 24 March 1922 discussional leaflet prior to the Eleventh Party Congress; see also RGASPI, f. 48, op. 1, d. 33, ll. 2–3.

Despite any resolutions issued by highly authoritative bodies, facts remain facts, irrefutably. Is it a fact or not that at the past Fourth Congress of the Metalworkers' Union, its central committee was selected [by the party leaders]? Is it slander or fact that nonproletarian elements dominate our party ranks overwhelmingly? Is it malicious fabrication by former, good-for-nothing 'dignitaries' [сановники] or fact, that there are hardly any workers among the leaders of local party organisations? Is it a fact or 'left SR chatter' that for a long time already a functionary [чиновник] spirit has made our party ill, and that all the medicines, which various RCP(b) congresses and conferences have prescribed for it, are not in stock? Hasn't it been a long time since we talked about the party's illnesses? Didn't we have a 'purge' a long time ago so that, like criminals on the run,[247] we could deny any trouble in the ranks of the RCP(b) and shift the blame to those comrades, who dared to say aloud that with which each comrade in the depth of his soul cannot agree?

Those who signed the declaration to the Comintern did not at all think about initiating 'struggle' with the RCP(b). This is an extremely unscrupulous and monstrous perversion of what is essentially an honest, revolutionary effort by a group of personnel to treat the illnesses, which eat away at the organism of our party, and to achieve unity in its ranks not just as a formality, but for the sake of iron-willed comradely cohesion.

But maybe the 'so-called' (a stupid irony!) Workers' Opposition (why did this corpse, buried by the Tenth Party Congress, need resurrection?) is nothing more than a herd of deceived people, who 'former dignitaries have made fools of'? Is it possible that the authors of the 7 March *Pravda* lead article, in complaining against comrades Shliapnikov, Kollontai, and Medvedev, on whom they bestow the title 'chiefs' of the Workers' Opposition, consider all the rest just simply representatives of 'less steadfast strata of the proletariat and of unreliable elements of our party'? It is most strange that the 'steadfast' orthodox communists turn out to be the legalists, the 'twenties generation' [двадцатники], and petty bourgeois types [мещанские], but not the proletarian elements of our party.[248] How is it that old party veterans, some of whom have

---

247   He uses the term Иван Непомнящий, literally Ivan who doesn't remember to whom he's related, which was a reference to tsarist-era escaped convicts who tried to conceal their identities.

248   By legalists, Kopylov probably meant those social democrats (mainly Mensheviks) who had disavowed underground work between the 1905 and 1917 revolutions and carried out only legal political activities. It is more difficult to decipher the meaning of the term 'twenties generation', which is my translation of двадцатники. It could refer to those who joined

been in its ranks for more than twenty years, have suddenly become unhinged and come close to betraying the international proletariat?

Of course, it's possible to celebrate noisily about how easily victory was won over an 'anarcho-syndicalist sect', but one shouldn't fall into foolish raptures to such a degree, lose one's head, and talk oneself into such absurdities, as does the author of the *Pravda* lead article. To listen to him, it's as if the Workers' Opposition is nothing other than the branch office of the firm 'Chernov, Martov, Miliukov & Co.', and that its representatives still stroll about freely, only thanks to the Cheka's unpardonable negligence.[249]

What is this in actual fact?

'They can exist only by grumbling and playing the oppositionist game. For them, it is the most attractive part of the old bourgeois-democratic regime, which they would like to salvage in Soviet Russia'.

The 'so-called' Workers' Opposition, no matter how much they make fun of it, is more than 90% workers, who are old members of the underground organisation, who struggled for years to achieve the triumph of the dictatorship of the proletariat. Yet, the *Pravda* lead article's malicious, stupid, and unscrupulous irony transforms these workers who appealed to the Comintern into mediocre followers of Chernov and into knights and worshippers of that rotten old lady the Constituent Assembly [старушонка-учредилка].

Not bad for polemical tricks! Further along, it gets even worse! Blame for 'Kronstadt' is bestowed upon the 'unhinged political intriguers'!!! Indeed, is this not cause for amazement: 'Our party will not forget the lessons of Kronstadt, where peasant elements who lacked political consciousness gathered under Left SR, semi-anarchic, semi-Kollontaist slogans with the goal of opening the doors to counterrevolution'. There are some things, which are so absurd, wild, and ridiculous, that it seems useless to argue against them! It is just sad that a professional journalist writing in the press organ of the CC RCP(b) in the name of the entire party, lost his head like a Gogolesque town mayor [городничий], and sees everywhere around him only White Guardist pigs' snouts, without going to the trouble of trying to distinguish between White Guards, who are distorted by spasms of spite, and comrades, who are devoted to the party with

---

the Russian Communist Party in 1920–2, when it was already clear the Bolsheviks would or had won the Russian Civil War, so these late joiners were suspected of having joined only for self-serving reasons. Another possible definition is petty functionaries. (Thanks to Gleb Albert, Aleksei Gusev, Lars T. Lih, Simon Pirani, Timofei Rakov, and Aleksandr Reznik for discussing this with me.)

249 SR ideologist Viktor Chernov, Menshevik leader Iulius Martov, and Constitutional Democrat (Kadet) politician Pavel Miliukov.

all their heart and soul and who sincerely suffer acute pain on account of all those disorders, which disconnect and destroy the old spirit of comradeship in the ranks of our party.

Is it really more noble to play the role of a cunning slave, a toady, and an obsequious yesman, who at all times follows the bosses' orders by saying black is white and shouting 'Hurrah!' during a fire? There are moments, which demand special exertion and sincere unity, in order to implement consistently all resolutions of the Tenth RCP(b) Congress, which designate measures to liquidate abnormalities in our party's life.

How could the party's central press organ nudge people to depart from the party, if it can be so expressed! How otherwise to evaluate such pearls, for example: 'Not having any ideological baggage, this opposition, understandably, does not even dare to think about departure from the party ... Be off with you, frankly, develop your policy openly before the working class without abusing the name of communist, but we in the RCP(b) will struggle against you with all our might and we will see who will have the victory'.

Rude, stupid, and excessively candid. It emerges that *Pravda* (the article is unsigned) regrets that the Workers' Opposition does not leave the party and does not advance any ideological disagreements. Besides that, they claim that this is due solely to poverty of thought and the absence of theoreticians and men of letters, who would take it upon themselves to formally elaborate the ideological disagreements, which *Pravda* sees as implied or understood.

Indeed, it is as if nothing other than 'Left SR chatter' were behind the name of this ill-fated 'opposition'. Then there is this nice candour, threats, and counterposing of the '22' to all the rest of the RCP! Indeed, it seems that the '22' have still not been excluded from the party. You can't represent the matter as if the 'Workers' Opposition' (those signing do not call themselves this) already went over to the other side of the barricade.

To write so, to place the question so, means in advance to force events into a certain spirit, which someone finds desirable, and to suggest to the authors of the appeal to the Comintern a tactic, of which they never even dreamed. We have identified ourselves with the party too long to leave it so easily. No, we are not oppositionists by profession. We are not a herd made into fools by 'one or another dignitary' [сановник] or 'one or another woman writer'. We act openly and we do not employ the name of communist as just a cloak [missing text].[250]

---

250   The lower right-hand corner location of this text is torn away, so some phrases are missing here.

Neither cowardice nor fear drives the opposition's refusal to call party policy incorrect. The opposition in fact does not disagree in principle with the RCP(b) line. That against which the 'opposition' struggles was condemned in many resolutions at the Tenth Party Congress and at prior party conferences. Only party higher-ups' lack of desire to understand the true character of the opposition leads to such awkward distortions of its goal. It is not a coincidence, of course, that some oppositionally-oriented workers within the party still are not organisationally united. The collective concept of the Workers' Opposition, which has now been resurrected and not by us, does not have the same content, which it had on the eve of and during the Tenth Party Congress. Those who have now come together have done so exclusively on the basis of rejecting and struggling against abnormal things in our party's life. Otherwise, they are too diverse to build a faction and are even less likely to create a new party. Indeed, there is not the slightest need for one.

The politics of inflaming passions and of making a mountain out of a molehill does not lead to anything good.

They push a group of RCP(b) members onto the path of a split, but not one old member of the party will take this path. They can't be allowed to cast a struggle for unity in the party ranks as if it were a struggle 'against the RCP(b)'.

The 'so-called Workers' Opposition' is not a faction, a new party, or some sort of well-designed whole. By no means is it a handful of Left SR-type chatterers and political intriguers, but it is a share of party members, who are vitally connected with the party. They are flesh and blood of the organised, revolutionary worker masses' flesh and blood. Those who courageously fought under the banner of the united communist party, both when it was persecuted and then when it was in power, do not deserve defamation, contempt, and a manifestly uncomradely attitude expressed toward them. He who lays it on thick in representing the struggle for a united party as a struggle against the RCP(b) intends to suppress voices of protest against patently abnormal things in our party's life.

We are for the RCP(b) and not against it. One proves that one is a revolutionary not by words but by actions. Only through the eyes of a bureaucratic [казённый] patriot can healthy criticism of unhealthy things be regarded as counterrevolutionary. For an old member of the party, struggle against the RCP(b) would be the same to struggle against one's own mother.

Of course, the moment could come, when the RCP(b) could become completely different from what it was and what it should be. (Remember the 'cleansed' comrades). But then we will speak in a different way. Right now, comrades who intentionally try to struggle against the RCP(b), rather than struggle against those who soil its glorious revolutionary banner, deserve only severe condemnation.

31   Eleventh Congress of the RCP(b), March–April 1922, Published
      Speeches at Open Sessions, Unpublished Speeches at 2 April 1922
      Closed Session, Published Resolution and other Materials Relating
      to the Former Workers' Opposition[251]

Preface by editorial commission: Due to a series of reasons, publication of the
protocols of the Eleventh Party Congress was delayed. Chiefly, this was because
stenographic reports of the protocols were not corrected by the authors themselves during the congress and the reports turned out to be in an unsatisfactory
condition (with inaccuracies, omissions and so forth). The editorial commission was unable to address some of these inadequacies. Consequently, the text
of the published protocols has not only lacunae in the form of insufficient corresponding quotations, but also some forced abridgements, some inaccuracies
and so forth (p. 3).

[Session one opens during the daytime on 27 March 1922. Lenin declares the
congress open.]

∙ ∙
∙

Session three, 28 March daytime session. Tomsky chairs.

[Miliutin, Ioffe, Shumiatsky, and Stukov speak.]

Shliapnikov (pp. 101–9). The Tenth Congress buried the Workers' Opposition.
But since its death, not one assembly or congress has passed without mentioning its name. This is done despite the fact that, as we heard our party
secretary declare authoritatively yesterday, we now have no groupings or factions. But obviously someone needs to create this Workers' Opposition. True,
Vladimir Ilich said yesterday, that this name needs to be changed now. We
cannot protest against this. You named it, so you can rename it. Right here
yesterday Vladimir Ilich said that we are sowing panic and that panic needs

---

251   RKP(b) 1961, pp. 101–9, 186–9, 244–5 (Shliapnikov), 118–21, 160–2, 191–6 (Medvedev), 196–
       201 (Kollontai), 325–9 (Kiselev), 450–3 (Kutuzov), 465–7 (Korzinov) 577–80 (resolution
       about some members of the former Workers' Opposition), 702–10 (Eleventh Party Con-
       gress Commission report about the Workers' Opposition), 748–56 (9 August 1921 CC
       plenum protocol, 15 February 1922 directive on Miasnikov, official notes, resolutions, and
       protocol); RGASPI, f. 48, op. 1, d. 14, ll. 14–24 (Kollontai), ll. 50–64 (Shliapnikov), ll. 65–7
       (Kubiak), ll. 126–31 (Medvedev). Zorky (ed.) 1926 published excerpts of some speeches.

to be fought with machine gun fire. This is already the second time I have heard this and have sensed machine gun fire aimed against me. Right now both machine gunners are sitting side by side. There they are, those machinegunners. (Laughter.) Ever since the Tenth Congress made me a hostage of the Workers' Opposition in the CC, they often judged me there. Back in August, when I was on trial in the CC,[252] Comrade Frunze promised to use machine guns to convince me of what was right. But we will speak more carefully. These pictures involving machine guns remind us of the history of other revolutions. True, there weren't yet machine guns then, but there were skirmishes among the vanguard of the revolution (not of communists, there were none of them then either). Everyone knows what this led to. I think that it would be best if we would not make reference to machine guns when we talk to one another.

There is panic now, but who created it? Our work creates panic. Comrade Stukov, who spoke before me, fully confirms this. Why does panic really occur in an army or anywhere else? In the army, any detachment starts to panic when it loses touch and when it does not know what is happening around it. It is exactly the same in the party. When party detachments lose touch and don't know what's going on and where they should go, then panic is what you get. We do have panic in the party right now, because the party as a whole, living organism does not participate in political life. As an illustration of this, I can introduce cases when among senior personnel in the Moscow discussion club[253] speeches ring out, which really have a panicky effect on the strata of workers who are in the Moscow party organisation.

---

252   Editors' footnote: He means the CC RCP(b) plenum session on 9 August 1921, with the participation of CCC, where on V.I. Lenin's suggestion it was discussed whether to exclude A. Shliapnikov from the CC and from the party.

253   Editors' endnote: The Moscow Committee of the RCP(b) organised a discussion club in August 1921. According to the 29 December 1921 decision of the Secretariat and the Bureau of the MC RCP(b), discussion clubs were created likewise in the districts of Moscow (see Archive of the Institute of History of the Party of MC and MGC KPSS, f. 3, op. 2, d. 29, l. 14). Among their tasks was discussion of party building, soviet building, and the economic policy of the Soviet Republic. Soon, however, various oppositionist groupings started using the tribune of the MC RCP(b) discussion club for propagandising their views. The CCC discussed the matter about the discussion club, established that 'recently discussions in the club have assumed a demagogic, unparty-like character', and recommended to the Moscow party committee to 'direct particular attention to the club's work'. On 20 February 1922, the Politburo of the CC RCP(b) examined the matter about the discussion club and recommended to the MC to do everything possible to make the discussion club 'an actual club for discussing questions of interest to the masses.' See also A.A. Solts's report for more on the discussion club (this edition, pp. 173–4).

I can tell you about some cases, when they discuss there questions, which go all the way up to leasing out Soviet power. People express notions about how it would be better for us to lose power now in order to take it anew after ten years. Not long ago they came to an understanding that had monstrous assumptions in regard to the CC. Unfortunately, the matter concerns the Genoa Conference. Therefore, I will not say what happened there, I will only note that for two days in a row, senior Moscow personnel discussed some questions. Discussions essentially led very nearly to accusing the CC of high treason. That's where the panic comes from. Panic is born from lack of information and absence of contact, directives, and leadership.

Next, one shouldn't forget that right now we are experiencing a collapse. I myself experienced and observed such a decline in 1907. When I arrive at our assemblies of senior personnel, oh, how it reeks there of 1907! We remember the moods of the intelligentsia and of the nonproletarian elements, which were close to it in those times. How much one is reminded of that time now! Our senior personnel, including comrade Lenin, comrade Kamenev, and others, provide the grounds for these moods. I made the rounds of several gubernias and I know how party members were confused by the lack of agreement about what mistakes have been made. When you speak about mistakes, you have to be precise or say nothing at all, since mistakes are supposed to teach us something, and not leave us in a fog. In that formulation, which we heard, mistakes cannot be instructive. In connection with the New Economic Policy we observe a reevaluation of values and quests for a different base of support, which would be a new [social] buttress outside the proletariat. The latter development calls forth alarm and it worries us to a high degree.

What have we seen and heard lately? They said to us that we workers, worker power, and the proletarian government, are in debt to the peasant (muzhik). This expression, which was made at the December party conference, acquires the political meaning that we should be the cheapest government possible for the peasant. Alongside this, they forget that we can only be an inexpensive government at the expense of the working class. Cheap government costs the proletariat dearly, for it leads to physical degeneration. All this troubles the minds not only of party members, but of all workers.

At the last Moscow conference,[254] Comrade Kamenev depicted NEP as a maneuver of the socialist revolution. He prefaced this with the thought that for the party there is no dogma either in relation to the old, or in relation to

---

254   Editors' endnote: He means the Eighth Moscow Gubernia Conference of the RCP(b), which took place 23–5 March 1922.

the new economic policy. This is not true. We have some dogmas, which were in the old economic policy. Under it, the socialisation of enterprises, the abolition of private property, and the introduction of universal labour obligations were carried out. There were also many other 'dogmas'. At that time, we tried to speak out against several 'dogmas' on labour questions. We were not against labour obligations, but against the system of labour armies. At that time, comrade Tomsky had had enough of comrade Trotsky. I had had enough of so-called 'freedom of labour', which they attributed to us because we warned then that these labour armies could not be symbols of our faith at all. They answered us that this is an inviolable dogma. Dogmas in the past were strong. If we want to get rid of dogmatism, then we have to proceed a little differently.

Current maneuvers in economic policy push us toward seeking a 'firmer base' than that which we have had up to now, while we still depended on the working class for support. At assemblies of senior personnel, I very often hear very unflattering opinions about our own class, of which we consider ourselves the vanguard, by people trying to justify the quest for new bases of support. Vladimir Ilich said yesterday that the proletariat as a class, in that sense which Marx had in mind, does not exist. Allow me to congratulate you [plural] with being the vanguard of a nonexistent class. They say that our proletariat is becoming declassed and that it has radically fallen behind. If you listen to comrade Kamenev's honey-tongued speeches, then it turns out that even the leading worker of Moscow expresses the interests of landowning peasants. At the December party conference, he declared that even our advanced Moscow metalworkers speak in the language of peasant interests. According to the words of comrade Zelensky, which he uttered at a conference in Moscow, the New Economic Policy generates proprietary instincts among workers.

Now you should add to this sum what the CC distributes in its informational letters about the working class, where it characterises those strikes which have occurred in some places (read the last letter, the eighth one). You will see there that the Zlatoustinsk strike and the strike of Briansk workers are the work of monarchist hands. When they tried to verify this by asking metalworkers about it, then it turned out that the strike was not the business of monarchists. Instead, it occurred because we did not supply workers or pay them their wages on time. Such an attitude toward workers forces one to suspect that by depicting the proletariat in uncharacteristic ways, comrades seek justification for political maneuvers and for seeking support in other social strata. Senior personnel speak such thoughts directly.

We are saying to the congress that the danger of principled differences threatens us. Up to now, we haven't had differences of principle in the party.

Now there is the danger that such differences may appear, because of the attitude taken toward the working class. We would like to hear from Vladimir Ilich how he regards such a type of ideological maneuver, which is a re-evaluation of values and a distorted evaluation of our activity. It's necessary once and for all to remind you that we will not have a different and 'better' working class. We need to be satisfied with the one we do have.

Vladimir Ilich circumvented the main question, which is about building socialism in large-scale industry. We hear more speeches about how we are indebted to the muzhik. The party is called upon to help the muzhik and to help the agricultural economy. The question about the need for union [смыкание] between industry and agriculture (peasant economy) is posed correctly. But this union [смычка] is not only the free market. Indeed, also the peasantry is not a unified whole. The peasantry is differentiated. In helping the landowning peasant, we should know how to help him who already ceases to be an owner. We have not found an answer to this from Vladimir Ilich.

Then there is the question, which worries all of us here. This is a question of extraordinary importance. For having had one doubt about it, I came to be tried by a court. This is the question about how it seems as if we are steering the car, but we are not going where we want to go. How is it, Vladimir Ilich, that this happens? These peculiarities occur because we sit too far from the chauffeur of our revolution, which is the proletariat. Can't we sit a little closer? Then there won't be such a lack of coordination, and we will go not where we are led, but where we need to go.

Our largescale industry has been cruelly neglected, for which I rebuke our CC. The attitude toward industry was beneath contempt. Official speeches discredit our proletarian base, which in practice translates into complete disdain toward our largescale industry. Just ask any director of our largescale factories and plants, of large glavki, and of large trusts. Everyone will confirm this. Vladimir Ilich spoke yesterday about largescale, mixed enterprises and about agreements which we concluded. The metalworkers sent me agreements. It is unknown who concluded these agreements, which bypass the economic bodies. There are 22 agreements for orders placed abroad for the approximate sum of 300 million gold rubles. Moreover, the gold went for objects, which could all be fully produced in our own country and two or more times more cheaply. That is the reality.

Comrade Miliutin said just now that we are suffocating for lack of circulating capital. They advance the slogan to learn how to trade. We have many who trade. It might be that we should even get rid of some of them. Yet the matter is not about merchants, Vladimir Ilich, but that the state of the market is such that it beats us down. We cannot hold out. We need money now. In pursuit of it, we create such anarchy even on the shortage-plagued [голодный] metals market that the sale price does not recover the cost of meager wages, so low have prices for manufactured wares fallen. Prices for metals, in comparison with bread prices, stand thus: metal in Moscow is about 2.5 million per pud, while bread costs 5 million per pud. Earlier these ratios were that one pud of metal was equal to a minimum two puds of bread. This is a difference of 400%. If you take even the norm during the famine year of 1892, then this difference is approximately 200%.

Thus, it emerges that the matter is not just that we don't know how to trade, or as some say, that we don't know how to manage. No, the problem is that we don't have the resources with which we could manage. For lack of capital, we are forced to close our factories. Yet this capital is given to Sweden, Germany, and a little to England, in order to construct new factories in which they will build locomotives for us. This occurs at a loss to our republic and lacks any kind of political sense. A stop should be put to this. Otherwise, we'll come to the point when factories and plants will emit smoke everywhere, except in our republic. Here I have very telling documents about this.

Chair: Your time has expired. Who is in favour of extending comrade Shliapnikov's time? For five minutes? I ask for a show of hands. Comrade Shliapnikov, continue your speech.

Shliapnikov. I will read to you this document, which was sent to the Politburo. It encompasses 22 agreements.[255]
1) Five agreements for one million puds of metal tyres for the sum of 8,434,665 Swedish crowns; that is eight-and-a-half crowns per pud.
2) Four agreements for 1300 puds of rails and ties for 50 dollars per ton; that is for the sum of 1,078,500 dollars, or one ruble and 66 kopecks per pud.
3) Five agreements for 372,000 puds of iron pipes; the price is in Reichsmarks and Czechoslovakian crowns.
4) Two agreements for 237 tons of copper pipes and brass pipes; the price is in Reichsmarks.
5) Three agreements for 1700 locomotives for approximately 144,000 rubles each.

---

255 Shliapnikov's interpretation of the agreements had a political goal. For a more objective and scholarly treatment of the agreements and to understand the context behind them, see Heywood 1999, p. 191. I am grateful to Anthony Heywood for help translating some of the specialised terms for railway equipment in Shliapnikov's speech.

6) Two agreements for 1500 tanker wagons for 750 British pounds sterling and 3925 Canadian dollars per tanker wagon.

7) One agreement for 200 locomotive boilers for around 40,000 rubles per boiler.

Glavmetall has no information about how close to being fulfilled are those orders, which have already exceeded deadlines.

Metal tyres

Around one million puds of these were ordered for delivery within a time frame, which our factories would find acceptable unconditionally. The productivity of Sormovsky and Kulebaksky factories alone is two-and-a-half million puds per year, not counting Dneprovsky, Briansky, Lugansky, and Taganrogsky factories. Undoubtedly, the price of four rubles and 25 kopecks, not counting the cost of transport, is inflated. It suffices to say that before the war, it fell to lower than one ruble and 50 kopecks per pud.

Even considering current changes, it would have been possible all the same to fulfil [these orders] for half the foreign price. Thus, at least around two million gold rubles were lost on this order. By the terms of the contracts, the agreements should have been concluded by now.

Rails and ties

One thousand and three hundred puds of rails and ties have been ordered.

The delivery times would be acceptable for our factories, because any of the southern factories, such as Dneprovsky, Russko-Belgiisky, Donetsko-Iurevsky, Iuzovsky or Saldinsky and Nadezhdinsky, could fulfil the order completely.

The price of one ruble and 60 kopecks per pud is not exaggerated, but is acceptable, reckoning with the current moment.

Before the war, rails cost up to one ruble and 12 kopecks per pud. From a cautious position, it is possible to consider the order not to be unprofitable in a monetary sense.

The agreements should have been concluded already.

Iron, copper and brass pipes

All these orders for pipes could be fulfilled in our factories, but not in such short time periods. It is difficult to say anything regarding the price, since the agreements are concluded in such banknotes as Reichsmarks and Czechoslovakian crowns, the currency of which fluctuates and is unknown to us.

The agreements already should be concluded.

Locomotives

One thousand locomotives were ordered from a Swedish factory and 600 locomotives from German factories through Swedish brokers.

A time frame of five years undoubtedly would be acceptable for our factories, given that our own factories can fulfil orders in less than five years [sarcasm]. The price, not considering the cost of transport and other overhead expenses, is around 144,000 rubles per locomotive, not taking into account that Swedish locomotives are paid for at cost, with an additional profitable sum of interest on the employed capital [занятый капитал] that was advanced, but not less costly than 140,000 gold rubles. German orders are not conditional upon the cost of manufacturing price [себестоимостью не обусловлены], and in this is their advantage.

The price is overstated at least twice, even considering existing conditions.

The prewar cost of manufacturing price of such a locomotive was around 42,000 rubles, and the sale price was 52,000 gold rubles.

According to Gomza's calculations, even taking account of the 20% rise in the price of materials, the manufacturing cost price of locomotives in Russian factories would not exceed 75,271 gold rubles with a 60% work intensity [интенсивность труда].

Thus, about 110 million gold rubles were overpaid for the order of locomotives from abroad.

Tanker wagons

One thousand and five hundred tanker wagons were ordered at a price of about 7,500 rubles per tanker wagon.

Such tanker wagons of the type taken from abroad were not made in Russia earlier. Therefore, it is impossible to give a precise comparison, but probably it is possible to say that the price is one and one-half times more expensive than before the war.

Delivery times are brief. They are seven months in all, which our factories could fulfil under normal conditions and under the condition of building a tank of our type.

The type of tanker wagons, which have been ordered from abroad, differs very much from ours. Therefore, you have to have special spare parts for these tanker wagons.

It is possible to calculate that 3,750,000 rubles were overpaid on this order.

Locomotive boilers

Two hundred boilers were ordered for a price of 797,000 pounds sterling. Considering the weight of the boiler type to be 185,000 puds, it comes out to about 43 gold rubles per pud.

Considering the prewar price to have been around seven rubles per pud, then 36 rubles per pud or 6,660,000 gold rubles were overpaid.

Delivery times would be difficult for our factories but acceptable.

Thus, not taking pipes into account and calculating conservatively, we overpaid 122,410,000 gold rubles.

Payment conditions were unprofitable for us. For the main order of locomotives, tens of millions of payments were made in advance in the form of interest-free loans and were issued for several years. Deposits were made at 20–25% of the price of manufactured wares. Further payments will be made as items are manufactured. All this creates very favourable conditions, which our own factories do not enjoy.

The chief evil, which still has not been overcome, is that when comparing prices between foreign factories and our factories, they desire to calculate the gold ruble according to the Narkomfin exchange rate, which lags at least three times behind the actual rate. For only this reason, we cannot so far compete with foreign orders.

If Glavmetall were to be presented with the same sums as those paid out abroad and for the same time period, our factories could turn production around, fulfil a huge majority of foreign orders, and cope with manufacturing locomotives without any special difficulties.

[signed by:]
Sudakov, member of the VSNKh Presidium
Tolokontsev, Assistant Chair of the Glavmetall Collegium
Tugarinov, engineer and Assistant [Head] of the Gomza Technical Section
Lepse, Chair of the All-Russian Union of Metalworkers central committee
Pudalov, Engineer and Director of the Production Section

This, comrades, no doubt clearly illustrates the situation, in which the vehicle of state goes not in the direction we would like it to go, although we are at the wheel. This document here is signed by VSNKh Presidium member Sudakov, Metals Department Assistant Director comrade Tolokontsev, and other comrades. I don't think that Vladimir Ilich can say that they are poorly informed. A Politburo decision was demanded in order to get this information. Only then did the door open and make it possible to receive these agreements. This clearly indicates that we need to sit closer to the chauffeur of our revolution. Then the vehicle will not be steered in a direction where we don't want to go. In conclusion I have to say that in our country, such things often become a weapon of the opposition. Don't think also that I saved this especially for the congress. No.

The apparatus of state management has to be improved by serious means in order to struggle against bureaucratism. A more attentive attitude and more trust toward one another are needed.

It would be preferable if Vladimir Ilich would define more precisely toward whom he wants to apply the methods of struggle against those who spread panic, about which he spoke. I also think that he recognises that we did not create this panic. If he means the appeal of the 22 to the Comintern, well we appealed not to a maneuvering army, but to the Comintern. A maneuvering army could only have learned about it through *Pravda*,[256] which is edited by CC appointees. If by this they created panic, well sure, panickers should be put on trial. (Applause.)

[Larin and Manuilsky speak.]

Medvedev (pp. 118–21). Comrade Lenin essentially did not present an annual political report about the CC's work. He delivered a very instructive political speech, which contributed something new toward explaining the New Economic Policy. Nevertheless, it was not a report as one ought to be. All the same, the CC for the course of a year carried out a definite line in all areas of our policy: industry, transport, agriculture, food supplies, finance and all other areas. What does this experience tell us? Vladimir Ilich told us nothing about experience, although in our opinion it is interesting. Vladimir Ilich's speech here at the Eleventh Congress bears all those features, which have already accompanied his speeches over the course of a rather long time.[257]

I take here an instruction about the problems of economic work, which very distinctly expresses the line, which was dictated to all economic bodies at the Ninth Congress of Soviets.[258] Our Party CC dictated it. It says, 'the Con-

---

256   Editors' endnote: Apparently he means no. 53 of *Pravda* from 7 March 1922, in which was placed the lead article 'Decision of the Comintern on RCP questions' with an evaluation of the antiparty essence of the 'Workers' Opposition'. In this issue were published: the statement of the 22 to the Comintern, the CC RCP(b) report about the Politburo's decision on this question, the resolution of the expanded plenum of the Executive Committee of the Comintern, the resolution of the RCP(b) faction of the Fifth All-Russian Congress of the Metalworkers' Union, and the CCC report.

257   Editors' footnote [not endnote]: According to the archived stenographic report, there follows further: 'During each major event – at a party congress, at a congress of soviets, at a conference – we hear everywhere, no matter how strange this might seem to us, but for some reason Vladimir Ilich constantly stands at attention before the tasks and needs of the peasant masses' (TsPA IML, f. 48, op. 1, ed. khr. 4, l. 146).

258   Editors' endnote: The Ninth All-Russian Congress of Soviets took place in Moscow 23– 28 December 1921. A total of 1991 delegates attended the congress. There were 1631 deleg-

gress of Soviets instructs all economic bodies to consider it their chief and urgent task to achieve in the shortest period possible, no matter what, enduring practical successes in supplying the peasantry with a large amount of wares, which are necessary to raise up agriculture and to improve the lives of the labouring peasant masses.' 'All industrial management bodies must not allow this most important goal to slip from their view.' 'The improvement of the situation of workers should be subordinated to this goal. This means that all worker organisations (first of all trade unions) are obligated to be concerned about such an industrial arrangement, which would quickly and fully satisfy the requirements of the peasantry. Moreover, industrial workers' wage increases and improvement of their living conditions should directly depend on the degree of achievements in this regard.' 'Narkomfin's activity should be subordinated to this goal', and so on, and so on. All senior comrades' speeches at all major events in party and soviet life bear such a character.

Comrade Shliapnikov already pointed out here what kind of character imbues all speeches regarding the worker masses. When you come into contact with broad circles of worker masses, while you are delivering reports that provide information about and explain our party's work, you often happen to hear deep distrust expressed toward our policy. From workers who are communists, we hear an explanation of many unhealthy phenomena, which we observe now in the party through the character of above-indicated party leaders' speeches. We see proletarians depart from our party. They are not those who came to the factories accidentally, for those 'proletarians' have been let go in sufficient numbers during personnel reductions. We are talking about the best workers leaving our party. They are the ones who worked for years in our party ranks, rendered enormous services to the party, and who sacrificed everything for it.

What explains these moods in our party ranks? Even on the pages of the central party press organ, we read about how the best party personnel, when resigning their membership in communist cells, declare that they feel like puppets when they vote in party elections. (Voice from the audience: Not true.) I don't know, maybe this is not true, but they tell about this on the pages of *Pravda*, and worker-communists are not satisfied with this situation. If you like, I will bring you irrefutable examples of these things. We feel that our party's attention toward the working class keeps weakening. This is especially appar-

ates with a deciding vote. Of them, 1522 were members and candidate members of the RCP(b). ... [List of questions examined at the congress.] V.I. Lenin delivered to the congress a report about the activity of VTsIK and Sovnarkom. ... [Discussion of congress's decisions.]

ent in regard to those questions of economic policy, which were the soul of all of CC policy for the past year.

Let's take the metals industry. Comrade Shliapnikov demonstrated to you the actual results of policy in the area of preserving the largescale metals industry, which is the steel framework of our whole national economy. In food supply policy, we see the very same picture of slackening attention to the situation of the worker masses, the same unhealthy phenomena, and the same negative results. Not long ago Narkomprod published a four-year report.[259] This report, which was composed not by the Workers' Opposition but by Narkomprod, showed to whom went the resources that had been allotted to workers. It demonstrated who took the lion's share of these resources and what amount went to the working class population. From these numbers, we see that only eight million workers were fed, while 35 million from the rest of the population. We collected resources by means of the colossal exertion of worker masses in food supply armies and by other such measures, which in many districts subverted the influence of our party among broad labouring masses in the countryside. Fatty foods, which were the more valuable part of these resources, went to satisfy not so much the proletariat as the other part of the population. Well, when we now say at worker meetings that our republic is impoverished and destitute, workers shake their heads distrustfully. This is because they see that some strata of the population have clothing and shoes and don't go around swollen from famine.

We do not want to say that the CC's ill will shaped these features of our food supply policy. We think that they took shape precisely because insufficient attention was paid to the situation of worker masses. During all this time, the party as a single whole organism did not participate in determining food supply policy, just the same as with other policies. It is no accident that you see all the time orators, who sit here in the centre, delivering the CC's political report. We learn from conversations with comrades, who have arrived from various places, that they do not know what policy the CC has carried out in all areas.

We see the kind of supreme disasters we experience from the depreciation of our ruble, thanks to issuing paper money in enormous, astronomical figures. The last conference and the Ninth Congress of Soviets resolved to try to reduce the issue of currency. What are the results of our party's financial policy? The results stand out in real numbers. We have trillions of unpaid wages in the rail-

---

259   Editors' endnote: He means the collection *Four Years of Food Supply Work* [Четырые года продовольственной работы] (Moscow, 1922).

way sector. Recently we received information that only a portion of metalwork-ers have debts equal to 800 billion [миллиард], which steadily grows month by month. Obviously, the issue of currency is being cut, but so that this reduction is made at the expense of not paying wages to the working class. You all know what kind of unrest we experience because of this.

Strikes arise more frequently not because of anarchist deviations and such, but because we are indebted to the workers. Read *Pravda* and you will see how it says there that workers go around all the institutions, leaving no stone unturned, but at the end of March salaries still had not been paid for January. This policy gives birth to ominous moods in the working class and in its atti-tude toward our agitation drives and our slogans. Against the background of these things, we see how an indifferent attitude toward their own fate begins to arise among the worker masses. We observe a mood of apparent disillusion-ment in those successes, which resulted from their supreme sacrifices during recent years. We see how the mood takes shape: 'it's all the same, you won't accomplish anything', 'it's useless to go', and so forth. This is the grounds for such phenomena, as when an individual proletarian starts to look for a way out of a difficult material situation through the speculative market or by applying individual efforts. These moods hack away at the root of our party's influence. You have to struggle skilfully with such moods. You can't struggle against them in the same way as has been done for the past few years. They thought that Politburo directives and orders could solve absolutely all problems. Now the Politburo itself declares that an end must be put to this state of things, this cir-cumstance ... [ellipses in text] (Voice: Who spreads this mood?). I will tell you who spreads it, if my time will be extended, and I will prove that you particip-ated in this.

For the past year, the party's communist cells have not participated in shap-ing, defining, and elaborating its policy. The Tenth Congress decided that com-munist cells should become 'the main fighting bodies of the party's economic work',[260] but where are such cells?! Are they the 'main fighting bodies of the party's economic policy'? And it is not only about economic work.

The party should live and act amicably and agreeably. Formal orders can't achieve this. Party cells should be the basic bodies in all areas of our politics and work. In the party itself, we often observe indifference and pessimism in regard to those tasks, which we so insistently shout about and which we put on the agenda of every meeting.

---

260 Editors' endnote: He means the resolution of the Tenth RCP(b) congress, 'On Party Build-ing'.

Not long ago *Pravda* in one of its leading articles[261] expressed concern that nothing was heard before the Eleventh Congress about what the party thinks regarding its agenda and which questions should be set before this congress. According to this editorial, 'this is a dangerous phenomenon'. It can confront the party with the need to convene an extra party congress after the Eleventh Congress, in order to reconsider or pose new questions, which deeply worry most of our party members.

We want for CC policy in the upcoming year not to be isolated from the party as a whole, as it was in the past year. We want maximal success in warding off dangers, which threaten us and about which comrade Lenin spoke, without denying the real danger that NEP conceals within itself the possibility of the working class gradually losing political supremacy. Therefore, we should emphasise that no matter what, we need to insure our party against even a weak loss of contact with the proletariat. More attention needs to be paid to proletarian everyday life [быт] and to the proletariat's creative strengths. Only the proletariat can give our party the strength to direct the vehicle of state along the path, which our party set out in its programme. Without trust in the proletariat, we will simply mark time in place and will not succeed in our struggle to solve the designated tasks.

[The chair calls for a break after Medvedev's speech. When delegates return, Lomov, Kosior, Trotsky, Krzhizhanovsky, Lenin, and Larin speak.]

∙∙
∙

Session four, 28 March, evening.

[Chair not identified. Molotov speaks first. Then Kharitonov, Nogin, and Frunze make briefer statements.]

Medvedev (pp. 160–2). I propose the following resolution on the report of the Central Committee and the Revision commission:

'Having heard the reports of the CC and the Revision Commission and debates on these reports, the Eleventh RCP(b) Congress considers:
1.   That for the period just ending, the CC's policy did not allot sufficient actual concern, energetic measures, communist forces, and material

---

261   Editors' endnote: He means the lead article 'To the Party Congress,' printed in *Pravda* no. 37, 16 February 1922.

resources to lift up largescale state industry. Without raising up and strengthening largescale state industry in actual fact and not just in resolutions, it will be completely impossible to consolidate the proletarian dictatorship under the conditions of the New Economic Policy and to overcome the attack of petty bourgeois forces and capital against our country, as well as the attack of international capital against the political supremacy of the proletariat in our first Republic of Soviets.

2. That this circumstance, moreover, directly caused the CC's inattention in its everyday work to the needs and the situation of the industrial proletariat. These needs were not satisfied to the degree to which they could have been, if more attention had been paid to them. Under the New Economic Policy, the influence of the conscious sector of the proletariat over the broad worker masses could not help but be undermined by this attitude of the CC toward the needs of the proletariat, accompanied as it was by systematic propaganda on the pages of central party press organs and speeches of the most prominent party leaders and personnel that reevaluated the creative strengths of the proletariat.

3. That in its interrelations with elected central trade union bodies, the CC frequently violated decisions of the Tenth Congress, which had precisely and correctly established these interrelations. The CC in fact created factional divisions among party members who were trade union personnel.

4. That a narrow circle of only the most prominent party leaders prepared and elaborated the most important party decisions in various areas of state building and party building. This unavoidably made the most important decisions of the CC a surprise for the whole party and made it impossible for all party members to rapidly assimilate and implement the CC's decisions.

5. That because of the character of CC decisions (as indicated above), the CC did not have systematic vital and organic links with all party provincial organisations. Therefore, its leadership's attempts to rapidly and amicably implement its decisions could not work.

6. That therefore the Eleventh Party Congress finds it necessary to propose to the new CC to decisively define all these phenomena, ensure the complete and utter influence of the proletarian vanguard, which means the RCP(b), over the broad worker masses, and finally overcome the CC's internal alienation from all provincial party organisations and from the party as a whole'.

Voice from seat: This is an entire declaration [декларация]!

Chair. Comrades, are there any more proposals regarding the CC's report? There aren't any more.

[Various delegations voice their approval for Frunze's resolution. Manuilsky and Solts speak. There is discussion. Riazanov and Sedoi speak.]

Shliapnikov (pp. 186–9). Comrades! That bill of indictment, which comrade Solts read to you here, is just as new to me as it is to you. Not one of the points, which are formulated in this indictment, as far as I know, was presented to us either collectively or individually. Do you need to be told that the odious character which they imparted to this business corresponds neither to our intentions nor the actual state of affairs! I most resolutely protest comrade Solts's declaration and I declare in turn that his accusations are baseless. I think that I will succeed also in proving this to the commission, which was selected. There was no factionalism or any special preparation for this so-called 'public appearance' [выступление]. The business proceeded in the following way. The Comintern discussed the united worker front. In our party, this question had been discussed comparatively little. We, a group of comrades, privately discussed this question. Moreover, we did so without any ulterior motives or any effort to create any platform on this basis. We especially attentively looked at how this business of the united front stands in our party, if this united front exists … [ellipses in text] You can't close your eyes to what we have had in reality since we declared unity in our party. Since the Tenth Congress, there has been no unity. Despite the fact that last year in this hall we had a big ideological brawl, if you will, even so we were more united than we are now. In some gubernias, some of which I have happened to visit and others about which comrades who came here informed me, an undesirable isolation, even differentiation, is noticeable. Perhaps this isolation usually has no ideological footing, but in any case it disrupts the unity of will, thought and actions, which we now need so much.

The working class now finds itself in a monstrously difficult position. In our party, we often hear thoughts about how our proletariat is declassed, without any explanation of the reasons. Still worse, they don't propose measures of struggle against this declassing. So, you see that there is something of a fissure in the ideological relationship between the proletariat and its vanguard, which is our party. We became extraordinarily worried about this reality which we saw, as well as about the thoughts uttered by broad circles. But how could we force the CC to pay attention to this? The CC's attitude toward me personally and toward many other comrades who had the misfortune or fortune to bear the label 'Workers' Opposition', which that same CC affixed upon us, was such that anything we proposed or any thought we had was already discredited in advance, just because it emerged from us.

Before me and others stood the question of how to go on [как всё-таки быть]? The party congress is being prepared. To speak out before a mass of members, even here, in Moscow, would mean creation of a platform and a grouping. From the standpoint of the resolution about unity, this would obviously be a criminal act. So we decided to go up the party hierarchy. To where? To the Central Committee? They don't pity us there. We decided to go to the Comintern. To the Comintern we went with the single task of resolving by this route those painful questions, which worry us. There we were judged and condemned. We recognise this and we accepted this decision, as all other decisions both of our congresses and of international congresses. Of all the signatories, no matter how they were defamed, there is not one on whose conscience lies the failure to carry out any of our party's decisions.

I should say to comrade Sedoi, who has either come very late to know our history or knows about only our recent history, you should be careful when defaming others. I will point out to you that you forget one person's history, in speaking about Medvedev, as if this fixture [гвоздь] of our opposition is very nearly an inveterate Menshevik. I should say to you that this is that same Medvedev, who went into exile on the case of organising strikes of protest against the trial of our deputies at the time, when you went, and you know where you went, against the will of our party as a volunteer into the French army. This same comrade Medvedev was sent on the case of comrade Petrovsky to Siberia because he wanted to organise a strike in Piter, a strike of protest against the case of Petrovsky and others. Such is the irony of fate, that the prosecutor in a case about violation of party directives is himself a person who is very tarnished in this sense. Comrade Sedoi, I warn you. There are not so many of us old party personnel [работники], and we will not sling mud at one another, but we will put the question in a political manner.

The Comintern censured us. We thought this decided the matter and we submitted to it. Does it suit you to examine it anew? We will submit to this, too. No matter what your sentence, no matter what, we will go to the working class all the same. This should not be forgotten. We came from there to this tribune here, but we will return there. We will meet with you, comrade Sedoi, in the ranks of the working class, no matter what sentence is pronounced upon us. Of course, I am extremely surprised that our Control Commission did not present this indictment and its decision to us in the usual way, as it does in regard to all who are accused. But I think that it will lay out to you its rationales on this account, especially in the concluding speech. Once more, comrades, I repeat that the letter did not intend what they try to attribute to it, that is to raise panic, with which the rather vulgar lead article in *Pravda* smeared us and this letter. If you compare the lead article to the text of our letter, then you will see a striking contradiction.

We wanted only one thing, which was to turn the attention of our CC to party members' state of suffering. It should not be forgotten, comrades, that the doubts, which tear us apart right now, also torment hundreds of thousands of party members who are workers. If little is said about them at the speakers' platforms, well very much is said on the floor [в партере]. We know this by the examples of some gubernias and by all our assemblies. I see here comrades from Gomel. Together with them I organised a provocation [провокация] against party members to get them to converse, because it is awful, in the end of it all, to have before oneself a silent auditorium of communists who act as if they agree with everything, but who actually think and say very much apart from us and not from the speaker's platform. This is an extraordinarily dangerous sign. I know it, I lived through it in 1907 in the Piter organisation, not in the Moscow one. At that time there was also a state of indifference and apathy toward our party's interests and toward the interests of the revolution.

(Voice from seat: That was another time.)

That was another time. True. Then this phenomenon was less dangerous for us than it is now. Right now this is fraught with very profound complications for us. Comrades, I should declare at this court that all of the 22 only desired to reinforce, strengthen, and invigorate the party. In vain do they separate us into sheep and goats, single someone out as organiser, someone else as leader, and see a great conspiracy underpinning it all ... [ellipses in text] The appeal was literally the result of several hours of conversation. I wrote it by hand on the spur of the moment, according to comrades' dictation. That is how it was. It was completely unconnected to any sort of preliminary preparation, organisation and so forth.

Someone, comrades, needs to create the Workers' Opposition. I have noticed this more than once. I should say, comrades, that here, let's say, comrade Solts asked a question about the Fourth All-Russian Congress of Metalworkers, at which we unanimously accepted the need to carry through the general party line and those theses, which were accepted at the Tenth Congress. We had no opponents. The report about the tasks of trade unions was completely withdrawn. We did not give any grounds to the Central Committee to say that we have any disagreement with it. The Central Committee itself started to divide us into sheep and goats and so created the situation that during roll-call voting 120 votes were for one list and 37 for another. The Central Committee supported the list that got 37 votes. Comrade Solts said here that we worked this up. Nothing of the sort was done. There was no kind of grouping at all. Comrade Molotov is correct in that there were neither groupings among us after the Tenth Party Congress, nor during the period before or after the Fourth Congress [of the Metalworkers' Union].

Further, comrades, it was not limited to this. There were still other attempts. Although the Workers' Opposition had died, they tried to revive it and drag it into the international orbit of associations of a fourth international.[262] No matter how strange, the organisers of this affair lived in the Hotel Lux on a Soviet expense account. They assembled people, held meetings, and sent couriers to me. I promptly informed the Central Committee, but these attempts were repeated. Not long ago, two weeks ago in fact, I also informed the Central Committee about this. The CC answered that it took my statement 'under advisement'. If that's how the matter will go, then you will see that I will very often be put on trial, probably, for others' cases, not for my own personal wishes. They claim that I am attempting to break up our party. Our desire is to see the party whole. We all with our own hands created the party together with thousands of workers both in the underground and during the revolution. It is not so easy for us to separate from this party and to wish for a split in it. Those who utter this thought and who attribute it to us are very unworthy comrades.

[The chair says it is time to end the session, but there are three brief statements by Sedoi, Kosior, and Riazanov.]

···

Session five, 29 March, daytime session.

[Unnamed chair announces that debate on the CCC report will continue. Medvedev is the first to speak.]

Medvedev (pp. 191–6). Comrades! Comrade Shliapnikov already cast enough light on the matter of how our appeal arose. I will supplement it only with a few strokes, which will show whether there is any basis to the Control Commission's accusation that our 'appeal to the Comintern was prepared in secret already long ago'. Comrade Shliapnikov told you how our appeal arose. I will add the

---

262   Editors' endnote: In 1922, the Communist Workers' Party of Germany attempted, without success, to unify anticommunist sectarian groupings of individual countries (Germany, Holland) under general leadership and to organise a fourth international.

following to his story. We had no need to prepare this appeal far in advance for the simple reason that half of the signatories are all close personal friends. Our friendship grew and was reinforced on the basis of more than ten years of joint work in the underground. All these comrades live here in Moscow. We talk on the telephone, we meet at work-related assemblies, and we had no need to prepare this step long ago. Of the other half, most are also personal friends, who had arrived for the Fifth Congress of the Metalworkers' Union. Just like us, some of them were members of the central committee of the Metalworkers' Union. In all our party and union work, we never came into conflict.

I agree with comrade Solts only about one thing, which is that in our party ranks we were always in the first category. We never were in the same category as one of our accusers. We did not defend the bourgeois fatherland in the trenches as volunteers, as comrade Sedoi did. However, he recovered, saying that he was not in the trenches, but worked for 'defence'. Thus, he reminded us of that feeling, which precisely this self-seeking element, which took cover in 'defence', elicited from all of us and from the masses. Thus, comrades, this first accusation, like all the accusations which comrade Solts formulated here, is absolutely unfounded. Comrade Solts says that we prepared this appeal long ago, but why does Solts bring you an unsubstantiated statement? Why did he not reveal to you those documents, which he should have had as confirmation, and say: 'Here is the evidence, which not one of the signatories can refute'? He does not have these documents. We understand the entire difficulty of Solts's position. He is forced to resort to the gambler's rule: 'When you don't have a match, then start with diamonds'.[263]

I should say directly that before assembling and writing our appeal, we first had personal meetings with almost every one of our 22 comrades and listened patiently to them tell about their concerns. Each of them came to me or to comrade Shliapnikov and told about what they observe in the provinces in all areas of state building, and chiefly what in the party deeply alarms them and summons forth their greatest fears for the fate of the proletariat and the revolution. On the basis of these discussions we arranged a get-together, in order not to keep talking one-on-one. We said: 'We all know one another, let's converse together, at least maybe our mistakes will become clear. Maybe those repulsive phenomena, which one comrade witnessed, can be seen only in one part of our republic, but not in our whole party.' When we assembled in order to verify jointly our evaluations of the state of things in our economy and in our party, we clearly saw and heard from comrades from the Donbas, from the south,

---

263   Когда не с чего, так с бубен.

from the Urals ... [ellipses in text] (Voice from seat: Miasnikov was with you.) Not only Miasnikov was with us. Also comrade Tashkin was with us. Neither here, nor in the commission, nor in the CCC have I heard anyone accuse him of what Miasnikov is accused of. I am confident that we will not hear this. So from these joint conversations, as comrade Shliapnikov said, arose this appeal of ours. What were we after with this appeal? Here they shout 'schism' at you and they play on this note, for they understand that it is the only thing on which our accusers can play. What has the CCC brought into evidence? In this regard the Central Control Commission remains true to itself. It simply accuses, but it obviously feels no obligation to prove its accusations to you.

No, we set ourselves one task. How are we to reduce those things in our party's life, which according to our deepest conviction, have led it especially recently toward the greatest danger, which is a breach with the proletariat? We never said that the proletariat is perfect. We know its weak aspects. We know its lack of culture not less than does Solts, but even more so than he or anyone else, for we live and work continuously with the proletariat. It is our deepest conviction that no matter how few in number, how disorganised, how poorly educated in communism, and how significant its weaknesses, only the proletariat is for our party that basic resolute force, on which it can depend in its struggle for consolidation and continuation of our revolution and for communism. The party can and should serve only the interests of the proletariat.

We regard as the most supreme danger the party's weakening attention to the needs and situation of the proletariat and the danger of a breach between the party and the working class that grows out of this. We assigned ourselves just one task. How are we to reduce this supreme danger? Two paths stood before us. We could go through the party by appealing to its rank and file on the eve of the Eleventh Party Congress and elucidate to them the most dangerous phenomena in our party. The alternative was to go to the highest communist court of appeal.

Before us arose the question of the form in which we could appeal to all party members. We clearly understood that we could do this only by offering theses, which undoubtedly would have turned right away into a platform. Posed in the framework of discussion, they would have distracted the party's forces from direct work. Although we did not begin the discussion before the Tenth Party Congress, we knew from our experience of it that the current discussion could also deeply undermine our party's already weakened influence over the broad worker masses. We said to ourselves that this path needs to be rejected, for we could not even consider any intentions to undermine our party's influence either within or outside of our republic. Indeed can any party member who knows us personally have any doubt of this? I personally never resigned from any party posts, which fell to my lot during more than twenty years. Therefore, we decided to appeal to the Comintern.

The Comintern was discussing the United Worker Front. We decided to put before it the problem that not all is well with us in this sense. We pointed out some things, which not one comrade can deny, if he does not want to deceive himself. Making this step, we did not have in mind the publication of our 'Appeal'. None of our documents, even the 'Appeal' and its goals, even formally bear an agitational character. They are not intended for broad masses of people. Indeed, if we had wanted to publicise these documents [достоянием гласности], we undoubtedly would have written and explained them in such a way, so that all party members would have found them comprehensible. That is why the accusation against us of the intention to produce a schism in our party is monstrous and is made in the greatest bad faith.

In this hall we will find dozens of comrades, who have known us since before the revolution. We met them while carrying out underground work. Not one of them would fling this accusation against us. At that moment, when you could observe a broad ebb of party members from party ranks due to difficult circumstances, many of those departing comrades found us in our apartments and in the union and asked us: 'What are we to do?'.[264] Each time we considered it our duty to say to them: 'Don't take this step. It is the most harmful and dangerous thing you could do for the revolution'. In all the cases of mass departure from the party (Briansk, Nikolaev) that are known to the CC, we attempted to persuade members to remain within the party. Ask the ill-starred comrade Paniushkin if anyone else warned him as much as we did not to leave the party? We knew him earlier, during the revolution. We told him that he was taking a most dangerous step and we tried to talk him out of it. If we had wanted a party split, why would we have needed to do this in regard to Paniushkin?

They say that the worst elements in the party are leaving it. I don't know if comrade Rykov is present here. He has frequently been quoted here and I will allow myself to cite him. He knows comrade Babkin, who has been a member of our party since 1903, is a former plenipotentiary of STO, and so forth. Even such a comrade as he came and said, 'I offer to resign from the party'. We told him that if he takes such a step, he should be regarded as the greatest criminal both in relation to the party and to the working class. After our conversation with him, he remained in the party ranks and carries out work that the party assigns to him. We know dozens of examples, when comrades such as he raised

---

264   Как нам быть?

this question. We considered it our duty to tell them that they were leading the party toward danger. Therefore I repeat that only the greatest lack of scruples can lead one to accuse us of intending a party split.

The CC Politburo, in its decision about our appeal to the Comintern, found that we did not violate party discipline. Now they say that we provided material, which White Guards could use. Well, it need not be forgotten that indeed we delivered our appeal personally into the hands of Comintern Executive Committee members. If this appeal subsequently landed among White Guards, as happens with some secret documents, it is impossible to accuse us of this. Senior CC leaders frequently have declared that classified CC documents end up in the White Guard press, yet no one accuses them of aiding White Guards. But someone needs to toss us out of the party. Someone has an interest in this. Therefore, they seek motives, which would serve as evidence that we are making the party weaker, not stronger.

That which we said in our appeal to the Comintern is not only our personal conviction, but is confirmed by entire assemblies of communists. In Novgorod gubernia, they discussed our declaration from 7 to 2:30 a.m., according to a Nizhegorod gubkom member's report. After a lengthy discussion, they declared our letter's characterisation of the intraparty situation to be correct. They pointed to a massive amount of evidence from their organisation that supports our position. All this proves that the only accusation that can be made against us is telling the Comintern about our party's illnesses. Yet even comrade Lenin has frequently emphasised that our party's virtue is that it, alone in the entire world, is not afraid to talk openly about its weaknesses. We never diverge from this exact thought. We see the strength of our party precisely in that it is not afraid of the truth. It does not fear to admit to itself that it is weak. We have said this frequently. We also thought that we had the right to say so to the Comintern, which is the highest communist court of appeal.

As for the accusation that I am one of the organisers, well, comrade Solts knows a good half of the signatories himself. He cannot confirm with a good conscience that these comrades can be 'worked over' [обработан]. He knows comrades Borisov, Bruno, and Pravdin rather well. He does not have the right to say that they can be 'worked upon' like little boys. That's why these accusations are unfounded, comrades.

Solts says that I did not trust the CCC. How was it really? During our discussion in the CCC, I was asked: why did you not appeal to the CCC? I answered that I don't believe that you [the CCC] can do something about this problem. I pointed out that *Pravda* on 7 March published a characterisation of us personally and of our political behaviour. You heard CC member comrade Trotsky, one of our most prominent leaders, state that he is not satisfied with this article. I said then: You should have said that such a policy demoralises the party. We asked the CCC: Why haven't you refuted the slander that was directed against us? We cannot include ourselves among aggrieved high officials, because not once has the CC refused to give us a senior appointment. I did not say during this conversation that we know there is no reason to turn to you. All the same you can't make any decision on this question, for it is a political matter. You frequently said in our practical work that you don't discuss political questions. If you want to accuse us of violating party discipline, well formulate this so, for you have not formulated it. We don't have any grounds to trust your assertions that you could change anything about the state of things, which we have characterised.

So that's what is behind comrade Solts's indication that I did not trust the CCC. He depicted it as if I place my own self far above everything else in general. If it were so, it stands to reason that very many others would have noticed this. I have worked in the party for 22 years and I have never pretended to any degree to aspire to the role of a chief, a leader, and such. No. Here there are very many comrades, who know me personally and know my work. They know that I never promoted myself. This accusation does not suit me at all. The entire indictment, which the CCC has advanced, is baseless. Its characterisation of us is only correct about one thing, which is that we always represented the first category in our party. If now Solts says that we are in the category of the party's good-for-nothings, well this is just his opinion.

About the Comintern's decision, we stated at all assemblies, where we were asked, that we recognise it as obligatory without conditions. The Comintern wants for us 'together with the party to acknowledge the difficulties facing it and shoulder to shoulder together with it to overcome these difficulties'.[265] We have done so and still do so. If it suits you now to reject our efforts in this direction, then do as you please, but it is slanderous to accuse us of striving to split our party. We did not do this. Only those who lack all conscience can accuse us of this.

Kollontai (pp. 196–201). Comrades, the case of the 22 is being examined here. I am 23rd on the list, as you know, as an associate. Nevertheless the CCC does me the honour of transferring me to the first category. Moreover, it claims that I was somewhat of a chief among our 22 comrades.

No matter how flattered I am by the title of chief, nevertheless I most categorically reject it, because I think that our remaining 22 comrades are so conscious.

---

265 Editors' footnote: The quote is not correct. See this edition, p. 752.

I cannot lead behind me such old comrades as Kopylov, Mitin, Tolokontsev and others. On the contrary, I learn much from them. In any case, I do not assume leadership over them. It seems to me that in this case the Control Commission acted just as it has become accustomed to act since our party has been ruled according to a military-type regime. There is a habit always to have a command structure and rank-and-file. Even in regard to the 22, it found a command structure and rank-and-file.

Next, comrades, the Control Commission finds it incriminating against me that my brochure 'About the Workers' Opposition', which was published last year, was reprinted in various press organs abroad. First of all, comrades, you know that no one is responsible for republication. When this brochure appeared in the KAPD newspaper, I formally requested that the brochure should not be reprinted. The Executive Committee of the Comintern has my declaration. Since I am a member of the Third International and the brochure was printed in an organ created by a fourth international, to which I have no relation, I requested that it cease printing the brochure. No one is safe from the reprinting of articles or brochures, which point out the party's flaws. Our enemies constantly do this. They even interpret toward their own ends the speeches of our top chiefs. I read that comrade Radek's speech was interpreted as meaning that Russia's policy was changing in a way that would suit the interests of England. No one is safe from this.

About the Control Commission's indications that I was at one time a Menshevik, well comrades, let's say this directly. If we start to exclude people for this, then we'll have to exclude not just me. We need to remember that among us there are many comrades, who in 1915 were not yet Bolsheviks, whose brochures in 1915 were not published by the CC, who in 1915 did not work together with us, and who did not help organise the Left Zimmerwald. Besides that, all comrades who work with me know my work. Recalling one's past Menshevism is first of all a polemical trick. The main thing is not about me. The main thing is the very statement of our 22 comrades, who I join as 23rd, but nevertheless I am transferred to the first category.

What, strictly speaking, incriminates the 22? Does the appeal to the Comintern incriminate them? No! Comrade Trotsky and even the CC pointed out that formally the 22 comrades had the full right to appeal to the Comintern. How was our statement conveyed to the Comintern? Since I conveyed it, then I can say how it happened. The statement was given exclusively to Comintern Conference Presidium members. Moreover, there were not even enough copies for all members of the presidium. Obviously, if the matter of presenting a statement had been thought out in advance, if it had been prepared in advance, then enough copies would have been prepared so that at least all members of the presidium would have had one. There weren't even enough for all presidium members, not to speak even of all members of the conference. Our declaration was translated only into French. There were not even translations into the remaining languages. That means that no preparatory work was made. So formally there was definitely no violation of party discipline. No comrade says that our step was criminal in a formal sense.

What brought forth our appeal? We saw the Comintern as our court of highest appeal. We deeply trust the Comintern as an institution. We appealed precisely to it, because we saw that something is not right in our party. I would say that right now an unhealthy, difficult process takes place in our party. Red blood cells are departing. What will remain then of our party, if its red corpuscles – the working class – leave it? Naturally, it will then become lymphatic, inert, inactive, and dull. Fear of this picture and process forced us to appeal to the Comintern: comrades, our higher-ups do not listen to words of caution, so turn their attention to what is happening. Maybe our speaking out will force our higher-ups to think more seriously about what is happening and to pay attention to workers' mass departure from the party, the decline of party activism, the party's isolation from the masses, and to the fact that the working class does not feel now 'at home' in our party. If the masses felt that they could find in the party a complete answer to their questions and the means for struggle against the dark forces that surround us, then workers would strive to join the party. Instead, the masses remain on the sidelines and workers leave the party. All these things forced us to appeal to the Comintern, since we regard it highly and we deeply respect it. We do not regard the Comintern as some chance meeting of comrades.

We appealed to the Comintern, because we regard the Comintern as the highest court of appeal, and because we expected from it a definitive decision of the question that worries us. The Comintern decided the question. At the Control Commission, I was asked, 'Do you submit to the Comintern's decrees?' 'Of course, we submit'. The Comintern declared definitively that we were wrong in this case. We didn't question everyone. We didn't present enough materials. Once the Comintern has said that one must observe unity and submit to party discipline, or else 'your deviation will lead to your exclusion from the Comintern',[266] then the business is over. In this sense, the Comintern gave a definite directive to warn the 22 comrades.

Not one word was said about excluding them.

---

266   Editors' note: The quotation is incorrect. See pp. 751–2 of the current edition.

When the Control Commission put to me the question, 'Do you submit to this decision?', I answered, 'Of course'. 'This means that you will not under any circumstances speak out and struggle in the same spirit?' To this I said definitively, 'I will not struggle in such a way as I have struggled up to now. When I see things that do not correspond to our party's decrees, I will appeal, protest, and criticise each time to the appropriate level of the party hierarchy. Not only that, but I think that you, as the Control Commission, should obligate me to do so. This is how I understand the duty of each party member: to appeal to the appropriate body, and we consider the Comintern our highest body, to point out to it where we see mistakes, and to demand that the appropriate party court should correct them. We should be and want to be not only voting members, but also active party members. Our comrades should find it possible to participate actively in our work'. That was my answer to the Control Commission. It means that formally the act of the 22 was not incriminating. Of what are the 22 accused? The appeal's content? But what precisely is the content? When I heard yesterday the speeches of comrades Kosior, Osinsky and many others, I thought: 'my god, they speak ten times more harshly than what was said in the appeal of the 22'.

Voice from the presidium: The matter is not about this.

Kollontai. If we had said something similar, then probably the 22 would have been treated even more severely. It follows then that something other than the content matters. The basic content of the declaration says, 'the party is isolated from the masses'. This isolation exists. It is obvious. No one denies it. This is our sorrow and our pain. When you come to a factory, where there are 900 workers and where during assemblies 22 vote for the party's resolution, four abstain, and the remainder simply does not vote, this demonstrates the inertia, the isolation, and those dark sides of our party life, with which one must struggle. Another thing shows the loss of contact. Indeed is it not typical that here at the congress in the political report we have not heard even a word about what, strictly speaking, the working class should do? What should the workers, namely the workers, do right now to struggle against unemployment? What is to be done about such things during the new policy, when ahead lies the resettlement of workers from apartments into basements? All this emphasises the fact that the party is isolated from workers.

Further, the statement says that the party's social composition is being altered. In 38 more-or-less industrialised gubernias, only 44% of party members are workers. This is already a threat. You know about all these things. Therefore, there's no need to repeat them. But you shouldn't blame the declaration for this. What can explain the isolation and the workers' weakening influence in the party? Objective conditions? No, comrades, not only objective conditions. Objective conditions are the basic and chief reason, but it's impossible to heap all the blame on objective conditions. Otherwise, there would not be a section for agitation and propaganda in our party. The more difficult are the objective conditions, the more necessary it is to make sure that the party will not be cut off from the workers. The main role in the party must be secured for workers, so that when it comes to union between peasantry and workers, political leadership would remain with the workers nevertheless.

They need to determine and take account of such things, but we see that they don't do this. Isolation from the worker masses is caused not only by objective conditions, but also by the decrease in party members' activism and by the stifling of thought within the party. Instead of actively participating in work, our cells study commercial geography. Indeed, was the congress's agenda discussed ahead of time? No. The 'Discussion Leaflet'[267] came out just a day before the congress. The reason can be found in the party regime. It needs to be changed so that workers would feel 'at home' in the party and could carry out their working-class policy. But indeed the CC wants this, too. It means that we should say directly that there is nothing criminal in the contents of the declaration of the 22. Where does the guilt lie?

We demanded that the Comintern should get our leading comrades to turn their attention to changing the regime in the party, the need to do something, and how to do it. There is no obvious crime, yet the exclusion of several comrades is on the agenda. Comrades, will this change that illness, which is felt in the party, that lymphatic disorder, decrease of activism, absence of critical thought and of the necessary stimulus to it? If we will not reason and think, then we will not know how to find an end. We will not know how to eliminate the isolation from the masses. The exclusion of these comrades will not end the illness, but will drive the illness inside. Let comrades think about how this will reverberate in the provinces. Workers should put their initiative to work, they should take part in the creativity of life, but such a measure will not facilitate this. On the contrary: won't this drive the illness within? After this, won't there

---

267   Editors' endnote: 'The "Discussion Leaflet" [Дискуссионный листок] is a nonperiodic
      publication of the CC RCP(b). It was first issued in January 1921, by decision of the Ninth
      All-Russian Party Conference. As a rule, it was published prior to party congresses. In 1921,
      two issues appeared before the Tenth Congress. Before the Eleventh Congress the "Discus-
      sion Leaflet" came out on 24 March 1922. Subsequently, the "Discussion Leaflet" did not
      appear as a separate publication, but was published in the newspaper *Pravda*.'

be still more silence, passivity, departure of workers from the party, and lack of faith by workers in their own strengths? Such a decision will not help to elevate the working class's faith in itself. It's necessary to change the regime in the party, so that workers would find it possible to show their initiative within the party. We support the Tenth Party Congress's resolution about worker democracy and freedom of intraparty criticism. We want for it to be implemented and we will do everything to confirm workers' democracy not just on paper and not just in words, but in fact. We want workers' role in the party to be confirmed and recognised as in fact the basic, chief, leading role. Our salvation lies in the creativity of the working masses!

[Tsifronovich speaks next.]

Chair. There is a proposal to cease debate and there are protests from the other side. Let's allow one person to speak in favour and another against.

Kubiak. This needs to be feared. When comrades were at gubernia conferences, they said not one word, when it was proposed that the presidium resolve all questions on the agenda. It's the very same thing now at the party congress.

Voice from seat: Not true.

Kubiak. What is not true! You Orenburgers didn't have a conference at all. The proletarian Urals also did not find it necessary to convene a conference before the congress. There was nothing to talk about. On our agenda are two essential questions for discussion. One question is about the staff of gubernia control commissions and the other is about the 22. This is not a simple conversation. Maybe it will be necessary to add someone to the 22. Therefore, I suggest that we take several minutes to discuss this question.

Voice from seat: I speak in favour of ending debate. The Eleventh Congress should not in any case take up the matter of gubernia control commission staff. We can talk about this in a purely businesslike commission, which will sufficiently clear up the matter. About the 22, there will be a special commission, which will make a report.

Chair. I am putting it to a vote. The majority supports ending debate.

[Solts speaks. He says much about Shliapnikov and the appeal of the 22 to the Comintern. Medvedev interjects several times with 'I didn't say that',

'I was not at the assembly', and 'Lie'. Myshkin, Zinoviev, and Tomsky speak. Vardin reads a statement.]

Chair. Comrade Shliapnikov will speak about a personal matter.

Shliapnikov (pp. 244–5). Comrade Solts brought to you an excerpt from comrade Cachin's notebook. Comrades, I know of some such excerpts from my speech yesterday. I did not dwell on them, because I supposed that the commission we chose would acquaint itself with the entire business. I am surprised that comrade Solts forgot about this. I declare right here and now that neither the tone nor the character of our discussion had that odious character, which they try to attribute to it. They say that someone spoke to him about our case, but I cannot speak about those doubts (I am grateful to comrade Zinoviev today), which comrade Cachin came and told me about. I mean that very same comrade Cachin who writes in his notebook things that I did not say.[268]

Chair. I cannot allow comrade Shliapnikov to cast aspersions upon comrade Cachin at this party congress. Comrade Cachin accepted world proletarian revolution after hesitating for a long time. Casting suspicion upon comrade Cachin's notes, which comrade Solts read aloud, cannot be permitted here.

∴

Session 7. 30 March, morning. Kamenev chairs.

[Sokolnikov, Preobrazhensky, Spunde, and Andreev speak.]

Kiselev (pp. 325–9).[269] Comrades! Sokolnikov's theses do not point out the main basic line, to which we should presently hold and which has colossal significance for our financial policy.

First of all, let's pay attention to the approach. Minor palliatives are given, which Narkomfin itself would be able to correct, since it is given enormous

---

268 Marcel Cachin's notebooks were published in four volumes as *Carnets de Marcel Cachin*, under the direction of Denis Peschanski (Paris: CNRS Editions, 1993–8). The entries to which Shliapnikov and Kollontai (below) refer were published in volume 3 (1921–1933), published in 1998, edited and annotated by Serge Wolikow and Jacques Girault, pp. 207–14).

269 A.S. Kiselev signed the theses of the Workers' Opposition, but not the Letter of the 22.

rights in this regard. If you will take a look at its activity, you will see that it made some mistakes.

Under current conditions, the financial question needs to be approached in the same way that a private capitalist would approach it. We say: business is not moving along, sound the alarm, and give us a lessee. When they've put a lessee in place, business takes off. Our business doesn't get off the ground, so let's put together a partnership [товарищество] with private capitalists, whether it be a foreign capitalist or a Russian. Why are the Russian capitalist and lessee successful? Why does the collective composed of Soviet representatives and private capitalists get things done? Why can't we ourselves do this? Because when the lessee leads the enterprise, he has a different financial policy than we do. If we put together a mixed partnership, it will conduct a different policy than we do.

There is not a word in comrade Sokolnikov's theses about what policy we will conduct. How does the capitalist approach each enterprise? He takes an accounting of all his holdings [хозяйство]: plants, factories, mines, railroads, and money. Then he says, 'I have 100 million rubles of capital. If I don't want to be engaged in any industry, then these 100 million will give me 3.5% interest in the State Bank'. He thinks, 'I will lie on the stove and each year I will receive 3.5 million rubles, while the capital will remain untouched'. Yet how do we do business? We do not take into consideration either the interest on capital or the amortisation of capital.

As confirmation, I will point to several examples. Take the post and telegraph. Narkompochtel [the People's Commissariat of Post and Telegraph] collected 378 billion in December, then collected 192 billion, and then 496 billion. If you convert this into real gold rubles, how much do you get? In December three and three-tenths million gold rubles, in January 700 thousand gold rubles, in February 600 thousand gold rubles, and just that. How much did Narkompochtel bring in before the war? Ten million gold rubles.

You will say that territory has been reduced in size, other revenue streams have been reduced, and conditions have changed. Narkompochtel tried to resolve the problem incorrectly, for it departed from economic calculations [хозяйственный расчёт]. If we lease out the post office, immediately there will be a profit, but we have a loss. Trade turnover [торговый оборот] was reduced and operations were reduced by 50%. Nevertheless, they should have brought in five million gold rubles, not 600 thousand rubles.

Take communal services [коммунальное хозяйство]. All you have to do is to travel in a Moscow city tram. You will see that although earlier they took seven kopecks, now they take 30,000, which is equivalent to one and nine-tenths kopecks. You will say that we are such geniuses and such good organisers that having received one and nine-tenths kopecks, we turn it into a profit. We do not run the economy well. Everything here is expensive, but wages are low. We see from our expenses that we currently run the economy more expensively.

Now, if you take pay for apartments, about which they just spoke, we will see the following. Under the New Economic Policy, the Moscow Soviet set pay for apartments at 90 kopecks per square *sazhen*.[270] If you take an apartment of 12 square sazhens, it will cost 10 rubles and 80 kopecks. This is a two-room apartment in the centre of the city, with heat, light, sewage, and plumbing. This is an apartment for the bourgeoisie, of which we have 27 thousand (this many licenses have been issued in Moscow for this number). There are already 27 thousand private manufacturers in Moscow. About two months ago, these private employers had approximately 55 thousand shop-assistants [приказ-чики] and workers employed in private manufacturing. If you take the apparatus of private tradesmen and artisans [ремесленники], they number in the hundreds of thousands of people receiving apartments. They receive for 10 rubles apartments which before the war cost 40–50 rubles. In such a way, these speculators and private employers are made equal to our state enterprise workers, but in practice it turns out that wages are falling. Remember that in 1910 Moscow collected 200 million rubles in pay for apartments. I don't have the information for the present. In any case, significantly less is collected.

Let's move on to the problem of our largescale railway economy. Again, you will see that we don't take the correct approach. We resolved the main, basic question of whether employer-entrepreneurial profit is permissible and if it needs to be taken. I think that it needs to be taken, for we have the Soviet, Narkomzdrav [People's Commissariat of Health], and Narkomvoen [People's Commissariat of the Military], which need to be maintained. Some comrades, who ask if it is necessary, do not take this into account. Essentially, this means that they don't have economic accounting. Accounting [расчёт] was established in the railway economy in or around August. Then the ruble was worth 20 thousand Soviet rubles. Based on such an exchange rate, pay for cargo and passenger travel was established on railways. Guilt lies not with Narkomfin [People's Commissariat of Finances], but with NKPS [People's Commissariat of Transport], which demanded to be given only ready money but did not want to do anything itself. But Narkomfin did not have ready money. It gave a printing press and some train cars which brought paper, a larger number each day. I don't know how much paper is demanded now, but in any case a considerable amount. If we examine the income receipts [доходы] of NKPS, then here

---

270   A *sazhen* was 2.13 meters.

is what we get. First of all, if you heard the numbers, it proposes to collect more than two trillion. But if you convert this amount to gold rubles, it will be equivalent to less than two million gold rubles. Now with the current exchange rate you see that this is equal to a million. Utter rubbish!

If one assesses the enormous railway economy, on which has been spent nearly 300 millions of gold, an enormous holding of train cars, locomotives, rails, and buildings, what enormous resources this comprises! In January the ruble was worth 20 thousand rubles, in March 270 thousand rubles, and we all carried on [возили] according to the same prices. Instead of 13 kopecks we received one kopeck for a railway ticket for local connections, and NKPS carried on. If it were based on economic accounting, a directive would be given to set and calculate the ticket price according to the private capitalist principle. We made a huge mistake, which we could have avoided.

Now, if you will recall the taxation policy, then you will say that the tax policy also reduces all that we have done to nothing.

Take, for example, our excise duty on wine. When the excise duty was set on wine, based on 20,000 rubles, we established that 75 gold kopecks should be taken from each bottle. Now, if we will take a look at what these 75 kopecks became, then it turns out that in January they turned into 25 kopecks, into five kopecks by February, in March three kopecks and so forth. If you look at spirits (alcohol), then 40 kopecks per degree were assessed. By February it was eight kopecks and in March five kopecks. On cigars two rubles and 50 kopecks were set. Then we received 50 kopecks in February and 31 kopecks in March. The tax on salt was set at one ruble per pud. Now we annually extract 50 million puds, while earlier we got 120 million puds. If we set the tax at one gold ruble, then realistically we should receive 40–50 million gold rubles. We do not receive this, because these rubles turned into 20 kopecks in February, and in March into 18.5 kopecks. In such a way, our taxation policy comes to naught.

Here is Narkomfin's grand total. In January seven billion and 16,000 were collected, in February one billion and 335 million, and in March three trillion. Realistically it turns out, according to the exchange rate, as follows. In January Narkomfin has 2,454,900 and in February 1,673,700. Thus, when Narkomfin totals everything up, it showers you with figures. If you compare them, however, it turns out that we collect very much paper, but realistically this comes to naught.

Thus, we should approach this problem completely clearly and not like it's been approached so far, which was not in the theses. We should say completely clearly and definitively that all enterprises and economic bodies should proceed from the principles of private capitalist reckoning, for we are encircled by capitalism. They will shower us with cheap goods from abroad, if Vneshtorg will not be capable of holding back this flood of goods and indeed if we will not cordon it off. We need to approach the business just like the private capitalist approaches it. Instead of saying 'lease it out', we ourselves need to base our economy on such principles. If it will turn out that this is not suitable, then we will see. If it will turn out that it competes with private enterprises and with mixed enterprises, then it is a different question. It seems to us that we have one way out, which is to attempt to rent out to others without fail.

We have theatres, which are cultural undertakings. They say that there should be more investment in these. Back under the tsars, they put one million rubles into the Bolshoi Theatre. Well, let's say we will give one million. But when we should give money to more than one theatre, this question needs re-examination. The Malyi Theatre received in February one million and 601,000 rubles, which means in gold rubles 1,855 rubles for the month. Maybe this is a cultural undertaking, but I should say that our approach is not at all as it must be. I don't want to blame individual commissariats, for this is our common sin. The commissariats are the guilty parties in this, as well as Sovnarkom and our party, which poorly looks after this. The Moscow Artistic Theatre received 3,283 rubles, one of the studios 84 rubles, and the studio of Maxim Gorky 16 rubles. If you count up all the actors, then on average 51 rubles per month goes to all theatres. I am sure that this does not come to more than 51 per person. Here it has to be said that we will pay extra, but it needs to be said precisely how much extra. This needs to be determined precisely, for we cannot construct a state budget without this.

I have very much material, but not enough time. I cannot demand too much of your attention. The clear and definite point that emerges is that if we will act according to purely capitalist considerations, then the theses about financial policy should say so without any ambiguity. This is the basic thing and we should proceed from this.

If we do not carry this out, then here, there, and everywhere we will lose. Instead of 100 million rubles, we will have 60 million rubles after a year. After another year, maybe there will be five million. Maybe, for example, NKPS needs to pay extra, so how much extra to pay? This needs to be established precisely. Without establishing this precisely and without such a directive, I repeat, we cannot at all emerge from the financial crisis.

[Lomov, Larin, and others speak next.]

∴

Session 8

[Kubiak delivers the report of the mandate commission, pp. 365–7.]

∴

Session 10, 1 April, morning session.

[The chair is not named. Iakovlev speaks first, and then others.]

Kutuzov (pp. 450–3). Comrades! Each time when a party congress or conference gathers, party building is posed as the most urgent question. This question is put on the agenda not simply to have something to talk about, but so that comrades from the provinces, who know local work, would discuss this topical question.

We see, nevertheless, that a fissure emerged as the result of raising the party building question before the Tenth Congress. We got the Workers' Opposition, the Trotskyists, the Leninists, the Tens, and whatever else. This means that something was unhealthy. Yesterday we heard comrade Zinoviev's report. Tell me, what did he say that was new in comparison to the last congress, when comrade Bukharin made the report? I will tell you. He said nothing new. It means that you have to give the Tenth Party Congress its due, for it discussed this question in detail. It decided to accept a resolution, which would have satisfied everyone, especially at that moment, and to build a coalition Central Committee of our party, bringing into it Kutuzov and Shliapnikov.

Some members of the Workers' Opposition thought that now things would be better. Comrades, I should say that at the first session of the party CC, at the first CC plenum, the mood was such that I thought the united front should go from above to below. I felt complete justice and love toward everything in which our party is involved. The letter to all party members was accepted in this same spirit.[271] But what became of this further? I assumed that any decision of the congress should be implemented and that local decisions should be coordinated with the CC, but what was done? What is happening in the provinces? I should say that one answer was heard from the provinces, one declaration: 'All is well, that is for sure'.

Comrades! From my personal experiences, I could give you some examples of how the decisions of the Tenth Party Congress were implemented. I worked

---

271   Editors' endnote: See the newspaper *Pravda* no. 64, 25 March 1921.

in the Bauman District Party Committee. What did the MC [Moscow Party Committee] do? It came to the point that at one meeting they did not allow me, a CC member, to speak. Besides that, the Moscow gubernia conference meets and discusses the MC's attitude toward the Bauman district.[272] Comrades submitted a declaration that such and such comrades, including Kutuzov, want to make a statement to the CC. The question about exclusion from the party was put to a vote. Only by one vote did it it fail. Otherwise everyone would have been excluded, including a CC member. This is a fact. (Objections from the delegates

---

272 Editors' endnote: In 1921 the leadership of the Bauman District Party Committee was in the hands of the Workers' Opposition. It did not obey the decision of the Tenth Party Congress to cease factional struggle and it continued to sabotage the implementation of the party's most important measures in the district. The group of ward [участок] organisers of Mostiazhartovsky, Voennyi, Syromiatnikovsky, Basmannyi and other wards, expressing the moods of the party masses of the district, demanded that the MC RCP(b) put a stop to the antiparty activity of the Workers' Opposition, which had built itself a nest in the Bauman District Party Committee (see the archive of the Institute of Party History of MC CPSU, f. 3, op. 2, d. 18, l. 17). The Moscow Committee of the RCP(b), having investigated the situation in the Bauman District, held an expanded plenum on 22 September 1921 and decided to qualify the circumstances of work in the district as 'representing a threat of a complete break between the party organisation and the working masses' (see Archive of the Institute of Party History of MC CPSU, f. 3, op. 2, d. 18, l. 14). The MC decided to rearrange cadres in the Bauman District. However, members of the District Party Committee, maintaining the views of the Workers' Opposition, did not obey. Their antiparty behaviour was discussed at a delegates' assembly of Bauman District on 27 September 1921. The assembly accepted a resolution, which condemned the work of the district committee. Eighty-three people voted for it and 22 voted against, with 10 abstentions (see f. 63, op. 1, d. 45, l. 2). However, members of the district committee from the Workers' Opposition group did not calm down. They brought their disagreements with the minority of the committee to the Seventh Moscow Gubernia Conference (29–31 October 1921), where they declared that they do not submit to the MC's decision and demanded that it be re-examined. The Seventh Gubernia Conference condemned the antiparty activity of the Bauman group of the Workers' Opposition. The conference accepted a resolution, which the delegation of Krasnopresnensky District proposed, in which it said, 'The Seventh Moscow Gubernia Conference, having heard the declaration of the group of comrades from Bauman District, where they complain about decisions of the Moscow Committee about Bauman District, regard: 1) the decision of the Moscow committee to be correct and subject to unconditional execution; 2) The content of the declaration submitted to the gubernia party conference is antiparty, and the fact of its preliminary distribution among party members introduces disorganisation and squabbles into the party ranks; 3) Based on such an evaluation, the conference calls to order all comrades in this group, proposes to them to submit without reservations to the decisions of the Moscow Committee that have already been made, and warns them that failure to implement party discipline and further disorganising acts will place them outside the ranks of the party' (see f. 3, op. 2, d. 12, ll. 5 reverse–6). See also V.I. Ivanov's speech (this edition, pp. 470–1).

in their seats.) I request that you not interrupt and that these interruptions not be included in my time. I spoke six minutes.

Besides that, I'll point to another example. On the one hand, it is said that you can't purge a member of the Party CC, for this is the holy of holies. To purge him is not permissible, but I, a sinner, was subjected to this purge [очищение]. Why did they not exclude me? Probably they did not find sins, although there was a fair amount. Comrades! I should say that after the Tenth Congress, we got a division into 'yours' and 'ours'. Someone's hand especially acted upon the provinces in some way. Some say, why did the Party CC not take measures? I want to say, why did you comrades sitting here not speak the whole truth about what you are doing? Why did you not speak? When you walk around the lobby, along the lanes, back alleys, and secluded corners, you lay it all on the line, explaining everything from top to bottom, yet here you act like in the military, with the response that 'all is well'.

Comrades, you are electing a new CC now. They always think that after this there will be something new and special. You need not close your eyes to the fact that the old foundation of the CC remains as it is. Are these comrades necessary? Yes, the majority of them are necessary, but in general and on the whole, comrades, the basic line remains as it was before. What is necessary for a newly-composed CC? You need to come and speak the truth, all the truth, without hiding anything. Here's what we have. In the provinces, there is the most enormous and most serious dissatisfaction. They start to look at one another like the Magician looks at Petrushka.[273] They begin to fear one another and speak in whispers, so that no one would overhear. That's what it's come to. If the same type of work will continue among party members, then we won't get very far. We talk about a United Front, but where is the United Front in our country? There are old comrades, who we always honoured at full voice,[274] and then we say: he left the party! What does this mean? This means that we sin when we frivolously call upon one another to go and show automatic approval to Zinoviev and Lenin! That's what it can come to. You can't joke like this with old activists [работники]. Will you tell on those who did something nasty, committed deception, cheated, or arranged a provocation? This is another question. If they've provided information, this is not a sin, comrades. Information needs to be provided here, there, and everywhere.

---

273   He actually says, 'like the devil looks at Petrushka' (как черт на петрушку). This is a reference to the popular puppet show Petrushka. See Kelly 2009 and Wachtel 1998.

274   во всю ивановскую.

Comrades, I think we also can't pass by in silence comrade Zinoviev's statement that we leaned for support only on cranks [чудаков]. Comrade Zinoviev expounded, of course, upon material that he received in his own hands. If he had stated this not at the conference, but in some other place, I would have straightened him out. I think that there is only one new thing in his theses, which is that worker-communists need to be sent back to plants and factories. I ask, who will remain in the central governing bodies? Who will remain in our bureaucratic institutions? If we sound the alarm now, if we shout now that there aren't enough workers, what will you say when you have dissipated the rest? Defeat this point in the most severe fashion! If you will accept it, if you will lean for support too much on cultured people, then consider me in the first category of those to be excluded ... [ellipses in text] For it is impossible, on the one hand, to shout: workers into management, workers should study! – and on the other hand, to say, you are not cultured, so study culture in the plants and factories. We humbly thank you [irony]. I think that if we will now go to the plants (I am not afraid), then they will say to us: my dears, everything is fine with us. But indeed, I know that there is not enough of this and not enough of that, and I should defend myself. Well then they'll say to me: 'Why in the devil did you come here, you should have remained there'. Therefore I consider this point to be mistaken.

Comrades, I should likewise declare here that after our purge, the theses accepted by the Tenth Congress must be corrected in the part about our attitude toward those, who we want to bring into our ranks and who again will come under surveillance for possible purging. But in general I think that theses and decisions need to be accepted just once, not 30 times. This one time they were accepted at the Tenth Party Congress. We do not need new theses, or else we will put together theses and decisions, and then we'll have to assemble legal experts in order to sort out what was decreed and in which year. You acted according to the resolution of the Eighth Congress, when you should have acted according to the resolution of the Tenth Congress.

In order for us to have a United Front, which is a closely united family, if you will, then you should state openly what dissatisfies you. There is much dissatisfaction to which attention needs to be paid. You shouldn't make prescriptions like the doctor does: don't drink, don't smoke! It shouldn't be that they would say to you: you preach about confiscating valuables, but a gold chain gleams on you, as this was stated to me in Ivanovo (well okay, my chain is not gold). Here is our way of doing things. They start to wear things that don't suit them,[275] but

---

275 Напяливать на себя.

they preach about confiscating valuables. It's necessary to struggle against this. That's where our danger lies. Attention needs to be turned to this danger. That, people of culture [культурники], is where we need to study. But what do we get? Peter, because he is cultured, will tell about how he organised, say, conferences and so forth, yet no matter what a backwoods redneck [Ванка рыжьий] does, they will not publicise it, because he is not cultured.

So that there would be a united, firm, unwavering front of the Russian Communist Party, and comrades, it should be firm in order to confront danger, at this session it needs to be said – (Voice from seat. Don't sign up [to speak]!) No, people should not be discouraged from speaking. They shouldn't be excluded.

Chair. Finish up, Ivan Ivanovich.

Kutuzov. So that there should be a United Front, those very same uncultured masses, on which you depend for support, need to sense that the situation is improving.

[Pikel and Smidovich speak, and then various others.]

G.N. Korzinov (pp. 465–7).[276] In his report about the results of the party purge, comrade Shkiriatov mentioned that those decisions, which the congress took earlier, in fact are not being implemented in the provinces. We know well that the Tenth Party Congress carried through the principles of worker democracy. In fact, it confirmed the principle of discussing all important political questions, which confront the party. Unfortunately, this did not happen in reality. Worker members of the party and even nonparty sympathisers declare that it is important for us to be party members not just on paper, not just when voting, and not just when stuffing our bellies. It is important to collectively work out a line, which our highest party organisations would implement. Unfortunately, after the Tenth Party Congress this either didn't happen or was very limited. Moreover, we say that the party should be more united at the current time. No one will deny this.

Our party should currently absorb as much as possible of the proletarian element, meaning the healthy worker element. The numbers tell us that the leading majority of the party, especially in the Moscow organisation as com-

---

276 Korzinov signed neither the Workers' Opposition's theses nor the Letter of the 22, but at the Tenth Party Congress, he voted against both the resolution condemning the Workers' Opposition and the one banning factions. As a supporter of Ignatov's views, he attended a meeting of the Workers' Opposition during the Tenth Party Congress.

rade Zelensky emphasised, is composed of those very elements, which emerged from among the fellow travelers. These elements are imbued with a vulgar, petty bourgeois psychology, do not properly assimilate, and do not want to carry out a strictly-defined Marxist line. There you have those abscesses and illnesses, which we need to get rid of. Comrade Zinoviev says that workers should present three recommendations and can be accepted after a six-month stage of candidacy. Workers don't especially love to go and collect signatures. It's another matter for petty bourgeois fellow travelers, who with pleasure will collect for you not only five, as comrade Zinoviev recommends, but ten signatures, because their goal is just to get into the party. They know very well how to genuflect [откланяться]. They know how to say, 'I will do as you command', so as to achieve a higher, more respected position. Like the majority of you, I worked in factories. During the course of 20 years, we rooted out workers who did not know how to work as required, but who knew how to run their mouths. Now that our party is in power, the most disgraceful tale-bearing, careerism, and favouritism are practiced. That is what ruins and breaks down our party ranks. We need to get rid of this. Only then will our party really be united and strong, like it was in October.

I propose that for workers we should keep the same two recommendations and three-month stage of candidacy. Fellow travelers, who are deserters from the petty bourgeoisie, should provide ten recommendations. Moreover, these recommendations should be from comrades, who have gone through the school of rigorous underground circles, for such comrades will not in vain hand out recommendations left and right. Then these fellow travelers will need to do a stage of candidacy not for one year, but for two years at least. During this candidacy, they should be required to perform physical labour in plants and factories. I remember that when we were working in the underground, many *intelligenty* who taught us came to the plants and factories and worked with us, either as unskilled labourers or as assistants to metalworkers and so forth, when they wanted to persuade workers to come into the party and move the revolution along. Workers supported them, they taught us, and they learned how to do physical labour. This needs to be done now, too.

According to point seven, people need to be driven out of soviet and economic organisations into the factories and plants. I would have no objection, if comrade Zinoviev actually had spoken about how to drive the entire petty bourgeoisie to the factories and plants, but to keep workers, who really do have a firm hand, there to lead economic policy. If one or another worker-communist or nonparty person served as a commissar [закомиссарился], then send him to a factory and promote a fresh comrade from below to his place. Then the atmosphere will be refreshed.

Point 10 speaks about squabbles [склока]. The question is serious. We say that it's necessary to struggle against squabbles. But how will we do this? Will it be by randomly choosing an individual comrade and setting him in the pillory [к позорному столбу], or by some other means? When we struggle against squabbles, then we need to approach the essential question dispassionately and to say that squabbles, quarrels [ccopa], and groupings are not permitted, either formally or informally. Those who squabble or create groupings should be expelled. Together with them that element, which gives rise to these squabbles and groupings and the like, needs to be chased out. We know that squabbles occur there in the provinces just because individual committee men [комитетчики], secretaries, and individual party functionaries make up reasons to squabble. This needs to be eradicated. Everyone who makes up these reasons should be thrown out ... [ellipses in text]

My last correction relates to cultivating party members. Here they say much, but further than conversations they do not go. We know that in connection with NEP, it is possible to get everything. You only have to put 'money on the barrel [бочка]'. Currently our cells give the entirety of membership dues to raikoms, leaving nothing for themselves, and they have no resources. I propose to act on this like we acted earlier. We left 50% of membership dues in the circle, while 50% went to the raion party organisation, the gubernia organisation, and the Central Committee. Then we will have resources in cells, raions and gubkoms. Then it will be possible for each party member to buy a book, read it, and study it, and at a future cell session to recite what they understood. In this way we will successfully put all comrades' party thought back into our work. If this will not happen, then everything will remain on paper with us. I propose that the Eleventh Congress discuss and accept these four corrections.

∴

Session 11, 2 April, morning.

At the end the chair states, 'Now we should move on to elections of the CC, the Revision Commission and the Control Commission. But before we move on to the question about techniques [техника], we have to take a break in order to fully clear the hall. After that only congress delegates with a full or consultative vote will be permitted to enter the hall. No guests at all should be located in the hall'.

[The chair cleared the hall for a closed session of the congress, which was devoted to discussing and voting upon the case of the appeal of the 22 to the ECCI. The translation of its proceedings is based on unpublished archival material documents.]

Speeches at the closed session of the Eleventh RCP(b) Congress on the case of the 22 members of the former Workers' Opposition, 2 April 1922, afternoon.[277]

Contents:
1. Supplements to the decision about control commissions (Sedoi).
2. About bringing Kotliakov before a revolutionary tribunal (Enukidze).[278]
3. Report of the commission on the case of the 22 members of the former Workers' Opposition (Lebed).
4. Debate about the commission's report. Speakers: Kollontai, Medvedev, Shliapnikov, Kubiak, Petrovsky, Antonov-Ovseenko, and Manuilsky.[279]
5. Acceptance of the resolution on the case of the 22 members of the former Workers' Opposition and corrections to it.
6. Read results of elections to the CC.
7. Comrade Lenin's speech about publishing an announcement in *Pravda*.
8. Comrade Riazanov's speech about publishing an announcement in *Pravda*.
9. Conclusion of the Eleventh Party Congress.
10. Corrections to Comrade Lenin's concluding speech, with Tovstukha's explanatory note attached.
11. Stenographic report of the closed session (and duplicate).

Lebed. Comrades, you remember that the commission was selected in relation to the CCC's proposal to exclude from the party some of the comrades, who signed the letter of the so-called group of the 22. The CCC charged them with frequent systematic violation of the Tenth Congress's decree on party unity. The commission you chose decided that first of all, it needs to be clarified as to whether factionalism really did take place. Was this group and were other comrades really linked by means of the ideology and platform, which were worked out before the Tenth Congress? Having acquainted ourselves with materials of the CCC, the Moscow Control Commission, the Comintern protocols, and

---

277 RGASPI, f. 48, op. 1, d. 14.
278 Kotliakov, a guest (not a delegate) from the Petrograd organisation, was sent before a revolutionary tribunal for having insulted a sentry.
279 According to the stenographic records, Medvedev's and Kubiak's speeches were not recorded in full.

other documents, and having interrogated personally Shliapnikov, Medvedev, Kollontai, Tolokontsev, Chelyshev, Bruno and other comrades, we came to the following conclusions:[280]

1) They prepared in advance and convened the meeting, at which they discussed and signed the statement of the 22. It did not just occur on the spur of the moment, but definitely illegal, factional work preceded it. This factional work was connected with the point of view and line of behaviour, which preceded the Tenth Congress.

2) Twenty-two comrades gathered at a certain time on a certain day. These 22 included not only comrades who live and work here in Moscow, but also comrades from other main centres of Russia. The main question on this meeting's agenda was to discuss unity within our party. In the course of five hours, they discussed this question [of party unity]. At the end of the session, they proposed to appeal to the Comintern with the declaration about which you know. Under questioning, comrades Iakhontov and Medvedev and some others denied that the meeting was organised. They explained that the meeting was completely coincidental. Coincidentally, 22 comrades assembled, started to talk about various problems of trade unions and the economy, and concluded that they needed to talk about the unity of the party front.

But comrades, a comparison of the answers given under interrogation by comrades from among the 22 does not convince us that the meeting was accidental. First, comrades Shliapnikov and Medvedev were not personal friends with all 22 comrades, as they stated to us in the commission. They counted about 12 people, with whom they were personally connected through old revolutionary underground work. As concerns the remaining ten people, well they did not have such a connection with them. They invited them knowing that they adhere to a certain grouping. The very character of the convocation was such that telephone telegrams [телефонограммы] and personal invitations were dispatched. This confirms still more that the meeting undoubtedly was organised. The meeting was organised by the initiative of Shliapnikov and Medvedev. The commission established this fact unanimously.

There was another matter we needed to clarify, because our Party CC and CCC have not denied the right of groups of comrades and of individual comrades to appeal to the Comintern about violations of order within our party. Since the matter stood so, we considered it necessary to clarify if this group

---

280   Handwritten and typed copies of the commission members' questions and the interviewees' answers are in RGASPI, f. 48, op. 1, d. 17.

met just once or was there systematic constant longterm factional work. From documents, which I will make public in good time, we established without a doubt that there was contact with the provinces. Letters written to comrades Shliapnikov and Medvedev definitely indicated that there had been such meetings earlier. For example, Mitin from the Donbas in his letter to comrades Shliapnikov and Medvedev very clearly and definitely asks if Shliapnikov and Medvedev fulfilled the assignment, which they were given at the previous meeting. Comrades Shliapnikov and Medvedev deny that they had meetings before this. About this meeting they say that it too was coincidental and was connected with resolving economic and general questions. Comrade Mitin expresses in his letter dissatisfaction with comrades Shliapnikov and Medvedev for inadequately fulfilling their tasks and he suggests that they transition to self-defence. Another letter from a certain O. Savichev in Rostov says very definitely, 'We, the Workers' Opposition, can win over the Rostov organisation, if we want this. But since we consider this to be inexpedient right now, then we will restrain ourselves'.

Significantly, both the first and the second letter talk about fulfilment of various factional directives, about group-type decisions, and about elaboration of a world view, a platform, and the ideology of this party. Comrade Mitin writes about our lads trying to win over factory committees, by means of them communist cells, then district conferences, and eventually the Donbas can be ours. He asks what it means to say the Donbas is ours. He makes relevant conclusions about the need to transition to self-defence. Savichev definitely writes in his letter about the need to elaborate a world view. As you see, the similarities between these two letters and the direction they take attest that these comrades obviously discussed exactly the same questions at their previous meetings. All this material convinced us that the last meeting, too, where they discussed the declaration to the Comintern and links with provinces occurred on the footing of a factional organisation.

Other documents likewise confirm without a doubt that comrades from this group of 22 carried out a nonparty line. We in the commission asked comrade Shliapnikov if he finds it permissible to make an unverified declaration to the Comintern and to point to unverified facts, which relate in part to the party wanting to create a provocation against the Workers' Opposition after the Third Congress. Allegedly, the Cheka agent Rubinov came to Shliapnikov's and Kollontai's secretaries with the proposal to create a group in a fourth international. The provocation consisted of trying to create grounds to exclude Shliapnikov and Kollontai from the party. Allegedly, there was a search of Shliapnikov's apartment in Moscow, even though he was a CC member. Also, someone unsealed a letter sent to comrade Shliapnikov from Revel, which contained a complaint about the customs mission there (reads.)[281] Next, comrade Kollontai declared, 'When workers go on strike, the Red Army carries out the role of strikebreakers' (reads). Shliapnikov declared, 'You foreigners are shown parades and formal state spectacles here. This is only for show, while in fact a powerful strike movement is occurring'. (reads)

We asked if it was possible to place before the Comintern commission completely unverified facts. Comrade Shliapnikov responded that the protocol was poorly composed and incorrectly formulated both in meaning and tone. Comrade Kollontai .... [ellipses in text] did not exactly deny what she said about boycotts. She pointed out that in her opinion, elections to the Moscow Soviet proceeded in the context of workers' apathy and indifference and that in some rare cases there was even a boycott. After this, the commission started to wonder whom to believe. Should we trust the protocol, which was signed by five members of the commission, which was selected by the Comintern conference, or should we believe comrade Shliapnikov? Both the facts and the character of comrade Shliapnikov's answers convinced us of the veracity of the protocol. We could not believe at all that comrade Shliapnikov speaks French so poorly that he was not understood. Moreover, we think that comrade Shliapnikov gave evasive, unclear, and vague answers to some questions. (Shliapnikov: For example?) Indeed, Shliapnikov says that he provided written answers after the Comintern's decision, so it follows that he could remember what he said to the Comintern. Yet in response to some questions which we asked, for example, 'who received the letter', Shliapnikov declared, 'I don't remember if it was Medvedev or I'.

Based on CCC materials, the commission established that Shliapnikov was repeatedly brought up for violating the decisions of the Tenth Party Congress. In a party cell, he declared, 'It is not workers' fault that they steal; it is the government's fault'. You know that by a majority of only one vote, the CC decided to warn but not exclude comrade Shliapnikov from the party. As concerns the conversation about a personal search, comrade Shliapnikov declared that obviously he was misunderstood, that it was not he who was searched, but that a letter addressed to him was intercepted.

Medvedev also declared that the first meeting was completely a coincidence. Comrades gathered completely on the spur of the moment and started to discuss party unity. Medvedev does not deny that he declared to the Control Commission that he did not organise this meeting. This was fixed in a protocol and he confirmed this in the commission.

---

281   Revel (alt. Reval) was the Russian name for the Estonian city Tallinn.

The matter about inviting comrade Miasnikov to this meeting interested us. All comrades, who signed the declaration to the Comintern, deny that they knew and even that comrade Medvedev knew that it had been decided to exclude Miasnikov from the party. However, some comrades confirmed that they knew about his brochure, in which he wrote about freedom from monarchists to anarchists inclusively. Under questioning, as I said, comrade Kollontai confirmed what she said about the boycott. About whether she considers a split of our party to be premature, she added that if the party does not correct certain procedures and does not take a certain line, then she thinks that a split will be unavoidable. She confirmed this in the commission. Further, when comrade Kollontai was asked if there had been meetings earlier and if she participated, she declared that she did not participate and that there were no such meetings and no organised contact. In her opinion, if there had been all of this, then our party's abnormalities would have been eliminated sooner and party thought would have been livelier.

Therefore, on the basis of documents and interrogations, the commission concluded that comrades Shliapnikov, Medvedev and Kollontai undoubtedly organised this meeting and other meetings. They without a doubt supported links with the provinces. The commission thinks that the decision of the Tenth Congress should be applied to such comrades.

Now, about comrade Mitin, who was asked why he sent this letter and if he thinks that by sending this letter, he violated the decision of the Tenth Congress about unity. He declared that he does not think so, because this letter is not about the party. It concerns the economy, trade unions and other things.

The CCC also proposed to exclude Kuznetsov from the party. First, he hid the length of time he had been in the party. He said that he joined in 1904, but the commission found out from old revolutionaries that even in 1916, when he was in exile, no one considered him to be a party member, nor did they draw him into any party work. He did not carry out party work on his own. It became completely clear that in 1908–9 this very same Kuznetsov maintained a grocer's shop, which he opportunely received as an inheritance. Just as unfortunate is the matter of his profession. He said that he is a metalworker. In the CCC, he declared that he was a metalworker for 22 years. He told us that that it was only 10 years in all. However, we established that he entered the factory for light work only during wartime, so as not to be called up for wartime service in the tsarist army.

Remaining comrades from the group of 22 do not acknowledge their mistakes. They do not recognise that it was incorrect to organise this meeting, to discuss at it the unity of the front, or to summarise unverified facts. They still do not admit mistakes, even though this act brought forth disorganisation and violated the unity we need. They do not even acknowledge errors after publication of the Comintern's and CC RCP's decisions. Having learned about the CCC's proposal to exclude from the party comrades Shliapnikov, Kollontai and Medvedev as organisers and leaders of the former Workers' Opposition group, some of these comrades submitted a declaration of solidarity. They requested that if the above individuals would be excluded by the congress, then they wish to be excluded as well. We asked what moved them to submit such a declaration, which we told them was an even greater violation of party discipline. But first of all, they think that they were generally correct. They do not perceive mistakes in their fait accompli. Second, they cannot reconcile themselves to the fact that some of their cosigners could be punished differently than others. We told them that the party has just one party discipline. There is no group discipline. If documents establish that comrades from the first category of those proposed for exclusion by the CCC really were leaders around whom the former Workers' Opposition grouped, then they are doubly guilty for violating a party directive. Therefore, they should be punished suitably.

In conclusion, comrades, I will read aloud the documents, which we have. I will read only the most significant excerpts from Savichev's letter (reads). Then further: The party organisation counts the year of its existence ... [ellipses in text] (reads excerpt from Savichev's letter). Another excerpt: 'Write about moods, perspectives, changes and concrete measures'. Savichev writes this. I just happen to know who Savichev is. He appeared, god knows from where, in 1917 in the Ekaterinoslav organisation. He is the son of a grand bourgeois, a homeowner, they say a lawyer. He is a young person and it is unknown how he got into the party. I remember that the Ekaterinoslav gubkom talked about excluding him. After liquidation of the Grigorevsk offensive, he was accused in part of having written an article against the Cheka and having yielded to a Menshevik mood. After that he was tried frequently for adventurist escapades. A comrade from Ekaterinoslav gubernia says that the question about him has just been resolved positively. This person wanted to create the world view of the former Workers' Opposition.

Then Mitin. He claimed to have been a party member since 1904. The commission found that he entered the party only in 1920. Before that he was a Menshevik and in 1919 he actively opposed Soviet power (reads excerpt from Mitin's letter). 'I remember that at our last meeting ... [ellipses in text]'.

Voice from seat: What is the date of Mitin's letter?

Lebed: This letter is undated. Comrades Shliapnikov and Medvedev told us that they don't remember when approximately this letter was sent.

Shliapnikov (from his seat): At the end of May, comrades.

Lebed: Comrade Shliapnikov said to us: 'I don't remember, I don't know'. Comrade Mitin declared that he also does not remember. But it would seem it would have been in June or July. On the basis of these documents and facts, the commission unanimously resolved to propose the following statement to the party congress: 'The Tenth Congress of the RCP instructed the CC' (reads). ... [ellipses in text]. In relation to the remaining comrades, the commission suggests to confirm the warning issued by the Comintern.

Kollontai. Comrades, they've dropped the previous accusation against the 22 comrades of submitting a declaration to the Comintern, but have raised a new accusation of a factional grouping. The entire accusation by the Eleventh Congress commission builds upon this very factional grouping. But before addressing the question about whether a factional grouping existed, I want to clear up some things about the previous accusations, which are connected to the 22 comrades' appearance at the Comintern Executive Committee's (Ispolkom's) expanded session. The commission's report has already been distributed to you. It is an entire brochure, which is a lot of material, but it is not exhaustive. For some reason, it did not include the statement, which I sent right after I received what they call the 'protocol of the Comintern commission'. I sent this statement to the Comintern Ispolkom, to our party Politburo, and to the Control Commission. This statement refutes two very important accusations that were brought against me personally and it provides some explanation. Nevertheless, this document did not land in the commission's report. But we will return later to these two points.

First of all, I want to turn your attention to page six, where it says that we bypassed the Russian delegation when we submitted the declaration to the Comintern Ispolkom. We delivered the declaration to the Presidium. Comrade Zinoviev was in the Presidium. He received the original Russian-language statement at exactly the same time when the other commission members received the text in French. Moreover, comrades, pay heed, this factional act was so superbly organised that there weren't even typed copies and not enough handwritten ones for all commission members. A rewritten copy had to be passed from hand to hand. True, I blundered when I did not think to give a copy to the Russian delegation, but I thought that comrade Zinoviev was the Russian delegation's representative.

Now the second thing, comrades, is about the Comintern's commission. As you see, there are 16 points laid out in the accusation against us. These points purportedly include our statements. But I must protest, first of all, against the text of these accusations. I protest, because no one recorded a protocol at the commission's session. Maybe we blundered, in that we did not insist upon the invitation of stenographers and protocolists[282] to this session of the Comintern commission. Then there would not have been misunderstandings and you would have a protocol, which would have precisely recorded the words of comrades Shliapnikov, Medvedev, and me. We approached this commission, however, as if going to dear comrades. We counted upon our words not being distorted and intentionally used against us as a notorious perversion of what we actually said. You know that each thought can be expressed in a different form. I assert that no one wrote down this protocol while we were there. Indeed, you will see this, comrades. Even here it says definitely how 'comrade [Vasil] Kolarov formulated these accusations from Shliapnikov and Kollontai in the following way'. It means they were formulated later. On the other evening, I requested of comrade [Karl] Kreibich that he send us the protocol, because this is usually done. If he composes it, then he should give it to those who spoke for their review.

Comrade Kreibich relayed to us that no one kept a protocol at the time. It was restored later by memory. According to what comrade Kreibich said, comrade Clara Zetkin restored it, but here it says that comrade Kolarov restored it. I ask you to pay attention to the fact that the protocol was not kept precisely. Therefore we are not responsible for each letter of its formulation.

Having read this thing, which they call a protocol, I protested two points: point 7 regarding the Moscow Soviet and a point further down about the Red Army. I protested in writing to the Comintern Ispolkom and I sent a copy to the Politburo. (She reads the text of her protest.) This is the first thing. This matter was brought up again at the session of the Eleventh Congress's commission and again not in the way that I formulated it. Here on page eight, it says that comrade Kollontai declared that she considers it to be a negative phenomenon that during re-elections to the Moscow soviet, there were almost no groupings which were opposed to the communists, and likewise that there were no groupings among the communists. I said that I thought it not to be an undesirable thing but instead a dangerous symptom that no groupings at all spoke out. When they were formulating the protocol more precisely, I drew attention to the fact that it did not express exactly what I said. Comrade Dzerzhinsky said, 'Comrade Kollontai, why do you insist so much on precise language? This has no significance'.

Moving on, there is the very important point regarding the Red Army. Here on page 22 it says, 'When the statement ended, comrade Marcel Cachin read

---

282   Uses feminine forms стенографистки and протоколистки.

the following entry from his notebook in order to supplement the accusation, which the commission set forth against Shliapnikov and Kollontai'. So, comrade Marcel Cachin's notebook appears on the scene. It reports that I said that when workers go on strike, Red Army men play the role of strikebreakers. When I read this in the materials, I was surprised. I said absolutely nothing about the Red Army to the commission, because this did not relate at all to the little report, which I made in presence of the commission. I was not a presenter at this commission's meeting. They invited Shliapnikov and me, whereupon I declared right away that I had come as an interpreter. We proposed that they invite other comrades who signed. I was there in case an interpreter was needed. Then, in addition to Shliapnikov's statement, I took the floor and provided some clarifications. How the Red Army came up, I could not understand.

But after I examined more carefully this bit about comrade Marcel Cachin's notebook, I remembered something, about which I wrote in the statement, which I sent to the Comintern Ispolkom and to the CC. For some reason, this statement did not land in this report. It said: 'In addition, I must protest against the supplement to the protocol, in which there is information that was collected from the notebook of a commission member'. At the session when the commission met, I said nothing about the Red Army. Marcel Cachin's notes are from my private conversations with him (reads). I lodge a protest, because I could not possibly speak so absurdly about the Red Army as this example purports. Just think about how nonsensical this is. Only a comrade, who is completely unfamiliar with our life, could write this, only a French comrade, who caught an accidental and isolated fact and wrote about it in a distorted form. Then I thought that we might find still more absurdities by searching the notebooks of our comrades. But this is a good lesson for us. You have to weigh every word when you speak. But the fact of the matter is not about weighing words, when you speak, but about .... [ellipses in text] there is no place for them, if they will distort our words and will try to use them against us. I protest, for I declare that I could not have uttered such nonsense.

Next, comrades, comrade Lebedev brought into his report yet a fifth point incriminating me. This is my speech at the Third Comintern Congress. I will not say what it was about, but it is strange that two days after this speech, the Comintern Ispolkom elected me to the International Women's Secretariat and confirmed my membership in the Comintern Ispolkom and later in the presidium, in which I remain for the time being. I think that if my speech had been antiparty, they would not have appointed me as International Women's Secretary and would not have elected me to the Comintern Ispolkom.

Now they talk about a new accusation of factionalism. They say that this was an organisation. I will repeat to you what I said to the commission, which is that there was no factionalism. A faction was not organised. Yet if there had been one, the party would have gained from this contact, in the sense that we would have met and debated among ourselves as close friends. But here is the misfortune and to what we have been reduced. When there are just two of us, we talk about a lot of things that cause us pain. But when a third person comes (laughter), we fall silent. We fear one another. We worry that this third person will think that we two are that very same Workers' Opposition, which brings about division in the party.

Chair. Your time is running out.

Kollontai. I request that the comrades give me 10 more minutes for what might be my final deathbed speech.

Chair. There are no objections.

Kollontai. The fact of the matter is that when close comrades gather, they speak cautiously with one another. I repeat here, as I did to the commission, that I think that it would be useful to discuss problems, which have become painful. For example, consider how little this congress has discussed party building and related matters. No matter how highly I regard comrade Zinoviev's report on party building, knowing his intellect and talent, nevertheless I will say that people from the provinces could give us considerably more practical supplements. That is, if only there had been earlier the possibility to talk through these questions in the provinces, if they could have allowed a clash of opinions there. You don't want to say how it was. There is no clash of opinions in the provinces, probably there was not. Indeed, speaking for myself, as soon as you express a definite opinion, which departs from certain directives, right away the talk about factionalism begins. That is why I think that it would not be terrible, if there were a greater possibility for exchange of opinions within the party.

Now I will address factionalism. If any kind of faction actually had been organised, would it have acted so clumsily? Indeed would it have issued a declaration, which only touched on the most general questions? It would have elaborated a factional proposal. This is the first thing. The second thing is that we would not have gone to a meeting of the Comintern Ispolkom. We would have prepared for the Eleventh Congress and would have brought forth a platform for it. Now that would have been factionalism. We all have struggled to prevent a party rupture. We think unconditionally that this is an undesirable phenomenon and that we should employ all our strengths now in order to make the party healthy. It would be a great misfortune, if our party would lead us and its life in such a way as to make this split actually possible. Therefore, we acted without meeting in a factional manner. So I categorically deny the accusation against us regarding factionalism and organisation of a faction.

The next accusation raised here is on page eight, where it says that neither comrade Kollontai nor comrade Medvedev thinks it was a mistake to appeal to the Comintern. They accuse us of being frightfully unrepentant. If we had sincerely repented, so they said to us in the Control Commission, then there would have been a different attitude toward us. Sincere repentance. They spoke very warm words to us about this, but it forces me to recall Saltykov-Shchedrin's tale about how they sent peasants into exile. Upon meeting these peasants, the author asks them: what are you being exiled for? They answer, 'For being unrepentant. The lord, the landowner [барин, помещик] teaches us what is good, intelligent, and reasonable. He even goes so far as to pull us by the hair, but we remain unrepentant. For our unrepentance, we are exiled'.

The third accusation is about efforts to create a split. They said very definitely that comrade Kollontai declared that the time will come for a party split, of course, if the party will not correct its line. Both here and to the commission, I have pointed out that I have become accustomed to look at things from a historical standpoint. Speaking exclusively for myself in this case, I personally took a conceptual approach. I am accustomed to regarding things from a historical standpoint. Unfortunately, historical materialism teaches me that the number of mistakes I see in our party, chiefly in its mode of operation [regime], shows me that many of our comrades will find it confining. There is discontent. Many find the stuffiness [духота] in the party suffocating. The impossibility of displaying one's initiative and thought puts off many. Historically, this forces them to gather in groups, although they would prefer to avoid this. What do we need to do?

First of all, we need to restore the health of the party regime. This is the most basic thing. Finally, what we have now, which is a small grouping of a few higher-ups who essentially make the decisions, should disappear. Passing resolutions alone will not change things. We pointed out that the Tenth Congress resolutions about worker democracy need to be implemented. As we also indicated, it is undoubtedly important, desirable and correct in a political sense to have union [смычка] with the peasantry, but equalisation of the entire political line [равнение всей политической линии] should follow the line of the working class. Right now, circumstances are difficult. The new bourgeoisie-in-creation is putting pressure on the party and the entire soviet apparatus. Pressure also comes from a different social stratum of the peasantry. Our party cannot come to be the servant of the soviet apparatus. On the contrary, the dictatorship of the proletariat should remain in full measure. Therefore, we need to try to create such a regime within the party, so that workers would strive to join it. We need to involve the working class, such as it is, in creating a foundation, which in actual fact would firm up the dictatorship of the working class. What kind of dictatorship of the working class is it, if we say that the working class does not exist? It is the kind of dictatorship in which we did not involve the working class.

Comrades, they will judge us now not for our deeds, but for our thoughts and for our attempt to realise within our party the resolutions, which our congresses accepted. I affirm that the regime within the party will not change after excluding several of us comrades. For change to occur, conscious will and judgement are needed. Speaking straightforwardly, we would find it difficult to be excluded. But if this heavy sacrifice is demanded in order to restore our party's health, I am ready to bear this blow, which would be the heaviest in my life. You should know what we want and what kind of thoughts we have. I will repeat it briefly once more. We want a leading role in the party for the working class, both within the party and outside of it. We want for Tenth Congress decisions about worker democracy to be carried out. We want a higher level of activism and the certain opportunity for exchange of opinions and criticism. But we also advocate the attraction of the working class into all areas of creative life. We are against the party's isolation from the working masses. We believe in workers' creativity. If there is no place for this in our party, then exclude me. But even outside the ranks of our party, I will live, work and struggle for the Communist Party.[283]

Medvedev.[284] I will begin with the commission's report about the 22, which you have in your hands. I request that you turn to the first page. First of all, I should say that during all my 22 years of work in the party, I have never been a cowardly person who hid my thoughts. Moreover, as we are here at a closed session, I give you my honest word that I will speak the pure truth (reads). I request of you to look here: 'The Comintern conference elected (reads)'. 'What did Shliapnikov, Kollontai and Medvedev say to this commission', further 'They informed members of the commission'. I am skipping over a few phrases 'about dissatisfaction and political apathy of the working class'. I confirm that this is an utter and intentional lie. I am not a CC member, nor am I a candidate member. When you write three times in a document, which will be distributed all

---

283   Documents in this file show that Kollontai made minor stylistic and grammatical changes to the version of her speech to be preserved, with some clarifications and elaborations.
284   Medvedev's speech is from the second copy of the stenographic report. It appears that he might not have corrected it.

across Russia, that I am a candidate member of the CC, well is this just a slip of the tongue? I think that this was done intentionally, in order to lift me up higher by the hair and throw me to my death.

Now I will move on to comrade Lebed's accusations. He said that I am the organiser and motivator. This document, which you have in your hands, does not provide my testimony. For half an hour I carefully put down in writing everything, for which I was willing to put my life on the line. The report mentions none of this. Kindly read this testimony. When comrade Dzerzhinsky asked me, 'How do you regard Kollontai's words', I said that it's not true, for I know of a case when workers were far more activist than was expected. ... [ellipses in text] They undermined our party bodies' decision. Our party body set up rules for elections, so that only those whose names had been given to the elections commission 24 hours in advance could be elected. I recalled one case in which workers disrupted this. I could not possibly have said what they have attributed to me in this document, which will travel all across Russia and far beyond Russia's borders.

I will move on to the accusations that I was motivator-organiser. Comrades, I have already declared that our meeting was accidental. I should decipher this here a little. Likewise, I requested that this be entered into the protocol precisely. I'm ready to recognise this at any time of day or night. I said that ten years of personal friendship and work in the underground link us to 12 of the 22, while most of the remaining ten had come to attend the Congress of Metalworkers. They were members of the central committee of the Metalworkers' Union, of which we also were members. Further, I will describe how the meeting came together. At a personal meeting, we, the members remaining here, heard about some sad resolutions. People spoke about how extremely difficult it is to show any kind of creative enterprise or initiative at any party assembly. Comrade Petrovsky points out that Comrade Medvedev and others are old members of our party and personal friends. I don't deny that we have worked a long time with these comrades and that we meet often. Twelve of us are members of the central committee of the Metalworkers' Union and heads of economic bodies. As such, we have turned to one another to resolve economic problems. Not only are we personal friends, but we work together all the time in relation to industry. It is not true that we summoned people by telephone-telegram. I adamantly deny this.

Further, Comrade Lebed asserts that the commission established the existence of factionalism. If there really had been factionalism, then how could comrade Molotov have reported to the congress that there are not numerous tendencies or groupings of any kind. Here is what he said in his report: 'recently it seems as if' (reads an excerpt from comrade Molotov's report). If the party's general secretary, whom you have elected, says this in a report, well you should dismiss him, for he's a bad secretary. During the course of a year, he was unable to catch us. All that time we were at his disposal. He dispatched us here, there, and everywhere to senior work assignments.

They say that I was an organiser and an inspirer. Allow me to say briefly what I have done recently. When the Czechoslovak uprising began in mid-1918, I was a member of VTsIK and as such was thrown into struggle for this Czechoslovak front. There I was until the beginning of 1919. I was a member of the division and of the Military Revolutionary Council (Revvoensovet) of the First Army, until we took Ufa and Orenburg. Then it was broken up into two independent parts and our body was liquidated. I was recalled to Moscow. In the beginning of 1919, I was at the CC's disposal and it immediately sent me to the Caspian-Caucasian Front. I was there in the field until our army was forced far back. The army was supposed to take the Caucasus from the direction of Astrakhan district. The Revvoensovet was disbanded.

After this I returned here to Moscow and was appointed chair of the Donskoi Executive Committee (Ispolkom). Many days, weeks, and months I spent in Donskaia oblast or in nearby districts, where I led work right up to the Seventh Congress.[285] The congress was 7 November. Then on 17 December 1919, I was sent close to Petrograd as a member of the Revvoensovet of the Seventh Army. Then I worked with Comrade Zinoviev. I stayed there until the last days of January [1920]. In the last days of January, I was recalled here. There was peace with Estonia and the army was transferred over to labour. I was recalled to Moscow and was assigned as a railway commissar in charge of repair of rolling stock, two bread lines (Moscow-Kazan and Kursk), one military line (Aleksandrovsk), and one fuel line (Northern). After this, I was transferred to the Kuban for party work. I returned from the Kuban in the end of 1920. After the Eighth Congress, I was returned to membership in the central committee of the Metalworkers' Union.[286]

From June to the end of July 1921, I worked part-time and was on partial leave. After that entire struggle, which I had to wage, I needed rest, and the central committee granted my request for leave. After a month, I went for six and a half months as a special representative [уполномоченный] of VTsIK to Iaroslavskaia guberniia. They say that I organised illegal organisations. Com-

---

285   The Seventh Party Congress was held in March 1918 and the Eighth Party Congress in March 1919. The Seventh Congress of Soviets was held 5–9 December 1919. Perhaps Medvedev was referring to the latter, but he or the stenographer placed it in the wrong month.

286   The Eighth Congress of Soviets was in December 1920.

rades from Iaroslavl are here. Nemsky is secretary of the gubernia committee. Tabakov and Mitkevich are also here. Say, please, did I convene illegal meetings and select likethinkers in your organisation and counterpose them to our general party organisation? This is not so, comrades. This accusation is a total fabrication, with the goal of undermining everything which we have accomplished.

The accusation against me of factionalism is totally baseless. Some of the questions about Mitin's letter were not presented to the commission. Mitin's letter was addressed to me, but I still declare right here and now that I had forgotten that. This happened right after the congress. I explained to the commission what 'ours' and 'our lads' mean. I said that we metalworkers use this expression for someone who is either a metalworker or a comrade with whom we worked a long time in the underground. They did not tell you that I said to the commission that the meeting about which Mitin wrote was among Metalworkers' Union central committee members. Mitin, Ptashkin, Lobanov, and some other comrades attended the meeting. Those from the provinces said that they get no information about union and party matters, so they told those of us in Moscow to keep them informed by sending materials about union and party matters. Shliapnikov and I assumed this responsibility. A comrade, with whom we have worked since the very beginning of the revolution, requested this. Comrade Lebed, why did you not reveal accurate evidence? Why did you not put it in print? You should have done this in the report, so that I would believe you. You did not do this.

During our discussion with the commission, they asked me why we did not appeal to the Control Commission. But the ccc does not resolve all political problems. In the course of further discussion, they told me: 'Indeed, the congress elected us'. Then I said, 'True, the congress elected you, but in fact you do not investigate these questions'. It is true that in private conversation I said, 'I don't believe you'. Why, comrade Solts, did you not bring a document that you put Medvedev on trial for violating party discipline? (Solts: We did not put you on trial.) For 22 years, I have worked in our party. I can recall no time when I was not an activist. I don't know if the representative of the Cherepovetskaia Control Commission is here at the congress.[287] Yes, there she is. She knows me. She knows that I have worked since the beginning of 1905, when I appeared before her at her apartment as the first candidate of a circle of agitators. Many comrades know that I was always among their ranks during the most difficult

---

287   I could not identify this person, based on the lists of delegates with full and advisory votes, but the organisation was represented at the congress.

periods for our party. Not once was I tried for violation of party discipline. The CC did not find anything in our behaviour that violated party discipline. This did not happen for 22 years, and it has not happened now.

Since the CC secretary said there are no factions, then the accusation falls away. If they do cast this accusation, well it is not based on anything. Thus the accusation falls away [отпадает]. Here is what they try to attribute to me. Supposedly, I am worn out from having been a roaming [кочующий] member of the party. I was in Astrakhan. I was in various places. No one has the right to tell me that I didn't work much. I was in the army. No one will dare to point to me and say that sometime and somewhere I created some kind of grouping, which was directed against our party organisation. I never did this. How will you decide? In this document, the commission proposes to exclude me from the party. If, in the course of a year, I will prove my devotion to the working class and that my devotion to the working class is higher than group interests, then the party will accept me back. I regard your decision without fear, because I don't feel that you will fatally wound me. When you heard the Control Commission's proposal for the first time, party members were present here as guests. Having heard this, these party members decided to place me before a court of the working class. Right now in Moscow, elections are proceeding for the congress of metalworkers. I received an invitation from the Radio Morse factory. Together with other comrades, I was elected to the Congress of Metalworkers.

Zelensky. So you will appeal to the workers.

Medvedev. Don't try to set me up. I'm not saying that my fearlessness is due to thinking that the workers will follow me. But I do reject the baseless accusation that I'm an enemy of the working class and an enemy of the party. Comrade Paniushkin's statement also confirms this (reads an excerpt from it). That's what was said when the comrade decided upon a senseless step. Here is how he characterises our attitude toward his wish. No one can say anything to us about our behaviour. I will regard your decision without fear. After all you've heard, you might decide that excluding us will make the party stronger and increase its forces. I speak sincerely in saying that I would exclude each of you, if I were confident that it would make the party stronger. I have told the truth and your business is to decide.

Handwritten note from Shliapnikov to comrade Vasilevsky:
    I am returning the stenographic reports. The last one was extraordinarily confused. Parts of speeches by comrade Medvedev, comrade Kubiak, and oth-

ers were inserted into mine. I had to fundamentally rework and rewrite them. I request that you follow the rewritten text. A. Shliapnikov, 7 April [1922].

Shliapnikov's speech with editing marks in his hand:

[Where the differences are significant, I enclose in parentheses the parts he adds and strike through those he marks for deletion]

Comrades, the very way in which this case is formulated here attests to deeply unhealthy relations within our party. Even if you exclude us from the party, I would be happy if you would use our example to halt all those outrages which take place within our party. Before dwelling on all the presenter's distortions and the documents he quoted, I permit myself to direct your attention to what we experienced after the Tenth Congress. You know about the conditions in which the Tenth Congress took place. Our desire to put an end to all kinds of factionalism was unanimous. Comrades here, who were in the Workers' Opposition and were delegates to the Tenth Congress, will confirm that our last meeting was dedicated not to creating any more factions or groupings in the provinces, but to work within the party. We agreed to direct any efforts along the party line, according to party procedures, and on common foundations, ~~without creating any groupings~~. Comrades Kubiak, Kutuzov, and others will confirm this.

It (the assertion) is not true that ~~right now this last~~ appeal (of ours) has ~~at least some kind of very remote~~ ideological link with what happened then (at the last congress). What the presenter quoted here has no relation to reality, either formally or actually. Comrade Presenter pointed to two letters. Mitin wrote one letter in May or June of last year. The second letter was written in May of last year. No one explained the origins of these letters. This report refers to the letters' origins thus: 'Some letters and documents, which Shliapnikov was forced to hand over the Party CC at the faction of the last Congress of Metalworkers'. This statement does not correspond to reality. I did not surrender these letters under any kind of pressure (and not at all at the location, where the act of indictment indicates). I handed over part of the letters (about 13) at the session of Moscow senior personnel ~~where comrade Zinoviev was present and I did so on his suggestion~~ (I gave the commission 13 more letters and documents in my apartment). (But how and for what reason did I hand over these 26 documents?)

In my report, I pointed to cases of persecution within the party on the basis of former factional divisions. From the perspective of party unity, this is impermissible. If we want unity, we can't separate out people on the basis of how they voted or what line they supported before or at the Tenth Congress. It is harmful to divide members in this way after we have accepted a resolution about unity. This is a splittist tactic. (At the meeting of Moscow personnel,) Comrade Zinoviev flung at me (the rebuke) that the facts I brought up were not true and that there were no such cases. ~~That these letters are in the briefcase.~~[288] The assembly of senior personnel selected a commission of five to seven people and (right there) I laid 13 documents on the table. When they came to my place, I gave them 13 more. Thus, 26 documents (were given over), (crying out about abnormalities in our party and about violations of unity).

~~Then they quoted here the letter of Savichev, a person who went crazy from factionalism, as comrade Solts confirmed.~~ (What are we seeing now? They use this letter to impart a 'criminal-punitive' character. The prosecutor spoke about Savichev's letter. If he had inquired of me in a comradely manner about this comrade, then he would not have relied upon his letters, I hope. Right around the same time when Comrade Savichev wrote his letter, he was being judged by the control commission, which together with a medical doctor forcibly dispatched him to a sanatorium. That is, they found in him signs of psychological disorder, which arose on the basis of last year's discussion. But our accusers think it is fine to use all means against us, including even letters from mentally ill people. Comrade Solts can confirm everything I've said.) Comrade Solts and I pitied this comrade, whose brains were addled by factional struggle. I received many letters from him. ~~In the CCC they investigated his case and Solts sent him to a sanatorium.~~ Yet this document here, you see, serves as evidence that we have links and a faction. Well, what could be more vulgar (more unconscionable than this?). If (the commission) took this seriously, then it should have studied all 26 documents, which I presented.

I receive a lot of letters. ~~Tokchak's letter: 'They accuse our party of Menshevism and that we betray the eight-hour work day'. The letter is addressed to Shliapnikov and to Tomsky.~~ (Just before coming here I received a letter signed by a comrade named Tkachko. I don't know him, but this does not stop the comrade from appealing to me and to Tomsky with a protest against eliminating the eight-hour work day). On the basis of this letter, one could say (likewise) that I am organising something. Comrade Lebed rebuked me, because I do not remember who wrote the letter he quoted, even though I remembered what I said in the Comintern and I refuted those distortions which entered the commission's questions. Imagine this for yourselves: they take from me an envelope

---

288   Что в портфеле эти письма.

containing 26 documents. They read an excerpt from a letter that they say comes from the Donbas. I ask if there is a signature. They answer 'no'. Moreover, you know, this letter was written a year ago, but the Comintern commission was just a month ago (and naturally it is easier to remember that which is closer in time). If it works the opposite way with comrade Lebed, that is, the further in time he departs from events, then the better he remembers them, then this is his fortunate nature. I am not distinguished by this quality.

The main point of the accusation is that we had systematic links. Facts are needed to prove this. But to prove our systematic contact on the basis of two letters, of which one is from a ~~crazy~~ (mentally ill) person and the other from a Metalworkers' Union central committee member, who writes about union matters (and paints a picture of monstrous outrages taken toward party members). Aren't comrades Andreev and Kubiak here? The Politburo assigned them together with us to work up a plan for downsizing the metalworking industry. We had to meet often (and the business in the letter is about that). (Alone and en masse, we often went to the Politburo). After the Tenth Congress, a shake-up began in the provinces. In some places, there were persecutions and expulsions from the party (in order to settle accounts for old disagreements). I was bombarded with letters. In going to the Politburo and the Orgburo, I left no stone unturned. I pestered everyone. I pointed out that unjust pressure occurred in the provinces. I spoke about how we don't acknowledge the resolution on unity that we accepted. Already in April and May, I brought protests to the CC. Unfortunately, nowhere did I receive satisfaction. (They seize upon the word 'meeting' and find fault.) I saved a large number of written complaints from the provinces. (The commission, which was selected at the assembly of Moscow senior personnel, should have paid close attention to the documents given over to it. It should have tried to correct those defects and flagrant violations of party unity, which are raised in those documents and which have not been refuted.)

~~Hiding nothing, I handed over these documents in good conscience, so that they should be studied.~~ We had no underground organisations. (Does it really need to be said?) If an underground organisation were needed, comrades, then we, who are all people with underground experience, could have organised it. I insist to you that this did not enter into our (intentions) ~~interests, nor into the interests~~ (was not dictated by the interests) of our party. Comrades from Gomel are here. I spent time with them from November to February. If I had been a factionalist, then it would have come to light during my work there. I made the circuit of a significant share of (uyezds of Gomel) gubernia, and as a special representative of VTsIK, I carried through the produce tax [продналог] there. Let comrades from Gomel say if I departed even one iota from the CC's line or from those decisions, which resulted from the Tenth Congress decree. I am confident that I will not receive even one rebuke from them. That is reality, while this /he points to the commission's materials/ is a fairy tale. There is no basis to the charge that we systematically carried out 'underground work'.

Such trivia have even been introduced, as if by means of telephone-telegrams we invited people to meet.[289] There was nothing of the sort, comrades. Here is how it was. Before the Congress of Metalworkers, comrades come to visit me and they sit for awhile, or I go to visit someone, without any previously outlined programme and without any agenda determined in advance. (Having dispersed our congress group), we decided at the Tenth Congress that we needed to remain within the party and not create any groupings. We strictly observed this decision, including the decision of the Tenth Congress about unity.

Comrade Lebed quoted here some phrases from the letter of one comrade, ~~Fokin~~ (Frolov) it seems (his letter served as the basis for a trial of me in August). The Electrical Factory (of the Station) of 1886 party cell has evaluated and disproved this whole letter. (In point 2 of its protocol no. 22, we read: 'Resolved to transfer the question about comrade Frolov's tactless step to the cell bureau for its investigation. The bureau will make a report about it at the next session of the cell. Having heard the oral statement of comrade Vasilev, who is the secretary of the Communist Faction of the district branch of the All-Russian Union of Metalworkers, the communist cell declares that comrade Shliapnikov did not make any factional statements in his report about economic policy, which he made on the cell's request'.) Both the Moscow Committee and the Party CC, to which this protocol was sent in full, know about this. This (Frolov) ~~Fokin~~ landed under investigation for having written the letter. So, I was put on trial on the basis of such information (in August, but now these tarnished and disproven facts are put forth in the name of the commission of the congress). ~~Comrade Fokin seems to be an electrical station worker, but who he really is, I well and truly do not know.~~

(Comrade Lebed declared that) the interrogation convinced (him) that we are not all personally connected. (Not) true. Comrade Medvedev pointed out (how and why we) were all personally connected (either through the Union of Metalworkers or in the underground). If anyone (of our comrade acquaintances) wants to see one another, to converse, you can (of course) come and bring along your comrade, please. To make a faction of this is just as difficult to do as from a tea party or pancake supper, which they arrange sometimes in Moscow, even in the Kremlin. It is not right to make a split and faction out of this (rendezvous of comrades) and to blow it up (into something criminal).

---

289   Telegrams sent by telephone.

Let's move on (now) to what I said to foreigners (who were communists). I made a rather detailed report about these matters to our CC. Just as soon as the article appeared in *Pravda* on 7 March, I sent the following declaration to the Politburo, which I introduce here fully, in order for you to be current about what I said and how I actually said it. In order to cut short unscrupulous commentary, /he reads/.[290] (This letter refutes all the insinuations contained in the accusation and it provides an important picture of how the matter actually stood.) In order to force the CC to carry out the decisions of the Tenth Congress, it was necessary either to transfer the question to the rank and file, as was done during the period of discussion, or to put pressure upon the CC through an external (international) body. We selected the latter path.

It was not our fault that the radio broadcast an intraparty matter and the press wrote about it. Many times I resolutely refuted the odious, unworthy distortions, which were derived from notebook entries and elsewhere, and were used to characterise our testimony to the commission.

Over the past year, there have been many attempts to set up a provocation around an organisation of the Workers' Opposition, including an attempt at a fourth international. At the Fourth All-Russian Congress of Trade Unions, they tried to 'unite' me in a group with the late Artem [F.A. Sergeev], textile workers, and others. This happened again at the Metalworkers' Congress. In August of last year, people whom I did not know sent couriers, who proposed that I enter a fourth international. I informed the CC about this right away. I delivered a negative answer to the courier and simultaneously sent a copy of it to the CC. But just imagine. The CC was not interested. I can read to you an extraordinarily revealing document about this business. (Questions to comrade Trotsky and his answer).[291] That is how they regarded my statements at the CC plenum. You see, I made the question directly about the Cheka. Why?

~~If any cell requests me [as a speaker or for other party work], it meets refusal and a ban on further requests for me. Comrades have brought up facts that a courier, who was a party comrade, carried a letter to me about shocking things going on in the Estonian mission. He was detained and the letter was confiscated, Athough the letter was addressed to a CC member, it was returned to the person about whom the complaint was made. The CCC is currently investigating this matter.~~

Now I will address the matter, which concerns comrade Miasnikov. Neither at the time of the Tenth Congress nor ~~after~~ (before it) was Miasnikov ever a

---

290   See document above.

291   See these documents below.

member of the former Workers' Opposition. He spoke out against us in the most resolute way. We knew that his case was being investigated (in the CC), but we did not know yet that they had already decided to exclude (him). He had not received this decision about exclusion. Otherwise, of course, he would not have numbered among those who signed. This is so elementary that it's hardly even necessary to think much about it. Who is comrade Miasnikov? Comrade Miasnikov is a proletarian (who has devoted his whole life to the party). There are (not) so many of these among us. He needs to be regarded somewhat differently and not just tossed overboard. We (the party) now have lost influence over him. (But does the matter really stand with him as the prosecutor informs us?) I have a statement from Perm gubkom (member) (comrade) Belov, who informs of the following: /reads/

Note from Perm gubkom member A. Belov to the Politburo, 1 March 1922. Upon my arrival in Moscow, I learned that comrade Miasnikov had been excluded from the RCP(b) and that he was accused of having published in Perm gubernia a brochure called 'Discussion Material'. I attest that the brochure was published not by comrade Miasnikov, but by the gubkom. The gubkom plenum decided to publish it. The proposal at the plenum to publish it was made by one of the conference participants, but not by comrade Miasnikov.[292]

Shliapnikov (speaking): That's the kind of picture that is revealed.

~~Now concerning a fourth international. That was an attempt to stage a provocation. There were many such facts. This also happened at the Fourth Congress of Metalworkers, when they wanted to make the Workers' Opposition out of Artem and me. The business did not end with this. There was an attempt to join~~ the Workers' Opposition to a fourth international. I protested at the plenum. I even have written evidence of my protest. I wrote the following to comrade Trotsky: /reads/

Note from Shliapnikov to Trotsky, 30 March 1922 (typed copy).
L.D. Don't you remember my protest, which I made at the CC plenum in the autumn of last year regarding Cheka (VChK) participation in organisation of a fourth international? They corrected me then that this was not VChK, but Registrud [labour registry]. You became interested and jokingly forced me to repeat the story about how a fourth international was organised in Moscow. I think you also remember my proposal to forbid the Cheka from organising a

---

292   RGASPI, f. 48, op. 1, d. 14, l. 60.

fourth international, which also met with laughter. Neither then nor afterwards did they deny the Cheka's participation.

A. Shliapnikov

Shliapnikov: So I said 'with Cheka participation'. I had facts. At that time they corrected me and said that this was not the Cheka, but Registrud. Nevertheless, I know that there is a bit of a resemblance. Here is comrade Trotsky's answer: /reads/.

Trotsky's reply:

A.G. I remember what you said in this regard. But I and all the others, I suppose, thought that this was simply a *boutade* (quip), a trick. It never entered my head that you could think seriously that the Cheka (Dzerzhinsky, Unshlikht?) are organising a fourth international. Trotsky.[293]

Shliapnikov (speaking):[294] Of course, I don't suspect either Dzerzhinsky or Unshlikht; it is lower down. Who knows? When I learned the details, then I was startled that all threads led to the Hotel Lux. Parenthetical 'comrades' gathered there and organised an international hostile toward us. One person, who was wrapped up in this affair, turned out to bear several names and to live in the very Hotel Lux. First one thing, and then another. All this forced me to say that

---

293　Both notes are from RGASPI, f. 48, op. 1, d. 14, l. 58.

294　The documents in this file include a page purportedly from Shliapnikov's speech, which was not in the version he corrected. The page was located between the section ending with the reading of Trotsky's letter and the page beginning with a statement about Dzerzhinsky and Unshlikht. Here:

　　... (reads) ... The New Economic Policy deepens this dissatisfaction, because well-fed people appear on the streets. All this places the proletariat in a completely different situation than it held two years ago. "NEP deepens this dissatisfaction ..." (reads up to the word порада). Of course, if you come to the factory, then your mood will be different than if you spend time in the Bolshoi Theatre or at our congress. This reason threatens a break between the party and the proletarian mass. "According to the last point" ... /reads/. Further you quoted completely inaccurately here some points, which it would seem I said, but since they are taken in isolation, they are absurd. Yet in fact I did not say them and did not even think them in such a way as they are arranged. I was asked: "What is your attitude". I will not talk, but will read what I wrote then under fresh impression of the matter. The first answer was about my attitude toward NEP: "My answer comes to the recognition ..." (reads). That which I read, you know all this, and there are not few such facts. /reads/. I think that this is so. If our people had been there, not in the factionalist sense, this would not have been. The second question concerned my situation in the CC and in the party. I brought up some facts related to this. Letters went missing. I did not receive some letters ... (laughter, noise). I did not complain about this (reads).

this was a Cheka agent. So I felt I had to confront the CC with the question (and there they corrected me, pointing out that it was not the Cheka, but Registrud). Then this affair (organisation of a fourth international) continued. In March the same people made the same type of proposal to me. As in the first case, I brought it to the attention of the CC. ~~I think this was on 30 August.~~ They didn't even ask me about it. Obviously the CC knew. It was informed (by others) that a fourth international is being organised. Neither in the Orgburo nor in the Politburo did anyone ask me about this.

Chair. Your time is running out.

Shliapnikov. ~~I will take another couple of moments.~~ I think that you will unburden us of oppressive nicknames [клички]. Vladimir Ilich promised to change our name. Obviously, he had in mind making us nonparty. But all the same, I have to say that if you will talk with us like we talk with you, there will be considerably more points of convergence than disagreements that push us apart. On our side, by me in particular, everything was done in order to restrain hot heads from making false steps. Molotov, Solts, and others know this. Frequently I directed entire groups of people on the Bauman, Briansk, Nizhegorod, and many other cases to the Party CC. For me, it was more important than anything that the party be united and intact. But we observed how this party unity was being realised in an extraordinarily strange way. In the provinces, people either pass into a rage over this unity or they close themselves off into small groups. We need to pay attention (to relate) to this danger very seriously.

If you think that our exclusion will make the party stronger – do it. But I should say to you, let comrade Zelensky not worry. While you were arranging a trial of us here, Moscow workers learned about this. Factory cells in four factories responded to this news by electing me to the gubernia conference of the Metalworkers' Union. /Voice from seat: From nonparty workers./ No, comrade, the party cells unanimously advanced me as a delegate. I have protocols confirming it. We need to reject those paths we have taken toward resolving the question about unity. Speaking for us and for myself in particular, we gave no reason at all during this time for allegations that I organised a nucleus within the party for the purpose of splitting it. There are no such documents, that is, if you don't count letters from a (mentally disturbed) ~~crazy~~ person and from Mitin, who speaks exclusively about our internal union matters that took place a year ago. (It is vexing that so much attention and strength has to be spent on refuting slander, insinuations and distortions, instead of talking about the essence of those problems which we raised in the letter. Once more I state that all accusations against us of factional groupings are false.) But if you find that we should be expelled because we had something to say to you at this congress and if our thoughts and concerns about the fate of the working class are foreign to you, well, go ahead, exclude us.

Chair. Comrade Kubiak will speak against the commission's proposal.

Kubiak. Comrades, this is not the first party congress, which has had to resolve struggle within our party. True, this is the first congress, which has put this question so acutely. I think that I will dwell on party history a little, comrades, as comrade Zinoviev did in his report on party building. Although representatives of the proletariat were on the bench of the accused, I think it's possible to spend a little time, nevertheless, on the proletariat.

Comrade Zinoviev is right that students[295] sat in our Bolshevik committees. What comrade Zinoviev didn't say was that already in 1903, we workers began conducting definite struggle against these student committees. We heard a similar attitude about Zalutsky, which was that he didn't know how to make reports and that he was illiterate. As has been indicated, the workers' party convened the Stockholm Congress. Comrade Voroshilov, who was its representative, now is sitting there in the Presidium. At the London Congress in 1904, there was also a workers' faction, in which I had the good fortune to be present. At this London Congress, for the first time, the question of worker parties' active work was placed acutely. We brought into the CC the first worker, who was comrade Foma as I recall. So, comrades, the struggle is not new, but it has a history. The history of the struggle goes back further than the Tenth Party Congress, even considerably further. Comrades, it's also necessary to understand the reasons for this struggle. I am not about to dwell on them, however, for I do not have enough time to do so.

We'll proceed to the essence of the document at hand. First, I need to remind you that comrade Lenin, comrade Zinoviev, and the commission said that the 22 bore no guilt for submitting a declaration to the Comintern, for each party member has the right to do this. Nevertheless, comrade Lenin in his report spoke chiefly about the appeal of the 22 to the Comintern. If it is forbidden to appeal, then we need to say so or be told outright. Otherwise, inasmuch as there was already a trial at the Comintern, let us forget about this fact to whatever extent possible. Now, comrades are charged with the crime of creating an organisation and preparing a party split. Comrade Medvedev spoke with great conviction. Medvedev is asked to prove his dedication to the working class. Of course, this can be imposed upon Mitin and Kuznetsov, but it is

---

295 He uses the terms студенчество and курсистки; the latter meant women students.

the purest nonsense to impose it upon Shliapnikov and Medvedev. I will not take the liberty of proving the opposite, for many of those here who worked in the underground know both Shliapnikov and Medvedev and know their dedication to party work and to the working class. What's the matter? Of what are they guilty?

They are blamed for Mitin's and Savichev's letters. Comrades, not only comrade Solts, but also the former CC secretary Mikhailov and others declare that Savichev is a mentally disturbed fellow, who has written many letters. Perhaps, even probably, he will write still more. I think that if you were to look in comrade Ilich's desk, we could find letters, of which the authors sit here and about which we likewise would need to talk. But where is the actual evidence that a split was prepared? So what if there was a meeting of the former Workers' Opposition. I had the fortune or misfortune to attend two such meetings. The Politburo itself christened us the former Workers' Opposition. In May, Medvedev, Shliapnikov, [ ][296] and I were invited to report to the Politburo about the New Economic Policy. Afterwards we were ridiculed, yet a VSNKh representative published our proposals almost in full a week later.

At this Politburo session, they recommended to us to work up this question. Yet you propose that we could have worked it up just over the telephone. I must confess, though, that we did not fulfil the Politburo's directive. Not once did we meet. That is, at least I personally was not once [at a meeting] and so I am guilty for not following party discipline. In the course of several months, I did much CC work in the gubernias. The CC has not accused me of supporting the Workers' Opposition. On the contrary, I dispersed the Workers' Opposition. For example, the Tambov organisation was strong before the Tenth Congress. Does it exist now? What about the Briansk organisation? Do they carry out work there? No. That means that it is impossible to set up links and to create an organisation. Therefore, I propose that the Party Congress should reject the commission's proposal by a large majority, if not unanimously. Let's just limit our resolution to agree with the Comintern's decision and leave it at that. I allow an exception in regard to Mitin and Kuznetsov. Also, in regard to Kuznetsov, the CC is guilty for having restored to him his rights. They can be excluded, but I propose that we limit ourselves to agreeing with the Comintern's decision on the others.

Petrovsky. Comrades, I would not have spoken about this matter, if a good ten years had not linked me with these comrades in the same common business

---

296   Only the first letter of the name is in the text. It appears to be a 'V', but according to a different source, Kutuzov accompanied Shliapnikov, Medvedev, and Kubiak to the Politburo meeting (see above).

of rigorous struggle and not only rigorous struggle, but also the joy of victory. Nevertheless, I cannot agree that these comrades can justify their actions by appealing to the ancient character of their party membership and to various services to the party. Entire parties, not just individual comrades, can make mistakes in the course of rigorous political struggle. When I heard comrade Medvedev enumerate his services to the party, well it seemed to me that you could say the same for any of those present here currently. Take my son, for example, who can count at least a dozen cities, where he pursued political struggle.

When I, comrades, sat in a Politburo session .... [ellipses in text] at that time I heard Krasin deliver a report on this question and comrade Stomoniakov was there. The question about concessions came up and it was explained that we haven't got any concessions. Around the same time, we heard in Kharkov that there was talk in a Moscow discussion club about the sale of Russia at the Genoa Conference. I am speaking about an actual fact, which should serve as a practical lesson for young party members. At a time when rumors circulated that Russia was being sold off, the 22 submitted a document to the Comintern. Then comrade Zinoviev said, 'Everything was fine until someone got some harebrained ideas'.[297] Rumours about the sale continued to circulate until even in remote provinces they said that Russia is being sold off. They asked if it was the beginning of the end. Of course, I had to explain that in our party, like in any part of society, there are simply rival opinions. I also pointed out that because the bureaucracy is concentrated in Moscow, they have nothing to do there and so they spend much time on conversation. /laughter/ I explained that it was all baseless and to no good end, and that was how one should regard it.

The declaration of the 22 comrades gave rise to concern that something was not right in Moscow. It conveyed the impression that the centre is not strong, that we are unstable, that there is discord in the party, and so forth. Comrades, this moment has passed. When I gave a report, I dwelled on the need to issue a last stern reprimand at the congress and a final warning. This how I thought about it, but the All-Russian Conference did not support this approach, after it became clear that when comrade Shliapnikov and other comrades of the group of 22 complained to the Comintern, they signed together with Miasnikov, no matter how they tried to extricate themselves from this. Chernov wrote an article in which he said: /reads quotation from article/. Then the newspaper *Rul* disseminates it as if it is society's general opinion [общественное мнение] that we are on the edge of ruin, that the Genoa Conference has no actual basis

---

297 In the text, the idiom reads, не бьют печали, да вот накачали. According to Krylov 1973, p. 243, the idiom goes, не было печали, так черти накачали.

to recognise Soviet power, and so forth.[298] When we arrived here and beheld this unfortunate commission, in which we sat in session, we formed a completely different impression.

I concluded that we need to follow a radical course of treatment, because if comrade Medvedev and comrade Shliapnikov (we are mainly talking about them), with whom we jointly achieved more than one socialist victory, could say: comrades, there was a time, when we could speak and act without directives and without advance permission. (Indeed did they have to speak to us so, indeed we were not gendarmes).

Without a doubt, they gathered with an objective in mind. There is nothing behind the rebuke for the document being printed, because if it had not been printed, the rebuke would have been twofold [суryboe]. Then they would have made the more severe accusation that the CC hid it. The matter is not about this. It would have been another matter if, after the entire republic and the congress rejected this act and when not one voice was raised in support of this resolution, the comrades had come to the commission and had said, 'We think that this was a mistake'. Permit me to backtrack a bit to the history of how the Workers' Opposition was conceived. I, too, participated in it, at the beginning. When we gathered, we discussed what Kubiak just talked about, which was about admitting more workers into the CC. Even now I support this and they tease me about being a Makhaevist. Our Ukrainian comrades say that in this I am a single-minded person, for I will always struggle for more workers to be brought into the CC. But why organise an entire opposition, create a programme on this basis, and so forth?

Then I saw that comrades, who could not be considered seasoned proletarians, were starting to come to our meetings. Former Mensheviks started to attach themselves to us last year. They had not shed their Menshevism. Then I said to Shliapnikov and Medvedev, look, an unsuitable element, which can spoil the whole business, is latching on to us. Then, when no measures were accepted to consolidate worker opinion, about which Kubiak spoke, I said that I will no longer go along with you.

Then there is comrade Kollontai. She spoke out at the Tenth Congress and comrade Bukharin brilliantly criticised her heretical rubbish, which had nothing to do with communism. Today you witnessed her argue that supposedly the party does not allow discussion, as if there was no discussion about party building and so forth. Well, comrade Kollontai is largely responsible for a group of unreliable people having begun to latch on to the tendency. More Menshevism than pure communism erupts from her speech.

---

298 *Rul* was a Russian-language newspaper published in Berlin from 1920 to 1931. It represented the views of Russian liberals (Constitutional Democrats – Kadets).

Well, suitable measures need to be taken. You can't look at all documents from a gendarme's point of view, as when Iaroslavsky mistakenly called Medvedev a candidate and now everyone swears about this. You need to take into account the entire aggregate of work, not just attend to how each 'i' is dotted. How does the statement of the Comintern appear in focus? That is why we have to speak of discipline to old party members. The fact that you are an old member of the party means that from you should be expected greater, stricter, and more unswerving discipline than from a young member.

Antonov-Ovseenko. I considered it my duty to speak here because, first of all, I carry out practical work together with those who were earlier members of the Workers' Opposition group. Samara was one of their centres, as is well-known, but we did not sense in Samara any organised connections with Moscow or any underground, antiparty work. We worked closely with these comrades while we resolved the most difficult problems, of which this starving gubernia has so many. We encountered from these comrades neither the slightest sabotage of our actions nor the slightest lack of desire to work. Therefore, I thought I needed to attest to this.

With the greatest anguish, I have come to speak at this tribune about what you too see and feel, which is that we have what we know to be defect in the party. This defect is isolation not only from broad strata of nonparty workers, but also from broad circles of workers who are in our party. Not without reason does the declaration of comrades, who face exclusion, meet with applause at this congress. It is clear that we have a hidden ulcer inside. There are various means for eliminating factionalism, but the means which they want to apply here are most harmful. The means we applied in Samara were more reliable and more correct. There we drew into work those who did not trust the party organisation. That's how we act toward the nonparty masses.

In connection with the resolution about the trade union movement, this is so easy to do right now, standing wholly on a party footing. In such a way, we draw closer to the broad masses and eliminate any kind of demagoguery by our party. We have the right to demand that our party should have a different attitude toward the heterodox. This attitude should be different than the one which was necessary when the acuteness of factional struggle justified intransigence. We have just emerged from this period and we can resolve questions with much more patience.

For what do they want to exclude comrade Kollontai? Look at how many falsehoods saturate[299] the documents about the declaration. If you start to ana-

---

299   Literally, he uses the Russian idiomatic construction 'sewn with white threads'.

lyse these documents of the commission, then you can see that unfounded accusations[300] run from beginning to end ... [ellipses in text]. Do we even need this document, in order to pass judgement on the case, such as it is? The Comintern, which is a highly authoritative organisation, judged these comrades. The Comintern Ispolkom plenum gave these comrades a warning that their actions could place them outside the party ranks. Why was it necessary then to propose the exclusion from the party of these comrades, without any new facts being introduced? This proposal did not come from the Comintern, which only subjected them to an ordeal.

I think that we have no reason to go further than the Ispolkom suggested. On the contrary, we think that such a decision would be a much greater blow against party unity than this group's activity and declaration. Exclusion of these comrades would be a much greater blow against the unity of the proletariat, because each member of the Workers' Opposition everywhere would be forced to define his attitude toward such a decision. Secondly, the contradiction in principle, which has already become sufficiently clear, would become even more sharply defined. I think that we will all agree now with that which comrade Molotov said in his report, which is that we have seen factional struggle diminish and become less acute and that differences of principle have been eliminated and we have party unanimity.

We value the opinions of nonparty workers and of the broad masses in general, but why should we rehash our differences of principle for their judgement? I think that there is no need for this and that this would be a deep tactical mistake, which we should not make, comrades. We should say that we unanimously recognise the Declaration of the 22 to be full of completely unfounded demagogic attacks, but because the Comintern Ispolkom plenum issued a definite decision and there are presently no new factors, which could interfere with implementation of this decision, we take under advisement the decision of the Comintern Ispolkom. We find it possible to keep the comrades within the party and we direct the CC to exclude them from the party if they violate party discipline in the future. We propose the following resolution: /reads a resolution/.

Manuilsky.[301] *It is a heavy moral burden for each of us here to judge meritorious figures of the workers' movement. Both Medvedev and Shliapnikov have rendered*

---

300   Again, 'sewn with white threads'.

301   The following is partially verbatim and partially paraphrased from my abbreviated notes. The paraphrased portions are italicised.

great services, but we need to examine what Shliapnikov, Kollontai and Medve-dev said at the commission's meeting from a political point of view. I assert that this group's activity will lead in fact to the formation of a liberal workers' party here. *The Mensheviks used the Declaration of the 22 to discredit our party. Their newspapers in Kharkov talk about a split. ... We might have to pay more dearly at Genoa for this appearance of division. ...* We, comrades, have decided that the worker masses will speak for themselves. First we heard from them in the Don-bas, which is that very centre, from where we hear the voices reacting to this act. The authors of the declaration apparently counted on the Lugansk organisa-tion to support them, but comrades, the assembly of the Lugansk organisation, at which were present up to 400 senior personnel, voted unanimously with nine abstentions to demand the comrades' exclusion from the party. A wave of similar demands rolled in from all of Ukraine and from many cities. ... *It would be mad to exclude all those who signed ... but we need to act severely in regards to frequent offenders.*

[Next are voting and discussion related to voting.][302]

Chair. The discussion has ended. Let's proceed to a vote. We have two resolu-tions, one from the commission and one from Antonov-Ovseenko.

Smirnov.[303] The [Northwest?] delegation proposes an amendment to the com-mission's resolution.

Chair. This can be introduced later.

Voice calls for rollcall voting.

Chair. A majority rejects rollcall voting. The vote count reveals a minimum of 227 and maximum of 245 for the commission's resolution and 215 for Antonov-Ovseenko's. The commission's resolution receives a majority.

Voice. The question is very important. It smacks of a split, so I propose rollcall voting.

---

302   The following is translated verbatim except for italicised sections, which are my para-phrased notes.

303   V.M. Smirnov and I.N. Smirnov were delegates. This was probably I.N. Smirnov, who was a delegate from Petrograd.

Chair. We'll now vote on the correction. No one is against the correction.

Voice. By how much of a majority is the question about exclusion from the party decided?

Chair. The statutes say that a simple majority decides all questions. The correction of the Petrograd delegation is edited in the following way: 'present to the cc the right to readmit to the party earlier than indicated those comrades excluded for one year, who, having been outside the party, will prove in fact that they go along the same path as the Communist Party'. The correction is accepted by a vote.

Kin suggests to exclude Kuznetsov and Mitin, but to apply the Comintern's decision to Kollontai, Shliapnikov, and Medvedev.

Chair. I must put to a vote the commission's resolution with the correction we have accepted.

Antonov-Ovseenko: I suggest holding a separate vote regarding each of the five. If the 22 are not all excluded, but only five are excluded, then each should be so for individual reasons. I propose we vote separately.

Chair: As long as a small group expresses doubt, I do not have the right to violate the congress's decision. So comrades, a majority of the Congress accepts a certain resolution. In this resolution it says: it is necessary to exclude such and such comrades. It is not possible for me to put comrade Antonov-Ovseenko's proposal to a vote, for this is a re-examination of the question. ... All I can do is put the resolution to a final vote.

Kin. I request that my suggestion be put to a vote.

Chair. Who is for Kin's correction? Kin's correction passes by 225–35 votes against 215.

Chair. ... We are now confronted with the following situation: we accepted the commission's resolution, which proposes to exclude certain comrades, as the basis of our resolution. After this the Congress accepted the Petrograd delegation's correction, which gives the cc the right to return them to the party ranks. Now we've agreed not to exclude three comrades. If we want to leave the Congress with a resolution which can be explained to Russian and foreign workers, then we should clear up the matter.

Osinsky. (not audible), (noise).

Tomsky. I suggest we add to the resolution: 'Regarding Shliapnikov, Medvedev and Kollontai, the Congress empowers the CC, in case they demonstrate a similar antiparty attitude in the future, to likewise exclude the aforementioned comrades from the party.' ... [ellipses in text]

Chair. I will put to a vote Tomsky's and Kin's corrections. We will accept the one which will receive a clear majority.

Mikoian suggests combining Tomsky's and Kin's corrections. The chair calls a vote and Tomsky's addition is accepted.

Chair. Allow me to make such a formulation. We'll accept as the basis the commission's proposal, but we'll replace the part about results with comrade Tomsky's correction. Regarding the three comrades Kollontai, Shliapnikov and Medvedev, the Comintern commission's decision remains in force. As for the remaining two, Kuznetsov and Mitin,[304] the commission's resolution remains in force. Who's opposed? An insignificant minority. There are few abstentions. This ends the matter. Now we can proceed to the results of elections to the CC.

Lenin also speaks at this closed session to protest against the congress's decision to ban advertising in Pravda. He asks how will Pravda get enough revenue so as not to fall behind Izvestiia. Riazanov says that the intention was to have the party press organ funded only by party organisations. They vote to send the matter to the CC for a second vote.

[The 12th and final session of the Eleventh Party Congress was on the evening of 2 April.]

Resolution about Some Members of the former Workers' Opposition, 577–80

1. The Tenth RCP(b) Congress charged the CC to 'carry out the complete destruction of any factionalism'. The Congress directed 'all groups, which formed on the basis of one or another platform, to promptly disperse without exception' and charged all organisations to 'strictly ensure that no factional acts are permitted'. The Congress decided that 'failure to imple-

---

304   A typographical error had 'Medvedev' in place of 'Mitin'.

ment this decision should lead to unconditional and prompt exclusion from the party'. The Tenth Congress elected to the CC two members of the former group of the so-called Workers' Opposition. Also, it promoted to senior soviet posts comrades who had earlier belonged to this group. The party as a whole took all measures so as not to allow any persecution of those who formerly engaged in factionalism. During the party verification and purge, the CC sent special circulars with special instructions to all organisations, confirming that former members of the Workers' Opposition should be treated most carefully and attentively. Many of them were put in charge of verification commissions at the gubernia and oblast levels. They were also appointed to the Central Purge Commission and to the control commissions. Thus, the party showed the greatest trust toward them.

2. Despite all this, former members of the Workers' Opposition frequently violated the decision of the Tenth Congress. They preserved and supported an illegal factional organisation within the party. Thanks to this, their factional speeches and acts in the centre and in the provinces introduced demoralisation into the party ranks, without a doubt. Frequently, they attempted to select the personnel of leading trade union bodies, as for example the Metalworkers' Union central committee, on a factionalist basis rather than on the basis of efficiency. Factionalist comrades conducted not only open struggle, but, as the commission established, also underground struggle to seize leading party, trade union and soviet bodies in the provinces. Speeches by members of the former Workers' Opposition at meetings often bore the character of opposition to the rest of the party: 'we and they'. Such speeches against party decisions forced the CC RCP(b) on 9 August 1921 to pose the question about excluding CC member comrade Shliapnikov from the party. More than half the number of CC members and candidate members, which was required in order to apply this measure, spoke out in favour of it already at that time.

Comrade Shliapnikov was not excluded only because one vote did not suffice to meet the minimum 2/3 of votes of full and candidate CC members required for application of this radical measure.

The 9 August 1921 decision, which was approved unanimously (with 3 abstentions), read as follows:

'Taking into consideration comrade Shliapnikov's frequent violations of party discipline, as a member of the CC, the assembly states that it is completely impermissible for Shliapnikov to continue to make speeches, declarations and criticisms, which are directed against CC policy and which counteract the decisions that actually do express the opinion of the party congress, outside of cc meetings. His further such behaviour will put pointblank the question of whether it is possible for comrade Shliapnikov to continue to work in the Central Committee. Taking this into consideration, the assembly categorically calls on comrade Shliapnikov to radically change all his political behaviour in this regard, in order to bring it into agreement with the cc's line, in the ranks of which he stands. If in the future comrade Shliapnikov will not change his behaviour, the cc is instructed to convene the same type of assembly (a plenum of members and candidate members of the cc and ccc) for a second examination of the question'.

Such behaviour by members of the former Workers' Opposition contributed to a situation, in which a group that was attempting to convene a fourth international addressed members of the former Workers' Opposition as if they were kindred in spirit. They called on them for support and to unite their forces. They reprinted and broadly distributed comrade Kollontai's brochure 'About the Workers' Opposition' and other such works. Moreover, comrades from the former Workers' Opposition did not give resolute rebuff to such groups, which harm the workers' movement. They did not distance themselves in public and officially from these groups, but only limited themselves to weak statements in this respect.

The Comintern unanimously passed a negative evaluation of Comrade Kollontai's public speech, which was given in an antiparty spirit at the Congress of the Comintern. All the press that is hostile to us made broad use of the speech.

The Eleventh Congress especially selected a commission, which was composed of 19 delegates, who represented local organisations. This commission established that factional meetings took place at various times. Those at these meetings made conspiratorial decisions and they charged the group leaders, comrades Medvedev and Shliapnikov, with executing these decisions. cc member comrade Shliapnikov and comrade Medvedev, having received letters of the most antiparty character from those who share their views (Savichev, Mitin), did not bring the problems broached in these letters to the cc for discussion, despite the fact that the letters were not at all personal but related entirely to nonparty moods and activity of former members of the Workers' Opposition.

3.   Finally, regarding the last meeting of members of the former Workers' Opposition group, as a result of which the appeal to the Comintern appeared, the commission established that comrades Medvedev and Shliapnikov convened a special meeting of some supporters of the former Workers' Opposition group; that G. Miasnikov, who was condemned and

excluded from the party, was involved in this meeting; and at this meeting, on the basis of completely unsubstantiated, unverified facts and information, they composed an indictment against the party. Moreover, as some who signed this declaration admitted, they didn't even know the contents of the document that well, but only signed for reasons of group solidarity.

4. In full agreement with the CC RCP(b), as it was composed on the eve of the Eleventh Congress, the congress considers that those comrades who signed the declaration did not violate party discipline at all by having submitted this declaration to the Comintern, which is the highest body of our class communist organisation. The comrades are not condemned for this. But the Congress considers to have been antiparty the preservation, for over the course of a year, of a factional grouping and factional meetings, and the continuation of factional struggle, which is contrary to the resolute, unconditional directive of the Tenth Congress. The Congress regards as completely impermissible the communication to the Comintern of information, the falsehood of which was established by a special commission, which the Comintern selected. The Congress most resolutely censures the behaviour of individual group members, who communicated false information about the party in their explanations to the commission of the Comintern and who distorted the actual picture of the entirety of relations between the RCP(b) and the working class as a whole.

5. The commission likewise considers it to have been established that the former Workers' Opposition group, which by its behaviour demoralised the party organisation from within, attempted simultaneously to consolidate its influence and considered it possible under certain conditions to break up our party. It waited only for the time to be ripe for a split. Comrade Kollontai in particular, in her brochure, which was published before the Tenth RCP(b) Congress, introduced the thought that the split is inescapable and that to bring it about only the right time is needed. After the Tenth Congress, she did not abandon this line of behaviour. In the explanations she gave to the commission of the Eleventh RCP(b) Congress, she confirmed that she considers a split inevitable, if the party will not change its line, by which she means if the party will not follow the mistaken views of comrades Kollontai, Medvedev, and Shliapnikov which are harmful for the working class.

When the commission asked her if there were other factional meetings similar to the last one, comrade Kollontai expressed regret that there were few such meetings. The congress considers completely impermissible the situation, which this group occupies in relation to the party, especially at this most difficult time for the working class. The economy is being restructured, capitalist elements are being strengthened to a certain extent, the country suffers from an unprecedented famine, there are threats of foreign intervention, and petty bourgeois moods are intensifying. The first condition for the victory of the working class is party unity and the strictest discipline in party ranks.

On the basis of all this, the Eleventh Congress, having heard the decision of the expanded Comintern Executive Committee (ECCI) plenum about the 22, the report of the 19-member commission which the congress chose to investigate the activity of some former Workers' Opposition members, and the explanations of comrades Shliapnikov, Medvedev and Kollontai, has decided:

1) To join in agreement with the ECCI decision in relation to comrades Shliapnikov, Medvedev and Kollontai and to instruct the CC, in case these comrades in the future manifest a similar antiparty attitude, to exclude the named comrades from the party.

2) Exclude from the party comrade Mitin as a malicious disorganiser. Having been for 16 years an active Menshevik party member and having entered into the RCP(b) in 1920, he organised a factional grouping and unswervingly conducted a demoralising line in the Donbas party organisation.

3) Exclude comrade Kuznetsov from the party as an element alien to the proletariat. He deceived the party's trust by means of false information about his past, about his length of time in the party, and about his time as a worker. He hid that he is a former grocer, who temporarily entered the ranks of workers in order to evade wartime military service.

Report of the Eleventh Party Congress Commission on the Workers' Opposition, pp. 702–10

Dear comrades!

The Eleventh Congress of the RCP(b) charged us to investigate all the circumstances connected with the activity of the former Workers' Opposition group, including the act of submitting a declaration to the Comintern by 22 comrades, who are former members of this group. The commission investigated all materials on the present matter that had accumulated in the Central Committee, the Central Control Commission, the Comintern and the Moscow Control Commission. It summoned the most activist comrades who signed this declaration and it posed to them some clarifying questions.

The commission's work led it to the unanimous conviction that it is dealing not with an accidentally composed grouping, but very much with a factional organisation. The commission considers it necessary to remind all party members that the Tenth Party Congress specially condemned the views and activity of the Workers' Opposition group. The Congress resolutely condemned any and all factionalist groups and passed a decision about party unity, in which it emphasised that 'unity and cohesiveness of its ranks, ensuring full trust between party members, and truly friendly work actually embodying the unity of the will of the vanguard of the proletariat are especially necessary at the current time, when some circumstances intensify vacillations among the country's petty bourgeois population'.

The Tenth Congress recognised as necessary 'that all conscious workers clearly would recognise the harm and impermissibility of any kind of factionalism, which inevitably leads in fact to the weakening of friendly work and to repeated and intensified attempts by enemies who attach themselves to the ruling party in order to deepen division within it and use it to further counter-revolution'. The Congress charged the Central Committee: 'to utterly destroy any factionalism'. The Congress prescribed: 'immediately and without exception to disperse all groups that have formed on any platform' and charged 'all organisations to most strictly enforce the impermissibility of any factional acts. Failure to execute this decision of the congress should entail unconditional and immediate exclusion from the party'.

In a special resolution about the syndicalist and anarchist deviation in our party, the Congress resolutely condemned as a syndicalist and anarchist deviation the views of the Workers' Opposition group, which had taken shape within the RCP(b) up to the Tenth Party Congress.

The Tenth Congress in actual fact implemented the decision about party unity, when it included two of the most prominent persons from the dispersed group, comrades Shliapnikov and Kutuzov, within the newly composed Central Committee. The congress chose two other prominent personnel from this group, comrades Medvedev and Kiselev, as candidate CC members. The party assigned comrade Kollontai to work in the Comintern. When verification and purge of the party's ranks began, comrade Shliapnikov was included in the central commission on verification of the party's membership. Some of those who shared his views were included in oblast, gubernia, and uyezd commissions on verification of the party's composition.

Comrades from the dispersed Workers' Opposition group were placed in senior party, trade union and soviet posts by means of systematic transfers, which in the interests of expediency and best use of personnel were carried out on the basis of Party Congress decisions. Thus, the party, both through its Central Committee and its provincial bodies, gave the comrades from the former Workers' Opposition group the full possibility to work to the greatest benefit of the proletariat.

But comrades from the dispersed group did not cease factional struggle. Some facts establish without a doubt that *an illegal factional organisation was preserved* and at the head of it stood its inspirers and leaders, who were comrades *Shliapnikov, Medvedev and Kollontai*.[305] Despite the fact that comrade Shliapnikov was a member of the Central Committee, his speeches at trade union congresses as well as at other party and nonparty assemblies bore the character of setting himself off against the party: 'we and they'.

Frequently they attempted to reinforce this factionalism in the most important bodies, such as the trade union of metalworkers. The letter, which this group's member Mitin from the Donbas addressed to Shliapnikov and Medvedev, inarguably proves the presence and preservation of a factional organisation and the arrangement of meetings at which resolutions were brought forth, the executors of which were Shliapnikov and Medvedev. Thus, Mitin writes: '*At our last meeting you and Shliapnikov were assigned to evaluate the New Economic Policy and to make our conclusions from it*'. In that same letter he writes that he has assigned himself the task to place 'our lads' in all factory committees (*zavkoms*), in order through them to win over factory cells and *along this line to conduct work toward the seizure of the district party committee (raipartkom) and the conference*. He attempted by similar means to win over the gubernia union, economic council, and trade union council. 'If I would succeed in carrying this out, the Donbas would be ours', he writes.

In another letter, which party members in Nikolaevsk received from Moscow and passed on to the CC of the Communist Party (Bolshevik) of Ukraine, a member of the Workers' Opposition writes, 'In the case involving the metalworkers, our comrades displayed complete incomprehension of the basic rules of politics, against which we *as a collective* should struggle'. Further, the writer recommends tactics of struggle: '*Our group should be resuscitated as a group*, first of all, to realise a new course of economic policy and expose the attitude toward it of the worker part of the Communist Party. This course, despite its inevitability and the need to further it, *does not signify that the policy of the worker part of the Communist party should be the same as the official line is now*. I think that if the group as a whole will set about clarifying its position on this question, then undoubtedly we will elaborate a common line'. Further the author recommends 'answering insolence with insolence and meeting attack

---

305   The italics here and below in the report reflect italics in the published Russian version.

with organisation and crossing over to the offensive'. 'Just avoid introducing sentiment into politics, as our comrades did at the congress of metalworkers'.

At the communist faction of the last congress of the Metalworkers' Union, comrade Shliapnikov was compelled to hand over some letters and documents to the Party CC. These letters and documents irrefutably establish that an organisation of the Workers' Opposition group was present within the party, that it even had a secretariat, that it distributed circular letters, supported work in the provinces that demoralised the party organisation, and that the attitude of members of this underground organisation toward our Party CC was very antiparty, subversive, and uncomradely. They were just preparing for the most propitious moment for a split, about which comrade Kollontai wrote in her brochure about the Workers' Opposition, when she indicated that the time had not yet come for this split. Mitin writes: 'If the seizure of party, soviet, cooperative and trade union bodies were successfully carried out, the Donbas would be ours. But what does "ours" mean? What is our ideological world view?' *Only people who belong to a grouping alien to our party, who do not share the party line, and who struggle against it, can write in such a way.*

Similar facts, and especially comrade Shliapnikov's speech, forced the Party CC at its 9 August plenum to convene a special meeting of all its full and candidate members present in Moscow and CCC members, in order to discuss what stance to take toward comrade Shliapnikov's violation of party discipline. Already at that time, more than half of those at this meeting spoke in favour of excluding comrade Shliapnikov, but a little less than 2/3 of those needed to apply this measure in accord with the Tenth Congress's special resolution. Then the CC issued the resolution which was supposed to stop comrade Shliapnikov, as well as all those who thought like him, from continuing the line they conducted that was unbefitting of party members. In actual fact, however, this did not happen.

The Central Committee soon had to examine the activity of one member of this group, comrade Miasnikov, who frequently attempted to carry through at party and nonparty meetings and likewise in the press views, which, after familiarisation with them, CC members recognised as antiparty. These views were the ideological reflection of moods, which seized the vacillating part of workers during the Kronstadt events in spring 1921. They attempted to make the vacillations of the petty bourgeoisie the banner of the party. At the same time when the entire bourgeois press aimed to organise the reviving petty bourgeois element that was hostile toward us, comrade Miasnikov proposed to proclaim freedom of speech and of the press 'from monarchists to anarchists inclusively'.

Despite the fact that on 22 August 1921 these views were identified as incompatible with the interests of the party, comrade Miasnikov continued to defend them, not only at party assemblies but also at nonparty assemblies, while remaining a party member. He interpreted the party's patience with his escapades as meaning: 'All is permitted to me'. Comrade Miasnikov answered comrade Lenin's letter thus: 'I received your letter, but I don't have time right now to write you an answer'. Only significantly later he answered: 'I still can't find the time to respond to your letter'. What kept comrade Miasnikov so busy at this time? Despite having been forbidden, he once again was speaking in defence of these views. He also used comrade Lenin's letter for further destructive work in the Perm organisation, having called forth the departure of almost the entire Motovilikhi delegation of 31 people from the all-city conference in August and having submitted a demagogic and antiparty protest against the gubkom.

Exactly the same as after the 22 August resolution, Miasnikov returned to Motovilikha anew and, without prior arrangement, gave a report on his time spent in Moscow, about his theses, and about the 22 August decision of the CC Orgburo. Finally, Miasnikov sent a letter to Kurzhner in Petrograd on 25 November 1921 and convinced him to win over at least two districts and thus unify all the disaffected under one banner. On 15 February 1922, a special commission comprising comrades Solts, the CCC chair, and CC secretaries Mikhailov and Molotov, resolved to exclude G. Miasnikov from the party. On 20 February, the CC RCP Politburo confirmed this decision (see the decision about G. Miasnikov).

After several days, as was precisely elucidated from interrogations of those who signed the declaration of the 22, comrades Medvedev and Shliapnikov convened those who shared their views. G. Miasnikov, who had already been excluded from the party, participated. At this meeting, they worked out the statement to the Comintern, which they addressed to members of the international conference of the Communist International, a copy of which they sent later to the CC RCP(b). They distributed copies of this statement to members of the ECCI (comrade Kollontai translated it into German), but they did not give it to the Russian delegation of the Comintern and did not even alert the Russian delegation about it. In this statement, they depict the situation in our party as so difficult that it appears as if the threat of a split looms over the party. It seems to us, dear comrades, that the resolution of our congress about the report of the Central Committee, which was unanimously accepted, serves as the best refutation of this declaration: 'There has never before been such unanimity in our party as we have now'.

Having received a copy of the 22 comrades' declaration, which was addressed to members of the International Communist Conference, the Politburo of the CC, without denying the right of individual comrades to appeal to the Comintern as to the highest court of appeal, assigned comrades Zinoviev and Trotsky to explain to the conference or to the commission, if the conference would create one, the true character of this statement and the distortions of reality permitted in it. At the same time, considering it completely impossible to hide from the party a similar type of accusation put forth against the party and its highest body the Central Committee, the RCP(b) Central Committee instructed the Secretariat to inform all gubkoms about the text of the appeal of 22 comrades to the Comintern and about the decision of the CC Politburo. It needs to be noted that G. Miasnikov, who several days previously was excluded from the party, signed this statement as if he were still a party member, although at the time he knew about his exclusion. Likewise, CC member Shliapnikov and candidate CC member Medvedev had to have known about it.

On 28 February the International Conference of the Communist International selected a commission to examine this statement. The commission was composed of the following comrades: Clara Zetkin, [Marcel] Cachin, [Jakob] Friis, [Vasil] Kolarov, [Karl] Kreibich, [Umberto] Terracini and [Arthur] Macmanus. What did comrades Shliapnikov, Kollontai and Medvedev tell this commission? They told commission members completely unverified facts. In the most unscrupulous way, they accentuated exclusively unfavourable aspects of our activity and they provided a completely distorted picture of relations between the party and the working class as a whole. So, they told about unprecedented political apathy of the working class and about a decline in the activism and energy of rank-and-file members. They illustrated this by pointing to the last elections in Moscow, which, in their opinion, workers boycotted. As all who conducted these elections know, however, it has been a long time since there has been such revolutionary enthusiasm and political activism among workers as there was during the last elections to the Moscow Soviet.

Shliapnikov frivolously talked about a search of his apartment, which in fact never happened. He said that the party wanted to stage a provocation of the Workers' Opposition involving creation of a group of a fourth international, in order to create grounds for excluding Shliapnikov and Kollontai from the party. He talked about workers leaving the party in large numbers, which contradicts the facts and numbers (see protocols of the Comintern commission's session). The Comintern commission informed an expanded ECCI plenum about the results of the investigation. The expanded plenum did not find the complaints of the 22 comrades to be valid. The ECCI likewise emphasised that these comrades' behaviour sharply contradicted the Tenth Party Congress's obligatory resolutions about party unity and the anarcho-syndicalist deviation. The ECCI reprimanded these comrades and seriously warned them that continuing the struggle they began will lead to defiance of the RCP(b) and its tasks and to a contradiction with the interests of the Russian proletariat. Moreover, continued struggle will place them outside the ranks of the Third International. It expects that consciousness and communist training will force comrades from the opposition in the future to take their place in the ranks of the party in a disciplined way and to conduct joint struggle against dangers arising from circumstances, which they together with the party will apprehend and overcome.

The attitude of the Communist Faction of the Fifth All-Russian Congress of Metalworkers toward the Declaration of the 22 makes it obvious how repulsed the most conscious strata of the working class were by the activity of members of the Workers' Opposition group. The faction heard the resolutions of the commission and of the Comintern plenum. It also heard the explanations of comrades Zinoviev, Shliapnikov and Clara Zetkin about the Declaration of the 22. The Communist Faction of the Congress of Metalworkers unanimously, with five abstentions, welcomed the decision of the Comintern plenum and warned the comrades not to repeat such acts, which threaten a split in the most disciplined communist party in the world (see the resolution of the Fifth All-Russian Congress of Metalworkers).

Finally, the Central Control Commission, which the Tenth Party Congress elected, attempted through comradely discussion to clarify the actual motives behind the Declaration of the 22, as well as the degree of conscious participation in this declaration by those who signed it. Moreover, some comrades who were summoned to explain their motives and actions to the Central Control Commission regarded it not as a comradely organisation, which was empowered by the party congress, but as an alien and hostile organisation of inquest. Comrade Medvedev declared outright that he cannot regard the CCC with full trust. Although it was elected by the congress, he (Medvedev) did not elect it. Among the signatories was one CCC member, comrade Chelyshev, who in the course of 10 months has worked jointly with other comrades in the CCC and has never complained of any serious disagreements with comrades there. He did not bring to the CCC's attention the fact that he submitted the declaration to the Comintern, although the CCC was chosen exactly in order to take care of eliminating those phenomena pointed out in the declaration of the 22 comrades, if such phenomena actually took place.

All these facts confronted the commission, which the Eleventh Congress selected to clarify all the circumstances around this declaration. The commission interrogated comrades Shliapnikov, Medvedev, Kollontai, Mitin, Kuznetsov, Bruno, Polosatov, Shokhanov, Chelyshev, and Tolokontsev. The commission also read comrade Ivanov's declaration that any measure to be applied to any of the signatories should also be applied to him; Paniushkin's statement that Shliapnikov and Medvedev at one time convinced him not to leave the party;

the declaration of Shokhanov, Polosatov and Bekrenev that was analogous to Ivanov's declaration; Korenevkin's testimonial about Kuznetsov's activity in 1916; the declaration of Chelyshev, Borisov and Bruno, which was analogous to Ivanov's statement; the declaration of comrades S.N. Smidovich, Golubeva, and Elizarova-Ulianova about the significance for the party of comrade Kollontai's actions; and the declaration of Medvedev from Briansk.

Despite the fact that the All-Russian Congress, which is the party's highest legislative body, authorised us to investigate this case, we did not perceive a comradely attitude in the behaviour of the comrades whom we summoned. They even behaved toward our commission as if it were a bourgeois judicial or investigatory body, whose functionaries were questioning them about some kind of illegal case. They explained that they had forgotten much, they did not wish to name names, and so forth. On the basis of stenographic reports and protocols and by attentively comparing the summoned comrades' explanations with the materials at hand, the commission became fully convinced that it faced members of an illegal organisation, who were conducting underground work destructive for the party and preparing for a time conducive to a split. They verbally declared their formal obedience to the Comintern's and RCP(b)'s decisions, but in fact they continued to conduct their previous line.

Comrade Shliapnikov declared that he could not foresee what results would emerge from presenting the declaration. He is dissatisfied with the turn the matter took, but he does not repent of having submitted the declaration, in fact far from it. In other words, he thinks that the Comintern made the wrong decision. Comrade Kollontai stated that she considered it to have been a bad thing that there were no groupings among communists and almost no groupings running opposed to the communists during re-elections of the Moscow Soviet. She declared that if the party will not correct its line, then of course the time should come to break with it. She regrets that there were no organised links among those who supported the views of the Workers' Opposition. Finally, she does not consider her declaration to have been a mistake, even after hearing the Comintern's decision. Comrade Medvedev, too, does not consider it to have been a mistake to bring completely unverified, false information to the attention of the Comintern.

Regarding comrade Mitin, who claimed to have been in the party since 1902, the commission established that in fact he stood in the ranks of the Menshevik Party for sixteen years. He was an active Menshevik, who spoke out resolutely against Soviet power and the Communist Party. Only in 1920 did he enter the RCP(b). From his letter to Shliapnikov and Medvedev,[306] comrades

---

306   Editors' footnote: See Mitin's letter in the book *Otchet komissii syezda* (Moscow: 1922), pp. 10–12.

can see what kind of depravity this malicious disorganiser, who wormed himself into our ranks, introduced into the party milieu and how leaders of this group deceived the Comintern, having claimed him as a party member since 1902.

The commission established that comrade Kuznetsov is a person completely alien to the proletariat. He is from the grocery trade with its mercenary-minded petty bourgeois habits and made a transition to the factory workbench in order to escape compulsory military service. His length of party membership, which was shown in the declaration as from 1904, does not correspond to reality. To the Central Committee, Kuznetsov could prove his party membership only since 1917, despite the fact that many comrades know him.

Regarding the remaining comrades who signed the declaration, the commission has no materials which would point to their factional and antiparty behaviour, except for their participation in the last meeting organised by comrades Shliapnikov and Medvedev at which they elaborated the Declaration of the 22.

The commission asked the comrades, among other things, about whether they would submit to the decisions of the Comintern and the RCP(b) congress.

The comrades' explanations did not convince the commission to any degree that the comrades actually can submit completely to these decisions. How comrade Miasnikov, who was excluded from the party, understands this subordination is obvious from the following fact. In his 6 August letter to comrade Lenin, comrade Miasnikov wrote: 'I am bound to the party by blood. I think that there has never been nor will there be a better party of the proletariat'. After signing the declaration to the Comintern, comrade Miasnikov set off for Motovilikhinsky factory, where he organised reelections of the factory committee and achieved the election of a nonparty factory committee. He organised an underground group, which nonparty people also entered, and he most energetically set about the further disorganisation of trade union, party and soviet bodies. The commission thinks that an end should be put to such activity. The Congress and the entire party should show unity before the most conscious, leading part of the Russian proletariat, its Communist Party, and the international proletariat. The Congress and party should show the same unity, which already found expression in the unanimous acceptance of the resolution, which approved the Central Committee's political and organisational line, and in the fact that not one delegate of the All-Russian Party Congress voted for comrade Medvedev's opposing resolution.

The commission finds it necessary to exclude forever from the party such people as Mitin and Kuznetsov, who are alien to the party and bring harm to it. The commission proposes to the Eleventh Congress to exclude from the party comrades Kollontai, Medvedev and Shliapnikov and to place them outside the ranks of the Comintern, in order to resolutely warn those who share their views not to continue making dangerous steps that are harmful for the party. Experience will show whether they will want to remain with the vanguard of the working class, or if they will continue destructive work to disorganise it. If they will prove in the course of a year that their dedication to the cause of the working class is higher than group and factional interests, then the working class will accept them back into the ranks of its Communist Party, having remembered their former services to the revolution. Along with that, the commission finds it necessary to declare that those who signed the Declaration of the 22 do not represent the views of all those members of the Workers' Opposition group, who belonged to it up to the Tenth Party Congress. During the past year, many prominent persons from this group, who formerly supported the views of Shliapnikov, Medvedev and Kollontai, were able to subordinate their groupist, factional views to the party line and to work in full agreement with the party, without violating the unity of will and of action, which the party of the proletariat of the RSFSR needs so much in unprecedentedly difficult conditions.

The commission, which the Eleventh RCP(b) Congress selected, calls upon all party members to more amicably close their ranks around the party banner for unity and to struggle most resolutely against attempts to violate this unity and against attempts within our party to create any kind of alien organisations, which would lead to demoralisation and weakening of its ranks.

Commission, selected by the Eleventh RCP(b) Congress

Published as a separate brochure under the title *Otchet komissii syezda* (Moscow, 1922); published here according to the text of the brochure

Materials about the Workers' Opposition Group, pp. 748–56
Protocol of 9 August 1921 CC plenum

All members and candidate members of the CC and CCC who were present in Moscow participated. The plenum convened on the basis of point seven of the Tenth Party Congress resolution on party unity.

Heard:
1. Comrade Sedoi's statement about the current assembly's authority.
2. About comrade Shliapnikov's violation of party discipline.

Decided:
1. After an exchange of opinions, the meeting unanimously recognised its own authority to resolve the question about comrade Shliapnikov.

2. In view of comrade Shliapnikov's frequent violations of party discipline while he was a cc member, the assembly finds it completely impermissible for comrade Shliapnikov to continue to make speeches, declarations, and criticism directed against cc policy and in opposition to decisions, which in fact express the opinions of the Party Congress, beyond the bounds of the cc. Should he do so, it will place point blank the question about whether it is possible for comrade Shliapnikov to work in the cc. With this in view, the assembly categorically calls upon comrade Shliapnikov to radically change all his political behaviour in this regard by coordinating it with the line of the cc, in the ranks of which he stands. In case comrade Shliapnikov will not change his behaviour in the future, the cc is authorised to convene just such an assembly for a second examination of the question.

∴

15 February 1922 Decision about G. Miasnikov

Decision about the case of Miasnikov by the commission composed of comrades Solts, Mikhailov and Molotov, 15 February 1922.

Having acquainted itself with the material about the case of Miasnikov, the commission composed of comrades Solts, Molotov and Mikhailov came to the conclusion that comrade Miasnikov committed antiparty acts.

1) Despite the fact that at the end of May 1921, the Perm Gubernia Party Committee (gubkom) determined that a report, which Miasnikov prepared to make at a general meeting of RCP(b) members, to be antiparty and forbade him to deliver it, he tried to speak both at the gubernia conference on 21 June 1921 and in Motovilikhinsky District. This led to squabbles in the party organisation.

2) When the Perm gubkom raised to the cc the case about Miasnikov, the cc Orgburo on 29 July 1921 found his theses to be antiparty both in direction and in spirit and created a commission composed of comrades Zalutsky, Bukharin and Solts.

Comrade Miasnikov, having received a letter from Vladimir Ilich dated 5 August about the questions he had raised, did not wait to hear the commission's decision but returned to Perm, where he used his trip to Moscow and comrade Lenin's letter for further destructive work in the Perm organisation. He brought about the departure of almost the entire Motovilikhinsky delegation (31 people) from the all-city August conference, which was accompanied by a demagogic and antiparty protest against the gubkom.

3)   When the CC Orgburo on 22 August 1921 agreed with the report of the commission composed of comrades Stalin, Solts and Mikhailov that Miasnikov's theses were incompatible with the interests of the party and forbade him to deliver them at party meetings, comrade Miasnikov again returned to Motovilikhi and without prior arrangement delivered a report about his presence in Moscow, about his theses, and about the CC Orgburo's 22 January decision.[307] His behaviour violated the Orgburo's decision and brought forth further ruin in the organisation, which was expressed in a new protest on 5 September 1921 by the Motovilikhi organisation connected with the CC Orgburo's decision.

4)   Comrade Miasnikov's destructive party work did not stop with this. In his 25 November 1921 letter to comrade Kurzhner in Petrograd, Miasnikov prevailed upon him to win over at least two districts, thus uniting under one banner all those who were dissatisfied. Simultaneously he urged Kurzhner to take measures and he himself also took measures toward printing and distributing his own articles, comrade Lenin's letters, and the Orgburo decisions. He did so, despite the fact that the CC Orgburo found it possible to print only one of his articles of that time and that only in the 'Discussion Leaflet'. Miasnikov did not receive permission to make public comrade Lenin's letter and the Orgburo's decision. He succeeded in doing this in Perm as well as in Moscow, where he himself arranged their distribution.

5)   The commission finds that comrade Miasnikov obviously and frequently violated party discipline, broke completely with the party, and uses his presence in the party only to facilitate his struggle against it and its decisions, by trying to organise a special grouping within it in direct violation of the decisions of the congress. Based on everything indicated above, the commission proposes to exclude comrade Miasnikov from the party.

Excerpt from the Politburo CC RCP(b) Protocol no. 100, 20 February 1922

Heard:

3)   About Miasnikov (the commission's report, delivered by comrade Solts)

Resolved:

3)   a)   Confirm the commission's decision and introduce into it a correc-

---

307   Editors' footnote: Obviously '22 August'.

tion allowing Miasnikov the right to petition for reentry into the party after a year.

b) To authorise the same commission to compose a brief memorandum about how it decided Miasnikov's guilt and punishment.

Party cc Statement about the Declaration of the 22

The cc informs party organisations the following:

The attached declaration of the group of 22 comrades, to whom comrades A. Kollontai and Z. Shadurskaia added their support, expresses the ideas and moods of the former so-called Workers' Opposition group, part of whom signed the document.

As is known, the Tenth Party Congress in special decisions (the resolution 'about party unity' and 'about the syndicalist and anarchist deviation in our party') resolutely condemned the ideas of the former Workers' Opposition group and gave instructions to immediately disperse all factional groups (including the Workers' Opposition faction) under the threat of exclusion from the ranks of the RCP(b).

The current declaration is addressed to members of the International Conference of the Communist International (with a copy to the cc RCP). The Central Committee (Politburo) of our party accepted on 27 February the following decision about the declaration:

a) Having received a copy of the declaration of 22 comrades, which was addressed to members of the international communist conference, the cc Politburo, without denying the right of individual comrades to appeal to the Comintern as to the highest court of appeal, instructs comrades Zinoviev and Trotsky to clarify to the conference or to the commission, if such will be created by the conference, the true character of this declaration and the distortions of reality permitted within it. In any case, the cc instructs comrades Zinoviev and Trotsky to present to the conference documents of the Tenth RCP(b) Congress, attesting to the fact that the party congress already last year condemned the views and factional organisation of those comrades, part of whom signed the current declaration.

b) Charge the Secretariat with informing all gubkoms (through the oblast party bodies) the text of the appeal of the 22 comrades to the Comintern and the decision of the cc Politburo.

c)   Publish this together with the decision of the Comintern.

For examination of this declaration, the International Conference of the Communist International on 28 February chose a commission composed of the following comrades: Clara Zetkin, Cachin, Friis, Kolarov, Kreibich, Terracini and MacManus. A supplement informing of the Comintern's decision will follow.

Resolution of the Expanded Plenum of the Comintern Executive Committee

A specially assembled commission of comrades Clara Zetkin, Cachin, Friis, Kolarov, Kreibich, Terracini and MacManus came to a unanimous conclusion regarding the complaint of 22 Russian comrades against the RCP(b). Having heard out the commission's conclusion, the expanded plenum of the ECCI declares the following:

We communists were not surprised that the difficult situation of Soviet Russia also created a difficult situation for the RCP(b). Such circumstances demand special cohesion, discipline, and the special effort of all the party's forces to secure the dominion of the proletariat, which is organised by the party, within as well as outside the country. The New Economic Policy, which entails unavoidable concessions to capitalism and to the small and middle peasantry, conceals in itself the danger of intensified petty bourgeois influence in state bodies as well as in the party.

The explanations, which the commission heard from representatives of part of the so-called Workers' Opposition led by Shliapnikov and Kollontai and from representatives of the CC RCP(b), showed that the leading centre of the RCP(b) was aware of these dangers from the very beginning. Likewise, it knew about the danger of bureaucratism. The leading centre of the RCP(b) spoke out resolutely against these dangers and it continues to conduct this struggle in unprecedentedly difficult objective conditions.

The criticism by those who signed this declaration knocks at an open door and lacks the necessary clarity not only in that part, which discloses the reasons for the existing disorder, but also in that part of it, which concerns investigating ways to eliminate them.

The position taken by the comrades who have brought the complaint has not helped the party at all in its struggle against objectively created abnormalities. Not only has it not strengthened the party, but on the contrary it weakened the party and simultaneously provided weapons against the party and against the proletarian dictatorship to the enemies of communism, meaning Mensheviks and even White counterrevolutionaries of the worst type.

Therefore, the expanded plenum of the Comintern Executive cannot acknowledge the complaint of the 22 comrades as correct. The plenum emphasises that these comrades' behaviour is sharply at odds with obligatory decisions of the Tenth RCP(b) Congress about party unity and the anarcho-syndicalist deviation. The Ispolkom seriously cautions these comrades and places them on notification that continuing the struggle, which they have begun, must lead to conflict with the RCP(b), its tasks, and the interests of the Russian proletariat. Therefore, it will place them outside the ranks of the Third International. The Ispolkom thinks that in the future, consciousness and communist training will force comrades from the opposition to take their place in the party ranks in a disciplined way, and, shoulder to shoulder, conduct general struggle against dangers, created by circumstances, which they will perceive and overcome together with the party. The conference regards any loss to the RCP(b) as harmful both to Soviet Russia and to the entire Communist International.

The conference hopes that precisely this serious situation will force the Russian proletariat to unite more closely and firmly around the RCP to defend Soviet Russia and the world revolution.

Resolution of the Communist Faction of the Fifth All-Russian Congress of the Metalworkers' Union

Having heard the unanimous decision of the commission and of the Comintern plenum and likewise the explanations of comrades Zinoviev, Shliapnikov and C. Zetkin about the Declaration of the 22 communists, the communist faction of the Fifth All-Russian Congress of the Metalworkers' Union completely welcomes this decision of the highest body of international communism and considers it the duty of any communist to submit to this decision without questioning it.

Simultaneously, the faction cautions the comrades not to repeat such actions, which threaten a split of the Russian Communist Party, which is the most disciplined one in the world.

In the name of this mighty unity, the faction of the congress summons those comrades who signed the document to observe greater discipline, self-restraint and order, especially at the current difficult moment, when the slightest unsteadiness within the Russian Communist Party, which rules the first labourers' republic in the world, intensifies the effrontery and certitude of the world bourgeoisie against the proletarian government and against the international working class.

Accepted unanimously with five abstentions.

From the Central Control Commission

In connection with the declaration, which 22 comrades submitted to the Comintern Ispolkom plenum, Comrade Shliapnikov said both to a meeting of Moscow senior party personnel and to the Communist Faction of the Union of Metalworkers that he frequently brought to the attention of the Central Control Commission those facts, about which the 22 comrades told in their declaration. The CCC finds it necessary to state that not once did comrade Shliapnikov nor any others of the signatories submit any such statement to the commission. The CCC did not even know about the submission of such a declaration. Not once did CCC member comrade Chelyshev, who signed it, utter even a word about it to the CCC.

Protocol of Comintern Commission Session

On 26 February 1922, the presidium of the expanded session of the ECCI received the following declaration in Russian and in foreign languages, without any warning to the Russian delegation or to the RCP(b) Central Committee [the editors refer the reader back to the pages on which the Declaration of the 22 is printed].

Comrade Kollontai gave this declaration to the presidium.

Having become acquainted with this document, the CC Politburo unanimously accepted the following resolution:

'Having received a copy of the Declaration of 22 comrades, which was addressed to members of the international communist conference, the CC Politburo, without denying the right of individual comrades to appeal to the Comintern as to the highest court of appeal, instructs comrades Zinoviev and Trotsky to clarify to the conference or to the commission, if such will be created by the conference, the true character of this declaration and the distortions of reality permitted within it. In any case, the CC instructs comrades Zinoviev and Trotsky to present to the conference documents of the Tenth RCP(b) Congress attesting to the fact that the Party Congress already last year condemned the views and factional organisation of those comrades, some of whom signed the current declaration'.

In response to the Declaration of the 22 and to the decision of the Politburo of the CC of the RCP(b), the expanded session of the ECCI unanimously elected a special commission to examine the above complaint. The commission was composed of the following comrades: Clara Zetkin (Germany), Marcel Cachin (France), [Jacob] Friis (Norway), [Vasil] Kolarov

(Bulgaria), [Karl] Kreibich (Czechoslovakia), [Umberto] Terracini (Italy) and [Arthur] MacManus (England).

Comrade Kolarov chaired this commission, which met in two sessions. To the first session were summoned representatives of the group, which submitted the complaint. Comrades Shliapnikov, Kollontai and Pravdin were summoned. Because of information they provided, comrade [Leonid] Serebriakov was questioned about one of the points of the complaint (about the order for locomotives abroad). The second session was dedicated to conversation with representatives of the CC RCP(b) (comrades Trotsky, Zinoviev and Rudzutak), who explained the accusations which were presented.

This last session proceeded in the following manner. In the presence of the entire commission, the commission chair, comrade Kolarov, proposed to CC representatives to write concisely, under his dictation, those accusations presented by comrades Shliapnikov and Kollontai, and then to provide point-by-point explanations.

Comrade Kolarov formulated these accusations by comrades Shliapnikov and Kollontai in the following way:

1. Free criticism is not allowed in the party. Even prior to accepting decisions, discussion is not permitted. The CC alone decides everything. The party is confronted with an accomplished fact. The most obvious examples are the party's decision about the tax-in-kind and the decision about the United Front tactic.

2. The Central Committee of the RCP(b) exerts constant pressure on local committees through its assignment of secretaries and other officials. The CC systematically sends to the provinces its own candidates as secretaries. If the gubernia party committees do not agree with the CC's suggestions, then the CC finds the means by which to force them to agree.

3. Stages of the party hierarchy [инстанции] ignore workers. Workers are not allowed the opportunity to participate seriously in the work of party organisations, trade unions, and soviets. Because of this, bureaucratism grows at an incredible rate. The party's composition is mostly petty bourgeois. Workers are increasingly quitting the party. The danger of social degeneration in the party is enormous.

4. The Central Committee of the RCP(b) exerts systematic pressure on communist factions of trade unions. Against the opinion and will of communist workers and trade unions, the CC composes its own lists [for trade union leadership] and simultaneously forces communist factions of trade unions to carry through these lists.

5. The party wanted to create a provocation against the Workers' Opposition. After the Third [Comintern] Congress, a Cheka agent named

Rubinov came to Shliapnikov's and Kollontai's secretaries and proposed to create groups for a fourth international. The provocation was intended to create grounds for excluding Shliapnikov and Kollontai from the party.

6. Shliapnikov's apartment in Moscow was searched, although he is a member of the party CC. Someone opened a letter, which was addressed to Shliapnikov, came from Revel, and contained complaints about the [Soviet] customs mission there. Instead of being delivered to Shliapnikov, the letter was redirected to that person, against whom the letter contained complaints. True, after Shliapnikov's report, the Party CC decided to investigate this incident, but so far nothing has emerged from the investigation. Apparently, the decision was taken only as a diversion.

7. Workers virtually boycotted the latest elections to the Moscow Soviet. Even those workers who voted for communists often did so only from fear that if they would not elect communists, then repression would follow and the elections would be annulled.

8. The Soviet government wastes gold. Orders of locomotives from Germany and Sweden caused enormous harm to the republic. Russian workers are left without work, although Russia has carriage-building works which could produce locomotives twice faster and two and one-half times cheaper than abroad. Before the war, Russia produced 1,200 locomotives each year.

9. The Workers' Opposition originated the idea of a party purge, but the purge has been spoiled to a significant degree. The Tsaritsyn organisation serves as an example.

10. Comrades who signed the complaint of the 22 have already been invitated to appear before the Central Control Commission. This, of course, is the beginning of repression against them.

11. At the All-Russian Congress of Metalworkers, someone hinted in advance that the commission, which the Comintern Ispolkom appointed in expanded session, is certain to condemn those who lodged the complaint.

12. Of 35 gubernia committee secretaries, only three are workers. The rest are not workers, but are journalists and the like.

13. A large number of workers quit the party. As an example, 306 workers and 185 who were not workers left the Moscow organisation from May to August. The situation is worse in other cities.

14. When comrade Miasnikov signed the Letter of the 22, he had not yet been excluded from the party. He received the letter about his exclusion two days later.

15. RCP congresses' resolutions are good, but the CC and local [местные] committees do not carry them out.

Conclusion: The RCP(b) is almost completely isolated from the workers. Workers are abandoning the party. The party is becoming petty bourgeois.

Shliapnikov declares that he does not want formation of a separate faction, but workers need to be given the opportunity to participate in the life of the party. Workerisation needs to be carried out.

Comrades Trotsky, Zinoviev and Rudzutak explained all these points in detail.

At the end, comrade Marcel Cachin read the following entry from his notebook, with the aim of supplementing the commission's accusations against Shliapnikov and Kollontai:

'Kollontai declared to us that when workers strike, Red Army men carry out the role of strikebreakers. Red Army men had to occupy plants and factories, which striking workers left, and had to carry out work in their absence.

Shliapnikov declared to us: you, meaning foreigners, are shown parades and state-funded spectacles, but this is only for show. In fact, a powerful strike movement is ongoing. The working class is breaking with the current government. The grounds for indignation, as you see, are very serious'.

These two additional declarations by Shliapnikov and Kollontai, which were quoted in the notes of comrade Cachin, naturally drew special attention from comrades Trotsky, Zinoviev and Rudzutak, who represented the CC RCP(b). They repeated once more their questions to the comrades. All commission members, who were present, confirmed that the declarations were made in this very form.

The following written declaration came to the commission from Shliapnikov and Kollontai:

'The goal of our appeal to the conference of the Comintern Ispolkom was:
1.   To caution the CC RCP(b) that its policy being implemented threatens the party with the greatest dangers, which are:
      a.   Loss of the party's unity with the proletariat.
      b.   Weakening of the proletariat's role and influence both in the party and in bodies of state power.
      c.   Complete social degeneration of the party as an inevitable consequence of these phenomena. This degeneration is already noticeable within the party now.
2.   To warn the party that the established regime in fact leads, in current circumstances and given its current social composition, to workers' mass departure from the party and to strengthening of nonproletarian elements' role and influence within it.

In order to protect the party from the dangers we have indicated, we propose the urgent need to:

1. Secure for proletarian party members the leading posts in the party and soviets and carry out mass recruitment of nonparty workers to work directly in government.

2. Propose to the CC RCP(b) to actually carry out the decisions of the Tenth Congress about worker democracy in the party and in the trade union movement.

3. Secure actual freedom for intraparty criticism, without which it is impossible to revive party life, to develop self-activity, to cultivate initiative, and to elevate party members' general level of consciousness and conscious discipline.

4. Cease persecution of those who demonstrate heterodoxy in party and official soviet work. Cease also the discrediting of worker communists by labeling as 'anarcho-syndicalism' any worker's disagreement with decisions made by higher-ups'.

After receiving these two declarations and after familiarisation with various letters and materials, the appointed commission of the Comintern unanimously accepted the following resolution:

'Regarding the complaint of 22 Russian comrades against the RCP(b) and the unanimous conclusion of the specially appointed commission composed of comrades Clara Zetkin, Cachin, Friis, Kolarov, Kreibich, Terracini and Mac-Manus, the expanded ECCI plenum declares the following: ...' [The text is the same as that translated above.]

For several hours, an expanded ECCI session discussed this resolution of 4 March. At this session, comrade Kreibich (from Czechoslovakia) spoke on behalf of the commission. Comrades Shliapnikov and Kollontai defended the views of the group of 22. Comrade Radek defended the view of the CC RCP(b) and comrade Clara Zetkin delivered the final words in the name of the commission. After debates the above resolution was accepted unanimously with four abstentions (two comrades from Switzerland and two comrades from Czechoslovakia).

Because comrade Shliapnikov (at a 5 March meeting of Moscow party organisation activists) declared that some of the accusations set forth in the 15 points above were incorrectly formulated (although neither he nor Kollontai said anything of the sort to the commission), the present statement is being given (in German and French translations) to the commission chair comrade Kolarov, the commission secretary comrade Kreibich, and to all commission members present, with the request that they verify in writing that what is set out above is correct.

Signatures of all commission members present:
Chair: Kolarov
Secretary: Kreibich
Members: Clara Zetkin, Terracini

Published in the brochure *Otchet komissii syezda* (Moscow, 1922), pp. 14–24; printed according to the text of the brochure

32   A.M. Kollontai's Diary Entries on the Appeal of the 22 and on the Eleventh Party Congress[308]

12 March 1922

A new period. Internal reconciliation in the very depths of my soul. Let there be on the surface agitation, vexation and bitterness but there is calm down below. There is no discord within myself.[309] Twenty-two comrades presented to the Conference of the expanded Executive Committee of the Comintern their declaration, which criticised intraparty relations. There was nowhere else where it could be submitted. To the CC? To the one which you consider the culprit for an incorrect line, a false course, and a harmful regime within the party? Why would you present a declaration to it? Rubbish. To the Eleventh Congress? Who would allow such a statement to be made? They would stifle it. They would not allow it to proceed.

It is true that our people (Shl[iapnikov], Medv[edev] and others) hurried a little. It should have been made into an 'act', which was prepared in advance. Delegates should have been 'won over' and corroborating signatures gathered. But our people surrendered to their mood. Impatience! I, too, on that memorable day of 26 February, was unable to assume a sobering tone. Everything coincided.

Debates proceeded about the United Front. We agreed with the idea and the principle, but the vague formulation was completely unsuitable. There were no boundaries. The line fluctuates. I decided to take the floor and speak in support of the French and Italians, who are demanding to render it more concrete. I signed up beforehand. In the morning I look at the list of orators, but I'm not

---

308   RGASPI, f. 134, op. 3, d. 37, ll. 33–9.

309   Новая полоса. На душе – примирённо внутренно, в самой глубине. Пусть на поверхности и волнения, и досада, и горечь, а на дне – тихо. Нет разлада с собою.

there. I ask to add my name. [Ludovic-Oscar] Fros[sard] inserts it. Zinoviev saw this and I notice a disturbance in the presidium. They run to the telephone.

Trotsky appears and comes toward me. He asks, 'Do you intend to speak for or against the United Front?' – 'For but with reservations, I demand concrete expressions'. – 'Hm ... Must I polemicise with you?' 'If you are wholly in favour of Zinoviev's theses, then yes'. – 'Does it mean that I have to beat you again?' (with a courteous smile) – 'You'll see'. Not less politely. We move on to something else, about Women's Day, about why I don't argue about the United Front at the Ispolkom session, but instead speak directly at the conference. We part peacefully.

Radek comes running up: 'What will you say about the United Front?' ... What is it with them? What are they afraid of? It's annoying.

After several minutes – Zinoviev. 'Do you want to speak against the United Front? But indeed the party's directive has been accepted, the Russian delegation should stand for the United Front. We don't know what you will say. I suggest to you not to speak'. I refuse. My explanation to Zinoviev is phrased less politely. They leave me in peace for five minutes. Again, Zinoviev descends from the rostrum and comes into the hall toward me. The delegates are curious. Zinoviev proposes 'to hold a consultation'.

Across the presidium and into the neighboring room hurried Trotsky, Radek, Zinoviev, Safarov, and I. They sit down. Silence. They exchange glances. Trotsky begins to speak. In the name of the CC, he inquires about what I will say: 'We don't know'. 'OK, I'll briefly inform you'. But after the first phrases, I see that their eyes are downcast and that obstinate dissatisfaction is on their faces.

Why this play-acting [комедия]? I interrupt myself to say, 'Tell me directly: does the CC forbid me to speak? If there is such a decree, I will obey, as a disciplined member of the party. But let this be a CC directive'.

Awkward silence. Trotsky says distinctly, 'Yes, we direct that you should not speak'. 'In that case, I request that you fix in a protocol that the CC forbids me to speak'. 'Safarov, write a protocol. Not just you personally, but all members of the Russian delegation should obey party directives. The matter of the United Front has been decided. Why did you not speak against it at the conference in December?'

I answer. We converse for several minutes. I throw out several 'truths' about the stifling of opinion and about nothing being discussed ahead of time. It occurred to them to try to discover if there were an 'organisation' behind this. They criticise, deny, and backtrack ... A familiar picture! ... The Tenth Congress was a year ago. But then it was worse and more difficult, because then our people Al[eksandr] and Med[vedev], abandoned and disavowed me ... The Workers' Oppositionists had themselves asked me to join them at the Tenth

Congress. If only there hadn't been this unnecessary blunder with Zoia's signature! ... That should not have happened.

They read it at the session. There is grave silence. They listened. They kept us waiting and wondering. They seemed afraid to move. Then they began intensely to 'attack' in private conversations.

They composed the commission. Here was the most vexing and painful thing. I had naively believed in the famous independence of [Marcel] Cachin, [Umberto] Terracini, and [Jakob] Friis. All of them followed Zinoviev's pre-arranged lead. They gathered once and hurriedly questioned Shliapn[ikov] and me. They sat for three hours with Tr[otsky] and Zin[oviev] and brought forth a censure of us. On the next day, the newspaper *Pravda* was completely devoted to us. The crusade was opened 'to smear'. Radek wrote a vulgar article from the gutter. This already was not painful.

It hurt to find out that everything I said in private conversations with Friis and Cachin reached Zinoviev and Carr and goes as material against me, as an 'accusation'![310] What is this? Is there really such demoralisation? They come to me, get information, and then inform about it? It was painful and unspeakably tormenting to wait for Kreibich to read the 'sentence' and pronounce an accusatory, prosecutorial speech, woven from cunning attacks against us (obviously, Radek was the author).

It hurt to sense that wall of hostility, which arose between us and the congress, when Shliapnikov and I spoke. It reminded me of 1917, a handful of Bolsheviks, and the seething hatred of a hall full of defencists ... But then it was easier, much easier!

Radek spoke insolently against us, but chiefly against me. He flung out: 'Here I am polemicising not with a lady, but with an enemy of our party'. And no one protested! Even the old lady Clara kept silent. Zinoviev has developed servility and cowardice to such an extent! ... Although those days of acute persecution were a tormenting experience, my soul became more peaceful. At least someone decided to speak the truth. I think that this act will not pass in vain. It will force some to think and to understand that it's not possible to continue further in this way. The main thing is that it will get easier for worker-communists. Not all of our people act like scoundrels and 'are silent, silent, silent' (in ECCI).

It has not been decided what they will do with us. There is hesitation at the top. They speak of excluding three at the Party Congress: me, Shl[iapnikov], and Medvedev. They threaten to do more. Not those at the very top, but the 'yes-men' [make threats]. Among those at the very top, there is a wait-and-see position.

---

310   Carr's birth name was Ludwig E. Katterfield. He was from the USA.

I talked my heart out [заговорилась]. I persistently attempted to get the floor. And it was strange. From the moment when the question erupted at the Congress, at once sympathy toward us appeared from some at the Congress. The atmosphere of deaf hostility was broken. All those 'dissatisfied' delegates, who to one or another degree oppose the cc's decision,[311] express obvious sympathy for us. They condemn our appeal to the Comintern, yet at the same time they essentially recognise our innocence.

On Wednesday morning I spoke. It was so-so. I was nervous. They applauded, so there was sympathy. And right there I started 'counterwork'. Zinoviev and Kamenev work on the stage by courting the delegates from their seats, but I go 'to the people', meaning into the hall and the corridor. They cluster round me, ask questions, and debate. There are more sympathisers for us than I thought. But the ECCI works without faltering. Our question is the central one of the congress. It arouses the most heated disputes and it worries [people]. They chose a commission. Of course, all are all appointees. Hand-selected. Not one sympathetic to us or, as I call them, 'liberal'. Nevertheless, the commission 'vacillated', but they pressed upon it and the commission obediently voted against us – for exclusion. In such a spirit [the page breaks off]

11 April 1922, Tuesday. Moscow.

A new notebook and maybe a new phase of life. The congress ended on the 2nd. We were not excluded! By 315 votes against 294, Antonov-Ovseenko's correction passed, leaving us in the party until new speeches! ... This is a victory, not ours personally, but of the worker [rest of page is cut off]

Manuilsky and P[et]rovsky were (weakly) opposed to us. Kubiak and Antonov were on our side. This was wonderful. As I was speaking, I understood that the congress was leaning toward us in sympathy. Our opponents only increased the sympathy toward us. Oh they made a lot of noise [rest of the page is cut off]

---

311   It appears as if the word 'decision' (rendering cc possessive) was added later. I cannot be sure how much later it was added. Apparently her first thought was to write that these delegates opposed the cc.

33   Letter from A.M. Kollontai to the Comintern Executive Committee,
        Copying the Politburo, 15 March 1922[312]

Having acquainted myself with the protocol of the Commission of the Conference of the Executive Committee, which examined the declaration of 22
comrades, I consider it necessary to introduce the following correction. In point
seven, where it tells of elections to the Moscow Soviet, it indicates that they
took place while workers boycotted them. I spoke about the elections as evidence of the growing rupture between the party and the masses. I cited the
example of workers' decline in morale, which was expressed in absenteeism
during the elections.

The editors of point seven of the protocol attribute to me thoughts about an
active boycott by workers.

Likewise, I must protest against the addition to the protocol of information,
which was obtained from the notebooks of commission members.

At the end of the protocol, there is the heading, 'Additional information from
comrade Cachin's notebook'. Here it refers to my words about the Red Army. I
categorically assert that at the commission's session, I said nothing about the
Red Army. Comrade Cachin's notes, obviously, relate to my private discussion
with him, which occurred approximately a week [illegible word] in my room.
In this discussion, by the way, I pointed to the danger of counterposing the
interests of the state to those of the worker masses, given the complexity of
the circumstances being created. For example, I pointed to the occasion, about
which I know, when military units were applied to work in place of striking
dock workers.

It is impermissible that a private conversation between comrades would figure as an accusation in 'supplement to the protocol'. Moreover, in connection
with the declaration of the 22, the given formulation distorts the entire meaning of my private conversation with comrade Cachin.

---

312   RGASPI, f. 134, op. 3, d. 37, l. 49, carbon copy.

34   Letter from A.M. Kollontai to the Editorial Board of the
      'Communist Worker Newspaper' of Germany, Requesting That It
      Cease Publication of Her Brochure, *Rabochaia Oppozitsiia*,
      22 September 1921[313]

[This document is handwritten and in Russian. It is followed by a typed copy in Russian and a typed copy in German.]

To the Editors of the 'Communist Worker Newspaper' of Germany.

As a member of the Comintern, I believe that any international grouping of the working class that exists beyond the bounds of the Comintern harms the proletariat and hampers the realisation of the historical task of the Third International. Therefore, I request the editors of 'Communist Worker Newspaper' of Germany to immediately cease publication of my brochure *Rabochaia Oppozitsiia* in a press organ, which is published by a party that stands outside the Comintern and sets as its goal the creation of an international grouping in counterweight to the Third International. Moreover, my brochure was intended only for a narrow circle of readers who were members of the Tenth Congress of the RCP(b).[314]

35   Iu.K. Milonov, 'On the Way to a Worker Encyclopedia: Instead of a
      Preface'[315]

[Bold-type words indicate text that was in bold typeface in the original.]

1.   *Elements of Proletarian Culture*
In our time, special mass organisations work to create proletarian culture. They are called proletcults. The proletarian culture, which they are creating, comprises the elements of proletarian art and proletarian science. That is how the leaders, theoreticians, and vanguard of the proletarian movement define its content. In their opinion, both of these elements are **equally** important parts of the proletariat's creative, cultural work. Both of them are of equal value.

---

313   RGASPI, f. 134, op, 3, d. 38, ll. 1–4.
314   According to KAPD member Bernhard Reichenbach, Kollontai had given him a copy of
       her *Rabochaia oppozitsiia* booklet in case it were confiscated by party officals. Although
       she requested it back shortly afterwards, he had already sent it to Germany, where it was
       translated and published (Clements 1979, pp. 204–5, 209; Farnsworth 1980, pp. 257–8).
315   'Na puti k rabochei entsiklopedii: vmesto predisloviia', in Bogdanov 1921, pp. iii–xxiv.

Rank-and-file proletcultists, who are the movement's practioners and its army, see this differently. The overwhelming majority of them are preoccupied **exclusively with art**. They completely forget about science. Possibly, many of them are not even familiar with the very concept of proletarian science. Only a small group of those, who engage most actively and deeply with the questions of the movement, understand this concept. However, their familiarity with the concept of proletarian science is exclusively theoretical and it does not have any impact upon their practical work. This group knows that creating proletarian science is a task no less important than creating proletarian art. It knows that accumulation and unification of such science will lead, as a result, to the appearance of a Worker Encyclopedia. This encyclopedia should consist of a strictly systematic interpretation of the entire circle of knowledge in that form in which it appears to the proletariat. But this small group does not take any practical steps toward creating proletarian science and a Worker Encyclopedia.

Such dissonance in the ranks of the proletcult movement leads to deplorable results in practice. In fact, our proletcultists' creative work bears an abnormally one-sided and half-hearted character. They prefer one element of proletarian culture over the other element. Art displaces and replaces science. In order to convince oneself of this, it is sufficient to compare the content of the leading journal *Proletarskaia kultura* with the content of local proletcults' work. Meanwhile, now more than ever, the business of creating a workers' encyclopedia is both completely **necessary historically** and completely **possible scientifically**.

2.   *Historical Necessity for a Worker Encyclopedia*

First of all, the experience of past social revolutions, and secondly, the experience of the revolution, which is unfolding before our eyes, confirm the need for a worker encyclopedia. Evidence need not come from an investigation of all social revolutions, which have taken place so far. It is quite sufficient to dwell only upon the most significant and typical social revolutions, which indeed hold within themselves everything that is most essential. Two such revolutions were the feudal and the bourgeois. Of course, their development should be traced along the line of actual events, which have come to a conclusion in one or another country. Here it is completely sufficient, however, to take only those countries, where the course of events was most characteristic for revolution of one or the other type. For feudal revolution, Judea is such a country, and for bourgeois revolution, it is France. When investigating the development of events, there is no sense in dwelling in detail upon each link in their long chain. Indeed, here it is necessary to clarify only the relationship between the **transformation** of a new class into the **ruling** class and the **appearance** of its class encyclopedia. For the purpose of this essay, clearly it is completely sufficient to take only these two links out of the entire chain of events.

Those are the necessary boundaries, within which we will investigate the experience of past social revolutions.

After these preliminary remarks, it is possible already to move on to the study itself, without any concern about serious misunderstandings. The feudal revolution in Judea envelops the period that begins between the fourteenth and the tenth centuries BCE and continues to the beginning of the Christian era.

By revolution, what is meant here is only restructuring social relations. First of all, the transition from nomadic herding to settled agriculture was completed during this period. Clan society was regenerated into neighborhood-based society. Patriarchal guardianship was replaced with exploitation by feudal lords. Feudal government developed on the ruins of communal self-government. Already after the stratum of patriarch-organisers completely transformed into a class of feudal lord-exploiters, the so-called Pentateuch of Moses (Torah) appeared in the 5th century BCE. Legends, songs, and traditions, which had accumulated over the ages, were gathered, unified, and edited into a compilation by high priests [жрецы]. That is how the complete and basic features finalising the expression of the feudal, authoritarian, religious world view appeared. Briefly put, this was the Feudal Encyclopedia.

The experience of the feudal revolution tells us that the class encyclopedia appears after the class created by the revolution transforms into a ruling class. For feudal society, if you please, it would be even more correct to say that it happened after this class appeared.

The bourgeois revolution in France occupied the period from the fourteenth to the eighteenth centuries of the current era. During this time, feudal relations were restructured into serfdom. Cities with handicrafts manufacturing arose. Commercial capital appeared and its development led to the formation of domestic capitalist industry. Then this industry [промышленность] became textiles manufacturing. The absolutist monarchy with its gentry-estate and bureaucratic-police state emerged from the collapsing feudal state. Quests for gold and markets caused the arising bourgeoisie to accumulate a large amount of technical knowledge. As this technical knowledge was systematised and analysed, great discoveries and new inventions appeared. In contrast to the dismal Christian culture of the Middle Ages, the forgotten, joyous culture of the ancient pagan world was reborn. This was expressed in the so-called Era of Enlightenment. Then numerous heresies rose against Catholicism, developed, and merged into one general stream of Reformation. Toward the end of the first half of the eighteenth century, all these new ideas and knowledge, which accumulated discretely, were collected and systematised by a group of philosophes, or literary men, from the bourgeois class. Their labour represented an integrated interpretation of the abstract [отвлеченно]-individualist world view. That is how the bourgeois encyclopedia, or as it is usually called, the French Encyclopedia, arose. In the beginning of the last quarter of the eighteenth century, the bourgeois intelligentsia led almost all the urban people and the majority of the rural population of France in overthrowing the rule of the nobility and clergy. This intelligentsia was the ideological heir of the philosophe-encyclopedists. It came to power and built a republic in place of an absolutist monarchy. The new authority destroyed serfdom and other remnants of feudalism and it separated the church from the state.

The experience of the bourgeois revolution speaks differently than the experience of the feudal one. Here the class encyclopedia appeared before the class that created the revolution transformed into the ruling class.

Generalising from the experience of both these revolutions, we inevitably arrive at such a conclusion. The process of a class's creation of **its own** encyclopedia **necessarily** interlaces **in one or another form** with the process of its transformation into the ruling class. This conclusion represents a simple generalisation or, more accurately, empirical law. It only sets up a link between things of interest to us, but it does not provide explanations. However, for our task, this suffices for the time being.

That's of what the experience of past social revolutions speaks. Now we'll turn to the revolution, which is unfolding in front of our eyes.

That phase of development of social relations, which Russia has already entered just now and which the entire capitalist world is preparing to enter soon, is the immediate threshold to the socialist system [строй]. In this phase, **the proletariat transforms from oppressed to ruling class.** At first and for awhile, it holds power together with the peasantry, which is its petty bourgeois fellow traveler. But later, as the revolution develops, the proletariat begins to rule completely alone. The dictatorship of the proletariat is realised. Once the class prepares to become the ruling class, and even more so when it actually becomes the ruling class, the experience of past revolutions makes it is completely **natural to expect** that it will create its own **class encyclopedia.** This alone tells of the great need to create a Workers' Encyclopedia in our time.

The facts of the Russian Revolution demonstrate that this is exactly so and not otherwise.

That is what they say.

During the imperialist war, the contradictions in the capitalist system were acutely revealed. This circumstance confronted the working class with the question about socialist revolution in all its magnitude and in a completely practical way. From that moment, the rapid revolution of the ideology of the working class began. This ideology began to transform from a vulgar, petty bourgeois one into a revolutionary socialist one. First of all, the fighting consciousness of the proletariat took shape. Along with it, the will to seize power and destroy the bourgeois system [строй] appeared. Then, organisational consciousness also gradually began to grow. A certain ability to build complex social relations accumulated, although very slowly. The first phenomenon characterised the ideology of the masses and the second one characterised that only of a small vanguard, which actively worked in various types of proletarian organisations.

In such a condition, the working class and its petty bourgeois fellow traveler, the peasantry, in the person of the army, found it necessary to seize power in practice. Simultaneously, the fighting consciousness of the proletariat turned out to have been fully formed already. Therefore, the very seizure of power was completed unusually rapidly and successfully. Just as successfully was the new authority defended from attack by hostile classes, despite unbelievable difficulties of various types. However, the picture significantly changed, when the business went as far as building and organising a new government and new production. Here it came to light that the masses and vanguard had **insufficient consciousness as organisers**. It turned out that the masses were not at all in the condition to participate in this construction. They needed to receive appropriate education in advance. The vanguard, willingly or not, was forced to take it up. However, it also could not build just by itself, so in this it enjoyed the aid of the old bourgeois intelligentsia. After the stability of the new power came to light, its labouring grassroots went into service to the worker-peasant government. The vanguard of the proletariat used them in its construction. But because its organiser consciousness was incompletely formed and insufficient to meet the enormous organisational tasks confronting it, then naturally it fell under the influence of the old bourgeois intelligentsia. The very essence of the bourgeois intelligentsia, its situation, and its role in social cooperation gave birth within it to such organisational methods as bureaucratism and anarchism. Indeed, it had to command and organise discrete parts of social life, not all of it systematically. The method of comradely cooperation is inherent in the proletariat, but its culturally dependent higher-ups use the first two organisational methods. The proletariat's unformed organiser consciousness explains this fact, which at first glance is completely incomprehensible, that in the Soviet state bureaucratism and departmental [ведомственный] anarchism are so strong, although indeed it essentially is not bureaucratic and not departmental [ведомственный].

So the business stands so far, while the republic of the working class and peasantry is found in the situation of a besieged fortress and an armed camp. At this time, it is busy organising an original military communism. Under such communism, there is equal distribution of what remains from production forces, which were destroyed by war. With these remnants, they feed the army and the labouring population. Likewise they support production, which serves military needs. So the matter stands, while the tasks of organisers do not increase or become more complex. In the best case, they remain unchanged.

The disarray in the proletariat's organiser consciousness appears still more acute, when these tasks increase in magnitude and become more complex. The need to restore and develop production forces is revealed in the process of revolution. It becomes clear that without complete and thorough technical revolution, the proletariat not only cannot build socialist production relations, but is not even in the condition to simply hold political power in its hands. Besides that, it cannot make this technical revolution on its own for reasons already explained. The working class itself, in the visage of the Communist Party, understands its unpreparedness and with full consciousness transitions to the organisation of the production relations of state capitalism. In this it collaborates even more broadly with the entire spectrum of the bourgeois intelligentsia and even with the old industrial and commercial bourgeoisie. Obviously, this cooperation is in fact only a modified form of struggle. Of course, its conditions are set by the proletariat itself. Nevertheless, it is a concession. In the conditions of cooperation, the defining moment is most likely not the strength of the proletariat, but its weakness. It has to concede up to that limit, beyond which it does not have the strength to step. And this limit marks a very small plot [клочок] of economic life. From the political aspect, the need to preserve the political union of the proletariat with the peasantry composed the base of the new course toward state capitalism, but it is possible not to dwell on this aspect, because our party literature sufficiently elucidates it. For the same reasons, there is no sense in speaking about what state capitalism is.

That is the experience of revolution, which is unfolding before our very eyes. What does this experience demonstrate?

It says that the **proletariat can be the organiser of the new society only to the degree to which it produced its own organisational methods.** Proletarian culture in general is composed of the entire sum of these methods and proletarian science of part of them. In other words, it says that during the revolution, the **proletariat** should in one way or another create a **Workers' Encyclopedia,** which will be the foundation for a Socialist Encyclopedia of the classless, stateless society of the future.

Thus, from this experience, it is likewise possible to arrive at an **empirical law. There exists a connection between a lack of structure [неоформлен-ность] of organisational methods original to the proletariat, a lack of structure in its consciousness as an organiser, and defects in its work as an organiser.** This is the situation it is coming to.

So far, we have operated only with the empirical law of cultural revolution. It set up contact between phenomena of interest to us, without having explained this contact, however. It does not provide the possibility to fully understand the general need for each class to have its own class encyclopedia and the partial need to create a Worker Encyclopedia now. Therefore, here it is expedient to also expound upon the **abstract law** [абстрактный закон] of such a revolution.

There you have it.

The ideology, which otherwise they call social consciousness or 'spiritual' culture, comprises speech, science, art, law, and morality.

It is **formed and takes shape** under the influence of technology and economics, the production forces of society, and production relations. Usually it is acceptable to say, 'Ideology is determined by the social existence of people', which means by their relations within production and toward production. Ideology is superstructure on the economic substructure. Thus, speech, science, art, law, and morality come together differently for different social classes during different eras of social development. However, this does not settle the question of contact between ideology on the one hand, and the economy and technology on the other.

Ideology is not only superstructure and in any case, it is not a useless adornment. It is formed under the influence of economics and technology. But at the same time it **regulates and organises them.** Art, law, and morality cultivate in people certain concepts, feelings, and desires, which determine their actions and behaviour in social life. Understandably, they are defined within the boundaries of their social situation and class interests. Science shows the path of difficult struggle against nature and class struggle in society. Speech unifies the efforts of individual people in cooperation.

So, ideology reminds one of an instrument, which by its form and hardness is adapted so as to make it possible to process material. Just exactly the same, the content and form of ideology is adapted to the economy and technology, so as then to organise both of them. **Ideology is an organisational instrument.**

The proletariat and its conscious vanguard always take account of the organisational role of ideology both in theory and in practice. Marxist ideologists of the workers' movement are such a vanguard. The doctrine about class (self-)consciousness of the proletariat occupies one of the most visible places in Marxist theory. The essence of this doctrine comes down to that the struggle of the working class develops only according to the degree to which it is aware of its situation in society, its interests, its tasks, and the means for resolving them. In Marxists' practical activity, work on class self-consciousness of the proletariat always took and still takes the most prominent place. Indeed, class self-consciousness is the ideology of the class.

Now, it is completely understandable why each class develops its own encyclopedia as it becomes the ruling class, meaning the organiser. It should have an organisational instrument for an organiser's work. This instrument should fit the material being processed and the strengths of the class working upon it. Ideology is such a weapon, as we already explained. Science represents an element and a unit of ideology. The encyclopedia is a complete and systematic exposition of science.

Several more words should be said about why right now, more than at any other time, a Worker Encyclopedia needs to be created.

Right now the working class has to organise state capitalism, which means that it has to construct essentially that which the bourgeoisie could not, did not know how, and did not want to build. Its collaborators in this work are and cannot help but be this exact bourgeoisie and the bourgeois intelligentsia. By necessity, the proletariat has to do that which is not its real business and at the same time, moreover, collaborate with its class opponent. It should make difficult and very unpleasant material concessions to its new colleague [сотруд-ник]. In such conditions, the proletariat should be maximally independent ideologically and culturally. Otherwise, it is threatened with the danger of even more difficult and unpleasant concessions, which are ideological. It may fall under the ideological influence of the bourgeoisie and begin to cooperate with it not only with its body, but also with its soul. The history of the workers' movement knows of such a case, which was the failure of the Second International. Only the availability [наличность] of an independent proletarian culture can safeguard the proletariat against hostile cultural influence. From this, it is completely obvious that right now it needs to apply as much effort as possible to create this general culture of proletarian science and the Worker Encyclopedia taken separately.

However this is not yet all.

It turns out that the bourgeoisie is not capable of building state capitalism. Such an assertion at first glance may seem strange. But in fact, so it is. Indeed, state capitalism is the organisation of commercial-capitalist production relations by the government within the framework of the entire state. Up to now, the bourgeoisie has built only an anarchic economy, which in the best case was organised only within the framework of united enterprises. It is an individualist class. The ideas of the collective and of an organised national economy are alien to it. Characteristic of it are such features as personal careerism and patriotism to one's factory, industry, or department. The social nature of the bourgeoisie appears in these features. Therefore, one more task still confronts the proletariat. It should counterpose its own organisational methods to those of the bourgeoisie. The proletariat should guide the bourgeoisie and the bourgeois intelligentsia during the period while state capitalism is built. **The proletariat is confronted by the task of struggling for the maximal organisation** against its new colleagues' anarchist, disorganising efforts. In order to resolve this task, the proletariat needs all the more to draw up and work out its own class-organised methods, which are proletarian culture in general and proletarian science in particular, especially a worker encyclopedia.

So, **the Worker Encyclopedia not only insures the proletariat against ideological influence from its collaborators in the economy, but also secures for it the real possibility for practical leadership by these collaborators in the business of building state capitalism.**

The general conclusion from everything, which has been laid out here, is that the creation of a worker encyclopedia for our time is **actually** a historical necessity. Thus, the negative conditions which work against its appearance in our reality are obvious.

3.   *The Encyclopedia's Scientific Potential*

This is also present in greater or lesser degree. This means that it is possible to speak about the presence of positive conditions.

The experience of past encyclopedias points to three such conditions. Here they are.

First of all, there is the concisely formulated cultural point of view of the class, which creates an encyclopedia. It is an instrument, which newly revises all knowable scientific material of the old society and class, which have departed from the historical scene. By its role, it reminds one of a sieve, which separates the necessary from the unnecessary. Only part of this old material can be accepted and only after revisions. The cultural point of view of the class contains all the material of the new encyclopedia, as if it were its ideological skeleton. Such is the authoritarian-religious point of view of Bible and the abstractly individualist one of French encyclopedia. When the creators of both these encyclopedias carried out their work, they took from the old cultures only elements, which corresponded to their point of view and discarded everything else. Jewish high priests took authoritarian elements of patriarchal culture, after having separated from them all remnants of the culture of primitive communism. Rejecting the feudal ideology of the Middle Ages, French philosophes accepted the individualistic culture of antiquity, but without the authoritarian elements that ran through it.

The precisely formulated cultural point of view of class is the first scientific condition for the appearance of its class encyclopedia.

The **second condition** is **to have on hand** a certain amount of scientifically knowable **material**, which has **already been revised** and understood from the **new point of view**. It usually is the foundation, or more truly, the core, around which all the rest then begins to grow out [нарост ать]. Indeed, to build something new, one needs material, which has been prepared and adapted for it. This is completely obvious. For the Bible, such material comprised songs, legends, and customs, which accumulated during the feudal revolution. For the French encyclopedia, it was the works by important people in the era of great inventions and discoveries, the Renaissance, and the Reformation. There you have the basic core of both of these encyclopedias.

Finally, the third and last condition is expressed in the need for a **certain number of scientifically prepared personnel from the ranks of the building class**. Given this, it is not important that their origins and social situation linked them to it. Of course, it would be better, if this were so. But another thing is far more important. They should firmly stand on its cultural point of view. Such a chief of the proletariat as Marx, for example, illustrates this fact and proves that it is true. He was not a worker, but he was the ideologist of the working class. For the Bible, high priests were such personnel and the philosophes were so for the French encyclopedia.

Such are three scientific conditions.

Now it is necessary to clarify the degree to which they are all sufficiently present at the current time, in relation to the new encyclopedia.

The cultural point of view of the working class is formulated completely clearly. This point of view is collectivist-labour. It is free from any fetishism, authoritarian religion, and abstract individualism. The founders of scientific communism, Marx and Engels, first formulated it in their works. They expressed it most distinctly in their doctrine about the historical materialism, which composes the substructure and pivot [стержень] of all Marxist theory. The essence of this doctrine is that it recognises that the technology of society forms its economy. Together, they both form ideology. After they have been formed, they regulate one another: ideology regulates economics and technology, and economics regulates technology. The relationship between them is identical to the relationship between the instrument and material. The previous chapter explained this in more detail.[316] It is possible to understand it

---

316 'Previous chapter' probably refers to the previous numbered section of this essay.

in this way only by looking at reality from the point of view of the labouring collective. Much does not have to be said about the collectivist-labour point of view, just exactly as about the class cultural point of view of the proletariat. This position is almost obvious. Indeed, it seems that the class's cultural point of view is a clot of its vital-labour experience. The proletariat, in this regard, is the labouring and collectivist class. It ought to be considered labouring, because in the production process, its activist energy overcomes the resistance of nature. It is collectivist for the reason that it works in enormous collectives, which means in conditions of broadly developed, systematically organised cooperation in plants and factories. It is completely clear that the collectivist-labour point of view is exactly the point of view of the proletariat.

The works of A. Bogdanov formulate this point of view even more precisely. He regards it as organisational. The entire universe, or otherwise the entire global process, consists of diverse units of elements.[317] Elements act [выступают] in combinations organised by various means and to a different extent, and not otherwise. From this point of view, the entire content of the life of humankind unfolds before us, like the organisation of the external forces of nature, the organisation of forces of the human collective, and the organisation of experience. The world lives and develops in the struggle of organisational forms. They come into conflict and disorganise one another. As a result, you get a more harmonious organisation. The struggle for existence in the world of animals and plants concludes in the survival of the fittest. As a result of the struggle of classes in society, it is restructured according to the condition of production forces. Unified theories grow out of the struggle between individual opinions. There you have particular cases of the struggle between organisational forms.

Actions and reactions [активности-сопротивления] are elements of the organisational processes of the universe. These are two sides of the same coin. That which in class struggle comes out for the bourgeoisie as its action [активность] turns out to be the reaction to the proletariat and vice versa. When a hammer splits a stone, the stone acts like a combination [сочетание] of reactions. But the stone represents a combination of actions, when it smashes a nut.

From this point of view, each phenomenon is regarded in its relationship to the surrounding environment and each element in its relationship to the whole. Social life represents such a picture. Ideology acts [выступает] like the

---

317   С неё вся вселённая, или иначе весь мировой процесс, представляется состоящим из различных частиц элементов.

organisation of ideas. It adapts to economics and technology, but then it organises them. Economics is the organisation of people. It adapts to technology in order then to organise it.

The ideological content of the organisational point of view is identical to that of the collectivist-labour point of view. It is also a clot of the vital-labour [жизненно-трудовой] experience of the proletariat. The labouring life of this class, as we already clarified, consists in its overcoming the resistance of nature by means of its activity. Therefore, it is completely natural for it to imagine elements of the world in the form of actions and reactions [активностей-сопротивлении]. Its labour consists of disorganising, destroying, and disuniting on the one hand and in organising, creating, and uniting on the other. It disorganises material so as to organise a product. This is the basis for imagining the world in the form of organisational processes. The organisational point of view only much more completely and simply formulates the labour experience of the working class.

Thus, the first condition of the scientific possibility for a worker encyclopedia exists.

Now let's turn to the second one. Is there enough scientifically knowable material, which has been revised from the cultural point of view of the proletariat?

First of all, the literary legacy of Marx and Engels needs to be pointed out here. It is a revision of political economy and philosophy. Criticising bourgeois political economy as it was explained by Adam Smith and David Ricardo, Marx thus laid the foundation for the proletariat's political economy. He made this criticism in his most important work, *Capital*. Together with Engels, he revised the bourgeois philosophy of the idealist Hegel and of the materialist Feuerbach. Their philosophical works resulted from this revision and they contained the basic core of proletarian philosophy. Besides that, Marx and Engels accomplished enormous work in that same direction in other areas of knowledge: history, studies of morality, law, and government. Later Marxists created an extensive literature about all these questions, which allows one to speak about proletarian political economy, philosophy, sociology, ethics, and proletarian law. However, this is not even all the material of proletarian science. The works of the proletarian philosopher [Joseph] Dietzgen in the area of logic need to be mentioned. The Russian Marxist scholar Bogdanov went even further. He recast biology and psychology from the proletarian point of view. He set to work upon the so-called pure sciences, such as astronomy and mathematics. He laid the foundation of the science of organisation, which generalises and unifies all material that is knowable from the proletarian point of view. He calls it 'tectology'.

There is sufficient material to make it **fully possible to speak about proletarian science and about the presence [наличность] of some elements of a worker encyclopedia. The second condition of scientific possibility [научной возможности] also is present.**

There remains the third and last thing. Are there scientists?[318]

This question can be answered in the following way. There are small groups of proletcultists, who are more or less acquainted with the idea of proletarian science. They work in proletcults, party schools, worker-peasant universities, worker faculties, courses of various types, and other cultural cells and bodies in our country. They more or less understand the tasks. However, there is insufficient knowledge of how to approach it in practice and there is no basic familiarity with all those sciences which have to be revised. Only a few individuals so far can be found with such knowledge, unfortunately. Undoubtedly, it must begin with these few individuals. But there can be confidence that new collaborators will be found as work proceeds. They will emerge from the broader strata of the groups of proletcultists already noted above. Indeed, the work itself is historically necessary. For very many Marxists, this will become clearer the further it goes. Thus, **right now and for the time being, there are only people who can be initiators, pioneers, and skirmishers [застрельщики] in the business of creating a new encyclopedia.**

It goes without saying, that it is absolutely possible scientifically to create the elements of this encyclopedia in our time. That is the general conclusion from the entire analysis made here.

4.   *Onto New Rails*

This is the slogan, under which the work of our proletcults needs to be restructured now.

Discord in the ranks of the proletcult movement should be destroyed. The army needs to be pulled up to the level of the vanguard and their positions aligned. Creation of a new proletarian science should be given the same priority as creation of proletarian art. In other words, **proletcults should take up work to create a worker encyclopedia.**

Active proletcultists, who are familiar with its exact idea and who have certain scientific skills and experience, should act precisely as initiators and pioneers of these truly great works.

Onto new rails. On the path to a worker encyclopedia. This is the practical conclusion from the analysis made above.

---

318   The word for 'scientists' could also be rendered as 'scholars'.

In order to take practical work in a new direction, however, some questions, which are connected with this encyclopedia, need to be clarified precisely. What are its tasks? By what methods will it be created? How should the work to create it be organised? How should the organisational apparatus be constructed? These are the elements, which need to be clarified before taking up this business.

5. *Basic Questions of the Worker Encyclopedia*

The basic questions have already been set out. It remains only to answer them. Here are the answers.

The tasks of the worker encyclopedia are bipartite. They are, on the one hand, **socialisation**, and on the other hand, **democratisation of science**.

The first consists of revision [переработка] and elaboration [разработка], from the proletarian point of view, of the scientific data of the entire scientific inheritance from bourgeois society. This point of view is collectivist-labourist. Its ideological content and social meaning is already explained in the chapter about the scientific potential of the new encyclopedia. From this point of view, science is the collectively organised labour experience of humankind, which has accumulated over generations and is the instrument for organisation of collective labour. Science is an instrument of the collective, just as a machine or a tool is not only of work-related but also knowledge-related. Such a revision of it comes down to the following. First of all, they explain in what way one or another science was born and developed from accumulating, processing [обработка], and organising labour experience. They determine what role it plays in organising the social life of labour. They establish the labour content of its concepts, methods, formulae, how all grew out of the labour process, and how they help to organise it. This revision of the scientific inheritance of bourgeoisie removes from its material all elements of fetishism, both authoritarian-religious and abstract-individualist. In other words, approaches to understanding science like divine revelation and abstract truth [отвлеченная истина] will disappear from it.

This is the first task of the workers' encyclopedia. It could also be called proletarianisation, because science is revised from the proletariat's point of view. But indeed, the proletariat is the builder of socialism. It represents the embryo of socialism within capitalist society. Its science is the embryo of socialist science. Therefore, we call revising it from the proletarian point of view the socialisation of science. Besides that, it can also be named so because in the process of revision, the point of view of the cognizant individual [познающий индивидуум] is replaced by the point of view of the social organism, which is the labouring and cognitive [познающий] society.

The second task is democratisation. It consists of the simplified and abbreviated explanation of the data of science, which has already been socialised, so that it would be comprehensible to the popular masses, which are the broad democratic strata of the population. However, such simplification and abbreviation should not cause detriment to the depth or precision of scientific theses [положения]. Moreover, it should not be so much the results and conclusions of science, which should be explained, as its methods. That's how democratisation differs from popularisation and vulgarisation of science. Of these two, the first emphasizes the people's familiarity only with the results and conclusions of science. It leaves them unaware of the methods and premises of science. The second adapts science to the understanding of masses, but often to the detriment of the depth and precision of scientific theses. It achieves this adaptation precisely at the expense of depth and precision. [Nikolai] Rubakin's general scientific brochures can serve as examples of vulgarization. The majority of so-called popular scientific booklets for the people are examples of popularisation. Both of them show how not to democratise science. Bogdanov's course on political economy serves as an example of works, which actually democratise science and prepare the majority of Russian Marxist workers for revolutionary work.

That's what the tasks of the Workers' Encyclopedia come down to. Now we will dwell upon the methods for fulfilling these tasks.

They are dual, just like the tasks, and they amount to the **review of all scientific data** and all knowable [познавательный] material **from the perspective of socialisation and democratisation.**

In the first sense, its review should be expressed by clarifying how entire branches of science and their concepts, methods, and formulae historically arose from collective labour. Further, it should be established in what way they developed, with some being replaced by others under the influence of the development of the labour process. In other words, the review from the perspective of socialisation should consist in **studying the history of science** from the collectivist-labourist, organisational point of view. As a result of such a review, we will receive a new illumination of and a new understanding of all the scientific material. We'll divide it into groups and redistribute it among the individual branches of science. We'll arrive at a new arrangement of these sciences in the encyclopedia of knowledge and a new classification of them. We'll rearrange individual branches of study within different scientific fields.

The method of democratisation attempts to explain scientific data systematically, deeply, and precisely enough, and at the same time make it clear, simple, understandable, and accessible to the popular masses. There need to be as **many** such attempts as possible and they need to be as **diverse** as possible. Of these, the most successful should be selected, consolidated, and the accumulated material should be processed [обрабатывать]. As a result, the formulations will be simpler and clearer, as well as deeper and more precise.

Such are the methods of work in general outline.

Finally, the last thing is their **organisation**, which is **expressed in the creation of worker universities, which are united into a socialist academy.**

The worker university is distinguished both from the universities of the old type, the so-called state universities, and from the new worker-peasant ones. Examples of it are the pre-revolutionary party schools in Capri and Bologna and the Moscow Proletarian University, which worked in 1919. The main characteristics of the worker university come down to the following.

First of all, there is the **proletarian class composition of students in attendance.** The need for such a composition is conditional upon the workers being exactly those, who are most receptive to the ideas of proletarian culture. Their life-work experience attests to this. In rare exceptions, members of the working [трудовая] intelligentsia and the working [трудовой] peasantry can fully assimilate these ideas. But the great bulk of the work experience of the latter is tightly influenced by individualist culture. In the worker university, science that has already been socialised will be democratised. It is patently obvious that it should be composed of the proletarian class. Other elements of society can be permitted there only as exceptions.

The second characteristic of the university is **its program**, which is determined by the general task of the university. This task is not simply preparing personnel who specialise in a certain branch, but primarily those who get work done. Chiefly, it will prepare organisers, leaders, and others who have a universal scope. They are such people, who can more or less freely orient themselves and make sense of various branches of work. Therefore, **the program needs a certain encyclopedic character** [энциклопедичность]. It should strive to envelop the entire circle of knowledge. Familiarisation with scientific methods and their historical development is especially important to include in it. Indeed, only under such conditions is it possible to produce doers [деятели] who are generalists [с универсальным размахом] and have the skills to be organisers.

As for the third characteristic, it concerns the **organisational set-up of work** and the form of collaboration among students, lecturers, and directors. In the Worker University, this **cooperation should be comradely.** On the basis of completely equal rights, students, lecturers, and directors should participate in directing the life of the university: putting together and changing programs, determining methods of work to fulfil programs, and the like. University bodies are to be constructed from various numbers of students and lecturers. In other words, their relations are those of less experienced comrades to more experienced ones.

Finally, the last characteristic is **creative methods of work such as you find in a laboratory**. Proceeding through the program, it would not be simply like in the plant [фабрика], with personnel stamped out according to a pattern prepared in advance. It would be exactly the contrary, for they would attempt instruct the students as deeply as possible and to approach each group of them by taking into account their particularities. Put succinctly, they would work like in a laboratory. This also means that when going through the program, they would not only master that which is laid out in it, but also the students themselves would advance questions and would independently attempt to provide an original answer. They would attempt to stimulate creative thought and work [творчество].

The Worker University is an instrument to democratise science, which has already been socialised. The **Socialist Academy** is the instrument for its further socialization.

First of all, it is not a self-contained corporation [корпорация] of high priests of science or of professional scholars. It can fulfill its task only if its **doors** will be **open freely** to all who are interested in scientific questions and who are adequately prepared to make a definite contribution to the enormous business of socialising science. Only thus is it possible to connect the revision of science with vital work experience. Only so is it possible to make this revision (pererabotka) the cause of the labouring and thinking collective.

Besides that, the Socialist Academy should be not simply scholarly, but an **instructional-scholarly** institution. In other words, it should simultaneously revise science and demonstrate the results of its work to circles of those interested in scientific questions. At the same time, it prepares new proletarian scientists in special studios [студия]. This is not a temple [храм] where priests hide away in the holy of holies.[319] This is something like a factory laboratory or a workshop of experimental science, where each interested and thinking worker can test his powers of invention, to verify in practice the results of his observations and work processes and to analyse these results.

That's how the main questions of the worker encyclopedia should be answered.

---

319 Священно действуют недоступные взорам смертных жрецы.

6.   *In Place of a Preface*

The role of this article in relation to the 'Essays in organisational science' is to explain the ideas of the author of the 'Essays' about proletarian science and a worker encyclopedia. A few words should be said about why and how a worker encyclopedia is connected with organisational science. Likewise, the practical task of this publication needs to be clarified.

Organisational science is the result of the socialisation of bourgeois philosophy and generalised abstract sciences. Thus, it **represents a small part**, but a very essential one, of the **new encyclopedia.** Therefore, it is necessary to become familiar with the question in a more general arrangement in order to set about the study of organisational science.

But besides that, this science is an **instrument of works which lie on the path to a worker encyclopedia.** Indeed, it contains a clearly defined, organisational-collectivist-labour formulation of the proletarian point of view. It explains organisational methods and basic concepts. It clearly points out the paths and results of the organisational revision of some bourgeois scientific methods, concepts, and laws.

Those are the reasons why the article 'On the path to a worker encyclopedia' prefaces the 'Essays'.

The practical task of this publication comes down to **directing the work of our proletcults onto new rails** and to directing our proletcultists on the path to a worker encyclopedia. It is intended for the more activist ones, who have a deep understanding and are the best prepared.

Therefore, the introductory article is written so that only minimal acquaintance with the history of culture and with basic questions of philosophy is needed to understand it. The book's appendices also demand a certain grounding in science. 'The science of social consciousness' and 'Philosophy of living experience' ['Наука об общественным сознании' и 'Философия живого опыты'), which also belong to the pen of the author of the 'Essays', are the rung on the ladder from which it is easiest to step into this book. The less prepared should start from there. But we are appealing to those, who already have the necessary preparation.

The appendices will serve as a practical guide on how to use organisational science in the most diverse branches of labour and cognition [познание]. The theses about mathematics point out the way to socialise one scientific field and provide a model and general contours of proletarian mathematics. Theses about social engineering [техника] and economics explain the causative dependence [причинная зависимость] between the condition of productive forces [провоздительные силы] and production relations [производственные отношения]. The report about the scientific organisation of labour shows the way to an actual scientific solution of the most complex economic questions.

We appeal to the leading proletcultists, who will understand us without difficulty and quickly. But they should carry these ideas into the very heart [глубина] of the proletcult movement by propagandising them in broad circles through their clubs, by acquainting the most promising workers with them, and by organising scientific workshops.

This publication sets itself the task of contributing toward turning the work of our proletcults onto new rails.

On the way to a worker encyclopedia!

Iu. Milonov
  Samara, 4 August 1921.

Former Worker Oppositionists in the Debates of the NEP Era and during the First Five-Year Plan, 1922–30

With its first phase completed by the end of 1922, NEP entered a second, when monetary taxation began to play a significant role in state revenue and banking was revived. A plentiful harvest in 1922 offered prospects for recovery from the deprivations of War Communism, yet it hardly assured stability.[1] Free to sell much of their crop on the open market, peasants could hold back their goods in order to force up prices, thus threatening Soviet workers with famine. With industry recovering more slowly than agriculture, an imbalance arose between industrial and agricultural prices, culminating in the October 1923 'scissors' crisis, when peasants withdrew from the market. Workers, who continued to suffer from unemployment in 1923–4, could hardly afford the food, clothing and services that had become widely available. They were not paid wages for months at a time, effectively lacked unemployment or sickness insurance and suffered frequent injuries in the workplace. Early NEP crises related to market phenomena set the context for strikes and oppositionism.

The years 1923–6 saw furious internal party debates on the course of NEP and on building socialism. Many party members worried that, under NEP, opponents of socialism would overwhelm the party. They saw rapid industrialisation as the only hope, while others believed that the triumph of socialism was dependent on NEP's continuation. Lenin intervened less often in party politics, as he suffered several strokes in 1922–3. Mute and paralysed through 1923, he died on 21 January 1924. The question of who would lead the party after his death was inseparable from debates over political and economic policies. Trotsky jousted with the ruling triumvirate of Zinoviev, Kamenev and Stalin until 1925, when political alliances and positions realigned. Trotskyists, Zinovievists and other politically active factions attempted to enlist former members of the Workers' Opposition for their own efforts, while Stalin and Bukharin pressured them to conform. Although the Workers' Opposition had disbanded, its leading figures held important positions in government and industry, cultivated union-wide networks of supporters and met to discuss politics and economics. The

---

1 Carr 1950–3, vol. 2, pp. 353–7.

ghost of the Workers' Opposition haunted the rhetoric of party control bodies and the political police.

Some former Worker Oppositionists, like Tolokontsev, Kiselev, and Kutuzov, foreswore further oppositionism and buried themselves in work. Others, like Shliapnikov, Medvedev, and Chelyshev, gradually came to realise that factionalism was a dead-end, yet they continued to voice critical views about developing Soviet policies of the 1920s. Their political views evolved in the 1920s in dialogue with contemporary events. Lutovinov maintained a critical stance until his suicide in 1924. Tracing Aleksandra Kollontai's turn from oppositionism to apparent loyalty to Stalin is more difficult, given her revisions to her diary.[2] Having lost their base in the Metalworkers' Union, former Worker Oppositionists from there transferred to diplomatic work, posts as economic administrators, research, editing and writing in the party and trade union historical commissions (Istparts), and other non-trade union positions. Writing the history of the revolutionary and trade union movements offered the opportunity to create important records of revolutionary history, which conveyed messages to workers to organise themselves, not to depend passively on party *intelligenty*. During the 1920s, when trade union Istparts concentrated on collecting and publishing historical documents, the contributions of former Worker Oppositionists like Shliapnikov and Milonov were highly valued. After 1930, however, the party's ideological agenda marginalised and stigmatised historians who refused to skew their analysis to support the party's political, social, and economic agenda during Stalin's revolution from above.[3]

Although by late 1922, many former Worker Oppositionists appeared to have bowed to the party's decisions on trade unions and reconciled with the need for NEP as a general policy, they continued to be troubled by their perception that workers did not prevail in the party, unions, higher education or the army. They claimed to stand steadfast in their desire for workers 'to hold all levers of management, in the party as well as in the government'.[4] Their concern for the role of workers in the party and industry resonated with the views of other oppositionists, especially Gavriil Miasnikov's 'Workers' Group' and another group called 'Workers' Truth'. Indeed, some former Worker Oppositionists met for conversations with members of Workers' Group in 1923–4. Nevertheless, key differences remained. Miasnikov elevated the soviets above the unions as economic managers, which Shliapnikov and Medvedev opposed, because they feared peasant influence in the soviets. While at the heart of the

---

2 Farnsworth 2010.
3 Gilmintinov 2019, pp. 233, 237, 242, 246–7.
4 TsA FSB, R33718, d. 499061, vol. 13, ll. 1–12.

Workers' Opposition program was the aim to achieve greater worker influence within the party, Miasnikov seemed prepared to create a new party dominated by workers.

Although 'Workers' Truth' claimed to be a Bogdanovist group that emerged from the Workers' Opposition, there is actually little evidence of organisational ties between 'Workers' Truth' and former members of the Workers' Opposition. Former members of the latter were informed through private channels of the former's perspectives, given that Medvedev possessed copies of Workers' Truth materials. Aleksandr Bogdanov denied any connection to Workers' Truth, although his biographer James D. White has claimed that Bogdanov's anti-authoritarian philosophical perspective fed into the programs of not only Workers' Truth, but also the Workers' Opposition and even the Democratic Centralists.[5] With a membership mainly composed of student youth of proletarian origins, its programme pertained more to culture than to economic management. Notably, some key leaders of Workers' Truth, Polina Lass-Kozlova and Fanya Shutskever, were women. Despite these differences, party leaders feared that workerist groups might link up.[6] Therefore, the OGPU (formerly Cheka) kept them under close surveillance. (In February 1922, the State Political Administration (GPU) replaced the Cheka, then became the OGPU in 1923 with the creation of the USSR. Lower-level political police administrations were still called GPU. The term GPU was often used interchangeably with OGPU.)[7]

OGPU head Dzerzhinsky suspected the Workers' Opposition of maintaining a faction, collaborating with Workers' Group and Workers' Truth and using their administrative posts in the metals industry in order to attract worker support for their positions.[8] Informants told Dzerzhinsky of several meetings in the first half of 1923 at which they perceived that the former Workers' Opposition might link up with Workers' Group. Among attendees were former members of the Workers' Opposition such as Vladimirov, Chelyshev, Pravdin, Orlov, Lutovinov and Tolokontsev. Allegedly, they discussed whom to elect to the CC and CCC, supporting a CC with Stalin, Zinoviev and Trotsky, but rejecting Kamenev, Dzerzhinsky and Molotov. They would have nominated Medvedev and Orlov to the CC and Shliapnikov to the CCC.[9] The report that attendees found Kamenev's and Dzerzhinsky's CC membership unacceptable, while accepting Stalin's and

5   White 2018, p. 418.
6   Pirani 2008, pp. 126–7; Bordiugov et al. 1995, kn. 1: 204–22; RGASPI, f. 82, op. 2, d. 181, 4; d. 182; TsA FSB, R33718, d. 499061, vol. 40.
7   Hagenloh 2009, Glossary and pp. xvii–xviii.
8   RGASPI, f. 82, op. 2, d. 175, l. 12.
9   RGASPI, f. 76, op. 3, d. 296, ll. 25–50.

Zinoviev's presence, departs significantly from the allegation of a speaker at the Twelfth Party Congress who claimed that the Workers' Opposition wanted the entire triumvirate removed from the CC. Informants often poorly understood the content of political discussions or had self-interested motives to distort it, but this informant seems to have been a highly placed and well-informed party member.[10] Participants also discussed Miasnikov's manifesto, which he wanted to present to the Twelfth Party Congress in April 1923. Mutual recriminations arose against Miasnikov 'for organising a new party' and against Shliapnikov for succumbing to the dispersal of the Workers' Opposition. Both informer reports and participant accounts confirmed that the majority sided with Shliapnikov, not Miasnikov. Thus, there was no factional agreement. On the contrary, their circles competed for members, with some overlap between them.[11]

Because he encouraged workers to strike, Miasnikov was arrested in May 1923. Forcibly dispatched to a diplomatic post in Germany, he struck up ties with German communists who were dissatisfied with Comintern policy. His supporter, N.V. Kuznetsov, attempted to carry on efforts to draw into their group former members of the Workers' Opposition, despite Miasnikov's contemptuous dismissal of Shliapnikov. Further meetings with Lutovinov, Ignatov, Medvedev and Shliapnikov in summer 1923, however, produced no agreement. Lutovinov objected to the plans of the Workers' Group to organise non-party workers and warned them that Dzerzhinsky had unsuccessfully attempted to recruit him (through Tomsky) to attack the Workers' Group.[12] Denying any harm in their familiarity with workerist oppositional groups, Shliapnikov and Medvedev reluctantly agreed to condemn the Workers' Group and Workers' Truth in the press, if the CC so instructed.[13] Without success, the Workers' Group attempted to bring Kollontai into its struggle, which came to the attention of party authorities. During brief returns to Moscow from her diplomatic posts abroad during the second half of 1923, her relations with her old comrades from the Workers' Opposition fluctuated.[14]

With Politburo sanction, the OGPU arrested key members of the Workers' Group in 1923, but leading former Worker Oppositionists emerged unscathed

---

10 Deutscher 1959, p. 96. Dzerzhinsky's 27 July 1923 notes were from the report of an informer named 'Foma', apparently a high-ranking party member (RGASPI, f. 76, op. 3, d. 296, ll. 1–2). Foma was the underground name of at least four prominent Old Bolsheviks: Petr Zalutsky, Dmitry Manuilsky, Aleksandr Smirnov and Nikolai Kozyrev.

11 RGASPI, f. 589, op. 3, d. 9103, vol. 3, ll. 41–3; TsA FSB, R33718, d. 499061, vol. 37, ll. 29–36.

12 TsA FSB, R33718, d. 499061, vol. 37, ll. 29–36.

13 RGASPI, f. 76, op. 3, d. 296, ll. 1–2.

14 RGASPI, f. 76, op. 3, d. 296, l. 41; f. 82, op. 2, d. 175, ll. 45–53; Kollontai 2001, vol. 1, pp. 156–7, 182–3.

from the case.[15] Bogdanov was arrested in September 1923 and detained for more than a month, but he convinced Dzerzhinsky of his innocence and was released.[16] Miasnikov was arrested only in the autumn, after Dzerzhinsky convinced him to return from Germany to Russia by insincerely guaranteeing his protection from arrest. Imprisoned until spring 1927, Miasnikov was then sent into internal exile in Erevan. He escaped from there to Iran in 1928, making his way to Paris, where he worked in factories. After the end of World War II, he was repatriated to the USSR, tried secretly and executed.[17]

Although nearly all party members disapproved of the Workers' Group's programme and methods, many of them criticised the OGPU's method of fighting such groups. Communist workers wrote letters to former leaders of the Workers' Opposition complaining of OGPU bodies gathering criminal evidence against dissenters. Former oppositionists asked them to intercede after they were arrested, imprisoned and interrogated by the OGPU. Interrogators charged former oppositionists with belonging to the Workers' Group and asked them if the Workers' Opposition was active. In party cells Shliapnikov and Kollontai were even accused of 'links with foreign counterrevolution'. Party leaders' response to such complaints constituted a warning not to contest the party's use of the OGPU against intraparty dissenters. Party committees relied increasingly on the secret police throughout the 1920s to monitor oppositionists and interpret their activities to party leaders. Russian historian G.L. Olekh has argued that the party 'oligarchy' used the secret police in the 1920s to serve factional interests, but that the police sometimes 'fabricate[d] reports to force the party nomenklatura to act under the Cheka's dictate'.[18] Such an atmosphere of secret police intimidation against party members, in addition to disillusion with NEP and marital tensions, may have contributed to Lutovinov's suicide in May 1924.[19] Despite use of police and party control bodies against dissenters, discontent continued to percolate in the party.

As Lenin's illness worsened and limited his role in the leadership, discontent grew within the party over its domination by Zinoviev, Kamenev and Stalin (the 'triumvirs') and in reaction to their policies. Some party members regarded Trotsky as Lenin's natural successor, but Lenin's choice was by no means clear,

---

15   RGASPI, f. 76, op. 3, d. 296, ll. 25–50.

16   White 2018, pp. 429–31.

17   RGASPI, f. 17, op. 162, d. 1, ll. 9–31; Alikina 2006, pp. 158–60.

18   RGASPI, f. 17, op. 2, d. 104, ll. 1–26; f. 589, op. 3, d. 9103, vol. 3, ll. 1–28, 38–46; Vilkova (ed.)
      2004, p. 103; Olekh 1999, p. 89.

19   Gurevich 1927, p. 5; RGASPI, f. 17, op. 2, d. 30 and op. 3, d. 71; and f. 593, op. 1, d. 9, ll. 23–4,
      and d. 10, ll. 2–3, 10–11, 18.

nor was it his right to designate a successor. Although Stalin, of all party leaders, saw Lenin most frequently in 1923, he and Lenin had recently sparred on nationalities policy and the formation of the USSR, with Lenin favouring federalism and Stalin centralism. Having dictated notes (later called his 'Last Testament'), in which he evaluated his potential successors as all lacking in some way and made proposals to enlarge the CC, restructure Gosplan and merge the CCC with the Workers' and Peasants' Inspectorate [*Rabkrin*], Lenin subsequently added the proposal to remove Stalin as General Secretary of the party because he was 'too rude'. This characterisation emerged partly from crude words Stalin spoke to Krupskaia and partly from his and Ordzhonikidze's intimidation of Georgian communists who sought their own republic within the USSR (Ordzhonikidze struck one of them). Lenin sought to enlist Trotsky to present his proposals to the party, but Trotsky agreed with the *triumvirs* not to attack them at the April 1923 Twelfth Party Congress in return for their permission to air his views on industrial planning and the concentration of industry within the context of NEP. By 'concentration of industry', he meant to close many unproductive factories and concentrate production in a few large ones, but this alarmed workers who were already suffering from unemployment and low wages.[20]

By autumn 1923, Trotsky's agreement with the *triumvirs* had disintegrated. In a letter to the Politburo in early October, he attacked party economic policy and appointmentism, and faulted the lack of intra-party democracy. Forty-six Russian communists subsequently signed the 'Declaration of the 46', echoing his views and calling for an extraordinary conference of the CC.[21] Preobrazhensky was likely the key author of the document, which also incorporated many ideas from the Democratic Centralists.[22] Worker Oppositionist Mikhail Lobanov has been misidentified as a signatory of the Declaration of 46 in 1923, due to a misreading of the first initial of the original Lobanov signature on the document. Rather than an 'M', it is an 'A'. The signature on the document is in a different hand than Mikhail Lobanov's signature as it appears elsewhere. Finally, he was never accused subsequently of having signed the Declaration of the 46.[23]

---

20   Lewin 1968, Chapters 4, 6, 7; Deutscher 1959, pp. 92–102. Sakharov 2003 disputes the testament's provenance, arguing that there is no evidence that it originated with Lenin and citing circumstantial evidence that Lenin's secretaries may have manufactured or tweaked it in order to aid Trotsky in the succession struggle.

21   Deutscher 1959, pp. 112–13; Day 1973, pp. 87–8.

22   Reznik 2017, pp. 32, 34.

23   Deutscher 1959 claims that members of the Workers' Oppositionists figured among the 46, but I did not recognise any of their names (Deutscher 1959, p. 114). According to Pirani 2008, one former Worker Oppositionist, Mikhail Lobanov, signed the Declaration of

On 25–7 October 1923, the CC and CCC discussed these documents, ultimately deciding to censure Trotsky and for the first time openly labeling supporters of the 46 'oppositionists'. Passions were high on all sides. Given increasing agitation in party cells over the declaration, party leaders decided to open the debate in early November, but Trotsky, laid low from malaria, could not engage in it until December.[24]

Meanwhile, foreign affairs intruded into the discussion. Soviet communists paid close attention to German leftist politics in 1923, the year of the famed hyperinflation in Germany. They had high hopes for a German revolution, so the failure of a Communist Party of Germany uprising in Hamburg in late November 1923 provoked debate in the circles of the Russian Communist Party. In December 1923 a German communist spoke to former members of the Workers' Opposition in Moscow. Declaring that it made no sense to conduct revolution in Germany as it was carried out in Russia, he or she pointed to contextual differences including the absence of war, a more formidable and better-organised bourgeoisie, a robust social-democratic party, a weak communist party and a fierce fascist movement.[25] The German comrade's interpretation likely influenced views expressed by these former Worker Oppositionists during the ongoing party debate.

With Trotsky's return to action and rising levels of criticism of domestic and foreign policies, the debate in party cells reached a fever pitch in December 1923. Trotskyists and Democratic Centralists decried the government's neglect of heavy industry and the lack of 'democracy' within the party. Trotsky tried to harness the energy of young party members and Komsomolists, claiming that a generational divide existed in the party. In this debate, Shliapnikov criticised both sides. Calling for an acceptance of intra-party criticism, state subsidies and orders for heavy industry and for more workers to join the party, he and his circle wrote and promoted a resolution in party cells, spoke at party meetings, and published in the press. The Metron factory party cell endorsed the resolution. Trotsky also called for a surge of workers into the party and criticised

---

the 46 (p. 217). According to Anon 1975, the signatory was A. Lobanov (p. 10). Likewise, on a copy of the signature sent to me from Aleksandr Reznik, the initial appears to be 'A', not 'M'. In the file on Mikhail Lobanov that I consulted in the Security Services Archive of Ukraine, there was no accusation against him of having signed the Declaration of the 46. If he had signed the document, surely the NKVD would have included this among the charges against him in the 1930s.

24   Vilkova (compiler) 2004, pp. 272–3; RGASPI, f. 17, op. 2, d. 104, ll. 1–26; Deutscher 1959, pp. 116–18; Reznik 2017, p. 41.

25   Albert 2011, pp. 111–42; TsA FSB, R33718, d. 499061, vol. 42, ll. 232–7.

the 'bureaucratic degeneration' he saw within the party. Yet Trotsky regarded mobilising not only the workers but also the youth as twin solutions to this crisis.[26] Sensitive to Trotsky's complicity in persecuting the Workers' Opposition in 1921, Shliapnikov nevertheless supported freedom of criticism for all party members, including Trotsky. Unlike Trotsky, he did not perceive a generational division within the party, but a social division. Insisting that it was necessary to change economic policy in order to attract more workers into the party, he expressed fear that heavy industry under NEP would die out, but he opposed Trotsky's plan to revive industry by closing small enterprises and concentrating industry in a few large ones.[27] He disagreed with Trotsky's assertion that bureaucracy should be destroyed, instead arguing that it had to be strengthened by electing its members.[28] Nevertheless, the opposition of Trotskyists and Democratic Centralists won a majority in the Khamovniki party district committee, at the conference of which Shliapnikov and many others voiced their criticisms and proposals. This largely intellectual party district was the only one where the oppositionists prevailed.[29]

Aleksandr Reznik argues that the Left Opposition of 1923–4 comprised an opposition of the leaders and one of the masses. He identifies its weaknesses as a too informal organisation and as excessive concentration on political questions, while neglecting economic problems that could have given workers a greater stake in the opposition.[30] The debate ended with the Thirteenth Party Conference, 16–18 January 1924, during which Trotsky again was weakened by malaria and forced to evacuate the stage. Few supported his views at the party conference, elections to which the triumvirate had manipulated in its favour. Trotsky was condemned, the triumvirate prevailed and Trotsky went south to recuperate. On the way, he heard of Lenin's death on 21 January, but did not return to Moscow for the funeral, which seems to have struck a blow to his prospects for the succession. Little concerned with Trotsky's health or his chances at the leadership, former Worker Oppositionists were more preoccupied with the conference's decision to admit a massive number of workers into the party. The number of one hundred thousand recommended by the conference was increased after Lenin died (the 'Lenin levy') – in February to May, two hun-

---

26   RGASPI, f. 589, op. 3, d. 9103, vol. 2, l. 2; TsA FSB, R33718, d. 499061, vol. 37, l. 27; Deutscher 1959, p. 122.
27   TsAODM, f. 88, op. 1, d. 168, ll. 65–83.
28   TsAODM, f. 88, op. 1, d. 168, ll. 29–42; Shliapnikov 1924, 'Our Differences', pp. 4–5; Zorky (ed.) 1926, pp. 144–57; RGASPI, f. 17, op. 71, d. 82, ll. 7–22.
29   Reznik 2017, p. 259.
30   Reznik 2017, pp. 256, 261, 382.

dred and forty thousand workers joined.[31] Yet many new entrants carried the baggage of political illiteracy and careerist ambitions. Reznik argues that the mood of grief in the party over Lenin's death and the influx of workers into the party both stifled the oppositionist mood and encouraged efforts toward unity.[32]

Despite Zinoviev's 1924 call to purge Trotsky from the party and to exert pressure on him to recant his views, Zinoviev and Kamenev moved closer to his evolving position on industrialisation and further from Bukharin's encouragement of peasant consumerism. Shliapnikov disagreed with Stalin's and Bukharin's policy formulations at the Fourteenth Party Conference in May 1925 and revealed his criticisms in a draft manuscript that probably circulated among his supporters in Moscow. On Stalin's theory of socialism in one country, he wrote: 'Stalin refuses to accept that socialism as an economic system cannot be contained by the borders of one country'. Addressing the 'turn to the countryside' announced at the conference, Shliapnikov declared it a continuation of earlier pro-peasant policy, only without socialist pretence.[33] His time abroad had thus not reconciled him to the leadership's policies. Nevertheless, Shliapnikov's commitment of his views to paper did not mean that he was ready to engage in political struggle. Victor Serge, a supporter of Trotsky at that time, recalled that in spring 1925: 'The militants of the old Workers' Opposition proved to be non-committal, since they believed us to be too weak and, as they said, distrusted Trotsky's authoritarian temper'.[34] Upbraiding Shliapnikov for passivity, one comrade outside Moscow expressed disappointment with him for being 'indecisive' and for failing to give directions.[35] In addition, Ivan Nikolaenko, the administrator of the Ukrainian Tobacco Trust in Kiev, wrote of his concern at having seen a photo in *Izvestiia* of Shliapnikov standing next to members of Stalin's circle. Worried that this meant he was politically close to them, Nikolaenko complained that Stalin's circle suppressed dissent and initiative. Specifically, he disparaged Lazar Kaganovich, secretary of the CC of the Communist Party of Ukraine, as possessing the 'boorishness of a shop clerk'. Replying that his positioning in the photo was accidental and had no political

---

31   Deutscher 1959, pp. 132–5.

32   Reznik 2017, pp. 73, 75.

33   TsA FSB, R33718, d. 499061, vol. 38, ll. 22–74.

34   Serge 2002, p. 210.

35   TsA FSB, R33718, d. 499061, vol. 13, ll. 101–3. Mariia Trifonova corresponded with Shliapnikov and Medvedev in the second half of the 1920s and the first half of the 1930s. In 1924, she and her husband, Ivan Pivon, had belonged to the 'workers' list' of delegates at the Eniseisk Gubernia Party Conference. The gubernia party control commission voted to exclude them from the party for factionalism (Demidov 1994, pp. 36–7).

significance, Shliapnikov noted that he had tried to enrol in the list of speakers at the congress, but Valerian Kuibyshev had told him that he would not be allowed to speak 'for your own good'.[36]

In December 1925, at the Fourteenth Party Congress, Stalin proposed his theory of 'socialism in one country', which Zinoviev and Kamenev openly opposed. At this congress, Zinoviev and Kamenev employed Lenin's 'Last Testament' in an attempt to undermine Stalin. Kollontai attended. She found that many of her old comrades supported Zinoviev and Kamenev. If her diary account can be believed, she supported Stalin as a more capable leader than his rivals. Noting that Shliapnikov and Medvedev 'lean towards the Leningraders' (Zinoviev and his supporters), she did not place them solidly in that camp.[37] Trotsky was opposed to 'socialism in one country', but did not immediately ally with Zinoviev and Kamenev. Nevertheless, Stalin feared that the oppositionists would join forces, so he took pre-emptive measures, beginning with removal of Zinoviev, Kamenev and their allies from important positions. Political tensions also increased at the local level, which had implications for former members of the Workers' Opposition. In January 1926 Shliapnikov received a letter from a comrade outside Moscow who reported that local officials in his area sharply criticised the 'Leningraders' and would not allow him and his associates to speak, charging that they were the 'Workers' Opposition' and were 'ganging up with the Leningraders'.[38] By April 1926, the United Opposition led by Trotsky, Zinoviev, and Kamenev had formed.

As Shliapnikov and his circle had developed their own fairly comprehensive critique of party policy independently of Zinoviev, Kamenev and Trotsky, these more prominent oppositionists attempted to sway the former members of the Workers' Opposition to their side. Stalin used various methods to divide and subdue the oppositionists, including CCC investigations. Shliapnikov and his comrade Medvedev became CCC targets due to a January 1924 letter Medvedev had sent to Valerian Barchuk, a former metalworker employed by the Commissariat of Enlightenment (Narkompros) in Baku, a major centre of the oil industry on the Caspian Sea and a pre-revolutionary nexus of revolutionary activity (Stalin had organised cells there). In response to Barchuk's inquiry about the views of former Worker Oppositionist in Moscow on NEP, workers and international revolution, Medvedev's so-called 'Baku letter' reiterated points that Shliapnikov had made in public discussion, but in more incendiary language. That he wrote on behalf of a group of people (Mikhail Mikhailov,

---

36   TsA FSB, R33718, d. 499061, vol. 14, ll. 5–10; vol. 12, l. 21.
37   RGASPI, f. 134, op. 3, d. 44, ll. 6–10.
38   TsA FSB, R33718, d. 499061, vol. 39, l. 31.

Chelyshev, Nikolaenko, Bruno, Pravdin and Shliapnikov) was conveyed through his signature 'from all of us'.[39] This letter, as well as the 1926 CCC investigation of it, are important for what they reveal about Shliapnikov's and his supporters' evolving views on NEP and the CCC's role in redefining key political concepts such as oppositionism, party loyalty, party discipline, bloc and faction.

Medvedev's letter expressed a fear that NEP was becoming established economic policy and voiced objections to the development of private agriculture and the stimulation of peasant consumerism. He called for the expansion of heavy industry by eliminating waste in the budget and imposing higher taxes on the peasantry. In international policy, he criticised the Comintern for applying the Russian model of centralised control to other European socialist and worker movements and for assuming that revolution in Western Europe would unfold according to the Russian pattern. He opposed the departure of communist minorities from trade unions, soviets and factory committees dominated by social democrats.

The letter and materials from the 1923–4 party discussion only reached Baku in early June 1924. The Azerbaijani Cheka, which had been keeping Communist Party members under surveillance since at least mid-1922, became aware of the letter in July 1924, when it infiltrated informers into the so-called 'Baku group of the Workers' Opposition'. (In Transcaucasia, Chekas remained in place until mid-1926, when they were replaced by GPUs.) Police reported that most of the group's dozen members were former workers who were employed in soviets, although a few were industrial workers at the time. The group had only two or three meetings. In October 1924 Baku party officials sent a copy of Medvedev's letter to the CCC, where it was greeted with mockery, yet was kept on file in case of future need.[40] There were hundreds, perhaps thousands, of such 'cases' in CCC files, but this letter became a weapon of Stalin's party leadership against the oppositionists.

The version of Medvedev's letter that Baku officials sent to the CCC was distorted. Uncharacteristic spelling mistakes and grammatical errors were not the only features that distinguished it from his original. The second version made it appear as if he sought large-scale industrial concessions and large foreign and internal loans as a means of gathering capital for intensive industrialisation. Moreover, it conveyed the impression that he had given up on the Western-European workers as revolutionary and proposed that the Western-European communist organisations dissolve and rejoin social-democratic parties.

---

39   Deutscher 1959, p. 138; Felshtinsky (ed.) 1990 vol. 1, pp. 90–101.
40   RGASPI, f. 589, op. 3, d. 9103, vol. 1, ll. 286–7, 293–300; Knight 1993, pp. 23, 29.

Bukharin, Stalin, Iaroslavsky and others based their attacks on the falsified version of the letter. References to the letter in secondary literature have been based on inaccurate information originating from these opponents.[41]

When Zinoviev (on Politburo assignment) discussed the letter with Medvedev in December 1924, he did not show him the version received from Baku, but Medvedev sensed that it diverged from the original. Expressing concern that the OGPU had doctored it, he requested its publication, explaining that the rumour mill had roused curiosity among many who were eager to read it. The Politburo considered demanding that Zinoviev write a denunciation of Medvedev's letter but Zinoviev did not do so. Nevertheless, that was not the end of the matter. The Azerbaijani Party Control Commission took up investigation of the 'group' in Baku in 1925.[42] Further developments were tied to intra-party political struggles, as Zinoviev and Kamenev went into opposition against Stalin.

Their struggle set the tone in which Shliapnikov and Medvedev received news of the Baku case. When the newspaper, *Bakinsky rabochy*, revealed the Baku affair in early February 1926, it described the group as a cell of the Workers' Opposition that had links with other oppositionist groups, had conducted work outside the party and included former Mensheviks and SRs. The newspaper warned that 'freedom of criticism' led inexorably to the formation of factional groups, and finally to 'direct counterrevolution'. In early February 1926, the Azerbaijani Party Control Commission found the 'Baku oppositionists' guilty of underground anti-party organisation and agitation. Four were excluded from the party, six were reprimanded or warned and six others were 'rehabilitated'. The investigation reportedly included physical abuse and intimidation.[43] Communist Party leaders in Baku accused Shliapnikov and Medvedev of having directed the group's activities.

After Shliapnikov and Medvedev saw the Baku newspaper article, they attempted face-to-face appeals to party leaders. Finally, they sent a letter of protest to the Politburo and the CCC. Framing the affair in terms of provocation, they insisted there was no Workers' Opposition in Baku, only mutual acquaintances meeting to discuss politics. Mounting an offensive, they accused party leaders in Baku of intent to frame 'old and meritorious party members' as counterrevolutionaries. They requested the publication of their protest letter and all

---

41   Daniels 1988, p. 279; Day 1973, pp. 158–60; Deutscher 1959, pp. 274, 277, 307; RGASPI, f. 589, op. 3, d. 9103, vol. 2, ll. 226–33.

42   TsA FSB, R33718, d. 499061, vol. 13, ll. 29–36; RGASPI, f. 589, op. 3, d. 9103, vol. 1, ll. 293–300.

43   RGASPI, f. 589, op. 3, d. 9103, vol. 1, ll. 290–300; and vol. 2, ll. 143–4; TsA FSB, R33718, d. 499061, vol. 39, l. 333.

the materials Medvedev had sent to Barchuk in 1924.[44] They aimed not only to reveal the documents' true contents, but also to provoke an open discussion of the issues raised in them.

Iaroslavsky fired off a memo to other CCC members expressing consternation that the Azerbaijani Party Control Commission had not coordinated its investigation with the CCC, given that prominent party members in Moscow were named. Tensions between central and local party control bodies were a persistent problem in the history of the CCC and of its successor, the PCC (Party Control Commission, 1934–8). The *de facto* subordination of local control commissions to local party committees, rather than to the CCC, exacerbated frictions. Iaroslavsky insisted on upbraiding the Azerbaijani and Transcaucasian party control commissions, to which the chief of the Transcaucasian control commission responded that he had not known about the case.[45]

After having sent a commission to conduct an on-the-ground investigation in Baku, the CCC initially concluded that there had been no oppositional group in Baku, despite an unsuccessful attempt to form one. Consequently, the CCC changed expulsions to stern rebukes with warnings or reprimands. Changing expulsions to milder punishments had become customary for control commissions at all levels. Nevertheless, Shliapnikov and Medvedev were forced to confront CCC investigators Aron Solts, Iaroslavsky and Maria Ulianova at the end of March. The meeting was tense, as Shliapnikov refused to believe that this case could have gone forward in Baku without someone in the leadership giving instructions, while the CCC investigators claimed to feel insulted by his implications.[46]

Questions to both concerned whether Shliapnikov and Medvedev held the views expressed in the letter, what was the purpose of the letter and exactly who had been involved in its drafting and dispatch. The investigation's subjectivity was underscored by a question characterising the letter's content as 'organisational and propagandistic directives'. Shliapnikov's and Medvedev's demands to publish all the documents, their insistence on answering CCC questions in writing (contrary to usual CCC procedures of oral examination) and their request to take investigatory materials home for examination all roused suspicions that they wanted to use the investigation for factional politics. Finally agreeing to submit questions in writing, CCC Shliapnikov and Medvedev to

---

44   RGASPI, f. 589, op. 3, d. 9103, vol. 1, ll. 75–115; vol. 2, ll. 33–4.
45   RGASPI, f. 589, op. 3, d. 9103, vol. 1, ll. 301–4; vol. 2, l. 36; Getty 1997, p. 2.
46   RGASPI, f. 589, op. 3, d. 9103, vol. 1, ll. 127–214; vol. 2, ll. 95–117; Getty 1997, p. 2. Mariia Ulianova supported Stalin and Bukharin in 1925–6 (Turton 2007, pp. 114–15).

leave without answering questions. Nevertheless, they refused to allow the men to take investigatory materials home, justifiably fearing that the two would duplicate and distribute them. They could only examine the materials in CCC offices.[47]

Through spring and summer 1926, the investigation was postponed. In late May, Stalin wrote to Molotov that he should press Bukharin to accelerate writing an article directed against the Workers' Opposition. Stalin recalled that Zinoviev had been assigned to write it, but had not done so and therefore had 'sabotaged the assignment from the Politburo'. Inferentially connecting Trotsky and Zinoviev to Shliapnikov, Stalin wrote to Molotov in mid-June: 'I think pretty soon the Party will punch the mugs of Trotsky and Grisha [Zinoviev] along with Kamenev and turn them into isolated splitters, like Shliapnikov'. In the meantime, more pressure was applied, including a corollary investigation of Medvedev, based on allegations that he had engaged in factional politics in Moscow oriented towards 'linking' with Zinoviev, who would 'give directives'. Finally, a 10 July *Pravda* editorial ('On the Right Danger in the Party', probably written by Bukharin) accused Medvedev of giving up on international revolution and favouring the lease of large-scale Soviet industry to foreign capitalists. Shliapnikov, who was on holiday in the south when the *Pravda* article appeared, declared to Medvedev his intention to appeal against 'Bukharinist distortions' and print the response he had composed as a pamphlet.[48]

At an important party plenum on 15 July 1926, Stalin called Medvedev's letter 'Menshevist' and accused Zinoviev of 'sabotage' in having delayed criticising it. Further, he accused Trotsky and Zinoviev of having formed a bloc with the Workers' Opposition. Objecting that the Politburo never 'assigned' him to write an article, Zinoviev claimed that he had thought the letter should be published and critically analysed in the journal, *Bolshevik*, and that he had thought Stalin and other Politburo members had agreed with him on this in 1924–5.[49] For his part, Medvedev objected that accusations made against him in the press and at the plenum were based on statements not even in his original letter, that his views on foreign leases had coincided with those of Lenin and that his opin-

47   RGASPI, f. 589, op. 3, d. 9103, vol. 2, ll. 102–17, 136–8.

48   RGASPI, f. 589, op. 3, d. 9103, vol. 1, ll. 149–214; vol. 2, ll. 139–40, 147–8, 154–5; Lih et al. (eds.) 1995, pp. 104–5,114–15; TsA FSB, R33718, d. 499061, vol. 43, l. 204. Lih et al. (eds.) 1995 also believed that Bukharin wrote the 10 July editorial in *Pravda* (Lih et al. (eds.) 1995, p. 104).

49   Lih et al. (eds.) 1995, pp. 104–5, citing RGASPI, f. 17, op. 2, d. 246, vyp. 1, ll. 75–6; and d. 696, ll. 46–7. Lih et al. (eds.) 1995 wrote that they found no Politburo decision assigning Zinoviev to write an article criticising Medvedev's letter.

ions were very different from those cited in the article. Shliapnikov joined him in sending a letter of protest to *Pravda* and the CCC, requesting the publication of Medvedev's original 1924 letter and a manuscript by Shliapnikov.[50]

Shliapnikov's manuscript eventually reached an audience by means of the United Opposition's distribution of it. Aware of their collaboration, Stalin wrote to Molotov in late September that the question of Medvedev could not be 'glossed over'.[51] In his manuscript, which was finally published in *Bolshevik* in September 1926, Shliapnikov delivered a sharp rebuttal to *Pravda*'s charges, a spirited defence of Medvedev's views and an attack on the motives of party leaders. He insisted that Politburo members were raising a political scandal around the letter merely in order to carry out reprisals against 'growing oppositional moods in the party'. Next he complained that the political slander of oppositionists had become a weapon of party struggle and a means of rapid promotion for party careerists. Supporting Medvedev's accusation that the worker-peasant alliance was turning into an alliance with wealthy peasants (kulaks), he concluded by calling for the 'triumph of workers' democracy' and for an end to the internal party system of 'criminal investigations, denunciations, public defamations, and threats'.[52]

Despite Shliapnikov's spirited defiance, the Opposition had already lost this round due to Stalin's reliance on 'rowdies' to 'disrupt' oppositionist meetings, his successful depiction of the Opposition as anti-peasant and the apparent appeal of the 'socialism in one country' doctrine to the rank-and-file. Trotsky, Zinoviev, Kamenev and other leaders of the United Opposition acknowledged their defeat and pledged to dissolve their opposition. The Politburo required them to denounce Shliapnikov's and Medvedev's 'Menshevik platform'.[53] In late October, Trotsky was expelled from the Politburo, after *The New York Times* published Lenin's 'Last Testament' and Trotsky hurled at Stalin the insult 'gravedigger of the revolution' at an expanded Politburo meeting.

---

50   RGASPI, f. 589, op. 3, d. 9103, vol. 2, ll. 186–91, l. 250. The CCC promptly conducted a comparative analysis of the two different versions of the 'Baku letter' (RGASPI, f. 589, op. 3, d. 9103, vol. 2, ll. 192–233). *Bolshevik* published Shliapnikov's manuscript in September 1926, but Medvedev's letter was only published in Russia in 1990.

51   RGASPI, f. 82, op. 2, d. 185, ll. 59–60; f. 589, op. 3, d. 9103, vol. 1, ll. 127–33, 149–214; Lih et al. (eds.) 1995, p. 129.

52   Shliapnikov 1926, 'O demonstrativnoi atake i pravoi opasnosti v partii', pp. 62–73. It closely follows the draft, which is in RGASPI, f. 589, op. 3, d. 9103, vol. 1, ll. 7–21 and 41–62. Shliapnikov's article in *Bolshevik*, the 10 July *Pravda* article and the *Bolshevik* response were all republished in book form (Slepkov (ed.) 1926).

53   Deutscher 1959, pp. 282–6; RGASPI, f. 17, op. 3, d. 592, 7 October 1926. Bukharin, Rykov and Tomsky signed the Politburo resolution.

The high tensions within the CC over this affair helped shape the context in which Shliapnikov and Medvedev had also come to terms with the CCC. Isaac Deutscher portrayed theirs as an abject submission, writing in error that both were expelled from the party and only re-admitted after making an 'exemplary recantation'.[54] On the contrary, they struggled determinedly to resist charges of anti-party factionalism.

Shliapnikov and Medvedev met 20–9 October in almost daily long sessions with the CCC and finally the Politburo. Initially defiant, they then began to negotiate over the wording of their statement to refute the most extreme charges of Menshevism and of having been in a bloc. The CCC members required them to completely reject their previously-held views on all important questions and to recognise that the accusations brought against them in the party press were justified. Significantly, the CCC required them to acknowledge that neglecting to distance themselves from the United Opposition was sufficient evidence of a bloc. Finally, the CCC demanded that they express regret that Medvedev's letter was used against their wishes as the basis for an anti-party attempt to organise a group.[55]

The case then went to the full CCC Presidium. Unfavourably comparing their intransigence to Trotsky's and Zinoviev's recognition of their errors (they in fact had also tried to negotiate), Kuibyshev objected that Shliapnikov 'thinks that he enjoys some kind of special moral authority in the party'. Indeed, some presidium members seemed sympathetic towards Shliapnikov.[56] Consequently, the CCC resolved to expel Medvedev from the party and to give Shliapnikov a stern rebuke and warning. Dismayed, the two men appealed to the Politburo. Still, they did not acknowledge mistaken views or condemn their allies. The Politburo assigned Ordzhonikidze and Ianson to work with them on a text. The final product fulfiled much of the CCC's request, stating that Medvedev's letter contained crudely erroneous views, that attacks in *Pravda* and *Bolshevik* were justified and that their previous statements to the CC and CCC regarding the Baku case were wrong. The letter acknowledged that they used methods of factional struggle and condemned these methods. It called on their allies to disperse any factional underground groups they might have formed. But it still did not acknowledge that they were in a bloc with Trotsky, Zinoviev and Kamenev, nor did it repudiate all their past views. After Ordzhonikidze and Ianson for-

54   Deutscher 1959, pp. 295–6; Deutscher 1966, p. 309.

55   RGASPI, f. 589, op. 3, d. 9103, vol. 1, ll. 70–115, 140–1.

56   RGASPI, f. 589, op. 3, d. 9103, vol. 1, ll. 149–214; Anderson et al. (eds.) 2007, vol. 2, pp. 345–415, 427–52.

warded the letter to Stalin, the CCC rescinded its warning towards Shliapnikov and conceded that Medvedev could remain in the party.[57]

Immersed in his work administering metals imports, Shliapnikov avoided factionalist intrigues after October 1926, but he still found much to criticise about party policy. When the Soviet-supported Chinese Nationalist Party crushed the Chinese Communists in April 1927, and when British trade unionists withdrew from the united front in September, the revived United Opposition disparaged Stalin's and Bukharin's apparent miscalculations in foreign affairs. Although members of the opposition may have tried to entice Shliapnikov to declare support for it, by signing its May 1927 declaration (the 'Declaration of the 83'), which criticised a broad range of foreign and domestic policy measures, he maintained an autonomous stance in intra-party discussions. Some of his own supporters pressured him to speak out. One (perhaps Maria Trifonova) wrote to him inquiring as to where he stood in the looming political struggle within the party. She scorned the programme of the United Opposition for incorporating 'too much democratic honey' and for weak 'formulas on workers and the economy'. Taking Shliapnikov to task for following 'old tactics of silence and inactivity', however, she warned that if he did not act, she and her confederates might join 'the left wing of the opposition'.[58]

Shliapnikov acknowledged that many Communists were 'surprised' that he did not come out in public support of the United Opposition. He explained that he supported the new opposition but without 'merging with it, not losing our political identity'. He did not sign its programme because he was not invited to help draft or revise it and because its leaders had not repudiated their 1926 condemnation of the Workers' Opposition. Although six thousand communists signed the Declaration of the 83, Shliapnikov seemed sceptical of its validity, concluding: 'Remember that "programmes" are elaborated during struggle that can last years'. Thus, he continued to elevate the initiative of workers above the direction of leaders. Shliapnikov afterwards confirmed sympathy for the leftist opposition, but denied ever having joined it. His comrades from among the most prominent members of the Workers' Opposition

---

57 RGASPI, f. 17, op. 162, d. 599, protocol 65, 29 October 1926, p. 2; f. 589, op. 3, d. 9103, vol. 1, ll. 148, 215–30, 241–2, 247, 25–30 October 1926. The final text was published in *Pravda*, 31 October 1926.

58 TsA FSB, R33718, d. 499061, vol. 40, ll. 168–74. Petr Zalutsky may have asked him to consider signing the 'Declaration of the 83' (TsA FSB, R33718, d. 499061, vol. 5, ll. 42–3). Somewhat confusingly, the 'Declaration of the 83' is occasionally referred to as the 'Declaration of the 84', but for consistency I have used 'Declaration of the 83'.

probably agreed with him. A CC statistical analysis shows that only one former member of the Workers' Opposition signed one of the United Opposition's petitions.[59]

When party leaders allowed oppositionists to publish in an official discussion supplement to *Pravda* in November 1927, Shliapnikov utilised this sanctioned means of expressing his views. Defending the Workers' Opposition as an advocate of heavy industry, he disputed claims in the party press of industrial recovery, asserting instead that in the metals industry 1913 levels had not been reached. Disputing the party leaders' distortion of the positions of the Workers' Opposition, he asserted that it had always advocated a stronger role for workers in the party and the improvement of their working and living conditions. Blaming disagreements within the party on the presence within it of 'an enormous number of petty-bourgeois elements' and their 'ideology and policies', he called for an influx of industrial workers into the party and for 'worker democracy' to replace the existing political culture.[60] Siding more unequivocally with Stalin's position, Kollontai published an article in *Pravda* in 1927 attacking the United Opposition.

The United Opposition was defeated at the Fifteenth Party Congress in December 1927 and 75 opposition leaders were expelled from the party. Zinoviev and Trotsky had been expelled earlier. In total, around eight thousand oppositionists were expelled in 1927–8. Nevertheless, some oppositionists continued to air criticisms into 1928.[61] Unknown persons continued attempts to involve Shliapnikov and Medvedev in oppositional politics, but they were increasingly suspicious of OGPU provocations.[62]

Stalin turned against NEP in the late 1920s, claiming that it put the USSR at risk of being overtaken by external enemies and undermined by internal ones. Having defeated the Right Opposition of Bukharin, Tomsky and Rykov, who wanted to continue the gradualism of NEP, Stalin and his men imposed forced collectivisation and rapid industrialisation on the Soviet Union. Stalin's 'revolution from above', or 'Great Break', was an unspeakable personal tragedy for millions of Soviet citizens. So-called 'wealthy peasant' (kulak) families were abruptly and forcibly exiled to remote regions, many of them dying *en route* or at their destinations, while famine devastated the lives of, and brought untold suffering to, huge numbers of Ukrainians and Kazakhs. Stalin's policies not only starved

59   TsA FSB, R33718, d. 499061, vol. 12, ll. 28–35; RGASPI, f. 82, op. 2, d. 186, l. 47.

60   RGASPI, f. 82, op. 2, d. 195, ll. 117–25.

61   Daniels 1988, p. 320; Gusev 2008, p. 153; Halfin 2007, Chapters 5–6.

62   TsA FSB, R33718, d. 499061, vol. 40, l. 1, 9.

the countryside, but put pressure on workers. Many inexperienced new workers lost their lives in workplace accidents on construction sites, in mines and in factories. The Stalinist economy born of the new five-year plans was deeply flawed, with bottlenecks, spoilage, statistical manipulation and neglect of the consumer sector becoming systematic. Nevertheless, Stalin's revolution created entirely new industries, new industrial centres and drastically increased the urban population and industrial workforce.[63]

Many former Left Oppositionists, including those from the Workers' Opposition, hoped that Stalin's drive for industrialisation, despite its flaws, would realise their goal of creating a highly productive and egalitarian economy and society that would assure a better quality of life for all Soviet citizens. They yearned to participate in the project for, as Deutscher wrote: 'It was a galling thought for the Trotskyists also that the great change, this "second revolution", might be carried out without them'. Former Worker Oppositionists, too, occupied important posts in planning, economic administration, and domestic and foreign trade. Although Stalin undertook to put his own men in control of the Soviet Union's economic and industrial administration, he was still forced to rely upon many former oppositionists to help carry out his policies. The continued high profile of former oppositionists in industrial and other posts troubled him, especially when labour unrest erupted in various regions as a result of food shortages, workplace injuries, long hours and pay delays. Many Trotskyists and Democratic Centralists had not reconciled with Stalin's policies, but maintained an underground political network. For them, the lack of intra-party democracy and the harnessing of workers to production tasks seriously flawed efforts to industrialise and collectivise.[64] Fearing that oppositionists might capitalise on worker unrest, Stalin directed renewed police attention to them as well as harassing them by means of persistent investigations by the CCC for both petty charges and more serious ones of factionalism.

Scapegoating technical specialists lingering from the old regime was another means by which Stalin's regime attempted to deflect workers' grievances from the top party leadership. This ran counter, however, to the importance Bukharin placed on accommodating this group. Stalin's turn against Bukharin's alliance with the technical intelligentsia surfaced during the Shakhty Trial, which took place in 1928 in the Donbas region of southern Russia. Employing methods later applied more effectively in the Great Terror of 1937–8, this show trial falsely

---

63   On Stalin's break with Bukharin and his revolution from above, the many important works include Tucker 1990; Cohen 1980; Fitzpatrick 1983; Kuromiya 1998; Lewin 1975 and Viola 2007.

64   Deutscher 1959, p. 411; Rossman 2005; Gusev 2008, p. 154.

charged Soviet and German engineers with industrial sabotage ('wrecking') and with being class enemies. Subjected to pressure and intimidation, some succumbed by making false confessions, but others resisted. Those on trial were sentenced to execution or imprisonment; following the trial, thousands more engineers were arrested. This trial threatened to derail trade with Germany, but Krestinsky worked together with Narkomtorg to smooth over relations.[65]

By 1929 Stalin perceived the need to break with NEP and commence intensive industrialisation, for which he would acquire capital by forcing the peasants to turn over more grain to the state. To mobilise the party to support his policies, he conducted a widespread campaign against former oppositionists and supporters of Bukharin. Having expelled Trotsky from the USSR in February 1929, in April Stalin defeated Bukharin's opposition to his industrialisation plan, yet many party members were still reluctant to abandon the worker-peasant alliance of NEP.[66] Stalin needed to neutralise potential opponents in the party. Despite Shliapnikov's and Medvedev's efforts to remain apart from political struggle, they were dragged into an investigation of an alleged group of oppositionist workers in Omsk, a city in south-western Siberia which had served as a capital for the Whites during the Civil War. In contrast to the Baku case, that regarding Omsk featured a far more visible OGPU role, yet at times played out with comical errors.

Omsk party officials and the CCC constructed a history of the 'Workers' Opposition' in that city; Shliapnikov and Medvedev disputed their narrative. A protracted dispute had unfolded in 1922 between groups in the Omsk party organisation, one of which was labelled the 'Workers' Opposition', and advocated elevating workers to party-leadership posts, while the other was loyal to the Sibbiuro. (Olekh concludes that the 1922 group was not truly kindred with the Moscow Workers' Opposition, but Tatiana Sandu disagrees.)[67] A Trotskyist detained and interrogated by the OGPU tried to deflect the attention of the authorities away from himself by providing evidence about a new 'Workers' Opposition Group' in Omsk in 1926–7. After the Trotskyists ceased opposition, he claimed, the Omsk Workers' Opposition continued it, by creating parallel party organisations, distributing a leaflet, obtaining a press to print Lenin's 'Last Testament' and seeking support among workers of the Anzhero-Sudzhensk and Kolchuginsk coal mines. This 'Workers' Opposition', however, consisted of office staff who, in their criticism of the 'intra-party regime', may

---

65   Kashirskikh 2006, p. 36. Documents on the Shakhty case were published in Krasilnikov et al. (eds.) 2010–11.
66   Cohen 1980, pp. 304–14.
67   Olekh 1994, pp. 101–23; Sandu 2006, pp. 156–9.

have been motivated by career-related grievances. Earlier informers had repor-ted on them, but the authorities ignored them until transport police arrested N.S. Krylov for drunken brawling at a railway station in mid-May 1927 *en route* from Omsk to Moscow. A search of him revealed letters allegedly of a political nature addressed to Nikolai Maksimov, an oppositionist who left Omsk after the 1922 conflict and then worked in Moscow in VSNKh. Conveyed to Moscow, Krylov was interrogated by Iakov Agranov, a prominent OGPU official, who coaxed him into confessing that he belonged to an 'underground' organisation linked to Shliapnikov and Medvedev through Maksimov. The centre's attention to this case led to the arrest of fifteen to twenty Omsk 'oppositionists', all of whom acknowledged having read and distributed oppositionist literature, but who denied accusations of having formed an 'underground organisation'. The investigation was halted due to insufficient evidence.[68] Despite the transfer of some accused conspirators away from Omsk, oppositionist texts continued to circulate in Siberia.

With Stalin's renewed struggle against his intra-party rivals in 1929, the 'poorly educated but fanatically devoted' first secretary of the new Siberian krai committee, Robert Eikhe, brought attention to alleged oppositionism by Trotskyists and members of the Workers' Opposition in Omsk. On his initiat-ive, thirteen people, including some accused of being members of the Workers' Opposition in 1922 and in 1926, were arrested in late August 1929 for having pos-sessed illegal literature and printing moulds and for having tried to link up with workers in other industrial centres. Given the allegation of long-term activ-ity, the OGPU and CCC, now led by Ordzhonikidze, resolved in autumn 1929 to investigate the Omsk group of the Workers' Opposition. Based in the Omsk rail-way workshops, the organisation reportedly had attempted, without success, to organise workers in the Anzhersk mines. The flimsy evidence consisted of Krylov's 1927 confession, letters to Maksimov that were found on him then and 'illegal leaflets' from 1927–8, criticising the doctrine of socialism in one country and party policy towards the peasantry. The OGPU alleged that five members of the Omsk group met several times in 1928–9 with Maksimov, Medvedev and Shliapnikov, who gave 'directives'.[69]

The OGPU weakly defined Shliapnikov's directives as advice to meet 'as if to drink tea' and 'to use only legally published literature about the "Work-ers' Opposition"'. Even Shliapnikov's and Medvedev's recommendations 'not to issue underground leaflets, not to participate in strikes and not to link up with

68   Demidov 1994, pp. 77–82.
69   Demidov 1994, p. 122; RGASPI, f. 589, op. 3, d. 9102, ll. 13, 34–7.

Trotskyists in the underground', were cast as particularly subversive attempts to avoid coming to the attention of the authorities. Shliapnikov allegedly said that enterprise directors in Moscow belonged to the Workers' Opposition and gave it funds, and Maksimov told them that groups of the Workers' Opposition existed in other Soviet cities. Medvedev's gift of money to several of the visitors for return tickets to Omsk was depicted as conspiratorial. The OGPU report also named Chelyshev, at that time chair of the Moscow regional court, and Nikolaenko, a former Chekist working in the Nonferrous Metals Syndicate, as being at the centre of the Workers' Opposition.[70]

Most of those arrested in 1929 were quickly released. Unemployed, most soon recanted their views. The few who did not were exiled. One of these was an Old Bolshevik, Mikhail Vichinsky, who had been taken prisoner and tortured by the Whites during the Civil War, and was toughened by this experience. Recantations were sent 'for correction' to Moscow, where central authorities, guided by Iaroslavsky, created a revisionist history of consistent and intensifying oppositionist factionalism in Omsk from 1922 to 1929, with links to Shliapnikov and Medvedev, who allegedly 'gave directives', were 'ideological leaders', 'supplied literature and money' and told workers to rejoin the party and 'conduct destructive work within it'.[71]

With Politburo endorsement, the CCC turned to investigating the role of Shliapnikov and Medvedev in the Omsk case.[72] In late November 1929 CCC investigators Krivov and Kaganovich interrogated them separately.[73] While Medvedev was sarcastic, combative and acerbic, Shliapnikov more carefully contested the charges. Of the Omsk workers who allegedly visited them, Medvedev recalled only Vichinsky, already ill and old, coming to Moscow in 1929 to appeal for a pension and asking for his and Shliapnikov's help in interceding with the CCC for one. Asked why he did not report this to the party, he asserted that he had no need to report his visitors, because those who kept him under surveillance were well aware of who he saw and under what circumstances.[74] Shliapnikov also claimed that he and those close to him were under OGPU surveillance during these years, about which he often complained to the OGPU.[75]

---

70   RGASPI, f. 589, op. 3, d. 9102, ll. 34–5. I did not have access to Chelyshev's CCC and NKVD files and was allowed to consult only some of Nikolaenko's materials.

71   Demidov 1994, pp. 130–1; RGASPI, f. 589, op. 3, d. 9103, vol. 3, l. 54.

72   RGASPI, f. 17, op. 162, d. 8, l. 2.

73   RGASPI, f. 589, opis 3, d. 9102, ll. 67–106.

74   RGASPI, f. 589, op. 3, d. 9102, l. 104–5.

75   RGASPI, f. 589, op. 3, d. 9102, l. 41.

Attempting to discover the evidence, Shliapnikov received only vague answers and concluded that this was an old case, already resolved, but his interrogators were not dissuaded. He therefore obligingly related that in 1927 several workers from Omsk had come to Moscow to appeal against their exclusion from the party. He recalled having strictly advised them not to engage in factionalism or to create a new party, or to attribute to him views that 'Trotskyists sowed under the guise of a united opposition'. Finally, he cast doubt on the possibility that Vichinsky, 'a very serious person', could have said and done what the CCC depicted. When asked why he received these men, he answered that it would have been rude to turn away a visitor or inquire as to his reasons for visiting. Moreover, he could not control how the other person interpreted the meeting. Regarding links, Shliapnikov found it natural that fellows from Omsk would visit their comrades who had been transferred to Moscow, including Maksimov. He declined to cast judgment on what Maksimov said to them, but only insisted that he himself gave no directive.[76]

Either in jest or feigned *naïveté*, Shliapnikov pointed out that these Omsk workers did nothing wrong in opposing 'Rightist' ideas and policies and he doubted that they had conducted any illegal work. When the interrogator suggested that Shliapnikov's 1926 articles could have been interpreted as 'directives', he objected that they were published by the party and had opposed factionalism. Moreover, he mischievously asserted, his proposals in 1924–6 differed little from 1929 party policies on industrialisation.[77] Humour and language emphasising his adherence to proper party conduct had become his chief means of defence against false accusations. Yet both CCC and OGPU officials were determined to fit his open, 'legal' forms of dissent into a uniform oppositionist framework.

Shliapnikov found it ludicrous that anyone could think that he and Medvedev would 'make a base of our illegal organisation somewhere in Siberia, the devil knows where'. When Krivov inquired as to whether he had expressed any 'doubts about the party line' to his visitors from Omsk, Shliapnikov drily replied that he would not have had such a subtle conversation with strangers. Despite Shliapnikov's conciliatory posture, Kaganovich doubted that he had only told supporters to work within the party. In fact, to him even this sounded subversive. Persistently, Krivov argued that Shliapnikov and Medvedev were to blame because they had 'not actively conducted the party line' in speeches or in the press. Krivov emphasised the importance of 'sincerity' and Kaganovich

---

76   RGASPI, f. 589, op. 3, d. 9102, ll. 77–84.
77   RGASPI, f. 589, op. 3, d. 9102, ll. 75–6.

warned: 'The time is coming, when one can't be silent'. Shliapnikov offered that he could use as the basis for a new article his 1925 manuscript, in which he had criticised Bukharin's and Zinoviev's proposals on agriculture. He found it relevant to the situation in 1929, a not-so-subtle reminder that he had been more consistent than Stalin in promoting industrialisation. The interview concluded with Shliapnikov's promise to write an article and his assurance that he wanted to preserve 'good relations'.[78]

In mid-December 1929, Shliapnikov published in *Pravda* an article supporting intensive industrialisation.[79] This did not mean that he approved of Stalin's approach to collectivisation, which was poorly planned and implicitly encouraged excesses, resulting in horrible human tragedy and enormous damage to agriculture. More than five million people from successful farming families (called '*kulaks*' and presumed hostile to Soviet power) were deported to Siberia and the far north as forced labour. Many died of hunger, cold or disease; children and elderly people were particularly vulnerable. Peasants killed over half their livestock rather than relinquish their animals to the collective. Even spring planting was threatened.[80] In his 2 March 1930 'Dizzy with Success' article in *Pravda*, Stalin condemned excesses, cautioning that collectivisation should be voluntary and suit local conditions. Shliapnikov then remarked in a private letter to Medvedev (sent through an acquaintance) that Stalin's article would have been timelier in October or November.[81] Such irony was hardly in keeping with the horror that had been visited upon the peasantry. For his part, Stalin disapproved of Shliapnikov being published in *Pravda*, even when he was writing in favour of party policy. He faulted the editors of *Pravda* for allowing Shliapnikov's article to 'slip through' and assured Molotov, who was on holiday, that he would '*straighten out* the Shliapnikov affair *today*' (Stalin's emphasis).[82] Shliapnikov and Medvedev had just written a letter to the CC in which they expressed disapproval of factionalism and denied having engaged in underground work.[83] Unsurprisingly, however, it was not published. The Bukharinists had been purged from *Pravda*'s editorial board in early autumn 1929, with Iaroslavsky numbered among the replacements.[84]

---

78 RGASPI, f. 589, op. 3, d. 9102, ll. 67–74.
79 Shliapnikov 1929, 'Za industrializatsiiu – za sotsializm', *Pravda*, 16 December, p. 2.
80 Viola 1996 and 2007; Fitzpatrick 1996.
81 TsA FSB, R33718, d. 499061, vol. 43, l. 207.
82 Lih et al. (eds.) 1995, pp. 185–6.
83 RGASPI, f. 589, op. 3, d. 9102, l. 4 has a reference to the letter, which I could not find.
84 Cohen 1980, pp. 297, 450, fn. 120.

In a letter to Ordzhonikidze, Shliapnikov asserted that the scanty materials he had been allowed to study on the Omsk case convinced him that the case had been conducted 'abnormally', that there was nothing new in it and that neither he nor Medvedev had violated party statutes. However, the authorities had interpreted their 'friendly party advice' as a 'directive' issued by a 'centre'. In his opinion, the resulting picture was a 'contradictory hodgepodge'. Further, he was offended that the OGPU and CCC had 'worked up' this case secretly since spring 1928, in violation of party regulations. Reminding Ordzhonikidze of his earlier assurances that the CC did not consider this matter important, Shliapnikov objected that the case was indeed being pursued seriously. As confirmation, he pointed not only to Maksimov's arrest, which had occurred around the time of Shliapnikov's and Medvedev's questioning by the CCC, his imprisonment for more than a month, and attempts by an OGPU employee to force Maksimov's wife to take a package to Shliapnikov or Medvedev. He requested that Ordzhonikidze help free Maksimov and halt 'provocational work'.[85]

In mid-January 1930, not having heard from Ordzhonikidze, Shliapnikov went to visit him at the CCC but found him away. After that he dropped in on Iaroslavsky to discuss the case. After taunting Shliapnikov a bit, Iaroslavsky placed his protest on the agenda of the CCC party collegium (board), but then it was postponed until Medvedev returned to Moscow from holiday in February. Upon his arrival, he was surprised to find an incriminating letter from Maksimov that appeared to him, Shliapnikov, and Maksimov's wife to have been forged. On 23 February 1930, the CCC again delayed deciding the Omsk case.[86] On that same day, CC and CCC members urged Shliapnikov to write a statement about the Omsk case. Responding promptly, with a document entitled 'About a big mistake by a small group in Omsk', Shliapnikov repudiated factionalism and denied that the Workers' Opposition had 'led underground work'.[87] Instructing Medvedev to deliver the statement, attempt to see Stalin about the case, and stay in touch by mail, Shliapnikov left for holiday.

While on holiday, Shliapnikov learned about Cossack uprisings in the North Caucasus, resulting from collectivisation and dekulakisation. Following these events with great concern, he worried that the press was not rebutting unspecified 'absurd rumours' that had spread about the events. He hoped that 'political tact' could help restore 'peaceful mutual understanding' in the wake of

---

85   RGASPI, f. 589, op. 3, d. 9102, l. 41; d. 9103, vol. 3, ll. 50–1.
86   RGASPI, f. 589, op. 3, d. 9102, ll. 40–1, 52; TsA FSB, R33718, d. 499061, vol. 43.
87   RGASPI, f. 589, op. 3, d. 9102, ll. 2–4.

numerous arrests.[88] There must have been a large measure of self-delusion in his assessment of the events unfolding around him, as it seems that he did not comprehend the full tragedy of forcible collectivisation at that time. Deeply immersed in writing his historical memoirs and preoccupied with avoiding prosecution on the Omsk case, perhaps he was not fully able to assess the meaning and impact of Stalin's radical new policies. Despite his failure to employ the language of class warfare in his private reflections on collectivisation, he surely saw it as a necessary and objectively 'progressive' measure, the only way to accomplish Soviet industrialisation in the existing domestic and international context of limited capital for investment and increasing hostility from the Soviet Union's neighbours.

While on holiday, Shliapnikov wrote to Omsk party leaders, asking them to print his statement about the Omsk case, which had not yet appeared in the party press. Instead, Omsk party leaders published in the newspaper, *Rabochy put*, a 'Letter of 10 Oppositionists' that implicated Shliapnikov and Medvedev in factionalism. The CCC, expressing dissatisfaction with Shliapnikov's and Medvedev's earlier statements, called on them to write another one. Nevertheless, Shliapnikov and Medvedev continued to complain that they could take no responsibility for people misunderstanding their views. Combatively, they argued that the CCC's logic would make even Iaroslavsky an accomplice of Omsk workers, because they had read his book about the Workers' Opposition.[89]

On 13 March 1930, the CCC voted to expel Maksimov from the party. Released from prison, he appealed against his purge from the party and three-year exile to Central Asia. Denying that he or the Omsk workers had been in the Workers' Opposition, he insisted that the only reading material he had given them was that approved by the CC, including Iaroslavsky's book and party-congress protocols. Complaining about OGPU threats to keep him in jail until he would confess to anti-party work, Maksimov wrote that he had refused to confess because he did not want to 'deceive myself, you, the party and history'.[90] He asked Shliapnikov and Medvedev for assistance in his appeal.[91] They were in a weak position to do so, yet they tried.

On 28 May the CCC concluded that Shliapnikov and Medvedev had been aware that people in Omsk had created 'an underground group of the Workers' Opposition' and were at fault for having failed to stop them and for having

88   TsA FSB, R33718, d. 499061, vol. 43, l. 210.
89   RGASPI, f. 589, op. 3, d. 9102, ll. 1, 4.
90   RGASPI, f. 589, op. 3, d. 9102, l. 57; ll. 15–19.
91   TsA FSB, R33718, d. 499061, vol. 43, ll. 162–7.

failed to tell party leaders. Despite this rebuke, Iaroslavsky, on 29 May 1930, confirmed their verification by the party purge that the Sixteenth Party Congress had ordered in 1929. On the same day, however, someone (perhaps Iaroslavsky) attempted to re-open the Omsk case and to ratchet up the charges. Depicting an evolution of the Omsk affair that linked worker opposition to peasant uprisings, the accusation now was that a counterrevolutionary group discovered in March 1930 in Omsk had sought to lead kulak uprisings to overthrow Soviet power.[92]

In the new narrative, oppositionists turned to the peasantry because they had become disillusioned in the working class, as if they were reverting from Marxism to Populism, except that they were linked to kulaks. Describing unsuccessful attempts to obtain arms, the unknown author wove unrelated groups and incidents into a narrative that purported to show an unbroken line of opposition that had evolved into counterrevolution. Resistance to collectivisation in Siberia had indeed grown rapidly. Hundreds of armed bands in Siberia attacked collective farms (kolkhozes). In 1930 the number of bands in Western Siberia alone had grown to eight hundred and eighty. Transit camps for kulak deportees in Omsk, Tomsk and Achinsk held people who had cause to be embittered against the Soviet regime.[93] Whether or not Omsk workers had sought to collude with peasant bandits, someone in the party and/or secret police intended to demonstrate links between intra-party opposition and counterrevolution. Rather than apply the 'tact' that Shliapnikov preferred in dealing with peasant disturbances, Stalin and his allies opted to scapegoat oppositionists.

Iaroslavsky introduced a resolution to the CCC Presidium calling for harsher measures against Shliapnikov. On 3 August, the CCC sternly reprimanded him for having 'support[ed] anti-party elements leading factional struggle against the party', of having 'covered up' the Omsk group's work, and of having slandered the OGPU. Formally disputing all the charges, Shliapnikov argued that Iaroslavsky had introduced no new evidence. He interpreted the latest charges as a response to his appeal on Maksimov's behalf and to his criticisms of the OGPU for having applied 'methods of provocation' in regard to Maksimov's wife. He clarified that his accusations were against individuals, not the OGPU as an institution, and were not universal, but pertained to the Omsk case specifically. Refusing to apologise for having defended Maksimov, he declared: 'I considered it my duty to stand up for him'. The CCC let stand the reprimand

92   RGASPI, f. 589, op. 3, d. 9103, vol. 3, ll. 56–61, 109; d. 9102, l. 5.
93   RGASPI, f. 589, op. 3, d. 9103, vol. 3, ll. 56–60; Werth 2007, pp. 37, 86.

and all the other decisions on the Omsk case. Moreover, Iaroslavsky continued to scour not only the USSR, but also peripheral regions, for evidence damning former members of the Workers' Opposition.[94]

Nevertheless, political dangers continued to haunt Shliapnikov, Medvedev, and other former Worker Oppositionists in Omsk and elsewhere. Omsk figured among the cities where the NKVD in 1935 accused Shliapnikov and Medvedev of having organised counterrevolutionary groups. For the Omsk workers, final consequences arrived even earlier. The NKVD alleged that in 1933 Omsk oppositionists had raided a collective farm, killed four collective farmers and stolen kolkhoz property. In July 1934 several Omsk oppositionists returned from prison camp and exile only to be accused of new counterrevolutionary work. They, along with nearly 40 other workers, were arrested and some were shot.[95]

Many former Worker Oppositionists were targeted in the 1933 party purge, removed from their positions, and transferred to less significant work. After the assassination of Leningrad party boss Sergei Kirov in December 1934, there was a wave of arrests of former oppositionists. A case was constructed against the former Worker Oppositionists, but on allegedly new material. A centre in Moscow was alleged to have links with groups in Omsk, Rostov-on-Don, Kiev, Odessa, Baku, and Kharkov. Charges accumulated over the course of 1935–7 to include terrorism and plots to assassinate Soviet leaders. Chelyshev died in a prison hospital during the interrogation phase of his case.[96] Sapozhnikov and Lobanov were transferred from Kiev to Moscow to stand trial, where they recanted testimony coerced from them in Ukraine.[97] Nevertheless, the case against the Workers' Opposition could not come to the conclusion the NKVD desired, because no major figures and very few minor ones confessed fully to the charges against them. A post-Soviet Russian historian described the Workers' Opposition as 'one of the most united organisations, a symbol of revolutionary steadfastness and unity of workers in the struggle against the authorities'.[98] To say that they were organisationally united still by the 1930s is an overstatement, but they were distinguished by an inability to accept that their confessions to false charges could help the party, by strong ties of loyalty that hindered them from tarring one another with false accusations, and

---

94   RGASPI, f. 589, op. 3, d. 9102, ll. 39–41, 44–56, 62, 108–9. For more on Iaroslavsky's attitude towards oppositionism, see Dahlke 2008.

95   Iakovlev (ed.) 1991, pp. 105–6; TsA FSB, R33718, d. 499061, vol. 5, ll. 28–31; Papkov 1997, p. 105.

96   Smirnov 2001, pp. 126–7.

97   Haluzevyi derzhavnyi arkhiv Sluzhba Bezpeky Ukrainy (SBU), Sapozhnikov's case file held in the Kiev branch and Lobanov's case file held in the Kharkov branch.

98   Papkov 1997, p. 104.

by a different understanding of the party than that promoted by Stalin and his supporters. Their firm convictions helped them resist Stalin's rhetoric and narrative of the party's past and to imagine an alternative to his vision of socialism.

1   **Letter from S.P. Medvedev in Berlin to A.G. Shliapnikov in Moscow, 26 September 1922**[99]

[On the left margin of the first page of the first copy, S.P. Medvedev wrote by hand on 4 February 1935 that the letter was written in 1922 and possibly taken to Shliapnikov in Moscow through A. Medvedev.]

Today, September 26, our friend who bears the same last name as I, comrade A. Medvedev, leaves us in Berlin for Moscow. He is the same one who collaborated with us in the 22. I'm forwarding this document [грамота] by him. There was no one reliable with whom to send this information previously, although the information does not represent anything criminal from any point of view.

1.   Of those friends you recommended, I found, saw and especially enjoyed discussions with comrades [Michael] Niederkirchner, Max Ziese, [Richard] Müller, Fanny Ezerskaya [Fanny Jezierska], and a few other personnel of the German Communist Party. The first three [Niederkirchner, Ziese, Müller] and comrade [N.R.] Krebs, who is also a metalworker, had much worthwhile to say about the situation in Germany, about the role and influence of the Communist Party among workers, and about the role and influence of workers within the party.[100]
      [Paraphrase: Ezerskaya could tell him little because she had been in Italy for the past year, but she acquainted him with a young worker-communist who informed him about 'rather interesting facts from the life of the German Communist Party'.]

2.   'What does the German Communist Party signify among the working masses?' I asked each of them. They all answered unanimously that it is still very, very weak. It has neither enough ideological influence on the masses now, nor does it have its very own apparatus which would be sufficiently capable of coping with leading the activity of its own members,

---

99   TsA FSB, R33718, d. 499061, vol. 13, ll. 1–23, three typed copies.
100   For more on these individuals, see Hoffrogge 2014.

at the very least, in various areas of the workers' movement of Germany. It still has not come together and taken shape ideologically, organisationally, or materially!! Max Ziese and Niederkirchner illustrated this especially well! [Paul] Levi reigned within it, in an ideological sense, before the March putsch! It was so organisationally weak that it immediately became overwhelmed by and surrendered to the indignant feelings of a sudden influx of circles of worker masses, which had been roused to fury. They were chiefly from among the more secure industrial workers and shop assistants! Another interesting circumstance is that all these comrades were against the tactics that Moscow dictated then! And so much so, that in the days of the putsch they did not even go out onto the street, despite the party's summons!

This putsch nearly killed the possibility of forming a strong communist party for many years. An insignificant number of members remained in the party. All leaders were so demoralised that they demoralised the workers, so that [the leaders] lost any sort of influence among [the workers] and [the leaders] threw themselves from the extreme left to the extreme right, including Rush [Oskar Rusch?]. Only workers' worsening living conditions during inflation saved the party from death. The Communist Party alone supported the efforts of the broadest circles of the masses to improve their situation through struggle. Likewise, there was a sloughing off [отслоение] in trade unions, although more slowly and not so broadly. Here an interesting story begins.

A significant exfoliation [отслоение] of communists in trade unions, primarily in the union of metalworkers, created a central faction of trade union personnel who were communists. At a special meeting, trade union personnel elected this faction to further lead the trade union movement. By the way, both Max Ziese and Niederkirchner entered into it. This entire faction immediately reserved for itself the right to have the last word in questions of the trade union movement and leadership of it. Understandably, this did not suit 'certain personages' and so struggle began to subordinate this faction to the party CC. Its leaders Ziese, Niederkirchner and others were accused of indecisiveness. This was done again in connection with escapades [авантюра] in the trade union movement. The CC decided to have its own kind of putsch here. It set forth the imperative to seize the Metalworkers' Union, where communists were stronger than in other unions. With this perspective in mind, it demanded convocation of a communist conference of Metalworkers' Union members on an all-state scale. The idea was either to elect a communist central committee, if there were enough communists, or to seize the union by forming a temporary bureau, calling a congress, and electing a new communist central committee for the union.

Ziese, Niederkirchner, and all the other best communist workers were against this adventure. They thought this route to be very dangerous and so they were branded as 'vacillators'.

The CC's decision went against the faction of trade union workers. The latter insisted on calling a conference as the party and not as the union. Otherwise, there would be disorganisation.

Now, take note of this, my dear. After the decision of the assemblies I described, Max Ziese, as a member of the union's central committee, was supposed to begin actually disorganising the union. He zealously followed 'party discipline'. They convened a conference. It turned out to be so poorly attended and even so ideologically diverse that the Scheidemanns did not let this opportunity slip. They excluded from the union all participants of the conference, including Ziese, one or two at a time. No workers anywhere defended those who were excluded for their line of action, which party 'chiefs' had foisted upon them.

After these trade union communists were excluded from trade unions, the Communist Party turned on them. Now there is not even one active, real trade unionist who would consider it correct for communists working in the trade union movement to subordinate themselves to the party and carry out its decisions rather than those of union bodies, when these two are in conflict. This is how the sprouts of independence [независим-щина] or syndicalism arise and grow.

3.   I asked them, 'What is your role in the party's decisions?' The answer was such: 'We play no role at all in its decisions'. Again, I asked them, 'How can you hold out against this? Indeed they will constantly arrange provocations against you to speak out in some way, and not from malice, but because of bad manners [невежество]'! The answer I received was: 'Well, no! That's enough! This was possible to do once and then just because of our imprudence! Now we will give no one the right to act like they're the bosses of the trade union movement'. During our discussion, when I pointed to the indications they gave that they and the party made different decisions on some questions, they answered very simply. 'We do not hinder the party committee in passing decisions, but we do not consider it obligatory to implement them'. When I asked if this means that these party committee decisions are not carried through, the answer was simple: 'These decisions are sent to Moscow, but they don't send them to us'. Right now all of them resolutely oppose the Profintern's direct dependence on the Comintern.

All the comrades whom I have singled out here clearly recognise that the CC lacks any sense of purpose and that it is entirely under the power of the Comintern. Worst of all is that it does not sense firm ground under its feet. [Point four is missing]

5. During our discussion, all the comrades declared that they do not know our position and do not understand it. They asked, 'Are you for NEP?' I said yes! 'You are for the fact that the last word belongs to the party, even in questions of the trade union movement?' I said yes! 'Then what's the matter?' I began to explain:

    a. In our republic, I said, 90% are peasants and petty bourgeois strata and no more than 10% are proletarians.

    b. In our party, 54% are petty bourgeois elements and only 46% are proletarians. All senior posts in the party are taken by journalists, teachers, clerks, and similar such petty bourgeoisie.

    c. In our trade union movement, the majority belongs not to production unions, but to professional corporative unions of petty bourgeois strata.

    d. In our soviets in ¾ of the republic, there are almost no proletarians. Bourgeois and petty bourgeois political careerists occupy all senior posts in them.

    e. In the Red Army, we have 90% peasants and no more than 10% proletarians.

    f. In its command staff, there are 67% peasants and 13% workers.

    g. In the higher education institutions, 70–75% is bourgeois and 25–30% workers.

    h. According to the report by the Chair of the Miners' Union at the August conference, our workers receive 2 ½ commodity [товар-ный] rubles.[101] It is the same across all of Russia with the exception of Moscow and Petrograd, where it is somewhat higher.

    i. They pay these wages to workers with a delay of from one to three months.

    j. There is no insurance. There are no measures for the protection of labour at all.

    k. There is an eight-hour working day at the factory and an eight or ten hour working day in the garden, in order to stay alive.

---

101   This was a unit of currency used during early NEP, before a 'hard' currency was introduced. See https://economy-ru.info/info/37822/.

l.   A strike is regarded as a counterrevolutionary act in state enterprises, where workers are no better off than in private ones.

m.   NEP is radically changing the role and influence of the working class
and its unification in the state.

Well when I reeled off to them this list, their eyes nearly popped out from
amazement! They had contemplated nothing of the sort. I had with me
the VTsSPS report, from which I quoted to them the literal text confirming what I had pointed out.

'How do you think to change such a situation?' Well, I again enumerated
everything that we put forth. They just declared that now they understand
us and what we want. They understood especially well and were outright
gratified that we want for the workers to hold in their hands all the reins
of management, both in the party and in the state!

They find this especially clear and comprehensible!

In a word, after our conversation, these comrades will be among our best
friends. In any case, they will not allow themselves to be fooled about our
character. Oh, by the way. When they tried to point out that we resemble,
as they say, syndicalists, I told them what syndicalists want in relation to
the party. I asked if indeed this could apply to them, for they don't want
union personnel to be subordinated to the party. They jokingly confessed
that they might be closer to syndicalism than are we. That is all for now.
You should send them right away from Russia brief letters, at the very
least, which would be addressed to them personally, chiefly to Max Ziese
and Niederkirchner. The latter jokingly told about how when you were
here, you said he was 'insufficiently disciplined'. Then after you left, he
said, we were purged at our congress for violating party discipline. Well,
he was pleased that they pinned this medal on your chest, too.

You must write to him about this!

They laughed out loud about how we were sent packing at important
moments in Russia. When I counted off to Ziese and to Niederkirchner
the republics assigned to you: Tatar, Kir[giz?], Bash[kir], they burst out in
laughter. They declared that similar such attempts are made here toward
them, but so far with no results! Ziese said to me that after your departure,
he wrote several letters to you, but he has not received an answer. If it will
be possible, I will see our friends again.

With best wishes, S.

2   Iu.Kh. Lutovinov's Speech at the Twelfth RCP(b) Congress,
     17–25 April 1923[102]

Comrades, let me say that comrade Zinoviev's report, especially the section
about the party's internal situation, made me deeply despondent. Allow me to
speak sincerely. Despite the fact that I personally did not expect much that was
new from comrade Zinoviev's report, all the same somewhere in the depths
of my soul a glimmer of hope flickered that comrade Zinoviev would more
closely, objectively, and concretely address the resolution of the problem of the
intraparty situation, which deeply worries all of us. But alas and oh! Hope has
deceived us this time, as it always does in such cases.

Comrade Zinoviev did not present the question in all its magnitude yesterday, comrades. He should have posed it in a Marxist way. Neither did he speak
about the extraordinary abnormalities taking place in our party, nor did he
reveal the main reasons for these things.[103] It goes without saying that such
a formulation of the question is incorrect and extremely harmful. Comrade
Zinoviev said that the party became healthier and that all groupings disappeared without a trace. Is that so, comrades? Is that so in the provinces and in
the centre? I know that groupings exist. Comrade Zinoviev attested to this in his
report. Comrade Zinoviev's threats, which are directed toward some anonymous authors, attest only to the fact that the CC does not desire to bring up this
question. The CC is like the ostrich, which hides its head in the sand.

Groupings exist. Comrade Zinoviev confirms this himself, when he speaks
about how some grumblers now are attempting to unite. Comrades from the
Democratic Centralist grouping now attempt to unite all from Workers' Truth to
the Workers' Opposition on the same platform, which would be the programme
of a future new party. Of course, comrades, none of this is new. Nevertheless,
an anonymous platform exists. No one knows who wrote it. Also, something
like a programme of the so-called Workers' Truth group exists. It is true that an
entire brochure was written. But all this attests to the fact that these groupings
not only have not disappeared without a trace, but that they were driven into
the underground, where they exist now. (Noise.)

Comrades, I strongly request that you not interrupt me. You will go and lay
hands upon [выйдёте и накладёте] not only Lutovinov, but all those who dis-

---

102   RKP(b) 1968, pp. 115–117.
103   Editors' footnote: Further in the stenographic report there followed: 'and became like the
       SR Kerensky, who shouted in his time and resolutely threatened each and every one. When
       some kind of danger threatened, he always declared: we will not tolerate it, we will smash
       it, and so forth. He even said: I won't stand for it, but will smash it'.

agree with you. Right now you don't have any right at all to prevent me from speaking. I want to say that, inasmuch as all these groupings and platforms exist, obviously there are foundations for this. If anonymous theses appear and anonymous authors feel they have to publish platforms, well this is only because in our RCP(b), there is no normal way to voice one's ideas and point of view on one or another question. This proves that if you are in the RCP(b) and you attempt to criticise just the purely practical implementation of the political line, not even this line itself, well right away you will be counted among the category of Mensheviks, or SRs, or whomever suits them. We heard this in comrade Zinoviev's report. I took down from his speech the following phrase: 'Under current conditions, any kind of criticism, even if from the left, inevitably will become Menshevist'.

What is this? (Voices: 'Correct!') I hear many people say 'correct'. But what does this mean? Is Zinoviev or the entire CC correct? (Voices: 'The entire party!') It's far from the entire party. Only the Politburo, as if it were the infallible pope, says: everything I do, I do correctly; don't dare to object; and no one has any right to criticise. Not only is this not Marxist, but it is an extremely dangerous practice, which inevitably leads to conflicts. I'm not about to stir up any kind of opposition here. I am just pointing out the existing state of things. If it will continue so further, then it is obvious that all sorts of groupings will be the result and the logical conclusion of all this.

Now extraordinarily difficult conditions confront the party. Unity, comrades, is necessary as never before. But by what means do we need to achieve this unity? By means of repression, meaning by shutting up the mouths of those who desire to speak out on one or another question or who introduce one or another concrete proposal? Such facts exist. Inasmuch as such facts exist and since it is not possible to struggle against them in the provinces or in the centre, then it is necessary to struggle at the congress itself. The party is called the party of the proletariat. Yet the proportion of its members who are workers is 40% in the gubernias, 30% in the uyezds, and 54% in the cities. It follows that workers are a minority compared to the other elements in the party. Those, who do not belong to the class of the proletariat and who now demoralise the party, present a great danger to the party. There is no doubt that the Congress must come to a halt before this great danger and turn the wheel a bit to the other side. It must relax the regime, in which all kinds of opposition now inevitably arise. Comrade Zinoviev's method of saving the party, which undoubtedly expresses the opinion of the entire CC, is unsuitable.

Such an exclusive right to save the party without the participation of all party members reminds me of our Vneshtorg's exclusive right to internal trade, without suitable specialists or organisation. I think that it should not be just the CC's exclusive right to save the party, but it should be the right of each active party member, who participated no less in creating and building this party, who worked in the party before the revolution, who has up to now remained to work in it, and who feels all its pain. There is no basis at all for denying to these active party members the right to save the party. Comrade Zinoviev here is completely wrong when he says that we will not allow, will not tolerate, and so forth. This method, which needs to be recognised as completely unsuitable, can have an impact while the party still more or less preserves its unity and still has not been riven by all sorts of discord into groupings. But the more groupings there are and the more dissatisfaction grows among broad worker masses, the less possible will it be to save the party and manage it by such methods.

I would like to say a few more words about the party's participation, or interference as comrade Zinoviev says, in our economic bodies. Comrade Zinoviev complains that when the CC interferes in some functions of economic bodies, the economic planners incorrectly state that the CC is not up to speed on this matter. Of course, the economic planners' point of view is incorrect. Right now you can't conceive of our economic planners, who have not learned how to manage, receiving the right to dispose of all industry and to expend available resources. This is completely impermissible, of course. It is completely wrong, but it needs to be said also that the CC's policy in this regard needs to be changed. Comrade Larin just spoke here rather picturesquely about this policy.

The Politburo includes only two people who actively participate in the country's economic life. If the Politburo will in practice resolve all economic problems from small to large, well of course it goes without saying that the Politburo could not completely resolve these matters without making mistakes, even if it were Solomon. Of course, this would be completely abnormal. The economic planners need to be given some rights, of course. I think that the situation will continue to be abnormal, until we unite the political work of our party with the purely economic. That is, there should be in the Politburo persons who connect both political and economic work. Only under such conditions can the correct resolution of all problems be conceivable. My time has run out. Therefore, I'm stopping.

3   S.P. Medvedev's Notes from 6 December 1923, Possibly from a
       Private Talk Given in Moscow by a German Communist[104]

About the general situation in Germany.

All analogies between German events and those of the Russian October make
no sense at all. The situation in Germany is incomparable. ... The bourgeoisie
is stronger and better organised than was the Russian bourgeoisie. Russia was
in a state of war, which is not so in Germany. Russia could use the contradictions of two imperialisms, but Germany can't do so. The financial situation is
completely different. The German SDs are stronger than were the Russian Mensheviks. The German trade unions are much stronger than the Russian ones
were. The mystical charm of the Soviet Union has become completely obsolete, thanks to events. But it is unfair to say that the German working class is
not revolutionary. This discredits it. The problem in Germany of weak soviets
is because we did not understand the significance of soviets and the need to
struggle within them. ...

In Germany we not only do not have soviets as bodies of proletarian revolution, but we don't even have an actually revolutionary communist party. But
then we have a strongly organised fascism, which is the master of the state
apparatus and holds in its hands the top brass [генералитет], officers, the
Reichswehr, and other armed forces of the country. These material forces suffice for them to become entrenched for the long term. ...

In order to have the right to leadership, a real communist party is needed, not
just that misunderstanding which now is called a communist party. ... Now, all
across the world, people are reevaluating all political values, parties are being
regenerated, and opportunism is spreading. ... At the last illegal congress of
factory committees, we even had such delegates as a member of the Stinnes
party and a delegate from [illegible].[105] At this congress we proposed resolutions which spoke not about factory committees but about soviets becoming
bodies of political dictatorship. But our CC did not approve and it spoiled this
resolution, which the Congress had unanimously accepted. Our CC substituted
'factory committees' for 'soviets'.

---

104   TsA FSB, R33718, d. 499061, vol. 42, ll. 232–7. The ellipses in this document's translation
       here indicate omissions in my transcription of Medvedev's notes.
105   Hugo Stinnes (1870–1924) was a German industrialist who profited immensely from World
       War I and became a media magnate after the war. He was elected to the Reichstag in 1920
       as a founding member of the liberal German People's Party (*Deutsche Volkspartei* – DVP).
       The illegible word may have been an abbreviation for one of the German peasant parties.

The Communist Party essentially behaves as if it is an adjunct to the right SDs. In the party we have direct opportunism in relation to the government. We are constantly reevaluating the forces of our political enemies. Now we consider them insignificant and ourselves the decisive force. So we acted in Saxony. It's necessary to point out that the revolution in Germany can't be made as a coup [переворот] in just two cities as this was done in Russia. ...

The conclusions are: dictatorship of the proletariat, nationalisation of large industry, and so forth. But no one believes in these conclusions any more. ... The party needs to stand for the soviets, for the dictatorship of the proletariat, and so forth ... Without this, there is the threat of a split.

4   N.A. Kubiak's Speech to the Thirteenth Party Conference,
       17 January 1924[106]

Comrades, the All-Union Party Conference is within its rights to demand an answer from people who for three months jerked the party around and who tried to undermine the party's authority among workers and peasants. They wanted to sap the Party CC's authority. They already undermined the Moscow Conference and they promise to undercut the All-Union Conference. After all these actions, it was supposed that comrades, who so disorganised the party, would come to us here and propose one or another line. What do we see, in fact?

Here, at this conference, comrades Preobrazhensky and Sapronov dwelled upon the history of the Moscow discussion. For the union-wide conference, it is not so important who said what, when, and how. The conference needs to know the response to the Document of the 46 and Trotsky's letter, about which the entire party knows. Do you support it or not? You should answer this. If you do not answer, then you are pitiful fighters for that line, which you want to advance as correct.

I can still understand Comrade Preobrazhensky, who said in advance that we are Old Bolsheviks, we know party history, and we will struggle within the party. Comrade Preobrazhensky, be careful around turns [тихо на поворотах]. [At that moment, when the Bolshevik Party waged the bitterest struggle against the Mensheviks, Comrade Preobrazhensky closely embraced the Mensheviks in the Far East. (Preobrazhensky: A lie.) Yes, this was in 1917, when you did so.

---

106   RGASPI, f. 51, op. 1, d. 7, ll. 199–202, consulted in the Hoover Institution Library & Archives.

It is true that it was not for long, about three weeks, but all the same you were in congress with [illegible] and Company.][107]

Instead of coming here with a platform, Comrade Sapronov keeps busy frightening and threatening the party about what will happen if the party will take any measures against the oppositionists, such as they turned out to be. I suggest that these threats have no significance for the party, as we have become accustomed to understand it, and it will not feel threatened.

Comrade Radek's speech is another curiosity at this conference. He says that the CC was unable to use the opposition like Comrade Lenin used the Workers' Opposition at the Tenth Congress. But why could Comrade Lenin use the Workers' Opposition? It was because the Workers' Opposition gave us something [illegible]. The question is different – was this correct or not? And what did the current opposition contribute? Radek here said that Trotsky is a good man. Who says that he is bad? But if this good man makes a mistake or thinks he will lead the party into making mistakes, then there is no doubt that the party, including the conference, should straighten out this good comrade.

Comrade Radek brought this statement of caution about good people and he warns that if the party will take repressive measures, then in the future it will be taught an unwanted lesson. It is strange to hear this from Comrade Radek, who proposes to the Politburo and CC to punch some mugs [мордо-битие] within the CC of the German Communist Party, yet here he calls for the schoolboyish method of influence [воздействие]. Comrades, here is a discrepancy. If you propose to knock heads [мордобитие] within the German party, then here in our country allow the Russian Communist Party, which is accustomed to struggle, to carry it out to the end. Now don't you sigh, for of course there is nothing terrible in this.

They say that they removed some military staff person, Boguslavsky, and others. Excuse me, how horrible! You are demanding renewal of the apparat? We are renewing it and are concerned about renewing it. You yourselves demand this. You say it's necessary to shake up everything. Secondly, comrades, you can't connect the removal of individuals to serious party discussion. We do not drag back out materials that we already withdrew. It's necessary to request that the CC report would provide information about why it was withdrawn. But this is not what the matter is about.

The conference gathered not to discuss why Antonov-Ovseenko was removed, but to summarise the results of three months of jerking the party around and to request a reply. You answered that you agree with the CC. Good.

---

107 Someone struck through the text shown in brackets here.

What are you thinking about doing now? At the Moscow Gubernia Conference, Comrade Preobrazhensky declared that there are no disagreements of any kind. Rafail, who spoke after him, said that the Moscow Gubernia Conference was tampered with [подтасована], its decisions are garbled [подтасованы], and it is not authoritative. They declare the same thing here, both in [illegible] and at the conference, that of course this conference of apparatchiks does not vote to approve our proposals.

First of all, there were no proposals aside from stupid ones, for which you can't raise your hand in approval. In this way, comrades set the conditions for a further struggle or a campaign to undermine the authority of the decisions of this party conference. Yet after this they are horrified that the conference proposes a resolution in which there will be a point defining the steadfastness of Communist Party members.

5   A.G. Shliapnikov, 'Our Differences', *Pravda*, 18 January 1924[108]

[The published version differs in some significant ways from the original draft, which was entitled 'About the Lost Deed: regarding discussion'. This draft, which Shliapnikov signed and dated 21 December 1923, is preserved in Communist Party archives (RGASPI). A second draft with some handwritten suggestions, which were probably made by either Shliapnikov or Medvedev, exists in NKVD files, among materials confiscated from S.P. Medvedev after his 1935 arrest (TsA FSB).[109]

In the document below, I have inserted in brackets the text found in the draft manuscripts, but not in the published version, and have provided the initials of the archive where the draft was found. I have also tried to indicate whether the differences stem from alternative wording, insertions, or omissions. 'Alt' means that there is a difference of wording between the published and archival version. 'Missing' or 'omits' indicates wording present in the published version but not in the archival version. 'Ins' indicates wording that appears in the archival version but not in the published version.[110] I do not know who altered the published version and whether this occurred with Shliapnikov's permission.]

---

108   'Nazhi rasnoglasiia', reprinted in Zorky (ed.) 1926, pp. 144–57.

109   '*O propavshei gramote: po povodu diskussii*' in RGASPI, f. 17, op. 71, d. 82, ll. 7–22 and in TsA FSB, R33718, vol. 40.

110   At first glance, these designations may seem counterintuitive, but my goal is to distinguish not only between the published and unpublished versions, but also to tie the differences to the separately archived unpublished drafts.

According to some comrades' assurances on the pages of the party press [RGASPI alt: assurances of our official circles and press], discussion of the most important questions of party life and politics, starting with intraparty democracy, is approaching a conclusion. These assertions, however, more likely express the comrades' [RGASPI alt: official circles'] personal wishes, but don't correspond to reality at all. Even within the perimeters of Moscow, the agitated party masses don't display the desire to retire and they suppose that discussion has far from settled the most important questions of party life. There are even some harbingers that the long-lived party 'calm' threatens to end stormily, not on worker democracy, but around it and in connection with it.

The polemics, which have just begun among individual members of the Central Committee, essentially are transitioning from worker democracy to other questions. All questions posed for discussion and related ones spill out from Moscow across the whole Soviet Union. Stopping this is out of the question. There should be concern only that the discussions at the local level should receive a principled direction. Fears about the harm of discussion should be rejected and all attention should be focused so that no one should forget about the party, even during terrible disputes over matters of principle, and no one would lower the discussion to the level of sensational disclosures and scandalous stories.[111]

We don't want to say by this that we support cover-ups of abnormal relations within the party and its leading bodies. However, trifling [RGASPI ins: personal] disputes, especially [RGASPI alt: even] between individual members of party institutions on the pages of the party press, should not be a subject of the broad party masses' attention and discussion. From our experience and from party history, we know that among the higher-ups we [RGASPI ins: always] had squabbles, intrigues, mutual bickering along with and more often in connection with principled disagreements in the party. But never did they engage the special attention of broad party circles.

On the other hand, the side that was not soundly Marxist always tried to distract the attention of broad party circles from the actual essence of political debate by creating outrageous scenes and issuing false shouts of indignation. The party as a whole has carried out its decisions only regarding political disagreements, and only these have defined its work. All the rest, like rubbish, was thrown into the wastebin of history. Now it's necessary to strive only so that this

---

111   Shliapnikov uses the phrase 'from the secrets of the Madrid court', probably in reference to a historical novel by Georg F. Bourne (Georg Fülborn (1837–1902)) entitled *Secrets of the Court of Madrid, or Isabella*. Translated into Russian in 1874, the novel was popular in Russia and the phrase was often used in jest.

unfolding discussion would serve to elevate the consciousness of party members and to divert attention as little as possible toward party-historical rubbish.

Recent party meetings devoted much attention to and displayed many passions concerning our central press organ *Pravda*'s polemical tactics toward the opposition. Without thinking of contending the right of the central press organ's editors to defend the CC and its line [RGASPI missing: 'and its line'], we join in protest against attempts to politically defame the opposition. Among those now protesting against such unworthy methods of polemics among party members, we see even those, who not so long ago worked hard to discredit and defame dissenters. We can only welcome their change of heart and express the wish that their lesson is not lost on those who now take up a similar trade.

A Historical Inquiry

We Bolsheviks never considered forms of party organisation and methods of party work without connecting them to conditions, time, and place. We always coordinated our methods of work with and subordinated them to the political tasks of the proletarian party. So the historical explanation, which official representatives of the organisation and some comrades from the opposition give, of why a 'democratic spring' appeared only in December 1923, suffers from incompleteness and imprecision. Some defenders of the CC [RGASPI alt: Bureaucratic [казённые] defenders of all lines of the CC] and of any other committee that poses as a defender of party unity, use such evidence that leading party bodies are correct in recognising the need to change the former CC line on party building, which leaves doubt in the minds of many party members [RGASPI ins: as to whether these comrades defend their salary and their position of command instead of the party].

Having opened discussion, the CC representatives offer in their speeches such explanations for the party's new turn, which show that certain thoughts of the 'Workers' Opposition' are not alien to them now, if one does not suspect them of having hired them out in order to master 'the element of democracy'. Our CC member comrades now have set out to defend the Tenth Congress resolution on intraparty democracy. They are delivering such speeches and uttering such thoughts and proposals, for which those very same CC members judged and condemned rank-and-file working-class members of the party just a few months ago.

Speaking on behalf of a certain section of the opposition, comrade Preobrazhensky shows solidarity with and justifies the CC's general line, resolutely disassociates himself from the thoughts of the former Workers' Opposition, and finds the CC's mistake only in that it [TsA FSB alt: finds the basic mistake in party policy in that the CC] was a little tardy in making the transition to intraparty democracy. His historical information [TsA FSB ins: about why the Tenth Congress directives on worker democracy became a 'lost deed'] doesn't elicit denials from the CC members involved in the discussion, because their interpretations do not differ [RGASPI alt: does not elicit denial from the official side, for it does not differ in any way from the bureaucratic interpretation]. The question about the past and about the reasons for the 'delay' in implementing the Tenth Congress's decisions is far from unimportant, for it is the key to understanding several aspects of the current situation.

Up to the time of the Tenth Congress, everyone understood that the cessation of war and the transition to peaceful economy building demanded changes in the party's organisational forms and its work methods. This became especially clear when the Congress accepted the New Economic Policy and demanded that each party member actively participate in implementing it. The resolution about intraparty worker democracy [TsA FSB ins: despite important limitations on its principles] to a significant degree satisfied all representatives of tendencies then at the congress [TsA FSB ins: including the Workers' Opposition].

Oppositionist tendencies [TsA FSB alt: Supporters of this last tendency] saw in the realisation of this resolution the possibility of drawing broad working-class circles into party life and the means of having influence upon party policy. However, along with this were accepted another two resolutions concerning the struggle against [TsA FSB ins: so-called] 'anarcho-syndicalism' and about unity [TsA FSB ins: in their content directed against proclaimed principles of workers' democracy]. After the congress, [TsA FSB ins: under cover of these two resolutions, right away] a battle was waged against 'deviation', that is, against delegates from the 'Workers' Opposition' at the congress, and likewise against all those who elected them.

Struggle was conducted not along an ideological line, but by denial of work assignments, expulsion from places of work, systematic transfers, and even expulsions from the party. Any party member, who defended the Tenth Congress resolution on worker democracy, was declared a supporter of the 'Workers' Opposition' and a demoraliser of the party and was subjected to all sorts of lashes of the command regime being consolidated within the party.

This struggle continued right up until recently, on the eve of the current discussion. Not only official leading party circles waged it bitterly, but also the leaders of the current opposition, many of whom were members of leading party bodies. In harmony with the 'apparatchiks', the present leaders of the 'opposition' intimidated party circles with shouts about the 'danger of the Workers' Opposition'. They also supported unconditionally all methods for intraparty suppression of [RGASPI alt: methods of intraparty terror against] any party member who, in attempting to speak in defence of the revitalisation of party ranks, referenced the Tenth Congress resolution, which now the leaders of the 'opposition' proclaim to be their 'symbol of faith'. There you have one of the most important reasons why Tenth Congress resolutions were not implemented.

Having received full approval and support from the current oppositionists to punish supporters of the 'Workers' Opposition', the CC felt strong enough after the Twelfth Congress to apply some of these measures toward those who, in the opinion of Politburo leaders, do not share its line of work and conduct against it open or hidden struggle [RGASPI omits 'and conduct against it open or hidden struggle']. The registration and assignment apparatus directed blows at unrepentant Trotskyists and Democratic Centralists. Supporters of these tendencies began to be removed from political posts. The struggle gave rise to conflicts both within and outside of the CC. These conflicts coincided with very alarming phenomena in the working class, which revealed our weakness.

Is this intraparty struggle accidental? Not only Old Bolsheviks but anyone who knows party history would say it is not accidental. Bolshevism as a tendency grew and became stronger through factional struggle. In the interests of the political goals it had set for itself, the Bolshevism of illegal times did not fear intraparty splits. Truth vindicated the Bolshevik position. In the days of the underground, our party vigilantly watched over its command staff, especially in the provinces, so that it was a well-rehearsed choir of one mind with the centre, fiercely fighting throughout the whole history of Bolshevism for the principles of revolutionary Marxism and consistently for the proletarian line in the general struggle.

And so these tried and true old traditions of selection and organisational skills revived with extra strength right after the Tenth Congress. However, our comrades failed to take into account two things: the radically changed general circumstances, in comparison with underground times, and the changes in the social and party composition of the RCP(b). Well-tested old traditions for selection of personnel and organisational methods filled it with alien content [RGASPI ins: that with time became an element directly hostile to the proletariat]. The composition of our party is socially heterogeneous and it radically differs from what it was during underground times. More than 85% of its members have no underground experience. Besides that, the party has a fair amount, higher than 22.5 thousand, of people who departed from other parties. A large share of them occupied leading party posts.

Our party waged and continues to wage struggle for a single party of the Russian proletariat. In these conditions, our old organisational skills turned out to be insufficient. They demand reinforcements and changes [RGASPI omission: they demand reinforcements and changes] [RGASPI ins: and have suffered defeat. History has not justified them. In this matter we have turned out to be correct, meaning those of us who do not pretend to regard ourselves as direct pupils of comrade Lenin, but who do not cease to be Bolsheviks]. That which the party endured and still experiences, we foresaw [RGASPI alt: many foresaw] already two years ago. All the dangers [TsA FSB ins: springing from the social diversity of the party's composition] which official CC representatives now do not hide, we frequently put before it, but the CC remained deaf to our warnings [RGASPI omission: we frequently put before it, but the CC remained deaf to our warnings].

The Situation within the Party

No one disputes the fact that our party is going through a crisis. Likewise no one disputes that the crisis we are experiencing demands such measures, which everyone calls 'a decisive turn to a new course'. But not everyone explains the reasons for the intraparty crisis in the same way, nor does everyone agree how hotly the crisis is burning. There is a variety of contributions toward understanding the new course. Those who express official 'party opinion' are preoccupied most of all with not allowing supporters of the opposition 'to acquire capital' for the new course. They try with all their strength to earn trust in themselves and to receive the CC's nod of approval for the announced new course and approval of its policy.

Oppositionist comrades Preobrazhensky and I.N. Smirnov, who defend the CC's general policy against our accusations about its mistakes, find CC policy incorrect only in the area of intraparty building. We consider the opposition's initial interpretation to be limited and incorrect. Never have Bolsheviks separated the party's 'general policy' from its organisational aspect. If the opposition thinks that the CC's general line of policy was incorrect, then the CC has all the grounds to prove and declare that it is also correct in intraparty policy [TsA FSB ins: since the latter was dictated by the former].

We do not agree with this opposition or with [RGASPI ins: official] supporters of other [RGASPI alt: any] courses either in defining the reasons or about the character of the crisis itself. Not sharing separate sections of the CC's policy, we consider it mistaken mainly in economic policy, in relation to which all CC policy [RGASPI alt: all other CC 'policies'], which is directed toward holding onto power, has become equated. This situation finds confirmation in that circumstance, in which the very appearance of discussion coincides with the economic crisis and as a matter of fact is called forth by it.

We formulated our accusations against the CC before the Tenth Congress, at that Congress, and at the Eleventh Congress. We expressed distrust toward

CC policy, because, mildly speaking, it in fact manifested little care and attention toward the interests of industry, which atomised cadres [RGASPI alt: monstrously atomised basic cadres] of the proletariat and called forth growth of unemployment in the country. Only this year have we heard recognition of the mistakes the CC committed in regard to large industry.

[RGASPI ins: Comrade Preobrazhensky, as they say, asked us in public if we want to say that under comrade Lenin policy in this direction was not correct. His phrasing attests that official representatives' methods for catching heretics are also not alien to comrade Preobrazhensky. These expressions remind us of the methods of 'orthodox' priests, when they disputed with sectarians during tsarist times. When debating the latter before an audience and 'orthodox' missionaries felt powerless to prove their correctness, they turned to their opponent and shouted out with pathos: 'And what will you say about the devoutly orthodox tsar?' Obviously, the opponent fell silent at such a turn in the debate.

But we are fortunate that our debate is conducted in significantly different conditions and that we can continue it fearlessly, even when our opponents phrase their questions in such a way. We ardently answer him that Bolsheviks have never regarded their leaders as sinless priests. We frequently expressed our disagreement with comrade Lenin directly to him and in public. Let comrade Preobrazhensky read speeches made at the Eleventh Congress. He'll see there that we did not agree with comrade Lenin's assertion that we do not have a proletariat and so forth. Proof of that which-]

[TsA FSB ins: Just let comrade Preobrazhensky read the speech at the Eleventh Party Congress, he'll see there that we did not agree (with this basic CC policy, without doubt at decisive moments dictated by comrade Lenin nor) with confirmation (of it) that we don't have a proletariat and so forth.]

We can see evidence that in recent years party policy has deviated away from the proletariat and its 'narrow' guild interests in that the party's social composition during these years also has unswervingly changed and not in the interests of the proletariat. The 1922 census yields 514,529 party members and candidate members. By social composition, they are then distributed in the following way: full and candidate party members of factory cells – 54,283 or 10.5% of the total, party members of transport cells – 36,626, or 7.1%, military cells – 122,542, or 23.8%, peasant [cells] – 154,228, or 30%, soviet cells – 97,571, or 19%, school [cells] – 49,279, or 9.6%. Thus, we have in all 17.6% proletarians and employees connected to production or transport.

Our everyday link with broad nonparty masses is expressed in this statistic. The same statistic tells about the degree of workers' actual trust in our party. This is not the first time we have seen the danger for the party in the prevalence of nonproletarian elements within it. Moreover, we do not consider this phenomenon to be accidental. Did peasant elements, service intelligentsia, and the petty bourgeoisie accidentally pour into our party? The fact that they found an expression of their interests in the party's policy explains their entry. Petty bourgeois elements' recognition of party policy as 'their policy' would not be so bad, if we had not observed alongside this the reduction in the party of the proportion and role of the proletarian element.

When nonproletarian elements show recognition of our party's policy and at the same time workers and the rural poor are not only estranged from the party but also depart from it, this should be considered an indicator that the policy of the party and of its leading bodies conceals great dangers. Not only statistics, but also recent events and the strike wave of workers indicate that this estrangement and departure of working masses happened. We find in the resolution of the Petrograd Gubernia Party Conference confirmation of the estrangement and departure of rural poor. Even comrade Kalinin notes this phenomenon in his speech in the Hall of Columns. The party should quickly take account of the political consequences of this. Such is the political side of the question.

The party's mistake in the main area of policy (economic) led to squabbles in the CC's organisational work. Not accidentally did we see the flourishing of that party regime which now encounters such sharp condemnation. The policy, which has been conducted up to now, could not lean for support on proletarian initiative [самодеятельность]. Nonproletarian party strata turned out, by their very psychology, to be rewarding elements for the command system of work. The methods of work being established did not make them indignant. They found satisfaction of their social-class interests in the CC's policy, which was implemented under this system, and its methods. But there is a limit to everything. The party regime, which was built on the suffocation of intraparty initiative and criticism, not only became obsolete long ago but also has placed the party recently on the edge of danger. This danger very acutely manifested toward losing contact with the proletarian and semi-proletarian masses and in losing leadership over them.

As we now see, all those who play at democrat come together to deny the 'old regime' in the party. Now all have become 'democrats'. They have finally remembered the lost deed [грамота] of the Tenth Congress. However, not all understand that this regime is tied to policy and from this they make the false step of accusing the party apparatus of all sins. There is a great share of truth that in the party apparatus there is an unsuitable element. There are former SRs, Bundovists, and Mensheviks, who are alien to it in spirit. There are not so many Old Bolsheviks any more. But where is our guarantee that this noisy anti-'apparatchik' struggle, which is raised now, will yield actual political results and not just lead to the replacement of some apparatchiks with others?

Bolsheviks have become accustomed not to beat around the bush, but to get to the point.[112] (This thing needs to be thoroughly thought out.) [TsA FSB: strikes the idiomatic expression and recommends: Bolsheviks became accustomed to thinking things through to the end]. Hatred of the apparatus is just an expression of dissatisfaction with the regime that has riven party members into two camps: those managing and those being managed. This can be overcome not simply by replacing some individuals with others, but only by implementing another system, which would establish correct relations between leading party bodies and the broad masses of party members. If we want to realise a new course seriously and for a long time, then least of all do we need a sensation in this matter. It should not be forgotten that the new course is being reduced only to the apparat. Among all the noise, it can turn out that the matter will be reduced to the simple replacement of some individuals with others [RGASPI alt: replacement of a crow with a magpie], with no benefit for worker democracy.

On Worker Democracy

Some comrades depict the intraparty dispute as a rivalry between the party's younger generation and its elders [RGASPI alt: party conservatives and liberals]. There is nothing more mistaken than such an assertion. No one has succeeded in creating any principled differences among intraparty organisations on the basis of age differences. The dispute began with questions about work methods, forms of organisation, and transitions to the basis of defining interrelations between party bodies and the entire party mass. [RGASPI omission: from 'There is nothing' to 'party mass' inclusively.]

[RGASPI ins: If you look at individual personalities, you see a picture of comrade Kamenev, the Moscow nobleman [дворянин], struggling with comrade Preobrazhensky, the liberal representative of financial state capital. Each of them praises 'his own democracy' and each is concerned only 'about his own people'. From history we know that when conservatives and liberals struggle among themselves, workers' democracy loses. So it has occurred among us. Both representatives, liberal and conservative]

Struggling for intraparty democracy, they [RGASPI: lower case 'struggling'; omits 'they'] forget to stipulate that in our party the business is not about democracy in general, but about worker democracy. This 'worker democracy' should not be understood as depriving nonworker elements in the party of the right to democracy. We understand worker democracy not only to mean the sum of

---

112   бить не по оглоблям, а по коню.

rights of each party member to participate in its affairs, but also to indicate the way in which questions are decided.

Some comrades [RGASPI alt: Conservatives and even some liberals in our party] are inclined to regard intraparty democracy as an instrument for suppressing voices or as a means for developing the orator's art in our party. We differ decidedly from such lovers of 'pure democracy'. We regard intraparty democracy only as the means to elevate party members' activity, reinvigorating the party ranks, and increasing its cohesion. But we consider it most important that worker democracy make it possible for the entire party collective to participate in deciding the party's political problems and influencing its character and direction.

At the same time we do not close our eyes to the fact that successful development of worker democracy is closely tied to radical changes in our party's social composition, so that proletarian elements would decidedly dominate. Moreover we understand the word 'proletarian' not in the abstract sense [RGASPI ins: of social estate [сословной]], and we place before the party the task of attracting into its ranks workers now occupied in production. This is not a technical task, and it cannot be decided by organisational-pedagogical measures, but should be realised politically.

Only by directing policy toward expansion and development of industry and elevating the material situation of workers and consumer services for them, not just in declarations but in actuality, can we count on the necessary flow of them into our party. Only the development of all branches of industry and the intensification of production of objects of mass use [RGASPI ins: and not SR Manilovshchina[113] to save small peasant farms from cheapening of bread] will allow us to successfully broaden the 'scissors' question and will create better conditions for further development of agriculture. Only this path will make it possible to absorb unemployment, bring together the revolutionary working class that has been dispersed through the years, raise its proportion in the government, and offer a way out to the rural poor groaning under the kulaks. This is what we contribute to the understanding of worker democracy and to its successful development at the current time.

We regard the CC and CCC decision only as the first step on the path toward realising the Tenth Congress resolutions on worker democracy, but in this decision we see many indications (concentration and so forth), which in their

---

113   This is probably a reference to the character Manilov in Nikolai Gogol's poetic novel *Dead Souls*. Shliapnikov is casting a derogatory and undeserved image of the SRs as impractical types who utter lofty phrases but who do nothing to improve the peasants' lives or the agricultural economy in practical ways.

very essence are directed not at consolidation and development, but toward undermining worker democracy. The party's current social composition does not give us confidence that the party will not further constrict the proletarian base in our country, and that this point about concentration will not be realised.

All vacillations in the party and beyond it, about which so much is now said, are only the result of the extreme weakening of large state industry, which is the main base of our dominion in the country, and of the extreme atomisation and material dissatisfaction of the working class. Its further weakening conceals in itself the deepest dangers of thorough weakening and even loss of our political supremacy. This danger has now become clear and understandable for everyone. If the CC, having taken the path of worker democracy, does not supplement it with policy in the direction indicated, it cannot successfully withstand these dangers and eliminate all disagreements within the party, including our own.

Party members worry about where is the 'guarantee' that the CC and CCC resolution will not turn out to be a 'lost deed' and that the 'apparat' will not swallow it up. The only answer there can be to these apprehensions is the activity and initiative of the rank-and-file without oppressive tutelage; the guarantee first of all is in this. All attempts by party functionaries to oppose or interfere with implementation of the 5 December resolution should be resolutely condemned and should meet the most energetic opposition from each rank and file party member. Those guilty of these attempts should be just as resolutely dismissed from leading posts.

Likewise, all those measures which aim to draw the entire mass of party members into discussion and decisions about party policy, guarantee against oblivion and loss of the deed. For this, barriers between the broad mass of party members and the leading bodies need to be abolished. There should be a practice of holding general assemblies not only of 'senior', 'active', and so forth, but of all party members, without dividing them into categories. [TsA FSB draft ends here.]

Party functionaries and executive bodies must be deprived of the right to decide party-political questions without proper authority to do so and over the heads of general assemblies, committees, and cells. We have allowed it to come to the point that organisers, 'group organisers', and secretaries think that their official position has awarded them the right to decide and express the opinions of organisations and cells without proper authority and without discussion. This must be ended.

Cells should be freed from importune tutelage and should have the right to assemble without the preliminary permission of official persons and committees. Simple notification of the committee fully ensures contact and orderly work.

Each of us has a single party identification card. We are members of the Russian Communist Party. We are deprived of the right to be present at assemblies of party members, however, if these assemblies do not occur in the 'courtyard', in which we are registered. This arrangement should be eliminated. Upon presenting identification, party members should be allowed at all party assemblies and even at open sessions of committees.

The system of secret work references and secret personal files of party members needs to be ended immediately. The general assembly of the cell should completely openly provide references about party members.

Make a transition from words to action about 'rapprochement' with production. Give party members the freedom to judge the management and work of institutions in which they labour.

Realisation of just these modest wishes would suffice to tear out by the roots the unhealthy formulation of the question about 'apparatchiks'.

The problem of material inequality among party members is inseparable from the question about intraparty worker democracy. It is utopian to dream about universal equality under the New Economic Policy. However, there is a way to eliminate the scandalous excesses, which demoralise not only on those who commit them, but also the surrounding milieu. To solve this problem, one needs to recall that once upon a time we decided this question correctly. After the October days, we decreed and implemented a statute about pay for senior government personnel. The regulation defined pay according to the wages of highly skilled workers. Why not take this route now? Why not ban holding more than one office, receiving multiple salaries, and similar 'sinecures'? This measure would create satisfaction not only within the party, but also far outside of it. It should be remembered that the Paris Commune took such a path.

About Factions and Groups

During discussion, representatives of the party's majority constantly confront the party masses with the question about groupings and factions. They indicate entirely correctly that, given the party's current composition, the creation of separate groups, which are linked organisationally and bound by special discipline, will inevitably lead to a party split. Now all adversaries from the opposition agitate and frighten rank-and-file party members with the real spectre of a party split. However, warning about the danger of a split doesn't accomplish much. One needs to think about how to avoid this danger.

The good intentions of just one side are not enough. We know this from our three-year experience. It doesn't take much to demand that any opposition would voluntarily refuse to consolidate into a faction. We need to create such conditions of work and interrelations within the party, which would not chase the opposition into complete isolation. The conditions, which existed in our party until the new course, pushed party members toward forming exclusive groups. The party's vital idea sought an outlet. It could flow only apart from official party paths.

We can relate much that is instructive from the experience of the CC's struggle against supporters of the Workers' Opposition and from the experiences of local committees that followed the CC's example. Since the Tenth Congress, thousands of comrades have been judged and condemned for thoughts about workers' democracy within the party and for a critical attitude toward economic matters. Dozens of party personnel [RGASPI alt: investigators up to the most important] were busy for months searching for factions of the Workers' Opposition, but all their searches failed pitifully.

After the Tenth Congress, despite the fact that no one could establish the presence of any organisational factional group of the Workers' Opposition within our party organisations, its supporters were constantly persecuted and judged precisely as organisers of groups and as demoralisers of party unity. Such measures painstakingly but unsuccessfully urged them to take the path of factional exclusivity [RGASPI ins: and when these methods did not produce results, then they tried direct provocation, but this was also unsuccessful].

It sounds monstrous, but we do have grounds to say that they attempted to provoke some supporters of the Workers' Opposition to speak out against the party. In order to politically discredit us, they systematically attempted to link us, as the former Workers' Opposition and a well-known ideological direction in the party, with Paniushkin and his party and with Miasnikov and his Workers' Group. Paniushkin and Miasnikov, however, never expressed the opinions of the Workers' Opposition. During the Tenth Congress Miasnikov supported the platform of the Ten. His departure from the RCP(b) has no bearing on or connection with the ideas of the Workers' Opposition. Miasnikov was no less hostile toward its ideas than was Iaroslavsky, who tries now to discredit us by linking us with 'Workers' Truth'. Miasnikov's signature on the Letter of the 22 serves as the best evidence that it was not a factional grouping.

In his 19 December article in *Pravda*, Iaroslavsky attempts to link the Workers' Opposition with Workers' Truth only on the basis that Workers' Truth considers Workers' Group the left wing of the Workers' Opposition. [RGASPI ins: But by no means does this attempt connect these tendencies; rather, it only justifies the strong word 'slanderer', which Riazanov flung at him. Iaroslavsky fulfills this unflattering role so enthusiastically that he doesn't see how this method can link even him to Workers' Truth.] Indeed, if Workers' Truth regards

Workers' Group so sympathetically, well the latter considers itself not simply Workers' Group, but Workers' Group of the RCP(b). According to Iaroslavsky's method, this leads indisputably to the conclusion that it is the direct and indissoluble kin of Workers' Truth.[114]

[RGASPI ins: 'Defending the Workers' Opposition is not my task, of course,' says Iaroslavsky in his article. We can reply to him that we have become accustomed to see him invariably in the role of our abuser and we think that 'abuse from you – that is a crown worthy of praise!'.][115]

Essentially, the direction that Workers' Truth takes is especially deeply hostile to the former Workers' Opposition. Workers' Truth characterises the Workers' Opposition as an objectively 'reactionary' group and as 'a wolf in sheep's clothing'. Iaroslavsky himself introduces the first of these characteristics in his excerpts from the 'Workers' Truth' documents.

Why, despite recognition of [RGASPI alt: if we all recognise] the danger of a split and of the universal desire for [RGASPI alt: if all wish] unity, the problem of the impermissibility of groupings is posed so acutely during the current discussion? In fact it is necessary to acknowledge that in our party there are objective pre-conditions for the disarray of party ranks and for the creation of groups and grouplets. This social and national diversity hides within itself these dangers. 'Good intentions', which they now call forth, are insufficient by themselves. Only by expanding the party's proletarian base is it possible to put an end to this spectre of a split.

Prior to reinforcing the party with proletarian cement, the danger of factionalism may be eliminated only by decisively realising intraparty workers' democracy. Realisation of workers' democracy will help the party reveal all those aspirations, which are now masked by the general cry about a new course. The direction of intraparty democracy along a worker line will keep the organisation from flying off the rails of the proletarian revolution. If in the process of realising worker democracy, the party will succeed in revealing that some parts of its social composition ('sectors') are determined to depart from the tasks of proletarian revolution, it is necessary to ease their path [RGASPI ins: by means of a purge. Since the Tenth Congress] Accusations of factional-

---

114   Throughout the article, 'Workers' Opposition' and 'Workers' Group' are in lower case in Russian, while 'Workers' Truth' is capitalised. 'Workers' is used as an adjective not as a possessive in the Russian.

115   The Russian expression is из уст его хула – достойный хвал венец and is from the satirical verses of Kondraty Ryleev, К временщику (Подражание Персиевой сатире 'К Рубеллию'). The translation in the text above is that of Sibelan Forrester (http://www .swarthmore.edu/Humanities/sforres1/translations/Ryleev.html).

ism, of the creation of groupings frequently have been formulated against the person writing these lines and hundreds of other comrades. We indignantly rejected these accusations, but not from fear of any measures directed against us.

Within the ideological tendency, which acquired the name 'Workers' Opposition', there were more than a few party members who had worked in the underground, who had observed factional splits, and who had made them. Bolsheviks [RGASPI alt: We in principle] were not afraid of a split, if they [RGASPI alt: we] recognised that it was useful for the revolutionary goals of the proletariat. In the circumstances we are experiencing now, we consider a split of the party disastrous for the proletariat [RGASPI alt: we do not consider a split to be a method capable of resolving the proletariat's and party's historical tasks]. It would confront the proletariat with the possibility of a new civil war in the most difficult conditions and would lead to the loss of its revolutionary conquests [RGASPI omission of text from 'It' to 'conquests'].

We have never hidden these thoughts. For this reason and from the clear awareness that the formation of groupings would inevitably lead the party to a split, we avoided factional consolidations. Despite being persecuted, like-minded individuals of the 'Workers' Opposition', who were proletarians, had been underground activists, and who lived in various cities, unanimously spoke out with the same line of thought. This is not evidence of factional links, but demonstrates the depth of their proletarian consciousness. There is no longer any basis for factional consolidations, given that it is becoming possible now to have intraparty discussion of party policy and consequently to influence the party's policy.

About the Apparat and Trotskyism

Political content is starting to fill the discussion about intraparty democracy. The slogan of changing the apparat crowns conversations about democracy. Comrade Trotsky's letter gave cause to speak of shaking up the apparat and reminded many of old disputes regarding Bolshevism's organisational principles. However, comrade Trotsky's letter alone does not provide us with enough material to exhaustively explain all the peculiarities of his position and the rebukes made to him for past 'trotskyism'. But we can judge comrade Trotsky's position according to how individual features of it have been expounded upon elsewhere.

We remember the trade union discussion [RGASPI ins: we hear him interpret economic tasks in such a way, with which we cannot agree]. In his formulation, the party should subordinate the 'apparat' to itself. We see in this an attempt to resolve the question of organisational order, without connecting it to the party's political tasks. In this way, organisational schemes substitute for party policy and the struggle for the apparat replaces the dispute about the essence of party policy. Moreover, this struggle is not connected with political goals. This allows one to conclude that in the current discussion, comrade Trotsky's and the opposition's single goal is just the seizure of the apparat.

We see this also in the question about the attitude toward Gosplan and its role, in connection with the Twelfth Congress's decision on this matter. We blame [RGASPI alt: accuse] the CC and the Politburo not for bypassing Gosplan and deciding one or another economic question without its final word, but because they in their decision surrender to the influence of elements alien to the proletariat [RGASPI ins: and often decide these questions to the harm of the interests of the working class. This circumstance notwithstanding, we do not have any grounds for trusting Gosplan more than the Politburo]. The question about the economy is primarily a political question, and as such it calls forth disagreements.

The whole sum of comrade Trotsky's proposals, which we know about from the press, can in relation to economic policy be reduced to the further concentration of state industry and to strengthening Gosplan's role. In order to more greatly reduce large state industrial enterprises, to further reduce our material and social base, and to strengthen only the regulating principle in this very industry, he proposes to seek the quickest exit from the unceasing industrial and economic crisis in the country for the past few years, especially the severe crisis in heavy state industry. We do not share his views and his hope to resolve these problems by concentrating industry. We support the certain extension and expansion of production of items for mass use and likewise of machines and equipment for reorganisation, and the elimination of our industry's and agriculture's technical backwardness.

The dispute about the apparat assumes a political character. Comrade Trotsky did not indicate what direction he would give to the work of a 'new' or renewed apparat. Many hands extend toward the party apparat. In part they reach out in resolute favor of concentrating our industry. In this gravitation toward the apparat, we see the danger of the substituting a technical measure for a political task. The question about concentration concerns both policy and the fate of the working class. No one will successfully depart from it by taking refuge in organisational measures. Up to this time, there have been no grounds for setting comrade Trotsky off from other CC members on policy matters. On all major policy questions, he was in solidarity with other CC members. Now in the course of discussion the question about direction of economic policy is placed anew. By the answers to this question we can judge how well-founded are the slogans about seizing the party apparat.

[RGASPI alt: now comrade Trotsky has brought up for discussion questions, which he should answer, in order to stop all false interpretations that that he is trying for factional isolations within the party or around it. Comrade Trotsky commands the pen and word well. His direct answers to questions should put an end to all those rumors and implications, which are passed from ear to ear and only clog up and complicate the course of discussion on tasks placed before the party. From answers to openly posed questions, we can judge how much of a basis there is for accusations made against him and if there really are disagreements between him and other members of the CC.]

6   Resolution Proposed by A.G. Shliapnikov and Others from the Former Workers' Opposition, [January] 1924[116]

Having heard the comrades' reports and the ensuing debate, the assembly of party members resolves that:

1) Refusal to implement the resolution about worker democracy, which the Tenth Congress proclaimed, created in the party a regime for suppression of intraparty criticism, enterprise [самодеятельность], initiative, and comradely links among party members ...[117]

2) The intraparty regime has turned the party of the proletarian revolution into someone who has taken a great vow of silence [мольчальница], which has helped isolate party members from broad circles of the non-party worker masses and the rural poor ...

3) The leadership has arranged party work according to a command system and has selected personnel who are suited only to obeying commands. This has limited intraparty enterprise [самодеятельность], strengthened bureaucratism, led to red tape [казенщина], and ousted workers from leading bodies ...

4) The 5 December decision of the CC and CCC about implementing intraparty democracy makes it possible to struggle against the dangers threatening the party, especially with the danger of an internal split into 'higher-ups and rank-and-file' [верхи и низы] ... This decision makes it possible to unify all forces, strengthen the party ranks, and restore their health.

5) This assembly insists upon steadfast implementation of this resolution. It recommends putting before a party court all those who try to delay or oppose the implementation of this resolution.

---

116   RGASPI, f. 589, op. 3, d. 9103, vol. 2, l. 2, parts missing. This resolution seems to have circulated in an unknown number of party cells.

117   The ellipses here and below seem to represent material I omitted when taking notes.

6)   [missing] ...
7)   The following measures are necessary ...:
     a)   abolition and reduction of the intermediate stages of appeal [ин-
          станции] within the party;
     b)   making a practice of holding general assemblies in party work;
     c)   depriving party officials and executive bodies of the right to decide
          questions without proper authority and over the heads of the party
          cells;
     d)   [missing]
     e)   presenting to the cells the right to assemble without needing ad-
          vance permission from officials and committees ...;
     f)   repealing secret reference-keeping and 'yellow tickets' for party
          members;[118] ...
     g)   bringing more workers into the party ....

7   **A.G. Shliapnikov's Speeches at the Second Khamovniki District
      Party Conference, Moscow, 7–10 January 1924[119]**

Shliapnikov's speech at the Second Khamovniki District Party Conference,
Moscow, 7 January 1924

[The original document is not separated into paragraphs and appears to be an
uncorrected part of the stenographic report.]

Comrades, I should disclose the real reason why intraparty democracy has not
been implemented. Some comrades in the group to which comrade Sapronov
belongs helped hinder its implementation. It should not be forgotten that when
the Tenth Congress discussed questions of intraparty construction, it did so in
the context of the Kronstadt uprising and all those difficulties confronting the
party at the moment of transition to the New Economic Policy. So a line of argu-

---

118   'Yellow ticket' was a term applied to prostitutes' personal identification documents in
      tsarist Russia. In this context, it was probably used ironically to refer to records that stig-
      matised oppositionist party members.
119   TsAODM, f. 88, op. 1, d. 168, ll. 65–83. The Khamovnichesky or Khamovniki District of
      Moscow was one of the city's six or seven districts (raions) in the early 1920s. Moscow
      gubernia also included 17 rural districts (uyezds) then. See Pirani 2008, p. 253. The district
      is home to the Cathedral of Christ the Saviour, Novodevichy Convent, and the Pushkin
      Museum. In 1924, it was also a location for a Red Army Military Academy, which was later
      named after M.V. Frunze.

ment from Kronstadt and peasant uprisings is historically incorrect. Another reason would be more accurate, but some reasons are rooted in the New Economic Policy itself.

Comrade Kamenev has touched upon the New Economic Policy a little. In economic policy, as the outgoing year demonstrated, the party is confronted by the need to implement measures relating to worker policy, which cannot be carried out within the party by means of worker democracy and initiative. When Comrade Kamenev passed over this question, he did so cunningly, in my opinion, and comrade Sapronov covered up his cunning. They forgot one crime they committed jointly after the Tenth Congress. Along with the resolution about worker democracy, the Tenth Congress also accepted two more resolutions. One was about unity and the other was about struggle against so-called deviations. It must be pointed out to you, comrades, that the latter two resolutions especially defined our intraparty construction. I know this from my own personal conversations with comrade Lenin, as well as from the struggle, which flourished behind the scenes of this party unity. Comrade Kamenev, we as Old Bolsheviks should be a bit more logical.

After the Tenth Congress, the party was confronted with the task of assembling that unity, which was violated before the Tenth Congress. No matter how we swore at the Tenth Congress that we are united as one, this unity was a lie. In fact there was no unity. If comrade Kamenev had said to us here that the task is to bring together hundreds and thousands of comrades, no matter what the sacrifice by any groupings, if you please, we would have regarded the comrades' explanations here a little differently. But there is no such approach as the one Comrade Lenin took during the time when I was a CC member. Although the Party Central Committee did not literally disperse the Congress of the Metalworkers' Union, it scandalously violated the rights of the communist faction of the congress.

The thoughts with which Comrade Kamenev begins and which Comrade Sapronov echoes explain why workers' democracy could not achieve victory in our country in 1921. The CC gave paramount importance to the liquidation of all those factional phenomena within our party, which took place before and during the Tenth Congress. These factional groupings were the Workers' Opposition, Trotsky's group, and some subgroupings. Well, at least Lenin did not hide this. When the question came up about drumming me out of the Metalworkers' Union, he said to me personally, 'your Union of Metalworkers is essentially nothing else than the party organisation of the Workers' Opposition. The Metalworkers' Union has 500,000 members. We do not have so many workers in the party. The entire party consists of about this many people. It is clear that we cannot leave you there'. That is what he said openly.

We struggled against such views. We in the Workers' Opposition did not regard ourselves as a faction. We just considered the Workers' Opposition to be a certain direction of thought. During the three years since 1921, we comrades have most of all avoided any possibility of consolidation. I say this especially gladly now, for Emelian Iaroslavsky's latest attempt to link me with Workers' Group and other sorts of illegal oppositions has ended in the most shameful failure. Comrade Kamenev himself will confirm that neither the Politburo nor the CCC has any materials from the history of our intraparty struggle, which could brand us with factional particularism [обособленность]. This false fear of factionalism also is present in the current debate, comrades. It is no coincidence that Comrade Kamenev is emphasising factionalism right now in all debates against Preobrazhensky and Sapronov. If, first of all, we do not dispel this basic danger in the presenter's thought, which is a pointed attack against the opposition, we will not resolve the problem of actually building relations within the party on the principles of worker democracy.

I think that we should not expect anything more from the policy that promotes fear of criticism and oppositionist phenomena. We should be reconciled. The CC especially should understand that not all criticism and not all oppositionism lead logically, historically, or necessarily to factions, a split of the party, and so forth. Everything depends on how the CC behaves itself. From my personal experience, I know that at the Eleventh Congress we were backed into a corner on the case of the 22. Comrade Kamenev cannot deny this. I should just say, comrades, the case of the 22 and earlier such cases were about implementing and realising intraparty worker democracy.

So it is nonsense, comrades Sapronov, Preobrazhensky, and Osinsky, that struggle for worker democracy within the party began with the Letter of the 46. It's the utmost nonsense. I will say why this is so. Your democracy begins from September [1923]. After the Tenth Congress, the majority of the CC saw in the Workers' Opposition the chief danger for the unity of the party. Without fail, we are depicted as factionalists, who attempt to demoralise the party, which I indignantly refute. Now in principle, we are not afraid of a split. During my lifetime, I have split organisations across the whole expanse of Russia. The Bolsheviks never feared a split.

Kamenev: Except in their own party.

Shliapnikov: Correct, comrade Kamenev. But don't forget that there are moments when not everyone agrees about what they consider to be their own. We disagreed with the Mensheviks over what to consider our own and we split.

So, comrades, it's necessary to look at it from the direction of struggle waged by the majority of the CC within the party. Then much of what was revealed in September last year will be clear. If the struggle waged against us since the Tenth Congress had made the party stronger and truly united, then I, your humble servant, would only welcome it. But I declare that it was waged by the most disgraceful, vilest methods, which have made the party unhealthy. I know that under the cover of unity, they took all possible measures of retribution against heterodox thinkers. In fact, unity has not existed and does not now exist. Therefore, these methods of struggle against so-called splittist factional elements did not withstand historical trial. They turned out to be false.

Comrades Sapronov, Preobrazhensky, and Osinsky, you were in that camp, which struggled against us and reviled us in all kinds of ways during these three years. Yet you felt you were in danger, when [V.G.] Knorin's Uchraspred [subdepartment of records assignments] apparat was directed against you. Comrade Sapronov here asserted that they began by transferring comrade Rakovsky, but he did not finish telling the story. There were also some former Trotskyists. Finally, they say, there are rumors that a campaign was waged against Trotsky within the CC. So far there are no written documents. I don't trust rumors. Comrade Kamenev, maybe in your concluding words you'll either confirm or deny this. But in any case, from this moment nostalgia for democracy begins. These comrades have seen that there is no other method of influencing the party's policy and its life, except for worker democracy, which so far has been linked only with the name of the Workers' Opposition. Indeed, they have just now stigmatised anyone who supported or spoke about worker democracy. Look in the archives of the CC and CCC. How many documents there expose people as being in the Workers' Opposition?

Such is my little correction to those historical truths, which resound from this tribune, and I would ask you to very much keep it in mind. Nevertheless, despite all that is odious in our party's internal daily life, the party has turned out to be a prisoner not of worker democracy, but of other methods. Some call this the military method, which is barrack-like and bureaucratic. Very many names exist. But why, dear comrades, has neither comrade Sapronov nor comrade Kamenev given an answer? I will help them. I will try to unite them on the basis of my thoughts. It is no accident, comrades, that in our country these methods have achieved supremacy. If we will address our party's social composition now, it would not be Makhaevshchina. If I had said this to you two years ago, then we would have been crucified in all directions. But now even comrade Kamenev has to join arms with the Workers' Opposition in order to struggle against an empty and often incoherent opposition. I can only salute the CC, if it will stand with us not only in defining phenomena, but will also make the corresponding political conclusions.

I believe that our party's social composition is the reason why our party has not yet pulled away from such methods of work. Some here have already discussed the party's social composition, which according to the 1922 census was: 10.5% (54,000) workers in factory cells; 7.1% (36,000) in transport work, counting candidate members; 23% (122,000) in military cells; 30% (154,000) in peasant cells, 19% (97,000) in soviet cells, and 9.6% (49,000) students. If you speak about worker democracy, it should be clear that is not simply about chatter or democracy as an instrument for training your voices or as a school of orator's arts, but about democracy as a definite system of intraparty policy. Well indeed, worker democracy can be nice only for this 17%, but the remaining 83% have been satisfied with that policy, which we have had. Only thus is it possible to explain why these methods survived in our country. I will go further. As long as the social composition is the same, everything remains as it has been, no matter how much noise will be raised about worker democracy.

Comrade Kamenev asked us why so much noise began after the CC resolution about worker democracy, but not before it. He explains that it happened because Trotsky wrote a letter stating views that his colleagues in the Politburo and the CC do not completely share. I read this letter and I do not attribute to it such great significance as comrade Kamenev does. I agree with comrade Kamenev that there is an incorrect formulation in this letter. Bolsheviks have not been divided by age, but by class if anything. Trotsky himself says that neither old men nor young ones will decide, but the social composition will do so. That is the main thing.

I can talk about something from CC history. Comrade Kamenev rebuked Trotsky for having erred in procedure when he appealed over the head of the CC to party members. I disagree with this. I think that CC members have the right to associate directly with party members, certainly not through the Orgpolitburo or some sort of Secretariat.[120] True, for such thoughtlessness I was once put on trial. In August 1921, when I was still a CC member, I spoke at a meeting in the Society of 1886 about some matters related to the CC's attitude toward our industry. I was put on trial. Moreover, the prosecutor was comrade Lenin. Trotsky supported the accusation and accused me of that exact same thing, with which those same colleagues are now charging him. There is some historical information for you.

---

120   The Orgburo, Politburo, and Secretariat were ostensibly separate bodies. Shliapnikov's reference to them here carries a mocking tone.

Kamenev: So we are consistent.

Shliapnikov: So it emerges that when you join the CC, you pledge that you have no right to speak without its consent. I spoke out twice and it put me on trial twice. This is my personal divergence and I cannot agree to censure Trotsky for it. It would be better if members of the Committee would take a formal position, both about my speech in a worker cell and about the essence of this letter, like they did very clumsily on the pages of *Pravda*. But to accuse Trotsky and to see this letter as counterrevolutionary is premature. There is no evidence for a trial of Trotsky. Such a letter is very meager as a factional platform, even for Trotsky. The two theses about old and young do not suffice to organise a new faction. Therefore, Comrade Kamenev, share with us something more substantive from the Politburo, only something which in principle and actual fact deeply differs from Trotsky's offering. This would be worthy of such an assembly, where you speak. Otherwise, it emerges that not only Sapronov turns the whole affair into a squabble, but that you also muddy the waters around this personal squabble.

Deeper in the party there are disagreements. The CC's task is first of all to reveal these disagreements. During this time of party calm, the party has not been accustomed to carry out Marxist analysis and to report about its own mood. The CC should have helped the party in this business, but we have not seen this. Comrade Kamenev exerted himself very much here on account of the CC's past errors, but he was very surprised by how we raise so much noise and flog ourselves over these errors, which the CC committed. Well, this is because the party elects the CC. I do not share this opinion. I think that we do not flog ourselves, but we flog someone. The situation, nevertheless, is such that the party did not participate in solving those problems and mistakes, which we have acknowledged from the tribune. This is the horror of our situation. If you and I would resolve all problems, about both the economy and intraparty life, then things would have turned out differently. Since our CC decided these questions especially clumsily, then we flog the CC. If the CC does not want to be flogged, well I fully understand that. The experience is familiar to me. (Kamenev: we request flogging for the case [просим сечь за дело].) We'll try, Comrade Kamenev. (Laughter.)

The CC and I have many disagreements, which I have always emphasised. Despite these theses about party building and economic policy, I am now trying to find it possible to agree with the CC on many points. During the past three years, I have tried not to disagree with the CC, but even so I still do not find full satisfaction about the main questions of economic policy. You know Zinoviev's and Kamenev's opinion about the international policy of the Russian revolution and lately about the German revolution. Our party has not forgotten its international tasks, contrary to White Guardist and Menshevik rumors about how we will become demoralised and will forget our international tasks as soon as we transition to peacetime construction. This has not occurred. This is a lesson about our international guiding star, but there is another star in domestic economic policy. This is largescale heavy industry. Since the beginning of NEP, the CC's policy toward large industry has not been simply mistaken. It has been completely criminal.

Comrade Kamenev probably knows that this is my sore spot. In the CC's theses, we find many such troubling places, which tell about how our comrades incorrectly imagine the alliance of largescale industry with the so-called peasant market. All this, if to take in mind also the practice of our last three years, places the further development and even the very existence of our large-scale industry under the deepest doubt. I am especially interested in that industry, which restores resources and tools of production, which means heavy industry, mining, metals processing, production of machines and tools for agriculture and other areas. This means, in other words, all that which creates constant capital [постоянный капитал] in the country and which gives a powerful jolt to developing productive forces.

Our main industry has been bruised year after year and systematically so during the entire time of the New Economic Policy. We made a mistake here, they say. In one of his reports, perhaps in the Hall of Columns, Comrade Rykov declared that yes, in 1920 a little mistake was committed in relation to large industry. The little mistake was that orders for locomotives, which our industry so craved, were given to Swedish and German factories. He says that this was committed in 1920. I should say that it was also committed in 1921, 1922, and 1923. If the wish of comrades Osinsky and Preobrazhensky will be fulfilled, well it will continue also in 1924.

Comrade Sapronov exposed comrades from the Politburo, who proposed a very large break-up [ломка], which verged on actual repeal of the monopoly on foreign trade. There you have the sum of extraordinarily deep disagreements, which we have in our party, some of which can be recognised. I would ask that our party be safeguarded from these disagreements. The resolution, which was printed in the 1 January issue, essentially says much in the same old spirit about economic policy, but it is poorly coordinated with our everyday practice. This everyday practice breaks up everything, even the good parts of the resolution which we have.

In this resolution, there are attempts to explain the crisis which we are now experiencing in relation to the imbalance between the development of agriculture and small-scale industry on the one hand and large-scale state-owned industry on the other hand. According to the theses, it emerges that right now we have overproduction and crisis, thanks to the disparity between tempos of agricultural and industrial development, which for the past year have reduced small scale industry almost to nothing, while largescale industry made a giant step forward. But this crisis has strange characteristics, which make it appear to be not a crisis of overproduction, but the opposite, for this crisis occurs at a time when there is an extraordinary rise in the price of foodstuffs [продукты]. As is known, prices rise as a result of goods shortages. Once again, they propose to us that concentration will cure this crisis.

Kamenev: Who?

Shliapnikov: Yes, comrade Kamenev, it is there in the theses. I took you at your word in the academy, when you said that you reject the system of concentration. But if you will look in the theses, it is there. Only you say that it has to be done more rationally. If it's assumed that the Putilov factory in Piter needs to be closed, then that would be a major political mistake. If Briansky will be closed, then supposedly it is a smaller political mistake. I think that no matter where we shut down a large enterprise, all the same we will undermine the basis of the proletarian revolution in doing so. I am not inclined toward favouring local interests. The theses, however, give full rein to this possibility.

Comrades, we think that our CC's main mistakes were in economic policy. These mistakes were made first at the end of 1920, then in 1921, and in 1922. We are still feeling the effects of what they cost us. Unfortunately, I do not have numbers, but overall during these years we spent more than 700 million gold rubles on large orders abroad. I could tell you even more about how we spent this capital and how we wasted it. I have a report of the Worker-Peasant Inspectorate, in which it says how we placed these orders. These mistakes become especially difficult to accept when you find out that they were committed despite protests from some CC members, worker organisations, and economic bodies, which are interested in lifting up our heavy industry, not in building new factories in Sweden and Germany. Essentially this is what occurred recently. You just think about it, we suffer because of a hundred million gold rubles (or hundreds of millions). We have no circulating capital. Yet we bound our already poor treasury to foreign orders in the hundreds of millions. Upon investigating this matter, the CC commission decided that from the point of view of formal soviet auditing, all these orders represent the thorough pumping out of our gold reserves in order to support and strengthen industry foreign to Russia. It contributes to the well-being of big bankers and is done at the expense of our industry. That is how the CC's past economic policy can be characterised in relation to our large-scale industry.

My fear for our largescale industry right now is based on some data, which is already available from the current year. Here before me is a memorandum on large-scale industry, which is composed by Dzerzhinsky. He is also a CC member and he probably does not diverge from comrade Kamenev on economic policy. Comrade Dzerzhinsky, who manages transport, now protests most energetically against orders that take resources from transport for locomotives, cars and all kinds of spare parts that it doesn't need. From the departmental [ведомственной] point of view, comrade Dzerzhinsky has demanded, probably in the CC, that they spare him from these expenditures and force our large-scale industry to work for the population in general. When you hear from such senior persons such pitiful and foolish yet telling proposals, about how to force large-scale heavy machine industry to work for the free market, it is tantamount, comrades, to the final closing of all of our metallurgical, metalworking, and machinebuilding industry. Even now it does not amount to much, but nonetheless it is still breathing. This is how comrade Dzerzhinsky puts the question, despite the obvious existence in the CC of other perspectives on our large-scale industry. I only want to say that comrade Dzerzhinsky did not protest when hundreds of millions were wasted on ordering locomotives abroad.

Kamenev: Who gave the orders?

Shliapnikov: The Politburo.

Kamenev: When?

Shliapnikov: The orders were given right up to 1922.

Kamenev: They began since 1920.

Shliapnikov: They began also in 1920. I guessed you right, comrade Kamenev. You want to say that V.I. was with us then (laughter). Comrades, could you be any more malicious? Comrade Kamenev wanted to ask me who was Commissar of Transport (Narkomput)? It was Trotsky. I will say more. I witnessed the vilest campaign, which sickened many railway workers. It was conducted over the course of months, on the pages of our newspapers, and at some congresses. The campaign was about how our railways will come to a halt in two months, if we will not order from abroad a minimum of 3,000 locomotives. That was their justification. Then when they went to make the orders, they made them with such a reckoning so that the first locomotive would appear in our country not in two months but in approximately three years. (Laughter). We guessed perfectly well that these were blackmailers and adventurers, but we could not convince the CC of this. The CC supported these adventurers against us, and stigmatised us. When questions are decided so, it is a bit more than a simple mistake. It is a crime.

Chair: Two minutes remain. (Voices: we request a continuance.) How much more time do you need?

Shliapnikov: I will try to finish by four o'clock. I will try to cut it short, so as not to trouble you too much with my speech. The resolution of these economic questions worries us. I very much depart from comrades Preobrazhensky and Osinsky on economic questions. I'm not sure about Comrade Sapronov. It seems as if I disagree less with Comrade Sapronov. It's not because of what Larin writes, but because Sapronov and I spoke with one another. It seems as if he and I evaluate concentration in the same way. But one CC member issues a published memorandum, which is entirely directed against our large-scale industry. Here is what he writes. (Voice: who?) Yes, Dzerzhinsky, who is also People's Commissar of Transport. That the metals industry should set as its main task the satisfaction of the needs of the broad population, keeping in mind its weak ability to pay. The production programme of the metals industry should be composed in conformity with this principal task.

Now comrades, in order to understand the demand of this so-called population for the products of large metalworking and metal extracting industry, I turned to the statistics of 1913. If you take a population of 130 million and expect each person to pay 25 kopecks, well we will have 30 million for the entire metals industry. Here it is proposed that we stake all our grandiose large-scale extracting and processing industry on these 30 million. It is hard to imagine anything pettier. Only a handicraftsman who knows the handicrafts market can reason in such a way. Never has large-scale industry been sustained by this market of the population. It was sustained chiefly on account of mill equipment, factories, and mines. That's how. It provides and creates the means and tools of production and of reproduction. That's what it provides, but it never has been maintained by producing teapots, samovars, pot covers, and similar wares. Comrade Kamenev asks from where to take the resources. I would ask Comrade Kamenev, why did you not think, when you hauled 700 million gold rubles across the border, why did you not think that these questions confront us? There also comes to mind one crank economist, who at one time said to me: comrade Shliapnikov, really do you not understand that for us in Russia, gold does not have any value? There was such an eccentric. If you want, I'll name him. They will name themselves. (Laughter.)

I have ten minutes left, comrades. As before, problems of large industry worry us. They continue to fester and CC resolutions will not resolve them. This chatter about the alliance of workers and peasants and about scissors will continue to be just chatter, if the CC will not take action by expanding industry. In order to close the scissors, that is to give cheap wares to our peasantry, only one path is possible. This is not the path of concentration of industry, but the path of seeking resources in order to develop it more powerfully. (Voice: How?) How, you want me to say. Comrades, I indicated what did not need to be done. Let's put the task before the CC. I am not sure that the resources we possess have been spent expediently. They would have been spent more expediently on developing our largescale industry, rather than to support handicrafts and all sorts of small-fry.

We need worker democracy not in order to exercise our voices, but in order to solve problems of economic policy as the first priority. I, for one, am less angry at the CC now for one reason. This is because it is possible now for me to develop before you views, which the CC has considered criminal. This gives me the opportunity to win over supporters of my views everywhere. I think that the CC will not see any factional intentions in my effort. Still the effort alone to have supporters of my views everywhere can serve neither for comrade Kamenev nor for comrade Iaroslavsky as grounds for accusing me of factional consolidations [закрепления], as they want to do to comrade Sapronov.

But comrades, let's nevertheless consider why is there is such a fuss about factions and groupings. Obviously, there are such dangers in our party. There are, but where are these dangers, where do they hide? Comrade Kamenev should have pointed to the mixed social composition and exceedingly small proletarian base in our party. If you want for worker democracy to fully triumph in our party, so that Comrade Kamenev should not have to prove next year why he could not gain it this year, we can propose only one measure. This is to conduct the policy of the CC and the policy of the entire party, so that it would attract workers to us. It is not accidental, comrades, that there turned out to be such a social composition in our party. What do you think? Did our blue eyes attract the peasants, the service intelligentsia, and the petty bourgeoisie [мещанство]? No, it is not accidental. Obviously, the party's policy attracts more people from those groups than from the mills and factories. That's where the solution to the problem is. It is utter nonsense to think that we can attract workers into our party simply by wishing for it to happen. Economic policy needs to change so that this million, who work with us now, would feel our party to be as near and dear to them as it was in bygone years of struggle. Yet we do not have this. We should also bear in mind the danger which threatens us from the direction about which they think least of all. For every million who are working, we have a million unemployed. More and more prominent on the list are those, who cannot get by on dwarfish plots of land. They arrive in towns, which are under the authority of the Communist Party, and where they do not find defence for their unemployed, poor-peasant interests.

Here are the questions in their entire expanse and we do not see any redress of them. The chief thing is that we do not see in the CC's theses any resolution of these contradictions in our economic policy and in our economic life. I wish that the CC would take initiative, not that individuals who do not belong to the CC would seek the way out. I am afraid that comrades, who seek the way out without doing so under the banner of the CC, would be perceived as striving to create a special platform. Therefore, I especially am careful not to propose anything like a resolution. I would like for comrade Kamenev in his concluding word to respond to all those disquieting thoughts, which I have shared with you and with the CC. Only by politically formulated answers is it possible to judge the CC, Comrade Sapronov, and the comrades who go along with him. In the light of this great policy, we can judge or condemn, reject or accept Comrade Trotsky's formulation or another one.

As for all these bits of information regarding who behaved how in which historical period, I can cover this briefly. In our party of Old Bolsheviks, we did not regard our leaders as priests. For us Comrade Lenin was not such a sinless priest. It happened that we and Comrade Lenin swore at one another [крыли] in our meetings and he did not take offense at this. Comrade Kamenev was sworn at. There is not such a person in the party who could say that he is without sin. Further, in the most difficult circumstances probably, there will be even fewer such people. But in order to sin and err as little as possible in the future, let's conduct party work and general policy together collectively. Then we will not flog Comrade Kamenev and comrade Kamenev will not judge others in the capacity of a priest. Only this formulation will make it possible, Comrade Kamenev, to avoid factionalism and groupings. Only under the light of general party discussion can we avoid possible groupings. Social heterogeneity provides a strong basis for these groupings. Of course, comrades, I can say from my personal experience that it is very easy to consolidate groupings, when within the party there is persecution of a certain part of it. One needs to be very experienced and disciplined, in order not to take this path. Comrade Kamenev is correct that there are such positions to which you are led not by your personal wish, but by objective circumstances.

If we do not want Comrade Sapronov and others to slip into particularism [обособленность], then those within the party should behave differently. In some districts, where official circles turned out to be in the overwhelming majority, they were so unwise as to completely isolate the opposition from elections to the congress. This phenomenon is fraught with the most profound danger. It is the kind of danger that can push a certain part of the party to consolidate into a grouping. From my personal experience, comrades, I can say that they drove me away. They linked me with a fourth international, which was connected to the GPU. Comrade Kamenev knows this. In my time in 1921–2, I informed the CC about this. I told it about many such efforts to create groupings around me, near me, with me, and without me. Right now I say to you sincerely: when they speak to me about factionalism and about this group's effort to create a faction, I see before me sad pictures. It is not only those who are accused who create factions. Factions can also be especially organised for them. I would like very much for no one in our party to take this second path.

Now I'd like to say two words about old and new party members. Comrade Kamenev and many others dwell very much on the old guard. Of course, no one suspects us of an unfriendly attitude toward the old guard, but to say that the opposition or Trotsky in particular is guilty of disrespect toward the old guard, in my opinion, is somewhat unjust. I happened upon an official booklet of the CC titled *Registration and Distribution of Work*, printed in 1923, in which I find a most extraordinarily disgraceful characterisation of our old guard. This was in an official publication, which was printed in many thousands of copies for our gubernia committees and so forth. This old guard, as depicted here, consists of those whose biographical questionnaires are registered with the CC. These are 1,680 people. Of these, approximately [illegible] are workers, [illegible] peasants, 30% office staff, and 12% are miscellaneous.[121] The CC characterises this old guard in such a way: 'Attempts to carry out' (reads).

What can be a viler characterisation of our old guard than that, which is given in an official press organ? Further, there is such a place, where they force young and old to knock heads [стукают лбами]: 'The reason is of somewhat a different order' (reads).

I have not even heard Sapronov set people off against one another so. Further, 'It would be risky to go too far' (reads).

I will make some proposals, which touch on questions of intraparty democracy (noise).

Chair: How much more time do you need? (Voices: Please, please.)

---

121   The percentages he gives for workers and peasants are illegible. I have not been able to find
        this publication, *Uchet i raspredelenie rabot*, by a search of Russian library online catalogs.

Shliapnikov: I need two minutes. I will not read any more excerpts. I just want to conclude with the following. If we want to think seriously about realising worker democracy in our party, then we need to remember once and for all that only radical change of the social composition of our party can make this possible. We need to enlarge our party to hundreds of thousands of workers very soon (applause). Only by this path can we avoid vacillations in our party. This is possible to do not by technical measures, but by making entry easier. The matter is not about reducing the number of questionnaires workers have to write upon entering the party. These are trivialities. If necessary, workers will write twenty times more questionnaires than have been written so far. No, it is necessary to solve this problem in a political way. Party policy must be changed so that workers would see it differently than in recent months, when workers demonstrated and struck against us in Petrograd. The class force must really be fulfilled within the party. The revolution would be realised in full. This call not to lose sight of the interests of the peasants is correct, but we should not transform our communist party into an appendage of the petty bourgeois element. (Applause.)

∴

A.G. Shliapnikov's closing words, Second Khamovniki District Party Conference, 9–10 January 1924[122]

[The translation below is of Shliapnikov's heavily edited version of the stenographic record of his speech.]

During these two days of the conference, I have observed how some comrades want to use intraparty democracy, which is unfolding, as a means for exercising their vocal chords. I think that the problems confronting our party will not be resolved in this way. Intraparty discussion should be based upon worker democracy. It should expose those deeply principled questions, which force the assembly to seethe with excitement. Comrades would display a passion that does not contradict the supposition that we all support unity of our party.

Yesterday proletarians carried out reconnaissance [поиски] in this hall and then delivered speeches. This pained me and others also, I think. Comrade Zinoviev was partially correct, when he pointed out in his first article on 7 November that our party proletarian, the worker from the bench, when

---

122   TsAODM, fond 88, opis 1, d. 170, ll. 29–42.

defending the party higher-ups at our plants and factories, has lost touch with nonparty, rank-and-file workers. Yesterday, what we heard here was graphic confirmation and illustration of this. Comrade Kamenev probably exploits speeches by some of the proletarians who spoke yesterday from this tribune. But we should warn him that we acknowledge as correct comrade Zinoviev's assertion about the backwardness [отсталость] of workers who are party members. We want to supplement his explanation by saying that the cc's intraparty policy is guilty for this backwardness of broad circles of proletarian masses in the party. Personally I have been luckier than comrade Zinoviev. Earlier I found and still find even now more than a few outstanding, developed workers among those who are in the plants and factories. But our party bodies do not welcome them. It is not enough to be developed. They also demand obedience. This is why we see sometimes only very backwards workers at our meetings.

The historical information, which has been given here, is incorrect. The Tenth Party Congress was held when disorder [стихия] raged in the country and when Kronstadt presented a terrible danger. We discussed intraparty democracy while cannons thundered. We regarded it as a means of strengthening, soldering, and developing our members. All historical information which is given here (about how it was specifically Kronstadt that interfered) does not stand up to criticism. This information is dictated only by the rather understandable effort to justify one's behaviour for the past three years. Warnings, which were sounded frequently from within our party against the policy of stifling any kind of criticism and any kind of initiative, inevitably met resistance from the cc. If I were inclined to dig among the garbage,[123] as they say here, I could remind you and Comrade Kamenev of very many bitter moments, but I have too little time to spend it reminiscing.

I disagree about much with comrades from the opposition Sapronov and Preobrazhensky. I perceive that they are insufficiently consistent and inconsistently logical when they divide the policy of the cc into various sections. While in general and on the whole it is correct, there are black holes [чёрные пятна] in parts of this policy. I think and will try to prove to you that in the economy, which is the main question, our cc has often committed the very same mistake during these years. This mistake is ignoring our large-scale industry and it reverberates across the entire economy, in the work of our party apparatus, and in intraparty building. We Bolsheviks never divided party policy into sections. If we are to speak about mistaken cc policy, well it consisted of incorrect analysis

---

123   I translate as 'dig among garbage' his phrase перетряхивание старого тряпя.

of the role of large-scale industry in our economy. The last theses, presented by the Central Committee and printed in *Pravda* on 1 January, also are guilty of this.

They want our basic heavy industry, which is extracting and processing, to ride on the footboard of a peasant cart. I should say that never has large-scale industry fit upon a peasant cart. Those comrades are deeply mistaken in thinking that if we want to develop our large-scale industry, then first we should prepare petty industry and help it transition from small to middle, from middle to larger, and from larger to largest. This is the deepest delusion. Never has our industry been built so. It has never developed anywhere in this way. Right now we note the growth in our country of small-scale industry, meaning handicrafts. In this lies a great threat to our large-scale industry, for this growth comes at the expense of the plunder of our large-scale industry. Comrade Kamenev indicated to us here that we are not grateful to our peasantry, that we fleece it, rob it, and even pillage it. This is how he expressed himself. I have heard more than once such words [словеса], I remember that Vladimir Ilich even used such a word [словечко], but later he nevertheless rejected it. We did not find it in the stenographic report. This is about the claim that all of us, including the working class, live at the expense of the muzhik. There is such a theory in political economy, which teaches that everything is from the land and everything is in the land. But you know that Marxism introduced some corrections to it, so that no traces remained from this theory. We know that the SRs also posited that everything is in the muzhik and all of socialism is in the peasantry.

Of course, our policy cannot ignore 85% of the peasant population. Only fools or blind men would close their eyes to the backwardness of our country and to its agrarian character. But, comrade Kamenev, those who want to murder our industry and cut off the smallest movement toward communism for the sake of our country's backwardness can be called something stronger than fools or blind men. We have carried out such a policy frequently over recent years. I already pointed out to you how we gave orders abroad not only for locomotives, but also for many other types of industrial products. During this time of foreign trade, we pumped abroad around one billion of gold, which was a direct loss. It was the outright murder of our large-scale industry. You will not discard this fact from history and politics. Right now, despite the fact that the CC's theses were written as if they oppose concentration and support large-scale industry, in practice everything continues to remain as it was of old. As before, one sees the policy of resolute concentration, contraction [сужение], and orders abroad.

Comrade Osinsky strongly supports concentration and goods [товарной] intervention. I never agreed with him and I don't believe at all in his democratism. I have many grounds for this, at least from the practical experience of his activity in Tulskaia gubernia. But the matter is not about this. We have had disagreements in the party. Opinions have changed. There is no misfortune in this. The misfortune is that intervention continues. Comrade Osinsky told us that now Gosplan and STO are also elaborating a plan for goods intervention. Some branches of industry, which would be affected by this plan, were mentioned here. Among these is scythe production. The production of scythes is one of the simplest types of production in the metals industry. We have scythe factories. We also have handicraftsmen in Vladimirskaia gubernia, who produce scythes. Our factories and our handicrafts artels could make millions of scythes in our country, if all government resources, which we fling over the border, would be dumped into our industry. The same thing can be said about sugar, leather, and other goods.

We know from the metalworkers' report how they complained to the People's Commissariat of Transport (NKPS) about Dzerzhinsky's policy of attempting to destroy our locomotive, machinebuilding, and train carriage manufacturing factories. Now all economic planners send abroad orders for equipment of midsize and light industry. They attempt to receive from abroad equipment, which requires immediate replacement, rather than order it from our factories. This is from official sources. Comrade Kamenev said to me that there cannot be talk about closing Putilov factory. He confirmed the same thing regarding Briansk factory. Of course he was surprised when I asked him: How do things stand in the Donbas? He expressed indignation at the very thought of closing the Donbas. Yet here the newspaper *Trud* from 6 January tells us that the coal industry administration now proposes to carry out reductions in the Donetsk coal mining industry.

This is done at a time when, as you know, demand for fuel is rising in our country as industry develops and grows. Simultaneously, some of our state institutions buy the very same fuel abroad. The newspaper *Ekonomicheskaia zhizn*, which is STO's most official press organ, writes that Petrograd needs 37,000,000 puds of mineral fuel. They decided to buy 15,500,000 puds in the Donbas and 15,500,000 puds in England. You know that in England we pay for delivery from the mines, we do the loading, we hire the steamers, and we unload them in our ports. The Petrograd Oblast Ekoso proposes such conditions to our Donbas: free delivery to us in Petrograd.[124] It follows that they are to pay for

---

124   Ekoso is the abbreviation of 'economic conference' or 'economic council'. Ekoso first appeared in 1920, when the Council of Labour and Defence (STO) was created at the Eighth All-Russian Congress of Soviets on 29 December 1920. It was in charge of coordinating the activity of institutions in securing the country's defence and economy building and working out a unified economic plan.

the railway carriage and delivery for nine months on credit. The English coal industrialists so far have not opened a nine-month credit for us. Indeed, they sell us this coal for cash. Payment is due on the day of loading it.

Comrade Kamenev, I would like to place this before you and to say that it's not much to write theses and pronounce big words about how important large-scale industry is for us. One needs to carry out policy which actually supports it. If we had in fact followed through on this, we probably would not observe such ruin in our large-scale industry. We would not see the skilled cadres of our working class so dispersed. Answering my question about industry, Comrade Kamenev retorted that right now our industry sits on the spine of the 'population'. That is what communists, who are our comrades, love to say now. Some of them adopt such a tone, as if they already speak in the name of 'the entire Russian people [народ]'. It is not true that our industry does not create value and is only held up by the backbone of the population. It would be more accurate to say that not all the value accrues to the government. Because industrial enterprises' capacity is still small, it does not permit the kind of profits, which could be had in capitalist times. But it cannot be said that our worker lives at another's expense and that he does not labour enough for his pitiful allotment of wages.

Comrade Kamenev was wrong, when he spoke about the 'robbery' of the muzhik, the heavy tax, and the consequent, emergent political danger. He indicated that the most 'predatory period' in our country was in 1920, on the eve of the New Economic Policy. I resolutely dispute his assertion. I never take anyone at his word. Comrade Lenin taught me this. He pronounced in my presence the phrase, 'only fools take people at their word'. Comrade Kamenev assures us that 1920 was a year when we robbed the peasantry of much. But do you know what share all of agriculture (raw materials, bread, labour, cartage, and various taxes) held in the general state budget for 1920? I will take the most official data from the collection *On New Paths*.[125] This book was published by the STO commission, of which Comrade Kamenev is the assistant chair. The budget at that time was about one billion, 600 million. Agriculture's share was less than 25% in prewar value.[126]

What came together in these one billion, 600 million in prewar rubles? Production, except for fuel, totaled 512 million, fuel in all forms was 350 million, food supplies together with raw materials composed 392 million, and railway

---

125   Possibly he is referring to Miliutin 1923.

126   В бюджете того времени составлявшем в общем около 1 миллиарда 600 миллионов, в довоенной стоимости доля сельского хозяйства была менее 25%.

transportation at 300 million.[127] If you count postal and telegraph services and other parts of the state-owned economy, then we come to approximately one billion, 600 million. From this it is clear that the peasantry, which is 85% of the entire population of the Republic, provides only 25% support for the government. Let Comrade Kamenev have this 25%, for it is dear to him. But this does not mean that we should, from the rostrum, cry out that it is hard for him [тяжко ему]. One needs to investigate for whom it is difficult and why. One needs to know that our agriculture has fallen behind. It still has not been drawn into the ongoing capitalist revolution. Many peasants come to be involved in the capitalist revolution when they are cast out of agriculture. This question is very complex. You won't resolve it by shouting about the low prices of agricultural produce. Shouting will only help to create favourable moral circumstances for the NEP bourgeoisie and all sorts of middlemen and kulaks, who become rich from the food supplies of the countryside.

Such was state revenue in what was, in comrade Kamenev's opinion, the most predatory period. You should know also that everything remains the same. I have in my hands Sovnarkom materials, which were just published in *Ekonomicheskaia Zhizn*. In these, we find some thoughts regarding the 1923–4 budget. From these materials, it emerges that state revenue received from agriculture through direct and indirect taxes was 385 million gold rubles, which is about 25% of the entire revenue [доходная часть] in the state budget. In such a way this supposedly extortionist [грабительское] ratio of 1920 remains apparent also for 1924.

We'll move on now to the nature of those burdens borne by our peasantry. Comrade Kamenev says that we suffocated the peasants with indirect taxes, in addition to direct taxes. [Cryptic sentence, which is difficult to translate.[128]] Indeed, we apply excise duties chiefly on industrial products. Consequently, it means seven-tenths of that falls not on the peasants, but on the urban population. Thus, he disproves himself here.

Nonetheless, what kind of burdens are these? We can compare these burdens only to the prewar period. Only by it can we judge how cruel the tax policy of our proletarian dictatorship is. Taking these data, we see that all of it together is about 50% of what the peasants paid before the war. This gives us the key

---

127 Toward the end of the conference, Shliapnikov introduced a correction, which might have related to this part of his speech: 'Comrade Kamenev rebuked me for carelessly using numbers. I will introduce precise information. The commission received credit for 300 mil. not at the end of 1919, but in October 1920.' (l. 98).

128 Несколько держится главным образом на семь десятах городским рынком, операется на городское население.

to understanding why we remain in power, given the supposedly extortionist nature of our power, about which shout not only Mensheviks and SRs, but also some eccentrics from our own party. Yes indeed, it is because the peasant sees that he profits most under us. It is only for that reason and not because the Politburo knows very well how to maneuver among the petty bourgeoisie.

If we still add to this that the peasants received land, meadows, forests, and property valued in the several billions of gold rubles as a result of the October Revolution, then you can easily explain why the peasants 'tolerate' us, as they say. It is thanks namely to this, rather than to any tricks and subterfuges.

Now I will address the topic of scissors. They say to us that if we cannot make these scissors meet, then the peasants will not tolerate us. I should like to restrain Comrade Kamenev's bellicose ardour and scaremongering. No, it will not lead to an armed uprising. The peasant will not seek cheap wares by means of the bayonet. However, this does not mean that there is no danger. The danger is that expensive industrial goods push the peasant toward products of small handicrafts industry. We can see how weavers' looms and garrets, where they make handicrafts, appear next to the largest textile factories. This is a direct return to handicrafts [кустарничество]. For us this is as dangerous as open armed struggle. But it is a pointless undertaking to struggle against this by making a noisy racket.

So how are we to struggle against the expensive prices of industrial wares? Well, two paths are taking shape. The path Comrade Osinsky proposed is that of 'goods intervention' [товарная интервенция], which was practiced earlier and killed our industry. Comrade Kamenev's solution, judging from the theses, is the same old song about 'making a base' [базирование] on the peasant market. Comrade Preobrazhensky tried to reconcile the two approaches. But neither of these proposals satisfies me.

I don't agree that we can eliminate the scissors gap by means of goods intervention or by some other maneuver in international trade. These scissors are a product of the lack of regulation [неналаженность] of our production. This lack of regulation of production is not so much technical as it is political. The scissors directly result from our industrial paralysis. The crisis came into existence not because we have too many wares, but because we produce too few wares. We cannot produce more industrial goods, because there isn't sufficient circulating capital. When the CC theses state that industry should strictly conform to the direct peasant market, I fear that this will be understood so that, if this directive is implemented, our industry will be compressed in order to match the purchasing power of today's peasant market.

The capacity of the peasant market is still poor. This path will force us into 'logical concentration'. According to some economists' plans, logical concentration will provide income to the government by closing all 'unprofitable' enterprises and throwing all resources into the so-called 'profitable' ones. This will leave one blast furnace in the south and two in the Urals. It will close Guzhon and other enterprises in Moscow. Clearly, this will stab our large-scale industry in the back. We cannot solve the scissors problem in this way, it stands to reason.

The scissors question is about the further development of our industry. At one assembly, Comrade Kamenev was wholly in solidarity with me on this question, but there is nothing new in the CC theses, which he is defending now, in comparison with what was said at the Twelfth Congress. At the Twelfth Congress, there were some positive achievements. Nevertheless, the resolution included a point, which we cannot reconcile with the new course and even less with the course toward worker democracy. This is the point about concentration, the significance of which I already spoke to you about. If we want to seriously resolve economic problems, then the solution can only be expanding all of our large-scale industry. In this way, we will also create a market for the grain, which our peasants produce.

Right now, some economists are attempting to solve the problem of the low price of grain by doing so in the countryside itself. This is a mistaken policy. The solution to this problem should not be sought there, but in the towns, and shouting about the low price of bread won't help. Escape from those inconveniences, which have accumulated in the countryside, is possible only by increasing the size of the urban population, the growth of the proletariat in our country, and its influx into our industry. What do we see now in the countryside? Here you heard comrade Solovev, whose speech needs to be remembered. It contained nothing as terrible as many people thought. One just needs to understand him. Maybe he spoke incoherently and his thoughts sometimes got confused. But his main idea was that in the countryside under NEP, a poor peasantry (bednota) was created, and that our party has given nothing to this poor peasantry. Pekar, who spoke in the name of the proletariat of Khamovniki district, asked the CC to satisfy the peasantry and the entire proletariat also after it.

We need to assimilate the old Marxist truth about what we can do for the bednota and explain it to these comrades, instead of supporting harmful illusions about giving a horse, a cow, and an agricultural machine to each peasant who seems poor. We cannot do this. We can only unify the bednota into collective farms in the countryside and present machines and tools to these farms on credit. This we can do. But to think that we can preserve their dwarfish farms in the conditions of kulak competition would betray basic Marxist concepts. I think that we should explain this to comrade Solovev and he will quickly understand. I suppose that Comrade Kamenev will not take this path, for he is too respectable a Marxist to support such errors. But can we return to creating committees of the poor in the form, in which Comrade Solovev proposed them? This means to create them as we did in 1918, with the plunder of the kulaks in mind. Of course not, because this path would return us to the beginning of 1921. We cannot go along that path. Currently, the committees of the poor in the countryside essentially should be collective farms of the rural poor. This is one of many questions around the peasantry, which demand the party's solution. The other is class policy in taxation.

Up to now, the rural poor have not been considered much in our country's taxation policy, so the kulaks have had the advantage. Many comrades have said so. On this matter, the CC probably will act fully in line with those proposals, which were introduced here. Probably we will not disagree about this. The main disagreements among us will be about the relationship between industry and other branches of the economy. We have not yet seen from the CC any clarity regarding this question. In part this serves to impede me and others who think like me from supporting the CC with all the energy, with which we always supported it during our party's illegal existence and during the revolution. There is no clarity. As far as we understand, this line regarding industry is obviously petty bourgeois. I have only five minutes remaining, according to what has been allotted to me as a democrat of a special brand.[129] I suppose you will allow me to finish up talking about intraparty democracy and will give me as much time as the others have had.

Voices: We request that his time be extended.

Chair: In agreement with the regulations, I present you ten minutes.

Shliapnikov: Thank you. I do not demand more. Now I will speak about worker democracy and non-worker democracy. Comrade Riazanov crashed upon me with the rebuke that he will not give us 'workers' democracy'. At the military academy, Comrade Radek voiced the opinion that the resolution of the Tenth Congress on intraparty democracy meant that it should be limited by the borders of the worker sector. Despite all my love for proletarians and all my 'so-called Makhaevshchina', I most resolutely reject such offers. We have not become accustomed to share out participation in our party work by social estate [посословно] as proposed by comrade Radek. Indeed, it is completely

---

129   Согласно урезанного для меня, как демократа особой марки.

impossible to carry this out organisationally. But the CC should give direction to this democracy, just like the Tenth Congress gave it.

It is no accident that the Tenth Congress did not speak about just intraparty democracy. I think that Comrade Kamenev cannot refute my point. The Tenth Congress posed the question about intraparty worker democracy. What does this truly mean? Does it mean depriving party members who are not proletarians of participation in party work? It means nothing of the sort. The Tenth Party Congress invested certain content in this formula for party work. Therefore, I think that it's necessary to fulfil worker democracy not simply by exercising one's vocal chords, which I have frequently heard here, but by adopting a definite policy to expand proletarian might and the proletarian base within our party and in the entire country beyond its borders. That's what this worker democracy means to me. It is a means for strengthening, unifying, and developing our party.

Comrade Solovev here expressed the wish that orators should be a little clearer. One comrade from among the workers declared that it seems as if everyone agrees that the party needs to be cleansed, but that he cannot understand why the speakers look at one another so maliciously, if they all agree. Twenty years ago, I also was very angry when I happened to be present in our party during a time of disagreements between Bolsheviks and Mensheviks. I was such a virtuous youth that I sincerely desired that all socialists would be brothers. It seemed to me that in arguing among themselves and rending apart the organisation, social democrats committed a crime. It took some time before I became convinced that the argument had a deep character and wouldn't be resolved virtuously. Then I took a definite position, so by the fifth year [1905] I was a Bolshevik.

Comrades who speak here propose that everyone should unify around a purge, but they have forgotten one thing, which is that it's also necessary to agree upon whom to purge from the apparatus. For example, Comrade Kamenev probably would like to purge the party of such members as me. He already expressed this desire rather intensely at the Eleventh Congress. Other comrades probably want to purge Comrade Sapronov or [three words marked out and illegible] the party from Comrade Sapronov. I personally bear no grudge against Comrade Kamenev or Comrade Sapronov. I do not want to purge the party of them. But I do want to deprive the CC of the possibility to purge the party of those with the temerity to have an opinion, which departs from that of Comrade Kamenev. (Applause) So far we have not had this in intraparty policy. I was once put on trial just for having disagreed with the CC on some questions. All attempts to find factionalism and groupings and to establish my participation in them ended in a pitiful fiasco here, there, and everywhere.

We know Comrades Zinoviev and Kamenev from past work in the illegal underground. When they and others warn here of factionalist danger and nominate Comrades Sapronov, Preobrazhensky, and me as dangerous characters, then we should resolutely reject such insinuations. We should indicate that we have not had such intentions in the past and do not have them now. Likewise, I do not consent to accuse Comrade Kamenev and the majority of the CC of factionalist actions. Since they have a majority, it is ridiculous to speak about factionalism. But I would like for the majority to not use its power in order to hang on us the labels of factionalism and to attempt to unify us into a faction. This they have tried to do and still try to do.

If we want to avoid groupings, we should make it impossible for the CC to act among us, so as to drive away party members who think differently from it on one or another question. The CC should not drive members into a faction by stopping at nothing in its attempts to maintain party unity. In my earlier report, I already spoke to you about how the so-called Workers' Opposition was frequently ill-treated after the Tenth Congress. This happened in Moscow and beyond, all with the CC's sanction. Here I rebuked Comrade Osinsky, who then rebuked me and declared that I am a political bankrupt. I can invite Comrade Drozhzhin as a witness, for he also judged me at the Eleventh Congress. Tell me if I have changed at all in the political sense. You will say no. In the past few years, Comrade Osinsky frequently changed his positions and his moods. He wrote in favour of democracy in 1918, yet in 1920 in Tula he tied this democracy into knots.[130] At the same time, he accuses me of bankruptcy. Well, I do not consider myself to be politically bankrupt. We think about and analyse the CC's line, particularly its economic policy. This does not attest to my bankruptcy. I frequently uttered these ideas earlier, I express them now, and I will struggle for them until I see that the CC actually will support and expand our large-scale industry, not just in words and resolutions.

Regarding intraparty construction, it's as if the CC's intention to carry out the 5 December resolution is supposed to smooth over any disagreements. But we have witnessed actions here and in other districts, which indicate that the CC is in a fighting mood. As before, it holds to the course of not allowing any criticism or heterodoxy. Of course, we should refuse to support its practical politics in this regard. The question about the apparat worries comrades very much, especially as Comrade Trotsky formulated it. This question is decided incorrectly. Obviously, we cannot smash the party apparat, but we can strengthen it in every way possible by building it on the principle of elections. If the oppos-

---

130   загибал этой демократии салазки.

ition will regard the matter so, then I will support it within limits, but while rejecting everything that is bad about the ways in which Comrade Osinsky and others interpret economic policy. [End]

After other concluding speeches:

Shliapnikov (l. 95): I should state a reservation [оговорок]. Comrades who are proletarians, metalworkers, and chemists have asked me if I am introducing a resolution, in order to divide the votes of the opposition, so that comrade Kamenev's resolution would pass. Comrades who were at the meeting have asked me this. In line with the fundamentals of proletarian dictatorship, I declare openly that I would not propose an entire resolution just to divide an assembly. But I do propose it with the support of the comrades from Kauchuk Rubber Plant, who agree not because they are elastic people but because they are proletarians. I ask that my resolution be accepted as a pillar that may be strengthened a little. Dissonant notes in it may be eliminated. My resolution is the following (reads).[131]

8   S.P. Medvedev, 'Letter to a Baku Comrade', 1924[132]

[Note about the document:

The document is translated here from the version published in the collection Felshtinsky (ed.) 1990, but with comparisons made to two different archival versions preserved in CCC files. One version was received from Baku and was never published in full, but it served as the basis for party leaders' criticism of the document.[133] S.P. Medvedev was not permitted to see that version, but he extrapolated from party leaders' statements that it had been doctored and he alleged that it distorted what he had actually written. In July 1926, Medvedev

---

131   His resolution receives very few votes, the exact count of which is not provided in the stenographic report.

132   Felshtinsky (ed.) 1990, vol. 1, pp. 90–101; RGASPI, f. 589, op. 3, d. 9103, vol. 2, ll. 226–33; TsA FSB, R33718, d. 499061, vols. 13, 41). The published version of Medvedev's letter is identical to documents among Medvedev's personal papers in the Central Archive of the Federal Security Service of the Russian Federation (TsA FSB). Shliapnikov's CCC file in the Russian State Archive of Socio-Political History (RGASPI) contains a comparative layout of both versions.

133   Bukharin wrote a 10 July 1926 *Pravda* editorial condemning the letter. Stalin denounced it at a 15 July 1926 party plenum (Lih et al. (eds) 1995, pp. 104–5).

delivered to the CCC a 'corrected' version, which was published in the collection cited above.

The version that Baku authorities sent to the CCC had stylistic, grammatical and spelling errors, which were uncharacteristic of Medvedev, and a few significant differences in content. One entire paragraph in the Baku version was missing from the version, which Medvedev offered in 1926 as a true copy of the original. I have not found any copy that was signed and dated by Medvedev in January 1924. Therefore, it cannot be certain how closely any of the surviving versions are to the original letter, which Medvedev mailed to Baku.[134]

There were substantive differences between the version received from Baku and the one Medvedev offered to the CCC as the genuine version. The version seized in Baku made it seem as if Medvedev had given up hope that European workers could be revolutionary. At the same time, he assessed Comintern methods in Western Europe as flawed. In the Baku version, Medvedev appears to disagree with the Comintern's assessment of European Social Democratic governments as bourgeois. Medvedev's version has no such statement. Finally, the Baku version presented him as an advocate of large-scale industrial concessions and foreign loans at the cost of major losses for the Soviet state. Because party leaders' published criticisms of the letter are reflected in the secondary literature, it is important to highlight the differences between the two versions when making the document available in English translation.

Below, I italicise the sections where Medvedev's purported original differs significantly from the version transmitted from Baku, and I place in brackets the relevant segment from the version authorities in Baku sent to the CCC.]

Sergei Medvedev's Letter to a Baku Comrade[135]
Dear comrade V.,

We[136] received your[137] letter and materials about the discussion in Baku. We saw and talked with comrade Kobyzev.[138] From the letter as well as from dis-

---

134   I have speculated elsewhere about the reasons for differences between the documents, but have not been able to consult archives in Baku, which might offer additional answers.

135   The translation was previously published in *The NEP Era: Soviet Russia, 1921–1928*, vol. 8 (2014), pp. 25–42.

136   'We' probably refers to himself together with Shliapnikov.

137   Uses formal 'you' [Вы].

138   According to Eldar Zeinalov (April 2017 correspondence), Kobyzev was a conspiratorial name for D.M. [or N?] Kolosov. Kolosov (b. 1874) had a technical education and had been a party member since 1904. A mechanic, Kolosov was working in 1924 for the Technical Supply Board of Azerbaijani Oil and was on a business trip to Moscow. According to the case

cussion with comrade Kobyzev it became clear that you still don't know about our article, which was published in *Pravda* on 18 January 1924.[139] It was written and submitted to the editors of *Pravda* on 20 December, when even here in Moscow the discussion was unfolding ever more broadly. All positions by that time had been defined. In our article we gave a clear stance toward all questions, which were placed for discussion. It's very unfortunate that this article didn't make its way to you. In any case you will now have it. We are sending it with comrade Kobyzev. Together with it, we are sending a clarification of our general positions: the stenographic report of comrade Shliapnikov's speech at the Khamovniki District Party Conference and a copy of the resolution which we introduced chiefly in worker cells. Examine these attentively and you will find answers to the basic questions in your letter. Keep in mind that in these materials we define only the basic direction of party policy, not touching on separate features of it in various areas. In this letter I treat only those aspects which perhaps *after familiarisation with the indicated material* [phrase omitted from version 2] will still be insufficiently clear for you.

1.   About your resolution it needs to be said that it incorrectly defines the role and significance of the CC's internal party policy. One should never forget that this area of party policy is a derivative, subordinate area. It is defined by the party's fundamental and all-defining economic policy. And this last, in the end, is the result of the correlation of *class forces in our country, their proportion and strength in the country's general economy. It is defined directly by the social composition of our party, where the working masses compose only one-sixth or one-seventh of its members* [class forces of our side, its proportion and the economic strength of each social class in the country's general economy, the result of the correlation of each group's proportion in our party's current composition, where worker groups, where the working masses compose just one-sixth or one-seventh of its members]. Thus we define the *dependence of intraparty policy* [significance of intraparty policy and so forth], clarifying it as such in our documents. It would be deeply incorrect to think that it's possible to divide various areas of party policy into separate – completely independent parts and then, sharing the basic economic policy of the CC – to

---

against him, upon his return to Baku he suggested making copies of Medvedev's letter and the other documents and reading them aloud to workers in factory shops (RGASPI, f. 589, op. 3, d. 9103, vol. 1, ll. 293–300, 8 February 1926, 'O gruppe Bakinskikh "oppozitsionerakh": rezoliutsiia plenuma partiinoi kollegii kontrol'noi komissii AKP(b), 12 January 1926').

139   This article was published under A.G. Shliapnikov's name as author. See document #4.5 ('Our Differences') above.

successfully and logically criticise those separate parts or features of its policy, which in their essence are a direct result of the content, character, and direction of this economic policy. This mistake is the basic flaw of your resolution. It is aggravated even more by the fact that in your attempts to defend your resolution, you emphasise that you are not criticising or, more accurately, are not linking your disagreements on questions of intraparty policy to the general policy of the CC. Here in Moscow we have the 'September Opposition' (comrades Preobrazhensky, Piatakov, Smirnov and others) – which on this basis was smashed and completely demoralised. You could possibly not escape this either, if in Baku in official party circles there were more *experienced* [propertied][140] politicians.

2. a) In questions about economic policy – we do not share the general character of it that the CC gives it in its resolution and *which it possesses in reality* [omitted from version 2]. I say 'general character' – not because we were supporters of all particular features of this policy. Far from it. But in this letter I must be brief and so, touching only on the fundamentals of this policy, I leave aside its individual features. The main all-defining feature in the CC's resolution 'on immediate tasks of economic policy' is that in this resolution all large state industry is designated as an appendage to the small peasant household. All that is doomed to *downsizing* [shattering], to so-called 'concentration' and only where such a reduction can elicit the outright indignation of the working masses who are doomed to long-term unemployment, only at that moment will this reduction or 'concentration' give way to considerations of a political character. But it's obvious, that this only eliminates the reduction itself, but not by one iota does it solve the question of the actual preservation and expansion of our centres of industry and of revolutionary proletarian forces. He who knows or is at least interested in the brief history of our industry, will easily see, that never in its chief areas, – metallurgy and machine building, coalmining and oil, fuel extraction in general – was it, in its origins and development, based on the peasant household but instead rested on railway, highway construction, on the *uninterrupted* [omitted] expansion of all *industrial* [omitted] branches of the economy, supplying them with materials, *machines, instruments* [omitted] and so forth, on the growth of the urban economy *and* [omitted] on enormous resources 'for

---

140 *Искушенные* [имущественные].

defence of the country' [quotation marks omitted]. The entire peasant world consumed an insignificant sum, in comparison with these consumers, and was not even a significant aid for these branches of heavy industry. And now when the CC proclaims, that for state industry this peasant market is the limit beyond which it cannot go, that namely in this direction it will solve all questions of industry, – we, naturally, see in such a policy a direct threat to heavy industry and to the very existence of the working class. And most of all to the *achievements of the working class, which it secured by means of the October seizure of power* [And most of all to all but for the working class, the conquerors of the October seizure of power].

I can give you here a concrete example of the situation in which such a policy puts, for example, the Baku oil industry. Since we now have *significant* [enormous] supplies of kerosene, gasoline and mineral oil, and since demand for them *for now* [omitted] is very limited, in accord with the general economic policy of the party which has been decreed – the entire Baku and Grozny oil refining and processing industry will be downsized and all oil extraction will be focused only on procuring unrefined oil. This means that we will have an inescapable reduction of worker cadres in the indicated branch of the oil industry, and together with that the *contraction* [improvement][141] of our material base. This is the basic character of the party's economic policy, *outlined in the CC's resolution* [omitted] for the immediate period of time in power. In it is concealed, in our opinion, a great danger to the interests of the working class and the further fate of Large State Industry.

b)   This danger will become even more threatening, if we look at still another feature of our intraparty policy, at the attitude of *party leaders, supported by* [omitted] the overwhelming majority of members – toward the 'new economic policy'. Until recently they have *portrayed* [associated] this policy as a maneuver in keeping with socialism. By means of this maneuver they meant temporarily, under the pressure of cruel necessity, to give some space to the petty bourgeois capitalist pressure of the peasantry and the *rural and urban* [omitted] bourgeoisie engaged in trade (which are inseparably linked to the peasantry), in order to revive and consolidate the material base of our supremacy, *large state industry*, [omitted] with

---

141   *Сужение* [улучшение].

maximum energy, and with the help of fortified state industry to begin to struggle against the inescapable growth of NEP and against private capital on the free market.

Now almost no one presents the question in such a way. On the contrary, now we hear almost entirely of near rapture over this policy, dictated to us by a force hostile to the proletariat and in this way attesting to the fact that 'from need this policy is transformed into the highest political virtue', that this policy ceases to be represented as a *forced retreat* [free-thinking attitude] from our conquests, by its very price to save them; rather, it increasingly is depicted as our only conceivable *economic* [and reasonable] policy, which would be the policy of strengthening all accomplishments of the working class as a result of the October Revolution, the policy which is directed toward and in essence consists of the consolidation of the dictatorship of the proletariat.

So, if you will pay attention to this criticism of the so called 'new economic policy', which in fact is a direct expression of the interests of the petty bourgeois peasant and urban masses, – whose political pressure it was proclaimed it would weaken, – then the emphasis on the transformation of large state industry is just an appendage to the economic policy of the small-holding peasant household, to the limited household uses and personal demands of the peasant masses themselves, – and [this course] becomes even more threatening to the fundamental conquests of the working class.

c)   We've come to the point that for every million employed, we have over a million unemployed. The further accelerated development of agriculture, *in the first instance* [omitted] of kulak and *more or less* [rather more] well-off[142] *or the so-called 'middle' ('serednyak')* [omitted] masses of peasants, *being* [was] a deeply progressive phenomenon for our exhausted economy, will inescapably lead to the displacement of the less economically *secure* [alleviated] peasant masses and former workers before anything else will flood cities and towns. Already now this influx is becoming more and more massive. Along with this, after the *impending* [omitted] recognition of us in Europe, we will enter into *closer* [greater] contact with the world market, and this means, that our own state economy must *catch up* [be equal] to economic development in Europe.

---

142   состоятельных.

As concerns the development of our agriculture, which is *largely* [overwhelmingly] based on the small peasant holder, it must catch up to *international* [omitted] markets, selling its products not only in Europe but also in America, and this will intensify the displacement, the self-expulsion of the weaker of these farmers in our countryside and will push toward the towns more and more masses of the ruined ones. If state industry seems to be in a bad situation *at this moment* [at one moment], when we cannot secure work even for the currently unemployed, well *it can be even worse, if* [at that moment we can seem thrown off from our current pedestal of power by] a small group of Bonapartist swine *would try to overthrow us* [omitted] and in attempting to do so might not meet the necessary resistance from those enormous unemployed masses *of the towns* [omitted], fragmented by poverty, which might in their situation seem not only passive, but in their suffering, might even relate sympathetically to such a confluence of events, in the hopes that the victory of private capital, although it would condemn them to cruel exploitation, would not allow them to expire from hunger. And such a mood could be found not only among unemployed workers, but even among those who work and who live under constant expectation of layoffs.

If such a misfortune were to befall us, we would still less be able to count on the rural poor supporting us. Not in vain was it indisputably established during discussion that these rural poor are leaving the ranks of the party. Thus, we do not share the policy of the CC, which in the main for the nearest period will be directed toward its own preservation, its reinforcement and even the development of the petty peasant economy; which bases all industrial policy only on its *current needs* [extirpations].

We think that the petty peasant household, under NEP and depending on the international market, is doomed to *stagnation in barbarian conditions and to inevitable* [omitted] ruin. All efforts to save it, to help it resist and even develop *in its current form* [omitted] – are reactionary-utopian attempts. The solution for these doomed peasant masses can lie only in developing state industry, where the rural masses could find application for their hands and strengths.

Any support of the illusions of small peasant holders that Soviet power must and will save them from destruction, while preserving capitalist competition and free trade, will only corrupt *them politically* [their consciousness] in so far as these illusions are confirmed;

[small peasant holders will make] constant demands on the government, to make up with various subsidies from its means the difference between the cost of the products of their labour, as it is defined on the one hand according to the world market and on the other by that minimum of resources, which are necessary to them for their personal and economic existence. These features in our economic policy exist right now. In the future under that economic policy, *which the cc outlines in its resolution* [omitted], confirming the possibility of a seemingly broad development for the small peasant economy, – these features will inescapably expand, will exhaust the already deficit state budget and will lay an even more colossal burden on the working class, for all these subsidies the government will spoon out chiefly, as the resolution of the cc says, 'from the income of state enterprises and state property', that is from increasing the exploitation of workers in state industry.

That part of the rural population, which remains, with the exception of the masses as indicated, is the rural kulak bourgeoisie, which is no less hostile to us than is the old sort of bourgeoisie. We can only conduct a cruel political struggle against it. This is the main essence of our disagreements on questions of party economic policy. We see in this policy the prevalence of the interests of that six-sevenths of its composition, which are petty bourgeois elements, and not the reinforcement of the dictatorship of the proletariat in the economy as well as in politics.

What do we offer as a counterweight to this policy:

a) the transfer of the chief centre of economic policy from the peasant economy to large industry, to its resurrection, to its expansion, its development, to the employment of all state resources particularly in this direction. This policy will serve the vital interests of the proletarian masses of the towns, as well as the interests of those semiproletarian masses of the countryside, who all the more will be ruined for the reasons shown above and as if in mockery of them – this expansion will be all the more destructive for them, the more plentiful the harvests, for particularly in these conditions the products of their labour will be more devalued. This policy will [further] serve our communist goals. It is the only *correct and really possible* [omitted] communist policy, capable of securing for us the most painless resolution of the question of the *petty* [omitted] peasantry *and of solidifying its political union with the working class in our republic* [omitted];

b)   when introducing such proposals, usually they frighten you with questions: where to get the resources for this? We don't have them. We answer thus: if we don't have enough resources for this, then we have in the current budget anyway such resources that go *not toward the development of the large state economy, but to support the petty bourgeois economy of the well-off part of the peasantry and to support the utopian illusions of the small-holding peasantry indicated above, which our party itself consolidates with this stratum of the peasantry* [to development of the policy outlined by us, and partially to support those utopian illusions of the small-holding peasant economy, which the overwhelming majority of our party supports in this stratum of the peasantry];

[We know, however, that these resources are insufficient. And we demand that the government search more energetically for resources by way of foreign and internal state loans and granting concessions, and with greater losses than those our government was prepared to allow for upon being granted such credits.]

c)   we think that in our country's current economic condition, with those perspectives *for it* [omitted], of which I spoke above, [which await us] great material sacrifices to international capital, which is ready to go toward the revival of our *dormant* [violated] industrial regions, – is a lesser evil, than that condition in which we are and can be found in recent years in the area of our industrial and agricultural economy, the condition, which can seem for us ruinous.

To think that we can with that [role and] specific gravity of the working class, which it has in state policy, gather the necessary masses of capital for the turn around of ruined industry by way of *income and property* [omitted] taxes, – means to amuse oneself with futile illusion. To think that these masses of capital we'll put together only *more protractedly 'penny by penny, nickel by nickel'* [out of nickels only more protractedly] *from that same industry* [omitted], this means to supplement the [former] illusion *of the small-holding peasantry* [omitted] with the illusion of petty bourgeois imitators *of the towns* [omitted]. For such a way of accumulation we would need half a century. We still don't know what period of time it will take for us to emerge from the deficit of our state budget. Only empty-headed windbags can speak in this circumstance about *actual* [omitted] accumulation.

These are our basic disagreements with the economic policy of our party and the existing policy in the countryside. The results of these policies at the current moment already bear down on the working masses as weights, in the future they will become heavier. To think that in the future they will patiently bend their backs, – means not to see surrounding phenomena, or not to understand their significance.

3. Our party's international policy – as is any party's such policy – is the continuation of our internal policy in the international arena. That which *distinguishes* [mitigates] our policy within the country, are the same features it brings to a significant degree to the international area. Its basic flaw consists in that it wants to see everything in the light of our country's experience. The so-called 'Worker-peasant government', coming to replace the 'Worker government' – is *an expression of* [omitted] a hopeless attempt to resolve the basic problems of the West European workers' movement by the means and methods of our country. This leads to failures, willingly or unwillingly, but this policy constantly discredits the role of the better organised and more conscious *masses* [circles] of the Western European proletariat and tries to find for itself support in its less conscious elements and in the 'peasantry' of the Western European countries. But such a peasantry, which we had up to the moment of our revolution, doesn't exist in Western Europe. It exists in the Near and Far East. But we now know what the attempt to rely on the peasantry came to, for example, in Bulgaria. This Comintern-dictated attempt led to the downfall of the Bulgarian Communist Party. We know just as well that even in peasant Finland the slogan 'worker-peasant government' has *fewer chances* [least liabilities] than anywhere else.

Such is the chief direction of our international policy. It also defined the character of Comintern tactics, which they tried to impose in Germany, Italy, and France. In all these central European countries, which have a decisive significance for the international revolution, this tactic led to the fact that from the general mass of the proletariat's organised forces, the forces of the communist part of it were torn out and were set in opposition to the remaining mass of the proletariat, as the more revolutionary parts against those supposedly incapable of conscious participation in the revolutionary demonstrations of the working masses. The more they disorganised the general working class movement and the communist part of it, the more they isolated it from the general mass of the organised proletariat and they deprived it of steady influence on the masses from outside their ranks. We are the bitterest opponents of this policy. We see no possibility to speed up the course of events in Western Europe toward revolution, while standing apart from and against the overwhelming mass of the organised working class. We are for the communist working masses to remain the constituent part of the working masses, organised in trade unions, cooperatives, soviets, factory committees and so forth, so that any attempts to seize power in these organisations, bypassing the will of the overwhelming mass of their members, or to create an organisation isolated from the masses would be decisively rejected, as a venture which disorganises the workers' movement.

This, in general outline, is our attitude toward international policy. If the support of the Western European proletariat was necessary for us up to now, then now, when our links with Europe are broadening and taking shape, this support is a hundredfold more necessary to us. But with that policy of constantly discrediting the more organised and conscious workers, which we defended and conducted through the Comintern, we arrived at full isolation of the working masses of our country from the proletariat of the Western European countries and to a similar isolation of the communist part of the latter from the bulk of the masses in Western Europe.

Attempts to artificially graft our methods of work onto all Western European countries lead only to what we see, for example, in Norway. From this example it's especially obvious, how these attempts have literally led to the disorganisation of that country's worker movement; to the emergence of materially feeble 'communist' sections and to their maintenance on the account of the Russian working masses, for which they paid with blood and sacrifices, but which they cannot use for themselves under current conditions. In fact there is being created a horde of petty bourgeois servants, *supported by Russian gold, depicting themselves* [which for Russian gold depict themselves] as the proletariat and allegedly as *representatives of* [representing] the 'revolutionary workers' of the Comintern.

Those methods, by which the Comintern tries to conquer the Western European working masses – are obviously hopeless. [But the soil, on which the Comintern feeds – the Western European working masses – is obviously hopeless.] They not only do not bring us closer to the organised international proletariat masses, but on the contrary, estrange us. Seeing these misfortunes, its leaders, in the persons of our party leaders, seek support for their policy outside of the masses and preach, for example, that American tenant farmers are more revolutionary, than the American organised working masses.

From here, naturally, it remains to take just one step toward these farmers, and they will turn out to be that fundamental base of "communism," on which must be staked the entire activity of American communists. Similar quests occur in all other European countries. They are evidence that the Comintern's policy, as guided by our party leaders, as a consequence of failure in the proletarian masses, is imbued with strivings toward the petty bourgeois property-owning classes. These classes are all the more often juxtaposed to working class associations, as the more capable of carrying out a socialist revolution, which lacks only organised leadership.

If such leadership is secured for them in the person of the communist party, they will be the first in completing a socialist revolution. This is the basic flaw of all our international policy. This flaw explains all the systematic persecution and discrediting of Western European proletarian-class associations, which still do not follow communist slogans. [It explains such a discrediting of social democratic government in general, such as the current labour government in England. The latter pretty often is depicted as a government of the bourgeoisie. We cannot agree even one iota with such policy and tactics.] It is disastrous for the cause of the real socialist revolution.

Our evaluation of Western European Social Democratic parties deeply departs from those evaluations, given by our leaders. They regard all leading cadres of these parties as traitors, lackeys of the bourgeoisie and so forth. And this relates to the German just as well as to other Social Democratic parties. This fact alone is enough to reject a similar characterisation of these *cadres as explaining nothing and to doubt that they are the* [peoples as the] chief reason why in Western Europe the bourgeoisie still reigns. It is obviously not Marxist and leads us to a dead end.

Given such an explanation of the bourgeoisie's supremacy, there is no ray of hope ahead, *since* [indeed] all the most conscious, organised and disciplined working class cadres, from which are organised all leading circles of Western European socialist parties, are traitors and so forth. *Then who is the actual bearer of the socialist revolution* [omitted]? In fact, these elements *in the eyes of the broad working masses of the Western European states* [omitted] not only do not betray any working class interests, but on the contrary, from the point of view of the proletarian masses, they are most devoted to their interests. Therefore Social Democrats are still strong and powerful. Therefore they still can utilise the deep trust of the proletarian masses.

Namely a Marxist analysis can easily explain such an evaluation of these parties and leaders *by broad masses of the workers* [omitted]. The entire solidity of their link with the working masses and the masses' wholly deep trust in them is explained by the fact that these Social Democratic party leaders never subordinated the working masses' overall everyday needs to various individual demands by the party regarding the interests of the revolution. On the contrary, they see their interests chiefly in the satisfaction of the everyday [improvements of the] needs of the working masses. At times they are willing to consider as a revolutionary goal the successful resolution of these *partial* [omitted] needs for broad circles of the worker masses through shortening work time, through raising their pay and through elevating their role in government or community administration. And since the international proletariat has many such needs, then there's nothing unnatural in entrusting the whole leadership in their struggle namely to those who present them not with red pipedreams in the form of a wider perspective, but to those who capably defend them from everyday adversities. That is the soil, on which is formed the Western European socialist parties' devilishly durable link with the working class of their countries, which we have so far observed, despite the occasionally really criminal behaviour of their parties' leading circles in *important* [separate] moments of these masses' struggle.

Departing from such an evaluation of the role of socialist parties and their leaders, we say that to conquer the Western European working masses, the Comintern does not need to constantly discredit as traitors the organisations that unite the proletarian class and their leaders. By such means you'll not win them over. To achieve this goal it is necessary to gather patience and skill to defend the everyday needs of the working masses, in order to reveal before them more intensively the whole illusion of proposals that the satisfaction of such needs will essentially change their social and material situation. It's necessary to resolutely reject all attempts to realise a socialist revolution by circumventing the conquest of Western European proletarian mass organisations. Finally, it's necessary to change decisively the relations with these organisations, which have formed up to now.

We think that the actual situation is such that our organisations such as Profintern, in fact are willingly or unwillingly, a weapon of alienation of both the Russian working masses and the Western European communist masses from resolute masses of all the proletariat. It is a direct obstacle, not at all justified in fact, on the path to formation of an actual unified front of the working class of each country and on an international scale. This is the basic thing that separates us from current party *leaders* [policy] in questions of international policy.

4.   Now regarding the death of comrade Lenin. His loss is, understandably, an important and painful event. But all is relative in this world. We are by no means in such a hopeless mood regarding the future, as some of our

party circles. And in this we are shored up by the fact of the mass entry of workers into the party ranks. This in our opinion coincided with comrade Lenin's death, but was not a direct consequence. This is the second act of that revival of Russia's worker masses which began in August and September with mass strikes aimed at the improvement of their desperate situation. In this act we perceive the more active mass elements' attempt to find in the party the lever for changing their difficult material situation, in which they are found even now, to force it to defend the interests of the mass of workers in its everyday policy and work. This factor we regard as cause for rejoicing not only for our country's working class, but also for the party and for us personally.

Regarding this phenomenon [omitted] we experience the deepest satisfaction with our efforts to make our party truly a workers' party. Whatever worker elements this movement captures, we see in it a boon. It doesn't concern us if these are not the most conscious elements. On the contrary, this confirms our rather great hopes that the party namely under the influence of these elements, which are perhaps less conscious but more broadly based, will have to rise to defend a policy which will link it more closely with workers' interests, since *namely these elements' direct interests are the interests of the working masses, and their direct pressure to a great degree is capable of securing today's immediate interests more so than the pressure of more conscious circles of these masses* [namely these elements' interests are the interests of the masses to a greater degree than we'll say the direct interests of today's more conscious circles of the masses].

This new entry must exert influence on the party's economic policy. To close a factory where there are 10–15 communists out of 500, for example is a lot easier to do than when 150–200 or even 60–100 are communists. This alone is enough to make us happy. It's necessary only, of course, not to be beaten down by that banality which is proposed in connection with this phenomenon, supposing that all these workers surged into the party 'in order to study Leninism,' and that it is necessary quickly to organise as many party lectures, courses, schools and so forth as possible. It's necessary to see a direct danger in such a welcome, which can quickly chase out of the party's ranks not only those entering now but also those who were in the party earlier.

Now about the results of the discussion. As with the 'new course', so the discussion and its outcome in no way were linked with Lenin's death. This course and discussion of it arose long before any suggestion of Lenin's possible demise, even *before* [at] the all-Russian conference. This means that it is impossible to connect all these events. You will find an answer to your main question – 'indeed has everything come to nothing', in our 18 January 1924 article in *Pravda*, where we clearly explicated, how it came to be that since the Tenth Party Congress worker democracy was laid to rest in the CC's depths. You'll find even more explanation in the stenographic report of Comrade Shliapnikov's paper. All this seems so simple and clear, as if there were no special need to explain this circumstance.

We perceive that already before the Tenth Congress our party became so socially differentiated, that it nearly fell apart as a result of bitter discussion. This is the first thing. The second is that at that same congress and afterwards the CC gave itself the task, no matter what, to create party unity, which, it was understood, was threatened from the outside by the possibility of a new civil war. Third, the 'Workers' Opposition' was the only faction, which had a future in the working class, therefore all whips and scorpions, stipulated by secret points of the resolution on 'unity' were directed precisely against supporters of the 'Workers' Opposition', [that is] against *supporters of the need to resolutely protect* [policy not in] the direct interests of the proletarian masses of our country.

Fourth, could the CC under such conditions implement within the party principles of workers' democracy? Of course not. Implementation of these principles would on the next day have confronted it with worker elements in the party uniting around the 'Workers' Opposition' and would have made absolutely impossible that economic policy which it mapped out at the congress itself and which in the future would assume such a character that it would be directly aimed against the interests of the masses, at least on the issues of loans for gold, bread and other things.

Implementation of principles of workers' democracy would not have allowed the implementation of that 'concentration', *which is the curtailment* [omitted] of the economy, which became the essence of the CC's policy already from that time.

Well all that to one side, but from the other – the overwhelming petty bourgeois composition of the party itself which could be an active supporter of bourgeois democracy but not of workers' democracy, that is, a democracy that would not only guarantee each party member's active participation in party activity, but would obligate it moreover to direct this activity toward working class interests, to infuse it with the workers' spirit and interests. These two basic conditions determined the fact that the resolutions of the Tenth Congress, despite the presence in it of essential limitations on the principles of worker democracy, nevertheless remained unrealised.

Ask yourself if any of these conditions essentially changed. If so, then in what direction, and then you'll give yourself a clear answer to your question. Now this circumstance, like a thunderbolt, struck all worker elements in factories and higher education, who in some places supported rather energetically the 'September opposition'. Now they've become bitterly disappointed in their illusions both in the possibility of implementing worker democracy, given the party's current composition, and in the 'September opposition'. But all this disillusionment and bitterness is just a result of their illusions and nothing else. It would be sad, if you were to yield to such illusions and would reap disillusion from them. We are convinced that it will not be difficult now for you, on the basis of these materials, to resolve all questions regarding the period just experienced and in the present.

With this I must finish my letter. I intended to write briefly, but in fact as you see it became a whole brochure, but if this will help elucidate questions still not clear to you, I will not regret that I spent two whole days writing you this letter. In conclusion I express our sincere desire that you would more solidly link up with those new worker cadres which doubtlessly are responding in your region to the all-Russian phenomenon of workers' entry into the party. If these writings did not clarify everything, don't pass up a convenient opportunity to get in touch, then it'll be possible to provide additional information to you.

With communist greetings from all of us[143]
  (Medvedev)

One last urgent and ardent request: If you need to preserve this letter, even for a little while, please try to type a copy of it for yourself on a typewriter and return this original to me no matter what. I did not write this letter quickly. This explains some carelessness, necessitating corrections. During the writing itself, I was interrupted and called away a hundred times, so you'll figure out for yourself what kind of insertion is called for and where. I can't rewrite the letter. I repeat, try to return it to me no matter what, and if possible, in a short time. [circa 20 January 1924]

---

143 Under NKVD interrogation in 1935, Medvedev named those he meant by 'all of us' as: Mikhail Mikhailov, Mikhail Chelyshev, Ivan Nikolaenko, Genrikh Bruno, Aleksandr Pravdin and Aleksandr Shliapnikov (TsA FSB, R33718, d. 499061, vol. 5, ll. 28–31). All these had supported the Workers' Opposition in 1920–1.

9   Letter from S.P. Medvedev in Moscow to A.G. Shliapnikov in France,
       27 December 1924, and A.G. Shliapnikov's Answering Letter, Dated
       7 January 1925, Written in Paris[144]

Yesterday, I saw Figatner, who will leave for Paris on Sunday, 28 December. I'll
send this letter with him. I have already received from you three missives: a
postcard, a note, and a typed letter. I haven't hurried to answer until today, since
they don't contain such questions as would demand a quick answer. I just didn't
have time to write about our everyday life in the spirit of my current letter and
send it by the usual diplomatic post. Only Figatner's departure presents the
possibility to send you a description of our life, with almost complete confidence that it will reach only you and will not fall into the hands of those to whom
I do not address it.

There haven't been any especially major events within our federation since
you departed from Moscow. The campaign against Trotsky has completely
faded. Already there is no longer that same passion on the newspaper pages
which they stirred up at the beginning around his speaking out. They have
transferred struggle against his political views and evaluations to brochures
about 'Leninism and Trotskyism', 'Trotskyism and Leninism', and so forth. Now
all those who have long needed a good reason to speak out, in order to rehabil-
itate themselves of worse sins, or to finally earn the bosses' favour and advance
their careers, are excelling at this field [поприще].

But then in the international area, right after your departure, we were
presented with a completely unexpected gift, verily, of a provocation in Estonia. It's completely obvious that we have nothing to do with this! The Estonian
government was vitally interested in such a provocation and summoned those
few cadres of the worker milieu who could no longer endure to participate in
it!

That's how the party communicated it. The only ones who will not believe it
are those, who do not know that all of our party reports are 100% correct about
reality.

Our friend, Vanya [Ivan] Chugurin, is working to bring our battleships into
the proper state! He has had to sweat a lot in exertion over this work, which
he was assigned! He endured the ordeal, although not exactly brilliantly! The
cruiser and torpedo boats proceeded into the waters of Revel and they looked
round. Fortunately they did not encounter danger and returned home!

---

144   TsA FSB, R33718, d. 499061, vol. 13, ll. 24–8, handwritten original, ll. 29–40, typed copy.

Don't be surprised by my joking mood about this! 'It is no sin to laugh at all that seems funny'![145] Indeed can you and I speak without laughing about this event and about the failure to implicate us in it, after all that we witnessed just a few days before your departure from Moscow! Indeed, we can allow ourselves to predict outright that the Latvian, Finnish, Lithuanian, and Polish governments will soon arrange similar provocations in their countries, without fail.

According to your agreement with comrade Zinoviev that he and I discuss my letter, I saw him on the Saturday, on which you and he set our meeting. The conversation lasted over one and one-half hours. We talked in his secretariat. The conversation was full of mutual trust on many questions. At the beginning of the conversation, comrade Zinoviev noted that my letter had not a trace of squabbling or personal [attacks?] and that this very circumstance moved him to talk with me about its content. He said that it was written sincerely and from the heart, without any intention to be made public, and that it has its own logic, which takes views on various questions and from them generalises a unified system of views on cardinal questions of policy. Despite all these positive qualities, he said, a bad spirit saturates the letter!

Right then I interrupted him with a question and a request. The question was about whether he and his closest companions have grounds even now to emphasise to everyone everywhere that I am especially embittered against Politburo members. The second expressed the desire that in the future these very members would not interpret their actual disagreements with us as if they were based on my special personal animosity toward them.

Zinoviev explained to me that it has seemed so to all of them up to now and that the reason for this was my outward appearance. But he said that the tone in which my letter was written makes it possible to converse in a completely calm manner about the essential areas where we disagree. Right then he listed all those points, about which he intended to exchange opinions.

He noted five such points.

1.   The assertion that all attempts to strengthen and consolidate smallscale peasant agriculture, and in like manner secure for it the possibility to develop, are reactionary-utopian efforts.

---

145   This phrase (Смеяться, право, не грешно / Над всем, что кажется смешно) appears to be from the verse 'Poslanie k Aleksandru Alekseevichu Pleshcheevu', written by N.M. Karamzin in 1796. According to one source, it is 'employed as a formula for justifying laughter, mockery, or irony when such a reaction may elicit reproach from someone' (http://dic .academic.ru/).

He does not agree with this. He thinks that this form of agriculture has still not reached the limit of its resources and that it composes a large share of peasant holdings. Therefore, he says, we cannot rule it out.

2. About large state industry, he agrees 50 %. When I asked about the remaining 50 %, he answered that I regard them as conscious opponents of large industry.

    Right away I assured him that I am ready to repeat three times that I have not accused you of this! I am prepared to acknowledge gladly that you consciously want to revive large state industry. But this won't change the facts. You are reducing large state industry to the role of an adjunct to the peasant homestead, yes even to the destitute homestead.

3. About concessions. He thinks that I'm pushing our country into such a gaping maw [хайло], which would swallow us up completely, and that on this question I have a Krasinist spirit. Regarding the last thing, I declared that I fully support my assertion that we're suffering immeasurably more from the failure of our large state industry than we would suffer from rather large sacrifices to European capital, which would be prepared to revive our extinguished industrial regions. I never have been nor will I be touched by a Krasinist spirit. He expresses this spirit in thinking that use of the weapons of October was premature in our country and by his opinion that we were bankrupted most of all in the management of the economy. From this, he concludes that the entire economy should be delivered into the hands of those who know how to manage it. This means not just the part of the economy, which is now ruined, but also the part which our forces lead. I absolutely cannot share this spirit, for it would mean for me to regard myself as nothing better than cattle. I said, 'Hardly do you, yourselves, admit that this is possible'.

    I said, 'if you are scared by the gaping maw of European large capital, well we are frightened to a much larger degree by a petty-bourgeois sea of peasants. If the gullet of European large capital succeeds in swallowing us up, then at least it will bring us tens or hundreds of thousands of people to continue our work. If a petty-bourgeois maw of muzhiks [мужлане] swallows us up, then it really will swallow us up without leaving anything behind, not even a trace of our existence'.

4. About Comintern policy. He pointed out that Lenin originated this policy. Without having attempted to discredit and having created schisms for the past period, we would not have succeeded in those reconquests we won from the 'yellows' and the SDs. Only now can we attempt to negotiate and agree with the socially conciliatory unions, because now we are sufficiently strong to confront them even within their own organisations.

5. I've forgotten just now what the fifth question was. I'll write about it later.

Zinoviev declared that my letter as a whole reminds him of the well-known 'Credo' of the Economists.[146] He said that it was written also from the heart and not for the press, but its heart was such that they were afraid to publish it. I interrupted him at this point and said that I not only am not afraid of its publication, but that I insist upon it. Right then I told him that many of my friends and old comrades, who do not even currently share our views, ask me to give them the letter to read, since they know about its existence as political news. I cited in genuine form my conversation with Glebov from Leningrad, which took place in the presence of some trade unionists at the congress of trade unions. Glebov smiled spitefully as he asked me, 'Well, what's up?' [Ну, что?]. I responded with the question, 'What do you mean?!' [А что такое?!]. Then he answered 'Still writing?!' I asked him in turn, 'And have you already read [it]?'! He answered, 'I read [it]!' Thus, I said to Zinoviev that many trade unionists, at least those in Leningrad, have come to know about my letter. Then he told me what happened in Piter with my letter. That Naumov, who works now in Baltflot [Baltic Sea Fleet], was the first who approached him [Zinoviev] at a conference and laid out his views on the state of things, which as it turned out, coincided in the main with the views in my letter. Right behind him some of the trade unionists started to express these same views. Zinoviev said that he then gathered the trade unionists together and showed them my letter as evidence that some of them were expressing views that resembled the point of view of the Workers' Opposition. Naturally, he frightened those who know what this can lead them into.

Concerning publication of my letter, I asked to be given it for review, since I am not confident that the GPU did not insert into it the thoughts it desired and did not given it such a character, which not long ago English agents gave to the letter attributed to you [Zinoviev]. I have not made up my mind to aspire to more than this, since I see clearly by Trotsky's example into what the party press has been transformed now. Nevertheless I do not conceal from you, I told him, that I reserve for myself the right to answer all our friends with a new letter regarding the former letter, since only by this method can we express our thoughts.

In connection with this, he asked if I think that they made a mistake by having a dispute with Trotsky. I answered, that I resolutely condemn those forms and means, in which they carry out the dispute against him. This dispute is

---

146   This is probably a reference to the 'Credo' written by E.D. Kuskova in 1899, and published in Lenin 1935, vol. 2, pp. 477–80. There is some disagreement as to whether it should be associated with the Economists in the social democratic movement. See Thatcher, 2007, pp. 729–30, 735.

onesided and essentially has been transformed into a situation in which the apparatchiks and party masses are stirred up against him. Meanwhile, the free exchange of opinions about the content of the questions posed by Trotsky could be rather fruitful for the class-oriented political education of working-class youth at the very least.

Right then he indicated that some districts of the Petrograd organisation demand not this, but the outright exclusion of Trotsky from the party, but he said that he was resolutely against this! Expressing great doubt, I stated to him that I could not imagine that leaders of so-called activist parts of any districts of the Leningrad [party] organisation would dare to carry through such a decision in the face of your [Zinoviev's] disapproval. They know too well who feeds them [whose meat they eat]! He indicated that assemblies of party masses carry such decisions and again he assured me that he is absolutely against it.

'Well, so what!' I answered him, 'Well indeed, if you can be believed, you have still not corrected your role in it'. 'How so?!' he asked. 'Well, how indeed! You say you don't want to apply these measures, but you stir up the party masses and set them upon Trotsky in this very direction. You reap from the party masses' decisions what you have sown! You will continue to pursue this path, until you will be forced either to submit to this mood, which you aroused, or to resign from your posts. Not one of the punitive measures against Trotsky, which have been proposed as a result of the character of the dispute, which your speeches against Trotsky inspired, can end the dispute about the questions he has posed. On the contrary! It can be considered that precisely this moment is the beginning of a new civil war!

Precisely due to all these considerations, we think that the way in which you set up the ideological political dispute with him is absolutely harmful. Besides all that, it does not allow even one party person who respects his own political dignity, yet who absolutely disagrees with the ideological, political, and tactical aspects of Trotsky's position, to openly speak out against his positions'. In concluding our exchange of opinions about this question, he declared that they discussed for a long time the question concerning the forms that the dispute should take.

A day after our conversation, I already did not see in *Pravda* the same fiery campaign for resolutions, which I had observed in each issue before this. Obviously, the instigators of this campaign did not find in it the results, which they wanted to achieve.

In conclusion, I'll note still one more circumstance, which became clear in conversation with comrade Zinoviev. He disclosed to me that Narkomzem [the People's Commissariat of Agriculture] shares our point of view about on whom in the countryside the wager should be placed, when it comes to offering help, whether it should be on large and middle peasant agriculture or on the small and smallest. Several days before my conversation with Zinoviev, Foma bitterly defended approximately the same point of view as mine.[147] I decided to verify how true Zinoviev's statement was. I gathered the necessary materials about Narkomzem's work and the questions it posed. I became convinced that 'it may seem the same but there is a big difference'![148]

Narkomzem really did bitterly criticise the proposals about putting a wager on the bedniak. It indicates that there is not any kind of aid to the small and smallest peasant holders in the countryside that will keep our transport or industry at full capacity or provide a massive amount of agriculture production for export, which is the only thing that would turn European governments resolutely on the path toward establishing stable relations with us. From this, it concludes that Narkomzem should help the large and middle peasants in the countryside! This is, so to say, a rural Krasin! Although we share to the utmost the first part of its opinions, clearly we cannot support its conclusions even one iota!

Ending the conversation, Zinoviev declared that the questions posed in the letter are those cardinal questions, around which disputes about our party policy strictly revolve and that the urgent obligation of all party members is to clarify these questions. With this in mind, he proposes the following. After discussion with Trotsky has ended, he will bring out a brochure for party members, in which he will publish my letter, after having discarded from it all that is connected with individual persons. He will provide a critique of it in a special article, which he will give to me to read. My objections will be published together with his article in a brochure. He agrees to do this no sooner than in two months, so that this brochure would not fan the flames of a new discussion. I expressed my full consent to all these proposals and with this, we finished our conversation. Zinoviev expressed the wish to exchange opinions about the questions we touched upon one more time, before any public speeches or acts. Naturally I expressed complete solidarity with this. That's the condensed version of this conversation. If you please, that is enough about it.

Of our friends, I have seen Pravdin, Bruno, and Lobanov together with the Krasinists. Pravdin's son accidentally shot himself and was paralysed in the legs for awhile.

---

147   Foma was a nickname for more than one Old Bolshevik.

148   Федот, да не тот.

Yesterday I saw Mikhail Chelyshev. He told much that was instructive from the realm of our courts, as an index of what is going on in the country. Criminal banditry grows inordinately, both in the cities and in the villages, despite the broad application of executions by shooting for such deeds. They exterminate counterfeiters in batches, several hundred per month. However, these types of crimes do not decrease, and it's obvious that they cannot decrease. But the most typical characteristic of the courts is that no one there poses questions about crimes in connection with social milieu, the degree of material deprivation, cultural conditions, and way of life. He points out that if things go on like this for the next ten years, there will not remain one person in the USSR, who has not been convicted by a court. Another characteristic feature to which he points is that the more helpless the leaders of the court feel in the struggle to end the growth of crime, the broader their instructions become to execute people by shooting and to confine them to prison for long sentences for these crimes.

The Ukrainians told me that the entire party-soviet leadership [верхушка] is informed, possibly through Mikhail Kalinin or possibly through others, about your declaration that you are in solidarity with the Politburo about everything. Pravdin said that he was interrogated about whether it is true that Shliapnikov voted for the resolution accepted at the meeting of the M[oscow] C[ommittee] with activist personnel, which is talked about in the districts. The Ukrainians, naturally, shake their heads regarding the news they get from leading circles, but seriously, did none of them really know what's going on here and on what such information is based? Brykov informed them so well about your statement, that they all only became fortified in the veracity of that information, which comes from party higher-ups.

Recently Lobanov said that this whole story about your supposed statement demoralised their milieu. Part of those who heard this information responded indignantly. Some of our acquaintances asked me if this is true. Even Serebriakov asked about this same thing. From the history of all this, one thing emerges without a doubt. Someone circulated this sensation broadly and used your assignment [abroad] successfully enough to add the ring of truth to it. To the Ukrainians and some of our other friends, I explained in detail our actual views and those few points of convergence, which we have with the views of those who officially lead our policy. But all the same, I have had an unpleasant feeling from this entire history.

Well, I'm finishing up! I wrote a whole tale. Many people ask, what is Shliapnikov up to and how is he getting along? I usually answer that I still don't know. Actually, I can't say anything about this. I hear already versions that Shliapnikov wrote something to T-m [Tomsky]! Obviously, he said something somewhere about this, and, if you please, even with a goal in mind! But he possibly did not say everything, but only that which corresponds to his goals.

A.G. Shliapnikov's Letter in Reply to Medvedev, 7–10 January 1925, Paris[149]

['To comrade Pravdin' is typed near the top, inexplicably.]

On 5 January 1925, I received your letter of 27 December 1924, which comrade Figatner passed on to me. I read about your conversation with great interest. I agree entirely with it. I'm extremely disappointed with the speculation involving my name, which occurs in connection with my trip to Paris. Although I have little available leisure time here, thousands of versts from our native Moscow, the distance has allowed me to validate our thoughts and our actions and I am even more convinced of their correctness. I am disturbed and surprised by conversations among our friends and acrimonious evaluations of my assignment.

This assignment does not inaugurate any new era in our situation. I see right now that I made a big mistake when I accepted the Politburo's proposal about temporary work abroad in negotiations with France. The mistake is that I believed that it would actually be possible to do useful work here, when the CC probably only sought to find me work beyond the borders of our country. My solidarity with the Politburo's views in this area of international policy did not play a decisive role, since the CC learned of my personal views only after it made the assignment.

My situation in Paris is extraordinarily false. For Narkomindel I am a very undesirable guest at its very hearth. Leaders of Narkomindel have not become accustomed to encounter objections to their actions and thoughts from its representatives abroad. Therefore, they meet my opinions and analysis with indignation, hysterics and complaints to the CC. I have no desire at all to polemicise with them, so I send my analysis and opinion about the situation directly to the CC. But doesn't it seem to you that such a situation is extraordinarily abnormal and that it cannot continue so for long?

You can imagine for yourself that Narkomindel and I have taken separate paths. More accurately, I parted with it, even in evaluating the simplification of those ceremonies, which fall to the lot of the diplomatic corps in France. They support everything medieval that has remained in the business of ambassadorial relations. Our attempt to simplify this operation summoned forth disap-

---

149   TsA FSB, R33718, d. 499061, vol. 12, original; vol. 13, ll. 41–9, copy.

proval and, it's possible to say, almost a rebuke [выговор] from the collegium of Narkomindel, despite the fact that we did not depart from the bounds of the published decree about simplifying such ceremonies.

I regard my activity here as very short-term. I already suggested to comrade Litvinov that he propose to the Politburo to replace me with a person whom they find more suitable. I am determined to do this myself also during my trip to Russia to deliver a report.

I think that I do contribute something useful here in one area, which is that of the workers' movement. Our doubts about what is happening abroad have been fully justified, as far as concerns French workers' organisations and parties. The trade union movement here is experiencing a period of stagnation. If we will compare French trade unions with those before the war, then we will be forced to recognise that they have not increased their influence significantly beyond what it was in 1914. Both of the existing Federations of Labour count no more than 700,000 members. You will understand the degree of each industry's organisation, if I take Paris as an example. Up to 200,000 metalworkers work in the suburbs of Paris, but only 6,000 people are united in unions belonging to both tendencies. If we add to this the bitter struggle between our party comrades on the one hand, and reformists, syndicalists, and such on the other, we find that this mutual fighting diminishes these giants. The employer, manufacturer, and factory owner are the absolute masters of the Republic. As you see, there is still much to do to unite workers and to create actual unity in the workers' movement. I already had a meeting with our comrades. They are still digging their heels in, but I am sure that unpleasant reality soon will force them to change their attitude. I also meet with reformists and talk with them about unity. They agree with the principle of unity from below, but not with simply combining existing organisations.

France is now experiencing an economic ascent. There is almost no unemployment. Employers in some branches of industry import cheap foreign labour. However, an end is foreseen to this economic wellbeing in the near future. A significant share of French industry works now for the internal market, which is expanded by the restoration of destroyed areas. As these works are completed, French industry will need foreign markets. This transition undoubtedly will entail crisis. The usual crisis at the moment is unemployment. The French government will struggle against unemployment by expelling all those foreigners, who arrived in this country in search of wages or who were brought in by employers' organisations.

Political struggle in France bears an extraordinarily exacerbated character. Bitter struggle goes on between the former nationalist bloc, which unites all that is reactionary in France (large property, large capital, landowners), and the leftist bloc, which won in the May elections in France and unites the petty bourgeoisie, socialists, and some of the middle-level industrialists. The rightwing press persecutes the Left Bloc government.

The Communist Party of France conducts its own independent policy, but I think that it makes some dangerous mistakes in evaluating its forces and selecting its means of struggle. According to some informants, the party has 13,000 members in the Paris district, while according to others it has 17,000. Of them, about half are foreigners. Outside Paris, they number about 50,000. The organisational forces are not great. But after a success the communists did not expect, which was during the street demonstrations connected with transferring [Jean] Jaures's ashes to the Pantheon, the heads of those in some party circles began to spin and they began to expect a French October very soon. Exploiting this mood, the reactionary press led a campaign to intimidate the petty bourgeoisie with the threat of the red spectre. In the course of several days, the weapons stores of Paris sold out all their stock. The petty and grand bourgeoisie became armed to the teeth. Some frightened parliamentarians demanded machine guns from the government for [defending] their apartments. The reactionary press achieved its goal and created an extraordinarily dangerous mood. The fright of the petty bourgeoisie began to disappear after the recent demonstration organised by the Communist Party, which revealed its actual forces as significantly smaller than during the government demonstration in honour of Jaures.

The Communist Party of France is switching over to Russian rails in an organisational sense. It is adopting a system of cells, but this transition is accompanied by a deviation toward illegality, which holds some dangers. The first danger is that the French workers are completely incapable of the illegal form of organisation. You yourself know perfectly well that even in our times, the workers in the factories knew who our party members were, but it is completely impossible to hide this in France. In that desperate struggle which now is waged against the Communist Party of France, there is the danger that factory worker communists, who are few in number and who are united in cells of a given factory, will be tossed out of this factory during the lay-offs soon to come.

In my opinion, the transition from a system of sections to cells is being made too hastily, without the necessary preparation. It is possible that in the future they will return to sections and groups. The very effort toward illegal existence is completely unjustified. You can't speak of fascism in France, at least not in the Italian sense of this word. There is not the main ingredient, which is unemployed and declassed soldiers, who in Italy played a decisive significance in the formation of fascist cadres. All cases of apparent fascism are just the usual conflicts with 'yellows', who want to undermine strikes. An example of this is the fighting and murder during the strikers' clashes in Douarnenez.[150] Milleranovite and royalist circles are attempting to create an organisation in the image of Italian fascism, but they do not have a mass following.[151]

I met with [Pierre] Monatte, who, as you probably know, was excluded from the Communist Party of France around the time we arrived in Paris. He was expelled for having published a brochure containing letters to the CC, in which he evaluated the condition of the party. Knowing Monatte and having some sympathy toward him, and likewise toward [Alfred] Rosmer and a third metalworker comrade who were excluded together with him, I am attempting to persuade them to appeal to the Comintern, but so far without success. Comrade Monatte, to whom I tried to prove the need to appeal to Moscow, points to the senselessness of this matter, because he entered the Communist Party of France without special enthusiasm. He was only carrying out the insistent wish of his political and trade union friends, who regarded his entry into the party as a revolutionary necessity. He himself was never a great fan of the political form of organisation. He did not hide this when he entered the party, but he did not expect that in the party they would slight him so, even forbidding him to write in the party's newspapers. He and his friends are thinking about organising a little periodical journal in Paris about the workers' movement. Our party comrades in France do not see in this any danger for themselves. I personally do not agree with their optimism. I regard the appearance of Monatte's journal as the beginning of the unification of former communists who do not agree with the party's current tactics. The appearance of such a group alongside the existing communist party in France will greatly hinder its work.

I have sought and found a large number of my comrades from the French Socialist Party and from the factories where I worked in and around Paris. A significant share of them numbered among party and trade union activists both before and after the war. After the war, when struggle went on in the socialist camp for creation of the Third International, my more activist friends organised the first cells of the Third International in France. Currently, all these comrades are outside our party, but they have not lost even one iota of their activism, which they have transferred exclusively into the trade union movement and

---

150   Douarnenez is a port town in Brittany. The fishing industry employed many people there in the early twentieth century. A strike, which was largely of women canning industry workers who wanted better working conditions, occurred there in 1924. See Martin 1994.

151   Shliapnikov is probably referring to Alexandre Millerand, who was a Republican-Socialist and who served as President of France in 1920–4.

education. This phenomenon, which is also familiar from Germany and from our country, offers rich fare for all sorts of philosophical conclusions. My French friends explain that they left the Communist Party, because they disagreed with its methods of work. It tries to imitate methods which were born from the conditions of revolutionary struggle in Russia and to implant these in France. We remain friends and I usually visit them for lunch or supper, during which five to ten workers gather. We converse and debate politics. On Sunday, 11 January 1925, I will host a reciprocal lunch for all my proletarians.

I received from some workers a questionnaire broaching the relationship of revolutionary Russia with West European parties and working class, and likewise the condition of industry and the situation of the working class of our country. I already answered all these questions orally in conversation and I think I will summarise them in written form for publication in the French press. Right now I am earnestly propagandising the idea of unity, but I meet stubborn resistance from the United General Confederation of Labour. True, this is not from its entire complement, but only from comrade [Gaston] Monmousseau who leads it. He disagrees with the principle of unity from below and instead promotes the slogan of unity from above, which essentially is a compact between leading elements of both tendencies. I am afraid that this tells of how they fear their own helplessness and of their weak influence upon the masses.

Already long ago I wrote the letter to Tomsky, about which you heard, but for some reason I still have not received an answer to it. Try to find out in passing why he for so long has not answered my letters.

Write me about how your housing problem was resolved. Have you moved to our apartment and how have you adjusted there? I will be very glad if you will write your tales more often.

10   A.G. Shliapnikov, 'Features of the Current Moment: About Results of the Fourteenth Party Conference', with S.P. Medvedev's Suggested Changes, May 1925[152]

Brief accompanying note from A.G. Shliapnikov to S.P. Medvedev, Moscow, 10 July [1925]

---

152   TsA FSB, R33718, volume 38, ll. 22–74, two drafts, with S.P. Medvedev's suggested changes, May 1925, excerpts.

Dear Sergei,

I'm sending you one uncorrected copy (on thick paper) and one that has been corrected.[153] The article is enormous. If you give it to anyone [illegible], warn them that it is a draft. Today I'm traveling through Nizhny [Novgorod]. At home, all is well.

Greetings and wishes,
A. Shliapnikov

S.P. Medvedev's suggested corrections
1.   On page two, correct the place about the conference's decisions about consolidation of power for the wealthy of the countryside.
2.   Further, it should be said that the economic growth of the peasantry [illegible phrase] toward the interests of development in a capitalist direction summons forth contradictions between the peasantry and working class.
3.   Following after this part, indicate that 'the resolution distinguishes'[154] and so forth and then already 'demands liquidation of the remainders [остатки] by all (com.)' and so forth.
4.   Replace the expression 'senior CC members' with 'members of the CC's leading group'.

Corrected draft: 'About Several Features of the Current Moment', typed with editing marks in Shliapnikov's hand[155]

Excerpts:

The slogan 'look to the countryside', which was proposed several months ago, elicited bewilderment and confusion in some ranks of our party. For many ... it was completely unexpected. Besides that, our party's recent policy was entirely and systematically adapted toward the interests of the petty bourgeoisie of the countryside. The interests of the countryside have directly dictated all large-scale measures since the transition to NEP, as well as NEP itself. Tax and credit policy, money reforms, lowering of prices on industrial goods ...

---

153   I did not take notes from the uncorrected draft, which was preserved in TsA FSB, R33718, d. 499061, vol. 38, ll. 41–74. My notes from the corrected version follow below.
154   The Russian word was either отличает or отмечает.
155   TsA FSB, R33718, volume 38, ll. 23–40.

Worker masses who are party members feel especially cruelly the impact of the character and content of all these measures upon themselves. They have clearly seen that the party looks toward the countryside and not toward them.
…

All party decisions of the past few years have favoured the peasantry, so the new slogan can't be viewed as a turn in new direction. It is only a continuation and development of the NEP of 1921 …

The Fourteenth Party Conference … tore away part of the ideological-political cloak, which had covered NEP up to then, and exposed its capitalist features. The same conference confirmed measures which led inevitably to the seizure of power by the prosperous and wealthy of the countryside. Simultaneously, it strengthened their hold on power during the 1924–5 electoral campaign.

In the resolution on party building, the conference notes that the union of workers and peasants, which began to take shape in 1917 and was created in the period of civil war, now no longer serves as a brace for the further existence of the bloc. The USSR's economic growth gives birth to contradictions between the proletariat and the peasantry.

… the resolution recognises the inevitability of capitalism's growth for the near future. The entire aggregate of directives of the Fourteenth Party Conference has disproved one of the legends, which was composed in praise of NEP … which is that it is a socialist maneuver …

[Begins to analyse Bukharin's and Stalin's speeches to personnel of the Moscow party organisation and Zinoviev's speech to the Communist Faction of the Third All-Union Congress of Soviets; also refers to Lenin's 1923 article about cooperatives when referring to Bukharin's use of it to justify policies of 1925]

One can ascribe this entire characterisation of the cooperative movement only to our worker cooperation, Tsentrosoiuz, which has its own enterprises. Comrade Bukharin became confused and so he confuses the reader. However, it would be frivolous to think that comrade Bukharin is simply mistaken. No, he is trying to put a foundation under today's petty bourgeois practice and make it stronger, as a matter of principle. This 'new' plan, which is attributed to V.I. Lenin, helps comrade Bukharin to make conclusions that are diametrically opposed to those of Lenin. If in 1921 he had in mind the use of state and private capital (concessionary and such types) against the petty bourgeois element, now in 1925 comrade Bukharin counterposes this petty bourgeois element 'against large capital (that is, essentially against state capital, since we have no other large capital – A. Sh.) and against the remnants of private capital'.[156] Lenin really does point out that it is possible to use the petty bourgeoisie

---

156   He refers the reader to *Bolshevik*, no. 8, p. 12.

against large capital, but only comrade Bukharin can show us the conjuror's trick of directing small capitalists and producers against themselves and that he can do only on paper.

[Criticises Stalin's report ...]

Comrade Stalin, in trying to shed light upon the fate of socialism in our country, begins with a reference to presently existing contradictions. He does not directly analyse or investigate the class essence of these contradictions, but limits himself only to confirming the existence and character of these contradictions ....

Comrade Stalin aims to overcome contradictions between the peasantry and workers by means of some special, socialist path for agricultural development. Comrade Stalin does not show where this path exists. Obviously, this path of development exists in his head, a hint of which is contained in this reference. Only one thing is clear from his speech. It is that this socialist path 'means development by means of steadily elevating the wellbeing of the majority of the peasantry'. The measures by which he is determined to achieve this well-being, and why this well-being of petty-bourgeois farming is called 'socialist', remain a secret known only to him. Comrade Stalin does not doubt that development of the small peasant economy will take the path he indicated, because, you see, the peasantry itself has an interest in this. Reasoning thus, comrade Stalin falls into populist generalisations and conceals the existing contradictions within the peasantry ...

Comrade Stalin slips close to servility toward the petty bourgeoisie, when he promises to save it and to elevate its wellbeing on the basis of small property holding. He makes agriculture, which is the more conservative sector of small-scale production, the foundation for building the future socialist society. Thirty years ago, French opportunists already attempted to promote such 'socialism', when they promised to support small property ownership, but the old man Engels evaluated this severely ....

The situation in Western Europe fully refutes him ... In France the majority of peasants are small holders ... This doesn't help the development of socialist ideas among them ... Only agricultural labourers and semiproletarians are inclined toward socialism ... This is populism .... These are SR lies about special paths for the development of agriculture. ... Stalin and Bukharin ... just raise old populist dust and cast it upon their heads. ...

Comrade Stalin is mistaken and confuses others, when he speaks about our country as if about a socialist country. We do not have socialism. A whole range of economic structures continue to coexist, beginning with peasant barter and transitioning to small handicraft production, regenerating private capital, and our state capitalism as a transitional step toward socialism. State industry is still too weak to resolutely define the economic structure of our country. The prevailing economic form is still small commodity production. An enormous share of the national economy, which is our country's agriculture, is built on private capitalist foundations. ...

We have no socialism. Therefore, it is still early to speak of contradictions existing between socialism in our country and capitalism over there.

The basic contradiction between our country and other capitalist countries is that we do not permit free entry and development here to large foreign private capital. The capitalist world system cannot be reconciled to a barrier placed to it in our country. The remaining contradictions with capitalist measures, including those which are called forth by the danger of 'a red specter' coming from the east, with rejections of old treaties, nationalisation of large property including foreigners' property, refusal to pay loans, and the right of each nation to self-determination, are of secondary significance.

Our active policy of attempting to secure allies against Anglo-American capitalist imperialism exacerbates these contradictions even more. Contradictions between colonial countries and capitalist powers give birth to forces, which also are allied to us, among the oppressed peoples of the East. Our socialist intentions and the struggle, which we wage and lead against capitalist countries, dispose the proletarian circles of the West toward us. All contradictions are linked by a chain of general policy. Therefore, only on paper is it possible to define them separately by taking each group in isolation. Such is the circle and the character of internal contradictions, when examined most closely. Comrade Stalin resolutely warns against replacing internal contradictions with external contradictions. ... He encloses socialism within purely Russian borders and rejects the understanding that socialism as an economic system cannot be limited and locked in by the borders of one country. ...

Agreement with the peasantry inside the country alone is insufficient for building socialism. ... In the last case, our socialist measures inevitably collide with the private-proprietary interests of smallscale peasant agriculture. We cannot close our eyes to this. It is possible to struggle against this danger by creating an industrial base in the very 'heart' [нутро] of agriculture.

It is mistaken and harmful to separate, by means of a Great Wall of China, our workers' movement and our struggle from the West European movement and struggle, when they are closely linked by their very essence ....

[Presents data about agriculture, compared with 1914 and 1916.]

As a result of such a subdivision (from 12 million peasant households before the war to 22 million in 1924), we have a large number of peasant holdings, which are 'self-sustaining' but completely weak economically ... Livestock holding quickly rises in growth ...

Unification into cooperatives cannot make the poor peasants' dwarfish and horseless agriculture stand on its own two feet. Peasants who are so poor can bring nothing into the cooperatives, except for their labour power ... Cooperatives can help the matter by transforming the smallest farms of the poor peasantry into a powerful, collective farm. But this task is not up to the means of the poor peasants. Without systematic economic aid from the government, this business will not move ahead. ... The suggestion to give horses to those who don't have them, and thereby lead their farming onto a stable path, will not resolve the issue on a mass scale. ... The peasant farm's basic need is not horsepower. For 37 % of the poor, who have less than two desiatinas of land per farm, a horse will not make their farming more productive.[157] A peasant cannot even sustain his horse on such a small amount of arable land. He needs at least three and a half desiatinas of land to sustain a horse in the central region .... The question of concentrating farms and of voluntary unification needs to be posed. These 'compacts' [уговоры] about the need to organise large farms will be too weak to overcome the proprietary and individualist prejudices of the poor. They will not hinder the natural process of concentrating the peasant economy. ...

In some places, the government can and should help poor peasants and farm-labourers (batraks) by buying them out or by longterm leasing of their plots of land. This would free them from the unprofitable conditions of leasing land to kulaks. By concentrating these plots of land, the government could consequently organise farms on them or rent out such plots to peasants.

The third series of measures, which are concealed under the general formula 'liquidating the remnants of military communism', mean the freeing of commodity circulation[158] in the countryside. In the countryside, until very recently, a single commodity was forbidden from 'freely' circulating. This was the rural workforce. At the same time when the exploitation of urban hired labour was not interrupted for even one day, various prohibitions encircled the use of hired labour in the countryside. However, these prohibitions could not eliminate the demand of a developing agricultural economy for 'strong' peasants when hiring temporary or permanent working hands, nor could they 'abolish' the presence of the rural poor who craved some sort of work. The presence of these two conditions led to the union of the exploiter and the exploited against the authority, who would forbid or limit the use of hired labour in the countryside. ... Under such conditions, the exploitation of hired labour went underground

---

157   Desiatina = 2.7 acres.
158   Развязывание товарного оборота.

and assumed severely difficult forms of bondage that were literally unheard of. The legalisation of hired labour in the countryside will benefit the rural poor, for it will make it easier to defend it as a seller of its own labour. ...

Not one proposal above goes beyond simple satisfaction of the needs of petty 'middle' peasant farming. In all the proposals, there is not one government economic measure, which could serve as a linchpin and which would be capable of really transferring peasant farming onto socialist rails. These measures consist of organising large state agricultural enterprises. These are the grain factories, which have sometimes been discussed. But the business of organising state plants [фабрики] for agricultural production frightens shortsighted politicians, who try first of all to dam the approach to proletarianising the countryside. Some circles even oppose creating such enterprises, as if they are undesirable competitors with small agriculture. The reference to our poverty is only an empty excuse. Our agricultural bank spent not a small amount of resources, but they were spent on those measures, which essentially waste state wealth outright. These measures need to be given a productive direction by being deployed for creating industry in agriculture. ...

The further development of agriculture should be bound to industrial development. He, who will attempt to resolve the problem of the rural economy separately, will inevitably come up against the urban, industrial economy. The problem of the poor will be resolved not so quickly in the countryside as in the city. Only the rapid, powerful growth of industry and further distribution of labour between town and countryside are capable of swallowing up those excess rural hands, of which some are so frightened and which call forth measures intended to delay the proletarianisation of the countryside. Preserving small-scale holdings in our country will lead to unprecedented contradictions. These will include extreme inflation, which would exceed by several times the cost of living in capitalist countries, and unprecedentedly low wages for the proletariat.

Besides that, the development of agriculture during four years of NEP has not eliminated the basic danger, which emerges from small proprietary farming. It would be mistaken to hope that raising the general wellbeing of the countryside can eliminate this danger. On the contrary, if smallscale peasant farming becomes better off, stronger, and more significant, it will only strive for power and force the existing authority to serve its interests. All that occurred in the countryside in connection with the past year's elections fully confirms this. Under such conditions, the leadership of the working class can be preserved only under the condition that our large industry will be rapidly lifted up.

Despite bureaucratic optimism, our country's industry is developing very painfully and slowly. At the same time when primitive agriculture is quickly moving toward achieving pre-war norms of arable land (90% of prewar) ... large industry has only reached 47% of the prewar level of production.[159] The quantity of the industrial workforce also has not exceeded 50% of that before 1917. Information in comrades Zinoviev's and Stalin's reports is incorrect and exaggerated. We do not have four million industrial workers. In March of this year, there were only 1,460,075 workers. Large state industry has not reached 75% of prewar production, as comrade Zinoviev claims. It is not even at 50%. In the mining industry, it is even less. In metals extraction and processing, it hasn't even reached 25% of prewar production. ... At the same time, when capitalist countries of Western Europe and America have raised their economy significantly higher than before the war, we are still marking time around the period of 1913, counting on achieving it in two or three years at best. Besides that, urban unemployment and proletarianisation of the countryside threaten outright pauperisation, so great is the 'surplus' population in the countryside and so insignificant is its absorption by industry and seasonal work. ...

Capitalism is emerging from the postwar crisis and developing further. ... Political unification of bourgeois forces around rightwing, conservative, and even reactionary parties accompanies the strengthening of capitalism in Europe. This bourgeois adjustment attests that the capitalist economy is now developing in the context of international contradictions so great that the bourgeoisie is determined to resolve them by military force. ... Militarist and nationalist circles and conservative parties are growing stronger ....

Working class forces now are found in a state of great moral and organisational disorder. In many countries, the forces of the proletariat are systematically weakened by the cruel internal struggle between two tendencies. ... Voices call out for unity ... but there are no results in most countries ... The overthrow of all feudal remnants and struggle for the eight-hour working day and other proletarian demands, which ease the situation of the working masses, dissipated the revolutionary scale of the workers' movement in the most leading countries. Such a historical coincidence of circumstances has not justified our expectations and our reckonings on international revolution. Some Comintern leaders, who are frequently mistaken in their calculations and predictions, have become so discouraged by such jokes of history that they regard the whole course of revolutionary events in Europe as a complete betrayal of the revolution by reformist leaders and the many millions of workers who support them.

---

159   His figures come from p. 8 of L.B. Kafengauz's annual periodical of Soviet economic statistics, *Gosudarstvennaia promyshlennost SSSR* (published by Promizdat), but it is not clear which issue he is citing.

Such an attitude ... and explanation do not provide the key to understanding the real reasons for the failure of the slogans of socialist revolution. ...

Speaking about objective signs of socialist revolution, our politicians and economists oversimplified the situation in European countries and completely left out of their calculations the condition of the working class. They took the working class as already completely prepared, as taught by war and its consequences, and as ready to go into struggle for socialism. According to this simplified scheme it emerged that only reformists and all possible kinds of compromisers from social democracy are the obstacle to this struggle of the West European proletariat for its power. ...

The question arises of why did the majority of European workers understand the voices of traitors better than the voices of their selfless friends. Throughout history, there still has not been a case when the majority of a class betrayed its interests. It is only possible to explain this by understanding the changes, which the war brought about in the working class. ...

Industrial cadres have been destroyed and replaced with women's and children's labour. The war drew the petty urban and rural bourgeoisie into industrial work and proletarianised them. The war years were extremely unfavourable for raising or developing the class consciousness of new strata, who poured into the proletariat. These elements are the support base of reformism and social betrayal ... France had seen especially marked changes. ... Now about three million foreign workers are there, mostly from backwards countries like Poland or African colonies. ...

They link the traitorous role of reformers in the workers' movement with the interests of the section of the working class called the worker aristocracy. The theory about the role of the 'worker aristocracy' represents a small attempt to 'correct' Karl Marx's tenet that as capitalism develops, it gives birth to broad circles of the proletariat, who have an interest in capitalist exploitation. This theory is deeply incorrect. It directly contradicts elementary tenets of Marxism and of reality and is saturated with antiworker thinking.

Who is considered the 'worker aristocracy' in Europe? This is usually defined as skilled workers, who are present in all branches of industry. Skilled workers are numerous in all types of metals and machinebuilding industry. Everywhere these cadres of workers are the most developed and the best organised. Skilled workers are exploited in conditions that are common to all workers, but as trained specialists, they have higher wages than untrained workers do.

Arising from this situation, they make conclusions about skilled workers having an interest in preserving capitalist exploitation, but they forget the basic position that it is not wages that decide, but the role of the worker in production. However, the progress of mechanisation, of automatization, and of division of labour levels out and leads to the decrease of the skilled workforce. Now nowhere is it an especially privileged caste. Nowhere abroad do highly skilled workers earn more than twice as much in wages as simple unskilled workers. If you judge the worker aristocracy by wages, then the most 'aristocratic' in comparison with unskilled were always our Russian metalworkers, of whom the wages of highly skilled categories exceeded by four or more times the wages of unskilled workers. In all European countries, skilled cadres of workers are the most conscious fighters and the best organised and advanced in relation to other categories of workers. Our communist parties found and even now find in this milieu the largest number of supporters and sympathisers. The theory of worker aristocracy was thought up only to justify and explain our failures among this milieu of workers. ...

The history of struggle in Russia refutes such an explanation of the role of skilled workers. ... Skilled workers were the leading force of our country's revolutionary movement and they remain so even now. ... The same analysis is applied to the trade union movement of the West ... Our information about the worker movement of the West is full of contradictions. The more worker leaders betray the organised masses, the stronger becomes their influence. All these phenomena taken together 'stabilise' and even aid the growth of social democracy. Revolutionary impatience often harmfully influences the analysis of reality and more often the logic of thought. The influence of reformist leaders and the growth of social democracy are the direct consequence of the adaptability of tactics, methods, and policy toward understanding and serving the interests of the broader masses of the proletariat. ... programmes addressing short-term needs and offering 'little deeds' are familiar to us from Menshevik practice in the worker movement of our country ... Communists' struggle against reformists on the basis of defending workers' economic interests turned into struggle against trade unions, and so European communists didn't know how to link short-term interests with the tasks of general struggle for power and for socialism.

But our senior Comintern leaders have still not learned anything from these persistent facts. As previously, we hear theories, which number significant strata of workers among the capitalists and explain European workers' trade unions as an outright weapon of counterrevolution. Such an approach to winning over worker masses and such a characterisation of mass worker organisations are false and harmful, since they cannot strengthen the Comintern's influence. On the contrary, they can elicit from workers no other feelings than dissatisfaction with any actions other than resolute resistance to carriers of such views.

In connection with the stabilisation of capitalism, a very dangerous situation is being created for workers in the whole world, including all European states. As capitalism grows stronger, various contradictions and armed conflicts grow even more greatly. ... Workers are not capable of using conflicts among their enemies in the active struggle for power. Worker revolutionaries and communists in all countries are confronted with the task of gathering forces and strengthening existing worker organisations, first of all trade unions. Unity of the trade union movement cannot remain just an agitational theme. Such a situation is taking shape in Europe now, so that further struggle of workers insistently demands unity of forces. Those parties or leaders who do not see or understand this necessity commit mistakes and are condemned to vegetate.

The same obstacle stands everywhere along the road to unity of the trade union movement. It is the struggle among various tendencies. ... A significant amount of resources is wasted on internal struggle. The way out of this is possible only through a conscious agreement between 'reformists' and 'revolutionaries' about unity on the basis of class struggle, the minority's support of the majority, and the minority's right to propagandise its views among members of the organisation. Past and present experience shows that this path is the only way to create unity among mass, nonparty workers' unions. Only in this way can European communists join together with broad worker masses and fill their criticism of reformism with more concrete educational content. Creating unity in the world trade union movement ... is the most vital need and revolutionary duty. ... Our party, acting through the Comintern, shouldn't throw the majority of the working class and its vanguard into the camp of counterrevolution, only because it does not share our views about current tasks.

When some theoreticians enter a certain part of the working class into the camp of the enemies of socialism, they are at the same time making a rather characteristic turn toward the petty bourgeoisie. In the revolutionary era during which we live, the petty bourgeoisie is now accorded an unprecedentedly decisive role. The role of the working class in ongoing socialist revolutions is reduced to that of 'instigator'. Simultaneously, the peasantry is brought in as the 'heavy infantry' of the socialist revolution. From the history of revolutionary struggle in the West, we know what became of the proletariat's role as 'instigator'. We witnessed and experienced the role of 'instigator' in our country, during the March 1917 Revolution. Workers played the role of instigator and overthrew the monarchy, but the large bourgeoisie started to make decisions. Now they introduce a change: the proletariat 'conceived' its revolution, but the petty bourgeoisie will decide it in the end.[160] What will be the end of such a

---

160   He refers the reader to Zinoviev's brochure, *Vazhneishie cherty sovremennogo momenta,*

'proletarian' revolution is not hard to imagine, for it will answer the interests of that class, which will finally decide the matter. The 'heavy infantry' and its role in our country, beginning from 1921 and up to the current day, can serve as an example.

In order to attract the petty bourgeoisie to support European communist parties, demands were advanced to divide large farms to satisfy petty bourgeois appetites. This was done even in those countries where the peasantry's weight in the economy was insignificant. In Germany, a similar demand was directed right against agricultural workers and could not achieve their support. Theories arise about the common interests of the petty bourgeoisie and the proletariat and about the small farm's vitality and revolutionary significance.

Our Comintern produces the theories and practice laid out above, in its attempt to transplant the experience of our revolution onto other countries. Transplanting our experience, which was a result of our country's historical particularities, in such a way can give birth to nothing better than a caricature, or to adventurism, which is worse. Moreover, this effort has nothing in common with Marxism. Use of our experience as a template for other countries, without any regard for their historical particularities, cannot bring the proletarian revolution closer. Instead, the opposite most likely will occur, which is that such methods will discredit it.

The communist parties of the West face the task of winning over the working masses, from whom they are still very remote. They will manage to win influence over the working masses only by means of determined and consistent propaganda and struggle against the national limitations of reformism. The task is enormous and demands protracted work, but there is no other way. In such a context, assigning them the task of drawing the petty bourgeoisie into the socialist revolution will force them to make substitutions not only for revolutionary forces, but also for revolutionary goals. The West European proletariat will not be seduced by such a 'revolutionary' perspective, which will be decided by the 'heavy infantry' of the petty bourgeoisie. The latter has grown fat on war and rural famine crises. The West European proletariat does not need the rural petty bourgeoisie, because the proportional weight of small farms in the European economy is comparatively smaller than in our country.

Arrogantly rejecting the proletariat of the 'rotten West', some comrades turn the party's policy around to the East. There, on the horizon of the semi-patriarchal and petty bourgeois East, they have seen the rising star of socialist

---

p. 16. This is probably *Vazhneishie cherty sovremennogo perioda*, which was translated into English as *Russia's Path to Communism* (London: Communist Party of Great Britain, 1925).

revolution. Revolutionary events in Eastern countries are said to be of 'decisive' significance for the fate of the proletarian revolution in the leading countries of Europe. The struggle of Eastern peoples against feudalism and the national oppression of imperialist powers are melded into one with the proletarian emancipatory struggle, which creates a bunch of contradictions and general confusion.

The emancipation of the East has enormous significance for the revolutionary proletarian movement, but there is no basis for giving it decisive influence over the proletarian revolution in the West. The peoples of the East still have their 1905 in front of them. In its struggle, the East is far from united. They have industry there, which became especially stronger during the war. There is also a working class. The latter is too weak to have a decisive influence on the world revolution. The forces of the bourgeoisie are large and they combine with the general capitalist system prevailing in other countries. The decline of feudal power and of imperialist oppression will not shake the capitalist system and will not destroy the power of capital. This decline will not bring essential changes in the correlation of class forces in the West. Capitalist rule will be destroyed in the East by those same forces, which will struggle against it in the West. There is no other path for the East.

11   A.M. Kollontai's Diary Notes, February 1926 and November [1927][161]

[It is possible that Kollontai later revised these entries.]

3 February 1926. Oslo, Norway.

[She arrived in Moscow on 23 December 1925 and was there for one and a half months. She attended the Fourteenth Party Congress.]

It was an utterly unprecedented congress, for it was nervous and difficult, with [illegible word] the designation [обозначение] of two tendencies. All of a sudden, Zinoviev is heading a Leningrad Opposition. Under NEP, of course, it was inevitable that peasant influence has grown and is becoming firmly established in the soviets. It weighs upon our policy. Our economy is better, but the peasantry is a danger. The peasantry already [illegible word] to puts forth its own ideology and its [illegible word] leaders, who [two illegible words] will direct

---

161   RGASPI, f. 134, op. 3, d. 44, ll. 6–10.

the country's policy toward securing [illegible word] peasant private property instead of toward communism. This is very dangerous and many of us foresaw it. But it had never even occurred to me that Rykov would come to lead the 'peasantisation' of Soviet power. This was impossible to imagine. And then there are all these young 'red professors' of the Bukharinist persuasion [толк]. Indeed, they are developing a petty-bourgeois ideology outright.

The Leningraders, with Zinoviev and Kamenev, essentially express the reaction of the 'hereditary proletarians' of Piter (Petrograd) against these peasant-like moods of Rykov and Co. Trotsky falls into another extreme [?]. As always, that one is for pressure, clamping down, urgent measures, and superindustrialisation. He cannot satisfy the workers and even less so the peasants. It was strange to see Trotsky sitting in the delegates' rows and not in the presidium. Stalin's intensifying popularity was very striking [illegible word] at the congress. He is impressive, restrained, and resolute. He personally was not with anyone but, together with Rykov, he beat Trotsky and beat the Leningraders. Stalin is correct from the governmental point of view. The kind of socialism that Trotsky wants will not be built in such a ravaged country. The peasantry needs to be allowed to 'recover its breath'.

Among the Leningraders, there are longtime party members, workers, so many acquaintances, and so many comrades-in-arms! Even Klavdiia Nikolaeva belongs to the opposition.

Kamenev acknowledged to me, 'We ourselves did not expect that we would go so far'. There is much dissatisfaction among the broad masses of workers. There is dissatisfaction with prices, bureaucratism, and our inability to lift their self-activity in the business of creating Soviet industry. They do not see anything new. But what do they want concretely? There is no clarity. There is only repudiation. Do they want better prices and different wage rates? Zinoviev and Kamenev attempt to impart a 'principled character' to all this. But everyone senses that they (not the workers) have much that is personal invested in this struggle. It is something personal against Stalin. He is stronger and braver than they. He has something which they precisely lack. This is that he is concerned not about himself, but about the party, for he is its personification, as Lenin was. For him the cause and the goal are more important than petty 'ambitions', as with Trotsky and Zinoviev. In this is his strength. The masses have not trusted Zinoviev and Kamenev for a long time.

The Stalinists (this is a new word in Moscow) were closer [illegible word] to me personally. Shl[iapnikov] and Medv[edev] lean toward the Leningraders. But this is a negative beginning![162] There is nothing concrete, nothing positive

---

162   Someone drew a marginal line along the previous two sentences.

there. Also, I could never be in solidarity with Zinoviev, I hate this petty, base creature too much for his mistaken [illegible word] and harmful policy in the Comintern.

Old friends and party members, who are not outright oppositionists but 'who criticise', say: 'Are you really speaking out against Trotsky? Now, when he is in such a difficult situation?' There are still strong remnants of a past upbringing and prerevolutionary morals: it is 'not honourable' to speak out at 'such a moment'.

But I listen to the voices of the masses. They more correctly take account of a party member's duty [?] in the Soviet government. Do they need to know where I stand? What is this, a game of hide and seek? I wrote an article for *Pravda* 'about how the masses are against the opposition'. In the morning, Mikoian called to say, 'You wrote well'.

On 7 November [1927], Trotsky's prestige among the masses suffered a great loss. The opposition behaved stupidly and became 'ridiculous'. I was in the People's Commissariat with Mikoian at night, when the Politburo decided to exclude Trotsky, Kamenev and Zinoviev.[163] We followed the course of the decision by telephone.

[written in a different pen] There was a tragic element in this inevitable and historically correct decision, especially for those, who lived through 1917 as activists.

12   Letter from I.I. Nikolaenko, Kiev [to A.G. Shliapnikov and
      S.P. Medvedev], circa 1926[164]

[omission] ... I am perturbed by two circumstances. A portrait of Aleksandr appeared in *Izvestiia VTsIK* along side, it is possible to say, the chiefs [вожди] of the working class, who were named above. I must acknowledge that this surprised me very much. I still had not fully processed the first thing, when in Kiev they convened a limited group of party activists [актив], at which the chief of the Kiev organisation made a report about a plenum of the CC VKP(b). From the report, it became clear that the plenum decided to lift the tax from those

163   Trotsky and Zinoviev were expelled from the party on 12 November. Kamenev was only expelled at the Fifteenth Party Congress in December 1927.
164   TsA FSB, R33718, d. 499061, vol. 14, ll. 5–8, handwritten copy, ll. 9–10, typed copy. His handwritten original contained misspellings and ungrammatical expressions, which the typist corrected. The typist also changed some of his word choices. At the time, Nikolaenko was manager of the Ukrainian Tobacco Trust.

peasants with few resources [маломощные] and to decrease prices for food supplies, fixing them to the level of wages earned.[165]

Of course, I took the floor, as they say in our Ukraine, 'to speak' [промову] and expressed satisfaction with the decision about the tax, while noting that this was done too late and that 'you were advised to accomplish this on time'. As concerns the lowering of prices, I recognised them as inappropriate [неумест-ными] and as a continuation of the old policy of strengthening kulak farming at the cost of wringing the sweat out of the workers.

The chief attacked me very maliciously. But because he did not have any facts with which to deflect my attack, he shouted until he was hoarse. Grisha actively supported me. No matter how strange it seems, we met with sympathy from the so-called constricted [суженный] group of activists.

The enumerated facts produce on me the impression that a political veteran is turning the CC's attention to our street, which is overgrown with grass. But I cannot find reasons, which have called this forth. Therefore, I request of you, if you will find it necessary and possible, to write me a couple of words about Moscow news.

In the party apparatus, there is unbelievable illiteracy. For example, all I have to do is speak out in public for representatives of various 'coms'[166] to jump on me. They carry in such rubbish [околесицу] that an ordinary party member is left with his mouth hanging open in surprise. An interesting incident occurred in one trust, into which a former colonel was accepted as deputy director of the warehouse. Party members found him suspicious, because until July 1917, he was a quartermaster and did not serve anywhere during subsequent years. The Trade Union of Chemists gave him a trade union card. Ostensibly, he joined the union. But it turned out that it is forbidden to accept unemployed people into the union. Then the wise union personnel took from him an entry fee and entered a note that he had been unemployed for six months. This circumstance still more worried party members, who had an interest in sending to this place their own party person. They moved to convene the trust's collective, but the chair of the trust declared that this is not their business. Then the party members went to the party committee. The party committee ordered them to keep quiet.

There are even greater curiosities. One military communist said something rude to the secretary of the district committee (raikom), which is named for the January Uprising. The raikom secretary called the corps commander. The

---

165   решено снизить цены на продукты закрепляясь на достигнутом уровне зарплаты.
166   'Com' is likely shorthand for committee, commission, commissariat, etc.

corps commander ordered the military communist to go apologise. The comrade appeared before the secretary, saluted, and stated: on the basis of the corps commander's order, I beg your pardon. I don't know, but they say that the secretary of the raikom was very dissatisfied with this.

I could introduce dozens of such cases, but I do not want to take up too much of your time. If you are following the Kherson case, you can form an impression about Ukraine. Or take the case of the Kiev militia. Was it worth raising such a din? Moreover, they arrested 60 party members on this case.

All this attests that the petty bourgeoisie leads our organisation. Unprecedented discrediting of Soviet power and the party is going on at such a crucial moment. In my opinion, in our Ukraine, narkomats are stagnating, even one such as VSNKh. There is not one popular person for Ukraine, Rabkrin, Narkomtorg. It is difficult to say what will happen next, but it won't improve under this leadership.

As concerns our trade union movement, well it goes along on its own way and the working class survives without any help.

You have taken note of the Kievsky Opb [?]. Their notes can be extended to all trade unions' work.

As you see, the situation is difficult. In party and trade union work, there is unprecedented indifference. They don't allow those who are capable of showing activism to speak. Personally, I was not allowed a nonvoting role at the last party conference, despite the fact that three days before it, I applied to participate actively. Second, in Kharkov, at the gathering of party activists, where Chubar made a report, they also did not let me speak. I appealed to the CC secretary, Kaganovich, who promised me, but he left and did not follow through. (It needs to be noted that this fellow is as extraordinarily boorish as a bailiff.)

Don't think that this information is the fruit of my sick soul. I feel cheerful and I am ready to take action at any minute.

13   Letter from A.G. Shliapnikov, Moscow, to [I.I. Nikolaenko], 12 May 1926[167]

Dear friend,

I received your letter, although it arrived with a delay, because the address was incorrect.

---

167   TsA FSB, R33718, d. 499061, vol. 12, l. 21–2.

First of all, I must resolutely refute the slanderous talk of the Zatonskys [?] and their ilk regarding my alleged refusal (under the guise of departure) to speak at the Fourteenth Congress.[168] The truth is that I tried to sign up already during Molotov's report, but was placed at the 100th spot on the list. Later they moved me down to the 120th position. I made numerous requests and tried to negotiate with individual Presidium members (comrades Rykov, Stalin, Kalinin, and Kuibyshev), but they joked in response and agreed to assign me as the 90th speaker. Finally, comrade Kuibyshev openly (in front of witnesses) told me that he would not allow me to speak, because this 'would be best for' me. It's not difficult to understand, that the tales of the Zatonskys [?] and similar types are filthy attempts to discredit us in general and me in particular.

Conversations about the photograph should be regarded in the same way. They snapped our picture during the TsIK session. We were photographed several times and sometimes without any desire to fall within the camera's scope. In my photograph, there are other comrades besides me. However, no political conclusion should be made from this. To rebuke me for having stood next to Voroshilov, who behaved so badly in Leningrad, makes as much political sense as to rebuke me for being a member of the same party as he. I am very happy with your information and will make from it the appropriate conclusions for the future. But you should disprove fabrications on the spot yourselves. Don't allow them to develop unchecked and don't yield to such ignorant provocations.

We know about the plenum and its decisions. However, I do not see in them any changes of our CC's policy. I don't know what exactly they reported to your group of party activists, but judging from the contents of the plenum's work, I don't see any radical turn in its decision about the economic question. [Illegible phrase]. The plenum's decisions are just as lacking in perspective as was the Fourteenth Congress. They have not identified a way out of the crisis.

All of the same tendencies struggled at the plenum as at the congress. As before, the petty-bourgeois deviation runs up against the timid resistance of the overwhelming minority, using Kalinin's words. Try to grasp the meaning of the plenum's decisions and think them over. You will see that they lack the turn toward that which you desire. Verify this in practice. Look closely at lived experience. How are those questions resolved in your parts? You will see clearly that everything stays the same. Nothing changes. The emancipation of the poor

---

168   Perhaps he is referring to Vladimir Petrovich Zatonsky (1888–1938), who at the time was secretary of the Central Committee of the Communist Party (Bolsheviks) of Ukraine. He was a Menshevik before the revolution and joined the Bolsheviks in 1917.

countryside from the tax cannot serve as an indicator of change, although the opposition put forth this proposal.

Your views about the policy of 'lowering prices' are correct. There is no turn toward the direction, which you favour. Prices on agricultural goods are rising. 'Socialist' agricultural cooperatives in fact are becoming syndicates for monopolistic sales of the foodstuffs produced by the rich men [богатеи] of the villages.

The incident you related about military personnel illustrates only the degree to which the party has become bureaucratised. As concerns the 'authorities' hesitation', well there are 'great politics' [большая политика] behind this. Look more attentively into this and you will see that for a long time already the method of 'discreditation' has existed in our party as a means for undermining authorities. Now this method is appearing as a means of political, group, and class struggle. Within the party and at the top of the soviets, these methods are used broadly. This system of discreditation facilitates the advancement to the 'leadership' and power of those 'needy' elements, which you encounter now at every turn. I cannot agree that all this is just 'a period of social stagnation' [безвременье]. No, essentially we are seeing political time-serving, which is carried out on the basis of the country's economy.

That which you note in trade union work can be seen in other branches of society and government. All worker organisations' activity is bureaucratised and leads to the loss of contact with the masses, about which you report. Indeed, can you not see the same thing in our party? It is now built upon and conducts its work along the same favourite bureaucratic path. All these phenomena conceal an enormous danger. But it is worth little to point out harm and danger. One also needs to point out the way to correct and avoid danger. This can only be implementation of the old slogan of worker democracy. But one needs to struggle for this. The 'party-union-soviet bureaucracy' taking shape in our country and merging now with the petty bourgeoisie, is firmly entrenched. The existing 'pressure' within the party supports it.

The case of the Kiev militia and hundreds similar to it, which extend all the way to embezzlement, are rooted in what you call 'stagnation'. But think about it. Why has it become such a 'good time' for the growth of such things? Why is the matter not about 'stagnation' in policy, but about the system for selecting people to carry out this policy? In fact, the existing order gives birth to the bureaucracy's complete lack of responsibility to the party grassroots. It is just the same in trade unions, where there is lack of responsibility to the workers of a given union. That's where that phenomenon comes from. They are the bosses and the bureaucracy. They are all out for themselves. Workers are left to their own devices, as you have noticed.

How is it in England? The greatest events, which are historically unprecedented, are happening. More than five million workers are on strike. Our 'leading' bodies have turned up at the tail of events. The strike arose 'in spite of' expectations and revealed the real level of our pretenders to international leadership.[169] No matter how this strike ends, it will have enormous political consequences, which go far beyond the borders of England itself. Write a note about how those in your area regarded the strike.

14 A.G. Shliapnikov, 'About a Demonstrative Attack and the Rightist Danger in the Party'[170]

Comrade Medvedev's personal letter to a Baku party proletarian is analysed in the article 'Rightist Danger in our Party', which appeared in the 10 July 1926 issue of *Pravda*. This letter relates to the 1923–4 period of intraparty discussion and it had an exclusively personal character. Nevertheless, it acquired public significance within the party and became known to Politburo members already in 1924, when the first cases against workers, who were party members in Baku, were arranged by provocation. Two years passed after CC members had received it. Then, suddenly, the editors of our central press organ saw in it the expression of a 'rightist danger' in our party and decided to pay attention to the questions it posed.[171]

We would be very grateful to *Pravda* editors even for belated attention to the questions posed in comrade Medvedev's letter, for excerpting it, and partially publishing it, if this had been done without intentional distortions. We have the right to demand from *Pravda*'s editors that distortions not be made. The editors themselves consider comrade Medvedev's personal letter, which was written at the request of a party comrade from Baku back in January 1924, 'an important political document'. Besides that, not only has it not become less interesting after two and a half years, but in the editors' opinion, this letter has 'even acquired urgent political topicality'. It would seem that defining the letter so would require the editors to treat it actually as an important political document and to publish it in full.

---

169 Shliapnikov's footnote: By the way, they say that Zinoviev is 'forbidden' to speak about the strike ... [ellipses in his text].

170 'O demonstrativnoi atake i pravoi opasnosti v partii', *Bolshevik*, no. 17, 15 September 1926: pp. 62–73; also published in Slepkov (ed.) 1926, pp. 74–84.

171 Nikolai Bukharin most likely wrote the editorial.

But the editors of *Pravda* have not published it in full, because publication of the letter's genuine contents would make it impossible for them to strike a typical political blow, which CC leaders devised, against comrade Medvedev's letter, against the author of this article, and through us against those comrades, who do not share the policy of the CC majority. Thus, the *Pravda* editors' sudden clarification and raising of the question about comrade Medvedev's letter suited the leaders of the CC majority. Their goal, however, was not to analyse and illuminate the questions posed in comrade Medvedev's letter, nor was it to inform the party about the rightist danger in its ranks, nor even to explain the mistakenness of the views laid out in it. Their goal was to politically defame us and frighten those, who do not share the policy of the current CC majority and who are afraid to acknowledge the genuine rightist danger they see in it.

Political slander of the Workers' Opposition and of opposition in general long ago became a weapon of party struggle and a means of rapid mobility for careerists, who attach themselves to the party. Alongside them, ignorant historians and political intriguers, who have an interest in group struggle, try to discredit us by referencing V.I. Lenin's ideological struggle against us, without understanding either its genuine motives or its political significance. We will tell the party about this struggle in our own time. Although he conducted struggle against us, V.I. Lenin also keenly listened to our statements of alarm about the fate of our revolution. Current VKP(b) leaders differ from Vladimir Ilich blatantly in their attitude toward opposition, for they long ago lost any genuine feeling of concern for the fate of our revolution.

Very frequently, slanderers try to lean for support on V.I. Lenin when they engage in dishonest means of political struggle. But their attempts should be resolutely exposed. V.I. Lenin did not resort to dishonest methods and references to him are dirty slander.

Our intraparty ideological struggle of 1920–2 differs from the current one by the depth of its content and its instructiveness. The lessons of that time have not been lost for the party or for us. But now is not that time. It's 1926, not 1921. The disagreements of our time deeply convince us that we would have stood with V.I. Lenin against the leadership of the current CC majority, as we were with him in the very first days of the February Revolution against the leaders of the current CC majority.[172]

Obviously, the desire of the article's author to gain favour with leaders of the CC majority induced him to resort to forgeries, false quotations, and cheating.

---

172   This is a reference to Kamenev's and Stalin's more moderate position toward the Provisional Government, in comparison to that of Lenin.

The party editorial board, apparently for the same motives, did not eliminate deliberate distortions in the document and the author's own fabrications about my and comrade Medvedev's alleged 'platform'.

II.

Falsehoods gush forth even in the first lines of the article about the 'Rightist Danger in our Party'. Beginning the article with a reference to the case of the 'Baku opposition', the editors do not cease distorting facts and even CCC directives to the Politburo on this case. The published CCC VKP(b) decision on the case of the 'Baku opposition' and comrade Solts's article state outright:

> No facts attested to the actual formation of a group. Therefore, there is no basis to assess these comrades' work as that of a group that took shape. That there was impermissible impulsiveness in this case is attested to by the facts that they were defamed as counterrevolutionaries and that non-party workers were warned that if they will again participate in similar underground organisations, their case will be transferred to the appropriate soviet bodies.

That is how comrade Solts wrote, although we think of him as extremely biased toward any case, where our names appear. But the party editorial board conveys the information in another way.

Pravda editors should know about the CCC decision, which mentions the reprimand [выговор] against the CC secretary and Azerbaijan KP(b) CCC chair for fabricating this case. Even the CCC presidium, after having examined this case in response to our protest, had to rescind the verdict, not mitigate it, as it says in the article. That is what the official documents say, but the editors overlook them and repeat many times in just one column that comrade Medvedev's letter was 'addressed to members of the Baku group' and so forth. They are obviously distorting facts.

In the first section of the article 'Rightist Danger in Our Party', when describing comrade Medvedev's attitude toward the party's economic policy, the author tries to elevate the dispute with us to the plane of principle, but quickly slips back onto the favourite, profitable path of distorting the quoted document.

Pravda editors transform the concern for the fate of our large state industry, which is expressed in the letter, into comrade Medvedev's unwillingness 'to coordinate' the development of large industry with the development of agriculture. The editors pass off comrade Medvedev's points about the limitations of the direct peasant market for products of heavy industry (metallurgy, machinebuilding, coal and so forth), as an effort to destroy the economic alliance of the city with the countryside.

Only malicious intent allowed the editors to interpret comrade Medvedev's worry about the condition of heavy industry as denial of the importance of the alliance. It suffices for us to point out to *Pravda*'s editors that in the year when the letter was written, the situation of large industry was extremely difficult. 'Departmental' [ведомственная] struggle against orders for large industry threatened its very existence. We will recall only a few moments from this struggle, which especially clearly come to light in the dispute between the People's Commissariat of Transport (NKPS) and VSNKh about railway orders. Who does not know that NKPS managed to completely 'emancipate' itself from orders for locomotives, train cars, rails, and such material, and demanded that VSNKh convert metallurgical and machinebuilding factories to directly serve the needs of the rural economy? Indeed, didn't the dispute about the need [нужность] for factories in Leningrad threaten the existence of the largest factories? Years of discussion have only confirmed comrade Medvedev's warning. Further events demonstrated to the entire party the need to pose the question about industrialising the country's entire economy. The Fourteenth Congress put the task of implementing industrialisation on the agenda. Our country's industrial backwardness is becoming an obvious threat to all the conquests made in the October Revolution.

Comrade Medvedev's argument about the instability of small-scale[173] peasant holdings in existing conditions of capitalist competition is common to all Marxists, who are Leninist-Bolsheviks, but the editorial board of our central press organ disputes it. Our entire programme of practical measures in the countryside, which include various types of cooperation, is founded on recognising the instability of such farms. But the editors are charmed by 'the alliance with agriculture' in general, not with the poor peasants (bednota) and middle peasants, so they do not see how the alliance becomes one with the kulak.

We remember well our old struggle against reactionary SR theories about the vitality of small farming. Since capitalist relations now exist in our agriculture, we do not intend to deceive the poor with promises to save their dwarfish 'self-sufficient' proprietary farming in the conditions of NEP and of cruel struggle in the market. The editors do not refute comrade Medvedev with facts proving that our petty proprietary agriculture develops along another path. Why do they not write that poor peasant (bedniak) farms go along another path?

---

173   Here and in some other places, he and Medvedev use terms мелький and мельчайший, which mean 'small' and 'smallest', but it seems superfluous to translate them into English literally.

Why do they not write that bedniak farms in the countryside have become firmly established on the basis of private property? No, they cannot do this, for everyone knows too well now that for the two years, which have elapsed since comrade Medvedev wrote his letter, stratification in the countryside made an enormous stride forward. Comrade Medvedev was interested most of all in the fate of these small holdings, and that is what he wrote about, not about development of 'peasant agriculture' in general, as the editors write. Yes, large-scale (kulak, and as is now said 'powerful-seredniak') farming has rich prospects. *Pravda* pleads for union with it, when it rebukes us for desire to break up the alliance. Indeed, we have not eliminated capitalist relations in the countryside. Because they are there, laws of capitalist competition continue to function. This should not be forgotten.

The editors point to cooperation as the path of development for small peasant holdings. They clearly do not understand that this path of development means renouncing prospects for development of self-sufficient small proprietary farming. It only confirms comrade Medvedev's stated position about the inevitable death of independent, small peasant farming. Only epigones of the kulak bourgeoisie can speak about bright prospects and a rosy future for bedniak farms. All these assurances can only conceal capitalist activity to the benefit of rural exploiters, who need to preserve such illusions among the poor.

In his personal letter, Comrade Medvedev addressed just the party's general task in agriculture. He noted the mistake in pursuing a policy, which tries to secure the independent development of small peasant holdings, for that will perpetuate relations, which are now forming in the countryside. This path was already tried a long time ago and condemned by history. The economic process of supplanting weak rural holdings needs to and can be carried out without bearing sickly fruit. The path can be eased to cooperative, fraternal associations. It would be a deception, however, to promise the poor peasants that their independent holdings will be preserved and even raised up, on the grounds of preserving private ownership. Attracting these elements of the peasantry through fraternal organisations, cooperation, and such to make the transition from individual, small forms of farming toward large ones is an important, urgent task. We have never denied it.

Comrade Medvedev's letter says little about 'alliance with the countryside', but it says enough, especially about alliance with the rural poor, which is where Bolsheviks stubbornly concentrated their attention in the countryside, in contrast to all those SRs and Mensheviks who promoted the 'peasantry'. Alliance with the middle peasant is decided more simply. It depends on the possibility for our state industry to become capable of satisfying the commodities famine [товарный голод]. For the rural poor, the alliance question is rather more acute and complex. Even cooperative societies are essentially helpless to render aid to the enormous mass of the poor. Comrade Medvedev's answer to this question is that the alliance of the rural poor with the city depends on the degree to which our industry is developed, on the capacity of state construction, and other large-scale works.

III.

All the lines of comrade Medvedev's letter show concern for the position and future of the working class and poor peasantry, which is linked to the sluggish development of our country's productive forces. The editors interpret this as an invitation to bow to international capital. The author of the article 'About the Rightist Danger' did not hesitate to engage in outright fabrication. As evidence of our error, he inserts his own thoughts as if they were quotations from the letter. This makes it seem as if 'we demand that the government search more energetically for these resources by means of foreign and internal state loans and allowing concessions with great losses and material sacrifices, than those that our government was ready to concede for the presentation to it of such credits.'

We categorically deny that there is any such place in comrade Medvedev's letter. The CC and CCC have the original version of comrade Medvedev's letter, so any party comrade can verify our assertion about the editors' mendacity. Where did the editors get this phrase? A good half of the entire accusation against us is built around nonexistent quotes from the letter. That is how the editors struggle against us. Why did the editors find such a forgery necessary? The editors needed this forgery and fabrication in order to depict us as supporters of a 'policy of concessions without limits'. That is how truthfully the editorial board of our central press organ communicates the document.

Setting aside their approach toward struggle by using dishonesty, lies, and slander, we dare to ask the editors if they have reviewed their attitude toward V.I. Lenin's proposals for concessions. We fully support his proposals and do not fear the implementation of the concessions policy, within the bounds he outlined. We are not confused by the author's clamour and his negative attitude toward concessions. We can remind phrase-mongers and chatterboxes about V.I. Lenin's words:

> By propagating state capitalism in the form of concessions, Soviet power strengthens large production over small, the advanced over the obsolete, and machine production over manual work. It increases the quantity of products of large industry available [деловое отчисление], and reinforces government economic relations in contrast to petty bourgeois

anarchic ones. A moderately and carefully implemented concessions policy, without doubt, will help us to quickly improve (to a certain small degree) the conditions of production and the situation of workers and peasants. Of course, this will be at the price of certain sacrifices, including payment to the capitalist of tens of millions of puds of the most valuable food supplies. The determination of that measure and those conditions, under which concessions are profitable and not dangerous to us depends on the correlation of forces and is decided by struggle. Concessions are also a sort of struggle. Concessions policy is the continuation of class struggle in another form. In no way does it replace class struggle with class peace. Practice will show the methods of struggle.[174]

We fully share V.I. Lenin's thoughts and demand nothing else from the party.

There is a portion of truth, however, in the editors' fabrication. Some supporters of expanding concessions policy go beyond the boundaries marked by V.I. Lenin, but they are in the Politburo. Already in the spring of last year, comrade Rykov moved through the Politburo a decision about expanding concessions policy. Although we do not share or support many of comrade Rykov's views and actions now, we still cannot accuse him of supporting 'concession policy without any limits'. We hope that when he carried the decision to expand concessions policy, he did not forget what V.I. Lenin said about acting 'moderately and carefully'.[175]

---

174   V.I. Lenin, 'The Tax in Kind: The Significance of the New Policy and its Conditions', written March-April, 1921, was published as a pamphlet in May 1921. For an alternative translation, see Lenin 1965, *Collected Works*, first English edition (Moscow: Progress Publishers), vol. 32, pp. 329–65: 'By "implanting" state capitalism in the form of concessions, the Soviet government strengthens large-scale production as against petty production, advanced production as against backward production, and machine production as against hand production. It also obtains a larger quantity of the products of large-scale industry (its share of the output), and strengthens state regulated economic relations as against the anarchy of petty-bourgeois relations. The moderate and cautious application of the concessions policy will undoubtedly help us quickly to improve (to a modest extent) the state of industry and the condition of the workers and peasants. We shall, of course, have all this at the price of certain sacrifices and the surrender to the capitalist of many millions of puds of very valuable products. The scale and the conditions under which concessions cease to be a danger and are turned to our advantage depend on the relation of forces and are decided in the struggle, for concessions are also a form of struggle, and are a continuation of the class struggle in another form, and in no circumstances are they a substitution of class peace for class war. Practice will determine the methods of struggle'.
175   Here the *Bolshevik* journal editor added a footnote: Neither comrade Rykov nor the CC ever accepted any decisions about 'expansion of concessions policy beyond the boundaries marked by V.I. Lenin'. On the contrary, the CC VKP(b) resisted any such attempts.

The editors distorted the entire meaning of the part of the letter, where it talks about industry and concessions. In accusing comrade Medvedev of wanting 'to liquidate self-sufficient Soviet state industry', the editors simply slander him. Two columns further, they refute their own accusation and even rebuke comrade Medvedev for wanting to develop our state industry too quickly. Analysing the fate of small farming and poor peasants, the editors say that comrade Medvedev 'thinks that there is only one way out for millions of inescapably ruined peasant holdings, which is maximally rapid development of large state industry.' So it is said – of large state industry, and not any other kind.

Correctly developing the thought taken from comrade Medvedev's letter, the editors further write that he thinks that 'the development of state industry should go at such a pace that it would employ the entire fatally ruined mass of rural folk [деревенщина]'. Is it possible to interpret these thoughts as comrade Medvedev's wish to lease our large industry to the Urquharts?[176] No, only malicious intent to defame us moved the editors to use the letter in such an obviously false way. Our 'platform' is not to lease out our state industry, but to develop it to the maximum and to attract internal resources and foreign capital into the business of creating new industrial branches and strengthening already existing ones, just 'moderately and carefully'.

The second part of that same article is devoted to investigating comrade Medvedev's 'international political course', as the author expresses it. Here the editors proclaim comrade Medvedev to be 'an enemy in principle of the Comintern's policy' and they use the favoured method of forgery. Toward this end, they represent a counterfeit excerpt as an argument: 'that soil, on which the Comintern is sustained – European working masses – is obviously hopeless'. Declaring that this was taken from comrade Medvedev's letter, they smear this lying fabrication over several columns. We declare that the given phrase is completely fabricated and forged. There is no such place in comrade Medvedev's letter.

The character of the fabrication and the direction of the false quotation will be especially clear, when we turn to the original. Comrade Medvedev's letter states that 'those methods, by which the Comintern tries to win over West European worker masses are clearly hopeless. Not only do they not bring us closer to the organised international proletarian masses, but on the contrary,

---

All decisions, which the party accepted, were only the preparation and practical application of those principled proposals, as V.I. Lenin stated them in his articles and speeches about concessions. They were directed toward eliminating inaccuracies and shortcomings, which were revealed in practice during implementation of concession policy.

176   He may have been referring to Leslie Urquhart, who was Chair of Russo-Asiatic Consolidated.

they drive us further away from them'. All it takes is to compare this place with the excerpt, which *Pravda* presents, in order to understand the difference.

The entire part of the article about comrade Medvedev's supposed 'international political course' is full of intentional distortions of the letter's content. That which the letter says about the situation in Norway after the split is intentionally applied to all parties within the Comintern. By the phrase 'horde of petty-bourgeois retainers' using the Comintern's resources, comrade Medvedev meant only 'servants' like [Andreas] Rudniansky and Co., who leech onto the communist movement. It does not correspond at all to the spirit or the content of the letter to characterise it as 'a rabid attack on the Comintern'. If this letter really was 'a rabid attack on the Comintern', then why did the CC keep silent about it for two years? Why was it silent about it at the Fourteenth Party Conference and even at the Fifteenth Party Congress? No, the *Pravda* editors' depiction of the letter only now became necessary and just to frighten those who are dissatisfied with the current policy, which the CC's leading majority is realising.

By the same route of counterfeiting, they accuse comrade Medvedev of 'undisguised defence of the Second International'. The editors took several words from comrade Medvedev's letter, diluted them with their own fibs, and added fabrications, as if comrade Medvedev protested against the discrediting of 'social-democratic government in general', for example, the MacDonald 'labour government in England'. We declare that there is not and cannot be such a protest in comrade Medvedev's letter regarding social democratic government in general, or MacDonald's in particular, for it does not even mention them. When comrade Medvedev's letter was written, MacDonald's government still did not exist. All that the author says about this instance is a complete lie, which is based on forgery and intentional distortion of the letter's text.[177]

Following their favoured method of juggling the facts, the editors attempt to prove further that comrade Medvedev 'recommends to liquidate independent communist parties, to close the Red International of Trade Unions', and even 'to return to the ranks of social democracy'. This is achieved very simply and easily. In that part of the letter, where it talks about how 'we stood and stand for communist worker masses remaining the constituent part of worker masses, who are organised into trade unions and cooperatives', the author of forgeries inserted two more words 'and socialist parties'. These little words, which are

---

177   Editors' footnote: The first newspaper notice about the formation of MacDonald's government appeared in our press only on 24 January 1924.

assembled in bold type, serve as the basis for accusing comrade Medvedev of 'liquidating the Comintern'.

The clamour about our intention 'to liquidate the Profintern' belongs to the arsenal of means by which they want to conceal actual liquidation. No, we are not liquidating the Profintern. This liquidation happened a long time ago. The editors should know that the 'united front' policy forced VTsSPS to try to achieve a connection to trade unions and worker associations by going around and over the head of Profintern. These actions, which circumvented Profintern, already undermined its authority and significance long ago, and could not help but do so. In fact, maneuvers surrounding the effort to turn the Anglo-Russian Committee into a new international centre reduced to nothing Profintern's activity and its international significance. This 'bypass' around Profintern went so far that the very words 'Red Profintern' were removed from the statutes of our all-union trade union organisations already long ago.

Our disagreements about Profintern do not lie on that plane to which the author of the article attempts to transfer the dispute. Our differences about Profintern and Amsterdam stem from the unprincipled narrow-mindedness [делячество], on which leaders of the CC majority built their attitudes toward Amsterdam. We are against such a policy.

We do not at all share the ideological capitulation, under the banner of which they prepare to liquidate Profintern. Comrade Stalin especially clearly expressed this already at the Fourteenth Party Conference. In the name of 'the average worker from the masses', he rebuked European communists: 'You want to destroy that business, which I created for decades, when you demonstrate to me that communism is better than trade unionism. I don't know, maybe you are correct in your theoretical computations regarding communism. How can I, a simple worker, figure out your theories, but I know one thing. My trade union fortresses led me into struggle. They defended me, for better or worse, from the capitalists' attacks. Anyone who intends to destroy these fortresses will destroy my own worker cause. Stop attacking my fortresses, enter into trade unions, work there five years or so, and then help to improve and strengthen them even more. I will have a look at what kind of fellows you are. If you turn out really to be suitable fellows, then of course, I will not refuse to support you'.[178]

No, we worked completely differently in our trade unions and did not win them over by such paths. We did not go to Menshevik worker politicians[179] for

---

178 Citation to I. Stalin, 'K itogam XIV konferentsii RKP(b)', pp. 23–4.

179 For 'politician' he uses the pejorative term политикан.

training and were not dragged along by their leash. We did not simply 'improve and strengthen' unions. We led struggle in them not only to improve workers' situation, but also in political struggle. We did not disdain trifling matters, but linked them to the main tasks and final goals of the working class. In this struggle, we were not simply 'suitable fellows', but party activists, who implement party policy and connected it with the union's everyday work. We did not enter into a bloc with social democratic Mensheviks, but voted them out from leading posts in the trade union movement.

IV.

All the editors' attempts to prove comrade Medvedev's 'liquidationism', as we already indicated, rest on distortions and false quotations. All these distortions are the basis for the third part of the article, which addresses the 'evolution of the Workers' Opposition'. But all of the author's contrived attempts to depict me and comrade Medvedev as Mensheviks are unsuccessful, because the accusations are built upon a false foundation.

The majority leaders of our CC know Menshevik opinions of us very well. If the Mensheviks had evaluated us in the way that *Pravda* claims, then these evaluations would already have been used against us a long time ago. The *Pravda* editors' references to Mensheviks are mistaken. The editors can find out how and what the Mensheviks think of us from their 'central organ' *Sotsialistichesky vestnik*. For a long time, *Sotsialistichesky vestnik* has considered us 'reactionary communist utopians'. Summarising the results of our Fourteenth Party Congress, *Sotsialistichesky Vestnik* assessed the congress's leading majority as realistic politicians. We know that Mensheviks always considered themselves to be such 'realistic' politicians and regarded us Bolsheviks as 'utopians'.

Reproaching us for 'lack of faith' in building socialism in 'one country', the editors essentially speak their minds against large industry under state control, while hiding their attitude under the declaration that 'not just any development of large industry in our country should be regarded as the success of building socialism'. The editors forgot the thing, which V.I. Lenin often reminded all phrase-mongers and which he wrote in his famous brochure *The Tax in Kind*, which is that in our conditions, 'State capitalism does not struggle here with socialism; rather, the petty bourgeoisie and privately owned capitalism struggle together and in concert, both against state capitalism and against socialism'.

V.I. Lenin preferred large enterprises 'under the control of owner-entrepreneurs' over petty bourgeois enterprises. He especially emphasised the threat of petty bourgeois economic elementalism [стихия] and believed that 'he who does not see this, just due to his blindness, reveals that he has become the captive of petty bourgeois prejudices'.[180]

We are not afraid to say that we regard any kind of large industry under state control essentially as a step, which brings us closer to socialism. That is compared to the patriarchalism and primitive handicrafts, which surround us.

The epigones of the petty bourgeois order prefer millions of small proprietors over large capital, because they consider the latter to be more politically dangerous. Like V.I. Lenin, we see danger where it is really obvious, which is precisely in petty bourgeois elementalism. Like Lenin, we think that 'either we subordinate this petty bourgeois to our control and regulation (we can do this, if we organise the poor peasantry, which is the majority of the population, or semiproletarians around a conscious proletarian vanguard), or it will inevitably overthrow our worker power, just like [Louis-]Napoleon and [Louis-Eugene] Cavaignac overthrew revolution, which sprouted up precisely on this small proprietary soil [in 1848 in France]. Thus the question stands and this is the only way the question stands', said and wrote V.I. Lenin.[181] We do not and will not forget this valuable instruction.

The accusation of liquidating 'proletarian internationalism' is also founded on fabrications. Slander, fake quotes, and distorted thought serve the author in constructing his accusation.

The editors wasted especially much ink on their indignant defence of the 'petty bourgeois hordes', who use up the Comintern's money. It is not comrade Medvedev who 'dances around gold', but the editors who slanderously disseminate his expression, which relates to a certain type of users, toadies, and careerists.

Just as monstrous a fabrication is the entire accusation built against us of 'liquidating the Bolshevik party and the course toward political democracy in the country'. By shouting about the 'course toward political democracy in the country' as if we advocated it, the editors in fact are distracting the party's attention from those who actually implement and ideologically defend it.

We are taking under advisement the editors' instructions that 'it is forbidden to fraternise with Amsterdam renegades'. We have to point out to them, however, that this rebuke should be directed not at us, but toward those who really fraternise with Amsterdam renegades. Clearly, the editors mistakenly accused us of this and we are returning it to them.

---

180   Citation to N. Lenin, 'O prodovolstvennoi naloge', pp. 5–6.
181   Citation to Ibid.

The editors incorrectly accuse us of holding a 'course toward political democracy'. In doing so, they are making scapegoats of us. In the same newspaper, which that party group edits, we recently read information about 'results of soviet re-elections', which eloquently illustrate that genuine bourgeois democracy is already celebrating its victories.[182] In vain do the editors heap blame on us for an alien course. By attacking us, they shield themselves. Neither comrade Medvedev nor the author of this article determines policy in our country. The dominion of bourgeois democracy is being prepared by those who especially zealously wage struggle against the opposition.

While the editors squinted their eyes at the 'Medvedev-Shliapnikovist danger', the direct bourgeois danger grew from the right and got moving. On 10 July, the editors thundered at us about a course toward 'political democracy', but on 8 and 9 July we read in the same newspaper *Pravda* that the danger of this course's realisation already confronts us. This course exists in political reality and it is being realised at the expense of workers and the rural poor.

V. Karpinsky's article in the same 8 July issue of *Pravda* leads to the conclusion that 'expansion of the circle of the countryside's voters at the expense of its exploiter elements occurs simultaneously with the constriction of semiproletarian and proletarian elements' participation in political life and a decrease in the party's influence over soviets'. Those are the results of the CC majority's policy in the countryside.

Matters do not go any better in the towns. The same author's article in *Pravda* on 9 July mentions that 'expansion of the voting population at the expense of the urban petty bourgeoisie occurs simultaneously with a decline in the proportion of proletarian voters among the general voting mass and with their decreasing political activity in comparison with new cadres of petty bourgeois voters'.

Yet at the same time, the editors thunder against us for our alleged 'course toward political democracy', although this course is implemented by those same circles, whose instructions the central press organ fulfills. The editors send the party in the wrong direction by calling on it to give 'a resolute rebuff' to comrade Medvedev and me and to our alleged accomplices and protectors.

The author of the feuilleton commits here the same mistake, as did the majority of compromisers and 'also socialists' of the limited national type in 1917, when they saw danger in the left sector of the revolution and did not notice it in the camp of the bourgeois counterrevolution. Refuting the accusations raised against us, which have been built on a foundation of fabrications, false

---

182   Citation to *Pravda*, 8 July 1926.

quotations, and distortions, we consider it our party duty to protest not only against such methods of struggle, but also against the policy, in the interests of which the current CC majority dictates struggle against us.

For the past year, the party has become an arena of monstrosities. The CC's currently dominating faction devastated the Leningrad organisation for expressing its apprehensions regarding the growing kulak danger in the country. Among the genuinely proletarian part of the Baku organisation, they discovered 'counterrevolution'. They persecuted 14 workers and three office staff, of whom a series of people who had joined the party in 1904–5 were expelled from it. Since the Fourteenth Party Congress, the party's entire life has adapted for the purpose of 'exposing' dissenters and struggling with all party members, who express dissatisfaction with the party's current policy.

As if directly added to this, there is literally an economic offensive against the working class. Nine years after the October Revolution, workers in our main industrial branches still dare not dream of their prewar wages.[183] In fact, the real wages, which workers already achieved, are reduced, under various pretexts (lowering wage rates, raising output norms, and so forth). The economising regime is distorted and directed along the line of intensified exploitation of workers. All this conceals a great danger for the party. They bombard us in order to distract the party's attention from the real dangers confronting it.

For two years already, our Party CC has known about the content of comrade Medvedev's letter. At the Fourteenth Party Congress, no one said a word about it. For the past year and a half, comrade Medvedev and the author of this article frequently saw and exchanged opinions with almost all members of the Politburo in its current composition. Not one of them regarded the letter as a 'rabid attack on the Comintern'. On the contrary, the CC General Secretary, comrade Stalin offered opinions, which confirmed the criticism of the Comintern's methods of work expounded upon in the letter.[184]

For the past year, those same CC leaders have frequently proposed work assignments to us. They have not demanded that we recognise their line or struggle against the Leningrad Opposition. As disciplined party members, we

---

183   Editors' footnote: This rehashes the usual articles from the Menshevik *Sotsialisticheksy Vestnik*, which repeat lies that workers dare not dream about prewar wages. Wages in some branches of industry have already surpassed the prewar norm and steadfastly grow in others. It is the same thing with the economising regime. Everyone knows the party's point of view about this from the recently published address, which comrades Stalin, Kuibyshev, and Rykov signed.

184   Editors' note: In a special letter, which was sent to Politburo members, Comrade Stalin pointed out the openly Menshevik-liquidationist line of Medvedev's letter and demanded rebuff of such 'platforms'. Comrade A. Shliapnikov here utters an outright lie.

agreed to work, but we declared that struggle against the opposition, which alerts the party to the kulak danger, would be disastrous. They tried to summon us to this struggle by aggravating our feelings of offence toward those who especially zealously struggled against us at the Eleventh Party Congress. They told us directly and indirectly about who inspired and led the assault on the Workers' Opposition. From those same circles, we learned that V.I. Lenin did not go along with some CC members' demand that he speak at the Eleventh Party Congress in favour of our exclusion from the party. But, no matter how bitter sometimes the personal offences and memories, we did not think it possible to submit to motives of political and personal revenge. All our lives we have been guided only by the interests of our proletarian party and its final victory.

No, it is not the presence of a 'rightist danger in our party' that forced the editors to publish an article about comrade Medvedev's letter two years later. It is not we who threaten the party with this danger. The article's tone, selection of quotations, and finally, use of counterfeit excerpts, tell of something else. Having chosen us as a target of attack, CC leaders decided to carry out reprisals against the oppositionist moods, which are growing in the party. All oppositionist moods among the party-proletarian milieu and those akin to it are directed now against the bureaucracy and formalism that suffocate the party, against bureaucratic disparagement of initiative and intraparty criticism, and against the suppression of party thought that develops independently of bureaucrats.[185] The party bureaucracy does not disdain any methods to achieve its goal of self-defence. But such methods should not be used to fight oppositionist phenomena. Defamation of us (or other individual comrades) can confuse and frighten only political cowards. Any proletarian who has worked with us or heard us, however, does not and will not believe slander against us.

The 'July threat' hangs over us anew. But we fearlessly lived through the July threat in 1917, and the author's July threats do not scare us. We are confident that revolutionary proletariat in our country will at last achieve victory over all petty bourgeois elements. We will do everything we can to ensure that 'worker democracy' will be victorious inside our party and that, in the interests of genuine unity, the system of intraparty criminal investigation [сыск], denunciations, defamation, and threats, which disrupts our ranks, will disappear.

---

185   Editors' note: Point by point these words are written in the article 'Kto khuzhe i kto luchshe', *Poslednie novosti*, 3 September 1926.

15   Letter from A.G. Shliapnikov and S.P. Medvedev to the CCC
        Presidium and the Politburo of the CC VKP(b), 17 September 1926[186]

On 10 July of this year, the central organ of our party *Pravda* published an editorial feuilleton entitled, 'Rightist Danger in Our Party', which slanderously distorted our views about the party's internal, economic, and international policies. The way in which this was done is unworthy of party members.

In reply to this article, we made written and oral statements to the CC and CCC. Our letter, which we sent on 17 July to the editorial board of *Pravda* and to the Politburo, has still not been published. In an article entitled 'About a Demonstrative Attack and the Rightist Danger in the Party', Shliapnikov wrote a detailed analysis exposing and refuting the slander raised against us. It was sent to *Pravda* and to the Politburo on 19 July, but it has not been published either.

With the present letter, we once more categorically declare that the accusation against us of efforts to let our heavy industry out for lease to capitalist concessionaires is entirely false and slanderous. Not less false is the accusation against us of liquidating communist parties and promoting entry into social democratic parties. Our attitude toward the Amsterdam International is just as slanderously and falsely depicted. The quotes, which are supposedly drawn from comrade Medvedev's letter, are fabricated. The letter does not contain them, so it follows that they are outright falsification.

This entire campaign of slander against us, as well as against all those who consider themselves to be our political friends, forces us to demand from you the strictest and most thorough investigation of the forgery and falsification of comrade Medvedev's letter. Both the Party and we should find out who committed the forgery and toward what ends. At the same time, we ask you to force the central press organ to print our 'Letter to *Pravda*' and the article 'About a Demonstrative Attack and the Rightist Danger in the Party', which refute the slander raised against us.

Signed by A.G. Shliapnikov and S.P. Medvedev

---

186   RGASPI, f. 589, op. 3, d. 9103, vol. 1, l. 40.

16   Letters from A.G. Shliapnikov and S.P. Medvedev to the Politburo,
        CC, and CCC VKP(b), October 1926

Letter from A.G. Shliapnikov and S.P. Medvedev to the Politburo CC
VKP(b) and the CCC VKP(b), 19 October 1926.[187]
Dear comrades,

'The CC VKP(b)'s Notice about the Intraparty Situation', which was published
in *Pravda*, no. 240, 17 October, made severe accusations related to party politics
against us. In the interests of our party and its genuine unity, we consider it our
duty to make the following statement.

1)   The CC's notice indicates that 'the July plenum of the CC and CCC an-
     nounced the unification of Trotskyists, the 'New Opposition', and the
     Shliapnikov-Medvedevist current into a common bloc against the party
     and outlined the splittist policy of this bloc'. We affirm that we did not
     belong to any kind of factional bloc and did not conduct any kind of split-
     tist policy.

2)   The CC's notice states that the United Opposition, meaning by this to
     include us, permitted 'some steps, which violated the party's unity and
     disrupted any number of party bodies' decisions'.

3)   The CC's notice accuses us 'of arranging illegal factional cells and com-
     mittees and the like'. We affirm that we did not create any sort of factional
     cells and committees, and that we are resolute opponents of organised
     consolidation of our ideological differences.[188]

4)   The CC's notice declares us to be supporters of a Menshevist platform,
     liquidators of the Comintern and Profintern, and supporters of unifica-
     tion with social democracy. We declare that during the 25 years we have
     been in the party, we were enemies of opportunism in all its forms, includ-
     ing Menshevism. We affirm that we are resolute and unconditional sup-
     porters of the Comintern and just as resolute opponents of the Second
     International, with which we began to struggle already in 1914. We are not
     and never have been supporters of simple liquidation of the Profintern.
     We support party decisions and maneuvers about unity of the interna-
     tional trade union movement.[189]

---

187   RGASPI, f. 589, op. 3, d. 9103, volume 1, l. 68.
188   They use the term идейные расхождении here and elsewhere and at other times. This
      phrase can also mean 'differences of principle'.
189   The word 'maneuvers' is underlined in red, unclearly by whom.

5)   The CC's notice demands an 'open statement' about obedience to all decisions of the party, the Fourteenth Congress, the CC, and CCC about unconditional implementation of these decisions. We always obeyed and now consider all decisions of party congresses, the CC, and CCC binding for ourselves and are prepared to implement them unconditionally.

With communist greetings,

S.P. Medvedev and A.G. Shliapnikov (signed)

Letter from A.G. Shliapnikov and S.P. Medvedev to the CCC VKP(b) Commission and to the CC VKP(b), 20 October 1926[190]

In reply to the questions put to us about comrade Medvedev's letter to a Baku comrade, we state the following:

1)   The letter answered the comrade's personal inquiries. As is evident from the letter, it was composed in conditions when the discussion was still not exhausted, it was not intended for publication or distribution, and it bore exclusively a private character. Therefore, it was not even recopied. It did not and could not bear the character of a factional platform. Moreover, it was accompanied by an article and stenographic record of a speech about our negative attitude toward the formation of factional groupings. That we then did not distribute the letter anywhere eloquently attests to the fact that the letter did not serve as a platform. It was delivered to the CC from Baku in a distorted form, with additions and insertions, which were not included in the genuine original. And it was obtained by special means.[191]

2)   The letter was not edited, because it was not a platform and it was not intended for publication and distribution. It contained some mistaken and crude formulations, which permitted ambiguous interpretations directed against the party and contradicting the general spirit of the letter. The most important place that is mistaken and lends itself to a hostile interpretation is where the letter points to the Comintern's methods in attempting to win over the West European worker masses. The letter introduced an example related to the situation in the Comintern in 1923–4 in connection with the split of the Norwegian Labour Party and did not in any case relate to the Comintern as a whole. Another such mistaken place is where its reference to the Profintern allows the possibility to accuse the author of the desire for its simple liquidation. We consider these formu-

---

190   RGASPI, f. 589, op. 3, d. 9103, vol. 1, ll. 69 (signed original), 72–3 (typed copy).

191   The previous sentence was underlined in brown pen.

lations to be crudely mistaken and unreflective of our genuine attitude toward the Comintern and Profintern.

Our actual attitude toward both international centres indicated above is laid out in some statements, including the last letter to the Politburo and CCC dated 19 October.

3) The polemical expression about a 'July threat' (in the article published in *Bolshevik* no. 17) was based only on the fact of the appearance in the month of July (in *Pravda* on 10 July) of an article discrediting us politically. This expression is very far from comparing the CC to Kerensky's government (*Kerenshchina*) and does not hint at civil war. Still, before *Bolshevik* no. 17 saw light, we expressed to CC secretary comrade Molotov our desire to remove the harsh polemics from the article, but there was no response.

4) In connection with the case of the 'Baku opposition', we made to the CC and CCC some harsh oral and written statements, which are impermissible in the conditions of normal party life. We gladly offer our excuses for the harsh polemics we allowed. We ask the CCC to ensure the possibility of a normal existence in the party for us and in this way help us to eliminate all the abnormal conditions surrounding us.

Text of the Statement to the CCC and Politburo of the CC VKP(b), Which the Commission Advised Comrades Shliapnikov and Medvedev to Accept, 21 October 1926[192]

In the notice of the CC VKP(B) about the intraparty situation, which was published in *Pravda*, no. 240, 17 October, severe party-political accusations were made against us. We stand accused of conducting factional work and of participation in splittist struggle jointly with the entire opposition against the decisions of the party and of its leading bodies. In the interests of our party and its genuine unity, we consider it our duty to make the following declaration.

We currently do not hold the sum of views as they are laid out in comrade Medvedev's letter and defended by comrade Shliapnikov's article. Currently we consider to have been mistaken our statement in this letter that we radically depart from the CC's policy on all basic questions: 1) of internal policy, economic, in regard to the working class and peasantry, 2) external international policy: about the attitude of the Comintern toward the peasantry, about the attitude to the Profintern and Comintern, and about the attitude toward social democratic parties of the Second International. In addition, we recognise that the formulations we gave in the letter (incorrect and insulting char-

---

192 RGASPI, f. 589, op. 3, d. 9103, vol. 1, l. 71.

acterisations of some sections of the Comintern, the characterisation of the leaders of social democracy, and our statement that the Profintern is an unjustifiable obstacle toward creation of a United Front) justify the many accusations advanced against it in the central organ of the party and in *Bolshevik*. We are resolute supporters of the Comintern and we support party decisions and maneuvers on the question about unity of the international trade union movement. We do not think that leaders of social democratic parties ever counterposed the everyday needs of the working class in general and partial demands of separate categories of them to the interests of the revolution.

Although we did not speak out jointly with the New Opposition either in the press or at meetings, the very fact that we did not dissociate ourselves from it at the time when there existed a community [общность] of hostile attitude toward the policy of [illegible] provided a basis for considering us to be in a bloc together with the opposition.

We declare that we are not supporters of the New Opposition. We resolutely and unconditionally condemn the methods of factional struggle and in general the organised consolidation of views, which diverge from party decisions. We consider as binding and are prepared to implement all decisions of party congresses, of the CC, and of the CCC.

We regret that, contrary to our wishes, comrade Medvedev's letter served as the foundation for an antiparty attempt to organise a grouping on the basis of views, which were laid out in this letter, although the letter itself bore a personal character and was not intended for distribution.

Letter from A.G. Shliapnikov and S.P. Medvedev to the Politburo and CCC, 21 October 1926[193]

In the notice of the CC VKP(b) about the intraparty situation, which was published in *Pravda*, no. 240, 17 October, severe party-political accusations were presented toward us. Along with this, the commission of the CCC VKP(b) put to us some questions in connection with Comrade Medvedev's letter. In the interests of our party and of its genuine unity, we consider it our duty to make the following statement.

1) Having been accused of participating in a common bloc against the party and of pursuing the splittist policy of a bloc, we declare that we have not been in any factional bloc nor have we conducted any splittist policy.

2) We stand accused of violating party unity and disrupting decisions of the highest party bodies. We state openly that we did not intentionally

---

193   RGASPI, f. 589, op. 3, d. 9103, vol. 1, ll. 140–1.

make one step to violate party unity or to disrupt the decisions of any party bodies.

3) To the accusation against us of illegal work and setting up illegal factional cells and committees, we respond that we did not create any factional cells and committees. We resolutely and unconditionally condemn methods of factional struggle and generally the organised consolidation of views, which diverge from party decisions. We consider as binding and are prepared to implement all decisions of party congresses, the CC and CCC.

4) On the basis of comrade Medvedev's letter, we are accused of supporting a Menshevist platform, liquidation of the Comintern and Profintern, and unification with social democracy. We consider it our duty to state the following:

  a) Comrade Medvedev's letter answered a comrade's personal inquiries. As is obvious from the letter, it was not intended for publication or distribution, even though it was composed when the period of intraparty discussion was still open and had not yet expired. It bore exclusively a private character and therefore it was not even rewritten. It did not and could not bear the character of a factional platform, because the documents accompanying it, which were Comrade Shliapnikov's 18 January 1924 *Pravda* article and the stenographic records of his speech at the Khamovniki District Party Conference, expressed categorically our negative attitude toward the formation of factional groupings. That we did not distribute the letter anywhere then eloquently attests that it did not serve as a platform. Likewise, it was delivered to the CC from Baku in distorted form, with additions and insertions, which were not included in the genuine version.

  b) Because the letter was not a platform intended for publication and distribution, it was not edited. If we had considered it to be a political platform to any degree, we would not have allowed this. We recognise that it contains some mistaken and crude formulations, which permit ambiguous interpretations directed against the party. However, these contradict the general spirit of the letter and the author's intentions. The most important place, which is mistaken and yields to hostile interpretation, is the place in the letter about the Comintern's methods of winning over the West European worker masses. The example drawn in the letter related not at all to the Comintern as a whole, but only to the situation in it in 1923–4, in connection with the split of the Norwegian Labour Party. Just as mistaken are the places mentioning the Profintern, which provide the possibility to accuse the author of the supposed desire for its immediate and unconditional liquidation, and the attitudes of SD parties' leaders toward the everyday needs of the worker masses and the interests of the revolution. We consider these formulations crudely mistaken, for they do not express our genuine attitude toward the Comintern, the Profintern and leaders of SD parties, and they make possible the accusations, which are advanced against us in the central organ of the party and in *Bolshevik*. In actuality we think that leaders of SD parties counterpose and replace struggle for revolution with struggle for the everyday minor needs of the broad worker masses. Our genuine attitude toward both above-indicated international centres already was laid out in some statements. To supplement them, we state once more that for the 25-year period of our presence in the party we were true enemies of opportunism in all its forms, including Menshevism. We declare that we are resolute and unconditional supporters of the Comintern and just as resolute opponents of the Second International, with which we already began to struggle in 1914 together with V.I. Lenin and under his leadership. We were not and are not supporters of unconditional and immediate liquidation of the Profintern. We fully support party decisions and maneuvers concerning the question about unity of the international trade union movement. We express regret that contrary to our desire, Comrade Medvedev's letter was given the character of a political platform and was made public.

5) The polemical expression about the 'July threat' (in the article placed in *Bolshevik* no. 17) is based only on the fact of the appearance in the month of July (in *Pravda* of 10 July), of an article, which politically discredited us. This expression does not hint at civil war and departs far from comparison of the CC with Kerensky's government (*Kerenshchina*). Already before *Bolshevik* no. 17 saw light, we declared to CC secretary comrade Molotov our desire to remove harsh polemics from the article, but we received no response.

6) In connection with the case of the 'Baku opposition', we made some harsh oral and written statements to the CC and CCC, which are impermissible in the conditions of normal party life. We consider them to be mistaken. Their appearance resulted from that abnormal situation, in which we were placed.

Signatures of S.P. Medvedev and A.G. Shliapnikov

Letter from A.G. Shliapnikov and S.P. Medvedev to the CCC Presidium, 23 October 1926.[194]

Dear comrades,

Today we learned that the CCC Presidium, having heard the report of the commission on the investigation of our case (in connection with the well-known case of the 'Baku opposition') and our explanations, decided to exclude one of us from the party and to declare a stern rebuke [выговор] with a warning [предупреждение] to the other.

We regard this decision as excessively severe. Neither is it justified by the nature of our views and our behaviour within the party, nor does it correspond to the interests of the party. Therefore, we appeal to you to overturn this decision.

At two sessions of the CCC commission, which investigated our case, we declared that we recognise all the mistaken places in this letter and in the article in *Bolshevik*. We made this acknowledgement in resolute form. We accepted any reprimand from members of the commission, who were comrades Solts, M.I. Ulianova and Iaroslavsky, and we introduced into our statement the essential words and phrases, which Comrade Iaroslavsky proposed.

We resolutely and unconditionally acknowledged the impermissibility of factional struggle and likewise the organised consolidation of views, which diverge from party decisions.

We declared that we consider it obligatory for us to implement all decisions of party congresses, of the party CC and CCC.

At the session of the CCC Presidium, we heard out comrades Ianson's and Kuibyshev's reprimands regarding for the polemical nature of our statement. Right then we expressed our complete readiness to remove all the polemical parts from our statement of 21 October. Simultaneously, we once more expressed our readiness to accept Comrade Kuibyshev's concrete proposals, although we felt that we had already expressed in that statement our recognition of mistakes and unconditional obedience to party decisions. Despite this, we learned about the above-indicated CCC decision.

We find this decision completely incomprehensible, for members of the commission, having investigated our case, seemed fully satisfied with our oral and written statements and they did not express any additional wishes.

We appeal to the Politburo to examine our case. If it considers the attached statement from 21 October to be insufficient, we declare that we are ready to

---

194   RGASPI, f. 589, op. 3, d. 9103, vol. 1, l. 148.

carry out additions and changes. We request that you not refuse to summon us to be present during the discussion of our case.

Signed by S.P. Medvedev and A.G. Shliapnikov

Letter from A.G. Shliapnikov and S.P. Medvedev to the Presidium of the CCC VKP(b), 25 October 1926.[195]

Having heard at the session of the CCC Presidium the party-political accusations put forth against us, we consider it our duty, in the interests of our party and its genuine unity, to state:

1. We recognise that comrade Medvedev's letter contains some crudely mistaken formulations, which allow an ambiguous interpretation directed against some party positions and contradicting the author's actual views and intentions and the general spirit of the letter.

2. The most important mistaken places in the letter are those formulations concerning the methods of work of the Comintern and Profintern. We consider these formulations crudely mistaken; they do not express our genuine attitude toward the Comintern and Profintern.

3. We are resolute and unconditional supporters of the Profintern and Comintern. Just as resolutely do we oppose the Second International. We think that leaders of present-day social democratic parties counterpose the struggle for the everyday and minor needs of workers to the revolutionary struggle for socialism and substitute the former for the latter.

4. We think that some similar crude mistakes gave cause for the accusations against us in *Pravda* and *Bolshevik*.

5. Comrade Medvedev's letter was not a platform. We regret that, contrary to the author's wishes, it was given the character of a political platform and made public in distorted form.

6. The polemical expression about the 'July threat' (in the article placed in no. 17 of *Bolshevik*) was based only on the fact that in July an article against us appeared in *Pravda* (on 10 July). This expression does not compare the CC to Kerensky's government (*Kerenshchina*) and does not hint at civil war.

7. In connection with the case of the 'Baku opposition', we made some harsh oral and written statements to the CC and the CCC, which were impermissible in the conditions of normal party life. We regard them to

---

195   RGASPI, f. 589, op. 3, d. 9103, vol. 1, l. 217.

have been mistaken and to have resulted from that abnormal situation in which we were placed.

8.   We resolutely and unconditionally condemn the methods of factional struggle and organised consolidation of views, which diverge from party decisions. We regard as binding for ourselves and are ready to implement all decisions of congresses, the CC and CCC.

Signed by A.G. Shliapnikov and S.P. Medvedev

CCC VKP(b) Secretariat Meeting, 28 October 1926, Protocol no. 82[196]
Secretariat members present were Ianson, Iaroslavsky, Shkiriatov, Ilin, and Chutskaev. From the CCC Presidium, Kuibyshev attended. Shliapnikov and Medvedev were present. The Secretariat deliberated on the case of Medvedev and Shliapnikov and examined their statements of 23 and 25 October 1926. Copies of the Secretariat's decision were sent to Stalin and Molotov.

Decided:
    Since Shliapnikov's and Medvedev's statement of 23 October states that they are ready to make changes in their statement, then the decision of 23 October 1926 of the CCC Presidium can be re-examined, if Shliapnikov and Medvedev will openly declare the following:
a)   They acknowledge that it was a mistake to send in 1924 to Barchuk, a member of the Baku organisation, a letter, which has become known to the party and contains some positions, which are deeply contrary to the fundamentals of Leninism and the principles of the Communist International.
b)   They regret that they did not accept measures against distributing among members of the Baku organisation this letter, which is directed against the party and which serves as a platform on the basis of which individual comrades attempted to create a factional grouping in Baku in 1924.
c)   They consider the sum of views on basic questions of internal, external, and international policy of the party and Comintern, as these views are laid out in the Baku letter, to be a crude mistake, which contradicts the basic line of the VKP(b) and of the Communist International. They recognise as mistaken the views expressed in the letter about relations between the working class and the peasantry, about concessions policy, about the role and activity of communist parties in various countries in relation to

---

196   RGASPI, f. 589, op. 3, d. 9103, vol. 1, ll. 219–20.

liquidation of the Profintern, and about social democratic parties of the Second International and their leaders.

d)   They regard as especially mistaken, intolerable, and insulting the letter's characterisations of individual sections of the Comintern, and likewise that place in the letter, where it says that the Profintern is the direct obstacle on the path to formation of an actual United Front of the working class, a view which in fact is totally unjustified.

e)   The letter contains crudely mistaken views, which are hostile to the decisions of the party and Comintern and which justify that sharp criticism, to which these views were subjected in the editorial article of the central organ, 'About the Rightist Danger in Our Party', and in the *Bolshevik* article, 'Once More About ...'.

f)   Comrade Shliapnikov's article in no. 17 of *Bolshevik* is incorrect and impermissible in tone and content, for it depicts the party like a ruling faction. They must ask pardon for the crude attacks permitted against the party in their letter and for their comparison of the party's criticism of them with the 'July threats' of 1917.

g)   They consider it to have been their mistake that they permitted factional methods in struggle against the CC and with the party. They must declare that they will not conduct any kind of factional work and that they call on those who support their views to take the same position. Likewise, where those who support their views have created factional underground groupings, they call upon them to immediate disperse such groupings.

h)   They must recognise as absolutely binding for themselves and will unconditionally implement the decisions of congresses and conferences of the party, its CC, and CCC.

The CCC Secretariat by no means insists that comrades Shliapnikov and Medvedev should meet these minimal demands, which would make it possible for the party to reconsider the decision taken by the CCC Presidium. The CCC Secretariat leaves it up to comrades Shliapnikov and Medvedev themselves to decide whether to submit an appropriate statement.

Letter of A.G. Shliapnikov and S.P. Medvedev to the Politburo and the CCC Presidium, 28 October 1926, with Brief Omissions[197]

... We received the CCC Secretariat's notification about reconsidering our case. We have been handed these written demands at today's session of the Secret-

---

197   RGASPI, f. 589, op. 3, d. 9103, vol. 1, l. 222.

ariat. We already met most of these demands in our 25 October statement. We eliminated those formulations which, in the opinion of comrades Ianson and Kuibyshev, ... bore a polemical or vindicating character.

The new demands overlook our last statement and force us only to recognise that the campaign of slander against us in the press and at meetings, which has continued since July, was justified ... We once more declare:

1) Comrade Medvedev's letter was not a platform and we did not distribute it. We regret that apart from the author's wishes it was given the character of a platform and that it was used in the press in a distorted form. We likewise regret that we could not take measures against its distribution in Baku.

2) The letter contains some crudely mistaken formulations, which permit ambiguous interpretation directed against some party positions and which contradict the author's actual views and intentions and the general spirit of the letter.

3) The most important mistaken place in this letter is where it points to the Comintern's methods of work and makes an insulting comparison to one of its sections. We regard this most important part of the letter as crudely mistaken and as not reflective of our genuine attitude toward the Comintern.

4) Just as mistaken is the place, where it refers to the Profintern and provides the possibility to accuse the author of the desire to liquidate it. We regard this formulation as mistaken. We support party decisions and maneuvers in regard to the Profintern.

5) We are resolute, unconditional supporters of the Comintern and just as resolutely oppose the Second International. We consider as mistaken the depiction of social democratic leaders as if they do not substitute everyday interests for the interests of the revolution. On the contrary, we think that leaders of present-day social democratic parties replace the revolutionary struggle for socialism with struggle for the everyday needs of workers, which they oppose to the interests of the revolution.

6) We acknowledge that some similar crude mistakes provided grounds for the accusations, which are advanced against us on the pages of *Pravda* and *Bolshevik*.

7) We regard the polemical tone and some harsh expressions in comrade Shliapnikov's article in no. 17 of *Bolshevik* to be impermissible in normal conditions of party life. The expression about the 'July threat' does not compare the CC with Kerensky's government and is not a hint about civil war, but is based only on the fact of the article's appearance in July in *Pravda*.

8)   In connection with the case about the 'Baku opposition', we made some harsh oral and written statements to the CC and CCC. We consider them to be mistaken. This resulted from that abnormal situation in which we are placed.

9)   We resolutely and unconditionally condemn the methods of factional struggle and organised consolidation on the basis of views, which diverge from party decisions. In those places, where those who share our views created factional underground groupings, we call on them to immediately disperse such groupings.

10) We recognise as unconditionally binding upon ourselves the decisions of congresses and conferences of the party, its CC, and CCC, and will implement them unconditionally.

Signed by A.G. Shliapnikov and S.P. Medvedev

Decision of the Presidium of the CCC VKP(b), 29 October 1926, on the Case of Comrades Medvedev and Shliapnikov[198]

To Ianson, Stalin, Molotov, and the Secretariat of the Bureau. S.P. Medvedev and A.G. Shliapnikov were present.

The statement presented by comrades Shliapnikov and Medvedev does not satisfy the demands, which the Secretariat of the CCC recommended to comrades Shliapnikov and Medvedev on 28 October 1926 (protocol no. 82, point 1), because it does not contain a direct and sincere acknowledgement by them of mistakes made toward the party. Therefore the CCC Presidium stands behind its decision of 23 October 1926 (protocol no. 81, point 2).

Letter from A.G. Shliapnikov and S.P. Medvedev to the CCC VKP(b) and Politburo, 29 October 1926[199]

In the interests of the party and its genuine unity, we declare openly that:

1.   Comrade Medvedev's letter to a Baku comrade (1924) contained some crudely mistaken views, which were directed against some party positions and which contradicted Leninism and the principles of the Communist International.

2.   The most important mistaken place in this letter is where it points to the Comintern's methods of work and makes an insulting comparison to one of its sections (a horde of petty bourgeois minions who are supported by

---

198   RGASPI, f. 589, op. 3, d. 9103, vol. 1, l. 230.
199   RGASPI, f. 589, op. 3, d. 9103, vol. 1, l. 227, unsigned.

Russian gold). We consider this most important part of the letter to be crudely mistaken and not reflective of our genuine attitude toward the Comintern.

3. Just as mistaken a place is the reference to the Profintern, which provides the possibility to accuse the author of the desire to liquidate it. We consider this formulation to be mistaken. We support party decisions in regard to the Profintern.

4. We are resolute, unconditional supporters of the Comintern and just as resolutely oppose the Second International. We think that the leaders of present-day social democratic parties, being agents of the bourgeoisie, betray the interests of the working class.

5. We recognise that some similar crude mistakes provided the grounds for the accusations, which are advanced against us on the pages of *Pravda* and *Bolshevik*.

6. We regard as impermissible the polemical tone and some harsh expressions in comrade Shliapnikov's article in no. 17 of *Bolshevik*.

7. In connection with the case of the 'Baku opposition', we made some harsh oral and written statements to the CC and CCC. We regard these as mistaken.

8. We condemn resolutely and unconditionally the methods of factional struggle, which we allowed, and likewise we resolutely condemn any kind of organised consolidation on the basis of views, which diverge from party decisions. In those places, where those who share our views created factional underground groupings, we summon them to immediately disperse such groupings.

9. We recognise as unconditionally binding for ourselves and will unconditionally implement the decisions of congresses and conferences of the party, its CC and CCC.

[The names of Shliapnikov and Medvedev are typed at the end, but there are no signatures.]

Memo from [Sergo] Ordzhonikidze and [Nikolai] Ianson to Stalin[200]
We are sending you a statement, which was signed by comrades Medvedev and Shliapnikov and which they hand-delivered to us today, 29 October 1926. We ask you to distribute it to members and candidate members of the Politburo and CCC Presidium and to schedule it for discussion by the Politburo tomorrow, 30 October.

---

200   RGASPI, f. 589, op. 3, d. 9103, vol. 1, l. 241.

CCC *Presidium decree of 30 October 1926* cancels its earlier decision to exclude Medvedev and warn Shliapnikov.[201]

'Comrades Shliapnikov and Medvedev Recognise Their Mistakes', Pravda, *31 October 1926, p. 1, cols. 7–8*:

Comrade Molotov's Report at the Morning Session of the 30 October Party Conference

Comrades, I am here to report the decision of the Central Committee and Central Control Commission concerning comrades Shliapnikov and Medvedev.

As a result of yesterday's Politburo session, to which comrades Medvedev and Shliapnikov were invited, the Politburo assigned two comrades, Ordzhonikidze and Ianson, to conduct the final negotiations with comrades Shliapnikov and Medvedev about the nature of the statement, which they should make in order to eliminate any grounds for accusing them of factional work and of those grossly and obviously mistaken views, which they defended and which found expression both in comrade Medvedev's well-known letter 'to a Baku comrade' and in comrade Shliapnikov's article, which was published in *Bolshevik*. As a result, we have the final text of these comrades' statement, which will be published in *Pravda* tomorrow. I will read this entire text, for it is not long. (Reads aloud the text of the statement, which follows below.) In connection with this statement, the CC and CCC decided to publish the following notification:

Notification from the CC and CCC

The CC and CCC are pleased to notify all party members that comrade Medvedev and comrade Shliapnikov addressed to the CCC and CC a statement, in which they not only acknowledge the harm of their factional work, but also reject the deeply incorrect views that they propagandised. The CC and CCC in such a way establish the further disintegration of the oppositionist bloc, which signifies the complete and categorical victory of the idea of Leninist unity of the VKP(b). Comrades Medvedev's and Shliapnikov's statement is printed today in the party's central organ (in *Pravda*).

Statement of comrades Shliapnikov and Medvedev
Moscow, 29 October 1926

---

201   RGASPI, f. 589, op. 3, d. 9103, vol. 1, l. 242.

To the Presidium of the CCC VKP(b)
To the Politburo of the CC VKP(b)

In the interests of the party and of its genuine unity we declare openly that:

1. Comrade Medvedev's letter to a Baku comrade (1924) contains some crudely mistaken views, which are directed against some party positions and which contradict Leninism and the principles of the Communist International.

2. The most important mistake in this letter is where it points to the Comintern's methods of work and compares one of the sections to a horde of petty bourgeois minions, who are supported by Russian gold. We consider this most important part of the letter to be crudely mistaken and to not express our genuine attitude toward the Comintern.

3. Just as mistaken is the part regarding the Profintern, which makes it possible to accuse the author of the desire to liquidate it. We consider this formulation to be mistaken. We support Party decisions in relation to the Profintern.

4. We are resolute, unreserved supporters of the Comintern and just as resolutely oppose the Second International. We think that leaders of present-day social democratic parties betray the interests of the working class and are agents of the bourgeoisie.

5. We acknowledge that some similar crude mistakes provided the basis for accusations put forth against us on the pages of *Pravda* and *Bolshevik*.

6. We consider the polemical tone and some harsh expressions in comrade Shliapnikov's article in no. 17 of *Bolshevik* to be impermissible.

7. In connection with the case of the Baku opposition, we made to the CC and CCC some harsh statements orally and in writing. We consider these to be mistaken.

8. We resolutely and unconditionally condemn the methods of factional struggle that we permitted and likewise resolutely condemn any kind of organised consolidation on the basis of views, which depart from party decisions. We call on those who share our views and who took the path of creating underground factional groupings to immediately disband such.

9. We acknowledge the decisions of party congresses and conferences and of the Party CC and CCC to be indisputably binding upon ourselves and we will unconditionally implement them.

With communist greetings,
A. Shliapnikov
S. Medvedev

17 A.G. Shliapnikov, 'Letter to the Editor'[202]

Dear comrade editor!

I request that you not refuse to publish the following letter in the newspaper you edit.

For the past few months of this year, in the press there have appeared some speeches, articles, and brochures, which contain inaccuracies about my activity in October–November 1917. Some of the false assertions about my role in October even entered into a textbook (the collection *Rabochaia oppozitsiia, materialy and dokumenty*, compiled by M. Zorky, with a preface by E. Iaroslavsky). This incorrect depiction forces me to warn student and worker youth, and likewise all party members who are studying the 'materials about deviations in the vkp(b)', about the authors' incorrect depiction of the October events and of my role in them.

Comrade Bukharin uttered the first falsehood about me at a meeting of Leningrad party organisation activists on 28 July 1926. Speaking about 'ideological sources of the oppositionist bloc', comrade Bukharin declared that 'comrade Shliapnikov was also among the October deserters; he also left his post during the October days'.[203]

Comrade Iaroslavsky writes the very same falsehood about me in some articles and in his brochure *Rabochaia oppozitsiia*,[204] in which he says that 'the party struggled and became stronger through struggle against such comrades as Shliapnikov, the future leader of the Workers' Opposition, who departed the Council of People's Commissars at the most difficult moment and declared that he refuses to take responsibility for the disastrous policy of Lenin and the Leninist Bolshevik Party, since he does not believe in the forces of the working class'. Comrade Iaroslavsky's assertion, just like comrade Bukharin's reference, is false from beginning to end. I never turned down party obligations, did not resign from posts during the October days, and never was a deserter.

In October 1917, I participated in some cc sessions with the activists of that time, I spoke out for the seizure of power and in favour of organising an uprising, and I voted for it. Through the Metalworkers' Union, I participated in implementing these cc decisions.

---

202 'Pismo v redaktsiiu', *Bolshevik*, no. 21–2 (30 November) 1926: 135–8.
203 *Bolshevik* footnote: See the brochure *Partiia i oppozitsionnyi bloc: speeches of comrades Rykov and Bukharin*, p. 87.
204 Bolshevik footnote: See the brochure E. Iaroslavsky, *'Rabochaia oppozitsiia', 'Rabochaia gruppa', 'Rabochaia pravda'*, published by Molodaia gvardiia, p. 6.

All comrades Bukharin's and Iaroslavsky's references to my desertion do not correspond to reality and result from incorrect use of some publications' imprecisely exposited facts and documents of that time. The document below serves as grounds for their accusation of me:[205]

I signed this document on 2 November, but with the reservation that in signing it, I subscribed only to the 'evaluation of the political moment about the necessity of coming to an understanding', but at the same time I stated that 'I consider it impermissible to relinquish my responsibility and duty'. So it says in the signed document. Comrades Bukharin and Iaroslavsky completely overlooked and forgot about my statement.[206] From this document, it is obvious that I agreed with the initiators of the statement only on 'the need to form a socialist government from all soviet parties'. In the conditions of that time, I interpreted this as entry by Left Socialist Revolutionaries, as representatives of the revolutionary peasantry, into the 'temporary worker-peasant government'. Left Socialist Revolutionaries then had influence among the masses, which is especially graphically obvious from the composition of VTsIK in those days. Then it had 62 members from our comrades the Social Democratic Bolsheviks, 29 Left SRs, and 10 people in all from the remaining factions (Internationalists, Ukrainian Socialists and Maximalists). The Right Socialist Revolutionaries and Social Democratic Mensheviks left the Second Congress of Soviets and so placed themselves against the soviets and declared themselves opponents of soviet power.

I supported coming to agreement with the Left Socialist Revolutionaries for two reasons. The most important reason why I supported agreement with Left Socialist Revolutionaries at that stage of the revolution was recognition of the need to agree with the revolutionary peasantry, which at that time followed the Left SRs, while our influence in the countryside was still weak. Majorities in peasant congresses in the provinces followed the Left SRs. The Congress of Soviets of Peasant Deputies, which opened at that time (11 November), was clear confirmation. Of more than 260 delegates to the congress, 110 were members of the Left SR faction and 40 were nonparty peasant delegates who sup-

---

205   He inserts a widely published statement written by Zinoviev, Kamenev, and signed by them and others who resigned their positions just after the October Revolution in order to protest against the lack of a coalition government composed of all parties in the Soviet. It shows that Shliapnikov signed the statement without resigning from his position.

206   Shliapnikov's footnote: Since comrade Iaroslavsky makes reference to a document, which was included in comrade Trotsky's book *1917*, I consider it necessary to point out that comrade Trotsky published this document not in full, but without my annotation, which was in the original.

ported them, not counting 50 delegates who were supporters of the Right SRs. Only 40 delegates supported us and 15 Ukrainians 'sympathised' with us.

The second reason, which motivated me to defend agreement with the Left SRs, was the effort to defeat the intrigues of all our opponents, who were depicting us simply as 'usurpers of power' behind the backs of the soviets who did not take into account other soviet parties. Not only our outright enemies, but also Internationalists, Maximalists, Left SRs, and all kinds of parties harped on this note that we 'usurped power' for our party only. This agitation found a response among workers, partially among the advanced metalworkers of Piter. Agreement with the Left SRs cut the ground out from underneath this agitation and exposed the enemies of soviet power.

Our Party CC, on V.I. Lenin's suggestion, dispatched me to the congress to discuss with peasant delegates this line of agreement with the Left SRs.

In that very month of November, our CC did come to agreement with the CC of the Left SRs, which I thought then to be necessary and correct. Following along after this, the Peasant Soviet merged with the Soviet of Workers' and Soldiers' Deputies in the body of the then-acting VTsIK of the Second Congress of Soviets.

Already in 1922, I told about how it happened that I signed the document. Any comrade who is interested in the truth can find this in no. 10 of *Proletarskaia Revoliutsiia*. My participation in this business is described in detail there and so far no one has disproved it. Here is what I wrote then about this: [inserts his statement published in *Proletarskaia Revoliutsiia*, no. 10 (1922)].

Everything I've said is easily confirmed by the facts and genuine documents. Any Petrograd metalworker, union board member, or member of a delegates' assembly of that time knows that I was not a deserter.

I did not abandon my posts either in October 1917 or later. In part in October 1917 to January 1918, on assignment from the CC and on the suggestion of the Sovnarkom chair V.I. Lenin, I fulfilled work in two commissariats: the People's Commissariat of Labour and the People's Commissariat of Trade and Industry, not even speaking about other party, soviet, and trade union assignments. And who, together with trade unions, organised the struggle against sabotage then? Just these facts are sufficient, in order to disprove the accusation brought against me of refusing work and responsibility for party policy.

I request of all comrades, who read and study the 'deviations in the VKP(b)', to keep in mind the explanations I have laid out above. I request that the authors of brochures, speeches, and articles containing falsehoods about me should correct the mistakes they have let through.

With communist greetings,
A. Shliapnikov

P.S. I request that all newspapers, which have published the articles mentioned above, will print this letter.

Moscow, 10 November 1926

18   Undated Letter from Unknown Person (Perhaps Mariia Trifonova), to Which Shliapnikov Replied in a 19 July 1927 Letter[207]

[The NKVD confiscated this letter during a search of Klychkova's apartment on 28 February 1935. It belonged to Sergei Medvedev, who wrote in the margin: 'I allow that it could have been written by comrade Trifonova, who is the wife of my comrade Pivon'.]

Intraparty events of great historical importance are quickly accumulating. They demand from you, dear comrades, a clear, precise, concrete, and unambiguous formulation of our attitude toward looming intraparty battles and a determination of our place in them.

The approaching moment of untying, more accurately, of cutting the Gordian knot of some cursed questions forces us also to confront you directly with questions and demand answers, which are just as direct.

For us, it is clear that the moment of the CCists' [Цековщина][208] triumph in the party is drawing nearer. Iaroslavsky and Manuilsky toured Ukraine, where they openly delivered insolent speeches. (It was probably not just they, who toured, and not just in Ukraine.) You probably have already heard about these. They made cynical statements at activist groups of major organisations about how the 'majority', in struggle against the opposition, will not stop at 'weak measures, like those applied to the Miasnikovists, but will apply more radical ones, which are appropriate to wartime conditions'.

In an organised way, apparatchiks worked up the opinion of so-called 'Old Bolsheviks' on the subject of carrying a resolution about excluding the opposition from the party. All these circumstances obviously attest to the unfolding of the first act of a multi-act tragedy of the working class. Its resounding achievements are to be plundered by the bourgeois and petty bourgeois swine of state, trade union, party, cooperative, and other apparats. They clamp down on the

---

207   TsA FSB, R33718, d. 499061, vol. 13, ll. 83–8.
208   The word as written appeared to be Цанковщина, but that does not make any sense.

proletariat and squeeze out its juices to benefit the 'socialist' construction of the peasant kingdom.

1) It is clear to us that excluding Trotsky, Zinoviev, Smilga, and the like **from the party** (the 'demands' of the Permsky, Artemevsky, and similar 'organisations', see *Pravda*) is the first step not only toward final liquidation of any sort of intraparty opposition, but also of the party as such. It is the first wide-open step of the approaching Thermidor. Therefore, we think that we should not remain observers on the sidelines in the developing struggle. Otherwise, we will be doomed to political death as a defined tendency in the party, not only to physical destruction.

We understand that not only should we not prematurely offer ourselves up to attack, but for considerations of strategy should – (there was more detail about this in the letter, which A., on the day of departure, gave to S., B. having returned).[209] But we do not doubt for a minute that all the same they will destroy us after the 'anti-Trotskyist' upheaval [переворот]. Why, and in the name of what, should we remain apart from the struggle now? Indeed, do you think that by remaining on the sidelines, we will save ourselves?

But if such an assumption would turn out to be justified, then in what capacity would we remain then in the Communist Party with Mussolini at the top?[210] Would it be as an underground opposition, or as a loyal opposition to his communist-fascist majesty? If not in one or the other capacity, well then surely not with those who are building the guillotine for the proletarian revolution, which now our primitive [доморощенные] Noskes are knocking together [сколачивают]?[211] Why and for the sake of what should we remain on the side of events?

2) If we should get involved in common struggle, then how should we base our actions in contact with other oppositionist tendencies?

3) If we should work, speak out, publish, and distribute [information], then in what capacity? Should we be accomplices [пидпихачев?] or an independent[212] unit?

---

209   I am not sure who A, B, or S are, or whether it was A or B who gave the letter to S.

210   I am not exactly sure of this translation, because of the grammar in the original: Но, *если такое предположение и оправдалось, то в качестве кого мы останемся тогда в партии коммунистического сверх Муссолини?*

211   This is probably a reference to Gustav Noske (1868–1946), a Social Democratic politician who was the first defence minister of the Weimar government in Germany. In 1919, he authorised violent force to suppress communist uprisings.

212   I translated самодавлеющая and самоопределявшаяся as the one word 'independent'.

4) If we should exist as organised groups in the provinces, then will you guarantee to us as much systematic, ideological leadership as possible? That is, if we cannot yet demand from you constant contact and regular illuminating information?

5) If, in your opinion, a) we should not work independently; b) we should not speak and vote against CC resolutions at party meetings ('in order not to expose ourselves'); c) we should not merge with the left flanks of the opposition; d) we should not demand guidance from you; and e) we should not communicate with one another ('so, as they say, not to disappear') –

6) Then indeed, what do you recommend to us to do, dear comrades? Should we climb into our shell and observe events from there? Or, in your opinion, is it futile even to observe?

7) Our worker public here has little memory of our historical existence and only due to the reminders of it in official reports. Here a month is like a year. If we will rest on the laurels of the past, then in still another couple of months, we will sink into a general pile of petty bourgeois, functionary, peasant manure, which goes by the name 'Stalinist *aktiv*', that is, if we remain in the party. Yes, we'll sink so far that not even our ears will be visible.

8) Further, here we became acquainted with a draft platform. (Do you know it? It's about 70 pages long.) We analysed it, pondered upon it, but did not sink our teeth into a detailed analysis of it. We only noted that it suffers from some defects: reticence [недоговорённость], imprecise formulations about the worker question, and an overload of democratic honey. We are interested in your attitude toward the possibility of constructing something like a minimum program on the basis of a similar platform, if there is not another one today, and if one is not foreseen in the nearest future, which, by the way, is not to be awaited?

9) We think it necessary to notify you that if you will continue the old tactic of silence and inaction (don't take offence, dear comrades, for the harsh words, but we have not sensed a different tactic), we will be forced to discuss merger with the left flank of the opposition (for the time being) in order not to be snapped apart into isolated individuals [перещёлкнуты по одиночке] then when unavoidable events crash upon us. We cannot be silent observers remaining on the sidelines (indeed, to do so would be criminal!). Yet we do not consider it possible to speak out in the name of our group, given the attitude our centre holds toward developing events. This letter, which emerges from our activist group, is dictated to us not only by objective demands of the current moment, but also by moods of

those comrades, who are workers and party members, who join our group and express discontent regarding the absence of direct instructions, firm directives, and ideological guidance from our leaders. We ask that you provide a firm answer to all the questions posed above as quickly, precisely, clearly, and in as much detail as possible.

P.S. My mother-in-law (or namesake?) [тёща or тёзка?] and B know about this letter. Being here, I acquainted them with it, moreover, I did not hear any objections from them.[213]

Signed with what appears to be initial 'M'

19   Letter from Aleksandr [Shliapnikov] to Unknown Person, 19 July 1927[214]

Dear comrade,

I received your letter, which I will now attempt to answer in more detail. First of all, it is clear from your letter that you're nervous and excited, but this is not suitable, especially now. One must not yield to emotions [чувства] and lose the capability for a dispassionate Marxist analysis of events.

I was extremely amazed by your questions about our place 'in the coming intraparty battles'. Indeed, do our past and present insufficiently clearly indicate where we stand? This place 'in battles' of the present and future we do and will occupy among the ranks of those who defend the positions of revolutionary Marxism and who struggle against the opportunism of our time. We already timidly set out on this path in 1920 and do not propose turning away from it now.

It would be useful if our friends would turn to the documents of that time for information about our 'place in battle', especially to the case of the 22 and the Eleventh Party Congress. These documents will help to restore memories and make it possible to conduct 'a historical accounting' of struggle prior to 1926.

---

213   Although 'we' is used throughout the letter, this last note is written in the masculine singular. The masculine form casts doubt on Trifonova's authorship, but it could have been added by her husband Pivon.

214   TsA FSB, R33718, d. 499061, vol. 12, ll. 28–35. Typed at the top of the document: 'The document belongs to A.G. Shliapnikov and was found during a search of Klychkova's apartment on 28 February 1935'.

Iaroslavsky's and Manuilsky's speeches and their threats about reprisals against the opposition do not surprise me. Just as unrealistic presently is the threat to 'exclude from the party' Zinoviev, Trotsky, and other CC members. They'll be expelled from the CC at the next plenum. The majority of CC members do not find it politically profitable now to exclude Trotsky and Zinoviev from the party. This would mean (for the majority) to assume responsibility for having begun a split. The majority will not go for this for the time being.

I was extremely startled by your idea about the impermissibility of standing on the sidelines of events. Who is that wise guy, who made you think about 'watching from the sidelines'? We never gave anyone such advice to remain on the sideline of events. Such behaviour would be deeply mistaken. One should not remain on the sidelines, just as one should not yield to the speculative frenzy [ажиотаж] of the Iaroslavskys and Manuilskys, who in the end are inveterate liars.

We frequently have talked to our friends about the need to support the new opposition in all kinds of ways. We warned only that support of the new opposition should not grow into simple unconditional merger and would not entail the loss of our political countenance. The latter danger appears in your letter. You tend to regard all events of intraparty life only from the point of view of the new opposition's moves. You don't attempt to critically analyse events in the same way that we do. This can lead you to allow yourself to be pulled along behind the movement [хвостизм]. We are opposed to this.

The absence of our signatures on the famous Declaration of the 83 disturbed many of our friends. This circumstance also surprised the majority of the CC. However, the smallest attempt to analyse the 'statement' and the circumstance that gave rise to it would make it clear to you that we could not sign it. The statement satisfies us neither in form nor in essence. Add to this the information that the statement's initiators appealed to us for our signatures already after it was composed, signed, and sent to the CC. Consequently, there could be no talk of any 'corrections'. Then you'll understand that such a manner of 'bloc' or 'contact' for us is completely unacceptable. We have the right to regard such actions as political cunning [лукавство] and as the consequence of fear of a genuine bloc of the New Opposition with the Workers' Opposition. We cannot forget the lesson of 16 October 1926, when the leaders of the new opposition came to an 'amicable agreement' with the majority and agreed to recognise the necessity for struggle against the Workers' Opposition.

We suppose that a genuine bloc will be possible only when the leaders of the New Opposition will reject struggle against us. Let the New Opposition's provincial grassroots demand from their leaders such a step. Without this condition, a genuine bloc and consolidation of the oppositional forces are impossible. As long as this does not happen, we will occupy a position in support of the New Opposition, but without merging with it and losing our political countenance.

The content of the Declaration of the 83 satisfies us very little in essence as well. There are many correct positions in it, but the basic class formulations are vague and incompletely prepared. We find completely unacceptable the position about changing the intraparty regime. The leaders of the New Opposition and all 83 signatories wish only one thing, which is return to intraparty democracy as it was 'under Lenin'. We know very well the degree of this democracy. It was tested on us. Proletarian party members know it well, too. No, the past is not an ideal for us and we will not return to it. As before, we unconditionally support workers' democracy in all its manifestations – workers' party, soviet, trade union, and social activity.

The desire of the 83 to return to the past is completely natural, for it is the past that belongs to them. But we will not struggle for such a past, which is their ideal. Here there should be complete clarity. However, this should not be understood as the wish to insure ourselves in the present and future against ideological struggle and criticism. No. We are proponents of comradely criticism and party ideological struggle, but we declare ourselves to be resolute opponents of those vile methods of defaming heterodox party members which took place in the past and are practiced widely now.

It would be very important and politically expedient if our old, experienced friends would look at the path we have taken and would study the experience of our struggle. It is possible to do using legal materials, for in the struggle against us edited collections have appeared, among which it is possible to find some of our documents. Studying our experience and our analysis will make it possible for you to defend your positions more steadfastly and not feel alone in the ongoing struggle.[215]

We intentionally did not hurry to write a platform, but this does not mean that we are against the exposition of our views about the current situation in the party and in the Comintern, inside the country and abroad. We have laid out our views frequently, although not in the way we would have wanted ourselves and not so fully as was needed.

Read 'Our Differences' in *Pravda* from 18 January 1924 and you will find answers there to many questions, which trouble you now. Finally, you should not ignore comrade Medvedev's letter and last year's argument around it, including our article in *Bolshevik* no. 17 (1926).

---

215   He uses the phrase Иваном не помнящим родства.

We will gladly inform you of political news and will provide our analysis of events. However, you should keep in mind the imperfections of the postal system and not present demands that exceed our strengths and capabilities. It is also very important to us to have your inquiries, your analysis, and the opinions of our friends in the provinces about all questions of party policy. Therefore, don't be stingy with letters. Use any occasion to transmit a letter through someone traveling here [оказия].

Regarding the Platform of the 15, I can't write anything so far, since I still haven't seen it and have not read it. We've had no genuine contact with the authors of this platform, despite desiring it.

After autumn 1926, this group of 'Democratic Centralists' kept to itself, closed up, and through third parties suggests a bloc to us, although all leaders of this group are acquainted with us and could have directly raised a bloc to us. However, they are taking other routes for some reason. We don't know the reason for that, but it is possible that it tells of their inner fear of being linked with the Workers' Opposition, of which the representatives of Democratic Centralism were very afraid earlier.

When I will become familiar with their platform, then I'll write an analysis of it. I can only say that the analysis by Slepkov, a 'specialist' on struggle against opposition, is very weak and pitiful.

That is what I can answer briefly to you to your general questions. Now I'll touch on details and 'trifles'.

Your arrangement of questions such as two, three, four, five, and six utterly surprised me. Who distorted to you our counsels? Not once have we thought in the way that you depict it. We never said to anyone that struggle should be waged against an incorrect policy line. In our opinion, struggle needs to be waged for a correct political line of the party. The question is more about how to struggle and against whom to struggle. On tactics just as much as in ideology, we support preservation of our independence (in the spirit of the 18 January 1924 article in *Pravda*).

We are for 'contact' with other tendencies and for coming to agreement with them about individual questions, but we are against merger with them. We are ready to go into a bloc under the condition of agreement about fundamental questions of the moment. We are not against merger with one or another tendency, under the condition of unified views about basic questions of domestic and foreign policy and about means for realising the goals we set. However, you in the provinces should not trust the words of the New Opposition and its readiness to come to some sort of agreement. Here is how matters in the centre have gone so far. Each of the groups (Democratic Centralists, Trotskyist-Zinovievists) has tried to acquire our names, but without a genuine political compact. This method smacks of political intrigue [политиканство]. So far we have not gone along with it and we don't intend to do so.

I agree with you that there is a demand for a 'platform', which generalises our positions. Sufficient material for it has accumulated in the past and at the present. But I think that in the period we are living through, you can't place a special programme on the agenda yet. This question can confront us only if our attitude toward being in the party changes and if things change within the party itself.

If comrades wish to exchange opinions on this theme once more, then write to us and we will discuss it. There is sufficient 'platform-like' material in our separate articles and speeches. Put them together and you will get the 'minimum', which you need now. The Democratic Centralists' intention to 'unify' all tendencies around their platform can lead to creating a political hodge-podge [окрошка], which should particularly be avoided. It is obvious from your thoughts that you grasped the 'optimism' in the Democratic Centralists' platform. This is just in passing. I will tell you my opinion in detail when I will read the platform.

I cannot give advice to use the Democratic Centralists' labour as a pivot [стержень]. This pivot needs to be worked up according to our documents and from our point of view. There are materials. Only some labour is required for their further generalisation [обобщение]. This should not be done in a hurry, but soundly and with calculation. Remember that 'programmes' are elaborated for years in the process of struggle and in the course of the movement. We discussed much in addition with the letter's bearer and he will be able to convey to you my attitude toward current events and so forth.

Aleksandr

20   A.G. Shliapnikov, 'Lessons of Intraparty Struggle'[216]

A new and most severe party crisis marked the end of celebrations of the ten-year anniversary of the October Revolution. At the top level of the party, there had been frequent outbursts by individuals and even entire groups, which the Central Control Commission invariably repressed. Then major differences of principle rose anew to the surface of the party's political life. Neither the

---

216   RGASPI, f. 82, op. 2, d. 195, ll. 117–25, 9 November 1927; 'Uroki vnutripartiinoi borby', *Pravda*, 22 November 1927, p. 6[?], cols. 1–6.

appearance of the crisis nor the existence of differences of principle within the party is anything unexpected.

Both the crisis and the disagreements are the direct consequence of the class forces that have taken shape and become stronger in the country in recent years. Along with this, class struggle became exacerbated in the country, the results of which are evident in the towns in the enormous queues for food and the huge influx of the unemployed. Because our party is composed of diverse social forces and is the only open political arena in the country, it now reflects especially vividly the struggle developing in the country.

Peasant agriculture [крестьянское хозяйство] now has achieved the prewar level of development. In some standards and types of farming, it has surpassed the prewar level. Further development of it is held up by the incapacity of large state industry at its present level to satisfy all the demands [нужды] of the peasantry. It is incapable of absorbing the 'superfluous' hands of the countryside, which 'hamper' the concentration of the economy and impede the growth of the middle peasant [середняк] and of its ideal, which is the 'powerful' proprietor [хозяин]. This exerts pressure on the 'town' through raw materials, bread and other food products.

Likewise, the excessively slow course of development directly places rural and urban poor, the generation of worker youth, and cadres of unemployed proletarians in a desperate position. Here you have the elements and the foundations, which now shake society's calm and its effort to achieve 'order'. However, this class struggle is refracted extremely distinctively in the party, through its traditions and its peculiarities.

During recent years, the party press has steadfastly and untiringly repeated warnings about the appearance of a right danger in the party. However, it found this right danger neither in the growth of a private property-owning petty bourgeois element, nor in its pressure on authorities, nor even in individual concessions to this element. Our party press and our party leaders saw this danger first of all in the party tendency, which has been known as the Workers' Opposition since the Tenth Congress. Now they call this alleged 'rightist danger' not only Worker Oppositionist, but also Trotskyist, Kamenevist, Zinovievist, and so forth.

Party members, especially those who are proletarians, should not take the press at its word, but should verify the disagreements by examining documents and materials, listening to both sides of the debate rather than just one, and decide for themselves if they who shout loudest and who defame others are correct. Those who are attacked want the party to bring up for discussion by as many party members as possible those questions, which our reality now pushes to the forefront of the agenda.

We consider it our party duty to defend ourselves from the calumnies and slander, which our party press, on its pages, has tirelessly poured forth onto the head of the Workers' Opposition during the past few years. Party comrades can easily receive reports of our party congresses, beginning with the Tenth, and see in them that the Workers' Opposition always spoke out in defence of large state industry and simultaneously tried to vindicate the interests of the working class and its organisations in the broadest sense of this word.

Already in 1920–1, the Workers' Opposition pointed out that the incorrect expenditure of hundreds of millions of gold rubles for orders placed abroad, at the expense of our heavy industry, expressed disdain toward large industry. Now there can hardly be found even one bold spirit [смельчак], who would justify such a policy, but for this we were called capitulators to European capital. In the years that have passed since that time, the lack of attention to large state industry became especially clear. As a consequence of this attitude, our heavy industry (coal, mining, and metals industry) has still not recovered or achieved the prewar level. The goods famine is felt especially acutely now.

Articles about industrialisation fill the party press. There are all kinds of agitational posters on the same theme, but the condition of the main branches of heavy industry still has not reached the level of 1913. A decade after the October Revolution, our metals industry has recovered only 71% (judging by iron smelting) in comparison with 1913. This sensation about industrialisation does not bear out in reality. Without iron and steel, there can be no industrialisation, no machinebuilding, and no replacement of human labour with machine labour.

The attitude toward large industry was the centre of disagreements between supporters of the Workers' Opposition and the Central Committee of that time. Our struggle for building large state industry was called first anarchosyndicalism, then capitulation before European capital, and now simply right deviation.

Along with this, we struggled to actually and radically improve the situation of the worker masses. For this, they declared us to be demagogues and defenders of 'narrow shop committeeism' [цековщина]. The best evidence that all these accusations against us were groundless is that the main mass of mineworkers and metalworkers, even ten years after October, do not have even those beggarly wages which they had before the war. In the preceding economic year, the wages of metalworkers on average reached only 83.4% in comparison to the prewar level. There are more than 600,000 metalworkers in our large industry. Coal industry, with more than 219,000 workers, pays workers only 75.2% of their prewar wages.

Thus, the main cadres of the proletariat, without whose initiative and labour enthusiasm you won't accomplish any industrialisation, are beaten down materially and morally. But to speak this truth in our conditions means to incur the accusation of 'right deviation', while those who embellish reality turn out to be among the 'leftists'. Such methods are taken from an alien, bourgeois camp. We know them well, but they do not frighten us.

In recent years, slander against the Workers' Opposition was disseminated in the party press especially zealously in connection with the so-called letter of comrade Medvedev. Comrade Medvedev's genuine letter has still not been published. A falsified letter was published in excerpted form. It did not come from his pen. Only on the basis of falsified excerpts and inaccurate quotations, can we be accused of right deviation.

Meanwhile, there is a genuine right deviation in the party. It is the deviation, which advances as its slogan, 'get rich' and

'accumulate while times are good', and even declares that 'each new factory is a burden for the peasant'.

But among the Workers' Opposition, there is not even one supporter of these or similar slogans. Supporters of such slogans are to be found in the Central Committee. There, among them one should search for the genuine right danger, which has placed the party on the verge of a split.

II.

Since the Fourteenth Party Congress, the attention of party members and of broad worker society [общественность] was riveted on the unfolding intra-party struggle, the banner of which was raised by the Leningraders. The essence of the debate, which was suddenly revealed at the congress, was little known and poorly understood for a long time and it is possible to say that it is still so for the enormous mass of party members. However, the character and circumstances in which this struggle unfolded, and especially its methods, attested to the extreme sensitivity of the debate.

The pages of reports about CC plenums, and recently the pages of the party press, bristle with an abundance of swear words, personal attacks, and abuse, which only pollute and obscure the debate and interfere with the correct understanding of it. Published stenographic reports show that the CC is becoming an arena for the display of such hostility, which is incompatible with its bearers' presence in the leading party body. Any party member, who has read these stenographic reports and the excerpts from them in the press, comes away with the impression that CC plenums have begun to resemble peasant gatherings [сходы], which are rent with contradictions and internal enmity and where people resort to curses and threats instead of arguments and attempts at persuasion.

Such a method of struggle is becoming a direct and immediate threat to party unity, in the name of which the majority of the Central Committee acts. But methods for mechanically suppressing heterodoxy and oppositionist moods in the party environment have turned out to be incapable of preserving even the appearance of this unity. The experience of the CC majority's cruel struggle against the Workers' Opposition after the Eleventh Party Congress is particularly telling about the bankruptcy of such methods.

Five and a half years ago, a group of worker members of the party, 22 in all, submitted a well-known declaration to the Comintern, which posed approximately the same questions, around which struggle now occurs within the party. The appeal of the 22 stated, 'At the time when bourgeois forces ... workers respond to this by leaving the party'].[217]

Our appeal to the Comintern was dictated by alarm about the party's unity. We were very close to the broad proletarian masses of that time, especially to metalworkers. We knew their attitude and mood. Together with them, we set this in motion. As a matter of principle, we did not repudiate our step at the Eleventh Congress. Already at that time, the danger coming from the petty bourgeois element [стихия] was revealed in the context of the New Economic Policy. True, this danger was in its embryonic state. Despite this or maybe because of it, we considered it our party duty to bring this to the attention of the communist centre. In acting so, we wanted [citing Letter of the 22] 'to warn the CC RCP(b) that the policy it is implementing threatens ... under the label of "anarcho-syndicalism".'

Although the Central Committee at that time recognised our right to appeal to the Comintern, it simultaneously sought 'ring leaders' and created against us a party judicial process, which culminated at the Eleventh Party Congress. However, the majority of delegates of the Eleventh Congress understood us better and turned out to be closer to us than was the CC majority and its proposal to exclude us from the party as 'instigators' was rejected.

Have all these exceptional measures of struggle against us in fact been justified? The bleak reality of our days shouts loudly about how such mechanical measures for struggle against heterodoxy bring only harm to the party's unity. More than five years have passed, since the time when exceptional measures were applied to us. We see now that the questions we posed then in the Letter of the 22, as well as other questions which have not been resolved normally, have now come to confront the party anew. The current CC majority, in its struggle against the New Opposition, is repeating old methods, which were especially vividly and instructively applied in the business of struggle against the Workers'

---

217   I have not included the entire excerpt here. He cites the text, which was published in *Pravda*, 7 March 1922. The Letter of the 22 is translated in this collection, above.

Opposition. Such methods bankrupted those who quite zealously implemented them. The CC intends to use all means to suppress the heterodox and to discredit them, but it will not allow open comradely discussion of those questions of principle, which are on the agenda and which worry a significant part of the party milieu. Only in this way is it possible to understand all that is done now under the guise of 'discussion' in our party.

Discussion, which was intended to help a broad circle of party members make sense of a complex network of disagreements, turned out to be completely disconnected from party cell discussions about elections to conferences and from the conferences themselves. Discussion was deformed from the start and began only after all preparatory work for the congress was finished. This circumstance leads directly to the mechanical 'erasure' of any kind of opposition from party legality and to its exposure to attack. These organisational 'blows' do not diminish differences and do not eliminate disputes, but only drive them deeper within.

The history of recent party teaches us to understand that the roots of intraparty disagreements lie in our country's economy, in class struggle, and in developing class contradictions. The party's heterogeneous social composition and the huge mass of petty bourgeois elements within it facilitate the permeation of this milieu's ideology and policy into the party. Along the same line and through the same stratum, the party's political leadership is also subjected to the direct pressure and influence of nonproletarian forces. The harmful consequences of this social heterogeneity may be weakened only by halting acceptance into the party of nonproletarian elements[218] and intensifying attraction into it of workers.

However, it would be an unfounded illusion to think that it is possible to eliminate disagreements and avoid intraparty debates. Disagreements and disputes of such an order which we observe now will disappear only along with class war and its contradictions. But with greater homogeneity in the party's composition, no disagreements or intraparty disputes can be dangerous, for they will not threaten it with a split along the line of class divergence. On the contrary, in the course of disputes and divergences, the alien and the nonproletarian will emerge more quickly onto the surface of political life. Struggle against nonproletarian phenomena will educate the party and its proletarian core and make them stronger.[219]

---

218 The published version adds here the phrase 'dispersal of nonproletarian cells and a purge of the entire party'.

219 The published version has the word 'masses' in place of 'core'.

It should be acknowledged that the currently existing order is obviously defective and is completely intolerable. Years of hidden struggle and outward silence are followed by weeks of discussion fever, which remind one of the vulgar hullabaloo[220] of elections in bourgeois countries. This situation needs to be radically changed. The tenth anniversary of the October Revolution has passed. We think that the time has come to set up a different order in the party, under which party members could discuss, decide, and act without bureaucratic tutelage and without asking the permission of secretaries.

Party members should be able to put on the agenda and discuss not only those questions, which the centre demands, but also those which interest and concern a given group of party members. Only when there is open discussion of all questions, on which differences arise, will the party and worker masses be able to correctly evaluate who goes to the right or to the left. Without these conditions, struggle against disagreements and heterodoxy will assume the character of reprisals. As it was in our case, we will see further at each step that reprisals will naturally summon resistance, which will entail violations of party discipline.[221]

However, punitive policy never resolved disagreements anywhere and it will not resolve them in our country. Instead of threats, the CC majority should find a means to avoid the danger of a split.[222] There is just one means to do so, which is by[223] setting up within the party such an order, which would allow all party members to discuss and resolve the political questions worrying their party and country. Until these conditions will be evident, periodic crises will haunt the party and the very threat of a split will not go away. Besides that, the consciousness of party members, especially of proletarians,[224] has grown and it cannot be reconciled with the currently existing order, when all is decided without their involvement and when periodically and 'suddenly' they are confronted with crises in the party.

We propose to the Central Committee to finally implement the principle of intraparty workers' democracy and in that way ease the party's exit from a dif-

---

220   The word he uses, *ажиотаж* or agiotage, can also be translated as stock-jobbing.

221   The published version has the phrase 'bears an acutely antiproletarian character' in place of the phrase 'will naturally ... party discipline'.

222   In place of 'find a means to avoid the danger of a split', the published version has 'take the path of resolutely changing the social composition of the party by making it 90% proletarian and changing its internal regime'.

223   In place of 'There is just one means to do so, which is by setting up', the published version has 'It is necessary to set up'.

224   The published version reduces the phrase 'of party members, especially of proletarians', to 'proletarian party members'.

ficult situation. We vote for workers' democracy, which we consider capable of bracing the party and avoiding further complications![225]

Obviously, a 'change of regime' alone is insufficient. A different policy is needed, but if the editors permit,[226] I will address this in another article.

21   A.G. Shliapnikov, 'For Industrialisation and For Socialism'[227]

Under the slogan 'to catch up and surpass' the industrial development of the capitalist countries, the Fifteenth Congress and the Party CC's subsequent decisions have in practice put the entire magnitude of problems of our country's industrialisation. Everyone attributes great significance to the party's measures to eliminate the country's economic backwardness, but there are still some insignificant circles of comrades who are afflicted by doubt. Recognising the need for industrialisation in general, they express misgivings that the party's projected timelines for realising its programme are too short, and they consider attempts to hasten them to be close to madness. Their scholarly opinions are that the tempos do not correspond to reality and so are doomed to break down. One would think that the preceding year of 1928–9, with its high indicators of industrial upsurge, would have sufficiently convinced the doubters of the correctness of the accepted tempo, but it was not so. 'Doubt' creeps in, clinging to the lingering goods famine. The tempo of heavy industry's development is set in contrast to the tempo for developing light industry, which works to satisfy the population's immediate needs.

Sometimes it is difficult to understand what hides behind this juxtaposition of light industry to heavy. Is it political cunning or incomprehension of how these branches of the unified economic organism are mutually interconnected? Likely it is political cunning, for now anyone, even the barely literate proletarian and the peasant, knows that our economy's further development depends on heavy industry in metal and coal.

Others doubt outright the entire volume of industrialisation tasks. They say, 'the burden is too great to bear'.[228] To doubt without trying to find a way and means to strengthen the case for industrialisation is a completely un-Bolshevik approach. The only way to do so in our country is through the per-

---

225   Exclamation mark changed to period in the published version.
226   The phrase 'if the editors permit' was omitted in the published version. I do not think he followed this up with another article.
227   'Za industrialisatsiiu – za sotsializm', *Pravda*, 16 December 1929.
228   The phrase he uses is *'Непосильна ноша, не по спине груз'*.

sistent and organised labour of many millions of workers and peasants. Our proletarian shows that he understands the tasks of industrialisation by steadfastly raising the productivity of labour, by subscribing to loans, and by actively supporting all measures for industrialisation. The poor and middle-income rural peasant masses, the urban service employees, and handicraftsmen need to come to the same understanding. The plan outlined by the party should be fulfilled by unifying all the efforts of the 'active population' of our Soviet country. Not one country in the world possesses similar potential. Indeed, the planned unification of the efforts of millions of labourers is completely unavailable to capitalism. Therefore, those who turn to the examples of the capitalist West in setting limitations to our tempos and tasks for building socialism are wrong.

Some say, 'But the countryside is not with the town, the peasant is not interested in such industrialisation'.

Are such assertions true? Not at all. First, you can't speak 'in general' about the countryside and the towns, for our population is not yet uniform in class composition in either place. Some in the countryside and some urban residents are dissatisfied with the town. But these sectors are so insignificant that even their direct opposition to industrialisation will not hinder it.

Only the exploiters in the countryside are dissatisfied with industrialisation, for it will deprive them of the possibility to use the cheap poor peasant work force, which will leave for seasonal work or to fill the cadres of the factory proletariat. The kulak element of the countryside is especially dissatisfied with industrialisation, because industrialisation makes agricultural machines and other equipment for working the land more accessible to broad peasant masses. This disrupts the kulak's exploitative power in the countryside.

Those, who talk now about dissolving the alliance between city labourers and those of the countryside, are completely wrong. Their speculation is based on temporary food supply difficulties and the party's extraordinary measures to secure food supplies for worker districts. Those, who make hysterical investigations, compare the 'requisitions' [продразверстка] of old times with present-day state procurement [заготовка], and rebuke the CC for applying measures of 'military communism' outside of wartime, are wrong. They forget the main thing, which is that the party never advanced extraordinary measures toward those lower down [привниз] and did not apply them maliciously, but due to special conditions at the time.

But the most important thing to especially note is that in lamenting extraordinary measures (these complaints came from both the right and the left), they've overlooked the main thing, which is that small-scale peasant farming is very weakly and slowly being raised to the level of a consumer economy.

Just three or four years ago, the slogan 'a horse to each poor peasant without one' was fashionable 'leftism'. No one even thought about whether he needed a horse for his dwarfish farm, or if he could maintain a horse on only two hectares of arable land. The general condition of agriculture in 1924 was that the area of land under the plough already approached that of the prewar time, with only 75% of draft horses (in comparison with 1916). Just as incorrect and limited was the well-known 'platform' demand to raise the price to the level of indefinite 'cost value' [себестоимость]. Such extreme leftism in the matter of aid to peasant agriculture essentially did not escape captivity to petty-property owning illusions.

Now the party has posed the question of lifting up agriculture onto industrial rails (getting agriculture going) in a genuinely Marxist way, a Leninist way. Even brief experience, rather a small amount of time in the history of agriculture, nevertheless speaks eloquently and convincingly of the superiority of large-scale farming over small-scale, dispersed holdings and of the possibility to build genuine industrial agriculture in our conditions. Only by industrialising agriculture and building large, state-owned grain, cattle, raw material, and other types of farming, will it be possible to implement a strong foundation of food supplies and raw materials under the five-year plan and simultaneously show the peasantry the path to liberation from all the adversities and instability of small-scale individual farming.

Collectivisation of agriculture is criticised indirectly and not in essence, but indirectly by means of 'rumours' and information about administrative pressure on the poor and middle peasant elements, as if they were being 'hounded' into the collective farms. Distortion is possible in any matter, but it is absolutely impossible to explain as 'administrative' pressure the mass entry into and formation of new collective farms which has taken place everywhere this year. The peasant is a great practitioner and a master, so why in the world would he refuse to use technical resources, which are given to him to farm better on amalgamated and collective foundations? He can only refuse on the basis of personal prejudice. The enormous mass of peasants already understand that there is no other way out from poverty, which verges on destitution. With all its resources, the party will help the poor peasantry surmount its personal prejudices. In the first place, it will provide the example of largescale farming, which entails improvement of their material situation. That will quickly succeed in clearly proving collectivisation's advantages and its superiority over individual farming.

The highway of industrialisation is marked out, the landmarks are placed, and millions of proletarian hands already are laying its foundation in response to the party's call. The path will not be without difficulties or potholes and furrows, but our country's proletariat will be able to overcome them, for its entire future and its final triumph depend on the success of industrialisation. The success of industrialisation and the surmounting of difficulties in its way depend to a great extent on our party's condition. The uninterrupted growth of the worker core in the party for the past few years serves to guarantee its unity and cohesion. The development of self-criticism and intraparty worker democracy will help the party and the working class of our country to quickly catch up with the leading capitalist countries of the West and once more to show the proletariat of the whole world its superiority over the capitalist system.

22   A.G. Shliapnikov, 'Letter to the Editor'[229]

Dear comrade editor,

After my article, 'For industrialisation – for socialism', appeared in *Pravda* on 16 December, I received both directly and through your editorial board many inquiries about my motives for speaking out in the press. For full clarity, I think it necessary to state the following:

1) One of my motives for speaking out in *Pravda* on 16 December in favour of the party's current line was to attempt to end the ambiguity around my silence, as if it hid some divergence from the party line.

2) From my 16 December *Pravda* article, it is clear that **I have no differences with the majority of our party's cc**[230] on the entire sum of political questions, which now stand on the agenda of party activity and are touched upon in my article, namely: a) industrialisation; b) giving top priority to heavy industry; c) industrialisation of agriculture by intensifying sovkhoz building and collectivisation of bedniak and seredniak farming; d) application of special or extraordinary measures in procurement of food supplies or raw materials for cities and industry; and e) struggle against the kulak.

3) On those questions, which served as the object of disagreements in 1925–6, **I remain on the footing of our** (mine and Comrade Medvedev's) **declaration of 29 [?] October 1926**, which condemned our views, and **I have no grounds or reasons to refute or re-examine it.** Here is the text of this declaration:

[1926 declaration follows – see above]

---

229 'Pismo v redaktsiiu', *Pravda*, 26 December 1929, p. 4(?).
230 The preceding and phrases below were printed in bold.

4) In my article in the discussion issue of *Pravda* on 22 November 1927, I
    really did **set forth and defend mistaken views** about intraparty life. The
    party's line was completely correct. The party did and does everything
    it can to develop intraparty democracy and self-criticism. My attacks on
    leading party bodies were mistaken and impermissible. I have nothing in
    common with the counterrevolutionary position of Trotskyism or with
    the opportunistic position of the Rightists, either on questions of intra-
    party life or on other questions.

5) I have no disagreements with the CC VKP(b) on the main questions of for-
    eign policy.

With communist greetings,
A. Shliapnikov
24 December 1929

23   **A.G. Shliapnikov's Letter to the Bureau of the Omsk District
        (Okrug) Party Committee, 4 April 1930**[231]

Dear comrades,

While I have been in Gagry for medical treatment, I have received information that the Omsk party press organ published a letter from ten former party
members, who were excluded for underground work, in which comrade Medvedev and I figure as 'ideological leaders'. The CCC acquainted me with this
affair and provided an exhaustive explanation, which I think you will find interesting.

   Already in February of this year, I wrote a short note in order to caution and
struggle against the use of my and comrade Medvedev's names and the banner of the former 'Workers' Opposition' for underground work. This was on the
request of CCC members. However, I could not transmit it personally, since my
poor health required me to go to a sanatorium. Therefore, I assigned dispatch
of this note to my comrade. I have no idea what happened to this note. I did
not see it in *Pravda*. I don't know if it was sent there or if it makes any sense to
dedicate a whole page of the central organ *Pravda* to the Omsk case.

   It is another matter for Omsk. I think it would be very useful and even obligatory to publish the note there, especially after the letter of the ten was pub-

---

231   RGASPI, f. 589, op. 3, d. 9102, l. 1.

lished. Therefore, I am sending the note under the title 'About a Big Mistake by a Small Group in Omsk'. I request you to publish it in your party newspaper.

At the same time, I ask you, for the sake of comradely kindness, to send the issue in which it will be published to the following address in Moscow: [provides his home address].

24 A.G. Shliapnikov, 'A Big Mistake by a Small Group in Omsk', 28 February 1930: Excerpts[232]

[Begins with a disclaimer telling Omsk workers that the Workers' Opposition has not led underground work within the party or outside of it.]

Sometimes, we have been forced to explain how we view factional work ... We have opposed it and still oppose it, because it leads to a split which would be a blow against the revolution.

We first encountered the 'Omsk case' at the end of 1927. Some workers, who were former party members, had arrived from Omsk and gone to the CCC. Then they saw us and told us that 'Trotskyists' had organised an illegal group in Omsk and had brought into it some of the workers (Tarasov, Kogin, Shulega, and others). The Trotskyists had distributed their literature through this group. ... We explained to these comrades their mistakes ...

But two years later, we learned that the mistake had been repeated. Using our names as cover, someone had involved workers of Omsk. We must warn the Omsk workers that we have not and do not participate in underground work. ...

25 Letter from A.G. Shliapnikov and S.P. Medvedev to the CCC, 28 April 1930, with a Copy to the Politburo[233]

On 25 April, I received your 13 April letter and the attached Omsk newspaper *Rabochy put*, no. 48. We already twice fulfilled the wish of CCC members (and of Politburo members) that we write a statement for the press. By demand of the CC, we did this on 24 December 1929. During its composition, we were told that no more statements would be demanded from us.

---

232   RGASPI, f. 589, op. 3, d. 9102, ll. 2–3, typed manuscript with Shliapnikov's signature.
233   RGASPI, f. 589, op. 3, d. 9102, l. 4.

At the session of the CCC party collegium on 23 February 1930, which was dedicated to the 'Omsk case', some comrades (members of the CCC and CC) proposed to us to write an article about our attitude toward this case. We also fulfilled this desire. The article was written on 28 February for publication under the title, 'About a Big Mistake by a Small Group in Omsk'. It was delivered to the CCC and handed personally to comrade Shkiriatov, who expressed his satisfaction that we fulfilled the CCC's wishes. We still do not know the fate of this article.

Upon receiving a copy of the Letter of Ten Oppositionists, which pointed to our alleged 'ideological leadership' of their group, we sent a letter addressed to the secretary of the Party District Committee (okruzhkom) in Omsk, with a copy of the brief article, which was written on 28 February and transmitted to comrade [Matvei] Shkiriatov. The okruzhkom was requested to publish it. The letter and article were sent by registered mail [заказный пакет] on 4 April, but we do not know if it was published. We ask you to require the Omsk Okruzhkom to publish this article.

The 'Letter of the Ten Oppositionists' essentially retold the same accusations, which comrade [Timofei] Krivov made against us at a 23 February CCC session. We explained in detail the baselessness of all the accusations, including those, which the 'Letter of the Ten' reproduced. To those explanations, we can now add more. We never had any personal, written, direct, or indirect relations or communications with any of those who signed the Letter of the Ten, nor do we know any of them personally.

As concerns comrade Iaroslavsky's wish that 'no one could consider us at the present time to be the ideological inspirations and leaders of the Workers' Opposition', well this circumstance is out of our control. For the past few years, we frequently stated in the press our negative attitude toward all factional groupings. We condemned any kind of factional work. We neither participated at all in forming groupings nor did we create a faction of the Workers' Opposition. However, this fact did not hinder the artificial creation of a 'new case' of the Workers' Opposition against us.

We were shown how easy it is to find oneself among the 'accomplices' of a factional case. At a 23 February session of the party collegium on our case, a presenter declared comrade Iaroslavsky's book *About the Workers' Opposition* to be a means of propagandising the ideas of the Workers' Opposition.[234] Consequently, the author was an accomplice of the ideological leadership of the Omsk group.

---

234   Iaroslavsky 1927.

We hope that the CCC and Politburo will put an end to the persecution of us, which deliberately rests upon tendentiously selected materials about our alleged factional activity.

Biographical Glossary

Andreev, Andrei Andreevich (1895–1971) was born into a poor peasant family in Smolensk gubernia. * His father was a textile worker and a yardman. Andreev completed two years of village school and began studying Marxism around 1910. He worked as a dishwasher in a Moscow restaurant and held various jobs in the Caucasus and southern Russia. In 1914 he joined the RSDRP(b) and began working in Petrograd artillery factories. He was a member of the Petersburg Committee in 1915–17 and secretary of the Union of Metalworkers in 1917–18. After the revolution, he chaired the Central Council of Factory Committees of the Urals. He was among leaders of the Metalworkers' Union of Ukraine and was elected chair of the Railway Workers' Union in 1920. A VTsSPS secretary in 1920–2, he became a Party CC member in 1920. Among his high positions were Party CC secretary in 1924–5 and 1935–46, CCC chair in 1930–1, Commissar of Transport in 1931–5, Politburo member from 1932–52, and Party Control Committee chair, 1939–52. He was treated for deafness in 1953–4 and was among the alleged 'victims' in the so-called Doctors' Affair. He retired in 1962 and lived in Moscow in the House of Government.

Antipov, Nikolai Kirillovich (1894–1938) was born into a peasant family in Novgorod gubernia; his father was a metalworker. He studied through four classes of technical school and worked at the World Admiralteisky shipbuilding factory in St. Petersburg. In 1911, he joined a Marxist circle, in 1912 the RSDRP(b), and in 1913 was arrested and exiled. Then he returned to St. Petersburg, where he worked in Novyi Aivaz. Arrested again in 1914, he was imprisoned for a year in a fortress. After his release and an interlude in Moscow, he returned to Petrograd to work in various factories and carry out underground party work. Arrested and imprisoned in 1914–15, he then worked at Dinamo factory in Moscow. In 1915–16 he was imprisoned in Butyrka prison in Moscow. Later in 1916 he served as a private in the tsarist army. From late 1916 to 1919, he worked in Petrograd, with a brief imprisonment in 1916–17. He carried out party organising work in 1917. After the October Revolution, he became a member of VSNKh, then worked in the Cheka. In 1919, he was secretary of the Kazan Gubernia Party Committee, chair of the gubernia executive committee, and a member of

---

*   Sources for entries are: Alikina 2006; Berlin 2006; Buketov 2015; Chugurin 2011; Clements 1979; Filippov 2018; Gambarov 1989; Lane 1995; Pauly 2014; Pirani 2008 (using biographical information from TsAODM, RGASPI, TsDAHO, and TsAGM); RKP(b) 1961; Riddell 2015; Rodionova (ed.) 1985; Slutskaia 2017; Smirnov 2001; Tostorff 2016; Weissman 1974; Zenkovich 2002; *Katorga i ssylka*; correspondence with Eldar Zeinalov, April 2017; Memorial Society Index; RGASPI, fonds 5, 99, 589, 671; *Bolshaia Sovetskaia Entsiklopediia*; http://www.hrono.info/; *Encyclopedia Britannica*; Marxists.org; www.famhist.ru; *Spravochnik po istorii Kommunisticheskoi partii i Sovetskogo Soiuza, 1898–1991*.

the Revolutionary Military Council of the Reserve Army of the Republic. Then he worked in Tsektran. In 1921, he joined the VTsSPS presidium and became a CC member at the Thirteenth Party Congress. In the 1920s, he held party secretary positions in Moscow, the Urals, and Leningrad province. He served in 1928–31 as People's Commissar of Post and Telegraph of the USSR. From March 1931 on, he worked in Rabkrin and was a member of the presidium of the Party CCC. Expelled from the CC in 1937, he was arrested shortly afterwards and executed in 1938.

Antonov, [Isaif Pavlovich?] spoke on behalf of the Workers' Opposition at the Fifth All-Ukrainian Communist Party Conference, 17–22 November 1920, Kharkov. He seems to have been a delegate from an army organisation in Kharkov.

Antonov-Ovseenko, Vladimir Aleksandrovich (1884–1939) was born in Chernigov as the son of a tsarist officer. After he finished the Voronozh cadet corps in 1901, he entered Nikolaevskoe military engineering school. When he refused to take an oath of loyalty to the tsar because he hated militarism, he was arrested, detained for eleven days, and released into his father's custody. He then became a revolutionary upon joining a Social Democratic student circle in Warsaw in 1901. He did unskilled factory work in St. Petersburg and drove a coach, until he entered Petersburg cadet school in 1902. Having continued to agitate for revolution, he became a Bolshevik in 1903 and was a professional revolutionary by 1904. He founded the Warsaw military committee of the RSDRP and entered the revolutionary underground in 1905. Arrested and imprisoned numerous times, he traveled during his periods of freedom outside of Russia to Austria and Paris. In Paris, before World War I, he was a Menshevik but cooperated with Bolsheviks and worked on the newspaper *Nashe Slovo*. At the end of 1914, he became a Menshevik Internationalist. After returning to Russia in May 1917, he returned to the Bolshevik Party. He carried out revolutionary work in Finland, led the seizure of the Winter Palace and the arrest of Provisional Government ministers during the October Revolution, and was a delegate to the Constituent Assembly. He became People's Commissar of the Military and Commander-in-Chief of the Petrograd Military District. During the Russian Civil War, he commanded a front in Ukraine, led food requisitions, and was a member of the NKVD RSFSR board. In 1920–1, he executed numerous special assignments for the Soviet Executive Committee and was assistant chair of Narkomtrud in 1920. In 1921–2, he chaired the Samara Gubernia Party Executive Committee and was a delegate from there to the Eleventh Party Congress. In 1922–4, he was on the Revolutionary Military Council. After 1924, he worked in the People's Commissariat of Foreign Affairs, serving as a diplomatic envoy to Czechoslovakia in 1924–8. In 1923–7, he belonged to the Trotskyist Opposition. He served as Soviet ambassador to Latvia in 1929–30 and to Poland in 1930–4. An RSFSR procurator in 1934–6, he was general consul of the USSR in Barcelona, Spain in 1936–7. Briefly RSFSR People's Commissar of Justice upon his return, he was arrested in October 1937 and shot in February 1938.

Artem (Sergeev, Fedor Andreevich) (1883–1921) was born into a peasant family in Kursk gubernia and grew up in Ekaterinoslav, where his father did construction work. First he studied in a private school and then in a modern (non-classical) secondary school. After graduating, he entered Moscow Higher Technical School in 1901. Having become a student revolutionary, he was arrested, expelled, and imprisoned. After release, he became a revolutionary agitator and organiser in Ekaterinoslav gubernia. Part of the *Iskra* network, he attended the Kovalevsky school in Paris in 1903. After his return to Russia, he was rejected for admission to Petersburg Polytechnic Institute because he was politically unreliable. He worked on the railways and as a professional revolutionary. Having led the revolutionary workers' movement in Donbas in 1905, he spent 1906 in St. Petersburg, then moved to the Urals, by which time he had become a Bolshevik. Arrest, imprisonment, and exile followed. Having escaped exile, he traveled to Australia via Japan and China. There he worked on the railways and carried out revolutionary work for six years, becoming a citizen there. After the February 1917 Revolution, he tried to return directly to Russia, but was prevented due to his foreign passport. He took an indirect route through China to Vladivostok and then to Kharkov, where he assumed a leading party role. He was in Petrograd during the October Revolution, after which he returned to the Donbas. In 1919, he became a member of the Ukrainian Communist government and participated in the Russian Civil War. After the Bolsheviks took Ukraine, he chaired the Miners' Union in 1920. He died in the crash of an experimental locomotive on the Kursk railway in 1921. Stalin fostered his son.

Arutiuniants, S. (?–?) signed the theses of the Workers' Opposition as a member of the central committee of the Miners' Union. He may have joined the RCP(b) in 1920.

Avanesov, Varlam Aleksandrovich (Suren Karpovich Martirosian) (1884–1930) was born into an Armenian peasant family in Kars oblast. He graduated from the University of Zurich in 1913, having studied medicine. He joined the RSDRP in 1903 and was a Menshevik until joining the Bolsheviks in 1914. In 1917, he became a member of the Presidium of the Soviet Executive Committee. He was Deputy People's Commissar of Workers' and Peasants' Inspection (1920–1924), a member of the Collegium of the Cheka, and later Deputy People's Commissar for Foreign Trade.

Babkin, I.P. (1885–1940), having joined the RSDRP in 1902, carried out revolutionary work in Rostov-on-Don, Saratov, Tsaritsyn and other cities. He participated in the 1905–7 Revolution in Rostov-on-Don and was frequently arrested and jailed by the tsarist government. He was elected to the Rostovo-Nakhichevansky soviet in 1917. He chaired the labour department of Narkomprod RSFSR in 1918–21. Afterwards, Sovnarkom and STO sent him as an extraordinary representative to the Volga-Caspian region. From September 1921, he was a member of the Tsentrosoiuz Presidium. He chaired the board of the All-Russian Cooperative Trade Union of Fishermen. Among his other responsibilities included chairing the STO commission on the transport of oil from Astrakhan, STO Supreme Arbitrage commission member, VSNKh RSFSR Presidium member, Karelian sovnarkhoz chair, and Eksportles assistant chair.

Barchuk, Valerian ( ) was a metalworker who worked for Narkompros in Baku in the early 1920s. While there, he founded a group of the Workers' Opposition among employees of Azerbaijani Oil (Azneft) in 1923–4. He was transferred to Moscow in 1924 to work as a Narkompros instructor in the RSFSR.

Barsky, [ ] was a Metalworkers' Union representative from Nizhny Novgorod at the Fourth Congress of the Metalworkers' Union in May 1921. He was elected to the congress's communist faction bureau.

Barulin, I. was a Petersburg metalworker who participated in the October Revolution. He signed the Workers' Opposition's theses as Chair of the Main Board of the Association of Mid-Sized Machine-Building Factories. Later in 1921, he was a member of the presidium of the Moscow Gubernia Sovnarkhoz and head of its Metals Department. He often carried political and economic work while accompanying Kalinin. An 'M. Borulin' signed the Letter of the 22; it is not clear whether this was the same person.

Belenky, Grigory Iakovlevich (1885–1938) was born into a poor family in Mogilevskaia Gubernia. His father died when he was age twelve. He claimed no formal education, but said he was self-educated. He became a revolutionary at age 14, started distributing *Iskra* in 1901, and joined the RSDRP that year in Minsk (another source dates his party membership to 1903). He studied in political literacy evening classes. Having been arrested in 1902, he was imprisoned for a year, and exiled to Arkhangelsk for three years. Upon his return to Minsk, he became a Bolshevik underground activist in Vilnius and St. Petersburg. Arrested and imprisoned in 1907, he was sentenced to serve in a military fortress, but he continued his revolutionary work in the army. He went to Paris in 1908 for a party conference and then into the revolutionary underground in Kovno and Dvinsk. After a 1910 arrest, he was exiled permanently to Eniseiskaia gubernia, but escaped from there and reached Paris, where he worked for four years as secretary of the Paris section of the RSDRP(b). Having returned to Russia in May 1917, he began working in the Moscow party organisation and became secretary of the Krasnopresnensky District Party Committee until 1925, when he began working as Director of Agitation and Propaganda for the Comintern. He was also a member of the All-Russian Soviet Executive Committee at various times. He joined the Trotskyist Opposition in 1925 and in 1926 was excluded from the party for Trotskyism. Restored to the party ranks, he was again excluded in 1936 as a Trotskyist. From 1936–7 he directed an institute for improving qualifications of forestry technical personnel. Then he was executed.

Beloborodov, Aleksandr Grigorevich (1891–1938) was born in Aleksandrovsky factory in Permskaia gubernia into a worker's family. He completed a primary school education and began work in 1905 as an apprentice to a master in the gas-electric shop of Nadezhdinsky factory. He then was transferred to office work. Having joined an SD organisation in 1907, he was arrested in 1908 and sent to an orphanage for young criminals. Because it was full, he was redirected to prison, where he read voraciously. Upon his release in 1912, he returned to work at Nadezhdinsky factory as an electrician. He continued revolutionary work with the SDs and was affiliated with *Pravda*. Arrested in 1914, he was imprisoned for a few months and then exiled away from his home gubernia. After having worked in Tiumen, he in 1916 returned to Perm gubernia. In 1917, he was elected to party conferences and congresses in the Urals and as a delegate from there to the centre. He was a member of the Constituent Assembly. In 1918, he held party leadership posts in Ekaterinburg and was elected to the RCP(b) CC at the Eighth Party Congress. He played a role in the decisions that led to the execution of Nicholas Romanov and his family. During 1919, he served in the Civil War on the Southern Front and held various other posts. In October 1921, he returned to Moscow and became Assistant People's Commissar of Internal Affairs (NKVD). He was promoted to NKVD Commissar in 1923, the same year when he joined the Left Opposition led by Trotsky and signed the Declaration of the 46. He remained NKVD Commissar until 1927, when he was expelled from the party and exiled to Siberia. He was readmitted to the party in 1930 and worked in state purchasing. Arrested in 1936, he was executed in 1938, apparently without having confessed.

Boguslavsky, Mikhail Solomonovich (1886–1937) was a typesetter who in 1905 joined the socialist Jewish Bund. In 1917, he was a member of the Kremenchug soviet in Ukraine. In 1918–19, his leadership responsibilities included Voronezh City Soviet and Bolshevik City Committee. He held short-term positions in the Ukrainian Soviet government and in 1920 as head of Glavpolitput. Upon his transfer to Moscow, he joined VTsSPS and led the Bolshevik alternative to the Menshevik-controlled Printers' Union. He joined the Democratic Centralists (DCs) as a leading member. In 1922–4, he was deputy chair of the Moscow Soviet. From 1924, he chaired the Little Sovnarkom. Having supported the United Opposition in 1925–7, he was expelled from the party. He headed the Siberian Planning Commission in 1928. After recanting in 1930, he returned to Moscow. He was arrested and executed in 1936–7.

Borisov, Pavel Semenovich (1892–1939) completed primary school. Having joined the RSDRP in 1913, he carried out party work in Petersburg, Tula, and Samara and was often arrested and imprisoned by the tsarist government. After the February 1917 Revolution, he worked for the party in Samara. After the October Revolution, he held economic sector responsibilities in Petrograd and Moscow. He led factory trusts and was a member of VSNKh. He signed the theses of the Workers' Opposition as a member of the central committee of the Central Board of Artilleries Factories. He also signed the Letter of the 22 to the Comintern. From 1933, he led the Main Board of Agricultural Machinery of the People's Commissariat of Heavy Industry. He was arrested and executed in 1939.

Bruno, Genrikh Ivanovich (1889–1937) joined the RSDRP(b) in 1906 and carried out revolutionary activism in Riga, St. Petersburg, and Irkutsk. He was often arrested and jailed for his activities. In 1917, he chaired the Minusinsky Okrug Soviet and helped overthrow the Provisional Government in Petrograd in October 1917. During 1918–19, he held military and Cheka posts. From 1920, he held positions in economic administration, including chair of the Artillery Industry Board, Glavmetall collegium member, chair of the Board of the Ukrainian Agricultural Machinebuilding Trust, chair of the Board of Selmash Syndicate, and employee of Orgenergo of the People's Commissariat of Heavy Industry. He signed both the theses of the Workers' Opposition and the Letter of the 22. He was purged from the party in March 1935 and arrested the same year on the case of the Workers' Opposition. His execution followed in 1937.

Brykov, [N.D.?] entered the RCP(b) in 1919 and was a full voting delegate from the third Briansk Gubernia Conference to the Tenth RCP(b) Congress in 1921. He voted for the resolutions on party unity and on the anarcho-syndicalist deviation. In May 1921, a Brykov from Briansk was elected to the central committee of the Metalworkers' Union. At the Fifth Congress of the Metalworkers' Union in 1922, a Brykov from Kharkov was on Skliznev's list of nominees for the union's central committee, which means he was acceptable to former members of the Workers' Opposition. It is not clear whether Brykov from Kharkov was the same person as Brykov from Briansk.

Bubnov, Andrei Sergeevich (1883–1938) was born in Ivanovo-Voznesensk into the family of a textile plant manager. He graduated from a realschule in Ivanovo-Voznesensk and attended but did not graduate from Moscow Agricultural Institute. Having joined the Bolsheviks in 1903, he was arrested thirteen times and spent over four years in prison prior to 1917. He carried out revolutionary work in St. Petersburg, Nizhny Novgorod, Sormovo, Kharkov, Samara, and other cities. Having participated in the 1905 Revolution, he attended the RSDRP Stockholm Congress in 1906 and its London Congress in 1907. In 1907, he became a member of Moscow Committee of the RSDRP. He worked for the party as a writer, editor, and statistician. When the February 1917 Revolution began, he was in Eniseisk, but he returned to Moscow and was elected to the Moscow Soviet. He became a Party CC member at the Sixth RSDRP(b) Congress. A member of the Military Revolutionary Committee, he participated in the October 1917 Revolution in Petrograd. He was a member of the Executive Committee of the All-Russian Soviet and was a Left Communist during the Brest peace negotiations. A party leader in Ukraine after the Seventh RCP(b) Congress, he carried out underground work in Kiev during the Russian Civil War, held military posts, and chaired Ukraine's Soviet. His Soviet-era posts included chief of the Red Army Political Administration, member of the USSR Revolutionary Military Council, and RSFSR Commissar of Enlightenment. He belonged to the Democratic Centralists in 1920–1 and signed the Declaration of the 46 (Trotskyists) in 1923. Party secretary in 1925, he was a candidate member of the Party Secretariat in 1926–30. He was People's Commissar of Education in the RSFSR from 1929–37. Arrested in October 1937 in Moscow, he was shot in August 1938.

Budniak, F.D. was a candidate member of the Metalworkers' Union central committee in May 1921. He chaired the collegium of the factory-technical department of the Central Auto Section of VSNKh (Zavtotsas) in 1921. He was president of the Motor Industry Trust in 1922–3. In 1927, as a representative of the automobile and aviation department of Glavmetall, he went in a delegation to Germany for negotiations with BMW. That same year, he served as assistant director of Glavmetall. In some records, it is difficult to distinguish him from Budnik (below).

Budnik, [Savva Mikhailovich?] may have been from Moscow. He spoke at the October 1921 plenum of the central committee of the Metalworkers' Union. He was also in the MRO of the All-Russian Metalworkers' Union.

Bukhanov, Aleksei Alekseevich (1891–1938) was born in Moscow gubernia into a poor peasant family; his father died when he was five years old. He finished primary school and worked as a carpenter in Moscow, 1903–11. He worked in Kolomna in 1911–24, also as a carpenter, but in the Kolomensky locomotive building plant in 1911–18. He joined the RSDRP(b) in June 1917. He held local leadership positions in the Metalworkers' Union in 1918–22, including chair of the Kolomensky Raion Committee of the Metalworkers' Union and member of the presidium of the central committee of the All-Russian Metalworkers' Union in 1919–22. He was apparently a nominee of the party leadership at the May 1921 Metalworkers' Union congress, because he did not support the Workers' Opposition. He chaired the Kolomensky Uispolkom in 1922–4, but worked in Moscow in 1924–34. His places of work included the Moscow Metalworkers' Union, the Moscow State Machinebuilding Trust, the All-Union Trust of Midsized Machine Building, and the People's Commissariat of Worker-Peasant Inspection. Arrested in 1937, he was executed in 1938 without having confessed.

Bukharin, Nikolai Ivanovich (1888–1938) was the son of a Moscow gymnasium teacher. Aside from four years in Bessarabia in childhood, he spent his youth in Moscow. He experienced deprivation while his father was unemployed for two years. He was introduced to socialist literature in gymnasium, participated in the 1905 revolution, and began illegal work as a Bolshevik in 1906. He attended but did not finish the Law Department of Moscow University, because he spent much of his time in revolutionary organising. Coopted into the Moscow RSDRP Committee in 1908, he was elected to it in 1909. He was arrested twice in 1909–10. Exiled to Onega, he escaped abroad to avoid hard labour. While abroad, he began a career as a writer for *Pravda*, *Prosveshchenie*, and *Neue Zeit*. He lived in Austria, Switzerland, Sweden, and Norway; he was arrested abroad at least twice. He traveled to the United States under a false identity and in New York City edited *Novyi Mir*. After the February 1917 Revolution, he returned to Russia through Japan. In Moscow in 1917, he belonged

to the Executive Committee of the Moscow Soviet, was a member of the Moscow
Party Committee, and an editor of *Sotsial Demokrat* and the journal *Spartak*. He was
elected to the Bolshevik Party CC at the Sixth RCP(b) Congress. He led the Left Communists in opposition to the Brest Peace. In the 1920s, he belonged to the Party CC
and Politburo, and the Presidium of the Executive Committee of the Comintern.
He edited *Pravda*. His numerous publications included works on economics and
political philosophy. An enthusiastic proponent of NEP and ally of Stalin against
the United Opposition, he was targeted by Stalin as a leader of the Right Opposition
in 1928–9, when Stalin ended NEP and launched collectivisation and rapid industrialisation. Harried by Stalin and his supporters through the 1930s, he was arrested in
1937 and put on public trial, where he may have subverted the process in an attempt
to reveal its falseness. He was executed in 1938, but left behind his prison memoirs.

Bulkin-Semenov, Fedor Afanasevich (1888–1937) was the son of an unskilled worker at
the Baltiisky Factory, where he attended factory school and then became a metalworker. A Menshevik from 1904, he was a founding member of the Metalworkers'
Union and served on its board. He went as a party delegate to the London Congress.
Arrested in 1910, he went into exile and then fled Russia. Having returned, he represented Samara on the War Industries Committee, but was arrested in 1916 and exiled
to Siberia. He led the Orenburg Mensheviks in 1917–18 and edited the newspaper
Zaria. He joined the RCP(b) in 1919 in Kharkov. He was a soviet organiser and assistant chair of a soviet executive committee. In the 1920s, he wrote books and articles
about the history of the Petersburg Metalworkers' Union. Purged from the party in
1922 for having belonged to the Workers' Opposition, he was restored to party membership in 1927, purged again in 1935, and executed in 1937.

Cavaignac, Louis-Eugène (1802–57) was born to a Jacobin father and became a repub-
lican general. During the Revolution of 1848, he brutally suppressed an uprising of
Parisian workers who had revolted against the liquidation of national workshops,
which had provided some relief during a period of high unemployment and high
food prices. He ran for president but lost to Louis-Napoleon Bonaparte.

Chelyshev, Mikhail Ivanovich (1888–1937) was born in Sablukovo village, Arzamassky
uezd, Nizhegorodskaia gubernia. Educated in a trade school, he joined the RSDRP(b)
in 1914. During 1917, he was secretary of the Kanavinsky District Party Committee, chief of the organisational section, and chair of the Nizhny Novgorod City
Party Committee. In 1921–2, he was in the CC of the RCP(b). A close comrade of
Shliapnikov and Medvedev, he signed the theses of the Workers' Opposition and
the Letter of the 22. At the Eleventh Party Congress, he represented the Central
Auditing Commission with a consultative vote. From 1922 on, he chaired the Criminal Appeals Collegium of the RSFSR Supreme Court, chaired the Moscow Gubernia
Court, and was assistant chair of the All-Russian Soviet Executive Committee Com-
mission on Amnesties. In 1935, he chaired the Scientific-Technical Council of Indus-

trial Construction Materials of Narkomtiazhprom. From 1935, he served as assistant chair of the Main Court of Dagestan ASSR in Makhachkala. Arrested on 6 July 1937 for having belonged to the Workers' Opposition, he was interrogated twice and died on 23 December 1937 in a prison hospital. The causes of death were listed as heart failure and nephritis.

Chernov-Grechnev, Andrei Semenovich (1881–1972) had a technical education and worked as an engineer-mechanic. He joined the RSDRP in 1905 when he was a teacher at a mining school in Gorlovka in the Donbas. During the 1905 revolution he led a fighting squad there. He left Russia in 1906 and remained in emigration into 1918. He arrived in Paris in 1909, worked in a factory as a mechanic, joined the French Mechanics' Union and was a longtime chair of the Russian Workers' Club there. He was closely acquainted with Lenin. In 1919–21, he directed Sormovo factory. In this capacity, he signed the theses of the Workers' Opposition. Afterwards, he chaired Glavmetall of VSNKh, was a member of the collegium of the Central Automobile Section, and chaired Gomza. From 1925 he held leading jobs in Narkomvneshtorg. In the mid-1930s he worked as an engineer in Moscow for the Associations of Heavy Industry.

Chubar, Vlas Iakovlevich (1891–1939) was born in Ekaterinoslavskaia gubernia to illiterate parents who had a small farm. He finished two years of primary school in 1897–9, worked on the family farm, and was a day labourer on other farms. In 1904, he went to Aleksandrovsk to study in a mechanical-technical school and around the same time became involved in revolutionary circles. In 1905, he went to the countryside to carry out revolutionary organising among peasants. Having joined the RSDRP in 1907, he affiliated himself with the Bolsheviks. After he finished mechanical-technical school in 1911, he went through periods of factory work, arrest, and unemployment. In Moscow, St. Petersburg, and other cities in Russia and Ukraine, he was active in strikes, the insurance campaign, and revolutionary work. He was conscripted for military service in 1915 and in 1916 was sent to work in a weapons factory in Petrograd. A metalworker until the February Revolution, he then helped organise workers' militias, factory committees, and other revolutionary bodies. He was in the Petrograd Council of Factory Committees. After the October 1917 Revolution, he belonged to the VSNKh presidium. From 1920 on, he led party, soviet, and economic work in Ukraine as a member of the Revolutionary Committee of the Ukrainian Soviet Socialist Republic (UkrSSR), chair of the Presidium of VSNKh of the UkrSSR, and chair of the UkrSSR Sovnarkom. The Donetsk party organisation of the CP(b)U delegated him to the Eleventh Party Congress. From 1923 he was a member of the CP(b)U CC Politburo and CP(b)U chair, including during the time of the Ukrainian Famine. From 1927, he was a candidate member of the All-Union Communist Party CC Politburo. He became deputy chair of the USSR Council of People's Commissars and deputy chair of the USSR Council of Labour and Defence in 1934. Made a full

Politburo member in 1935, he served as USSR People's Commissar of Finance in 1937–8. Appointed chief of Solikamsk construction in the NKVD Gulag, he was arrested there in 1938 and executed in 1939.

Chugurin, Ivan (1883–1947) was born in Sormovo to a father who was a factory worker and began working at the Sormovo plant in 1894. He joined the RSDRP in 1902 and became a Bolshevik after the party split. He participated in the 1905 Revolution in Sormovo. He attended the Longjumeau School in 1911 and was a member of the Petersburg Bolshevik Committee in 1916–17. As secretary of the Vyborg Party Committee in 1917, he greeted Lenin at the Finland Station and delivered to him his party card. He participated prominently in the October 1917 Revolution. During the Russian Civil War, he held a high position in the Cheka and carried out political work in the Red Army. From 1921, he served as deputy director of the Krasnoe Sormovo Plant, chaired the board of Siberian Coal (Sibugol), directed the Northern Shipyard, and directed the Elektropribor Plant. He died near Moscow in 1947.

Dietzgen, Peter Joseph (1828–88) was a self-educated tannery worker who lived and worked in Germany, Russia, and the United States. Having become an atheist under the influence of Ludwig Feuerbach's writings, his interest in dialectical materialism led him to strongly support Marx and Engels. An original thinker, he contributed to Marxist philosophy in the area of epistemology. Matter, he explained, was eternal and constantly in movement; it produced an ideal consciousness containing that which was natural and social. He regarded thought as derived from the senses and imagination and in movement toward absolute truth.

Drozhzhin, I.V. ( ) entered the RCP(b) in 1917. At the Eleventh Party Congress in 1922, he was a voting delegate from the Riazan party organisation. He attended the Second Khamovnichesky District Party Conference in Moscow, 9–10 January 1924.

Dzerzhinsky, Feliks Edmundovich (1877–1926) was born into a minor Polish gentry family. He studied in gymnasium, but dropped out of the eighth class to become a fulltime revolutionary agitator. He first entered a social democratic circle in 1894, from which he joined the Lithuanian Social Democratic Party in 1895. He carried out party work in Poland and Russia and participated in the 1905 Revolution in Poland. He spent a total of eleven years in prison, exile, and at hard labour for illegal revolutionary activity. In 1917, he participated in party work in Moscow, was elected to the Bolshevik Party CC at its Sixth Congress, and entered its secretariat. He was a leading Petrograd Military Revolutionary Committee member during the October Revolution. Afterwards, he became a member of the Executive Committee of the All-Russian Soviet, chair of the Cheka, People's Commissar of Internal Affairs, People's Commissar of Transport, chair of the OGPU of the USSR, and chair of VSNKh of the USSR. From June 1924, he was a candidate member of the RCP(b) CC Politburo and a full member of the Orgburo. He died of a heart attack in 1926, not long after having denounced the United Opposition in a two-hour long speech.

Fedorov, Grigory Fedorovich (1891–1936) was born in St. Petersburg and joined the
RSDRP in 1907. Arrested twice, he was exiled from St. Petersburg in 1914. In 1917, he
was a member of the Executive Committee of the Petrograd Soviet, the Petersburg
Committee of the RSDRP(b), the CC RSDRP(b), the Petrograd Military Revolutionary
Committee, and chair of the Central Council of Factory Committees of Petrograd.
After the October Revolution, he was in the collegium of the People's Commissariat
of Labour. In 1918, he chaired the Nizhegorod Gubernia Executive Committee of
the Soviet and the Nizhegorod Gubernia Military Revolutionary Committee. In 1919,
he chaired the Saratov Gubernia Executive Committee of the Soviet. In 1919–20, he
directed the political sections of the Southern Front, the Thirteenth Army, and the
Fourteenth Army. In 1921, he helped crush the Kronstadt Uprising and worked in Petrograd trade unions and government in the 1920s. He was expelled from the party in
1927, reinstated in 1928, appointed as assistant chair of Metallosindikat, led the All-
Union Cartographic Trust in the early 1930s, purged from the party and arrested in
1934, given a ten-year prison sentence in 1935, and rearrested and shot in 1936.

Figatner, Iury Petrovich (Iakov Isaakovich) (1889–1937) was born in Odessa, where he
joined the RSDRP in 1903. He carried out revolutionary activism in Odessa, Warsaw,
and Moscow. He spent 1906–8 in France and Belgium. After returning to Russia in
1909, he was arrested, sentenced to seven years hard labour in 1911, and served out
his term in Butyrka prison. Freed in March 1917, he worked in party and trade union
organisations. His positions included Zakavkazsky Krai Party Committee member,
CC Caucasus Bureau secretary, VTsSPS Caucasus Bureau chair, CC RCP(b) Siberian
Bureau member, VTsSPS Siberian Bureau chair, VTsSPS Presidium member, and
after 1924, chair of the central committee of the Union of Soviet Retail Employees.
He was a member of VTsSPS Presidium in 1924–9, and a member of the Party CCC
in in 1925–34. In 1930–2, he was a member of the presidium of VSNKh USSR. From
1932, he served in the collegium of the People's Commissariat of Heavy Industry. In
1935–7, he held various positions in the forestry industry and commissariat. He was
arrested and executed in 1937.

Fokin [Vasily Ivanovich] was the name of an apparent Worker Oppositionist referenced
in Mitin's letter. A person by this name signed a petition asking for Medvedev to be
allowed to speak at the Fifth Congress of the Metalworkers' Union. The surname
was used to refer to the informer Frolov who reported on Shliapnikov's speech in
the party cell of the Moscow Hydroelectrical Station. It is not clear whether these
were all the same or different people.

Friis, Jacob (1883–1956) was a socialist journalist who belonged to the Norwegian
Labour Party. He took both internationalist and pacifist positions during World
War I. In 1919, his party joined the Comintern and he served as a delegate to the
Second and Third World Congresses of the Comintern. He was in its Executive Com-
mittee in 1920–1, but in 1923 he supported the Norwegian Labour Party's decision to

withdraw from the Comintern. He belonged to the Communist Party of Norway in 1928–33, whereupon he rejoined the Labour Party.

Glebov-Avilov [sometimes Avilov-Glebov], Nikolai Pavlovich (1887–1937) was born to a cobbler in Kaluga and experienced a childhood of poverty. At age twelve, he began working in a print shop. Around age seventeen (1904), he began attending political meetings and reading revolutionary pamphlets and newspapers. He joined the Kaluga Social Democratic party organisation and participated in the 1905 Revolution. Upon moving to Moscow in 1906, he worked in *Borba*'s underground printshop. He participated in the illegal All-Russian Railway Workers' Union and in party circles in factories. The Moscow Party Committee dispatched him to the Urals in 1907. Around 1910–11, he traveled to Italy to study in the higher party school. In Petersburg before the war, he edited the Metalworkers' Union's newspaper and wrote for *Pravda*. He met Lenin in Cracow in 1914. He was arrested, imprisoned and exiled numerous times in his revolutionary career. Places of his revolutionary underground activity included Moscow, St. Peterburg, Baku, Nikolaev (Kherson gubernia), and Ekaterinoslav. Among his places of exile were Kaluga, Tobolsk gubernia, and Narymsky krai, from which he twice escaped. When the February Revolution began, he agitated for revolution in Tomsk and then went to Petrograd. First he worked in the Petersburg Bolshevik Committee, then in the Petrograd Bureau of Trade Unions and its Presidium, and then in the VTsSPS Presidium. After the October Revolution, he served briefly as People's Commissar of Post and Telegraph. He served briefly in the Civil War on the Southern Front, but failed to carry out his duties responsibly. His positions in the 1920s included VTsSPS Presidium member, People's Commissar of Labour of Ukraine, chair of the Leningrad Trade Union Council and NorthWest Bureau of VTsSPS. He was a candidate member of the Party CC. Having supported Zinoviev in the United Opposition, he was reassigned to diplomatic work in Rome in 1926. He directed the Rostov Agricultural Machine factory from 1928 to 1936, when he was arrested and executed in 1937.

Goldberg, [ ] ( ) attended a small meeting of Worker Oppositionists during the Fifth Congress of the Metalworkers' Union. He represented Kharkov and Nikolaev. He may have become a Trotskyist later.

Guchkov, Aleksandr Ivanovich (1862–1936) was a moderate liberal from a wealthy family. A co-founder of the Octobrist Party, he chaired the Central War Industries Committee during World War I and served as Minister of War and the Navy for a few months under the Provisional Government. After the October Revolution, he emigrated from Russia to Paris.

Gurevich, Aleksandr Iosifovich (1896–1937) was born in Belostok. He graduated from a private gymnasium, but was not permitted to enter Moscow University due to the quota placed on Jews. He studied in the Moscow Commercial Institute while he was a revolutionary activist. He joined the RSDRP in 1916. He took a vocal line against the

Workers' Opposition and was elected to the Metalworkers' Union central committee in May 1921 as a candidate of the party leadership in place of Skliznev, who was a
former Worker Oppositionist. Until 1927, he remained among the leadership of the
Metalworkers' Union. From 1927 to 1930, he was in the presidium of the Party CCC.
From 1930–6 he held positions in economic administration. He was arrested and
shot in 1937.

Hempel (Appel), Jan (1890–1985) became a German Social Democrat in 1908. He carried out revolutionary agitation and organisation in Hamburg during World War I
and in 1919 joined the Communist Party of Germany. An ultraleftist, he helped found
the KAPD. He was a delegate to the Third World Congress of the Communist International. Imprisoned in 1923–5, he moved in 1926 to Holland, where he belonged to
the Internationalist Communist Group. From 1948 on, he was a Spartacist.

Iakovleva, Varvara Nikolaevna (1884/5–1941/4) graduated from gymnasium at age sixteen and enrolled in Higher Women's Courses in Moscow (the Gere courses) in the
Physics-Math Department, with a focus on astronomy. After a long period of studying social problems and participating in discussion groups, she decided to become
a Marxist. In 1904, she joined the RSDRP and later that year committed to Bolshevism. At first, she worked on the technical aspect of revolutionary work, then moved
into propaganda and organising. Although her home base was in Moscow, she was
often arrested and exiled. In 1910, she lost her job as a teacher in a Moscow city
school due to her illegal political work. From 1910–12, she was in exile in Narymsky Krai, but escaped to carry out illegal activism in the Central Industrial Region of
Russia. She was an agent of the RSDRP(b) CC and a member of the oblast bureau.
Arrested again in 1913 and returned to Narym, she fled to Petrograd, was arrested
thrice more, and sent to Astrakhan and then Enotaevsk. In spring 1916, she settled
in Moscow and became secretary of the Moscow Oblast bureau of the RSDRP(b) CC.
She had an attack of appendicitis during the February 1917 Revolution. She attended the Bolshevik CC meeting in Petrograd that planned the October overthrow of
the Provisional Government and she helped organise and lead the Moscow uprising in October 1917. Her post-revolutionary work included positions in the Cheka,
the Siberian Bureau of the RCP(b) CC, the Presidium of the Commissariat of Food
Supply, Narkompros, and as Moscow Party Committee secretary. She was a delegate
to the Seventh, Tenth, Eleventh, Fourteenth, Sixteenth, and Seventeenth Party Congresses. A Left Communist in 1918, she sympathized with the Democratic Centralists
in 1920, and signed the Platform of the 46 in 1923. From 1922–9, she served as Deputy
People's Commissar of Enlightenment and then as Commissar of Finance, 1929–37.
In 1937, she was arrested and in 1938 was given a twenty-year prison sentence. She
may have been shot in Orel Prison.

Ianson, Nikolai Mikhailovich (1882–1938) was born in St. Petersburg into a working-
class family of Estonian nationality. He studied in schools affiliated with the church

and with Kronstadt port. He began metals work in 1901 and joined the RSDRP(b) in 1905, carrying out party work in Petersburg and Revel. A member of the Revel (Tallinn) Committee of the RSDRP(b), he chaired the Revel Soviet of Workers' Deputies in 1905. Arrested in 1906, he was exiled to Tobolsk Gubernia. From 1907 to 1917, he was in the United States, where he was secretary of the Socialist Federation of Estonian Workers. He participated in the 1917 revolution in Estonia, but was arrested and deported to Russia when the Germans occupied the territory in 1918. In 1918–21, he directed a factory and then chaired the Samara Gubernia Trade Union Council. He was secretary of the Metalworkers' Union CC in 1921–3. From 1923 to 1934, he was a member of the Presidium of the Party CCC, serving as its secretary in 1923–30 and playing a key role in the purge of oppositionists from the party. His other leading roles were in Rabkrin (1925–8), in which he advocated use of prisoner labour in remote territories, and as People's Commissar of Justice of the RSFSR (1928–30). He served as People's Commissar of Water Transport from 1931–4, but was demoted in 1934 and dismissed in 1935. Arrested in 1937 and accused of spying for Estonia, he was executed in 1938.

Ignatev, [ ] ( ) from Izhevsk became a member of the Metalworkers' Union central committee in May 1921, apparently as a nominee of the former Workers' Opposition. He does not seem to have been the same person as N.S. Ignatev from Vitebsk who was at the Tenth and Eleventh RCP(b) Party Congresses.

Ignatov, Efim Nikitovich (1890–1938) joined the RSDRP(b) in 1912. He was among Moscow Soviet leaders in 1917; in 1919 he took over the party organisation in the Gorodskoi District of Moscow. He led his own group of communist industrial workers in 1920–1 in several districts of Moscow. They advanced proposals on party building and trade unions and cooperated with the Workers' Opposition at the Tenth Party Congress in March 1921. Subsequently, he was sent to Vitebsk to serve as chair of the Vitebsk Soviet Executive Committee. Later a historian of the soviets, he worked in higher education from 1929–38 as an administrator and professor of courses on soviet building. He was arrested and executed.

Iurenev (Krotovsky), Konstantin Konstantinovich (1888–1938) was born in Dvinsk to a railway station guard. He attended Dvinsk modern school and participated in illegal circles of students in 1904. In 1905 he joined the Dvinsk RSDRP organisation. It is not clear when he became a Bolshevik. Arrested in 1908, he spent three years exile in Arkhangelsk Gubernia and was released to St. Petersburg in 1911. In 1912, he went underground, but was rearrested the same year and expelled from St. Petersburg. He worked for *Pravda* outside of Petersburg city limits, in 1913 went to Bobruisk, and returned to live illegally in St. Petersburg. He helped to organise Mezhraionka, the interdistrict committee of SDs in Petrograd during World War I, was arrested in 1915 and tried in 1916, but released. He traveled to Simferopol as a party activist, was arrested and sent to serve in the army, but escaped. After a month in Crimea, he returned to Petrograd and worked in the revolutionary underground until the February 1917 Revolution. Then he joined the Executive Committee of the Petrograd Soviet and later the All-Russian Soviet. He chaired the Red Guards' main command. In 1918, he helped organise the Red Army and was a member of the Collegium of the People's Commissariat of the Military. In Moscow, he chaired the All-Russian Bureau of Military Commissars. In spring 1919, he was appointed to membership in the Revolutionary Military Council of the Eastern Front. He was a member of Simbirsky Gubernia Party Committee and carried out food requisitions in Kostromskaia Gubernia in autumn 1919. Then he became a member of the Revolutionary Military Council (RVS) of the Western Front. He was in the Smolensk City Party Committee and left the military for party work in early 1920. As a member of the Moscow Party Committee, he worked in Zamoskvoretsky and Bauman Districts. In summer 1920, he chaired the Kursk Gubernia Executive Party Committee. He wrote about party history for *Proletarskaia Revoliutsiia*. From June 1921, he worked for the People's Commissariat of Foreign Affairs as an ambassador to Bukhara (1921), Latvia (1922), Czechoslovakia (1923), Italy (1924), Persia (1925–6), Austria (1927–?), Japan (1933–7), and Germany (1937).

Ivanov, I. ( ) of Moscow participated in the Workers' Opposition and signed the Letter of the 22. Shliapnikov proposed him as a candidate member of the central committee of the Metalworkers' Union in May 1921. At the Eleventh Party Congress, I. Ivanov was identified as a member of the Workers' Opposition in the glossary to the stenographic record. At the Tenth Party Congress, I.A. Ivanov (Kiev Military Okrug Party organisation), who had been a party member since 1918, voted against the resolution on party unity but for the one on the anarcho-syndicalist deviation. He participated in the suppression of Kronstadt rebels. He spoke at the Tenth Party Congress about education, propaganda, agitation, and the anarcho-syndicalist resolution. Also at the Tenth Party Congress, I.N. Ivanov of the Siberian bureau of CC RCP(b), who had joined the party in 1918, voted for the resolutions on party unity and anarcho-syndicalist deviation., I.N. did not speak at the Congress. It is likely that I., I.A., and I.N. Ivanov were all different people

Ivanov, Vasily ( ) was a candidate promoted by party leaders for membership in the central committee of the Metalworkers' Union in May 1921. He was a member of the Kharkov Gubernia Committee of the Metalworkers' Union.

Jaures, Jean (1859–1914) was born into a French middle class family in the Tarn region. He was educated in Paris and was a university lecturer and historian. First elected to the French national assembly in 1885, he was a socialist by 1893. He became the leader of the French Socialist Party in 1902. A moderate socialist who was opposed to imperialist war, he was assassinated in Paris when World War I began.

Jezierska [Ezerskaia], Fanny (1887–1945) was a socialist born into a middle-class family in Poland. She spoke Russian and German, received an engineering education in Germany, served as Rosa Luxemburg's secretary, and was well known to many leading socialists across Europe. She was a Socialist Revolutionary from 1905–9 and joined the SPD in 1909. Having worked as an engineer during World War I, she served the Soviets in the diplomatic corps and in the Comintern bureaucracy in Moscow from 1918–28. She also helped translate Lenin's works into German. In 1928, she was permitted to leave the USSR for medical treatment abroad. She lived in Paris, 1933–40, fled to the south of France when Germany invaded, and arrived in New York City in 1941, traveling further to reunite with family members in California, where she lived until her death in 1945.[1]

Kalinin, Mikhail Ivanovich (1875–1946) was born in Tver gubernia into a peasant family that was not well-off. After he completed a zemstvo primary school, he went to work as a servant in St. Petersburg. He was permitted to read many books in the library of the family in whose house he served. At age sixteen, he took employment in a cartridge factory while he studied in a factory evening school. He became a metalworker at Putilov factory and joined the RSDRP in 1898. He participated in the 1905 Revolution and carried out party work in St. Petersburg, Tiflis, Revel, Moscow, and other cities. He often was a member of the Petersburg Committee of the RSDRP(b) and was frequently arrested and imprisoned. In 1912, he was a candidate CC member and later belonged to the Russian Bureau of the Bolshevik CC. He helped organise *Pravda*. A participant in both the February and October 1917 Revolutions, he remained in Petrograd for a time after 1917. Beginning in 1919, he was a candidate member of the Politburo, chaired the All-Russian Executive Committee of the Soviet of the RSFSR, and was chair of the Central Executive Committee of the USSR from 1922. He became a full member of the Politburo in 1926. Beginning in 1938, he chaired the Presidium of the Supreme Soviet of the USSR, until a few months before his death in 1946.

Kalnin, Ans Ernestovich (1883–1950) was born into a Latvian peasant family in Kurliandskaia gubernia. He joined the Latvian Social Democratic Party in 1904, was first arrested in Riga in 1906 and spent two years in prison. Having lived in Australia during 1912–17, he returned to Russia to join the RCP(b) and serve in posts including Labour Commissar of the Far Eastern Republic during the Civil War. He chaired the Miners' Union in Donbas in 1921 and supported Trotsky's views on the role of trade unions. He was in the Executive Bureau of the Red International of Labour Unions in 1922 and 1924. His later career included soviet economic posts. He was arrested in 1937 as a Trotskyist and sentenced in 1938 to eight years in a prison camp in Komi.

Kamenev (Rozenfeld), Lev Borisovich (1883–1936) was born in Moscow. His railway mechanic father later became an engineer. Well-educated radicals, his parents allowed him to play with factory children. He attended gymnasia in Vilensk and

---

1 Luban 2003.

Tiflis, where he joined Marxist circles. Arrested in 1900, he was soon released, whereupon he enrolled in the Law Department of Moscow University. Having been expelled from there, he was arrested, but exchanged exile for living in Tiflis under police supervision. In 1902, he arrived in Paris, met Lenin, went to Geneva, and returned to Russia in 1903. He entered the Petersburg Technological Institute, but did not finish. He largely worked in the revolutionary underground for periods of time punctuated by arrests, exiles, and imprisonments. Having participated in the 1905 Revolution in Minsk and St. Petersburg, he spent 1906–7 in St. Petersburg. Arrested and released in 1908, he departed for Geneva. He was in Cracow in 1913 and in 1914 went to Petersburg, where he edited *Pravda* and led the Bolshevik faction in the Fourth Duma. After the police closed *Pravda*, he relocated to Finland, but was arrested, tried in 1915, and exiled to Siberia, where he lived in Turukhansk, Eniseisk, and Achinsk. After the February 1917 Revolution, he was released and returned to Petrograd, where he resumed the editorship of *Pravda* and took a position in the Executive Committee of the Petrograd Soviet. At the April 1917 Bolshevik Party Conference, he was elected to the RSDRP(b) CC. He became a member of the Bureau of the All-Russian Soviet. After the July Uprising failed, he was arrested. He was a member of the Preparliament and the Constituent Assembly. During the October Revolution, he and Zinoviev disagreed with Lenin about the composition of the revolutionary government. He served in the Brest-Litovsk peace negotiations delegation and carried out a diplomatic mission to England and France in 1918. Arrested by Whites and imprisoned, he was exchanged in August 1918 and returned to Moscow, where he was elected chair of the Moscow Soviet. He had some duties on the front during the Civil War in 1919. He was a member of the ECCI. In 1922, he was assistant chair of Sovnarkom and STO, which he chaired after Lenin's death. While Lenin was ill, he transferred his personal archive to Kamenev, who became director of the Institute of V.I. Lenin. A member of the ruling triumvirate until he and Zinoviev parted ways with Stalin, he lost his high positions in 1926 and was appointed People's Commissar of Trade. Along with Trotsky and Zinoviev, he led the United Opposition. Expelled from the party in 1927, he recanted and was reinstated in 1928. Expelled again in 1932, he was condemned to death and executed in 1936 after the first Moscow show trial of the Great Terror.

Kaplan, Fanny Efimovna [Feiga Faivelovna Roitblat] (1887?–1918) was born in Volynskaia Gubernia. She participated in the 1905 Russian Revolution as an anarchist. Arrested in Kiev in 1907 after a bomb went off in her hotel room in Kiev, she confessed to having obtained and kept explosives and was found guilty of having prepared a terrorist attack on the life of Kiev General-Governor V.A. Sukhomlinov. She was sentenced to life imprisonment in Eastern Siberia, where she associated with SRs, Mensheviks, and other anarchists. She began to lose her sight in 1909. After the February Revolution, she was released from imprisonment and came to Moscow.

Having undergone an operation in Kharkov to partially restore her eyesight, she returned to Moscow. She was accused of and executed for an attempt on the life of Vladimir Lenin in August 1918, although her guilt and ability to shoot accurately have been disputed by some historians. The Bolsheviks identified her as a Right SR in 1922, but her political affiliations in 1918 are unknown.

Kariakin, I.I. ( ) from the Urals was the first 'Red Director' of Motovilikhinsky factory. A member of the Metalworkers' Union central committee, he supported the Workers' Opposition and reportedly said he would have signed the Letter of the 22 if he had been able to travel to Moscow to do so. When he was not elected as a delegate to the Eleventh Party Congress, he offered his resignation from the party. He was not a backer of Miasnikov. Sometimes his name appears as Koriakin.

Kerran [Kehrhahn], Ferdinand Lewis (1883–1949) was born to a German father in Britain, where he became an antiwar socialist who was imprisoned for four years during World War I. In 1920, he was a founding member of the Communist Party of Great Britain, a member of its Executive, and a delegate to the Third World Congress of the Comintern. He left the CPGB in 1923 in order to participate in elections as a Labour Party candidate. His later career was colorful, with an advisory role to King Zog of Albania, travels to Hong Kong and San Francisco, and perhaps a role in smuggling Jews out of Nazi Germany.

Kharitonenko [ ] ( ) was a delegate from Briansk to the Metalworkers' Union Congress in May 1921, where former Worker Oppositionists nominated him to be a candidate member of the central committee of the Metalworkers' Union. The party leadership opposed his candidacy.

Kiselev, Aleksei Semenovich (1879–1937) was born in Avdotino, Vladimir Gubernia, near Ivanovo-Voznesensk. His father worked in spinning mills, but also had a small plot of land, so A.S. worked in agriculture from an early age. He completed a church parish school and wanted to continue his education in seminary, but his father did not allow it. In an attempt to make him into a village teacher, the priest kept him in school two more years to teach the younger students. He began working at age fourteen in a printing plant as a metalworking apprentice. Meanwhile, he studied math, drafting, mechanics, and other technical subjects in evening classes and in Sunday school in Ivanovo-Voznesensk. Around age 18–19, he was given socialist literature to read by SD party members and in 1898 he began to attend illegal meetings and to recruit fellow workers. When the RSDRP split, he joined the Bolsheviks. Arrested first in 1900, he was arrested, imprisoned and exiled many times. Places of exile included Arkhangelsk Gubernia and Eniseiskaia Gubernia. He was imprisoned in Vladimir Gubernia, He worked in the revolutionary underground in Ivanovo-Voznesensk, Moscow, Kharkov, Nikolaev, Odessa, Batum, Tiflis, and Baku. He was a member of the Party Committee in Sokolnichesky District of Moscow and participated in elections to the State Duma in Ivanovo-Voznesensk. Among the factories where he worked were Gopper and Mikhelson in Moscow and Aivaz and Erikson in St. Petersburg, where he was elected chair of the Metalworkers' Union and worked as an insurance organiser before the war. He sold Singer sewing machines in Ivanovo-Voznesensk in 1909. In 1914, the party sent him to Austria, where he met Lenin and was coopted into the CC. After returning to St. Petersburg, he along with other Pravdaists was arrested in July 1914, imprisoned and exiled to Siberia. He fled military conscription and roamed Siberia illegally. Having participated in the February 1917 Revolution in Siberia, he then returned to Ivanovo-Voznesensk, where he was elected chair of the City Soviet, a member of the City District Party Committee, and a member of the City Executive Board. In summer 1917, he was elected to the Party Congress and to the CC as a candidate member. In 1917, he also was elected to membership in the All-Russian Soviet Ispolkom and to the Constituent Assembly from Vladimirskaia Gubernia. In 1918, he was elected chair of Tsentrotekstil in Moscow, a member of the Presidium of VSNKh, and a member of various other bodies. He participated in military actions against Kolchak, was chief of the Orenburg Defence Group, and in 1919 was delegated from the Red Army to the All-Russian Congress, where he entered the All-Russian Soviet Ispokom Presidium. From the end of 1919 to the beginning of 1920, he worked in Moscow, then he was elected chair of the Miners' Union and a member of the Party Committee of Zamoskvoretsky District. He went to Norway and Germany on trade union work in 1920. He signed the theses of the Workers' Opposition, but not the Letter of the 22. In 1921, he was appointed chair of the Little Sovnarkom. He was elected a candidate member of the CC RCP(b) and a member of the CCC Presidium, then was appointed People's Commissar of Worker-Peasant Inspection of the RSFSR and Assistant Commissar of Worker-Peasant Inspection of the USSR. From 1924 to 1937, he served as secretary of the All-Union Soviet Ispolkom. Arrested in 1937, he was executed shortly thereafter.

Klinov, [Iakov Ilich] (1882–1928) joined the RSDRP in 1905. He was a candidate member of the Metalworkers' Union central committee from Petrograd in May 1921. Among his positions were chair of the Petrograd Union of Metalworkers, Director of Factory #1, Manager of the "Banner of Labour" Trust of Factories in Leningrad, and member of the Party CCC, 1924–8.

Kolarov, Vasil (1877–1950) was born in the part of the Ottoman Empire that would become Bulgaria. His father was a shoemaker. He graduated from high school in Varna and worked as a school teacher in Nikopol, 1895–7. He joined the Bulgarian Social Democratic Party in 1897 and its revolutionary section in 1903. During those years, he studied law in France and Switzerland and worked as a lawyer in Bulgaria. He headed his local party organisation in 1904–12, attended the Second International Congresses in 1907 and 1910. He saw military combat in the Balkan Wars and was elected to the Bulgarian National Assembly in 1913. A participant in the Zimmerwald Conference in 1915, he did not hold a revolutionary left position. In 1919–23, he served as secretary of the Bulgarian Communist Party. From 1921, he was a member of the Comintern Ispolkom until it was dissolved in 1943. Having failed to carry out a revolution in Bulgaria in 1923, he lived in the USSR until 1945. While there, he was president of the Peasant International (1928–39). Having returned to Bulgaria at the end of World War II, he served as its President in 1946–7, then Deputy Prime Minister and Minister of Foreign Affairs in 1947–8, and Prime Minister in 1949–50.

Kolesnikov, Boris Leonidovich (1898–1937) was a Menshevik in 1917–18 in Kharkov. He joined the Bolsheviks in 1919. He was at private meetings of the Workers' Opposition and the Twenty-Two, worked for the Southern Bureau of the Metalworkers' Union in Ukraine, and was associated with Mitin and Lobanov in Ukraine. Later, he worked for the Commissariat of Heavy Industry. In 1930, the Krasnopresnensky Party Control Committee reprimanded him for being an irresolute party member. From 1932–6, he directed the Taganrog Metallurgical Factory named after Andreev in Azovo-Chernomorsky krai. He lost his position in 1936 due to accusations of Trotskyism and was executed in 1937.

Kollontai [née Domontovich], Aleksandra Mikhailovna (1872–1952) was born into a noble family; her father was a general of Ukrainian descent and her mother was from the Finnish peasantry. Growing up in St. Petersburg and Finland, she studied privately and began attending lectures at age sixteen. Her first husband was an engineer. She took his name and they had a son, but after a few years she left him to educate workers. As a member of the Political Red Cross, she collected money to support the 1896 textileworkers' strike. This activism encouraged her to become a Marxist. She began writing about politics in 1898 and went to Zurich to study. She traveled to England in 1899, then returned to Russia and joined the RSDRP. She participated in the 1905 Revolution and was a Menshevik from 1906–15. In emigration from 1908–17, she wrote books and articles about socialism and the emancipation of women. She began a relationship with Aleksandr Shliapnikov in 1911. In 1915, she joined the Bolsheviks in support of Lenin's position on World War I, during which she traveled between Scandinavia and the United States. Having returned to Russia after the February Revolution, she became a member of the Petrograd Soviet Ispolkom. She was a popular speaker and agitator among Baltic Fleet sailors and Petrograd Garrison soldiers and continued her work as a writer, although she was arrested and imprisoned in the wake of the unsuccessful July 1917 uprising. After the October Revolution, she held the post of People's Commissar of State Welfare. She was among the Left Communists who opposed the Peace of Brest-Litovsk in 1918. She became head of the Women's Department (Zhentodel) of the CC RCP(b) in 1920. From 1920–2, she mentored the Workers' Opposition, spoke on its behalf, wrote a pamphlet about it for the Tenth Party Congress, and signed the Letter of the 22 to the Comintern. She served in 1921–2 as secretary of the International Women's Secretariat of the Comintern. From 1923–45, she was a high-ranking diplomat in

Scandinavia, with a two-year interlude in Mexico from 1926–7. She played a pivotal role in ensuring Swedish neutrality during the Soviet invasion of Finland. In 1945–52, she was a Counsellor of the People's Commissariat and Ministry of Foreign Affairs of the USSR. She died of natural causes in 1952.

Kolosov, [D.M.?] ( ) was a former Socialist Revolutionary who assumed leadership of the Baku group of the Workers' Opposition after Valerian Barchuk was transferred to Moscow. His conspiratorial name was Kobyzev.

Kopylov, Nikolai Vasilevich (1889–1938) was born in Tula into a working-class family and was educated in a trade school-orphanage, where he stayed until he was age fifteen. Then he worked in factories and small craftshops in Tula, where he participated in the 1905 Revolution. He became active in the Metalworkers' Union in 1910 and in the RSDRP(b) in 1912. Beginning in 1914, he worked in Petrograd as an agitator, circle organiser, and propagandist. He was arrested in March 1916 after a citywide strike. After spending two to three months in jail, he was drafted into a disciplinary batallion, but he escaped and went to Ekaterinoslav. He moved to Kharkov in January 1917 just ahead of the police. After the February Revolution, he was a member of the Ekaterinoslav Party Committee and edited the party newspaper *Zvezda*. He was also a member of the Donetsko-Krivorozhsky Oblast Party Committee and secretary of the Party Committee of Novyi Lessner in Petrograd. After the October Revolution, he went to Tula to agitate, edit the newspaper *Revoliutsionnyi vestnik*, and chair the gubernia party committee. The Tula party organisation directed him to fight the Czechoslovakian forces in late August 1918, but in Moscow the Party CC intercepted him and assigned him to soviet work. He headed the Central Library Commission and worked for the publisher 'Kommunist', returning to Tula only in 1920. There he was first assigned to manage an arms factory, then he became a member of the gubernia party committee. Having traveled abroad to a congress of metalworkers, he worked upon his return in 1921 as a propagandist for the Metalworkers' Union central committee in Moscow. There he participated in the Workers' Opposition and signed the Letter of the 22 to the Comintern. He helped edit the newspaper *Bednota* in 1922–4. Beginning in 1924, he worked as a VSNKh special representative to France. In 1932–6, he managed Dormashtrest and the All-Union Association Orgenergo under the People's Commissariat of Heavy Industry of the USSR. He was arrested in 1936 and shot in 1938.

Korzinov, G[rigory?] N. (1886–1926) joined the RSDRP in 1904, participated in the 1905 Revolution, and carried out party work in St. Petersburg, Riga, Helsingfors, and Moscow, during which time he was arrested and jailed. He participated in the October 1917 armed uprising in Moscow. Then he carried out various work for the party, soviets, and in the economy. He belonged to the Moscow Soviet Ispolkom and the Moscow Party Committee. In 1921, he became director of the Proletarsky Trud factory. He was in Ignatov's group during the 1921 trade union discussion.

Kotliakov, Ivan Efimovich (1887–1929) was born in Kursk to a working-class family. He worked in his youth in the Martens iron foundry and became involved early in the revolutionary movement, joining the Bolshevik Party at age fifteen. He fled police surveillance to Kharkov, where he worked at the machine building factory Gelferikh-Sad. There he met the Bolshevik underground revolutionary Artem, who led the uprising of Kharkov workers in October 1905, in which Kotliakov participated and was wounded by the police. Having relocated to Moscow, he carried out party work in the Sokolniki district among tram workers. He was arrested and sent away from Moscow. In 1909 he made his way to St. Petersburg and went to work at a tram station, but was let go after he participated in a strike, which he helped begin. He worked at the Franco-Russian factory and the Erikson factory. Fearing arrest for strike activity he left for Tula, where he continued revolutionary agitation. He was elected a member of the board of the Metalworkers' Union. Having returned to Petrograd and gone to work at the factory Aivaz, he became acquainted there with M.I. Kalinin. He participated in the February Revolution on the streets, worked in the Vyborg District Uprava and in the Central City Duma. He also was active in organising the Vyborg Red Guard. After the October Revolution, he chaired the Petrograd Sovnarkhoz, briefly chaired the Central Board of Heavy Industry (in which capacity he signed the theses of the Workers' Opposition), directed city and oblast finance departments, and was a member of the Leningrad Oblast Party Committee, TsIK USSR and VTsIK. He suffered from deafness. He may have been the same Kotliakov who was sent before a revolutionary tribunal for having insulted a sentry at the Eleventh Party Congress, at which he was a guest of the Petrograd organisation, not having been elected as a delegate.

Krebs, N.R. (1890–1937) was the pseudonym of Nikolai or Verner Rakov, who also operated under the names Felix Wolf and Inkov. He was born in the Baltic territory of the Russian Empire, but was educated in Germany and worked in a bank there until early 1914, when he returned to Russia to work as an accountant in a factory. As a German, he was relocated to Perm after World War I began. He participated in the October Revolution in Omsk and joined the Bolsheviks in 1917. He was a partisan in Siberia and the Urals in 1918. Dispatched from Russia to Germany in 1919 to help lead the Communist Party of Germany, he also worked in the Soviet embassy in Vienna and in the Central European Bureau of the Red International of Labour Unions in 1921–3. He carried out Soviet foreign intelligence work after that. He was executed during the Stalinist terror as a Trotskyist.

Kreibich, Karl (1883–1966) was born in Zwickau and became an Austrian Social Democrat in 1902. He edited socialist periodicals and organised youth. When World War I began, he aligned his views with Lenin's position on the war. In Sudetenland, he mobilised radical leftists in the Socialist Party and then founded the Sudeten German section of the Czechoslovak Communist Party, which he represented at the Third World Congress of the Comintern. He was in the Czechoslovak CP Politburo in 1921–4 and 1927–9. The Comintern employed him in 1924–7 and 1929–33. In 1938, he moved to London and worked with the Beneš exile government during World War II. In 1950–2, he was ambassador from Czechoslovakia to the USSR. He was recalled and marginalised after he criticised the Slansky show trial.

Krestinsky, Nikolai Nikolaevich (1883–1938) was born in Mogilev on the Dnepr into the family of a gymnasium teacher. His nihilist father and populist mother were Ukrainians who left revolutionary politics after they had children. Late in his gymnasium education, he began to read revolutionary literature and entered the revolutionary movement in 1901. He became a nonfactional Social Democrat in 1903, but aligned with the Bolsheviks in 1905. After he graduated from the Law Department of Petersburg University in 1907, he worked first as a legal assistant and then as a lawyer until 1917. His legal work was punctuated by numerous arrests, exile from St. Petersburg, and periods spent in Vilno and the Urals. The February 1917 Revolution found him in the Urals, where he joined the Ekaterinburgsky and Uralsky Oblast committees of the RSDRP(b). At the Sixth Party Congress, he became a Party CC member. Other positions he held were Ekaterinburg Soviet Ispolkom member and Constituent Assembly delegate from Perm gubernia. In Petrograd, he was in the collegium of the People's Commissariat of Finance and Assistant Commissar of the People's Bank. In 1918, he was a Left Communist. He served as Commissar of Justice of the Petrograd Labour Commune and of the Union of Communes of the Northern Oblast. In 1919–21, he was a Party CC secretary, but lost his position dues to his support for Trotsky's position on trade unions in 1920–1. He was acting People's Commissar of Finance from August 1918 to October 1921, but served nominally until the end of 1922. From October 1921 until 1930, he was Soviet ambassador to Germany. From 1930–7, he was Assistant People's Commissar of Foreign Affairs of the USSR. He was briefly Assistant People's Commissar of Justice of the USSR, before being purged from the party in 1937 and executed in 1938.

Krivov, Timofei (1886–1966) was born in a village in Samara Gubernia. He finished the Simbirsk teachers' seminary in 1899, joined the RSDRP in 1905, participated in the 1905 Revolution, and was often arrested and imprisoned. He spent some time as an émigré, but also five years at hard labour. After the February Revolution, he was a member of the Ufa Soviet Ispolkom and the Ufa District Party Committee. His soviet and party work continued in Ufa after the October Revolution. During the Civil War, he carried out political work on the Eastern Front. In 1920–2, he was Party CC Urals Bureau secretary and in 1922 a CC instructor. From the 1920s through the early 1930s, he was a member of the CCC and PCC. In 1927–34, he was Assistant People's Commissar of Worker Peasant Inspection of the RSFSR. In the late 1930s, he was Assistant People's Commissar of Finance for the RSFSR, carried out trade union work, and chaired the central committee of the Union of Employees of Communal Enterprises. He retired after 1940 and worked in the Museum of V.I. Lenin.

Krol, Samuil Iakovlevich (1894–1937) was born in Mogilevskaia Gubernia into a merchant family, but he grew up in Moscow. He had a higher education. By 1914 he had joined the RSDRP(b). Arrested in 1916, he was exiled to Aktiubinsk, where he remained until the February 1917 Revolution. After his return to Moscow, he led the Union of Confectionaries and then chaired the Foodworkers' Union. He played a prominent role in the International Union of Foodworkers in the 1920s. A Trotsky supporter, he was removed as chair of the Foodworkers' Union in 1927 and given work in VTsSPS and economic assignments in Novosibirsk. As one of the most vocal and unrepentant oppositionists, he was sent to prison camps in Krasnoiarsk and northern Kazakhstan and remained in the Gulag until his execution.

Krupin [ ] ( ) was a candidate of the party leadership for the central committee of the Metalworkers' Union in May 1921.

Kubiak [also Kubiako, Kubiaka], Nikolai Afanasevich (1882–1937) was born into a working-class family in Meshchovsk, Kaluzhskaia Gubernia. After having finished a church parish school in 1895, he worked in a steam-engine factory and joined the party in 1898. Unemployed in Bezhitsa in 1900–3, he was a private in the Russian Imperial Army in Warsaw in 1903–4. He participated in the 1905 Revolution in Briansk and carried out party work in St. Petersburg. Arrested and exiled in 1907, he was released in 1911 and and worked from then until 1917 as an electrician at the Electrical Society of 1886 in Petrograd. After the February 1917 Revolution, he managed Beloostrov Station. During 1917, he became a member of the Petrograd Soviet, chaired the Sestroretsk District Party Committee, and chaired the Sestroretsk Zemskaia Uprava. In October 1917, he was a member of the Petrograd Okrug Committee of the RSDRP(b). After October 1917, he chaired the Sestroretsk Soviet, was Commissar of Agriculture of the Northern Oblast, secretary and chair of the Petrograd Gubernia Party Committee, chair of the Ispolkom of the Petrograd Gubernia Soviet, and chair of the central committee of the Union of Forestry Workers. He also worked for the People's Commissariat of Education. A Party CC instructor in 1921–2, he belonged to the Workers' Opposition in 1921. He served as CC Dalbiuro secretary in 1922–5 and secretary of the Far Eastern Krai Party Committee in 1925–7. He was a Party CC member from 1923–34, Party CC secretary in 1927–8, and in the Orgburo from 1927–30. He was People's Commissar of Agriculture of the RSFSR from 1928–9. He chaired Energotsentr of VSNKh USSR and from 1929–31 was in the Presidium of VSNKh USSR. He chaired Ivanovsky Industrial Oblast Soviet Ispolkom in 1931–2. From 1933–7, he chaired the All-Union Council of Communal Cooperatives and Communal Households under the Presidium of the Central Ispolkom of the USSR. From 1934–7, he was a candidate member of the All-Union Party CC. He was arrested and executed in 1937.

Kubyshkin, Iakov ( ) was a Petrograd metalworker who belonged to the Mezhraionka before the 1917 Revolution and was active in the Vasileostrovsky District, where he worked in a pipe factory. Not long after World War I began, he was called up into the tsarist army. He signed the theses of the Workers' Opposition when he was a member of the Central Board of Artilleries Factories. Later in 1921, he was a leader of the Metalworkers' Union in Crimea. He stuttered and suffered from tuberculosis. A Kubyshkin-Maltsev from the Donbas attended and spoke at a private meeting of the Workers' Opposition in 1921 or 1922, but it is not clear if he was the same person.

Kurzhner, [B.A.] was a Communist engineer in Petrograd and an ally of Gavriil Miasnikov.

Kutuzov [Zakharov], Ivan Ivanovich (1885–1937) was born into a poor peasant family in the village Novoselka of Smolensk Gubernia. He attended church school. In the winters, his father worked in Moscow factories. At age 14, he went to Moscow where he found work in a textile factory. There he read illegal revolutionary literature and joined the RSDRP in 1906. He helped organise the Moscow Textileworkers' Union in 1907. He joined the Bolshevik Party in 1917. After the February 1917 Revolution, he was a member of the Moscow Soviet, the Moscow Lefortovo District RSDRP(b) Committee, and the All-Russian Union of Textileworkers Bureau. He chaired the Moscow Oblast Union of Textileworkers and then the central committee of the All-Russian Union of Textileworkers from 1918–26. During those years, he also was a member of the VTsSPS Presidium. He was a candidate member of the All-Russian Soviet Ispolkom Presidium in 1919–20 and a member of it in 1920–35. He signed the theses of the Workers' Opposition, but not the Letter of the 22. At the Tenth Party Congress, he was elected to membership in the Party CC and remained there until the Eleventh Party Congress in 1922. He was a candidate member of the Party Orgburo during the same time. He was a candidate member of the Presidium of the All-Union Soviet Ispolkom in 1924–7 and a full member from 1927–37. In the 1930s, he also worked in the commission for struggle against juvenile crime and he chaired the All-Union Soviet Commission on Assistance to State Credit and Savings. He was arrested and executed in 1937.

Kuznetsov, Nikolai Vladimirovich (1884–1937) was born into a peasant family in Orlovskaia Gubernia, where he finished a three-year primary school. He may have joined the RSDRP in 1901 and spent a total of seven years in prisons. In 1917, he may have been a Soviet delegate and Constituent Assembly participant. In 1920, he worked in the cooperative movement. When he signed the Letter of the 22 and claimed there that he joined the RSDRP(b) in 1904, a commission of Old Bolsheviks determined that he had not even been a member in 1916, when he was in exile. He had only joined in 1917. Moreover, it was found that he had exaggerated his time as a metalworker, that he had owned a grocery shop in 1908–9, and he had only worked in metals factories during World War I to avoid conscription. He was excluded from the party at the Eleventh Party Congress in 1922. In 1923, he was a founding member of Workers' Group together with Miasnikov. That year, he worked in Glavmetall VSNKh. He was arrested again in 1926 for belonging to Workers' Group and given a prison camp sentence. In the 1930s, he worked as a technical director in Kurgansky textile factory. He was arrested in 1936 in Bataisk and executed in 1937 in Rostov-on-Don.

Kviring, Emmanuil Ionnovich (1888–1939) was born in a village in the area of Samara and Saratov, but he moved to town at age eleven and studied there until he was fifteen. When the 1905 Revolution occurred, he was at home in the village. In 1906, he began working in a Saratov pharmacy. As an independent socialist, he helped organise a trade union of pharmacy workers. When he went to St. Petersburg in 1912 and took courses on commercial economy in a polytechnical school, he became a Bolshevik, wrote for *Pravda*, and became secretary of the Bolshevik Duma faction in 1913. He was arrested and exiled first to Ekaterinoslav in 1914 and later to Irkutsk, from which he returned in 1917 to Ekaterinoslav. He spent the entire year of 1917 in Ukraine, where he was secretary of the Ekaterinoslav Party Committee and chair of the Ekaterinoslav Soviet. After the October Revolution, he chaired the All-Ukraine Economic Council. He was secretary of the Donetsk Gubernia Party Committee in 1920–2. From 1922, he served as secretary of the CC of the CP(b)U. He was elected to membership in the CC RCP(b) in 1923. After 1925, he left Ukraine, because he opposed Ukrainisation. In Moscow, he served as assistant chair of VSNKh of the USSR, assistant chair of Gosplan of the USSR, and Assistant Commissar of Communications. From 1934, he was Assistant Chair of Gosplan of the USSR.

Lavrentev, Pavel Fedorovich (1892–) had a primary school education and joined the RSDRP(b) in 1915. He was a member of the central committee of the All-Russian Metalworkers' Union. He supported the Workers' Opposition in 1921. Both the party leadership and the former Worker Oppositionists nominated him for the Metalworkers' Union central committee in October 1921. He was director of the factory of drilling machines in Kharkov oblast, 1934–6.

Lazzari, Constantino (1857–1927) was an artisan who joined the trade union movement in his youth. He helped organise the Italian Socialist Party in 1892, was a founding member of its central committee, and served as its political secretary in 1912–19. In the revolutionary socialist wing of the party, he attended the Zimmerwald and Kienthal Conferences during World War I and was sent to jail for most of 1918 for having spoken out against the war. He suffered repression under Benito Mussolini's Fascist government.

Lebed, Dmitry Zakharovich (1893–1937) was born to peasants in Ekaterinoslavskaia Gubernia. His father turned to unskilled factory work not long after he was born. D.Z. started working at age twelve and fell under influence of anarchists. He received some minimal education in a railway school. In 1908, he worked in a die factory, and contacted Mensheviks and SRs in a study circle. After joining the Bolsheviks in 1909, he carried out party work in Ekaterinoslavskaia Gubernia. After the February 1917 Revolution, he was a member of the ispolkom of its gubernia soviet. After the October Revolution, he edited the journal *Vestnik Narkomvnudel* and worked for the party and soviets in Ekaterinoslav and Vladimir. From late 1920, he was a central committee secretary of the CP(b)U, chair of the CP(b)U CCC, and People's Commissar of Worker Peasant Inspection in Ukraine. At the all-union level, he was Assistant People's Commissar of Worker-Peasant Inspection and a member of the CCC presidium. In 1930, he was assistant chair of Sovnarkom RSFSR. When he was arrested in 1937, he was accused of Ukrainian nationalism, although he had been strongly opposed to the milder policy of Ukrainisation in the 1920s.

Lenin, Vladimir Ilich (1870–1924) was born in Simbirsk into a well-educated, middle class family. His father, a school inspector, achieved hereditary nobility. His older brother was executed for participation in a conspiracy to assassinate the tsar. He studied in the law department of Kazan University but was expelled. After having studied further at home, he graduated from the law department of St. Petersburg University. He joined the Social Democratic movement in 1893 and the RSDRP in 1898. Having been arrested and exiled numerous times, he moved abroad in 1900. He wrote many important Marxist theoretical works, cultivated conspiratorial skills, and co-founded the newspaper *Iskra*, which served as the means to organise an underground, revolutionary network. He was instrumental in splitting the RSDRP into Bolshevik and Menshevik factions in 1903 and asserted editorial control over party periodicals. He returned to Russia during the 1905 Revolution, but fled to Switzerland in December 1907. He also lived for awhile in Paris and Cracow. Having returned to Russia in April 1917, he was the key figure in the Bolshevik seizure of power in October 1917. As the recognised leader of the party, he was in the Politburo. He also chaired Sovnarkom and the Council of Labour and Defence. Becoming increasingly ill by the end of 1921, he suffered several strokes in 1922–3 that left him incapacitated. He died in January 1924.

Lepse, Ivan Ivanovich (1889–1929) joined the RSDRP(b) in 1904 and worked in machine-building factories in Riga and St. Petersburg, where he also engaged in party organisation. He participated in the 1905 Revolution in Riga. He was conscripted into the army in 1914. In 1917, he held posts in the Bolshevik Party and the Metalworkers' Union in Petrograd. After the October Revolution, he was secretary of the Petrograd branch of the Metalworkers' Union and a member of the union's central committee. After the Workers' Opposition was ousted, he chaired the central committee of the Metalworkers' Union until 1929. He also was a member of the VTsSPS Presidium and a member of the Executive Bureau of the Profintern. He served in the Civil War.

Levit [ ] ( ) was a secretary of the KAPD delegation who sent a letter to Shliapnikov in
August 1921.

Liul, Adolf Petrovich ( ) was a Latvian from Riga. He came to Kharkov from Riga in
1915, when the VEK factory where he worked was evacuated. He was secretary of
the Kharkov Metalworkers' Union in 1921 and seems to have supported the Workers'
Opposition. He participated in the October 1917 Revolution and the Civil War.

Lobanov, Mikhail Ivanovich (1887–1938) was born in Rechka, Kolomensky District,
Moscow Gubernia to parents who worked in weaving and woodcarving, He was educated at home and in revolutionary study circles. He first witnessed a strike in 1901;
this and the Zubatov police-organised trade union movement made impressions
upon him. He joined the Bolshevik Party in 1903–4 and the Metalworkers' Union
in 1905. He participated in the 1905 Revolution in Moscow and was arrested several times in 1907–9. Chosen to attend Maxim Gorky's school at Capri in 1909–10,
he subsequently went to Paris for seven months and attended Lenin's lectures (he is
referenced as 'Stanislav' in Lenin's *Sochineniia*). Upon his return to Russia in 1910, he
was arrested and exiled to Arkhangelsk. He spent the next three years either working
in Moscow factories or under arrest. He was in Riga in 1914 and in the Vyborg District of Petrograd in 1914–16. Having returned to Moscow in 1916, he helped organise
the party and trade unions in Moscow in 1917. After the February Revolution, he
chaired his factory committee. He served as assistant chair of the Metalworkers'
Union and was a member of the Moscow Bureau of the Council of Trade Unions.
After the October Revolution, he worked at the Moscow telephone factory and as
head of the Conflicts Department of the Moscow Oblast Commissariat of Labour.
He was a delegate to the Soviet and a member of the central committee of the
All-Russian Metalworkers' Union, 1918–20. He spent some time on the Civil War
front in 1919. Having arrived in Ukraine in mid-1920, he chaired the Southern Bureau of the Metalworkers' Union central committee until late 1922, when he was
transferred to the presidium of the Ukraine Economic Council. He supported the
Workers' Opposition and signed the Letter of the 22. Secondary sources stating that
he signed the Declaration of the 46 along with Trotsky's supporters are incorrect.
A. Lobanov signed that document. M.I. continued to work in union, party, and economic bodies in Ukraine until 1929. Along with sovnarkhoz work, he was a member
of the collegium of the Trade Commissariat in Ukraine and was in the presidium of
VTsIK of Ukraine. During the First Five-Year Plan period, Lobanov was transferred
from Ukraine for economic work in the Urals, but he returned in the early 1930s
to Kharkov. He worked in an economic trust (Gorzavtrest) there. On the eve of his
arrest, he managed the wage rates claims bureau of Heavy Industry in Kharkov. Lobanov was arrested in Kharkov in August 1936 on the fabricated case of the Workers'
Opposition, and sent by special convoy to Kiev, where he was interrogated and formally charged in November. The NKVD accusation against him of terror claimed he

confessed to the charge. Transferred to Moscow, he was condemned there in March 1937 by the Military Collegium of Supreme Court. But when he appeared before the court, he retracted the part of his confession about terrorist activity. He said he had not belonged to the Trotskyists, but that he was among leaders of the Workers' Opposition in Ukraine, which he claimed had created a bloc with Zinovievists but not with Trotskyists.

Loriot, Fernand (1870–1932) was a teacher who joined the French Socialist Party in 1901 and was treasurer of the Teachers' Union in 1912. A opponent of World War I, he helped found the French Communist Party in 1920. Imprisoned in 1920–1 for his political activism, he attended the Third Congress of the Third Communist International in Moscow upon his release. He disagreed with mid-1920s attempts to reorganise the French Communist Party along Bolshevik lines and later became a revolutionary syndicalist.

Lutovinov, Iury Khrisanfovich (1887–1924) was born in Lugansk, Ekaterinoslavskaia Gubernia. He had a primary school education, began factory work in childhood, and became a metalworker. He joined the RSDRP(b) in 1904. He carried out revolutionary organisation and agitation in Lugansk, Aleksandrovsk, St. Petersburg, and other cities, usually as a member of local Bolshevik party committees. As a trade union activist, he attended the Petersburg Conference of Metalworkers in 1912. Arrested nine times, he spent a total of five years in confinement. He was exiled to Arkhangelsk Gubernia and Iakutskaia Oblast, but escaped both places. He was assigned to organise party conferences in the Donbas in 1916 and was there when the February Revolution broke out. In 1917, he chaired the Lugansk Metalworkers' Union and was a member of the Lugansk RSDRP(b) Committee. In 1918, he chaired the Donetsk-Krivorozhsk Oblast Committee of Trade Unions and the Sovnarkom of Lugansk Oblast. He participated in Russian Civil War actions against General Krasnov. During the Hetmanshchina in Ukraine, he was in the CP(b)U CC. Returning then to trade union work, he was a member of the central committee of the Metalworkers' Union and the VTsSPS presidium, serving as secretary of the latter in 1920–1. He also was a candidate member of the All-Union Soviet Executive Presidium. He was a key founding member of the Workers' Opposition, after which he served as assistant chair of the Soviet trade mission in Berlin in 1921–2. Before he died, he chaired the Union of Communications Workers. He committed suicide on 7 May 1924 (perhaps for both personal and political reasons) by shooting himself in front of his comrades while they were out drinking together. He left no suicide note.

MacDonald, Ramsay (1866–1937) was born in Scotland as the illegitimate son of a farm labourer and a domestic servant. He worked as a teacher, a clerk, and a journalist before becoming a fulltime politician. He led the British Labour Party in 1911–14 and in 1922–31 and was a Second International Ispolkom member. An opponent of British entry into World War I, he also opposed the Bolshevik seizure of power in 1917.

He was the first British Prime Minister from the Labour Party in 1924 and served again in 1929–35, although he was expelled from the Labour Party in 1931.

Mamchenko, Nikolai S. ( ) was a Worker Oppositionist in Murom to whom Shliapnikov wrote in July 1921. He helped organise a Bolshevik Party Committee in 1917 and met with Shliapnikov in Murom in 1918. I.S. Mamchenko was assistant chair of the Murom Scientific Society in 1919, but it is not clear if they were related.

Mann, Tom (1856–1941) was born near Coventry, England to a clerk at a coal mining operation. After three years of formal education, he did odd jobs around the colliery and later became an apprentice metalworker in Birmingham. As he became more interested in socialism, he educated himself through reading. A member of the Amalgamated Society of Engineers (ASE) and the Social Democratic Federation, he helped lead the 1889 London dock strike and participated in setting up the International Transport Workers' Federation. From 1901–10, he was in Australia, where he was exposed to syndicalism. He tried to establish a syndicalist movement in Britain. He belonged to the British Socialist Party during World War I and was ASE secretary from 1919–21.

Manuilsky, Dmitry Zakharevich (1883–1959) was born in a village in Volynskaia Gubernia into a family of peasant origins. His father was either an Orthodox priest or a volost clerk. D.Z. attended primary school in the village, then enrolled in Ostrozhskaia gymnasium. To support himself, he tutored other students. When he organised self-education circles in the gymnasium, the teachers hounded him. Nevertheless, he graduated in 1903 and entered St. Petersburg University. There he fell in with circles of revolutionaries and joined the RSDRP. In 1904, he joined a demonstration on Nevsky Prospect against the Russo-Japanese War. Arrested, he was severely beaten. Among the places where he carried out party work were St. Petersburg, Kiev, Dvinsk, and Kronstadt. He used the underground aliases Mefody and Foma, under the latter of which he joined the Petersburg Bolshevik Committee. He participated in the 1905 Revolution. After having helped organise an uprising in Kronstadt in July 1906, he was arrested, imprisoned and exiled first to Arkhangelsk gubernia and then to Iakutsk. He escaped prison before a looming military trial. Having departed Kiev in autumn 1907, he became an émigré in Paris, where he joined the Bogdanovist group 'Vpered'. He took an internationalist stance during World War I and in 1917 he belonged to Mezhraionka. In 1920–1, he served as People's Commissar of Agriculture of the Ukrainian Soviet Socialist Republic, was a secretary of the CC CP(b)U, and edited the newspaper *Kommunist*. From 1924, he belonged to the ECCI presidium, of which he was secretary from 1928 to 1943. In 1944, he became assistant chair of Sovnarkom and People's Commissar of Foreign Affairs of the Ukrainian SSR. He represented Ukraine at the United Nations Security Council in 1948–9. From 1946 to 1953, he was assistant chair of the Council of Ministers of the Ukrainian SSR. He retired in 1953.

Maslennikov, Sergei I.(?) (–1937) was a metalworker who joined the RSDRP in Moscow in 1911. He may have been the Maslennikov of Tula who was on Skliznev's list for the Metalworkers' Union congress presidium in May 1921. S.I. Maslennikov, who was accused on the 1935 case of the Workers' Opposition, may have been the same person.

Medvedev, Aleksandr Nikolaevich (1892–1944) was born in Bezhitsa, Kaluzhskaia Gubernia. His father did skilled work in a rail-rolling and mechanical factory owned by Prince Tenishev. A.N. joined the RSDRP(b) in 1912. In the same year, he was expelled from his sixth year at Orlovskaia realschule and sent back to Bezhitsa under police supervision, where he began to work in the Tenishev factory. He and his younger brother Dmitry participated in the 1917 Revolution. A.N. was elected chair of the Briansk Factory Council and then became a member of the district and gubernia RCP(b) committees. Both brothers joined the Red Guard in 1918. While Aleksandr remained in Briansk, Dmitry was sent to the Eastern Front. In 1918, he chaired the Briansk uezd Cheka in Orlovskaia gubernia. In 1919–20, he chaired the Briansk gubernia Cheka. As a Chekist, he crushed an anarchist uprising in Briansk and a mutiny in the Briansk garrison. He suppressed anarchists, Mensheviks, SRs, Ukrainian nationalists, and criminal bands in various areas. Upon being appointed chair of the Novgorod Gubernia Cheka in 1920, he was no longer directly involved in repressive operations. In 1922–4, he directed the supply section of Glavenergo and often traveled to Germany on business for it. He signed the Letter of the 22 and wrote a letter to Stalin in support of G.I. Miasnikov. Having participated in a political demonstration in Germany, he lost his accreditation there and was sent back to Russia. He was expelled from the RCP(b) in 1924, but then restored to membership in 1926. He worked in the Society of Old Bolsheviks, but was still subjected to CCC investigations and reprimands. In 1925–33, he studied at the Industrial Academy. He also worked as assistant director of factory no. 18 and as an engineer at factory no. 39, and held administrative posts at other Moscow enterprises. He managed the All-Union Autogenous Trust. Purged from the party in 1935, he was arrested and sentenced in 1937. He was executed either in 1942 or 1944, without having confessed to any crimes.

His younger brother, Dmitry Nikolaevich, worked in the administration of the Baltic-White Sea Canal and other NKVD projects in the 1930s, but lost his position in 1939 because of his brother's alleged political crimes. He led a partisan brigade during World War II and was named a Hero of the Soviet Union. Other brothers also redeemed themselves in the eyes of the state through their World War II service.

Medvedev (-Stebalin), Sergei Pavlovich (1885–1937) was born into the peasantry in a village in Podolsk District, near Moscow. He grew up partly there and partly near St. Petersburg, receiving a four-year primary school education. His father was a policeman in St. Petersburg Gubernia. S.P. worked at the Obukhov factory from 1898 to

1904 and participated in the 1901 strike while there. He joined the RSDRP in 1900 and was part of the Iskra network. He was in St. Petersburg in December 1906–October 1907, during which time he worked at the Electrical Station of 1886. He also carried out revolutionary work in Sevastopol. He was frequently arrested and exiled. Places of exile included the far north, his home village near Moscow, Turukhansky Krai, Krasnoiarsk, and Achinsk in Eniseiskaia gubernia. In 1912–13, he traveled to Finland, Berlin, and Cracow, where he met Lenin, Krupskaia, Zinoviev, and Stalin. During World War I, he worked as an insurance organiser. He was in Siberian exile in 1915–16. In March 1917, he helped organise a soviet in Achinsk and was elected its chair, and he co-founded a Bolshevik party organisation in Krasnoiarsk and the newspaper *Sibirskaia Pravda*. Because he had been conscripted into the military in 1916, he was transferred to the Northern Front near Riga at the end of March 1917 and remained stationed there until November 1917. As a delegate from the RSDRP(b) Siberian Oblast Bureau, he attended the April conference of the Bolsheviks. He chaired the Ispolkom of the Twelfth Army. He was sent to the Pskov Front in January 1918. He was elected to the All-Russian Central Ispolkom of the Soviet in March 1918 and was assigned to the Bureau of VSNKh. He was an investigator on the case of the Left SRs' assassination of Mirbach. In July 1918, he was sent to Penza to the Czechoslovakian front and became a division commissar. In September 1918, he became a member of the Revolutionary Military Council of the First Army of the Eastern Front, where he was a political commissar. In 1919, he was assigned to membership in the Revolutionary Military Council of the Caspian-Caucasian Front and as commissar of the Caspian Fleet. In August 1919, he was sent to chair the Don Soviet Ispolkom. He attended the Seventh Congress of Soviets in Moscow in October 1919. In November, he was assigned to the Revolutionary Military Council of the Seventh Army (Petrograd). In 1920, he was in the central committee of the All-Russian Metalworkers' Union, carried out assignments for the People's Commissariat of Transport, and was sent to be secretary of the Kuban Oblast Party Committee. Although he was elected unanimously to the position, the Caucasus Bureau (Ordzhonikidze, Stasova, Beloborodov and others) rejected him as unacceptable. At the end of 1920, he returned to Moscow to work in the Metalworkers' Union. He was among the leadership of the Workers' Opposition, signing its theses and the Letter of the 22. He authored the letter, 'To a Baku Worker' in 1924. He worked in Nonferrous Metals under the People's Commissariat of Heavy Industry in the late 1920s and was in its reserves in the early 1930s. Investigated by the Party CCC on the Baku, Omsk, and Riutin cases, he was purged from the party in 1933, sent to work in the administration of the White Sea Baltic Sea Canal in 1934, arrested in 1935, and executed in 1937.

Meshchersky, Aleksei Pavlovich (1867–1938) was educated in military school and at the St. Petersburg Mining University as a mining engineer. He organised and led the

Sormovo-Kolomna Industrial Association. In April 1918, his factories were nationalised and he was arrested and jailed. His civil wife arranged his release, they both escaped from Russia across the Finnish border, and they settled in Paris.

Miasnikov, Gavriil Ilich (1889–1946) was born in the village Berezovka in Kazanskaia Gubernia. He joined the SRS in 1905, but switched to the RSDRP(b) in 1906. Under the tsarist regime, he was often arrested and sent into exile, from which he usually escaped. In 1913, he was sentenced to six years hard labour in Orlov Prison, but was amnestied in March 1917. In 1917–18, he chaired the Motovilikhinsky Soviet in Perm Gubernia and was a Left Communist opposed to the Brest peace. As assistant chair of the Perm Gubernia Cheka in 1918, he became infamous for having murdered that year Tsar Alexander III's youngest son Grand Duke Mikhail, who had rejected the throne in March 1917. In 1920, he became chair of the Perm Gubernia Committee of the RCP(b). In 1922, he was assistant director of the Motovilikhinsky arms factory. He was not a member of the Workers' Opposition, having voted for Lenin's platform on trade unions at the Tenth Party Congress, but he signed the Letter of the 22. He was purged from the party in February 1922, arrested, and soon released. As leader of Workers' Group, he advocated freedom of speech for all workers and management of the economy by producers' soviets. Arrested again in 1923, he was sent to Berlin, where he engaged in political factionalism. Consequently, he was returned to the USSR, where he was arrested and sentenced to three years of imprisonment. Freed in 1927, he was exiled to Erevan, from which he escaped to Persia in 1928. He lived in Turkey from 1929 to 1930 and then in France from 1930 to 1941. He was arrested in Paris in 1941, escaped, and arrested again in Toulouse. He escaped in 1943, but in 1944 he was returned to the USSR, arrested in 1945, and executed late that year in Moscow.

Mikhailov, Mikhail Flegontovich (1892–1942) was born either in St. Petersburg into a working-class family or in the countryside near Kostroma, according to different records. He either finished only primary school or had a middle school education. Bilingual in Polish and Russian, he was a metalworker at Lessner and Feniks. Having joined the RSDRP(b) in 1913, he was exiled for protesting against the death penalty. During World War I, he served in the tsarist-era army as a private and was wounded in 1915. He helped organise the Red Guard and was a member of the Petrograd Soviet, the Petrograd Metalworkers' Union, and the Petrograd Gorodskoi District Soviet in 1917. He belonged to the Oblast Committee of the Metalworkers' Union in 1918, and in 1920 chaired the Raikom of the Metalworkers' Union. At some point, he was in the central committee of the All-Russian Metalworkers' Union. When he signed the theses of the Workers' Opposition, he led the Directorate of Aviation Factories (Glavko-avio). He did not sign the Letter of the 22. In 1922, he managed Aviation Factory no. 4. He was arrested on the case of the Workers' Group in 1923 while he directed the Metron factory in Moscow. In 1926, he directed a factory that made fire extinguishers and was drawn into the CCC investigation of the Baku case of the Workers' Opposition. He was arrested on the fabricated case of the Moscow group of the Workers' Opposition in 1935 while at work as a factory director in Moscow. He was rearrested in 1940 while he was already in the camps. Having served his sentences in Kolyma, he died in 1942 in the camp zone.

Mikhailov, Vasily Mikhailovich (1894–1937) was born in Moscow Gubernia into the family of a bookbinder and completed a village school. He worked as a factory apprentice in 1903–6 and from 1906–18 worked in Moscow printing houses; he took evening courses in 1913. He joined the RSDRP(b) in 1915. worked in the Sytin printing house from 1912 on. In 1917, he was a member of the Moscow Soviet and of the Moscow Committee of the RSDRP(b) and chaired the Gorodsky District Cheka in Moscow. In 1918–20, he carried out political work in the Red Army. In 1920–1, he worked in the Moscow Gubernia section of the Union of Printers. He was a member of the Orgburo and secretary of the CC RCP(b) in 1921–2. In 1922–3, he was a candidate member of the CC RCP(b) and a member of the Secretariat of the Moscow Gubernia RCP(b) committee. In 1923–4, he was senior secretary of the Zamoskvoretsky District Party Committee in Moscow, a candidate member of the Orgburo and Secretariat of the CC RCP(b). From 1923 to 1930, he was a member of the Party CC. In 1924–5, he served as a member of the Secretariat of the Moscow Gubernia Party Committee. From 1925–9, he chaired the Moscow City Council of Trade Unions. In 1926–30, he was a candidate member of the CC Orgburo. In 1929–32, he was first assistant director of Dneprogas. From 1930–7, he was a member of the CP(b)U CC and a candidate member of the All-Union CP(b) CC. From 1934–7, he was chief of Dneprokombinat. In 1937, he served as chief of construction of the Palace of Soviets in Moscow prior to his arrest and execution.

Miliukov, Pavel Nikolaevich (1859–1943) was born in Moscow and educated at Moscow University. A historian, he also led the liberal Constitutional Democratic (Kadet) Party. He served the Provisional Government in March–May 1917 as foreign minister and supported the continuation of the war. After the Bolsheviks took power, he left for the south of Russia, where he advised the Whites on politics. He died in France.

Millerand, Alexandre (1859–1943) was educated as a lawyer. A French Socialist Party leader, he became Minister of Commerce in 1899. His action provoked debate in the Second International about whether socialists should join bourgeois governments. In 1909, he was appointed Minister of Public Works. As such, he suppressed a railway strike in 1910. In 1912, he was appointed Minister of War. He served as French premier in 1920, and president in 1920–4. He stifled revolutionary strikes and favoured conservative appointees.

Milonov, Iury Konstantinovich (1895–1980) was born in Nizhny Novgorod. He joined the RSDRP(b) in 1912. In 1915, he studied in the Law Department of Moscow University, but was expelled, arrested, and sentenced to administrative exile under police supervision in Saratov. While in Saratov, he served as secretary of a hospital fund for print shop workers and as secretary of the agricultural census commission of the Saratov Gubernia Zemstvo. He was arrested twice and sent into administrative exile in Turgaiskaia Oblast, where he worked in a savings and loan bank. Amnestied after the February 1917 Revolution, he served as secretary of the Samara Soviet, as a member of the editorial board of the newspaper *Soldatskaia Pravda* (Samara), and as Commissar of the Military Revolutionary Committee of the Railway Telegraph. In early 1918, he chaired the Samara Gubernia Council of Factory Committees, served as Commissar of Labour of Samara Gubernia, and as provisional chair of the Samara Gubernia Cheka. Because power changed hands quickly there during the Civil War, he had to carry out underground work in Samara in mid-1918. From October 1918 to March 1919, he chaired the Samara Gubernia RCP(b) committee. Beginning in late 1918, he edited the newspaper *Privolzhskaia Pravda* and led the Samara Gubernia labour department. Among his positions in 1919–20 were Chair of the Samara City Soviet Ispolkom, Assistant Chair of the Samara Gubernia RCP(b) Committee, Chair of the Samara Gubernia Party Committee, Chair of the Samara Gubernia Council of Trade Unions, editor of the newspaper *Kommuna*, and political economy teacher at the Samara Gubernia Party School. He served as senior secretary of the Samara Gubernia Party Committee in mid-1920 and again in early 1921 and was a member of its presidium from late 1920 into 1921. At the same time, he served as rector of the Samara Worker-Peasant University. After having supported the Workers' Opposition, his posts shifted from party work into education. His positions in 1921–2 included head of the School of Social Sciences of Samara State University, academic secretary of the Chief Board of Political Enlightenment of the RSFSR People's Commissariat of Enlightenment, and Russian history teacher at the Higher Military School of Communications. He studied at the Plekhanov Institute of the Economy in 1922–4 and was chair of the Commission on Aiding Self-Education of the Main Board of Political Enlightenment of the People's Commissariat of Enlightenment of the RSFSR. From 1922–30, he was assistant director and then director of the VTsSPS Section on the History of the Trade Union Movement. In 1922–3, he taught political economy in the workers' department of the Moscow Higher Technical School named after N.E. Bauman. In 1923–5, he taught political economy and dialectical materialism at the Moscow Institute of Transport Engineers. From 1923–30, he taught the history of Russia and of the trade union movement at the Communist University named after Ia.M. Sverdlov and at the Higher School of the Trade Union Movement under VTsSPS. He was assistant director of the State Historical Museum in 1926–30 and director of it in 1930–1. In 1931–2, he was assistant director of the Institute of Technology under the Communist Academy and director of technology and technical policy of the Institute of Red Professors. In 1932–4, he headed the Scientific Research Sector of the All-Union Council of Scholarly Engineering Technical Societies. In 1934–6, he was senior scientist of the Office of Building Technology and chief editor of the Academy of Architecture publishing house. Having been promoted to the rank of Professor in 1932, he received a Ph.D. in Economics in 1937 and led the Department of History of Building Technology of the Moscow Engineering-Construction Institute named after V.V. Kuibyshev. From 1937–8, he was in the Academy of Architecture. In 1938, he was arrested and sentenced to ten years in an NKVD labour camp in the far north. After his release in 1948, he worked as a laboratory assistant and engineer for the All-Union Scientific Research Institute of Gold and Rare Metals in Magadan, chief of the Section of Labour and Quality of the Office of Local Construction Materials of the Construction-Assembly Administration of the Main Administration of Construction of the Far North of MVD USSR in Magadan; chief of the laboratory for testing new construction materials of the Main Administration of Construction of the Far North of MVD USSR in Magadan. In 1949–50, he taught analytical geometry and physics at the Magadan branch of the All-Union Correspondence Polytechnical Institute. His whereabouts in 1951–3 are unknown. In 1954–5, he taught mathematics at Magadan evening school. His party membership was restored to him in 1957 and he retired. He died in Moscow in 1980.

Mitin, Flor Anisimovich (1882–1937) was born into a peasant family in Kasimov, Riazan Gubernia. Having joined the RSDRP in 1902, he was a Menshevik from 1903–19, joining the Communist Party in 1920. He was a member of the board of the Vasileostrovsky branch of the Metalworkers' Union in St. Petersburg in 1911–12. He did metalworking at the Aivaz factory in Petrograd and in Ekaterinoslav. In Tula, he chaired the hospital fund and the Metalworkers' Union. He also lived in Kharkov, Lugansk, and Bakhmut. In Donetsk Gubernia, he chaired the Metalworkers' Union and Trade Union Council. He was a member of the Petrograd Soviet Ispolkom, chaired the Central Board of Heavy Industry, chaired the Krai Bureau of the Metalworkers' Union in Kharkov, and chaired the city hospital fund and the Metalworkers' Union in Ekaterinoslav. A participant in the Workers' Opposition, he also signed the Letter of the 22 to the Comintern. The Eleventh Party Congress purged him from the party in 1922 for factionalism and for demoralising the RCP(b) organisation in the Donbas. He may have been a member of Workers' Truth and may have associated with Workers' Group. He worked in a metallurgical trust in Ukraine in the 1920s. In the mid-1930s, a nonparty peasant named Mitin was a candidate member of the Board of Tsentrosoiuz. In the late 1930s, he lived in Moscow and worked as chief of the section of capital construction of Orgmetall. He was arrested and died of cancer in prison in 1937, before his sentence could be carried out.

Molotov (Skriabin), Viacheslav Mikhailovich (1890–1986) was born in Kukarka settlement, Viatskaia Gubernia, to a father who was a shop-assistant. He joined the RSDRP(b) in 1906, finished Kazan realschule in 1908, and studied at the Petersburg Polytechnical Institute, but he was expelled. Arrested numerous times, he was exiled to Vologodskaia Gubernia and Irkutskaia Gubernia. Among the cities where he carried out underground party work were St. Petersburg, Kazan, and Moscow. He worked on the Bolshevik newspapers *Zvezda* and *Pravda*. Aleksandr Shliapnikov coopted him into the RSDRP(b) CC Russian Bureau in late 1916. In 1917–18, he was a member of the Petrograd Soviet Ispolkom and of the Petersburg Committee of the RSDRP(b). He participated in the October 1917 Revolution as a member of the Petrograd Military Revolutionary Committee. In 1918, he chaired the Sovnarkhoz of the Northern Oblast. He was a special representative of the CC RCP(b) and Sovnarkom RSFSR in the Povolzhe in 1919. In 1919–20, he chaired the Nizhegorodsky Gubernia Soviet Ispolkom. In 1920–1, he was a candidate member of the CC RCP(b). He was senior secretary of the Donetsk Gubernia Party Committee in 1920. A member of the CC of the CP(b)U 1920–1, he also was its first secretary and a member of its Politburo and Orgburo. From 1921 to 1957, he was a member of the CC of the RCP(b) and then VCP(b) and its secretary from 1921–30. A candidate member of the Politburo of the RCP(b) in 1921–5, he became a full member in 1926–52. He belonged to the Orgburo, 1921–30. In 1924, he chaired the CC RCP(b) commission on work in the countryside. From 1926–43, he belonged to the ECCI; in 1926–8, he was a candidate member of its Presidium and Secretariat and in 1928–43, a full member of both bodies and secretary of the Ispolkom. He was senior secretary of the Moscow Gubernia Party Committee in 1928–9. He chaired the Party CC organisational bureau on the Central Industrial oblast in 1923–9. He chaired the USSR Council of People's Commissars in 1930–41 and the Council of Labour and Defence of the USSR in 1930–7. He held many other high positions in the 1930s–50s, the most prominent of which were People's Commissar and Minister of the Foreign Affairs of the USSR in 1939–49 and 1956–7. Expelled from the party in 1962, he retired in the same year. He was restored to party membership in 1984.

Monatte, Pierre (1881–1960) was an anarchist who by occupation was a proofreader. In 1904, he joined the leadership of the General Confederation of Labour (CGT). In 1907, he argued at an anarchist congress that anarchists should work within trade unions. He co-founded the revolutionary syndicalist journal *La Vie ouvrière* in 1909. When the CGT leaders supported France's war effort in 1914, he left the party and maintained an internationalist position on the war. He supported the Bolshevik government, despite harboring reservations about the subordinate role of trade unions under the Communist regime. In 1919, he became a secretary of the Committee for the Third International. He was imprisoned for nine months in 1920. He joined the Communist Party of France in 1923, but was expelled in 1924 for Trotskyist sympathies. He founded and edited the revolutionary syndicalist journal *La Révolution prolétarienne* and participated in the resistance under Nazi occupation of France.

Monmousseau, Gaston (1883–1960) was a railway worker in France, who at first was an anarchist member of CGT and later became a communist. He opposed World War I.

He became editor of *La Vie ouvrière* in 1921 and was the General Secretary of the United General Confederation of Labour (CGTU) from 1922–32. He belonged to the Executive Bureau of the Red International of Labour Unions (RILU), but worked in it little. In 1933, he directed the European Secretariat of RILU. He joined the French Communist Party (PCF) in 1925 and became a Politburo member of it in 1926. He sat in the French parliament from 1936–40. During the Nazi occupation of France, he helped lead communist trade unions in the resistance. He remained a leading member of the CGT and the PCF after World War II.

Müller, Richard (1880–1943) was a metalworker, a trade union leader, an editor, and a historian. First a German Social Democrat, he later became a Communist, He led the Turners' Section of the Berlin organsation of the German Metalworkers' Union (DMV) from 1915 and was an oppositionist within the union. He helped organise the Revolutionary Shop Stewards. During the November 1918 Revolution in Germany, he was one of the leaders of the workers' council movement. He was prominent within the Communist Party of Germany (KPD) until he left it. He did not join another party, but turned to writing history. His three-volume history of the German revolution was published in 1924–5.

Niederkirchner, Michael (1882–1949) was born in Hungary and was a machinist and trade union official in Germany. After four years of schooling, he carried out unskilled labour for a few years and at age fourteen, became a metalworking apprentice. Having been a trade union member since 1900, he joined the Hungarian Social-Democratic Party in 1903 and carried out military service in Austria-Hungary. He moved to Germany in 1905 and joined the SPD. As a conscript, he fought in the Austro-Hungarian Army during World War I. He participated in the October Revolution in Russia and remained in Moscow until 1919, when he returned to Germany and from 1921–30 managed the publishing house of the Red International of Labour Unions. He belonged to the Communist Party of Germany in 1926–7 and by 1928 he led a trade union opposition within the party. He held positions in Moscow in 1929–30. After the Nazis took power in Germany, he was arrested and imprisoned, and then deported to the USSR, where he lived until 1945. His son died in the Stalinist Terror and his daughter was executed in a Nazi concentration camp.

Nikolaenko, Ivan Ignatevich (1886–1937) was born in Lugansk, Ekaterinoslavskaia Gubernia. Although of Ukrainian nationality, his native language was Russian. An iron worker, he was self-educated. He joined the RSDRP(b) in 1905 and was arrested more than once for revolutionary activities. During the 1917 Revolution, he chaired the Railway District RSDRP(b) Committee in Lugansk. He was in the Red Guard and the Red Army. He served in the Don Bureau of the CC RCP(b) and as assistant chair of the Cheka of the Northern Caucausian Front in 1919. He chaired the Tambov Gubernia Cheka in 1919–20 and the Donetsk Gubernia Cheka in 1920. In 1920–1, he was assistant chair of the Donetsk Gubernia Soviet Ispolkom and a member of the

CC CP(b)U. In 1921, he chaired the Lugansk Cheka. As a delegate to the Tenth Party Congress in 1921, he supported the Workers' Opposition and voted against the resolutions 'On Party Unity' and 'Anarcho-Syndicalist Deviation.' In 1921–2, he chaired the Volynsk Gubernia Soviet Ispolkom. From 1921–3, he was a candidate member of the CC CP(b)U and a full member of it in 1923–4. He worked as People's Commissar of Internal Affairs in the Ukrainian SSR in 1923. In 1924–6, he managed the Tobacco Trust in Kiev. From 1927–[30], he chaired the Tobacco, Salt, and Preserves Syndicate. In 1931–2, he managed the Moscow branch of Soiuzkoks, which was responsible for coke used in iron ore smelting. In 1932–5, he was commercial director of the Gazoochistka Trust, which oversaw materials and processes for cleansing impurities from industrial gases. Arrested in 1935 on the case of the Moscow group of the Workers' Opposition, he was sentenced to five years confinement, but was executed in Cheliabinsk in 1937.

Nikolaeva, Klavdiia Ivanova (1893–1944) was born in St. Petersburg into a working class family; her mother was a washerwoman. She finished a three-year primary school in St. Petersburg in 1904, worked there 1905–11, usually in printing houses, and joined the RSDRP(b) in 1909. She was a political exile in 1911–13 in Veliky Ustiug. Upon her release, she worked in St. Petersburg until she was sentenced to administrative exile in Eniseiskaia Gubernia in 1915. Amnestied after the February 1917 Revolution, she became an editor of *Rabotnitsa*. She led the Women's Department of the Petrograd Gubernia Committee of the RCP(b) in 1918. In 1924, she led the Agitation-Propaganda section of the Petrograd Gubernia Party Committee. She served as head of the women workers' and peasants' section of the Party CC in 1924–6. She was a member of the CC RCP(b) and of the Orgburo and a candidate member of the Secretariat in 1924–5. Having supported the Leningrad and United Oppositions in 1925–7, she was demoted to candidate membership of the Party CC in 1925–34. She took classes on Marxism-Leninism under the CC in 1926–8 and led the agitation-propaganda section of the North Caucasus Krai Party Committee in 1928–30. In 1930–3, she led the Party CC section for agitation and mass campaigns. She served as second secretary of the Western Siberian Krai Party Committee in 1933–4. From 1934–44, she was a member of the Party CC. In 1934–6, she was second secretary of the Ivanovsky Industrial Oblast Party Committee. She was VTsSPS secretary and a member of the VTsSPS presidium in 1937–44. She died in Moscow.

Noske, Gustav (1868–1946) was born in Brandenburg, Prussia. Although a Social Democratic member of the Reichstag, he often favoured imperialist and colonialist policies, such as when he took a patriotic stance behind Germany during World War I. While the Kaiser still ruled, he was assigned to restore discipline after the Kiel sailors mutinied in October 1918. As Defense Minister of the Weimar Republic in 1919–20, he violently suppressed a communist uprising in Berlin, but resigned due to criticism after a failed right-wing coup (Kapp Putsch). From 1920–33, he was governor of Hanover province. In July 1944, he and others attempted unsuccessfully to overthrow Adolf Hitler. He died in Hanover, Germany.

Ordzhonikidze, Grigory 'Sergo' (1886–1937) was born into the Georgian nobility in Kutaisskaia Gubernia. He studied in medical school in Tiflis in 1901–5. After joining the RSDRP in 1903, he carried out party work in Western Georgia, Abkhazia, Baku, and other cities. He was often arrested, imprisoned, and exiled. He spent 1906–7 in Germany and 1910–11 studying at the Longjumeau party school in France. He was elected to membership in the RSDRP(b) CC in 1912 at the Sixth (Prague) Party Conference, but was arrested later that year and exiled to three years of hard labour in Shlisselburg prison and administrative exile in Iakutskaia Oblast. After the February 1917 Revolution, he was amnestied. Then he carried out revolutionary work in Iakutia, becoming a member of the Iakutsk Soviet Ispolkom. In summer 1917, he became a member of the Petersburg Bolshevik Committee and of the Petrograd Soviet Ispolkom. He carried out party work in Tiflis and Baku in late summer and early autumn, but returned to Petrograd to serve as a detachment commander in October 1917 to January 1918. In this role, he participated in the October Revolution. In 1918, he served as an extraordinary commissar of Sovnarkom in Ukraine and Southern Russia, a special representative of the party in Ukraine, chief of the Extraordinary Defence Headquarters of the Don Soviet Republic, and a partisan operative in the North Caucasus. In 1919, he chaired the Committee of Defence of the Terskaia Soviet Republic and the Caucasus Revolutionary Committee, and was a member of the Revolutionary Military Council (Revvoensovet) of the Sixteenth Army of the Western Front. In 1919–20, he was a member of the Revvoensovet of the Fourteenth Army of the Southern Front. In 1920–1, he was in the Revvoensovet of the Caucasus Front and chaired the North Caucasus Revolutionary Committee. A member of the Caucasus Bureau of the CC RCP(b) in 1920–2 and its senior secretary in 1921–2, he helped engineer Bolshevik power in the Caucasus. In 1921–7 and 1934–7, he belonged to the Party CC. He held leading party and military posts in the Caucasus in 1921–6. In 1924–7, he was a member of the USSR Revolutionary Military Council. A candidate member of the Politburo in 1926, he was a full member of it in 1930–7. He chaired the Party CCC and was USSR People's Commissar of Worker Peasant Inspection in 1926–30. He continued to be a member of the CCC until 1934, chaired VSNKh in 1930–2, and was USSR People's Commissar of Heavy Industry in 1932–7. He committed suicide.

Orlov, Kirill Nikitich (1879–1943?) was born in the village Khotetovo in Orlovskaia Oblast and had a middle school education. He became a revolutionary in 1901, when he participated in the Briansk general strike. His RSDRP(b) membership dated to 1903, when he was in Orel. He was arrested and jailed multiple times. He was conscripted into the Black Sea Fleet in autumn 1903. In 1905, he participated in the

mutiny that started on the Battleship Potemkin while he served on the Ekaterina
II. He was arrested and barely escaped the death penalty. He first met Lenin in 1905
in Moscow and then in Paris in 1914. He was a member of the Petersburg Committee
and the Red Guard. After the October Revolution, he led the Kronstadt Garrison, was
Commissar of the Tula Arms factories, and chaired the Council of Military Industry.
When he signed the theses of the Workers' Opposition, he was assistant chair of
the Council of Military Industry. He was a member of the central committee of the
Metalworkers' Union in 1921. By the late 1930s, he had been purged from the Communist Party and worked as a senior inspector in Auto Repair and Supply. He was
suspected of being a 'concealed Trotskyist'. Arrested in Perm Oblast in June 1941,
where he was working as a mechanic at an automobile depot, he was sentenced to
ten years confinement.

Osinsky, Nikolai (Obolensky, Valerian Valerianovich) (1887–1938) was born either in
Moscow or in Beklemeshevy Byki village in Kursk gubernia into a veterinarian's
family. He completed gymnasium in Moscow in 1905 and studied at Moscow Uni-
versity in 1905, in Germany in 1906, and finished the Law Department of Moscow
University in 1916. Having joined the RSDRP(b) in 1907, he worked for it in Moscow
and Tver. He was arrested several times. He served in the Russian Army in 1916–17.
After the February 1917 Revolution, he joined the Moscow Oblast Bureau of the CC
RSDRP(b). In 1917–18, he was a candidate member of the CC RSDRP(b). During the
October Revolution, he was a member of the Kharkov Military Revolutionary Committee. After the October Revolution, he managed the State Bank of the RSFSR and
chaired VSNKh. In 1918, he was in the VSNKh RSFSR Metals Section and on the editorial board of *Pravda*. He went as a Soviet special representative to Penza gubernia
and Tula gubernia in 1919. He chaired the Tula Gubernia Soviet Ispolkom and was
a member of the collegium of the People's Commissariat of Food Supplies in 1920.
In 1921–2, he was Assistant People's Commissariat of Agriculture and a candidate
member of the Party CC. He was assistant chair of VSNKh in 1923. He spent 1923–
4 at a diplomatic post in Sweden. A Left Communist opposed to the Brest Peace in
March 1918, he was a prominent member of the Democratic Centralists in 1920–1,
and in 1923 he belonged to the Trotskyist Opposition. He carried out Soviet business
in the United States in 1924–5. He held various positions in state planning, statistical
administration and VSNKh in 1925–35, was a Party CC candidate member in 1925–
37, a Presidium member of the Communist Academy in 1928–9, an *Izvestiia* editorial
board member in 1931, an academician in the USSR Academy of Sciences Branch of
Social Sciences in 1932, an academician in the All-Union Academy of Agricultural
Sciences named after V.I. Lenin in 1935, and Director of the Institute of the History
of Science and Technology of the USSR Academy of Sciences in 1935–7. He served as
chair of a grain-related agricultural commission in 1932–7, was arrested in 1937, and
was shot in 1938.

Paniushkin, Vasily Lukich (1888–1960) was born in Kochety, Tula Gubernia to a poor
peasant family. He finished primary school and apprenticed with his father as a
metalworker. In 1907, he joined the RSDRP(b) and carried out party work in St.
Petersburg and in the Baltic Fleet, in which he served from 1909. He was arrested
and in 1914 was sentenced to the death penalty, but survived. He escaped from confinement in 1916. After the February 1917 Revolution, he was in the Kronstadt and
Petrograd soviets and edited the newspaper *Krestianskaia Pravda*. A story circulated
among Mensheviks that he was among a group of Bolsheviks who killed seven military cadets. During the Civil War, he was a member of the Cheka collegium and was
an extraordinary military commissar in Tula Gubernia, Povolzhe, and the Urals. He
was also on the Eastern Front. After the war, he carried out work for the party in
Tula and Simbirsk. In 1919–20, he was a senior organiser and instructor for the CC
RCP(b). In 1920, he led the Bauman District Opposition in the Moscow Communist
Party organisation. A supporter of the Workers' Opposition, he resigned his party
membership after its defeat in 1921 and attempted to organise a Worker-Peasant
Socialist Party, for which the party expelled him. In June 1921, he was arrested and
sentenced to two years of hard labour, but he was amnestied six months later. After
meeting with Lenin, he was readmitted to the party. He worked in VSNKh from 1922,
in the Orel Party Committee in 1925–6, and in the Soviet trade delegation in Berlin in
1927–30. He was an industrial administrator and a collective farm manager in 1931–
7. Arrested in 1937, he was sentenced in 1940 to eight years of confinement and in
1944 to ten years of confinement. He retired in 1956 and died in Moscow in 1960.

Parov [ ] ( ) from the Urals was a supporter of the Workers' Opposition in the Metalworkers' Union.

Pavlov, A. ( ) joined the party in 1917. A member of the Metalworkers' Union central
committee, he signed the theses of the Workers' Opposition and spoke vocally at
meetings in support of it. He may have been from Petrograd or Moscow.

Pekar [ ] ( ) was a speaker at Khamovnichesky District Party Conference in 1924.

Perepechko, Ivan Nikolaevich (1897–1943) was born in Kiev. He joined the RSDRP(b) in
1914 and worked for the party in Moscow. He was often arrested and exiled. After the
October 1917 Revolution, he was secretary and assistant chair of the Southern Bureau of VTsSPS. During the Civil War, he served in the Red Army and worked in the
underground in Kiev. He was chief of the Military and Partisan sections and secretary of the underground Odessa Gubernia Committee of the CP(b)U. He was arrested
but freed. He served as secretary of the Odessa Gubernia Council of Trade Unions
and chief of the Political Section of the 27th Omsk Rifle Division. In 1920, he was
secretary of the Southern Bureau of VTsSPS. In 1921, he was chief of the Cultural-
Enlightenment section of VTsSPS and a member of the Presidium of VTsSPS. He
belonged to the Workers' Opposition in 1921–2. He was assistant chair of the Southern Bureau of VTsSPS in 1922, a member of the Revvoensovet of the Western Front

in 1922–3, and carried out political work in the Red Army. In 1927–8, he chaired the Central Council of Trade Unions of Belorussia and was a member of the Bureau of the CC CP(b) of Belorussia. He was first secretary of the Far East Krai Party Committee in 1928–31 and a member of the Revvoensovet of the Independent Far East Army in 1929. He was a candidate member of the Party CC in 1930–4, VTsSPS secretary in 1931–3, and a presidium member of VTsSPS in 1931. In 1933, he was chief of the political section of the October railway and from 1934–7 assistant chief of the Riazan-Urals railway. In 1937 he was arrested and in 1939 given a twenty-year sentence. He died in 1943 in Krasnoiarsk corrective labour camp.

Petrovsky, Grigory Ivanovich (1878–1958) was born in Kharkov into a peasant family. His father, who worked as a tailor, died when he was three and his mother, who worked as a laundress, remarried to an abusive alcoholic. G.I. studied in a model school operated under a seminary, but was expelled for inability to pay tuition. After being let go from a metalworker apprenticeship for complaining of abuse, he joined his brother in Ekaterinoslav and began working at Briansk factory in 1892. By 1897–8, he was a skilled metalworker. St. Petersburg workers who were exiled to Ekaterinoslav in 1897 introduced him to socialism. In 1899, he went to Nikolaevsk to help form an RSDRP committee, but was expelled from there in 1900 for strike activity. After returning to Ekaterinoslav, he was arrested and held in solitary for a year. He was in Ekaterinoslav during the 1905 Revolution, belonged to the Ekaterinoslavsky RSDRP committee, and was elected secretary of the soviet formed there. After the 1905 Revolution, he went to work for three months in Saarbrucken, Germany. In 1907, he worked in Mariupol factories. He was a Bolshevik deputy to the Fourth Duma in 1912–14 and worked on the newspaper *Pravda*. Arrested for opposition to Russia's participation in World War I, he was arrested, tried, and exiled to Siberia. He spent his exile in Turukhansk, Eniseisk, and Iakutsk. After the February 1917 Revolution, he was a commissar of Iakutsk Oblast and chaired the Committee of Social Security there. He also carried out revolutionary work in Petrograd and Ukraine. After the October Revolution, he became People's Commissar of Internal Affairs of the RSFSR, then in 1919, he was elected Chair of the All-Ukrainian Soviet Central Ispolkom, which he remained until 1938. As such, he was a central figure in imposing the grain requisitions that contributed to famine in Ukraine in 1932–3. Ekaterinoslav was renamed Dnepropetrovsk in 1926 to honour him. He was a member of the CC of the RCP(b) and the VKP(b) from 1922 on. He was a candidate member of the Politburo in 1926–39. He lost his high positions for having 'protected enemies of the people'. In 1940, he was appointed assistant director of the Museum of the Revolution of the USSR.

Piatnitsky, Iosif Aronovich [Tarshis, Iosif Oriolovich] (1882–1938) was born in Vilkomir village, Kovenskaia gubernia and joined the RSDRP in 1898. Arrested in 1902, he escaped and emigrated to Germany, but returned to Russia. He was arrested and released twice more in 1906 and 1908 and emigrated to Switzerland. Arrested in

1914, he was sentenced to three years of administrative exile in Fedino village, Eniseiskaia Gubernia. After the February 1917 Revolution, he was amnestied. In 1917, he was a member of the Moscow Committee of the RSDRP(b). He served in the Moscow Soviet Ispolkom in 1918–20, was a member of the Secretariat of the Moscow Gubernia Party Committee in 1920, and chaired the central committee of the Railwayworkers' Union in 1919–20. He was a candidate member of the CC RCP(b) in 1920–1, a full CC member in 1927–37, a member of the Orgburo in 1922–6, and a member of the Party CCC in 1924–7. Having created the conspiratorial technical apparatus of the Communist International in 1921, he belonged to the ECCI secretariat in 1922–37, was secretary of it in 1923–35, a candidate member of its presidium in 1926–8, and a full presidium member in 1928–35. In 1935–7, he led the political administrative section of the Party CC. Perhaps having expressed skepticism about the charges against Old Bolsheviks at a CC plenum during Stalin's terror, he was arrested in 1937, and he was executed in 1938.

Pleshkov, V. ( ) joined the RCP(b) in 1918 and was a member of the central committee of the Metalworkers' Union. He signed the theses of the Workers' Opposition and the Letter of the 22.

Plokhotnikov ( ) was a member of the Presidium of the Metalworkers' Union Congress from Kharkov in May 1921.

Polosatov, A. ( ) joined the party in 1912 and numbered among the Metalworkers' Union's leading members. He may have been a Party CC inspector in Iuzovka and Perm. A member of the Workers' Opposition, he also signed the Letter of the 22.

Prasolov, [Aleksei Grigorevich?] ( ) was apparently a metalworker and a Worker Oppositionist.

Pravdin, Aleksandr (Iosif) Grigorevich (1879–1938) was born in Annenkovo village in Kursk Gubernia. He worked as a carpenter and joined the RSDRP in 1899. He carried out work for the party in Odessa, St. Petersburg, Lugansk, and other cities. He participated in the 1905 Revolution and experienced arrests and exile. He was a member of the Northern Oblast Bureau of the RSDRP(b) CC in 1912, became a CC member in 1913, and contributed to *Pravda* in 1912–14. He had an important contact in railway engineer Iury Lomonosov, who often found him railway jobs in various cities of the Russian empire, including the capital. A.G. was arrested in 1916, but was released through the efforts of Lomonosov, who then found him a job in Ust-Katav. After the February 1917 Revolution, he conducted party work in the Urals and was a member of the Ufa Committee of the RSDRP(b). He was a candidate CC RSDRP(b) member in mid-1917. After the October Revolution, he was Assistant Commissar of Internal Affairs until 1919. He served in 1919 as a special representative of the Party CC and VTsIK on mobilisation in Gomel Gubernia and on grain requisitions near Kazan, Ufa, Viatka, railway districts and the Kama and Belaia rivers. He was a special representative of the Council of Labour and Defence and of VTsIK to the Western Front in

1919. In 1920, he belonged to the Ufa Gubernia Revolutionary Committee, chaired the Administration of Northern Railways, and was a member of the Revolutionary Military Council of the Turkestan Front. A member of the Workers' Opposition in 1920–2, he signed the Letter of the 22. In 1921–4, he directed the Institute of Civil Engineers. He was a CCC member from 1923–7. He served as Assistant People's Commissar of Communications of the USSR in 1924–5, worked in the USSR People's Commissariat of Foreign Trade in 1930–3, and led the Transport Group of the People's Commissariat of Worker Peasant Inspection of the USSR in 1933–4. In 1936, he was assistant chief of the transport group of the Commission of Soviet Control under the USSR Sovnarkom. He retired from that position in 1936, was arrested in 1937, and was executed in 1938.

Preobrazhensky, Evgeny Alekseevich (1886–1937) was born in Bolkhov, Orlov Gubernia. His father was an Orthodox priest.[2] He completed gymnasium in Orel and attended the Law Department of Moscow University, but did not finish. Having become a Bolshevik in 1903, he carried out party work in Orel, Briansk, Moscow, the Urals, and Siberia. Exiled to Irkutsk Gubernia in 1909, he was freed after the February 1917 Revolution, whereupon he became assistant chair of the Chita Soviet. He also worked in the Urals and was a member of the Presidium of the First Eastern Siberia Congress of Soviets. During the Brest peace talks, he was a Left Communist. A candidate member of the Party CC from 1917 to 1918, he was also a candidate member of the Urals Oblast Party Committee in 1918 and chaired the Presidium of the Urals Oblast Party Committee in 1918–19. He joined the *Pravda* editorial board in 1919 and was sent by the VTsIK to Orlov Gubernia as a special representative. In 1920, he chaired the Ufa Gubernia Party Committee and led the agitation and propaganda section of the Party CC. When he was a member of the Party CC, CCC, and Orgburo and a Party CC secretary in 1920–1, he supported Trotsky's platform on trade unions. He held other top positions in those years, too. He actively supported Trotsky's political and economic positions from 1923 on. Until 1926, he held senior positions overseeing sectors of the economy and education. In 1926–8, he was on the editorial board of the *Great Soviet Encyclopedia*. In 1927, he was excluded from the Party, exiled to Uralsk, and restored to party membership in 1930. He worked in state planning in 1929–32 and in 1932–3 was a member of the collegium of the People's Commissariat of Light Industry of the USSR. Arrested and purged from the party in January 1933, he was sentenced to three years exile but was restored to the party in December 1933. Until 1936, he assisted in the oversight of grain-growing and livestock-raising sovkhozes. Arrested in 1936, he was shot in 1937.

Primerov [ ] ( ) chaired the Metalworkers' Union podraikom near or in Enakievo.

---

2 Orthodox clergy are allowed to marry.

Radek (Sobelson), Karl Berngardovich (1885–1939) was born in Lemberg in the Austro-Hungarian Empire and graduated from the History Department of Cracow University. In 1902, he joined the Polish Socialist Party and he became a member of the RSDRP in 1903. He was especially active and prominent in Polish and German left wing movements and for a time belonged to the Social Democratic Party of Germany. Although he only joined the Bolsheviks in 1917, he collaborated with Lenin during World War I and shared an internationalist position on the war, but on the national question he differed with Lenin before the revolution. He arrived in Russia in October 1917 and became a Bolshevik CC member that year, remaining so until 1924. He was a Left Communist during the Brest peace. He held numerous party and soviet roles supervising contacts with foreign communists. In 1918, he was assistant Commissar of Foreign Affairs, in 1920–4 a member of the ECCI, and a member of its presidium in 1921–4. He was arrested in Berlin in 1919, but was released and returned to Russia at the end of the year. In 1923–4, he led the Eastern Section of the ECCI and in 1925–8, he was rector of the Communist University of Peoples of the East named after Sun Yat-sen. Among the leadership of Trotsky's Left Opposition after 1923, he was expelled from the party and exiled in 1927 to three years in Tobolsk. He was freed in 1929 after recanting and restored to the party ranks in 1930. He was an editor of *Pravda* and *Izvestiia* in 1929–30 and assistant editor of the journal *Za rubezhom* in 1930–2. From 1932–6, he led the Bureau of International Information under the Section of Culture and Propaganda of the Party CC. Excluded from the party again in 1936, he was arrested, convicted in the 1937 Moscow trial, and given a ten-year prison sentence. He was murdered in Verkhneuralsk prison in 1939.

Rafail [Farbman, Rafail Borisovich] (1893–1966) was born in Kursk and entered the RSDRP in 1910, but he only became a Bolshevik in 1919. Arrested in 1914, he was exiled to Tobolsk Gubernia. In 1917, he belonged to the Kiev Committee of the RSDRP(b) and chaired the Kiev Council of Trade Unions. In 1918–20, he was a member of the CC CP(b)U and served as its secretary in 1920. In 1920, he became secretary of the party cell and a member of the bureau of the party committee of the factory 'VEK' in Moscow, as well as chief of the Moscow Department of Education. He may have been a member of the Moscow party committee. He was a Democratic Centralist in 1920–1, a member of the Left Opposition in 1923, and a member of the United Opposition in 1927, at which time he was purged from the party. In 1930–2, he held various leadership posts in the VSNKh trusts Rudmetalltorg and Metallolom. Restored to the party ranks in 1932, he was arrested the same year, excluded from the party again, and sentenced to five years of imprisonment. He was freed in 1956.

Rakovsky, Khristian Georgievich [Stanchev, Kriestiu Georgiev] (1873–1941) was born in Kotel, Bulgaria and exiled in 1890. Beginning in 1889, he participated in social democratic movements in Bulgaria, Switzerland, Germany, France, Romania, and Russia. He co-founded the Socialist Party of Romania. From 1890–7, he studied medicine

in Geneva, Berlin, Zurich, and Nance, and finally earned a degree at Montpelier. He
served in the Romanian army in 1898–1900. In 1901–3, he studied in the Law Department of the Sorbonne. He held an internationalist position on World War I. He
arrived in Russia in 1917 and joined the Bolsheviks. He was a member of the Odessa
and Petrograd Soviets in 1917, but spent the late months of that year in Stockholm.
In 1918, he chaired a collegium on struggle against counterrevolution in the south of
Russia and the Soviet delegation to peace talks in Kiev, was the RSFSR diplomatic
representative in Austria, and was chief of the Balkan Department of the People's
Commissariat of Foreign Affairs of the RSFSR. In 1919–23, he held various positions
of power in Ukraine, including Sovnarkom chair, CP(b)U CC and Politburo member, Ukrainian Economic Council chair, and People's Commissar of Internal Affairs,
Health, and Foreign Affairs. He was also a member of the CC RCP(b) and All-Union
Party CC in 1919–27 and an RCP(b) Orgburo member in 1919–20. He held military positions as assistant chief of the Political Administration of the Red Army in 1919–20
and member of the Revvoensovets of the Southwest and Southern Fronts in 1920.
He chaired the Revvoensovet of the Ukrainian Labour Army in 1920–1. In 1923–
7, he was Assistant People's Commissar of Foreign Affairs of the USSR. He served
as a USSR diplomatic and trade envoy to Great Britain in 1923–5 and to France in
1925–7. Along with Trotsky, he was a leader of the Left Opposition. For that he was
purged from the party in 1927 and exiled to Astrakhan, then Western Siberia. In exile,
he worked in planning commissions. Although he confessed his errors in 1934 and
was restored to the party in 1935, he was rearrested in 1937. During his remaining
years of freedom, he had been employed by the RSFSR People's Commissariat of
Health and he chaired the All-Union Societies of the Red Cross and Red Crescent.
He was tried and convicted along with Bukharin in 1938, and executed near Orel in
1941.

Riazanov (Goldendakh), David Borisovich (1870–1938) was born in Odessa to a trades-
man and belonged to the urban estate. Although he attended gymnasium, he was
expelled. Having become a revolutionary in 1887, he carried out revolutionary activities in Odessa and St. Petersburg. Arrested in 1895, he was sentenced to three years
of exile in Kishinev. From 1900 to 1905, he lived in France and Germany. He joined
the RSDRP in 1903 and was known as a nonfactional Social Democrat who co-
founded the group *Borba* and engaged critically with the theoretical approaches
published in *Iskra*. Having returned to Russia in 1905, he was arrested in 1907 and
freed the same year. He spent the years 1907–17 in emigration. He lectured at the
party school in Longjumeau, France, in 1911. After returning to Russia in April 1917,
he became a member of the Ispolkoms of the Petrograd Soviet and of the All-Russian
Soviet. He joined the Bolsheviks in July 1917. He was a member of the VTsSPS Presidium, the Preparliament, and the Constituent Assembly. After the October Revolution, he supported a coalition government with Mensheviks and Socialist Revolu-

tionaries. He resigned from the Bolshevik Party in disagreement over the Brest peace, but returned the same year. In 1918–20, he headed the Central Archive of the RSFSR. He promoted his own platform in the 1920–1 trade union discussion, so the party removed him from work in trade unions. From 1921–31, he directed the Institute of Marx and Engels under the Socialist Academy of the USSR. In 1929, he became an Academician in the Department of Humanities (History) of the Academy of Sciences of the USSR. In 1931, he was purged from the party, arrested, disenrolled from the Academy of Sciences of the USSR, and sentenced to three years of exile in Saratov, where he worked at Saratov State University. Arrested in 1937, he was executed in Saratov.

Roland-Holst, Henriette (1869–1952) was born in The Netherlands into a wealthy middle class family. At first, she had private lessons at home, then she studied for four years in a boarding school. Her education focused on literature and music. She became a writer of poetry, history, politics, and philosophy. In 1897, she joined the Dutch Social Democratic Workers' Party and was on its left wing. During World War I, she held an internationalist position against the war and was in the Zimmerwald left. She helped found the Dutch Communist Party in 1918 and attended the Third World Congress of the Communist International in 1921, but left the Communist Party in 1927 due to her disagreement with Stalin's policies. She remained an unaffiliated socialist who disseminated socialist ideas in her writing. During World War II, she participated in the resistance movement against the Nazis. The University of Amsterdam in 1947 awarded her an honorary doctorate.

Rosmer, Alfred (1877–1964) was born to French immigrants living in New York. His family returned to France, where he worked as a civil servant and a proofreader. A revolutionary syndicalist, he participated in the editorial board of *La Vie Ouvrière*. He led French internationalist opposition to World War I and became close to Trotsky during the war. A strong supporter of the October Revolution in Russia, he was elected to the ECCI in 1920. He attended the Second, Third, Fourth, and Fifth Comintern World Congresses. He was expelled from the French Communist Party after he and Pierre Monatte took a public stance of disagreement with the party's campaign against Trotsky in 1924. He co-founded the journal *La Révolution prolétarienne*. He organised the Left Opposition in France in 1929–31. Although he broke with Trotsky in 1931, he resumed working with him after 1936 and was with him in Mexico in 1939. During World War II, Rosmer lived in the United States, but he returned to France in 1947 and published his memoirs in 1953.

Rozental, Iakov Ivanovich ( ) was a metalworker from the Urals, who worked more in trade unions than in the party. He chaired the commission on repair of railroad transport under the Metals Section of VSNKh around 1921.

Rubakin, Nikolai (1862–1946) was a bibliographer who promoted the education of the Russian people through booklets he wrote and his manuals on setting up and maintaining village libraries. Although he wrote legal articles published in Marxist journals and illegal pamphlets issued by revolutionary parties, he emphasized education over revolutionary violence. He began living in Switzerland in 1907 and established a library in Montreux of Russian materials. Vera Figner, Georgy Plekhanov, Vladimir Lenin, and other Russian emigres used his library. In 1920, he and his library moved to Lausanne. After he died, his collection of about 100,000 books was deposited in the Lenin Library.

Rudniansky, Andreas [Endre Rudnyánszky] (1885–1943?) was born in Hungary and was a lawyer by profession. He served as a cavalry officer in the Austro-Hungarian Army during World War I, until the Russians captured him. He became a Communist and stayed in Russia to organise a Hungarian Communist group; in 1919, he served there as representative of the Hungarian Soviet Republic. He participated in the first two Comintern congresses, but then embezzled Comintern money and went missing. He may have returned to Soviet Russia in 1926, been arrested, and then imprisoned for fifteen years.

Rudzutak, Ian E. (1887–1938) was born into a working-class family in a village in Latvia (Kurlandskaia Gubernia). He joined the Latvian Social Democratic Workers' Party in 1905 and carried out party work in Riga and Vindava. Having participated in the 1905 Revolution, he joined the RSDRP in 1906. In 1907, he was given a prison sentence of ten years hard labour, which he served in Butyrka Prison and Rizhsky Central Prison. Amnestied after the February 1917 Revolution, he became a member of the Presidium of the All-Russian Textile Workers' Union Central Council and secretary of VTsSPS. After the October 1917 Revolution, he was appointed to the VSNKh presidium. In 1918, he belonged to the Presidium of the Moscow City Council of Trade Unions, chaired the Moscow Oblast Sovnarkhoz, and was a member of the Presidium of VSNKh RSFSR until October 1921. He chaired Tsentrotekstil until 1920. In 1919, he was appointed chief of the Main Board of Water Transport of the RSFSR People's Commissariat of Transportation and later chaired the Union of Transport Workers. In 1920, he briefly chaired the Sovnarkom of the Autonomous Turkestan SFR and in 1921 chaired the Turkestan Commission of VTsIK. He was VTsSPS secretary and General Secretary of the Trade Union International (Profintern) in 1920–1 and VTsSPS general secretary in 1921–2. A member of the Party CC from 1920–37, he was an Orgburo member in 1921–2. He was sent to Germany for medical treatment in 1922. From 1922–4, he chaired the Central Asia Bureau of the CC RCP(b). He was a secretary of the CC RCP(b) in 1923–4, an Orgburo member in 1923–4, a candidate member of the Politburo in 1923–6, and a full member of it from 1926–32. He served as USSR People's Commissar of Transport, 1924–30. From 1926–37, he was assistant chair of Sovnarkom USSR and assistant chair of the Council of Labour and Defence of the USSR. In 1928–31, he chaired the Committee on Chemicalisation of the Economy. He chaired the Party CCC and was People's Commissar of Worker-Peasant

Inspection of the USSR in 1931–4. From 1934–7, he was a candidate member of the
Party Politburo. Arrested in 1937, he was executed in 1938.

Rukhimovich, Moisei Lvovich (1889–1938) was born in Kagalnik village in the Donbas,
graduated from Groznenskoe realschule, studied but did not graduate from Kharkov
Technological Institute, and joined the Jewish Bund in 1904 and the RSDRP(b) in
1913. From 1906–9, he lived in emigration in Turkey, Egypt, Greece, and Bulgaria. He
served in the Russian Army in 1914–17. After the February 1917 Revolution, he became
a member of the Kharkov committee of the RSDRP(b). He chaired the military section of the Kharkov Soviet and the Kharkov Military Revolutionary Committee. After
the October Revolution, he led the Kharkov Red Guard and was a member of the
Kharkov Gubernia Revolutionary Committee. In 1918, he was Military Commissar of
the Donetsk-Krivorozhskaia Republic and chair of the Central Command of Defense
of Donetsk-Krivorozhskaia Republic. He was also chief of the Department of Military Property of the People's Commissariat of Army and Navy Affairs of the RSFSR
in 1918. From 1918–19, he was commissar of the Central Administration on Formation of the Red Army of the Ukrainian People's Republic. In 1919, he became People's
Commissar of Military Affairs of the Ukrainian People's Republic, chief of the mining department of the Sovnarkhoz of the Ukrainian People's Republic, a member
of the Sovnarkom of the Ukrainian People's Republic and Soviet Socialist Republic, military commissar of the 41st Rifle Division of the 14th Army, chief of supply
of the 14th Army on the Southern Front, and a member of the Kharkov Revolutionary Committee. In 1919–20, he was a member of the Revvoensovet of the 14th Army
of the Southern and Southwestern front and a member of the Revvoensovet of the
Ukrainian Soviet Socialist Republic. He chaired the Ispolkom of the Donetsk Gubernia Soviet in 1920–2. He managed the Don Coal Trust in 1920–1 and from 1923. He
helped suppress the Kronstadt Uprising in 1921. He was a member of the CP(b)U CC
in 1921–7 and a member of its Politburo in 1924–6. A member of the All-Russian and
All-Union Party CC from 1924 to 1938, he was in its Orgburo in 1927–30. He chaired
the Ispolkom of the Bakhmut Uezd Soviet in Donetsk gubernia in 1922–3. In 1925,
he managed the Khimugol Trust. He chaired VSNKh of the Ukrainian SSR in 1925–6
and was assistant chair in 1926–8. He was assistant chair of the USSR VSNKh in 1928,
People's Commissar of Communications of the USSR in 1930–1, and manager of the
Kuzbass Coal Trust in 1931–4. In 1934–6, he was chief of the Main Administration
of Coal Industry of the People's Commissariat of Heavy Industry of the USSR and
Assistant People's Commissar of Heavy Industry of the USSR. He served as People's
Commissar of the Defence Industry in 1936–7, before he was arrested in 1937 and
executed in 1938.

Rusch, Oskar (1884–1935) was a metalworker in Berlin who led the Berlin branch of
the Union of German Metalworkers. He joined the Independent Social Democratic
Party of Germany leadership after having left the Social Democratic Party of Ger-

many in 1918. An opponent of the Revolutionary Shop Stewards movement, he was radicalised in 1919 street battles and after the murder of Rosa Luxemburg. Nevertheless, he did not work well with German communists. After visiting Russia in August 1920 in an official delegation, he became a supporter of the Bolshevik regime and joined the Communist Party of Germany (KPD). A member of the Red International of Labour Unions, he also belonged to the Berlin bureau of the International Trade Union Council when Max Ziese was its secretary. He seems to have resigned from the KPD in October 1921.

Rutgers, Sebald Justius (1879–1961) was born in Holland in 1879, was an engineer, and worked in Indonesia. He joined the Dutch Social Democratic Workers' Party before 1914. During World War I, he lived in the United States and moved further to the left. He supported the Bolshevik Revolution and was a member of the U.S. Bolshevik Bureau. He went to the First Congress of the Comintern in 1919 as the only Dutch delegate. He set up a bureau of the Comintern in Amsterdam and helped lead it. After the bureau was closed later in 1920, he went to Russia, where he worked as an engineer in the Kuzbas coal and chemical industry from 1921–6. He later held other scientific and economic posts in the USSR.

Rybak, D[mitry] I[vanovich] (1897–1938) was born in in Vitiazevka village in Kherson Gubernia, Ukraine. He joined the RSDRP(b) in 1916 and in 1921 was a delegate to the Tenth Party Congress from the party organisation in Nikolaev. When arrested by the NKVD in November 1937, he was an assistant shop director at Rybinsky factory no. 26 in Rybinsk, Iaroslavskaia Oblast. He was executed in 1938.

Rykov, Aleksei Ivanovich (1881–1938) was born into a peasant family in Kukarka settlement, Saratov Gubernia. He graduated from gymnasium in Saratov and studied in the Law Department of Kazan University, but did not finish. He joined the RSDRP in 1898 or 1899 and became a Bolshevik in 1903, but was not a hardcore Leninist in how he viewed and worked with members of other factions. He was arrested multiple times. He was a member of the RSDRP CC and its Foreign Bureau in 1905. A member or candidate member of the RSDRP(b) CC in 1906–11, he lived in France in 1910–11, was arrested in 1912, and lived in exile in 1912–14. From May 1917, he was a member of the Moscow Soviet Ispolkom. Later in 1917, he was a member of the CC RSDRP(b) and of the Petrograd Soviet Ispolkom, a member of the Preparliament, and a delegate to the Constituent Assembly. After the October 1917 Revolution, he served as People's Commissar of Internal Affairs of the RSFSR and was a member of the Party CC in 1917–18 and 1920–34. He chaired VSNKh RSFSR from 1918–21 and in 1923–4. He was assistant chair of the Council of Labour and Defence, 1921–4, and chair of it in 1926–30. In 1920–4, he was a member of the Party CC Orgburo and in 1922–30 a member of the Politburo. He was assistant chair of the RSFSR Sovnarkom in 1921–4 and of the USSR Sovnarkom in 1923–4. He chaired the RSFSR Sovnarkom in 1924–9 and that of the USSR in 1924–30. He belonged to the ECCI in 1924–35. In 1928, he chaired

the Central Council of the Society of Assistance to Defence, Aviation and Chemicals Construction (Osoaviakhim) of the USSR and RSFSR. In the same year, he figured
together with Bukharin and Tomsky in the defeated Politburo faction labeled the
'Right Opportunists' for their position favouring the continuation of NEP. Removed
from his high leadership positions, he served as People's Commissar of Post and Telegraph and of Communications of the USSR in 1931–6. He was a candidate member
of the All-Union Party CC in 1934–7. Arrested in 1937, he was executed in 1938.

Ryskin-Rysko, [Iakov Aleksandrovich?] ( ) was a Metalworkers' Union central committee member.

Sadoul, Jacques (1881–1956) was a lawyer and army captain from France who had socialist sympathies early in life. Serving in the Ministry of Armaments during World
War I, he played the role of envoy to the Russian Provisional Government and
attempted to encourage pro-Entente sentiments among Russian socialists in 1917.
After the Bolsheviks came to power, he attempted to discourage them from pursuing the Brest Peace, but through his contacts with them, he became a communist.
He remained in Russia during the Civil War, set up a French communist group there,
and advised Red Army leaders on its organisation. In Ukraine, he encouraged rebel-
lion among French interventionist troops and in Germany, he organised communist
cells. Living outside of France, he recruited members for the Communist Party of
France and wrote for *L'Humanité*, while he was under a death sentence in France.
In 1924, the death sentence was lifted and he returned to France. He was faithful to
the Stalinist line, wrote for *Izvestiia*, and served as an unofficial liaison between the
Soviet and French governments. After serving the Vichy government during World
War II, he became a communist again after the war. His last job was as a town mayor.

Sapozhnikov, Grigory Lvovich (1887–1937) was born in Rechitsa in what later became
Belarus. He had a primary school education. He was in the youth section of the Jewish Bund in 1904–6, but he joined the RSDRP(b) in 1906. At some point he served
in the infantry. He worked as a tailor and belonged to the clothing industry trade
union. His travels included Nizhny Novgorod, Odessa, Kharkov, and Kiev. He spent
six months in an Odessan prison. He was in Odessa in the Needleworkers' Union
in 1917–18 and went to Kharkov in 1918. He served in the Donetsk Gubernia Party
Committee in 1920 and was a candidate member of the Kiev purge commission in
1921. He supported the proposals of the Workers' Opposition in 1920–1. Prior to his
arrest during the Great Terror, he lived in Kiev and was chief of the Clothing Industry
Board of the People's Commissariat of Local Industry of the Ukrainian SSR. He was
a key figure charged and interrogated on the case of the Workers' Opposition in Kiev
during the Great Terror. During his closed trial in Moscow, he recanted much of the
confession extracted from him in Kiev. He was executed in 1937.

Sapronov, Timofei Vladimirovich (1887–1939) was born into a peasant family in Mos-
taushka village, Tula Gubernia. He studied in primary school for about a year, but at

age eight he was assigned to herd livestock. At age twelve, he was sent to St. Petersburg to serve the gentry landowner's family. When at age 13 he asked to be paid, they returned him home. He resumed tending cattle, but at age fifteen he painted houses for hire. Other jobs included mill work, groundskeeping, and stevedore work. During the 1905 Revolution, he participated in street demonstrations in Moscow. He was in contact with Bolsheviks but did not join the party then. He joined the Construction Workers' Union in 1907, before it was closed. He remained politically passive until 1912, when he joined the RSDRP(b) and helped organise party and trade union groups. He worked in the party underground in Moscow, Petrograd, Saratov, Nizhny Novgorod, and Tula during World War I. He was in Tushino when the February Revolution began. During 1917, he organised factory committees, soviets, and party cells. He chaired the Tushino-Guchkovsky District Soviet and the Moscow Uezd Soviet. After the October Revolution, he chaired the Moscow Gubernia Soviet Ispolkom until the end of 1919. He was a Left Communist opposed to the Brest peace and was a leader of the Democratic Centralists. In 1919–20, he chaired the Kharkov Gubernia Revolutionary Committee. In 1920, he was a member of the CP(b)U CC, chair of the RSFSR Little Sovnarkom, and senior secretary of the Samara Gubernia Party Committee. In 1920–1, he chaired the central committee of the Union of Construction Workers. In 1921, he chaired the Main Committee of State Construction under VSNKh RSFSR and was assistant chair of VSNKh RSFSR. He was secretary of the Party CC Urals Bureau in 1922, CC RCP(b) member in 1922–3, VTsIK secretary in 1922–4, and a member of the Main Concessions Committee in 1925–6. Having continued his oppositionist politics, he was purged from the party in 1927 and exiled to the Crimean ASSR in 1928. Arrested in 1935, he was confined to Verkhneuralsk Prison and shot in 1937.

Scheidemann, Philipp Heinrich (1865–1939) was born in Germany and died in Copenhagen, Denmark. A journalist and Social Democratic politician, he supported Germany's participation in World War I. He proclaimed the Weimar Republic in 1918 and was its first chancellor, but he resigned to protest the Versailles agreement. He served as a town mayor in 1920–5 and left Germany when the Nazis took power in 1933.

Semkov, Semen Moiseevich [Kogan, Samuil Moiseevich] (1885–1928) was born in Odessa and joined the RSDRP in 1902. He was arrested and exiled to Vologodskaia Gubernia. In 1909, he fled abroad but he returned to Russia in 1910. He left Russia again in 1911 to attend the party school in Longjumeau. After having returned to Russia, he was arrested in 1913 and sentenced to administrative exile in Uskul, but he fled abroad, ending up in the United States. From 1914–17, he was secretary of the New York section of the RSDRP and a member of the Russian section of the Socialist Party of the USA. He returned to Russia in November 1917. In 1918, he was Russia's envoy to Germany to discuss prisoners of war. From 1918, he served as a political commissar, chair of the administration of Izhevsk arms and steel factories, and as a member of the Revolutionary Committee and Revvoensovet of Ufimsk Fortified District. From 1921–5, he was secretary of the Moscow City Council of Trade Unions. He chaired the Zakavkazsky Council of Trade Unions in 1925. He was a member of the Party CCC in 1925–8. He died in Leningrad.

Serebriakov, Leonid Petrovich (1890–1937) was born in Samara to a father who was a metalworker, who moved often for work and took his family with him. Among the places L.P. lived in childhood were Ufa and Lugansk. He attended a two-year school in Lugansk and later was self-educated. His brothers introduced him to socialist literature and in 1905 he became a member of the Lugansk Committee of the RSDRP(b). He was arrested and fired from his factory job in 1906–7. In 1908, he was exiled for two years to Vologodskaia Gubernia. He traveled around many parts of Russia in 1910–11 for underground party work. In 1912, he was exiled to Narym for three years, but escaped and went to St. Petersburg. From there, the party sent him to Baku to lead a strike. From Baku, he journeyed on to Tiflis, Sukhumi, Nikolaev, and Odessa. Arrested, he was returned to Narym, but escaped again in 1914 and went to Moscow. There he was arrested and sent back to Narym. When his exile ended in 1916, he went to Tomsk. From there he went to Petrograd, participated in January 1917 demonstrations, and then went to Rybinsk. There he was taken into military service and stationed in Kostroma. In Kostroma, he helped organise the Kostroma Soviet. Then he moved to Moscow to be a member of the party oblast committee. After the October 1917 Revolution, he was in the presidium of the Moscow soviet until 1919 and chaired the Moscow Oblast Bureau of the Party CC in 1918. He was in the Party CC from 1919–21, the Orgburo in 1919–21, and secretary of the CC in 1920–1. He was a member of the Revvoensovet of the Southern Front, chair of the Southern Bureau of VTsSPS, and VTsIK secretary in 1919–20. He worked for the Commissariat of Transportation in 1921–7 and 1929. A supporter of Trotsky's trade union proposals and a signatory of the Declaration of the 46, he also played a crucial role in the formation of the United Opposition. He was purged from the party and exiled to Semipalatinsk in 1927 and restored to the party in 1930. In 1931–5, he was chief of the Central Administration of Highways and Automobile Transport of the USSR, under Sovnarkom, and in 1935–6 was demoted to assistant chief. Arrested in 1936, he was shot in 1937.

Sergeev, N.K. ( ) voted against the resolutions on party unity and censuring the Workers' Opposition. A Sergeev was on party leaders' list for the Metalworkers' Union central committee in May 1921, but it is unlikely they were the same person.

Shadurskaia, Zoia Leonidovna (1874–1939) was a very close friend of Aleksandra Kollontai since their childhoods in the Russian community of Sofia, Bulgaria. From 1900, she participated in the revolutionary movement. Sometimes resident in St. Petersburg, she also lived long periods abroad in Europe. During several periods in her life, she lived in the same household as Kollontai. She worked in trade missions and on the editorial board of the *Great Soviet Encyclopedia*.

Shats [ ] ( ) was a member of the Metalworkers' Union central committee in 1921.

Shipillo [ ] ( ) was secretary of Nizhegorodsky District Committee and a trade union activist. Party leaders opposed him for candidate membership in the Metalworkers' Union central committee in May 1921; he probably supported the Workers' Opposition.

Shkiriatov, Matvei Fedorovich (1883–1954) was born in Vishniakovo village in Tulskaia Gubernia. He finished primary school and took evening courses in Moscow, where he worked from 1906–11. He joined the RSDRP in 1906 and worked for the party in Moscow and Rostov-on-Don. Often, he was arrested. In 1915–17, he served in the army. After the February 1917 Revolution, he was a member of the Moscow Soviet Ispolkom. He belonged to the Bureau of Military Organisations under the Moscow Committee of the RSDRP(b). During the October Revolution, he was a member of the Tula Military Revolutionary Committee and a member of the Tula Soviet Ispolkom. In 1918, he was secretary of the central committee of the Union of Sewing Industry Workers and by 1920, he had become chair of the Moscow branch of the Sewing Industry Workers' Union central committee. In 1921, he chaired the Central Commission on Verification and Purge of Party Ranks of the CC RCP(b). He held various positions in the Party CCC in 1922–34. He was a member of the collegium of the People's Commissariat of Worker Peasant Inspection of the USSR from 1927–34. He held similar membership and positions in the Committee of Party Control from 1934–39. He was a member of the International Control Commission of the Comintern from 1935–43. From 1939–54, he was a member of the Party CC. He was assistant chair of the Commission of Party Control under the Party CC in 1939–52. He was a member of the Presidium of the CC CPSU in 1952–3 and chaired the Committee of Party Control under the CC CPSU in 1952–4. He died in Moscow.

Shliapnikov, Aleksandr Gavriilovich (1885–1937) was born in Murom, Vladimir province into an Old Believer family. His father, an unskilled worker of the urban estate, drowned when he was three years old. His mother took in washing to support her four children. He completed a three-year primary school, carried out odd jobs, and became an apprentice metalworker at age thirteen. He worked in Murom, Sormovo, and then St. Petersburg, where he participated in the 1901 strike and was blacklisted. He joined the RSDRP the same year and the Bolsheviks in 1903. He carried out party work in Sormovo, St. Petersburg, Murom, and Moscow. During the 1905 Revolution, he led an armed demonstration in Murom. Arrested and imprisoned several times between 1904 and 1907, he went underground in Moscow and St. Petersburg, became a member of the Petersburg Committee, and was sent abroad in early 1908. He met Lenin in Switzerland and moved on to Paris, where he worked in factories and participated in revolutionary socialist politics and trade unions. He began an intimate relationship with Alexandra Kollontai in 1911 that lasted until 1916. He traveled about Western and Northern Europe and re-entered Russia several times during World War I to reconstitute the Russian Bureau of the Bolshevik Party CC and to re-establish communications between Bolshevik leaders abroad and those in Russia. He was coopted into the Party CC. He was the most senior Bolshevik on the scene in Petrograd when the February Revolution began and he helped create the Petrograd Soviet. In 1917, he belonged to the Petrograd Soviet Ispolkom, and he chaired the Petrograd and All-Russian Metalworkers' Unions. After the October Revolution, he was named People's Commissar of Labour and carried out other tasks, of which grain requisitions took him to the south of Russia in summer 1918. This work led to his appointment as Chair of the Revvoensovet of the Caspian-Caucasian Front in 1918–19. He remained chair of the Metalworkers' Union until 1921 and worked in it between his military assignments, one of which took him to the Western Front in late 1919. In 1920, he went abroad to Central and Northern Europe on a trade union mission. Along with some other prominent trade union and industry leaders, he co-organised and co-led the Workers' Opposition in 1920–2; it promoted trade union management of the economy and workerisation of the RCP(b). He served in the Party CC in 1921, but lost his position as chair of the Metalworkers' Union that same year. In 1922, he helped lead an appeal to the Comintern to protest the suppression of worker heterodoxy within the RCP(b). Subsequently, he wrote memoir-histories of the revolutionary movement, held a Soviet diplomatic post in Paris in 1924–5, chaired the Metalloimport Board from 1926–9 which took him on business trips to European countries, led Rosmetizprom in 1931, and worked in Gosplan RSFSR in 1932–3. He was purged from the Party in 1933, arrested in 1935, imprisoned in Verkhneuralsk, exiled to Astrakhan in 1936, rearrested the same year, and executed in 1937 without having confessed.

Shmidt, Vasily Vladimirovich (1886–1938) was born in St. Petersburg, where his mother was a domestic servant. Parts of his childhood were spent in the countryside, as a foster child, or in an orphanage. In 1904, he finished a four-year town school. He participated in the 1905 Revolution and became a Bolshevik by the end of that year, when he also began work as a railway agent and then as a metalworker in railway workshops. He left Russia for Finland in 1907 to escape arrest. In Germany, he did unskilled work and then became a house painter, at which he worked until 1911. Toward the end of 1911, he returned to St. Petersburg, Russia to work for the party, in factories, and participate in the Metalworkers' Union. At the end of 1913, he was arrested but released. In 1914, he was elected secretary of the Petrograd Union of Metalworkers and he joined the Petersburg Committee of the RSDRP(b). After an arrest and two months in jail in 1914, he went to Ekaterinoslav, having been forbidden to live in Petrograd and 26 other cities. There he did factory, insurance, and party work. The Ekaterinoslav party organisation was busted up by the police in the

summer of 1915, but he escaped to Petrograd, where he worked illegally. He served
as secretary of the Petersburg Committee from 1915–17, when not in prison. During
the same period, he was also a Metalworkers' Union leader. Arrested at the end of
1915, he was released in August 1916 and went to work in a factory. At the end of
1916, he was arrested again and freed during the February Revolution. Still serving in
the Petersburg Committee, he was also secretary of the Petrograd Council of Trade
Unions. After the October 1917 Revolution, he served variously as VTsSPS secretary and presidium member, Commissar of Labour, assistant chair of Sovnarkom,
VTsIK member, CC RCP(b) member and candidate member, Director of the Dalugol
Trust. He figured in the Right Opposition of the late 1920s. In 1930–4, he served con-
secutively as assistant USSR People's Commissar of Agriculture, Chief State Arbiter
under Sovnarkom of the USSR, chief of the Khabarovsk Krai Communal/Municipal
Department. In 1934–6, he served simultaneously as chair of the Khabarovsk City
Soviet Ispolkom and as chair of the Primorsk Oblast planning commission. Arrested, purged from the party, and given a ten-year sentence in 1937, he was executed
in 1938.

Shokhanov, G.V. ( ) joined the party in 1912. Perhaps based in Moscow, he signed the Letter of 22. A T.K. Shokhanov joined Miasnikov's Workers' Group, according to Sandu,
but she also provides initials G.K.

Skliznev, Pavel Andreevich (1897–) joined the RSDRP(b) in 1917. Among his positions
after the October 1917 Revolution were board member of the Moscow department
of the Metalworkers' Union, brigade commander and commissar, All-Russian Metalworkers' Union central committee secretary and secretary of the Southern Bureau of
the All-Russian Metalworkers' Union central committee. He supported the Workers'
Opposition.

Skvortsov (Stepanov), Ivan Ivanovich (1870–1928) was born in Maltsevo-Brodovo village in Moscow gubernia and graduated from the Moscow Teachers' Institute in
1890. A revolutionary since 1892, a Social Democrat from 1896, and a member of
the RSDRP since 1898, he was first arrested in 1901. He became a Bolshevik in late
1904. His primary revolutionary work was as a writer and lecturer about history
and economics and he was based in Moscow after 1905. He sought to reconcile the
Bolshevik and Menshevik factions. In 1911, he was exiled to Arkhangelsk Gubernia.
In 1917, he edited *Izvestiia* of the Moscow Soviet and was on the editorial board of the
newspaper *Sotsial-Demokrat*. During the October Revolution, he participated in the
Military Revolutionary Committee in Moscow. After the Bolsheviks took power, he
was the first Commissar of Finance. Then he was on the editorial boards of *Pravda*
and *Kommunist*, and served as assistant chair of the All-Russian Council of Workers' Cooperatives, assistant chair of the State Publishing (Gosizdat) collegium in
1919–20, and chair of Gosizdat in 1921–5. He was senior editor of *Izvestiia* in 1925–
7, assistant senior editor of *Pravda* in 1927–8, and senior editor of *Leningradskaia*

Pravda in 1926–8. Around 1924, he was a member of the board of the Central Union of Consumer Societies of the USSR, a member of the Central Auditing Commission in 1921–5, and a member of the Party CC in 1925–8. He directed the Institute of Lenin under the Party CC in 1926–8, and belonged to the Socialist Academy Presidium. Among his published works was a Russian translation of Marx's *Capital*. He died in Sochi in 1928.

Smilga, Ivar Tenisovich (1892–1938) was born into the family of a farmer who also served as a forest warden in Latvia. He attended realsschule. His father was shot in 1906 as a revolutionary. I.T. became a Bolshevik in 1907. He attended Moscow University, but was expelled. He was arrested and exiled to Siberia in 1915, then freed after the February Revolution. In 1917, the Petersburg Committee of the RSDRP(b) assigned him to do revolutionary work in Kronstadt, where he was a member of the Bolshevik Committee in Kronstadt. He also was a member of VTsIK and of the Party CC (1917–19). During 1917, he belonged to the oblast ispolkom of army, fleet, and workers in Finland. After the Bolshevik seizure of power, he served as a Sovnarkom RSFSR special representative in Finland, a member of the RSFSR Revvoensovet, and as a member of Revvoensovets on many Civil War fronts in 1918–21. He supported Trotsky's proposals on trade unions in 1920–1. He was assistant chair of VSNKh in 1921–3 and in charge of fuel under it. Assistant chair of the State Planning Commission in 1925–6, he served as Rector of the Institute of National Economy named after G.V. Plekhanov in 1925–7. A candidate member of the Party CC in 1922–5, he was a full member in 1926–7. He was purged from the party in 1927 for Trotskyism, exiled to Narym, returned in 1929, and restored to party membership in 1930. He belonged to the VSNKh USSR Presidium in 1930–2 and from 1932–4 was assistant chair of Gosplan USSR. In 1934, he was assistant chair of Gosplan of Central Asia. In 1935 he was arrested and executed in 1938.

Sokolnikov (Brilliant), Grigory Iakovlevich (Girsh Iankelevich) (1888–1939) was born in Poltavskaia Gubernia. His father was a doctor on the railway. He learned to read at home and when his family moved to Moscow, he attended a five-class gymnasium, where he studied Latin and Greek. Harassed by gymnasium administrators for being Jewish, he became radicalised. First he joined self-study circles on political questions and then Marxist circles. He studied at Moscow University Law Department, but did not finish then. He joined the Bolsheviks in 1905 and participated in the December uprising in Moscow. He carried out propaganda work in 1906 and then joined the military-technical bureau of the Moscow Party Committee. Arrested in 1907, he was detained in Butyrka prison and in 1909 permanently exiled to Eniseiskaia Oblast in Siberia. After six weeks, he escaped, fled to Moscow and then Mariampol, and emigrated to Paris in autumn 1909. He lived abroad in France and Switzerland from 1909 until 1917. He met Lenin, went to émigré meetings, and led the worker club *Proletary*. He finished law school in 1914 and earned a doctorate in economics at the Sorbonne in Paris. Later he went to Switzerland. During World War I, he took an internationalist position. He also worked on Trotsky's newspaper *Nashe slovo*. He returned to Russia after the February Revolution together with Lenin, Zinoviev, and others on the sealed train that passed through Germany. He went to Moscow, where he became a member of the Moscow Oblast Bureau of the RSDRP(b) and then joined the editorial board of *Pravda*. He was a member of the CC RSDRP(b) in 1917–18 and of the CC RCP(b) in 1918–19. In 1917, he was a member of the Petrograd Soviet Ispolkom and assistant commissar of the State Bank of the RSFSR. In 1918, he chaired the Soviet delegation to the negotiations with Germany and signed the Brest peace. In 1918, he belonged to the Presidium of VSNKh RSFSR. During 1918–19, he was a member of Revvoensovets of the 2nd army of the Eastern Front, of the Southern Front, and of the 9th Army of the Southern Front. He commanded the 8th army of the Southern-Southeastern Front in 1919–20 and the Turkestan Front in 1920–1. He chaired other party and soviet bodies relating to Turkestan in 1920–2. From 1921, he worked in the Commissariat of Finance of the RSFSR, first as a collegium member, then as first assistant commissar, and subsequently as RSFSR and USSR People's Commissar from 1922–6. He was a member of the Party CC in 1922–30. He also commanded the Turkestan Front in 1922–3. A candidate member of the Politburo in 1924–5, he was also a candidate member of the Ispolkom of the Comintern in 1924–8. He belonged to the New Opposition in 1925 and to the United Opposition in 1926. Assistant chair of the State Planning Commission of the USSR in 1926–8, he chaired the Oil Syndicate of the USSR in 1928–9. From 1929–32, he was ambassador of the USSR to Great Britain. He was a candidate member of the Party CC in 1930–6. He was Assistant Commissar of Foreign Affairs of the USSR in 1933–4. In 1935–6, he was appointed first assistant People's Commissar of the Forestry Industry of the USSR. He was arrested in 1936, given a ten-year sentence in 1937, and murdered in prison in 1939 by other inmates, probably on the initiative of the secret police.

Solovev [ ] ( ) led both the Party Committee and Metalworkers' Union committee in Vyksa. He was nominated by the Vyksa Urban District for membership in the central committee of the Metalworkers' Union in 1921. Party leaders opposed his candidacy and removed him from his leadership post in Vyksa.

Solts, Aron Aleksandrovich (1872–1945) was born in Solenikas in Vilensk Gubernia and studied law at St. Petersburg University until he was expelled in 1899. Having joined the RSDRP in 1898, he carried out party work in St. Petersburg, Vilno, Ekaterinoslav and other cities. He belonged to the Bolshevik Petersburg Committee in 1912–13. The tsarist government arrested him in 1898, 1899, and twice in 1901. He was exiled to Irkutsk Gubernia in 1902 but escaped, only to be arrested again in 1903. After having been freed in 1905, he was arrested again in 1906 and exiled to Tobolsk Gubernia in 1907. Arrested in 1908, he was freed after a month, only to be arrested again in 1909 and freed the same year. Arrested in 1913, he was exiled to Turukhansky Krai, from which he escaped in 1914, was arrested again and sentenced to two years of hard labour. Freed in 1916, he joined the Moscow Bureau of the CC RSDRP(b). In 1917, he was a member of the Moscow Committee of the RSDRP(b) and was on the editorial board of the newspapers *Sotsial-Demokrat* and *Pravda*. He participated in the October Revolution in Moscow. He belonged to the Left Communists in early 1918 on the issue of the Brest peace negotiations. He held high positions in the Party CCC and Supreme Court of RSFSR and USSR from 1921 to 1934. In 1938, he was in the USSR Procurator's office. From 1924–43, he was a member of the CCC of the Communist International. He died in Moscow.

Sosnovsky, Lev Semenovich (1886–1937) was born in Orenburg. He grew up in the bookbindery where his brothers worked; there, he learned to read from an early age. His father had been a Nikolaevsky soldier who served nearly 25 years, who was often beaten and pressured to convert to Orthodoxy, but he remained Jewish. His father was an alcoholic and barely literate, but practiced law in a bar. Possibly mentally abused by his father, his mother was institutionalised for mental illness. L.S. attended gymnasium, but did not finish. He went to work as a pharmacy apprentice after his family split up and his mother died. Work for a very demanding boss stirred in him an interest in Marxism. He started reading *Iskra* and carried out party work in 1903, moving around to various cities and working in pharmacies. He became a Bolshevik in in 1904 in Ekaterinburg. Arrested in 1909, he was taken into the Russian army from 1909–10. Arrested twice in 1913, he was sentenced the second time to exile in Cheliabinsk and freed in 1916. In 1917, he chaired the Urals Oblast Committee of the RSDRP(b) and the Ekaterinburg City Soviet. From 1918–24, he belonged to the VTsIK Presidium. In 1918 and 1924, he edited the newspaper *Bednota* and he was senior director of the Russian Telegraph Agency in 1918–19. He chaired the Ekaterinburg Gubernia Revolutionary Committee in 1918–19 and the Kharkov gubernia RCP(b) committee in 1919–20. He edited the newspaper *Gudok* in 1920–1 and chaired the Agitation-Propaganda Department of the Party CC in 1921–2. He supported Trotsky's position on trade unions in 1920–1. From 1923–4 a member of the Party CCC, he was also on the editorial board of *Pravda* in 1924–7. Having remained a supporter of Trotsky, he was excluded from the party in 1927 and spent 1927–35 in exile. He was arrested in 1929 and freed in 1934. A member of the editorial board of the newspaper *Sotsialisticheskoe zemledelie* in 1934–6, he was restored to the party in 1935, but was purged and rearrested in 1936, and executed in 1937.

Sovetov, Aleksey ( ) served in the Civil War, suffered from tuberculosis, worked in various factory party cells, and belonged to the Bauman District group of oppositionists in the Moscow RCP(b) organisation. He was expelled from the party in 1921.

Stalin (Djugashvili), Iosif Vissarionovich (1878–1953) was born in Gori, Georgia to a shoemaker father. He was of Georgian nationality. He attended but did not finish seminary. He joined the RSDRP in 1898 and became a Bolshevik after the party split. Much of his early career as a revolutionary was in the Caucasus, but he was often arrested and exiled to Siberia or to the north of Russia. Often he escaped from exile. From 1912–53, he was a member of the Party CC. He spent the years 1913 to early 1917 in exile in Eniseisk Gubernia of Siberia. Released from exile after the February 1917 Revolution, he returned to Petrograd to join the Russian Bureau of the Party CC. He was a member of the Party Politburo and Orgburo from their formation until October 1952. He was People's Commissar of Nationalities Affairs from 1917–23. During the Russian Civil War, he belonged to the Revvoensovets of the Southern Front, the Western Front, and the Southwestern Front. He was also a member of the Republic Revvoensovet. In 1918–19 he was in the CC CP(b)U and in 1918 chaired the Central Bureau of Muslim Organisations of the RCP(b). In 1919–22, he was People's Commissar of State Control and Worker-Peasant Inspection. He held many other top positions, among which the most important were General Secretary of the Party CC from 1922–34 and Secretary of the Party CC from 1934–53. From October 1952 to his death in 1953, he was a member of the Bureau of the Presidium of the CC CPSU.

Stepanov [ ] ( ) asked to withdraw his name as a candidate for the Metalworkers' Union central committee in May 1921 on both the lists of the former Workers' Opposition and of the party leadership.

Sulimov, Daniil G. Egorovich (1890–1939) was born into the family of a metalworker in a village attached to the Miniarsky metals factory near Cheliabinsk. After he joined the RSDRP in 1905, he carried out party work in the Urals and was arrested several times by the tsarist government. He served in the Russian army in 1915–17. In 1918–19, he held multiple positions: member of the Presidium of the Oblast Administration of the Urals factories, collegium member of the Mining-Metals Department of VSNKh RSFSR, chair of the Perm City Soviet Ispolkom, member of the Samara Sovnarkhoz, assistant chief of the political section of the 5th Army, chair of the Cheliabinsk Gubernia organisational bureau of the RCP(b), and chair of the Cheliabinsk Gubernia Sovnarkhoz. In 1919–20, he chaired the Cheliabinsk Gubernia Party Committee. He chaired the Southern Urals Factory Administration in 1920–2. He was a candidate CC RCP(b) member in 1921–3 and a full member from 1923–37. In 1921–2, he chaired the Urals Industrial Bureau and was a member of the Urals Bureau of VTsSPS and of the Urals Bureau of the CC RCP(b). He was appointed chair of the Urals Economic Conference in 1923 and chaired the Urals Oblast Soviet Ispolkom in 1923–6. From 1926–7, he was first secretary of the Urals Oblast Party Committee. He was first assistant People's Commissar of Communications of the USSR and a member of the Party CC Orgburo from 1927–30. He chaired the RSFSR Sovnarkom in 1930–7. He was arrested and executed in 1937.

Tarasov, Georgy Fedorovich (1884–1938) was born in Podzolovo village in Moscow region. He was educated to a primary level. He joined the RSDRP(b) in 1914. A member of Dinamo factory committee in 1917, he was elected to Dinamo management board in 1918. He chaired the Moscow branch of the Metalworkers' Union in 1920–1. A supporter of the Workers' Opposition in 1920–2, he was among several people charged with binge drinking by the Moscow Party Control Commission in September 1922. The episode took place at the Moscow offices of the Metalworkers' Union and one worker died from excessive drinking. He faced expulsion from the party, but was given a pass due to his record as a revolutionary. He was not given leadership positions for two years. He worked as deputy head of the council of co-operatives for the disabled in the 1930s. He was arrested and executed in 1938.

Another Tarasov sometimes mentioned in the records about the Workers' Opposition was V.E. Tarasov from Omsk.

Tarygin [ ] ( ) was a member of the central committee of the Metalworkers' Union in May 1921 from Tula. He seems to have sided with party leaders in the conflict within the Metalworkers' Union leadership in May 1921.

Tashkin, A.M. (1892–1942) joined the RSDRP(b) in 1917. After the October 1917 Revolution, he worked in trade unions in the Urals and Siberia. After that, he was an instructor for the central committee of the Metalworkers' Union. Still later, he worked in the People's Commissariat of Heavy Industry and carried out work in economic bodies in the Urals and Leningrad. He belonged to the Workers' Opposition in 1921 and signed the Letter of the 22 to the Comintern in 1922. He was purged from the party in 1937.

Terracini, Umberto (1895–1983) was born in Genoa. He became a socialist in 1911 and joined the Italian Socialist Party (ISP) in 1916. He studied law at the University of Turin, but was arrested and imprisoned for agitating against World War I. After release from prison, he was drafted into the army and served until early 1919. He became a Communist after October 1917 and co-edited the weekly *L'Ordine Nuovo* in Turin. Among the leaders of the ISP from 1920, he joined the leadership of the Italian Communist Party after the split from the ISP in 1921. His first trip to Russia was for the Third Congress of the Comintern in 1921, when he was elected to its Ispolkom and served until 1922. He criticised United Front tactics. He remained in the ECCI leadership until 1924. An Italian parliamentary deputy in 1922–4, he was arrested in 1926 and imprisoned until 1937, when he was deported to the islands Ponza and then Ventotene, where he was freed in 1943 and joined the resistance. Still a communist, he held more moderate positions that brought reprimands from party leaders. He served in the Italian parliament after the war and was elected its president in 1947. He made more trips to the USSR in the 1960s.

Tikhonravov, Nikolai Mikhailovich ( ) voted against resolutions on party unity and anarcho-syndicalist deviation at the Tenth Party Congress. He authored a document that sympathised with the platform of the Workers' Opposition but Shliapnikov did not endorse it.

Tolokontsev, Aleksandr Fedorovich (1889–1937) was born into a peasant farming family in Roskino village in Cherepovetskaia Gubernia. He attended a village school and finished a trade school in 1904. Until age 16, he worked in agriculture, then as an apprentice (1907–10) in artisan shops and small factories in the town Cherepovets. From 1910–12, he worked in a technical school demonstrating work processes. He joined the Metalworkers' Union in 1912 and the RSDRP(b) in 1914. In 1913, he began metals work in St. Petersburg as a skilled metalworker. He worked at various factories, but mainly the Izhorsk factory in 1916–17. He became assistant chair of the Izhorsk factory committee in 1917 and joined the central committee of the Metalworkers' Union in the same year. In 1918–19, he directed the Izhorsk factory and was a member of a district soviet and district party committee in Petrograd. He was assistant chair of the Council of Military Industry and chair of the Central Board of Artilleries Factories from 1919–20. He was a presidium member of VSNKh of the Ukrainian SSR in 1920 and assistant chair of the collegium of the Main Board of the Metals Industry of VSNKh RSFSR in 1921. He was a member of the Workers' Opposition in 1920–1 and signed the Letter of the 22 to the Comintern in 1922. A candidate member of the Party CC in 1924–5, he was a full member from 1925–34. In 1925–6, he chaired the Central Board of State Unified Machinebuilding Factories. He chaired the Chief Military Industry Board of VSNKh USSR in 1926–9 and he was a VSNKh USSR Presidium member in 1926–32. In 1929–30, he chaired the Association of General Machinebuilding of VSNKh USSR. In 1930–2, he was chief of the Main Administration of Machinebuilding and Metalworking Industry of VSNKh USSR and Manager of the All-Union Association of Heavy Machinebuilding of VSNKh USSR. From 1932–4, he was a member of the collegium of the People's Commissariat of Heavy Machinebuilding of the USSR. A factory director from 1934–7, he was also chief of the Main Military Industry Board of the People's Commissariat of Heavy Industry of the USSR. He was arrested and executed in 1937.

Tomsky (Efremov), Mikhail Pavlovich (1880–1936) was born into a poor family of the urban estate in Kolpino, Petersburg Gubernia. His father was a metalworker, but his mother divorced him due to his alcoholism and abuse of her. Tomsky was registered as illegitimate, because he was born after the divorce. He finished a three-year primary school in St. Petersburg, then went to work in a box factory, where he lost a finger and was let go. He worked in a tobacco factory, returned to the box factory, and then became employed in a metalworking factory. He participated in a strike as a metalworker, then became an apprentice chromolithographer. By age 21, he was a skilled chromolithographer. He began reading socialist literature in 1903 and joined a Bolshevik circle in 1904. He participated in the 1905 Revolution in St. Petersburg and Revel, where he was elected to the Revel Council of Elders to negotiate with factory bosses. He helped organise the Revel Soviet of Workers' Deputies and the Metalworkers' Union there. Arrested in 1906, he was imprisoned and then exiled to

Narymsky Krai in Siberia. He escaped to Tomsk and returned illegally to St. Petersburg, where he was a union organiser. He was elected to the RSDRP(b) Petersburg Committee in 1907, went to the London Party Congress, and returned to Russia, where he was arrested, imprisoned and released. He was arrested again in 1908. He went to Paris in 1909 to participate in a meeting of the editorial board of *Proletary*. After that, he went to Moscow, where he revived the Bolshevik party organisation. Upon returning to St. Petersburg from Odessa at the end of 1909, he was arrested again and sentenced to hard labour in Butyrka Prison. There he studied Marxism. In 1916, he was exiled to Irkutsk Gubernia. After the February Revolution, he went first to Moscow and then to Petrograd, where he was a member of the Petersburg Bolshevik Committee. In mid-1917 he returned to Moscow to edit the journal *Metallist*. In December 1917, he was elected chair of the Moscow Council of Trade Unions. He also edited the VTsSPS journal *Professionalnyi vestnik*. In 1918, he was elected to the VTsSPS presidium and then was elected chair of VTSPS until 1921. In that year, he was sent to chair the Turkestan commission of the VTsIK and Sovnarkom RSFSR. Upon his return in December 1921, he became secretary of VTsSPS. Later in 1922, he resumed his position as VTsSPS chair and remained such until 1929. He was a member of the Council of Worker and Peasant Defence of the RSFSR in 1918–20 and a member of the collegium of the People's Commissariat of Labour in 1918. From 1919–34, he was a Party CC member. He was a member of the Party Orgburo in 1921 and from 1922-4. He was a Party Politburo member from 1922–30. He was General Secretary of the International Council of Trade Unions and a member of the ECCI in 1920–1. He led a trade union delegation to London in 1924. From 1923–9, he was in the Council of Labour and Defence of the USSR. After being removed from VTsSPS for his participation in the 'Right Opposition' together with Bukharin and Rykov, he chaired the All-Union Association of Chemicals Industry and was assistant chair of VSNKh of the USSR from 1929–32. He was chief of Gosizdat from 1932–6 and a candidate member of the Party CC from 1934–6. Fearing arrest, he committed suicide in 1936.

Tretiakov [ ] ( ) was a trade unionist from Tula.

Trotsky (Bronshtein), Lev Davidovich (1879–1940) was born in Ianovka village, Kherson gubernia, Ukraine. He studied at Odessa realschule and finished his secondary education in Nikolaev. He became a socialist in 1897 and joined the RSDRP in 1898. In 1898, he was arrested and exiled to Irkutsk Gubernia for for years. In 1902, he fled abroad. He sided with the Mensheviks in 1903. In 1905, he returned to Russia. During the 1905 Revolution, he chaired the St. Petersburg Soviet. He was arrested again toward the end of the year and exiled to Tobolsk Gubernia in 1906, but he escaped in 1907. During World War I, he took an internationalist position against the war and supported the Zimmerwald movement. He returned to Russia in 1917, joined the Bolsheviks, and was elected to their CC, of which he remained a member until

1927. Imprisoned after the July 1917 uprising, upon release he was soon elected chair of the Petrograd City Soviet Ispolkom. He chaired the Petrograd Military Revolutionary Committee. After the October Revolution he was People's Commissar of Foreign Affairs in 1917–18, a member of the Politburo in 1917–26, Chair of the Supreme Military Council in 1918, People's Commissar of War and People's Commissar of the Navy in 1918–23, chair of the Revolutionary Military Council of the Republic and the Union in 1918–25, an Orgburo member in 1919–20, temporary People's Commissar of Communications in 1920, chair of the central committee of the Union of Transport Workers in 1920–1, People's Commissar of Food Supply in 1921, People's Commissar of Military and Navy Affairs of the USSR in 1923–5, and Party CC Orgburo member in 1923–4. He was in the ECCI in 1920–4 and a member of the Communist International's Presidium until 1927. He chaired the Chief Concessions Committee of the USSR in 1925–7 and was a VSNKh USSR presidium member in 1925–6. In 1925, he was chief of the Electrotechnical board of VSNKh USSR and chair of the scientific-technical board of industry. In 1926, he chaired the Politburo's commission on China. Perhaps the leading oppositionist figure in the RCP(b) and VKP(b) from 1923–7, he was expelled from the party in 1927, exiled to Alma-Ata in 1928, and expelled from the USSR in 1929. He lived in Turkey from 1929–33. His Soviet citizenship was taken away in 1932. He called for a new international in 1933. From 1933–5, he lived in France and in Norway from 1935–6. In 1937, he co-founded the Fourth International and moved to Mexico, where he lived until he was assassinated by Stalin's agent in 1940.

Tsiurupa, Aleksandr Dmitrievich (1870–1928) was born in Aleshkakh, Tavricheskaia Gubernia, into the family of an office worker of the Aleshkakh town authority. He finished primary school and the town school. His family moved to Kherson, where he studied at the agricultural school and joined a revolutionary circle. He was active as a revolutionary in Ufa, Kharkov, Tula, and other cities. In 1893, he was sentenced to six months in prison and four years under police supervision. He was imprisoned again in 1895. He moved to Simbirsk in 1896, where he worked as a statistician in the gubernia zemstvo. In 1897, he was in Ufa, where he worked with exiles and met Lenin for the first time. He joined the RSDRP in 1898. More arrests and exiles followed, interspersed by work as an agronomist in Ufa for the city food supply board. His places of exile included Olonetskaia Gubernia. He was in Ufa when the February 1917 Revolution occurred and became a member of the Ufa Unified Committee of the RSDRP, a member of the Ufa Soviet Ispolkom, chair of the Ufa City Council, and chair of the Ufa Gubernia food supply committee. During the October Revolution, he participated in the Ufa Military Revolutionary Committee. Afterwards, he became assistant People's Commissar of Food Supply and in early 1918 the People's Commissar of Food Supply, which he remained until the end of 1921. Also in 1918–21, he served as Director of the Food Requisitions Army of the People's Commissariat of Food Supply. From late 1921–8, he was assistant chair of Sovnarkom and of the Council of Labour and Defence of the RSFSR and then USSR. He served as People's Commissar of Worker-Peasant Inspection of the RSFSR in 1922–3. A member of the Party CC from 1923–8, he simultaneously was assistant chair of Sovnarkom. He chaired the State Planning Commission in 1923–5 and was People's Commissar of Foreign and Internal Trade for several months in 1925–6.

Uglanov, Nikolai A. (1886–1940) was born in Fedoritskoe village in Iaroslavskaia Gubernia. He became a member of the RSDRP in 1907 and worked for it in St. Petersburg. He served in the Russian army from 1908–11 and 1914–16, when he was wounded and demobilised. In 1917, he was secretary of the Petrograd Union of Commercial and Industrial Employees and worked in the Petrograd Military Revolutionary Committee. After the October 1917 Revolution, he chaired the commission on organising food requisitions brigades and the Petrograd Okrug commission on struggle against deserterism. He was a military commissar during the Russian Civil War. In 1921, he worked as senior secretary of the Petrograd Gubernia Party Committee. He participated in suppressing the Kronstadt Uprising as military commissar of the Northern group of forces of the Kronstadt Front. In 1921–2, he was a member of the Northern Oblast Bureau of the CC RCP(b) and chair of the Petrograd Council of Trade Unions. He was a candidate Party CC member in 1921–2 and a full member from 1923–30. In Nizhegorod in 1922, he was chief of the organisational department of the Nizhegorod Gubernia Party Committee and assistant senior secretary of the Nizhegorod Gubernia Party Committee. He served as senior secretary of the Nizhegorod Gubernia Party Committee, 1922–4. He served as senior secretary of the Moscow Gubernia Party Committee, 1924–8 and as a secretary of the Party CC, 1924–9. He was an Orgburo member in 1924–9 and a candidate member of the Politburo from 1926–9. From 1928–30, he served as People's Commissar of Labour of the USSR. As a prominent member of the Right Opposition, his fate took a downturn after 1930. He served from 1930–2 as chair of the Astrakhan State Fishing Trust and in 1932 as a lower-level official in the People's Commissariat of Industry of the USSR. In 1932, he was purged from the party, because he was suspected of involvement in the Riutin group. He worked briefly in early 1933 at Znamensky mines in Western Siberian Krai, before he was arrested, yet was soon released. From 1933–6, he managed the Fishing Trust Association in Tobolsk. Restored to the party ranks in 1934, he was expelled again in 1936, arrested the same year, and executed in 1937.

Urquhart, John Leslie (1874–1933) was born to Scottish parents in the Ottoman Empire, where his father was involved in trade. J.S. was educated in engineering and chemistry. He moved to Baku in 1902 to manage a petroleum company and served as British Vice-Consul there during the 1905 Revolution. Together with Herbert Hoover, he was involved in mining operations in Russia before World War I as chair of the Russo-Asiatic Corporation. Although he strongly opposed the Bolsheviks and advocated for Allied intervention in the Russian Civil War, he attempted unsuccessfully in 1921 to obtain a mining concession from the Soviet government to restore control over properties the Russo-Asiatic Corporation had leased before 1917. He continued to seek concessions during the NEP Era, but shifted his attentions to Australia later in the 1920s. He died in London.

Vainberg (Veinberg), Gavriil Davydovich (1891–1946) was born in Podolskaia Gubernia into the urban estate. In 1903–8 he was a metalworking apprentice and metalworker in Mogilev. He joined the RSDRP(b) in 1906. He worked as a candy maker in a confectionery in Kiev in 1908–11. From 1911–15, he made furniture in a factory, made plywood, and was a confectioner in Kiev, Odessa, Mogilev, and Ekaterinoslav. He served 1915–17 in exile in Eniseiskaia Gubernia. Having been released in February 1917, he went to Petrograd to work as a metalworker in Petrogradsky pipe factory Prometei. From December 1917 to March 1918, he was secretary of the central board of the Union of Metalworkers in Petrograd. He was in the VSNKh presidium 1918–20, a VTsSPS instructor 1920–1, and head of the economic department of the Metalworkers' Union central committee in Moscow. In 1921–8 he worked in Petrograd, then Leningrad, in Metalworkers' Union and VTsSPS positions. He returned to work in Moscow in 1928, first as chair of the central committee of the Foodworkers' Union and as secretary of VTsSPS from 1929–37. He directed a pasta industry organisation from 1937–42. He retired on disability in 1942 and died in Moscow in 1946.

Vasilev, Antony Efimovich (1885–1970) was born to a poor peasant family in Pskov gubernia and completed a three-year primary school. When he was thirteen, he followed his father into work at the Putilov factory, becoming a skilled metalworker after some time there. He joined the RSDRP(b) in 1904 and participated in the 1905 Revolution. From 1908–13, he was in the Narvsky Raikom, the committee of the factory Aivaz, and a member of the Petersburg Bolshevik Committee. Often arrested, he was in Arkhangelsk, Riga, and Finland, but he left Petrograd for Rostov-on-Don in 1916 and worked at the Aksai factory. When the February Revolution occurred, he returned to Petrograd to chair the Putilov factory committee, in which capacity he assured sufficient fuel supplies to keep the factory working. He was in the Narvsky-Petergofsky District Committee of the RSDRP(b) in 1917 and a delegate to the 7th All-Russian Conference of the RSDRP(b). He helped organise Red Guard detachments, was a member of the Military Revolutionary Committee of his district, and participated in the attack on the Winter Palace. When the Bolsheviks nationalised the Putilov factory, Vasilev became its provisional director under the tutelage of the engineer A.P. Serebrovsky. It was not long before he returned to lead the factory committee and an engineer became factory director. During the Civil War, he participated in the defence of Petrograd. Later, he chaired the board of heavy industry factories in Petrograd, was a member of the collegium of the Council of Military

Industry in Moscow, and he chaired Gomza in Moscow. He was a member of VTsIK. He signed the theses of the Workers' Opposition, but continued to work in economic posts. He retired in 1931 due to a nervous system disorder.

Veprintsev, Nikolai Aleksandrovich ( ) was in P.P. Smidovich's Marxist circle and then in N.K. Krupskaia's circle in St. Petersburg. He joined the RSDRP(b) in 1903; he soon became a professional revolutionary under the name 'Peterburzhets'. He was directed to Baku for revolutionary work and there he met Stalin, with whom he may have had a conflict. Arrested and exiled, he headed the Metalworkers' Union of the Urals after the October Revolution. He left the party due to his disagreement with the dispersal of the Constituent Assembly. He apparently was merciful to former government officials in Zlatoust, for which he was arrested and sentenced to be shot, but saved by a telegram from Lenin. He returned to the party in 1921. He led the All-Union Energy Commission in the 1920s. Arrested in 1932, he was exiled to Barnaul, given another sentence and sent to Vorkuta, from which he was released in 1940 due to illness. He was permitted to live in Livna (Brod) and died in a hospital in Morshchansk in 1941, having fled the German attack.

Vladimirov, Mikhail Petrovich (Mednichikhin) (1880–1938) was born into a peasant family in Belavka, Nizhegorodskaia Gubernia. He studied in a church parish school. While he was working in Sormovo factories in 1899, he joined the RSDRP. He was first arrested in 1901, imprisoned, and then released under police supervision. He participated in a 1 May 1902 demonstration in Sormovo. He came to the attention of the police again in 1903 and was exiled to Vologodskaia Gubernia for three years. He escaped in January 1905, was arrested in February in Ivanovo-Voznesensk, and returned to Vologodskaia Gubernia to serve out his sentence. He was freed in the October 1905 amnesty. He went to Moscow in November 1905 and participated in the December armed uprising. Arrested afterwards, he spent three months imprisoned. He worked in the Metalworkers' Union and the Union of Town Workers and Office Personnel from 1906. He participated in strikes in 1906–7 and joined the Central Bureau of Trade Unions. In 1907, he moved to St. Petersburg and in early 1908 was arrested and sent to Nizhny Novgorod under police supervision. He left there and went to Baku. In December 1908, he was arrested in Grozny and in July 1909 sentenced to hard labour for four years. He was permanently resettled in 1913 in Eastern Siberia, from which he escaped in 1914. He lived in Riga and Petrograd, and worked in a factory in the Urals. He became a member of the Petersburg Committee of the Bolshevik Party. Several months before the February 1917 Revolution, he arrived in Moscow and entered the bureau of the Moscow Committee of the Bolshevik Party. During the February Revolution, he participated in a general political strike, helped organise the Moscow Soviet and joined its Ispolkom. At the end of June 1917, he was elected to the temporary central committee of the All-Russian Union of Metalworkers. Relinquishing his position in the Moscow Soviet Executive, he transferred to

Petrograd for work in the central committee of the Metalworkers' Union until 1922. He chaired the central committee of the oblast bureau of the union in the Urals. In 1923, he was transferred to work in the economy. He was assistant chair of the Main Administration of the Metals Industry (GUMP) for eleven months. Then he was a member of the board of Tsentrosoiuz and of the Presidium of Tserabsektsiia. In 1924, he was elected to the VTsSPS Presidium. Until 1927, he led the wage rates department in VTsSPS. At the same time, he replaced Tomsky as a member of the Council of Labour and Defence. He was a candidate member of the Presidium of VTsIK until 1931. In 1927, he was elected chair of the central committee of the Union of Local Transport Workers. From February 1930, he was a member of the board of Soiuzstankoinstrument. From 1932, he worked in the Party CCC and Worker Peasant Inspectorate. He was chief of the sector of abrasives of Glavstankoinstrument of the People's Commissariat of Heavy Industry of the USSR. He was arrested and executed in 1938.

Vorobev, [Mikhail Aleksandrovich?] ( ) was a member of the Metalworkers' Union central committee in 1921. He seems to have been acceptable to both party leaders and the former Workers' Opposition.

Voroshilov, Klim Efremovich (1884–1969) was born in Verkhee village in Ekaterinoslavskaia Gubernia. His father was a railway guard who had been a soldier and moved from job to job often, because he had conflicts with his bosses. Voroshilov had to work hard as a young child. He was beaten badly by a group of adult peasants at one job, because he was chosen for an assignment over one of the peasants. He could not read before he started a two-year zemstvo school at age twelve, but he progressed quickly, learning to read Russian classical literature and science. He remembered being the teacher's favourite. After he began factory work in 1896, he continued reading. His political work started in 1897–8, then he led a strike in 1899 and was arrested. Blacklisted, he could not be hired anywhere in the Donbas for three years. In 1903, he finally found work at Gartman factory in Lugansk, but police expelled him from the town after several months. He joined the party officially in 1903 and entered the Lugansk party committee in 1904. In 1905, he got work at Gartman factory again and led the factory's Bolshevik organisation until 1907. He participated in a strike in 1905 and was elected chair of the factory council. Arrested, beaten badly, and imprisoned, he went underground upon his release. In 1906, he attended the party congress in Stockholm and met Lenin there. In 1906–7, he was involved in transporting arms from Finland and set up bomb labs in Lugansk. He went to the party's London Congress in 1907 and in the same year attended the All-Russian Conference of Metalworkers' Unions in Moscow. Arrested again and exiled to Arkhangelsk, he fled exile and went to Baku to work for the party. There he worked with Stalin. Upon arriving in St. Petersburg, he was again arrested and returned to Arkhangelsk. Released in 1912, he was re-arrested and sent to Cherdynsky Krai. Freed in 1914, he worked at the Tsaritsynsky arms factory. He had to leave for Petrograd to avoid conscription and went into hiding in the underground. After the February 1917 Revolution, he was a member of the Petrograd Soviet and the Russian Bureau of the RSDRP(b) CC and edited the newspaper *Donetsky proletary*. He was a delegate to the Sixth Party Congress and chaired the Lugansk Soviet, City Duma, and Party Committee in 1917. He was a delegate to the Democratic Assembly and a member of the Constituent Assembly. He entered the government of Ukraine in 1918. His military work began in March 1918 and included the posts of commander of the 5th Ukrainian Army and the 14th Army. He was also on the Tsaritsyn Front. At the end of 1919, he was a member of the Revvoensovet of the 1st Cavalry. In 1921, he became a member of the CC RCP(b). He commanded the North Caucasus Military District in 1921–4. In 1924, he was in the Presidium of the USSR Revvoensovet. In 1924–5, he commanded the Moscow Military District. From 1925 on, he was People's Commissar of Military and Naval Affairs and chair of the All-Union Revvoensovet. He became a Politburo member in 1926. Other positions included membership in the Bureau of the Moscow Party Committee, Presidium member of the Moscow Soviet, chair of Moscow Aviation and Chemical Defence and Industry Society (Aviakhim), and assistant chair of Aviakhim RSFSR. From 1940, he was assistant chair of Sovnarkom USSR and chaired its Committee of Defence. From 1946, he was assistant chair of the Council of Ministers of the USSR. From 1953–60, he was a member of the Presidium of the Supreme Soviet of the USSR. From 1952–60, he was a member of the Presidium of the CPSU CC. Having been forced out of the party leadership along with Molotov et al in 1960, he retired and died in 1969.

Zalutsky, Petr Antonovich (1887–1937) was born into a peasant family in Krucha township, Mogilev Oblast and studied in school for one year. He became a metalworker and joined the RSDRP in 1904, becoming a Bolshevik in 1907. At some point, he was close to the Socialist Revolutionaries. Arrested in 1912 and exiled to Vologodskaia Gubernia, he escaped in 1914, was rearrested in 1915 and exiled to Irkutsk Gubernia, from which he escaped in 1916. He was a member of the Russian Bureau of the Bolshevik Party CC in 1916–17. In 1917, he also belonged to the Bolshevik Petersburg Committee, the Petrograd Soviet, and the Petrograd Military Revolutionary Committee. He did political work for the Red Army in 1918–20. From 1919–20, he chaired the Kursk Gubernia Revolutionary Committee. In 1920, he chaired the Kherson Gubernia Revolutionary Committee and the Kherson Gubernia Committee of the CP(b)U, both centred in Nikolaev. He also was a member of the Temporary CC CP(b)U in 1920. A candidate member of the RCP(b) CC in 1920–2, he was a member of the CC Orgburo in 1921–2. He was also a member of the VTsIK Presidium in the same years and was secretary of VTsIK in 1921. He led the Organisational Instructor Department of the CC RCP(b) in 1921–2. In 1922, he was secretary of the Urals Bureau of the CC RCP(b). From 1922–5, he was senior secretary of the Petrograd (then Leningrad) Gubernia Committee of the RCP(b) and secretary of the Northwestern Bureau of the Party CC. He was a Party CC member in 1923–5 and a candidate member of the CC Secretariat in 1924–5. In 1927, he was excluded from the party, but was restored to its ranks in 1928. He chaired the Nizhne-Volzhsk District Sovnarkhoz in 1928–32. In 1932–3, he was chief of construction of the Shaturskaia State District Electrical Station (Kashira) and in 1934 manager of the 'Stroimashina' Trust. Arrested in 1934 after the Kirov murder, he was given a five-year sentence in 1935, rearrested in December 1936, and executed in 1937.

Zatonsky, Vladimir Petrovich (1888–1938) was born in Lysets village in Podolsk Gubernia. His father was a volost clerk who helped begin the cooperative movement in Kamenets. During his years in gymnasium, he joined a student RSDRP organisation in 1905 and carried out party and trade union work among tailors' apprentices. He facilitated the flight of fellow RSDRP members abroad. After finishing gymnasium, in 1906 he enrolled in Kiev University, where he studied physics and chemistry. Although he was arrested several times and expelled from the university twice, he graduated in 1912. Having first worked as lab assistant, he was then invited to to teach physics in Kiev Polytechnical Institute. By 1914, he headed the chemistry laboratory in addition to teaching. During World War I, he was not very active in the party, but was neither a pacifist nor a defencist. In February 1917, he joined the Kiev organisation of Bolsheviks and by May 1917 was elected to the Kiev RSDRP(b) Committee, becoming its chair by the end of the year. Around the same time he belonged to the Kiev Military Revolutionary Committee and was appointed People's Secretary of Enlightenment of the Ukrainian People's Republic. In 1918, he served as People's Secretary of Foreign Affairs of the Ukrainian People's Republic and subsequently that year chaired the Central Ispolkom of the republic. In 1918–21, he held leadership roles in various military councils. A member of the CC CP(b)U from 1918–27, he was a CC CP(b)U Politburo member from 1924–7, Orgburo member from 1925–7, and secretary from 1925–7. His other top positions in the 1920s included chair of the All-Ukrainian Union of Cooperative Societies, People's Commissar of Enlightenment of the Ukrainian SSR, and member of the USSR Revolutionary Military Council in 1924–5. He became an academician of the Academy of Sciences of the Ukrainian SSR in chemistry in 1929. From 1927–33, he chaired the CCC of CP(b)U, served as People's Commissar of Worker Peasant Inspection of the Ukrainian SSR, and was assistant chair of Sovnarkom of the Ukrainian SSR. He also served in the presidium of the CCC of the VKP(b) from 1927–34. Chief editor of the journal *Chervonyi shliakh* from 1927–30, he chaired the Committee on Chemicalisation of the Ukrainian SSR from 1928–34 and was People's Commissar of Enlightenment of the Ukrainian SSR from 1933–7. A Politburo and CC member of the CP(b)U from 1933–8 and a candidate CC member of the All-Union Communist Party during the same years, he was arrested in 1937 and shot in 1938.

Zelensky, Isaak Abramovich (1890–1938) was born in Saratov into a tailor's family and received a primary school education at home, after which he began working in a hat-making workshop. He joined the RSDRP(b) in 1906 and carried out revolutionary work in the underground. Arrested multiple times, he was confined for a total of eight years. His places of exile included Orenburg Gubernia, Narymsky Krai, and Irkutsk Gubernia. In 1915, he was secretary of the hospital fund in Sormovo. He escaped from exile in Irkutsk in January 1917 and made his way to Moscow. After the October Revolution, he chaired the Basmanny District Soviet in Moscow until August 1918. In 1918–20, he led the Department of Districts of the Moscow Soviet, the Moscow Food Department, was a member of the collegium of the People's Commissariat of Food Supply of the RSFSR, and was senior secretary of the Moscow Gubernia Party Committee. He was a member of the collegium of the People's Commissariat of Food Suply of the RSFSR in 1920–1. In 1921–2, he was a candidate member of the Party CC and a full member, 1922–37. He was a candidate Orgburo member in 1922–4 and a candidate Secretariat member in 1923–4. He was a CC secretary in 1924 and a full member of the Orgburo in 1924. In 1921–4, he was senior secretary of the Moscow Gubernia Committee of the RCP(b). He chaired the Central Territorial Commission on National State Border Demarcation of Central Asia in 1924. From 1924–31, he was chair and senior secretary of the Central Asian Bureau of the Party CC. In 1925, he was a member of the Revvoensovet of the Turkestan Front. He was CC Secretary of the Communist Party of Uzbekistan, 1929–31. Tsentrosoiuz president from 1931 until his arrest in 1937, he was executed in 1938.

Zetkin, Clara (1857–1933) was born in Saxony, where her father was a teacher. She studied in Leipzig to become a teacher, but in 1878 became involved with a socialist group. Among her comrades was her first husband, Osip Zetkin, a Russian. She lived in exile in Switzerland and Paris in the 1880s and co-founded the Second International in 1889. She returned to Germany in 1890. A vocal proponent of women's emancipation, she worked closely with Rosa Luxemburg in the left wing of the German Socialist Party (SPD). An internationalist during World War I, she joined the USPD upon its founding in 1917 and left it in 1919, when she joined the German Communist Party. She attended the Third Congress of the Comintern in 1921 and was a member of the ECCI from 1922 on. Although she did not always march in step with Soviet Communist Party policies toward the international communist movement, she was not forced out of the Comintern or forced to renounce her views. She served as a deputy in the Reichstag from 1920–32, but left Germany around the time of Hitler's rise to power. She died in a Moscow sanatorium.

Zheltov, I.I. (1890–1939) joined the party in 1917 and participated in the armed uprising in Moscow during the October Revolution. Afterwards, he carried out work in soviets, trade unions, and economic bodies. Among his positions were Moscow Bauman District Soviet chair, factory director in Bezhitsa, Moscow Gubernia Trade Union

Council chair, assistant chair of the Uzbekistan Sovnarkom, and Narkomtrud USSR collegium member. In 1931, he was appointed director of factory construction in Cheliabinsk and Ufa and manager of Tsentrorud trust.

Ziese, Max (1882?–?) was active in the Union of German Metalworkers through its Berlin branch and belonged to its plumbers' section. In the early 1920s, he served as secretary of the Central European Bureau of the International Trade Union Council, which was the predecessor of the Red International of Labour Unions (Profintern). Only in 1930 did he join the Central Council of the Profintern. He may have worked at Profintern's Moscow headquarters in the 1930s. He may have left the communist movement by 1936 or he may have assumed covert activities. If, as some secondary sources report, Ziese was really an alias for Solomon Vladimirovich Mikhelson-Manuilov ('Uncle Max' or 'Black'), he may have become a Comintern agent in the United States in the 1930s. Mikhelson-Manuilov was born in Latvia in 1893.

Zinoviev (Radomyslsky), Grigory Evseevich (Ovsei-Gersh Aronovich) (1883–1936) was born in Elisavetgrad, Khersonskaia gubernia. His father owned a small dairy farm and he received his early education at home. At ages 14–15, he worked as a tutor and office clerk. He became a revolutionary in the late 1890s. Having joined the RSDRP in 1901, he went abroad in 1902, spending time in Berlin, Paris, and Switzerland. He became a Bolshevik in 1903, the same year when he met Lenin. He studied in the Chemistry and Philosophy Departments of the University of Bern in Switzerland and worked in a chemistry laboratory in Bern. Having returned to Russia in 1903, he left again at the end of 1904. He studied at Berlin University. He returned to Russia in 1905 to participate in the revolution in St. Petersburg, fell sick, and went abroad again. He studied in law school, but quit in 1906 and went to St. Petersburg, where he carried out party work among the metalworkers. He was elected to the Petersburg Bolshevik Party Committee and to the CC in 1907. In 1908, fellow party members sent him abroad, where he remained until 1917. An internationalist and Lenin's collaborator during World War I, he served on the editorial boards of *Proletary* and *Sotsial Demokrat*. Returning to Petrograd with Lenin in April 1917, he joined the Ispolkoms of the Petrograd Soviet and of the All-Russian Soviet. He chaired the Petrograd (then Leningrad) Soviet from 1917 to 1926, chaired the Comintern from 1919 to 1926 and was a Politburo member. After Lenin died, he was in the triumvirate of leaders along with Kamenev and Stalin, but he fell out with Stalin in 1925 and in 1926–7 allied with Trotsky. He was expelled from the party in 1927, readmitted in 1928 after recandation, and expelled again in 1932 and 1934. Tried in the first Moscow show trial of the Great Terror, he was executed in 1936.

Bibliography

Newspapers and Journals

Bolshevik
Izvestiia
Izvestiia TsK RKP(*b*)
Luch
Metallist
Pravda

Archives

Hoover Institution Library & Archives, Stanford University, California. Archives of the Soviet Communist Party and Soviet State: Microfilm Collection, Russian State Archives of Social and Political History (Rossiiskii gosudarstvennyi arkhiv sotsialno-politicheskoi istorii – RGASPI).

State Archive of the Russian Federation (*Gosudarstvennyi Arkhiv Rossiiskoi Federatsii –* GARF)

fond 130   Council of People's Commissars (Sovnarkom)
fond 382   Commissariat of Labour (Narkomtrud)
fond 5451   Bureau of the Communist Faction of the All-Russian Council of Trade Unions
fond 5469   Central Committee of the All-Russian Union of Metalworkers

Central Archive of the Federal Security Service of the Russian Federation (*Tsentralnyi arkhiv Federalnoi Sluzhby Bezopasnosti Rossiiskoi Federatsii –* TsA FSB)
R33718, d. 499061, Moscow Group of the 'Workers' Opposition' (56 vols.)
vols. 3–4, investigatory materials on A.G. Shliapnikov
vol. 5, investigatory materials on S.P. Medvedev
vol. 12, material evidence on A.G. Shliapnikov
vol. 13, material evidence on S.P. Medvedev
vol. 14, material evidence on I.I. Nikolaenko, Shliapnikov, Medvedev, and others
vols. 36–43, materials confiscated from S.P. Medvedev

Russian State Archive of Social-Political History (*Rossiiskii Gosudarstvennyi arkhiv sotsialno-politicheskoi istorii –* RGASPI)

fond 2   Lenin (Ulianov) Vladimir Ilich, 1870–1924
fond 5   Secretariat of V.I. Lenin, 1917–24
fond 17   Central Committee of the Communist Party of the Soviet Union, 1898,
          1903–91
fond 44   Ninth Conference of the Russian Communist Party, 1920
fond 47   Eleventh Conference of the Russian Communist Party, 1921
fond 48   Eleventh Congress of the Russian Communist Party, 1922
fond 76   Dzerzhinsky, Feliks Edmundovich, 1877–1926
fond 82   Molotov, Viacheslav Mikhailovich, 1890–1986
fond 95   Communist Faction of the All-Russian Central Council of Trade Unions,
          1918–24
fond 99   Communist Faction of the Central Committee of the All-Russian Metal-
          workers' Union, 1918–25
fond 134 Kollontai, Aleksandra Mikhailovna, 1872–1952
fond 304 Shliapnikov, Aleksandr Gavriilovich, 1885–1937
fond 589 Commission of Party Control, 1934–52;
          Committee of Party Control (KPK), 1952–91
          opis 3, delo 9102 Medvedev, Sergei Pavlovich
          opis 3, delo 9103 Shliapnikov, Aleksandr Gavriilovich
fond 593 Twenty-Third Congress of the Communist Party of the Soviet Union, 1966
fond 671 Ezhov, Nikolai Ivanovich, 1895–1938

Central Archive of Social Movements of the City of Moscow (*Tsentralnyi arkhiv obsh-
chestvennykh dvizhenii goroda Moskvy* – TsAODM)
fond 3   Moscow Committee of the Russian Social Democratic Workers' Party (Bol-
          sheviks), 1917–29
fond 63   Bauman District Committee of the All-Union Communist Party, city of
          Moscow
fond 88   Frunzensky (fmr. Khamovnichesky) District Committee of the All-Union
          Communist Party, city of Moscow
fond 267 Primary VKP(b) organisation, Moscow State Hydroelectric Station, Kirov
          raion

Central State Security Archive of Ukraine (*Galuzevy Derzhavny arkhiv Sluzhbi Bezpeki
Ukraini* – GDA SBU).
fond 13   Investigative materials on cases
          delo 1078 Investigative materials on the case of the counterrevolutionary
          organisation 'Workers' Opposition' in Ukraine, Kiev, 1937

Central State Archive of Public Organisations of Ukraine (*Tsentralnyi derzhavnyi arkhiv
hromadskykh obiednan Ukrainy* – TsDAHO)

fond 1   Central Committee of the Communist Party (Bolshevik) of Ukraine
fond 23   Society of Former Political Prisoners and Exiles

Party Congresses and Conferences

Kommunisticheskii Internatsional 1922, *Tretii vsemirnyi kongress Kommunisticheskogo Internatsionala: stenograficheskii otchet*, Petrograd: Gosizdat.

RKP(b) 1933, *Desiatyi syezd RKP(b), 8–16 marta 1921 goda: protokoly*, Moscow, Partizdat.

RKP(b) 1934, *Deviatyi syezd RKP(b), mart–aprel 1920 g., Protokoly syezdov i konferentsii Vsesoiuznoi Kommunisticheskoi partii (b)*, edited by N.L. Meshcheriakov, Moscow: Partiinoe izdatelstvo.

RKP(b) 1959, *Vosmoi syezd RKP(b), mart 1919 goda: protokoly*, Moscow: Gospolitizdat.

RKP(b) 1960, *Deviatyi syezd RKP(b), mart–aprel 1920 goda: protokoly*, Moscow: Politizdat.

RKP(b) 1961, *Odinnadtsatyi syezd RKP(b), mart–aprel 1922 goda: stenograficheskii otchet*. Moscow: Politizdat.

RKP(b) 1963, *Desiatyi syezd RKP(b), mart 1921 goda: stenograficheskii otchet*, Moscow: Politizdat.

RKP(b) 1968, *Dvenadtsatyi syezd RKP(b), 17–24 April 1923: stenograficheskii otchet*, Moscow: Politizdat.

RKP(b) 1972, *Deviataia konferentsiia RKP(b), sentiabr 1920 goda: protokoly*, Moscow: Politizdat.

Primary Sources: Published Documents, Autobiographies, and Memoirs

Anderson, Kirill et al. (eds.) 2007, *Stenogrammy zasedanii Politbiuro TsK RKP(b)-VKP(b): 1923–1928 gg.*, 3 volumes, Moscow: ROSSPEN.

Anon 1922, *Materialy po voprosu o gruppe rabochei oppozitsii na XI syezde RKP(b), otchet komissii i rezoliutsiia XI syezda RKP o nekotorykh chlenakh byvshei 'rabochei oppozitsii'*, Moscow: Izdatelstvo TsK RKP(b).

Anon 1975, *Documents of the 1923 Opposition*, London: New Park Publications.

Bogdanov, A.A. 1921, *Ocherki vseobshchei organisatsionnoi nauki*, Samara: Gosudarstvennoe izdatelstvo.

Bogdanov, A.A. 1980, *Essays in Tektology: The General Science of Organisation*, translated by George Gorelik, Seaside, CA: Intersystems Publications.

Bordiugov, G.A. et al (eds.) 1995, *Neizvestnyi Bogdanov v 3-kh knigakh*, Moscow: AIRO.

Bunyan, James (ed.) 1967, *The Origins of Forced Labor in the Soviet State, 1917–1921*, Stanford: The Johns Hopkins Press.

Cachin, Marcel 1993–8, *Carnets de Marcel Cachin*, vols. 1–4, edited by Denis Peschanski, Paris: CNRS Editions.

Chugurin, Ivan 2011, 'The Memoirs of Ivan Chugurin', translated by James D. White and Vladimir P. Sapon, *Revolutionary Russia*, vol. 24, no. 1, pp. 1–12.

Daniels, Robert V. (ed.) 1993, *A Documentary History of Communism in Russia: From Lenin to Gorbachev*, 3rd rev. edn, Vermont: University Press of New England.

Fedorov, Ivan Nikolaevich and Sergei Vladimirovich Tyrin 2016, *Istoriia Rossii: Nachalo XX–nachalo XXI veka; khrestomatiia, 10 klass*, Moscow: Drofa, pp. 79–80.

Felshtinsky, Iury (ed.) 1990, *Kommunisticheskaia oppozitsiia v SSSR, 1923–1927*, 4 vols., Moscow: Terra. Reprint of Benson, Vermont: Chalidze Publications, 1988

Fischer, Ruth 1982, *Stalin and German Communism: A Study in the Origins of the State Party*, New Brunswick: Transaction Books.

Gambarov, Iu. et al (eds.) 1989 [1927–9], *Deiateli SSSR i oktiabrskoi revoliutsii: avtobiografii i biografii*, 3 parts, Moscow: Granat; reprinted Moscow: Kniga.

Iakovlev, A.N. (ed.) 1991, *Reabilitatsiia: politicheskie protsessy 30–50-kh godov*, Moscow: Politizdat.

Iaroslavsky, Emelian 1927, *'Rabochaia oppozitsiia', 'Rabochaia gruppa', Rabochaia Pravda'*, Moscow: Molodaia gvardiia.

Institut marksizma-leninizma pri TSK KPSS, 1975, *V.I. Lenin i VChK: sbornik dokumentov (1917–1922 gg.)*, Moscow, Politizdat.

Kollontai, A.M. 1921a, 'Pora proanalizirovat', *Pravda*, 1.

Kollontai, A.M. 1921b, *Rabochaia oppozitsiia*, Moscow: Vosmaia Gosudarstvennaia Tipografiia.

Kollontai, A.M. 2001, *Diplomaticheskie dnevniki, 1922-1940*, 2 volumes, Moscow: Academiia.

Kovalchenko, I.D. (ed.) 1993, *Neizvestnaia Rossiia XX vek*, Moscow: Mosgorarkhiv.

KPSS SSSR 1954, *KPSS v resoliutsiiakh i resheniiakh: syezdov, konferentsii i plenumov TsK*, ch. 1 (1898–1924), seventh edition, Moscow.

Krasilnikov, S.A. et al (eds.) 2010–11, *Shakhtinskii protsess 1928 g.: podgotovka, proizvedenie, itogi*, 2 volumes, Moscow: ROSSPEN.

Krylov, Constantin 1973, *Russian Proverbs and Sayings in Russian and English*, NY: US Army Russian Institute.

Kvashonkin, A.V. et al. (eds.) 1996, *Bolshevistskoe rukovodstvo: perepiska, 1912–1927*, Moscow: ROSSPEN.

Lane, A. Thomas (ed.) 1995, *Biographical Dictionary of European Labor Leaders*, 2 volumes, Westport, CT: Greenwood Press.

Lenin, Vladimir Ilich 1926–35, *Sochineniia*, second edition, edited by V.V. Adoratsky et al, Moscow: Partizdat.

Lenin, Vladimir Ilich 1958–65, *Polnoe sobranie sochinenii*, 55 vols., fifth edition, Moscow: Politizdat.

Lenin, Vladimir Ilich 1960–70, *Collected Works*, 45 volumes, edited by Iurii Sdobnikov, fourth English edition, Moscow: Foreign Languages Publishing House.

Lih, Lars T. et al. (eds.) 1995, *Stalin's Letters to Molotov*, New Haven: Yale University Press.

McNeal, Robert H. (ed.) 1974, *Resolutions and Decisions of the CPSU*, Toronto: Univ. of Toronto Press.

Mikoian, Anastas 1970, *Mysli i vospominaniia o Lenine*, Moscow: Politizdat.

Obolensky, V.V. (N. Osinsky) 1918, 'Iz pervykh dnei VSNKh', *Narodnoe khoziaistvo*, 11: 11–14.

Pavlov, Evgeni and David Rowley (eds.) 2015–, *The Alexander Bogdanov Library*, edited by Evgeni Pavlov and David Rowley, 10 volumes, *Historical Materialism Book Series*, Leiden, The Netherlands: Brill.

Petrov, F.N. et al (eds.) 1963, *O Vladimire Iliche Lenine: vospominaniia, 1900–1922*, Moscow: Gosudarstvennoe Izdatelstvo Politicheskoi Literatury.

Riddell, John (ed. and trans.) 2015, *To the Masses: Proceedings of the Third Congress of the Communist International, 1921*, Leiden, The Netherlands: Brill Academic Publishers.

Rudzutak, Jan (ed.) 1927, *Diskussiia o profsoiuzakh: materialy i dokumenty, 1920–1921 gg.*, Moscow/Leningrad: Gosizdat.

Serge, Victor 2002, *Memoirs of a Revolutionary*, translated by Peter Sedgwick, Iowa City: University of Iowa Press.

Sh[liapnikov], A.G. 1917, 'Zadachi rastsenochnykh komissii', *Metallist*, no. 3: 3.

Shliapnikov, A.G. 1924, 'Nashi raznoglasiia', *Pravda*, January 18: 4–5.

Shliapnikov, A.G. 1982 [1923], *On the Eve of 1917*, translated by Richard Chappell, London/New York: Allison & Busby.

Shukman, Harold (ed.) 1988, *The Blackwell Encyclopedia of the Russian Revolution*, Oxford: Blackwell.

Slepkov, A. (ed.) 1926, *Put 'Rabochei oppozitsii': sbornik statei*, Moscow: Izdatelstvo Pravda i Bednota.

Tivel, A. and M. Kheimo (eds.) 1967 [1929], *Desiat' let Kominterna v resheniiakh i tsifrakh*. Milan: Feltrinelli.

Trotsky, Leon 1921, *O zadachakh profsoiuzov: doklad prochitannyi na sobranii 3 dekabria 1920 goda*, Moscow: Gosizdat.

Vilkova, V.P. (ed.) 2004, *RKP(b): vnutripartiinaia borba v dvadtsatye gody, dokumenty i materialy 1923*, Moscow: ROSSPEN.

Voline (Vsevolod Mikhailovich Eikhenbaum) 1974, *The Unknown Revolution, 1917–1921*, NY: Free Life Editions.

VTsSPS 1918, *Pervyi vserossiiskii syezd professionalnykh soiuzov, 7–14 ianvaria 1918: polnyi stenograficheskii otchet s predisloviem M. Tomskogo*, Moscow: Izd. VTsSPS.

Zinoviev, Grigory 1921a, *O roli professionalnykh soiuzov v proizvodstve: doklady tt. Zinoveva i Trotskogo, rech t. Lenina, sodoklady tt. Bukharina, Nogina, Shliapnikova i Riazanova i zakliuchitelnye slova tt Trotskogo i Zinoveva na soedinennom zasedanii del-*

egatov 8-go syezda sovetov, VTsSPS i MGSPS, – chlenov RKP 30-go dekabria, 1920 g., Moscow: VTsSPS.

Zinoviev, Grigory (ed.) 1921b, *Partiia i soiuzy (k diskussii o roli i zadachakh profsoiuzov): sbornik statei i material*, Petrograd: Gosizdat.

Zorky, Mark Solomonovich (ed.) 1926, *'Rabochaia oppozitsiia:' materialy i dokumenty, 1920–1926 gg.*, preface by E.M. Iaroslavsky, Moscow: Gosizdat.

Secondary Sources

Aksiutin, Iu. 1990, 'Aleksandr Shliapnikov', *Fakel*, Moscow: Politizdat: 132–55.

Albert, Gleb 2011, 'German October is Approaching: Internationalism, Activists, and the Soviet State in 1923', *Revolutionary Russia*, 24, 2: 111–42.

Albert, Gleb 2014, '"Comrade Speaker!" Zapiski as Means of Political Communication and Source for Popular Moods in the 1920s', *The NEP Era: Soviet Russia, 1921–1928*, vol. 8: 43–54.

Alikina, Nadezhda Alekseevna 2006, *Don Kikhot proletarskoi revoliutsii: dokumental-naia povest o tom, kak motovilikhinskii rabochii Gavriil Miasnikov borolsia s TsK RKP(b) za svobodu slova i pechati (1920–1922 gody)*, Perm: Pushka.

Allen, Barbara C. 2002, 'The Evolution of Communist Party Control over Trade Unions: Alexander Shliapnikov and the Trade Unions in May 1921', *Revolutionary Russia*, 15, 2: 72–105.

Allen, Barbara C. 2008, 'Transforming Factions into Blocs: Alexander Shliapnikov, Sergei Medvedev, and the CCC Investigation of the "Baku Affair" in 1926', pp. 129–52 in *A Dream Deferred: New Studies in Russian and Soviet Labour History*, edited by Donald Filtzer, Wendy Goldman, Gijs Kessler, and Simon Pirani, Bern: Peter Lang, 2008.

Allen, Barbara C. 2015, *Alexander Shlyapnikov, 1885–1937: Life of an Old Bolshevik*, Leiden, The Netherlands: Brill Academic Publishers.

Allen, Barbara C. 2019, 'The Workers' Opposition and the Specialists', *Canadian-American Slavic Studies*, vol. 53, issue 1–2: 5–23.

Aves, Jonathan 1996, *Workers against Lenin: Labour Protest and the Bolshevik Dictatorship*, London: Tauris Academic Studies.

Avrich, Paul 1970, *Kronstadt 1921*, Princeton: Princeton University Press.

Avrich, Paul 1976, *Russian Rebels, 1600–1800*, W.W. Norton & Company.

Avrich, Paul 1984, 'Bolshevik Opposition to Lenin: G.T. Miasnikov and the Workers' Group', *Russian Review*, vol. 43: 1–29.

Belenkin, B.I. 1989, ' "Im net chisla, razlichnym litsam ...": O sudbe bolshevika, revoliutsionera – podpolshchika A.G. Shliapnikova', *Znanie-sila*, no. 4: 55–64.

Belenkin, B.I. 1991a, 'Narodnyi komissar truda A.G. Shliapnikov'. *Pervoe sovetskoe pravitelstvo: oktiabr 1917–iiul 1918*, Moscow: Politizdat, 8?–104.

Belenkin, B.I. 1991b, ' "Rabochaia oppozitsiia": Post scriptum', *Oni ne molchali*, Moscow: Politizdat, 44–67.

Berlin, Valery 2006, 'Rovesnik veka', *Vecherny Kharkov*, 21 July.

Brandenberger, David 2011, *Propaganda State in Crisis: Soviet Ideology, Indoctrination, and Terror under Stalin, 1927–1941*, New Haven, CT: Yale University Press.

Brovkin, Vladimir 1990, 'Workers' Unrest and the Bolsheviks' Response in 1919', *Slavic Review*, 49, 3: 350–73.

Buketov, Kirill 2015, 'Piat shtrikhov k politicheskoi biografii Samuila Krolia', speech at the conference *Rabochee i profsoiuznoe dvizhenie Rossii: iz proshlogo v budushchee*, Moscow, 18–19 April 2015, published on http://www.iuf.ru/2/21/1757.html

Burdzhalov, Eduard N. 1987, *Russia's Second Revolution: The February 1917 Uprising in Petrograd*, translated and edited by Donald J. Raleigh, Bloomington, IN: Indiana University Press.

Carr, Edward Hallett 1950–3, *The Bolshevik Revolution, 1917–1923*, 3 volumes, London: Macmillan.

Chase, William J. and Vadim Staklo (eds.) 2001, *Enemies Within the Gates?: The Comintern and the Stalinist Repression, 1934–39*, New Haven, CT: Yale University Press.

Chernobaev, A.A. 1999, 'The Shliapnikov-Stalin Duel: From the History of the Intra-Party Struggle in the vKP(b) in the 1920s', *Revolutionary Russia*, vol. 12, no. 1: 103–114.

Clements, Barbara Evans 1979, *Bolshevik Feminist: The Life of Alexandra Kollontai*, Bloomington, Ind.: Indiana University Press.

Cohen, Stephen F. 1980, *Bukharin and the Bolshevik Revolution: A Political Biography, 1888–1938*, Oxford: Oxford University Press.

Dahlke, Sandra 2008, 'Le soufflé lointain de la révolution et la terreur du quotidian: Le bolchevik Emel'jan Jaroslavskij dans les annees 1930', *Cahiers du monde russe*, 49, 4: 581–603.

Daniels, Robert V. 1988 [1960], *The Conscience of the Revolution: Communist Opposition in Soviet Russia*, Cambridge, Mass.: Harvard University Press; revised edition, Boulder, Col.: Westview Press.

David-Fox, Michael 1997, *Revolution of the Mind: Higher Learning among the Bolsheviks, 1918–1929*, Ithaca, NY: Cornell University Press.

Day, Richard 1973, *Leon Trotsky and the Politics of Economic Isolation*, Cambridge: Cambridge University Press.

Demidov, V.V. 1994, *Politicheskaia borba i oppozitsiia v Sibiri: 1922–1929 gg.*, Novosibirsk: Izdatelstvo Sibirskogo kadrovogo tsentra.

Deutscher, Isaac 1959, *The Prophet Unarmed, Trotsky: 1921–1929*, NY: Oxford University Press.

Deutscher, Isaac 1966, *Stalin: A Political Biography*, second edition, NY: Oxford University Press.

Enteen, George M. 1978, *The Soviet Scholar Bureaucrat: M.N. Pokrovskii and the Society of Marxist Historians*, University Park, PA: Pennsylvania State University Press.

Farnsworth, Beatrice 1980, *Aleksandra Kollontai: Socialism, Feminism, and the Bolshevik Revolution*, Stanford, Calif.: Stanford University Press.

Farnsworth, Beatrice 2010, 'Conversing with Stalin, Surviving the Terror: The Diaries of Aleksandra Kollontai and the Internal Life of Politics', *Slavic Review*, vol. 69, no. 4 (Winter): 944–70.

Figes, Orlando 1989, *Peasant Russia, Civil War: The Volga Countryside in Revolution, 1917–1921*, London: The Clarendon Press.

Filippov, S.G. 2018, *Rukovoditeli tsentralnykh organov VKP(b) v 1934–1939 gg.: spravochnik*, Moscow: ROSSPEN.

Filtzer, Donald, Wendy Goldman, Gijs Kessler and Simon Pirani (eds.) 2008, *A Dream Deferred: New Studies in Russian and Soviet Labor History*, Bern: Peter Lang.

Fitzpatrick, Sheila 1983, *The Russian Revolution*, London: Oxford University Press.

Fitzpatrick, Sheila 1988, 'The Bolsheviks' Dilemma: Class, Culture, and Politics in the Early Soviet Years', *Slavic Review*, 47, 4: 599–613.

Fitzpatrick, Sheila 1992, *The Cultural Front: Power and Culture in Revolutionary Russia*, Ithaca: Cornell University Press.

Fitzpatrick, Sheila 1996, *Stalin's Peasants: Resistance and Survival in the Russian Village after Collectivisation*, London: Oxford University Press.

Fomichev, V.S. (ed.) 1984, *Vladimir Ilich Lenin: biograficheskaia khronika, 1870–1924*, 12 volumes, Moscow: Politizdat.

Gambarov, Iu. et al (eds.) 1989 [1927–9], *Deiateli SSSR i oktiabrskoi revoliutsii: avtobiografii i biografii*, 3 parts, Moscow: Granat; reprinted Moscow: Kniga.

Gatrell, Peter 1995, 'Big Business and the State in Russia, 1915–1918', pp. 7–14 in *Soviet History, 1917–53: Essays in Honour of R.W. Davies*, edited by Julian Cooper, Maureen Perrie, and E.A. Rees, London, Macmillan Press.

Getty, J. Arch 1997, *Pragmatists and Puritans: The Rise and Fall of the Party Control Commission*, Carl Beck Papers in Russian and East European Studies, Pittsburgh: University of Pittsburgh/CREES.

Getzler, Israel 1983, *Kronstadt 1917–1921: the Fate of a Soviet Democracy*, NY: Cambridge University Press.

Gilmintinov, Roman 2019, '"We Can and We Must": The Scientificity of Trade-Union History-Writing in the Soviet Union in the 1920s', *Studia Historiae Scientarum*, vol. 18: 219–54.

Gurevich, A. 1927, 'Desiat let VSRM', *Metallist, 1917–1927, iubileinyi nomer*: 5.

Gusev, Aleksei 2008, 'The "Bolshevik Leninist" Opposition and the Working Class, 1928–1929', in Filtzer, Goldman, Kessler and Pirani (eds.)

Hagenloh, Paul 2009, *Stalin's Police: Public Order and Mass Repression in the USSR, 1926–1941*, Washington: Woodrow Wilson Center Press.

Halfin, Igal 2007, *Intimate Enemies: Demonizing the Bolshevik Opposition, 1918–1928*, Pittsburgh, PA: University of Pittsburgh Press.

Hasegawa, Tsuyoshi 1981, *The February Revolution: Petrograd, 1917*, Seattle: University of Washington Press.

Heywood, Anthony 1992, 'The Armstrong Affair and the Making of the Anglo-Soviet Trade Agreement, 1920–1921', *Revolutionary Russia*, vol. 5, no. 1: 53–91.

Heywood, Anthony 1999, *Modernising Lenin's Russia: Economic Reconstruction, Foreign Trade and the Railways*, Cambridge, UK: Cambridge University Press.

Heywood, Anthony 2011, *Engineer of Revolutionary Russia: Iurii V. Lomonosov (1876–1952) and the Railways*, Surrey, UK/Burlington, VT: Ashgate Publishing.

Hirschkowitz, Nafthali et al (eds.) 2005–17, *Spravochnik po istorii Kommunisticheskoi partii i Sovetskogo Soiuza, 1898–1991*, http://www.knowbysight.info/

Hoffrogge, Ralf 2014, *Working-Class Politics in the German Revolution: Richard Müller, the Revolutionary Shop Stewards and the Origins of the Council Movement*, Leiden: Brill, 2014.

Holmes, Larry E. 1990, *For the Revolution Redeemed: The Workers Opposition in the Bolshevik Party, 1919–1921*, The Carl Beck Papers in Russian and East European Studies, University of Pittsburgh/CREES.

Humbert-Droz, Jules 1967 [1922], *Die Taktik der Kommunistischen Internationale gegen die Offensive des Kapitals; Bericht über die Konferenz der Erweiterten Exekutive der Kommunistischen Internationale, Moskau, vom 24. Februar bis 4. März, 1922*, Milano: Feltrinelli.

Iarov, Sergei Viktorovich 1999, *Proletarii kak politik: politicheskaia psikhologiia rabochikh Petrograda v 1917–1923 gg.*, St. Petersburg: Dmitrii Bulavin.

Kaliagin, A.V. 2003, '"Rabochaia oppozitsiia": ideino-kontseptualnyi aspekt (k voprosu o rozhdenii nepa)', *Istoriia i istoriki v meniaiushchemsia mire: sbornik statei*, Samara: NTTS. Pp. 221–228

Kan, Aleksander 2007, 'Upolnomochennyi Ispolkoma Kominterna A.G. Shliapnikov v Skandinavii, mart-iiun 1920', *Istoricheskii arkhiv*, no. 4: 162–71.

Kashirskikh, O.N. 2006, 'Krizis v Sovetsko-Germanskikh ekonomicheskikh otnosheniiakh 1928 goda', *Voprosy istorii*, 9: 35–48.

Kelly, Catriona 2009, *Petrushka: The Russian Carnival Puppet Theatre*, Cambridge: Cambridge University Press.

Kiselev, A.F. 1990, 'Partiinye diskussii o profsoiuzakh (1917 g.–nachalo 1920 g.)', *Diskussii v RSDRP(b) – RKP(b) 1917–1920 gg.*, Moscow: Institute of Marxism-Leninism under the CC CPSU, 326–47.

Kiselev, A.F. 1993, 'Rossiiskie profsoiuzy: ot nezavisimosti k ogosudarstvleniiu', *Vlast i obshchestvennye organisatsii v pervoi treti XX stoletiia*, Moscow: MIL 'NV Magistr', pp. 19–47.

Klehr, Harvey et al 1996, *The Secret World of American Communism*, New Haven, CT: Yale University Press.

Knight, Amy 1993, *Beria: Stalin's First Lieutenant*, Princeton: Princeton University Press.

Koenker, Diane P. 1985, 'Urbanization and Deurbanization in the Russian Revolution and Civil War', *Journal of Modern History*, 57: 424–50.

Koenker, Diane P. et al (eds.) 1989, *Party, State, and Society in the Russian Civil War: Explorations in Social History*, Bloomington, IN: Indiana University Press.

Komarenko A.L.O. 1992, 'Aleksandr Shliapnikov – istorik rossiiskogo rabochego dvizheniia v gody pervoi mirovoi voiny', *Otechestvennaia istoriia*, no. 6: 81–94.

Kuromiya, Hiroaki 1998, *Stalin's Industrial Revolution: Politics and Workers, 1928–1931*, Cambridge: Cambridge University Press.

Landauer, Carl 1983, *Corporate State Ideologies: Historical Roots and Philosophical Origins*, Berkeley, CA: Institute of International Ideologies, University of California.

Lewin, Moshe 1968, *Lenin's Last Struggle*, NY: Pantheon Books.

Lewin, Moshe 1975, *Russian Peasants and Soviet Power: A Study of Collectivisation*, NY: W.W. Norton & Co.

Lewis, Ben and Lars T. Lih (eds.) 2011, *Zinoviev and Martov: Head to Head in Halle*, London: November Publications.

Lih, Lars T. 2011, 'Zinoviev: Populist Leninist', in Lewis and Lih (eds.).

Long, James W. 1992, 'The Volga Germans and the Famine of 1921', *Russian Review*, 51, 4: 510–25.

Luban, Ottokar 2003, 'Fanny Thomas-Jezierska (1887–1945) Von Rosa Luxemburg zu Gramsci, Stalin und August Thalheimer – Stationen einer internationalen Sozialistin', *Jahrbuch für Historische Kommunismusforschung*: 286–319.

Malle, Silvana 1985, *The Economic Origins of War Communism, 1918–1921*, Cambridge: Cambridge University Press.

Mally, Lynn 1990, *Culture of the Future: The Proletkult Movement in Revolutionary Russia*, Berkeley and Los Angeles, CA: University of California Press.

Martin, Anne-Denes 1994, *Les Ouvrières de la Mer: histoire des sardinières du littoral breton*, Paris, L'Harmattan.

Mawdsley, Evan 1978, *The Russian Revolution and the Baltic Fleet: War and Politics, February 1917–April 1918*, London: Macmillan.

Mendelsohn, Ezra 1965, 'Worker Opposition in the Russian Jewish Socialist Movement, from the 1890's to 1903', *International Review of Social History*, vol. 10, no. 2: 268–82.

Miasnikov, G.I. 1995, *Filosofiia ubiistva, ili pochemu i kak ia ubil Mikhaila Romanova*, compiled by B.I. Belenkin and V.K. Vinogradov, *Minuvshee: istoricheskii almanakh*, vyp. 18, Moscow: Atheneum; St. Petersburg: Feniks.

Milchakov, A. 1991, 'Za inakomyslie k rasstrelu: naideno mesto zakhoroneniia pervykh dissidentov – Shliapnikova i Vuiovicha', *Vecherniaia Moskva*, July 12, p. 4, cols. 1–7.

Miliutin, V. 1923, *Na novykh putiakh: itogi novoi ekonomicheskoi politiki 1921–1922 gg.*, Moscow: Izdatelstvo Soveta truda i oborony.

Mitina, Daria 2009, http://kolobok1973.livejournal.com/834816.html

Naumov, V.P. 1989, 'Iz rossiiskikh rabochikh: stranitsy zhizni A. Shliapnikova', *Sovetskie profsoiuzy*, no. 19: 24–6; no. 20: 30–2.

Naumov, V.P. 1991, *Aleksandr Gavriilovich Shliapnikov: stranitsy politicheskoi biografii, Novoe v zhizni, nauke, tekhnike: seriia politicheskaia istoriia xx veka*, no. 8, Moscow: Znanie.

Naumov, V.P. 1993, 'Aleksandr Shliapnikov', *Istoricheskie portrety*, Moscow: Prosveshchenie, pp. 133–58.

Nove, Alec 1984, *An Economic History of the USSR*, NY: Penguin Books.

Olekh, G.L. 1994, '"Omskoe delo" 1922 g.: khronika i smysl sobytii', pp. 101–22 in *Iz proshlogo Sibiri*, vyp. 1, ch. 1, *Mezhvuzovskii sbornik nauchnykh trudov*, Novosibirsk: Novosibirsky gosudarstvennyi universitet.

Olekh, G.L. 1999, *Krovnye uzy: RKP(b) i ChK/GPU v pervoi polovine 1920-kh gg.*, Novosibirsk: Novosibirskaia gos. akademiia vodnogo transporta.

Oppenheim, Samuel A. 1973, 'The Supreme Economic Council, 1917–1921', *Soviet Studies*, 25, 1: 3–27.

Papkov, Sergei Andreevich 1997, *Stalinskii terror v Sibiri, 1928–1941*, Novosibirsk: Izdatelstvo Sibirskogo otdeleniia Rossiiskoi Akademii Nauk.

Pauly, Matthew D. 2014, *Breaking the Tongue: Language, Education, and Power in Soviet Ukraine, 1923–1934*, Toronto: University of Toronto Press.

Pavliuchenkov, S.A. 2008, '*Orden Mechenostsev': partiia i vlast posle revoliutsii, 1917–1929 gg.*, Moscow: Sobranie.

Pipes Richard 1994, *Russia under the Bolshevik Regime*, NY: Vintage Books.

Pirani, Simon 2008, *The Russian Revolution in Retreat, 1920–1924: Soviet Workers and the New Communist Elite*, London/NY: Routledge.

Pogorelskin, Alexis 2007, 'Kamenev in Rome', *The NEP Era: Soviet Russia, 1921–1928*, vol. 1, 101–18.

Pokrovsky, A.S. 2001, *Pervyi raboche-soldatskii parlament Rossii: I Vserossiiskii syezd Sovetov rabochikh i soldatskikh deputatov (3–24 iiunia 1917 g.)*, Moscow: Institute of Russian History of the Russian Academy of Sciences.

Pokrovsky, Mikhail Nikolaevich 1910–13, *Russkaia istoriia s drevneishikh vremen*, 5 vols., Moscow: Mir.

Pokrovsky, Mikhail Nikolaevich 1922–3, *Russkaia istoriia s drevneishikh vremen*, 4 vols., 2nd edition, Moscow/Petrograd: Gosudarstvennoe izdatelstvo.

Porter, Cathy 2014 [1980], *Alexandra Kollontai: A Biography*, London: Virago Press; revised edition, Chicago, IL: Haymarket Books.

Priestland, David 1997, 'Bolshevik Ideology and the Debate over Party-State Relations, 1918-1922', *Revolutionary Russia*, 10, 2: 37–61.

Rabinowitch, Alexander 1976, *The Bolsheviks Come to Power: The Revolution of 1917 in Petrograd*, NY: W.W. Norton.

Rabinowitch, Alexander 2007, *The Bolsheviks in Power: The First Year of Soviet Rule in Petrograd*, Bloomington, IN: Indiana University Press.

Raleigh, Donald J. 1986, *Revolution on the Volga: 1917 in Saratov*, Ithaca, NY: Cornell University Press.

Raleigh, Donald J. 2002, *Experiencing Russia's Civil War: Politics, Society, and Revolutionary Culture in Saratov, 1917–1922*, Princeton, NJ: Princeton University Press.

Rees, E.A. 1987, *State Control in Soviet Russia. The Rise and Fall of the Workers' and Peasants' Inspectorate, 1920–1934*, Basingstoke: Macmillan.

Reznik, Aleksandr 2017, *Trotskii i tovarishchi: Levaia oppozitsiia i politicheskaia kultura RKP(b), 1923–1924*, Sankt-Peterburg: European University in Saint Petersburg Publishing.

Riddell, John (editor and translator) 2015, *To the Masses: Proceedings of the Third Congress of the Communist International, 1921*, Leiden, The Netherlands: Brill Academic Publishers.

Rodionova, N.I. (ed.) 1985, *Soratniki: biografii aktivnykh uchastnikov revoliutsionnogo dvizheniia v Moskve i Moskovskoi oblasti*, Moscow: Moskovskii rabochii.

Rosenberg, William G. 1985, 'Russian Labor and Bolshevik Power after October', *Slavic Review*, 44: 213–39.

Rosenberg, William G. 1989, 'The Social Background to Tsektran' in Koenker, Rosenberg and Suny (eds.).

Rossman, Jeffrey 2005, *Worker Resistance to Stalin: Class and Revolution on the Shop Floor*, Cambridge, MA: Harvard University Press.

Ruble, Blair 1981, *Soviet Trade Unions; Their Development in the 1970s*, Cambridge: Cambridge University Press.

Ruble, Blair 1983, *The Applicability of Corporatist Models to the Study of Soviet Politics: the Case of the Trade Unions* Pittsburgh, PA: University of Pittsburgh/REES.

Sakharov, V.A. 2003, *'Politicheskoe zaveshchanie' Lenina: realnost istorii i mify politiki*, Moscow: Moscow Univ. Izd.

Schapiro, Leonard 1956, *The Origin of the Communist Autocracy: Political Opposition in the Soviet State, First Phase, 1917–1922*, Cambridge, Mass.: Harvard University Press.

Senn, A.E. 1977, *Nicholas Rubakin. A Life for Books*, Newtonville, Mass., ORP. Cited on International Institute of Social History web site.

Shkliarevsky, Gennady 1993, *Labor in the Russian Revolution: Factory Committees and Trade Unions, 1917–1918*, NY: St. Martin's Press.

Shliapnikova, I.A. and A.A. Chernobaev (eds.) 2002, '"My ne reshaem nyne dazhe svoei sudby": vospominaniia i pisma A.G. Shliapnikova, 1934 g.', *Istorichesky arkhiv*, no. 1: 3–31.

Slutskaia, T.K. 2017, 'Chekist Aleksandr Medvedev', website of the Unechsky Kraevedchesky Museum, http://museum-unecha.ucoz.net. Last accessed 29 April 2017.

Smirnov, N.G. 2001, *Repressirovannoe pravosudie*, Moscow: Gelios ARV.

Smith, Scott B. 2011, *Captives of Revolution: The Socialist Revolutionaries and the Bolshevik Dictatorship, 1918–1923*, Pittsburgh, PA: The University of Pittsburgh Press.

Smith, Stephen A. 1983, *Red Petrograd: Revolution in the Factories, 1917–1918*, Cambridge: Cambridge University Press.

Sochor, Zenovia A. 1988, *Revolution and Culture: The Bogdanov-Lenin Controversy*, Ithaca, NY: Cornell University Press.

Sorenson, Jay 1969, *The Life and Death of Soviet Trade Unionism: 1917–1928*, New York: Atherton Press.

Thatcher, Ian D. 2003, *Trotsky*, London/NY: Routledge.

Thatcher, Ian D. 2007, 'The First Histories of the Russian Social-Democratic Labour Party, 1904–6', *The Slavonic and East European Review*, vol. 85, no. 4: 724–52.

Thompson, John M. 1981, *Revolutionary Russia, 1917*, NY: Scribner.

Thorpe, Wayne 1989, 'The Workers Themselves': Revolutionary Syndicalism and International Labour, 1913–1923*, Dordrecht, The Netherlands: Kluwer Academic.

Tostorff, Reiner 2016, *The Red International of Labour Unions (RILU), 1920–1937*, translated by Ben Fowkes, Leiden, The Netherlands: Brill.

Tsakunov, S.V. 1994, *V labirinte doktriny: iz opyta razrabotki ekonomicheskogo kursa strany v 1920-e gody*, Moscow: Rossiia Molodaia.

Tucker, Robert C. 1990, *Stalin in Power: The Revolution from Above, 1928–1941*, NY: W.W. Norton & Co.

Turton, Katy 2007, *Forgotten Lives: The Role of Lenin's Sisters in the Russian Revolution, 1864–1937*, NY: Palgrave Macmillan.

Viola, Lynne 1996, *Peasant Rebels Under Stalin: Collectivisation and the Culture of Peasant Resistance*, London/NY: Oxford University Press.

Viola, Lynne 2007, *The Unknown Gulag: The Lost World of Stalin's Special Settlements*, London/NY: Oxford University Press.

Wachtel, Andrew 1998, *Petrushka: Sources and Contexts*, Evanston, IL: Northwestern University Press.

Wade, Rex 1984, *Red Guards and Workers' Militias in the Russian Revolution*, Stanford: Stanford University Press.

Wade, Rex 2000, *The Russian Revolution, 1917*, Cambridge: Cambridge University Press.

Weissman, Benjamin M. 1974, *Herbert Hoover and Famine Relief to Soviet Russia, 1921–1923*, Hoover Institution Press.

Werth, Nicholas 2007, *Cannibal Island: Death in a Siberian Gulag*, translated by Steven Rendall, Princeton, NJ: Princeton University Press.

White, James D. 2018, *Red Hamlet: The Life and Ideas of Alexander Bogdanov*, Leiden, The Netherlands: Brill.

Wildman, Allan 1967, *The Making of a Workers' Revolution: Russian Social Democracy, 1891–1903*, Chicago, IL: University of Chicago Press.

Zenkovich, Nikolai 2002, *Samye zakrytye liudi: entsiklopediia biografii*, Moscow: Olma-Press.

Zguta, Russell 1978, *Russian Minstrels: A History of the Skomorokhi*, University of Pennsylvania Press.

Zhuravlev, Sergei 2000, *Malenkie liudi i bolshaia istoriia: inostrantsy Moskovskogo Elektrozavoda v sovetskom obshchestve 1920–1930-kh gg.*, Moscow: ROSSPEN.

Unpublished Works

Memorial Society Index, Moscow, Russia.

Rakov, T.N. 2012, *'Rabochaia oppozitsiia v RKP(b)'*, diplomnaia rabota, Iaroslavsky gosudarstvennyi universitet.

Sandu, Tatiana Anatolevna 2006, *'Rabochaia oppozitsiia' v RKP(b) (1919–1923)*, kandidatskaia dissertatsiia, Tiumensky gosudarstvennyi universitet.

Spencer, Scott Sherwood 1981, 'A Political Biography of Alexander Shliapnikov', M. Litt. thesis, Oxford University.

Index

This index includes entries for people, institutions, places, and subjects discussed in the main text of the book. From the biographical glossary, only key entry names are indexed. If a person assumed a different name by which they were better known, the assumed name is indexed and the birth name is inserted in brackets. Brackets also envelop first names and patronymics or initials of which I am unsure. Parentheses are used for abbreviations and acronyms of institutions, shortened forms of personal names, and information identifying individuals whose first names are not known.

CPSIA information can be obtained
at www.ICGtesting.com
Printed in the USA
JSHW041532180822
29111JS00002B/2